Contemporary
Literary Criticism

Guide to Gale Literary Criticism Series

For criticism on	Consult these Gale series
Authors now living or who died after December 31, 1999	*CONTEMPORARY LITERARY CRITICISM (CLC)*
Authors who died between 1900 and 1999	*TWENTIETH-CENTURY LITERARY CRITICISM (TCLC)*
Authors who died between 1800 and 1899	*NINETEENTH-CENTURY LITERATURE CRITICISM (NCLC)*
Authors who died between 1400 and 1799	*LITERATURE CRITICISM FROM 1400 TO 1800 (LC)* *SHAKESPEAREAN CRITICISM (SC)*
Authors who died before 1400	*CLASSICAL AND MEDIEVAL LITERATURE CRITICISM (CMLC)*
Authors of books for children and young adults	*CHILDREN'S LITERATURE REVIEW (CLR)*
Dramatists	*DRAMA CRITICISM (DC)*
Poets	*POETRY CRITICISM (PC)*
Short story writers	*SHORT STORY CRITICISM (SSC)*
Literary topics and movements	*HARLEM RENAISSANCE: A GALE CRITICAL COMPANION (HR)* *THE BEAT GENERATION: A GALE CRITICAL COMPANION (BG)*
Asian American writers of the last two hundred years	*ASIAN AMERICAN LITERATURE (AAL)*
Black writers of the past two hundred years	*BLACK LITERATURE CRITICISM (BLC)* *BLACK LITERATURE CRITICISM SUPPLEMENT (BLCS)*
Hispanic writers of the late nineteenth and twentieth centuries	*HISPANIC LITERATURE CRITICISM (HLC)* *HISPANIC LITERATURE CRITICISM SUPPLEMENT (HLCS)*
Native North American writers and orators of the eighteenth, nineteenth, and twentieth centuries	*NATIVE NORTH AMERICAN LITERATURE (NNAL)*
Major authors from the Renaissance to the present	*WORLD LITERATURE CRITICISM, 1500 TO THE PRESENT (WLC)* *WORLD LITERATURE CRITICISM SUPPLEMENT (WLCS)*

ISSN 0091-3421

Volume 203

Contemporary Literary Criticism

Criticism of the Works
of Today's Novelists, Poets, Playwrights,
Short Story Writers, Scriptwriters, and
Other Creative Writers

Jeffrey W. Hunter
PROJECT EDITOR

THOMSON
★
GALE

Detroit • New York • San Francisco • San Diego • New Haven, Conn. • Waterville, Maine • London • Munich

Contemporary Literary Criticism, Vol. 203

Project Editor
Jeffrey W. Hunter

Editorial
Jessica Bomarito, Kathy D. Darrow, Jelena O. Krstović, Michelle Lee, Thomas J. Schoenberg, Lawrence J. Trudeau, Russel Whitaker

Data Capture
Francis Monroe, Gwen Tucker

Indexing Services
Laurie Andriot

Rights and Acquisitions
Denise Buckley, Emma Hull, Sue Rudolph

Imaging and Multimedia
Dean Dauphinais, Leitha Etheridge-Sims, Lezlie Light, Mike Logusz, Dan Newell, Christine O'Bryan, Kelly A. Quin, Denay Wilding, Robyn Young

Composition and Electronic Prepress
Kathy Sauer

Manufacturing
Rhonda Dover

Associate Product Manager
Marc Cormier

LIBRARY OF CONGRESS CATALOG CARD NUMBER 76-46132

ISBN 0-7876-7973-9
ISSN 0091-3421

Printed in the United States of America
10 9 8 7 6 5 4 3 2 1

Contents

Preface

Named "one of the twenty-five most distinguished reference titles published during the past twenty-five years" by *Reference Quarterly,* the *Contemporary Literary Criticism* (*CLC*) series provides readers with critical commentary and general information on more than 2,000 authors now living or who died after December 31, 1999. Volumes published from 1973 through 1999 include authors who died after December 31, 1959. Previous to the publication of the first volume of *CLC* in 1973, there was no ongoing digest monitoring scholarly and popular sources of critical opinion and explication of modern literature. *CLC,* therefore, has fulfilled an essential need, particularly since the complexity and variety of contemporary literature makes the function of criticism especially important to today's reader.

Scope of the Series

CLC provides significant passages from published criticism of works by creative writers. Since many of the authors covered in *CLC* inspire continual critical commentary, writers are often represented in more than one volume. There is, of course, no duplication of reprinted criticism.

Authors are selected for inclusion for a variety of reasons, among them the publication or dramatic production of a critically acclaimed new work, the reception of a major literary award, revival of interest in past writings, or the adaptation of a literary work to film or television.

Attention is also given to several other groups of writers—authors of considerable public interest—about whose work criticism is often difficult to locate. These include mystery and science fiction writers, literary and social critics, foreign authors, and authors who represent particular ethnic groups.

Each *CLC* volume contains individual essays and reviews taken from hundreds of book review periodicals, general magazines, scholarly journals, monographs, and books. Entries include critical evaluations spanning from the beginning of an author's career to the most current commentary. Interviews, feature articles, and other published writings that offer insight into the author's works are also presented. Students, teachers, librarians, and researchers will find that the general critical and biographical material in *CLC* provides them with vital information required to write a term paper, analyze a poem, or lead a book discussion group. In addition, complete biographical citations note the original source and all of the information necessary for a term paper footnote or bibliography.

Organization of the Book

A *CLC* entry consists of the following elements:

- The **Author Heading** cites the name under which the author most commonly wrote, followed by birth and death dates. Also located here are any name variations under which an author wrote, including transliterated forms for authors whose native languages use nonroman alphabets. If the author wrote consistently under a pseudonym, the pseudonym will be listed in the author heading and the author's actual name given in parenthesis on the first line of the biographical and critical information. Uncertain birth or death dates are indicated by question marks. Single-work entries are preceded by a heading that consists of the most common form of the title in English translation (if applicable) and the original date of composition.

- A **Portrait of the Author** is included when available.

- The **Introduction** contains background information that introduces the reader to the author, work, or topic that is the subject of the entry.

- The list of **Principal Works** is ordered chronologically by date of first publication and lists the most important works by the author. The genre and publication date of each work is given. In the case of foreign authors whose works have been translated into English, the English-language version of the title follows in brackets. Unless otherwise indicated, dramas are dated by first performance, not first publication.

- Reprinted **Criticism** is arranged chronologically in each entry to provide a useful perspective on changes in critical evaluation over time. The critic's name and the date of composition or publication of the critical work are given at the beginning of each piece of criticism. Unsigned criticism is preceded by the title of the source in which it appeared. All titles by the author featured in the text are printed in boldface type. Footnotes are reprinted at the end of each essay or excerpt. In the case of excerpted criticism, only those footnotes that pertain to the excerpted texts are included.

- A complete **Bibliographical Citation** of the original essay or book precedes each piece of criticism. Source citations in the Literary Criticism Series follow University of Chicago Press style, as outlined in *The Chicago Manual of Style,* 14th ed. (Chicago: The University of Chicago Press, 1993).

- Critical essays are prefaced by brief **Annotations** explicating each piece.

- Whenever possible, a recent **Author Interview** accompanies each entry.

- An annotated bibliography of **Further Reading** appears at the end of each entry and suggests resources for additional study. In some cases, significant essays for which the editors could not obtain reprint rights are included here. Boxed material following the further reading list provides references to other biographical and critical sources on the author in series published by Thomson Gale.

Indexes

A **Cumulative Author Index** lists all of the authors that appear in a wide variety of reference sources published by Thomson Gale, including *CLC*. A complete list of these sources is found facing the first page of the Author Index. The index also includes birth and death dates and cross references between pseudonyms and actual names.

A **Cumulative Nationality Index** lists all authors featured in *CLC* by nationality, followed by the number of the *CLC* volume in which their entry appears.

A **Cumulative Topic Index** lists the literary themes and topics treated in the series as well as in *Literature Criticism from 1400 to 1800, Nineteenth-Century Literature Criticism, Twentieth-Century Literary Criticism,* and the *Contemporary Literary Criticism* Yearbook, which was discontinued in 1998.

An alphabetical **Title Index** accompanies each volume of *CLC*. Listings of titles by authors covered in the given volume are followed by the author's name and the corresponding page numbers where the titles are discussed. English translations of foreign titles and variations of titles are cross-referenced to the title under which a work was originally published. Titles of novels, dramas, nonfiction books, and poetry, short story, or essay collections are printed in italics, while individual poems, short stories, and essays are printed in roman type within quotation marks.

In response to numerous suggestions from librarians, Thomson Gale also produces an annual cumulative title index that alphabetically lists all titles reviewed in *CLC* and is available to all customers. Additional copies of this index are available upon request. Librarians and patrons will welcome this separate index; it saves shelf space, is easy to use, and is recyclable upon receipt of the next edition.

Citing *Contemporary Literary Criticism*

When citing criticism reprinted in the Literary Criticism Series, students should provide complete bibliographic information so that the cited essay can be located in the original print or electronic source. Students who quote directly from reprinted criticism may use any accepted bibliographic format, such as University of Chicago Press style or Modern Language Association (MLA) style. Both the MLA and the University of Chicago formats are acceptable and recognized as being the current standards for citations. It is important, however, to choose one format for all citations; do not mix the two formats within a list of citations.

The examples below follow recommendations for preparing a bibliography set forth in *The Chicago Manual of Style,* 14th ed. (Chicago: The University of Chicago Press, 1993); the first example pertains to material drawn from periodicals, the second to material reprinted from books:

Morrison, Jago. "Narration and Unease in Ian McEwan's Later Fiction." *Critique* 42, no. 3 (spring 2001): 253-68. Reprinted in *Contemporary Literary Criticism.* Vol. 169, edited by Janet Witalec, 212-20. Detroit: Gale, 2003.

Brossard, Nicole. "Poetic Politics." In *The Politics of Poetic Form: Poetry and Public Policy,* edited by Charles Bernstein, 73-82. New York: Roof Books, 1990. Reprinted in *Contemporary Literary Criticism.* Vol. 169, edited by Janet Witalec, 3-8. Detroit: Gale, 2003.

The examples below follow recommendations for preparing a works cited list set forth in the *MLA Handbook for Writers of Research Papers,* 5th ed. (New York: The Modern Language Association of America, 1999); the first example pertains to material drawn from periodicals, the second to material reprinted from books:

Morrison, Jago. "Narration and Unease in Ian McEwan's Later Fiction." *Critique* 42.3 (spring 2001): 253-68. Reprinted in *Contemporary Literary Criticism.* Ed. Janet Witalec. Vol. 169. Detroit: Gale, 2003. 212-20.

Brossard, Nicole. "Poetic Politics." *The Politics of Poetic Form: Poetry and Public Policy.* Ed. Charles Bernstein. New York: Roof Books, 1990. 73-82. Reprinted in *Contemporary Literary Criticism.* Ed. Janet Witalec. Vol. 169. Detroit: Gale, 2003. 3-8.

Suggestions are Welcome

Readers who wish to suggest new features, topics, or authors to appear in future volumes, or who have other suggestions or comments are cordially invited to call, write, or fax the Associate Product Manager:

Associate Product Manager, Literary Criticism Series

Thomson Gale

27500 Drake Road

Farmington Hills, MI 48331-3535

1-800-347-4253 (GALE)

Fax: 248-699-8054

Acknowledgments

The editors wish to thank the copyright holders of the criticism included in this volume and the permissions managers of many book and magazine publishing companies for assisting us in securing reproduction rights. We are also grateful to the staffs of the Detroit Public Library, the Library of Congress, the University of Detroit Mercy Library, Wayne State University Purdy/Kresge Library Complex, and the University of Michigan Libraries for making their resources available to us. Following is a list of the copyright holders who have granted us permission to reproduce material in this volume of *CLC*. Every effort has been made to trace copyright, but if omissions have been made, please let us know.

COPYRIGHTED MATERIAL IN *CLC, VOLUME 203, WAS REPRODUCED FROM THE FOLLOWING PERIODICALS:*

Academic Questions, v. 9, winter, 1995-96. Copyright © 1996 by Transaction Publishers. Republished with permission of Transaction Publishers, conveyed through Copyright Clearance Center, Inc.—*America*, December 7, 1991. Copyright © 1991, www.americamagazine.org. All rights reserved. Reproduced by permission of America Press.—*American Theatre*, v. 19, March 1, 2002. Copyright © 2002, Theatre Communications Group. All rights reserved. Reproduced by permission.— *The Antioch Review*, v. 59, summer, 2001. Copyright © 2001 by the Antioch Review Inc. Reproduced by permission of the Editors.—*Chicago Review*, v. 42, spring, 1996. Copyright © 1996 by *Chicago Review*. Reproduced by permission.— *The Christian Science Monitor*, June 29, 1995 for "Summer Reading: A Time for Fiction and Fantasy" by Merle Rubin. Copyright © 1995 by Merle Rubin. Reproduced by permission of the author.—*College Literature*, v. 25, winter, 1998. Copyright © 1998 by West Chester University. Reproduced by permission.—*Commentary*, v. 99, January 1, 1995 for "From Schnitzler to Kushner" by Edward Norden. Copyright © 1995 by the American Jewish Committee. All rights reserved. Reproduced by permission of the publisher and author.—*Commonweal*, v. 125, April 10, 1998. Copyright © 1998 Commonweal Publishing Co., Inc. Reproduced by permission of Commonweal Foundation.—*Comparative Literature*, v. 46, spring, 1994 in a review of "Love's Knowledge" by Donald G. Marshall. Copyright © 1994 by University of Oregon. Reproduced by permission of the author.—*Critical Quarterly*, v. 36, spring, 1994; v. 37, autumn, 1995. Copyright © 1994, 1995 Basil Blackwell Ltd. Both reproduced by permission of Blackwell Publishers.—*Dissent*, fall, 1998. Copyright © 1998 by Dissent Publishing Corporation. Reproduced by permission.—*Essays in Arts and Sciences*, v. 30, October 2001. Copyright © 2001 by the University of New Haven. Reproduced by permission.—*ETC: A Review of General Semantics*, v. 57, winter, 2000. Copyright © 2000 by the Institute of General Semantics. Reproduced by permission.—*Ethics*, v. 111, October 2000; v. 111, July 2001. Copyright © 2000, 2001 by The University of Chicago. All rights reserved. Both reproduced by permission.—*Florida English*, v. 1, 2003 for "Aristotle and Angels: Tragedy in the Age of Anomie" by Stephen Aiello. Copyright © 2003 Florida English. Reproduced by permission of the publisher and the author.—*GLQ: A Journal of Lesbian and Gay Studies*, v. 1, 1994. Copyright, 1994, Gordon and Breach Science Publishers S.A. All rights reserved. Used by permission of Duke University Press, on behalf of the original publisher.—*Hudson Review*, v. 55, summer, 2002 for "Free Association" by Richard Hornby. Copyright © 2002 by The Hudson Review, Inc. Reproduced by permission.—*International Philosophical Quarterly*, v. 34, September, 1994 for "Transcending the Human: A Kierkegaardian Reading of Martha Nussbaum" by Ronald L. Hall; v. 37, March 1, 1997 for "'Divinity Must Live within Herself': Nussbaum and Aquinas on Transcending the Human" by Daniel McInerny. Copyright © 1994, 1997 by Foundation for International Philosophical Exchange. Both reproduced by permission of the publisher and the respective authors.— *Journal of Aesthetics and Art Criticism*, v. 50, winter, 1992. Copyright © 1992 Basil Blackwell Ltd. Reproduced by permission of Blackwell Publishers.—*Journal of Dramatic Theory and Criticism*, v. 16, fall, 2001 for "'A Kind of Painful Progress': The Benjaminian Dialectics of *Angels in America*" by Roger Bechtel. Copyright © 2001 by the Joyce and Elizabeth Hall Center for the Humanities and the Department of Theatre and Film at the University of Kansas, Lawrence, Kansas 66045, U.S.A. Reproduced by permission of the author.—*Journal of Philosophy*, v. 97, August 2000 for a review of "Sex and Social Justice" by Miranda Fricker. Copyright © 2000 by The Journal of Philosophy, Inc. Reproduced by permission of the publisher and the author.—*Lambda Book Report*, July-August, 1994 for a review of "Try" by Drew Limsky; v. 8, January 2000 for "Brilliantly Psychotic?" by Michael Thomas Ford. Copyright © 1994, 2000 Lambda Literary Foundation. Both reproduced by permission of the respective authors.—*Literature and Medicine*, v. 19, fall, 2000. Copyright © 2000 The Johns Hopkins University Press. Reproduced by permission.—*London Review of Books*, May 21, 1998. Appears here by permission of the *London Review of Books*.—*Los Angeles Times Book Review*, July 16, 1989; June 30, 1991; July 3, 1994; June 8, 1997; April 30, 2000. Copyright © 1989, 1991, 1994, 1997, 2000 by Los Angeles Times. All reproduced by permission.—*Metaphilosophy*, v. 29, October 1998. Copyright © 1998 Basil Blackwell Ltd. Reproduced by permission of Blackwell Publishers.—*Mississippi Quarterly*, v. 49, winter, 1995-96. Copyright © 1996 Mississippi State

University. Reproduced by permission.—*MLN*, v. 110, September 1995. Copyright © 1995 The Johns Hopkins University Press. Reproduced by permission.—*Modern Drama*, v. 39, spring, 1996; v. 41, winter, 1998. Copyright © 1996, 1998 by the University of Toronto, Graduate Centre for Study of Drama. Both reproduced by permission.—*Nation*, July 1, 1991; June 16, 1997. Copyright © 1991, 1997 by The Nation Magazine/ The Nation Company, Inc. Both reproduced by permission.—*National Review*, June 17, 1996. Copyright © 1996 by National Review, Inc, 215 Lexington Avenue, New York, NY 10016. Reproduced by permission.—*New Criterion*, v. 20, February 1, 2002 for "Goin' to Afghanistan" by Mark Steyn. Copyright © 2002 by Mark Steyn. Reproduced by permission of the author.—*The New Leader*, v. lxxx, September 22, 1997. Copyright © 1997 by The American Labor Conference on International Affairs, Inc. Reproduced by permission.—*New Republic*, October 12, 1992; v. 209, December 27, 1993; v. 220, March 8, 1999; v. 226, March 18, 2002. Copyright © 1992, 1993, 1999, 2002 by The New Republic, Inc. All reproduced by permission of *The New Republic*.— *New Statesman*, October 9, 1998; March 27, 2000; November 20, 2000; May 6, 2002. Copyright © 1998, 2000, 2002 New Statesman, Ltd. All reproduced by permission.—*New Statesman and Society*, September 30, 1994. Copyright © 1994 New Statesman, Ltd. Reproduced by permission.—*New York Review of Books*, December 4, 1986; August 17, 1989; January 13, 1994. Copyright © 1986, 1989, 1994 by NYREV, Inc. All reproduced with permission from The New York Review of Books.—*Novel*, v. 30, fall, 1996. Copyright NOVEL Corp. © 1996. Reproduced with permission.—*Political Theory*, v. 27, June 1999; v. 29, October 2001. Copyright © 1999, 2001 by Sage Publications, Inc. Reproduced by permission of Sage Publications, Inc.—*Publishers Weekly*, March 21, 1994; v. 250, November 3, 2003. Copyright © 1994, 2003 by Reed Publishing USA.. Reproduced from Publishers Weekly, published by the Bowker Magazine Group of Cahners Publishing Co., a division of Reed Publishing USA., by permission.—*Review of Contemporary Fiction*, v. 11, fall, 1991; v. 14, summer, 1994; v. 18, spring, 1998; fall, 2000. Copyright © 1991, 1994, 1998, 2000 *The Review of Contemporary Fiction*. All reproduced by permission.—*Social Theory and Practice*, v. 25, summer, 1999 for a review of "Sex and Social Justice" by Gardner Fair; v. 28, July 2002 for "Political Morality and Culture: What Difference Do Differences Make?" by Monique Deveaux. Copyright © 1999, 2002 by Social Theory and Practice. Both reproduced by permission of the publisher and the respective authors.—*The Spectator*, v. 271, October 30, 1993; v. 273, August 27, 1994; v. 275, September 9, 1995; v. 278, April 19, 1997; v. 284, April 1, 2000; v. 284, April 8, 2000. Copyright © 1993, 1994, 1995, 1997, 2000 by *The Spectator*. Reproduced by permission of *The Spectator*.—*Theater*, v. 29, 1999. Copyright, 1999, Yale School of Drama/Yale repertory Theatre. All rights reserved. Used by permission of the publisher.—*Theatre Journal*, v. 47, May 1, 1995; v. 48, March 1996; v. 55, March 2003. Copyright © 1995, 1996, 2003, University and College Theatre Association of the American Theatre Association. Reproduced by permission of The Johns Hopkins University Press.—*Tikkun*, v. 10, May-June, 1995. Copyright © 1995 Institute for Labor and Mental Health. Reproduced by permission of *Tikkun: A Bimonthly Jewish Critique of Politics, Culture & Society.*—*Times Literary Supplement*, July 4, 1986; May 27, 1994; April 25, 1997; June 23, 2000; October 27, 2000; May 31, 2002; June 7, 2002. Copyright © 1986, 1994, 1997, 2000, 2002 by The Times Supplements Limited. Reproduced from The Times Literary Supplement by permission.—*The Washington Post Book World*, November 25, 1990 for "The Heart Has Its Reasons" by Bernard Knox; May 4, 1997 for "Tea and Empathy" by Benito Rakower. Copyright © 1990, 1997 Washington Post Book World Service/Washington Post Writers Group. Both reproduced by permission of the respective authors.—*World Literature Today*, v. 72, autumn, 1998; v. 77, April-June, 2003. Copyright © 1998, 2003 by *World Literature Today*. Both reproduced by permission of the publisher.—*Yale Journal of Criticism*, v. 16, spring, 2003. Copyright © 2003 The Johns Hopkins University Press. Reproduced by permission.—*The Yearbook of English Studies*, v. 31, 2001. Copyright © Modern Humanities Research Association 2001. Reproduced by permission of the publisher.

COPYRIGHTED MATERIAL IN *CLC*, VOLUME 203, WAS REPRODUCED FROM THE FOLLOWING BOOKS:

Fisher, James. From "Introduction: The Feathers and the Mirrors and the Smoke," in *The Theater of Tony Kushner: Living Past Hope*. Routledge, 2002. Copyright © 2001 by Routledge. All rights reserved. Reproduced by permission of Routledge/Taylor & Francis Books, Inc., and the author.—Frantzen, Allen J. From *Before the Closet: Same-Sex Love from 'Beowulf' to 'Angels in America'*. University of Chicago Press, 1998. Copyright © 1998 by The University of Chicago. All rights reserved. Reproduced by permission.—Kruger, Steven F. From *Approaching the Millennium: Essays on 'Angels in America'*. University of Michigan Press, 1997. Copyright © 1997 by the University of Michigan. All rights reserved. Reproduced by permission.

PHOTOGRAPHS AND ILLUSTRATIONS APPEARING IN *CLC*, VOLUME 203, WERE RECEIVED FROM THE FOLLOWING SOURCES:

De Botton, Alain, photograph. David Levenson/Getty Images.—Kushner, Tony, photograph. AP/Wide World Photos.— Nussbaum, Martha C., photograph. Copyright © Jerry Bauer.

Thomson Gale Literature Product Advisory Board

The members of the Thomson Gale Literature Product Advisory Board—reference librarians from public and academic library systems—represent a cross-section of our customer base and offer a variety of informed perspectives on both the presentation and content of our literature products. Advisory board members assess and define such quality issues as the relevance, currency, and usefulness of the author coverage, critical content, and literary topics included in our series; evaluate the layout, presentation, and general quality of our printed volumes; provide feedback on the criteria used for selecting authors and topics covered in our series; provide suggestions for potential enhancements to our series; identify any gaps in our coverage of authors or literary topics, recommending authors or topics for inclusion; analyze the appropriateness of our content and presentation for various user audiences, such as high school students, undergraduates, graduate students, librarians, and educators; and offer feedback on any proposed changes/enhancements to our series. We wish to thank the following advisors for their advice throughout the year.

Dennis Cooper
1953-

American novelist, poet, short story writer, playwright, and editor.

The following entry presents an overview of Cooper's career through 2002.

INTRODUCTION

Cooper has earned cult status and critical distinction for his deeply disturbing fiction, which explores the furthest limits of morality and desire through graphic descriptions of sadism, necrophilia, and ritualized abuse in the homosexual underworld. Drawing upon the dehumanizing violence of horror films and hardcore pornography, Cooper's writing revolves largely around extreme acts of sexual assault, pedophilia, physical degradation, and gratuitous murder. His protagonists—disaffected gay adolescents, drug addicts, and predatory pedophiles and pederasts—are motivated by destructive sexual obsessions or shocking passivity that underscores the impossibility of intersubjective understanding, self-knowledge, or transcendence. In the tradition of the Marquis de Sade, Jean Genet, and William S. Burroughs, and influenced by a nihilistic punk-rock aesthetic, Cooper's fiction chronicles the various horrors, mutilations, and indignities that the physical body may suffer in the vain pursuit of truth and meaning. Though beginning his career as a poet, Cooper is best known for his loosely connected quintet of novels, *Closer* (1989), *Frisk* (1991), *Try* (1994), *Guide* (1997), and *Period* (2000).

BIOGRAPHICAL INFORMATION

Cooper was born in Pasadena, California, and grew up in nearby Arcadia, California. His father, Clifford Cooper, was a wealthy entrepreneur who owned a company that built missiles for NASA. Cooper's parents were friends with Richard and Pat Nixon, who visited often when Cooper was a teenager. Family life in the Cooper home was traumatic, however, and the protracted divorce of his parents impacted Cooper significantly. From an early age, he often stayed with friends to avoid the difficult atmosphere within his own home. During grade school Cooper met George Miles, an unstable boy whom Cooper befriended and served as a caretaker; Miles, who committed suicide in 1987, would become the inspiration for Cooper's quintet of novels.

After eighth grade, Cooper transferred from public school to a boys' school. He was expelled from Flintridge Preparatory School in eleventh grade for his poor academic record. Cooper, however, has attributed his dismissal to his drug use and open homosexuality. At age fifteen, Cooper discovered de Sade's *The 120 Days of Sodom,* a book whose subversive subject matter resonated with him. In addition to de Sade, Cooper became fascinated with other writers such as Genet, Burroughs, Charles Baudelaire, and Andre Gide, all of whom have shaped his work. Cooper attended Pasadena City College and later Pitzer College in Claremont, California, where a poetry teacher encouraged him to continue writing. Cooper began writing during the mid-1970s and published poems in several gay literary magazines. Finding the hippie movement unappealing, Cooper immersed himself in the burgeoning punk scene and moved to England in 1976. He also became interested in the avant-garde films of French director Robert Bresson. Upon Cooper's return to the West Coast, he established *Little Caesar,* an underground fanzine that embraced the spirit of punk art, literature, and music. The magazine's success enabled him to found Little Caesar Press in 1978, which featured the work of alternative artists such as Brad Gooch, Amy Gerstler, Elaine Equi, Tim Dlugos, and Eileen Myles. He soon published his first volume of poetry, *Tiger Beat* (1978), and, during the same year, became director of programming at Beyond Baroque, an alternative poetry project in Venice, California. His poetry collection *The Tenderness of the Wolves* (1981) was nominated for the *Los Angeles Times* poetry prize. Cooper moved to New York City in 1984 and, in 1987, followed a Dutch boyfriend to Amsterdam, where, while attending to his own drug addiction, he matured as a writer and developed work in various forms, including his first novel, *Closer.* After returning to New York, Cooper wrote *Frisk,* a novel that attracted notoriety and death threats from a gay-rights group for its unflattering portrayal of its gay characters. *Frisk* was adapted into a film by director Todd Verow in 1995. Cooper has worked as an art critic for *Art Forum* and *Art Scribe* and has also contributed articles to the *Village Voice* and *Spin* magazine.

MAJOR WORKS

Cooper arrived on the punk literary scene as a poet with *Tiger Beat* and *Idols* (1979), which focused on Cooper's obsession with boys he knew in his youth. He also published *The Tenderness of the Wolves,* a collection that included the notable short story "A Herd," which describes the homosexual rape, mutilation, and murder of teenaged boys by a calculating psychopath, thus establishing a dark and recurring theme in Cooper's fiction. Cooper's works are typically filled with characters—usually attractive, angst-ridden gay teens—who are so emotionally stunted that ordinary relationships cannot overcome their stultifying boredom and sense of isolation. Only violence, death, and dismemberment—discovering what is actually inside the body—can connect these characters in any real sense to fellow humans. To convey this perspective, Cooper's prose is decidedly spare, fragmentary, elliptical, and infused with the banal colloquialisms and shallow observations of drugged and disenchanted adolescents. It is set largely in the urban milieu of Los Angeles and against the backdrop of punk music and bohemian youth culture, and adults, except for pedophiles, are pointedly absent.

Closer revolves around the relationships of several teenaged boys, principally David, a narcissist with rock-idol aspirations and a profound disdain for human flesh, and George, a drugged and dangerously submissive aficionado of Disneyland. George is eventually enticed into a relationship with a Frenchman, Philippe, who, along with another psychotic friend, Tom, enact their fantasy of sedating and dissecting an attractive young boy. In *Frisk* Dennis is haunted by the pornographic "snuff" photographs of a mutilated boy (later revealed to have been an elaborate fake) that he viewed as a young teenager. Obsessed with fantasies of murdering and disemboweling one of his young male sex partners, Dennis travels to Amsterdam, where he records the details of his heinous—albeit imaginary—serial murders in letters sent home. *Try,* the third novel in the series, revolves around Ziggy, a confused, drug-abusing teenager who is sexually brutalized by his two gay foster fathers. Seeking to cope with his molestation, Ziggy befriends—and is rebuffed by—Calhoun, a straight heroin addict who hates all emotion. Attempting to cope in other ways, Ziggy turns to publishing a magazine, *I Apologize,* for sex abuse victims. Though Ziggy is portrayed more sympathetically than characters in Cooper's previous fiction, redemption is not a possibility, the innocent and defenseless—including the freshly deceased—are callously sodomized, and Ziggy's pathetic search for genuine affection, culminating in consensual sex with one of his fathers, goes unrewarded. The narrator of *Guide* is Dennis, a self-conscious projection of Dennis Cooper the author, and the narrative is a loose amalgam of real-time observations and recollections dealing with rough sex, drugs, pornography, and alternative music—all staples of Cooper's fiction. The novel is nominally concerned with Dennis's infatuation with two younger men, Chris and Luke, and is peopled by the author's circle of wayward acquaintan-

ces—teenaged hustlers, addicts, and pornographers—as well as thinly disguised appearances by actual members of British bands Blur and Silverchair, one of whom is drugged and raped. *Period,* the final installment in the five-book series, involves Nate and Leon, two teens who have made a pact with the devil in order to fulfill Leon's fantasy of raping a deaf-mute boy. Nate later travels with a satanic Goth band, The Omen, that roams about in a van, picking up and murdering runaway boys. The narrative is further complicated by various doppel-gängers and a parallel story involving Outsider artist Bob and author Walker Crane, who has written a cult book, called *Period,* a tribute to his dead lover, George.

In *My Loose Thread* (2002), Cooper returns to the bleak landscape of damaged high school boys in urban California. The narrator, a dazed teenager named Larry, engages in an incestuous relationship with his younger brother and becomes involved with a group of mercenary Neo-Nazi classmates who plot to kill another student and steal his diary. The story concludes with an episode of anarchic violence reminiscent of the Columbine High School shootings. Cooper has also published *Wrong* (1992), a volume of previously published short stories and sketches, including "A Herd," *He Cried* (1984), and the novella *Safe* (1984); this collection also includes Cooper's oft-quoted remark, "AIDS ruined death," by which he suggests that the real-life disease nullified death as an aesthetic or romanticized statement. He served as editor of *Discontents* (1992), an anthology of experimental short fiction by gay writers, and has collaborated with artists on several works: *Jerk* (1992), a mock children's book featuring Cooper's trademark motifs and photographs of puppet displays by conceptual artist Nayland Blake; and *Horror Hospital Unplugged* (1996), a parody of a rising rock star named Trevor Machine and Los Angeles-based popular culture, illustrated with surreal drawings by Keith Mayerson. Cooper has also written two plays, *The Undead* (1989) and *Knife/Tape/Rope* (1989). *The Dream Police* (1994) is a collection of Cooper's erotic verse from previous volumes of poetry, along with ten new poems.

CRITICAL RECEPTION

While Cooper's harrowing fiction has, not surprisingly, failed to gain a mass readership, he has attracted a cult following and consistently respectful reviews. His work is favorably compared to that of de Sade, Genet, and Burroughs, and even critics who find his subject matter unpalatable concede that Cooper manages to probe the darkest recesses of the human psyche with unflinching artistry and purpose. Cooper's work has drawn inevitable comparison to Bret Easton Ellis's *American Psycho,* which describes the gratuitous serial murders committed by an affluent white male. However, most critics are quick to note the superiority of Cooper's fiction, which derives from the author's frightening powers of imagination and distinct, claustrophobic prose. His five-novel series, concluding with *Period,* was hailed as a major achievement by reviewers, who praised Cooper's audacity and uncompromising commitment to the subversive literary project that he set for himself. Though marginalized as an avant-garde gay writer, many critics insist that Cooper's concern with gay relationships and deviant homosexual couplings—albeit central to his work—belies a greater interest in the problem of human alienation and the fundamental inadequacy of language. Furthermore, despite the depravity and ruthlessness of his characters, many critics discern an underlying morality in Cooper's work that, though repeatedly refuted and undermined by ever-greater acts of inhumanity, is revealed in the genuine desire for pure feeling, perfection, and transcendence repeatedly expressed by Cooper's protagonists. Nevertheless, Cooper's detractors maintain that his explorations of such abhorrent subjects—notably pedophilia, necrophilia, and coprophilia—offer little redeeming merit, even in the service of art. Moreover, the difficulty of separating Cooper from his fictional creations, a problem that arises from Cooper's semi-autobiographic appearances in his novels and his casual, matter-of-fact descriptions of the most malignant acts, have caused some critics to question Cooper's authorial distance and, consequently, his moral position. Though few would dispute that his work is shocking and often repugnant, it is in such extremity that Cooper has challenged the limits of artistic expression and established a voice and aesthetic uniquely his own.

PRINCIPAL WORKS

Tiger Beat (poetry) 1978

Idols (poetry) 1979

The Tenderness of the Wolves (poetry) 1981

He Cried (short stories) 1984

Safe (novella) 1984

Closer (novel) 1989

Knife/Tape/Rope (drama) 1989

The Undead (drama) 1989

Frisk (novel) 1991

Discontents: New Queer Writers [editor] (short stories) 1992

Jerk [illustrated by Nayland Blake] (novel) 1992

Wrong (short stories) 1992

The Dream Police: Selected Poems, 1969-1993 (poetry) 1994

Try (novel) 1994

Horror Hospital Unplugged: A Graphic Novel [illustrated by Keith Mayerson] (novel) 1996

Guide (novel) 1997

Period (novel) 2000

My Loose Thread (novel) 2002

CRITICISM

John Ash (review date 16 July 1989)

SOURCE: Ash, John. "The City of Lost Angels." *Los Angeles Times Book Review* (16 July 1989): 7.

[*In the following review, Ash acknowledges the pornographic and violent passages in* Closer, *but asserts that the work retains powerful and original writing.*]

Although I'm sure he'd cringe at the thought, Dennis Cooper's bleak and brilliant novel of gay teens in the affluent Los Angeles wastelands could be read as a cautionary tale concerning the advisability of stricter parental supervision. Parents, find out what your son is doing with his buddies in that locked bedroom! According to Cooper, sodomy and drug-abuse are the least of it, which is why—unlike *Less Than Zero*—**Closer** will never be made into a movie, even though there are terrific parts for Robert Downey Jr. and other bratpackers. But things are permitted in writing that could never be enacted for commercial cinema, and readers with a passing acquaintance with Sade, Burroughs or Genet will probably be able to get through Cooper's account of relentlessly mechanistic couplings, coprophilia, voyeurism, mutilation and near-murder without losing their lunches. His characters are not so lucky; they vomit frequently and copiously.

Bodily wastes and fluids are a key to the ruling obsession of **Closer**. Cooper's lost angels and the older men who prey on them are utterly unable to come to terms with the human body. They are obsessed with the thought of what its beautiful, "airbrushed" exterior might conceal. It is the fractured reiterations of this two-note theme that lend Cooper's prose its peculiar, poetic intensity.

John (would-be artist with punk affectations) is dating George, the novel's haplessly passive central character. John feels something "that could have been love but it was too manageable and kind of coldly interesting," and he is disturbed by the fact that, despite his "cuteness," George is "just skin wrapped around some grotesque-looking stuff." So much for the tender, romantic notions of the blank generation. David, who has paranoid fantasies of being an adored rock star (a kind of white, suburban Michael Jackson), worries that he's "just a bunch of blue tubes inside a skin wrapper."

The only thing these boys are sure of is that they look good. Their alienation enables them—via Cooper's astonishing prose—to see themselves with absolute clarity: "My body's short, thin, but healthy. It hangs from my shoulders like a clean leotard." David hates "the fact that human bodies are warm. I think they should be ice-cold or have no temperature whatsoever, like pieces of paper."

George, with his roomful of pathetic Disney souvenirs, and his inarticulate grief over his dying mother, is the link between all these characters. He seems to understand nothing other than the fact that men find him attractive, and in consequence will submit to anything, almost including his own murder. His older French lover, Philippe, fantasizes about beauty and death: "This particular fantasy nagged him. He'd stroll through streets, eat, bathe, weed his rose garden. And it would gather strength over his head, an insidious halo, as black as dried blood, glittering with the thunder of snapping bones." Philippe's psychopathic friend Tom plans the ultimate, ignorant investigation of the body, by opening it up and contemplating the entrails. Inevitably, *Closer*'s climactic image is the crushed body of a young man. The unspeakable mysteries of the interior are finally exposed and the result "looks like a flower bed." It is only at this point that someone belatedly calls out "Get help!" and the police arrive.

Edmund White has described this novel, in what may be a back-handed compliment, as being "as morally repugnant as it is esthetically seductive." In fact, it is completely in keeping with American puritan values. It is puritanism that has made the natural functions of the body an enigma and a problem, puritanism that has forced a break between consciousness and sensation, and these are Cooper's central themes.

Like most "serious" novels that make extensive use of pornographic materials, *Closer* implies a surprisingly conventional moral stance. We are left in no doubt as to what the wages of sin might be—one lost boy ends up paralyzed from the waist down, another is killed, while our bemused hero finds something resembling true love. He does so in the arms of Steve, the only character in the novel who is capable of taking effective action to protect himself and his friends. He is also the pampered child of rich parents, and an ambitious young entrepreneur. He could thus be regarded as a typical, successful product of the Reagan years. If this casts some doubt on Cooper's iconoclastic credentials, there can be no doubt about the power and originality of his writing. Sheer force of style raise *Closer* to the level of (at least) a minor classic.

Thomas R. Edwards (review date 17 August 1989)

SOURCE: Edwards, Thomas R. "Sad Young Men." *New York Review of Books* (17 August 1989): 52-3.

[*In the following review, Edwards presents a favorable review of* Closer.]

Dennis Cooper's **Closer** shows young lives not beginning but on the verge of ending in California, here conceived as "the end of the world" in a sense that *Moon Palace* [by Paul Auster] doesn't suggest. Cooper, whose purposes are anything but "regional," doesn't call it California, but the big roads are "freeways," and one of the characters has clearly spent more time at Disneyland than anyone probably should. The center of the action is a high school in a well-to-do suburb; all the main characters are homosexual; the time seems to be around 1980, since a teen-ager is reported remembering that. The Doors were a popular group when he was "a little boy," and AIDS seems unheard of.

Closer is a kind of homosexual *La Ronde,* following the interconnected couplings of six high-school boys and an older pederast. The novel seems meant to be, as it indeed is, shocking, at least for most readers, abundantly clinical in erotic details and unsparing in its portrayal of the depressing tone of a subculture. At sixteen, seventeen, eighteen, Cooper's youngsters are coolly and ruthlessly committed to fulfilling their desires, to which their ambiance offers unexpectedly little resistance. The few straight schoolmates who appear seem wholly tolerant and understanding of their friends' deviance; parents are determined to know as little as possible about their sons' private lives; the only teacher to make an appearance in the book is not just a fool but a drug user who is in the closet; explicit homosexual and sadomasochistic magazines and splatter and snuff movies are as readily accessible to the young men as *People* magazine or *Star Wars*; minors have no difficulty finding and being admitted to gay bars; and of course soft and hard drugs are everywhere. None of this may be surprising, bit by bit, but the bits are added up into a kind of sensual utopia where effort or regret is quite unknown, and I imagine that while some readers will be outraged by the book, some others will enjoy it as pornography.

This would be too bad, since Cooper's intentions appear to be more interesting and honorable. *Closer,* I think, is intended to be a story about the imagination under the direst kind of pressure, about how desire can persist to the brink of self-destruction and beyond. Certainly all these sad young men have some creative interests. John draws, David fantasizes that he's a rock star, George, who keeps LSD in a Mickey Mouse hat and wishes he lived in Disneyland, describes his perplexities in a diary, Cliff is a photographer and Alex a would-be filmmaker, and Steve, more a managerial type, contrives an elaborate disco in his parents four-car garage. None of them may have serious talent, but their dreams of creativity, like their devotion to sex and drugs and general nonconformity, seem to reach toward some better life that indifferent families, "youth culture," or the predatory world of adult pedophilia can't give them.

But beyond the unpleasantness of their surroundings waits something even worse. "I'm only sincere when I forget who I am," the nearly insane David reflects, and his illusion that he's a "gorgeous" rock idol embodies a despair about the self that the others feel only somewhat less extremely. "Everything but good looks should be pointless," thinks Alex, the film student, and their obsession with being physically attractive, or possessing others who are, moves the book in two directions at once.

One direction, an obvious one, is toward comment on the general culture, where the dream of perfection in the body afflicts not only young people of every sexual persuasion, whose uncertainty about their ability and worth at least gives them some excuse, but also a remarkable number of their elders, who really ought to know better. The other is toward a psychic pathology in which death is the mother of beauty in a sense Wallace Stevens may not have meant. The book's main adult figure, Philippe, once joined a club of men who "wanted to kill someone cute during sex," and both Philippe the alcoholic coprophiliac and his alarming friend Tom, who's bent on mutilating and killing his partners while observing the punctilio that they must consent, clearly associate desire with the destruction of its object. The body, the seat of "cuteness," is also the seat of primal self-disgust, and such a sexuality, as Sade told us, aims at transcending not only the sexual act but everything else as well. But then, in a world where all is possible and no conceivable sensation goes unfelt, literal death may be no more than a closing formality anyway. "Kill me, I can't feel anything," one of the characters begs, and the logic of his request has been made clear.

Closer is a noncommittal, rigorously descriptive, un-moralizing book, painful or even emetic in effect. But it seems an attempt to face squarely what Cooper sees as the implications of homosexuality's darkest corners. If this is so, it is a work of considerable courage.

Michael Silverblatt (review date 30 June 1991)

SOURCE: Silverblatt, Michael. "Tales from the Crypt." *Los Angeles Times Book Review* (30 June 1991): 2, 11.

[*In the following review, Silverblatt offers a positive assessment of* Frisk.]

To frisk is to "search a person for something concealed, especially a weapon," *Frisk* is about a man who wants

to kill someone and find what the body conceals. Spiritually, the thing that remains of the body after death is the soul. Physically, the thing that remains is only splatter.

The narrator of Dennis Cooper's novel *Frisk* also is named Dennis; whether he represents the author remains a question. The narrator seems to be interested in carnage; Dennis Cooper himself seems engaged in a search for the soul.

The narrator is fascinated with sex and death. As a child, he has seen some pornographic photographs of a murdered boy. The photographs turn out to be elaborately faked, but Dennis, hooked, becomes fascinated by the idea of killing. The images of death thrown up by punk rock, by horror and splatter films, by Stephen King novels, stake their claim on him. The line between art and life becomes blurred.

Frisk is ultimately a coming-of-age novel about a young man learning the difference between representation and reality, between pornography and art. Dennis chooses representation over reality; that is to say he becomes an artist rather than a killer, but the art he chooses, is dark and horrific.

The book's vantage point is entirely homosexual. The safe world is left behind, leaving a cast of pornographers, hustlers, drug users and sex addicts. The world displayed is unhealthy in the extreme. Nevertheless, the book is the work of a real writer, classical and aesthetic. The issues raised are moral and spiritual, the treatment austere, rigorous and contemporary. *Frisk* is an art novel but with the voltage and luridness of the most degraded thriller. It is a portrait of the artist in a world that has outgrown "nice" art.

Gertrude Stein has interesting things to say on the ugliness of the destined classic: "When it is still a thing irritating annoying stimulating then all quality of beauty is denied to it. . . . If every one were not so indolent they would realize that beauty is beauty even when it is irritating and stimulating, not only when it is accepted and classic."

Stein also says, "The creator of the new composition in the arts is an outlaw until he is a classic." *Frisk* certainly lays claim to being the work of an outlaw; that it is destined to classic status is upheld by its extraordinary vileness, the psychotic imagination of its violence and its bracing ugliness. Unlike some recent "transgressive" fiction, which we grow inured to but we don't really enjoy or admire, *Frisk* exhilarates by the intensity of its language, and by the suggestion of a spiritual radiance at the core of its dark vision.

Many may ask, Why dignify with the word *classic* a work that willfully betrays civilized values? Why is the high level of disgust this work causes worthy of so elevated a claim?

This is an odd question that has recently re-raised its conservative head: Why this emphasis on the ugly and the inhuman? One hesitates to answer the question this late in the day, after we have heard the answer again and again in reference to Flannery O'Connor's deformities or Beckett's cripples. It isn't enough to say, "The world is mean, and man uncouth." But more likely the case is that in extremity the artist finds the clarity to define his vision of the world. By clearing the page of the clutter of acceptable pieties and garden-variety realism, the artist is freed to discover moral and aesthetic connections. The artist need not beautify the world, he may do service by bringing purity and order to its ugliness.

The first and decisive test is the quality and originality of *Frisk*'s language. Yes, it is extremely profane, foul even, so foul that it cannot be quoted at any length in a publication such as this, but its structure and syntax reveal a real ear for what speech has become and a poet's ear for the elegance of modern cadence. The book is about the process of taking forbidden materials and transforming them into art.

Cooper's language lurches about, simulating now the jerky intensity of a hand-held camera in an after-hours club, now the startling disorientation of a jump-cut, representing a lapse of consciousness or the momentary aphasia of a drug-induced blackout. This is the syntax of discontinuous contemporary consciousness; any one who has ever taken a mind-clouding chemical has felt physically the stammer and slash of these madhouse sentences. The disfiguring buzz of *ums* and *uhs* and verbal hesitations, the sentences that just stop because the speaker cannot remember what it was that he was saying, the blur of obscenities, slurred and half-meant; these are the daily banalities of language that Cooper converts into the austere rhythms that shape and distort his English.

It's a commonplace to complain about the inarticulateness, not to say illiteracy, of the current generation of Americans. Cooper turns these excrescences to aesthetic purpose, making an art form out of what is available to him: in this case, the "dead" language of people who claim to be aesthetes of the spirit while engaging in anonymous sex. These connoisseurs interrogate the body, finding the odor of the armpit "too blatant." "Crotch, overrated. Mouth, profound." They sample the body's secretions, verging on cannibalism. The body is being asked to speak, but it is not being asked to use words.

As Dennis begins to recognize the slightly stuporous, dark-haired boy who is his "type," the reader begins the descent into the mind of the serial killer. Bodies become clues, valued for the secrets they have locked inside. Dennis loses track of his actual behavior, telling himself

he's "perfecting his feelings," "dissecting their physical perfection." We witness, awed, the ongoing process of alienation from the physical world. Intimacy, physical and emotional, is replaced by a bizarre quest for ultimate knowledge, a knowledge that can only be satisfied when the body has been torn open and frisked.

Dennis, like the adult admirer of teen idols or the obsessive who fixates on porn stars, is unlikely to address the object of his desire—the result is an elaborate fantasy life that fastens upon the body. The body necessarily has no connection to personality or mind. No wonder Dennis examines orifices looking for "information"— smells, textures, tastes. The body's secretions substitute for language; revulsion and attraction substitute for emotional exchange. When Dennis begins to buy hustlers and talk to them about death and the secrets their bodies hold, the reader is held in the twin grip of repulsion and fascination. The fascination is more interesting than the repulsion, because Cooper manages to subordinate the descent into terror to the quest of the holy.

Slowly, the strategy of the book becomes clear. The faked snuff photos of the opening provide the key. It will calm no one's nerves to say so, but there is no actual murderer in *Frisk*. Just as the pornographer simulates a victim, using dyed cotton to manufacture a vicious-looking wound, Dennis Cooper has simulated a killer, effectively using the language of sexual compulsion to draw us in.

This is not a book that leaves one with the feeling of ease or edification. Dennis the killer mutilates the bodies of his victims, leaving only a mess behind. Dennis Cooper, a disturbing and transcendent artist, enters the mind of a killer and comes out with a genuine revelation.

David Kaufman (review date 1 July 1991)

SOURCE: Kaufman, David. "All in the Family." *Nation* (1 July 1991): 21-5.

[*In the following review, Kaufman provides a generally favorable review of* Frisk, *finding both merit and dissatisfaction in the novel's experimental approach.*]

The very ambition to categorize so-called gay literature may be something of a self-defeating proposition: By reflecting the larger world, certainly the better examples of the "genre" transcend any categorical limitations we might infer. To insist otherwise would be to reject the assimilation captured so well in a number of new novels, and to hazard stereotypes that they deny.

This emerges as an inescapable message now that the world of commercial publishing is embracing a range of gay male novelists who refuse to depict the world according to an outmoded dualistic convention of "gay" and "straight" (as if it ever really were that) but rather as a more varied whole, the better to describe the ways in which people lead their lives, regardless of sexual orientation. In this light, what tends to be most remarkable about the fiction of David Leavitt, Paul Monette and even newer comers such as John Weir and Michael Cunningham is how unremarkable their gay characters are. These authors demonstrate that, to pervert the cliché, fiction has always been straighter than truth. (The primary exception in mainstream publishing was to allow for gay coming-of-age novels. But in comparison with the concerns of the new generation, consider how quickly even so fine an example as Edmund White's *A Boy's Own Story* has acquired an Uncle Tomish aura.)

Whether relieved by gallows humor or in relentlessly somber prose, AIDS is of course also a ubiquitous presence in today's fiction, where it has arrived with the same vehemence it has in our lives. Even Alice Hoffman had to get in on the act with *At Risk,* an exploitative and mawkish, summer-breezy novel about an 11-year-old girl ("from a perfectly average middle-class family," as Caryn James wrote in a related profile on Hoffman for *The New York Times*) who contracted AIDS from a blood transfusion. By now it is a truism that, along with playwrights, novelists are keeping pace with the evolution of the virus and its social ramifications in ways that Hollywood and television have been avoiding like the proverbial plague it is.

The less obvious but more intriguing point is that the twin *leitmotifs* of assimilation and AIDS are related: The real common denominator, whether the virus is treated explicitly or not, is a coming to terms with lost possibilities, a better understanding of the life that was or might have been, in order to get the most out of the one that remains. This is true not only of so-called AIDS novels such as Weir's *The Irreversible Decline of Eddie Socket,* Monette's *Afterlife* and *Halfway Home,* and David B. Feinberg's *Eighty-Sixed* but also of Ken Siman's *Pizza Face,* set in the 1970s, before AIDS was recognized, and novels such as Cunningham's *A Home at the End of the World,* which treats AIDS peripherally. Deliberately or not, Cunningham's novel and *Halfway Home* are part of a literary movement that testifies that nothing less than a new definition of the American family is in order, one that is more dynamic and capacious, more cognizant of the extended possibilities that have already permeated the society.

Although novels invested in eliminating long-held barriers between gay and straight were earlier apparent in fiction from small presses, only recently have they secured the support of commercial publishers. A turning point in literature was marked less than a decade ago by David Leavitt, with his first collection of short stories, *Family Dancing,* and his first novel, *The Lost*

Language of Cranes, neither of which dealt with AIDS per se. (Nor, surprisingly, did Leavitt's second novel, *Equal Affections,* published in 1989, although his more recent story anthology, *A Place I've Never Been,* does to some extent.) But while Leavitt clearly emerges as a pivotal figure for a legion of writers with visions of an increasingly homogenized world, he also asks the question, At what price, penetration? Though he was seized as a gay writer to be reckoned with by the straight literary aristocracy early in his still-young career, the signs already indicate that Leavitt, in the way of most pioneers, may be sacrificed to the unavoidable concessions he made: In Leavitt's fiction, one still finds an opposition between gay and straight sensibilities, perpetuating the clash by default; this begins to explain why some militants consider Leavitt to be more "straight" than "gay."

It is rather in the post-Leavitt landscape that the status has become even more difficult to define, the quo harder to locate—exactly the development worth celebrating. Phrased another way, it's the difference between a gay character and a character who happens to be gay, which is a lot less subtle a distinction than it may at first appear. And although Leavitt was welcomed specifically for making that leap, his mission has thus far been too self-conscious to achieve the results of some of his disciples, most notably Michael Cunningham. . . .

Though *Halfway Home* revolves around AIDS, which figures only as a hovering presence (and then, only in the later part) in *A Home at the End of the World,* it would appear to be a vacant topic in Dennis Cooper's latest novel, *Frisk.* But vacancy is a key to any appreciation of *Frisk.* And even though Cooper's notorious obsession with a connection between sex and death precedes AIDS (as Cooper himself has written elsewhere, "AIDS ruined death"), sooner or later it brings to mind grimmer aspects of an epidemic that has been permitted to flourish for too long.

Considering its arrival in the wake of the vacuous *American Psycho,* there will probably be a temptation to dismiss *Frisk* as imitatively sensationalistic. Unquestionably, it is equally grotesque and disturbing to read. But if Bret Easton Ellis's irredeemably disgusting claptrap has become merely the latest rallying point for a rebellion against its type of content, it would be a shame to lose sight of Cooper's more meaningful accomplishment. It is a far more worthwhile literary exercise, even as it brings to mind much earlier literary curiosities and ventures into gay sadomasochism—such as Alfred Chester's *The Exquisite Corpse,* and *The Story of Harold,* which was published under the pseudonym Terry Andrews and prompted wild speculation as to who the author really was.

Cooper has never enjoyed Ellis's popularity or success (nor will he, in view of his propensity for subversive literary experimentation and his eschewal of standard narrative formats), but he has been forging his de Sade-like investigations since the 1970s and was writing about psychosexual serial murders at least by 1982, when *Tenderness of the Wolves* was published. In *Frisk,* Cooper achieves precisely the virtues that Ellis apparently sought in *American Psycho.*

Frisk is unequivocally concerned with what happens after you've "stopped feeling anything," what remains on the other side of excess, the emptiness that needs to be filled. Or as another character says, "You can get used to anything. Then you stop feeling, you just respond, your brain reduces the world to . . . whatever."

On its most forthright level, the story traces the path of a first-person narrator who happened upon some pornographic photos as an adolescent that "went on to completely direct or destroy my life in a way." We follow him as he moves from Los Angeles through New York and finally to Amsterdam, into ever creepier recesses of his own sick mind. He becomes "totally removed from almost everyone," investing all of his energies in an intense, suppressed "interest in sexual death."

Along the way, he meets various hustlers and punks who, via the deadening effects of drugs, become passive accomplices to his heinous acts. "My perfect type," says the narrator, named Dennis no less, "tends to be distant, like me. I don't mean matter-of-fact, I mean shut tight. Like he's protecting himself from other people or pain or both by excising himself from the world in every way, apart from the obvious physical stuff you need to get by such as walk, talk, eat, etc."

Cooper is indeed matter-of-fact, and it is precisely the chilling effect of his deadpan tone, his relentless objectivity, that captures our attention and retains it through the extensive pornographic passages. The sex itself somehow becomes incidental to the pathology that motivates it. His obsession inevitably leads to episodes of repugnant murders, described in grisly detail that seems designed to stretch human comprehension.

After his first of a series of murders, Dennis reflects, "I guess I'd fantasized killing a boy for so long that all the truth did was fill in details. The feeling was already planned and decided for ten years at least." In Amsterdam, he hooks up with two German thugs who periodically accompany him to the windmill he lives in, where the unspeakable acts are committed. "They're as fucked up as I am, just not as intelligent. They kill guys because it's a kick, whereas for me it's religious or something."

Throughout the narrative, Dennis refers to his intention of better understanding his obsession by writing a book about his fantasies, which obviously becomes the one

we're reading. Though in the end, the murders are exposed as fabrications, S&M tales within S&M tales, Cooper has made his point just the same: The effect of reading *Frisk* is to make us impervious to our own disgust at a profusion of violence, possibly mimicking our long-term response to TV and the daily news.

Perhaps the most telling and truly autobiographical passage is one that indirectly alludes to AIDS:

> I just realized the major reason I'm so nonchalant about death is that no one I knew ever died until the last few years, when I was already pretty removed and amoral. Before then, someone else dying was strictly a sexual fantasy, a plot device in certain movies I liked. When people died in those contexts, the loss or effect or whatever was already laundered before it reached me. It was a loss to a particular storyline, say, but nothing personal. So now that ex-boyfriends have started to die off, the situation is really unique, even incomprehensible. The only thing I can do, friends and journalists tell me, is cry. But the idea of death is so sexy and/or mediated by TV and movies I couldn't cry now if someone paid me to, I don't think.

What is *Frisk,* finally, if not an indictment of a generation left to drown in a flood of images? As Bataille once wrote regarding his notion that literature is evil, "This concept does not exclude morality: on the contrary, it demands a 'hypermorality.'" But while Cooper is most intriguing for the heavy dose of morality he divulges through his perfectly amoral or numb tone, *Frisk* remains less than satisfying as a novel, which may be unavoidable for an author who repeatedly sets out to mock the novel as a form.

Though the world that Cooper portrays is exclusively gay, *Frisk* still subscribes to the current batch of novels that document coming of age in the past few decades—its chapter titles are dated, 1969-89.

Indeed, AIDS has not only eclipsed but also intensified the process of this thing we call life, for an entire generation of writers old before their time. It is a matter of supreme irony that gays should be coming to life in such numbers on the page, assimilated into mainstream publishing, just as we are dying in such numbers on the street.

Jack Byrne (review date fall 1991)

SOURCE: Byrne, Jack. Review of *Frisk,* by Dennis Cooper. *Review of Contemporary Fiction* 11, no. 3 (fall 1991): 280.

[*In the following review, Byrne discusses the perverse themes and obsessions in* Frisk.]

"When Dennis is thirteen, he sees a series of photographs of a boy apparently unimaginably mutilated. Dennis is not shocked, but stunned by their mystery and their power; their glimpse at the reality of death. Some years later, Dennis meets the boy who posed for the photographs. He did it for love" (jacket). *Frisk* is about what happens between Dennis's first look at such "snuff" shots and his last look at the reality behind the "snuff" and things created for the boys in the back room: "The wound is actually a glop of paint, ink, makeup, tape, cotton, tissue, and papier-mâché sculpted to suggest the inside of a human body." Is murder the ultimate experience? Dennis Cooper goes beyond the question; he asks "What is it to touch skin, smell it, taste the body's secretions? This is not possession. The lungs, the intestines, the brain: to hold them in bloodied hands—that is it. What is it to murder a trick, a punk, a yuppie, a boy?" Cooper's narrator, also called Dennis, wrestles with this problem throughout the novel, hoping to exorcise the overwhelming desire to experience firsthand the murder of a certain type of victim: "Over the years I've decided or figured out that there's a strain of the human race I'm uncontrollably drawn to. Male, younger, lean, pale, dark-haired, full-lipped, dazed looking." Clearly, for Dennis, this is the prelude to incipient necrophilia accompanied by latent homosexuality, and a growing interest in the usual laundry list of the pervert's dream of Turkish delights—"three ways, rimming, and drugs," s & m, booze, mescaline, massage parlors, hardcore and soft-core sex magazines, porn videos, splatter films, marijuana, hash, crack, *Tie Me Up! Tie Me Down,* buckle me with belts, belt me with buckles, all leading to the fantasy of fantasies, murder, dramatized in recent years as snuff movies, those little-seen attempts to market the ultimate horror—the "murder" of helpless victims to satisfy some of those who live for the love that dare not speak its name, in Wilde's phrase, many of whom "see homosexuality as a journey with stages—beginning with humiliation and ostracism, proceeding to glamour and sprezzatura and (after the boyfriends), either seeking a sort of domesticity or rotting in lechery." *Frisk* is about the lechery of the mind, the obsession with murder and death acted out in fantasy and bordering on the possibility of actually murdering the victim, ending with the ultimate snuffing out of life. Poor Dennis's apologia of sorts comes when he pouts, "Maybe . . . if I hadn't seen this . . . snuff. Photographs. Back when I was a kid. I thought the boy in them was actually dead for years, and by the time I found out they were posed photographs, it was too late. I already wanted to live in a world where some boy I didn't personally know could be killed and his corpse made available to the public, or to me anyway. I felt so . . . enlightened?" We should remember that in this fantasy world a real snuff film is like the abominable snowman—we have yet to see a real yeti!

David Van Leer (review date 12 October 1992)

SOURCE: Van Leer, David. "Beyond the Margins." *New Republic* (12 October 1992): 50-3.

[*In the following review, Van Leer discusses the problematic categorization of gay literature and offers a tempered review of* Discontents, *which he praises for its subversive angle but criticizes for its inclusion of banal experimentalism.*]

Homosexuality in literature takes many forms. A teacher suspects his motives for wishing to separate a pupil from his parents. A black American sees his affection for a bisexual African as a kind of economic exploitation. A transvestite dishes the writer Brett Easton Ellis and teases the nipples of the rock star Adam Horovitz. The diversity of these stories might lead some to wonder whether there is such a thing as "gay literature." Indeed, the meaning of the category is the subject of a vigorous if implicit debate in the new anthologies promoting gay fiction. (In recent years the anthology has become the preferred method for introducing gay literature to a wider readership. Publishers want to demonstrate the variety of gay writing, and to do it quickly before more of the writers fall to AIDS.) Despite their admirable motives, however, the new anthologists have found it harder to tie together such a diverse body of material. . . .

A more confrontational sense of the relation between sexuality and literature is offered in Dennis Cooper's ***Discontents: New Queer Writers.*** For Cooper, both sex and fiction are sites of political struggle. Recently some activists have begun to attack the '60s notion of homosexuality, objecting that the post-Stonewall liberation movement, in promoting a "gay sensibility," really addressed only the white middle-class males in the community. The most obvious sign of such prejudice was the hostility toward women and black men in the gay meccas of the Castro, West Hollywood, Greenwich Village, and Fire Island. Substituting the word "queer" for the tainted word "gay," the new activists dissociate themselves from what they decry as the racism and the sexism of "gay" culture, and from the nonconfrontational political tactics of the Gay Liberation movement.

It is in the general context of this furious debate between older liberal gays and younger radical queers that Cooper locates his authors. His collection stands as a "wake-up call" to traditional gay anthologies, with Cooper playing rebel leader to White's role of elder statesman. As with Queer Nation, the activist group most concerned with revolutionizing "gay" politics, the debate begins as one about minority representation. White's authors [in *The Faber Book of Gay Short Fiction*] are almost exclusively white middle-class urban males. Cooper's "queer" collection is more diverse. It includes work by women, and by men who are neither white, middle-class, nor on the Castro-Village circuit.

These differences concerning race and gender originate in a fundamental disagreement about literature. For Cooper, the true villain is not the elitism of White's stories but their aesthetics, their belief that fiction should realistically describe human emotions and situations. Rejecting the careful plotting and the elegant prose of the conventional short story, Cooper's fictions are self-consciously experimental—both "ultraliterary" and "postliterate." Few are concerned with character development, or with narrative. Many challenge the distinction between fiction and non-fiction by presenting themselves as whacked-out autobiography. Playlets and odd typography interrupt even the most straightforward narratives. "Alternative" cartoons are interspersed amidst the prose. And the whole is peppered with violence and vulgarity—sadomasochism, disembodiment, and excrement.

Such experiments can seem like just business as usual among the terminally hip. Writers like Dorothy Allison and Gary Indiana temper their vulgarities with poetic cadences. But many aspire so little to a high literary style that their works seem less postliterate than preliterate, less cutting edge than dull. At its best, what saves the indifferent prose from degenerating into verbal assault is its humor. The wittiest piece in Cooper's collection is "Myself Sexual," Vaginal Creme Davis's diatribe against L.A. trendoids, a camp monologue that is two-thirds drag review and one-third *Finnegans Wake*.

But the barbs strike deeper when they are directed inward. Halfway through the book, Canadians Johnny Noxzema, G. B. Jones, and Jena von Brucker meet for their "Naked Lunch," a trashing of everything about the gay punk scene from William Burroughs and trust fund performance artists to this book itself. The grumpy dialogue forgoes the high wit of the Algonquin for the low dish of the ladies who lunch. But whatever the conversation's strictly literary merit, it is admirable for refusing to dignify with high seriousness the supposedly solemn topics of coming-out and the "broad scope" of gay literature. Cooper's feisty collection offers a welcome antidote to the apologetic stateliness of the traditional gay anthology.

Still, it is possible to wonder what part queerness plays in these fictions. In such a surreal setting, of course, sexuality does not surface as anything so pedestrian as an identity crisis. These writers reject coming-out anxiety as just more middle-class angst. "Queerness" need not even imply sexual activity at all. In these stories it resides not in plot, but in tone and style. Homophobes frequently use negative adjectives of extravagance, like "outrageous" and "flamboyant," to characterize homosexuals, but this anthology turns that cliché on its head by implying that, yes, extravagance and homosexuality *are* the same. Queerness is (as the back cover of Cooper's anthology announces) inherently "transgressive," and transgression is naturally queer.

The differences between the anthologies, then, reflect the two ways in which minorities have traditionally related to the dominant culture. White reassures his readers that homosexuals are not so bad as people say, that "we are just like you." Cooper, playing Malcolm X to White's King, or Terminator to his Shane, counters that gays are worse than people think, that they do indeed defy everything that the mainstream holds dear.

Yet however different their rhetoric, in one important respect both editors agree. Cooper and White believe that the character of the literature derives from the nature of the individual writers. That is, gay literature is different because gay people are different. To some degree, this is common sense: whatever else gay literature might be, it is literature written by gay people. Still, this particular truism is also misleading. It implies that gay writers imbue their writing with something special that makes the literature essentially gay, and encourages us to search for this essence in people rather than in writing. Defining literature as an outgrowth of personality, Cooper and White ignore a fundamental danger of minority studies: that a certain way of describing the special character of gay literature may reinforce cultural clichés about who gay people are. Sometimes it is hard to distinguish a positive cultural characteristic from a negative cultural stereotype. No definition of minority literature can be any better than the concept of minority that underlies it. It is no less discriminatory to say that gays are naturally transgressive than to say that they are naturally hairdressers.

Neither Cooper nor White has fully considered how sexuality or any other special interest informs literature—or more generally, what it means to write minority fiction. Minorities do not write minority fiction because they cannot write as well as "major" writers; though he was doubly "minor," Baldwin was undeniably among the finest American writers of his generation. Nor does the minority status of their work arise from the fact that it deals only with issues relevant to a small subsector of the population: all writers depict general truths through specific experiences, and only later does rafting down the Mississippi or bullfighting in Pamplona seem universally significant.

In a sense, minorities do not write "minority" fiction at all. The minority label originates not with individual writers, but with a culture that makes a priori judgments that some subjects are universal and other subjects are merely personal. And superior literary skill does not really transcend these prejudices. In those masterpieces—*Moby-Dick* or *Remembrance of Things Past*—that contain elements of both the major and the minor, readers simply repress those aspects that seem like special interests. We remember the whiteness of the whale, but we forget Ishmael and Queequeg's night in bed.

Writers who self-consciously accept the minority (and minoritizing) label are faced with an additional problem. They wish to suggest that certain material not often represented in fiction is worthy of literary consideration. Classic gay novels like Gore Vidal's *The City and the Pillar,* Baldwin's *Giovanni's Room,* and more recently Andrew Holleran's *Dancer from the Dance,* Larry Duplechan's *Blackbird,* and Jack Fritscher's *Some Dance to Remember* all introduce readers to settings and psychologies that had not previously been depicted in literature. In so doing, they enlighten straight readers, but they also have a more particular mission for gay readers, which is to reassure them. They tell people who might otherwise have thought themselves abnormal that many share their sexual interests.

Yet this admirable desire to explore new literary material can itself turn limiting. In depicting homosexuality, novelists tend to focus on the small percentage of gay people's lives that is different, and to diminish the emphasis on the larger part of those lives that is presumably the same as everyone else's. The unintentional result is to reinforce the stereotype of gay difference, even to exoticize the sexual practices that they mean to naturalize. Novels about being gay have very little time to be about anything else. In putting homosexuality into literature, they tend to leave the world out of homosexuality.

The question remains, then, whether we can have a gay literature that is not merely about its own gayness, but is true to the variety of ways in which gays relate to each other and to the world. It is interesting to note that at present the possibility of such a complete representation is more fully realized outside the literary tradition of the novel. Science-fiction writers such as Samuel R. Delaney and Thomas M. Disch, mystery novelists such as Richard Stevenson and Michael Nava, and humorists like Joe Keenan place homosexual characters at the center of otherwise traditional genre situations. The very fact that these works are about other things—exploring worlds, solving murders, getting laughs—requires their authors to make their sexual points indirectly. Homosexuality in these popular works is simply taken for granted. And while the result is a fairly conventional use of the genres, these stories do manage to portray more fully the experience of gay people in the world than many more self-conscious works of gay literature. . . .

After Stonewall, gay writers were impatient with the accommodations that previous generations had made in order to be permitted to discuss sexuality at all. With their new candor and their confrontational style, gay writers and queer writers of the past twenty years managed to open up literature to a serious examination of non-traditional sexual desires. But any opening up can become its own kind of trap. Once gay writers could

not talk about sexuality. Now that seems to be all that they can talk about. Gay authors today face not only the commercial challenge of whether to write for a crossover market; they face also the aesthetic challenge of how to depict a world beyond the narrow confines of the individual consciousness. Such scope, which is the beginning of real literature, requires a more inclusive understanding of the ways in which people are gay, and a wider social sense of the environments in which homosexuals must live. If gay literature fails to address the diversity of which sexuality is only one facet, it truncates the experience of the homosexual life. Far from liberating ourselves, we may find that we have exchanged the closet for the pigeonhole.

Dennis Cooper and Jonathan Bing (interview date 21 March 1994)

SOURCE: Cooper, Dennis, and Jonathan Bing. "Dennis Cooper: Adolescent Rebellion Propels His Dystopian Vision." *Publishers Weekly* (21 March 1994): 48-9.

[*In the following interview, Bing provides an overview of Cooper's life, literary career, and thematic concerns and relays comments from Cooper regarding his work and critical reception.*]

In the tradition of the best grass-roots art, Dennis Cooper has been publishing his poetry and fiction at the margins of the cultural marketplace, in fanzines, chapbooks and obscure literary journals, since graduating from high school in the early 1970s. Yet many of Cooper's readers only know of his most recent work, a series of slim and startling books from Grove Press—the novels, **Closer** and **Frisk,** and the short-story collection **Wrong**—each an ice-cold glimpse of gay teenaged sexual turmoil, drug abuse and obsessive violence rendered in his signature spare and meticulous narrative style.

At once clinical and creepily meditative, Cooper's fiction has been championed by some as a bold, dystopian vision of sexual desire and moral laxity in contemporary life, but it has also proven too unsavory for others. Even Cooper's books with Grove have until now remained cultish and marginal: his emotionally drained, gay teen and 20-something characters are hustlers, punk rockers, artists and loners who fill their time with anonymous sex, horror films, amateurish artistic ventures and random acts of self-mutilation.

With the publication of **Try** this month by Grove/Atlantic, Cooper may finally win over a much wider audience. **Try** is a wrenching portrait of a manic teenager named Ziggy who is sexually brutalized, in excruciating detail, by his two gay foster fathers. Spaced out, deeply confused and magnetically sexy, Ziggy ditches high school, struggles to articulate his own emotional turmoil by publishing a fanzine about his sexual abuse and devotes himself to his best friend, a hopelessly strung-out writer. *Try* presents a broader spectrum of male, female, gay and straight characters, and a far more compassionate view of the complexities of human relationships than any of Cooper's previous books, broadening the horizons of his fictional world while retaining its stylistic tautness and its power.

Cooper receives *PW* in his modest East Hollywood apartment on a sunny Saturday a few days after the Los Angeles earthquake. Compared to the malevolent look of his publicity photos, the 41-year-old author, dressed casually in a T-shirt, black jeans and white Converse sneakers, is genial, with pale, angular features that give him a lanky and ascetic appearance. Asked how he's weathered the earthquake and its aftershocks, Cooper admits, "I'm really enjoying it. I know it's terrible, but I grew up with it."

Like the disaffected teens of his fiction, Cooper came of age, in his own estranged and unhappy fashion, in Arcadia, Calif., an improbably named, affluent Los Angeles suburb. "I was raised very badly," he points out. "I was a mess and miserable and did a lot of drugs." Cooper attended a private boys' school and began writing obsessively after discovering Baudelaire and the Marquis de Sade at the age of 15. At that stage, he explains, "I was writing these weird parodies. I wrote this whole novel that was based on *The 120 Days of Sodom,* and I took all the guys in high school that I wanted to sleep with and I cast them in it and just killed them off."

Cooper was expelled from private school in 11th grade, which raises the question of whether his subsequent fixation with high school reflects a desire to come to grips with whatever trauma he experienced at that age. "There's no literal event it's about," he shrugs. "I set them in high school because I like young people, and because I just resist the adult world." Cooper's voyeuristic fascination with adolescent runaways, punks and social castoffs has led some to view him as the Jean Genet of the American suburbs. Indeed, the glory that Cooper, like Genet, finds in social abjection reflects a relentless revolt against authority, and adults appear in Cooper's fiction in the most reprehensible roles—as serial killers, cold-blooded fetishists or drunk and neglectful parents. "I always hated adults, and I still do," he observes nonchalantly. "Most of my heroes were rock stars or writers, so I had imaginary adult mentors more than real mentors."

But, according to Cooper, the conflicted desires and hang-ups of adolescence make the strongest grist for his fiction. "It's a point at which your childhood's eating at you and adulthood's eating at you and you're just in chaos. I feel like that's the truth or something. People in that state are in touch with what the world's really about."

Cooper's work is also about the ephemeral, awkward beauty of teenaged boys, and throughout his fiction, there is one recurrent physical type, a thin, pale, sleepy-eyed figure with smooth skin and untidy dark hair who tends to subsume all others. Cooper acknowledges that many of his friends are much younger than he is and that the cadences of adolescent slang and the linguistic turmoil of teenagers attempting to give weight to authentic emotions without sounding clichéd remain a powerful source of inspiration. 'What I love about living in L.A. is that type of inarticulate grasping for clarity. The way those kids talk, it's very poetic. I find them incredibly sympathetic."

Choosing to emulate literary rebels like Rimbaud and Genet, Cooper dropped out of school after a year at Pitzer College in Claremont, Calif. A prolific period of writing and publishing followed, and in 1976, Cooper launched *Little Caesar,* a literary journal which he sought to infuse with the anarchic spirit and do-it-yourself ethic of the nascent punk scene. He also began publishing volumes of his own poetry, including *Tiger Beat* (Little Caesar Press, 1978), *Idols* (Seahorse Press, 1979) and *The Tenderness of Wolves* (Crossing Press, 1981). In 1983, he composed a prose poem called **"My Mark,"** a gritty, Petrarchan reverie for an estranged lover that was incorporated into *Safe,* a novella published a year later by Seahorse Press. Shortly thereafter, he stopped writing poetry altogether.

Cooper reflects with some dismay on his early writing and is not eager to see much of it reprinted. *Safe* was reissued by Grove/Atlantic last year in the short-story collection *Wrong,* a hodgepodge of older sketches and stories which Cooper now wishes had never been assembled. "*Wrong* has a bunch of horrible old stuff in it," he says. "I wish it hadn't happened. My agent did *Wrong* as a two-book deal to get me a little extra money. I like about five things in it and the rest just embarrasses me."

When *Safe* was first published, however, in 1984, Cooper suddenly gained the attention of mainstream New York publishers. Jonathan Galassi, then an editor at Random House, expressed interest in his next project, so Cooper moved to Amsterdam and confidently began work on *Closer.* "I was so naive. I thought, wow, this is pretty much a guarantee he's going to publish it, so I wrote it for him. And I sent it to him as soon as it was finished and he didn't like it at all." Unagented and still living in Amsterdam, Cooper persuaded his friend, the late Chris Cox, then an editor at Ballantine, to pitch the manuscript to Michael Denneny and other major editors of gay fiction. "Nobody wanted it," he explains. "And I was pretty despairing." Eventually Ira Silverberg, then publicity director of Grove, showed it to Wait Bode, Grove's editor-in-chief, who bought the manuscript for $2000 on the condition that Cooper rewrite the first chapter. Silverberg has been Cooper's agent ever since.

Closer is an ingenious conceptual study of a circle of solipsistic high school boys centering around the angelic, drugged-out George Miles, who is seduced by an older man whose fetish is to inject his lovers with novocaine and dissect them. Cooper claims to have derived the pitiless, uninfected style of *Closer* from the French filmmaker Robert Bresson. "No one's seen his work but he's like my god. There's a kind of monotony to it and a kind of hermeticism. In *Closer,* what I was trying to do was to flatten everything out into these equal paragraphs so it's almost like you're watching a train track, so it would numb everything out."

Closer also relates the serial iconography of the mass media to the repetition-compulsion of serial murder, a theme Cooper explored fully in his next novel, *Frisk,* published by Grove two years later. "By the time I was finishing *Closer,* I knew what I didn't like about it anymore," Cooper explains. "I wanted to work on the violence more. That's what *Frisk* came out of." *Frisk* depicts the fantasy life of a character named Dennis, who at age 13 encounters some snuff photos of a disemboweled teenager. Obsessed with the notion of killing the boys he picks up for casual sex, Dennis later moves to Amsterdam and pens a letter home describing a series of ritualistic murders he claims to have committed, but which prove to be imaginary.

More thoroughly than his previous work, *Frisk* evinces Cooper's fascination with human flesh and with the sexually laden pathological desire to open the body up to explore its secret interior. "I believe Sade," Cooper states bluntly. "The information about life was there, the horror and power abuse. The idea that the body is this package, there's no spirit or anything, it's just this machine and if you take apart the machine then you'll understand it, but you'll never understand it even then. Life's so hopeless. *Frisk* was a confrontation," he adds. "*Frisk* seduced you into believing something was true, and then left you with your own pleasure or whatever you got out of that experience."

Although Cooper has avoided the denunciation one might expect from the political right (as Edmund White observed, "This is the very stuff of Jesse Helms' worst nightmares"), he has been the target of much criticism from gay-rights activists. During the book tour for *Frisk,* says Cooper, "People would come up to me and say:

you have no right to do this." The most shattering attack followed a reading at A Different Light in San Francisco, where Cooper was approached by two men who handed him a pamphlet headlined "Dennis Cooper must die." It consisted of drawings and quotes from the savage reviews in area gay papers. "I freaked out," Cooper recalls. The pamphlet had been produced by a faction of Queer Nation, which had conducted a literal-minded reading of his work and deemed it politically dangerous. "The idea was that fiction was real, and that by killing them in my fiction I had really tried to kill them. It didn't make a lot of sense." Cooper eventually found a mutual friend who put him in touch with the director of the group, and the death threat was officially lifted.

Nevertheless, he is still dogged by criticism that his work is sadistic and politically irresponsible. "My response is that for better or worse, gay identity doesn't interest me. It never has. Everybody in my work, until the new book, has been gay. It's a hermetic world, it's a closed system. And they're not interested in their sexual identity. It's one of the few things that isn't a problem for them. They're totally happy about being gay. I'm totally happy with being gay. If anything, being gay should allow a massive amount of freedom in terms of the imagination. So I feel like that's just pure policing."

Cooper contends that such literal interpretations often fail to grasp the experimental ideas and complex aesthetic effects he seeks to achieve in his books. "I always want them to come from a place that's not conventional and then only get conventional when they absolutely have to make a point or to keep the eye moving down the page." In *Try,* however, Cooper avails himself of more traditional narrative techniques, and as a result, Ziggy is one of the most nuanced and sympathetic case studies in child abuse in recent fiction. Cooper acknowledges that when he wrote the novel, he was breaking off a long-term relationship and, like Ziggy, was trying to care for a friend who was addicted to heroin. "It was a really deep fucked-up period in my life. The book was kind of to ground myself in the real world." He adds, "Ziggy's the first character I've ever done who is trying to understand what's happening to him. And he hasn't gotten very far, but he's trying, and that's like a big step."

Although pleased with the security he's found at Grove, Cooper is wary of attracting too much attention with his new book. "It's tricky. I like the margins. I've always admired artists who've made an incredibly narrow, obsessive body of work. I feel like I'm mining this stuff that's really like a psychosis for me. It's really personal, and I'm gonna keep doing it until I'm bored with it."

Matias Viegener (essay date spring 1994)

SOURCE: Viegener, Matias. "Men Who Kill and the Boys Who Love Them." *Critical Quarterly* 36, no. 1 (spring 1994): 105-14.

[*In the following essay, Viegener examines the American fascination with psychosexual murderers and the portrayal of homosexuals as calculating, deviant criminals, drawing attention to* Frisk *and* Jerk *for examples of the pathological, anti-social gay killer. Viegener contends that Cooper's depictions of sexual violence are not a strategy for transgression, but suggest the extreme limits of experience, self-identity, and intersubjectivity.*]

The homosexual killer sits at the juncture of two great social obsessions, homosexuality and criminality. The homosexual criminal has a long history, epitomised in life in the case of Oscar Wilde and in representation in his novel *The Picture of Dorian Gray.* Jean Genet made this perilous equation the centrepiece of his life's work, such that criminal desire (specifically the desire to steal, though also to kill) is not only the analogue but the very constituent of homosexual desire. In this essay, I'd like to site the work of gay writer Dennis Cooper within this tradition of homosexual pathology, linking sexual or gender difference to criminality and illness. In taking up this spectrum of destructive desire, or lustmord—murderous joy—Cooper has not only won the opprobrium of the gay community (for his nostalgia for the pathologised homosexual) but he also undermines the very basis of contemporary gay culture's identity-formation both in terms of representation and of self-image. This subject has been simmering in much recent gay culture, such as Tom Kalin's film *Swoon,* Todd Hayne's *Poison,* Fassbinder's *Querelle,* and in the more mainstream *Apartment Zero* and *Silence of the Lambs.* At its core is a quest for limit experiences that surpass the safety of bourgeois sexuality and a resistance—through forms of violence—to unified subjectivity.

Of all the specimens of criminality, the serial killer, heterosexual *or* homosexual, receives the most intense exposure in the media. He, for so he is gendered, is unlike all other criminals in that his acts are never marked by necessity; he is the only criminal whose motives are without self-interest. Since 'motive' is a fundamental category for convicting criminals, serial killers are a conundrum for the legal and medical professions. Incapable of ascribing 'natural' criminal motives to these killers, we are directed by sociologists, policemen and even true crime books to the theoretical fringes: sexual pleasure and desire are presented as the best tools to interpret their crimes. Madness is usually judged by a model of medical dysfunction—criminality as disease—much as homosexuality was once addressed as an infection or an illness. More tailored to examining

the individual than his context, professional discourse can only see madness as analogous to cancer or disease, rather than as a culturally programmed dialogue.

Serial killers are spoken of as the 'aristocrats' of crime reporting, strangely admired both in the prisons and in the media. Better educated and with a higher IQ than most criminals, their methods are usually coldly systematic; they are able to manipulate social, media and police interactions and psychological profiles generally rate them high in ambition. Both popular wisdom and analytic culture face a profound aporia in explaining the serial killer. If sanity is primarily judged in our culture under the precepts of illness, i.e. by disorders of thought or affect, or by the incapacity to function, these killers are profoundly capable. Most of the killers in the research seem highly nuanced in their interpretation of the signifiers of desire, identity, gender and sexuality.

Crime has been the province of three major disciplines, sociology (an academic discourse), criminology (within the framework of legal and penal systems) and pathology (as determined by the medical and specifically psychoanalytical professions). These institutions are supposed to bring meaning to the crime which is beyond mere moral condemnation or superstitious fancy. One of the current sociological interpretations (Leyton, p. 14) is that sex crimes are a consequence of class difference and that murderous desire is always focused on members of the upper-middle class (ignoring the fact that many women who are killed are prostitutes, and that killers generally seem to kill within their own class and race). The most prevalent is the feminist view that considers all sex crimes as driven by hatred for the female; they are at the structural core of patriarchal ideology (Caputi, Morgan, Brownmiller). Men killed by men are assumed to be feminised, despite much evidence that it is their phallic status (autonomy, desirability) that is literally and symbolically attacked. What emerges most profoundly in the studies is that their statistic bases are always inadequate, and that all of the theorists have an underdeveloped sense of the textual nature of sex crime, of murder as a form of writing. My project here is to establish that murder is always a media(ted) act, with its partial object being the representation of desire and representation of murder itself.

It is no understatement to say that American culture is both violent—the USA has the highest homicide rate in the industrialised world—and fascinated by violence, whether in the form of the gratuitous spectatorship of highway fatalities, sensationalised reporting or aestheticised representations of violence. As Edmund Burke says in his essay on the sublime, 'we delight in seeing things, which so far from doing, our heartiest wishes would be to see redressed' (p. 47). Our culture famously regulates the representation of violence far more than violence itself. Writing on Genet, Sartre says that 'it is the specter of murder, even more than murder itself, that horrifies people and unlooses base instincts' (p. 485). Actual instances of social violence are generally presented to us in mediated form, as highly mediated objects, and we learn to read them aesthetically—take, for example, the Holocaust, or more recently, the Gulf War.¹ Rather than focus on the way in which representations influence behaviour and experience, which seems to be how both conservative and liberal critiques are pointed, my course will be to look at how acts of violence are a kind of reading of crime and of the nature of desire.

The more I've read, the less I find serial killers interesting at all. They are surprisingly banal. It is the fascination with serial killers which is interesting. My interest is less in drawing a psychological profile of such a killer than in what his representation tells us about the construction of the homosexual. What motivates our fascination with him? In what ways does this figure countermand the positive identity politics of the post-Stonewall generation? Can he be said to be attacking (with vastly different agendas, from within the gay world and from the homophobic straight world) precisely this fixed identity?

Dennis Cooper's novel *Frisk* opens and closes with a series of five snuff photographs, a kind of haunted frame; this prologue and epilogue are titled with an infinity sign, signalling their positions as the beginning and end of the narrative universe. The first five are what haunt the first-person protagonist Dennis throughout the novel; they culminate in the victim's crater-like anus, 'as if someone had set off a bomb in his rectum' (p. 27). Though these photographs are later alleged to be staged, they haunt the narrator so profoundly that his only resolution in the end is to restage them. The specularity of this frame, centred around the image of the damaged anus, forms a 'small tunnel entrance, too out-of-focus to actually explore with one's eyes, but too mysterious not to want to try' (p. 4). This opening and closing plays on the very nature of illusion and its role in constructing both our desires and our representations of them. Desire is always preceded by representation and acting on our desires—destructive or not—is an aesthetic production: we create our objects of desire. *Frisk* is centred on an elaborate feint, in which Dennis the narrator deceives his ex-lover and friend into believing he's begun to actually murder young men (one of their favourite fantasies); thus the whole text starts to limn how narrative constructs desire.²

The serial killer's relationship to representation calls into question representation itself. Sexual murders (probably because they are so publicised) are among the crimes most likely to inspire copycat killings and false confessions. Serial killers, most memorably Ted Bundy, often report (to the media, of course) that pornography and/or violent pornography have inspired their crimes. Their media careers are marked by excess, by a spectacular nature that forces even the reserved, anti-sensationalist *New York Times* to revel in details such as Jeffrey Dahmer's frying 'his victim's biceps in Crisco vegetable shortening'. Tabloid murders have often been the only way in which homosexuality has entered public consciousness. Rarely has the notoriously homophobic *New York Times* tried to render this explicitly what it is that homosexuals *actually do*.

What is the significance of sexual violence, as it emerges in both popular discourse (e.g. the Jeffrey Dahmer case) and the gay artist's work? Dennis Cooper focuses on homosexual gay violence with a singular vigour; his stories centre on disaffected suburban male teenagers, with their apparent inability to connect either to a normative heterosexual family or to the existing gay community. Steeped in sex, rock, drugs and violence, these recalcitrant narratives often culminate in images of murder or disfigurement against a backdrop strangely denuded of women, parents, teachers or policemen. Often excoriated by the gay community, Cooper's work is centred on the abject homosexual. Sexuality is no longer a positive self-affirming act, but a profound disruption of identity and psychic comfort. Both in Cooper's imaginary and in popular representation, the sex killer is the apex of disaffection, the killer who 'chopped what was beneath him until no owner could claim it' (**'A Herd'**, p. 14).

Imagine wanting to speak of language and identity, of psychic mechanisms of masochism, homosexuality, subject and object, identification and desire; imagine wanting to speak of all the abject potentialities of existentialism, and to choose to do so in the language of the average Californian teenager. To do this because the intellectual language of the adult world seems even more evacuated than that of the everyday, and to do so while also avoiding the temptations of allegory—of using simple terms to tell transcendental or moral lessons. Dennis Cooper's style avoids polysyllabic words and subordinate clauses; most of his sentences are declarative and one finds hardly a latinate word. The style flattens all affect; the spiritual emptiness of this work is cast against a faint backdrop of the television as a distant spectator to the character's black mirror of desire. Cooper's characters are mostly inarticulate, their words peppered with ums, 'etc.', 'like . . .' and 'whatever'. There are few metaphors and no elaborate descriptions—except in the case of sex or death—and the writing might be said to bear a relationship to American minimalism except for Cooper's absolute disdain for the kind of petty-bourgeois content of minimalism.

In the general alienation of Cooper's teenager, sexual stimulus is modulated into information, rather than desire. Explaining why he wants a hustler to leave his shit unflushed in the toilet, he tells him that the 'information' will 'create a mental world . . . uh, wait. Or a situation where I could kill you and understand . . .' (*Frisk*, p. 69). Desire for the other becomes the desire to know the other, to see past the limitations of 'skin'. The narrator of *Frisk*, the first person 'Dennis', describes his perfect type, hairless, pale, thin:

> My usual. Now I'm at the part in the fantasy that always fucks me over. I want him, specifically his skin, because skin's the only thing that's available. But I've had enough sex in my life with enough guys to recognize how little skin can explain about anyone. So I start getting into this rage about how stingy skin is. I mean, skin's biggest reward, which is sperm, I guess, is only great because it's a message from somewhere inside a great body. But it's totally primitive.

(p. 53)

Dennis sits and scribbles in his journal, masturbating, 'but inside my head the most spectacular violence is happening. A boy's exploding, caving in. It looks sort of fake since my only models are splatter films, but it's unbelievably powerful' (p. 54). The representation of violence is inseparable from violence itself; slasher, splatter, snuff or horror films (*Nightmare on Elm St, Friday the Thirteenth*) are among the only cultural touchstones in Cooper's fictional universe. Cooper's characters are post-punk aesthetes whose aestheticism consists of finding a few reliable guideposts to get them through the night of everyday life. The scenario in a typical Cooper narrative always involves male adolescents in a world without adults or women. As in the world of Bataille's *Story of the Eye*, the adults are ineffectual or absent, forming an empty backdrop to the world of adolescent desire. Its severe minimalism, antimelodrama, an almost-camp seriousness, and anti-bourgeois, vanguard apocalypticism are all inflections of the punk movement.

In Cooper's short story about serial killer Ray Sexton, **'A Herd'**, a similar kind of alienated desire is focused on magazine stars. They 'were Ray's angels, freed from the limits of IQ and coordination . . . Teen stars' perfections haunted him, and a vague resemblance to one or another could, more often than not, be gleaned from the face of a boy he had killed . . . A boy chained up or tied down, in the midst of whatever torture, might turn his head sideways and an idol's look would appear in one feature or another. . . . More often, he wouldn't see any resemblance until the boy died . . . Then what Ray had done took on meaning' (**'A Herd'**, pp. 10-11).

It is only death which provides the ultimately empty object on which to cathex one's desires, but this death takes the physiognomy of the television character imprinted as the object of desire in the first place. This object is oddly blank, like Garbo's face on the Sphinx,

which Roland Barthes describes as a blank screen, a profound selflessness which engenders desire (p. 70). This central concern of Cooper's allies him with a major concern of many postmodern theorists. Planted in a hyper-real culture without a space for resistance, negation, or political change, writers and artists endeavour to unveil a *real* which escapes simulacra. Foucault holds fast to a notion of counter-discourse which recovers subjugated constituencies, and, in other registers, Deleuze's rhizomatic and nomadic wanderings over and under codification, and even Baudrillard muses on secret knowledge and seduction. These might be subsumed into Lyotard's retrenchment to the sublime, as they dematerialise the subject within the fantasmatic pleasure of the text, and as they are ultimately anti-narrative and demonstrate a dissolution of language and representation itself. However, I believe that Cooper is both never outside representation and rather polemical in his position regarding identity and (homosexual) desire.

In the recent novella *Jerk*, Cooper's text unfolds over four levels of discourse. Accomplice killer David Brooks speaks to us 'live' about his experiences 'as a drug-addicted, psychotic teen murderer in the early seventies'. On the second level he hands the audience a file of two 'non-fiction' stories, which introduce serial killer Dean Corll and his other accomplice, Wayne. Corll soon articulates the central impasse of the 'intellectual' murderer: how can one really *know* one's object? The inner life of the victim, his sensations, remain inaccessible. Is the victim ever 'ours'? Corll asks his accomplices. 'They're not ours . . . not even dead.' This disquisition is answered by a Mephistophelean knock on the door: a teenager fascinated by Dean's dark magnetism. Like the other victims, he virtually offers himself. These are figures whose life is so empty, death seems possible, the most ultimate experience. 'The worst that could happen', says one, 'is nothing.'

The third discourse emerges in David's puppet show, given to us in script form. Here the freakish turnaround occurs in which Dean Corll begins to speak as the voice of his victim, 'Dean-as-corpse'. This provokes the conceptual crisis of the story: identity becomes so permeable that it is merely an act of will, as permeable as fabric. Dean tries to overcome the innate distance between killer and victim by projecting the victim as one of his television love-idols, the boy from *Flipper* or *Dennis the Menace*. This resolves the problem of interiority, since television stars have no inner lives, as Dean explains: they are only what is onscreen, pure surface. This mimicry, the ultimate act of making the corpse into a puppet, provokes Wayne into killing Dean and finally, after a third murder, David into killing Wayne. But this is not a conventionally moral judgment about the limits of murder. It is as much, as in all of Cooper's work, about the limits of representation. An appended 'paper' from a student in a course on 'Freudian Psychology as Refracted through Post Modern Example' forms the fourth layer of discourse. In an analysis of David's puppet show, the student diagnoses a loss of meaning at the core of the show, that the closer David tries to convey the events, the more distant their meaning becomes. Intelligence gives the feeling of mastery over things, but one nevertheless cannot possess those things.

While being logically arrayed, none of these four levels of discourse are privileged over the others. They form a kind of elegant double (triple or quadruple) mirroring, a kind of Jacobean play-within-a-play. During the puppet sequences, David's job is also to film the murders in Super-8, which becomes yet another layer of simulacra. The third murder is inspired by viewing these films, and the final death—David killing his fellow accomplice and lover, Wayne—occurs when he throws the camera at Wayne's head. *Jerk* is thus a meditation on the nature of illusion, desire and representation, and on their manifestation in the real world, as identity.

These murderers are guilty not just because they kill, but because they overidentify with their desired prey. Their sadism is a form of masochism. In his 1915 'Instincts and their Vicissitudes', Freud constructs a three-step process to explain the relationship between violence and desire. Masochism is descended from sadism by a process of reversal: all the subject's instincts include aggressive components which are directed upon its object. In a secondary stage, both the object and the aim change: the impulse to mastery is turned upon oneself and turned from active to passive. Finally, the impulse returns to an object in the world, and another person 'has to take over the role of the subject' (p. 232). Freud is not content with saying that masochism is a reversed form of sadism, since he still maintains that sadism is a projected form of masochism, as the sadist could not take pleasure in other's pain without having experienced masochistically the link between pleasure and pain. Within psychoanalysis, this argument is further elucidated; for our purposes, what is vital here is that Freud holds to the primacy of sadism.[3] The suffering is 'enjoyed masochistically by the subject through his identification of himself with the suffering object' (p. 235).

If identification is at the core of Freud's ambiguity around sadism, it is also at the genesis of Cooper's characters' self-destructions. Their emptiness is self-driven, a search for a limit experience which (like ecstasy, horror, rage, hunger, fear, repulsion) is always located at the boundaries and orifices. But these limits are not the typical 'heightened experience' of realism or classical tragedy; they are abject. Julia Kristeva points out that they are precisely those things which break down distinctions, an abjection within which looms

'one of those violent, dark revolts of being, directed against a threat that seems to emanate from an exorbitant outside or inside, ejected beyond the scope of the possible, the tolerable, the thinkable' (p. 1).

If anything, Cooper's work is anti-psychological, opposed to any depth model. By literally showing us what's inside the body, and entering through the anus, he demystifies interiority. By reproaching the exterior/false against the interior/truth, he also takes on the identity formation of the mainstream post-Stonewall gay community. Cooper's work inhabits the stereotype of the pathological homosexual as an aesthetic strategy against endemic homophobia, though to him the gay community as it exists is also deeply homophobic and normative—in particular in framing the ideal homosexual relationship in the terms of mutuality.[4] What Cooper's novels do not resemble are the critical anti-homophobic work of much of (the eighties) gay activist art. His novels invoke characters who seek loss and oblivion, who are 'beyond good and evil' or 'neither good nor evil', as Foucault put it. They are also beyond the oppositional strategies of activist art, which in this context become interpreted as merely reactive and over-rationalised.

The homosexual is suspended within a certain paradox: as manifesting either an excess of passion (which is more commonly held and somehow more forgivable—one sees this in apologies for gay promiscuity) or a strange conscious *dispassion,* a moral sang-froid which enables him to cross boundaries the 'decent' human upholds.[5] Alfred Hitchcock's *Rope* is exemplary in this respect. The homosexual couple is manifestly repressed, over-controlled, and they see themselves as beyond the law, outside the limits; their amorality is a kind of Nietzschean anti-morality, which compels them to kill a schoolmate as a living proof of their superiority to the common laws of civilisation. When not seen as the subject of criminal *passion,* the homosexual serial killer is more generally represented in the media as a *calculating* psychopath. This is the terror of the serial killer: not his excess of passion, but his dispassion, his systematic strategies. This paradigm of sexuality evacuates the notion of sex as fulfilment, as truth or comfort; sex becomes an inadequate expression, a site in which power relations are deployed to negate an inadequate fixed identity toward a kind of existential anti-truth.

All existentialist writers begin with the premise that the ontological dimension (Being) has been forced out of consciousness by the institutions and systems of a society that overvalues rationality. However, Cooper is no existentialist. His interests are no more in authenticity than they are in transgression; his novels are if anything a meditation on the inability to transgress, both literally and figuratively, on how it is impossible to murder someone without losing one's identity through an invasion of representation—all the murders that came before—just as it is impossible to 'really know someone'. Thus his subject at base is banality, not transgression.

And if banality can be 'overcome', or displaced, it must be through what Bataille has termed expenditure. A rationalised cultural economy is limited to activity which is either productive or self-preservative, while expenditure reflects the thrall society has in loss, 'in catastrophes that, while conforming to well defined needs, provoke tumultuous depressions, crises of dread, a certain orgiastic state'. Expenditure is linked to the logic of sacrifice, and examples of it include 'luxury, mourning, war, cults, the construction of sumptuary monuments, games, spectacles, arts, perverse sexual activity (i.e., deflected from genital finality' (p. 118). The stress in Bataille which so aptly applies to Cooper is that it considers the problem of surplus, of what a society does with its surplus resources: the circular ritual of destruction in *Jerk* is a form of unproductive social exchange, 'generous, orgiastic and excessive'. Moral retribution would require a form of social rationalism, a coherence of the subject over narrative space. Cooper's novels are not moral tales. His notion of heterogeneous experience is on the order of the Marquis de Sade: one which disrupts the demands of the utilitarian, of an ordered and rationally productive society. Heterogeneity in this sense is a form of madness, since it evaporates the distinctions of interior and exterior central to the subject, thus demanding the dissolution of the (in this case homosexual) subject.

Notes

1. Walter Benjamin ('On the Work of Art in the Age of Mechanical Reproduction') comes to mind here: the aestheticisation of violence is the avant-garde of the aestheticisation of politics.

   One might argue that the Holiday/Rodney King tape escaped this dynamic; much was made of the crudeness of the video format (a kind of aesthetics of authenticity) as essential in provoking such a strong, i.e. violent, response.

2. Elizabeth Young argues that at the centre of Cooper's work is the sadomasochistic anal taboo, around which he defies prurience and rejects obscenity 'in favor of clarity and understanding' (236). It seems to me that this disregards the element of the subject central to Cooper's fiction.

3. Deleuze resolves the problem of masochism in psychoanalysis by the invocation of a sadistic superego and a masochistic ego; pp. 123-34.

4. See David Bergman, p. 40. While discussing Joseph Allen Boone's interpretations of American quest romances, he notes therein an 'elevation of mutuality—rather than polarity—in the male bond [which]

presents a conceptual alternative to the gender inequality institutionalized by marriage in heterosexual relations'.

5. Both terms of this paradox are homophobic, of course. Most gay artists and writers defend or excuse the excess of passion (and seek normative patterns for it), while relatively few defend dispassion.

Bibliography

Roland Barthes, 'Le visage de Garbo', in *Mythologies* (Paris: Editions du Seuil, 1957).

Georges Bataille, 'The Notion of Expenditure', in *Visions of Excess,* trans. A. Stoekl (Minneapolis: University of Minnesota Press, 1985).

David Bergman, *Gaiety Transfigured: Gay Self-representation in American Literature* (Madison: University of Wisconsin Press, 1991).

Edmund Burke, *A Philosophical Inquiry into the Origin of Our Ideas of the Sublime and Beautiful,* ed. J. T. Boulton (London: Routledge & Kegan Paul, 1958).

Jane Caputi, *The Age of Sex Crime* (Bowling Green, Ohio: Bowling Green Press, 1987).

Dennis Cooper, *Frisk* (New York: Grove, 1991).

Dennis Cooper, *Jerk* (San Francisco: Artspace Press, 1993).

Dennis Cooper, 'A Herd', in *Wrong* (New York: Grove, 1992).

Gilles Deleuze, 'Coldness and Cruelty', in Deleuze and Sacher-Masoch, *Masochism* (New York: Zone Books, 1989).

Sigmund Freud, 'Instincts and Their Vicissitudes', *Standard Edition,* vol. XII.

Julia Kristeva, *Powers of Horror: An Essay on Abjection* (New York: Columbia, 1986).

Elliot Leyton, *Hunting Humans: Inside the Minds of Mass Murderers* (New York: Pocket Books, 1986).

Robin Morgan, *Demon Lover: On the Sexuality of Terrorism* (New York: Norton, 1989).

Jean-Paul Sartre, *Saint Genet: Actor and Martyr,* trans. Bernard Frechtman (New York: George Braziller, 1963).

Elizabeth Young, 'Death in Disneyland: The Work of Dennis Cooper', in Elizabeth Young and Graham Caveny, *Shopping in Space: Essays on American 'Blank Generation' Fiction* (London: Serpent's Tail, 1992).

Times Literary Supplement (review date 27 May 1994)

SOURCE: Review of *Wrong,* by Dennis Cooper. *Times Literary Supplement* (27 May 1994): 21.

[*In the following review, the critic discusses Cooper's portrayal of the emotionally bereft in* Wrong *and* Closer.]

Talking of recent fiction, the narrator of one of Dennis Cooper's short stories in **Wrong** observes that "The sharpest new writers tend to appropriate either the language or sheen of pornography . . .". This is certainly true of Cooper's own work, which is not only arrestingly well written but graphically obscene. Where Cooper parts company with the pornographic imagination is in the traumatized humanity of his writing, and in his attempt to explore the buried emotion under the shiny surface. As the title of **Wrong** suggests, Cooper is something of a moralist—in the most urgent and least puritanical sense of the word—and his explorations of the further fringes of homosexual life carry a sense of lost emotional and moral bearings. The title-story features a sex killer who comes to feel: "After death, what's left. . . . Once you've killed someone, life's shit. It's a few rules and you've already broken the best." This is radically unlike the more familiar tendency in late twentieth-century culture which stresses the blankness and inconsequentiality of the experience, and Cooper's work seems directed against the prevalent anaesthesia of a world which is too hip, too jaded or just too plain stupid to feel that something has gone badly astray. George Miles, the young protagonist of Cooper's most recent novel, **Closer,** is a case in point. George is a drug-gobbling cipher, an unusually beautiful but emotionally numb all-American kid whose inner life revolves around Disneyland rides. Cooper explores the link between vacuity and obscenity as George's "friends"—who include a phoney artist, a coprophile, and a snuff-movie enthusiast,—lust after his advert-like perfection. The porno-world that Cooper meatily dissects is one where real emotions are out of place; "they don't belong here, any more than a man's fist belongs in a boy's ass". As the Cooper persona in one of the stories writes, it was only recently "I knew love's function, understood its context, put my reaction to it in quotes when it reared its ugly head. Now I'm holding it under this work like it's something I'm intent upon drowning."

Alexander Laurence (review date summer 1994)

SOURCE: Laurence, Alexander. Review of *Try,* by Dennis Cooper. *Review of Contemporary Fiction* 14, no. 2 (summer 1994): 222.

[*In the following review, Laurence offers a positive assessment of* Try.]

The writer Robert Hardin has noted "Dennis Cooper will be remembered as the most prophetic writer of his time." These are strong words, and one can keep them in mind when reading Cooper's latest post-punk novel **Try.** The main character, Ziggy, is the adopted teenage son of two gay fathers with illusions of becoming respectable. Ziggy spends his time putting together a magazine called *I Apologize.* His two fathers abuse Ziggy sexually and otherwise. For comfort, he turns to his uncle, an overweight man who makes porn films, and to his best friend, Calhoun, who is a junkie. This deceiving little narrative shifts in point of view as it traces the lives of these strange people. Cooper fuses minimalism with new narrative techniques, references to film and video, and musical familiarity with Hüsker Dü and Slayer helps.

Cooper's fiction has always been a metaphysical struggle to fully possess the body. There is no human soul in Cooper's universe, or better yet, the body and soul are equal. When his characters try to act their wishes on the body, to produce its truth, they are sadists bordering on the impossible. **Try** is proof that Dennis may be the legitimate heir to William S. Burroughs. **Frisk, Wrong,** and **Closer** are an interesting counterpoint to Burroughs's earlier novels. But Cooper still hasn't written his *Naked Lunch.*

Michael Cunningham (review date 3 July 1994)

SOURCE: Cunningham, Michael. "Oh for a Little Despair." *Los Angeles Times Book Review* (3 July 1994): 3, 8.

[*In the following review, Cunningham offers a positive evaluation of* Try.]

If Jean Genet and Paul Bowles could have had a child together, he might have grown up to be a writer like Dennis Cooper. I've learned not to push Cooper's work on just anybody, but if a friend seems even halfway receptive I usually prepare him or her by saying something like, "Cooper is appalling, but so is the modern world." I go on to remind him or her that *Lolita* was generally considered perverse to the point of dangerousness when it first appeared. As was *Madame Bovary.*

Try, Dennis Cooper's third novel, is the story of a ravaged, omnisexual 16-year-old named Ziggy and his hopeless romance with Calhoun, a straight heroin addict who, in his own words, "hates all emotion." The book traces their impossible love through a world so fried by drugs and brutality that a feeling as concrete as despair would be a relief. **Try** is a true original, full of perversely moving moments and a bleaker-than-bleak, strangely comic vision. It may be some kind of screwed-up American classic.

In his grungy L.A. loft, Calhoun floats above emotions on an icy little cloud of heroin. Ziggy, stuck in the suburbs, crackles with emotions so electric and unpredictable he can scarcely stand upright. As a "hyper-active, hard-to-place two-year-old" he was adopted by Roger and Brice, two gay men making a "stab at heterosexual-style bliss." The bliss thinned out quickly, Roger moved to New York, and Brice started molesting Ziggy the year Ziggy turned 8. Now Roger has decided it's his turn with Ziggy. He flies back to Los Angeles from New York with sedatives and a pair of skintight Lycra bikini shorts for his adopted son.

Ziggy copes as best he can by fixating on Calhoun, by sleeping with a kind and pretty rich girl named Nicole, and by insisting that every new atrocity practiced on him is good material for his homemade magazine, "I Apologize: A Magazine for the Sexually Abused." To sidestep the avalanches of terror and self-hatred that periodically overwhelm him, he writes up his tales of abuse—sometimes as they're happening—with avid detachment. He's like a journalist blandly reporting his own murder.

Calhoun, roughly equally damaged, depends on Ziggy's devotion but will not, can not, respond. For Calhoun, an actual emotion would be too ragged and harsh. It's better to shoot up and drift away. He's ostensibly writing a novel, which appears only as a spectral presence on his laptop, "that glimmering rectangular blueness, that spooky night light." The laptop is always turned on but never, ever, used.

Dennis Cooper has been charting the course of scarred, nervous lives like these for almost a decade and a half now. His novels, stories and poetry work and rework a few essential . . . the word *themes* is probably too mild. The word *obsessions* may even be too mild.

In Cooper's fictional world, love and torture are so closely related as to be nearly indistinguishable. Emotional connection is too difficult, so Cooper's characters invade their loved ones' bodies in search of the fundamental human essence that's getting blocked on every other channel. Cooper's lust objects tend to be young boys, and I mean young boys. By age 10 or so, they're viable. By 16 or 17, they're over the hill.

Try is Cooper's least horrifying novel, and it may also be his best. In his last novel, *Frisk,* a character fantasized about torturing a little boy in such salacious detail that I remember thinking, as I read it: "This is a fascinating book, and when I'm finished reading it, I don't want it in the house." Cooper is a scary guy, and reading him doesn't feel particularly safe. One moment you feel as if you're in the company of a significant artist who doesn't flinch over the numbed violence of our lives right now. The next moment you feel like a kid who's hitched a ride with John Wayne Gacy.

In *Try,* Cooper lightens up a little without sacrificing any of his edge, though anyone who reads *Try* without knowing the larger body of Cooper's work may be hard pressed to imagine that it involves a "lightening up" of any kind. In Cooperland, when a 13-year-old overdoses,

the man he's been sleeping with doesn't call the hospital; he calls a gentleman who'll pay top dollar for a few hours alone with the corpse. At least in *Try* he closes the bedroom door.

Cooper's fiction bridges a gap between the behavior chronicled in Literature with a capital L and the behavior chronicled in the juicier newspapers, the ones that keep us informed about serial murders and fetishes that end in death. Cooper is important because he aims his flashlight beam toward the darkest places; he's frightening because he admits to having an appetite for whatever he finds there.

Cooper's voice is full of a zoned-out adolescent poetry, at once brimming with emotion and reticent about showing any emotion at all. He's Mr. Cool—grand passions are for geeks. The most he'll allow his characters is scraps of intimacy and a vaguely apologetic devotion to highly diluted beauty.

There are times when Cooper's vision feels as grimly, impenetrably romantic as an adolescent's, and subject to adolescent limitations. Even as a fan I've found myself growing impatient with a world so resolutely centered on the young, white and miserable. It can feel like a cramped little universe, more generously filled with morbid curiosities than actual truths. It can be hard to remember that this is the same planet and species that produced Tolstoy, Dickens, Garcia Márquez, Toni Morrison.

With *Try,* however, Cooper extends his range. Women (well, girls) appear for the first time as sympathetic characters and as objects of desire. Love exists beyond the worship of the flesh, and some kind of grubby, compromised redemption might even be possible. The limitations imposed on the characters in *Try* are not wholly different from the limitations of the culture in general, in that soaring emotions aren't all that easy to maintain in the face of assorted addictions, endless violence and a sorrow so large it doesn't really have a name. After reading *Try* you might feel, at least for a while, that almost every other contemporary American novel is a little forced and melodramatic, full of wishful thinking rather than hard human facts.

Cooper is an important and highly idiosyncratic writer, with a nose for some of the least presentable living odors. In *Try* he has produced a harrowing, intricately accomplished work of art. It should be read. It might even endure, if that doesn't sound too geeky.

Drew Limsky (review date July-August 1994)

SOURCE: Limsky, Drew. Review of *Try,* by Dennis Cooper. *Lambda Book Report* 4, no. 5 (July-August 1994): 35.

[*In the following review, Limsky judges* Try *as overly self-conscious and redundant.*]

It's not easy to care about a cast of characters composed of junkies, pedophiles and necrophiliacs, and who are continually described in terms of their filth, yet readers may develop a grudging affection for Ziggy, the hapless protagonist of Dennis Coopers third novel, *Try.*

The product of an abusive upbringing, Ziggy is a mess. One of his two gay fathers, Brice, has been molesting the eighteen-year-old since childhood, and Roger, Brice's ex and Ziggy's other father, habitually fantasizes about rimming his son; he writes Ziggy a series of letters delineating his proficiency in this and other anal-related activities. Disturbingly, every male character over thirty in *Try* is preoccupied by the anuses of adolescent boys; in fact, the novel is so replete with references to that orifice, that to accurately describe the story's action one would quickly deplete his store of synonyms for "asshole" and have to invent new ones.

Ziggy is in love with the straight Calhoun, who has shot up so much heroin that he can no longer locate receptive veins; Ziggy doesn't register the fact that his intermittently catatonic "best friend" is incapable of having a relationship with anything other than a syringe: "'You mean so much to me,'" Ziggy tells his day-tripping pal. "'You mean a lot to me too,'" Calhoun responds, "'but you know, shut up.'" "'Right.' Ziggy responds, smacking his lips together." Rebuffed by Calhoun, Ziggy falls into bed with his classmate Nicole, the transsexual Cricket, and eventually, one of his fathers (voluntarily, this time). It soon becomes clear that the scarred teenager is looking for love wherever he can find it; he's so emotionally available and so sexually accommodating that he's a parody of neediness.

Yet Ziggy—who spends his free time publishing a magazine for victims of childhood abuse, called *I Apologize*—emerges as a figure of not insubstantial resourcefulness and pathos, particularly when he's holding forth on his feelings. In a moment of uncharacteristic assertiveness, Ziggy exclaims to one of his sex partners, "'If you loved me . . . you wouldn't rim me while I'm crying.'" Cooper makes Ziggy funny in spite of himself, though one can't help feeling that neediness is an easy target.

The author of the novels *Closer* and *Frisk* continues to push the envelope, not only in subject matter, but also in language. Cooper's voice is edgy and crisp, and his sensibility is unshockable, full of been-there-done-that attitude. His exhausting prose is characterized by etceteras and ellipses and loose-cannon sentences that go on for eight or ten lines, then snap into place, or not. He is often darkly funny, but his writing is too studied, too self-consciously post-post-modern in a Douglas Coupland sort of way, to seem truly free-associative, as is his intention. Too often the jazzy rhythm of his sentences remain in the reader's mind while content evaporates.

And many readers will simply find the book's rewards too scant for all the repellent acts—the necrophilia scenes are as clinical and odious as in *American Psycho*—one must endure. Cooper conveys an utter disgust with the human body in general, and one might tire of the sameness of the characters, who all seem obsessed with bodily scents, pausing at length to contemplate their own fetid armpits. Cooper wants to let us know that we're all dirty, disgusting, and guilty of abusing each other, and all that may reverberate with some readers; then again, it's conceivable that one could plod his way through *Try* just waiting for someone to bathe.

Guy Mannes-Abbott (review date 30 September 1994)

SOURCE: Mannes-Abbott, Guy. "Far Out." *New Statesman and Society* (30 September 1994): 56.

[*In the following review, Mannes-Abbott offers a positive assessment of* Try.]

Dennis Cooper's urgent and uncompromising fiction reduces the critical mainstream to bemusement, and draws polemical support from admirers who recognise its rhythms. This is true of all cultish writing, but Cooper deserves more than cultishness because his work is genuinely innovative and draws from wide cultural sources to develop its confrontational poise.

Baudelaire wrote of three pursuits "worthy of respect" in *My Heart Laid Bare*: "to know, to kill and to create", and these are Cooper's parameters too. Books like *Wrong, Closer* and *Frisk* are full of violent sex but for Cooper, though "sex is the ultimate intimacy . . . it's not enough." In all his writing, sex contains transcendent possibilities in the form of a metaphysics of desire punctuated by death. Divinity takes the form of a kiss, the rectum is a source of profundity and, in *Frisk,* he has the character Dennis write about "killing cute guys" as "some kind of ultimate truth."

Cooper's antecedents are clear; from Nietzsche and Sade through Bataille, Burroughs and contemporary cultural theory. He knows exactly what he is doing in his fiction, the boundaries he crosses and those he balances on, and his direct, taut prose rarely snags on itself. But it is the audacity of the writing, perfectly mirrored in its subject, that propels Cooper towards the rank of high stylist.

Try has Cooper's familiar ingredients but in different proportions. Less extreme, it is also more complex and accomplished. It is about teenage Ziggy and his relationships with his estranged adoptive fathers, his snuff movie-making "Uncle" Ken, his experiments with Nicole and his love for heterosexual novelist and heroin-using Calhoun. Ziggy lives with his "main dad" who has beaten and raped him since he was eight, and the novel follows what happens when his "other dad" Roger, a music journalist, arrives in LA after Ziggy agrees to have sex with him, "which is probably this huge mistake". The soundtrack is Husker Du and Slayer, but the book's rhythm is taken from Céline's triple dot device: tick, tick, tick, pump, pump, pump, tick, tick, tick.

Try gradually accumulates tangential fragments until they form a tightly assembled whole with the fragility of a burnt book. A pivotal scene involves Ken filming his abuse of a drugged boy who later ODs, Ziggy interviewing both for his magazine for the sexually abused (*Slayer*), Impressionism and a violent necrophiliac. The whole thing is a "revelation" and "cool" for Ziggy, who leaves early with the Slayer tape. Ken says "I had a great time. I did." The scene is grotesquely funny, clever and unsettling, and exemplifies Cooper's gambit.

His writing represents and does not analyse desire; the only flaw here is the overtly ridiculous voice of Roger, who is too articulate about his fantasies. But Cooper's triumph in *Try* is to be able to write about extreme experience and even recover a redemptive vocabulary without relying on ironic strategies or the easy collapse into satire.

Earl Jackson Jr. (essay date 1994)

SOURCE: Jackson, Earl, Jr. "Death Drives across Pornotopia: Dennis Cooper on the Extremities of Being." *GLQ: A Journal of Lesbian and Gay Studies* 1, no. 2 (1994): 143-61.

[*In the following essay, Jackson studies the interrelationship of sex and death in Cooper's fiction and the author's explorations of the limits of self-knowledge and metaphysical longing, as depicted in scenes of ritualized sexual violence and physical degradation and mirrored in the simulacra of voyeurism and pornographic images.*]

> You go not till I set you up a glass
> Where you may see the inmost part of you.
> *Hamlet* 3. 5. 19-20

> Perhaps our true sexual act consists in this: in *verifying to the point of giddiness the useless objectivity of things.*
> Jean Baudrillard

Like Jean Genet and William S. Burroughs before him, Dennis Cooper writes consistently within predominantly male homosexual contexts, but his subject is rarely "homosexuality" *per se.* Moreover, the sexual practices thematized in Cooper's work are not part of an identity politics, but are rather subordinated to an investigation into the interior of the body, a movement of objectification and obsessive violation of the body's contours, a peering inside the costume of the person to his real location. Of the generally accepted erotogenic zones, the penis receives far less attention than the anus and the mouth: orifices, ruptures between the surface of "personality" and the murky labyrinths within, apertures into the more tenebrous realities of the organism.

Cooper's concerns, however, are decidedly inflected and nuanced by the sexual orientation of his male characters. The violence in his writings can be articulated "as a kind of studying the self" without participating in or extending the history of male violence against women that complicates similar themes in heterosexual literature and film (qtd. in Meyer 64). Furthermore, the AIDS epidemic is often a non-explicit horizon of Cooper's writing—a terrible historical accident that imposes an unanticipated literalness upon the risks to the body and the self that sex constitutes in much of his work.[1] As he writes in **"Dear Secret Diary"**: "When I'm fucking someone and he accidentally falls off the bed I like to pretend he's about to be shot for trying to defect. Or I did before AIDS ruined death" (5). The present essay is an attempt at a critical account of Cooper's meditations on sexuality and death in his major works, and of how their dynamics not only delimit but also inform human experience.

THE MELANCHOLIA OF DESIRE: "SQUARE ONE" AND "A HERD"

Cooper's early work celebrates the boys who were the targets of his youthful sexual obsessions (*Tiger Beat, Idols*). From *The Tenderness of the Wolves* on, however, there is a shift to an exploration of the vagaries of desire itself—its nature and its location in and among the bodies of both its subject and its objects. Cooper's meditations on the enigma of desire are perhaps most densely encapsulated in **"Square One,"** a highly personal essay on pornographic film as both a rehearsal of that mystery and a clue to its intractable solution. Here Cooper demonstrates how fantasy and memory condition sexual experience and give reality its lie. **"Square One"** has three foci: Jeff Hunter, "star of half a dozen videos and films . . . [whose] physical makeup fits my master plan for the 'ideal sex partner,' a guy I've refined from my 15 or more years of fucking and fantasizing" (83); George M., a "long-lost friend and Jeff lookalike . . . the most focused part of what I'd fashioned into a sex life in '71" (85); and "Ron, Rod, or Rob," someone Cooper "had sex with in a dark hall behind the screen" (89).[2]

Cooper retraces the history of his interest in Jeff Hunter from his first viewing of *Pacific Coast Highway* to finding Jeff accidentally several years later, burnt out and being fistfucked in a porno magazine. In reflecting on his attraction to Jeff, Cooper realizes that it stems from Jeff's resemblance to Cooper's "long-lost friend," George. At the point of this recognition, the narrative scene alternates between a porn theater where a Jeff Hunter film is playing and memories of seducing George as a teenager. Cooper attempts to extricate memory from fantasy through a real sexual encounter in the theater:

> I just had sex in a dark hall behind the screen. I stretched out on a filthy mattress with someone named Ron, Rod, or Rob. . . . I don't know who I expected to fuck but it wasn't a poorly lit man whose name I couldn't catch. . . .
>
> I felt like saying, "You're sweet," but it didn't suit the occasion. So I said, "Bye, Ro-," muffling the last consonant to be safe.
>
> When I was with Ro- I thought of someone else. First Jeff reared his jaded head. I grabbed Ro-'s ears, shoved my cock up his ass until George's face came up for breath.

> ("Square" 89-90)

"Real sex" seems to obfuscate the mechanisms of desire more than it illuminates them. In fact, the real experience on "the filthy mattress" gained its significance parasitically from the fantasy and the memories that circumscribed it. The relation between Jeff and George is clearer, but no more consoling:

> They're distinct. George is the beauty. Jeff's the statue erected of him in a public place, so he'll remain aloft. . . . Jeff's just the shadow that falls across us when we're at certain points in our lives. By now we know what we've missed and become depressed. I'm a man brushing tears, imaginary or not, from my face.

> (86)

The despair comes from a network of intersecting dead-ends: a fantasy/film image that is unfathomable because it has no depth; a memory whose essence is the sense of loss it shapes; and a genital event that can neither correspond to the power nor fulfill the promise of either of the former.

The alternation in the narrative between the Jeff Hunter film and the memories of George figures the vacillation in the modalities of the narrator's desire between mourning and melancholia, with a decided emphasis on the latter. George is the object of Cooper's mourning, Jeff of his melancholia. Mourning is the process of reconciling oneself to the loss (usually the death) of a loved one (Freud, "Mourning" 243-44). Melancholia may be triggered by a similar loss, but often with more tenuous relations to external circumstances. Often the loved one "has not actually died, but has been lost as an object of love," as when one is "jilted" (245). Cooper's relation to Jeff maintains the logic of melan-

cholia, but reverses its symptom: rather than the object not really being absent, here the object is not really present. Introducing Jeff into his fantasies creates an attainment that is a form of loss, which at once ameliorates and reiterates the real loss of George.

Melancholia can also arise when the subject is not conscious of whom he/she has lost, or when the subject knows whose loss he/she is mourning, but cannot understand what it is in that person that the subject has lost by losing that person (244). Much of this applies to Cooper's object-relations to both Jeff and George, even when George was present. In fact, the conditioning factors of melancholia describe some of the pervasive features of desire as Cooper elaborates them throughout his works. What Cooper lost in George is that which one needs from the object of desire, but Cooper characterizes his sexual relationship with George with the same melancholic inability to ascertain what that is and for what loss its attainment will compensate. Pierre, the porn star in Cooper's novel *Frisk,* reflects on the mysterious qualities of sexual motivations from the perspective of the "object" of melancholic desire: "[T]he way men deal with me is like I'm a kind of costume that someone else, someone they've known or made up, is wearing" (67). Recalling a client who had been sexually enthralled with him, Pierre said his lovemaking was "like if I was where someone had buried some sort of treasure or antidote to something malignant in him" (87).

The riddle that is incessantly posed to the desiring subject is the nature of the attraction, and the relation of the body desired to the person desired, a riddle whose frustration is most dramatically expressed in **"Square One"** when Cooper admits that "It was [George] I imagined my cock entering each night, not just his flimsy ass, though that's the first thing I opened when I got the chance" (85). The plots and themes in Cooper's texts often involve the same operative paradox: the persistence of obsessive metaphysical gestures within a radically demystified world, gestures expressing a longing for that X which seems to inhere within a human object of desire that is nevertheless not coextensive with the physical body in which that desire is given shape and through which the desire is brought under control. A desire to know that X—that essence of the person—is overliteralized in acts of mutilation and murder. As Cooper continues to learn nothing of his own desire in reviewing memories of sex with George, he muses, "If I'd sliced into George I'd have been covered with blood at least. There'd be evidence, if no answer" (88).

Cooper's earliest sustained prose exploration of the relations among sexual desire, the transcendence of beauty, and horror is the story **"A Herd,"** which chronicles several weeks in the life of Ray Sexton, a

John Gacy-like serial killer of teenage boys. Sexton begins his ritual as a voyeur, the images of the boys framed in their bedroom windows analogous to the movie screen in porno theaters:

> When a boy was undressing in his room . . . he was relaxed. And if he was watched through a window, cut in three parts by the partly closed shades, by a viewer who had nothing gentle or worthy to do, it was very much like that boy was performing a striptease. . . . Everything was seen and judged from the window.
>
> The man outside mulled an aesthetic to fit the occasion and fashioned rewards from these limits.
>
> ("Herd" 53)

The visions of boys seen through the windows are an accidental and intermediate instantiation of those commodified images of desire that porn perpetuates, as do other, more pervasive media, such as the fanzines of teen idols who configure Sexton's obsessions: "[Teen magazine] stars were Ray's angels, freed from the limits of IQs and coordination, whose distant looks had a cloudy, quaalude effect." Sexton transforms the compromise "aesthetic" of voyeuristic/consumer passivity into an active and destructively creative one through the slaughter of the boys he desires. The "star" quality that originally attracted him to his victims appears sporadically in their faces during the ordeals he inflicts—"an idol's look would appear. . . . Then what Ray had done took on meaning" (56).

Sexton's practices suggest a kind of dark Platonism, a searching for absolute beauty by destroying the individual accidents of its corporealizations. Diotima rhetorically asks Socrates a question to which Sexton provides a horrifying answer: "How would it be . . . if someone could see the Beautiful itself, pure, clear, unmixed—not infected with human flesh and color, and a lot of other mortal nonsense—if he were able to know the divinely Beautiful itself, in its unique form?" (*Symposium* 211E). Whatever and wherever a boy is once Sexton is finished with him, he is not "the thing on the table." Diotima's prescribed ascent to the Beautiful requires serial experiences of the physical beauty of boys, leading to increasing generalization and abstraction. Sexton liberated the ideal from the boys' bodies, and kept it within him, checking his memory of each victim with the newspaper photographs after the bodies had been found: "Ray looked at the face of a boy in the newspaper. The young man had put his lips close to a camera and pouted. The camera had focused, flashed. The face had slid through a hole in its side, unfogging slowly" (73).

The essence of a person becomes something which radiates from the body, as a numinous simulacrum of the face that had held it captive. This version of the ideal gives it a shape intelligible to its worshippers, transform-

ing the boys at times into idols who look down from incomprehensible distances—at once fully accessible and absolutely unattainable (like Jeff Hunter's image on the movie screen). This is also the principle of Cooper's volume of poetry, *Idols,* panegyrics to boys in high school he loved or longed for, and to teenybopper heartthrobs of the '70s. In the prose poem **"Teen Idols"** Cooper reflects on the pop-culture processes of mass-market image cathexis:

> Teen idols are the best boys on the block. . . . Always romantic, they sign their photos "I think of you and you're beautiful" and then "love always" and then their first names. They know how to please us, to keep us hanging on.
>
> (*Idols* 58)

Note the similarity of this description to Sexton's of a boy called Jay: "Ray wished he could hand this boy his photo to autograph. The boy would write, 'loved you, kissed me, I'm yours . . . let's fade away' then his first name" (**"Herd"** 73). Sexton made Jay a celebrity—an "idol"—by negating his existence—reducing it to the fleeting fame of a newsphoto—a photo of "someone who didn't exist." Sexton's action is complemented by Craig in the title story of Cooper's collection *He Cried,* who made enlargements of the newsphotos of a serial killer's victims: "He tacks it next to the others, across his bedroom wall. Ten corpses stare through the grain like hallucinations he used to worry he'd never come down from" (*Cried* 30).

If Sexton represents a homicidal extension of the idealism of the *Symposium,* the porn theater in **"Square One"** is a site for a psychoanalytic inversion of the epistemology of the *Republic.* In Book VII, Socrates likens the unenlightened to people chained in a cave, forced to look only forward at the wall. Behind them is a flame and between the flame and the prisoners, people walk continually holding up puppets and images of animals and other objects. The only knowledge of objects those restrained have is of the shadows of the puppets projected onto the wall of the cave; such "knowledge"—*eikasia*—the acceptance of images as reality—is the only option for these unhappy prisoners (514 a-c). The men in Cooper's porno theater have consciously induced a state of *eikasia* in themselves.[3]

In Plato's allegory, there are at least two more levels of reality beyond that of the shadow play. The unshackled prisoner could turn from the shadow of the bull-image on the wall to see the real bull-image casting the shadow. The freed prisoner could be led out of the cave to see a real bull. No parallel options exist for Cooper's moviegoers. If the need for the real incited a revolution in the porn audience, the Platonic paradigm could not provide a basis for any reasonable or satisfactory action (in fact all actions arising from such a need would destroy the possibility of the type of satisfaction obtained by viewing the film): "[T]he screen hangs between paying customers and our ideal lovers. If we charged, ripped it down, we'd find a wall of unsupported brick" (**"Square"** 88).

Cooper's theater does not possess the escape exits of Plato's cave, because its patrons retain the pessimism and frustration caused by idealism, but have discarded the faith in any metaphysical system that would support the epistemological teleology of Plato's allegory. The transition from shadow, to icon, to real object parallels the transition Socrates urges us to make when he condemns art in *Republic* X: from an artificial representation (a painting of a bed) to a tangible object (an actual bed) to the intelligible object (the Form of 'bed'). The images on the movie screen hold no guarantee of an accession to higher forms of objects of which they are emanations. The ontological saturation of the film image itself is an ontology by default, due to a technology that can only reproduce a reality that no longer exists by the time of its re-presentation.

Unlike Plato's cave dwellers, the porno spectators actually know the difference between image and reality, but have consciously repudiated this knowledge in order to maintain a fantasy that feeds their desire. In fact, the men in the audience suspend their disbelief precisely because *they know that the referent of the image does not exist.* The suspension of disbelief in film spectatorship is often compared with the "split belief" of the subject's defensive disavowal of castration.[4] But this contradictory belief can also reflect aberrations in the mourning process. When the subject's resistance to the reality of the object's loss is particularly great, the subject may reject "reality" and retain the object in a "hallucinatory wishful psychosis" (Freud, "Mourning" 244-45). Hallucination nullifies the distinction between a presentation in consciousness and a perception (*Interpretation of Dreams* 565-66); such states appear to be regressions to an earlier phase in which the child imagined objects of satisfaction not really present (*Interpretation of Dreams* 544-46), a habit gradually overcome by the adaptation to "reality testing" ("Two Principles" 219-21). Hallucinations are not actually brought about by a regression, but rather by the ego's withdrawal of cathexis in external reality ("Metapsychology" 231). Dreams represent a non-pathological form of this renunciation (232); film viewing is a culturally sanctioned and controlled version of this deliberate withdrawal from reality testing. The realism of a film concretely produces an analogous experience to the identification of ideation and perception. If the structural dynamic of spectatorial belief resembles a refusal to complete the work of mourning, the spectator's cathexis to the screen image enacts melancholia in its epistemological and ontological contradictions. Claiming possession of the desired object through its image is also acknowledging the impossibility of that possession. The image is object as non-existence. The spectacle of the porn-image is no longer a subject but a memorial to the abnegation of subjectivity (the *subject's* deliberate becoming-object of the gaze); but it is also a sign of that *object's* absence as well. Guy Debord writes that "the spectacle is *affirmation* of appearance and affirmation of all human life . . . as mere appearance. But the critique which reaches the truth of the spectacle exposes it as the visible *negation* of life, as a negation of life which *has become visible*" (10). Cooper's texts are one such critique of the "truth of the spectacle." In exposing that spectacle as the "visible negation of life," Cooper also lays the groundwork for reconceiving representation as a concrete cultural elaboration of the death drive. In his increasingly psychomythic narratives in which his characters embody and enact this representational tragedy, Cooper delineates the death drive as a force whose symbolization "allows for an intuition of the unconscious, even though it is already at the level of discursive thought: a theoretical exigency, the refracted derivative of desire" (Laplanche 109).

The inevitable temporal and spatial disjunction between the scene of filming and the scene of projection gives any film a potentially elegiac aura: even in mainstream cinema, the film often shows stars no longer young or long dead, times and places no longer possible to experience as they are depicted. The mortality of the depicted real that the film image both denies and demonstrates is magnified to its most nightmarish extreme in gay male porn. Since the onset of the AIDS pandemic, there is a macabre likelihood that a significant number of the cast of any gay porno film is dead. The porn actor, who, like any film actor, gives himself up to the camera, allowing the cinematic apparatus to produce an image of him that will bracket (and thus negate) his biosocial individual particularity, may also be participating in his actual (extrafilmic) obliteration. The acts engaged in in the films also suggest the actual occasion of the infection: porn videos made since 1980 that feature unprotected anal sex may be delayed reaction snuff films. Therefore, the general paradoxes of the cinematic situation (the viewer's deliberate ascription of reality to flickering images; the cognitively full representation of a non-present world) become intensely imbued with death in the gay male porn that Cooper discusses. The films hybridize the qualities of the pop star posters, in the glamorization of male beauty, and the newsphotos of the murdered boys in **"A Herd"** and **"He Cried,"** in the funereal quality of these images. In both cases physical attractiveness is an indirect cause of death. (*Eidolon,* from which "idol" is derived, means both a representation of a god and a phantom of a dead person.)

The other major form of disavowal operative within the split belief of film spectatorship is the fetish. Because

Cooper writes outside of heterosexual presumption, he returns "fetish" to a pre-Freudian meaning—independent of the castration complex and male fears of sexual difference. Instead the fixation on representation in lieu of referent becomes akin to a more traditional religious meaning of fetish: "An inanimate object worshipped by savages on account of its supposed inherent magical powers, or as being animated by a spirit. A fetish differs from an *idol* in that it is worshipped in its own character, not as the image, symbol, or occasional residence of a deity" (*OED*; see also Pietz).

Cooper's search for an absolute that would at least *justify* the vehemence of human need (most viscerally expressed in sexuality), if not *satisfy* it, recalls earlier attempts to rediscover the numinous in the phenomenal as a response to a loss of faith. In his concentration on the physical beauty of men, Cooper betrays a nostalgia for certain patterns of Western transcendence. Equating in *Safe* the "truth" of Mark's body to a skeleton is a virtually medieval gesture both in its iconography and in its repudiation of the flesh. In **"Teen Idols"** he posits the teen stars as entities "behind" their photos. In **"Square One"** Cooper ventures behind the screen to have "real" sex with Ro-. Reality is behind the veil, but it is a disconsolate discovery, and one that leaves the ineffability of the screen images intact. It is interesting too that instead of following Plato's cavemen out into the sun, Cooper goes further into the theater, to find that the "real" is banal, and only tolerable when punctuated and screened over by the images of irrecoverably lost objects.

Although in this scenario the belief in the reality of images seems to borrow its pathos from the traces of idealism in a post-idealist world, the involvement with non-real figures acquires additional meaning from a psychoanalytic discovery not to be found in premodern thought: Freudian "psychical reality"—the legitimation of unconscious fantasy, and hence of phantasmatic representations (Laplanche and Pontalis 8-9). The psychical realities (unconscious wishes) that find shape most vividly in dreams allow the embodiments of the fantasies (porn stars, strippers, hustlers, movie stars, and rock musicians) to be replaced as primary objects by the visual records of their allure: these are fantasies whose gratification no longer presupposes even potential physical contact with the bioenergetic entities the icons memorialize:

> There are magazines to present them endlessly, in love and lonely. . . . The boys lounge suggestively each moment of their lives. Pictures prove that. In some ways these photos are the idols, not the boys behind them. . . .
>
> (*Idols* 58)

Visual images become an end in themselves, because of the recognized unattainability of the stars who had posed for them, and because of the perfection possible within these representations that life cannot offer.[5] While pornography aids in concretizing and confirming fantasies through its maximalization of the visible, it is also predicated upon the impossibility of the "total fulfillment" it depicts. Furthermore, the transparency of pornography to its object exposes the secrets of the body, but not the mysteries of the body's fascination for the viewer. Desired bodies can be documented, but what makes those bodies desirable cannot be so easily accounted for. The frustration involved in desire arises from the contradictory ontological status that physical beauty is assigned. Beauty is both immediately accessible and ultimately indefinable, at once apodeictic and arcane. Beauty and sexual allure take on transcendent roles within pornographic film, at once manifest as the visible surfaces of the bodies, but also functioning to hypostasize the significance of those bodies beyond the very physical limitations that the film insistently exposes:

> Beauty . . . [is] the deity panning for gold in these wasted stars' used up bodies. It creates dreams out of people the cat wouldn't drag in, aiming our cocks at, averting our minds from "the ditch of what each one means," as Bob Dylan whined. . . .
>
> (**"Square"** 92)[6]

Although the director, as high priest of the fetish-religion, controls the basic structure and sequence of the images in the film, there is something inherent in the body those images depict, something before which the director "is as powerless as the trained dog running alongside a herd of cattle, each of whom could crush him with a misstep. He is merely the right man at the right place, right time" (**"Square"** *Soup* 71). The reality of the porn film ("they're *really* doing it") is still a delayed—posthumous—one: those "real people" "really doing" it are no longer there. In fact they perform in a non-existent space, one Cooper finds essentially morbid: "I have faith that the man who composed [the scene] has managed an accurate portrait of what it would be like to stand in a place far beyond mine, one I compare to death" (**"Square"** *Soup* 72). But the plane in which fantasy and reality, desire and satisfaction coincide is limited to the movie screen, and has no correlate in "real life"; there can be no change of venue, and all attempts to construct a materialist compromise, a spatialization of the ideal, result in a despondent parody (the hall behind the porno screen in **"Square One"**), in paralyzing hallucinatory refuges (George's Disneyland in *Closer*), in psychotic parodies of childhood whimsy (Gary's playroom in *Frisk*), or in sheer life-denying chambers of horror (Ray's crawl space in **"Herd"**).

Robert Glück has called Dennis Cooper a "religious writer" who, "like Poe," uses "the horror genre . . . to test the boundaries of life, generate feelings of wonder and awe" ("Running"). Glück's observation also indicates the affinity both writers have for the work of Georges Bataille, who viewed sexuality and religion as two manifestations of a "disequilibrium in which the being consciously calls his [*sic*] own existence in question" (*Erotism* 31). Glück's interest in "the sublime" and Cooper's definition of "God" are both unquestionably Bataillean in character. Glück describes the "sublime" as "nothing, . . . a catastrophe, a violent orgasm . . . anything that expresses a void which our communities have filled with religions and monsters in order to understand the absence of ground" ("Truth's Mirror" 41-42). Cooper first distinguishes his conception of "God" from the ordinary Christian one, which he dismisses as "that simple and rickety projection into which our ideas about death tend to focus when we get lazy" (**"Smoke"** 1). He lists the probable locations of his more awesome and seductive "God" in "sleep, hallucinations, daydreams, orgasms, comas, one's own body, others' bodies, the dark, the sun . . ." and suggests that it is not only aligned with death, but is a powerful temptation toward death, drawing the living out of the boundaries of life. God is a "Siren" and is disruptive of life in ways that inform sexual desire and aesthetic inspiration: "[W]hen we want to see God we might as well get specific—seduce someone, make art, commit suicide, masturbate. . . ." (**"Smoke"** 2)

The means by which Glück and Cooper depict sexual access to "the sublime" or "God," respectively, differ in ways that reflect each writer's schematics of the relations between sexual ecstasis and intersubjectivity. Although Glück's narrator "Bob" in *Jack the Modernist* is the penetrated spectacle for the involved onlookers in the baths, the orgasm he achieves is his own, through the others but not with them. And sexual culmination is as much an evocative negativity for Glück as it is for Cooper: "I felt a soldier's fidelity to the orgasm . . . singled out from all the orgasms in the flux. . . . [T]he spasms that were not me overtook and became me along with a sense of dread. I felt like a tooth being pulled. . . . I relinquished the firm barrier that separated us—no, that separated me from nothing" (*Jack* 55-56). In Cooper's system, the subject of desire is never the object of desire; the unidirectionality of desire is modelled on the relation of the spectator to the screen, which also figures both the subject's melancholia and his fetishistic awe of the object.[7]

Desire is further schematized throughout Cooper's individual works in oppositions between subject-meaning (meaning as an intentional act) and object-meaning (meaning as effect/affect). "Subject-meaning"—what the subject intentionally means by what it does/desires—is one of the themes of Cooper's poem, **"Poem for George Miles"** (the "George M." of **"Square One"**), which is an elegy both for the object of desire and the quality of that desire. The lyric voice is a twenty-nine-year-old "I" looking back at a poem written for George when that "I" was 19 (the nostalgia and the temporal discontinuities of the speaking subject are reminiscent of Beckett's "Krapp's Last Tape"):

> When I first sharpened a
> pencil in purpling language
> and drew my first poem
> from its raveling depths
> it "poured my heart out"
> as thoroughly as I would,
> make that could, at 19. . . .
> The poem is now cleaned
> out of power, as bed is
> once sunlight has entered.
> I see its mathematics: lines
> built as an ornate frame
> around a skeletal feeling
> that's faded from sight.
> Who knows what I meant?
>
> (*Cried* 24)

On object-meaning, any number of illustrations could be selected. For example, Cooper's musings on Jeff Hunter:

> It's not Jeff who moves me, like I said. He's the part I can relate to. It's as though some concept way over my head has taken human form so we can communicate. . . . It's as if Jeff is moaning, "This is as much as you'll grasp," and not, "Fuck me," continuously.
>
> (**"Square"** 84)

In his prose, the object of desire (the object-meaning) often proves impermeable to revelation while it remains the focal point of the narrative. The narrative itself becomes the flux of desire and is what gets revealed (the subject-meaning), illuminated in contrast to the opacity of its object. This is the dynamic of Cooper's first full-length novel, *Safe*, a triptych, three separate views of the same enigmatic young man, Mark Lewis. The meaning and nature of the desired object's power is as resistant to explication as Mark is ultimately rejecting of the love of his three suitors in these narratives. At times the subjectivity of the viewer becomes "entangled" (a word Cooper likes) with the object, in the attempt to excavate the secret of the object's power. In the "My Mark" section of *Safe*, the first-person narrator, "Dennis," deconstructs a photograph of Mark in which intentional and affective meanings coalesce over Mark's absence (or the absence which Mark embodies) and the enigma of Mark's erotic power:

> A head that has power over me. A globe lightly covered by pale flesh, curly black hair, and small, dark eyes whose intensity's too deeply meant to describe or remember the color of, seemingly smeared and spiraling.
>
> I fill a head with what I need to believe about it. It's a mirage created by beauty built flush to a quasi-emotion that I'm reading in at the moment of impact: its eyes on mine, mine glancing off for a second, then burrowing in.
>
> (62)

What Mark reveals to his lovers, his beauty—as captured in the narrator Dennis's photo of Mark's face—is also what conceals his "true self" from them. The fascination Mark held for Rob, Dennis, and Doug drew them to him but ultimately kept him a secret. Dennis's truths are always finally elegiac, his meanings trivial when compared to the inarticulate radiance of the desired object. "My Mark" is both exploration and resignation:

> What's left behind is Mark's beauty, safe, in a sense, from the blatant front lighting of my true emotion, though it creeps in. I'm moving stealthily closer, I think, to the heart of the matter, where Mark's body acts as a guide to what he has been feeling. That's his, like great art is the century's it was created in, though still alive in the words of a man who speaks well of him.

> (*Safe* 58)

POSTMETAPHYSICAL SACRIFICE: *CLOSER*

Cooper's characters have a resentful fascination with the body's limitations, without the option of cyberspace (as in William Gibson); they act on a suspicion of the body's truth, without the promise of a supraphysical plane (as in writings of religious mystics and in ghost stories). The characters in Cooper's fiction often either embody or act out a paradox central to any sexual desire and practice, no matter how refined and urbane. Roland Barthes comments on the irony in the great care he lavishes on his appearance to arouse his lover to engage in acts of passion that will ruin that very highly groomed self which had been designed to incite its own destruction. This observation on the contradictory nature of the "toilet" he performs on himself in preparation for the "encounter" leads him to investigate the etymology of the word "toilet," where he discovers two obscure meanings:

> "the preparations given to the prisoner condemned to death before he is led to the scaffold"; . . . "the transparent and oily membrane used by butchers to cover certain cuts of meats." As if, at the end of every toilet, inscribed within the excitation it provokes, there were always the slaughtered, embalmed, varnished body, prettified in the manner of a victim. In dressing myself, I embellish that which, by desire, will be spoiled.

> (127)

In *Safe* Rob discusses Ray Sexton with his lover, "equating the shambles Sexton left high school gymnasts in to the flushed, dripping wet mess Mark becomes in his arms"(20). The contradictory impulses of self-assertion and self-abnegation that cofunction in sexual desire also subtend the parallels of violence and sexual intercourse in the (usually unwelcome) threat that violence constitutes to the physical integrity of the body and the (often sought after) threat to the ego-boundaries

in sexual union. These parallels, as well as the similarities between orgasm and death as annihilations of the discrete self, inform the sense of erotic horror that permeates Cooper's work.

Just as the movie screen concretizes a heaven that evacuates all metaphysical longing, the mass media problematizes the structure of the psycho-physical self—particularly in terms of the relations between the external and internal "person." The boys in Cooper's work live in a media-ocracy in which the ultimate significance of a person is flattened out into a form of celebrity (as in Warhol), absolutely exteriorizing the self through a radical identification between the "self" and its public persona (the "Sean Cassidy" and "John F. Kennedy, Jr." poems in *Idols,* for example). The real boys experience contradictions between external self and internal life that never disturb the blissful sheen of their cult heroes's posters. Furthermore, the literalization of space described in **"Square One"** and **"A Herd"** is paralleled here in the pervasive interest the characters take in the difference between the beauty of the visible body and the awful "truth" of the internal organs. "Interiority" loses its mystical and psychological meanings of soul and mind, and is transposed onto viscera. Jeff Hunter's "heart" cannot even nostalgically suggest a center of human emotions, as it is simply "a lump of confusing blue tissue two feet up his asshole" (**"Square"** 89). This dualism renders the human fundamentally inexplicable. The beauty, personality, and actions of the boys are a veneer whose interior reality is simply a complex of body parts that would be disgusting to most people, and meaningful only to medical specialists.

Closer concerns a half dozen wealthy gay high school students in a suburb of Los Angeles, all of whom are sexually obsessed with one another, and in particular with George Miles. The boys are divided into subjects and objects of desire, the subjects being at least relatively articulate, and the objects either dazedly incommunicative, like George, or immersed in a fantasy world, like David, who believes he is a rock star. The key actors in the novel each have a specialty that involves a particular manipulation of the body: John is an artist who sketches the boys, Alex is an aspiring filmmaker who documents some of the sexual activity central to the plot, and Steve is an entrepreneur who fills his converted garage nightclub with bodies and sets them dancing. These would represent the positive creative urges, matched by the negative creative urges of the two adults in the novel, Philippe, who dreams of mutilating and murdering young men, and Tom, who actually does.

The body in *Closer* is repeatedly demythologized. John conceives of his drawings as a means to disable the beauty of his subjects, to "reveal the dark underside, or whatever it's called, of people you wouldn't think were particularly screwed up" (5).[8] Even sex does not allow the body to elude the sense of its grisly facticity. When John has sex with George, he wonders at the fact that "George's skin felt so great. That was the weirdest part, feeling how warm and familiar George was and at the same time realizing the kid was just skin wrapped around some grotesque-looking stuff" (7).

David's biologist father decorated the walls of their house with pictures of semi-dissected adolescents. At dinner David cuts his "quiche into eight thousand pieces," trying to keep his eyes averted from a poster above his father's head of a boy roughly David's age, whose "back is turned and where his ass used to be there's this thing that looks half like drawn curtains and half like what's left of a cow once it gets to the butcher's shop" (28). Such brutal reality may be one of the factors that had driven David into his rock star delusion and his obsession with his own beauty that he admits "helps me believe in myself and not worry that I'm just a bunch of blue tubes inside a skin wrapper" (22).[9]

Both of these sentiments suggest the incorporation of an ego that is as entirely surface as the posters and movies that have formed it. Such an ego bears a striking resemblance to Didier Anzieu's notion of the "skin ego," which is part of his adjustments of Freudian psychoanalytic models to empirical changes in predominant pathologies. When Freud was practicing, the majority of patients were suffering from "straightforward neuroses," but in Anzieu's own practice he notes a significant increase in "borderline cases" between "neurosis and psychosis" in which the patient suffers

> from an absence of borders or limits . . . uncertain of the frontiers between the psychical and bodily Egos, between the reality Ego and the ideal Ego . . . unable to differentiate erogenous zones, [the patient] confuses pleasant experiences with painful ones, and cannot distinguish between drives, which leads him [sic] to experience the manifestation of a drive not as desire but as violence. The patient . . . experiences a diffuse sense of ill-being . . . of watching the functioning of his body and mind from outside, of being a spectator of something which is and at the same time not his [sic] own existence.
>
> (7)

These borderline states lead to a profound sense of emptiness in attempts at meaning that produce, instead of an ego-object relation, an ego-abject relation (Kristeva, "Within" 43-44; and Barzilai 295). "Abjection" is the dread of that which was once part of the body but was expelled as "unclean" or "disgusting." These abjects however continue to threaten the integrity of the subject with a chaotic dissolution of the boundaries of inside and outside (Kristeva, *Powers* 3-4). The

precarious balance between the skin ego and the viscera in John and David's psychic structures should be clear from the above passages. The balance is displaced as the narrative progresses.

Within this wasteland of self-preempted youths, George becomes deeply involved with Philippe, an older Frenchman with bizarre tastes. Their sex involves necrophiliac fantasies, beatings, and coprophagia. Eventually Philippe introduces George to Tom, another older man who examines George matter-of-factly and brutally, forcing a hand down his throat and up his anus. After a particularly violent threesome, Tom drives George home, and tells him if he ever considers suicide, to call him. George makes note of that invitation, and its ambivalence. He then goes into his room to examine his ass, to see if he can understand what these men find so attractive about it. Here George attempts to assimilate the inexplicable pleasure of the Other into his assessment of his own value as a person. He mistakes Philippe's and Tom's objectification of him as a confirmation of him as a subject (it is exactly the opposite).[10] This is the same error that Henry makes in *Frisk* when he describes a recent sexual experience and his interpretation of it:

> [L]ast weekend I slept with two . . . guys. . . . They kept calling me "that." One would ask, "What does that taste like?" and "What's the temperature inside of that?" . . . It made me realize I'm important to certain people.
>
> (*Frisk* 7)

The boy's need to reduce thought to neurological quiescence through excessive drug use, and their compulsive fashioning and delimiting of the self to fit the desire of the Other, are expressions of the death drive that takes George to Tom's house after George's mother's death. As he writes in his diary before leaving for Tom's, "It's like a party or something to say my goodbye to the person I am" (*Closer* 98). George did not realize how true that might have become: Tom no-vocained him and began "chopping him down" in his basement. When Tom asked him if he had "any last words" George intoned the words of the Disneyland ride, "Dead . . . men . . . tell . . . no . . . tales," which brought on the tears that literally saved his life: disgusted at this display of emotion, Tom threw him out of the house (99-100).

The importance of Disneyland to George cannot be dismissed as a *deus ex machina*. It locates the kind of pervasive vacuum in which George lives and which he particularizes in both his self-apprehension and his willingness to subject himself to dehumanization.[11] George becomes a (necessarily) inarticulate embodiment of the postmodern environment that engendered him. For Baudrillard, Disneyland is "a perfect model of all the entangled orders of simulation. To begin with it is a play of illusions and phantasms: Pirates, the Frontier, Future World, etc." (*Simulations* 23-24).[12]

George becomes as much a simulation of a person as the automated denizens of the Disney pavilions, or the inexhaustibly available images of the porn stars. Alex describes George's "hyperreal" state best when he compares George's looks to "the real boy that Pinocchio was forced to become" (*Closer* 62). When Philippe sees George fall on the street, he reacts in a way that explains why he can use George as he does: "When Philippe pictured George's expression approaching the ground, he saw pretend pain, the look that would creep over dolls' faces when children left them alone in the dark" (105). George's beauty taken to be an unreal perfection of reality suggests Baudrillard's "automaton"—particularly in the kind of deadly curiosity George arouses in his adult admirers: the automaton is "an interrogation upon nature, the mystery of the existence or non-existence of the soul, the dilemma of appearance and being. It is like God: what's underneath it all, what's inside, what's in the back of it?" (*Simulations* 93). These are precisely the questions that Tom and Philippe (and before them Ray Sexton, and after them the "Dennis" of *Frisk*) attempt to answer.

Philippe's melancholia reverses the disavowal of the hallucinating mourner and the average moviegoer; he looks at a real person (George) and disavows his reality. George and Philippe share a disorder that is necessary for hallucinations, and that is analogically enacted in film spectatorship: the failure to distinguish consistently between what is internal and what is external to the ego.[13] Philippe and Tom sought the secret of George through literal invasions and excavations of George's body. George (like the other boys) confused his inner self with his "innards," in a detour of abjection, which according to Kristeva is an attempt to individuate the self by demarcating the divisions of inside and outside (*Powers* 60-61).

Even when more successfully accomplished than in George's case, abjection leaves a residue of the contingency of identity in the materiality of its biological components—that which can be expelled or incorporated, but which signifies the morass into which the subject can re-devolve (*Powers* 9-11; 70-71). The vehemence with which George was handled and literally reduced to bodily secretions/excretions in his encounter with Philippe and Tom actually galvanized his need for these men. The materials they forced from his body made him realize that his interior offered no support for an articulatable self. Furthermore, these "abjects" attest to the "precariousness of the subject's grasp of its own identity," foreboding the return to "the chaos from which it is formed." George's dependence on the adults' objectifying lust to fortify his exterior-

ized ego against this anxiety is a will-toward-death as subject, but it is also a defense against the abjection he experiences at their hands, since this abjection itself is "one of the few avowals of the death drive, an undoing of the processes constituting the subject" (Grosz 74). The dissonance between the scatological horrors of George's sex life and the ethereality of mass media ego-ideals only perpetuates the cycle, since abjection itself constitutes a dual acknowledgment of the necessity and impossibility of the subject's "desire to transcend corporeality," in which the subject rejects yet affirms "the defiling, impure, uncontrollable materiality of [its] embodied existence" (Grosz 72).[14] Neither George nor Philippe understand what Glück calls the "disjunction between self and body" ("Truth's" 41-42). The sublimations of this disjunction Cooper's characters effect, inaugurate the melancholy mystery of desire and its often tragic resolutions.

The central obsessions of the novel are figured most graphically in Philippe's memories of a snuff film made by one of the members of Philippe's circle:

> He'd picked up the hitchhiker, coerced him home, got him drunk, numbed his body with Novocaine, led him into a basement, started the film rolling, mutilated his ass, asked if he'd like to say any last words, to which the boy had said, "Please don't." Then he killed him.
>
> The only sound in the room was the clicking projector. Sometimes the clicks and the stabs matched for a few seconds. . . . Then the boy made a very bland face. "Is he dead?" someone asked. "No," the man answered. "Not yet. Watch." . . .
>
> . . . At what seemed a haphazard point, everyone in the room heard a brief, curt announcement. "Now," it said. . . .
>
> The film ended. It flapped like a bat. People redid their pants.
>
> (*Closer* 108-09)

Like the more innocuous porno audience in **"Square One,"** these men share a fascination with what the images reveal and what mysteries they mark but mask. The boundaries among living individuals and between the living and the dead are concatenated in this awful ritual, which recalls Bataille's explanation of sacrifice in a less self-conscious historical period of human evolution: "The victim dies and the spectators share in what his death reveals. This is what religious historians call the sacramental element" (*Erotism* 82). Note the striking similarity in tone and theme in Glück's description of spectator sex in the baths:

> Men stood around, serious, watching us. . . . [O]thers tended me respectfully because the one who is fucked induces awe by his extreme exposure. . . . [T]heir collective mind said *he's doing it* which my finite mind repeated. Although they masturbated themselves to

obtain immediate knowledge of my excitement, *it was as spectators that they solemnly shared in what my pleasure revealed.*

(*Jack* 54-55 second emphasis added)

Each of the passages above concerns the communal witnessing of an event that makes intensely present an extreme boundary of human being: death and orgasm, each an incontrovertible "now" which absolutely interrupts the continuity of consciousness. The mediation of film makes the situation in **Closer** significantly different. The temporal and spatial divisions between the viewers and the center of attention structures the non-reciprocity of subject-object relations (the object cannot return their look). The boy's murder forecloses the possibility of a full knowledge of what is seen: the onlookers in the baths or in the audience can experience orgasm but not death. The spectatorial situation exemplifies the intersubjective limits of these men's desire; conversely, the transitive negativity of their desire (sexuality as annihilation of the object) informs a theory of representation that is practically an occult reverence for representation as an endlessly iterable expression of this outwardly directed death drive. The snuff film implicates representation, because the filming and screening of the murder are integral aspects of the crime.[15] The film incites a religious awe as a memorial of the point at which the person ceases to be. This, however, is only a peculiar variation on the logic of filmic practice, since any film or photograph is also a record of the absolutely lost, a testament to the absence of the object it represents. Film and photography are thus perfect techniques for realizing and preserving the de-entification of the living person. Film/photography becomes the postmodern version of the functions Bataille discerns in the cave paintings of Lascaux: "The cave drawings must have been intended to depict that instant when the animal appeared and killing, at once inevitable and reprehensible, laid bare life's mysterious ambiguity" (*Erotism* 74).

The corpse—in its hideous resemblance to the living person now gone—is an obscene subversion of personhood (Kristeva, *Powers* 9-10; Blanchot 256; Gallop 45); the photographic or filmic image is an attempt to retain what is already gone, which is informed with the death that the corpse literally embodies.[16] Sexual fantasies, either those "within" the person or those expressed in pornographic media, instigate a coalescence of the simulacrum of the corpse with the retention of the lost object. Bazin suggested that "the plastic arts" might owe their real impulse to the "practice of embalming the dead" (*What Is Cinema* II, 9). Art historians tell us that realistic human portraiture began with death masks (Ariès 257-58).[17] Cooper's work insistently exposes the relation between representation and death—the negation of the real in the image; the self-alienation within desire; the internal negation of the

referent of the metaphor—all based on the resemblance of the corpse to the person who has died. The trajectories among representation and reality, life and death, desire and its ends, are dramatized in Cooper's work as passion plays in a childlike world where childhood has always already been invaded by the negativity of adult sexuality (Ferenczi 156-57).

The sacrificial quality of sex, in which the object becomes an opacity of negation and the subject disincorporates itself within the image of the desired object, finds an ancestral model in the cave painting of a man with an erect penis before a dying bison, a paradoxical image which (in Bataille's assessment) asserts the "essential and paradoxical accord between death and eroticism," a truth that "remains veiled to the extent that the human mind hides from itself" (*Tears* 53). This is a truth or an awe-filled intuition of the truth that Dennis Cooper explores, most recently emblematized in the entranced gaze at the fake snuff photo in the opening section of **Frisk**, in which the plaster-of-paris wound on a boy's supposedly shot-open anus takes on the forbidden fascination of death and sexuality itself—an uncanny sight that lures one into the abyss, something which, in Cooper's words, is "too out-of-focus to actually explore with one's eyes, but too mysterious not to want to try" (4).

ACKNOWLEDGMENTS

I would like to thank Dodie Bellamy, Robert Glück, Bo Huston, David Jansen-Mendoza, and Kevin Killian, for their conversation and support.

Notes

1. "I think in my work there's always been a sort of terror about sex. The desire for sex that you could have with someone you objectify but the terror of having to deal with a real person. . . . Sex is a really scary thing, you've got to choose your partners carefully, and what to do. . . . I always think the sex in my books is so unsexy, because they're nervous about each other, and it's so much about just wanting to get something out of this body they're with and some idea they have about this person. . . . [And since AIDS] it's just a general terror that's come over sex. And I think it's reinforcing that in my work" (qtd. in Meyer 64).

2. "Square One" was originally published in *Soup 4: New Critical Perspectives,* ed. Bruce Boone (1985): 70-72. When I quote a passage that appears only in that version and was not included in the later version, printed in *Wrong,* it will be cited as "Square Soup."

3. "An audience made up of men like me has surrendered its collective will to a filmmaker's. Like a cheap spaceship prop in an old sci-fi flick, a grungy

theater scattered with hopeful, upturned faces seems to speed toward its destination—giant bodies composed of light" ("Square" 83).

4. Freud, "Fetishism," and "Splitting"; Mannoni 175-80; Mulvey.

5. Even people with "real" sex lives often prefer the numb and numbing refuges of the world without consequences provided by pornographic media: "The life pornography pictures is ordered. . . . Doug wants to live in this one-dimensional world. . . . If someone he fucked died he'd never hear about it and if he did the world wouldn't compute or feel real to him. He'd be involved in his latest orgasm, face drawn so tight nothing else could get under" (*Safe* 84-85).

6. The Dylan quotation, from "The Gates of Eden" (*Bringing It All Back Home*), which also refers to the "object-meaning," is used again parodistically in *Closer* (5).

7. The only major symptom of melancholia as Freud describes it that is not directly evident in Cooper's narrative personae is the tendency to berate the self as morally inferior ("Mourning" 246-48). A desiring subject in Cooper's texts does, however, tend to disregard his corporeal self as a meaningful part in any sexual encounter. In other words, these subjects never wish to see themselves as objects of desire. The "Dennis" narrator of *Frisk* states that sexual reciprocation makes him "very uncomfortable," noting that his tricks "must pick up on my tastes right away, since they almost never want to explore me. They just lie back, take it from me. . . . Usually I don't notice my body. It's just there, working steadily. I wash it, feed it, jerk it off, wipe its ass, and that's all" (50).

8. John "subtracts from" his subjects by defacing their drawings (*Closer* 4). "In porn a director can only add or subtract from what exists outside his control—attractiveness" ("Square" *Soup* 71).

9. Or the clue David—despite himself—in *Closer* gives the reader of the origin of his rock star delusion: "Once upon a time I was a little boy. I rode my bike constantly. I wandered everywhere. bought stuff, sang songs to myself. I stopped in a mall. This man came up to me. He was an A & R man for a big record company. He told me I was amazing. I said okay and we went back to his house. He tried to fuck me. I bled all over the place. Then he showed me the door and said, 'Thanks for being so well designed, kid'" (*Closer* 37).

10. Other characters also assess their bodies' attractiveness in the mirror, attempting to see it as others do: Mark in *Safe* (41) and Julian and Henry in *Frisk* (13; 16-17).

11. During George's first encounter with Philippe, he envisioned it as an exploration in a mineshaft in a Disneyland western fantasy geography (50). When examining his wounded anus for its "charm" to Philippe and Tom, he compares the swollen opening to the "painted mouth" of "Injun Joe's Cave," a Disneyland ride whose entrance always gave him "goose bumps" (90-91). The macabre cross-hybridization of child's play and horror in Disneyland becomes clearer when comparing the boys with the adults. George's Disneyland LSD hallucination is strangely similar to a vision Philippe has as he explores his own murderous feelings toward George. George's trip: "Over his head, a Milky Way of skulls snapped like turtles" (88). Philippe's vision: "Philippe lay in bed imagining George's death. . . . The world he saw rang with percussion. Skeletons snapped" (106).

12. The "Dead . . . men . . . tell . . . no . . . tales" line comes from the "Pirates of the Caribbean" ride. See also Marin, on the postmodern dilemma of Disneyland.

13. A child learns this distinction through noticing that a stimulus that can be removed by motion is external (outside, perception), and one that is not effected through movement is internal (in consciousness) (Freud, "Instincts" 119-120).

14. David also acts this out in his fantasy of being skinned alive during a rock concert he stars in (*Closer* 26-27).

15. Stephen Heath discusses the relation of filmic representation to death and crime in his expansion of Cocteau's characterization of film as "death at work" through a reading of an Apollinaire story concerning the filming of a real murder (Heath 114). Film inaugurates a representation organically related to death, while becoming the epitome of the depthless surface of the psychotic subject—the "skin ego" (note that in many Romance languages the word for "film" is related to the word for skin).

16. "The image does not, at first glance, resemble the corpse, but the cadaver's strangeness is perhaps also that of the image. What we call mortal remains escapes common categories. Something is there before us which is not really the living person, nor is it any reality at all. It is neither the same as the person who was alive, nor is it another person, nor is it anything else. . . . Death suspends the relation to place, even though the deceased rests heavily in his spot as if upon the only basis that is left him. . . . Where is it? It is not here, and yet it is not anywhere else. Nowhere? But then nowhere is here. The cadaverous presence establishes a relation between here and nowhere" (Blanchot 256).

17. I am indebted to Robert Glück for bringing this passage to my attention.

Works Cited

Anzieu, Didier. *The Skin Ego*. Trans. Chris Turner. New Haven: Yale UP, 1989.

Ariès, Phillippe. *L'homme devant la mort*. Paris: Editions du Seuil, 1977.

Barthes, Roland. *A Lover's Discourse*. Trans. Richard Howard. New York: Farrar, Straus & Giroux, 1977.

Barzilai, Shuli. "The Borders of Language: Kristeva's Critique of Lacan." *PMLA* 106 (1991): 294-305.

Bataille, Georges. *The Tears of Eros*. Trans. Peter Connor. San Francisco: City Lights, 1989.

————. *Erotism*. Trans. Mary Dalwood. San Francisco: City Lights, 1986.

Baudrillard, Jean. *Simulations*. Trans. Paul Foss, Paul Patton, and Philip Beitchman. New York: Semiotexte, 1983.

————. *The Ecstacy of Communication*. Trans. Bernard and Caroline Schutze. New York: Semiotexte, 1988.

Bazin, André. *What is Cinema?* Trans. Hugh Gray. 2 vols. Berkeley and Los Angeles: U of California P, 1967-71.

Bellamy, Dodie. "Digression as Power: Dennis Cooper and the Aesthetics of Distance." *Mirage* 1 (1985): 78-87.

Blanchot, Maurice. *The Space of Literature*. Trans. Ann Smock. Lincoln: U of Nebraska P, 1982.

Cooper, Dennis. *Idols*. New York: Sea Horse, 1979. Rev. ed. New York: Amethyst, 1989.

————. "A Herd." *The Tenderness of the Wolves*. Trumansburg: Crossing, 1981. 51-75.

————. *Tigerbeat*. New York: Little Caesar, 1983.

————. *He Cried*. San Francisco: Black Star, 1984.

————. *Safe*. New York: Sea Horse, 1984.

————. "Square One." *Soup 4: New Critical Perspectives*. Ed. Bruce Boone (1985): 70-72.

————. "Dear Secret Diary." *Against Nature: a group show of work by homosexual men*. Ed. Richard Hawkins and Dennis Cooper. Los Angeles: L.A.C.E., 1988. 5-7.

————. "Smoke Screen." *They See God*. New York: Pat Hearn Galleries, 1988. 1-2.

————. *Closer*. New York: Grove Weidenfeld, 1989.

————. *Frisk*. New York: Grove Weidenfeld, 1991.

————. *Wrong*. New York: Grove Weidenfeld, 1992.

Debord, Guy. *Society of the Spectacle*. Detroit: Black and Red, 1983.

Ferenczi, Sandor. "The Confusion of Tongues between Adults and the Child." 1933. *Final Contributions to the Problems and Methods of Psychoanalysis*. London: Hogarth, 1955. 156-67.

Freud, Sigmund. "The Splitting of the Ego in the Process of Self Defense." 1939. *The Standard Edition of the Complete Psychological Works of Sigmund Freud*. Vol. 23. 271-78. 24 vols. Trans. and ed. James Strachey. 1953-74.

————. "Fetishism." 1927. *The Standard Edition*. Vol. 21. 147-57.

————. "Mourning and Melancholia." 1917. *The Standard Edition*. Vol. 14. 239-58.

————. "A Metapsychological Supplement to the Theory of Dreams." 1917. *The Standard Edition*. Vol. 14. 219-35.

————. "Instincts and their Vicissitudes." 1915. *The Standard Edition*. Vol. 14. 111-40.

————. "Formulations on the Two Principles of Mental Functioning." 1911. *The Standard Edition*. Vol. 12. 215-26.

————. "The Interpretation of Dreams." 1900. *The Standard Edition*. Vols. 4-5.

Gallop, Jane. *Intersections: A Reading of Sade with Bataille, Blanchot, and Klossowski*. Lincoln: U of Nebraska P, 1981.

Glück, Robert. "Running on Emptiness." *San Francisco Chronicle* 4 June 1989: 9.

————. "Truth's Mirror is No Mirror." *Poetics Journal* 7 (1987): 40-45.

————. *Jack the Modernist*. New York: Gay Presses of New York, 1985.

Grosz, Elizabeth, *Sexual Subversions: Three French Feminists*. Sydney: Allen & Unwin, 1989.

Heath, Stephen. *Questions of Cinema*. Bloomington: U of Indiana P, 1981.

Kristeva, Julia. *The Powers of Horror: An Essay in Abjection*. Trans. Leon S. Roudiez. New York: Columbia, 1982.

————. "Within the Microcosm of 'The Talking Cure.'" Trans. Thomas Gora and Margaret Waller. *Interpreting Lacan*. Ed. Joseph H. Smith and William Kerrigan. New Haven: Yale UP, 1983. 33-48.

Laplanche, Jean. *Life and Death in Psychoanalysis*. Trans. Jeffrey Mehlman. Baltimore: Johns Hopkins UP, 1976.

Laplanche, Jean, and J.-P. Pontalis. "Fantasy and the Origins of Sexuality." *Formations of Fantasy*. Ed. Victor Burgin, James Donald, and Cora Kaplan. London: Methuen, 1986. 5-35.

Mannoni, Octave. *Clefs pour l'imaginaire ou l'autre scène*. Paris: Editions du Seuil, 1969.

Marin, Louis. "Disneyland: A Degenerate Utopia." *Glyph* 1 (1977): 50-66.

Meyer, Richard. "Interview: Dennis Cooper." *Cuz.* Ed Richard Meyer. New York: The Poetry Project, 1988. 52-69.

Mulvey, Laura. "Visual Pleasure and Narrative Cinema." *Screen* 16.3 (1975): 6-18.

Pietz, William, "The Problem of the Fetish, I." *Res* 9 (1985): 5-17.

Dennis Cooper and Kasia Boddy (interview date autumn 1995)

SOURCE: Cooper, Dennis, and Kasia Boddy. "Conversation with Dennis Cooper." *Critical Quarterly* 37, no. 3 (autumn 1995): 103-15.

[*In the following interview, Cooper discusses the development of his thematic concerns and stylistic approach, his literary influences, the significance of representative characters in his fiction, and his interest in studying the notion of bliss in future works.*]

[*Boddy*]: *I'd like to start by asking you about what seems like a dominant concern of your work—both thematically and stylistically—the relationship between inside and out, the exterior and the interior of things.*

[Cooper]: I'm always trying to construct that dichotomy.

But sometimes it's not clear which is more desirable—the surface or the interior. Sometimes it's one, sometimes the other.

Well, confusion is central to the work—lured by the surface, then horrified by the interior, or disappointed. It's a battle within the work over which has the more information in it, whether what the surface suggests to your imagination is the truth, or whether there's some hidden meaning.

It often seems that surfaces are beautiful but not meaningful, or that there's a very easy meaning in the surface, while the truth is inside. This suggests that beauty and truth are not compatible—you can have only one or the other.

But then truth is always a projection of the writer or the characters. There is never an actual truth.

A word that comes up a lot is 'perfect' or 'perfection'.

I was really influenced by the film-maker Robert Bresson. His films are so . . . well, they're perfect. They're so tight, they're perfect. I'm always trying to create something so tight that it becomes perfect, thinking that some truth might then emanate from it. That's one of the reasons I write the way I do, why the process is as labour-intensive as it is. To get the work absolutely . . .

Perfect! Is the tension you describe similar to that tension within the stories that, while you enjoy the skin, you can't have what's underneath? The idea that an airtight skin doesn't let anything out or in?

It's the idea that, if you organise something well enough, somehow it will have within it *that thing*. Organising something really carefully or elaborately is all you can do. Then it's up to whoever to decode it, and that's where it gets vague, the part you can't control.

There are moments in different stories when characters want to talk about what's important—about love or death—and language fails them. They resort to 'blah, blah' or 'etc.' You talk about film, but as a writer you depend on language. You've worked in dance, and in **Jerk** *you combined your words with Nayland Blake's pictures, while the central character supplemented his words with a puppet show. Do you sometimes feel that language is not enough? That you'd rather be using some other medium? What about film?*

I don't feel frustrated with writing. I feel frustrated that you can't articulate or you can't understand . . . it's not that language is too limited, but that it's impossible to really pinpoint things or understand things completely because you're constantly reassessing everything. So it's a matter of trying to get to some point. And making the characters inarticulate, that's just an acknowledgment . . . it's a kind of respect for them—that their uncertainty is what's important.

You don't really use the first person very much.

Well, very carefully. I also switch tenses all the time—I have a sense of how each of them work, so it's a kind of distancing, having someone more immediate, having someone less so. Actually characters who use the first person are usually less enterable than those that are in the third person, because that's just the way fiction works. But in *Try* the character who uses the first person acts as sort of a red herring. You enter through him, and then you realise that that's not where you are, that's not where you're supposed to be. I'm interested in throwing people off, in disorienting them. In *Frisk,* for instance, I had the 'I' in there because I wanted to take responsibility for the material, because it would have been too easy otherwise to write a horror novel.

In part two of **Frisk,** *'Tense', you use quite a straightforward first person, while in 'Wilder', at the end, the first person is really weird in comparison. It seems to challenge the easy first person of 'Tense'.*

I don't want it to be easy. I don't want people to attach it too much to me, to locate the 'I' too much. In all the books there's the 'I', and then there's the third person perspective on the 'I' as well, so it doesn't locate them in one sensibility.

You also explore how characters construct themselves through other sources—if you see yourself as a TV character or in terms of the lyrics of a song you are seeing yourself in the third person, on the level of a character in a fiction which makes it easier to deal with unruly emotions, etc.

Right, yeah. It depends on the situation. In *Frisk* I wanted there to be a character who threw his identity around, who treated himself in the same way that he treated other characters, suddenly entering a character who wasn't the 'I' to get an objective view of himself, which of course is impossible and psychotic. That book especially was trying to disorient, to create a puzzle of fictional and nonfictional elements.

It's very theatrical.

Yeah, well it seemed like the only way to do it. I wanted to try to mimic horror films, some kind of genre thing, to keep people on the subject.

The tone seems to shift all the time, which also confuses the reader. One minute you're encouraged to feel compassion, the next it's very satirical. Critical responses to your work don't seem to pay much attention to the comedy.

Yeah, I know. You can imagine why that's true. Comedy is a great sedative, it's a great relaxer, it's a great way for people to enter something, for you to catch them off guard.

It must be frustrating then when people don't pick up on the comedy.

It's only frustrating when people say 'Is this supposed to be funny?'

Roger's first person narration is one of the most openly satirical parts of **Try.**

He's a super aesthete.

He reminded me of Humbert Humbert.

Yeah, maybe subconsciously. I used this really over-aestheticised voice all the time in my early work, and I wanted to turn it to candy. I wanted to get away from that way of thinking about things. At one time it seemed like a good way to look at things, and now it seems like a very faulty and simplistic way of looking at things. So I wanted to kill that perspective off because it

becomes so ridiculous and boring and repellent and all these things. I sense that one gets kind of tired of Roger after a while, you know 'oh here's one of these sections again, can I skip it?'

He's also interesting, with Brice, in terms of ideas of parents and how a family operates. Compared with the parent characters in your other books, they are the most visible. In the other books the parents are always in other rooms, they don't seem to notice their kids coming and going. Do you want to write more about parents and families?

Maybe I'll write more about adults. It's sort of one of my goals to accept that I am an adult and write about it. I don't feel very comfortably an adult, I don't relate to it very much. So they're still villains, they have been villains, hopefully they won't be villains any more.

In **Try** *they're certainly more fleshed out than in your previous work.*

Well I'm trying to enter them. I still think that they're a bit too much cartoons. But in *Try,* I wanted to place my sympathies within the work. There had been a lot of misunderstanding of *Frisk,* and I wanted my sympathies to be clear. So I wanted the adult characters to be understandable, and in a way sympathetic, but, in contrast to Ziggy and Calhoun and some of the other characters who are more thoughtful or inherently kind or respectful of one another, there's a loss of humanity, a loss of perspective that ultimately is troubling.

How much are the parents just cartoon baddies and how much are they really responsible for what happens to their children in your work?

In *Try* they are responsible. I was kind of exploring stuff that therapy tells you, seeing what I like or don't like about it.

Ziggy quotes his therapist all the time, but at one point he realises that the reason he doesn't kill Brice is because what his therapist calls abuse he actually thinks of as love.

He seems willing to listen to his therapist, and he checks with what the therapist has said all the time, but one doesn't have a sense that he's absorbed it yet. I don't think his therapist would say he should be friends with Calhoun either! Therapy is a very limited thing . . . I mean I'm in therapy so I'm trying to figure out what I like about it or don't like about it, what's useful about it or not.

Does it interfere with your writing?

No it doesn't interfere at all. It's true that there's a limit. Therapists see you in a certain way, and they do perpetually pinpoint your parents. You can't say anything without them saying, 'well don't you think that's because . . . your parents'. Every time you talk about someone you know, it's like 'oh he or she is like your father or your mother' and stuff like that. I mean that's too simple, things aren't that simple.

Is writing a kind of therapy?

Well, it has been, it has been. I grew weirdly and my parents were really horrible and all that stuff, but I've sort of changed lately. I often feel sort of alienated and isolated and on my own, and I've gone through periods of being very remote and blank—like things I write about. Writing helped me in my real life to be a bit more sensible. With *Try,* while I was writing it a close friend got addicted to heroin and I sort of devoted my life to helping him get off—almost twenty-four hours a day for around a year. I was writing at the same time. I wrote that book partially to figure out what was going on. Like Calhoun, my friend wasn't able to do anything, but there was a kind of inherent, understood gratitude that I was actually still staying with him even though he was totally fucked up. He and *Try* helped me understand that love is important.

Does your control over the language and structure— that perfect airtight quality—help?

Yeah, sure. You're examining, editing, rewriting your thoughts.

Do the formal demands of the writing interfere with your sense of what really happened?

Well, writing *Try* was really peaceful. My friend would be like convulsing, and I'd be watching over him and writing. It was something I could completely control. In most situations you shouldn't want to control your relationships with other people, they should just happen, but in that situation my friend was really sick and in pain and I couldn't really do anything—all I could do was just be there—and keep myself well because he needed me to be really clear. He needed me to be absolutely stable every second. Writing kept me from losing it.

What you say about spending a year with your friend in his room comes across in **Try.** *In many ways it's a very claustrophobic novel. You're either in Ziggy's room or Calhoun's room. There is a tension between these rooms being oppressive and being safe. But nobody goes outside very much.*

Yeah. The writing's like that.

Your work seems to be drawing on a French tradition rather than an American one.

Almost exclusively French.

How does that mesh or adapt to an American context?

Almost all the things that I was influenced by when I was young were French—writing, art, film. But I don't know. I'm obviously a really American writer. I love how American English is so messed up and fluid.

Do you see links between your work and that of other contemporary American writers? Your stories appear in anthologies like Between C & D *or* High Risk, *so people make connections. Is that just a publishing thing?*

Well, some of the people in those books I feel close to. Both those anthologies were kind of like 'bad boy' stuff, and I don't really . . . we were lumped together because we write about drugs or young people or violence, basically. There was a time when I really liked Kathy Acker's work. She was important to me when I was first writing, seeing her out there. But there aren't many . . . I mean I like a lot of people's work, but in terms of relating to it, there aren't many writers whose work I feel is on a similar track. I guess I feel more and more as if I'm on my own track. And the writing's changing now. I'm trying to get away from some of the subject matter that I've used before. I don't think it interests me as much. I think I'm on to other things.

When did you finish writing **Try***?*

Let's see. When did it come out? It came out last year. So I think around spring of ninety-two.

Quite a while. So you've been writing other stuff?

Well, I'm working on a couple of things. I'm co-writing a nonfiction book with my friend, Joel Westendorf. We're writing a book about the history of sensory overload in the arts. That's one thing I'm doing, and then I'm working on a book, a novel, but it's too early. It's kind of mulchy, it's going to be kind of different though, I think. Hopefully more blissful. I want to write about bliss, I'm interested in bliss now.

Bliss in the sense . . . ?

Well, I'm not sure yet. I'm just figuring out . . . I'm trying to step somewhere.

Your work seems to be becoming more openly romantic.

Yeah, I guess, but to me it's all really romantic.

The romance is nearer to the surface in **Try.**

To me *Try* was about friendship. That was what really interested me. Now I want to talk about . . . I used to do a lot of LSD, like *a lot,* and I had some weird experiences. I want to talk about where they took me, and somehow represent them in language—somewhere I was, and somehow use that in the language—how when you're high on psychedelics, you're isolated but you feel peace, you feel a kind of benign interest in things. And my books are always for specific people, and this one will be about a friend of mine, and what he inspires in me, which is a lot more happiness or something. So at this point I have all these different senses of things and I'm just writing all this stuff and then I'll kind of edit, edit, edit and work, work, work and then it'll become something. That's the way it always is.

Parts of **Closer** *appeared in journals before the book came out. Did you write the sections separately and then they developed into a book, or did you originally start with the idea of the book?*

There's a piece in **Wrong** called 'Wrong'—which has the George character in it. I'd written that, and originally I thought that I'd do something with that, because I didn't think it was quite right yet. So originally that was going to be the ending or conclusion of **Closer.** But once I started working on **Closer,** it was very much of a piece.

To come back to what you were saying about the new work. There is almost a religious sense in it, in some ways, with some characters who talk about God quite a lot. Do you think that you are describing, in some way, religious experiences?

Well, that's one of the things that interest me—I mean, not *God*—but maybe I'm beginning to sense where one finds spiritual comfort or spiritual information, and maybe it's in some place I never thought it would be. I think in a way my work has always been about that kind of locating . . . The guy in **Frisk** is, in a way, trying to reach a transcendent state, and so is George in **Closer**—all that LSD and Disneyland stuff is all an attempt to go somewhere else, to completely disorder himself, to leave the world.

You often cut down those escapes, you don't allow them to last too long!

Well, I don't know. In **Try,** Ziggy and Calhoun still have a lot of things to figure out—Calhoun is still a heroin addict. But I think, with all sincerity, you know, when the last line of the book is 'Fuck everything else', that's not just a joke. I mean it's stupid to say and it's a kind of . . . I don't know. But the love that Ziggy and Calhoun have for each other . . . it may not be an escape exactly, but . . .

But at the end of **Try** *it's starting?*

Yeah, it's starting. I think I have a better sense now that there is a kind of serenity or something, and I don't know why, or how it works, or what, but that there is a way that you can live with a kind of peace. It's not something . . . I've not lived in a peaceful state for most of my life, so it's interesting. It's too early to tell, but I'd like to write about peace. I'd really like to get away from the things that people call nihilistic in the work.

I don't really find it nihilistic because whatever happens there's always a striving for something else.

Yeah, well, they want the sublime, they just have their own way . . . the direction they've chosen to do it . . . I mean it's possible to understand why someone would want to reach the sublime through murdering someone, I mean it's a powerful thing to do. It's not a good choice, necessarily! But it's understandable why someone would think murder was the most amazing thing you could do. I don't think that's the most amazing thing you could do . . . any more! I don't know if I ever did, but I was interested in the idea for a long time.

There's a moment in **Wrong** *where a character says that, since AIDS, this kind of romantic idea of death can't work any more.*

'AIDS ruined death.' Yeah, I don't know. I may have thought so when I wrote that piece but actually it turns out that AIDS makes death more interesting. If you have friends dying all the time, you start to wonder what death is, and where they are.

It's changed it.

Yeah, it's changed it, it hasn't ruined it. I don't remember why I was thinking that, but everybody always quotes that line. AIDS did ruin a particular kind of romantic notion of death, a notion of death that a lot of my early work perpetuates, I guess.

Death in your work is very controlled—whether you're the killer or being killed in a very controlled environment—and disease isn't like that.

Giving up control is more interesting than trying to have absolute control. I mean in the work, I'll always want absolute control in terms of the text, but I think it's important to acknowledge that everyone is autonomous, and that everyone has control, and that everything you do is part of a combination of controls. I'd like to make my work less psychotic.

Another kind of tension that I find in your work is one between realism and what might be called anti-realism. On the one hand, there is abundance of realistic detail and dialogue; on the other hand, you and your characters are always pointing out how mediated our experience of all that is. So you find yourself seduced into the realism and then jolted out of it.

Yeah, hopefully. In **Frisk,** where I guess I was using that tactic most elaborately, there's so much set up for everything to be false. Perspectives shift. There's so much hearsay. A character is killed by an actor in an old set from the *Twilight Zone* TV show.

Although you're also encouraging readers to think it's real.

Yeah, yeah—of course I want that too! So I can't have it both ways—if you make your strategy too obvious on the surface, the work will become artsy, and I really don't want that. I mean, I like the nouveau roman and that sort of stuff, but I wouldn't want to just work from an objective standpoint, however complexly.

Because?

Because I think that truth comes from other people and not from books or art, ultimately I do, and that's why I make a decision to prioritise emotion. Even if the characters are fake the work's always about trying to get to another human, with all these things in the way, I want to communicate. I have problems with a certain kind of avant-garde writing where style becomes too much of an interference. I don't have much to say. I mean I have things that I'm interested in, things I want to study, but I don't have any statement. I have nothing to say about any of it. It's all confused and I'm just trying to instigate a thought, or to create a relationship with the people reading me.

Lynne Tillman too has talked about wanting to write in a way that was experimental but didn't announce itself as experimental; that work which announces itself is ultimately not that experimental because you can easily dismiss it.

Yeah, it's a fine line though. For instance, Kathy Acker—her earlier work is extremely experimental but actually I think you can transgress all those strategies very quickly and get in to what she's talking about.

You talk about how your work is changing, and how **Try** *has a more conventional structure. Is your new work like that too?*

No, the next one's going to be much more complicated. It will be very accessible in the sense that it will have a certain narrative sensibility and characters you're supposed to think about, but I want it to be much more disruptive. I want it to be much more psychedelic. I think it will be a much more difficult book, in that sense.

I'm not getting interested in conventional writing. I resist it. Even in **Try,** I think it's my favourite thing I've done, but I can see that there are things I had to do to have it cover forty-eight hours where something is happening every minute. There are parts that just function as filler. And I'm terrified of flab, so I certainly don't want to go more in that direction. I went as far in that direction as I could go and now I feel I want to pull away! But I learned some things about how to move a narrative along, which is not something I really knew how to do before. I didn't grow up reading novels, I grew up reading poetry. My first books were all poetry. I always wrote prose but it was very poetic, and I don't know how to do plot and character development and all that stuff—I don't want to know! I'm not interested in work that does that very much. It seems like I'm being lied to all the time.

In terms of prose, the short story seems closer to poetry than the novel.

Yeah, but there's so much more room to move in the novel.

Your novels are often like short story montages or collages.

Yeah, they're always broken up.

Do you still write poetry?

No, I hadn't written poetry since around 1985 and then somebody asked me to write some poetry for an anthology. So I wrote ten new poems, some were old ones I polished up though! I wanted to write about River Phoenix who'd just died. His death really affected me, and those feelings seemed more suited to poetry than to fiction.

Is it because you're writing prose now that you don't write poetry?

Yeah, I'd been writing both and then I got sick of writing stanzas and I didn't think I had much to say, I was so tired of playing around in tiny little spaces. I just started making paragraphs. My first novella, **Safe,** was very much like a prose poem. It was interesting to write these new poems, but I don't think I'll be doing more. I never think, 'I'll write a poem' like I used to.

Because poetry is more . . . ?

I mean I admire John Ashbery and people like that but I don't think I'm a skilful enough poet to be able to do what I want to do in the form. My poems of the early eighties were very elaborate and very complicated but they just seemed so . . . self-involved.

But when you wanted to write about River Phoenix you thought that poetry was right?

Yeah, well they're like love poems, in a really loose sense.

What's the anthology that they're in?

It's called *Uncontrollable Bodies: Testimonies of Identity and Culture.* It's a Bay Press anthology. Lynne's in it, some other people. It came out in the States a few months ago. It's no big deal.

A character in **Wrong** *says, 'He wanted one fresh perception.' Do you think one can have a fresh perception within the language of the genres that you draw on such as horror or pornography, or do you have a sense of there being some kind of pure language?*

Pure perception. I suppose I feel that one should aspire to that, I don't know if it's possible. There's definitely a lot of language pollution I'd like to avoid. But it would also be too utopian to think I could eliminate all of literature's tropes. Still, that's the idea, the Rimbaud thing.

Most contemporary writers seem not to try to strip language down in the modernist way, but simply to play different languages off against each other.

Yeah, me too. But I'm not interested in all that standard postmodernist interconstructing of texts. I don't have much interest in that sort of thing.

Ziggy's prayer at the end of **Try** *collapses.*

Because he doesn't have a language. Well, that's it. That prayer's about love, or I don't know if it was about love, but it was about wanting to be loved, and how you ask for love, and how you can't ask—either it exists or it doesn't. You can't say anything that would make someone love you. It just has to happen. I don't know how it happens. That's like a prayer, when you're asking for something and you don't know how to ask for it, and you don't know what to ask for. You're asking for an abstraction, for something that you can't even see or understand, for something that you don't know if you deserve. Wanting love from someone is like asking for divine intervention.

Bliss is always silent, without language.

Exactly. So I've just got to figure out how to write about bliss! It will be a challenge.

I'm glad you're moving toward bliss.

I don't want to be unhappy any more. You can easily decide that everybody's horrible, you're alone, and hate that you need other people—and I've done that. I thought happiness was ridiculous, a lie. I went through many years thinking that love and all that stuff just meant you were weak, and that happiness was a sedative, just something that Christianity constructed to keep you from pursuing the truth. I'm struggling against that belief now. I'm thinking that maybe there is a kind of pure happiness, maybe there's a kind of peace or something that's not a compromise. The other option is to just go crazy! So we'll see. The great treasure hunt.

James Gardner (review date 17 June 1996)

SOURCE: Gardner, James. "Transgressive Fiction." *National Review* (17 June 1996): 54-6.

[*In the following excerpt, Gardner provides a negative review of* Try.]

Thirty years ago the art of fiction began to undergo a change similar to one that had already befallen the theatrical arts. Though theater had once been the best loved form of mass entertainment, it yielded that title to film and then turned inward, catering to an elite taste that saw theater as art rather than diversion. As a result, these two factors, which had formerly been united, increasingly went their separate ways. Fiction also used to fulfill the Horatian injunction to delight as well as to edify. But in recent years it too has split, not into different media, as theater and film have done, but into different forms of fiction. On the one hand Stephen King and Jackie Collins are widely read for their entertainment value. On the other, novelists like Thomas Pynchon and William Gass intentionally and provocatively suppress the element of pleasure, as if it were incompatible with serious fiction. . . .

Fortunately, most contemporary fiction of the artistic kind is somewhat more rewarding. Often its vanguardism consists less in the sorts of formal difficulty that were characteristic of Gass and Pynchon than in the freshness of the authors' identities. Amy Tan, for example, writes about being a Chinese-American woman, Bharati Mukherjee about being an Indian woman in Iowa, Dale Peck about being homosexual, and Ernest J. Gaines about being black. Such literature falls within the modern liberal tradition of embracing difference and being open to other experiences. But both of these undertakings imply a core of shared values, so that, even as this literature asserts the difference between author and reader, it usually has the reassuring subtext of a common humanity that unites us all.

Despite the primacy of this kind of "nice" literature, there is another kind of literature that increasingly exhibits, and sometimes even advocates, very different values. Such fiction is often termed "transgressive," and there are correlative developments in film and the visual arts. Like the humanistic literature of Amy Tan, it is seen as being somehow liberal or leftist because it seeks the distinction of radical "otherness" and because it aspires to threaten the status quo that writers like Amy Tan and Bharati Mukherjee seek only to correct. The two strains converge from different angles of assault on a center allegedly dominated by a white, Anglo-Saxon, heterosexual, right-handed patriarchy.

The roots of transgressive literature, of literature that violently attacks the center of a culture, are ancient, reaching all the way from Euripides's *Bacchae,* through Marlowe and Webster and the Marquis de Sade, to Huysmans and Celine. This literature of self-defined immorality, anguish, and degradation is constantly waxing and waning in our culture, as, for its part, is the humanistic strain. Thus the ages of Fielding, George Eliot, Sinclair Lewis, and Saul Bellow were in a general way humanistic, whereas those of Byron and Wilde and the Surrealists tended in the other direction. At the present time—and this is perhaps a unique occurrence—the two strains exist side by side, as different faces of the same coin. Four recent and critically celebrated novels—Susanna Moore's *In the Cut,* A. M. Homes's *The End of Alice,* Dennis Cooper's *Try,* and Bret Easton Ellis's *American Psycho*—exemplify this development, each from a different angle.

What unites all these novels, aside from their almost unimaginable gruesomeness, is the peculiar relation in which they stand to the straitlaced center of society. . . .

In contrast to the sexual awakening of the narrator which is the main theme of *In the Cut,* we see in *The End of Alice* by A. M. Homes, another woman writer, and in Dennis Cooper's *Try,* sexual license presented not as a dilemma but as an accepted fact. The protagonist of the former novel is a 56-year-old man who has spent the past 23 years in prison and whose affected utterances recall Hannibal Lector minus the cannibalism. The plot is fairly simple: this murderous pedophile recounts his past adventures in a correspondence with a young woman who sees him as a role model, except that she is interested in young boys whereas he is interested in young girls. Many graphic scenes of child molestation, sodomy, and murder, follow. "All three boys," the female correspondent recalls, in a fairly typical passage, "were at that age of supreme softness where muscles waiting to grow are coated in a medium-thick layer of flesh, highly squeezable. They were at the point where if someone were to take such a child, to roast or bake him, he would be most flavorful."

If anything, Dennis Cooper's *Try* manifests an even greater level of sexualized violence, but this time from the perspective of male homosexuality. The protagonist,

Ziggy, is a victim of child abuse at the hands of the gay couple who adopted him. Though child abuse is very much in the news these days and is always reprehended in the strongest terms, Cooper's take on the problem is one of ambivalence, when not verging on enthusiastic endorsement. *Try* is an extended fantasy of unbridled sexual license in which those whom society sees as the victims are willingly acquiescent if not entirely complicit in their own sexual exploitation. In this voided world, there is no family structure to speak of. Parents are absent, or else they are ersatz, like Ziggy's. Likewise, school is only a place for trysting and for the purchase of drugs. Crimes go shockingly unpunished. When, in a subplot, Uncle Ken sodomizes the corpse of a 13-year-old who overdoses on the drugs Ken supplied, he simply disposes of the body and that's that. There would be little point in attempting to cite a passage, as it would not get past the judicious editors of this publication.

These two novels are intended for two groups of readers, pedophiles on the one hand, and "normal" people on the other. This loaded term "normal" is used advisedly for the simple reason that the authors themselves implicitly draw the same distinction. One senses that their gaze is always steadily fixed on the reader, as though asking, "Are you revolted yet? Are you shocked?" If this work were marketed as pornography, the term being used not in reproach but simply for purposes of description, we should be forced to acknowledge its usefulness to those whose fantasy life comprises the sodomizing of children, necrophilia, and coprophilia. What is entirely unpalatable is the squeamishness of *Try*'s reviewers, squeamish not in the sense of opposing so off-color a work, but in the sense of being too timid to call it by its name. The reviewer for the *New York Times* states that "Dennis Cooper has written a love story, all the more poignant because it is so brutally crushed." The reviewer for *Spin* calls it "Painfully poignant . . . beneath the queasy surface, no novelist empathizes more with the pathos of put-upon youth." Of course opinions may differ. But suffice it to say that I found no trace of poignancy at any level.

What is it then about the three books I have discussed that has granted them absolution from the censure that ordinarily would accompany such unbridled lubricity? The answer is clear. Sexual aggressiveness is traditionally defined in our society as the province of the straight white male. To the extent that each of these books attacks this center, it appears to acquire a contemporary relevance which exempts it from the moral scrutiny that a straight white male would receive. Furthermore, in its implicit threat to the patriarchy, and all that this threat implies of traditional liberal egalitarianism, it seems to take the moral high-ground. Susanna Moore and A. M. Homes display women who are as sexually predaceous as any man. Dennis Cooper displays homosexuals and even child molesters as spirited crusaders against a hypocritical middle class. It is in this light that they gain their relevance for those who read "quality literature," and it is this that makes them morphologically identical to Amy Tan and Bharati Mukherjee, however different their content. . . .

One crucial difference between these authors and the authors of ordinary novels, such as Stephen King and Jackie Collins, is that, whereas the latter are content to preserve the traditional protocols of fiction, these newcomers would have us believe, as they themselves believe, that they have penetrated to an all-important and long-hidden truth about human society. And in a general way we, their readers, do believe them. We believe them because in our relativistic age, we have lost the spiritual resources to confront that potent error which they lack either the intellectual honesty or the intellectual power to oppose: the error of supposing that, because everything indeed is not right with the world, everything must accordingly be wrong with the world; the error of supposing that, because we are plainly not a race of angels, we must perforce be a race of beasts. But in the end, they are still fiction writers after all, and this morbid fascination of theirs, this confidence that the center cannot hold, that all of morality is a sham, is the supreme fiction.

Gary Indiana (review date 8 June 1997)

SOURCE: Indiana, Gary. "Monster Mash." *Los Angeles Times Book Review* (8 June 1997): 14.

[*In the following review, Indiana offers a positive evaluation of* Guide.]

Since his writing first appeared in chapbooks in the late '70s, Dennis Cooper has been a uniquely disturbing presence in American literature, a major voice shunted to cult status by mainstream squeamishness, flawlessly fluent in the lingua franca of youthful alienation and its coolest, least affected recording angel. His early poems and short prose were memorably hailed by Edmund White as sounding like "Aeschylus with a mouthful of bubble gum." When Cooper's first full-length novel, *Closer,* appeared in 1989, Lynne Tillman wrote that the book "translates the moments and feelings for which we don't really have a vocabulary."

Cooper's work claims the bleakest regions of American affluence with the sureness of Faulkner staking out Yoknapatawpha County. Widely imitated by writers such as Brett Easton Ellis and A. M. Homes, Cooper lacks their dazzling commercial appeal and desperate wish to shock; he lives where they go vogueing. His novels are peopled by all manner of rock 'n' roll burnouts, drug casualties, juvenile porn stars, aspiring serial killers, artists and geeks, materially comfortable or willfully marginal malcontents living way beyond the edge. Shock Cooper does, but not because he tries to. Like the scorpion in the fable, it's his nature.

The burnished youths Cooper writes about—gorgeous on the outside, twisted on the inside—could have stepped out of Lauren Greenfield's recent Hollywood photo essay "Fast Forward." (One of Greenfield's 13-year-old subjects reports, "My point of view in life was going out, getting messed up and staying out till the late hours of the night, having a big social life.") In Cooper's novels, the kids are complemented by equally messed-up grown-ups who are eager to consume them like candy. Their goals are hilariously fetishistic and short-term, utopian in the sense that *The Hundred and Twenty Days of Sodom* is a utopian book. (In *Frisk,* the main character invites an old friend to join him in Amsterdam: "I want you to live here with me and participate in . . . this major transcendence or answer I've found in killing cute guys.")

Cooper conjures his human wreckage revue with wildly flexible, intimate prose that offers occasional flashes of the author at his desk, a la Jean Genet, cooking everything up as he goes along, sometimes lowering a squeezed-out character through the trapdoor of nonexistence. Murder often happens as sexually assisted suicide, doubling as the killer's effort to "really know" his victim. The author invites us to identify his proto-Sadean heroes' proclivities as his own and to read his books as intricate acts of self-therapy. This probably has a sincere element—Bunuel said that an artist has to kill his father, rape his mother and betray his country once a day to flex his imagination—but the idea that the book is only therapy is also a put-on. Cooper's assaults on the novel form are far too strategic to scan as memoirs. Think of a master tailor ripping a Chanel dress apart and reassembling it as a faux-Carnaby Street three-piece suit or a cape-and-codpiece ensemble.

Unlike Genet, Cooper has a genial, albeit bizarre, sense of humor about the ideas obsessively reiterated in all of his works, a major plus, because the material explores the anus as a magic keyhole into a hidden world. Body odors and excreta are privileged information, and intergenerational rough sex a presiding comic metaphor. (In *Guide,* Cooper reflects on why a guy he's interested in doesn't read his books: "As Luke has explained, he doesn't understand why anyone would want to write about the subjects my novels recapitulate so automatically. Neither do I, so we're even.") The comparison to Faulkner seems truer: Cooper fashions unchanging content into one-of-a-kind containers, albeit his content may be intrinsically less digestible than Faulkner's.

It isn't quite accurate, though, to say the content never changes. Each novel carries some residua from the one before it, and the terrain is so unmapped by other fiction that its nuances take time to register. Cooper's narratives play out in micro-worlds in which vocabulary attaches itself to sensation in startling ways, language itself being barely adequate for the dire events and mental states he describes. Acid trips and heroin highs, coprophagic snacks and dismemberments are all standard fare. Starting with *Closer*'s Schnitzler-esque rondelet of drug-inflected sex among Los Angeles latch-key teens, the author has been charting ever-larger quadrants of terra incognita that bring the reader queasily close to his or her worst nightmare. *Closer*'s precocious, self-absorbed adolescents read their dark fates in the brutally dysfunctional adult world around them; in their milieu, where being conscious and being stoned are synonymous, parents either molest their kids or ignore them entirely.

Cooper takes us into a world where the only attractive options are dangerous or lethal forms of self-transcendence, via drugs, death and/or other people's bodies. This world looks a lot like America as depicted on afternoon talk shows without the healing jargon. Its culture is inscribed in Cooper's teens and vulpine adults as weirdly nuanced death wishes and ingenious predatory impulses, acted out in a bath of rock music. (These books, somewhat frustratingly for older readers, can be time-framed in alignment with successive indie-rock trends.) In the novel *Frisk,* a narrator named Dennis, imprinted at an early age by bogus snuff photos he thinks are real, grows up with a compulsion to literally get inside the youths he's attracted to, in the belief that their eviscerated bodies will reveal something important about them. He views his ultimate failure to act out murderous wishes as both cowardice and a defining moral threshold.

The remote possibility of nontoxic love sometimes holds a wistful attraction for Cooper's protagonists, who nevertheless deflect situations in which feelings (as opposed to manias) threaten. While each of his books has a large, variegated cast, everyone in them shares a protective numbness that functions as self-control. They're terrified to expose their emotions, so acclimated to abuse that they'd rather be beaten to death than risk romantic rejection. Cooper's third novel, *Try,* twists the pattern of earlier books; Ziggy and Calhoun, though even more extravagantly damaged than Cooper's previous heroes (Calhoun's a junkie; Ziggy's been molested by two fathers and an uncle since he was 8), muddle their way through acres of psychic *grand guignol* to a place of tentative mutual trust.

Cooper's new novel, *Guide,* really is a guide, or gloss, that revisits most of the places where Cooper's fiction has been, laying out a multi-tracked plot with brisk efficiency, then scattering the pieces like so many colored tiles in a graffiti-enhanced mural. The narrator calls himself Dennis Cooper and tells us he's writing the book we're reading; his previous work is familiar enough to his teen characters that it's the butt of numerous jokes. ("You're not going to kill Luke, right?" a boy with "five little barbells through each eyebrow" asks Dennis anxiously. "Look," Dennis explains, "I'm like you. Only you put scary decorations on your outsides, and I put scary decorations on my insides.") Like *Try, Guide* has a platonic gay love story at its center, a familiarly semi-abject attachment of an older for a younger man. These lovers edge toward each other, sort of, while a circus of drug overdoses, kiddie porn videos and violent deaths swirls around them. *Guide* reveals how much a novel really is a wish construction: Chris, the boy Dennis discards to make room for Luke, his new obsession, gets castrated and dismembered by an insane dwarf (consensually, one hastens to add).

The dwarf is one of the book's most inspired bits of pathology, a pure extract of the ravening id that powers so much of Cooper's mental theater. Another wonderful narrative device is a comic strip drawn by a minor character named Scott that depicts Dennis' inamorata menaced by a cave-dwelling monster, which Cooper scatters in verbal close-ups, a few frames at a time, throughout a long section of the novel. There's also Mason, Dennis' cohort, shown raping the adored bass player of Smear after putting Rohypnol in the guy's Pepsi; Pam and Sue, lesbian pornographers, trying to dump the body of a kid who's died from natural causes in their studio; and Drew Baldwin, a much-adored teen who succumbs to Mason's charms after the latter knocks him unconscious with a skateboard. ("But he told me why he did it and . . . I understand, and . . . I'm cool with it.")

This book's form achieves what a lot of contemporary novels try and fail at, a kind of pull-focus effect that blurs past and present, not so much by jump-cutting across chronology as by eliminating time as an overall narrative element. Each episode has its discrete temporality. *Guide* is structured in musical intervals, with recurring dominant chords and minor motifs, a scheme that allows Cooper's first-person narrator to fold in events he's not involved in, even introducing himself in certain scenes from inside other character's heads. It's an extraordinarily risky method, continually reminding the reader that the supposedly obsessive author he's reading is placing things before him with a high degree of calculation. "Punk's bluntness," Cooper wrote in *Closer,* "edited tons of pretentious shit out of American culture. . . ." Cooper does the same kind of editing job on the modern novel's conventions, especially in the area of verisimilitude. In a sense, Cooper has sliced such a big window into his own prodigious fantasy life, which is also ours in one or another variation, that it no longer matters if events in his theater of cruelty seem "believable" or not. The fact that he exposes them is more than enough.

Guide is much broader farce than Cooper's previous novels; a small but plangent part of its intention is to revise the scary image of its author those other books have created (". . . even though my imagination's a freezer compartment for violent thoughts, I'm a wuss"). Happily, this revision doesn't approach the drastic self-bowdlerization John Waters accomplished with "Crybaby" and "Serial Mom" if anything, *Guide* amplifies the horror that is Cooper's specialty by further breaking down the glass wall between the imaginary and the real. I don't want to take anything away from this book's outrageousness by saying that it's the most seductively frightening, best-written novel of contemporary urban life that anyone has attempted in a long time; it's the funniest, too, and does for Clinton America what "The Tin Drum" did for postwar Germany.

Bruce Hainley (review date 16 June 1997)

SOURCE: Hainley, Bruce. "Body English." *Nation* (16 June 1997): 34-5.

[*In the following review, Hainley offers a positive assessment of* Guide.]

This is the problem: how to convey the realness of the world, of the guy so beautiful he "white[s] out" vision, when language is often recalcitrant to the point of shutdown, when the only fact that has a sort of truth—even when you are deep in the middle of exploring the terrain of that mystery called someone else's body—is basic human aloneness: the strange opacity of the other, whose distance from you is similar to the distance (that close, that far away) between things and the words for those things. In his work, Dennis Cooper returns again and again to such conundrums—distances—especially when they inhabit a particular type of fine young man who thwarts and also weirdly reiterates the fascinations and lapses of cognition:

> It's strange what goes on in your head when you're attracted to someone—I mean, so turned on that your thoughts are just a twisted narration to his day-to-day life, and then by some fluke or fated twist or whatever you get the chance to fuck him whenever you want, and you start to realize that his sublimity's just your own imaginative garbage, period, and that all you're going to get out of him is a new set of needs, body odors, opinions, emotions, et cetera, all of which you completely recognize from your other relationships, and you start thinking, So why am I prioritizing him again?

With *Guide,* Cooper has provided a handbook to his complex concerns while shattering what too many have come to think of as his only hallmarks. He is often mistaken as the postmodern disciple of Sade and Genet (from whom, unquestionably, he has learned), but the daring of *Guide* is how clearly he shows his interests in extremity to be a way of getting at the precariousness of living through language stripped down to its most vulnerable, tender and sweet.

Vulnerable, tender and sweet—Dennis Cooper? Yes. (The narrator admits, "my favorite cup . . . changes color according to the temperature of its contents," and describes a guy's antics when coming this way: "He yells—I mean, loudly—like his dick is a band that has just started playing his favorite song.") By breaking the structure of the novel into journal-like sequences and by having the narrator, "Dennis," pay attention to those people and things (music foremost among them: lines from songs by Guided by Voices, early Donovan, Blur and others float through the novel) that try "in various ways to attract [him] back into the real," Cooper allows his own pleasure and sadness to shine through. Dennis both is and is not Cooper, but there are clues as to why this shouldn't be read as a *roman à clef.* Band members' real names are used (Alex James of Blur, Daniel James of Silverchair), while the bands' names slip to Smear and Tinsel-tool. The distance between things keeps everything lively by showing how fantasy (fairy tales, porn, drugs) can map real life and how real life can mess up fantasies.

One of Cooper's goals is to make his novel a safe haven for what and whom he cares for; when Luke, a guy whose looks more than satisfy all of Dennis's requirements for distraction, moves in, Dennis finds that their relationship may be better than his fantasies, and it may provide him with a definition of love. At the beginning of almost every chapter there is a brief paragraph giving the lowdown on what has happened and what is happening; by providing the basic coordinates of the narrative, it lets the reader focus on the miraculously precise yet austerely casual language that, aside from Dennis's complicated emotions, is the only thing holding the safe haven together.

> Pam's fucked. Sue, too, for the moment. They're in a holding cell. Chris, Robert, Tracy, and Goof are abstractions at this point. You can basically forget them. Their bodies are gross to one degree or another. Drew is at Mason's. The latter has come on the former's face several times. Luke's getting stoned with some friends at his soon-to-be former apartment. Scott's at my place. We're sober. It feels kind of nice.

Forgoing the plot, one can relax into the book's meditations on drugs, sex, music. Ponder how Cooper shirks almost every responsibility of narrative and description (notice his use of "whatever" and how Dennis announces early on, "The details don't matter") and yet moves forward and holds on to what may matter more—

the blurring that occurs when life is transmuted into words in order to get back into the real. Cooper's accuracy, even when the writing fades away to something pale and doubting, amazes. About David, whom Dennis met while writing an article for *Spin* (for which Cooper is a contributing editor) on homeless teens, many of whom hustle themselves for money (*Guide*'s chapter "The *Spin* Article" is like but is not the article Cooper published in *Spin* using the same material):

> Word has it that David allowed himself to be kept by some rich older man. Then he got really, really sick. I mean, way too gaunt to turn anyone on anymore and . . . here the story gets blurry . . . he went somewhere else . . . blurriness . . . death. I don't know what to do with that story. It's not exactly fact, and it's not quite a fairy tale, either. Me, I plan to believe what I want to believe. Here's how it starts: Once upon a time, David had a bizarre energy that made excellent copy, and a physical beauty that made one hang on his thoughts, and a violent temper that undercut one's attraction to him, and an AIDS diagnosis that gave his life great symbolism. That's as far as I've gotten.

Somewhat cold, coming close to giving up, indifferent and/or resigned, the language is also hauntingly direct and tender.

Dennis is no easier on himself. Soon after revealing that his "imagination's a freezer compartment for violent thoughts," he admits:

> I'll say this once. I'm extremely fucked up. It doesn't show, but I am. Over the years I've developed a sociable, generous side, which I train on the people I know. It makes them feel grateful, which makes me feel purposeful. But secretly, I'm so confused about everyone and everything. Sometimes these moods will just come out of nowhere and lay me out. I'll curl up in bed for long periods of time, catatonic and near-suicidal. Or I'll space into a murderous sexual fantasy wherein some cute young acquaintance or stranger is dismembered in intricate detail, simply because he's too painfully delicious, i.e., through no fault of his own.

All of which means what? Gertrude Stein wrote a long time ago—who was paying attention?—that "if every one were not so indolent they would realise that beauty is beauty even when it is irritating and stimulating not only when it is accepted and classic." Of all of Cooper's work, this novel is the most irritating and stimulating: It is a beauty. His stunning prose borrows stylistics from the most vacuous genres available (self-help manuals, New Age tomes, substance-abuse rehabilitation pamphlets, porn). At times I shook my head in disbelief because of the risks he was taking to get everything in and hold it together. He admits the real (and necessary) possibility of failure; he allows his prose to get L.A. hazy; he trusts his admiration for certain bands enough so that to explicate not only something about himself

but also something about the experience of reading, writing and being he keeps the lyrics just as they are— part of the drift of living. "Guided by Voices: I can't tell you anything / you don't already know." Those lyrics are vitally true and Cooper believes them, but he also, with this novel, refutes them.

Matthew Roberson (review date spring 1998)

SOURCE: Roberson, Matthew. Review of *Guide*, by Dennis Cooper. *Review of Contemporary Fiction* 18, no. 1 (spring 1998): 230.

[*In the following review, Roberson comments on the metafictional aspects of* Guide.]

In *Guide,* the fourth book of his five-novel cycle, Dennis Cooper charts passage between a variety of seeming oppositions: desire and its fulfillment, reality and fiction, life and death, bodily knowledge and the language with which we express it. This middle-space seems to be Cooper's preferred subject because, as his character Chris puts it, it is only there that one can truly achieve a simultaneous understanding of both a thing and its opposite; "drugging himself in death's general direction," so as to move between existence and its extinguishing, Chris believes that only in such a location can we hope to grasp briefly what might be "everything there is to know about human existence."

Cooper's novel is itself a performance of this general idea. It is narrated by Dennis, who is self-consciously "writing a novel" about his friends; of *Guide,* he says, "This is it." Like Cooper, a writer for *Spin* magazine, and like Cooper, the author of a *Spin* article on homeless teens (which is included, and is significantly similar yet different from Cooper's), Dennis is both Cooper and a self-consciously fictional projection. This metafictional turn nicely illustrates *Guide* as a medium between the "real" world and the kinds of fiction we use to describe it. The novel's characters are effective mediums for the music lyrics, movie plots, and pervasive, seemingly communal fantasies of sex and violence that flood the Los Angeles setting. Absorbing and enacting and reshaping this pop culture, they come alive in often disturbing but always strikingly contemporary ways, functionaries of the fin-de-millennium hyperreal.

Guide is not for the (even remotely) squeamish. Although Dennis refuses to indulge his own murderous homosexual fantasies, his friends/characters/creations are not so restricted. It is not without reason that Cooper has been called a postmodern disciple of Sade and Genet.

Andy Beckett (review date 21 May 1998)

SOURCE: Beckett, Andy. "Whatever." *London Review of Books* (21 May 1998): 34-5.

[*In the following review, Beckett provides a favorable assessment of* Guide, *but expresses reservations over Cooper's indefinite morality.*]

Reading Dennis Cooper can make you queasy. This short novel is the fourth in a five-volume cycle concerned almost exclusively, so far, with sexual violence. *Closer* (1989) subjected an American teenager to anal mutilation; *Frisk* (1991) concerned the butchery of young Dutch boys; and *Try* (1994) in which one critic detected 'a gentler maturity', saw an adopted son greedily penetrated by his father. In each book, and here, too, such episodes are not just a quick splatter on the page, or the stuff of hints and ambiguity, but drawn-out, physical descriptions. And, all the while, amid the broken bottles and bruised buttocks and the entire 'fireworks display of blood', as one of his murderers puts it, Cooper feels no need to emote.

The gaze of his sentences is quite blank. This is from a section in *Frisk* called 'Numb':

> I think I was fucking him dog-style. He was stunning. I think he was moaning. I was about to come. I picked up an empty beer bottle without even thinking and hit the guy over the head. I don't know why. The thing broke. He fell off the futon. My cock slid out. He shit all over my legs . . . which made me weirdly furious. I grabbed hold of his neck and ground the broken bottle into his face, really twisting and shoving it in. Then I crawled across the room and sat cross-legged, watching him bleed to death.

Bret Easton Ellis tried the same kind of scenes in *American Psycho*. Yet Ellis's protagonist killed with glee, and thrilled at getting away with it. He was a wealthy and successful New Yorker; his crimes were acts of self-regard. Cooper's men of violence are close to anonymous; they are not proud of, nor even stirred by, their actions. They live in barely-described suburbs, and rarely eat or leave or have a long conversation. They just pursue their obsession, which is always the same: the violation of thin young men. The victims are never hard to come by. There is no chase, no tense entrapment, and no rescue. There isn't really a plot at all. Appetites and sustenance simply drift into alignment for fifty pages or so, then they get together in some empty living room, then the novel stops. After three years, another volume takes off from Cooper's small publisher, flies under the *Daily Mail*'s radar and flashes past his persistent admirers—Irvine Welsh and, inevitably, Ellis, who calls Cooper 'the last literary outlaw in mainstream American fiction'.

Increasingly, under variations of this billing, interviews with and reviews of Cooper are slipping into magazines and news. But this small fame—like most cult reputations—can seem opaque: only converts write about him. For non-believers, there are consolations, though. The strongest is the writing. *Guide* is so spare and conversational that, at first, it looks like carelessness. Someone's hair is 'chocolatey'; a spoon of heroin over a flame 'blackened, crusted up, et cetera'. When Cooper can't find the right word, he doesn't bother: 'As Luke drove, the freeway lost . . . something.' Such omissions and limitations come to seem suggestive. Luke is vacant, unable to concentrate, and views a blurry Los Angeles through a screen of drugs. He is 25, but his moral sense is as fogged and sluggish as his conversational skills. And his attractiveness to Cooper's older narrator, Dennis, flows from precisely these attributes. Luke's reply to any request is always: 'Whatever.'

Cooper has learnt from Joan Didion, the great flat-toned chronicler of California, that there is menace in repetition and restriction, in leaving out. By dispensing with the palm trees and the traffic snarl and all the state's surface noise and danger, he depicts a private, indoor California: low-lit, pale rooms with the blinds tight shut, the blue sky forgotten outside and the neighbours too busy with the television to notice anything. And in the quiet, Cooper's occasional efforts at imagery—'a beer bottle gasp', a dollar bill 'smashed' into a pocket—are amplified, and linger. When Luke sneaks into Dennis's study to look at his pin-ups, Dennis notices immediately: 'I heard his T-shirt brush over my can of pens and pencils.'

Such an ear can catch whispery social nuance, too. Dennis is not just interested in Luke; there is Chris—'slight, androgynous . . . drugging himself in death's general direction for years'. Dennis goes to the record shop where Chris works, offers him money for heroin, and takes him home. Early the next day, Luke comes round to Dennis's bungalow and finds them—they have taken acid. All three flop onto the couch; Dennis flicks glances between his lovers:

> I'm watching Luke, who is clearly alarmed. When he's tense, his eyes enlarge, and his lips stabilise . . . He probably hopes this expression is sturdy enough to read as cool and detached. But he's too pure a person, so it doesn't read as anything but self-protective and scared, at least to someone as thrilled by his every emotional minutia as I am.

Here and elsewhere, Cooper comes close to soap opera. Each character is a first name and a jumble of jealousies. Everybody keeps running into everyone else. But there is a relentlessness about the descriptions of faces, the mesh of anodyne phone calls, the paragraphs of gossip. Dennis and Chris and Luke; Mason, who lusts after English rock musicians; Pam, who makes 'pornos', and Goof, who's '12 and a half' and stars in them, all live in each other's bedrooms and fantasies—nowhere else. Their one remaining interest in the outside world is shared and cultish, too. Dennis and his friends love rock bands; in particular, bands on little-known labels—most of all, one called Guided By Voices—which are so esoteric and erratic in their output that even the NME barely covers them. Cooper drops lyrics by Guided By Voices into his dialogue like Shakespeare quotations. Their wisdom seems limited to a laid-back nihilism—'Everything fades from sight / because that's all right with me'—but his characters revere the words, like the posters and CDs that fill their bedrooms, with the ardour of sixth-formers.

Cooper, who is 45, is a rock critic in his spare time. He writes for *Spin,* a glossy American version of the NME, and all his years scrutinising the sleeve notes of Hüsker Dü, the Replacements, Pavement and the like have generated a dark thought: this kind of fandom, with its closed-off codes, its quests for perfect rarities, and its overwhelming maleness, makes a good metaphor for a kind of predatory sexuality. Halfway through **Guide,** Dennis comes across the perfect quarry.

Luke and Chris are not quite enough for him; on his pin-up board, Dennis has stuck up a picture of Alex, the bass player for an English band called Smear. Alex is 28, 'an insecure, self-involved, artsy borderline alcoholic' and 'cute beyond belief'. His band are playing in Los Angeles. One bleary morning, he shuffles out of his hotel to get some cigarettes. As he lollops along the sun-struck sidewalk in his stained T-shirt and baggy jeans—Alex is the only character whose clothes are described—he is recognised by the worst possible person: Mason. None of the shops sells cigarettes, but Mason has some. He lives nearby. Alex makes the mistake. While he stands around in Mason's living room, Mason gets two cans of Pepsi, drops 'several' tranquillisers in one of them, and gives Dennis a call. He comes straight round. Alex is unconscious on Mason's floor; Mason has flopped him onto his stomach, loosened his jeans a little. Back in their hotel, the rest of Smear are starting to wonder why Alex is taking so long. The next dozen pages are creepily amusing. The band stand around, waist-deep in the rooftop pool, talking to MTV ('It's meant to make them look Beatlesesque, probably'). Dennis has ten minutes alone with Alex, but is so awestruck he doesn't dare touch him. Then it's Mason's turn: 'He fucked Alex harder than he'd fucked anyone in his life.'

When Alex wakes up, 'His ass feels too . . . there. Normally, it's just unassumedly doing its job.' He tells Smear's singer, his best friend, 'something rather . . . untoward has happened.' There is only so long, though, that the surprise and the novelty of the situation can keep at bay what has actually occurred. And Alex's rape is just the start. The rest of the book is a long corridor of horrors. Chris decides he wants to die during sex. Dennis is too squeamish to oblige him, so Chris

contacts a porn-film veteran, who happens to be a dwarf, to do the job. It takes some determination to follow the knife-work closely. Then Goof dies, too, during one of Pam's 'pornos'. A pair of policemen find the body on some waste ground; one of them recognises it from a video he rented. By now, the couplings and disembowellings are coming as fast as in a cartoon or video game. Cooper has stopped bothering with calm scenes; the effect is numbing, almost absurd.

In all his novels, death is presented as a surprise. One minute, the victims are writhing, or mute but quite alive, the next their bodies have given up, leaked their contents away. Cooper's killers reel back in surprise, like children with broken toys. Their desires so possess them that other considerations—getting caught, extending the moment, let alone morality—are obliterated. The narrator of **Frisk** knows the feeling:

> I've got this long-standing urge to really open up someone I'm hot for. The Dutch boy in this case, because he's the latest example. The thought has me sweating and shaking right now . . . If he were locked in this toilet with me, and if I had a knife, I guess, or claws would be better, I'd shut up that minuscule part of my brain that thinks murder is evil, whatever that means . . . Inside my head the most spectacular violence is happening. A boy's exploding, caving in.

Cooper's killers, predictably, find the body both endlessly appealing and shiveringly grotesque. In **Closer,** a victim's skin is 'like plastic or candy', then, a few moments later, his flesh is 'just a bunch of blue tubes inside a skin wrapper'. In **Frisk,** 'human bodies are such garbage bags.' In **Guide,** 'their bodies are gross to one degree or another.' They can't be blank and perfect once they have been opened up. But the people here keep probing and peering inside, as if each 'wrapper' might contain some untasted delight. Cooper has a sly phrase for this: 'same old apocalyptic porno'.

His books are nimble with such self-mockery, and internal jokes and references, and get-out clauses from accusations of brutality. The butchery scenes are often sliced up into pieces, and scattered with blander chunks of relationship talk and domesticity. Cooper draws attention to the artificiality of his stories. At the same time, he likes to hint at the presence of a certain amount of autobiography—a frisson, as one of his porn connoisseurs might put it, of 'snuff' quality. **Guide** has a character called Dennis, so does **Frisk.** And Cooper, in interviews, admits he finds an English rock star called Alex attractive: Alex James, bass player of Blur, turns out to be the inspiration for Alex Johns, bass player of Smear. The bands are meant to be the same—and Cooper quotes Blur lyrics as Smear lyrics. Alex's few stunned words in the novel exactly mimic Alex James's contributions to music paper interviews.

Two months ago, the *Idler* magazine arranged for Alex James to interview Cooper. James didn't turn up. 'I don't want to hurt Alex,' Cooper insisted afterwards. There was satisfaction to be had in the episode, though—in a rock star embarrassed, and, more lastingly, in the sight of a would-be bohemian terrified by the possibility of actual depravity. Cooper in person would probably worry most of his fans. His justifications of his subject-matter are not terribly reassuring. 'When I saw kiddie porn in Amsterdam,' he said in *Melody Maker* recently, 'I didn't know what I thought.'

That, in a sentence, is how his books operate. They speak of the barely speakable, and conclude, 'whatever.' There is plenty in them to damn Cooper: the relish of the charnel-house chapters, the preying on the underage and vulnerable, the extreme rarity with which the word 'paedophile' appears. At times, these novels work purely as reminders of the randomness of censorship laws—the same stuff published in sex magazines would have the policemen stamping round. Yet Cooper's novels are brave. To portray cruelty and extremity so plainly, without a justifying backdrop of general degradation or poverty, is a difficult and esoteric task. Like Irvine Welsh's recent writing, it can feel airless and pointless. So far, though, Cooper remains compelling.

Michael Thomas Ford (review date January 2000)

SOURCE: Ford, Michael Thomas. "Brilliantly Psychotic?" *Lambda Book Report* 8, no. 6 (January 2000): 24.

[*In the following review, Ford comments on Cooper's blurring of the lines between fiction and reality as expressed in his novel* Period.]

Sometimes it's difficult to tell if an artist's success is really deserved or if he's simply developed a dedicated following because his work is so peculiar that people can't decide if it's brilliance or pretension. Dennis Cooper's success has certainly been accused of being both things. To some he is a master stylist, exploring the worlds of violence, sex, and desire in shocking ways that challenge readers to re-evaluate their views of morality and to confront their own, perhaps frightening, obsessions. To others his work seems nothing more than the psychotic visions of a mind fixated on young men, murder, gratuitous sex, and violence just for the sake of getting himself and readers off and/or shocking them.

Cooper's latest will undoubtedly add fuel to the debate. *Period* is the fifth, and last, book in the cycle he started with his novel *Closer* and continued in *Frisk, Try,* and *Guide.* Like the book's predecessors, *Period* centers on a tale of sex, murder, and obsession. This time, though,

Cooper has also thrown Satanism, the Internet, and goth subculture into the mix. The end result is a story that takes readers into a world in which reality and imagination are blurred and where truth is a slippery figure darting through the shadows—there one moment and gone the next.

Initially, the story seems straightforward. Nate and Leon, two teenage boys obsessed with Satanism and a goth rock band called The Omen, decide to make a deal with the devil so that one of them can have sex with a deaf-mute boy who spends his days observing life and writing about it in a notebook. It works, but the object of desire ends up dead when the boys decide that sacrificing him to their dark master will make them immortal. A fight ensues between Leon and Nate, and Nate ends up bloodied and confused at the shack of Bob, an eccentric Outsider artist (an artistic movement in which art is created by people who have no formal artistic training and who are, generally, outsiders because they live in non-urban areas or are mentally ill, prisoners, or otherwise removed from mainstream society) with whom he sometimes has sex. Shortly after, he improbably finds himself traveling on a bizarre road trip with the members of The Omen, who spend as much time murdering young male fans as they do seducing them with their music.

On the surface, things are not so different here than they are in many Cooper books. People are killed to get other people off. Boys are used for sex and use one another in turn. Everyone is obsessed with everyone else. But there's more to this book. Much more. The house in which Leon and Nate kill the deaf-mute boy is one of Bob's art projects—a series of black-painted rooms behind a perfectly-realized facade of a typical American home. After his supposed death, the deaf-mute continues to "speak" to readers in a series of minute-by-minute diaries detailing his thoughts as he wanders through the black rooms of the house. He is, in effect, a disembodied consciousness roaming through Bob's Outsider art project and reporting what he finds.

So, too, is Cooper's novel a wandering through the rooms of the mind, through the imagination of Outsiders/outsiders everywhere. His story, which at first seems deceptively like the most overdone and infantile of Goth rock fantasies, is really an intricate musing on the nature of reality, dreams, and obsession. As the story, such as it is, unfolds, we find that Nate and Leon are (maybe) characters in a book (called *Period*) written by one Walker Crane. A cult following has sprung up around the book; and various young men are desperately trying to figure out what it means and who the real people are who inspired it.

Among the players are George (Crane's ex-lover who may or may not have killed himself), Nate (a young man who has become Walker's new lover), Leon (who has named himself after a character in Walker's book and who was also George's lover), Bob (who has created a web site devoted to Crane's work), and various online personalities (including two boys who form a band called The Omen after reading *Period*) who interact with one another via e-mail and chat rooms as they try to unravel the mystery of *Period*, its creator, and its subjects.

No one in the book ever really does find out what's true and what isn't, which is exactly Cooper's point. *Period* is a novel about the realities we create when we become totally obsessed with someone or something. The characters take on various identities depending upon who they're interacting with and which story they're a part of at any given moment. They tell different versions of the truth, all or none of which may be accurate. Maybe the book is the fevered dream of one or more teenage boys high on drugs and bad rock music. Maybe it's the work of a writer obsessed with these same boys and the things they love. Or maybe it's equal parts all of these things. The work is a comment on the nature of art and its effects on both the creator and the audience, and in creating this ever-shifting world, Cooper questions whether life creates art or vice versa, and whether it matters in the end anyway.

Period is not an easy read, nor is it meant to be. The publisher classifies the book as poetry but refers to it as a novel in the jacket copy. Both are correct. Cooper's prose in this book is his most lyrical. Like the deaf-mute boy scribbling his vision of the world in his notebook, Cooper weaves a tangle of truth and lies. There's no lifeline to keep you tethered to reality as you stumble through his funhouse maze of words and ideas. In the end, he leaves you back where you began, with two boys observing a third and thinking up a way to have him sexually. Only instead of being Nate and Leon, they're Etan and Noel. Like Alice stepping into the looking glass, they've passed through the mirror in which Cooper's world is reflected and come out the other side. Or maybe that other side was the real one all along. Cooper leaves it up to the reader to decide.

Gregory Howard (review date fall 2000)

SOURCE: Howard, Gregory. Review of *Period*, by Dennis Cooper. *Review of Contemporary Fiction* 20, no. 3 (fall 2000): 147.

[*In the following brief review, Howard offers the opinion that* Period *is a "deeper and darker" work than its predecessors, and that the book contains a complex structure and extensive vision.*]

Period explores themes and motifs familiar to Cooper's readers. Here again is a world of boys bored with everyday life, stimulating themselves with drugs, sex,

and violence; here again is sexual confusion, thwarted desire, and misdirected affection. This book, however, is a deeper and darker work than its predecessors, more complex in its structure and more expansive in its vision. Gone is any locational detail, replaced by stark and desolate landscapes—an unnamed, rural town, the highway, an unnamed city. Much of the "action" takes place in virtual spaces like the Internet, the telephone, and radio. Gone, too, is any sense of linear narrative; this book bends back on itself, fragments, and puts itself back together.

The novel begins with two teens, Nate and Leon, sacrificing a cat to Satan so that Leon, who is infatuated with Nate, can instead have Dagger, a mute who looks exactly like Nate. The boys then decide to sacrifice Dagger inside of a "hellmouth," built by a local artist in memory of his boyfriend George, another Nate doppelgänger. Later, Nate is picked up by a Goth band driving around the country, picking up look-alike boys and killing them in an attempt to revisit their first kill. Cut to a city and a group of men whose lives revolve around Walker Crane's book *Period,* a tribute to *his* lover George, who was raped and beaten, a book which may be the book we have been reading. Unless the entire book is the fantasy of Etan, a Nate doppelgänger introduced at the end of the book, itself a revision of the beginning, in which Etan, infatuated with Noel, tries his luck with a Noel replica named George. In *Period*'s circular, looking-glass structure replete with multiple doppelgängers, Dennis Cooper has finally found a form to suit his content. *Period* is a startling work of fiction.

Henry Hitchings (review date 27 October 2000)

SOURCE: Hitchings, Henry. "Perverts and Their Prey." *Times Literary Supplement* (27 October 2000): 23.

[*In the following review, Hitchings alleges that* Period *fails to take a clear stand, and that Cooper's intentions are obscure and "illegible."*]

For twenty years, Dennis Cooper cultivated a reputation as a subversive, stylish, gay poet. Then, in 1994, he published **Closer,** the first in a series of loosely connected novels. His new book, **Period,** concludes this quintet of edgy, risk-taking volumes. As the title suggests, it is intended to bring the sequence to a definitive close; but Cooper, who is seldom content with the standard formulae of narrative fiction—its tired resolutions and coy denouements—chooses to complicate this composed but malignant last installment with self-reflexive ironies and technical sleight of hand. The implicit aim is to show the reader that the idea of closure is merely a construct; there can be no such thing as a final, decisive, determined ending.

The novel's dramas are psychological. Its opening paragraph suggests a precise geographical setting—"A little town made up of rickety shacks largely hidden away in some humongous oak trees that this thick fog enclosed"—but it is the fog, not the little town, that persists during what follows. The deliberately murky story concerns the efforts of a cultish goth band to secure human victims for its wayward creative project, an essay in the poetry of death. Rather than being shown events, we pick up tremors of forewarning and inklings of appetite; events consist of a series of conversations and musings, played out on the Internet, and in the form of disembodied dialogues, befuddled diary entries and cinematic vignettes.

Cooper's is a world instantly recognizable to any aficionado of online dalliance. Perverts and their prey hide behind assumed identities, explore their cravings with inarticulate candour, and feast on prospects and memories of transgression. The young male characters are interchangeable; they have no personality, existing merely in order to be the props of violence and fantasy. Cooper unflinchingly depicts a blandly hedonistic underworld, and evokes with skill the intellectual and emotional emptiness of chat-room dialogue, the dissolute vagueness of pornographic fanzines, and the tawdry sexuality around which so much cyber-fantasy revolves.

Contrary to what his fans might have one believe, Cooper's feel for the subtleties on English prose is only modest. Occasionally he musters an ingenious image—one character has "a malignant brain tumour the size of an alarm clock"—but for the most part the semi-literate vacuity of his characters serves as a convenient excuse to employ a muckily colloquial style. His writing thrives on stagy inverted commas, phrases such as. "Long story short" (as in "to cut a long story short"), and words like "scaredy-cat", "creepy", "nondesigned" and the necessary but overused "weird" and "strange".

With its numbly violent prose and moral opacity, *Period* is the quintessential "blank" novel. It avoids committing itself to any explicit standpoint; the narrator covers his tracks at every turn, and Cooper's own intentions are illegible to the last. Sickness and depravity are portrayed in a casual fashion, and though the characters who perpetrate the novel's evils are by any conventional standard unsympathetic, it remains unclear whether the reader is supposed to recoil in shock from the dystopian spectacle or enjoy its brutality.

There is a craven tendency to describe writing of this kind as "courageous", on the grounds that it knows no boundaries. We are supposed, it seems, to nod and reflect that "this is how things are". But Cooper's corner of the world, though larger than one might wish, remains obscure. Fans of his work scarcely need critics

to switch them on to its macabre delights; such is its samizdat appeal, they no doubt commune with his ideas at source, online, rather than after they have been mediated by formal publication. And, for the rest of us, Dennis Cooper's writing constitutes the sort of wake-up call that our beleaguered modern conscience barely needs.

Elizabeth Young (review date 20 November 2000)

SOURCE: Young, Elizabeth. "On the Buttocks." *New Statesman* (20 November 2000): 52.

[*In the following review, Young discusses Cooper's series of five novels, offering a positive evaluation of* Period. *Young acknowledges the base and sordid elements, but lauds the "grace and elegance" and "ethical torment" within the works.*]

When Dennis Cooper began his quintuplet of novels in 1989, of which *Period* is the last, he was no more than a minor poet on the Los Angeles avant-garde gay scene. But as the novels appeared with relentless regularity, and Cooper became more widely known, critics competed to garnish his work with ever more elaborate encomia: the novelist Edmund White wrote that Cooper was "reciting Aeschylus with a mouthful of bubble-gum"; Bret Easton Ellis called him the "last literary outlaw in mainstream American fiction"; the *New York Times* opined that "this is high-risk literature. It takes enormous courage for a writer to explore the extreme boundaries of human behaviour and amorality." Even I contributed my two cents worth, writing in the *Guardian*: "If Georges Bataille had been stranded in Disneyland, he might have written like Dennis Cooper." At the same time, the extreme sexual nature of Cooper's fiction resulted in his receiving death threats and being attacked by literal gay activists.

So what is the big deal about Dennis Cooper? In person, he seems to be anything but the heir to a great Continental tradition of licence and abandon. He may be aware of the transgressive tradition in which his work is located—de Sade, Poe—but he speaks (and often writes) in a deliberately dumbed-down Californian teen demotic. This is informed not only by the time he spends among deviant teens, but also by the compassion he feels for abused kids and, through association, by memories of his own unhappy childhood. Reading him is a bit like eating an apple full of razor blades.

The five novels in this series—*Closer, Frisk, Try, Guide,* and now *Period* (all published by Serpent's Tail)—concentrate on Cooper's own sexual fantasies. Each novel is a nightmarishly complex knot of predatory homosexual desire, murderous longing and rampant pedophilia. These are shot through with shards of romanticism, nurturance and moments of tenderness. Cooper is obsessed with a certain type of passive, abused, drugged teenage boy. The novels depict grotesque scenes of murder and mayhem.

Central to Cooper's fantasies is a compulsive buttock worship: "Goof's ass is this splayed, perfect, shimmering, televised orb"; "Junkies' asses are perfect, so constipated, such weird treasure chests"; "One of my fingers was up Chris's ass. There was this hard rock of shit stuck in there like a horrid antique."

Should people doubt that this is serious art, let me direct them to three books published recently by imprisoned US serial killers, one of whom was trained in creative writing and was quite talented. These books, with their endless, thudding scenes of sadistic torture, are utterly devoid of the grace and elegance of Cooper's work, his empathy and longing, his ethical torment.

Cooper is tormented, pre-eminently, by the inadequacy of language as a medium through which to express extreme emotions. "Words have this awful, downsizing effect on your thoughts"; "Luke's eyes are greenish . . . no, hazel—no, aquamarine with a spray of brown speckles and kind of, uh, yellowy smears."

In terms of animating one's deepest sexual fantasies, Cooper has something in common with William Burroughs. Burroughs wrote of the "courage" required of an author—"the courage of the inner exploration, the cosmonaut of inner space. The writer cannot pull back from what he finds because it shocks or upsets him, or because he fears the disapproval of the reader." Cooper has certainly felt very frustrated by those who (unfamiliar with the sentiments expressed here by Burroughs and similarly elsewhere) persist in misreading him. "I'm seen as this person who wants to kill boys and I'm NOT. They think I'm a monster." In *Period,* the narrator explicitly rejects any idea that he wishes to embrace his fantasies in real time: "I'm a wuss"; "I'm not an evil man"; "I'm sick. But I'm doing my very best, really."

Cooper has said that he detests the sexual exploitation of children; and yet he can "understand the impulse— the horror of it is very sexy or something". This presumably accounts for his wilful flouting of strong taboos: all the novels feature pornography, kiddie porn, child sexual abuse and snuff films.

The first book in the series, *Closer* (1989), supports a Lacanian pre-Oedipal reading with its creation of George Miles, beautiful and benumbed. Scared, self-destructive, he is Cooper's archetypal teenage muse. In *Frisk* (1991), a doomed flirtation with the reader, the narrator claims actually to have enacted his most extreme murderous impulses. *Try* (1994) is less

solipsistic and, mercifully, more plot-driven. In it, Cooper describes the damage sustained by Ziggy, the adopted son of an abusive gay male couple. After the publication of this book, Cooper went into therapy.

By the time *Guide* was published in 1997, I found that, with the best will in the world, I could read no more novels about boys' bottoms. In any event, they weren't a particular interest of mine. Yet I have since returned to *Guide,* and have found, as in *Period,* a deeper, more mature work. Both novels, unlike their predecessors, focus on other forms of love and tenderness; they are not simply cruel, exploitative depictions of extreme sexuality.

Elliptical and strange, *Period* is a worthy finale. George Miles reappears, providing a unity of thematic purpose. All the current appurtenances of Californian teendom are here: drugs, Goths, death metal, Satanism, the net, disturbed psychic states. And Cooper has at last achieved a certain distance from his implacable, airless fantasies. The prose is gentler, sadder and more resigned than in the earlier, sexually frenetic books. It is far more stylistically complex, too. Identities dissolve—and meld.

For Cooper, the body is itself a "text", something to be "read". He speaks of reading the body "like braille". Roland Barthes has written of how the "text can reveal itself in the form of a body, split into fetish objects"; that texts arise out of our history, "leaving the trace of a cut". Barthes calls them "texts of bliss"—or *jouissance.*

Cooper's texts are unequivocally part of this tradition. In this sense, his concentration on the buttocks is crucially important, signifying as it does all the divisions in his own nature. His achievement, in the end, is to illuminate ways in which we are all at psychic odds with ourselves, but remain trapped within the inescapable contours of our own hard corporeality.

Kevin McCarron (essay date 2001)

SOURCE: McCarron, Kevin. "'The Crack-House Flicker': The Sacred and the Absurd in the Short Stories of Dennis Cooper, Denis Johnson, and Thom Jones." *Yearbook of English Studies* 31 (2001): 50-61.

[*In the following excerpt, McCarron examines Cooper's depiction of existential angst, irreligion, and the impossibility of transcendence in his short fiction and series of novels, offering comparison to the work of the Marquis de Sade.*]

> Even an image he'd thought religious this morning is just a snap of some junkie on hands and knees, beckoning over one shoulder, eyes drugged to pitch-black, asshole fucked so many times it resembles an empty eye socket.
>
> —*Safe,* Dennis Cooper

His chest was like Christ's. That's probably who he
was.

> —'Dirty Wedding', Denis Johnson

'You heard a voice from God?' 'Seemed like I did', Ad
Magic said.

> —'Quicksand', Thom Jones

In his essay 'The Nature of Knowledge in Short
Fiction', Charles E. May cites Lionel Trilling to draw a
useful distinction between the novel and the short story:

> Whereas the novel is primarily a social and public form,
> the short story is mythic and spiritual. While the novel
> is primarily structured on a conceptual and philosophic
> framework, the short story is intuitive and lyrical. The
> novel exists to reaffirm the world of 'everyday' reality;
> the short story exists to 'defamiliarize' the everyday.
> Storytelling does not spring from one's confrontation
> with the everyday world, but rather from one's
> encounter with the sacred (in which true reality is
> revealed in all its plenitude) or with the absurd (in
> which true reality is revealed in all its vacuity).[1]

In Robert Stone's 'Miserere', from his collection of
stories *Bear & His Daughter,* the alcoholic protagonist
lays the bodies of several aborted children on the floor
before the altar of a Catholic church:

> Finally, she was alone with the ancient Thing before
> whose will she stood amazed, whose shadow and line
> and light they all were; the bad priest and the question-
> able young man and Camille Innaurato, she herself and
> the unleavened flesh fouling the floor. Adoring, defiant,
> in the crack-house flicker of the hideous, consecrated
> half-darkness, she offered It Its due, by old command.[2]

The memorable phrase 'crack-house flicker' here links
religion with narcotics, and the encounters with the
sacred and the absurd in the short stories of Dennis
Cooper, Denis Johnson, and Thom Jones are invariably
associated with the heavy usage of various drugs;
indeed, the actual conflation of drug abuse and religion
provides a crucial dynamic to the work of all three
writers.

The short story is particularly well-suited to an interrogation of religious presence or absence, in large part
because of its form. Although much contemporary critical thought accounts for the development of literary
forms materially,[3] it can also be suggested that the form
of the short story is the primary narrative form. May
writes: 'The short story from its beginning is primarily
a literary mode which has remained closer to the primal
narrative form that embodies and recapitulates mythic
perception' (p. 139). May cites Frank O'Connor to suggest: 'The short story has always been detached from
any concept of a normal society, remaining by its very
nature remote from the community—romantic, individualistic, and intransigent; consequently, always in the
short story there is a sense of outlawed figures wander-

ing about the fringes of society' (p. xxv). The alienation
Cooper's characters experience, in particular, can also
be seen formally represented in his work. It can be
argued that all that separates Cooper's novels from his
short stories is marketing: all his writing is episodic and
fragmented. As with Irvine Welsh's *Trainspotting,*
Cooper's novels can be read as groups of short stories,
even sketches or vignettes, thereby formally representing the alienation and estrangement experienced by the
characters. Cooper, in effect, has only ever written short
stories. Cooper's characters, as well as those of Jones
and Johnson, move through a fragmented America
presumably unrecognizable to the majority of their readers. Andrew Levy writes:

> From the 1830s and 1840s, when Eastern magazines
> and newspapers published anecdotes of frontier life
> gathered from papers and readers in the South and
> Southwest, the short story has always been a site of
> discourse in which a comparatively well-educated,
> middle-class audience could read about the fictional-
> ized lives of the more marginal participants in the
> American political project. (pp. 108-09)

Strikingly, the characters in the stories of Cooper, Jones
and Johnson are unconcerned at their lack of integration
into the 'American political project'; their desires lie
elsewhere.

In a review of Cooper's books **Wrong** and **Closer,**
Elizabeth Young wrote: 'Cooper's writing spirals as
tightly as DNA around death, perversity, tenderness and
desire. Its intensity and excess stem from his attempts
to find language that will encompass perverse eroticism
and transcendence within a world in which feelings has
[*sic*] been numbed'.[4] That Cooper's work is 'excessive'
few readers would contest, but its 'intensity' is considerably less easy to evaluate. Young's attribution of a literary motive to Cooper, her suggestion that she understands him and his work, is characteristic of her
appraisals of him. In her comprehensive book *Shopping
in Space* she writes: 'Cooper [. . .] is transcendent,
timeless. He has extraordinarily clear unconscious
drives and these tend to animate and energize every
aspect of his text whether he wishes them to or not.'[5]
Significantly, however, she quotes from Cooper's work
very infrequently. Even a claim such as the following is
unsubstantiated by any textual evidence: 'For all the
extremes and grotesqueries of his content, Cooper is a
tender, lyrical and very romantic writer' (*Shopping,* p.
257). This may be true, but it must also be taken on
trust by the reader unfamiliar with Cooper's work. Still
without quotation, Young places Cooper in a tradition:
'His works cannot be described as pornographic in that
they are not intended to excite the reader to orgasm, but
he certainly has affinities with the French erotic tradition represented by, among others, de Sade, Lautréa-
mont and Bataille.'

James Annesley, in his valuable book *Blank Fictions,* also links Cooper, among other contemporary American writers, with de Sade and Bataille: 'This familial resemblance is strengthened by a common interest in the kinds of subjects that obsessed William Burroughs, Georges Bataille and the Marquis de Sade.'[6] However, while the work of Bataille does provide a useful perspective from which to consider Cooper's writing, the comparison with de Sade is less easily maintained. Certainly it is not difficult to envisage a phrase such as the following, from a critique of de Sade's *Justine,* published in *Petites-Affiches* in 1792, being applied to Cooper's work in the 1990s: 'If the imagination that produced such a monstrous work is indeed deranged, it must be conceded that it is rich and brilliant of its kind.'[7] Less ambivalently, however, a journalist called Villeterque commented upon de Sade's *Les Crimes de l'amour* in phrases that could also equally be applied to Cooper's writing: 'A detestable book [. . .]. What possible utility is there in these portraits of crime triumphant? They stimulate the wicked man's maleficent inclinations, they elicit cries of indignation from the virtuous man who is firm in his principles, and in the weak man they provoke tears of discouragement.'[8] A similar reception, however, does not necessarily demonstrate a useful connection. Cooper's writing differs from de Sade's in far more ways than it is like it, and the most crucial difference occurs in their different representations of religion.

Simone de Beauvoir, in her introduction to *The One Hundred and Twenty Days of Sodom,* writes of Sade: 'His nature was thoroughly irreligious.'[9] De Beauvoir reads de Sade's work from a Marxist perspective, seeing it as exemplary of materialist philosophy, and in particular of Hobbes's views on nature. Angela Carter, like de Beauvoir, is interested in assessing the principles of exchange that underline de Sade's writing: 'Pleasure is a hard task-master. *The Hundred and Twenty Days at Sodom* offers a black version of the Protestant ethic but the profit, the orgasm obtained with so much effort, the product of so much pain and endeavor—the pursuit of the profit leads directly to hell. To a perfectly material hell.'[10] Although de Beauvoir refers to de Sade as 'thoroughly irreligious' there is too much sacrilege and blasphemy in his work for this to be the case. Maurice Lever writes of de Sade's fascination with sacrilege that it is rather surprising and more than a little odd in a man who throughout his life denied the existence of God. Blasphemy makes sense only as transgression of a recognized value. The true atheist is not the person who combats God by denying that he exists but the one that never thinks about his existence. Such a contradiction raises doubts about the reality of Sade's atheism. (p. 121)

De Sade's characters are haunted by the loss of God. The scenes of unspeakable degradation, the episodes depicting sequences of escalating atrocities, all point to an absence—the absence of God. By performing the most abominable acts imaginable, de Sade's characters seem to wish to attract the attention and the intervention of a divine agency, to finally provoke Him to show Himself, but all that looks back at them is the impassive face of a totally indifferent universe. It is rage at this absence that animates de Sade's work, but, crucially, the same cannot be said of Cooper's writing.

Cooper never has his characters speak of 'God' in anything but the most sceptical and vague terms. In **'Spaced'**, the narrator says: 'I mean, I know there's no God. People are only their bodies, and sex is the ultimate intimacy, etc., but it's not enough.'[11] In the first story, **'A Herd'**, from his first collection of stories, *Wrong,* which features a child rapist and serial killer, the narrator notes: 'If there was a God . . .'[12] In the final story in the collection, **'Epilogue'**, the narrator informs us: '"God" is the adjective I like to use when describing Joe, as it implies beliefs in the years since' (p. 160). In *Frisk,* the narrator, who is describing in graphic detail the abduction, rape, murder, and disembowelment of a succession of young boys, says of his partners in crime: 'They kills guys for a kick, while for me it's religious or something' (p. 94). The assumption here that religion has an equivalent, 'or something', is a characteristic belief of Cooper's characters, most of whom speak in a similarly vague and imprecise manner. Cooper's characters' attitude to religion is thoroughly contemporary: 'God', 'spiritual', 'religious', and similarly oriented words are just that in Cooper's work—words. They possess no stable, historical, or theological meaning; they are just nouns and adjectives that can be used as validly in one context as in another. This is not the case in de Sade's writing. De Sade's universe is one in which 'God' is a stable signifier, and transgression has a purpose.

Cooper's work articulates the end of the humanist ideal, the post-Enlightenment drive to place all meaning and all value in the human. In an essay on Bataille, Julia Kristeva writes: 'It is clear today, at a time when our culture is no longer the only center of the world, that since the bourgeois Revolution, the essential adventure of literature has been to take up again, dissolve, and displace Christian ideology and the art that is inseparable from it'.[13] Cooper's work is in the vanguard of this 'project':

> Mike dragged Keith down the hall by his hair. He shit in Keith's mouth. He laid a whip on Keith's ass. It was a grass skirt once Mike dropped the belt. Mike kicked Keith's skull in before he came to. Brains or whatever it was gushed out. 'That's that'. [. . .] He thought of offing himself. 'After death, what's left?' he mumbled. He meant 'to do'. Once you've killed someone, life's shit. It's a few rules and you've already broken the best. [. . .] He stared out at the Hudson. He put a handgun to his head. 'Fuck this shit.' His body splashed in the river, drifted off. (*Wrong,* pp. 63-65)

The authorial intrusion 'He meant "to do"' in this passage emphasizes Mike's lack of belief in an afterlife, while it is also clearly implied that 'the rules' are nothing but cultural constructions and that, therefore, there is absolutely no reason to obey them.

Sex and drugs fuel the lives of even Cooper's most amiable characters. Drugs, usually heroin, but often cocaine, LSD, and amphetamines, are a presence in virtually everything Cooper has written. It is the triviality of life, the encounter with the absurd, that Cooper's characters use drugs to avoid confronting. While amphetamines produce cranked-up sexual extravaganzas, which are never depicted joyously or sensually, LSD is capable of imparting a significance to incidents which they do not actually possess: 'George liked how acid could blow up the flimsiest topic.'[14] Heroin, the most ubiquitous narcotic in Cooper's writing, offers a blissful abdication from the pointlessness of existence: 'Across town, Calhoun sits in his fake-antique desk chair injecting a huge dose of heroin. [. . .] He unties his arm, blinks, and a subsequent rush, though it's more like an ease—warm, slightly sensual, trancy—crossfades the world around him into a vague, distant backdrop as well as it can, for a minute anyway.'[15] However, this ease is purchased at considerable cost: indeed, when humanity has been placed at the centre of existence, the ultimate cost. Cooper's work is actually anti-drug; the absence of sensuous description is reinforced by numerous characters' absolutely unequivocal condemnations of drugs. In *Closer,* the first-person narrator says: 'We decide to have sex again. As we do, I take occasional snorts from Keith's cocaine supply. Coke creates distances between its users and others, especially other users' (p. 130). In *Try,* Calhoun, high on heroin, wishes Annie to stay in his room but is unable to communicate this desire: 'Calhoun wants to say, Stay, or something to that effect. Instead, his mouth just sort of falls open, hangs there, a reddish black, roughly triangular slot, at the far back of which are some inventive emotions that don't have a chance against the shit heroin throws over everything in the world except its own . . . whatever. Slam' (p. 70). Later, Calhoun meditates on what heroin has done to him: 'God, things used to seem so potentially amazing re: Josie and love and all that before heroin moved in. [. . .] According to books he'd admired, heroin was supposed to make certain outdated necessities like love, friendship, sex obsolete, and it works in a way. Josie abandoned him, thanks to it' (p. 150).

With the absence of God, humanity is now at the centre of existence, but drugs, often taken to avoid confronting the pointlessness of an absurd world, create an inability in the user to form relationships with other human beings, leaving nothing but the drugs. This cruel circle of despair is central to Cooper's writing and lies behind many of the more bizarre and horrifying incidents in his

books. In *Frisk,* the narrator, Dennis, writes a letter to his old friend, Julian, describing in horrifying detail his abduction, rape, and killing of a number of young boys, some as young as ten or eleven:

> I pressed the point of the blade into the base of his throat and made a long, straight slit all the way down his chest, stomach. [. . .] It opened up. I pulled back the halves of white stomach flesh and saw his jumbled yellow guts, which had a weird strong stench. [. . .] I wiped the blood off his ass as best I could, grabbed the calf of his one intact leg and bent it way forward, opening the ass-crack. I licked it out for a long time. [. . .] His hole tasted metallic. I stretched it open and sniffed. The bowels reeked as harshly as I've ever known. I spat on the hole and fucked it brutally, which wasn't easy [. . .]. Stomp the kid's head, I said. Jorg jumped up, did. It was really horrific. The back of the head just caved in. The hair got all goopy with blood and brain tissue or something. Jorg pulled down his pants and dropped some shit on the crushed head. [. . .] God human beings are such garbage bags.

(pp. 105-06)

Later in the book it is made clear that this sequence of killings is a fiction, and Young draws a connection between Brett Easton Ellis's *American Psycho* and *Frisk*: 'Descriptions of murder have exactly the same effect linguistically, whether the murders are "realities" or "fantasies" in the book. They cannot be *more* or *less* real according to the plot. It is only fictional convention that makes them seem so. They are all just words' (*Shopping,* p. 257). Perhaps one of the most disturbing aspects of Cooper's work is precisely this sense that there is nothing left but words. Annesley, who also stresses that these horrifying descriptions are 'fictions', writes of this particular incident: 'There is no sense here that the corpse is any way connected to human life. It is just a thing to be mutilated' (p. 30). However, it could equally be argued that it is precisely *because* the boy is human that he is a 'thing to be mutilated'. Annesley suggests, with a particular focus on Cooper's fascination with excrement in his work: 'The casual brutality described in *Frisk* is thus linked to a dehumanizing transaction that generates "dead matter" in economic terms (the commodity), in psychological terms (excrement) and in real terms (murder)' (p. 32). Certainly, 'rimming', homosexual anal sex, and coprophilia are all portrayed as routinely in Cooper's writing as is drug abuse, but as Geoffrey Hartman observes of Walter Benjamin's analysis of Baudelaire: 'Benjamin was tempted to give his analysis at the price of occluding a radically religious perspective. The socioeconomic interpretation is not so much wrong as incomplete.'[16]

Intimations of something mysterious occasionally flicker through the minds of Cooper's characters, as occurs in a coprophiliac incident in *Closer,* for example, in what is possibly the most memorable image in all of Cooper's writing: 'He did a sharp nosedive and smelled something rancid but rich, like the trace of perfume in a king's tomb. He flattened his face on the butt, sucked and chewed at the hole, but his treasure was stuck in its vault' (p. 80). Bataille writes: 'It is clear, in any event, that the nature of excrement is analogous to that of corpses and that the places of its emission are close to the sexual parts. [. . .] Moreover, life is a product of putrefecation, and it depends on both death and the dungheap.'[17] Specific religious imagery is actually pervasive throughout incidents that focus on the anus. In *Try*, Ziggy reads a letter Roger has sent him, in which Roger details his fascination with young boys: *'As for what I like to do with them, rimming's the technical term for it. "Eating ass" is a lowlier synonym. Don't think for a moment that this brand of sex has any relationship at all to the "sex" Brice imposes on you. It's far more like worship, if anything'* (p. 19). In *Safe,* from *Wrong*, Mark examines himself: 'God knows his ass pays back all eye contact in spades—creamy white, small and firm, almost no hair in the crack. [. . .] Mark thinks his own even slightly resembles the Shroud of Turin' (p. 122). In *Try,* Ziggy's gay foster-father, who has been having sex with Ziggy since he was eight years old, says in a list he is compiling of Ziggy's physical attributes: 'Ass: In short, it emitted a stench I'd best leave in absentia, or at least to the discretion of listeners, as you would recognize this smell to which I obliquely refer from your own, well, *experiences*. Yet I'm positive you would agree that within its rottenness was a flowering so sweet and spicy [. . .] a secret, addictive ingredient that made one inevitably return' (pp. 160-61). What is being 'worshipped', what is 'addictive', is confirmation of humanity's eventual carrion status. In Cooper's world, human beings, who are no longer even connected to one another, who have no spiritual, moral, or intellectual value for one another, are nothing but sacks of blood and shit. In *Closer,* John is having sex with George and thinks: 'That was the weirdest part, feeling how warm and familiar George was and at the same time realizing the kid was just skin wrapped around some grotesque-looking stuff' (*Closer,* p. 7). In 'David', the narrator says: 'That's why I'm happy I'm famous for what I'm so famous for. Being gorgeous, I mean. It helps me believe in myself and not worry that I'm just a bunch of blue tubes inside a skin wrapper, which is what everyone actually is' (*Closer,* p. 22).

Cooper is by no means, however, a completely pessimistic writer and the salvation he does, guardedly, offer is both thoroughly contemporary and almost certainly the reason he is very highly regarded by critics such as Young and Annesley. Young wrote of *Closer* in her review, for example: 'Like all serious art, *Closer* falls exquisitely, effortlessly, into the little we know about art, language and the unconscious' (p. 42). Charles E. May writes: 'The short story as a genre has always

been more apt to lay bare its fictionality than the novel, which has traditionally tried to cover it up. Fictional self-consciousness in the short story does not allow the reader to maintain the comfortable cover-up assumption that what is depicted is real; instead the reader is made uncomfortably aware that the only reality is the process of depiction itself—the fiction-making process, the language act.'[18] Cooper often draws attention to the fiction-making process. In **'My Secret Diary'**, from *Wrong,* the narrator notes of a character called Kenny who is dying in hospital: 'No one bothers to visit him, not even me and I made him up' (p. 96). In *Safe,* from the same collection, Rob tries to account for the necrophilia fantasies his gay lover has discovered written down and hidden in his pornography collection: 'He claims it's research for his novel. He says his sentences are like bars on a cage that holds dangerous animals' (p. 109). Later in the same story, the narrator says of his own face: 'It had two poorly made, gentle, and endlessly flickering eyes that would scare me when I was innocent, although I'd carved them myself' (p. 133). He also writes of another character: 'Mark sleeps his way through the rest of this story' (p. 129). In a writer with Cooper's reputation for violence and nihilism there is something curiously old-fashioned, as well as élitist and disingenuous, in his faith in the importance of art, although it is, of course, the inevitable result of his creation of a thoroughly desacralized world: all we have left is the ability to describe the horrors. The perspective offered by Cooper throughout his work is that of those great brooding eyes in *The Great Gatsby*; it is as though those eyes were capable of detachedly recording the death throes of a degenerate and rapidly decaying culture. . . .

In a review of Tobias Wolff's collection of stories, *The Night in Question,* Robert Stone argues that Wolff's writing is 'fundamentally religious [in] nature.'[19] Stone further suggests that, in addition to the presence of redemption as a motif in Wolff's work: 'Another element that decisively demonstrates the religious element in Wolff's work is the repeated rendering of his characters' pathetic attempts to act morally.' Morality and religion, however, are not synonyms, although Cooper and Jones, particularly, often construct an equivalence between the two words. Both Cooper and Jones create a range of characters who seem able to envisage God only as a prescriptive presence, or absence, not as a supernatural or numinous force. They are contemporary writers not just in their graphic depictions of sexuality and drug abuse, but also in their belief that the most important, indeed the only, element of religion is the moral. Both writers also consistently imply that while transcendence is desirable it is unattainable without narcotics, and equally impossible to recapture without them. Only Johnson's characters have retained a sense of the centrality of the irrational or supernatural to religion, and they are often able to integrate a sacred experience into their predominantly secular lives.

Notes

1. *The New Short Story Theories,* ed. by Charles E. May (Athens: Ohio University Press, 1994), p. 133.

2. Robert Stone, *Bear & His Daughter* (London: Bloomsbury, 1998), p. 24.

3. See, with specific reference to the American short story, Andrew Levy, *The Culture and Commerce of the American Short Story* (Cambridge: Cambridge University Press, 1993).

4. 'The King of Cool', *Guardian,* 12 April 1994, p. 42.

5. *Shopping in Space: Essays On American 'Blank Generation' Fiction* (London: Serpent's Tail, 1992), p. 240.

6. James Annesley, *Blank Fictions: Consumerism, Culture and the Contemporary American Novel* (London: Pluto Press, 1998) p. 2.

7. Cited in Maurice Lever, *Sade: A Biography,* trans. by Arthur Goldhammer (New York: Harcourt Brace, 1994) p. 384.

8. Lever, *Sade: A Biography,* p. 510.

9. 'Must We Burn Sade?', introduction to the Marquis de Sade, *The One Hundred and Twenty Days of Sodom,* trans. by A. Wainhouse and R. Seaver (London: Arrow, 1991), p. 42.

10. *The Sadeian Woman* (London: Virago, 1979) p. 148.

11. Dennis Cooper, *Frisk* (London: Serpent's Tail, 1991), pp. 69-70.

12. *Wrong* (London: Serpent's Tail, 1992) p. 8.

13. 'Bataille, Experience and Practice', in *On Bataille,* ed. by Leslie Anne Boldt-Irons (Albany: State University of New York, 1995), p. 237.

14. Dennis Cooper, *Closer* (London: Serpent's Tail, 1989), p. 47.

15. Dennis Cooper, *Try* (London: Serpent's Tail, 1994), p. 2.

16. Cited in Douglas Tallack, *The Nineteenth-Century American Short Story: Language, From and Ideology* (London: Routledge, 1993), p. 158.

17. George Bataille, 'Death', in *The Bataille Reader,* ed. by Fred Botting and Scott Wilson (Oxford: Blackwell, 1997), p. 242.

18. 'Chekhov and the Modern Short Story', in *The New Short Story Theories,* p. 216.

19. Robert Stone, 'Finding Mercy in a God-Forsaken World', *TLS,* 15 November 1996, p. 23.

FURTHER READING

Criticism

Bahr, David. "Hannibal Lecture." *Advocate* (9 May 2000): 88-9.
    Provides discussion of Cooper's disturbing thematic preoccupations and literary style, relates Cooper's comments on his work, including his decision to turn to new subjects after the publication of *Period.*

Boddy, Kasia. "Boyzone Love." *Guardian,* (9 May 1998): 10.
    A brief, generally favorable assessment of *Guide.*

Ebershoff, David. "Bad Moon Rising." *Los Angeles Times Book Review* (7 July 2002): 3.
    A positive review of *My Loose Thread.*

Harris, Michael. Review of *Wrong,* by Dennis Cooper. *Los Angeles Times Book Review* (8 March 1992): 6.
    A brief, tempered assessment of *Wrong* in which Harris commends Cooper's audacity but questions his range of subject matter.

Innes, Charlotte. "Emerging from the Scary Shadows of Human Behavior." *Los Angeles Times* (9 October 1994): E13.
    Provides an overview of Cooper's life, fiction, and critical reception, along with the author's comments.

Reynolds, Susan Salter. Review of *Period,* by Dennis Cooper. *Los Angeles Times Book Review* (5 March 2000): 11.
    Offers brief comment on the plot and shocking content of *Period.*

Santella, Andrew. Review of *Period,* by Dennis Cooper. *New York Times Book Review* (9 April 2000): 23.
    Provides a brief summary of *Period.*

Shattuck, Kathryn. "How Nightmarish Childhood Events Became a 5-Book Series, Now Finished." *New York Times* (2 March 2000): E9.
    Offers discussion of Cooper's life, formative experiences, and literary career.

Taylor, Nick. "Creepy Uncle Psychotic." *Independent* (22 March 1998): 32-3.
    Provides an overview of Cooper's literary career and thematic concerns, along with Cooper's comments on his work, upon the publication of *Guide.*

Viegener, Matias. Review of *Jerk,* by Dennis Cooper. *Artforum International* 31, no. 10 (summer 1993): 102.
    Offers a positive assessment of *Jerk.*

Wilson, Charles. Review of *My Loose Thread,* by Dennis Cooper. *New York Times Book Review* (11 August 2002): 7.

Offers a brief summary and mixed evaluation of *My Loose Thread.*

Additional coverage of Cooper's life and career is contained in the following sources published by Thomson Gale: *Contemporary Authors,* **Vol. 133;** *Contemporary Authors New Revision Series,* **Vols. 72, 86;** *Gay and Lesbian Literature,* **ed. 1;** *Literature Resource Center;* **and** *St. James Guide to Horror, Ghost, and Gothic Writers.*

Alain de Botton
1969-

Swiss-born British novelist, critic, and essayist.

The following entry presents an overview of de Botton's career through 2003.

INTRODUCTION

De Botton is recognized as a distinctive postmodern voice in contemporary British literature. He has garnered critical and popular acclaim for fiction and nonfiction writings that utilize cultural allusions, literary criticism, philosophy, self-help jargon, travel literature, and other elements to explore relationships and offer guidance for living in the modern world. Critics view de Botton's application of philosophy and literary classics to circumstances within contemporary life as an attempt to make complex ideas more accessible, popular, and relevant to his readers.

BIOGRAPHICAL INFORMATION

De Botton was born on December 20, 1969, in Zurich, Switzerland. He attended Gonville College and Cambridge University in England, where he studied philosophy. He has worked as a television reviewer for the *New Statesman* and as a journalist for the *Sunday Telegraph*. He published his first novel, *Essays in Love,* in England in 1993; it was released in the United States a year later as *On Love*. The book attracted wide critical attention and earned him a reputation as an engaging and witty young author. He continues to write fiction, essays, and nonfiction, drawing on his interest in philosophy, literature, and travel, and serves as director of the graduate philosophy program at London University.

MAJOR WORKS

Essays in Love chronicles the doomed love affair of a nameless male narrator and a woman named Chloe. De Botton blends quotations from and allusions to the works of a myriad of prominent philosophers and authors—for example, Stendhal, Plato, Johann Wolfgang Goethe, Immanuel Kant, and Sigmund Freud—with self-help jargon, diagrams, graphs, and a numbering system for the paragraphs of the novel that is

reminiscent of the style of a philosophical treatise. *The Romantic Movement* (1994) follows the same thematic and structural pattern as his previous novel and is a straightforward love story between a young man and woman, presented with philosophical commentary. In his 1995 novel *Kiss & Tell,* de Botton employs a first-person narrator to relate the story of a man who attempts to prove that he is not narcissistic by writing the biography of an ordinary young woman named Isabel. *How Proust Can Change Your Life* (1997) is regarded as part literary criticism and part self-help book. The work gleans inspirational and self-help passages from Marcel Proust's *Remembrance of Things Past* and applies them to problems of contemporary life. De Botton takes a similar approach in *The Consolations of Philosophy* (2000), which focuses on the ideas of such philosophers as Socrates, Epicurus, Seneca, Montaigne, Schopenhauer, and Nietzsche. The book pairs the work of each philosopher with a particular personal problem, with the aim of providing insight into and solutions for issues such as unpopularity and despair. *The Art of Travel* (2002) draws on de Botton's personal vision and experiences as well as on the travels of such figures as Gustave Flaubert, Edward Hopper, and William Wordsworth to reflect on the nature, purpose, and benefits of travel.

CRITICAL RECEPTION

De Botton's incorporating of ideas, excerpts, and personae from literature and philosophy into his works has garnered a mixed critical reception. Most commentators have considered his work erudite, witty, and often illuminating, pointing out his use of humor and irony, his respect for his readers' intelligence, and his ability to portray complex ideas effectively. Other reviewers have derided his attempt to make philosophy more accessible, perceiving his approach as overly simplistic and accusing him of "dumbing down" philosophical thought in his effort to make it entertaining and pertinent to his readers. Moreover, such detractors have found his narrative devices tiresome and contrived and his humor uneven. In spite of these comments, de Botton is a popular author whom most reviewers have recognized as an intelligent and engaging voice within British literature.

PRINCIPAL WORKS

Essays in Love (novel) 1993; published as *On Love*, 1994

The Romantic Movement: Sex, Shopping, and the Novel (novel) 1994

Kiss & Tell (novel) 1995

How Proust Can Change Your Life: Not a Novel (literary criticism) 1997

The Consolations of Philosophy (nonfiction) 2000

The Art of Travel (essays) 2002

CRITICISM

Gabriele Annan (review date 30 October 1993)

SOURCE: Annan, Gabriele. "The Proper Study of Mankind Is Books." *Spectator* 271, no. 8625 (30 October 1993): 41.

[*In the following positive review, Annan finds* Essays in Love *to be "witty, funny, [and] sophisticated," and asserts the book is full of insightful observations.*]

On a BA flight from Paris to London the narrator picks up Chloe who happens to be sitting in the next seat. He takes her out to dinner, they go to bed together, fall in love and begin a serious affair. After a while Chloe loses interest. On the BA flight back from a weekend in Paris, she confesses that she has slept with the narrator's American friend Will. The narrator is devastated. Chloe follows Will to California. The narrator botches a suicide attempt (vitamin C instead of sleeping pills) and falls into a long depression from which he emerges three pages from the end while sitting next to Rachel at a dinner party. The following week and in the last paragraph, Rachel accepts his invitation to dine.

That's the whole plot [of *Essays in Love*] and it holds one's attention. The characters live: the narrator, introvert, analytical, fastidious, alarmingly well-read and indefinably old-fashioned; and Chloe, modern, extrovert, relaxed, relentlessly unsentimental. He loves the films of Eric Rohmer, she hates them. The author is very good at getting across what it is that attracts the hero (his alter ego?) to Chloe: her generosity, her self-deprecation, her throw-away charm, expressed through the way she talks. The dialogue is convincing and engaging.

But the plot is not the whole story by any means. The chapters have headings like 'Romantic Fatalism', 'Romantic Terrorism', 'Intermittences of the Heart'. The book is a psycho-philosophical treatise on love, the paragraphs numbered and ironically illustrated with diagrams; the first one is a mathematical calculation of the chances of Chloe and the narrator being seated side by side on the plane, the last a graph of her orgasmic contractions. There are quotations from and references to Plato, Kant, John Stuart Mill, Groucho Marx, Nietzsche, Wittgenstein, Pascal, La Rochefoucauld, Stendhal, Goethe, Freud, Barthes, and finally Dr Peggy Nearly, a Californian psychoanalyst whose do-it-yourself manual, *The Bleeding Heart,* was published in 1987. Botton invents a consultation between Dr Nearly and Madame Bovary in which the good doctor urges Flaubert's heroine to choose more suitable lovers and

> to make an effort to look inside yourself, to go over your childhood, then perhaps you'll learn that you don't deserve all this pain. It's only because you grew up in a dysfunctional family.

Emma isn't interested: she just wants Rodolphe back; and for the third week running she hasn't got the money for Dr Nearly's fee.

The narrator's self-analysis throughout the book is a lot more subtle than Dr Nearly's offerings, and he develops it into magisterial generalisations. The result is something like La Rochefoucauld's maxims crossed with *Adolphe,* with jokes and against a background of luggage reclaim areas and breakfast cereal packets. The narrator writes his suicide note at the kitchen table 'with only the shivering of the fridge for company'. The desolation of it! Ingeniously pinpointed mundane details stop the novel from getting too abstract. It is witty, funny, sophisticated, neatly tied up, and full of wise and illuminating insights. With so many illustrious names dropped, it is difficult to tell whether the insights are original or not: but they are certainly organised into a very entertaining read. For people who mind about that kind of thing, *Essays in Love* is also quite unusually optimistic.

Francine Prose (review date 27 December 1993)

SOURCE: Prose, Francine. "Habits of the Heart." *New Republic* 209, no. 26 (27 December 1993): 38-9.

[*In the following review, Prose finds parallels between de Botton's* On Love *and Stendhal's* On Love, *and judges de Botton's work as sharp, funny, and well written.*]

In the preface to his treatise *On Love,* Stendhal breezily takes off running past those indolent earlier writers who dropped out of the game after cataloging only "400 or 500 of the successive emotions, so difficult to recognize, which go to make up this passion." Stendhal way overshot the 500 mark in his own effort to categorize and to analyze, to qualify and to refine, to collect every anecdote and trenchant word ever uttered about *l'amour.*

Now, in a smart and ironic first novel, also entitled *On Love,* Alain de Botton picks up the torch, so to speak, more or less where Stendhal left off. De Botton's *On Love* reads as if Stendhal had lived into the '90s, survived modern critical theory (as he clearly has), thought it was funny (as he likely would have), but retained a novelist's sympathy for the impulse—which he shared—to deconstruct and to dissect in search of some higher understanding.

Divided into titled chapters ("Romantic Fatalism," "The Subtext of Seduction," "False Notes," "Romantic Terrorism" and so on) and brief, numbered sections separated by space breaks, de Botton's novel is a mock and serious philosophical inquiry into the grand passion that Stendhal compared to the Milky Way, "a bright mass made up of thousands of little stars, each of which is often itself a nebula." What launches the novel's obsessive, self-conscious and rather sweetly cerebral narrator on his own astral explorations is an intense and ill-starred love affair with a woman named Chloe.

He and Chloe meet on a shuttle from Paris to London and have a flirty conversation over the airplane safety diagram card. They dine in restaurants with names like Les Liaisons Dangereuses and Lao Tzu, seduce each other, make love, fall in love, partly combine their busy London lives (he is an architect, she a graphic designer) into a sort of third life with a history of its own and recurrent leitmotifs based on shared experience (a corpse they discover in the street, a stranger who passes Chloe a mash note in a bagel shop). They go on lovers' holidays that are at first ecstatic, then markedly less idyllic as their passion falters, until their romance crashes and burns on a flight from Paris, slyly written as the evil twin of the flight on which they met.

One of the novel's nervy jokes is how perfectly ordinary, how unexceptional, all this is. (The course of this affair would doggedly follow the parabola we can imagine the narrator drawing along with the visual aids—diagrams and charts—that he scatters throughout the text.) De Botton is well aware of this. And the narrator knows it, too. But that doesn't keep him from making his textbook-case romance the center of his life, and the improbable springboard for his metaphysical triple flips. So each mini-step forward or setback in his love moves him to microscopic analysis or flights of heroic abstraction.

At moments he succumbs with almost giddy abandon to passages of loony post-structuralist rhetoric, sheer bombast and quasi-academic absurdity. Fearing that Chloe has begun to fake orgasm, he plots a logarithmic measure of the sincerity of her response:

> It was at first hard for me to imagine an untruth lasting 3.2 seconds fitted into a sequence of eight 0.8-second contractions, the first and last two (3.2s) of which were genuine. It was easier to imagine a complete truth, or a complete lie, but the idea of a truth-lie-truth pattern seemed perverse and unnecessary.

Alternately, he is capable of keen observation, flashes of genuine lyricism, acuity and depth:

> However happy we may be with our partner, our love for them necessarily prevents us . . . from starting other romantic liaisons. But why should this constrain us if we truly loved them? Why should we feel this as a loss unless our love for them has already begun to wane? The answer perhaps lies in the uncomfortable thought that in resolving our need to love, we may not always succeed in resolving our need to long.

The great minds of the past—Saint Theresa of Avila, Darwin, Freud, the Oracle at Delphi—are quoted and consulted, as if for second opinions on the state of his love for Chloe.

What lends *On Love* its sprightliness is the satisfying way in which these philosophical test-balloons are repeatedly sent up and almost immediately punctured by little pellets of reality: here, the phenomenally banal events that mark this love affair's milestones. Deflated, theory collapses into fiction, into elegantly taut and deftly paced comic scenes. So, intent on seduction, the narrator resolves to obliterate his personality and remake himself in the image of someone Chloe might love. "My idea of what she wanted from a lover could have been compared to a tight-fitting suit and my true self to a fat man, so that the evening was a process resembling a fat man's trying to fit into a suit that is too small for him."

The problem is, he doesn't know enough about Chloe to know what she might want, until at last Chloe reveals a fondness for chocolate cake and he orders the sweet dessert—to which he is allergic. A meditation on the reality of Chloe's apparent perfection ends abruptly when she refers to a Bach cantata as "impossible yodeling." A dream of perfect union with one's Platonic "other half" ends when Chloe brings home a new pair of truly hideous shoes, "a platformed sole rising sharply up to a heel with the breadth of a flat shoe but as tall as a stiletto," and a "faintly rococo collar, decorated with a bow and stars and framed by a piece of chunky ribbon." In the midst of a convoluted meditation on the differences between political terrorism—Japanese Red Army members mowing down airplane passengers—and romantic terrorism—"a gamut of tricks (sulking, jealousy, guilt) that attempts to force the partner to return love, by blowing up (in fits of tears, rage or otherwise) in front of the loved one"—these lovers have a hilarious, grimly quotidian squabble in which each accuses the other of having locked their hotel key in the room.

It is a tricky novel, but to de Botton's credit the tricks are never cloying, and they are almost always amusing, not least because we sense the writer's own exhilaration in being able to make them work. This, of course, is quite different from watching a writer show off. Unusual things *do* work in this book; somehow de Botton is able to draw Chloe's character sharply even through the myopic lens of her self-obsessed lover, to make us sympathize with him and with her, and at the same time understand why she can't stand him, forever. (What woman would want to stay with a man who could so drastically doubt his love simply because he thinks that she has bought an awful pair of new shoes?)

It is a tricky thing to construct a novel on the framework of a plot that is, by design, ordinary and predictable. But it is precisely because we know it all so well—that first blush of attraction, that last quarrel about the keys—that the novel is so credible and so funny. And de Botton plays a daring game with how seriously we are meant to take this: we are mostly willing to agree that this romance is a matter of life and death, even though the narrator never loses his ironic distance or his self-conscious rationality, not even in the midst of sex or a half-serious suicide attempt. We come to feel, as he

does, that his love is a matter of consequence, even though we are told from the start, "Until one is actually dead (and then it must be considered impossible) it is difficult to consider anyone as the love of one's life."

The book's success has much to do with its beautifully modeled sentences, its wry humor, its unwavering deadpan respect for its reader's intelligence. A wonderful chapter, titled "Marxism," takes its text from "the old joke made by the Marx who laughed about not deigning to belong to a club that would accept someone like him" and, blithely assuming we will understand that this Marx is Groucho, not Karl, goes on to discuss *this* Marxism, a theory that addresses the problem of continuing to love someone even though that person loves us. Only very rarely does de Botton's nerve slip, as it does near the end, when he anxiously makes certain that we know precisely how far all this hard mental labor has finally gotten his narrator:

> Love taught the analytic mind a certain humility, the reason that no matter how hard it struggled to reach immobile certainties (numbering its conclusions and embedding them in neat series) analysis could never be anything but flawed—and therefore never stray far from the ironic.

One can't blame de Botton for stating the obvious, and not just because he's a first novelist. Some might suggest that this is not the ideal moment in literary history in which to stake everything on the reading public's intelligence, on its awareness of subtlety, even on its ability to read. One hopes that *On Love* will find its readers, the ones who get the joke, who understand that fiction can be funny *and* serious, who don't mistrust irony as an elitist trick; who can, without prompting, distinguish Groucho from Karl.

P. N. Furbank (review date 13 January 1994)

SOURCE: Furbank, P. N. "Marshmallowing." *New York Review of Books* (13 January 1994): 35.

[*In the following review, Furbank discusses the genre and unifying thematic concerns of* On Love.]

On Love is a first novel by a young writer living in London who has had the bright idea of tracing the course of an "ordinary" love affair—initial conflagration, ecstasies, domesticities, break-up, suicide attempt, beginning of new cycle, with new lover—breaking it up into numbered paragraphs (as in Wittgenstein's *Tractatus*) and enclosing it in a dense network of cultural allusions. Dante Flaubert, and Proust are at hand, but more pervasively the currently fashionable literary theorists and postmodernists: Saussure, Barthes, Bakhtin, Lacan, and Heidegger.

The restaurant was of no help, for its romantic setting made love too conspicuous, hence insincere. The romantic weakened the bond between authorial intent and language, the signifieds kept threatening infidelity.

Intimacy did not destroy the self/other slash.

Is it really *her* I love, I thought to myself as I looked again at Chloe reading on the sofa across the room, or simply an idea that collects itself around her mouth, her eyes, her face? In extending her expression to her whole character, was I not perhaps guilty of mistaken metonymy?

The "ordinary" couple are young, professional class, semi-affluent—she is a graphic designer on a fashion magazine and he, the narrator, is an architect—and, the "I" character contends, it is difficult for them to have a *story.*

Chloe and I were moderns, inner-monologuers rather than adventurers. The world had been largely stripped of capacities for romantic struggle. The parents didn't care, the jungle had been tamed, society hid its disapproval behind universal tolerance, restaurants stayed open late, credit cards were accepted almost everywhere, and sex was a duty, not a crime.

Indeed they do not achieve much of a story. Their self-doubts and quarrels, and even their intimacies, are made deliberately to run to type, and all the life and adventure is reserved for the mock-philosophic commentary. The rigidity of the author's Cartesian or Wittgensteinian form invites some neat deadpan devices, like the reemployment of the same sentences, with a few changed epithets, to render both the scene where love dawns and where it gloomily grinds to its end.

I was [*Chloe and I were*] sitting in the economy section of a British Airways jet making its way [*our way back*] from Paris to London. We had recently crossed the Normandy coast, where a blanket of winter cloud had given way to an uninterrupted view of brilliant blue waters [*dark waters below*]. . . . There was something comforting [*threatening*] about the flight, the dull background throb of the engines, the hushed gray interior, the candy smiles of the airline employees. A trolley carrying a selection of drinks and snacks was making its way down the aisle and, though I was neither [*both*] hungry nor [*and*] thirsty, it filled me with the vague anticipation [*nausea*] that meals may elicit in aircraft.

How shall one classify this novel? One is tempted at first to suppose its genre is philistinism: the vindictive philistinism of the campus novel (a tiresome genre) or of "Tom-Stoppardism"—a matter of getting your own back on culture "knowingly" (much as Gilbert and Sullivan, so "knowingly," got their own back on grand opera).

But actually, I think what may be involved is something else altogether. One has always vaguely puzzled over the habit of Augustan authors, Addison and Steele and their contemporaries, of bedecking their writing with quotations from Virgil and Horace and Lucan and Ovid. What puzzles is that more analysis has not been made of this all important socio-cultural sign. For the most part, *Spectator*- and *Tatler*-type quotations serve no intellectual use at all, proving no more than (if they prove so much) that the classical world also had views on a given subject. Their function is wholly social and "connotative," in Barthes's sense, and they are, for a writer of this period, as indispensable as a wig. Both the educational system and the promotion system are geared to this feature of the printed book or essay. In how many anecdotes does a poor boy rise from the plough to become bishop or prime minister because some benevolent clergyman or squire overhears him repeat a Latin tag. Even the gender system is supported by it. (When Fielding's Amelia recites a line from Virgil, her landlady faints from terror.)

This, I think, is the model for de Botton's dealings with Heidegger, Lacan, and the deconstructionists. He is making a genial unspoken joke to the effect that these, their theories and the tags from them, now constitute a social orthodoxy as Horace and Virgil did for the Augustans. They are a shibboleth for a now very large "quality" paper-reading, university-educated club or in-group, the cultured many. He knows these thinkers well enough to quote them accurately and appositely, but he is not pretending, any more than Addison and Steele really pretended, to put them to more than ornamental use. When he gives us a diagram, in the Barthesian or Lacanian style, he is careful to make it quite childish (for instance a row of regular teeth, and another row with a gap in them, like Chloe's, to illustrate the difference between the Platonic and the Kantian aesthetic). Fun with the structuralists and poststructuralists, and the actual look of their books, keeps him going in a sustained, rather engaging, and certainly wonderfully slick exercise in facetiousness. It is one in which he is depending, like other facetious writers in the past, on making the reader exclaim, enjoyably, "How true!"

In a way, the best chapter in the book is the one entitled "Marxism," the Marx in question being not Karl but Groucho. It turns on Groucho's brilliant though well-worn joke that he wouldn't want to join a club that would have him as a member. The narrator's first visit to Chloe's flat turns out miraculously successful. They sleep together (though he had been planning no more than a polite social kiss and exit), and next morning he finds prepared for him a complete feast of a breakfast. It seems to him, causing him panic, that he not only loves but is loved. Upon which he instantly picks a perfectly outrageous quarrel over there being no strawberry jam. There are five other kinds of jam on the table, but no decent jam, no strawberry, and he oafishly leaves the breakfast to get cold while he goes out to buy some.

The (Marxist) principle is clear:

> We fall in love because we long to escape from ourselves with someone as beautiful, intelligent, and witty as we are ugly, stupid, and dull. But what if such a perfect being should one day turn around and decide they will love us back? We can only be somewhat shocked—how can they be as wonderful as we had hoped when they have the bad taste to approve of someone like us?

The thought leads the narrator to a survey of the whole theory and tradition of romantic love. Is there something in Albert Camus's theory that we fall in love with people because they look, from the outside, so "whole," as against our own incoherence and dispersedness? Was Denis de Rougemont right in saying that the most serious obstruction to our passion is the one to be preferred above all others? Or Anatole France, that "it is not customary to love what one has," "Marxist" logic seems at first sight undefeatable, and the Marxist moment in relations, when it becomes clear that love is reciprocated, ought to be fatal; but in fact, in the short run at least, the novel asserts, self-love can sometimes get the better of self-hatred. "If self-love gains the upper hand, both partners may accept that seeing their love reciprocated is not proof of now low the beloved is, but of how lovable they have themselves turned out to be."

This chapter is the key to the book in more ways than one. The book's theme throughout is the utterly cliché nature, in these days, of the concept "love." In one of its best scenes, the narrator and Chloe, wanting to say they love each other and desperately racking their brains for some way that is not pure cliché, at last hit on a solution: noticing the complimentary sweet the waiter has left beside their plate, they agree that they "marshmallow" each other. "And from then on love was, for Chloe and me at least, no longer simply *love*. It was a sugary, puffy object a few millimeters in diameter that melts deliciously in the mouth."

It is for something of the same reason, however, that the book does not get very far as a story or novel, if indeed it intends to. For *automatic* Groucho-esque self-hatred, mechanical irony, is an awkward piece of equipment for a novelist. We read that, after the narrator and Chloe, with "apologies, insults, laughter, and tears," have got over their breakfast row, "Romeo and Juliet were to be seen together later that afternoon, mushily holding hands in the dark at a four-thirty screening of *Love and Death* at the National Film Theatre." Now the tone of that does not seem quite right. Some basic sense of decorum tells us that, at this point, a novelist ought to render the lovers' feelings straight and as they felt them, not translate them into cliches ("Romeo and Juliet," "mushily holding hands")—otherwise we are not reading a story. Again, when, after a failed effort at suicide (by mistake he grabs not sleeping pills but ef-

fervescent vitamin C tablets), the narrator restores his self-love by defecting from Marx to Jesus, it would be funnier if the tone for a moment became Jesus-like and not Groucho-like. Illusions have to be rendered before there is much point in puncturing them.

De Botton's novel is itself dedicated to a cliché, of the "How true!" type about how little we know ourselves, despite Freud. La Rochefoucauld, Roland Barthes, and Heidegger; but he has worked it up into all sorts of bright jokes and nice silly-clever ploys. This is not the last we shall hear of him.

Maria Januzzi (review date summer 1994)

SOURCE: Januzzi, Maria. Review of *On Love* by Alain de Botton. *Review of Contemporary Fiction* 14, no. 2 (summer 1994): 224-25.

[*In the following review, Januzzi contends that* On Love *is an inconsistent novel.*]

"Trop penser me font amours—love makes me think too much," sings a fifteenth-century troubadour in Roland Barthes's *Fragments of a Lover's Discourse.* Or, as the narrator of Alain de Botton's first novel [*On Love*] claims, "The philosopher in the bedroom is as ludicrous a figure as the philosopher in the nightclub." In telling the story of his failed love affair with a woman named Chloe, the narrator quotes or alludes to Plato, Montaigne, Goethe, Marx, Proust, Nietzsche, Freud, Lacan, Denis de Rougemont, and finally, the metabeloved, Barthes himself. The particulars of the relationship, in the end, are far less vivid than its author's love affair with French literature and literary theory.

The signs and signal-fires of love are (re)read by this narrator, grouped chronologically, numbered within chapters, and sometimes accompanied by diagrams. The diagrams are a disarming touch; they also help flesh out the obsessional character of the narrator, who is an architect. "Desire had transformed me into a decoder of symbols, an interpreter of the landscape," he says, and he means it. The reader must be willing to grant that a love affair might be reread as a text rather than retold as a history, and prepare to sacrifice light and heat for analysis.

Not that analysis is without its pleasures: the narrator is often a precise, astute commentator on his own situation. Recalling the chameleonic "Not who am I, but who am I for her?" mode of his first dinner with Chloe, he notes that "in the reflexive movement of that question," his "self could not help but grow tinged with a certain bad faith and inauthenticity." This is a most delicate anatomy of what happens, what has happened when someone finds himself eating an allergen to impress a date. The progress of love is also economically described: "Intimacy did not destroy the self/other slash. It merely moved it outside the couple. Otherness now lay beyond the apartment door, confirming suspicions that love is never far from a conspiracy."

Lacking the leaven of irony, the analyses occasionally fall flat. After describing their first argument (which he had gratuitously instigated), the narrator asks, "What had turned me into such a monster? The fact that I had always been something of a marxist." If the discourse **On Love** took shape as a Marxist critique of love stories, posing as a love story, this might have been interesting. Also, the author neither relishes nor deconstructs the gender-specificity of his two characters. I couldn't help thinking that the narrative would have been truer to its philosophical heart, and more welcoming, had the author followed Barthes in according the lovers sexual anonymity. Yet the book is almost lovable for its unevenness, its excesses. "Trop penser me font amours" . . . I'm looking forward to seeing what de Botton comes up with next, now that he's gotten this out of his system.

Tom Hiney (review date 27 August 1994)

SOURCE: Hiney, Tom. "The Mechanics of Love in the Nineties." *Spectator* 273, no. 8668 (27 August 1994): 35-6.

[*In the following mixed review of* The Romantic Movement, *Hiney asserts that de Botton "eschews any story line or character-drawing in favour of presenting the author as a sociological raconteur."*]

It seems that we have more to thank Douglas Coupland for than we first imagined. Not only did he give us the now completely redundant expression 'Generation X', but also a new format for the post-Postmodernist novel. Characterised by short chapters, regular digressions from the 'plot' and lots of ironic cartoons, 'Novelisation X' eschews any story line or character-drawing in favour of presenting the author as a sociological raconteur. All of which can be fun; when Alain de Botton hits the target, **The Romantic Movement** is a delight to read. But when he's bad, he's awful.

De Botton's speciality is love and relationships, and in **The Romantic Movement** he gives himself what he considers an archetypal contemporary relationship to play with. Alice is 24 and in advertising. Eric is 31 and in banking. They meet at a party, go out with each other for about 12 months and then split up. They're not particularly beautiful, nor amusing, nor temperamental; in his meticulous efforts to present an 'ordinary'

relationship, de Botton gets perilously close to writing a dull book. Alice and Eric operate like faceless crosses on a soccer coach's blackboard, and it is the arrows, squiggles and set-play movements between the two that interest the author.

When we meet 'Philip' (the man whom Alice will eventually turn her affections to) we get an even more thinly sketched character than those we already had. On page 247, where Eric unsuspectingly introduces the couple to each other, he tells Alice that

> Matt's got this friend of his, Philip. He works as a sound engineer on classical recordings. He's really nice and I remember he likes antiques, so maybe you should get along with him.

Twenty pages later, Philip is telling his friend Peter about this nice girl he's met 'through Matt's flatmate Suzy'. But Suzy lives in a two-bedroomed flat with Alice: Eric has no flatmate and Matt is never heard of again.

None of this is criminal in itself, but it does help dismantle the idea that **The Romantic Movement** is anything other than 'De Botton On Relationships'. As in his first book, **Essays in Love,** it is in exploring the mechanics of love in the Nineties that the author's own obsession lies. Every phase and shift in Eric and Alice's affair is itemised and turned into simile, with accompanying diagrams to bang the point home: 'Alice thought bitterly of how she was split into a bewildering range of moods, akin to a number of TV channels'; 'one could liken conversational potential to a tree-shaped structure'; 'one could have likened the scenario of love-permanence to a suspension bridge'; 'the result was a constant meteorological struggle, warm fronts struggling against cold fronts and forming unstable alliances in occluded fronts'; 'depending on her state of mind, Alice's outlook on life . . . alternated between two schools: that of the staircase and that of the tumble-dryer'.

Tumble-dryers apart, **The Romantic Movement** does provide some depressingly accurate reminders that most of us will always be closer to the Erics and Alices of this world than anything approaching Heathcliff or Cathy. And if Eric and co. had been allowed out of de Botton's test-tube long enough to achieve some sort of character, then the whole experience would have been even more depressing and far more enjoyable.

Merle Rubin (review date 29 June 1995)

SOURCE: Rubin, Merle. "Summer Reading: A Time for Fiction and Fantasy." *Christian Science Monitor* (29 June 1995): B1, B4.

[*In the following excerpt, Rubin lauds* The Romantic Movement *as witty, intelligent, and insightful.*]

Summer, it's been said, is the season of romance, and not only the moon-June kind of romance promised by popular song lyrics, but also that category of literature including everything from verse narratives of medieval troubadours and Shakespeare's *Cymbeline* to Melville's *Omoo* and Hawthorne's *The House of Seven Gables.*

For those who may remember the archetypal literary criticism of Northrop Frye, every season has its genre: tragedy for fall; for spring, comedy; winter, irony; and summer (the season of fulfillment and freedom from workday contingencies), romance—a rich, green dream world where imagination runs riot.

For Frye's devotees, the perfect summer reading list might include titles such as Scott's *Ivanhoe,* Keats's *Endymion,* Shelley's *Alastor,* Ovid's *Metamorphoses,* and Tennyson's *Idylls of the King.* For those whose tastes are a little more contemporary, however, there's plenty of summer fiction to offer a timely, perhaps even romantic, excursion into the green realms of the imagination. . . .

Returning to the present, Alain de Botton's **The Romantic Movement: Sex, Shopping and the Novel** is the tongue-in-cheek tale of a young woman looking for love in modern-day London. A dreamer and romantic, Alice is more in love with the idea of love than with anything or anyone else, and this lack of realism makes it hard for her to figure out whether the current handsome man on the horizon is Mr. Right or simply another Mr. Mistake.

The author of a previous novel called **Essays in Love,** de Botton has a flair for combining a diverting storyline with lashings of commentary that reads like a cross between a pop psychology guide to romance and a collection of Jane Austin-like ironic asides. To wit: "Shockingly incongruous in a romantic conception of love is the idea one might embark on a relationship not for the richness of another's eyes or the sophistication of their mind but simply to avoid contemplating a diary full of evenings alone." Succinct, bright, witty, replete with aphorisms, insights, even funny charts and graphs, the story of Alice and her quest will have readers nodding with rueful recognition.

Philip Glazebrook (review date 9 September 1995)

SOURCE: Glazebrook, Philip. "Portrait of a Lady and Little Else." *Spectator* 275, no. 8722 (9 September 1995): 41-2.

[*In the following review, Glazebrook explores the genre of* Kiss and Tell, *maintaining that "all deviations from the conventional forms in fiction are attempts to side-step some of the difficulties of novel-writing," claiming de Botton both gains and loses certain elements by using a biographical method in this book.*]

This engaging and delightful book [**Kiss & Tell**] is the history of a love affair told by the boy in the form of a biography of the girl. She, Isabel, is middle-class, middle twenties, a London girl with an office job. There is nothing remarkable about her except that she is an individual; and the biographical form in which the novel is cast—not so much a story as a straightforward shot at telling us what someone is really like—sets out her individuality in multifarious and lively detail.

As his reason for undertaking a biography, the narrator (recoiling from his last girl friend's accusation of narcissism) cites 'the impulse to know another fully'. It is an impulse by which love often discloses itself to the smitten one, but here love between the two of them is not spoken of, is not the subject under the biographer's microscope; yet every stage and every detail of their love affair is transmitted to the reader with a deft indirectness which is marvellous to read. The scene in which the biographer, whilst cross-examining his subject on her past affairs, manages also to get her into bed with him is beautifully done.

All deviations from the conventional forms in fiction are attempts to side-step some of the difficulties of novel-writing, and it is interesting to see what Alain de Botton gains and what he loses with his biographical method. It is legitimate, for instance, for the biographer to feed his reader raw undigested information about his subject—strings of 'facts' about her tastes or her past, even her answers to questionnaires—without obeying the novelist's obligation to make information seem to surface of its own accord on the current of the story. This facility has its dangers: in **Kiss & Tell** Isabel sits now and then so unnaturally still under questioning, like someone who has agreed to have her portrait painted, that forward movement and development are lost. Mostly, though, the questions are ingenious and the answers revealing.

But they reveal the character of an individual only. Here is the weakness of the 'biography' idea, that the focus must be so tight. From a good novel you learn about humanity as it is exemplified by a set of characters interacting and developing around carefully constructed and deliberately positioned events. From a biography you learn all there is to know about an individual, with perhaps a few other faces glimpsed in reflected light.

I wasn't sure just how deliberately the author of this book, though focusing on the biography of Isabel through the narrator's eyes, was meanwhile semaphoring to the reader the sly sketch he was making of the narrator himself. Whilst they are discussing chocolate-eating they are playing chess; is it significant that Isabel seems to be winning? When the biographer tells his subject he likes or dislikes her dress, of course she pays him no attention, for we already know he can't tell one dress from another. Again, it is a fact that the inside of Isabel's head—her thoughts, her phraseology—resembles a little too closely the inside of the narrator's head; does that show us the narrator's unregenerate narcissism creating Isabel in his own image, or does it show us a shortcoming in Alain de Botton?

The book is so cultivated and witty and self-aware that it's safe to assume that all its effects are intended and the author's control perfect. Such a writer could write the biography of a broomstick, as Dr Johnson suggested, and it would come alive under his pen.

Teresa Waugh (review date 19 April 1997)

SOURCE: Waugh, Teresa. "In Search of a Better Self." *Spectator* 278, no. 8803 (19 April 1997): 38.

[*In the following mixed review, Waugh derides* How Proust Can Change Your Life, *contending the work contains a contrived and patronizing tone, although she concludes the book paints a vivid picture of Marcel Proust.*]

Lurking in the world of letters there must somewhere be someone who could write a kindly introduction to Proust's *In Search of Lost Time,* whereby the reader would be taken by the hand and led gently through the text, skipping a paragraph here, a page or two there, until he or she, like all true admirers of Proust, is swept into the maelstrom of his great circular novel, fearful of ever again missing one word. For there are those, both well-educated and well-read, who still, after numerous attempts, fail to be captivated and thus, missing out on one of life's great pleasures, never manage to progress beyond the first or perhaps the second volume.

Might Alain de Botton's new book, **How Proust Can Change Your Life,** fulfil this function? Alas, that is not its purpose.

De Botton's intentions are somewhat different. He, I suppose, presumes that his readers will already be familiar with the master's work and so he sees it as his job, through an appreciation of the novel and some biographical sketches of Proust himself, to interpret for us how, if we properly understand *In Search of Lost Time,* we will be able to improve our spiritual quality of life.

With this in mind, he divides the book into chapters with headings such as 'How to be a Good Friend', 'How to Express Your Emotions' and 'How to Suffer

Successfully' and then extrapolates from the behaviour of the characters in Proust's novel and from other various writings (with no references given), how Proust, albeit unhappy himself, would have advised us to behave in order to be happy.

At intervals throughout the book, the reader may well wonder what audience de Botton sees himself as addressing. It is hard to imagine that an intelligent person who has read Proust—or indeed who hasn't—really needs to be told that dukes are not better than dustmen—or, come to that, duchesses than dustwomen; nor that it is possible to seek beauty in the modern world, beyond the confines of a Carpaccio or a Veronese.

Of whom, outside Form 5a, can de Botton ask, 'Why do we kiss people?' and reply:

> At one level, merely to generate the pleasurable sensation of rubbing an area of nerve endings against a corresponding strip of soft, fleshy, moist skin tissue . . .

This reviewer was, unfortunately, intensely irritated by many aspects of de Botton's thesis, finding it superficial, often contrived and at times patronising.

In the chapter on suffering successfully, de Botton takes a number of 'patients'—characters of Proust's who suffer because of some inability to cope with a problem, then analyses the problem and posits a solution. Thus, Françoise, the narrator's cook, becomes a know-all to cover up her own lack of education. Had she asked when she didn't know something, she might have had fewer problems and been a happier person.

Does it lie within the realms of possibility that Proust might have expected the reader to pick up a few details of this kind on the evidence of the text alone? And does any reasonably mature person really need to be told that suffering 'opens up *possibilities* for intelligent, imaginative enquiry', which possibilities, according to de Botton, are 'most often overlooked or refused'. Thank you.

Another peculiar and rather whimsical aspect of this book lies in the way it is illustrated, so that besides some reproductions of paintings by Monet or Chardin, there are illustrations of young girls skipping and hopping and swinging their arms, reproduced from Proust's doctor father's self-help book, entitled *Elements of Hygiene* (1888). All of which, whilst droll, feels somewhat self-conscious.

But it ill becomes the critic to be too harsh, and there are some excellent things too in this book. Most particularly de Botton manages to paint, through what are often no more than sketches, a very vivid picture of Proust the man. What appears to be the essence of this sick, neurotic, fur-coated, talkative, at times apologetic genius, is brilliantly conveyed. Little snippets of information, like the fact that Proust, as a mature man, once asked who wrote *The Brothers Karamazov*, combined with the occasional anecdote about, for instance, Proust sharing a taxi with Joyce, help to bring him very much to life. Interesting, too, is de Botton's exploration of the effect Proust had on Virginia Woolf.

So where do we go from here? Back perhaps to the pages of *In Search of Lost Time*. Can de Botton after all have achieved the almost impossible? Can he take the doubter by the hand and lead him through the tangled wood out into the sunny glades?

Graham Robb (review date 25 April 1997)

SOURCE: Robb, Graham. "Marcel the Moralist." *Times Literary Supplement* (25 April 1997): 36.

[*In the following review, Robb discusses* How Proust Can Change Your Life *and the purported intent of such chapters as "How to Be a Good Friend" and "How to Suffer Successfully."*]

What does a man who spent fourteen miserable years in bed have to teach us about happiness? What life-enhancing precepts can we hope to extract from the works of a mouse-fearing, hot-water-bottle-clutching Mummy's boy who was tormented by indigestion, constipation, a neurotic need for tight underpants and a chronic suspicion of doctors?

Alain de Botton's patchwork portrait [in *How Proust Can Change Your Life*] makes Proust sound like a Job in the hands of an unusually inventive Satan: he hated the cold and central heating, suffered from altitude sickness after a trip to Versailles, and was so acutely aware of neighbours' noise that he almost died from the installation of a WC next door. Even his stock-broker accused him of hypochondria, obviously recognizing a poor exponent of the art of probabilities. Proust died a few months later. He also, more famously, suffered from critical failure and a conviction that his writing resembled a piece of indigestible nougat. But he consoled himself with the seemingly contradictory belief that he had been "endowed with the power to procure the happiness of others", and it is this belief that de Botton sets out to justify.

Teasing Proust's nougat into a nine-part instruction manual on "how to stop wasting, and begin appreciating one's life", he enables Marcel to measure up to his incongruously healthy father and brother. Proust senior was a vast, unstoppable man devoted to the eradication of brain-softening and bubonic plague. "I have been happy all my life", he confessed. A staunch opponent of the spine-crushing corset, Dr Proust published a self-

help book for young ladies, samples of which are quoted along with their stodgily explicit illustrations, explaining how to balance on one foot and jump off a wall. "Ah, Céleste", Marcel is reported saying to his maid, "If I could be sure of doing with my books as much as my father did for the sick", presumably not referring to the anatomical benefits of balancing the seven volumes of *A la Recherche du temps perdu* on one's head.

Marcel's indestructible brother Robert was an expert on genitalia in whose honour prostatectomies are apparently still known as *"proustatectomies"*. De Botton points out with characteristic optimism that Robert's ability to survive being run over by a 5-tonne coal truck came at a price: an inability to notice things.

This, indeed, is the continuous moral: suffering sensitizes the mind. "Wisdom", ironically enough, is best acquired "painfully via life", not "painlessly via a teacher". Each chapter—"How to Take Your Time", "How to Suffer Successfully", "How to Be a Good Friend", etc—offers a useful Proustian axiom: do not "deny the bread on the sideboard a place in your conception of beauty"; do not "evaluate people on the basis of conspicuous categories"; do maintain marriages with the threat of infidelity and friendships with hollow words; do read books in order to nullify the numbing effects of habit, but do not ignore the lesson of "perhaps the wisest person in Proust's book", Mme Leroi: "Love? I make it often, but I never talk about it."

Those who do ignore Mme Leroi's lesson and find Proust's precepts somewhat puny when divested of their syntax might use the book as a do-it-yourself Proust kit. A Pascal *pensée* is set alongside an advertisement for Pears' toilet soaps so that we can test Proust's assertion that the imagination can feed on anything. For a similar reason, the current Paris-Le Havre timetable appears on page 46, happily evoking, for anyone who has sat on the train with a sense of lost time, the sleaze of Paris-St Lazare and the dismal mockery of Mantes-la-Jolie.

It is refreshing to be invited to identify Proust's characters with people from our own lives (the author's smiling girlfriend, "who has never read Proust", is winningly depicted in a photograph above the caption, "Kate/Albertine"), and to be reminded that Proust, like Pascal and Alain de Botton, is an example of that notorious *faux ami*: a "moraliste"—not to be confused with a "moralisateur".

Ultimately, *How Proust Can Change Your Life* suggests that the pleasure of Proust lies not so much in discovery as in recognition, and even that all these moral niceties are simply pretexts for those wonderful, serpentine sentences.

Proust's tail-chasing novel ends with the narrator's decision to write it, and although Alain de Botton ends his with an invitation to cast this and all other books aside, he has after all written a book of his own. A cautionary tale in the final chapter—ambiguously titled "How to Put Books Down"—describes Virginia Woolf's unhappiness with her own writing after becoming "embedded" in Proust. De Botton's *causerie* is an object-lesson in ridding oneself of an obsession with Proust. In effect, a *proustectomy*.

Benito Rakower (review date 4 May 1997)

SOURCE: Rakower, Benito. "Tea and Empathy." *Washington Post Book World* (4 May 1997): 8.

[*In the following review, Rakower deems* How Proust Can Change Your Life *a "brilliant tour de force."*]

Marcel Proust, a perpetual invalid who rarely left his cork-lined room, lived as no sane man could even imagine, while writing a novel that only the most determined readers have been able to finish. Some readers have felt like Mallory and Irving, 500 feet from the summit of Everest, gasping for breath in an increasingly rarefied atmosphere. But despite its enormous difficulty, *In Search of Lost Time* (*Remembrance of Things Past*) dominates the literary horizon as a supreme peak.

Alain de Botton has written what seems, at first, a whimsical "self-help" manual based on Proust's 3,000-page novel. His book [*How Proust Can Change Your Life*] is at once a brilliant tour de force and a seriously legitimate guide for the perplexed, amply fulfilling the promise of its title.

We are informed that "Proust was born into a family where the art of making people feel better was taken very seriously indeed." Proust *pere* was a doctor who wrote more than 30 books on all aspects of health and hygiene. To de Botton, Marcel was dutifully following in his father's footsteps while appearing to be an asthmatic invalid.

How can a man who made illness into a consecrated profession be trusted, and his implicit recommendations taken seriously? De Botton dismisses this problem easily in a typically urbane sentence: "It seems that such knowledge has usually been the privileged preserve of, and the only blessing granted to, the violently miserable." The telling word is "miserable." With deftness and wit, de Botton makes it evident that Proust was a Houdini of self-immurement, so accomplished that the scent of a lily drifting somehow into his hermetically sealed, cork-lined bedroom could induce a life threatening crisis.

"The happy few" who read Proust realize quickly that his novel examines relentlessly all the causes of human misery and unhappiness yet becomes an exhortation to seize the true bliss within us—Proust's celebrated *"la vraie vie."* De Botton's judicious excerpts show how the novel can teach us to suffer successfully, to express our emotions, to be a good friend, to open our eyes, to be happy in love, and to put books down.

In one of his finest passages, de Botton observes that for Proust the value of betrayal and jealousy is "its ability to generate the intellectual motivation to investigate the hidden sides of others." The good use to which we put the people who cause us pain is one of the novel's dominant motifs. Thus, the book becomes one of "the profound testimonies of what it means to be alive."

Proust, like Tolstoy, Stendhal and Flaubert, assiduously read the newspapers for ways to stimulate and sharpen his creative faculties. In one May 1914 newspaper there appeared the brief account of a horse who had leapt into the carriage of the tram in front of it, seriously injuring several passengers. De Botton suggests what Proust would have done with this simple story in a droll and facetious manner. No doubt the "somersault into the tram [was] provoked by misjudged nostalgia for a show-jumping career or vengeance for the omnibus that had recently killed its brother in the market place, later put down for horse steak."

De Botton is really pointing to the way Proust transformed his frivolity into a method for undertaking his greatest search, the search for lost time.

Perhaps the most fascinating episode in this erudite book is the meeting of Proust and English diplomat Harold Nicholson (a delegate to the Paris peace conference) at a party. The writer wanted to know what a diplomat's day was like. When Nicholson started to sum it up. "Well we generally meet at 10 . . ." Proust interrupted: *"Vous allez trop vite."* (You're going too fast.) According to his diary, Nicholson began again: "So I tell him everything. The sham cordiality of it all: the handshakes: the maps: the rustle of papers: the tea in the next room: the macaroons."

Macaroons? Proust famously decocted his childhood, and an entire French village, from a cookie dunked in a cup of lime tea. How confirming of his genius that a peace conference that prepared the way for Hitler would be precisely remembered for its macaroons and "tea in the next room." These sorts of ironies were never wasted on Proust, though no one could have anticipated the Second World War coming out of those tea cups.

After reading de Botton's book, one will savor Proust with fresh wonder and gratitude.

Brooke Allen (review date 22 September 1997)

SOURCE: Allen, Brooke. "The Power of Positive Proust." *The New Leader* 80, no. 15 (22 September 1997): 15-16.

[*In the following review, Allen argues that although* How Proust Can Change Your Life *might initially strike readers as a superficial, one-joke story, it is a serious, complex work that offers useful insights.*]

Marcel Proust as self-help maven? Alain de Botton's often amusing new book, ***How Proust Can Change Your Life,*** is indeed full of chapters with headings like "How to Suffer Successfully" and "How to Express Your Emotions." He contends that the great modern novelist was at heart one of the earliest proponents of the self-improvement mania. In de Botton's view, the multivolume masterpiece *In Search of Lost Time* (as he accurately translates its title) is not "a memoir tracing the passage of a more lyrical age"; it is "a practical, universally applicable story about how to stop wasting time and start to appreciate life."

The novelist's father, Dr. Adrien Proust, was a specialist in the field of public health whose work went far toward eradicating cholera and bubonic plague in France. He also wrote guides to physical fitness, making him "a pioneer and master of the keep-fit self-help manual." His son admired his achievements extravagantly. "Ah," he said to his maid, "if I could be sure of doing with my books as much as my father did for the sick."

De Botton's premise is a clever one, allowing him to sneak a rather slight literary study onto the most prominent display tables in the bookshops with the backing of a mainstream publishing house. It may seem to make the book a one-joke story, easily put down after flipping through a chapter or two. But in fact it expands naturally into the more serious theme that a great work, properly read, will offer invaluable insights. Or, as Proust expressed it: "Every reader is, while he is reading, the reader of his own self. The writer's work is merely a kind of optical instrument which he offers to the reader to enable him to discern what, without this book, he would perhaps have never experienced in himself."

At first glance Proust might not appear to be the ideal guide for those seeking health and happiness. An invalid, he suffered from severe asthma, inexplicable allergies, poor digestion, dizziness, and chest pain. He seldom arose before evening, and wrote all of *In Search of Lost Time*—a task that took him 14 years—in bed. He was accused of being a hypochondriac, but his death from pneumonia at the age of 51 lends credence to his self-description: "suspended between caffeine, aspirin, asthma, angina pectoris, and, altogether between life and death every six days out of seven."

Proust's love life, too, was far from satisfactory. Gradually realizing that the young women his mother produced for his inspection would never interest him, he accepted his homosexuality. But he was not ever to enjoy what modern self-help writers would call a "fulfilling relationship," except for a very brief period with a taxi driver who died in an air crash. "Love is an incurable disease," he wrote. "Those who love and those who are happy are not the same." It is an opinion unforgettably illustrated in his fiction.

In the Proustian scheme to feel is, to a large extent, to suffer. How then can we suffer successfully, to use de Botton's catchy phrase? Well, we must learn something from our pain—learn, at the very least, that it is useless and possibly meaningless. Here, for instance, is Proust on jealousy: "It is one of the powers of jealousy to reveal to us the extent to which the reality of external facts and the emotions of the heart are an unknown element which lends itself to endless suppositions. We imagine that we know exactly what things are and people think, for the simple reason that we do not care about them. But as soon as we have a desire to know, as the jealous man has, then it becomes a kaleidoscope in which we can no longer distinguish anything."

Friendship, unlike romance, was something Proust excelled at. His countless friends attested to his affectionate nature, his generosity, his invariable tact and kindness. Yet he was no warmer in his appraisal of friendship than of love, characterizing it as "a lie which seeks to make us believe that we are not irremediably alone." And he cautioned in his writing: "The artist who gives up an hour of work for an hour of conversation with a friend knows that he is sacrificing a reality for something that does not exist (our friends being friends only in the light of an agreeable folly which travels with us through life and to which we readily accommodate ourselves, but which at the bottom of our hearts we know to be no more reasonable than the delusion of the man who talks to the furniture because he believes that it is alive)."

While those might sound like the words of a hopelessly depressed and misanthropic person, Proust was not one to sink into a despair or throw himself off a bridge. His way of coping was cheerfully pragmatic; he decided that friendship, however unsatisfactory, was nevertheless important and he devoted considerable time and effort to its cultivation. His success was perhaps due to the fact that he entertained no unrealistic expectations; since he did not expect to find a soul mate, he could satisfy himself with simple affection. "I do my intellectual work within myself," he wrote, "and once with other people, it's more or less irrelevant to me that they're intelligent, as long as they are *kind, sincere, etc.*"

Proust so showered his friends with flattery that they invented a verb, "to Proustify," meaning to show a flowery, verbose geniality. He made it a rule to refrain wholly from unkind comment, and thought the pursuit of affection incompatible with the pursuit of truth. How different from our modern self-help gurus, who claim that honesty between friends is of paramount importance. Taking his cue from his hero, de Botton observes that "though the dominant view of grievances is that they should invariably be discussed with their progenitors, the typically unsatisfactory results of doing so should perhaps urge us to reconsider." How true; just think of the friendships you've known yourself that have foundered upon an excess of "honesty."

The imperatives of friendship and of art, of course, are not at all the same. Proust described artists as "creatures who talk of precisely the things one shouldn't mention." De Botton suggests, in turn, that we look at *In Search of Lost Time* as "an unusually long unsent letter, the antidote to a lifetime of Proustification . . . the place where the unsayable was finally granted expression."

Still, Proust's art has a good deal to teach us not only about personal relations but about that rarest of talents, the simple enjoyment of life. He advised that we pay close attention to the great painters who open our eyes to the world, and singled out for especial praise the work of Jean Baptiste Siméon Chardin, pointing to "the charm and wisdom with which it coats our most modest moments by initiating us into the *life* of still life."

Chardin chose to give the ordinary and the homely meaning, just as Proust himself did in writing about the village of Illiers, where he spent summers as a boy. Specific objects, or people, or existence itself is never trivial; what is trivial is the quality of our memories of these things. "We don't believe that life is beautiful because we don't *recall* it," Proust wrote, "but if we get a whiff of a long-forgotten smell we are suddenly intoxicated, and similarly we *think* we no longer love the dead, because we don't remember them, but if by chance we come across an old glove we burst into tears."

The glove, the smell inspire not so much recollection as appreciation. Works of art, including books, are also valuable insofar as they provide opportunities for appreciation. Otherwise, Proust stressed, their virtue is dubious: "As long as reading is for us the instigator whose magic keys have opened the door to those dwelling-places deep within us that we would not have known how to enter, its role in our lives is salutary. It

becomes dangerous, on the other hand, when, instead of awakening us to the personal life of the mind, reading tends to take its place. . . ."

The art, then, lies not in an artist's experiences but in the quality of his perceptions and his ability to convey them. De Botton illustrates this truth by recounting his visit to Illiers (fictionalized as Combray, it is now officially Illiers-Combray in honor of the novel). Arriving full of eager anticipation, he finds, not the timeless beauty of Proust's evocation, but a dull. dusty little town; the rooms of his Tante Leonie's house, where de Botton takes a guided tour, "re-create in its full esthetic horror the feel of a tastelessly furnished, provincial bourgeois 19th century home." As Proust said of the landscapes painted by Millet and Monet, the beauty is not in the scenes themselves. it is in the mind and eye of the artist.

While ostensibly this book concerns Proust's lessons on life. ultimately it probably reveals more about what he has to tell us regarding art. Be that as it may, even de Botton's smart, sometimes annoying, postmodern irony cannot obscure a sincere affection for his subject that few readers will fail to share. Who, after all, could resist a man who called his maid "Plouplou" and urged her to call him "Missou"? *How Proust Can Change Your Life* performs a valuable service in reminding us of the manifold allurements of a "great modernist" too often considered heavy and daunting.

Leslie Schenk (review date autumn 1998)

SOURCE: Schenk, Leslie. Review of *How Proust Can Change Your Life,* by Alain de Botton. *World Literature Today* 72, no. 4 (autumn 1998): 844-45.

[*In the following mixed assessment, Schenk explores stylistic aspects of* How Proust Can Change Your Life.]

You would imagine that any author clever enough to think up such a sure-fire title [*How Proust Can Change Your Life*], destined to make it a best seller in belletristic circles, could do no wrong. Well, he could and did, and so did I, for I bought a copy sight-unseen—that is, without opening the covers, and I suspect myriad Proustians the world over will be doing the same. It has been a long time since George Painter's superb biography came out, and we Proustians cannot get enough of what is now almost universally acclaimed as the greatest novel of the century, *Remembrance of Things Past,* the only possible contender being James Joyce's *Ulysses.*

When we do open the covers of *How Proust Can Change Your Life,* what we find is an amiable ramble through snippets of bright sayings by Marcel Proust accompanied by considerably lengthier and less bright sayings by Alain de Botton. Fair enough, I suppose, and something I suspect most of us could do and indeed already have done to some extent. I defy anyone to read Proust *without* finding passages to underline or copy. Most of us would not have the brass, though, to explain Proust's carefully expounded, transcendentally eloquent ideas by putting them into our own leadenly thudding words. Visconti's film *A Death in Venice,* a passable dramatization of Thomas Mann's novella, drew great power from the music of Gustav Mahler, no less, and Botton's book is a similar case of riding to glory on the coattails of a genius.

Nevertheless, Alain de Botton—who, despite his name, is English—has certainly done his homework very well indeed. He has even categorized his citations into nine chapters: "How to Love Life Today," "How to Read for Yourself," "How to Take Your Time," "How to Suffer Successfully," et cetera. The way these chapter headings are capitalized already seems a bit dubious to me, but never mind. However, one does have to ask: when this book was accepted for publication, was there no copy editor available? Proust is easier to read in French than in English, true, but one must admit he is not *really* easy to read in any language, especially when a sentence goes on for more than a page. But consider Botton's mangled style:

> A good way of evaluating the wisdom of someone's ideas might be to undertake a careful examination of the state of their own mind and health. After all, if their pronouncements were truly worthy of our attention, we should expect that the first person to reap their benefits would be their creator. Might this justify an interest not simply in a writer's work, but also in their life?

In Britain today, the unisexist *their* is commonly used to avoid the sexist and therefore supposedly derogatory *his* or *her* and is accepted equally willingly as singular or plural, *whom* is fading out of existence, and the unsplit infinitive is an utterly lost cause; but still, how many antecedents can the same *their* have within one paragraph? I count five here. The antecedent of the first *their* may be *whoever* is doing the evaluating, unless it be the *one* who has ideas, but in that case why *own*? The second *their* definitely refers to the *someone* who has ideas, although its placement could suggest it was *mind and health.* The third *their* clearly belongs to *ideas.* The fourth *their* refers to the *writer* called *someone* in the first sentence, as does the first *their,* but the latter might instead refer to *work. If* does not always call for a *were;* here *are* would be preferable.

Well, this is not exactly what we call careful writing. Even I can humbly propose a clearer version: "A good way for us to evaluate the wisdom of ideas might be to undertake a careful examination of the state of their

writer's mind and health [at the time of writing?]. After all, if such pronouncements are truly worthy of our attention, we should expect the first person to reap their benefits would be their creator. Might this justify an interest not simply in a work, but also in its author's life?" We can now understand the question, banal to the utmost, and answer it: "Yes, life sheds light on a work, work sheds light on a life, but the two are forever connected and separate"—so obvious it is embarrassing to have to state it.

Still, Botton unearths all sorts of fascinating Proustiana. For example:

> In 1922 [James Joyce and Marcel Proust] were at a black-tie dinner given at the Ritz for Stravinsky, Diaghilev and members of the Russian Ballet, in order to celebrate the first night of Stravinsky's *Le Renard.* Joyce arrived late and without a dinner jacket, Proust kept his fur coat on throughout the evening and what happened once they were introduced was later reported by Joyce to a friend:
>
> Our Talk consisted solely of the word 'Non.' Proust asked me if I knew the duc de so-and-so. I said, 'Non.' Our hostess asked Proust if he had read such and such a piece of *Ulysses.* Proust said, 'Non.' And so on.

This gives rise to Botton's speculations on what-might-have-been: "Proust: [*while taking furtive stabs at an* homard à l'américaine, *huddled in his fur coat*] Monsieur Joyce, do you know the Duc de Clermont-Tonnerre? / Joyce: Please, *appelez-moi* James. Le Duc! What a close and excellent friend, the kindest man I have met from here to Limerick." And so on, for another ten lines. Now, I ask you, what is the value of *that*? It only demonstrates the chasm of *mièvrerie* (soppiness, vapidity) that yawns between Proust's sensibility and that of this mini-Proust who even quotes his Master, in a fashion reminiscent of Flaubert's Bouvard et Pecuchet with their farcical dissection of clichés, on how to express things at once innovatively and incisively, and then plods on in a stale, flat style all his own. In a word, Botton's talent as a writer is simply not up to the task he has set himself.

I am surprised that Botton constantly refers to *In Search of Lost Time,* and never mentions the only truly controversial episode in the history of Proust's publication in English. As I once wrote in London's *Times Literary Supplement:*

> The prime example of well-meaning but misguided attempts . . . to improve on professional translators' work is the recent attempt to "get closer to the original" by changing *Remembrance of Things Past* into *In Search of Lost Time.* Any non-French-speaking person can look up *temps* and find "time" and look up *perdu* and find "lost" but surely any literate speaker of English ought to know that "lost time" means "pay deducted for unauthorized absences," and what has that to do

with Proust? . . . Clearly Scott Moncrieff's leap of the imagination in finding the little phrase in a Shakespeare sonnet to fit Proust's masterpiece should not be tampered with. . . . [Translation] is *not* to find word-for-word dictionary equivalents, but to recreate the original in another tongue.

C. K. Scott Moncrieff's original and flawed translation was revised by Terence Kilmartin, who also inserted missing passages, and then ditto by D. J. Enright. Well, Enright wrote to me as follows: "In fact I fought to keep the title *Remembrance of Things Past,* arguing that *In Search of Lost Time* sounded like one of those prehistoric movies featuring Raquel Welch, or at best Jules Verne—but failed. . . . The reasons for the change seem to be (a) the dissatisfaction with the old title long voiced by 'Proustians,' and (b) a factor (I suspect) which you can imagine for yourself." I imagine that "factor" was a purely commercial one suggesting, if not a different work, a translation vastly different from the skillful touching up it actually was. Not a word of all this (unless my eyes glazed) is mentioned in Botton's book, purportedly to be all about Proust's oeuvre. Proust himself did not like the Shakespearean title, but perhaps he too belonged to the school which holds that translation is a word-for-word chore. Well, I would point out that *recherche* really means *research,* the same way you can *entrer* somewhere you've never been but *rentrer* when you go home. And what is delving into the past if not *remembrance?*

Despite my various grievances, I must admit there is one enormous benefit to be derived from this little book, for Proustians and not-yet-Proustians alike. If it leads the literate public either back to rereading Proust or even more desirably to reading Proust for the first time—and I fully believe it inevitably will do both—that is already a most praiseworthy accomplishment.

Edward Skidelsky (review date 27 March 2000)

SOURCE: Skidelsky, Edward. "Comforting, but Meaningless." *New Statesman* (27 March 2000): 53-4.

[*In the following negative review, Skidelsky contends that* The Consolations of Philosophy *fails because "the conception of philosophy that it promotes is a decadent one, and can only mislead readers as to the true nature of the discipline."*]

I don't want to be accused of intellectual snobbery when I say that **The Consolations of Philosophy** is a very bad book. It is bad not because it makes unsupported generalisations, fails to define its terms, or any of the other conventional academic failings. All these are perfectly legitimate in a work of popular philosophy. It is bad because the conception of philosophy that it promotes is a decadent one, and can only mislead readers as to the true nature of the discipline.

This is all the more dangerous because the decadent notion of philosophy as "consolation" is actually very close to the true conception of philosophy. Philosophy—and to this extent Alain de Botton is correct—is not something that can be separated from life itself. It is not something that you do between nine o'clock and five o'clock, after which point "life"—dinner parties and flirtation—resumes. Life is continually thrusting philosophical questions upon us, and our answers to those questions make demands upon life. What carries on in universities under the name of philosophy has only an accidental relation to philosophy itself, just as what carries on in church has only an accidental relation to religion.

Socrates is commonly revered as someone who took philosophy seriously, who lived and died according to its demands. He is to philosophy what Christ is to Christianity. Like Christ, Socrates was completely misunderstood by his contemporaries. They viewed his endless questions about the nature of justice and beauty as a kind of childish game, unconnected to the serious business of life. (This is how most people still see philosophy.) The truth, as Socrates said again and again, is precisely the opposite. These are the most serious and practical questions that anyone can ask; compared to them, the "serious business of life" is a childish game. Christ made a similar point when he described the Pharisees as men who "strain at a gnat and swallow a camel". The things that most people take seriously are in fact ludicrously trivial. In moments of lucidity or remorse, they perceive this but find it hard to keep the perception in mind. Hardest of all is to live according to this sense of what really matters, as the biographies of Socrates and Christ demonstrate.

This austere conception of philosophy is inverted by de Botton. For Socrates, philosophy makes demands on life; for de Botton, life makes demands on philosophy. Philosophical theories are no more than ointments that we apply to soothe our various ailments. A remark by Epicurus, on the back cover of the book, sums it up: "Any philosopher's argument which does not therapeutically treat human suffering is worthless, for just as there is no profit in medicine when it does not expel the diseases of the body, so there is no profit in philosophy when it does not expel the diseases of the mind."

Not only is this conception of philosophy decadent in the popular sense of being effete, but it is also decadent in the precise sense of belonging to a period of cultural decline. The Epicurean view of philosophy as therapy was shared by all the main schools of late antiquity. This was a period in which the material and spiritual resources of classical civilisation were running dry. Barbarians harassed the frontiers, while a swollen administration stifled civic life. Unemployed mobs congregated in the imperial capitals, and were pacified with bread and circuses. Creative literature gave way to rhetoric and pastiche, and the official religion declined into an empty cult. Frustrated and dispirited, the educated retired to their libraries and found consolation in philosophy.

If you rewrite the above description, substituting "welfare and football" for "bread and circuses", and "psychotherapy" for "philosophy", you gain an approximate portrait of the modern west. The idea of philosophy as therapy appeals today for the same reason it appealed in late antiquity: it promises respite from insoluble problems. Even within "serious" philosophy, the therapeutic paradigm has proved seductive. Wittgenstein saw an analogy between his method, in which philosophical problems are "dissolved" into linguistic misunderstandings, and Freudian psychoanalysis. And relativism is often commended on the grounds that it encourages a tolerant, chilled-out attitude to life—an argument that can be traced back to ancient scepticism.

This conception of philosophy is not only distasteful; it falsifies its object. The first virtue of a philosophical theory is truth, just as the first virtue of a law is justice. Truth and justice cannot be traded for anything less. If a philosophical theory is false, it must be rejected, no matter how many therapeutic benefits derive from believing it. If a law is unjust, it should be repealed, however salutary its political or economic consequences.

De Botton ignores this obvious truth. He recommends Schopenhauer's misanthropic theory of sexual love—the theory, in brief, that all sexual love is a delusion created by the biological imperative of reproduction—for no better reason than that it can help cheer you up after a failed seduction attempt. It is true that misanthropy can be cheering—Schopenhauer himself was essentially a cheerful person—but that is not a reason to espouse it. The function of philosophy is not to pander to wounded vanity.

De Botton attributes his therapeutic conception of philosophy to thinkers who would themselves have rejected it. Apart from Schopenhauer, he deals with Socrates, Epicurus, Seneca, Montaigne and Nietzsche. Of these six, only Epicurus and Seneca would have endorsed the notion that philosophy is therapy. Socrates would never have suggested philosophy as a "consolation for unpopularity", because he did not think of unpopularity as something for which one needed to be consoled. Philosophy does not console one for popularity: it makes one indifferent to it. Similarly, Nietzsche's philosophy is not a "consolation for difficulties"; it is, rather, an injunction to seek out and triumph over dif-

ficulties. In both cases, de Botton is using philosophical ideas in ways for which they were never originally intended.

But it is Montaigne who suffers the greatest indignity at the hands of de Botton. Montaigne's remark, "If man were wise, he would gauge the true worth of anything by its usefulness and appropriateness in his life", is glossed as "Only that which makes us feel better may be worth understanding". Not only is this a miserable conception of intellectual endeavour, it is quite clearly a misinterpretation of Montaigne. Something may be useful or appropriate in your life without necessarily making you feel better. Once again, philosophy has been surreptitiously corrupted into flattery.

The medical analogy is misleading in another way. Different medicines may be incompatible in their effects, but they cannot strictly be said to contradict one another. This is because medicine refers to nothing outside itself. Philosophical theories, on the other hand, make claims about the world, and these claims can come into conflict. By treating philosophical theories as medicines, you abolish any sense of conflict between them. A little Epicurus for your money worries goes quite nicely with a bit of Seneca for your frustrations; that Epicurus and Seneca disagree with one another hardly matters. Ultimately, you lose the sense that philosophy refers to anything beyond the human psyche and its needs. It is transformed into a series of sound bites, all equally comforting and equally meaningless.

Perhaps some readers will find de Botton endearing, with his cocoa, holiday snaps and sexual hang-ups. But I failed to be charmed by these autobiographical touches, because they seemed like a calculated attempt at ingratiation. Philosophy has clearly not helped de Botton overcome the "indiscriminate desire for affection" he admits to in the opening chapter. But perhaps it has provided consolation for it.

Paul Ferris (review date 1 April 2000)

SOURCE: Ferris, Paul. "A Guided Tour Round Wisdom." *Spectator* 284, no. 8956 (1 April 2000): 53-4.

[*In the following review, Ferris examines the major philosophical figures discussed in* The Consolations of Philosophy.]

This stroll through the lives and works of half a dozen philosophers [*The Consolations of Philosophy*] is engagingly done, and as a bonus the publisher promises that the book will help us with 'some of our most familiar woes'. As I read I did try applying advice to myself and seeing where that got me. Botton does much the same. He is in and out of the book, giving us glimpses of his visits to bookshops, his travels and his love life.

Epicurus (b. 341 BC) is presented as being helpful to those who don't have much money. Botton supplies a knowing wish-list for a 21st-century zillionaire of taste (a Gulfstream IV jet, 'a half-moon commode by Grevenich' etc), by way of contrast with the simple life that Epicurus apparently advocated. He and friends occupied a rural commune, lived in freedom, ate vegetables from the garden, and found all the love and respect they needed from one another.

This raises problems for oneself. Friends, certainly, but friends alone? Didn't Epicurus (and most philosophers) find consolation in their reputations? Most of them were always scribbling books, aware of the interest of strangers, which is always refreshing. Simple victuals, yes, but what exactly constitutes 'simple'? I could sing the praises of grilled non-supermarket kippers, eggs boiled within hours of laying and home-made soup using stock from beef bones, but these simple foods are rarely available on demand.

A photograph, confusingly captioned but evidently chosen to illustrate the simple pleasures of life in a hut—mansions being unnecessary—shows a rear view of a line of young people in casual clothes, arms linked. Those of us who are that way inclined notice at once that a couple of the girls have attractive bottoms. Sex is another of the simple pleasures being advocated, except that it is usually far from simple, as others among Botton's Six attest.

Montaigne (b. 1533), whose wry nature saw that the weakness of cerebral philosophy was its failure to appreciate how an ingrowing toenail can sabotage reason, wrote sympathetically of life's physical embarrassments, the untoward fart, the attack of sexual impotence. What makes Montaigne attractive, at least in Botton's friendly account, is not a statement of principles but an example of believable fortitude and good humour. He was still grieving for the loss of a friend, whom he loved because 'he alone had the privilege of my true portrait,' 18 years after his death.

Seneca the Roman (d. AD 65) would have sniffed at such a waste of emotion. His stoicism relied on the expectation that the worst was always likely to occur: 'Reckon on everything, expect everything,' or, as Larkin growled, musing on mortality, 'Most things may never happen: this one will.' Seneca (categorised by Botton as offering 'Consolation for Frustration') deplored anger, too, because it achieved nothing: which is not strictly true. Before writing this (I am sorry these personal interludes are less exotic than the author's) I dropped an Ordnance Survey map in the kitchen which landed on the edge of a bowl of cat food, sending a shower of Felix everywhere. I shouted at map, bowl and myself, and immediately felt better.

The Romans of course hadn't heard of the unconscious, so that Seneca thought he was on the right lines when he saw anger as an error of reason, not a dark force erupting from below. Botton suggests, as one of his own pieces of useful advice, that we should not get angry when people are disturbing us with noise, but rather tell ourselves that they are not doing it on purpose to annoy. Doesn't that rather miss the point? A few years ago I lived in a flat near a madwoman, who would start screaming at her husband at 3 am. Obviously it wasn't directed at me, but knowing that this was true didn't reconcile me to the racket. The non-philosophic solution was to go out and buy earplugs. Or perhaps that *was* the philosophic solution.

The 'guide to living' side of the book, though, is a bit of a delusion. What we have are old-fashioned Brief Lives, succinct and lucid, with pretentious touches that mar but can be passed over quickly. By the time we reach Schopenauer (b. 1788), modern times are approaching, and the unhappy philosopher is concluding that we have an unknown self, a 'will-to-life,' that drives us towards our biological, sexual destiny.

Freud is being prefigured, though he denied having been influenced by Schopenhauer or even by Nietszche (b. 1844), the last of Botton's sages, who once remarked that all philosophical systems reflect the personal lives of the philosophers. Nietszche knew Freudian things before Freud, about the instincts and their repression. His insights failed to make him happy; to Botton he is the brave man committed to life, to being someone who 'no longer denies'.

Among the innumerable small illustrations printed alongside the text is a sports watch of the kind that a woman whom Botton fell in love with on a train from Edinburgh to Euston was wearing. It is that sort of book. But it manages to rise above its affectations.

James Delingpole (review date 8 April 2000)

SOURCE: Delingpole, James. "Alain and Me." *Spectator* 284, no. 8957 (8 April 2000): 51.

[*In the following review, Delingpole provides a laudatory assessment of de Botton's television series,* Philosophy: A Guide to Happiness.]

If Alain de Botton weren't a friend of mine, I think I would probably hate him. In fact, I know I would hate him because even when he wasn't as disgustingly famous and successful as he is now, I found myself loathing his guts on principle. I hated the fact that he was always on *Tatler's* 100 most eligible bachelors list; that he'd had two awesomely well-received, nauseatingly precocious novels published by the time he was 25; that he was younger, more intelligent, better looking and a zillion times richer than me . . .

Then, one day, I got to meet him and discovered that he was even worse than I'd feared: not only was he brilliant, handsome, youthful and rich, but the bastard was charming, modest and impossibly likeable too. I realised then that the only way of dealing with such a monster was to tame it and make it my friend. So we arranged to have tea at Fortnum & Mason's where we bonded so well that for days after I silently congratulated myself on my sublime genius: 'That Alain de Botton's no fool. If he likes me, it must mean I'm pretty damned wonderful.'

One of the good things about being Alain de Botton's friend is that in literary circles you can refer to him casually in conversation as 'Alain' and people tend to be quietly impressed, rather as they would in Hollywood circles if you started dropping Christian names like Bobby, Marty or Quentin. Another is that when you hear him performing brilliantly on *Start the Week,* or discover he's written another masterpiece or that he's a total natural on TV, you don't think 'tosser!' Rather, you root for him all the way.

I suppose now that I've said all that, you're not going to take seriously my remarks about his wonderful new TV series *Philosophy: A Guide to Happiness.* But, let me assure you, there are few things that make me more uncomfortable than heaping undue praise on the work of friends. If I hadn't liked the series, I would have found an excuse not to review it. (And, for the record, I found the recent TV adaptation of his *How Proust Can Change Your Life* ineffably tedious, so there.) *Philosophy: A Guide to Happiness,* though, is great. In theory, it sounds like yet another example of TV's relentless dumbing down. Each week, de Botton takes the work of a great philosopher, strips it down to a few handy soundbites and suggests how it might still be considered—ugh!—relevant to the modern world: how Seneca can cure road rage, for example. In practice, though, it's astonishingly clever and illuminating. Just as *How Proust Can Change Your Life* managed to make you feel not only that you really understood Proust but that you were now ready to tackle his oeuvre for real, so it is with de Botton's introduction to the great philosophers. You no longer see them as daunting figures whose work you're far too old and stupid to try comprehending now, but as wise old friends whom you'd very much like to get to know better.

Yes, I'm sure I must once have learned—and then swiftly forgotten—that Seneca was Nero's tutor and that he met his end with admirable dignity. But never before have I heard his life and work described so succinctly and sympathetically. On location in Rome, de Botton explained how Seneca's philosophy was born of its context: a world so riddled with treachery, cruelty and random violence that you woke up fully prepared for the possibility that this day would be your last.

What does this have to tell us about road rage? Why, that if you begin each car journey fully expecting to encounter traffic jams and bad driving, then you will be able to greet such horrors with philosophical indifference. But if you don't, when the inevitable happens, you're going to end up getting very, very cross.

The series is funny too. I particularly liked the scene where de Botton illustrated Seneca's view that man's predicament was akin to that of a dog being pulled by a chariot. His budget wouldn't run to a chariot, he explained, so instead he was shown pulling the dog along by a bicycle. Quite a hard thing to do, I imagine, while looking to one side and delivering a long, cogent piece to camera. But, as I say, the boy's a TV natural.

Whenever I ring up Alain these days for one of our regular chats, I always make sure to ask him first whether he's yet reached that stage of celebrity where he's too grand to talk to me. He always says no and, rather sweetly, when I told him I was going to review his series, he said he hoped that I would write more about our relationship than I would about the programme.

And I meant to, I really did. I was going to tell you about the long phone conversations we have about life, love and how much we hate writing books; about how weirdly secretive Alain is when talking about his background; and about how it was partly thanks to Alain's advice—'just make it like one of your *Spectator* columns, only more so'—that I managed to write the novel which, I've a strange suspicion, is going to make me almost as famous as he is. But I can't because I'm out of space.

Sylvia Brownrigg (review date 30 April 2000)

SOURCE: Brownrigg, Sylvia. "Dr. Feelgood." *Los Angeles Times Book Review* (30 April 2000): 6.

[*In the following review, Brownrigg asserts that de Botton's anti-philosophical approach in* The Consolations of Philosophy *does not do justice to his subject matter.*]

Let's be honest: None of us has enough time to read everything we ought to or even want to. As the stack of books we should read to be culturally literate grows ever higher, competing as it does with CDs everyone seems to be listening to and movies it would be good to have an opinion about, even the weight of the Sunday papers pushes us dangerously close to the question: Can I really fit this in?

In an increasingly servant-based culture, we do the sensible thing: Pay other people to read for us. The cheapest way to do this, of course, is to buy a book review. (My job as reviewer is essentially to be a reader-for-hire.) Here we can find out, at the very least, what's out there and how much of what's out there is considered worth reading. Incidentally, we can pick up enough information on a book to hold up our end of a conversation if someone should happen to refer to it. At the higher end of the market, we can buy and read an author who reads other authors for us and offers up tasty nuggets of their thought for his own time-strapped readership.

The English writer Alain de Botton has set up a neat line for himself in this racket. His perky 1997 volume, *How Proust Can Change Your Life,* was a well-researched but light-handed gloss on *In Search of Lost Time,* which interspersed biographical sketches of Proust with quotations from his great work, leaving readers not just entertained and enlightened but also with a slyly flattering sensation that they had themselves read Proust or at the very least understood the important things he had to say. One could enjoy Proust's views on "How to Be Happy in Love" or "How to Express Your Emotions" in a book that was accessible and short, even illustrated. Who knew Proust could be so breezy?

In his new book, *The Consolations of Philosophy,* De Botton takes the same approach with six philosophers, from Socrates to Nietzsche, with less happy results. De Botton stashes a justification for his method in one of the book's best chapters, on Montaigne, where he writes that clever people should get their ideas "from people even cleverer than they are. They should spend their time quoting and producing commentaries about great authorities who occupy the upper rungs of the tree of knowledge." To take on six philosophers is very different from taking on one novelist, however, and if in *How Proust* the author's wry lovelorn sensibility seemed reasonably matched with his subject (though his cute faux-naif tone threatened to sound precious), here the benign guide simply seems out of his depth.

That De Botton directs a graduate program in philosophy in London is bewildering—as he sounds nothing like a philosopher—to the great relief of his publishers, no doubt. He writes not only as if there were no contemporary discipline of philosophy, with figures such as Richard Rorty or Bernard Williams producing thought-provoking works, but also as if he were unaware of what makes philosophy exciting: its promise to tell us something about what the world is (metaphysics) or how to behave (ethics) or what we can know (epistemology). For De Botton, none of this is of interest. In his view, philosophers are united by "a common interest in saying a few consoling and practical things about the causes of our greatest griefs." It is philosophy as therapy, and truth—surely philosophy's own holy Grail—does not get a look-in. Williams' view, that "if philosophy, or anything like it, is to have a

point, the idea of 'getting it right' must be in place," is rejected by De Botton in favor of the pragmatic question: But does it help?

This deliberately anti-philosophical approach—in which the investigation is only important insofar as it might provide solace say, for heartbreak—might not pall so if the wisdoms De Botton discovered were genuinely helpful or, as he would put it, consoling. He is setting out to write a lay person's book, after all. Yet, though there are moments when De Botton stumbles upon a nicely humanist wisdom—in both Epicurus and Montaigne he finds lovely hymns to the value of friendship—on the whole his conclusions are remarkably banal, as is suggested by his chapter headings ("Consolation for Difficulties." "Consolation for Frustration").

Thus, De Botton examines Socrates not for his many views on politics or justice or even love but for how he might provide "Consolation for Unpopularity." De Botton focuses on Socrates' being condemned to death by fellow Athenians who distrusted his unconventional questioning stance and allows this to lead, with almost comic deflation, to his own reflection that "social life is beset with disparities between other's perceptions of us and our reality." To follow Socrates, De Botton tells us, we must learn to think for ourselves. (Isn't Apple Computer constantly telling us something similar?) Later, De Botton summarizes Nietzsche's complex thoughts on the value of difficulty and struggle in our efforts toward fulfillment with the lines: "Not everything which makes us feel better is good for us. Not everything which hurts us may be bad." Compare this with De Botton's similar, but altogether more graceful, reading of Proust: "We suffer, therefore we think, and we do so because thinking helps us to place pain in context, it helps us to understand its origins, plot its dimensions and reconcile ourselves to its presence."

In taking a *USA Today* approach to his selection of philosophers—peppering the text with tables, pictures (of a goat he saw near Montaigne's chateau; of the decorations he would choose for his private jet, if he had one) and randomly enumerated thoughts and including brief autobiographical anecdotes along the way (such as how reading Montaigne made him feel better after a brief episode of impotence)—De Botton seems to be trying to jolly us along. He writes with appealing frankness of his own tendency toward ingratiation and of his lack of self-confidence, and you can see both at play in this work, in which he tries to distract us from any consideration of his book's intellectual content. You begin to sense that De Botton is apologizing for the fact that he's writing a book at all, that he is trying to write something that will seem as easy as, say, television.

Then again, it *is* television. In Britain, the series based on this book has started to air. It seems by far the more appropriate medium for it (if not quite as good as the recent BBC version of De Botton's Proust book, which benefited from Ralph Fiennes' handsome performance as the melancholy Marcel). Driving around London with a van driver frustrated by bad traffic, De Botton benevolently dispenses Seneca's advice on dealing with anger, lounging in a young woman's room, discussing her boyfriend's abrupt walking out on her, De Botton sympathetically shares Schopenhauer's wisdom on a broken heart. De Botton explains Schopenhauer's view on the Will-to-Life and how her boyfriend must have rejected her not for any personal failings but rather because on a biological level he did not want to have children with her. "But isn't that sad?" the woman asks reasonably; whereupon the amiable De Botton can only admit that it is sad and then sweetly offer his last best consolation: an invitation to dinner.

If this volume is half as successful as the Proust book, we can surely expect other future De Botton readings of the great works. It's tempting to guess which authors might be next in line for his illustrated self-help treatment (Joyce was from Mars, Woolf was from Venus, perhaps?). I would say that De Botton, himself a novelist, has more to offer with his readings of literature than with any further philosophical excursions.

In *The Consolations of Philosophy,* it is in De Botton's passing readings of Stendhal, or Goethe that his prose comes to life and his eye finally sharpens, and we begin to suspect that under this elaborately constructed authorial persona is a passionate reader—one who turns to great novels when he is seeking consolation.

Mary Margaret McCabe (review date 23 June 2000)

SOURCE: McCabe, Mary Margaret. "Who Wants to Be a Millionaire?" *Times Literary Supplement* (23 June 2000): 14.

[*In the following negative review of* The Consolations of Philosophy, *McCabe argues that de Botton's attempt to make philosophy practical and more accessible fails.*]

Socrates' question, "How best to live?", might easily be misunderstood. He could have been asking, not what is the best life, but how, given that the best life is what we want, we are to get it. We might equally misunderstand his answer, that the unexamined life is not worth living, as advice about the means—examination, or philosophy—to what is worth having. From here it is a short step to imagining that philosophy is a practical skill, designed to provide us with the good things in life.

And this short step is a disaster for philosophy, thrust thus into the competitive world of consequences, for which it is manifestly unfit. In the culture of the market economy, we miss the fact that philosophy is valuable in and by itself; and this is the culture which will destroy not only the independence of philosophy, but the humanities entire.

It is deeply dispiriting, then, that the latest attempt to popularize philosophy—that is to say, to make philosophy into televisual fodder—does so precisely on the basis that philosophers can provide us with useful tips, convenient attitudes to strike in the muddle of our practical lives. Alain de Botton's *The Consolations of Philosophy* presents six philosophers—Socrates, Epicurus, Seneca, Montaigne, Schopenhauer and Nietzsche—as, in his version, means to combat the ills of human life. Socrates was put to death because his methods of philosophy were unpopular; but those methods themselves show us how to reason, and so (here, de Botton maintains, is the good consequence) how to resist the misguided opinions of others. Epicurus' odd hedonism allows us to see that happiness is not the possession of great resources, but the satisfaction of the right sorts of desire; so (the consequence) it doesn't matter if we don't have much money. Seneca the Stoic, who died painfully on the crazy instructions of Nero, shows us how to care less for the slings and arrows of outrageous fortune—and so, de Botton claims, to deal with frustration [*sic*]. Montaigne's broad view of the relativism of culture allows us to acknowledge, and to live with, our own frailties, while his attack on an intellectual elite should encourage us to foster wisdom, not academic show. Schopenhauer explains how love is the consequence of the species' desire to procreate; so disappointment in love is to be explained, and borne, by reflection on its natural origins. And Nietzsche insists that greatness is achieved through adversity, so (the consequence again) we may transcend failure for the sake of the success that is to come. Philosophy, on this view, is the self-help science, the art of success, whose imperatives are heard throughout the book against barely disguised autobiographical themes of social awkwardness, disastrous sexual activity and failure in love.

De Botton fails entirely to see that if reflection is to be thus directed, then, corrupted by the exigencies of practicality, it ceases to have the kind of reflective distance which makes it work. Even the more practical aspects of philosophy are not there to be harnessed to some immediate decision, or, worse, brought in to justify some decision after the event: ethical reflection matters because when we act, we should act for the right reasons, not because the right reasons should be hooked to the act after it is done. He fails to see that philosophy, to be philosophy at all, needs to be disinterested; and that two at least of his philosophical heroes died in making just that point. Indeed, philosophy, on his view, seems to be just what is said by philosophers, who utter generalizations about the human condition, or about wisdom.

But is that right? Surely philosophy has two vital concerns: reasons and reason. It asks "why?", and inquires about reasons—and so cares for well-structured argument. And it asks why this or that answer to the question "why?" is a good one: so it is reflective upon the reasons, it is about reason. This is so, of course, even if the conclusion of the reflective process is that reflection is inadequate, or that well-structured arguments are themselves a poor account of the giving of reasons. But of this sort of philosophical reflectiveness, de Botton's philosophers are innocent. Thus his account of Socrates misses entirely the point of the Socratic method (to expose and to reflect on the inconsistency in the beliefs of his interlocutor) and imagines it, instead, as a rather tedious business of finding counter-examples to a generalization, a process which easily degenerates into the kind of eristic which Plato's Socrates brings under attack.

The Stoics—whom de Botton portrays as rather whimsical ascetics, explaining bad luck by appeal to the goddess Fortune—had good reason to propose that the world is fully determined. Their ethical theory, consequently, involves a subtle account of how determinism is consistent with morality. The death of Seneca, then, should not be understood merely as a case of Stoic courage (the Stoics, we should recall, imagined that all sorts of frightful things might happen, so that when they did, they should strike with less force) but as the exemplar of the Stoic view that there is in fact only one thing that matters: rational virtue.

All of this is missing from ***The Consolations of Philosophy.*** Instead, we have a motley collection of Interesting Things said by Philosophers (despite their variously ghastly lives), presented in a format suitable for television (this is, after all, the book of the series). Thus the opening remarks about David's "Death of Socrates" are illustrated by a photograph of the chocolate milk the author was drinking at the time he first saw the picture. Or the analysis of the Epicurean account of pleasure is explained by a graph to show how happiness is not increased by greater luxury; and Montaigne's account of cultural relativism is accompanied by a map of "what is considered abnormal where". This is not the dumbing down of philosophy, it is a dumbing out. Nothing in this travesty deserves its title; Boethius must be turning in his grave.

Nora Miller (review date winter 2000-2001)

SOURCE: Miller, Nora. Review of *The Consolations of Philosophy,* by Alain de Botton. *ETC: A Review of General Semantics* 57, no. 4 (winter 2000-2001): 496-98.

[*In the following review, Miller maintains that* The Consolations of Philosophy *provides an invaluable insight into philosophical thought and deems the book enjoyable and worthwhile.*]

Alain de Botton believes we should use philosophy in daily living, that ideas from philosophy can provide consolation for a variety of typical human complaints such as inadequacy and unpopularity. In ***The Consolations of Philosophy,*** de Botton backs up his argument with the writings of six well-known philosophers: Sophocles, Epicurus, Seneca, Montaigne, Schopenhauer, and Nietzsche. To my surprise, I found that this book exploded several of my misconceptions regarding the philosophers in question. As I read on, it became apparent to me that my college-course exposure to these philosophers focused on just a small part of their total belief structures, and that the course *distorted* those parts severely. I would have counted this book worthwhile for that discovery alone.

Alain de Botton goes beyond mere description of ideas and shows how the life experiences of these thinkers produced the concepts he describes. The philosophers did not set out to develop large answers to large questions, but rather they acquired for themselves a set of hard-earned tools for living a successful or happy life. These days, philosophy has become detached from daily life, and most modern philosophers seem to believe that their work consists only of finding the large answers, not of improving the lot of the average person—that job belongs to psychologists. De Botton, a philosopher himself, contends that philosophy only matters as it applies to daily life and the living thereof.

More importantly, for our purposes, many of the concepts de Botton describes could have come directly from a text on general semantics. For example, in the section on Seneca, we read that Seneca believed that,

> . . . anger results not from an uncontrollable eruption of the passions, but from a basic (and correctable) error of reasoning. . . . if fingers are flicked over our eyes, we have to blink, but anger does not belong to (this) category . . . it can only break out on the back of certain rationally held ideas; if we can only change the ideas, we will change our propensity to anger.

In the section on Montaigne, de Botton says the philosopher traveled widely, partly to develop a broader and more conscious sense of "normal" and "abnormal," and that he decried the parochial belief of so many people that there could exist only one possible view of things—their own. De Botton presents several examples that show Montaigne embraced situational ethics and valued a relativistic orientation.

In the last section of the book, we come to Nietzsche, usually iconically linked to the Nazis and their beloved Superman (which of course bears little more than the name in common with his original concept of Ubermensch). Ask a college graduate who, like me, took only an overview course on philosophy, to name one concept Nietzsche developed besides that of the Superman and many will say "Pain is good." Some might conclude that this puts him in a league with the Marquis de Sade, but de Botton shows that the philosopher believed that to prosper, a person must not avoid the difficulties inherent in the climb towards success and achievement (not that pain "is good" but that it comes with the territory and acts to fertilize the soil in which pleasure grows). De Botton says that to Nietzsche,

> . . . every pain is an indistinct signal that something is wrong, which may engender either a good or bad result depending on the sagacity and strength of mind of the sufferer. Anxiety may precipitate panic, or an accurate analysis of what is amiss. . . .

In general semantics terms, one might say Nietzsche valued the ability to control one's semantic reactions and properly evaluate a difficult situation. To Nietzsche, the superior person embraces difficulties and gladly learns from them and thereby qualifies as Ubermensch.

I think readers of *ETC* will find this book worthwhile and enjoyable. The author has a somewhat whimsical style that might not please everyone, but the underlying information will probably appeal to those familiar with the concepts of general semantics, especially those who seek tools for a saner life.

Antioch Review (review date summer 2001)

SOURCE: Review of *The Consolations of Philosophy*, by Alain de Botton. *Antioch Review* 59, no. 3 (summer 2001): 641.

[*In the following review, the critic offers a mixed assessment of* The Consolations of Philosophy.]

De Botton, *enfant terrible* of the upper crust literary set in Britain, has produced a mildly entertaining discourse on the usefulness of Western philosophy [*The Consolations of Philosophy*]. His gentle and unassuming analyses are a mixed lot. For example, Socratic questioning may well help us to rationally test cultural assumptions and norms, but De Botton's one-

dimensional portrayal of Socrates provides none of the emotional depth necessary to construct a satisfying "consolation of unpopularity." His discussion of poverty, which centers on a lovely analysis of Epicurus' life, is much more successful. The other sections—Montaigne as the source of consolation for inadequacy, Schopenhauer as consolation for broken heart, etc.—are rarely successful, although each is written with considerable wit and charm. Helping readers to understand the deep connections between philosophical abstractions and issues of deep concern in their own lives is an important task. Unfortunately, De Botton's work is not nearly as edifying as he takes it to be. One hopes that this volume—as well as the popular companion British television series—will lead De Botton's many admirers to consult their libraries for the genuine article.

Julian Gitzen (essay date October 2001)

SOURCE: Gitzen, Julian. "How to Be Postmodern: The Fiction of Julian Barnes and Alain de Botton." *Essays in Arts and Sciences* 30 (October 2001): 45-61.

[*In the following essay, Gitzen compares the works of de Botton, particularly* How Proust Can Change Your Life, *with the fiction of Julian Barnes.*]

One of the most inventive English novelists to have emerged in the past decade is Alain de Botton. His stylistic originality is all the more striking in view of his youth (b. 1969). His background and his work notably resemble those of Julian Barnes, who is twenty-three years his senior. In addition to fiction, both writers have produced journalism and criticism. Coincidentally, both have served as television critics or reviewers for the *New Statesman*. The two men share Francophile tendencies, as reflected in the fact that Barnes's best known work is a fictional biography of Flaubert, while de Botton has recently produced a study of Proust, entitled ***How Proust Can Change Your Life*** (1997). Furthermore, while both are novelists, each evinces a strong interest in nonfiction, particularly biography and the analytic or argumentative essay, and both incorporate these forms into their fiction. The hybrid works which result perhaps should not be described as novels, their unconventionality being sufficient to position both Barnes and de Botton squarely among the avant-garde postmodernists.

Self-reflexivity or self-consciousness has long been accepted as a prominent feature of postmodernist art. In his *Critical Essays*, Roland Barthes champions self-reflexive literature, arguing against "realistic" or mimetic fiction on the grounds that fiction by its very nature is unrealistic. Fiction consists of language, or in the terms of Saussure, of signs and signifiers, rather than signifieds. As Barthes emphasizes, however realistic it affects to be, all fiction is necessarily selective; it *is* artifice, shaped in the interest of narrative, theme, and character portrayal. Furthermore, "Literature is never anything but language. . . . In other words, in relation to objects themselves, literature is fundamentally, constitutively unrealistic; literature is unreality itself. . . . The 'truest' literature is the one which knows itself as essentially language."[1] Barthes speaks approvingly of a "double-literature," which is "at once object and scrutiny of that object, utterance and utterance of that utterance, literature object and metaliterature."[2] Literature suitable for the present, Barthes maintains, is not content with illusory verisimilitude, but instead parades its own artifice and functions as "a mask which points to itself."

In addition to being conspicuously self-reflexive, the art of Barnes and de Botton exemplifies other postmodernist characteristics, as outlined by Frederick Jameson and Ihab Hassan. In his essay "Postmodernism, or the Cultural Logic of Late Capitalism" Jameson notes that postmodernists have been "fascinated precisely by this whole 'degraded' landscape of schlock and kitsch, of TV series and *Reader's Digest* culture, of advertising and motels, of the late show and the grade-B Hollywood film, of so-called paraliterature with its airport paperback categories of biography, the murder mystery and science fiction or fantasy novel: materials they . . . incorporate into their very substance."[3] Jameson's remarks provide a strikingly accurate description of several elements contained in the work of both de Botton and Barnes. For his part Hassan stresses the fragmentary and formally incomplete structure of postmodern art: "As an artistic, philosophical, and social phenomenon, postmodernism veers toward open, playful, optative, provisional . . . disjunctive, or indeterminate forms, a discourse of ironies and fragments."[4] "Playful, disjunctive, ironic, fragmentary": all four descriptive terms may be applied to the fiction of both Barnes and de Botton.

Julian Barnes had already published two novels, *Metroland* and *Before She Met Me,* when the appearance of *Flaubert's Parrot* in 1984 brought him worldwide acclaim. It was unlike any previous novel in English, though several reviewers likened it to Nabokov's *Pale Fire.*[5] Unlike *Pale Fire,* however, this novel incorporated some features of genuine biography: i.e., incidents in the life of Flaubert. On the other hand, equal importance was accorded to the character and past life of the biographer and narrator, Dr. Geoffrey Braithwaite. Readers familiar with *Madame Bovary* would quickly recognize parallels between the lives of Flaubert's married couple, the Bovarys, and the lives of Dr. Braithwaite and his late wife.

While the narrative presents elements of the life stories of both Flaubert and Dr. Braithwaite, its structure is fragmented and unsystematic. Considerable information about Flaubert is supplied, but it is not given in chronological format. Of the fifteen chapters which comprise *Flaubert's Parrot* only the second provides a brief chronological resume of the author's life and work, and it assumes the form of subjective contrast: a positive or optimistic account of Flaubert's life, balanced by an equally negative or pessimistic summary. For example, the first capsule biography refers to only one death, that of Flaubert himself in 1880, at which time he is said to have expired "full of honour, widely loved, and still working hard to the end," while the second biography commences with reference to the deaths of two Flaubert children before the birth of Gustave and also records the death of a third child when the author-to-be was only one year old. It continues with a relentless litany of deaths, including those of Gustave's father and his beloved sister Caroline, the deaths of his dear friends, Alfred le Poittevin and Louis Bouilhet, his mistress Louis Colet, his mother, and eventually of Flaubert himself, in this instance portrayed as "impoverished, lonely, and exhausted." Similar discrepancies mark the two accounts and estimates of Flaubert's work. Alluding to the publication of *L'Education Sentimentale* in 1869, the first biography notes that "Flaubert always claims it as *un chef-d'oeuvre,*"[6] whereas the second describes the book as "a critical and commercial flop." The first account makes no mention of Flaubert's play, *Le Candidat,* while the second dismisses it as "a complete flop," forced to close after only four performances. These pointedly contrasting life-summaries dramatically illustrate the manner in which biographies may be colored by the writers' attitudes toward their subjects. Two biographers possessed of more or less identical evidence and documents may produce widely differing accounts.

The parallel and contrasting miniature biographies constituting Chapter Two are, of course, ironically self-reflexive in character. *Flaubert's Parrot* continues in this self-reflexive vein, inquiring what sort of evidence biographers should collect and which facts they should consider as salient and worthy of mention. Dr. Braithwaite likens a biographer to a trawling fisherman. Having collected a net full of facts about the subject, the fisherman/biographer then "sorts, throws back, stores, fillets and sells." It is inevitable, however, that some fish will elude the trawler's net. Dr. Braithwaite encounters one such elusive creature in the form of a series of letters, supposedly recently discovered, which were exchanged between Flaubert and Juliet Herbert. The latter was an English governess, who lived for a time in Flaubert's house at Croisset while instructing his niece, and is believed by some experts on Flaubert to have been his mistress. To Dr. Braithwaite's mortification and rage, the discoverer of the letters blandly informs him that he has recently burned them in accordance with Flaubert's directive to Ms Herbert that they should be burnt.

Though he does not succeed in gathering as much evidence as he would like, Dr. Braithwaite remains tireless in his pursuit of any facts, however recondite, which may shed light on either Flaubert's work or his life. He alludes, for instance, to the scene in *Madame Bovary* during which Emma first surrenders to her second lover, Leon, while riding through the streets of Rouen in a closed cab. Having distinguished this scene as "probably the most famous act of infidelity in the whole of nineteenth-century fiction," he adds that it may well be misrepresented in the imaginations of readers because of an erroneous preconception about the shape of the cab in question. To clarify the matter, he quotes several lines from an obscure work by G. M. Musgrave, who visited Rouen around 1850, less than a decade prior to the publication of *Madame Bovary,* and who observed of the cabs of that city that they were "the most dumpy vehicles . . . of their kind in Europe. I could with ease place my arm on the roof as I stood by one of them in the road."(92) Emma's seduction would therefore have been even more cramped and uncomfortable than most readers have assumed.

One fact which Dr. Braithwaite has labored diligently to establish concerns the identity of a certain stuffed parrot. While composing *Un coeur simple,* Flaubert borrowed one such bird from the Museum of Rouen and kept it perched on his desk. Presumably this bird served as the model for "Loulou," the parrot which features prominently in that story. What is claimed as Flaubert's original parrot-companion is now housed in the Hotel-Dieu of Rouen, the hospital where Flaubert's father worked as head surgeon and where the writer spent his childhood. A second claimant, however, is ensconced at Flaubert's adult home of Croisset. Dr. Braithwaite seeks unsuccessfully to determine which of the two is the genuine parrot, only to reveal at the narrative's conclusion that at one time the Museum of Rouen possessed as many as fifty stuffed parrots, any one of which might have graced Flaubert's writing desk. The novel thus ends on a wry, indeterminate note appropriate to postmodernist fiction. Dr. Braithwaite's soberly industrious but fruitless pursuit of the authentic parrot, has, of course, its comic dimension, since the successful identification of the bird in question would have had no significance either for Flaubert's life or his work. The very impossibility of the task, however, highlights a matter of concern not only to Dr. Braithwaite but to all biographers: i.e., the insurmountable difficulties of recapturing the past. Some facts about the lives of even the most famous individuals have long been forgotten or will never be known. Consequently, no biography, regardless how lengthy, can be definitive.

A noteworthy similarity between *Flaubert's Parrot* and Alain de Botton's biographical novel **Kiss and Tell** (1995) is that both volumes feature biographers who are forthcoming about themselves. Most biographers are self-effacing, obeying Flaubert's dictate that, "The author in his book must be like God in his universe, everywhere present and nowhere visible."(88, FP) Flagrantly disregarding this convention, the narrators of Barnes and de Botton disclose important facts about themselves alongside of facts about their subjects. Dr. Braithwaite is particularly candid, and his self-revelations point to significant parallels between his own life and that of Flaubert's widower, Charles Bovary. Both men are medical doctors, general practitioners. Both have had unfaithful wives who subsequently committed suicide by swallowing poison. Both were devoted husbands and were (or are) inconsolable in their grief. As for the two wives, similarities between them began with their names. Emma Bovary and Ellen Braithwaite shared the same initials. Neither woman loved her husband, and both repeatedly lied about their adulterous affairs. Coincidentally, both used the excuse of attending the theatre to conceal the pursuit of their liaisons. Despite these resemblances, Dr. Braithwaite also notes significant differences. For instance, Emma Bovary was a reckless spendthrift, eventually undone by her unpayable debts rather than by her love affairs, while Ellen, in contrast, "didn't run up bills." Emma followed a downward path as her personality coarsened, and she became corrupted by lust, whereas Ellen "wasn't corrupted; her spirit didn't coarsen." Did Ellen find happiness or fulfillment in her "secret life," or did she, like Emma, "rediscover in adultery all the platitudes of marriage"? The doctor answers, "We didn't talk about it."(164) A significant irony underlies this cryptic reply. Dr. Braithwaite has previously expressed great admiration, even love, for Flaubert, yet despite his best efforts, he cannot assemble a satisfactory account of Flaubert's life. The facts for which he is searching appear to him like "a piglet . . . smeared with grease," evading all attempts at capture. The doctor also loved his wife deeply and intensely, but he had no knowledge of her "secret life," particularly because her only allusions to it apparently consisted of lies. Consequently, in order to account for his wife's decision to take her own life, he is forced to "hypothesise a little . . . fictionalise . . . invent my way to the truth." This affectionate but desperate expedient serves as a timely reminder of the necessary subjectivity of all biographies.

Like Barnes, Alain de Botton had published two novels prior to the appearance of his volume of biographical fiction. His two preceding works were **Essays in Love** (1993) and **The Romantic Movement** (1994), followed in 1995 by **Kiss and Tell**. While *Flaubert's Parrot* offers a unique blend of authentic biography and fiction, **Kiss and Tell** adopts the traditional form of fictional biography, i.e., a novel presented as the biography of a fictional character. The novel as biography or autobiography is as old as the English novel itself, as exemplified by Defoe's *Robinson Crusoe* and *Moll Flanders.* *Kiss and Tell* differs from all previous fictional biographies in English (with the exception of Sterne's brilliantly unorthodox *Life and Opinions of Tristram Shandy*), however, in being narrated by a biographer preoccupied not merely with the facts in the life of his chosen subject but also by the questions of *which* facts to present and in what order. In brief, his perspective and methods are comically self-reflexive. As biography *per se, Kiss and Tell* is unusual also in that its subject is neither famous nor exceptionally accomplished, though at only twenty-five, she *is* remarkably youthful. As the narrator is keenly aware, from Boswell to the present, biographers customarily have chronicled the lives of the famous from birth to death, whereas he has selected a young woman unknown to the public at large and presumably with as much as two-thirds of her life ahead of her. The individual in question, Isabel Jane Rogers, was born into a middle-class London family in 1968. She is the eldest of three children, brought up in "a small house in Kingston." After graduating from London University, she found work as a production assistant with a stationery company, where she has remained for the past four years. She now lives alone in a flat "in a street off Hammersmith Grove" in London.[7] The biographer's task is to enlarge and extend this simple profile. While rendering this undertaking considerably less arduous than usual, Isabel's extreme youth serves also to highlight a peculiarity of de Botton's work to date (which is perhaps accounted for by his own youth): the fact that he has as yet undertaken to portray no major character appreciably older than himself. The few older characters present in his fiction play minor roles there and are likely to appear as comic caricatures.

Although this constitutes his maiden attempt at biography, de Botton's narrator is well acquainted with the genre. He has read or is at least familiar with James Boswell's *Life of Samuel Johnson,* the works of Lytton Strachey, and such twentieth century landmarks as Richard Ellmann's *James Joyce.* He quotes Richard Holmes, the biographer of Shelley and Coleridge, to the effect that it is necessary for biographers to love their subjects if they are to follow patiently in their footsteps (a precept with which Dr. Braithwaite presumably would heartily agree). While the narrator does not actually express love for Isabel, he certainly is very fond of her and lives with her for a time (thus the appropriateness of the novel's gossip-promising title). In sharing Isabel's apartment, he follows the example of Boswell, who spent months in the company of Dr. Johnson (though not actually residing with him). The narrator has read enough biographies to recognize that Boswell is an unusual biographer in that he frequently recounts both his own activities during his companionship with

Johnson and remarks exchanged between Johnson and himself. In this regard also the narrator's methods resemble those of Boswell, while he shares Dr. Braithwaite's willingness to call attention to problems confronting the biographer. How, for instance, should a biographer order the events in the life of a subject? The customary method is to commence with the individual's birth and to progress chronologically to death, but the narrator protests that this practice disregards both the manner in which subjects experience or recall their own pasts and the process by which a biographer acquires information. Only after an eight-month acquaintance with Isabel has he obtained a clear picture of the events of her early childhood. The better to reflect this non-chronological development, he withholds until the seventh chapter a systematic account of her earliest years, by which point in the narrative the reader has already learned the details of her adult love affairs.

Another issue confronting biographers (and one also grappled with by Dr. Braithwaite) is that of selectivity. A conscientious researcher is almost certain to have knowledge of numerous facts or details which possess little claim to be included in a biography. For instance, de Botton's narrator recognizes as a comically insignificant piece of trivia an occasion witnessed by himself when Isabel ordered for her lunch an avocado, bacon, and turkey sandwich. While such details clearly are irrelevant, the narrator astutely observes that food *is* a vital feature of anyone's life, and that a subject's preferences in food are not to be totally disregarded. In his support he quotes Dr. Johnson's pronouncement that "Nobody can write the life of a man but those who have eaten and drunk with him." The narrator conveniently fails to mention that in his own *Lives of the Poets* Dr. Johnson sketched the careers of numerous writers, such as Milton and Dryden, with whom he had neither eaten nor drunk. Nevertheless, Isabel's preferences in food are not overlooked. She is said to have a marked fondness for pasta and chicken, the latter being "the thing she most liked to cook for dinner."

Central to the issue of selectivity is the question of approximately how long a biography should be. As the narrator points out, biographers have before them two sharply contrasting precedents: on the one hand the single-page *Brief Lives* of the seventeenth-century wit, John Aubrey, and at the other extreme Boswell's biography of Dr. Johnson, the unedited version of which runs to 1,492 pages. While inclined to favor brevity, the narrator recognizes that the omission of vital material may result in a caricature rather than an accurate portrait. He also perceives that in order to produce a balanced account of Isabel's life, he needs considerably more information than he possesses at present, but Isabel forestalls all further biographical endeavors by suddenly proclaiming herself to be weary of the narrator's inquiries and unwilling to answer any further questions or to supply any additional information about herself. As a result, her life story is abbreviated, its 246 pages falling far short of the 875 pages estimated by the narrator as the average length of biographies published from 1990 to the present.

When his subject refuses any further co-operation, the narrator is indeed at a stand, particularly because from the outset Isabel has been virtually the only person whom he has consulted in his quest for information. Her father, mother, and sister all reside in London and presumably are within easy reach, yet the narrator questions none of them, nor does he interview any of her friends, lovers, teachers or work-mates. His sole approach to a second person occurs when he accidentally encounters Flo Youngman, who for the past two decades has assisted in cleaning the Rogers' house. He draws Flo into conversation, anticipating "a fountain of stories with which to enrich [his] portrait." Although Flo proves amusingly garrulous, she makes only a brief, passing reference to Isabel, centering her attention instead upon her family members and neighbors.

The narrator's virtual negligence of all possible sources of information save Isabel herself ensures that what he eventually produces is less a biography than an extensive profile. The volume contains an Index such as might form part of a conventional biography, and it is instructive to consult the entry there for "Rogers, Isabel Jane." This item occupies three full columns of print, and its numerous subheadings, ranging from "aggression" to "vulnerability" and from "cynicism" to "warm personality," bespeak a wide ranging survey of Isabel's character, attitudes, and behavior. The book's two lengthiest chapters are the sixth and the ninth. The former recapitulates Isabel's various love affairs. As the subject of romantic love is de Botton's special province, it is no surprise to find him devoting extensive attention to Isabel's romances. The ninth chapter consists of a tongue-in-cheek review of various experiments in psychology, a field described by the narrator as "a myriad of incompatible theories of the antics of the human mind." Nevertheless, he maintains that "We are all psychologists in interpreting the behavior of others."(179) In so saying, he speaks not only for his own biographical methods, but also for the author, who in the two volumes preceding *Kiss and Tell* has supplied extensive psychoanalytic explanations of the conduct of his major characters, especially their reactions to being in love.

Philip Glazebrook, among the more perceptive reviewers of *Kiss and Tell,* regards the book as less than a novel because it portrays only one character: "From a good novel you learn about humanity as it is exemplified by a set of characters interacting and developing around carefully constructed . . . events. From a biography you learn all there is to know about an individual, with perhaps a few other faces glimpsed in reflected light."[8] Glazebrook is no doubt aware that his distinction is not strictly accurate, since a number of "good novels," among them Malcolm Lowry's *Under the Volcano,* Samuel Beckett's *Malone Dies,* Anthony Burgess's *Clockwork Orange,* and J. M. Coetzee's *Life and Times of Michael K.,* do focus upon a single character.

Nevertheless, his remarks highlight a limitation of *Kiss and Tell* and, indeed, of de Botton's fiction as a whole: each of his novels to date has centered upon the interaction of a single couple. His first novel, *Essays in Love,* revolves around the love affair between an unnamed narrator and a twenty-four-year-old graphic designer named Chloe. The affair commences after the two meet while occupying adjoining seats on a flight from Paris to London. Their romance continues for one year and ends suddenly (and symmetrically) during a second flight from Paris to London, when Chloe confesses that she has recently been seeing another man. The simplicity of the plot—its focus upon a relatively brief love affair between one couple—is somewhat offset by the commentary which insistently accompanies these events. A major innovative feature of this novel is that the majority of its text consists of nonfiction, most of it psychoanalytic in character. The commentary which constitutes the bulk of each chapter represents the efforts of an unusually thoughtful or introspective narrator to understand and explain the emotional experiences which he is sharing with Chloe. *Essays in Love* is recognizably postmodern precisely because it is less a conventional novel than a series of informal essays and as such a hybrid or "indeterminate" form. The book's essay-like format engenders a resemblance between its narrator and the speaker of *Kiss and Tell,* both of whom exist essentially as speaking voices, thinking and analyzing presences, rather than as fully formed characters. We learn nothing whatever about this narrator's physical appearance or characteristics and relatively little about his professional life (he is an architect) but much about his thoughts on the subject of love.

Prominent among the narrator's cogitations are explorations of several fundamental dichotomies, such as body/mind and real/ideal. His reflections upon the former center upon the sex act, traditionally assumed to be largely a physical rather than a mental function. Indeed, readers of the chapter in question, "Body and Mind," are likely to be recall the tireless fulminations of D. H. Lawrence against "sex in the head" (self-aware or self-conscious sex). For his part the narrator implicitly acknowledges that his lengthy analysis of sexual activity may expose him to ridicule: "If the mind has traditionally been condemned, it is for its refusal to surrender control to causes supposedly beyond analysis; the philosopher of the bedroom is as ludicrous a figure as the philosopher in the nightclub.'"[9] Having initially postulated that "few things can be as antithetical to sex as thought,"(46) the narrator eventually reaches quite a different conclusion. He acknowledges that "the mind can never leave the body," and that therefore, so long as one remains conscious, it is impossible to have a totally mindless experience. In any event, active minds are vital to lovers during sexual intercourse, since only through the agency of thought can each partner anticipate what will afford pleasure to the other. The achievement of sexual harmony is dependent upon mutual thought.

As for de Botton himself, one of the trademarks of his writing is the extensive attention which he devotes to matters of the intellect. (In a sense he qualifies as a successor to Aldous Huxley as a "novelist of ideas.") His frequent philosophical allusions have attracted the notice of several reviewers.[10] *Kiss and Tell,* for instance, makes reference to the thoughts or activities of Nietzsche, Bertrand Russell, Wittgenstein, Hobbes, Adam Smith, Kierkegaard, Rousseau, and Sartre. The narrator of *Essays in Love* also possesses a background in philosophy, which he brings to bear upon the subject of aesthetics. Evidently Chloe cannot be persuaded to believe herself beautiful. She assumes the existence of an objective standard of feminine beauty embodied in the models of *Vogue* magazine. When measuring it against this standard, she finds little to admire in her own appearance. The narrator describes Chloe as a follower of Plato, who postulated the existence of an ideal Form of beauty, conferred in part upon all beautiful earthly bodies. In contrast, the narrator embraces Kant's belief that the "determining ground" of aesthetic judgments must necessarily remain subjective. According to this view beauty resides first and foremost in the eye of the beholder. As it happens, Chloe is gap-toothed, prompting the narrator to supply one of his numerous explanatory diagrams or visual illustrations, of the sort favored by the linguistic theorists Saussure, Lacan, and Barthes, whom de Botton obviously knows well. The narrator presents two drawings: one features a gracefully formed set of "Platonic teeth," while the second gap-toothed drawing is labeled as "Kantian teeth." Chloe's lover claims to be attracted to the latter precisely because of their imperfections.

When seized by a desire to declare his love for Chloe, the narrator is thrown into doubt by postmodernist linguistic theory. Evidently he has read enough of Derrida and others to appreciate that the most common of terms lack fixed or universally shared meanings, and that any word may convey as many different meanings as it has recipients. If he were to express "love" for Chloe, what would she make of such an utterance? Her previous romances must have colored the term "love" for her. As for himself, several prior affairs have combined to shade that term of endearment with personal associations. He could not speak to Chloe of love without involuntarily recalling these past affairs, which would be an act of disloyalty to her. The chief noteworthy fact here is that the narrator proves to be incapable of a simple, unreflective, spontaneous expression of love. Just as he cannot make love without pondering about his actions and eventually concluding that such thoughts are not to be despised, so too he cannot announce his love without first considering the possible reactions of his beloved to such a declaration. He reviews the differing uses to which the word has been put in various historical eras and in differing societies. He acknowledges the distinction between sacred and profane love and between Eros and agape. He reflects that "the Troubadours equated love with unrequited passion" and that at least one tribe in New Guinea possesses no word for love. This thoroughgoing analysis leads the narrator to conclude that he requires a new and different word with which to convey his feelings. Amusingly, "marshmallow" strikes him as peculiarly apt for the purpose, and he assures us that when she was informed that he "marshmallow[ed]" her, Chloe understood him perfectly, describing his tribute (apparently without irony) as "the sweetest thing anyone had ever told her."

The psychoanalytic commentary which his readers have come to associate with de Botton is present abundantly in those passages in which the narrator assesses individual features of Chloe's personality and supplies an account of her conduct. He establishes, for instance, that it is a "deep seated and pervasive feature of Chloe's character" to blame herself for occasions on which she suffers. Even when violently ill, she prefers to remain silent, since she is loath to "load responsibility" upon another by expecting that person to care for her. He notes also her generosity, her creativity, her awkwardness in the company of other women, and her fierce loyalty to her friends. He acknowledges, however, that his portrait is incomplete and subjective, neglectful of certain features of Chloe's character and conduct. He has registered her "talent for baking bread . . . social anxiety . . . love of Beethoven . . . hatred of laziness [and] claustrophobia," while largely overlooking her "love of outdoor markets . . . mathematical talent . . . thoughts on God . . . relationship with her brother [and] taste for Victorian architecture."(149)

While the narrator's psychological insights of Chloe are perceptive, his later self-analysis is considerably less so. This lame attempt at self-understanding is prompted by Chloe's sudden departure. He searches for a reason for her desertion of him, finding it with overmuch alacrity in "rejection compulsion" syndrome, the origin of which he traces to his parents' divorce. In fairness to the narrator, during this discussion his voice assumes a decidedly ironic tone, indicating that he recognizes his self-psychoanalysis for what it is—glib and superficial.

It is of a piece with his comically inept suicide attempt, during which, in place of sleeping pills, he mistakenly swallows "twenty effervescent vitamin C tablets." This last is a spontaneous act, perhaps his only one since the moment of his falling in love with Chloe, and it has the merit of sobering him and convincing him of the folly of suicide. He now recognizes as a just censure the prediction of another woman whom he had once loved that he would "never be happy in love because I 'thought too much.'" At length, the narrator draws a closely related conclusion, his pointedly self-reflexive statement constituting a wry self-assessment by the author of his idiosyncratic undertaking in writing this essay-like novel (and in numbering each of its paragraphs in the manner of a philosophical treatise): "Love taught the analytic mind a certain humility, the lesson that however hard it struggled to reach immobile certainties . . . analysis could never be anything but flawed—and therefore never stray far from the ironic."(249)

Prior to de Botton's exploration of the subject, the "analytic mind" of Julian Barnes had already addressed the dimensions and powers of love in *A History of the World in 10 and ½ Chapters* (1989), another hybrid work mingling fiction with informal essays. As in *Flaubert's Parrot,* the focus here is upon issues relating to the search for historical truth. Once again Barnes acknowledges that historical facts are elusive and beyond the power of any individual to assemble in full. Although knowledge of history is indispensable to us, much of it remains forever beyond our grasp. Frustrated by his inability to encompass the facts of Flaubert's life, Dr. Braithwaite has been tempted to claim that "History is merely another literary genre: the past is autobiographical fiction pretending to be a parliamentary report."(90, FP) In *A History of the World in 10 and ½ Chapters* greater blame is accorded to human weakness than to the intractability of historical evidence. Barnes accuses historians of selectivity, of deliberate omission or distortion of facts, owing to their need to "fabulate": "We make up a story to cover the facts we don't know or can't accept; we keep a few facts and spin a new story round them. Our panic and our pain are only eased by soothing fabulation; we call it history."[11] Against history's everlasting obscurity, Barnes marshals the intangible power of love, which, he argues, affords the clarity of vision necessary to assimilate vital historical facts.

It has been the form, however, rather than the theme of *A History of the World in 10 and ½ Chapters* which has elicited the majority of critical comments. While the book has frequently been described as a novel, it hardly qualifies as such. The text does not consist of a single unified and extended narrative. Instead, it is composed largely of a series of chapter-length short stories, each with different settings and characters, but grouped around common subjects or themes. Interspersed among these stories are three chapter-length essays or reminiscences. The subject underlying these episodes is survival, especially at sea or on water. Barnes's approach to the subject is three-fold: the review of actual historical events, the conferring of historical significance upon fictional events, and the revisiting of pertinent myths, particularly that of the Flood and Noah's Ark. The author's implicit assumption is that much of human history has consisted of a struggle for survival. Therefore, by portraying selective instances of this struggle, he supplies representative illustrations of history in the making. To lend increased authenticity to this enterprise, several fictional episodes are based or modeled upon historical incidents. The second chapter, for instance, portrays the hijacking of a cruise liner at sea by a group of Palestinians, who execute a number of the ship's passengers before being overpowered by counter-terrorist commandos. This incident is reminiscent of the actual hijacking of the liner "Achille Lauro."

Several chapters of the book recall Frederick Jameson's observation that postmodern art frequently appropriates to itself the genres of science-fiction or fantasy. The opening chapter, for instance, consists of an account of the Flood and Noah's role in it from the viewpoint of a stowaway termite which voices indignation at the ill treatment and slaughter of many of the animals entrusted to Noah's protection. At least half of the book's chapters, however, possess standard features of fictional verisimilitude: carefully detailed settings, specific frameworks of time and place, plausible actions which are graphically depicted, and characters endowed with distinctive identities and expressing themselves in idiomatic language. One such chapter is "Upstream!", consisting of a series of letters written by a British film actor to his sweetheart in London. He is on location in the rainforests of Venezuela for the filming of a story about an exploratory journey up the Orinoco River by two Jesuit priests some two hundred years ago. The situation resembles that in a British film, *The Mission* (1986), directed by Roland Joffe and starring Jeremy Irons and Robert de Niro, which also depicts the experiences of a Jesuit missionary who was dispatched to the jungles of Brazil in the mid-eighteenth century. Barnes's descriptions of the jungle surroundings, the appearance and behavior of the native Indians, and the activities of the film crew are all detailed and credible, thoroughly consistent with the mimetic conventions of realistic fiction.

Perhaps because of the text's pervasive realistic atmosphere, the occasional authorial intrusions register with greater force. By interrupting his narrative in order to address related issues, Barnes violates a central tenet governing the composition of realistic fiction: that in the interest of verisimilitude, authors must as nearly as possible efface themselves from their texts. One such intrusion occurs in the chapter entitled, "Three Simple Stories," in which Barnes seeks to substantiate two premises related to his main theme. The first premise, common enough among historians, is that history repeats itself. The second (far less commonly maintained) is that myths eventually will be enacted as fact, will become history. The conclusion implied by these two premises is that the study of myths as well as of history will assist us to anticipate future events.

As a comic example of history repeating itself. Barnes relates an anecdote about an Englishman named Lawrence Beesley, who survived the sinking of the "Titanic." On the strength of a book which he subsequently wrote, entitled *The Loss of the Titanic,* he came to be regarded as an authority on that shipwreck, and forty years afterward he was engaged as a consultant for the film "A Night to Remember." As the sinking of the vessel was about to be filmed, Beesley went on board as an uninvited extra, apparently with the intention on this occasion of going down with the ship. The director spotted him, however, and ordered him off of the set. He was thus spared for a second time, and, in a farcical manner, history repeated itself.

To demonstrate how myth will eventually manifest itself as actuality, Barnes relates a modern version of the forty-year odyssey in the wilderness of Moses and the Israelites. This particular journey was undertaken in 1939 by 937 Jews aboard the liner "St. Louis." On May 13 of that year they sailed from Hamburg, expecting to be temporarily resettled in Cuba before eventually migrating to the United States. Upon arriving at Havana, however, they were refused entry. The ship then sailed up and down the coasts of North and South America, but without finding any country willing to give the passengers asylum. In despair, the ship's captain eventually turned back to Europe, where the passengers were dispersed to Holland, Great Britain, and France. On June 21, the British contingent reached Southampton, at which time "They were able to reflect that their wanderings at sea had lasted precisely forty days and forty nights."(188)

Barnes reserves his most personal statement for "Parenthesis," a chapter which consists of an argumentative essay enumerating the merits of love. The better to link this discussion to the theme of survival, he inquires at the outset whether or not the love of human beings will survive their deaths. Not surprisingly, he answers in the negative. What, then, are love's capabilities? Does it bring happiness? Not necessarily, Barnes replies, but it makes possible increased happiness and greater zest for life, because love's "primary effect is to energize." Love also enhances confidence and confers increased clarity of vision and discrimination: "Love and truth, that's the vital connection. . . . Have you ever told so much truth as when you were first in love?

Have you ever seen the world so clearly?"(240) While acknowledging that no entirely objective account of history is humanly possible, Barnes remains adamant that it is imperative to strive for greater enlightenment and that "43 per cent objective truth is better than 41 per cent." Not only can love serve as a helpful instrument in the quest for valid historical knowledge, but it can also supply an anti-materialist, anti-mechanical counter force to the materialistic tyranny of history. In light of this conclusion the witty didactic strategy of *A History of the World in 10 and ½ Chapters* becomes fully apparent. While exemplifying in its own narrative the "fabulation" of history which it deplores, at the same time the book exhorts its readers to strive for greater historical truth.

Barnes makes perhaps grander claims for love than does de Botton, but, like the narrator of **Essays in Love,** he is drawing upon his personal experiences, describing and analyzing the features of love and exemplifying its manifestations and its effects. However unconventional their techniques, both authors are addressing traditional features of fiction. The better to facilitate the portrayal of character, for instance, in *Flaubert's Parrot* and **Kiss and Tell** each adopts the guise of a self-reflexive narrator. As a means of developing theme, in **Essays in Love** and *A History of the World in 10 and ½ Chapters* each turns to nonfiction. In the latter two works both writers are concerned with love, from Boccaccio to the present a favorite subject of fiction. The pleasures and pains of love were depicted by Flaubert and Proust, two novelists highly esteemed by both Barnes and de Botton, but the fictional methods adopted by those two great novelists differ widely from the postmodern techniques employed by Barnes and de Botton.

Notes

1. Roland Barthes, *Critical Essays,* trans. Richard Howard (Evanston: Northwestern University Press, 1972) 159-160.

2. Barthes 97-98.

3. Thomas Docherty, ed., *Postmodernism: A Reader* (New York: Harvester/Wheatsheaf, 1993) 63.

4. "Toward a Concept of Postmodernism," Docherty 154.

5. Cf. John Updike, "A Pair of Parrots," *The New Yorker* 61.22 (July 22, 1985): 86-96, and Wendy Lesser, "Bloated and Shrunken Worlds," *The Hudson Review* 38.3 (Autumn 1985): 463-472.

6. Julian Barnes, *Flaubert's Parrot* (London: Picador, 1985) 26. Page numbers of all subsequent quotations from this edition are included in the text between parentheses.

7. Alain de Botton, *Kiss and Tell* (London: Picador, 1996) 37. Page numbers of all subsequent quotations from this edition are included in the text between parentheses.

8. "Portrait of a Lady and Little Else," *The Spectator* 275 (September 9, 1995): 42.

9. Alain de Botton, *Essays in Love* (London: Picador, 1994): 49. Page numbers of all subsequent quotations from this edition are included in the text between parentheses.

10. Cf. Andrea Ashworth, "Isabel Encounters Her Biographer," *Times Literary Supplement* 15 September, 1995: 20, and Lisa Zeidner, "Post-Modern Love," *New York Times Books Review* 11 June, 1995: 35.

11. Julian Barnes, *A History of the World in 10 and ½ Chapters* (London: Picador, 1990): 242. Page numbers of all subsequent quotations from this edition are included in the text between parentheses.

Jan Morris (review date 6 May 2002)

SOURCE: Morris, Jan. "Don't Be Ashamed to Go on a Bus Tour." *New Statesman* (6 May 2002): 44-5.

[*In the following review, Morris views* The Art of Travel *as "an elegant and entertaining evocation of all the sensations of travel," and as a manual for maximizing the travel experience.*]

This entirely delightful book [*The Art of Travel*] has an ambiguous title. Does it refer to the skill of travelling properly, or does it mean the matter of travel as the subject of art? A bit of each, it turns out, but it might better be called *The Philosophy of Travel*, because I think that's what it is really meant to be.

Most philosophers, in my experience, write a modicum of rubbish, and de Botton is no exception. He is a genuine master of the truism, a virtuoso of the obvious. I doubt if he has written a dull sentence in his life, but when he draws didactic conclusions, or talks about motives and suchlike, he does sometimes put one toe over the fringe of bunkum. That the reality of travel does not always live up to the anticipation; that painters can often tell us more about a place than photographers; that personal anxieties, brought from home, can encroach upon the mind even when you are lazing on a tropic beach somewhere—such thoughts could well be expressed by anyone who has been on a package holiday to Benidorm.

But away from the generalisations, this book is really an elegant and entertaining evocation of all the sensations of travel, and a manual of how to get the best out of it. Half of it concerns de Botton's own reflections; half of it is about the attitudes of great writers, painters and, yes, philosophers towards the whole business of going away from home. I have made a profession of the practice, so perhaps I may be forgiven for offering a few travelling techniques of my own, and seeing how de Botton conforms to them. Here they are:

> Wherever you go, pretend to yourself that you have never been there before.

> Remember that any experience, of any sort, even going to the dentist or losing a passport, is grist to the proper traveller's mill.

> Keep in mind E M Forster's advice about the best way to see Alexandria—"to wander aimlessly about"—or Lord Salisbury's theory of an ideal foreign policy—"to float lazily downstream, occasionally putting out a diplomatic boat-hook to avoid collisions".

> Don't set out to see what other people see.

> Take a sketchbook, not a camera.

> Don't be ashamed to go on a bus tour.

> Travel alone.

Almost all these simple precepts crop up in one form or another in this book, and de Botton graphically describes putting them to the test. He is fine, and fun, when he follows the travels of celebrated predecessors: Flaubert to Egypt; Humboldt to Peru; Edward Hopper into the service stations and late-night cafés of America; van Gogh among the wind-flustered cypresses of Provence; or Wordsworth amid the Cumbrian sublime. He is best of all, however, when discussing his own detailed and intimate responses to the making of journeys.

Pretending he has never been there before? He often goes down to Heathrow, he tells us, just to watch the aeroplanes go by, but nobody has ever described the take-off of a loaded 747 with such freshness and amazement, and I am prepared to bet that nobody ever will—in particular, that always thrilling moment when the lumbering progress of the aircraft along the tarmac suddenly becomes, with "the controlled rage of the engines" and "a slight tremor from glasses in the galley", a breathtaking release into the Elysian freedom.

Is everything grist to his mill? Of course. Absolutely everything. De Botton is as interested in the conversation of a man with a mobile telephone on a train as he is in the typography of public notices—as curious about the compulsion of deserts as he is about the different designs of front doors in England and Holland. I feel sure he would welcome, just for the experience, an interrogation at a Paraguayan immigration office, or the extraction of a tooth in a Rwandan dental surgery.

Wandering aimlessly? Well, he is perhaps too analytical to be quite authentically serendipitous, but he is certainly no conventionally organised traveller. He ignores guidebook itineraries, and indeed toys with the idea of writing his own subjective handbook to

Madrid—drawing attention, for instance, to the lack of vegetables in the city cuisine (three stars for interest, in his guide), to the smallness of Spanish male feet and to the extraordinary length of Madrileño surnames.

Not seeing what other people see? Bless you, he doesn't even try. De Botton's vision is entirely his own. Who else would observe that the cry of a black-eared wheatear has no effect on a caterpillar "walking strenuously across a rock"? Has anybody else ever noticed that the texture of Amsterdam brickwork is like that of halva from a Lebanese delicatessen?

De Botton takes both a camera and a sketchbook, it seems, but he quotes Ruskin on the value of drawing as a way of seeing places, however primitive your technique, and says that he began to appreciate the identity of oak trees after spending an hour drawing one in the Langdale Valley—my own experience exactly, after spending interminable coffee breaks trying to get the Doge's Palace right.

"Don't be ashamed to take a bus tour." Alain de Botton would never be. He doesn't give a damn, I'm sure, what other people think, and when he goes on a tour along the Van Gogh Trail, led by a lady guide from the tourist office at Arles, he carries his camera along, too, to take holiday snaps.

And does he travel alone? Not always, it seems. Somebody called M often accompanies him: but he proves my precept all the same, because on page 24 of this book, when the two of them are eating lunch in the shade of a tulip tree beside the Caribbean, they fall out over who should have the larger portion of crème caramel, and don't make up till nightfall.

So in all respects, this book gratifyingly confirms my own travelling criteria. De Botton probably prefers to be thought of as a philosopher, and I myself would rather categorise him (if he must be categorised) as an essayist; but the sparkling, profound and exuberant quality of *The Art of Travel* betrays him not just as an admirable traveller, but as one of the very best contemporary travel writers—an artist in the genre, in fact, in both senses of his title.

Annette Kobak (review date 31 May 2002)

SOURCE: Kobak, Annette. "Financial Alarm under the Palms." *Times Literary Supplement* (31 May 2002): 32.

[*In the following review, Kobak places* The Art of Travel *within de Botton's literary oeuvre and praises his unconventional approach to his subject matter.*]

"Bad art", Alain de Botton suggests in *The Art of Travel,* "could be defined as a series of bad choices about what to show and what to leave out." By this criterion, de Botton's own writing is getting to be better and better art. In his last three books, *How Proust Can Change Your Life, The Consolations of Philosophy* and now *The Art of Travel,* he has shed the sometimes gawky concern about "where it's at", and the fiction where philosophy kept breaking out, like Dr Johnson's cheerfulness, to create a form of belles-lettres which is unique to him: polished, contemporary, full of wit and intelligence, helpful and above all illuminating.

All de Botton's books, fiction and non-fiction, deal with how thought and specifically philosophy might help us deal better with the challenges of quotidian life—returning philosophy to its simple, sound origins. Satellite themes are given more or less spin in each book: how to be happy, courageous, just and good; how to deal with the eddies of anxiety provoked by others' misreading of us, and by our own paralyses and confusions; how to navigate the right course between chaos and order; how to live honestly in a materialistic culture; how to be a good friend; how to open our eyes.

Because he is in spirit an artist and craftsman rather than a storyteller (as well as a kind of inspired curator of the past), this revisiting of themes isn't repetitious but enriching, like Monet's revisiting of waterlilies. The new form de Botton has forged is in time with the times: linked, finely honed essays within which voices from the past such as Socrates, Seneca, Flaubert, Proust and Nietzsche are put in conversation with us and with each other, like some online conference call. Snippets of visual information—diagrams, blurry reproductions of paintings, likenesses of his protagonists, the odd snapshot he has taken, a goldfinch here, an isosceles triangle there—have burst out of the text from the start, even in a supposed novel like *The Romantic Movement.* The late W. G. Sebald breaks form in a similar way in his books, with more gravitas, more personal hinterland, but less accessibility. Yet de Botton's lightness of touch and concern about the humiliations of everyday life shouldn't be read as banality, just as Montaigne's shouldn't (though they were at the time). If each generation corrects for the mistakes of the previous one, perhaps the author is reinstating a concern with ethics as a guide to how to live life for a generation reacting against the ethical gap in its parents' mainstay, psychotherapy.

Sometimes the self-help manual "we" can feel a little presumptuous—"we" do not all feel alike—but, on the whole, de Botton does us the favour of presenting himself as being that much more timid than most. Stymied as he is by over-refined thought processes in the face of risk, like a calm Woody Allen, the essentially risky business of travel is a natural next step in his oeuvre. As you would expect, however, his concerns do not lie with how to cut the bristles on your toothbrush, or how to tense your muscles against mosquitoes. What interests him is how the search for happiness is caught on the wing in travel, and how thoughtful study of this impulse might tell us in what ways—if at all—travelling helps "human flourishing". There are many approaches he might have taken to this, including considering how much of a nomadic component is hardwired into us, but he takes an idiosyncratic route, seeing travel through the eyes of J. K. Huysmans, Baudelaire, Edward Hopper, Flaubert, Wordsworth, Edmund Burke Job, Nietzsche, Van Gogh and Ruskin, and venturing out randomly to Barbados, the odd airport and service station, Amsterdam, Madrid, the Lake District, Provence, the Sinai Desert and Hammersmith. The only conventional traveller included is Alexander von Humboldt, and he is only brought in to show how the manic fact-finding of his travels to South America is no longer open to us, now that the globe is charted. What is open to us is to consider what impulses drive us to travel, what psychological baggage we take with us on our journeys, and what is genuinely life-enhancing about the experience, as opposed to our expectations of what ought to be so. The book's own journey meanders back thrillingly on itself between the idea that "journeys are midwives to thought" and the idea that, with the right frame of mind, you can do that journey just as profitably on your own doorstep as in distant regions.

The inspirational aspects of journeying are such things as the "relief from the fake comforts of home", or—as Wordsworth and others discovered—that the mere fact of walking, let alone within a rich landscape, stimulates the brain. As de Botton says, "The mind may be reluctant to think properly when thinking is all it is supposed to do". The more adventurous aspects of travelling, in search of wild landscapes or what the eighteenth century called "the sublime", teach us that "sublime places repeat in grand terms a lesson that ordinary life typically introduces viciously: that the universe is mightier than we are, that we are frail and temporary and have no alternative but to accept limitations on our will". Or, put another way, "There are concerns which seem indecent when in the company of a cliff." Thus wilderness helps us with our humiliations in the world of man. However, de Botton has more fun with the opposite idea: that, as Pascal put it "the sole cause of man's unhappiness is that he does not know how to stay quietly in his room".

This idea surfaces in the book in many guises: in the author's decision to take a day off to wander round his home patch of Hammersmith with his eyes open and no agenda—no shopping, no trying to get anywhere—or in his approval of the underachieving peregrinations of Joseph de Maistre's brother, Xavier, who went on an epic journey in 1790 and gave his account of it in

Journey around My Bedroom. "Gratified by his experiences, in 1798, de Maistre undertook a second journey. This time he travelled by night and ventured out as far as the window-ledge, later entitling his account *Nocturnal Expedition around My Bedroom.*"

De Maistre explained how helpful his pioneering efforts would be: "Millions of people who, before me, had never dared to travel, others who had not been able to travel and still more who had not even thought of travelling will now be able to follow my example." He "particularly recommended room-travel to the poor and to those afraid of storms, robberies and high cliffs".

But these home-hugging insights are hard won. *The Art of Travel* starts with the dissatisfaction with the local weather and environment that usually precedes travel, what Baudelaire called "that appalling disease the Horror of Home". "Life", Baudelaire continued morosely, "is a hospital where every patient is obsessed by changing beds. This one wants to suffer in front of the radiator, and that one thinks he'd get better by the window." One steely grey winter's day in London, de Botton finds himself seduced by a brochure into thinking he would like a change of radiator, and takes off for Barbados. He does indeed find palm trees at an angle to a white beach, and, at the edge of the sea: "small lapping sounds beside me, as if a kindly monster was taking discreet sips of water from a large goblet".

However, his imagination hadn't reckoned with other things that were also there: luggage carousels, BP petrol stores, immigration paraphernalia, tour guides, stray dogs, electronics factories, and most of all the "momentous but until then overlooked fact . . . that I had inadvertently brought myself with me to the island". So a petty quarrel over supper with his companion renders the whole idyllic scenario null and void—worse than a grey day in Hammersmith because his expectations were so much greater, the let-down more oppressive, his pocket emptier. In spite of the radical change of scene, his mind "revealed a commitment to anxiety, boredom, free-floating sadness and financial alarm"—just as Flaubert's had, Job-like, in Egypt: "What is it, oh Lord, this permanent lassitude that I drag about with me?"

These observations are not new, of course. Others have been there before, including Sterne and Robert Louis Stevenson, but de Botton recasts them freshly and sensitively. He also tries to solve them, by giving us mental baggage more appropriate to contemporary travel: the ability to see poetry in liminal places like service stations and airports, an understanding of why art can be a good guide and why guidebooks can be very bad guides, cameos of men from the past who can be good companions on our journeys, even if we travel alone, or only from our armchairs. De Botton not only writes about these things, but demonstrates them through the text and illustrations. So the only passages in the book where the eyes glaze over are quotes from a Madrid guidebook, quietly proving the author's point that Goethe was right in saying "I hate everything that merely instructs me without augmenting or directly invigorating my activity". And a virtuoso piece on Van Gogh's painting of cypresses shows us why the flame-like turbulence that Van Gogh saw in them is actually the structural characteristic of cypresses in Provence, not part of the artist's own turbulence. This textual interactivity is something de Botton did to good effect in *The Consolations of Philosophy,* where he set up an "acquisition list" for happiness of such detail and sophistication—including a private jet ("Dassault Falcon 900c or Gulfstream IV"), with a picture on its tail-fin of a still-life of "three lemons by Sánchez Cotán from the Fruit and Vegetables in the Prado"—that you find yourself inhabiting this fantasy in some awe before he demolishes it and you realize you have been lured into ludicrous materialism.

In the end, like the company of good friends, travel emerges as a way of discovering truths about ourselves: "It is not necessarily at home that we best encounter our true selves." If this is not so in quite the same way for women, then it points up the fact that philosophy has been almost exclusively the preserve of men, and all de Botton's *compagnons de route* from the past are, as it happens, men. For although the challenges of life and travel are common to all human beings, some of them are different for women. Sometimes we are different "we's". Half of the human race could probably do with such witty, freewheeling advice for travelling dames, whether in the boudoir or Barbados.

Liedeke Plate (review date April-June 2003)

SOURCE: Plate, Liedeke. Review of *The Art of Travel,* by Alain de Botton. *World Literature Today* 77, no. 1 (April-June 2003): 111-12.

[*In the following review, Plate compliments de Botton's "light, humorous prose" in* The Art of Travel, *but feels that the author's comparisons between art and travel are often "contradictory."*]

Prodesse Et Delectare, "to teach and to delight," could indeed be de Botton's motto. For in *The Art of Travel,* as in *How Proust Can Change Your Life* (1997) and *The Consolations of Philosophy* (2000), he tackles some of life's Big Questions in light, humorous prose, reflecting on the assumptions behind holiday-making, probing our motives and desires for going on a journey, and questioning what we think we do when we travel with the help of a handful of (all-male, mostly French and English nineteenth-century) writers and painters.

The selection of guides to thinking about travel, no less than the topics chosen to explore, reveal de Botton's romantic inclinations. In a series of essays on the exotic, on the sublime, on Wordsworthian "spots of time," and on walks through one's own neighborhood in the spirit of de Maistre's *Journey around My Bedroom,* de Botton instructs us to "notice what we have already seen," echoing Shelley's claim that art "strips the veil of familiarity from the world, and lays bare the naked and sleeping beauty."

There's much to like in *The Art of Travel.* At times taking us over familiar (narrative, visual, or geographical) ground, de Botton is at his best when arguing for journeys at or close to home. The juxtaposition of Baudelaire's poetry and Hopper's painting reveals a captivating poetics of *attente,* of waiting and expectation; the demonstrations of the ways in which art can open our eyes to our surroundings—Van Gogh's paintings pointing the traveler's eyes to the cypresses, the olive trees, and the wheat fields of Provence, Ruskin's use of a sketchbook enabling them to remain "alive to the smallest features of the visual world"— hold the irresistible appeal of the reflective life wherein there's time to attend to and delight in the details of the quotidian. To compare the fascination the Orient held for Flaubert and de Botton's own enthusiasm for Amsterdam, containing for this reader the delight of the familiar made strange, also indicates the ways the reader is situated.

There's something discomforting about the "we" evoked throughout the text, that comes to insight on tropical islands, that is lured to travel by photographs of "a sandy beach fringed by a turquoise sea, . . . a palm tree gently inclining in a tropical breeze" yet to whom the landscapes of Provence are revealed through kindred artistic processes of selection. And there's something disturbing about the passing in silence over the fact that it is the same tourist industry that spoils the very picture it sells on "Winter Sun" brochures (think of Jamaica Kincaid's scathing description of the effects of tourism in *A Small Place*) and that uses art to tell us what to look for in a landscape, what counts as interesting. Despising guidebooks for telling us what's worth seeing yet applauding art for doing exactly that, de Botton looks at travel through an art that regrettably forgets it is itself ideological, and that the pleasures of the aesthetic are vested with many, sometimes contradictory, interests.

FURTHER READING

D'Aquila, Ulysses. Review of *How Proust Can Change Your Life,* by Alain de Botton. *Lambda Book Report* 6, no. 8 (March 1998): 29.

Provides a review contending that *How Proust Can Change Your Life* is an engaging and intelligent work, but warns that it should not be seen as a substitute for reading the work of Marcel Proust.

Edmundson, Mark. "Advice for the Lovelorn." *Washington Post Book World* (2 July 2000): 8.
Presents a review classifying *The Consolations of Philosophy* as a self-help book.

Moloney, Daniel P. "Happy Thoughts." *National Review* 52, no. 15 (14 August 2000): 69-70.
Review arguing that de Botton's observations in *The Consolations of Philosophy* are "charming," but ultimately too banal and eclectic for their own good.

Additional coverage of de Botton's life and career is contained in the following sources published by Thomson Gale: *Contemporary Authors,* **Vol. 159;** *Contemporary Authors New Revision Series,* **Vol. 96; and** *Literature Resource Center.*

Tony Kushner
1956-

American playwright.

The following entry presents an overview of Kushner's career through 2003. For further information on his life and works, see *CLC,* Volume 81.

INTRODUCTION

Kushner established himself as an internationally celebrated playwright with the critical and popular success of his epic two-part Broadway production, *Angels in America: A Gay Fantasia on National Themes* (1991, 1992). *Angels in America* explores issues of gay identity in America, set within the cultural context of the AIDS epidemic, Reagan/Bush administration politics, and the ending of the Cold War. Kushner's interweaving of dramatic interpersonal relationships, harsh political realities, and fantastical flights of imagination won him widespread critical acclaim and many prestigious accolades, including the Pulitzer Prize for Drama, the Antoinette Perry ("Tony") Award for Best Play, and the New York Drama Critics Circle Award for Best New Play, all for Part One of *Angels in America,* subtitled *Millennium Approaches,* and the Antoinette Perry Award for Best Play for *Part Two: Perestroika.* Kushner earned the 2004 Emmy Award for best writer in a miniseries for the television adaptation of *Angels in America.* Kushner's play *Homebody/Kabul* (2001), set in Afghanistan, received an Obie Award in 2002.

BIOGRAPHICAL INFORMATION

Of Jewish descent, Kushner was born July 16, 1956, in New York City, and grew up in Lake Charles, Louisiana. Both of his parents were classical musicians. Kushner became aware of his homosexuality at an early age, but attempted to change his sexual preference during his college years with psychotherapy. Eventually, he came to accept his sexuality, which has become a central focus of his theatrical writings. Kushner graduated from Columbia University, earning a B.A. in medieval studies in 1978. While working as a switchboard operator at the United Nations Plaza Hotel, he enrolled in the graduate program in directing at New York University, completing his M.F.A. in 1984. Since 1985, Kushner has maintained a successful career in theater as a playwright, director, and educator. He has served as as-

sistant director of the St. Louis Repertory Theatre from 1985 to 1986, artistic director of the New York Theatre Workshop from 1987 to 1988, director of literary services for the Theatre Communication Group in New York from 1990 to 1991, playwright in residence at the Juilliard School of Drama from 1990 to 1992, and as a guest dramaturge in the theater programs of New York University, Yale University, and Princeton University.

MAJOR WORKS

Angels in America includes over thirty characters and numerous interconnected subplots, totaling seven and a half hours of performance time. *Millennium Approaches,* Part One of *Angels in America,* introduces a smorgasbord of characters—fantastical, historical, and fictional—including an African-American drag queen, the oldest living Bolshevik, the ghost of Ethel Rosenberg, a rabbi played by a gentile actor, and an angel. The five central characters of *Angels in America* include Roy Cohn, a figure from the era of Senator Joseph Mc-

Carthy, who promulgated the "red scare" trials of the 1950s; Prior Walter, a young man with AIDS; Louis Ironson, a Jewish man who is Prior's lover; Joe Pitt, a bisexual Mormon; and Harper Pitt, Joe's wife. *Millennium Approaches* explores the impact of Prior's diagnosis of AIDS on the interrelationships among these characters. In one subplot, Cohn, a ruthlessly ambitious political player intent on gaining power within the ranks of the Reagan administration, defines homosexuality as a position of powerlessness; because he holds political power, Cohn argues, he himself is not a homosexual but is simply a heterosexual man who has sex with men. Further, although a doctor has just informed him that he is HIV-positive, Cohn argues that, since he is not a homosexual, it is not possible for him to have AIDS. Another set of subplots focuses on the loss experienced by Prior and Harper when each is deserted by his partner, while Louis and Joe develop a new relationship with each other. Kushner makes use of fantastic and hallucinatory elements in *Millennium Approaches,* such as Harper's fantasy that she is in Antarctica and a scene in which two characters meet and dance in each other's dreams. *Millennium Approaches* ends with a sense of apocalypse as an angel appears to Prior.

Part Two of *Angels in America,* titled *Perestroika,* follows the personal struggles of each of the central characters as they come to terms with the various changes and losses they experienced earlier. While many of the characters transform these crises into positive experiences, Cohn dies of AIDS, steeped in self-hatred, without truly learning anything from his experience. Cohn's ghost later appears as God's attorney. In the final scene of *Perestroika,* Prior addresses the audience directly with the personal gospel he has developed as a result of his experiences. *Perestroika* ends on a positive, hopeful note, emphasizing the power of the imagination to transform tragedy into beauty. A made-for-television film adaptation of *Angels in America* premiered as a miniseries on Home Box Office (HBO) in December 2003, earning Emmy Awards for Kushner, director Mike Nichols, stars Al Pacino, Meryl Streep, Jeffrey Wright, and Mary-Louise Parker and an Emmy for Best Miniseries. *Slavs! Thinking about the Longstanding Problems of Virtue and Happiness* (1995), which Kushner considered his coda to *Angels in America,* is set amid the dissolution of the Soviet Union and the end of the Cold War. In *Slavs!* a character named Aleksii Antedilluvianovich Prelapsarianov, who originally appeared in *Angels in America,* raises questions about the relationship between individual action and the forces of history. In an epilogue to *Slavs!* the characters who have died find that even in Heaven there are no conclusive answers to the "longstanding problems of virtue and happiness."

Kushner's exploration of the relationship between political circumstances and the personal lives of his characters

frequently includes fantastical elements such as angels, devils, and other spirits. An early play, *Hydriotaphia, or, The Death of Dr. Browne* (1987), is an imaginary reconstruction of the last day in the life of the historic figure Sir Thomas Browne, a seventeenth-century scientist and writer. Described as an "epic farce," *Hydriotaphia*—a word which means "urn-burial"—takes its title from an essay by Browne in which he concludes that God does not promise an afterlife to human beings. While lying in his deathbed, Dr. Browne is visited by characters such as his Soul, the Devil, a witch, and a grave-digger. In addition to treating gay themes, Kushner's works also address issues of Jewish culture, identity, and history. *A Bright Room Called Day* (1987) is set in Germany during the early years of Hitler's rise to power. In this play, a group of friends is dispersed under the pressures of the Nazi regime; some flee into exile, others retreat into hiding, and one woman is left alone, vulnerable to persecution. Zillah Katz, a young American woman living in contemporary times, is the narrator of the play. In commenting on the actions of the drama, Zillah draws parallels between the oppressive forces of the Nazi regime and current events. Kushner originally wrote Zillah's perspective with the provision that he would periodically update her commentary in keeping with the national context and current events of the play's production.

Kushner's other works continue to explore interpersonal dramas situated in a larger social, cultural, and political context of national and international events. *Homebody/Kabul,* written before the terrorist attacks of September 11, 2001, on the United States, was first produced a few months after the attacks. Because the play is set partly in Afghanistan and raises issues of Western powers in relation to Afghan politics and history, *Homebody/Kabul* was considered to be a prescient work. Set in 1998, Act I of the play introduces the Homebody, an elderly English housewife who recites an hour-long monologue in which she reads from an outdated travel book on Afghanistan and fantasizes about going to Kabul, where she makes love to an Afghan man. Act II takes place in a hotel room in Kabul, after the Homebody has traveled to Afghanistan and possibly been beaten to death for failing to observe the strict cultural codes of the Taliban regime. *Caroline, or Change* (2003), a musical, is set in the South during the Civil Rights era of the early 1960s, and concerns the relationship between a Jewish family and their African American maid, Caroline. Recent changes within the family structure are examined in the context of changes brewing in the South as a result of the Civil Rights Movement.

Kushner has also written a number of adaptations of plays by other authors. *Stella* (1987) is an eponymous adaptation of a play by German writer Johann Wolfgang von Goethe. *The Illusion* (1988) is adapted from the work by French playwright Pierre Corneille. *Widows*

(1991), co-written with Ariel Dorfman, is adapted from the novel by Dorfman. *The Good Person of Szechuan* (1997), adapted from a play by German playwright Bertolt Brecht, emphasizes the relevance of the original story to contemporary American society. *Dybbuk, or Between Two Worlds* (1997), adapted from the Yiddish play by S. Ansky, addresses questions of the impact of history on the notion of individual choice. The story concerns Leah, the daughter of a wealthy man who wishes to marry her off in the most profitable match he can find. In the end, the Dybbuk, a spirit character from Jewish mythology, possesses Leah's body and confronts her father about his moral failings.

CRITICAL RECEPTION

The initial critical response to *Angels in America* was overwhelmingly positive. Reviewers were impressed with Kushner's ability to address serious, current social and political issues—particularly gay identity politics in the era of the AIDS epidemic—while providing entertaining, humorous material that is accessible to mainstream Broadway audiences. The initial wave of essays on *Angels in America* from academic critics was equally laudatory. These critics explored the complexities of Kushner's representation of gay identity in the broader context of American domestic and international politics. Kushner was applauded for his representation of the intersections of gay and Jewish identity, as well as his examination of the relationship between individual experience and the collective interests of the broader human community. Critics were also impressed with Kushner's examination of the historical past in relation to current political issues. More recent criticism of *Angels in America* from the academic sector, however, has pointed out contradictions in its ideological underpinnings. Some have censured what appears to be a subversive political message in *Angels in America,* asserting that the play ultimately expresses a complacent political attitude that is easy for popular audiences to accept without truly challenging their values. Some feminist critics have argued that *Angels in America* relegates women to marginal status as opposed to the privileging of gay male identity. Despite these criticisms, however, Kushner is widely recognized as one of the most important playwrights of his generation—an openly gay, Jewish, and political writer unafraid of addressing contentious social issues with ambitious productions that offer a sense of hope for the future of humanity.

PRINCIPAL WORKS

Yes, Yes, No, No (play) 1985
A Bright Room Called Day (play) 1987
Hydriotaphia, or, The Death of Dr. Browne (play) 1987

Stella [adapted from the drama by Johann Wolfgang von Goethe] (play) 1987
The Illusion [adapted from the play *L'illusion comique* by Pierre Corneille] (play) 1988
Angels in America: A Gay Fantasia on National Themes, Part One: Millennium Approaches (play) 1991
Widows [co-adaptor with Ariel Dorfman from the book by Dorfman] (play) 1991
Angels in America: A Gay Fantasia on National Themes, Part Two: Perestroika (play) 1992
Plays by Tony Kushner [comprised of *A Bright Room Called Day* and *The Illusion*] (plays) 1992
Slavs! Thinking about the Longstanding Problems of Virtue and Happiness (play) 1995
Thinking about the Longstanding Problems of Virtue and Happiness: Essays, a Play, Two Poems, and a Prayer (miscellany) 1995
Dybbuk; or, Between Two Worlds [adapted from Joachim Neugroschel's translation of the original play by S. Ansky] (play) 1997
The Good Person of Szechuan [adapted from the play *Der gute Mensch von Setzuan* by Bertolt Brecht] (play) 1997
Tony Kushner in Conversation [edited by Robert Vorlicky] (interviews) 1997
Henry Box Brown, or the Mirror of Slavery (play) 1998
Plays by Tony Kushner [comprised of *A Bright Room Called Day*; *The Illusion*; and *Slavs! Thinking about the Longstanding Problems of Virtue and Happiness*] (plays) 1999
Death and Taxes: Hydriotaphia and Other Plays [comprised of *Hydriotaphia*; *Reverse Transcription*; *Terminating, or Sonnet LXXV, or, Las meine; Schmerzen nicht verloren sein, or Ambivalence*; *East Coast Ode to Howard Jarvis*; and *David Schinne in Hell*] (plays) 2000
Homebody/Kabul (play) 2001
Caroline, or Change (musical) 2003
Brundibar [illustrated by Maurice Sendak] (children's book) 2003
The Art of Maurice Sendak: 1980 to the Present [with illustrations by Maurice Sendak] (nonfiction) 2003

CRITICISM

Edward Norden (essay date January 1995)

SOURCE: Norden, Edward. "From Schnitzler to Kushner." *Commentary* 99, no. 1 (January 1995): 51-8.

[*In the following essay, Norden discusses the ideological implications of Jewish gay identity in* Angels in America.]

The good-looking young men cruising the aisles were putting on a show of their own. "Questionnaires!" they sang as they handed out pink forms to everybody. "Get your questionnaires!" The curtain of the Walter Kerr theater on Broadway would not be going up on this performance of **Millennium Approaches,** Part 1 of **Angels in America,** before everyone in the audience did his or her duty. If the **Angels** scripts, T-shirts, and baseball caps in the foyer were yours to buy or not, the questionnaire verged on mandatory.

And so the Jewish Long Islanders making up the bulk of the house, plus the corn-fed Midwesterners and Japanese tourists glad to be at this first half of Tony Kushner's seven-hour "Gay Fantasia," the hottest thing for two seasons running; yielded up the desired information as cheerfully as if they were doing a painless good deed. "Where," for example, "do you currently reside?" Followed by: "Please indicate which of the following factors or sources of influence you were aware of regarding **Angels in America,** and then the degree each factor was influential to your decision" to come. Tony Award for Best Play of 1993? Of 1994? Personal recommendation? Advertising?

Only after the mainly straight audience finished complying, and the ushers, at least one of them wearing a *yarmulke,* gathered the data, would the lights be killed.

One of the few audience members not cooperating, I was musing instead about the life, times, and work of a long-dead playwright as I waited. That playwright was Arthur Schnitzler, who used to be mentioned in the same breath as his fellow turn-of-the-century Jewish Viennese trailblazers: Theodor Herzl, Sigmund Freud, Gustav Mahler. But today, if Schnitzler's name rings any bell at all in pre-millennial America, it is as the author of *Dance in a Circle,* and this because a harmless travesty of his play entitled *La Ronde* was filmed in 1950 by Max Ophuls.

The idea of *Dance in a Circle/La Ronde* is fairly uncomplicated—The Prostitute meets The Soldier meets The Housemaid meets The Young Gentleman, and so on, the before-and-after dialogues of ten loveless heterosexual couplings up and down the social pyramid until with The Count and The Prostitute we are back again where we started. The copulations are never enacted on stage, needless to say, but only indicated with blackouts. Among the post-copulatory exchanges:

THE ACTRESS:

Count, you have done me a great honor.

THE COUNT:

I kiss your hand, *Fraulein.*

Probably few Americans who saw *Hello Again,* a short-lived musical by Michael John LaChiusa Off-Broadway recently, knew that his daisy chain of gay and lesbian

brief encounters was modeled on the same little Schnitzler play which first was banned and then, when put on, caused riots in Vienna and Berlin. Of course, the situation today is different in both those cities. There, unlike here, Schnitzler is well enough known, although it is an open question how much of his popularity is on account of his various works and how much due to nostalgia for a culture and its makers run out of town or exterminated by the grandparents of today's Viennese and Berliners themselves.

Was there anyone bending over a questionnaire in the Walter Kerr who did not know that *Angels* is the great AIDS play? Hard to imagine, even of the visitors from Osaka. As for Schnitzler and his contemporaries, they had something else to worry about. Public-health statistics a century ago were not what they are today; nevertheless, the overall incidence of syphilis in the capital of the Hapsburg empire in 1895 was probably between 15 and 30 percent.

"He who knows syphilis," William Osler had declared, "knows medicine." In other words, because the infection could hide for years before exploding in any organ of the body, and could impersonate diseases from mononucleosis to ringworm, it seemed the disease of diseases, the master disease. The filthy part, for Victorians, was its principal mode of transmission, and the hideous part, for anyone, was that mothers-to-be infected their unborn children.

Fifty years later, Stefan Zweig, a famous Jewish humanist and pacifist in his day, would write in his memoirs of Vienna:

> To the fear of infection was added the horror of the disgusting and degrading forms of the erstwhile cures. . . . For weeks on end the entire body of anyone infected with syphilis was rubbed with mercury, the effect of which was that the teeth fell out and other injuries to health ensued. The unhappy victim of a severe encounter felt himself not only physically but spiritually spotted, and even after so horrible a cure, he could never be certain that the cunning virus might not at any moment awake from its captivity and paralyze the limbs from the spine, or soften the brain.

Never in his many plays on the ways of heterosexuality in a bad society does Schnitzler more than very fleetingly hint at syphilis. Himself a doctor and a doctor's son, a Jew in terrifically anti-Semitic Vienna, the playwright had enough on his hands without breaking the VD taboo, *à la* Ibsen uniquely in *Ghosts.* It would have been very unwise for him to lay out how each character in the dance could well have infected the next, as foolish as it would have been to dig into the interconnected subjects of homosexuality, treason, and hatred of Jews in the upper reaches of the army of the emperor.

Schnitzler was brave, not crazy. As it was, he was put down as a decadent Jew for these sex plays, and as a pacifist traitor for his treatment of the near-holy institution of dueling. There was really nothing of the demon about Schnitzler, as there certainly was about his Viennese contemporaries Karl Kraus, the gemlike Jewish anti-Semite, or about the ineffable Otto Weininger, dead at twenty-three by his own hand—or, for that matter, as there was about Strindberg or Wedekind or Ibsen. The feeling about his plays, even when they climax in suicide as they often do, is sadder than it is tragic. A Schnitzler play is nicely-made, deceptively casual, oppressive rather than shattering. His virtues are those of rationality, detachment, humaneness: the perishable virtues of a doctor, with a strong dash of wit and implicit loathing for bourgeois hypocrisy thrown in.

But this did not keep his public or his enemies from misunderstanding him with a vengeance. That public, Schnitzler's core hometown audience flocking to what it liked to think were his amoral sex plays, was mostly Jewish. As Zweig was to remember: "The Jewish bourgeoisie . . . were the real audience, they filled the theaters." This audience was not especially interested in treatments of the anti-Semitism it tried to live with, and Schnitzler, having a good enough instinct for self-preservation, brought the topic up on stage only once, in *Professor Bernhardi.* Since (in contrast to Freud) he loved Vienna more than he hated it, one might say it was a good thing he died in 1931, seven years before a certain syphilophobic ex-tramp rode back into the city to the joy of that majority of its citizens which had always thought Schnitzler and his kind were dirty wreckers.

In *Mein Kampf,* without naming Schnitzler or any other writer, Hitler had labeled the Viennese theater of his youth "trashy . . . awful . . . unclean . . . obscene." Summed up the Nazi paper *Der Völkischer Beobachter* on Schnitzler's death: "Refined Jewish decadence."

Showtime finally on West 48th Street. The curtain goes up on a white-bearded hasidic rabbi, played by an actress. So intensively has **Angels in America** been publicized that the only revelations are going to be seemingly minor touches like this one, plus the feel of the production, including the currents passing back and forth between stage and audience.

Projected over the stage is the date of Act 1: October-November 1985. The bearded woman stands next to a coffin draped with a Star of David. In an unconvincing Yiddish accent, she (he?) is eulogizing one Sarah Ironson:

> . . . not a person but a whole kind of person, the ones who crossed the ocean, who brought with us to America the villages of Russia and Lithuania—and how we

struggled, and how we fought, for the family, for the Jewish home, so that you would not grow up *here,* in this strange place, in the melting pot where nothing melted. Descendants of this immigrant woman, you do not grow up in America, you and your children and their children with their *goyische* names. You do not live in America. No such place exists. Your clay is the clay of some Litvak *shtetl,* your air the air of the steppes—because she carried the old world on her back across the ocean, in a boat, and she put it down on Grand Concourse Avenue, or in Flatbush, and she worked that earth into your bones, and you pass it to your children, this ancient, ancient culture and home.

To repeat: the audience to whom Rabbi Isidor Chemelwitz addresses himself (herself) as to the family of the deceased is three-fourths suburban-Jewish. But on the whole this audience does not seem to understand how to take him (her) or the speech. As irony? As camp? As given? But this opening note will turn out to have been struck deliberately, for both the veil of ambiguity and the Jewish element are going to figure throughout both parts of the marathon *Angels.*

The very next scene gives us the excellent F. Murray Abraham as the late Roy Cohn, working the phones while tempting a young blond Mormon law clerk named Joe Pitt to take a job at the Justice Department in order to help block Cohn's disbarment. It is first-class *shtick.* By ten minutes into *Millennium Approaches,* several things have been established: a rapid-fire, high-decibel campy wisecracking performance style which the audience usually manages to love; the widest possible terms of reference on the part of the playwright, Tony Kushner; and the aura of some kind of existential affinity between gayness and Jewishness, at least today's native American Jewishness.

On this last point: if the devilish Cohn with his Yiddishisms will provide the most delectable moments of two long evenings out, another chief thread of a very tangled plot is introduced when the lead character, Louis Ironson, after the funeral service for his grandmother, is overwhelmed by the sight of his Wasp lover's first lesion. Will Louis ditch Walter Prior? Or will he be a *mentsh* and stay? The great play of AIDS is also going to be Jewish, in its way.

So what else is new? Though Kushner is more ambitious than his predecessors, his "fantasia" is but the latest in a tidal wave of homosexual New York plays by Jewish sons, going back almost a quarter-century.

True, not all the gay plays of the past 25 years have been written by Jews. An incomplete list of the nots would include Mart Crowley's pioneering *The Boys in the Band*; the works of Terrence McNally; David Drake's *The Night Larry Kramer Kissed Me*; *T-Shirts* by Robert Patrick; *Fifth of July* by Lanford Wilson; and the late Robert Chesley's raunchy *Jerker, or The Helping Hand* and his *Night Sweat,* the first AIDS play.

However, when in the Roaring 70's a new industry of unmasked, self-respecting, innocent, or agitational homosexual plays, based in Greenwich Village but with Shubert Alley in its crosshairs, was founded, this was done mainly by writers of Jewish extraction doing nothing to pass.

There was, for instance, *Passing By,* a 1972 Off-Broadway work by Martin Sherman. The new innocence and naturalness here are such that when Toby gives Simon hepatitis, they savor being ill together, getting well, and splitting, no hard feelings and close to none of the usual suicidal impulses. Toby is given to exclaiming, "Feh!" Sherman's equally didactic *Bent* (1979) has Max, a prisoner at Dachau, exchanging his yellow star for a pink triangle before walking into the electrified fence. *Bent* made it to Broadway, where the *Times*'s Walter Kerr found it "strong."

Harvey Fierstein also carried the message of gay self-acceptance uptown to the straight audiences, first in his *Torch Song Trilogy,* then in the smash drag musical for which he wrote the book, *La Cage Aux Folles* (1983). His Arnold Beckoff in *Trilogy* is a vulnerable, feisty queen in love with Ed, a bisexual Gentile who is unwilling, at first anyway, to leave his wife.

Among the memorable scenes in *Trilogy,* which first played downtown in 1978, is one where Arnold is penetrated anally in the orgy room of a bar while keeping up his patter and smoking a cigarette. The scene is played in the dark but is supposed to have nothing grim about it. Even his mother, "the Rita Hayworth of Brighton Beach," finally has to accept Arnold for what he is, the avatar of an overdue change in our society. Fierstein himself, in the role of Arnold, netted Tonys for both best play and best actor when the show moved to Broadway in 1982. There it joined *Falsettos* by William Finn and James Lapine, a tale in *Sprechstimme* of a New York husband and father, Marvin, who leaves his wife and child for the half-Jewish, very athletic Whizzer.

None of these Jewish-homosexual plays, where *kvetching* is in and self-loathing and menace out, is dramatically in the same league as Crowley's *The Boys in the Band,* not to mention closeted works like Tennessee Williams's *A Streetcar Named Desire* or Edward Albee's *Who's Afraid of Virginia Woolf?* They are, *Bent* included, more akin to second-rate cabaret, with or without music, and the Jewish element never goes much beyond the simple matter of fact and a certain domesticated style. But they served a vital function in the rise of the "crossover" play. Broadway producers ascertained that straight audiences would shell out, not to patronize or sneer at but to empathize with uncloseted stage gays who bled a little when pricked a little, and laughed when tickled.

So long, that is, as the "life-style" of gay liberation was not depicted too realistically. The cocaine snorting and no-tomorrow sadomasochistic orgying, down to which liberation was boiling, and which the Jewish writer-activist Larry Kramer fixed with disapproving eye in his in-group novel *Faggots* (1978), did not travel uptown. What traveled, and began disarming the general culture, was the schmaltzy version which Jewish boys were better at cooking up than *goyim.*

It therefore was not so astonishing that when the AIDS virus crashed the party, and a different type of crossover play had to be written, it turned out even more "Jewish" than before. The AIDS dramas by Jews which have come out so far, and which *Angels* epitomizes while aiming to transcend, make a genre topical as the obituary page, stylized as the Passion plays of Oberammergau.

Always the scene is Manhattan. The homosexual couple nearly always consists of a Jew and a Gentile, and conventionally the Gentile is the one who falls ill. (Exceptions: the suicide Reuben in Jean-Claude van Itallie's *Ancient Boys*; the interfaith lovers in Fierstein's *Safe Sex,* both frightened but neither yet sick; the yuppies Peter and Drew in Richard Greenberg's *Eastern Standard,* both of indeterminate ethnicity.) Will the Jewish partner in the conventional scheme obey the golden rule? Or will he run? From this problem springs the genre's dramatic tension, such as it is, beginning with the problematical Larry Kramer's own *The Normal Heart* (1985).

In that play, the emotional Ned Weeks, Kramer's alter ego, does stick by the dying Felix. In fact, they "marry" in the final scene in the hospital. In *As Is* by William Hoffman (also 1985), Saul not only tells Rich, "I'll be here for you no matter what happens," but in the last hospice scene climbs into bed with him, albeit behind a drawn curtain. Likewise in the 1990 sequel to *Falsettos* entitled *Falsettoland,* set in a time when "something very bad is happening"; there, Marvin not only comforts the dying Whizzer but is joined by his understanding ex-wife, her new shrink husband, and the lesbian neighbors for the bar mitzvah of the son, performed as a rousing finale around the hospital bed. No second thoughts, no true irony, no bad feelings.

By 1993 and *Jeffrey,* whose author is the self-described "nice Jewish boy" Paul Rudnick, it was predictable that the talkative, brave, sensitive, HIV-negative hero, fearfully pledged to abstinence and transparently disguised as a Roman Catholic, would see the light and go with buff, HIV-positive Steve. In short, when Felix, Rich, Whizzer, and Steve die, Ned, Saul, Marvin, and Jeffrey are going to have the right, the moral right, to publish their names in the obituary notices as loyal companions.

What about Louis Ironson? This is a question that remains unanswered for most of the combined 420 minutes of *Angels.*

Louis is a *shmendrick.* He is given to such talk as

> *Jeane Kirkpatrick* for God's sake will go on and on about freedom, when she talks about it, or human rights; you have Bush talking about human rights . . . these people don't begin to know what, ontologically, freedom is. . . . And what I think is that what AIDS shows us is the limits of tolerance.

The question whether Louis will stand by Walter Prior, his Wasp lover, and then whether, having abandoned him, he will be allowed to return, is one of three plots set in motion in **Millennium Approaches** and clumsily developed into the year 1986 in Part 2, **Perestroika.** Intersecting this is the story of Joe Pitt, the closeted Mormon Reaganite living in Brooklyn, his psychotically heterosexual wife, and his mother who flies in from Salt Lake City attempting to save the marriage after Louis guesses Joe's true nature. Third and foremost is the story, and presence, of Roy Cohn as quintessential McCarthyite and gay-bashing New York closet homosexual *macher.*

As biographies by Sidney Zion and Nicholas von Hoffman tell us, the real-life Cohn during his final months was indeed preoccupied with escaping disbarment, and was indeed claiming to be dying of something other than the gay disease. In *Angels,* when informed by the doctor that he has AIDS, he replies: "Homosexuals are not men who sleep with other men. Homosexuals are men who . . . have zero clout." Hence it is not possible for Cohn to have AIDS. This by-now famous line is one of Kushner's inventions.

Another is the ghost of the atom spy Ethel Rosenberg, who shows up at Cohn's hospital deathbed to taunt him for his role in the prosecution of her and her husband Julius more than 30 years before. Still another is the trademarked angel, descending over Walter Prior's bed with the words: "Greetings Prophet!" to close Part 1.

The sequel has Prior saying, "Maybe I am a prophet. Not just me, all of us who are dying now." During this evening he is befriended by the mother of Joe Pitt; Joe leaves his wife for Louis and refuses to help Cohn; Joe is left by Louis, who is guilt-ridden over having abandoned Prior. Cohn is ejected from the bar and noisily dies, the very sick Prior wrestles the angel for a blessing, curses God during a visit to heaven for "all the terrible days of this terrible century," and in an epilogue dated 1990 apparently has permitted Louis to return to keep him company.

Dramatically, *Angels* is much wind-up, little delivery. The play's champions have touted its grab-bag formlessness as itself definitively American, and it is true that everything including the kitchen sink gets in before the final curtain, giving the impression not only of expansiveness but even of a tolerant ambiguity on religion and unbelief, selfishness and loyalty. Right and Left. Even those puzzled by the seeming chaos get a lot for their money. Both evenings move along, thanks to director George C. Wolfe, to much stage business, and especially to the character of Roy Cohn—a Jewish monster beyond good and evil.

Cohn is the only really interesting figure in *Angels,* the only nontype. An anti-*shmendrick,* the opposite of Louis, he runs away with the show. Louis, meanwhile, is Kushner's alter ego, a gay, hyper, Jewish liberal-radical tripped up only occasionally by a hospital nurse, a flaming black queen with a perfect ear and great campy lines.

Although he blathers a great deal, and is sometimes a hypocritical coward, Louis's politics and sexual behaviors are, as far as Kushner is concerned, and we are supposed to concur, right on. The general rule in this play is that Kushner's ambiguities are quite studied—one understands where the playwright stands. A single lapse in the park aside, Louis could not be wiser or more generous sexually, as when he rescues Mormon Joe from the closet and they finally get together on the Lower East Side, the same neighborhood. Louis does not fail to say, where "the Jews lived when they first arrived." Joe has come to him but still hesitates. Louis is gently implacable. "Sometimes," he reassures the uptight conservative lawyer, "even if it scares you to death, you have to be willing to break the law." Kushner's stage directions: "Louis slips his hand down the front of Joe's pants . . . Louis pulls his hand out, smells and tastes his fingers, and then holds them for Joe to smell."

Rapt silences from the dark side of the footlights alternate with hurricanes of friendly laughter throughout *Angels.* Thus, when actor Dan Futterman as Louis elaborately follows the stage directions here, the audience is captivated. And no one has earlier protested, much less rioted, when Louis kneels, spotlighted, pants down, to be taken by a Central Park stranger in leather. "Infect me," he says not very wisely. "I don't care."

But that is the weak Louis. The strong Louis is the one who leads Joe with a firm hand out of the wilderness of heterosexual marriage into the promised land of homosexual lovemaking.

LOUIS:

> I don't believe in God. I think you should know that before we fuck again.

To which Joe, with him in bed, responds, "I love you."

No one makes a demonstrative exit from the theater during this scene, either. Or any other. A collective intake of breath for the naked, wasted Christ-like body of Prior (Stephen Spinella) with its painted-on sores. Laughter for the punch-line when Louis asks Isidor Chemelwitz: "Rabbi, what does the Holy Writ say about someone who abandons someone he loves at a time of great need?"

RABBI:

> . . . You want to confess, better you should find a priest.

LOUIS:

> But I'm not a Catholic, I'm a Jew.

RABBI:

> Worse luck for you, bubbelah. Catholics believe in forgiveness. Jews believe in guilt.

Or again, when his baffled, earnest, desperate wife is telling Joe about her day: "I heard on the radio how to give a blow job. . . . It was a little Jewish lady with a German accent." A tremendous knowing shriek, no one pausing to wonder how Dr. Ruth's size can be inferred from the radio.

And delight for the burning letters of the Hebrew alphabet, part of the stage design. Readers of the Sunday *New York Times* entertainment section have been instructed by Kushner that

> Hebrew is a language of great antiquity and mystery, and of great compression. Each letter, each word encompasses innumerable meanings, good and evil. The physical letters are themselves totems, objects of power. The Torah, the Book, is to be treated with veneration. Here is another Mormon-Jewish connection: both are people of the Book—only very different books.

If anyone in the theater thinks Kushner treats either the Jewish or the Mormon book with less than veneration, and is upset by that, he keeps it to himself. More laughter for a diorama at the Mormon visitors' center, where Joe's mother drags his wife. And the hugest laugh of all, for this:

BELIZE [THE BLACK QUEEN]:

> Guess who just checked in with the troubles? The Killer Queen Herself. New York's number-one closeted queer.

PRIOR:

> *Koch?*

The laughter has a more knowing edge to it than at *Millennium Approaches.* This is because, although suburban Jews predominate on both evenings, a much larger cohort of with-it Manhattan gays shows up for

Perestroika. No doubt all have already seen Part 1, and every bit of camp is picked up instantly. But more ghosts hover during Evening Two than Evening One. These are the spirits of the youngish men, often beautiful to look at, sometimes gifted, who died piteously in the past decade, just as some in the audience who knew, loved, abandoned, were unfaithful or faithful to, and nursed and wept over them know they also will die in the next decade unless a cure is found. The air especially at Evening Two is consequently shot through with grief, dread, and bravely stylish good humor, with sentiments of community, and also of resentment of something out there in America.

The mood, improbably, embraces the dying Roy Cohn as well. Throughout Part 2, anticipation of the next scene with him offsets incipient longueurs.

ROY:

> I don't trust this hospital. For all I know Lillian fucking *Hellman* is down in the basement switching the pills around.

A thunderclap of laughter. "I pleaded till I wept to put her in the chair," Cohn tells Joe. "Her" is Ethel Rosenberg again, whose ghost, like the Commendatore's in *Don Giovanni,* materializes to say, "Be seeing you soon, Roy. Julius sends his regards. . . . History is about to crack wide open." Having enjoyed him, the audience relishes Cohn's writhing exit quite as much as does Ethel, whom Kushner has say: "I came to forgive but all I can do is take pleasure in your misery. . . . And when you die all anyone will say is: better he had never lived at all."

What follows is probably as definitive a first on Broadway as the mimed sodomy earlier. Asked by the black nurse to do the right thing and say kaddish over the body, Louis is willing but ignorantly unable. Whereupon the shade of Ethel Rosenberg, played by the same actress who did the hasidic rabbi, intones the entire Aramaic prayer, Louis with a Kleenex on his head stumbling behind. You can hear a pin drop.

The epilogue, set at the Bethesda Fountain in Central Park, with its stone angel, has the ill but surviving Prior, Louis, the black queen, and Joe's mother, all reconciled. "This disease," Prior says to the audience in an envoi shedding the last veil of ambiguity and reminiscent of Clifford Odets at his agitprop best, "will be the end of many of us, but not nearly all, and the dead will be commemorated and will struggle on with the living, and we are not going away . . . *MORE LIFE* . . . The Great Work Begins."

Triggering a long stormy ovation and many curtain calls and leaving the dense and the unconverted to figure out what it all means.

Jewish homosexuals, famous and obscure, there have always been, including those who in the bad old days found ways to live unrepressed. The composer Ned Rorem, a non-Jew, tells in his memoirs of going home with one Morris Golde, "a brash, short, swarthy, muscular presence" from the Bronx, in prehistoric 1943. Later Rorem, who estimates having gone to bed with 3,000 men and several women, refers to "unsentimentally" obliging the anarchist poet-philosopher Paul Goodman, who "smelled of his baggy sweater and pipe smoke."

But this is old stuff. The art, fashion, music, publishing, and theater scenes were known by those who knew anything to be disproportionately Jewish and importantly gay many decades before Tony Kushner. Often enough, as in the Aaron Copland-Leonard Bernstein-Marc Blitzstein set, to which Rorem as a non-Jew won only partial entrée, the attributes of Jewishness and gayness overlapped, and were spiced by political fellow-traveling. The phenomenon is not new. The extent perhaps is.

Has the number of Jewish homosexuals taken a quantum leap, or is the increase simply apparent, the result of the closet having been vacated? Any bitterly unmarried, straight, non-Orthodox Jewish woman in the New York area yearning to marry in the faith and have children probably believes she can answer that one. It is not just that the closet is not what it used to be, she will tell you. No, the gay life has become positively fashionable among her generation of male Jews, and the absolute number of Jewish homosexuals has gone through the roof.

Here we enter uncharted territory. All the experts say that no matter what the group, and regardless of time and place, of repression or liberation, the ratio of men preferring men to those preferring women stays constant, and statistically minuscule. But what, our childless Jewish woman lawyer with a brother in the Village might ask, do they know? If the experts are right, how can it be that on any given Friday night, there may well be more worshippers at Beth Simchat Torah, the gay and lesbian *shul* downtown, than at any other synagogue or temple in the Diaspora? Go to the West Village after services on Friday night and see all these Jewish men having dinner with each other in candlelit Italian restaurants!

Don't get her wrong, she will add: a basher of homosexuals is the last thing she is. She retains a Jewish heart, she can't help admiring their stylish courage—her brother, thank God, remains HIV-negative. Moreover, her work takes her to other cities, where she has discovered smaller islands of the gay archipelago boasting a high percentage of Jews and has been told how these are raising property values in neighborhoods formerly given over to blight. Nevertheless, she's unhappy. She has the money, but not the time, for *Angels.*

Behind her and her frustration, and her brother, loom their parents, and one does not want to get her going on them. But there are many like her, you cannot avoid them unless you have nothing to do with Jewish women, and unless you pin everything on genetics; this raises a double question: has the American Jewish family of the last generation, a family more and more often with the father vanished, become a nursery for homosexual sons? And why have the many playwrights among them, with the exception of the intrepid Larry Kramer, shunned the family topic as if *it* were the real plague?

Kramer's *The Destiny of Me* (1992) is a sequel to *The Normal Heart.* In that first play, his *nudnik* of an alter ego, Ned Weeks, says, "We have simply fucked ourselves silly for years and years, and sometimes we've done it in the filthiest places." Now his Gentile lover has died, Ned himself is sick, and it is time to remember in a series of flashbacks what the playwright calls his own "journey to acceptance" of gayness. This means unearthing himself as a boy, unearthing his parents, and later the shrinks with names like Schwartz and Grossman who tried to "cure" him.

The Destiny of Me, like *The Normal Heart,* reveals that Kramer is no dramatist—his primary subject is himself, and he cannot get much distance from it. But at least he rummages openly in the past, agonizing over what he finds—something the ideology frowns on. It turns out Ned Weeks's father was hated by his artistic son, while the smothering mother was adored.

Ideological homosexuals were bound to give *The Destiny of Me* tepid reviews, despite Kramer's political standing as founder of ACT-UP. This dwelling on childhood and parents, like his earlier sermonizing against promiscuity, is extremely incorrect. It raises doubts whether he has truly told Drs. Schwartz and Grossman to go to hell. Much better for gay playwrights to leave childhood and puberty, mom and especially dad strictly out of their work.

This has so far been done by Tony Kushner, although he has confessed in one of numberless interviews that his own coming-out initiated "a family battle," and that his father took much longer to adjust than his mother, doing so only when *Angels* struck gold. In the play, Louis Ironson of course has parents and siblings—they are present in front of Rabbi Chemelwitz at the funeral of the grandmother. Explaining to Prior why he never visited this old lady at her nursing home, Louis says: "She looked too much like my mother."

And that is all, in seven hours, concerning his family. "Vast, sprawling, inclusive, wordy," Michael Feingold gushed in his review of *Angels* in the *Village Voice.* But while Ma Pitt comes on at length, and her deceased professional soldier husband, Joe's father, is thoroughly dissected, the Ironsons are kept out of sight and mind. Besides sparing Kushner's own family, this makes dramatic and ideological sense. The dramatic interest in *Angels* is Cohn, and the ideological message is that AIDS is more than a disease and that a homosexual perspective best comprehends reality and history. Bringing in Louis's family would have jeopardized everything.

In fact, in the beginning, *Angels* was to be a play about Cohn. The attractions for an ideological gay like Kushner are self-evident. What less obviously yet also compellingly makes Cohn's last days almost too good to be true is that he was such an anti-Communist.

Born three years after the Rosenbergs were electrocuted, Kushner is something of a red-diaper baby. Anyone with a nose in these matters can sniff it from *Angels,* but the playwright has come entirely clean in a credo published recently in—where else?—the *Nation.* It reads like nothing so much as one of Louis's expostulations. If American "capitalism" were to accommodate homosexuals by giving them equal rights, as it has every capability of doing, and if that were that, this in Kushner's eyes would be a tragedy. What profit from the struggle if gays end up with the same rights as heteros while the "free market" goes on savaging the world?

> Poverty, war, alienation, environmental destruction, colonialism, unequal development, boom/bust cycles, private property, individualism, commodity fetishism, the fetishization of the body, the fetishization of violence, guns, drugs, child abuse, underfunded and bad education (itself a form of child abuse)—these things are key to the successful functioning of the free market.

Homosexuals like Andrew Sullivan of the *New Republic* who are satisfied with tolerance are put down by Kushner as "assimilationists." This is quite a dirty word in some Jewish lexicons—but Kushner's teacher is neither Herzl nor any *rebbe.* It is Oscar Wilde, the preceptor of socialism with a gay face, "a socialism of the skin."

The notion that decadence is in the eye of the beholder, no more than an epithet for anything new in a culture which is feared by reactionaries, is always beguiling. "Decadence," said the critic Richard Gilman back in the 70's, in much the same words the ordinary professor of communications would use today, "is not a fact but a value judgment"—a judgment passed on the most forward-looking, actually the best, healthiest, most useful artists of the day. As for sex, conservatives always get hung up on this, naively or cynically identifying the sex in "decadent" art with paganism, and paganism with social breakdown.

To this, the straight butch lesbian Camille Paglia has entered a ringing plea of guilty: "Judeo-Christianity never did defeat paganism, which still flourishes in art, eroticism, astrology, and pop culture." According to Paglia, the eternal hallmark of decadence is the celebration of sexual perversion; and such decadence, long may it wave, continues to be with us because Christianity failed to destroy paganism, including "all theater, which is pagan showiness."

Paglia exaggerates. Not merely the celebration of perversion but blanket approval of the instincts and the love of death are what you have in truly pagan theater, and what you do not have in Shakespeare, Jonson, Chekhov, Schnitzler, Beckett, etc. Nevertheless, when Paglia vouches for a culture war going back 2,000 or 4,000 years and continuing into the future, attention should be paid. And we might remember, too, that Gore Vidal, saluted by Kushner as his mentor, has identified the great enemy today as homophobic monotheism. If such as Paglia and Vidal not only acknowledge paganism, but affirm the life-enhancing qualities of a pagan consciousness which squares, conservatives, and Bible-thumpers call decadent, where does Kushner's play fit in?

He implies the answer in his interviews—*Angels* is a play of gay ideology. Professors of that ideology agree that if straights are to be reeducated, their noses are going to have to be rubbed in it. They must be forced to look, not only at males kissing, but at the act itself, sex being the essence of this yet-to-be-fully-accepted way of life. "Sexual desire," states John Clum, a member of the deconstructionist and neo-Marxian English department at Duke, "is not the only dimension of the homosexual experience, but it is the core." To assert gay pride, and desensitize the heteros into acceptance, the lineaments of that desire gratifying itself have to be made visible. Among the beauties of *Angels* for Clum is that here, it happens.

But homosexual agitprop must not only render the gay way nonobjectionable. On this Clum is a more honest ideologue than Kushner. "In the past twenty years," writes the former, "homosexuality in drama has moved from shame-filled hints to proud assertion. Heterosexism, which used to be upheld as the norm, is now driven offstage." In other words, in order to accept gayness, the straight has to be led to the realization that his own way is a not-so-good one. Neither a good way of sex, nor a good way of imagining, of seeing and being in the world.

The ideology propagated directly by academics like Clum and indirectly by Kushner avows that imagination and sexuality grow one from the other, and that a distinctively homosexual imagination possesses the future. Gays, when free, *see* more clearly, powerfully, and inclusively than straights. No crossover play will do the job unless it sends the audience home with this new understanding. *Angels* is especially fine, says

Clum, because it "challenges the heterosexuals . . . to see with gay eyes."

What Clum somehow misses is that Kushner goes farther. He does to AIDS what Arthur Schnitzler, M.D. would never have dreamed of doing to any illness, let alone syphilis—he metaphorizes it. AIDS is shown as ghastly, but Prior comes to believe that having it endows him with the faculty of prophecy, is evidence of some kind of grace for "all of us who are dying now." And nothing believed in by this brave, together Wasp is to be dismissed by us.

It would be nice to know how many of those flocking to *Angels,* straights and for that matter homosexuals alike, buy the prophecy of a gay millennium. But one does not need an audience poll to feel that, ideological though *Angels* is, it is not, finally, pagan. A *New Yorker* profile reports that Kushner keeps a teddy bear among his possessions, and that seems right. Mimed homosexual acts notwithstanding, the fascination with Cohn notwithstanding, this play, like others of the genre, has a basically soft and cuddly, not a hard and Greco-Roman, feel about it.

However, *Variety* reports that the master director Robert Altman is bringing *Angels* to the screen. The Kushnerian view of America, sex, and the Jews is thus soon going to be available to the masses, and no doubt with its squishiness taken care of. At every multiplex where *Schindler's List* played last year, Americans will be offered the adventures of Roy, Louis, Joe, Prior, Ethel & Co., probably excluding the sodomy but including subtitled Yiddish, burning Hebrew letters, the f-word every 30 seconds, lesions, and kaddish, the whole *megillah* artistically riveting. Will the Academy of Motion Picture Arts and Sciences have the intestinal fortitude to bestow on the Altman version the Oscars guaranteeing it long, profitable, influential runs? Hard to say.

Uncertain, too, given this country's irritable mood, is the popular reception awaiting the movie when it opens. It is not inconceivable that at some malls the clean-cut will be out picketing what they apprehend is the brilliant glorification of pagan decadence. Should this happen, the ACLU will cite the First Amendment, while Jewish defense organizations, known among other things for their dutiful advocacy of gay rights, abortion-on-demand, and sex education, and for their reasoned opposition to prayer in school, will see no need but to keep mum.

For here is a salient difference between Europe in 1895 and our uniquely forgiving country 100 years later: Godfearing Christians, even the Puritans and the worse-than-uptight among them, those for whom AIDS is retribution from heaven, do not, whatever they mutter among themselves, publicly blame "the Jews" for anything. The ancient hateful conflation of homos, atheists, feminists, abortionists, Communists, and Jews is limited to the remoter gulches of Idaho that harbor the likes of the Aryan Nation. Everywhere else it is, and one hopes it will remain, beyond the American pale.

David Savran (essay date May 1995)

SOURCE: Savran, David. "Ambivalence, Utopia, and a Queer Sort of Materialism: How *Angels in America* Reconstructs the Nation." *Theatre Journal* 47, no. 2 (May 1995): 207-27.

[*In the following essay, Savran examines the ideological underpinnings of* Angels in America *in terms of the cultural, historical, and political context in which it was produced.*]

Critics, pundits, and producers have placed Tony Kushner's *Angels in America: A Gay Fantasia on National Themes* in the unenviable position of having to rescue the American theatre. The latter, by all accounts, is in a sorry state. It has attempted to maintain its elite cultural status despite the fact that the differences between "high" and "low" have become precarious. On Broadway, increasingly expensive productions survive more and more by mimicking mass culture, either in the form of mind-numbing spectacles featuring singing cats, falling chandeliers, and dancing dinner-ware or plays, like *The Heidi Chronicles* or *Prelude to a Kiss,* whose style and themes aspire to "quality" television. In regional theatres, meanwhile, subscriptions continue to decline, and with them the adventurousness of artistic directors. Given this dismal situation, *Angels in America* has almost singlehandedly resuscitated a category of play that has become almost extinct: the serious Broadway drama that is neither a British import nor a revival.

Not within memory has a new American play been canonized by the press as rapidly as *Angels in America.*[1] Indeed, critics have been stumbling over each other in an adulatory stupor. John Lahr hails *Perestroika* as a "masterpiece" and notes that "[n]ot since Williams has a playwright announced his poetic vision with such authority on the Broadway stage."[2] Jack Kroll judges both parts "the broadest, deepest, most searching American play of our time," while Robert Brustein deems *Millennium Approaches* "the authoritative achievement of a radical dramatic artist with a fresh, clear voice."[3] In the gay press, meanwhile, the play is viewed as testifying to the fact that "Broadway now leads the way in the industry with its unapologetic portrayals of gay characters."[4] For both Frank Rich and John Clum, *Angels* is far more than just a successful play; it is the marker of a decisive historical shift in American theatre. According to Rich, the play's success is in part the result of its ability to conduct "a searching and radical rethinking of the whole esthetic of American political drama."[5] For Clum, the play's appearance on Broadway "marks a turning point in the history of gay drama, the history of American drama, and of American literary culture."[6] In its reception, *Angels*—so deeply preoccupied with teleological process—is itself positioned as both the culmination of history and as that which rewrites the past.

Despite the enormity of the claims cited above, I am less interested in disputing them than in trying to understand why they are being made—and why *now*. Why is a play featuring five gay male characters being universalized as a "turning point" in the American theatre, and minoritized as the preeminent gay male artifact of the 1990s? Why is it both popular and "radical?" What is the linkage between the two primary sources for the play's theory of history and utopia— Walter Benjamin and Mormonism? And what does this linkage suggest about the constitution of the nation? Finally, why has queer drama become *the* theatrical sensation of the 1990s? I hope it's not too perverse of me to attempt to answer these questions by focusing less on the construction of queer subjectivities per se than on the field of cultural production in which *Angels in America* is situated. After all, how else would one practice a queer materialism?

THE ANGEL OF HISTORY

The opposite of nearly everything you say about *Angels in America* will also hold true: *Angels* valorizes identity politics; it offers an anti-foundationalist critique of identity politics. *Angels* mounts an attack against ideologies of individualism; it problematizes the idea of community. *Angels* submits liberalism to a trenchant examination; it finally opts for yet another version of American liberal pluralism. *Angels* launches a critique of the very mechanisms that produce pathologized and acquiescent female bodies; it represents yet another pathologization and silencing of women. A conscientious reader or spectator might well rebuke the play, as Belize does Louis: "you're ambivalent about everything."[7] And so it is. The play's ambivalence, however, is not simply the result of Kushner hedging his bets on the most controversial issues. Rather, it functions, I believe—quite independently of the intent of its author—as the play's political unconscious, playing itself out on many different levels: formal, ideological, characterological, and rhetorical. (Frank Rich refers to this as Kushner's "refusal to adhere to any theatrical or political theory."[8]) Yet the fact that ambivalence—or undecidability—is the watchword of this text (which is, after all, *two* plays) does not mean that all the questions it raises remain unresolved. On the contrary, I will argue that the play's undecidability is, in fact, always already resolved because the questions that appear to be

ambivalent in fact already have been decided consciously or unconsciously by the text itself. Moreover, the relentless operation of normalizing reading practices works to reinforce these decisions. If I am correct, the play turns out (*pace* Frank Rich) to adhere all too well to a particular political theory.

Formally, *Angels* is a promiscuously complicated play that is very difficult to categorize generically. Clum's characterization of it as being "like a Shakespearean romance" is doubtlessly motivated by the play's rambling and episodic form, its interweaving of multiple plotlines, its mixture of realism and fantasy, its invocation of various theological and mythological narratives, as well as by its success in evoking those characteristics that are usually associated with both comedy and tragedy.[9] Moreover, *Perestroika*'s luminous finale is remarkably suggestive of the beatific scenes that end Shakespeare's romances. There is no question, moreover, but that the play deliberately evokes the long history of Western dramatic literature and positions itself as heir to the traditions of Sophocles, Shakespeare, Brecht, and others. Consider, for example, its use of the blindness/ insight opposition and the way that Prior Walter is carefully constructed (like the blind Prelapsarianov) as a kind of Tiresias, "going blind, as prophets do."[10] This binarism, the paradigmatic emblem of the tragic subject (and mark of Tiresias, Oedipus, and Gloucester) deftly links cause and effect—because one is blind to truth, one loses one's sight—and is used to claim Prior's priority, his epistemologically privileged position in the text. Or consider the parallels often drawn in the press between Kushner's Roy Cohn and Shakespeare's Richard III.[11] Or Kushner's use of a fate motif, reminiscent of *Macbeth,* whereby Prior insists that Louis not return until the seemingly impossible comes to pass, until he sees Louis "black and blue" (2:89). Or Kushner's rewriting of those momentous moral and political debates that riddle not just classical tragedy (*Antigone, Richard II*) but also the work of Brecht and his (mainly British) successors (Howard Brenton, David Hare, Caryl Churchill). Or the focus on the presence/absence of God that one finds not just in early modern tragedy but also in so-called Absurdism (Beckett, Ionesco, Stoppard). Moreover, these characteristics tend to be balanced, on the one hand, by the play's insistent tendency to ironize and, on the other, by the familiar ingredients of romantic comedies (ill-matched paramours, repentant lovers, characters suddenly finding themselves in unfamiliar places, plus a lot of good jokes). Despite the ironic/comic tone, however, none of the interlaced couples survives the onslaught of chaos, disease, and revelation. Prior and Louis, Louis and Joe, Joe and Harper have all parted by the end of the play and the romantic dyad (as primary social unit) is replaced in the final scene of *Perestroika* by a utopian concept of (erotic) affiliation and a new definition of family.

Angels in America's title, its idea of utopia, and its model for a particular kind of ambivalence are derived in part from Benjamin's extraordinary meditation, "Theses on the Philosophy of History," written shortly before his death in 1940. Composed during the first months of World War II, with fascism on its march across Europe, the darkness (and simultaneous luminosity) of Benjamin's "Theses" attest not only to the seeming invincibility of Hitler, but also to the impossible position of the European left, "[s]tranded," as Terry Eagleton notes, "between social democracy and Stalinism."[12] In this essay, Benjamin sketches a discontinuous theory of history in which "the services of theology" are enlisted in the aid of reconceiving "historical materialism."[13] Opposing the universalizing strategies of bourgeois historicism with historical materialism's project of brushing "history against the grain" (257), he attempts a radical revision of Marxist historiography. Suturing the Jewish notion of Messianic time (in which all history is given meaning retrospectively by the sudden and unexpected coming of the Messiah) to the Marxist concept of revolution, Benjamin reimagines proletariat revolution not as the culmination of a conflict between classes, or between traditional institutions and new forms of production, but as a "blast[ing] open" of "the continuum of history" (262). Unlike traditional Marxist (or idealist) historiographers, he rejects the idea of the present as a moment of "transition" and instead conceives it as *Jetztzeit:* "time filled by the presence of the now" (261), a moment in which "time stands still and has come to a stop" (262). Facing *Jetztzeit,* and opposing all forms of gradualism, Benjamin's historical materialist is given the task not of imagining and inciting progressive change (or a movement toward socialism), but of "blast[ing] a specific era out of the homogeneous course of history" (263).

The centerpiece of Benjamin's essay is his explication of a painting by Paul Klee, which becomes a parable of history, of the time of the Now, in the face of catastrophe (which for him means all of human history):

> A Klee painting named "Angelus Novus" shows an angel looking as though he is about to move away from something he is fixedly contemplating. His eyes are staring, his mouth is open, his wings are spread. This is how one pictures the angel of history. His face is turned toward the past. Where we perceive a chain of events, he sees one single catastrophe which keeps piling wreckage upon wreckage and hurls it in front of his feet. The angel would like to stay, awaken the dead, and make whole what has been smashed. But a storm is blowing from Paradise; it has got caught in his wings with such violence that the angel can no longer close them. This storm irresistibly propels him into the future to which his back is turned, while the pile of debris before him grows skyward. This storm is what we call progress.

[257-58]

In Benjamin's allegory, with its irresolvable play of contradictions, the doggedly well-intentioned angel of history embodies both the inconceivability of progress and the excruciating condition of the Now. Poised (not unlike Benjamin himself in Europe in 1940) between the past, which is to say "catastrophe," and an unknown and terrifying future, he is less a heavenly actor than a passive observer, "fixedly contemplating" that disaster which is the history of the world. His "Paradise," meanwhile, is not the site of a benign utopianism but a "storm" whose "violence" gets caught under his wings and propels him helplessly into an inconceivable future that stymies his gaze.

Benjamin's allegory of history is, in many respects, the primary generative fiction for *Angels in America.* Not only is its Angel clearly derived from Benjamin's text (although with gender reassignment surgery along the way—Kushner's Angel is "Hermaphroditically Equipped"), but so is its vision of Heaven, which has *"a deserted, derelict feel to it,"* with *"rubble . . . strewn everywhere"* (2:48; 121). And the play's conceptualizations of the past, of catastrophe, and of utopia are clearly inflected by Benjamin's "Theses," as is its linkage between historical materialism and theology. Moreover, rather than attempt to suppress the contradictions that inform Benjamin's materialist theology, Kushner expands them. As a result, the ideas of history, progress, and paradise that *Angels in America* invokes are irreducibly contradictory (often without appearing to be so). Just as Benjamin's notion of revolution is related dialectically to catastrophe, so are *Angel*'s concepts of deliverance and abjection, ecstasy and pain, utopia and dystopia, necessarily linked. Kushner's Angel (and her/his heaven) serve as a constant reminder both of catastrophe (AIDS, racism, homophobia, and the pathologization of queer and female bodies, to name only the play's most obvious examples) and of the perpetual possibility of millennium's approach, or in the words of Ethel Rosenberg (unmistakably echoing Benjamin), that "[h]istory is about to crack wide open" (1:112). And the concept of utopia/dystopia to which s/he is linked guarantees that the vehicle of hope and redemption in *Angels*—the prophet who foresees a new age—will be the character who must endure the most agony: Prior Walter, suffering from AIDS and Louis's desertion.

Within the economy of utopia/dystopia that *Angels* installs, the greatest promise of the millennium is the possibility of life freed from the shackles of hatred, oppression, and disease. It is hardly surprising, therefore, that Roy Cohn is constructed as the embodiment and guarantor of dystopia. Not only is he the paradigm of bourgeois individualism—and Reaganism—at its most murderous, hypocritical, and malignant, but he is the one with the most terrifying vision of the "universe," which he apprehends "as a kind of sandstorm in outer space with winds of mega-hurricane velocity, but instead of grains of sand it's shards and splinters of glass" (1:13). It is, however, a sign of the play's obsessively dialectical structure that Roy's vision of what sounds like hell should provide an uncanny echo of Benjamin's "storm blowing from Paradise." Yet even this dialectic, much like the play's ambivalences, is deceptive insofar as its habit of turning one pole of a binarism relentlessly into its opposite (rather than into a synthesis) describes a false dialectic. Prior, on the other hand, refusing the role of victim, becomes the sign of the unimaginable, of "[t]he Great Work" (2:148). Yet, as with Roy, so Prior's privileged position is a figure of contradiction, coupling not just blindness with prophecy, but also history with an impossible future, an ancient lineage (embodied by Prior 1 and Prior 2) with the millennium yet to come, and AIDS with a "most inner part, entirely free of disease" (1:34). Moreover, Prior's very name designates his temporal dislocation, the fact that he is at once too soon and belated, both that which anticipates and that which provides an epilogue (to the Walter family, if nothing else, since he seems to mark the end of the line). Prior Walter also serves as the queer commemoration of the Walter that came before—Walter Benjamin—whose revolutionary principles he both embodies and displaces insofar as he marks both the presence and absence of Walter Benjamin in this text.[14]

Throughout *Angels in America,* the utopia/dystopia coupling (wherein disaster becomes simultaneously the marker for and incitement to think Paradise) plays itself out through a host of binary oppositions: heaven/hell, forgiveness/retribution, communitarianism/individualism, spirit/flesh, pleasure/pain, beauty/decay, future/past, homosexuality/heterosexuality, rationalism/indeterminacy, migration/staying put, progress/stasis, life/death. Each of these functions not just as a set of conceptual poles in relation to which characters and themes are worked out and interpreted, but also as an *oxymoron,* a figure of undecidability whose contradictory being becomes an incitement to think the impossible—revolution. For it is precisely the conjunction of opposites that allows what Benjamin calls "the flow of thoughts" to be given a "shock" and so turned into "the sign of a Messianic cessation of happening" (262-63). The oxymoron, in other words, becomes the privileged figure by which the unimaginable allows itself to be imagined.

In Kushner's reading of Benjamin, the hermaphroditic Angel becomes the most crucial site for the elaboration of contradiction. Because her/his body is the one on which an impossible—and utopian—sexual conjunction is played out, s/he decisively undermines the distinction between the heterosexual and the homosexual. With her/his "eight vaginas" and "Bouquet of Phalli" (2:48), s/he represents an absolute otherness, the impossible

Other that fulfills the longing for both the maternal and paternal (or in Lacanian terms, both demand and the Law). On the one hand, as the maternal "Other," s/he is constituted by "[d]emand . . . as already possessing the 'privilege' of satisfying needs, that is to say, the power of depriving them of that alone by which they are satisfied."[15] On the other hand, "[a]s the law of symbolic functioning," s/he simultaneously represents the "Other embodied in the figure of the symbolic father," "not a person but a place, the locus of law, language and the symbolic."[16] The impossible conjunction of the maternal and the paternal, s/he provides Prior with sexual pleasure of celestial quality—and gives a new meaning to safe sex. At the same time, s/he also fills and completes subjectivity, being the embodiment of and receptacle for Prior's "Released Female Essence" (2:48).

Although all of these characteristics suggest that the Angel is constructed as an extratemporal being, untouched by the ravages of passing time, s/he comes (quite literally for Prior) already culturally mediated. When s/he first appears at the end of *Millennium,* he exclaims, "*Very* Steven Spielberg" (1:118). Although his campy ejaculation is clearly calculated as a laugh line, defusing and undercutting (with typical postmodern cynicism) the deadly earnestness of the scene, it also betrays the fact that this miraculous apparition is in part the product of a culture industry and that any reading of her/him will be mediated by the success of Steven Spielberg and his ilk (in films like *Close Encounters of the Third Kind* and *E.T.*) in producing a particular vision of the miraculous—with lots of bright white light and music by John Williams. To that extent, the appearance of the Angel signals the degree to which utopia—and revolution!—have now become the product of commodity culture. Unlike earlier periods, when utopia tended to be imagined in terms of production (rather than consumption) and was sited in a preceding phase of capitalism (for example, in a preindustrial or agrarian society), late capitalism envisions utopia through the lens of the commodity and—not unlike Walter Benjamin at his most populist—projects it into a future and an elsewhere lit by that *"unearthly white light"* (1:118) which represents, among other things, the illimitable allure of the commodity form.[17]

Although the construction of the Angel represses her/his historicity, the heaven s/he calls home is explicitly the product (and victim) of temporality. Heaven is a simulacrum of San Francisco on 18 April 1906, the day of the Great Earthquake. For it is on this day that God "[a]bandoned" his angels and their heaven "[a]nd did not return" (2:51). Heaven thus appears frozen in time, *"deserted and derelict,"* with *"rubble strewn everywhere"* (2:121). The Council Room in Heaven, meanwhile, *"dimly lit by candles and a single great bulb"* (which periodically fails) is a monument to the past, specifically to the New Science of the seventeenth century and the Enlightenment project to which it is inextricably linked. The table in the Council Room is *"covered with antique and broken astronomical, astrological, mathematical and nautical objects of measurement and calculation. . . ."* At its center sits a *"bulky radio, a 1940s model in very poor repair"* (2:128) on which the Angels are listening to the first reports of the Chernobyl disaster. Conflating different moments of the past and distinct (Western) histories, Heaven is a kind of museum, not the insignia of the Now, but of *before,* of an antique past, of the obsolete. Its decrepitude is also symptomatic of the Angels' fear that God will never return. More nightmare than utopia, marooned in history, Heaven commemorates disaster, despair, and stasis.

Because of its embeddedness in the past, the geography of Heaven is a key to the complex notion of temporality that governs *Angels in America.* Although the scheme does not become clear until *Perestroika,* there are two opposing concepts of time and history running through the play. First, there is the time of the Angels (and of Heaven), the time of dystopian "STASIS" (2:54) as decreed by the absence of a God who, Prior insists, "isn't coming back" (2:133). According to the Angel, this temporal paralysis is the direct result of the hyperactivity of human beings: *"YOU HAVE DRIVEN HIM AWAY!,"* the Angel enjoins Prior, "YOU MUST STOP MOVING!" (2:52), in the hope that immobility will once again prompt the return of God and the forward movement of time. Yet this concept of time as stasis is also linked to decay. In the Angel's threnody that ends the Council scene, s/he envisions the dissolution of "the Great Design, / The spiraling apart of the Work of Eternity" (2:134). Directly opposed to this concept is human temporality, of which Prior, in contradistinction to the Angel, becomes the spokesperson. This time—which is also apparently the time of God—is the temporality connected with Enlightenment epistemologies; it is the time of "Progress," "Science," and "Forward Motion" (2:132; 50). It is the time of "Change" (2:13) so fervently desired by Comrade Prelapsarianov and the "neo-Hegelian positivist sense of constant historical progress towards happiness or perfection" so precious to Louis (1:25). It is the promise fulfilled at the end of *Perestroika* when Louis, apprehending "the end of the Cold War," announces, "[t]he whole world is changing!" (2:145). Most important, the time of "progress, migration, motion" and "modernity" is also, in Prior's formulation, the time of "desire," because it is this last all-too-human characteristic that produces modernity (2:132). Without desire (for change, utopia, the Other), there could be no history.

Despite the fact that this binary opposition generates so much of the play's ideological framework, and that its two poles are at times indistinguishable, it seems to me

that this is one question on which *Angels in America* is not ambivalent at all. Unlike the Benjamin of the "Theses on the Philosophy of History," for whom any concept of progress seems quite inconceivable, Kushner is devoted to rescuing Enlightenment epistemologies at a time when they are, to say the least, extremely unfashionable. On the one hand, *Angels in America* counters attacks from the pundits of the right, wallowing in their post-Cold War triumphalism, for whom socialism, or "the coordination of men's activities through central direction," is the road to "serfdom."[18] For these neoconservatives, "[w]e already live in the millennial new age," we already stand at "the end of history" and, as a result, in Francis Fukuyama's words, "we cannot picture to ourselves a world that is *essentially* different from the present one, and at the same time better."[19] Obsessed with "free markets and private property," and trying desperately to maintain the imperialist status quo, they can only imagine progress as regression.[20] On the other hand, *Angels* also challenges the orthodoxies of those poststructuralists on the left by whom the Marxian concept of history is often dismissed as hopelessly idealist, as "a contemptible attempt" to construct "grand narratives" and "totalizing (totalitarian?) knowledges."[21] In the face of these profound cynicisms, *Angels* unabashedly champions rationalism and progress. In the last words of *Perestroika*'s last act, Harper suggests that "[i]n this world, there is a kind of painful progress. Longing for what we've left behind, and dreaming ahead" (2:144). The last words of the epilogue, meanwhile, are given to Prior who envisions a future in which "[w]e" (presumably gay men, lesbians, and persons with AIDS) "will be citizens." *"More Life"* (2:148), he demands.

Kushner's differences with Benjamin—and the poststructuralists—over the possibility of progress and his championing of modernity (and the desire that produces it) suggest that the string of binary oppositions that are foundational to the play are perhaps less undecidable than I originally suggested. Meaning is produced, in part, because these oppositions are constructed as interlocking homologies, each an analogy for all the others. And despite the fact that each term of each opposition is strictly dependent on the other and, indeed, is produced by its other, these relations are by no means symmetrical. Binary oppositions are always hierarchical—especially when the fact of hierarchy is repressed. *Angels* is carefully constructed so that communitarianism, rationalism, progress, and so forth, will be read as being preferable to their alternatives: individualism, indeterminacy, stasis, and so forth ("the playwright has been able to find hope in his chronicle of the poisonous 1980s"[22]). So at least as far as this string of interlocked binary oppositions is concerned, ambivalence turns out to be not especially ambivalent after all.

At the same time, what is one to make of other binarisms—most notably, the opposition between masculine and feminine—toward which the play seems to cultivate a certain studied ambivalence? On the one hand, it is clear that Kushner is making some effort to counter the long history of the marginalization and silencing of women in American culture generally and in American theatre, in particular. Harper's hallucinations are crucial to the play's articulation of its central themes, including questions of exile and of the utopia/dystopia binarism. They also give her a privileged relationship to Prior, in whose fantasies she sometimes partakes and with whom she visits Heaven. Her unequivocal rejection of Joe and expropriation of his credit card at the end of the play, moreover, signal her repossession of her life and her progress from imaginary to real travel. Hannah, meanwhile, is constructed as an extremely independent and strong-willed woman who becomes part of the new extended family that is consolidated at the end of the play. Most intriguingly, the play's deliberate foregrounding of the silencing of the Mormon Mother and Daughter in the diorama is symptomatic of Kushner's desire to let women speak. On the other hand, *Angels* seems to replicate many of the structures that historically have produced female subjectivity as Other. Harper may be crucial to the play's structure but she is still pathologized, like so many of her antecedents on the American stage (from Mary Tyrone to Blanche DuBois to Honey in *Who's Afraid of Virginia Woolf?*). With her hallucinations and "emotional problems" (1:27), she functions as a scapegoat for Joe, the displacement of his sexual problems. Moreover, her false confession that she's "going to have a baby" (1:41) not only reinforces the link in the play between femininity and maternity but also literally hystericizes her. And Hannah, despite her strength, is defined almost entirely by her relationship to her real son and to Prior, her surrogate son. Like Belize, she is given the role of caretaker.

Most important, the celestial "sexual politics" (2:49) of the play guarantees that the feminine remains Other. After his visitation by the Angel, Prior explains that "God . . . is a man. Well, not a man, he's a flaming Hebrew letter, but a male flaming Hebrew letter" (2:49). In comparison with this masculinized, Old Testament-style, "flaming" (!) patriarch, the Angels are decidedly hermaphroditic. Nonetheless, the play's stage directions use the feminine pronoun when designating the Angel and s/he has been played by a woman in all of the play's various American premières. As a result of this clearly delineated gendered difference, femininity is associated (in Heaven at least) with "STASIS" and collapse, while a divine masculinity is coded as being simultaneously deterministic and absent. In the play's pseudo-Platonic—and heterosexualized—metaphysics, the "orgasm" of the Angels produces (a feminized) "proto-matter, which fuels the [masculinized] Engine of Creation" (2:49).

Moreover, the play's use of doubling reinforces this sense of the centrality of masculinity. Unlike Caryl Churchill's *Cloud 9* (surely the locus classicus of genderfuck), *Angels* uses cross-gender casting only for minor characters. And the crossing of gender works in one direction only. The actresses playing Hannah, Harper, and the Angel take on a number of male heterosexual characters while the male actors double only in masculine roles. As a result, it seems to me that *Angels,* unlike the work of Churchill, does not denaturalize gender. Rather, masculinity—which, intriguingly, is always already queered in this text—is produced as a remarkably stable, if contradictory, essence that others can mime but which only a real (i.e., biological) male can embody. Thus, yet another ambivalence turns out to be always already decided.

THE AMERICAN RELIGION

The nation that *Angels in America* fantasizes has its roots in the early nineteenth century, the period during which the United States became constituted, to borrow Benedict Anderson's celebrated formulation, as "an imagined political community, . . . imagined as both inherently limited and sovereign."[23] For not until the 1830s and 1840s, with the success of Jacksonian democracy and the development of the ideology of Manifest Destiny, did a sense of an imagined community of Americans begin to solidify, due to a number of factors: the consolidation of industrialization in the Northeast; the proliferation of large newspapers and state banks; and a transportation revolution that linked the urban centers with both agricultural producers and markets abroad.[24]

It is far more than coincidence that the birth of the modern idea of America coincided with what is often called the Second Great Awakening (the First had culminated in the Revolutionary War). During these years, as Klaus Hansen relates, "the old paternalistic reform impulse directed toward social control yielded to a romantic reform movement impelled by millennialism, immediatism, and individualism." This movement, in turn, "made possible the creation of the modern American capitalist empire with its fundamental belief in religious, political, and economic pluralism."[25] For those made uneasy (for a variety of reasons) by the new Jacksonian individualism, this pluralism authorized the emergence of alternative social and religious sects, both millennialist evangelical revivals and new communities like the Shakers, the Oneida Perfectionists, and, most prominently and successfully, the Mormons.[26] As Hansen emphasizes, "Mormonism was not merely one more variant of American Protestant pluralism but an articulate and sophisticated counterideology that attempted to establish a 'new heaven and a new earth. . . .'" Moreover, "both in its origins and doctrines," Mormonism "insisted on the peculiarly American nature of its fundamental values" and on the identity of America as the promised land.[27]

Given the number and prominence of Mormon characters in the play, it should come as little surprise that Mormonism, at least as it was originally articulated in the 1820s and 1830s, maintains a very close relationship to the epistemology of *Angels in America.* Many of the explicitly hieratic qualities of the play—the notion of prophecy, the sacred book, as well as the Angel her/himself—owe as much to Mormonism as to Walter Benjamin. Even more important, the play's conceptualization of history, its millennialism, and its idea of America bring it startlingly close to the tenets of early Mormonism. Indeed, it is impossible to understand the concept of the nation with which *Angels* is obsessed (and even the idea of queering the nation!) without understanding the constitution of early Mormonism. Providing Calvinism with its most radical challenge during the National Period, it was deeply utopian in its thrust (and it remains so today). Indeed, its concept of time is identical to the temporality for which *Angels in America* polemicizes. Like *Angels,* Mormonism understands time as evolution and progress (in that sense, it is more closely linked to Enlightenment epistemologies than Romantic ones) and holds out the possibility of unlimited human growth: "As man is God once was: as God is man may become."[28] Part of a tremendous resurgence of interest in the millennium between 1828 and 1832, Mormonism went far beyond the ideology of progress implicit in Jacksonian democracy (just as *Angels*'s millennialism goes far beyond most contemporary ideologies of progress).[29] Understood historically, this utopianism was in part the result of the relatively marginal economic status of Joseph Smith and his followers, subsistence farmers and struggling petits bourgeois. Tending "to be 'agin the government,'" these early Mormons were a persecuted minority and, in their westward journey to Zion, became the subjects of widespread violence, beginning in 1832 when Smith was tarred and feathered in Ohio.[30] Much like twentieth-century lesbians and gay men—although most contemporary Mormons would be appalled by the comparison—Mormons were, throughout the 1830s and 1840s, attacked by mobs, arrested on false charges, imprisoned, and murdered. In 1838, the Governor of Missouri decreed that they must be "exterminated" or expelled from the state. In 1844, Smith and his brother were assassinated by an angry mob.[31]

The violent antipathy towards early Mormonism was in part the result of the fact that it presented a significant challenge to the principles of individualist social and economic organization. From the beginning, Mormonism was communitarian in nature and proposed a kind of ecclesiastical socialism in which "those entering the order were asked to 'consecrate' their property and belongings to the church. . . ." To each male would then be returned enough to sustain him and his family, while the remainder would be apportioned to "'every man who has need. . . .'" As Hansen emphasizes, this organization represents a repudiation of the principles of laissez-faire and an attempt "to restore a more traditional society in which the economy was regulated in behalf of the larger interests of the group. . . ."[32] This nostalgia for an earlier period of capitalism (the agrarianism of the early colonies) is echoed by Mormonism's conceptualization of the continent as the promised land. Believing the Garden of Eden to have been sited in America and assigning all antediluvian history to the western hemisphere, early Mormonism believed that the term "'New World' was in fact a misnomer because America was really the cradle of man and civilization."[33] So the privileged character of the nation is linked to its sacred past and—as with Benjamin—history is tied to theology. At the same time, this essentially theological conceptualization of the nation bears witness to the "strong affinity," noted by Anderson, between "the nationalist imagining" and "religious imaginings."[34] As Timothy Brennan explains it, "nationalism largely extend[s] and modernize[s] (although [does] not replace) 'religious imaginings,' taking on religion's concern with death, continuity, and the desire for origins."[35] Like religion, the nation authorizes a reconfiguration of time and mortality, a "secular transformation of fatality into continuity, contingency into meaning."[36] Mormonism's spiritual geography was perfectly suited to this process, constructing America as both origin and meaning of history. Moreover, as Hans Kohn has pointed out, modern nationalism has expropriated three crucial concepts from those same Old Testament mythologies that provide the basis for Mormonism: "the idea of a chosen people, the emphasis on a common stock of memory of the past and of hopes for the future, and finally national messianism."[37]

This conceptualization of America as the site of a blessed past and a millennial future represents—simultaneously—the fulfillment of early nineteenth-century ideas of the nation and a repudiation of the ideologies of individualism and acquisitiveness that underwrite the Jacksonian marketplace. Yet, as Sacvan Bercovitch points out, this contradiction was at the heart of the nationalist project. As the economy was being transformed "from agrarian to industrial capitalism," the primary "source of dissent was an indigenous residual culture," which, like Mormonism, was "variously identified with agrarianism, libertarian thought, and the tradition of civic humanism." These ideologies, "by conserving the myths of a bygone age" and dreaming "of human wholeness and social regeneration," then produced "the notion of an ideal America with a politically transformative potential." Like the writers of the American Renaissance, Mormonism "adopted the culture's *controlling* metaphor—'America' as synonym for human possibility," and then turned it against the dominant class. Both producing and fulfilling the nationalist dream, it "portray[ed] the American ideology, as all ideology yearns to be portrayed, in the transcendent colors of utopia."[38] A form of dissent that ultimately (and contradictorily) reinforced hegemonic values, Mormonism reconceived America as the promised land, the land of an already achieved utopia, and simultaneously as the land of promise, the site of the millennium yet to come.

I recapitulate the early history of Mormonism because I believe it is crucial for understanding how *Angels in America* has been culturally positioned. It seems to me that the play replicates both the situation and project of early Mormonism with an uncanny accuracy and thereby documents the continued validity of both a particular regressive fantasy of America and a particular understanding of oppositional cultural practices. Like the projects of Joseph Smith and his followers, *Angels* has, from the beginning, on the levels of authorial intention and reception, been constructed as an oppositional, and even "radical" work. Structurally and ideologically, the play challenges the conventions of American realism and the tenets of Reaganism. Indeed, it offers by far the most explicit and trenchant critique of neoconservatism to have been produced on Broadway. It also provides the most thoroughgoing—and unambivalent—deconstruction in memory of a binarism absolutely crucial to liberalism, the opposition between public and private. *Angels* demonstrates conclusively not only the constructedness of the difference between the political and the sexual, but also the murderous power of this distinction. Yet, at the same time, *not despite but because of these endeavors,* the play has been accommodated with stunning ease to the hegemonic ideology not just of the theatre-going public, but of the democratic majority—an ideology that has become the *new* American religion—liberal pluralism.[39]

The old-style American liberalisms, variously associated (reading from left to right) with trade unionism, reformism, and competitive individualism, tend to value freedom above all other qualities (the root word for liberalism is, after all, the Latin *liber,* meaning "free"). Taking the "free" individual subject as the fundamental social unit, liberalism has long been associated with the principle of laissez-faire and the "free" market, and is reformist rather than revolutionary in its politics. At the same time, however, because liberalism, particularly in its American versions, has always paid at least lip service to equality, certain irreducible contradictions have been bred in what did, after all, emerge during the seventeenth century as the ideological complement to

(and justification for) mercantile capitalism. Historically, American liberalism has permitted dissent and fostered tolerance—within certain limits—and guaranteed that all men in principle are created equal (women were long excluded from the compact, as well as African American slaves). In fact, given the structure of American capitalism, the incommensurability of its commitment both to freedom and equality has proven a disabling contradiction, one that liberalism has tried continually, and with little success, to negotiate. Like the bourgeois subject that is its production and raison d'être, liberalism is hopelessly schizoid.

The new liberalism that has been consolidated in the United States since the decline of the New Left in the mid-1970s (but whose antecedents date back to the first stirrings of the nation) marks the adaptation of traditional liberalism to a post-welfare state economy. Pursuing a policy of regressive taxation, its major constituent is the corporate sector—all others it labels "special interest groups" (despite certain superficial changes, there is no fundamental difference between the economic and foreign policies of Reagan/Bush and Clinton). In spite of its corporatism, however, and its efficiency in redistributing the wealth upward, liberalism speaks the language of tolerance. Unable to support substantive changes in economic policy that might in fact produce a more equitable and less segregated society, it instead promotes a *rhetoric* of pluralism and moderation. Reformist in method, it endeavors to fine tune the status quo while at the same time acknowledging (and even celebrating) the diversity of American culture. For the liberal pluralist, America is less a melting pot than a smorgasbord. He or she takes pride in the ability to *consume* cultural difference—now understood as a commodity, a source of boundless pleasure, an expression of an exoticized Other. And yet, for him or her, access to and participation in so-called minority cultures is entirely consumerist. Like the new, passive racist characterized by Hazel Carby, the liberal pluralist uses "texts"—whether literary, musical, theatrical or cinematic—as "a way of gaining knowledge of the 'other,' a knowledge that appears to replace the desire to challenge existing frameworks of segregation."[40]

Liberal pluralism thus does far more than tolerate dissent. It actively enlists its aid in reaffirming a fundamentally conservative hegemony. In doing so, it reconsolidates a fantasy of America that dates back to the early nineteenth century. Liberal pluralism demonstrates the dogged persistence of a *consensus politic that masquerades as dissensus.* It proves once again, in Bercovitch's words, that

> [t]he American way is to turn potential conflict into a quarrel about fusion or fragmentation. It is a fixed match, a debate with a foregone conclusion: you must have your fusion and feed on fragmentation too. And

the formula for doing so has become virtually a cultural reflex: you just alternate between harmony-in-diversity and diversity-in-harmony. It amounts to a hermeneutics of laissez-faire: all problems are obviated by the continual flow of the one into the many, and the many into the one.[41]

According to Bercovitch, a kind of dissensus (of which liberal pluralism is the contemporary avatar) has been the hallmark of the very idea of America—and American literature—from the very beginning. In this most American of ideologies, an almost incomparably wide range of opinions, beliefs, and cultural positions are finally absorbed into a fantasy of a utopian nation in which anything and everything is possible, in which the millennium is simultaneously at hand and indefinitely deferred. Moreover, the nation is imagined as the geographical representation of that utopia which is both everywhere and nowhere. For as Lauren Berlant explains, "the contradiction between the 'nowhere' of utopia and the 'everywhere' of the nation [is] dissolved by the American recasting of the 'political' into the terms of providential ideality, 'one nation under God.'"[42] Under the sign of the "one," all contradictions are subsumed, all races and religions united, all politics theologized.

DISSENSUS AND THE FIELD OF CULTURAL PRODUCTION

It is my contention that *Angels*'s mobilization of a consensual politic (masquerading as *dis*sensual) is precisely the source not only of the play's ambivalence, but also of its ability to be instantly recognized as part of the canon of American literature. Regardless of Kushner's intentions, *Angels* sets forth a project wherein the theological is constructed as a transcendent category into which politics and history finally disappear. For all its commitment to a historical materialist method, for all its attention to political struggle and the dynamics of oppression, *Angels* finally sets forth a liberal pluralist vision of America in which all, not in spite but because of their diversity, will be welcomed into the new Jerusalem (to this extent, it differs sharply from the more exclusionist character of early Mormonism and other, more recent millennialisms). Like other apocalyptic discourses, from Joseph Smith to Jerry Falwell, the millennialism of *Angels* reassures an "audience that knows it has lost control over events" not by enabling it to "regain . . . control," but by letting it know "that history is nevertheless controlled by an underlying order and that it has a purpose that is nearing fulfillment." It thereby demonstrates that "*personal* pain," whether Prior's, or that of the reader or spectator, "is subsumed within the pattern of history."[43] Like Joseph Smith, Tony Kushner has resuscitated a vision of America as both promised land and land of infinite promise. Simultaneously, he has inspired virtually every theatre critic in the U.S. to a host of salvational fantasies about theatre,

art, and politics. And he has done all this at a crucial juncture in history, at the end of the Cold War, as the geopolitical order of forty-five years has collapsed.

Despite the success of the 1991 Gulf War in signaling international "terrorism" as the successor to the Soviet empire and justification for the expansion of the national security state, the idea of the nation remains, I believe, in crisis (it seems to me that "terrorism," being less of a threat to individualism than communism, does not harness paranoia quite as effectively as the idea of an evil empire). If nothing else, *Angels in America* attests both to the continuing anxiety over national definition and mission and to the importance of an ideological means of assuaging that anxiety. In *Angels,* a series of political dialectics (which are, yet again, false dialectics) remains the primary means for producing this ideological fix, for producing dissensus, a sense of alternation between "harmony-in-diversity and diversity-in-harmony." The play is filled with political disputation—all of it between men since women, unless in drag, are excluded from the political realm. Most is centered around Louis, the unmistakably ambivalent, ironic Jew, who invariably sets the level of discussion and determines the tenor of the argument. If with Belize he takes a comparatively rightist (and racist) stance, with Joe he takes an explicitly leftist (and antihomophobic) one. And while the play unquestionably problematizes his several positions, he ends up, with all his contradictions, becoming by default the spokesperson for liberal pluralism, with all *its* contradictions. Belize, intriguingly, functions unlike the white gay men as an ideological point of reference, a kind of "moral bellwether," in the words of one critic.[44] Because his is the one point of view that is never submitted to a critique, he becomes, as David Román points out, "the political and ethical center of the plays." The purveyor of truth, "he carries the burden of race" and so seems to issue from what is unmistakably a "white imaginary" ("[t]his fetishization," Román notes, "of lesbian and gay people of color as a type of political catalyst is ubiquitous among the left").[45] He is also cast in the role of caretaker, a position long reserved for African Americans in "the white imaginary." Even Belize's name commemorates not the Name of the Father, but his status as a *"former drag queen"* (1:3), giving him an identity that is both performative and exoticized. He is the play's guarantee of diversity.

The pivotal scene for the enunciation of Louis's politics, meanwhile, is his long discussion with Belize in *Millennium* which begins with his question, "Why has democracy succeeded in America?" (1:89), a question whose assumption is belied by the unparalleled political and economic power of American corporatism to buy elections and from which Louis, as is his wont, almost immediately backs down. (His rhetorical strategy throughout this scene is to stake out a position from which he immediately draws a guilty retreat, thereby making Belize look like the aggressor.) Invoking "radical democracy" and "freedom" in one breath, and crying "[f]uck assimilation" (1:89-90) in the next, he careens wildly between a liberal discourse of rights and a rhetoric of identity politics. Alternating between universalizing and minoritizing concepts of the subject, he manages at once to dismiss a politics of race (and insult Belize) and to assert its irreducibility. Yet the gist of Louis's argument (if constant vacillation could be said to have a gist) is his disquisition about the nation:

> this reaching out for a spiritual past in a country where no indigenous spirits exist—only the Indians, I mean Native American spirits and we killed them off so now, there are no gods here, no ghosts and spirits in America, there are no angels in America, no spiritual past, no racial past, there's only the political.

[1:92]

For Louis, America hardly exists as a community (whether real or imagined). Rather, for this confused liberal, America is defined entirely by its relationship to the "political." With characteristic irony, Kushner chooses to present this crucial idea (which does, after all, echo the play's title) in the negative, in the form of a statement which the rest of the play aggressively refutes. For if nothing else, *Angels in America*—like *The Book of Mormon*—demonstrates that there are angels in America, that America is in essence a utopian and theological construction, a nation with a divine mission. Politics is by no means banished insofar as it provides a crucial way in which the nation is imagined. But it is subordinated to utopian fantasies of harmony in diversity, of one nation under a derelict God.

Moreover, this scene between Louis and Belize reproduces millennialism in miniature, in its very structure, in the pattern whereby the political is finally subsumed by utopian fantasies. After the spirited argument between Louis and Belize (if one can call a discussion in which one person refuses to stake out a coherent position an argument), their conflict is suddenly overrun by an outbreak of lyricism, by the intrusion, after so much talk about culture, of what passes for the natural world:

BELIZE:

> All day today it's felt like Thanksgiving. Soon, this . . . ruination will be blanketed white. You can smell it—can you smell it?

LOUIS:

> Smell what?

BELIZE:

> Softness, compliance, forgiveness, grace.

[1:100]

Argumentation gives way not to a resolution (nothing has been settled) but to the ostensible forces of nature: snow and smell. According to Belize, snow (an insignia of coldness and purity in the play) is linked to "[s]oftness, compliance, forgiveness, grace," in short, to the theological virtues. Like the ending of *Perestroika,* in which another dispute between Louis and Belize fades out behind Prior's benediction, this scene enacts a movement of transcendence whereby the political is not so much resolved as left trailing in the dust. In the American way, contradiction is less disentangled than immobilized. History gives way to a concept of cosmic evolution that is far closer to Joseph Smith than to Walter Benjamin.

In the person of Louis (who is, after all, constructed as the most empathic character in the play), with his unshakable faith in liberalism and the possibility of "radical democracy," *Angels in America* assures the (liberal) theatre-going public that a kind of liberal pluralism remains the best hope for change.[46] Revolution, in the Marxist sense, is rendered virtually unthinkable, oxymoronic. Amidst all the political disputation, there is no talk of social class. Oppression is understood not in relation to economics but to differences of race, gender and sexual orientation. In short: *an identity politic comes to substitute for Marxist analysis.* There is no clear sense that the political and social problems with which the characters wrestle might be connected to a particular economic system (comrade Prelapsarianov is, after all, a comic figure). And despite Kushner's avowed commitment to socialism, an alternative to capitalism, except in the form of an indefinitely deferred utopia, remains absent from the play's dialectic.[47] Revolution, even in Benjamin's sense of the term, is evacuated of its political content, functioning less as a Marxist hermeneutic tool than a *trope,* a figure of speech (the oxymoron) that marks the place later to be occupied by a (liberal pluralist?) utopia. *Angels* thus falls into line behind the utopianisms of Joseph Smith and the American Renaissance and becomes less a subversion of hegemonic culture than its reaffirmation. As Berlant observes, "the temporal and spatial ambiguity of 'utopia' has the effect of obscuring the implications of political activity and power relations in American civil life."[48] Like "our classic texts" (as characterized by Bercovitch), *Angels* has a way of conceptualizing utopia so that it may be adopted by "the dominant culture . . . for its purposes." "So molded, ritualized, and controlled," Bercovitch notes (and, I would like to add, stripped of its impulse for radical economic change), "utopianism has served . . . to diffuse or deflect dissent, or actually to transmute it into a vehicle of socialization."[49]

The ambivalences that are so deeply inscribed in *Angels in America,* its conflicted relationship to various utopianisms, to the concept of America, to Marxism, Mormonism, and liberalism, function, I believe, to accommodate the play to what I see as a fundamentally conservative and paradigmatically American politic—dissensus, the "hermeneutics of laissez-faire." Yet it seems to me that the play's ambivalence (its way of being, in Eve Sedgwick's memorable phrase, "kinda subversive, kinda hegemonic"[50]) is finally, less a question of authorial intention than of the peculiar cultural and economic position of this play (and its writer) in relation to the theatre, theatre artists, and the theatre-going public in the United States. On the one hand, the Broadway and regional theatres remain in a uniquely marginal position in comparison with Hollywood. The subscribers to regional theatres continue to dwindle while more than half of Theatre Communications Group's sample theatres in their annual survey "played to smaller audiences in 1993 than they did five years ago." Moreover, in a move that bodes particularly ill for the future of new plays, "workshops, staged readings and other developmental activities decreased drastically over the five years studied."[51] On the other hand, serious Broadway drama does not have the same cultural capital as other forms of literature. Enmortgaged to a slew of others who must realize the playwright's text, it has long been regarded as a bastard art. Meanwhile, the relatively small public that today attends professional theatre in America is overwhelmingly middle-class and overwhelmingly liberal in its attitudes. Indeed, theatre audiences are in large part distinguished from the audiences for film and television on account of their tolerance for works that are more challenging both formally and thematically than the vast majority of major studio releases or prime-time miniseries.

Because of its marginal position, both economically and culturally, theatre is a privileged portion of what Pierre Bourdieu designates as the literary and artistic field. As he explains, this field is contained within a larger field of economic and political power, while, at the same time, "possessing a relative autonomy with respect to it. . . ." It is this *relative autonomy* that gives the literary and artistic field—and theatre in particular—both its high level of symbolic forms of capital and its low level of economic capital. In other words, despite its artistic cachet, it "occupies a *dominated position*" with respect to the field of economic and political power as whole.[52] And the individual cultural producer (or theatre artist), insofar as he or she is a part of the bourgeoisie, represents a "dominated fraction of the dominant class."[53] The cultural producer is thus placed in an irreducibly contradictory position—and this has become particularly clear since the decline of patronage in the eighteenth century and the increasing dependence of the artist on the vicissitudes of the marketplace. On the one hand, he or she is licensed to challenge hegemonic values insofar as it is a particularly effective way of accruing cultural capital. On the other hand, the more effective his or her challenge, the less economic capital

he or she is likely to amass. Because of theatre's marginality in American culture, it seems to be held hostage to this double bind in a particularly unnerving way: the very disposition of the field guarantees that Broadway and regional theatres (unlike mass culture) are constantly in the process of having to negotiate this impossible position.

What is perhaps most remarkable about *Angels in America* is that it has managed, against all odds, to amass significant levels of both cultural and economic capital. And while it by no means resolves the contradictions that are constitutive of theatre's cultural positioning, its production history has become a measure of the seemingly impossible juncture of these two forms of success. Just as the play's structure copes with argumentation by transcending it, so does the play as cultural phenomenon seemingly transcend the opposition between economic and cultural capital, between the hegemonic and the counterhegemonic. Moreover, it does so, I am arguing, by its skill in both reactivating a sense (derived from the early nineteenth century) of America as the utopian nation and mobilizing the principle of ambivalence—or more exactly, dissensus—to produce a vision of a once and future pluralist culture. And although the text's contradictory positioning is to a large extent defined by the marginal cultural position of Broadway, it is also related specifically to Tony Kushner's own class position. Like Joseph Smith, Kushner represents a dominated—and dissident—fraction of the dominant class. As a white gay men, he is able to amass considerable economic and cultural capital despite the fact that the class of which he is a part remains relatively disempowered politically (according to a 1993 survey, the average household income for gay men is 40% higher than that of the average American household).[54] As an avowed leftist and intellectual, he is committed (as *Angels* demonstrates) to mounting a critique of hegemonic ideology. Yet as a member of the bourgeoisie and as the recipient of two Tony awards, he is also committed—if only unconsciously—to the continuation of the system that has granted him no small measure of success.

A QUEER SORT OF NATION

Although I am tempted to see the celebrity of *Angels in America* as yet another measure of the power of liberal pluralism to neutralize oppositional practices, the play's success also suggests a willingness to recognize the contributions of gay men to American culture and to American literature, in particular. For as Eve Sedgwick and others have argued, both the American canon and the very principle of canonicity are centrally concerned with questions of male (homo)sexual definition and desire.[55] Thus, the issues of homoeroticism, of the anxiety generated by the instability of the homosocial/homosexual boundary, of coding, of secrecy and disclosure, and of the problems around securing a sexual identity, remain pivotal for so many of the writers who hold pride of place in the American canon, from Thoreau, Melville, Whitman, and James to Hart Crane, Tennessee Williams, and James Baldwin—in that sense, the American canon is always already queered. At the same time, however, unlike so much of the canon, and in particular, the canon of American drama, *Angels in America* foregrounds explicitly gay men. No more need the reader eager to queer the text read subversively between the lines, or transpose genders, as is so often done to the work of Williams, Inge, Albee, and others. Since the 1988 controversies over NEA funding for exhibitions of Mapplethorpe and Serrano and the subsequent attempt by the Endowment to revoke grants to the so-called NEA four (three of whom are queer), theatre, as a liberal form, has been distinguished from mass culture in large part by virtue of its queer content. In the 1990s, a play without a same-sex kiss may be entertainment, but it can hardly be considered a work of art. It appears that the representation of (usually male) homosexual desire has become the privileged emblem of that endangered species, the serious Broadway drama. But I wonder finally how subversive this queering of Broadway is when women, in this play at least, remain firmly in the background. What is one to make of the remarkable ease with which *Angels in America* has been accommodated to that lineage of American drama (and literature) that focuses on masculine experience and agency and produces women as the premise for history, as the ground on which it is constructed? Are not women sacrificed—yet again—to the male citizenry of a (queer) nation?

If Kushner, following Benjamin's prompting (and echoing his masculinism), attempts to "brush history against the grain" (257), he does so by demonstrating the crucial importance of (closeted) gay men in twentieth-century American politics—including, most prominently, Roy Cohn and two of his surrogate fathers, J. Edgar Hoover and Joseph McCarthy. By so highlighting the (homo)eroticization of patriarchy, the play demonstrates the always already queer status of American politics, and most provocatively, of those generals of the Cold War (and American imperialism) who were most assiduous in their denunciation of political and sexual dissidence. Moreover, unlike the work of most of Kushner's predecessors on the American stage, *Angels* does not pathologize gay men. Or more exactly, gay men as a class are not pathologized. Rather, they are revealed to be pathologized circumstantially: first, by their construction (through a singularly horrific stroke of ill luck) as one of the "risk groups" for HIV; and second, by the fact that some remain closeted and repressed (Joe's ulcer is unmistakably the price of disavowal). So, it turns out, it is not homosexuality that is pathological, but its *denial*. Flagrantly uncloseted, the play provides a devastating critique of the closeted gay man in two medicalized bodies: Roy Cohn and Joe Pitt.

If *Angels in America* queers historical materialism (at least as Benjamin understands it), it does so by exposing the process by which the political (which ostensibly drives history) intersects with the personal and sexual (which ostensibly are no more than footnotes to history). Reagan's presidency and the neoconservative hegemony of the 1980s provide not just the background to the play's exploration of ostensibly personal (i.e., sexual, marital, medical) problems, but the very ground on which desire is produced. For despite the trenchancy of its critique of neoconservativism, *Angels* also demonstrates the peculiar sexiness of Reagan's vision of America. Through Louis, it demonstrates the allure of a particular brand of machismo embodied by Joe Pitt: "The more appalling I find your politics the more I want to hump you" (2:36). And if the Angel is indeed "a cosmic reactionary" (2:55), it is in part because her/his position represents an analogue to the same utopian promises and hopes that Reagan so brilliantly and deceptively exploited. Moreover, in this history play, questions of male homosexual identity and desire are carefully juxtaposed against questions of equal protection for lesbians and gay men and debates about their military service. Louis attacks Joe for his participation in "an important bit of legal fag-bashing," a case that upholds the U.S. government's policy that it's not "unconstitutional to discriminate against homosexuals" (2:110). And while the case that Louis cites may be fictional, the continuing refusal of the courts in the wake of *Bowers v. Hardwick* to consider lesbians and gay men a suspect class, and thus eligible for protection under the provisions of the Fourteenth Amendment, is anything but.[56] Unilaterally constructing gay men as a suspect class (with sexual identity substituting for economic positionality), *Angels* realizes Benjamin's suggestion that it is not "man or men but the struggling, oppressed class itself [that] is the depository of historical knowledge" (260). More decisively than any other recent cultural text, *Angels* queers the America of Joseph Smith—and Ronald Reagan—by placing this oppressed class at the very center of American history, by showing it to be not just the depository of a special kind of knowledge, but by recognizing the central role that it has had in the construction of a national subject, polity, literature, and theatre. On this issue, the play is not ambivalent at all.

Notes

My thanks to Rhett Landrum, Loren Noveck, John Rouse, and Ronn Smith for their invaluable contributions to this essay.

1. Joseph Roach has suggested to me that the closest analogue to *Angels* on the American stage is, in fact, *Uncle Tom's Cabin,* with its tremendous popularity

before the Civil War, its epic length, and its skill in addressing the most controversial issues of the time in deeply equivocal ways.

2. John Lahr, "The Theatre: Earth Angels," *The New Yorker,* 13 December 1993, 133.

3. Jack Kroll, "Heaven and Earth on Broadway," *Newsweek,* 6 December 1993, 83; Robert Brustein, "Robert Brustein on Theatre: *Angels in America,*" *The New Republic,* 24 May 1993, 29.

4. John E. Harris, "Miracle on 48th Street," *Christopher Street,* March 1994, 6.

5. Frank Rich, "Critic's Notebook: The Reaganite Ethos, With Roy Cohn As a Dark Metaphor," *New York Times,* 5 March 1992, C15.

6. John Clum, *Acting Gay: Male Homosexuality in Modern Drama* (New York: Columbia University Press, 1994), 324.

7. Tony Kushner, *Angels in America: A Gay Fantasia on National Themes. Part One: Millennium Approaches* (New York: Theatre Communications Group, 1993), 95. All further references will be noted in the text.

8. Frank Rich, "Following an Angel For a Healing Vision of Heaven and Earth," *New York Times,* 24 November 1993, C11.

9. Clum, 314.

10. Tony Kushner, *Angels in America: A Gay Fantasia on National Themes. Part Two: Perestroika* (New York: Theatre Communications Group, 1994), 56. All further references will be noted in the text.

11. See, for example, Andrea Stevens, "Finding a Devil Within to Portray Roy Cohn," *New York Times,* 18 April 1993, section 2, 1-28.

12. Terry Eagleton, *Walter Benjamin, or Towards a Revolutionary Criticism* (London: Verso, 1981), 177.

13. Walter Benjamin, "Theses on the Philosophy of History," in *Illuminations,* ed. Hannah Arendt, trans. Harry Zohn (New York: Schocken Books, 1969), 253. All further references will be noted in the text.

14. Tony Kushner explains: "I've written about my friend Kimberly [Flynn] who is a profound influence on me. And she and I were talking about this utopian thing that we share—she's the person who introduced me to that side of Walter Benjamin. . . . She said jokingly that at times she felt such an extraordinary kinship with him that she thought she was Walter Benjamin reincarnated. And so at one point in the conversation, when I was coming up with names for my characters, I said, 'I had to look up something in Benjamin—not you, but the prior Walter.' That's where the name came from. I had been looking for one of those WASP names that nobody gets called anymore." David Savran, "The Theatre of the Fabulous: An Interview with Tony Kushner," in *Speaking on Stage: Interviews with Contemporary American Playwrights,* ed. Philip C. Kolin and Colby H. Kullman (Tuscaloosa: University of Alabama Press), forthcoming.

15. Lacan, "The Signification of the Phallus," in *Ecrits: A Selection,* trans. Alan Sheridan (New York: Norton, 1977), 286.

16. Elizabeth A. Grosz, *Jacques Lacan: A Feminist Introduction* (London: Routledge, 1990), 74, 67.

17. Benjamin maintained a far less condemnatory attitude toward the increasing technologization of culture than many other Western Marxists. In "The Work of Art in the Age of Mechanical Reproduction," for example, he writes of his qualified approval of the destruction of the aura associated with modern technologies. He explains that because "mechanical reproduction emancipates the work of art from its parasitical dependence on ritual, . . . the total function of art" can "be based on another practice—politics," which for him is clearly preferable. Benjamin, "The Work of Art in the Age of Mechanical Reproduction," *Illuminations,* 224.

18. Although one could cite a myriad of sources, this quotation is extracted from Milton Friedman, "Once Again: Why Socialism Won't Work," *New York Times,* 13 August 1994, 21.

19. Krishan Kumar, "The End of Socialism? The End of Utopia? The End of History?," in *Utopias and the Millennium,* ed. Krishan Kumar and Stephen Bann (London: Reaktion Books, 1993), 61; Francis Fukuyama, *The End of History and the Last Man,* quoted in Kumar, 78.

20. Friedman, 21.

21. Aijaz Ahmad, *In Theory: Classes, Nations, Literatures* (London: Verso, 1992), 69. Ahmad is summarizing this position as part of his critique of poststructuralism.

22. David Richards, "'Angels' Finds a Poignant Note of Hope," *New York Times,* 28 November 1993, II, 1.

23. Benedict Anderson, *Imagined Communities: Reflections on the Origin and Spread of Nationalism* (London: Verso, 1991), 6.

24. See Lawrence Kohl, *The Politics of Individualism: Parties and the American Character in the Jacksonian Era* (New York: Oxford University Press, 1989).

25. Klaus J. Hansen, *Mormonism and the American Experience* (Chicago: University of Chicago Press, 1981), 49-50.

26. See Ernest R. Sandeen, *The Roots of Fundamentalism: British and American Millenarianism 1800-1930* (Chicago: University of Chicago Press, 1970), 42-58.

27. Hansen, 52.

28. Joseph Smith, quoted in Hansen, 72.

29. See Richard L. Bushman, *Joseph Smith and the Beginnings of Mormonism* (Urbana: University of Illinois Press, 1984), 170.

30. Hansen, 119.

31. For a catalogue of this violence, see Jan Shipps, *Mormonism: The Story of a New Religious Tradition* (Urbana: University of Illinois Press, 1985), 155-61.

32. Hansen, 124-26.

33. Hansen, 27, 66.

34. Anderson, 10-11.

35. Timothy Brennan, "The National Longing for Form," in *Nation and Narration,* ed. Homi K. Bhabha (London: Routledge, 1990), 50.

36. Anderson, 10-11.

37. Hans Kohn, *Nationalism: Its Meaning and History* (Princeton: Van Nostrand, 1965), 11.

38. Sacvan Bercovitch, "The Problem of Ideology in American Literary History," *Critical Inquiry* 12 (1986): 642-43; 645.

39. Despite the 1994 Republican House and Senate victories (in which the Republicans received the vote of only 20% of the electorate) and the grandstanding of Newt Gingrich, the country remains far less conservative on many social issues than the Republicans would like Americans to believe. See Thomas Ferguson, "G.O.P. $$$ Talked; Did Voters Listen?," *The Nation,* 26 December 1994, 792-98.

40. Hazel Carby, "The Multicultural Wars," in *Black Popular Culture,* a project by Michele Wallace, ed. Gina Dent (Seattle: Bay Press, 1992), 197.

41. Bercovitch, 649.

42. Lauren Berlant, *The Anatomy of National Fantasy: Hawthorne, Utopia, and Everyday Life* (Chicago: University of Chicago Press, 1991), 31.

43. Barry Brummett, *Contemporary Apocalyptic Rhetoric* (New York: Praeger, 1991), 37-38.

44. Lahr, "The Theatre: Earth Angels," 132.

45. David Román, "November 1, 1992: AIDS/*Angels in America*," from *Acts of Intervention: Gay Men, U.S. Performance, AIDS* (Bloomington: Indiana University Press, forthcoming).

46. This is corroborated by Kushner's own statements: "The strain in the American character that I feel the most affection for and that I feel has the most potential for growth is American liberalism, which is incredibly short of what it needs to be and incredibly limited and exclusionary and predicated on all sorts of racist, sexist, homophobic and classist prerogatives. And yet, as Louis asks, why has democracy succeeded in America? And why does it have this potential, as I believe it does? I really believe that there is the potential for radical democracy in this country, one of the few places on earth where I see it as a strong possibility. It doesn't seem to be happening in Russia. There is a tradition of liberalism, of a kind of social justice, fair play and tolerance—and each of these things is problematic and can certainly be played upon in the most horrid ways. Reagan kept the most hair-raising anarchist aspects of his agenda hidden and presented himself as a good old-fashioned liberal who kept invoking FDR. It may just be sentimentalism on my part because I am the child of liberal-pinko parents, but I do believe in it—as much as I often find it despicable. It's sort of like the Democratic National Convention every four years: it's horrendous and you can feel it sucking all the energy from progressive movements in this country, with everybody pinning their hopes on this sleazy bunch of guys. But you do have Jesse Jackson getting up and calling the Virgin Mary a single mother, and on an emotional level, and I hope also on a more practical level, I do believe that these are the people in whom to have hope." Savran, 24-25.

47. See Tony Kushner, "A Socialism of the Skin," *The Nation,* 4 July 1994, 9-14.

48. Berlant, 32.

49. Bercovitch, 644.

50. Sedgwick used this phrase during the question period that followed a lecture at Brown University, 1 October 1992.

51. Barbara Janowitz, "Theatre Facts 93," insert in *American Theatre,* April 1994, 4-5.

52. Pierre Bourdieu, "The Field of Cultural Production, or: The Economic World Reversed," in Bourdieu, *The Field of Cultural Production: Essays on Art and Literature,* ed. Randal Johnson (New York: Columbia University Press, 1993), 37-38.

53. Randal Johnson, Ed. Introd., Bourdieu, 15.

54. *Gay & Lesbian Stats: A Pocket Guide of Facts and Figures,* ed. Bennett L. Singer and David Deschamps (New York: The New Press, 1994), 32.

55. See Eve Kosofsky Sedgwick, *Epistemology of the Closet* (Berkeley: University of California Press, 1990), 48-59.

56. It is not the subjects who comprise a bona fide suspect class (like African Americans) that are suspect, but rather the forces of oppression that produce the class. For an analysis of the legal issues around equal protection, see Janet Halley, "The Politics of the Closet: Towards Equal Protection for Gay, Lesbian, and Bisexual Identity," *UCLA Law Review* (June 1989): 915-76.

Jyl Lynn Felman (essay date May/June 1995)

SOURCE: Felman, Jyl Lynn. "Lost Jewish (Male) Souls: A Midrash on *Angels in America*." *Tikkun* 10, no. 3 (May/June 1995): 27-30.

[*In the following essay, Felman examines the parallels between Jewish and gay identity as presented in* Angels in America. *Felman asserts that Kushner's play is ultimately about "Jewish male self-loathing in the twentieth century."*]

Tony Kushner's 1993 Pulitzer-Prize-winning play, *Angels in America,* is very gay. And Jewish. It's about assimilation, self-loathing, and men with lost souls; the betrayal of the faith and the abandonment of a moral vision. Depending on who the viewer is, there are two versions of the play, playing simultaneously. There's the deeply moving, virus-infected, *goyishe*-gay-who-divinely-hallucinates; plus Mr. married-Mormon-coming-out-of-the-closet to pill-popping-straight, soon-to-be-happy-ex, Mrs. Mormon—AIDS version. Then there's the culturally lost, wondering-in-secular-exile, ambivalent *treyf,* quasi-civil-libertarian-melting-pot-mess, full-of-self-deception, painfully revealing Jewish version, located in the extremely bizarre triumvirate of Roy Cohn, Ethel Rosenberg, and the imaginatively invented totally believable (character of) Louis Ironson. Ultimately, one plot informs the other as the characters move in out of their tightly woven, inter-related narratives. But *Angels in America* will always be my *Jewish Fantasia on National Themes.* It resounds in my ears like the long, hard, final sound of the *shofar* calling the People Israel to worship in a postmodern, Hillary Clinton-reconstructed, school-prayer-reinstated, third-wave-neo-Newt-Gingrich era. Where, lying at the foot of the Statue of Liberty, Jewish identity is in fragments while lost Jewish (read male) souls seek solace in the exact same, singular, superclean anus of a closeted, self-righteous, God-fearing married Mormon faggot. Yes, *Angels* is about Jewish male self-loathing in the twentieth century held tightly within the ever expanding embrace of Miss Liberty's very tired, porous hands.

Angels opens with a quintessential, North American Jewish moment: A very old rabbi with a heavy Eastern European accent, long beard, and stooped shoulders presides over the funeral of a woman who has spent the last ten years of her life at the Bronx Home of Aged Hebrews without a visit from her grandson, who lives minutes away. At the funeral, the rabbi reads out loud the names of the family mourners whose roster by the third generation is generously sprinkled with one Gentile appellation after another. For the Jew who dies alone without family or community, Kushner has written the new "Diaspora *Kaddish.*" Rabbi Chemolwitz publicly admits that he doesn't know the deceased Sarah Ironson or her family. But he knows Sarah's journey

and the meaning of that journey, which in the end is more important than knowing the person herself. For it is in the irreversible departure from Eastern Europe to the climactic, but culturally dislocating arrival at Ellis Island where Jewish continuity is affirmed. Listen to the rabbi:

RABBI:

> (He speaks sonorously, with a heavy Eastern European accent, unapologetically consulting a sheet of notes for the family names): . . . This woman. I did not know this woman. . . . She was . . . (He touches the coffin) . . . not a person but a whole kind of person, the ones who crossed the ocean, who brought with us to America the villages of Russia and Lithuania—and how we struggled, and how we fought, for the family, for the Jewish home, so that you would not grow up here, in this strange place, in the melting pot where nothing melted. . . .

By using the plural "we" rather than the singular "she," the rabbi purposefully includes himself in the historic crossing of Ashkenazi Jews from the old country to the "new" country. And with the public insertion of himself into his "eulogy for the unknown," he affirms Jewish continuity in spite of the fact that he is presiding over the funeral of a Jew he did not know for a family he does not know. Then, through the brilliant use of the second-person "you," Kushner personalizes the impersonal space of the estranged Diaspora Jew from his/her cultural roots. Alone in the middle of a pitch-black stage with the coffin of our ancestors, the stooped rabbi stands facing the void. At the exact same moment, the audience is dramatically transformed into the future generations—not only of Sarah Ironson's family, but of the Jewish people in general. Then to us, as Jews, the rabbi speaks:

> Descendants of this immigrant woman, you do not grow up in America, you and your children and their children with the *goyische* names. You do not live in America. No such place exists. Your clay is the clay of some Litvak *shtetl,* your air the air of the steppes—because she carried the old world on her back across the ocean, in a boat, and she put it down on Grand Concourse Avenue, or in Flatbush, and she worked that earth into your bones, and you pass it to your children, this ancient, ancient culture and home. *(little pause.)*

When the audience is secured as the next generation, the rabbi ends his eulogy with a bitter, painful admonition:

> You can never make that crossing that she made, for such Great Voyages in this world do not any more exist. But every day of your lives the miles that voyage between that place and this one you cross. Every day. You understand me? In you that journey is. . . .

In *us* that Journey *is.* Even if we want to forget where we came from, we can't. It's impossible. The journey lives in us, in spite of us; not only as cultural, but also as spiritual inheritance.

By opening *Angels* with this scene, Kushner claims his rightful place in the Jewish lexicon of post-Holocaust writers confronting secular Jewish identity in the Diaspora. Yet the questions *Angels* ask around sexuality, autonomy, and cultural preservation belong within the ethnic, narrative tradition that began in the old country with Sholem Aleichem's Tevye, asking *The Almighty* for guidance in raising his Jewish daughters in a secular world. And that particular ethnic tradition continues on today (in the New World) with the "all-American, Jewish everyman" plays of Arthur Miller, Paddy Cheyefsky, Nathanael West, and Neil Simon's *Broadway Bound.* But Kushner, writing in a post-structuralist age, explodes the boundary of tribal sensitivities. He uses a sexuality clearly constructed outside of procreative, nuclear, heterosexual marriage as the postmodern metaphor for the new, self-loathing Willy Loman. Willy has become "Nelly," and so very fey at that.

Louis Ironson is the post 'Nam, civil rights redux, contemporary Jewish Nelly. Not a likeable, hardly sympathetic liberal, Jew-boy fella. The son of good Jewish lefties and a failure by his own admission, he's a word processor working in the courthouse basement of the Court of Appeals in Brooklyn. (He never made it to law school.) After his grandmother's funeral, he confides to his *shiksa* boyfriend Prior Walter that he hasn't visited Bubbe Sarah for ten years; she reminded him too much of his mother. With this confession, Kushner appears to play into the Philip Roth/Norman Mailer, Metro-Goldwyn-Mayer, hate-your-mother-yiddische-mamma's-boy stereotype.

But Louis's absence from his family must also be read in the context of the historical abandonment of an entire people and the shame that abandonment produced. Louis doesn't visit Sarah because he is afraid of his mother's shame; the shame of the little *feygelah* who leaves home not to marry and make a fortune, but to fuck other little *feygelahs,* Jew and Gentile alike. Louis has internalized the family shame and projects this shame onto his grandmother. So he cannot visit her out of fear of revisiting his own (Jewish male) self-loathing. This singular act of abandonment of an immigrant grandmother, by a self-loathing Jew, forms the controlling metaphor upon which Kushner seeks to negotiate the question of morality in human relations in the age of AIDS.

Louis Ironson abandons his virus-infected lover just as he abandoned his grandmother. Ignorant of Jewish tradition and afraid of what he's about to do, Louis checks with the rabbi after Sarah's funeral.

LOUIS:

> Rabbi, what does the Holy Writ say about someone who abandons someone he loves at a time of great need?

RABBI:

> Why would a person do such a thing?

LOUIS:

> Maybe because this person's sense of the world, that it will change for the better with struggle, maybe a person who has this new-Hegelian positivist sense of constant historical progress towards happiness or perfection or something, who feels very powerful because he feels connected to these forces, moving uphill all the time . . . maybe that person can't, um, incorporate sickness into his sense of how things are supposed to go. Maybe vomit . . . and sores and disease . . . really frighten him, maybe . . . he isn't so good with death.

RABBI:

> The Holy Scriptures have nothing to say about such a person.

For Kushner, speaking rabbinically, abandonment is an act of moral as well as spiritual impotence. For Jews—Israeli and Diaspora—abandonment is not only a twentieth-century (Jewish) *leitmotif,* but also a historical obsession. And, in the age of AIDS, both public: medical, governmental, and religious, and private: family, friends and colleagues, abandonment has become a controlling metaphor for gay suffering. Appropriately then, Kushner uses a gay Jew as cultural icon, representative of the "desertion dilemma," so central to both the Jewish and gay communities.

Out of his internalized self-loathing, Louis abandons his grandmother—his roots. Because of his shame, he is unable to comprehend that he is about to abandon his lover, Prior, in the exact same way. With the creation of Louis Ironson—secular Jewish faggot that he is—Kushner locates the question of abandonment outside a religious context. Throughout *Angels,* Louis seeks to locate moral justification for the immoral abandonment of those he loves.

Enter the character of Roy Cohn, who has built a career on the totally fallacious moral justification of the stupendously grotesque, immoral act. Kushner uses Roy Cohn's assimilated, self-loathing Jew-boy persona to mirror the self-loathing Louis Ironson. Are they identical characters? In the play, Louis abandons his literal family, the-mother-of-his-mother. And he deserts his life-partner, sick with AIDS. Roy abandons his metaphoric mother, Ethel Rosenberg. And he forsakes his homosexual brothers by always fucking in a locked closet. Both men are isolationists, living in *Galut*—contemporary Jewish exile. Louis lives outside Jewish communal life, whereas Roy is completely acommunal. Thus, the narrative function of Roy Cohn in *Angels* is to create an alter ego for Louis, a point-counterpoint from which Kushner positions assimilated and estranged, very middle-class, Jewish male identity. In this context, the audience sits as the *Bet Din,* a Jewish court, judging the morality of Louis Ironson—the newly wandering, perpetually meandering, Diaspora Jew. Next to Roy Cohn, Louis looks good, or so it would appear.

But why make the central characters of your play self-loathing gay Jews? Because Kushner, himself a gay Jew, employs one identity to inform dramatically upon the other. Ultimately he uses the condition or state of Diaspora, male "Jewishness," as cultural signifier for "gayness." He draws thematic parallels between assimilation and self-loathing within the Jewish male psyche, and location and dislocation within the gay male psyche. (The only women in the play are dead, angels, or crazy.) And—for the first time in contemporary, mainstream, *Broadway* theater—Kushner dares to use the homosexual persona to reveal Jewish male neurosis. Thus, there is a certain post-structuralist symmetry being constructed around the social identities of Jewish and Queer. Kushner exposes the vices of one identity with the other, and vice versa.

The challenge, then, lies with the heterosexual audience, both Gentile and Jew. As innocent bystander, the Gentile must resist the desire to distance the self from these characters precisely because of their Jewishness and/or their homosexuality. But for the male, heterosexual Jew to identify himself with either Louis Ironson or Roy Cohn is a far more difficult predicament. To identify with them as Jews is to locate the exiled self in a pattern of familiar, albeit uncomfortable, neurosis about "Hebrew" circumcised maleness and to face the internalized shame of the classic pariah.

The queerness of Roy Cohn and Louis Ironson does not invalidate their Jewishness; on the contrary, it illuminates. For the author, the social (not to mention historical) link between Jew and homosexual is clearly potent. He knows personally that it is in the intersection between assimilation and self-loathing that both Jews and homosexuals are caught.

Kushner then collapses the borders between sexuality and ethnicity: A fragmented id becomes a fluid ego, although often a despised one at that. Finally, as if he is writing *responsa* to Harvey Fierstein's "mother" in the groundbreaking *Torch Song Trilogy,* when she forbids her son to mention Jewish and gay in the same *Kaddish,* Kushner refuses to split off the self. The problem is that what he offers in the characters of Louis and Roy, point-counterpoint, are too easy to reject precisely because they are so full of self-loathing. So Kushner strategically introduces (into the play) the "sacred" secular Jewish mother, Ethel Rosenberg, who was betrayed by all the prodigal Jewish sons: Irving R. Kaufman, Irving Saypol, Roy Cohn, and her own brother David Greenglass. She is the final link between the men, Jewish identity, assimilation and self-loathing.

It is the presence of Ethel Rosenberg in *Angels in America* which calls into question Jewish male morality in the postmodern era.

The first scene when Ethel appears, Roy is very sick—so sick he can barely function and is about to collapse. In a chilling moment that leaves the audience psychically suspended, Ethel Rosenberg calls 911 for an ambulance to take Roy Cohn to the emergency room. Throughout *Angels,* Cohn reflects on his proudest moment; his greatest singular accomplishment—according to him—the epitome of his power (and the height of his assimilation and self-loathing) was when he persuaded Judge Kaufman to sentence Ethel to death in the electric chair. Kushner successfully exposes Roy's misogyny and internalized anti-Semitism. So when Ethel calls for the ambulance, it becomes apparent that she has come back to haunt her executioner and witness his demise. Kushner has made Roy Cohn, in the last weeks of his life, dependent on Ethel Rosenberg. Face to face, the Jewish son meets the (Jewish) mother he ruthlessly betrayed.

Ethel appears next at Cohn's hospital bedside. She announces that the end is near. Cohn is about to be disbarred, and Ethel has come back for the hearings. Slowly, almost imperceptibly, the balance of power shifts between the abandoned mother and the son who abandoned her. Until now, Roy was in charge. But with his impending disbarment, his total collapse, political and physical, is imminent.

At the same time, Louis has taken a lover, left the lover, and (near the end of Part Two) begged Prior to take him back. Tightening the symmetry in the play, Kushner parallels Roy's disbarment with Prior's refusal to take Louis back. Because of their immoral and unethical behavior, both Louis and Roy are thrown out and rejected by their own people. But unlike Louis, Roy has no shame. Thus, by the play's end, the characters of Louis Ironson and Roy Cohn are distinguishable. The audience slowly develops a limited sympathy (but never compassion) for Louis, whose lover will not take him back. But for Cohn, there is nothing. Ethel is there to witness it all. Her appearance at Roy Cohn's hospital bed, in the middle of the AIDS epidemic, is a *coup de théâtre.* Kushner has brought Ethel back to say *Kaddish* for Roy—the "infected" Jew for whom there is no prayer.

Framing the "Jewish Play" within the play, Kushner begins and ends *Angels* with a *Kaddish.* The first *Kaddish* was not just for Sarah Ironson, Louis's grandmother, but rather for an entire era, including a lost sense of Jewish peoplehood. The last Prayer For The Dead, coming almost at the end of Part Two in *Perestroika,* is truly a restructuring of the post-immigrant Jewish experience. The *Kaddish* has been transformed into a postmodern mourning prayer for lost Jewish souls. And it is in the final act of *davening* that Louis, Ethel, and Roy become the unholy triumvirate.

At the request of Prior's nurse, Belize (who stole Cohn's personal supply of AZT), Louis has come unwillingly to say *Kaddish* for Cohn. When he begins, Louis mixes up several Hebrew prayers until, out of nowhere, Ethel appears at the foot of the bed to lead Louis in the *Kaddish*. In this moment, Kushner exposes the true condition of the exiled Jew. Louis is the post-Holocaust Jew who quotes Hegel, but does not even know the *Kaddish*. He is truly lost; the product of his own shame and self-loathing, he cannot mourn properly. And Ethel, dead already forty-two years and for whom we still say *Kaddish*, is the only one who knows the words.

The scene is both emotionally satisfying—Roy Cohn is disbarred and finally dead—and disquieting. The new Diaspora Jew wanders around in *Galut*, intellectually informed, but culturally ignorant, sexually despised, and profoundly isolated. This, then, is the consequence of Louis's abandonment of those he loves. Having been only for himself—who is he? A combination of Willy Loman redux and Tevye's nightmare of a son-in-law. And who are we, Jews, Gentiles, and heterosexuals who disassociate ourselves from Louis Ironson, as though his dilemma is not ours? In the Diaspora, as Tony Kushner deftly shows with his "Gay Fantasia on National Themes," the question of abandonment simmers in the melting pot, boiling over whenever the temperature gets too hot, scalding everybody in sight.

James Fisher (essay date winter 1995-96)

SOURCE: Fisher, James. "'The Angels of Fructification': Tennessee Williams, Tony Kushner, and Images of Homosexuality on the American Stage." *Mississippi Quarterly* 49, no. 1 (winter 1995-96): 12-32.

[*In the following essay, Fisher compares the representations of homosexuality in Kushner's* Angels in America *and the plays of Tennessee Williams.*]

> Who, if I were to cry out, would hear me among the angelic orders?[1]
>
> —Rainer Maria Rilke

> Still obscured by glistening exhaltations, the angels of fructification had now begun to meet the tumescent phallus of the sun. Vastly the wheels of the earth sang Allelulia! And the seven foaming oceans bellowed Oh![2]
>
> —Tennessee Williams

For centuries, Angels have been symbols of spiritual significance. Residing in a realm somewhere between the deity and his creations, they watch over humanity as unspeakably beautiful harbingers of hope and of death. Such rich and profoundly unsettling icons are central to Tennessee Williams's poem "The Angels of Fructification," in which his angels provide a vision of homosexual eroticism comparatively rare in his dramas. Williams was the theatre's angel of sexuality—the dramatist most responsible for forcefully introducing sexual issues, both gay and straight, to the American stage. The fruit of his labor is particularly evident in the subsequent generations of playwrights who present gay characters and situations with increasing frankness, depth, and lyricism. Such works bloom most particularly after the 1960s, and most richly in Tony Kushner's epic *Angels in America,* which has been described by critics as one of the most important American plays of the past fifty years.[3]

There are significant parallels to be found in Kushner's two *Angels in America* plays, *Millennium Approaches* and *Perestroika,* and the dramas of Williams. Both playwrights feature classically inspired epic passions; both depict dark and poetic images of the wondrous and horrifying aspects of existence; both create a kind of stage language that is at once naturalistic and lyrical; both ponder the distance between illusion and reality; both explore the nature of spirituality from a grounding in modern thought; and both deal centrally and compassionately with complex issues of sexuality from a gay sensibility. Although Alfred Kazin has written of homosexuality that "'The love that dare not speak its name' (in the nineteenth century) cannot, in the twentieth, shut up,"[4] the emergence of Williams, and those dramatists like Kushner following in his footsteps, says much on a subject about which the stage has been silent for too long.

In reflecting on the history of homosexuals in American theatre, Kushner believes that "there's a natural proclivity for gay people—who historically have often spent their lives hiding—to feel an affinity for the extended make-believe and donning of roles that is part of theater. It's reverberant with some of the central facts of our lives."[5] It is not surprising that, in a society in which homosexuals were firmly closeted before the 1960s, the illusions of the stage provided a safe haven. Williams could not be as open about his sexuality in his era as Kushner can be now, and thus had to work with overtly heterosexual situations and characters. Williams's creative achievements grow out of a guarded self-awareness and desire for self-preservation, as well as the constraints of the prevailing values of his day.

Donald Windham believes that Williams "loved being homosexual. I think he loved it more than he loved anybody, more than he loved any thing except writing,"[6] and Edward A. Sklepowich seems to agree when he writes that "Williams treats homosexuality with a reverence that at times approaches chauvinism."[7] In fact, Williams was often ambivalent about homosexuality—either his own or anyone else's—in his writings. Although his sexuality was well known in the theatrical community, it is unclear when Williams first "came out" publicly. His 1970 appearance on David Frost's television program seems the earliest public declaration. When Frost asked him to comment on his sexuality, Williams replied, "I don't want to be involved in some sort of a scandal, but I've covered the waterfront."[8] He also told Frost that "everybody has some elements of homosexuality in him, even the most heterosexual of us" (p. 40), but a few years later he wrote, "I have never found the subject of homosexuality a satisfactory theme for a full-length play, despite the fact that it appears as frequently as it does in my short fiction. Yet never even in my short fiction does the sexual activity of a person provide the story with its true inner substance."[9] A couple of years later, in an interview in the *Village Voice,* Williams made the point with bluntness: "I've nothing to conceal. Homosexuality isn't the theme of my plays. They're about all human relationships. I've never faked it,"[10] and in 1975 he stated, "Sexuality is part of my work, of course, because sexuality is a part of my life and everyone's life. I see no essential difference between the love of two men for each other and the love of a man for a woman; no essential difference, and that's why I've examined both. . . ."[11] In his novel, *Moise and the World of Reason* (1975), Williams is franker in his depiction of homosexuality than in any of his plays. However, more important than issues of homosexuality, the characters in the novel feel the absence of love and a need for connection—constant themes in all of Williams's work. There is no question that, as a rule, Williams was writing about love and not gender. He criticized sexual promiscuity as "a distortion of the love impulse,"[12] and for him, this impulse, in whatever form, was sacred.

In retrospect, Williams's cautious exploration of homosexuality—or at least his unwillingness to be more overt about it in his plays—pales by comparison with the defiant openness of Kushner's work. Williams balked at writing what he called gay plays, but Kushner says, "I feel very proud that **Angels** is identified as a gay play. I want it to be thought of as being part of gay culture, and I certainly want people to think of me as a gay writer. It does also seem to speak very powerfully to straight people."[13] To understand, in part, why Williams obscured homosexuality in his plays, Gore Vidal explains that Williams "had the most vicious press of almost any American writer I can think of. Fag-baiting was at its peak in the fifties when he was at his peak and it has never given up, actually."[14] Donald Spoto believes that Williams's ambivalence had to do, in part, with the fact that he wanted "to be controversial—the hard-drinking, openly homosexual writer with nothing to hide—and at the same time, a man of *his own time,* a Southern gentleman from a politer era who would never

abandon propriety and privacy."[15] This view might indicate why Williams seemed uncomfortable with public displays of drag or campiness, which, he writes, are

> imposed upon homosexuals by our society. The obnoxious forms of it will rapidly disappear as Gay Lib begins to succeed in its serious crusade to assert, for its genuinely misunderstood and persecuted minority, a free position in society which will permit them to respect themselves, at least to the extent that, individually, they deserve respect—and I think that degree is likely to be much higher than commonly supposed.[16]

And it was in the arena of the arts, Williams believed, that the gay sensibility was most likely to first engender such respect. In his *Memoirs* he states, "There is no doubt in my mind that there is more sensibility—which is equivalent to more talent—among the 'gays' of both sexes than among the 'norms' . . ." (p. 63). At the same time, Williams wished to attract a broader audience than gays for his work and seems to have believed that a so-called gay play would limit his access to universal acceptance.

Williams's concern about acceptance was not without some justice. He did not have to look too far back into the preceding decades of American drama to see that the audience was, at best, uncertain about its willingness to accept homosexual characters and issues. The first American play to deal openly with homosexuality is believed to be Mae West's *The Drag,* which generated so much controversy that it closed before completing a tumultuous pre-Broadway tour in 1927. A few other curiosities appeared in the subsequent decades, most notably Lillian Hellman's *The Children's Hour* (1934), in which the question of a lesbian relationship is at the center. Of course, secondary homosexual characters appear in a few plays of the 1930s and 1940s, but they are rarely identified as such. Simon Stimson, the alcoholic choir master of Thornton Wilder's *Our Town* (1938), is a vivid example of such types, typical in that he is comparatively unimportant to the plot and that he is seen mostly as a tragi-comic victim. With the appearance of Robert Anderson's *Tea and Sympathy* (1953), in which a sensitive young man is viewed by his peers as a homosexual (even though it later becomes clear that he is not), gay issues and characters slowly come out of the shadows.

During the 1950s, other playwrights introduced gay characters and issues, but often not in their most visible work. William Inge, inspired to become a playwright by Williams's example, did not feature openly homosexual characters in any of his major plays, but in a few lesser-known one-acts he does so vividly. Inge's *The Tiny Closet* (1959), for example, features a man boarding in a rooming house where the nosy landlady has been attempting to break into a padlocked closet in his room.

As soon as the man goes out, the landlady and her friend manage to break in and discover an array of elegant women's hats. The landlady's violation—and the presumption that she will cause him public disgrace—leaves the man's ultimate fate in question. Inge's blunt attack on intolerance[17] was written in the aftermath of the McCarthy era and was a forerunner of later gay plays, particularly those written after the late 1960s, which argue for greater acceptance for homosexuals.

Mid-twentieth century dramatists employed various techniques to present gay characters and situations. One device often used is "transference," the act of hiding gay viewpoints and situations behind a mask of heterosexuality. Edward Albee, often accused of using transference in the writing of such plays as *Who's Afraid of Virginia Woolf?* (1962), is a gay dramatist who also emerged in the 1950s. With the homosexual triumvirate of Williams, Inge, and Albee dominating the non-musical Broadway stage—and despite the fact that none of them had publicly acknowledged their own sexuality—*New York Times* drama critic Stanley Kauffmann "outed" them in 1966. Although he does not give their names, it is clear to whom he is referring in his article "Homosexual Drama and Its Disguises." Kauffmann implies that homosexual writers have no right to write about anything but gay characters—an attitude which would logically imply that men are unable to write about women and vice versa. Kauffmann's notion, undoubtedly all too prevalent in the mid 1960s, becomes clearer when he writes:

> Conventions and puritanisms in the Western world have forced [homosexuals] to wear masks for generations, to hate themselves, and thus to hate those who make them hate themselves. Now that they have a certain relative freedom, they vent their feelings in camouflaged form. . . . They emphasize manner and style because these elements of art, at which they are often adept, are legal tender in their transactions with the world. These elements are, or can be, esthetically divorced from such other considerations as character and idea.[18]

Albee firmly refutes the idea that he, or Williams, employs transference in his plays: "Tennessee never did that, and I can't think of any self-respecting worthwhile writer who would do that sort of thing. It's beneath contempt to suggest it, and it's beneath contempt to do it."[19] Gore Vidal's explanation of the centrality of women characters in Williams's plays seems a valid alternative to understanding his work and the reasons critics see transference in his plays. Vidal believes that for Williams, a woman was "always more interesting as she was apt to be the victim of a society."[20] Williams understood, as Strindberg did, that there are many aspects of the female in the male and vice-versa. And, also like Strindberg, Williams's pained, driven, poetic, and passionate characters are unquestionably extensions of his own persona regardless of their gender.

For surviving life's vicissitudes, Williams believed that "romanticism is absolutely essential" (Frost, p. 35) and felt that the "ability to feel tenderness toward another human being, "the ability to love" (Frost, p. 35) was paramount and that people must not let themselves "become brutalized by the brutalizing experiences that we do encounter on the *Camino Real*" (Frost, p. 35). Romanticism, however, must co-exist with self-awareness and a clear sense of the difference between illusion and reality. The characters who suffer most in Williams's plays do so less because of any deviance from accepted norms than because they are, somehow, self-deluded. There is no doubt that constraints on sexuality in the American society of his time meant that Williams's sexually driven characters were often outlaws who could only be fulfilled through some kind of transgression. His characters were often shocking to audiences and even more so in the world they inhabited. Aggressive in their pursuit of fulfillment, they can destroy and be destroyed as Williams undoubtedly hoped to destroy constraints and mores that prevented the survival of a romantic view and the ability to love. Reflecting on Williams's plays, Edward Albee suggests that the drama itself is "an act of aggression. It's an act of aggression against the status quo, against people's smugness. At his best, Tennessee was not content with leaving people when they left a play of his the way they were when they came in to see a play of his."[21]

Williams's first Broadway success, *The Glass Menagerie* (1944), is rare among his works in that the sexuality of his characters is not a significant factor. However, beginning with his next produced play, *Summer and Smoke* (1947), the sexual personas of his characters become central and visible—and would remain so for the rest of his career. In *Summer and Smoke,* Alma Winemiller fears and rejects sexuality, which she equates with bestiality, and she places a high value on spiritual love. However, she is physically drawn to young Dr. John Buchanan, her neighbor, whose view of sexuality is purely biological. "I reject your opinion of where love is," she tells John, "and the kind of truth you believe the brain to be seeking!—There is something not shown on the chart."[22] However, what is missing from John's biological chart frustrates Alma—a creature of desire. John is similarly trapped behind his awe of Alma's purity. He admits to her that "The night at the casino—I wouldn't have made love to you. . . . I'm more afraid of your soul than you're afraid of my body. You'd have been as safe as the angel of the fountain—because I wouldn't feel decent enough to touch you . . ." (p. 222). For much of the play Alma hides behind her propriety and the safety of her weak suitor, Roger Doremus, an unacknowledged gay may who, she instinctively understands, poses no sexual threat to her. Ultimately, Alma's despair leads her to abandon her resistance to sexuality. In the final scene of the play she is discovered near the same angel of the fountain John mentioned, picking up a traveling sales-man who refers to her as "angel." Williams acknowl-edged that Alma's startling liberation mirrored his own move "from puritanical shackles to, well, complete profligacy."[23] Profligacy, as he describes it, represents "Liberation from taboos" (Gaines, p. 27). To Williams, sex is ultimately a welcome and potentially joyful release, and as a playwright he endeavored not to "make any kind of sex dirty except sadism" (Gaines, p. 27).

Roger Doremus is one of several shadowy gay charac-ters Williams includes in his early plays; in fact, in the next play the gay character would not even appear on the stage. *A Streetcar Named Desire* (1947) was a seismic event in contemporary theatrical sexuality. Blanche DuBois, raised in a genteel family of the Old South, faces so many burdens of physical and emotional death that she begins to believe that the opposite of death is sexual desire, which she seeks promiscuously. The most harrowing death in Blanche's past is the suicide many years before of her young husband, Allan Grey. Allan's repressed homosexuality can only be read as weakness by the immature and frustrated Blanche. As she recounts it to Mitch,

> There was something different about the boy, a nervous-ness, a softness and tenderness which wasn't like a man's, although he wasn't the least bit effeminate look-ing—still—that thing was there. . . . He came to me for help. I didn't know that. I didn't find out anything until after our marriage when we'd run away and come back and all I knew was I'd failed him in some mysteri-ous way and wasn't able to give the help he needed but couldn't speak of! He was in the quicksands and clutch-ing at me—but I wasn't holding him out, I was slip-ping in with him! I didn't know that. I didn't know anything except I loved him unendurably but without being able to help him or myself. Then I found out. In the worst of all possible ways. By coming suddenly into a room that I thought was empty—which wasn't empty, but had two people in it . . . the boy I had mar-ried and an older man who had been his friend for years. . . .[24]

Later in her story, Blanche recounts the events of the same evening at the Moon Lake Casino, after Allan has killed himself: "It was because—on the dance-floor—unable to stop myself—I'd suddenly said—'I saw! I know! You disgust me . . .' And then the searchlight which had been turned on the world was turned off again and never for one moment since has there been any light that's stronger than this—kitchen—candle . . ." (p. 115). The deep root of Blanche's sexual dysfunction can be found in Allan's homosexuality and her inability to understand or accept it. Despite her desperate dalliances with countless other men, she is tragically unable to reignite the light of love snuffed out by her treatment of Allan.

The issue of transference consistently emerges in criti-cal discussions of *A Streetcar Named Desire* and Blanche's character. Among others, Robert Emmet

Jones describes the play, remaking Blanche as a homosexual male; he finally concludes, however, that it is not the femininity of Blanche but the masculinity of Stanley Kowalski that ultimately provides *Streetcar* with a "very homoerotic element . . . in a convincing heterosexual situation."[25] Before Williams, the male body was not depicted in American drama as erotically appealing, but Stanley, particularly as embodied by the young Marlon Brando, is a sexual catalyst for both sexes. Stanley, a character defined by his appetites, ultimately uses his sexual power as a weapon against Blanche, but learns, as Blanche has, that sex for its own sake is inevitably destructive—only when it is mixed with love and compassion can it redeem.

In terms of Williams's homosexual characters, his next important play was *Camino Real* (1953), a drama that failed to attract an audience in its original production, more because of its startling theatrical innovations than because of its subject matter. *Camino Real,* a play of fanciful metaphysics pleading for a romantic attitude about life, depicts the crosscurrents of history as described by a particularly literary sensibility. Williams intermingles such characters as Don Quixote, Kilroy, Camille, Casanova, and Lord Byron in a fantastic world drawn from elements of Spanish folklore and traditional Christianity. Although it is relatively unimportant in the action of the play, the character of Baron de Charlus, borrowed from Proust, is an avowed homosexual and pointedly effeminate—a trait Williams himself disliked. When these types appear in his plays they are often objects of ridicule, Williams showing strangely less compassion for effeminate men than for the more masculine homosexuals he often depicted. Such masculine characters of ambiguous sexuality appear more frequently in Williams's plays of the mid-to-late 1950s. In *Orpheus Descending* (1957) Williams makes use of the myth of Orpheus, who descends into the underworld to rescue his lover Eurydice from the King of the Dead. Williams introduces Val Xavier as his Or-pheus, a sensual and poetic hero inarticulately yearning for some vaguely understood form of transcendence, either through art or sex. A rather less poetic version of this type can be found in Chance Wayne, the young male hustler of *Sweet Bird of Youth* (1959), but it is with Brick Pollitt, the alcoholic ex-athlete of *Cat on a Hot Tin Roof* (1955), that Williams takes another important step in his depiction of homosexuality.

Brick shares Williams's repugnance at what he calls "fairies," mocking the deceased former owners of the family estate, who were two gay men. Brick's past triumphs in sports are taken by all as a sign of masculin-ity, but his family, particularly his sexually frustrated wife, Maggie, are distressed by his reckless and relent-less drinking. He does not drink, however, because his athletic career is over, as all but Maggie think, but because he fears that his confused feelings for his deceased best friend, Skipper, who he now knows was a homosexual, haunt him. In response to the question, Williams explained that Brick "went no further in physical expression than clasping Skipper's hand across the space between their twin beds in hotel rooms—and yet his sexual nature was not innately 'normal'."[26] Brick is also disgusted by the "mendacity" he sees around him and finally recognizes in himself. Here character and author meet, for certainly Williams understood as a gay man in 1950s America that mendacity, as Brick explains, is "a system that we live in."[27] Hellbent on destroying himself, Brick drinks to oblivion but learns in the final scenes that the act of love is more important than anything—including the gender of those involved. Maggie becomes an angel of salvation for Brick and, as the play concludes, she succeeds in drawing him back to her bed through her compassionate wish to create an heir—a son of Brick's—to whom a dying Big Daddy can leave his vast fortune and estate.

There are no such saving angels to be found in *Suddenly Last Summer* (1958), in which Williams sketches a vision of a predatory universe. Following the violent and mysterious death of her son, Sebastian, the imperious Violet Venable tries to convince young Dr. Cukrowicz to perform a lobotomy on her disturbed niece, Catherine, who has witnessed Sebastian's death. Mrs. Venable does not want Catherine's version of Sebastian's death to prevail. However, Cukrowicz encourages Catherine, who painfully recounts the final hours of the voraciously homosexual Sebastian, who died at the hands of a mob of predatory youths he had used sexually. In a sense, Sebastian, who is apparently incapable of real love, is devoured by his own promiscuous appetites in a frightening cosmos where only the most efficient predators survive.

The last stage of Williams's depiction of homosexuality is the most significant in his dramatic canon. At the time of the play's initial New York run, Walter Kerr described *Small Craft Warnings* (1972), which is set in a down-and-out bar, as a play of "Talkers, drinkers, losers getting ready for one or another kind of death."[28] Frequently considered by critics to be a lesser play in the Williams canon, it is, in fact, the most important work in understanding Williams's dramatic depiction of homosexuality. Critics have generally claimed that Williams offers a dark and embittered view of homosexuality through the character of Quentin, a middle-aged gay screenwriter. The play, which is written in a series of connected confessional arias for the major characters, permits Quentin, in a speech Williams himself considered the best in the play, to reflect on his way of life:

> There's a coarseness, a deadening coarseness, in the experience of most homosexuals. The experiences are quick, and hard, and brutal, and the pattern of them is practically unchanging. Their act of love is like the jab-

bing of a hypodermic needle to which they're addicted but which is more and more empty of real interest and surprise.[29]

Quentin also expresses his amazement at Bobby, the young hustler from Iowa he has recently picked up. Williams describes Bobby as having "a quality of sexlessness, not effeminacy" (p. 240), and Quentin is moved by his discovery that Bobby has "the capacity for being surprised by what he sees, hears and feels in this kingdom of earth" (p. 261), and painfully notes that he himself has "lost the ability to say: 'My God!' instead of just: 'Oh, well'" (p. 261). Bobby presents an image of youthful wonder and a joy in his sexuality that balances Williams's portrayal of Quentin's dulled sensibilities. Another angle is supplied by Leona, the self-described "faggot's moll," a drunk and habitué of the bar, who recalls the experiences of her deceased brother to Quentin:

> I know the gay scene and I know the language of it and I know how full it is of sickness and sadness; it's so full of sadness and sickness, I could almost be glad that my little brother died before he had time to be infected with all that sadness and sickness in the heart of a gay boy. This kid from Iowa, here, reminds me a little of how my brother was, and you, you remind me of how he might have become if he'd lived.

> (p. 254)

At the time *Small Craft Warnings* was first produced, critics were eager to believe that Williams was condemning homosexuality—or regretting his own—in this play, and that Quentin's bitterness and disillusionment were some sort of final statement on the subject by Williams. In fact, Williams shows several faces of homosexuality in the play and Quentin's and Leona's views, if indeed they are speaking for Williams, may well have more to do with the author's personal unhappinesses and addictions than with a desire to make a universal statement on homosexuality. Williams, who played the role of Doc in the off-Broadway production of *Small Craft Warnings* for part of its run, believed that Quentin was close to his own persona because he, too, had

> quite lost the capacity for astonishment. . . . I'm not a typical homosexual. I can identify completely with Blanche—we are both hysterics—with Alma and even with Stanley. . . . If you understand schizophrenia, I am not really a *dual* creature; but I can understand the tenderness of women and the lust and libido of the male, which are, unfortunately, too seldom combined in women.[30]

Williams's interest in androgyny and bisexuality also becomes clear in his depiction of Bobby's exuberant love life in *Small Craft Warnings*. Bobby has lost none of the aforementioned capacity for astonishment, and at one point in the play he describes an experience that literally caught him between the sexes:

On the plains of Nebraska I passed a night with a group of runaway kids my age and it got cold after sunset. A lovely wild young girl invited me under a blanket with just a smile, and then a boy, me between, and both of them kept saying "love," one of 'em in one ear and one in the other, till I didn't know which was which "love" in which ear or which . . . touch. . . . The plain was high and the night air . . . exhilarating and the touches not heavy.

(p. 264)

In his letters and his *Memoirs,* which were written at about the same time he was working on *Small Craft Warnings,* Williams writes with similar eroticism about his own sexual history. Perhaps his ultimate public stance is best expressed by Monk, the owner of the bar in *Small Craft Warnings,* who opines of gays, "I've got no moral objections to them as a part of humanity, but I don't encourage them in here" (p. 264).

The theatre in general was catching up with Williams's depictions of homosexuality in this same era. With the appearance of Matt Crowley's *The Boys in the Band* (1968), gay theatre, and the inclusion of homosexual characters and issues in mainstream American drama, increased significantly. Between 1960 and the 1980s, however, gay characters were often reduced to peripheral status in the plays—or were seen most vividly in musicals like *La Cage aux Folles* (1983), boulevard comedies like *Torch Song Trilogy* (1981), or in broad stereotypes in straight plays. There were exceptions, including Albee's *Everything in the Garden* (1967), Le-Roi Jones's *The Toilet* (1964), and the inspired grotes-querie of Charles Ludlam's Theatre of the Ridiculous, but at the outset of the AIDS epidemic an important change occurred in the depiction of gays. Homosexual plays became either scathing indictments of American society's failure to respond adequately to the AIDS crisis, as in the plays of Larry Kramer, or dark depictions of the oppression of gays, as in Martin Sherman's *Bent* (1978), which dramatizes the brutal oppression of homosexuals during the Holocaust. However, no gay dramatist seems logically to follow Williams, who, as Delma Eugene Presley writes, "made serious efforts to explore the subjects of reconciliation and redemption"[31] in their work. Before Williams, only Eugene O'Neill faced such questions; after Williams, only Tony Kushner.

Despite many similarities between Williams and Kushner, there is at least one obvious difference: Kushner is a dramatist with a strongly political perspective. Williams is rarely thought of as political and believed that it was "only in the case of Brecht that a man's politics, if the man is an artist, are of particular importance in his work" (*Memoirs,* p. 178). In recalling his political awakening, Williams wrote in his *Memoirs* that he came of voting age while working at Continental Shoemakers and "cast my first and last political vote. It was for Nor-man Thomas: I had already turned Socialist" (p. 46). Late in life, his political interests became inflamed by "the atrocity of the American involvement in Vietnam, about Nixon's total lack of honesty and of a moral sense, and of the devotion I had to the cause of Senator McGovern" (*Memoirs,* p. 120), and he continued to long for the emergence of "an enlightened form of socialism" (*Memoirs,* p. 118). Otherwise, Williams's drama is certainly not overtly political, but Kushner, who also calls for reconsideration of socialism in light of the collapse of the Soviet model, argues that "All theater is political. If you don't declare your politics, your politics are probably right-wing" (Blanchard, p. 42). The AIDS epidemic had, in essence, pushed gay dramatists toward a more politicized view—even more than had been inspired by the Stonewall era. A politicized gay theatre, for Kushner, is a positive direction, and he believes that "America watching the spectacle of itself being able to accept homosexuality is good for America" (Blanchard, p. 42).

Kushner's political awakening began when he was in college. He was inspired, in part, by the writers and artists emerging from the Stonewall generation, by ACT UP and Queer Nation, whose chant, "We're here, we're queer, we're fabulous," pervades Kushner's plays. He acknowledges some debt to dramatists like Larry Kramer and Harvey Fierstein, but more directly significant to his development as a dramatist is his deep admiration for Williams: "I've always loved Williams. The first time I read *Streetcar,* I was annihilated. I read as much Williams as I could get my hands on until the late plays started getting embarrassingly bad. . . . I'm really influenced by Williams."[32] Kushner also admires the plays of John Guare, who "Like Williams, has figured out a way for Americans to do a kind of stage poetry. He's discovered a lyrical voice that doesn't sound horrendously twee and forced and phony" (Savran interview, p. 24). Kushner aims for a similar sort of lyricism in **Angels in America,** weaving a tapestry of the crushing human and spiritual issues of the Reagan era—and beyond—with poignance (in the Williams sense) and epic stature (in both the O'Neillian and Brechtian senses). John Lahr writes of Kushner, "Not since Williams has a playwright announced his poetic vision with such authority on the Broadway stage. Kushner is the heir apparent to Williams's romantic theatrical heritage: he, too, has tricks in his pocket and things up his sleeve, and he gives the audience 'truth in the pleasant disguise of illusion.' And, also like Williams, Kushner has forged an original, impressionistic theatrical vocabulary to show us the heart of a new age."[33]

At the very least, if Williams's plays dramatized homosexuality from the 1940s through the early 1970s, Kushner's plays clearly provide the next chapter. In technique, particularly in his lyricism, scope, humor, and compassion for his characters, Kushner is clearly in Williams's debt. There are also distinct differences. For example, all of the major male characters in *Angels* are gay—some are "out" and others are "closeted"—but all must deal with their sexuality centrally in the action Kushner provides. Whereas Williams's gay characters are forced by their times to the periphery of mainstream society, Kushner's characters have broken through to the center—but not without great cost. In *Small Craft Warnings,* Williams provides Quentin and Bobby equal time to reveal their differing perspectives, and Kushner similarly allows each of his characters ample opportunity to share their private journeys of self-discovery within the complexities, contradictions, and hypocrisies he sees in modern American life.

Drama critics like John Simon, often accused of homophobia, disliked the plays, particularly finding them to plead "not just for homosexuality but also and especially for transgression, a life-style of flouted complaisance and flaunted socially unacceptable excess,"[34] but the plays have been highly acclaimed by any standards. One of the great ironies of the success of *Angels in America* is the enormous mainstream audience that has embraced the play, despite the fact that its politics, moral universe, and sexuality are, at least as measured by whom we elect to public office, the opposite of what American society claims to believe in. It is perhaps in this irony that some of the questions that both Williams and Kushner explore meet. As Kushner wonders, "What is the relationship between sexuality and power? Is sexuality merely an expression of power? Is there even such a thing as 'sexuality'?" (Savran interview, p. 100).

There is a sense of Greek fatality in *Angels in America* that can be felt in *The Glass Menagerie, A Streetcar Named Desire,* and *Suddenly Last Summer,* but also an Ibsenite element—the idea that humanity is on the wrong road and that the souls of the past and future will demand retribution. Like Ibsen—and certainly Williams—Kushner believes that personal tragedy, both real and fictional, teaches and profoundly changes people. The *Angels in America* plays are feverish historical dramas about our immediate and current history, but it is the questions Kushner asks that are of greatest significance. What claim can we make to humanity in a nation racially, politically, morally, and sexually divided? Has America chosen an uncompassionate path as part of an inevitable movement toward spiritual decline and death or can this course be changed and renewal be achieved? For Williams, tragically inspired plays "offer us a view of certain moral values in violent juxtaposition" (*Where I Live,* p. 53), and Kushner provides such conflicts in *Angels in America.* Despite the political predilections of its author, *Angels in America* attempts to allow both sides to have their say. Its most lovable character is dying of AIDS, but so

is its most detestable; both conservative and liberal characters have admirable moments and reprehensible ones; the strong become weak and the weak become strong. Kushner seems to believe what Williams once said of human experience: "I don't believe in villains or heroes—only right or wrong ways that individuals have taken, not by choice but by necessity or by certain still-uncomprehended influences in themselves, their circumstances, and their antecedents" (*Where I Live,* pp. 91-92).

It is in this vein that Kushner's "gay fantasia" begins. The first play, *Millennium Approaches,* opens on a somber scene as an elderly rabbi stands over the coffin of Sarah Ironson, a woman whose difficult life embodies the immigrant experience of her generation. The rabbi ominously warns that "Pretty soon . . . all the old will be dead."[35] And with them will go the values and certitudes that shaped their lives and our times. Kushner then focuses his gaze on a married couple, Joe and Harper Pitt, and a gay couple, Prior Walter and Louis Ironson, the grandson of the deceased woman. These two relationships are both at points of primal crisis when they intersect with the life of a McCarthy-era hatchet man and shark lawyer Roy Cohn. Joe is a Mormon lawyer whose conservative politics lead him to Cohn, who would like to place Joe in the Justice Department as his man in Washington. Joe, however, is caught up in a personal struggle with his long repressed homosexuality. He has lived according to the rules by which he was raised—to be a family man, to be devoutly religious, and to be a conservative Republican. However, he is also miserable. In an agonized plea to Harper, who demands that Joe tell her whether or not he is in fact a homosexual, Joe says what Williams's Brick Pollitt might have said with a greater sense of self-awareness: "Does it make any difference? That I might be one thing deep within, no matter how wrong or ugly that thing is, so long as I have fought, with everything I have, to kill it" (p. 40). Joe's life-long conflict with himself is most potently illuminated in a later speech to Harper that is reminiscent of Reverend Shannon's struggle with his vision of a predatory god in *Night of the Iguana* (1959):

> I had a book of Bible stories when I was a kid. There was a picture I'd look at twenty times every day: Jacob wrestles with the angel. I don't really remember the story, or why the wrestling—just the picture. Jacob is young and very strong. The angel is . . . a beautiful man, with golden hair and wings, of course. I still dream about it. Many nights. I'm . . . It's me. In that struggle. Fierce and unfair. The angel is not human, and it holds nothing back, so how could anyone human win, what kind of a fight is that? It's not just. Losing means your soul thrown down in the dust, your heart torn out from God's. But you can't not lose.

(pp. 49-50)

Later, Joe encounters Louis, who is in a desperate flight of fear from his long-time lover, Prior, who is suffering from the initial stages of AIDS. Racked with guilt at his faithlessness, the liberal Louis reflects on the era, which he sees as a metaphor for his own behavior. He describes himself, and Joe, as "Children of the new morning, criminal minds. Selfish and greedy and loveless and blind. Reagan's children" (p. 74). Louis has a brutal, punishing sexual encounter with a stranger in Central Park in a situation that mirrors Quentin's description of the "coarse" experience of homosexuals in *Small Craft Warnings*. The stranger asks, "You been a bad boy?" Louis can only sardonically reply, "Very bad. Very bad" (p. 55).

Meanwhile, Joe's wife, Harper, seriously addicted to Valium, and Prior, often delirious as he becomes sicker with AIDS, meet in each other's hallucinations. These scenes have a mystical quality but are also filled with the sort of campiness Williams preferred to avoid. Some critics of *Angels* similarly found the campiness unfortunately stereotypical, but Kushner believes that there is something empowering for gays in drag and a camp sensibility. Kushner's use of various forms of humor with all of his characters, but most particularly with Prior, is remarkably similar to the ways in which Williams typically broke the unspeakable tension of his most unsettling scenes to expose the absurd and grotesque sides of a character's circumstances. As Williams told Dick Cavett in a television interview: "Much of my pleasure in life comes from the fun, you know, the funny side of people. And if you omit that from them then they don't seem quite real. I don't find people lovable unless they're somewhat funny."[36]

Kushner uses a quite different brand of humor with the character of Roy Cohn. Cohn's gleefully bitter corruption is both comic and frightening. One of the most remarkable aspects of *Angels*—and something that is typical of Williams as well—is the way in which Kushner achieves sympathetic moments for even his most monstrous and transgressing characters. Roy is a rapacious predator, who is first discovered in his command module juggling phone calls and wishing he had eight arms like an octopus. It is Roy's self-loathing that is most unsettling and is most vividly shown in his scathing denial of his homosexuality: "Homosexuals are not men who sleep with other men. Homosexuals are men who in fifteen years of trying cannot get a pissant antidiscrimination bill through City Council. Homosexuals are men who know nobody and who nobody knows. Who have zero clout" (p. 45).

Roy represents a kind of trickle-down morality in *Angels*—Kushner's notion that if there's corruption, greed, and bad faith at the top, it will ultimately seep down to each individual in the society. As Robert Brustein writes, there are "no angels in America, only angles,"[37]

and *Angels* depicts a moral combat represented at various points by the opposing poles of conservative and liberal, gay and straight, transgressor and victim. Also, as in many of Williams's best plays, *Angels* deftly captures a convergence of past, present, and future. The past, as previously indicated, is symbolized by the death of an elderly Jewish woman; the present by the greed of the Reagan era, by Cohn, and by a general loss of faith and loyalty, as demonstrated in the behavior of Joe and Louis. The future is represented by a choice between destruction and change best exemplified at the end of *Millennium Approaches* by the startling appearance of an angel, who may be bringing news of either salvation or apocalypse.

As a dramatist with a decidedly political bent, Kushner is perhaps closer to a George Bernard Shaw or a Bertolt Brecht than to Williams. However, both Kushner and Williams offer a view of a changing socio-political environment, with their characters caught between two worlds: one that is dying and one that is being born. Although Kushner himself is certainly of the left-wing of the political spectrum, it is in Prior's human and personal politics, more than Roy's or Louis's polemics, that Kushner's sympathies lie. Prior grapples with the politics of existence with a profoundly humane and compassionate viewpoint. Fearful of his future, Prior recounts a story of one of his ancestors who was forced to escape in a lifeboat with seventy other passengers when a ship foundered. Whenever the lifeboat sat too low in the water or seemed about to capsize, crew members aboard would hurl the nearest passenger into the sea. Dying of AIDS, Prior says

> I think about that story a lot now. People in a boat, waiting, terrified, while implacable, unsmiling men, irresistably strong, seize . . . maybe the person next to you, maybe you, and with no warning at all, with time only for a quick intake of air you are pitched into freezing, turbulent water and salt and darkness to drown.
>
> (pp. 41-42)

At the end of *Millennium Approaches,* an angel appears to a delirious Prior, who is frightened but with moving courage resists his fears: "I can handle pressure, I am a gay man and I am used to pressure, to trouble, I am tough and strong and . . ." (p. 117). At this point, Prior is overwhelmed by an intense sexual response as the angel crashes through the ceiling of his room. The angel, calling Prior a prophet, announces that "The Great Work begins" (p. 119).

In the second play, *Perestroika,* the characters continue their individual journeys in a darker and even more intellectually complex drama. Where *Millennium Approaches* depicts faithlessness and selfishness with compassion while offering a glimpse of the retreating conscience of American society, *Perestroika* finds Kushner's indomitable characters moving tentatively toward the feared changes. Despite the overall grimness of much of **Perestroika,** the play finally, and with a moving humanism typical of Kushner's—and Williams's—work, brings several of the characters to some measure of forgiveness and a settling of accounts. Most shattering of all may be the scenes in which Belize reluctantly but compassionately nurses the delirious and dying Cohn, despite hateful taunts and threats. In another moving sequence, Louis, appalled to find himself at the bedside of Cohn, reluctantly gives in to compassion and joins a ghostly Ethel Rosenberg to chant the "Kaddish" over Cohn's corpse. Similarly, Joe's mother, Hannah, cares for the abandoned and increasingly disturbed Harper. While working at her volunteer job at New York's Mormon Welcome Center, Hannah leaves Harper alone with a life-size diorama of a nineteenth-century Mormon pioneer family. Harper thinks she sees her errant spouse in the image of the "Mormon Father," and she pleads for guidance from the "Mormon Mother." When the figure comes miraculously to life and grimly leads Harper toward the next stage of her personal journey, Kushner achieves a transcendent meeting of past and present not at all unlike that in Williams's *Camino Real,* a magical road where the fictions of history and literature converge with reality.

Hannah has lost her son Joe as a result of her rigidity, but visiting Prior in the hospital teaches her acceptance for the "otherness" of homosexuality. She asks Prior if she should come see him again, and Prior, borrowing Williams's most famous—and campiest—line, becomes Blanche DuBois for a moment. "Please do," he says, "I have always depended on the kindness of strangers." Hannah, unfamiliar with the reference, can only reply, "Well that's a stupid thing to do."[38] Hannah does return and is no longer a stranger, either to Prior or herself, for she too has been visited by Prior's angel and experienced a similarly orgasmic encounter with the angel that has transformed her.

The final scene of **Perestroika** is set at the Bethesda fountain in Central Park, with a statue of an angel in its center. It is not at all unlike the one where Williams's repressed Alma Winemuller had her sexual awakening. At the fountain a newly created family including Prior, Hannah, Belize, and a repentant Louis meet. A stronger, wiser Hannah asserts Kushner's view of the interconnectedness of all humanity—regardless of race or sexual preference—and the primacy of loyalty and commitment to others. Prior points out the angel of the fountain, Bethesda, a figure commemorating death but suggesting "a world without dying" (p. 147). Prior, the prophet, whose AIDS symptoms have stabilized, notes that the healing waters of Bethesda's fountain are not flowing now, but that he hopes to be around to see the

day they flow again. And in a final statement, this indomitable gay character speaks for all those who have come before, from the plays of Williams through Kushner:

> This disease will be the end of many of us, but not nearly all, and the dead will be commemorated and will struggle on with the living, and we are not going away. We won't die secret deaths anymore. The world only spins forward. We will be citizens. The time has come.

(p. 148)

Notes

1. Rainer Maria Rilke, "Duino Elegies. The Ninth Elegy," in *Selected Works, Vol. II. Poetry,* trans. J. B. Leishman (Norfolk, Connecticut and New York: A New Directions Book, 1960), pp. 244-245.

2. Tennessee Williams, "The Angels of Fructification," in *In the Winter of Cities. Selected Poems of Tennessee Williams* (New York: New Directions, 1956, 1964), p. 34.

3. Kushner's theatrical output thus far includes the plays *Yes, Yes, No, No* (1985; children's play). *Stella* (1987; adapted from a play by Goethe), *A Bright Room Called Day* (1987), *Hydriotaphia* (1987), *The Illusion* (1988; freely adapted from a play by Pierre Corneille), *Angels in America. Part One. Millennium Approaches* (1990), *Angels in America. Part Two. Perestroika* (1991), *Widows* (1991; written with Ariel Dorfman, adapted from Dorfman's novel), *Slavs* (1994), and *The Dybbuk* (1995; adapted from S. Ansky's play).

4. Alfred Kazin, "The Writer as Sexual Show-Off: Making Press Agents Unnecessary," *New York Magazine,* June 9, 1975, p. 38.

5. Bob Blanchard, "Playwright of Pain and Hope," *Progressive Magazine,* October 1994, p. 42.

6. Donald Windham interviewed in "Tennessee Williams. Orpheus of the American Stage," a film by Merrill Brockway broadcast on "American Masters" (PBS-TV), 1994.

7. Edward A. Sklepowich, "In Pursuit of the Lyric Quarry: The Image of the Homosexual in Tennessee Williams' Prose Fiction," in *Tennessee Williams: A Tribute,* ed. Jac Tharpe (Jackson: University Press of Mississippi, 1977), p. 541.

8. David Frost, *The Americans* (New York: Stein and Day, 1970), p. 40.

9. Tennessee Williams, "Let Me Hang It All Out." *New York Times,* March 4, 1975, Section II, p. 1.

10. Tennessee Williams interviewed by Arthur Bell, *Village Voice,* February 24, 1972.

11. Tennessee Williams interviewed by Robert Berkvist, *New York Times,* December 21, 1975.

12. Tennessee Williams interviewed on "The Lively Arts" program (BBC-TV), 1976.

13. Gerard Raymond, "An Interview with Tony Kushner," *Theater Week,* December 20, 1993, p. 17.

14. Gore Vidal interviewed in "Tennessee Williams. Orpheus of the American Stage," a film by Merrill Brockway for "American Masters" (PBS-TV), 1994.

15. Donald Spoto, *The Kindness of Strangers, The Life of Tennessee Williams* (Boston/Toronto: Little, Brown and Co., 1985), p. 292.

16. Tennessee Williams, *Memoirs* (New York: Doubleday, 1975), p. 63.

17. Inge's one-act *The Boy in the Basement* (1962) makes a similar plea for tolerance.

18. Stanley Kauffmann, "Homosexual Drama and Its Disguises," *New York Times,* January 23, 1966. Section 2, p. 1.

19. Edward Albee, cited in *The Playwright's Art. Conversations with Contemporary American Dramatists,* ed. Jackson R. Bryer (New Brunswick, New Jersey: Rutgers University Press, 1995), p. 21.

20. Gore Vidal interviewed in "Tennessee Williams. Orpheus of the American Stage," a film by Merrill Brockway for "American Masters" (PBS-TV), 1994.

21. Edward Albee interviewed in "Tennessee Williams. Orpheus of the American Stage," a film by Merrill Brockway for "American Masters" (PBS-TV), 1994.

22. Tennessee Williams, *The Theatre of Tennessee Williams. Volume 2* (New York: New Directions, 1971), p. 221.

23. Jim Gaines, "A Talk About Life and Style with Tennessee Williams," *Saturday Review,* April 29, 1972, p. 27.

24. Tennessee Williams, *A Streetcar Named Desire* (New York: New Directions, 1980), p. 114.

25. Robert Emmet Jones, "Sexual Roles in the Works of Tennessee Williams," in *Tennessee Williams: A Tribute,* ed. Jac Tharpe (Jackson: University Press of Mississippi, 1977), p. 554.

26. Tennessee Williams, *Where I Live. Selected Essays,* ed. Christine R. Day and Bob Woods, with an introduction by Christine R. Day (New York: A New Directions Book, 1978), p. 72.

27. Tennessee Williams, *The Theatre of Tennessee Williams. Volume 3* (New York: New Directions, 1971), p. 127.

28. Walter Kerr, "Talkers, Drinkers and Losers," *New York Times,* April 16, 1972, Section 2, p. 8.

29. Tennessee Williams, *The Theatre of Tennessee Williams. Volume 5* (New York: New Directions, 1976), p. 260.

30. Tennessee Williams interviewed by C. Robert Jennings, *Playboy* (20, April 1973).

31. Delma Eugene Presley, "Little Acts of Grace," *Tennessee Williams: A Tribute,* ed. Jac Tharpe (Jackson: University Press of Mississippi, 1977), p. 579.

32. Tony Kushner Considers the Longstanding Problems of Virtue and Happiness. An Interview by David Savran," *American Theatre,* October 1994, p. 24.

33. John Lahr, "Earth Angels," *New Yorker,* December 13, 1993, p. 133.

34. John Simon, "Angelic Geometry," *New Yorker,* December 6, 1993, pp. 130-131.

35. Tony Kushner, *Angels in America. Part I. Millennium Approaches* (New York: Theatre Communications Group, 1992, 1993), p. 11.

36. Tennessee Williams interviewed on "The Dick Cavett Show," 1974.

37. Robert Brustein, "Robert Brustein on Theater: Angles in America," *New Republic,* May 24, 1993, p. 30.

38. Tony Kushner, *Angels in America. Part II. Perestroika* (New York: Theatre Communications Group, 1992, 1994), p. 141.

John R. Quinn (essay date March 1996)

SOURCE: Quinn, John R. "Corpus Juris Tertium: Redemptive Jurisprudence in *Angels in America*." *Theatre Journal* 48, no. 1 (March 1996): 79-90.

[*In the following essay, Quinn argues that the concept of law is central to both the national and spiritual themes running through* Angels in America. *Quinn asserts that, in Kushner's play, the law emerges as a kind of secular religion.*]

"In the beginning was the Word; . . . [then] The Word became flesh."

—John 1:1,14

Law, at least the contemporary American concept of it, is a nerve running through nearly every organ and extremity of the body of Tony Kushner's ***Angels in America: A Gay Fantasia on National Themes.*** The abundance of ***Angels*** passages that address or refer to the law demonstrates the subject's ubiquity in the plays. Among other things, two of the plays' central characters, Roy Cohn and Joe Pitt, are not only closeted homosexuals but also attorneys (Cohn is a seasoned practitioner, whereas Joe Pitt researches and drafts opinions for a federal judge). Their presence, as I discuss in greater depth below, saturates the plays' dialogue with the vocabulary and cultural referents of American legalspeak. Legal metaphor and allusion are also part of the everyday discourse of non-lawyers Louis and Prior: for example, Prior renders a "verdict" on Louis's failings in love,[1] Louis and Prior debate the merits of the judicial tasks of deliberating and rendering judgment (*MA* 38-39), and Louis's masturbatory intellectualism includes speculations on the relationship among law, "Justice," and the Constitution.[2] Law enters into countless other lay settings as well; to name a few, Mr. Ties reminds Harper of the "by-laws" (*MA* 102) of the International Organization of Travel Agents, Belize speaks of the "law" of love (*MA* 100), Roy urges Joe to find some "law" that he can break (*MA* 110), and the "Law for real" busts Harper's imagination (*P* 21). Legal places, such as the ironically named Hall of Justice in Brooklyn and Department of Justice in Washington, loom large in the plays' landscape. Lastly, many of the plays' pivotal dramatic moments are or involve momentous legal events, such as the trial of Ethel Rosenberg, Cohn's disbarment proceedings, and Louis's discovery of the conservative opinions that Joe Pitt ghostwrote for Judge Wilson.

In this essay I argue that law is more than subtext or local color. Instead, law is intricately intertwined among the "national" themes Kushner handles, significantly advancing the urgent and weighty messages about spirituality and apocalypse that *Angels* so poignantly delivers. Ultimately, law acquires the salient characteristics of a secular religion in the America that Kushner brings to the stage.

Many of the plays' principal characters embody different types or distinctive components of law. We know this by the stark difference between Joe Pitt's and Roy Cohn's legal ethics: they disagree strongly about the "legality" and necessity of Cohn's having accepted a loan from his client (*MA* 66) and about Cohn's having engaged in private, ex parte conversations with the judge during the Rosenberg case (*MA* 108). (Cohn and Joe clash equally in lay ethics as well, as evidenced by their argument over Joe's refusal to go to Washington without his wife Harper [*MA* 106-8]). Roy Cohn's ogreish, grotesque, scene-stealing command of *Angels* demands that his character be first in an interpretation of law's function in the plays.

Kushner employs Cohn, the "famous lawyer" (*MA* 112), as a stereotype of the successful lawyer in capitalist, materialist, litigious America. Like many of the other characters in the plays, however, Cohn's stereotypicality is only superficial; in reality, he is a subversion, or more accurately for Cohn, a perversion, of the familiar type. Cohn's lawyering is conspicuous for its mangling of truth, its shoot-from-the-hip, get-away-with-whatever-you-can impudence, and the ensuing lability of the governing rule of law. My focus here, however, is the extent to which Cohn's lawyering differs from the garden-variety, ethically compromised practice of the stereotypical American lawyer. As many readers and theatregoers probably would concur, a skillful attorney, if paid to do so, can argue that black is white or the Pope is Jewish. Increased media coverage of sensationalistic trials has stimulated American appetite to near insatiability and encouraged popular belief that success as a defense lawyer in particular seems to be a function of antics, gamesmanship and manipulation—a kind of legaltheatre. Delineation of the important though subtle difference between Cohn and the American stereotype first requires an accurate measure of the amount of truth-mangling and procedural impudence American jurisprudence regards as healthy, and an appraisal of the extent of ensuing preceptive instability it tolerates.

Truth's status in the epistemology of American jurisprudence is equivocal. On the one hand, fledgling lawyers are taught that truth is the pearl that advocacy and the adversary-based standard of American legal procedure are supposed, at the end of the day, to unearth. Most of the rules of evidence and procedure governing trials are specific applications of the general goal of promoting the reliability and trustworthiness of proof.[3] Even an accused's right to have an attorney, and to cross-examine witnesses, both of which are constitutional guarantees, are repeatedly justified by the Supreme Court on the ground that adversariness promotes truth.[4] When not abused, the procedural rules maximize the chance, though do not guarantee, that truth will emerge, that the judge or jury will ascertain the correct version of the historical events at issue in a case. On the other hand, even in their unabused application, the legal rules frequently endorse implicit departures from truth. Examples are the notorious legal fictions known as the presumption of innocence and the related distinction between legal guilt and factual guilt. Legal guilt is established by a sufficient quantity and quality (i.e., probativeness) of evidence; qualitative or quantitative deficiency results in acquittal, a concept the law carefully does not equate with factual innocence. Acquittal happens solely by operation of the presumption—not affirmative proof—of innocence and often may occur even when factual but inadequately proven guilt exists. Thus, "legal truth" equals not "factual truth," but only that which can be proven according to the standards of the law.

Cohn's conduct, however reprehensible, at first appears to be within the letter of this code. For example, we know that Cohn accepted a loan from a client, but in Cohn's words, unless the event can be "proven" (*MA* 66) it did not occur. On closer inspection, however, Cohn's disregard for truth is more serious, flagrant, and conscious than that committed by the American lawyer's opportunistic capitalization on an adversary's meager proof at trial. For Cohn, the law's presumption of innocence and distinction between legal and factual guilt lose their tolerable fictional nature because he applies them not only to his courtroom practice but to his lay existence. He so consistently professes belief in what are in fact untruths—for example, he denies he is homosexual even though he sleeps with men (*MA* 45), he tells Joe he has cancer, not AIDS, and then denies he is ill at all (*MA* 109), and he evades admitting he accepted a loan from a client—that his version of truth seems to be grounded entirely in courtroom epistemology rather than in lay standards. In a word, Cohn lives too literally and exclusively by the letter of the law, a provision of which is the law's tolerance of the fictitious "legal" fact.

By contrast, the stereotype of which Cohn is a corruption exhibits at least some residual regard for the factual truth underlying the evidence and some recollection of the original goals of the system. Even when evading the rules, the ethically compromised stereotype does so with less impudence than Cohn. In short, the stereotype may practice the law's fictions inside the courtroom, but does not live by them outside. Cohn, however, takes the law's fictions and loopholes outside the arena of the courtroom and lives his life by them. The symptom of Cohn's pathological internalization of legal standards of truth is a sense of complete randomness and chaos; he loses any ability even to know when he is indulging legal fictions. Ranting at his doctor over the telephone, Cohn aptly summarizes his evidentiary non-principles: "*I* don't even know what all I know. Half the time I just make it up, and it *still* turns out to be true!" (*P* 31, emphasis in original). Thus Cohn divorces the law (here, the evidentiary law, the way to truth) from its context, its spirit, the place where it has authority, by the consensus of the system and its participants. Disease and putrefaction inevitably ensue.

That Cohn's procedural jurisprudence is a diseased version of the norm is less subtly portrayed in the plays. Prototypically, aggrieved citizens do not have duels in the street but take their disputes to court, where judges and juries resolve them (and even the government prosecuting a criminal must proceed likewise). The same framework exists in Cohn's world, but it is contaminated by abuse. Again, it is fair to say that from even the typical lawyer we nowadays tolerate or even expect some procedural abuse in the name of zealous advocacy (i.e., the resort to last minute motions, undisclosed witnesses or other kinds of scheming mischief or disruptive harassing malpractices) when diligent research, copious documentation or rhetorical acumen fail. Still, Cohn's transgressions are far more substantively egregious. He does not merely file more last minute motions or harbor more undisclosed witnesses, but instead contaminates the entire framework, employing such litigation strategies as "schtupping" (*MA* 14), securing theatre tickets for judges (*MA* 12), and improperly conversing ex parte with them (*MA* 108). In really "big" cases he exploits the assistance of

a "well-placed friend" in the Department of Justice (*MA* 67). Cohn practices not law but a debased, Boss Tweed politics masquerading as law, conduct that even American audiences long exposed to indictments of the conniving antics of the successful American lawyer find appalling. In short, Cohn's abuse of procedure, like his disregard for truth, is a perversion of the original, a mutation of the prototype, a desecration and defilement. To call his victory in any given legal matter a "legal result" would be profoundly ironic by any standard but Cohn's.

Like an incipient cancer, Cohn's corruption, however destructive, is nonetheless insidious. It infiltrates and draws on the body's internal systems to spread, eventually overtaking and destroying the host—Cohn or the law. Importantly, Cohn continues to operate within the framework even as he contaminates it. Although he corrupts the method by which judges decide cases (by sleeping with them and the like), he does not try to have cases decided any other way. He instead seeks to spread his tainted kind of judge: tellingly, Cohn approvingly describes the Reagan appointees on the federal bench as "land mines" (*MA* 66), lying in wait to destroy affirmative action and other civil and constitutional protections. In short, Cohn is a diseased version of the norm.

The ensuing instability of the rule of law that Cohn's lawyering engenders is, like his ailing regard for truth and sickly abuse of procedure, a diseased amplification of the norm. Delineating the typical lawyer's tolerance for law's instability is best accomplished in terms of the concept of "determinacy." Determinacy—i.e., susceptibility to a more or less single correct reading—is a concern in legal scholarship because law usually takes the form of a written text, such as the Constitution, a statute, or a regulation, that requires interpretation (the interpretations often taking the form of judicial opinions that, in turn, also become texts to interpret). Like truth, determinacy has both an "official" and an "unofficial" position in the law. On the one hand, determinacy has long been supposed to be a sine qua non of the law: if the citizenry wishes to avoid prison, individuals must be able to know what the rule of law is and what it requires of them. Various doctrines, reliance on precedent, and reason decide individual cases or occasions for interpretation.

On the other hand, sensitive readers of United States law have always known that other factors affect the outcome and the rule of law. Oliver Wendell Holmes is an early spokesperson of legal realism, acknowledging that we are, after all, only human beings, and not machines, deciding legal cases and writing legal rules, so the social, political or other "attitude" of the decision-maker also influences the outcome.[5] More recently, a movement in the legal academy known as

Critical Legal Studies has made these factors, especially the political attitude of legislators and the original Constitution drafters, rather than doctrine, the focus of legal study.[6] Currently, the debate about determinacy has taken on greater intensity as the emerging law and literature movement has gained momentum.[7] In that debate, defenders of the distinction between literary and legal interpretation argue that law is unlike literature because literary texts tolerate or even prize plurivocality and multiple meaning, as argued by famous spokespersons of literary ambiguity (Cleanth Brooks), plurivocality (Roland Barthes) and indeterminacy (Derrida).[8] In response, it has been argued that law is not as hermeneutically determinate as has been commonly supposed, but instead has determinacy superimposed on it for necessary political ends.[9] Relying, moreover, on Robert Crosman's assertion that something that might be regarded as a single correct meaning is "negotiated" by collections of individual readers' interpretations, one might also argue that literature is itself less indeterminate than legal scholars suppose.[10]

Against even this backdrop, Cohn exhibits a more perverted indeterminacy. The indeterminacy that occupies legal scholars is a by-product of the effort to arrive at a rule of law, of the process that at times may only afford lip service to justice, fairness, consistency and so forth. For Cohn, on the contrary, the indeterminacy of the rule of law is a central tenet of his creed of life. Cohn's directive to Joe Pitt—"[m]ake the law or subject to it" (*P* 108)—is telling. Cohn sees only two possible relations to the law, and because he seeks to avoid, at all costs, ever subjecting himself to the law, Cohn ceaselessly works to change it. In other words, indeterminacy for him is the governing principle, rather than the unavoidable consequence, of human lawmaking. Indeterminate, alterable rules are the staple of his existence.

Thus, the indeterminacy that Cohn amplifies virtually disables law from continuing to carry out its principal function—i.e., to govern people, to define their rights and obligations, to advise them how to behave. In Cohn's world, the law follows the deed, merely rubber stamps the transpired events. To paraphrase Balzac, Cohn's actions are the author, and law is merely the secretary,[11] a relationship that strips law of its ability to prescribe, or describe, what ought to be.

Such a law is absolutely meaningless, form without substance, letter without spirit. If Kushner were Milton, Cohn would be Satan—impudent, conniving, master of words and tongues, insatiable sovereign of Chaos. For Kushner, of course, Cohn is the bad "Angel" battling the forces of good for the soul of America.

Cohn continues pathetically to profess a belief in the very system he has corrupted, frequently using legal vocabulary that he has stripped of meaning. For example, he insists on his "constitutional right" to be attended by a white nurse, describes Belize's attempt to steal his AZT supply as "illegal," and threatens to "report" him for it (*P* 60). Cohn himself, though an attorney, lacks any real knowledge of substantive law. In the hospital, a complete reversal occurs and Cohn becomes the client-like recipient of legal advice from Belize, even though the ostensibly omnipotent Cohn at first cannot induce Belize, the "butterfingers spook faggot" black drag queen nurse, even to sit with him (*P* 30). Belize ultimately brings law to its knees, as Cohn resorts to begging Belize for his company, and it turns out that Belize in fact knows more about the legal aspects of AZT than Cohn and more about its medical aspects than Cohn's "very qualified, very expensive WASP" doctor (*P* 29).[12] In Cohn's world, the Department of Justice in Washington and the Hall of Justice in Brooklyn dispense anything but true justice—there is only corruption in Washington (*MA* 63), and Judge Wilson's opinions denying homosexuals constitutional protection and narrowly construing federal environmental protection legislation (*P* 109) exemplify the injustice issued in Brooklyn.[13] In what are mere words, collections of letters devoid of meaning and spirit, these designations have the hollow ring of labels adorning the mock-equivalent institutions and monuments in totalitarian regimes.

Cohn's deviation from the jurisprudential norm is indeed like that of a cancer, ravenous in its hunger, growing and operating at a rate independent of the rest of the body of which it is a part, destined to overtake and kill the very body that sustains it. But the corrupt, diseased, tumorous nature of Cohn's lawyering also has important textual and thematic links with the physical infection and ensuing "corruption" of Cohn's flesh and blood with AIDS. In a telling speech in which Cohn again describes the indeterminacy of law, he also reveals an important link between the law and corporeality. Feigning indifference to the disbarment committee charges, Cohn defends his disregard for the "fine points" (*MA* 63) of the law, explaining: "I don't see the Law as a dead and arbitrary collection of antiquated dictums, thou shall, thou shalt not, because, because I know the Law's a pliable, breathing, sweating . . . *organ*" (*MA* 66; emphasis in original). (This motif is echoed later, when Cohn complains that with only one telephone line in his hospital room he cannot "perform basic bodily functions" [*P* 31].)

In another context or from another speaker, Cohn's characterization of law as pliable and breathing would be entirely unobjectionable. Popular disapproval of law tends to increase the more the laity perceives law to be a collection of technicalities, antiquated dictums, and "fine points," so Cohn's declaration has some superficial appeal. For Cohn, however, the speech is another clever, lawyerly elocution to justify his own lawless conduct.

The speech is also an important indicator of Cohn's thematic function.

Cohn's corporealization of the law reverberates in his own life and death. Law is Cohn's lifeblood, as vital to his existence as his actual circulatory system. Therefore, it is fitting that he dies as soon as he learns he is disbarred. Counterfeit prophet, Cohn actually foresaw the events; when first receiving the disbarment committee charges, Cohn defiantly insists that he will be a lawyer "till my last bitter day on earth . . . until the day I die" (*MA* 69). Cohn's prophecy has the ironic literalness of those voiced by three witches to Macbeth,[14] as Cohn's death occurs immediately after, and on the same day as, his disbarment. Indeed, his rejoinder to Ethel Rosenberg's announcement of his disbarment is the query "Am I dead?" (*P* 113).

The coincidence of Cohn's disbarment and death is important. Both events exemplify the triumph of the true spoils of corruption. Both also signify the death of Cohn's corrupted, hollow, spiritless, unprincipled law. Cohn's brand of law fails as a way to salvation; he and it are both destroyed.

By allusion to biblical conceptions of law, prophecy, and salvation, Kushner uses Cohn's life, law practice and death by HIV infection to illuminate his message about spirituality and apocalypse. The ubiquity of law in the world of **Angels in America** is roughly akin to law's omnipresence and stature in the everyday life of the Jewish world portrayed in the Old Testament. Like the original law of Moses, Cohn is the old law that became corrupted as people lived by its letter but ignored its spirit. The sacred monuments of his law (the Hall of Justice and the Department of Justice) have become places of injustice, overrun with blasphemers, like the Temple in Jerusalem. And like that Temple and the old law, those monuments and Cohn must be destroyed and rebuilt or supplanted by a new covenant.

At the same time—and this is Kushner's accomplishment in the plays—the corporeality of Cohn and of Cohn's law are also inverted representations of the new law, a sort of Satan resurrected. John's Gospel tells us that "in the beginning was the Word"[15]—the old law—and then the Word "became flesh"[16]—Jesus Christ, the new law. Cohn's Satanic fiendishness and spiritual barrenness make him the antithesis of Christian values or the new covenant Christ was supposed to inaugurate, yet Kushner's text shrouds some of Cohn's moments with Christ references. For example, Cohn's heart is a "[t]ough little muscle" that "[n]ever bleeds," (*P* 27), the opposite not only of a political liberal's figurative bleeding heart, but also of Christ's; Cohn's hospital stay begins as a kind of crucifixion by IV needle, during which his combative but spare uttering of "I *hurt*" (*P* 27; emphasis in original) antithetically echoes Christ's

similarly unadorned "I thirst."[17] Like Christ, Cohn believes he is misunderstood by his own people (fellow lawyers) and handed over by them for trial and condemnation by outsiders. Cohn expressly compares the disbarment committee to a foreign sovereign: he describes the committee members as "genteel gentleman Brahmin lawyers, country-club men," who probably think of him as "some filthy little Jewish troll," and so complains that he is being tried by a jury that is not comprised of his "peers" (*MA* 66-67). Cohn is thus a Christlike sacrificial lamb. At the same time, however, he is Satan ousted from Heaven.

Cohn, then, is simultaneously Satanic and Christlike. He is Satanic in so far as he appears like a fallen prophet at the end of the world. He is, however, structurally similar to Christ in that he brings a new, or *successor,* law that is supposed to supplant a *former* law. But Cohn-as-Christ is as corrupted as the old law that the scriptural Christ was sent to destroy, and so Cohn too must be destroyed. Before the Angel appears to Prior, a voice echoing John the Baptist's repeatedly urges Prior to "prepare the way" (*MA* 35), the announcement that prophets will follow, and, like the biblical declarations, an admonition that the prophets may be good or false. Cohn, preacher of blindness, not vision, is a false prophet. In this way Cohn simultaneously signifies both the old and the new law. Through such a doubly endowed figure, Kushner makes the point that the successor—i.e., the current—regime, has features in common with the one it succeeded: the new, like the old, has run its course, has been corrupted, is also at its end.

Lawyering's inherent theatricality, and the fascination of audiences with legal drama, naturally makes law fruitful material for the stage. But law functions thematically, and especially effectively, as Kushner's material because his plays are a fantasia on *American* themes. In Kushner's America, secular law is a kind of religion, in much the same way scriptural law was religion in the world of Old Testament Judaism. Numerous legal scholars have theorized constitutional law as a kind of civil religion for America.[18] Kushner renders this same concept theatrically.

A cornerstone of the law-as-religion argument is the notion that the United States Constitution is, like the Torah, the Koran, and the New Testament, a "sacred text,"[19] a document having both rules and great symbolic value for the people it governs and "dispens[ing] not just social order but spiritual identity."[20] Further, like the Torah, the Koran, and the New Testament, the Constitution has spawned a body of secondary texts commenting upon and interpreting the primary text which accrue to and become part of the text. Judicial opinions interpreting the Constitution—including the one Joe Pitt ghostwrote for Judge Wilson denying homosexuals protection under the Equal Protection

Clause—are like Talmudic commentary on the Torah, or the apostles' epistles or contemporary priestly sermons interpreting the Gospels. Cohn is absolutely correct when he explains to Belize that: "Lawyers are . . . the High Priests of America. We alone know the words that made America. Out of thin air. We alone know how to use The Words. The Law . . ." (*P* 89). The point is underscored theatrically: onstage, the massive desk that dominates Cohn's office and opening scene functions as a kind of secular temple or altar.[21] Continuing the metaphor, Cohn urges Belize to "[h]ire a lawyer, sue somebody" because "it's good for the soul" (*P* 89), a line through which Kushner seems to mock the sincerity of Cohn's claim that litigation has soul-enhancing properties. The line also conveys the playwright's overt indictment of America's blindness and spiritual death; its law lacks any spiritual dimension. It is hardly "good for the soul."

By juxtaposing Cohn, the lawyer whose body is infected, with the plays' other lawyer (Joe Pitt) and other infected body (Prior), Kushner poignantly reveals his vision of America. Pitt is loyalty, belief, hard work, idealism, discipline, institutional religion. Not a bad guy if you agree with his politics, but the point is that he fervently believes in "the system." Pitt is the non-corrupted, non-infected version of Cohn. Pitt's law, like Roy Cohn's, is also "not justice" or "an expression of the ideal" but only "power" (*P* 110); it is not as corrupt in its process as Cohn's ex parte communications and favors, but it is every but as lacking in real justice because it fails to connect with principles, consequences, real people, or a coherent vision of the common good. The legal opinions Pitt wrote for Judge Wilson (*P* 109-10) show that the "restored" law (*MA* 26) in which Pitt believes is, like Cohn's corrupted version, all letter and no spirit, form over substance. It is a jurisprudence that allows him to conclude that the federal Air and Water Protection Act "doesn't protect *people,* but actually only *air* and *water*" (*P* 109; emphasis in original).[22] Pitt's law cannot be literally regarded as "corrupted" for the simple reason that it is altogether devoid of flesh and blood. Pitt's internal deadness emphasizes that his law-religion is no more the path to salvation than Cohn's.

Prior, by contrast, is not institutionally religious, and not a lawyer, but he is the path to salvation. Kushner gives Prior only a handful of lines of overtly legal dialogue, but collectively they are telling: Prior by implication disagrees with Louis's preference for the "shaping of the law" and instead endorses the judgment and "execution" that Louis rejects (*MA* 38-39), expressly rendering a "verdict" against Louis's deficient heart (*MA* 78-79). He also complains that Louis's departure was "criminal," something he had "no right"

to do (*MA* 77). When Prior takes his final leave of the angels, he urges them to "sue God for abandonment" (*P* 136), echoing Cohn's earlier flippant advice to Belize (*P* 89).

Collectively, these lines reveal that Prior, like other prophets, is in some ways a product of his culture (namely, the United States, where law is an influential cultural referent), and, like many Americans, he often expresses his thoughts and feelings in legal jargon and metaphor. Individually, the lines reveal the dissimilarities between Prior's law-religion and Cohn's. Unlike Roy's law, Prior's is avowedly determinate. Deliberations must result in verdicts, and must proceed according to principles; Prior's law prizes the justice and truth lacking in Cohn's (and, for that matter, Pitt's). Prior is also a spiritual character, marked from the outset as one with vision, sensitivity and strength, which sets him apart from Cohn. (He is often referred to literally as a "prophet" [e.g., *P* 85].) A seer, Prior is a Jacob figure who ascends, undergoes transformation, and descends; the true prophet in polar opposition to Cohn's false prophecy. The union of law and religion that Cohn aggressively forges and appropriates is innate to Prior, whose name, after all, denotes judge in both secular and religious settings.

Returning to matters of flesh, Cohn and Prior differ in a subtle but important way. Both have HIV infection, but Cohn's body deteriorates more quickly and substantially than Prior's, which exhibits symptoms, to be sure, but seems to have reached a détente with the virus. Because the disease is AIDS, one cannot state that Prior "has survived," or "is cured," but he nonetheless is surviving, and has been "living with" (*P* 146)—not dying from—the disease for what Kushner wants us to regard as a long time (at least five years, longer than Prior lived with Louis [*P* 146]). Furthermore, what suffering and deterioration Prior does experience engenders his visionary development, whereas Cohn's persona retains all its manipulative mean-spiritedness in the face of fatal illness, such as when he tricks Ethel Rosenberg into thinking he is dead (*P* 115). It is no coincidence that Prior affirmatively chooses "more life" (*P* 136), whereas Cohn welcomes death, glad to be "finally done with this world, at long, long last" (*P* 113). If the physical corruption of Cohn's body and his corrupt lawyering—or the death of his body and lack of spirituality—go hand in hand, then so do the survival of Prior's infected body and his spiritual growth. Simply put, Prior's physical life continues only because he transcends mere physicality and develops spiritually, whereas Cohn dies seeking only physical remedies and materiality. Flesh follows spirit. (Onstage the inversion is carried further, as Prior and Cohn's appearances contrast with each other and subvert ordinary expectations. Prior, the endorser of life, wears a black, hooded cloak during much of **Perestroika,** while Cohn, the embodiment of death, wears hospital-patient white.)[23]

The spiritual nature of Prior's law is underscored further by its dissimilarity from Louis's. Louis, whose Jewishness is featured throughout the plays, is the textbook rabbinic figure; yet he, too, is not the correct law or path to salvation. He exists *completely* in the rational world, the verbal world, is capable of endless speechifying (*MA* 89-92). The deliberative process is never-ending; indeed, he declares Justice to be an "immensity" (*MA* 39), presumably as immense as the body of Talmudic commentary. His preference for the process over the verdict (*MA* 38), a desire for excessively individualized justice, is his way of avoiding ultimate responsibility as Cohn does, an attitude consistent with his flight from Prior's illness. He does not see the law as indeterminate in theory; in practice, however, he is, as Belize observes, so "ambivalent" (*MA* 95) about everything that he will never move through the deliberative stage and arrive at a judgment. Louis is overly rational; his "law" is all in the mind, all "Big Ideas" (*P* 96), a process of words only (living up to his occupation, a word processor).[24] His law, like Cohn's, lacks any spiritual dimension. Not only flesh, but also the mind, must follow spirit.

If Prior has any disciple or spiritual comrade in the plays it is Belize. Like Prior, Belize has imaginative capacities (e.g., he does drag) and is emotional; he lacks neither mind (recall that he advises Cohn) nor body, but he exemplifies most the "law of love" (*MA* 100), exhibiting a kind of unassuming spirituality. In contrast to Louis's assertion that Justice is "immensity," Belize insists, with the unadorned wisdom of an apparent fool figure, that "Justice is simple" (*MA* 100). Unlike Louis, he can "smell," and what he smells is "[s]oftness, compliance, forgiveness, grace" (*MA* 100).

Prior's religion, if he can be regarded as representing one, is a sort of secular, modern-day American gnosticism. Following Ronald Garet, I use the term in a metaphoric sense, uncapitalized, to refer to ideas about salvation comparable to those of the traditions of Hellenistic culture known as Gnosticism.[25] I suggest that Prior exemplifies a gnostic interpretive position toward the law. As Garet has argued, the interpretive feat characteristic of gnosticism is a revisionist approach to creation stories in order "to privilege radical proposals and to relativize the claims of the orthodox."[26] Typically, the "radical proposal" is a "retelling" of the creation story, of man's beginnings (Garet, 102). Substantively, Garet's uncapitalized "gnosticism" is "an account of redemption as a final overthrow of the limits inherent in the creaturely state" (102).

Through Prior, Kushner exemplifies a jurisprudential hermeneutics and substantive theme about salvation that are gnostic. Unquestionably, Prior demonstrates the gnostic triumph of spirituality over corporeality, the "final overthrow" of the "limits inherent in the creaturely state," the flesh of Cohn's world. Yet Prior does this without in fact forsaking his body.

The spirit of gnosticism is best understood as the Latin *anima,* as distinguished from *animus*. Both are soul, or spirit, but *anima* is soul as the principle of life, whereas *animus* is soul as a principle of intellection and sensation. Prior exemplifies the triumph of *anima* over *animus*. Joe Pitt might be said to exhibit *animus,* a soul, but his is belief in the mind only. Prior exhibits spiritual knowledge, not the mere belief of Joe Pitt, nor the over-rationalized kind of knowledge Louis pursues. Prior's knowledge, by contrast, is intuitive, wisdom based on experience and observation rather than books and deliberation. His intuition is often a kind of clairvoyance; at many moments in the play, he sees beyond mere appearances to the hidden truth. For example, when he sees Harper for the first time, he knows that her husband Joe is homosexual, without her saying anything (*MA* 33). Finally, Prior's choice to come back down to earth and not remain in that "other" place where angels traditionally reside is kind of gnostic gesture, a belief that salvation comes from within the individual person.[27]

In Kushner's gnostic jurisprudence, the "radical proposal" is not a retelling of the creation story so much as it is a revision of redemption, a retelling of the orthodoxy's claims about salvation. If in the beginning the law was the word, and the word then became flesh, then in the gospel according to Kushner, the spirit must now transcend as it coexists with the flesh, as the new and final law, the new way, truth and life.

Notes

My thanks to James Haigney of the Department of Theatre Arts at the State University of Stony Brook for an insightful introduction to Kushner's complex opus and for helpful comments on an earlier draft of this essay, and to Brian Gempp for continued trustworthy editorial assistance.

1. Tony Kushner, *Angels in America: A Gay Fantasia on National Themes. Part One: Millennium Approaches* (New York: Theatre Communications Group, 1993), 78. Subsequent references will be included parenthetically in the text, preceded by the abbreviation *MA* (for *Millennium Approaches*).

2. Tony Kushner, *Angels in America: A Gay Fantasia on National Themes. Part Two: Perestroika* (New York: Theatre Communications Group, 1994), 35, 67. Subsequent references will be included parenthetically in the text, preceded by the abbreviation *P* (for *Perestroika*).

3. For example, the Supreme Court has characterized cross examination as the "greatest legal engine ever invented for the discovery of truth." *California v. Green,* 399 U.S. 149, 158; 90 Sup. Ct. 1930, 1935 (1970). Addressing procedure more generally, the Court has explained, "the procedural rules which have been fashioned from the generality of due process are our best instruments for the distillation and evaluation of essential facts from the conflicting welter of data that life and our adversary system present. [The rules] enhance the possibility that truth will emerge from the confrontation of opposing versions and conflicting data. 'Procedure is to law what "scientific method" is to science.'" *In Re Gault,* 387 U.S. 1, 21; 87 Sup. Ct. 1428,1440 (1967) (Fortas, J., quoting Henry Hubbar Foster, "Social Work, the Law and Social Action," in *Social Casework* [1964], 386).

4. The Sixth Amendment to the United States Constitution guarantees a criminal defendant the rights, among others, "to be confronted with the witnesses against him" and "to have the Assistance of Counsel for his defence." U.S. Constitution, amend. 6. The Supreme Court, in justifying the concept that the right to counsel necessarily includes the right to effective assistance of counsel, has explained that competent advocacy is essential to the truth-finding process of the adversary system. *United States v. Cronic,* 466 U.S. 648, 656; 104 Sup. Ct. 2039, 2045 (1984) (Stevens, J.). The Confrontation Clause, according to the Supreme Court, guarantees two separate rights: the right to physically face the accuser and witnesses, and the right to cross-examine those witnesses; its "central concern" is to "ensure the reliability of the evidence against a criminal defendant by subjecting it to rigorous testing in the context of an adversary proceeding." *Maryland v. Craig,* 497 U.S. 836, 845; 110 Sup. Ct. 3157, 3163 (1990) (O'Connor, J.).

5. Oliver Wendell Holmes, "The Path of the Law," *Harvard Law Review* 10 (1897): 457, 467.

6. For general reference, see Duncan Kennedy and Karl E. Klare, "A Bibliography of Critical Legal Studies," *Yale Law Journal* 94 (1984): 461-90 (1984) and James Boyle, ed., *Critical Legal Studies* (New York: New York University Press, 1994).

7. The "law and literature" enterprise has two branches: the reading of literary texts with special attention to their treatment of law, and the effort to import literary theorists' insights about reading into the project of interpreting legal texts. Examples of the former include the collection of legal readings of *The Merchant of Venice* gathered in *Cardozo Studies in Law and Literature* 5.1 (1993) and Brook Thomas's *Cross-Examinations of Law and Literature: Cooper, Hawthorne, Stowe and Melville* (New York: Cambridge University Press, 1987). The latter I have discussed in greater depth in my recent article, "The Lost Language of the Irishgaymale: Textualization in

Law and Literature," *Columbia Human Rights Law Review* 26 (1995): 553-678.

8. Seventh Circuit Court of Appeals Judge Richard Posner is a major opponent of the law and literature movement. He details his position in *Law and Literature: A Misunderstood Relation* (Cambridge: Harvard University Press, 1988), 247-57.

9. See Paul Kahn, "Interpretation and Authority in State Constitutionalism," *Harvard Law Review* 106 (1993): 1147.

10. Robert Crosman, "How Readers Make Meaning," *College Literature* 9 (1982): 207-15.

11. Honoré de Balzac, *Introduction to The Human Comedy* 15 (1842).

12. Belize is also the name of a South American nation whose laissez-faire regime makes it popular among tax-shelter seekers in the United States.

13. Just as Roy Cohn was a real person, much of Kushner's legal material is real, or realistic. As most know, there does exist a unit of the executive branch of the federal government known as the Department of Justice, and it is in Washington. There does not exist, however, a "Hall of Justice" in Brooklyn, but we know this is the label for a federal courthouse (*P* 92). A federal courthouse does exist in Brooklyn but it houses only trial-level judges, not appellate-level federal judges like the one for whom Joe Pitt is a clerk. A much more imposing courthouse, and one that houses both trial-level and appellate-level federal judges, exists in lower Manhattan and likely was Kushner's model.

14. Shakespeare, *The Tragedy of Macbeth,* act 4, scene 1, lines 80-81 and 92-94.

15. John 1:1 New American Bible.

16. John 1:14.

17. John 19:28.

18. See, e.g., Ronald R. Garet, "Comparative Normative Hermeneutics: Scripture, Literature, Constitution," *Southern California Law Review* 58 (1985): 35; Thomas C. Grey, "The Constitution as Scripture," *Stanford Law Review* 37 (1984): 1; Sanford Levinson, "The Constitution in American Civil Religion," *Supreme Court Review* (1979).

19. E. L. Doctorow, "A Citizen Reads the Constitution," in Doctorow, *Jack London, Hemingway, and the Constitution: Selected Essays, 1977-1992* (New York: Random House, 1993), 126. The document probably also falls within the category of "Classic Texts" that the world's oldest living Bolshevik complains no one reads anymore (*P,* 14).

20. Doctorow, "A Citizen Reads," 126.

21. George C. Wolfe, director, *Angels in America: Millennium Approaches.* By Tony Kushner. With Larry Pine (Cohn) and Daniel Jenkins (Prior). Walter Kerr Theatre, New York. 14 October 1994.

22. Although it sounds absurd, the theatrical opinion is not hyperbole, but a realistic portrayal of the kind of letter-over-spirit way in which real-life Republican appointees read the Constitution. A flagrant example is Justice Clarence Thomas's reasoning in a case involving the claim of a transsexual inmate who argued that his incarceration with male inmate invited assaults and abuse and was therefore "cruel and unusual punishment." Justice Thomas concluded that because the "unfortunate attack that befell" the transsexual "was not part of his *sentence,* it did not constitute *'punishment'* under the Eighth Amendment." *Farmer v. Brennan,* 114 Sup. Ct. 1970 (1994) (emphasis added).

23. George C. Wolfe, director, *Angels in America: Perestroika.* By Tony Kushner. With Larry Pine (Cohn) and Daniel Jenkins (Prior). Walter Kerr Theatre, New York. 15 October 1994.

24. James Haigney first called to my attention the significance of Louis's occupation.

25. For general background on Gnosticism, see Elaine Pagels, *The Gnostic Gospels* (New York: Random House, 1979) and Giovanni Filoramo, *A History of Gnosticism,* trans. Anthony Alcock (Cambridge: Blackwell, 1991).

26. Ronald R. Garet, "Gnostic Due Process," *Yale Journal of Law and the Humanities* 7.1 (1995): 97, 102-3. Garet offers a fascinating reading of Justice Douglas's opinion in *Griswold v. Connecticut,* 381 U.S. 479 (1965) (the important precursor to *Roe v. Wade,* 410 U.S. 113 [1973]) arguing that it is a gnostic text.

27. Although this essay addresses religious themes in *Angels* it expressly does not discuss Mormonism because, *inter alia,* my point of entry is law, not religion; each strand in Kushner's complex thematic tapestry warrants discrete attention; and because Kushner's use of Mormon material has received notable treatment by David Savran in "Ambivalence, Utopia, and A Queer Sort of Materialism: How *Angels in America* Reconstructs the Nation," *Theatre Journal* 47 (1995): 207, 216-21.

Charles McNulty (essay date spring 1996)

SOURCE: McNulty, Charles. "*Angels in America*: Tony Kushner's Theses on the Philosophy of History." *Modern Drama* 39, no. 1 (spring 1996): 84-96.

[*In the following essay, McNulty examines Kushner's representation of the AIDS epidemic in* Angels in America *in the context of American politics and history. McNulty asserts that while* Millennium Approaches *offers fresh insight into the workings of history,* Perestroika *retreats from this radical historical revisioning through the fantastical element of the angel descending from heaven.*]

AIDS plays have come to be thought of as a phenomenon of the 1980s, as Happenings were of the 1960s. Though the epidemic still rages, the bravely furious genre that began with William Hoffman's *As Is* and Larry Kramer's *The Normal Heart* has for the most part receded into the paragraphs of theater history textbooks. Nicholas de Jongh identifies the central mission of these plays as the fight against "an orthodoxy that regards AIDS as a mere local difficulty, principally affecting a reviled minority."[1] It is not entirely surprising, then, that the category has been said to have drawn to a close. The disease, after all, has been acknowledged, albeit belatedly, to be a widespread calamity; only the morally deaf, dumb, and blind have resisted this assessment, and they most certainly remain beyond the pale of agitprop, no matter how artfully conceived. To make things official, an obituary of the genre appeared in *American Theatre* in October of 1989:

> Recently, AIDS has fallen off as a central subject for new drama. It's no wonder. When, for instance, spectacle and public ritual are so movingly combined in the image and action of the Names Project Quilt, conventional theater seems redundant—at best a pale imitation of the formal, mass expressions that help give shape to real grief and anger. Time and again the spirited protestors of ACT UP have demonstrated that the theater of AIDS is in the streets.[2]

The cult of Tony Kushner's **Angels in America,** by far the most celebrated play of the 1990s, would appear, however, to have rendered all this premature. Subtitled **A Gay Fantasia on National Themes,** Kushner's two-part epic features a deserted gay man with full-blown AIDS battling both heaven and earth. But **Angels** represents not so much a revival of the category as a radical rethinking of its boundaries. For the playwright, the question is no longer what is the place of AIDS in history, but what of history itself can be learned through the experience of gay men and AIDS.

Kushner's angels were inspired not from any Biblical ecstasy but from the great twentieth-century German-Jewish critic Walter Benjamin's "Theses on the Philosophy of History."[3] Benjamin, writing in the spring of 1940 in France only a few months before he was to kill himself trying to escape the German occupation, borrows Paul Klee's 1920 painting *Angelus Novus* to convey his rigorously anti-Hegelian understanding of the movement of history:

> This is how one pictures the angel of history. His face is turned toward the past. Where we perceive a chain of events, he sees one single catastrophe which keeps piling wreckage upon wreckage and hurls it in front of his feet. The angel would like to stay, awaken the dead, and make whole what has been smashed. But a storm is blowing from Paradise; it has got caught in his wings with such violence that the angel can no longer close them. This storm irresistibly propels him into the future

to which his back is turned, while the pile of debris before him grows skyward. This storm is what we call progress.[4]

The movement of history is conceived not in terms of a dialectical narrative intent on progress, but as a steadfast path of destruction. All, however, is not lost. For Benjamin, the present represents a crisis point in which there is the opportunity to take cognizance of the homogeneous course of history, and thereby shift a specific era out of it.[5] For Kushner, a gay activist and dramatist enthralled by Benjamin's brooding analysis of history, the present crisis couldn't be more clear. Surveying five years of the first decade of the AIDS epidemic, the playwright casts a backward glance on America's domestic strife, and with it something unexpected flickers into view—the revolutionary chance to blast open the oppressive continuum of history and steer clear into the next millennium.

To realize this Benjamin-inspired vision, Kushner follows the lives of two couples and one political racketeer from the annals of the American closet—all in the throes of traumatic change. Louis, unable to deal with the fact his lover Prior has AIDS, abandons him; Joe, an ambitious Mormon lawyer, wants to abandon the homosexual part of himself, but ends, instead, abandoning his valium-popping wife Harper, and last, but not least, Roy Cohn, sick with AIDS, abandons nothing because he holds onto nothing. In an age in which shirkers of responsibility are encouraged to unite, Louis, the obstructed New York Jewish intellectual, and Joe, the shellacked all-American Mormon protégé of Cohn, spend a month together in bed, while their partners are forced to find ways of coping alone. "Children of the new morning, criminal minds. Selfish and greedy and loveless and blind. Reagan's children," is how Louis characterizes Joe and himself, in this most troubling trouble-free time. "You're scared. So am I. Everybody is in the land of the free. God help us all,"[6] he says to Joe, sincerely, though at the same time still groping for a way to move beyond guilt and self-consciousness into the intoxicating pleasures of sexual betrayal.

Kushner provides a quintessential American framework for the current historical dilemma in the play's opening scene, which features Rabbi Isidor Chemelwitz's eulogy for Louis's grandmother. Not knowing the departed too well, the Rabbi speaks of her as "not a person but a whole kind of person, the ones who crossed the ocean, who brought with us to America the villages of Russia and Lithuania—and how we struggled, and how we fought, for the family, for the Jewish home, so that you would not grow up *here,* in this strange place, in the melting pot where nothing melted" (1:10). Referring to the mourners as descendants, Rabbi Chemelwitz admits that great voyages from the old worlds are no longer possible, "[b]ut every day of your lives the miles that

voyage between that place and this one you cross. Every day. In you that journey is. [. . .] She was the last of the Mohicans, this one was. Pretty soon . . . all the old will be dead" (1:10-11). For Kushner, the past's intersection with the present is inevitable, a fact of living; what disturbs him is the increasing failure of Americans to recognize this, the willful amnesia that threatens to blank out the nation's memory as it moves into the next millennium.

This fugitive wish to escape the clutches of the past is concentrated most intensely in Louis, who is faced with the heavy burden of having to care for his sick lover. An underemployed, hyper-rationalizing word processing clerk in the court system, he is unable to come to terms with his current life crisis. In a conversation with his Rabbi, he tries to explain why a person might be justified in abandoning a loved one at a time of great need:

> Maybe because this person's sense of the world, that it will change for the better with struggle, maybe a person who has this neo-Hegelian positivist sense of constant historical progress towards happiness or perfection or something, who feels very powerful because he feels connected to these forces, moving uphill all the time . . . maybe that person can't, um, incorporate sickness into his sense of how things are supposed to go. Maybe vomit . . . and sores and disease . . . really frighten him, maybe . . . he isn't so good with death.
>
> (1:25)

Louis is determined to "maybe" himself out of his unfortunate present reality—and he's not beyond invoking the heaviest of nineteenth-century intellectual heavyweights to help him out. This peculiar trait is only magnified after he eventually leaves Prior for Joe. One of the more incendiary moments occurs at a coffee shop with Prior's ex-lover and closest friend, Belize. Wishing to ask about Prior's condition, Louis launches instead into a de Tocqueville-esque diatribe. "[T]here are no gods here, no ghosts and spirits in America, there are no angels in America, no spiritual past, no racial past, there's only the political, and the decoys and the ploys to maneuver around the inescapable battle of politics" (1:92), he explains breathlessly over coffee to Belize, who appears unimpressed by all the academic fireworks. In fact, Belize makes clear that he can see right through Louis's highbrow subterfuge. "[A]re you deliberately transforming yourself into an arrogant, sexual-political Stalinist-slash-racist flag-waving thug for my benefit" (1:94), he asks, knowing all too well from his experience as a gay African American drag queen that history is not simply some dry-as-dust abstraction, but an approximation of the way individuals lead both their public and private lives.

Though Kushner is critical of Louis, he in no way diminishes the gravity of what this character is forced to deal with. Louis has, after all, good reason for wanting to flee. When he confronts his lover on the floor of their bedroom, burning with fever and excreting blood, the full horror of this disease is conveyed in all its mercilessness and squalor. "Oh help. Oh help. Oh God oh God oh God help me I can't I can't I can't" (1:48), he says to himself, mantra-like, over his fainted lover— and who could be so heartless to argue with him? Louis's moral dilemma is compelling precisely because what he has to deal with is so overwhelming. Still, the playwright makes clear that all the talk of justice and politics will not free us from those terrifying yet fundamental responsibilities that accompany human sickness and death. All the Reaganite preaching of a survival-of-the-fittest creed will not exempt us from our most basic obligations to each other. Belize knows this, and he brings the discussion back to the matter at hand, Louis's desertion of his lover at a moment of profound need. "I've thought about it for a very long time, and I still don't understand what love is," he says before leaving Louis alone outside the coffee shop. "Justice is simple. Democracy is simple. Those things are unambivalent. But love is very hard. And it goes bad for you if you violate the hard law of love" (1:100).

Though stalwartly behind Belize's felt wisdom, Kushner observes an analogy between the ambivalence of love and the working out of democracy and justice, the bedroom and the courtroom not being as far apart as most would assume. Louis and Joe's ravenous infidelity, for example, is seen to be in keeping with the general dog-eat-dog direction of the country. During the warm-up to their affair, Joe tells Louis of a dream he had in which the whole Hall of Justice had gone out of business: "I just wondered what a thing it would be . . . if overnight everything you owe anything to, justice, or love, had really gone away. Free" (1:72). Louis, whose motto has become "Land of the free. Home of the brave. Call me irresponsible" (1:72), has found the perfect soulless mate for a self-forgetting fling. "Want some company?" he asks. "For whatever?" (1:73). Later, in Part Two of *Angels,* when the two men get involved, they help each other get over the guilt of leaving their former lovers behind. First Joe:

> What you did when you walked out on him was hard to do. The world may not understand it or approve it but it was *your* choice, what *you* needed, not some fantasy Louis but *you.* You did what you needed to do. And I consider you very brave.

And then, somewhat more reluctantly, Louis:

> You seem to be able to live with what you've done, leaving your wife, you're not all torn up and guilty, you've . . . blossomed, but you're not a terrible person, you're a decent, caring man. And I don't know how that's possible, but looking at you it seems to be. You do seem free.[7]

Joe, giving a new American spin to the phrase the "banality of evil," admits to being happy and sleeping peacefully. And so all would seem to be well in the couple's new-founded East Village love nest, except that Louis has bad dreams.

"In America, there's a great attempt to divest private life from political meaning," Kushner has said on the subject of his play's vision. "We have to recognize that our lives are fraught with politics. The oppression and suppression of homosexuality is part of a larger agenda."[8] In fact, nearly everything under the sun, from valium addiction to VD, is considered part of a larger agenda. For Kushner, politics is an intricate spiderweb of power relations. His most singular gift as a dramatist is in depicting this skein, in making visible the normally invisible cords that tether personal conscience to public policy. The playwright does this not by ideological pronouncement, but by tracking the moral and spiritual upheavals of his characters' lives. AIDS is the central fact of *Angels,* but it is one that implicates other facts, equally catastrophic. Racism, sexism, homophobia, moral erosion, and drug addiction come with the Kushnerian territory, and, as in life, characters are often forced to grapple with several of these at the same time.

Kushner uses split scenes to make more explicit the contrapuntal relationship between these seemingly disconnected narrative worlds. Roy's meeting with Joe, to discuss the junior attorney's future as a "Roy-Boy" in Washington, occurs alongside the scene in which Louis is sodomized in the Central Park Rambles by a leather-clad mama's boy. Louis's mini-symposium at the coffee shop is simultaneous with Prior's medical checkup at an outpatient clinic. Dreams, ghosts, and a flock of dithering, hermaphroditic angels are also used to break through the play's realistic structure, to conjoin seemingly disparate characters, and to reveal the poetic resonances and interconnectedness of everyday life. In a mutual dream, Harper, tranquilized and depressed, travels to Prior's boudoir, where she finds him applying the last touches of his Norma Desmond makeup. In a febrile state known portentously as the "[t]hreshold of revelation" (1:33), the two are endowed with clairvoyant insight, and it is here that Harper learns for sure that her husband is a "homo," and Prior understands that his illness hasn't touched his "most inner part," his heart (1:33-34). Even in his characters' most private, most alone moments, the "myth of the Individual," as Kushner calls it, is shot through with company.[9]

Nowhere is this merging of social realms more spectacularly revelatory, however, than in the presentation of Cohn. Though much is based on the historical record, Kushner publishes a disclaimer:

> Roy M. Cohn, the character, is based on the late Roy M. Cohn (1927-1986), who was all too real; for the most part the acts attributed to the character Roy [. . .] are to be found in the historical record. But this Roy is

a work of dramatic fiction; his words are my invention, and liberties have been taken.

(1:5)

Cohn, however, would have nothing to complain about: Kushner does the relentless overreacher proud. All Nietzschean grit and striving, Kushner's Cohn is forever trying to position himself beyond good and evil. "Transgress a little, Joseph," he tells his Mormon acolyte. "There are so many laws; find one you can break" (1:110). Power alone concerns him. Politics, the game of power, "the game of being alive," defines every atom of his being—even his sexuality, which refuses to be roped into traditional categories. Identity and other regulatory fictions are decidedly for other people, not for Cohn, who informs his doctor that labels like homosexuality

> tell you one thing and one thing only: where does an individual so identified fit in the food chain, in the pecking order? Not ideology, or sexual taste, but something much simpler: clout. Not who I fuck or who fucks me, but who will pick up the phone when I call, who owes me favours. This is what a label refers to.

(1:45)

Cohn's own claim to transcendental fame is that he can get Nancy Reagan on the phone whenever he wants to. How different this is from Prior's relationship to his own sexuality; on his sickbed, he steels himself with the words: "I am a gay man and I am used to pressure, to trouble, I am tough and strong" (1:117).

But it is Louis, as Ross Posnock has noted, who is Cohn's true emotional antithesis.[10] Though the two share no scenes together, their approaches to the world represent the thematic struggle at the center of Kushner's play. Yes, Louis transforms himself into a Cohn wannabe, but in the end he proves too conscience-ridden to truly want to succeed. Early on, when he asks his Rabbi what the Holy Writ says about someone who abandons a loved one at a time of great need, it is clear that he will have trouble following Cohn's personal dictum: "Let nothing stand in your way" (1:58). "You want to confess, better you should find a priest," his Rabbi tells him. On being reminded that this isn't exactly religiously appropriate, his Rabbi adds, "Worse luck for you, bubbulah. Catholics believe in forgiveness. Jews belief in Guilt" (1:25). Louis is a would-be Machiavelli hampered by the misgivings of his own inner-rabbi. "It's no fun picking on you Louis," Belize tell him; "you're so guilty, it's like throwing darts at a glob of jello, there's no satisfying hits, just quivering, the darts just blop in and vanish" (1:93). An exemplary neurotic, Louis internalizes the play's central conflict: the debt owed to the past vs. the desire for carte blanche in the future. Or as Louis himself puts it, "Nowadays. No connections. No responsibilities. All of us . . . falling through the cracks that separate what we owe to ourselves and . . . and what we owe to love" (1:71).

AIDS brings this dilemma to a rapid and painful reckoning. Grief has come into people's lives earlier in the late 1980s, occurring where it normally would have been postponed. Kushner believes this sad fact may very well force Americans to confront the consequences of their blind individualism. The trauma of AIDS holds for him the greatest potential source of social change. Early death, governmental back-turning, and whole populations of enraged mourning have created what Kushner would call a state of emergency. The conditions, in other words, are ripe for revolution. Communal consciousness, provoked by loss, has translated into militancy and activism. What's more, Kushner has convinced himself of Benjamin's prerequisite for radical change—the belief that "*even the dead* will not be safe from the enemy if he wins."[11] Haunting **Angels in America** is the restive ghost of Ethel Rosenberg, the woman Cohn famously prosecuted and had ruthlessly sentenced to death. "History is about to crack wide open" (1:112), she cries out with a vengeful laugh at her ailing enemy, who taunts her with the idea of his immortality. Indeed, "Millennium Approaches" has become the dead's battle-cry as well as that of the living.

To make clear that the forces of light are rallying against the forces of darkness, Kushner entitles the last act of **Millennium Approaches** "Not-Yet-Conscious, Forward Dawning." Even level-headed Belize shares this fervent sense that revolutionary change is coming. Outside the coffee shop, he assures Louis that "[s]oon, this . . . ruination will be blanketed white. You can smell it-can you smell it? [. . .] Softness, compliance, forgiveness, grace" (1:100). It is on this hopeful note that the playwright ends the first part of his epic saga. An angel, crashing through Prior's bedroom ceiling, announces:

> Greetings, Prophet;
>
> The Great Work begins:
>
> The Messenger has arrived.

(1:119)

The Great Work, however, begins with a nay-sayer. Aleksii Antedilluvianovich Prelapsarianov, the world's oldest living Bolshevik, begins **Part Two: Perestroika** declaring:

> The Great Question before us is: Are we doomed? The Great Question before us is: Will the Past release us? The Great Question before us is: Can we change? In Time?
>
> And we all desire that Change will come.
>
> (*Little pause*)
>
> (*With sudden, violent passion*) And *Theory?* How are we to proceed without *Theory?* What System of Thought have these Reformers to present to this mad swirling planetary disorganization, to the Inevident Welter of fact, event, phenomenon, calamity?

(2:13-14)

Kushner himself doesn't have a theory to offer before the lights come up on Prior cowering in bed with an Angel hovering over him. What the playwright has instead is an insight into the workings of history. "As Walter Benjamin wrote," the playwright reminds, "you have to be constantly looking back at the rubble of history. The most dangerous thing is to become set upon some notion of the future that isn't rooted in the bleakest, most terrifying idea of what's piled up behind you."[12] Kushner understands that the future needs to have its roots in the tragedies and calamities of the past in order for history not to repeat itself. The playwright's very difficult assignment, then, in *Perestroika* is to somehow move the narrative along into the future, while keeping history ever in sight; he must, in other words, find the dramatic equivalent of Klee's *Angelus Novus,* and bring us either to the threshold of a fresh catastrophe or to a utopia that throws into relief the suffering of the past.

Surprisingly, and in most un-Benjaminian fashion, Kushner rushes headlong into a fairy tale of progress. Tom between the reality of protracted calamity and the blind hope of a kinder, gentler millennium, the playwright opts for the latter, hands down. Kushner says of himself that he "would rather be spared and feel safer encircled protectively by a measure of obliviousness."[13] To that end, Prior not only survives his medical emergencies, but the playwright has him traipsing up a celestial scaffolding to heaven. Louis and Joe's torrid affair ends when Louis finds out the identity of Joe's boss. Calling Cohn "the most evil, twisted, vicious bastard ever to snort coke at Studio 54," Louis explodes at his month-long bedfellow, "He's got AIDS! Did you even *know* that? Stupid closeted bigots, you probably never figured out that each other was . . ." (2:111). After Joe punches him in the nose, Louis goes back to Prior, who lovingly tells him it's too late to return. Cohn, at long last, kicks the bucket, only to have Louis and Belize (with help from the ghost of Rosenberg) say Kaddish over him. "Louis, I'd even pray for you," Belize admits, before explaining the reason for his unusual benevolence:

> He was a terrible person. He died a hard death. So maybe. . . . A queen can forgive her vanquished foe. It isn't easy, it doesn't count if it's easy, it's the hardest thing. Forgiveness. Which is maybe where love and justice finally meet. Peace, at last. Isn't that what the Kaddish asks for?
>
> (2:124)

Though the two men end up ransacking the undearly departed's stockpile of AZT, it is Cohn who has the last laugh. In a fleeting moment of monstrous irony, Kushner grants Cohn his dream of immortality by letting him serve as God's defense attorney. Harper, tired of traveling through her own drug and-loneliness-induced

Antarctica, demands Joe's charge card and leaves for the airport to catch a night flight to San Francisco. "Nothing's lost forever," she says before making her final exit. "In this world, there is a kind of painful progress. Longing for what we've left behind, and dreaming ahead" (2:144).

The action concludes in a final pastoral scene in Central Park, in which Prior, Louis, Belize, and (somewhat implausibly) Hannah, Joe's Mormon mother and Prior's newest friend and sometimes caretaker, bask in the sun of a cold winter's day. "The Berlin Wall has fallen," Louis announces. "The Ceausescus are out. He's building democratic socialism. The New Internationalism. Gorbachev is the greatest political thinker since Lenin" (2:145). (Thus the title *Perestroika.*) The soothing story of the healing angel Bethesda is told, after which Prior sends us all contentedly home:

> This disease will be the end of many of us, but not nearly all, and the dead will be commemorated and will struggle on with the living and we are not going away. We won't die secret deaths anymore. The world only spins forward. We will be citizens.
>
> The time has come.
>
> Bye now.
>
> You are fabulous creatures, each and every one.
>
> And I bless you: *More Life.*
>
> The Great Work Begins.
>
> (2:148)

We won't die secret deaths anymore? The world only spins forward? Such uncritical faith in Progress would have been anathema to Benjamin, and to the Kushner of the first part, who so cogently applies the German's uncompromising historical materialism to America's current fin-de-siècle strife. The playwright has quite emphatically turned his attention away from the past and present turmoil, to a future that seems garishly optimistic in contrast. What happened?

There is a definite movement in *Perestroika* away from historical analysis towards a poetics of apocalypse. The pressure of reality seems to have induced an evangelical fervor in Kushner, in which social and political reality has become subordinate to religious fantasy. "The end of the world is at hand," Harper declares, while standing barefoot in the rain on the Brooklyn Heights Promenade. "Nothing like storm clouds over Manhattan to get you in the mood for Judgment Day" (2:101), she adds to the timely accompaniment of a peal of thunder. If that is not enough to convince us, Kushner whisks us around the heavens to hear the angels sing:

> We are failing, failing,
> The earth and the Angels.
> Look up, look up,

It is Not-to-Be Time.
Oh who asks of the Orders Blessing
With Apocalypse Descending?

(2:135)

As Frank Kermode points out in *The Sense of an Ending: Studies in the Theory of Fiction,* "[I]t seems to be a condition attaching to the exercise of thinking about the future that one should assume one's own time to stand in an extraordinary relation to it. . . . We think of our crisis as pre-eminent, more worrying, more interesting than other crises."[14] This is, of course, in large part a way to distract from the urgency of the present. Cultural anxiety is often transmuted into the myth of apocalypse; society, too, has its defense mechanisms for dealing with uncomfortable reality. On this point Savran agrees: "Regardless of Kushner's intentions, *Angels* sets forth a project wherein the theological is constructed as a transcendent category into which politics and history finally disappear."[15]

Ironically, though the play is set in a tragic time (a "murderous time" implies the Stanley Kunitz epigraph to **Millennium Approaches**), Kushner steers clear of tragic death, preferring instead to finish on a Broadway upnote. What makes this ending particularly hard to accept is that the playwright hasn't provided any convincing evidence to suggest that the state of emergency has let up in the least. Instead, he focuses on the gains in Prior's inner struggle, his will to live and general spiritual outlook. "Bless me anyway," Prior asks the angels before returning to a more earthbound reality. "I want more life. I can't help myself. I do. I've lived through such terrible times, and there are people who live through much much worse, but. . . . You see them living anyway. [. . .] If I can find hope anywhere, that's it, that's the best I can do" (2:135-36). New Age self-healing now takes precedence over politics, the spirit of individualism infects AIDS, and anger becomes merely an afterthought directed at God. "And if He returns, take Him to court," Prior says in a huff before leaving the cloudy heavens behind. "He walked out on us. He ought to pay" (2:136).

The situation parallels almost exactly the course of public response to AIDS in America. In the second decade of the epidemic little has changed, except for the fact that there is a diminishing sense of crisis. Activism has lulled, militancy has subsided into earnest concern, while conservatism, fundamentalism, and Jesse Helms-style homophobia are on the rise. AIDS, though still deadly, has been symbolically tamed. "Nothing has made gay men more visible than AIDS," Leo Bersani observes in *Homos.*[16] "But we may wonder if AIDS, in addition to transforming gay men into infinitely fascinating taboos, has made it *less dangerous* to look."[17] Troubled by the enormous success of **Angels,** Bersani argues that it is yet another sign of "how ready and

anxious America is to see and hear about gays— provided we reassure America how familiar, how morally sincere, and particularly in the case of Kushner's work, how innocuously full of significance we can be."[18]

Bersani offers these comments as part of a larger critique on the Queer movement's spirited, if often hollow, rhetoric of community building, which has come in response to AIDS, and which he views as dangerously assimilationist. Sharing Louis's belief in "the prospect of some sort of radical democracy spreading outward and growing up" (1:80), Kushner insists on the possibility of this kind of Queer (i.e., communal) redemption. Indeed, the playwright has said (with no trace of self-irony) that he finds *Benjamin's* sense of utopianism to be in the end profoundly apocalyptic.[19] Savran explains that, "[u]nlike the Benjamin of the 'Theses on the Philosophy of History,' for whom any concept of progress seems quite inconceivable, Kushner is devoted to rescuing Enlightenment epistemologies."[20] That is to say, "*Angels* unabashedly champions rationalism and progress."[21]

Benjamin's vision, however, seems ultimately far less bleak than either Kushner's or Savran's wishful idealism. Bertolt Brecht's remark on "Theses on the Philosophy of History" seems peculiarly apt: "[I]n short the little treatise is clear and presents complex issues simply (despite its metaphors and its judaisms) and it is frightening to think how few people there are who are prepared even to misunderstand such a piece."[22] Progress was for Benjamin a debased term primarily because it had become a dogmatic expectation, one that left the door open to very real destruction:

> One reason why Fascism has a chance is that in the name of progress its opponents treat it is as a historical norm. The current amazement that the things we are experiencing are "still" possible in the twentieth century is *not* philosophical. This amazement is not the beginning of knowledge—unless it is the knowledge that the view of history which gives rise to it is untenable.[23]

Kushner's brand of progress, in fact, seems dangerously close to that uncritical optimism on which Social Democratic theory, the antagonist of Benjamin's entire vision, relies:

> Progress as pictured in the minds of Social Democrats was, first of all, the progress of mankind itself (and not just advances in men's ability and knowledge). Secondly, it was something boundless, in keeping with the infinite perfectibility of mankind Thirdly, progress was regarded as irresistible, something that automatically pursued a straight or spiral course.[24]

For Benjamin, history is essentially the history of trauma. It is the sequence of violent breaks and sudden or catastrophic events that cannot be fully perceived as they occur, and which have an uncanny (in the rich

Freudian sense of the word) tendency to repeat themselves. His essay is above all an inducement to consciousness, a clarion call to the mind to wake from its slumber and apprehend this persistent cycle of oppression and the mountain-high human wreckage left in its wake. Benjamin doesn't so much believe, as Savran suggests, that the present is doomed by the past, as that paradoxically in order for a society to free itself to move in a more utopian direction, the fundamental inescapability of the aggrieved past must be vigilantly acknowledged.

In her essay "Unclaimed Experience: Trauma and the Possibility of History," Cathy Caruth makes the crucial point that "the traumatic nature of history means that events are only historical to the extent that they implicate others . . . that history is precisely the way we are implicated in each other's traumas."[25] This insight provides a way to understand not only the sweeping synthesis of Kushner's political vision in Part One, but also what may have gone awry in Part Two. From the vantage point of the traumatic experience of gay men and AIDS, Kushner taps into a much larger pool of American trauma, from the McCarthy witch hunt and Ethel Rosenberg to Reagan and neoconservatism. That Kushner is able to reveal from such an unabashedly gay, indeed flaming, position these indissoluble political bonds may be surprising to those who cannot conceive of sharing anything in common with men who imitate Tallulah Bankhead. But through the intimate concerns of Prior and Louis's relationship, Kushner opens up historical vistas onto generations of America's oppressed. The question is: were the almost unbearable scenes of Prior's illness, the pain of his and Harper's abandonment, and the punishing hypocrisy of Roy Cohn and his kind so overwhelming, so prolific of suffering, that they forced the playwright to seek the cover of angels?

By the end of *Perestroika,* Kushner stops asking those pinnacle questions of our time, in order to dispense "answers" and bromides—Belize's forgiveness of a rotten corpse; Harper's comforting "[n]othing's lost forever"; Louis's paean to Gorbachev and the fall of the Iron Curtain. By the final scene, Prior learns that "[t]o face loss. With Grace. Is Key . . ." (2:122). This is no doubt sound knowledge. But to be truly convincing it must be passed through, dramatized, not eclipsed by celestial shenanigans peppered with *Wizard of Oz* insight. Surrounded by loved ones, Prior sends us off with hearty best wishes. AIDS has become an "issue" and all but vanished from sight. After convincing us brutally, graphically, of the centrality of AIDS in our history, and of the necessity of keeping the traumatic past ever in sight, the playwright abandons the house of his uncommon wisdom. *Millennium Approaches* may

be the most persuasive and expansive AIDS play to date, but, as the silent backtracking of *Perestroika* suggests, the genre needs continuous reinforcing.

Notes

1. Nicholas de Jongh. *Not in Front of the Audience: Homosexuality on Stage* (London, 1992), 179.

2. Alisa Solomon, "AIDS Crusaders Act Up a Storm," *American Theatre* (Oct. 1989), 39.

3. David Savran, "Tony Kushner Considers the Long-standing Problems of Virtue and Happiness," *American Theatre* (Oct. 1994), 22-23.

4. Walter Benjamin, "Theses on the Philosophy of History," in *Illuminations,* ed. Hannah Arendt, trans. Harry Zohn (New York, 1968), 257-58.

5. Benjamin, 265.

6. Tony Kushner, *Angels in America; A Gay Fantasia on National Themes. Part One: Millennium Approaches* (New York, 1993), 74. Subsequent references will be included in the text, preceded by the numeral 1.

7. Tony Kushner, *Angels in America: A Gay Fantasia on National Themes. Part Two: Perestroika* (New York, 1994), 38. Subsequent page references will be included in the text, preceded by the numeral 2.

8. John Lahr, "Beyond Nelly," *New Yorker* (23 Nov. 194), 127.

9. Kushner, "Afterword," *Perestroika,* 150.

10. Ross Posnock, "Roy Cohn in America," *Raritan,* 13:3 (Winter 1994), 69.

11. Benjamin, 257.

12. Savran, "Tony Kushner," 25.

13. Kushner, "Afterword," 155.

14. Frank Kermode, *The Sense of an Ending: Studies in the Theory of Fiction* (London, 1966), 94.

15. David Savran, "Ambivalence, Utopia, and a Queer Sort of Materialism: How *Angels in America* Reconstructs the Nation," *Theatre Journal,* 47:2 (1995), 221.

16. Leo Bersani, *Homos* (Cambridge, MA, 1995), 19.

17. Ibid., 21.

18. Ibid., 69.

19. Savran, "Tony Kushner," 26.

20. Savran, "Ambivalence," 214.

21. Ibid., 214.

22. Bertolt Brecht, *Journals* 1934-1955, trans. Hugh Rorrison (London, 1993), 159.

23. Benjamin, 259.

24. Ibid., 262.

25. Cathy Caruth, "Unclaimed Experience: Trauma and the Possibility of History," *Yale French Studies,* 79 (1991), 192.

Steven F. Kruger (essay date 1997)

SOURCE: Kruger, Steven F. "Identity and Conversion in *Angels in America.*" In *Approaching the Millennium: Essays on "Angels in America,"* edited by Deborah R. Geis and Steven F. Kruger, pp. 151-69. Ann Arbor: University of Michigan Press, 1997.

[*In the following essay, Kruger examines the intersection of individual identity and collective history in* Angels in America.]

The titles and subtitles of Tony Kushner's **Angels in America** emphasize its status as political drama, announcing its exploration of "national themes" at a particular moment in global and cosmic history—the moment of "perestroika" as "millennium approaches." At the same time, these titles and subtitles call attention to the personal and psychological as crucial terms for the play's political analysis. This is a *gay fantasia on national themes,* an intervention in American politics that comes from a specified identity position and that depends somehow upon fantasy. The "angels" of the play's main title condense the political and personal in a particularly efficient manner: evoking at once Walter Benjamin's "angel of history"[1] and the guardian angel who watches over a particular individual, Kushner's Angel is both Prior Walter's fantasy creation and "the Continental Principality of America," one of seven "inconceivably powerful Celestial Apparatchik/ Bureaucrat-Angels" who preside over the continents and the ocean.[2] Like the "angel of God" whose appearance to Joseph Smith is explained in **Perestroika** ("He had great need of understanding. Our Prophet. His desire made prayer. His prayer made an angel. The angel was real. I believe that" [2:103]), the Angel in Kushner's play is both evoked by individual desire and somehow "real," speaking simultaneously to one person's needs ("For behold an angel of the Lord came and stood before me [Joseph Smith]. It was by night and he called me by name and he said the Lord had forgiven me my sins") and to collective historical circumstances ("He revealed unto me many things concerning the inhabitants of the earth which since have been revealed in commandments and revelations").[3]

CONSTITUTING IDENTITY

Written, as Kushner makes explicit, out of a "Left politics informed by liberation struggles . . . and by socialist and psychoanalytic theory" (2:154), **Angels in America** is at least in part the product of gay identity politics, and central to its political argument is a consideration of sexual identity. The play explores Harper's troubled marriage to Joe, the ways in which this confines both her and him, and the ways in which Harper's fantasy life recapitulates but also enables a certain escape from the unsatisfactory heterosexual relation. The play depicts the closeted figures of Roy and Joe struggling to *dis*identify from gayness. And it displays complex, indeed contradictory, definitions of gayness as, for instance, both strength and weakness—in Roy's words: "Homosexuals are men who know nobody and who nobody knows. Who have zero clout" (1:45); in Prior's: "I can handle pressure, I am a gay man and I am used to pressure, to trouble, I am tough and strong" (1:117).

Closely wrapped up with the play's analysis of sexuality is a recognition of how AIDS—identified in the popular imagination with a gayness conceived of as always already diseased and weak—becomes not just a category of health or illness but also of identity. Roy's disavowal of gayness is simultaneously a disavowal of identity as a person with AIDS: "AIDS is what homosexuals have. I have liver cancer" (1:46). Prior, unlike Roy, claims despised identities, but his bitter assessment of the world's treatment of "faggots" and people with AIDS echoes Roy's: "We don't [count]; faggots; we're just a bad dream the real world is having" (2:42).

Race, ethnicity, and religion are similarly prominent, and similarly conflicted, categories of analysis in the play. Belize's and Louis's political positions are shown to differ particularly around the question of race, in ways clearly connected to their differing experiences of racial identity (1:89-96). Jewishness and Mormonism figure importantly in constituting a sense of identity for most of the play's characters—Louis and Roy, Hannah, Harper, and Joe. The marginality of each of these religious traditions is shown to contribute to the individual's sense of his or her place (or lack of place) in the structures of power. Even Roy, despite his self-confident assertions, feels Jewishness as an obstacle to maintaining political centrality: "The disbarment committee: genteel gentleman Brahmin lawyers, country-club men. I offend them, to these men . . . I'm what, Martin, some sort of filthy little Jewish troll?" (1:66-67). Prior Walter's identity as "scion of an ancient line" (1:115) is bodied forth onstage in the figures of the prior Priors who serve as the Angel's heralds; the stability of the Walter family seems a crucial factor in shaping Prior's emerging identity as (reluctant) prophet for the Angel's deeply conservative political project—"YOU MUST STOP MOVING!" (2:52)—a project that Belize suggests is Prior's own fantasy: "This is just you, Prior, afraid of the future, afraid of time. Longing to go backwards so bad you made this angel up, a cosmic reactionary" (2:55).[4]

While a gender analysis is less prominent in the play than the consideration of sexuality, AIDS, race, religion, and ethnicity,[5] it nonetheless remains important for the depiction of Harper, who, especially in her engagement with the fantasy figure of the Mormon Mother, recognizes something about her own silencing and disempowerment: "His mute wife. I'm waiting for her to speak. Bet her story's not so jolly" (2:70). And gender is important in the politics of some of the men's self-identifications—particularly those of Belize and Prior as ex- (or ex-ex-) drag queens; thus, though Belize himself suggests that "All this girl-talk shit is politically incorrect. . . . We should have dropped it back when we gave up drag" (1:61), he responds with anger to Louis's assessment of drag as "sexist" (1:94).

The play also importantly, if playfully, suggests that the very taking of political positions—Joe's being a Republican, for instance—may be an act of self-identification not unlike the claiming, or disclaiming, of a sexual identity, such as Joe's disavowal of gayness (see 1:29).

* * *

As this sketch of some of the play's identity concerns should suggest, *Angels in America* does not arise from or depict a politics that consists simply in embracing an identity position like gayness as the sufficient basis for a political movement. We might indeed see the play as in part a response to criticism, particularly from within feminism, of an identity politics that fails to recognize the multiple determinants of identity; in the words of Elizabeth Spelman, for instance:

> Dominant feminist theory locates a woman's true identity in a metaphysical space where gender is supposed to be able to roam free from race and class. . . . [T]hough doing this appears to be necessary for feminism, it has the effect of making certain women rather than others paradigmatic examples of "woman"—namely, those women who seem to have a gender identity untainted (I use the word advisedly) by racial or class identity, those women referred to in newspapers, magazines, and feminist journals simply as "women," without the qualifier "Black" or "Hispanic" or "Asian-American" or "poor."[6]

Kushner's interrogation of gayness similarly recognizes the nonunitary nature of such a category, its differential constitution in relation to other determinants of identity. The play presents us with gay men who are white and black, Jewish and Mormon, conservative and liberal, butch and femme, and certainly not easily unified or unifiable under a single political banner. Thus recognizing the differences within identity categories, the play

furthermore emphasizes that any individual's identity is potentially contested and riven: sexuality, gender, and race do not come together without conflict and contradiction. Harper must negotiate between being a thoughtfully articulate woman and being a Mormon woman of whom silence is expected. Joe must navigate the rift between homoerotic desire and political and religious beliefs that insist on the repudiation of that desire. Roy, committed to Republican, McCarthyite political positions and to the political "clout" these bring him, denies as strongly as possible the potentially marginalizing force of his Jewishness and homosexuality. And so forth.

The complexity of identity in *Angels in America* also arises from Kushner's conception of it as social and relational: one is not oneself in isolation but only in contrast to, in solidarity and negotiation with a variety of other selves. This is obviously true among the main characters of the play, in which, for instance, Prior's state of health reveals or even determines much about how Louis thinks of himself or in which Joe's and Harper's decisions are crucially related to their sense of the other's identity. The others who shape the self may also be internalized figures from the past—an Ethel Rosenberg who returns punishingly to urge Roy on to death. They may be powerful historical presences like the Priors of Prior's heritage or like Louis's grandmother. And they may, most "bewilderingly" (1:30), be a complex mixture of the "real" and the fantastic, as when Prior and Harper, who have never met, somehow appear in each other's dreams/hallucinations to reveal crucial information about each other that each has not, at least consciously, realized (1:33-34, 2:68, 2:121-22). In such scenes even a character's fantasies and imaginations are conceived of as not solely his or hers. These gather their full meaning only in relation to, even interpenetration with, one another—just as, in Kushner's stagecraft, the "split scenes" suggest that discrete actions must, if we are to understand them fully, be read together: Harper and Joe's relationship defines Prior and Louis's, and vice versa, as both couples appear simultaneously onstage.

Identities so complexly defined entail certain *political* possibilities—cross-identifications like Harper's and Prior's and renegotiations of identity and difference that might make certain shifts in power relations possible, might, for instance, allow Joe to move from a simple disavowal of homosexuality to a reconsideration of it that also entails rethinking political and religious alignments. But the play also is careful not to depict identity simply as fluid and thus subject to easy, volitional change; nor does it attach a utopian political fantasy to the belief that identity might be renegotiated. Despite the presentation of identity as complex, as multiply determined, as relational, identity stubbornly remains identity, a marker of something unique to—given and intractable in—the person. Roy evokes "the immutable heart of what we are that bleeds through whatever we might become" (2:82), and, while Roy should by no means be taken as a reliable spokesman, the belief in such a "heart" is not his alone. A similar notion is at work when Harper reassures Prior that, despite his having AIDS, his "most inner part" is "free of disease" (1:34) or when Joe reassures Louis that, despite his having left Prior, he is "in [him]self a good, good man" (2:38) with "a good heart" (2:75). All of these assessments *may* be erroneous—they are each challenged elsewhere—but they nonetheless express a strong sense of the depth and stability of identity. The first speech of the play, Rabbi Isidor Chemelwitz's eulogy for Sarah Ironson, calls attention to a material heritage that is inescapable, "the clay of some Litvak shtetl" worked into her children's bones (1:10). The self may be always on a "voyage" and a "journey" (1:10-11), it may move somewhere new, but it also returns continually to a place of origin in a movement beyond the control of individual will, a function of constraints placed on the self by the history into which it is born.

If the self is not constituted by some simple, unconflicted claiming of identity, if, as well, it is not formed in isolation from others but, rather, responds to a whole variety of (political) pressures, it also is not so easily changed or reshaped. Indeed, having recognized, in Kushner's conception of identity, the potential for political change, we must also recognize that the *how* of that change is problematic. The "Great Question" with which *Perestroika* begins is "Are we doomed? . . . Will the Past release us? . . . Can we Change? In Time." Here, as stated by Prelapsarianov, the "World's Oldest Living Bolshevik," the question is explicitly political, and its "we" is the we of world history, not of identity politics or personal psychology (2:13). But in Kushner's play, with its insistence on the merging of the political and the personal, the question does not only resonate with the grand narratives of international politics. Indeed, the same Great Question reappears later in *Perestroika,* transposed into the language of the individual: Harper asks her fantasy figure, the Mormon Mother, "How do people change?" (2:79). Whether raised by Harper with personal urgency or by Prelapsarianov as he searches for the next "Beautiful Theory" to "reorder the world" (2:14), this is perhaps the play's central political question.

CONVERTING IDENTITY?

Angels in America is in many ways a play about conversion. The experience of HIV illness is often conceived as involving a conversion of the self (we speak, e.g., of "seroconversion"), and Prior's discovery that he has AIDS is depicted in part as making him a new person: "I'm a lesionnaire" (1:21). The Angel's visitation to Prior takes the form of a mission of conver-

sion: given a new identity, Prior is, like Joseph Smith, to become Prophet of a new dispensation. Indeed, in the course of the play all its characters undergo startling shifts in identity. Hannah is not only physically transplanted to New York but becomes *"noticeably different—she looks like a New Yorker"* (2:145). Roy, who clings tenaciously to his professional status as a lawyer, is disbarred just before his death. Harper moves through a period of dysfunction to strike out on her own, choosing "the real San Francisco, on earth," with its "unspeakable beauty" (2:122), over her unsatisfying life with Joe, a fantasized Antarctica, and a "depressing" Heaven, "full of dead people and all" (2:122). Belize re-embraces a discarded drag identity (1:94) and, in *Perestroika,* works through his hatred for Roy Cohn toward some kind of "Forgiveness" (2:124). Louis and Joe each move out of "marriages" and into a new relationship with each other, a movement that, for both, entails a radical rethinking of the self. Louis is forced to consider whether he is capable of truly loving; when he decides that he is and tries to return to Prior, he finds that he "can't come back" (2:143), that the relation to Prior is now essentially changed. The couple that Prior and Louis once formed is replaced by the play's final argumentative, but communal, quartet of Prior, Louis, Belize, and Hannah. And Joe, the character whose fate is left least resolved at the end of *Perestroika,* is also perhaps the character who has undergone the most radical conversions. He admits his at first denied homosexuality. He moves from a heterosexual to a homosexual relationship, from a commitment to Reaganism and Mormonism to a willingness to "give up anything" for Louis (2:74), from "never [having] hit anyone before" to a violent attack on Louis (2:111-12). By the end of the play his relation to Harper has been precisely reversed. She is leaving him, having slapped him as he has just beaten Louis. He, not she, is now the one in need of psychological support that is not forthcoming, and, as she leaves, Harper transfers to Joe the Valium she herself once used in substitution for his missing support (2:143). As (a fantasized) Harper earlier suggests to Joe, "You're turning into me" (2:40).

It is not surprising, given the play's emphasis on such radical changes in self and self-conception, that it focuses so much attention on Mormonism and Judaism, both religions whose originary moment is a conversional one that involves a movement of dis- and relocation.[7] This is true in Mormonism not only in the revelation to Joseph Smith and the westward movement that this initiated but also in the opening visions of *The Book of Mormon,* in which Lehi is "commanded" to separate himself from the corrupt Jews of Jerusalem by "tak[ing] his family and depart[ing] into the wilderness" (1 Nephi 2:2). This founding moment of course echoes the founding of Judaism in God's command to Abraham: "Get thee out of thy country, and from thy kindred, and from thy father's house, unto a land that I will shew thee"

(Genesis 12:1).[8] (The echo is intensified in the names of Abraham's and Lehi's wives—Sarai/Sarah and Sariah.) Mormonism is indeed explicitly recognized as a religion of conversion in *Angels in America*; in the play's only use of the word *convert* Prior responds to Hannah's unexpected solicitude toward him by saying, "Please, if you're trying to convert me this isn't a good time" (2:100).

But, while both Judaism and Mormonism originate in a radical movement away from a prior religious tradition, both also express a strong resistance to change. We remember, for instance, the words of the Rabbi that open the play and that make the Great Voyage of Jewish migration both an enormous dislocation and a refusal of "this strange place," a preservation of the "ancient, ancient culture and home" (1:10). Later Louis will recognize, comically, a circular movement enacted by Jewish immigrants and their descendants: "Alphabetland. This is where the Jews lived when they first arrived. And now, a hundred years later, the place to which their more seriously fucked-up grandchildren repair. . . . This is progress?" (2:15). Mormon social conservatism and traditionalism—"People ought to stay put" (1:82)—stands starkly against the radical break of its originary moment and founding mythos. Such ambivalence is already present in *The Book of Mormon.* Here the most radical conversions can occur; the black-skinned Lamanites can, with spiritual reform, turn white (see 3 Nephi 2:15-16). At the same time, however, the conception of Lamanite identity as essentially marred remains unchanged. The converting Lamanites *become* Nephites; the idea of a white Lamanite or of a morally upright black-skinned person is not admitted.[9]

An ambivalence similar to that present in both Judaism and Mormonism characterizes all the conversionary movements in *Angels in America.* The Angel's promise to undertake "a marvelous work and a wonder," to abolish "a great Lie," to correct "a great error" (1:62), turns out to be a call not for change but for its opposite, a project intended not to transform established identity categories or structures of power but, instead, to secure these with "Deep Roots": "Neither Mix Nor Intermarry . . . If you do not mingle you will Cease to Progress" (2:52). In the depiction of Prior it is an active question whether AIDS accomplishes a transformation of the self, with the play giving two contrasting answers: Prior's "I don't think there's any uninfected part of me. My heart is pumping polluted blood. I feel dirty" (1:34) posed against Harper's "deep inside you, there's a part of you, the most inner part, entirely free of disease" (1:34), which Prior later echoes—"my blood is clean, my brain is fine" (1:117). Louis changes position frequently in the play, but his movement is ultimately circular, a return to where he began. With characters like Belize, Hannah, and Harper, one wonders if apparent conversions might not be better understood as assertions of an identity "essential" to the self that has been temporarily suppressed. Belize, like Louis, moves in a circle, giving up drag only to reembrace it; his forgiving Roy Cohn alongside their agonistic relation echoes his simultaneous antagonism and concern for Louis. Hannah is perhaps poised, from her earliest moments in the play, to move away from her Mormon "demographic profile" (2:104): Sister Ella Chapter tells her, "you're the only unfriendly Mormon I ever met" (1:82). Harper's identity as a "Jack Mormon," her "always doing something wrong, like one step out of step" (1:53), may similarly be seen as conditioning the change she ultimately makes in her life. Roy, though "defeated" (2:114), moves one last time to assert his power, using the pathos of his impending death to reaffirm "clout": "I fooled you Ethel . . . I just wanted to see if I could finally, finally make Ethel Rosenberg sing! I WIN!" (2:115). Indeed, the last words he speaks while alive in the play exactly echo his first (cf. 1:11 and 2:115).

At the same time that the play displays each of its characters undergoing major changes, it thus also asks whether these in fact represent real changes in the self or, rather, express or reaffirm a preexisting, stable identity. This double movement is especially evident in the treatment of the changes that Joe undergoes. On the one hand, we may see Joe as radically transformed in the course of the play. On the other, we might legitimately ask whether his behavior, even as he comes out and becomes involved with Louis, *really* changes. Isn't the concealment of his homosexuality from Harper simply replaced by the concealment, from Louis, of his Mormonism, the meaning of his work as chief clerk in the Federal Court of Appeals, and his connection to Roy Cohn? Just as much of *Millennium Approaches* is devoted to Harper's uncovering of Joe's homosexuality, so *Perestroika* traces Louis's discovery of Joe's concealed religious and political identities. Harper and Louis in essence "out" Joe's secrets, but Joe himself continues to behave much as before, returning repeatedly to Roy and, when his relationship with Louis fails, trying to return to Harper.

SKIN AND BOWELS

The problem of identity and its possible conversion is worked out in *Angels in America* particularly through a dialogue between external and internal self, a thematics of skin and bowels. Skin recurs repeatedly in the play as necessary to the integrity of a self, both macro- and microcosmic. Thus, Harper, in her opening speech, sees the "ozone layer" as "the crowning touch to the creation of the world: guardian angels, hands linked, make a spherical net, a blue-green nesting orb, a shell of safety for life itself" (1:16-17). "Safety from what's outside" is central to her positive vision of the millennium, and the flip side of that vision is the failure of protective covering: "the sky will collapse" (1:18). Harper also makes clear that "people are like planets, you need a thick skin" (1:17), and the decay of the ozone layer is matched at the level of individuals by the loss of bodily integrity attendant upon AIDS, a loss marked in the play (as in the popular imagination) particularly by the skin lesions of Kaposi's sarcoma (1:21). Harper's "systems of defense giving way" (1:17) reappear in Henry's description of the action of HIV, which depends upon both a failure of the skin and damage to the internal "skin" of immunity (see 1:42).

Susceptible to decay and invasion, the skin becomes a complex site—protective, yes, but also the place at which the self is endangered and at which one self may threaten another. Prior self-protectively insists that Louis not touch him, but immediately after, having *"shit himself"* and bled, he must warn Louis away: "Maybe you shouldn't touch it . . . me" (1:48). His breached, fragile skin presents pain and danger both for himself and for others. Elsewhere, the vulnerability of skin is recognized in ways not directly connected to physical risk. Louis, feeling guilty for having abandoned Prior, warns Joe not to touch him: "your hand might fall off or something." And, when Joe in fact touches Louis, he sees himself as violating a certain dangerous boundary: "I'm going to hell for doing this." As this scene also demonstrates, however, skin and the crossing of its boundaries provide the opportunity not only for wounding but for connection—here, the sexual connection between Joe and Louis: "I . . . want . . . to touch you. Can I please just touch you . . . um, here?" (1:116). Later Joe will also imagine the dissolution of a political boundary between himself and Louis: "Freedom is where we bleed into one another. Right and Left. Freedom is the far horizon where lines converge" (2:37). And the "ragged" skin that Harper imagines precariously protecting the earth, in her most hopeful vision, becomes a place of human interconnectedness:

> Souls were rising, from the earth far below, souls of the dead, of people who had perished, from famine, from war, from the plague, and they floated up, like skydivers in reverse, limbs all akimbo, wheeling and spinning. And the souls of these departed joined hands, clasped ankles, and formed a web, a great net of souls, and the souls were three-atom oxygen molecules, of the stuff of ozone, and the outer rim absorbed them, and was repaired.
>
> (2:144)

Here Harper sees the merging of human efforts across the barrier of self, the paradoxical coming together of those who have lost bodily integrity, whose own protective skins have been stripped from them, to replenish the skin of the world.

Implied, of course, in the image of a skin that insures integrity but is vulnerable, that guarantees separate identity but allows interconnection, is a depth, the contents that the skin holds together and that are threatened by its potential collapse. The decay of the ozone layer helps make possible a more general "dissolving of the Great Design" (2:134), which the Angel comes to announce and which Prelapsarianov recognizes as "mad swirling planetary disorganization" (2:14; also see 2:45). A cosmic "searing of skin" and "boiling of blood" (2:52), external and internal destruction, occur simultaneously. And, for the individual, the attack on protective skin—most strikingly, the damage to the immune system in AIDS—leads to an emptying out of bodily contents: Roy says, "Now I look like a skeleton" (1:111).

Buried depth, and particularly a depth of internal organs, of heart and blood and bowels, is in the play as constitutive of humanness, of human institutions, and of the world as is the protective skin. Though the skin may be breached, life stubbornly holds on: "When they're more spirit than body, more sores than skin, when they're burned and in agony, when flies lay eggs in the corners of the eyes of their children, they live. Death usually has to *take* life away. I don't know if that's just the animal" (2:136). The human being is, at least in part, a "DISGUSTING SLURPING FEEDING ANIMAL" (1:104), and the life of that "animal" in the world, including its institutions, involves a messy corporeality. Thus, in Roy's view "the Law" is not "a dead and arbitrary collection of antiquated dictums" but, rather, "a pliable, breathing, sweating . . . *organ*" (1:66); "this is gastric juices churning, this is enzymes and acids, this is intestinal is what this is, bowel movement and blood-red meat—this stinks, this is *politics,* Joe, the game of being alive" (1:68).[10] Roy's perspective on the world is the opposite of Harper's, though it too makes the leap from macro- to microcosm; Roy looks at things from their bloody "heart" rather than their celestial skin: "Unafraid to look deep into the miasma at the heart of the world, what a pit, what a nightmare is there—*I* have looked, I have searched all my life for absolute bottom, and I found it, *believe* me: *Stygian*" (2:81).

Though the depths Roy describes mirror his own "brutal" and opportunistic misanthropy (2:81), the play also shows how such depths participate in loving human relations. If connections among people occur through the skin, true attachments depend upon a deeper, more intimate, mingling. Louis describes "smell" and "taste" as the "only two [senses] that go beyond the boundaries . . . of ourselves" and that thus allow an interpenetration of self and other: "Some part of you, where you meet the air, is airborne. . . . The nose tells the body—the heart, the mind, the fingers, the cock—what it wants, and then the tongue explores" (2:17-18). Desire is a matter of the whole body, its depths as well as its surfaces. As Harper suggests, "life" is "all a matter of the opposable thumb and forefinger;

not of the hand but of the heart; we grab hold like nobody's business and then we don't seem to be able to let go" (2:122). Even when the heart's grasp fails, as Harper also recognizes, the rest of the body continues doggedly to desire: "When your heart breaks, you should die. / But there's still the rest of you. There's your breasts, and your genitals, and they're amazingly stupid, like babies or faithful dogs, they don't get it, they just want him" (2:20).

While transformation of the self, and of the world, is sometimes imaged in the play as operating on the skin's surface—"If anyone who was suffering, in the body or the spirit, walked through the waters of the fountain of Bethesda, they would be healed, washed clean of pain" (2:147)—equally crucial to the play's conception of conversion is a penetration of the self's depths. The heart that serves as "an anchor" for Harper must, the Mormon Mother insists, be left behind (2:71). The cosmic repairs that the Angel undertakes represent an attempt to transform the "battered heart, / Bleeding Life in the Universe of Wounds" (2:54), by paralyzing life's messy process, emptying out the self and the world. And the play several times brings internal and external change together. At the same moment that Roy advises Joe to live differently in the world by exposing himself, baring his skin ("don't be afraid to live in the raw wind, naked, alone" [1:58]), Louis self-destructively yearns to be penetrated ("fuck[ed]," "hurt," "ma[d]e [to] bleed," [1:54], even "infect[ed]" [1:57]). Roy himself will later ask Belize to "squeeze the bloody life from me" and to "open me up to the end of me" (2:76).

When Louis returns to Prior to "make up" with him (2:83), Prior insists that neither external nor internal change alone is sufficient to demonstrate Louis's conversion. He accuses Louis of presenting a surface that reflects no depth: "You cry, but you endanger nothing in yourself. It's like the idea of crying when you do it. / Or the idea of love" (2:85). But he is also suspicious of claims to internal change that fail to manifest themselves externally. When Louis tells him not to "waste energy beating up on me, OK? I'm already taking care of that," Prior responds, "Don't see any bruises" (2:83), and, having exacted from Louis the confession that he is "really bruised inside" (2:88), Prior insists on external proof: "Come back to me when they're visible. I want to see black and blue, Louis, I want to see blood. Because I can't believe you even *have* blood in your veins till you show it to me" (2:89). Louis, having been beat up by Joe (2:111-12), "made . . . [to] bleed" (2:127), indeed returns to Prior with "visible scars" (2:141), which stand for a change in his way of being in the world. In the economy of the play it is not enough for Louis to leave Joe; he must also confront him, in the scene that leads to violence, with what he has discovered about Joe's decisions for the Court of Appeals, his relation to Roy Cohn, and his

consequent entwinement in the history of McCarthyism. Louis's making external of his own internal change here operates through his "outing" of Joe's secrets, and, just as Louis's internality—the fact that he does "have blood in his veins"—is made literally visible, so the violent injustices of Joe's concealed political history are brought out in the violence he visits on Louis, a violence later explicitly approved by Roy: "Everybody could use a good beating" (2:127).

The play of surface and depth in *Angels in America* is particularly crucial in the depiction of Joe and his problematic conversions. At a moment when he is still fighting against his homoerotic feelings, Joe thinks of these as constituting something "deep within" that might be concealed or even expurgated: "I have fought, with everything I have, to kill it" (1:40). Joe's model of identity, the wished-for perfection of the "saints," is one in which internal and external selves correspond simply, unconflictedly, to each other: "Those who love God with an open heart unclouded by secrets and struggles are cheerful; God's easy simple love for them shows in how strong and happy they are" (1:54). (This is the flip side, or the positive image, of Roy's identification with "lower" life forms like HIV and "pubic lice," beings "too simple" to be killed, self-identical and transparent to themselves: "It [HIV] knows itself. It's harder to kill something if it knows what it is" [2:28].)

But, while Joe sometimes imagines that he has conquered his buried secret, made inside and outside concur, this is at the expense of both inside and outside. Joe sees his internal battle, his "secret struggles" (1:54), as leading not to a plenitude encompassing "heart" and worldly behavior, as with the "saints," but, rather, to an emptying out of the self, a "killing" of internal identity that leaves the external devoid of meaningful content: "For God's sake, there's nothing left, I'm a shell. There's nothing left to kill" (1:40). Joe's disavowal of an unwanted depth, his attempt to hide and kill his secret self, in fact fails. The "heart" has a power that cannot simply be denied or suppressed: "I try to tighten my heart into a knot, a snarl, I try to learn to live dead, just numb, but then I see someone I want, and it's like a nail, like a hot spike right through my chest, and I know I'm losing" (1:77). Joe's disavowed depth makes itself known not just internally but externally; he develops a "bleeding ulcer" (1:106) that forces the messiness hidden inside to appear on the surface, with blood coming from his mouth (1:80).

One kind of attempt to convert the self, through the stifling of an unwanted internality, thus fails, and Joe moves toward a different sort of self-conversion—"I can't *be* this anymore. I need . . . a change" (1:73)— another attempt to make external and internal selves concur, but this time through a "coming out" that would bring the heart to the surface. For such a conversion to occur, however, Joe imagines that his skin, the "outside" that "never stood out" (1:53) and that has concealed his disavowed depth, cannot remain: "Very great. To shed your skin, every old skin, one by one and then walk away, unencumbered, into the morning" (1:72-73). But, just as the attempt to disavow his buried homosexuality involves a violence against the internal self, so Joe's coming out, his shedding the skin of his prior life, involves a violence against the self and its history: "I'm flayed. / No past now" (2:75). Here the skin represents the individual's connections and commitments in the world—"everything you owe anything to, justice, or love" (1:72)—and Joe's imagination of shedding his skin is an attempted disavowal of such commitments. In order to stay with Louis, Joe declares himself ready to shed his "fruity underwear," his "temple garment"—"Protection. A second skin. I can stop wearing it." When Louis objects—"How can you stop wearing it if it's a skin? Your past, your beliefs" (2:73)—Joe reiterates his willingness to shed not just this "second skin" but "anything. Whatever you want. I can give up anything. My skin" (2:74).

Though stripping off one's skin and strangling one's heart seem diametrically opposed models of conversion, each depends upon a radical denial of part of oneself—whether the depth of uncontrollable desire or a surface of connections and commitments, whether the repressed content of a secret self or the historical sediments of the self's past. Indeed, Joe's first fantasy of shedding his skin follows immediately upon his imagination of a certain emptying out of depth:

> It just flashed through my mind: The whole Hall of Justice, it's empty, it's deserted, it's gone out of business. Forever. The people that make it run have up and abandoned it. . . .
>
> I felt that I was going to scream. Not because it was creepy, but because the emptiness felt so *fast*.
>
> And . . . well, good. A . . . happy scream.
>
> I just wondered what a thing it would be . . . if overnight everything you owe anything to, justice, or love, had really gone away. Free.
>
> It would be . . . heartless terror. Yes. Terrible, and . . .
>
> Very great.
>
> (1:72)

Just as the strangling of the heart leaves a self that is only a "shell," so the shedding of the skin depends upon an emptying out—a literalized heartlessness—that might leave the self "free" but also leaves it content-less, without past or history. Indeed, the impossibility or monstrousness of such a conversion is voiced not only by Louis but by Joe himself when he (homophobically) imagines, even as he claims "no past now," that his sexual relation with Louis has given him a new past—

"Maybe . . . in what we've been doing, maybe I'm even infected" (2:75)—and a past that reinvests him with an internality felt (as with his buried homosexuality) to be out of his control. And, just as Joe's disavowed internality reasserted itself through his bleeding ulcer, so his disavowed political and religious connections, supposedly shed as a skin, return in the form of blood. When Joe visits Roy, from whom he never makes a definitive break, to reveal that he is "with a man" (2:86), Roy orders him to return to his prior life: "I want you home. With your wife." In order to reach Joe, Roy pulls the IV tube from his arm and ends up *smearing [Joe's shirt] with blood."* Whereas Joe, despite his coming out, continues to imagine (not un-like Roy) that the greatest danger to himself comes from his homosexuality ("maybe I'm even infected"), the real danger is shown to be from his continued con-nection to Roy and his refusal, despite his conversion from closeted Mormon Republican to out gay man, to grapple with the meaning of that connection. Belize warns Joe to "get somewhere you can take off that shirt and throw it out, and don't touch the blood," an injunc-tion that Joe cannot understand because Roy continues to conceal that he has AIDS, and because Joe himself continues blindly to dedicate himself to Roy (2:87). Though Joe claims that he has jettisoned his past, Roy's blood, and Joe's own political actions and commit-ments, continue to stain him; they are not so easily shed. One might indeed see Joe's skin as not sloughed off but, rather, pushed inward, replacing the secret of homosexuality with a heart that Roy can celebrate—"His strength is as the strength of ten because his heart is pure! *And* he's a Royboy, one hundred percent" (1:64)—but that must now be concealed from Louis. Indeed, though the image of the bloodied shirt continues to represent the past as surface, this is also seen as depth, and a depth susceptible to infection; in revealing to Louis the relationship between Joe and Roy, Belize says: "I don't know whether Mr. Cohn has penetrated more than his spiritual sphincter. All I'm saying is you better hope there's no GOP germ, Louis, 'cause if there is, you got it" (2:95).

In the depiction of Joe and the changes he undergoes, then, two seemingly opposed models for conversion—the strangling of the heart in the service of the skin and the shedding of the skin at the demand of the heart—come together, each shown to be inadequate, a killing of vitality, a denial of the past. Joe's strongest statement of the desire for conversion—"I pray for God to crush me, break me up into little pieces and start all over again" (1:49)—indeed denies both internal and external selves, both the depth of feeling that for Joe is identi-fied with his homosexuality and the history of the self's relations in the world. Joe attempts first to deny feeling then to jettison the past, but he makes no real attempt to think how *both* surface and depth, skin and heart, constitute the self. In his last scene in the play, as he attempts to hold on to Harper, to return to a life he had seemingly left behind, he once again disavows a certain past—"I have done things, I'm ashamed"—but *which* past, whether his commitment to Roy or to Louis, remains unclear. He claims to "have changed," but, as he himself says, "I don't know how yet" (2:142). In some sense, for all his searching, Joe never finds a self of which *not* to be "ashamed"; for all his "changing," he never grapples with the self or its past history in such a way as to effect real change. Late in the play Harper can describe Joe much as he himself did before his "coming out": "sweet hollow center, but he's the nothing man" (2:122).

"TO MAKE THE CONTINUUM OF HISTORY EXPLODE"

If Joe's changes in the play represent failed rather than successful attempts at conversion, they nonetheless point the way toward a conception of what it would mean truly to undergo conversion.[11] This would involve grappling with an internality, a depth, a passionate desire, in such a way as neither to deny its power nor to follow it without consideration for its effects on others. It would also mean shedding one's skin, changing one's way of being in the world, without merely throwing off the "past" and the "beliefs" imbedded in that skin (2:73).

Perhaps the play's most powerful image of a conversion that goes beyond what Joe is able to accomplish comes in the Mormon Mother's response to Harper's question, "How do people change?" (2:79). Her answer suggests that real change is difficult, painful, and violent and that its difficulty arises precisely because it does not follow the easier paths toward conversion that others in the play attempt to pursue. It does not reach for a simple obliteration of the self ("break me up into little pieces and start all over again" [1:49]) or an emptying out of a disturbing depth; nor does it operate through a sloughing off of "everything you owe anything to" (1:72) or an embracing of (angelic) "STASIS" (2:54). Addressing Harper's question, the Mormon Mother suggests that change "has something to do with God so it's not very nice":

> God splits the skin with a jagged thumbnail from throat to belly and then plunges a huge filthy hand in, he grabs hold of your bloody tubes and they slip to evade his grasp but he squeezes hard, he *insists,* he pulls and pulls till all your innards are yanked out and the pain! We can't even talk about that. And then he stuffs them back, dirty, tangled and torn. It's up to you to do the stitching.

HARPER:

> And then get up. And walk around.

MORMON MOTHER:

> Just mangled guts pretending.

HARPER:

> That's how people change.

(2:79)

Nothing here is simply cast off or emptied out. The skin is breached and remains to be stitched up; the bowels are "mangled" but remain themselves. A prior self is not left behind—commitments remain, desiring continues, the history of the self travels on with it—and yet change somehow occurs through a violent rearrangement over which one may have no control but also through patching one's own wounds, living with what is "dirty, tangled and torn," "pretending" to go on and thus in fact going on.

Harper herself moves into a new life and not by simply rejecting the past: "Nothing's lost forever. In this world, there's a kind of painful progress. Longing for what we've left behind, and dreaming ahead" (2:144). Torn open by Joe's lack of love, "heartbroken," she nonetheless "return[s] to the world" (2:121) and without denying her "devastating" experience or her pain:

> I feel like shit, but I've never felt more alive. I've finally found the secret of all that Mormon energy. Devastation. That's what makes people migrate, build things. Heartbroken people do it, people who have lost love.

(2:122)

Here, of course, the play again connects one individual's movement to a broader social/political phenomenon, and, as in its treatment of individual conversion, it shows a real ambivalence about whether and how true historical change might occur. If Louis can claim that "both of us are, right now, too much immersed in this history . . . and there's no real hope of change" (1:91), just a few scenes later Ethel Rosenberg can announce that "history is about to crack wide open. Millennium approaches" (1:112). Again, as with individual conversion, there is deep skepticism about a project of historical transformation that would address either depth or surface alone. The Angel's project is ultimately shown to be bankrupt because it is an emptying out and arresting of the messiness that constitutes life itself. And, as Prelapsarianov warns at the beginning of *Perestroika,* the simple shedding of the past, without preparation of a new skin, without "the Theory . . . that will reorder the world," without the deep, transformative work— "the incredible bloody vegetable struggle up and through into Red Blooming" (2:14)—necessary to prepare the new, will lead to dissolution:

> If the snake sheds his skin before a new skin is ready, naked he will be in the world, prey to the forces of chaos. Without his skin he will be dismantled, lose coherence and die. Have you, my little serpents, a new skin? . . . Then we dare not, we *cannot,* we MUST NOT move ahead!

(2:14-15)

Something like the Mormon Mother's prescription for change, something that would slit open the skin of the present, grapple with the world's messy violences, with the deep traumas of its history, without obliterating or denying these, seems to be called for. As the play draws to an end, Louis argues, contra Prelapsarianov, that "you can't wait around for a theory" (2:146), but Hannah corrects him, in a way that brings together his and Prelapsarianov's ideas about how to change the world: "You need an idea of the world to go out into the world. But it's the going into that makes the idea. You can't wait for a theory, but you have to have a theory" (2:147). The new skin cannot precede the world's new demands; it can only develop as those demands—messy, traumatic, life-threatening but also the conditions of any new life—are lived.

One must "mak[e] a leap into the unknown" but a leap informed by theory and by the past (2:146): casting off the skin cannot be a rejection of the history that formed it. Indeed, the "leap into the unknown" with which **Angels in America** ends evokes Walter Benjamin's "tiger's leap into the past" even as it is a movement into the future.[12] As Benjamin suggests, the revolutionary move is to discover in the past those moments that speak to the present, resonate with it, allow the vision of history as an uninterruptible "continuum" to be rent. In some sense this is the work of **Angels** itself. Asking how to move forward in a world whose present and past are both deeply traumatic, it insists that whatever "painful progress" (2:144) might be possible will be achieved not by moving beyond trauma but by grappling with a traumatic present and by recalling past traumas as a way of being released from these, just as the play itself grapples with the crises of its present moment (AIDS, environmental disaster, Reaganism) *and* reinvents the vexed, complex, and disturbing elements of the past (McCarthyism, the Mormon experiment, family histories) in order to facilitate a movement beyond these into an uncertain but promising future.

Notes

1. See Walter Benjamin, "Theses on the Philosophy of History," in *Illuminations,* ed. Hannah Arendt, trans. Harry Cohn (1955; reprint, New York: Harcourt, Brace and World, 1968), 259. On Kushner's use of Benjamin, see Scott Tucker, "Our Queer World: A Storm Blowing from Paradise," *Humanist* 53 (November-December 1993): 32-35; and the essays by David Savran, Michael Cadden, Art Borreca, and Martin Harries in this volume.

2. Tony Kushner, *Angels in America: A Gay Fantasia on National Themes. Part One: Millennium Approaches* (New York: Theatre Communications Group, 1993), 3; *Angels in America: A Gay Fantasia on National Themes. Part Two: Perestroika* (New York: Theatre Communications Group, 1994), 3, 4. Future references will be given parenthetically in the text.

3. Joseph Smith, *The Essential Joseph Smith* (Salt Lake City: Signature Books, 1995), 28. Also see the more elaborate account in *The Book of Mormon: An Account Written by the Hand of Mormon upon Plates: Taken from the Plates of Nephi,* trans. Joseph Smith Jr. (1830; reprint, Salt Lake City: The Church of Jesus Christ of Latter-Day Saints, 1950), prefatory material: "Origin of the Book of Mormon." Future references to *The Book of Mormon* will be given parenthetically in the text.

4. See Allen J. Frantzen, in this volume, for a reading of the play's depiction of Prior's ethnic identity.

5. Class identity is less fully interrogated through the depiction of the play's characters than are other identity categories, though the play certainly shows itself aware of the centrality of class in U.S. politics during the Reagan era.

6. Elizabeth V. Spelman, *Inessential Woman: Problems of Exclusion in Feminist Thought* (Boston: Beacon Press, 1988), 186.

7. See Kushner's comments on the "interesting similarities between Mormonism and Judaism" (101), in David Savran, "Tony Kushner Considers the Longstanding Problems of Virtue and Happiness: An Interview," *American Theatre* 11:8 (October 1994): 20-27, 100-104, esp. 101-3.

8. I quote from the King James Version, *The Holy Bible* (New York and Scarborough, Ont.: New American Library, 1974).

9. Also see 2 Nephi 5:21 and Alma 3:6 in *The Book of Mormon.* Joseph Smith's own views on race and slavery seem to have shifted; see Smith, *Essential Joseph Smith,* 85-90, a letter of 1836 speaking against abolitionism; and 213-25, a statement of 1844 against the abuse of federal power that calls the "goodly inhabitants of the slave states" to "petition . . . your legislators to abolish slavery by the year 1850, or now" (221).

10. Roy's language here brings the play's doctrinaire McCarthyite/Reaganite together with its Bolshevik, Prelapsarianov (cf. 2:14).

11. This section's title is taken from Benjamin, "Theses on the Philosophy of History," 263.

12. Ibid.

Benilde Montgomery (essay date winter 1998)

SOURCE: Montgomery, Benilde. "*Angels in America* as Medieval Mystery." *Modern Drama* 41, no. 4 (winter 1998): 596-606.

[*In the following essay, Montgomery examines the similarities between Kushner's* Angels in America *and the tradition of medieval religious mystery plays.*]

Although highly praised in the popular press when it first appeared and officially canonized soon thereafter by Harold Bloom,[1] Tony Kushner's *Angels in America* has now come under the scrutiny of critics of a more suspicious gaze. Among these less than enthusiastic critics are the notorious Arlene Croce, who, if only indirectly, includes *Angels* as an instance of "victim art"; Leo Bersani, who finds the play "muddled and pretentious"; and David Savran, who unravels the play's ambivalences to show not only that it is seriously at odds with its own apparent intentions, but that its immense popularity can be accounted for in the way it supports the "binary oppositions" of the status quo and thereby implicitly supports the Reaganite agenda that it would otherwise subvert.[2] More positively, however, Savran also notes that "the play deliberately evokes the long history of Western dramatic literature and positions itself as heir to the traditions of Sophocles, Shakespeare, Brecht, and others."[3] Among these others, I suspect that an important tradition to which Kushner is also the heir is that of the medieval mystery cycles. To read *Angels in America* in the light of this tradition may help dispel Savran's suspicion that Kushner is as much the victim of Enlightenment categories as are his political enemies.

It should first be noted that although Kushner was a student of medieval culture (he graduated from Columbia with a degree in medieval studies),[4] he has little interest in the specific Christian contents of the cycles. Indeed, in an early interview with Savran, Kushner makes his ambivalence about the Middle Ages clear. On the one hand, he dismisses them as "of no relevance to anything" only to praise them later on for the "great richness [that] can come from societies that aren't individuated."[5] Kushner's use of the Corpus Christi plays in *Angels in America* is consistent with this ambivalence. While he is interested in the cycle plays because of their dramatic structure and internal form, his own agenda demands that he distance himself from their theological contents in favor of what appears to be a highly secularized humanism. To use Thomas M. Greene's language, Kushner "force[s] us to recognize the poetic distance traversed"[6] between the hierarchic world of the cycles and our own postmodern experience.

If, as Savran suggests, Walter Benjamin's "Theses on the Philosophy of History" (an essay written in 1940 in an attempt to account for the emergence of Hitler's new order) is "the primary generative fiction for *Angels in America*,"[7] we have an important instance of Kushner's abiding interest in the question of redemptive history, an interest first apparent in his *A Bright Room Called Day* (1985). Kushner himself admits that his protagonist, Prior Walter, is named for Benjamin and that his angel is modeled on Paul Klee's painting *Angelus Novus*, discussed in Benjamin's essay. Significantly, however,

the medieval mystery cycles are also attempts to come to terms with questions similar to those raised by Benjamin and of interest to Kushner. Developed in the late fourteenth and fifteenth centuries, during what Martin Stevens calls "some of the most disruptive upheavals of the social order," including economic depression and plague, the mystery cycles developed when, not unlike Benjamin four hundred years later, medieval Christians were re-examining the nature and meaning of redemptive history in an effort to redefine their own newly emerging social order. The plays helped, as Stevens suggests, to create "a reinvigorated sense of morality."[8] As such, the cycles would seem to be particularly hospitable to Kushner's postmodern didactic project, written at the end of the millennium and during the age of AIDS.

Moreover, Benjamin's theory of redemptive history is similar to that expressed in the medieval cycles. A student of Jewish mysticism, Benjamin felt that "the moral duty of criticism was to 'redeem' the past, to save it from oblivion by revealing its concealed truth."[9] Once revealed, the truth of the past, particularly as it is embodied in the "oppressed," might then provide some hope for the future. "The past," Benjamin says, "carries with it a temporal index by which it is referred to redemption." He notes that "for the Jews . . . every second of time was the strait gate through which the Messiah might enter." In his scheme, the contemplation of the whole of tradition "teaches us that the 'state of emergency' in which we live is not the exception but the rule."[10] No doubt selected in a way that would distress Benjamin, the events of the mystery plays show, nonetheless, the world in a similarly constant state of "emergency." These "emergencies" (the fall, a fratricide, the flood, the murder of children, etc.) are, moreover, presented in a way that links past "emergencies" to present realities. In the mysteries, each past event conceals some sign of Christ's redemptive action: an action made necessary by the initial cosmic "emergency," the fall of men and angels, with which the cycles begin; made possible by the death of Jesus, the central and ubiquitous emergency of the cycles; and, for those who have heeded the prefigurements, fulfilled in the ultimate emergency of "Doomsday."

While Kushner's use of multiple locations is obviously consistent with medieval practice, his arrangement of incidents in *Angels in America* closely imitates the structural outline of the mystery cycles. As the cycles trace an arc from Genesis to Doomsday, so, too, does Kushner's play. As the cycles begin with the Creation and Fall, Kushner's play also begins with allusions to a more perfect and, significantly, Jewish past, now fallen from grace. At the funeral of Sarah Ironson, Rabbi Chemelwitz notes that her grandchildren "with the goyische names" have become so assimilated into the modern world, a world fallen from the primal Eden of "the clay of some Litvak shtetl," that they are no longer capable of embarking on a "Great [Voyage]."[11] Moreover, as in the cycles, the individual incidents of *Angels in America* culminate in an epilogue whose apocalyptic imagery suggests the "doomsday" scenes of traditional mystery cycles. In Kushner's final scene, dominated by a statue of an angel, Hannah and Prior speak of a time "[w]hen the Millennium comes"—"[n]ot the year two thousand, but the Capital M Millennium" (II, 147). The scene focuses on another family, now newly constituted and prepared to do what the old Rabbi despaired of: to begin again, "to go out into the world" (II, 147). Sarah is replaced here by a new matriarch, Hannah, named for the Biblical prophet who praises Yahweh for defeating the powerful and raising up the poor and oppressed.[12] This newly constituted family has been gathered and redeemed not, as in the medieval cycles, because they have been chosen by Christ, but rather because its members have loved Prior Walter—the "prophet" of the new postmodern times whose wounded and dying body dominates each part of *Angels in America* as ubiquitously as the body of Christ dominates "every second of time" of the Corpus Christi cycles.

As in the cycles, all other action takes place within this Biblical are, an are that encompasses all time and understands it as redemptive history. In setting out the genealogy of Louis Ironson (grandson of Sarah, son of Rachel), Kushner positions one of his principal characters within the Biblical narrative of the Ur-family. In fact, Louis, full of self-loathing, later identifies himself with Cain ("now I can't see much and my forehead . . . it's like the Mark of Cain" [I, 99]), and he is the one character whose name and genealogy are invoked by the Rabbi at the "Fall" in scene one and who reappears throughout the play until the "Doomsday" of the final scene.

Among the other characters are, of course, angels, and also a devil, a devil whose particular traits are rooted in medieval practice. Even in George C. Wolfe's very unmedieval New York production, few critics failed to recognize the devil in Ron Liebman's out-of sync performance as Roy Cohn.[13] While in the cycle plays Lucifer's fall generally precedes Adam and Eve's, Kushner's devil appears first in the second scene, but is very much like the Lucifer of the Chester plays. There the devil sits in God's throne exclaiming, "Here will I sitt nowe in this steade, / . . . / Beholude my bodye, handes and head— / the might of God is marked in mee."[14] Similarly, Cohn sits in a throne of his own invention wishing he were a formidable monster: "an octopus, a fucking octopus. Eight loving arms and all those suckers" (I, 11). Like the Lucifer of York who gloats in a power that "es passande my peres" (is passing my peers),[15] Cohn claims, like God, to "see the universe" (I, 13), curses all with "God-fucking-dammit to hell" (I, 14), blesses chaos (I, 15), and, in a tempta-

tion scene (I, 52-58), tries to lure the faithful Christian, Joe, with the promises of similar power: "Let nothing stand in your way" (I, 58). By his own admission, he's "an absolute fucking demon with Family Law" (II, 138).

To counterbalance the devil, Kushner's principal angel, who may owe some inspiration to Benjamin's "Angelus Novus,"[16] also bears some additional resemblance, as Rob Baker points out, to the angels of medieval alchemy whose "Great Work" is to transform by fire base lead into pure gold.[17] Kushner's text, however, also associates his angels with Biblical angels. Perhaps playing with the frequent use of "Mary" in gay parlance, Kushner writes an "Annunciation" scene in which Prior exclaims, just before a Gabriel-like angel appears, "Something's coming in here, I'm scared, I don't like this at all, something's approaching and I. . . . OH! [. . .] God almighty . . ." (I, 118, stage directions omitted). Most frequently, though, Kushner associates his angel with Jacob's angel in Genesis 32. First, Joe, a closeted Mormon homosexual, alludes to Jacob's angel when he defends himself to his wife: "Jacob wrestles with the angel. [. . .] The angel is not human, and it holds nothing back, so how could anyone human win [. . .]?" (I, 49-50). Despairing of spiritual victory, Joe, who, nonetheless, had desired to be "Blessed" (I, 54), then seeks the approval of the angel's opposite. On his deathbed, Roy Cohn blesses Joe:

Roy:

> [. . .] You don't even have to trick it out of me, like what's-his-name in the Bible.

Joe:

> Jacob.

Roy:

> [. . .] A ruthless mother fucker, some bald runt, but he laid hold of his birthright with his claws [. . .]

> (II, 82-83)

Under the tutelage of Joe's Mormon mother, however, Prior, fully human and living with AIDS, literally "wrestle[s]" with the angel and wins, demanding, "bless me or whatever but I will be let go," after which he *"ascends"* to heaven on a *"ladder of [. . .] light"* (II, 119-20).

More importantly, the correspondence Kushner establishes between Prior Walter and Joe around their relationship to the Jacob story is typical of the kind of "[i]nterconnectedness" (to use Hannah's word [II, 146]) that characterizes the internal structure of the entire play. Specifically, these correspondences might more properly be named "analogies," and they, like the structuring are of the play, further situate *Angels in America* within a medieval dramatic tradition, a tradition developed when "resemblance . . . organized the play of symbols, made possible knowledge of things visible and invisible, and controlled the art of representing them."[18] David Tracy, a modern theorist of "analogy," defines it as "a language of ordered relationships articulating similarity-in-difference. The order among the relationships is constituted by the distinct but similar relationships of each analogue to some primary focal meaning."[19] Here, Prior and Joe are not simply opposites, as Savran's observations about "binary oppositions" would suggest. At one and the same time, they are both similar (in their homosexuality and their need of a blessing) and different (in that [a] one is closeted and the other is out and [b] one wrestles with the angel, the other spars with the devil). As analogues rather than paired opposites, each relates in a unique way to the story of Jacob's redemption. This pattern of relationships is precisely the kind that V. A. Kolve notes at work in the cycles. Like Erich Auerbach, who notes that medieval "figural interpretation changed the Old Testament from a book of laws and a history of the people of Israel into a series of figures of Christ and the Redemption,"[20] Kolve shows how events and characters in the "Old Testament" plays (Noah's flood, the sacrifice of Isaac, for example) prefigure events and characters of the "New Testament" plays (John the Baptist, the crucifixion of Jesus, for example). He notes further that this prefigurement occurs in such a way that "the differences between figure and fulfillment are as important as the similarities."[21] In other words, the ordered relationships among events and characters in the cycles preserve the principle of analogy: their similarity-in-differences is maintained, each achieving significance from a common relationship to some prime analogue. In the cycle plays, the prime analogue is Jesus Christ; in *Angels in America* it is, of course, Prior Walter.

Although analogy is most clearly evident in the "split scenes" placed strategically throughout the play, Kushner uses analogy most significantly as the metaphoric expression of the profound similarities-in-difference that his meditation on contemporary politics and AIDS has led him to discover abounding in all reality. Like Louis and Joe, Prior (male, gay, worldly) and Harper (female, straight, Mormon) only seem opposites. Meeting around a common table, they recognize each other at "the very threshold of revelation" (I, 33). They soon speak in parallel sentences ("I'm a Mormon"; "I'm a homosexual"; "[Mormons] don't believe in homosexuals"; "[Homosexuals] don't believe in Mormons"). They share not their partners' disembodied and "Enlightened" myth of progress but a more concrete understanding of human finitude and a conviction that imagination is limited because bound to memory. They so clearly comprehend each other that they can reveal truths about the one that the other did not suspect: Prior can tell Harper that Joe is gay; Harper can tell Prior that his "most inner part" is "entirely free of disease" (33-34).

Significantly, following these specific revelations and the larger implicit revelation that characters as diverse as Harper and Prior are not simply independent and opposing characters but fully implicated in each other's lives, the angel manifests itself for the first time.

Further, Kushner's analogies create an ordered series of relationships among God, self, and world and thereby give shape to the otherwise disparate elements of the play. If in the Corpus Christi plays the prime analogue is the suffering body of Christ, in *Angels in America,* the prime analogue is the suffering body of Prior Walter. Both bodies dominate their plays not simply as graphic images of physical pain and suffering but primarily as interpretive paradigms. Positing the wounded body of Christ as an analogue for, among other things, the woundedness of the social body, of the body politic, and of the individual physical body, the cycles teach that the destinies of these separate bodies are in fact interconnected. As each of these bodies (social, political, individual) suffers in its own way, its suffering also participates in Christ's suffering and in that participation achieves a significance inaccessible to the same suffering considered in isolation: as Christ must die to rise again, so too must all else that is. As the analogical design of the medieval plays redefined their own emerging new social order, so the similar design of *Angels in America* helps to redefine whatever sense of order Kushner sees emerging not only from the AIDS pandemic but also from the collapse of modernism itself. Rather than only exploring AIDS and its metaphors, as Susan Sontag does,[22] Kushner offers AIDS as the primary analogue by means of which he seeks to recover meaning not only in the wake of AIDS but also out of the ruins of the entire postmodern collapse.

When Roy Cohn's doctor says that in the "presence" of the HIV virus, "[t]he body's immune system ceases to function" (I, 42), he is describing for a single human body the woundedness that, by analogy, is typical of all the defenseless bodies in what Kushner's Angel calls a "Universe of Wounds" (II, 54). As Prior's body can no longer defend itself against death, Harper notices from the outset that all around her

> beautiful systems [are] dying, old fixed orders spiraling apart . . .
>
> [. . .] everywhere, things are collapsing, lies surfacing, systems of defense giving way. . . .
>
> (I, 16-17)

During the wrestling match with Prior at the end of the play, the angel remarks on the same events:

> The slow dissolving of the Great Design,
> The spiraling apart of the Work of Eternity,
> The World and its beautiful particle logic
> All collapsed
>
> (II, 134)

The separate elements in Kushner's design of a "Universe of Wounds" are the individual, the nuclear family, the American justice system, international diplomacy, the physical integrity of the planet, and the Judeo-Christian tradition itself.

In Kushner's design, these separate wounds form an ever-widening series of concentric circles radiating from a single wounded center, Prior Walter. In a vision of his own family history (I, 85-89), for example, the prior Priors teach him that "[i]n a family as long-descended as the Walters there are bound to be a few carried off by plague." While Prior's AIDS remains unique, suffering from plague, pestilence, "[t]he spotty monster," he learns, has an analogue in the common suffering of all that is human (86-87). Prior understands himself not only as an isolated, purely psychological entity, but as a member of the human family. On the other hand, Roy Cohn, unlike Prior, remains trapped in a thoroughly modern and "monological consciousness."[23] His disease, like Joe's homosexuality, must remain a secret, private, "closeted" business. Like Dante's Satan, he is the ultimate isolationist and last appears *standing waist-deep in a smoldering pit, facing a volcanic, pulsating red light* (II, 138). Moreover, the body of the traditional family is also wounded: Sarah Ironson's grandchildren have become assimilated; Joe's father could not love him (I, 76); Joe abandons Harper; Roy's "fathers" are "Walter Winchell, Edgar Hoover. Joe McCarthy most of all" (I, 56); even the Reagans are "not really a *family* [. . .] there aren't any connections there, no love, they don't ever even speak to each other except through their agents" (I, 71). In addition, like Prior, the body politic is wounded: justice is confused with power; "ipso facto secular humanism" has given way to "a genuinely American political personality. Modeled on Ronald Wilson Reagan" (I, 63); Washington is a "cemetery" (I, 23); "The whole Hall of Justice," Joe fears "it's empty, it's deserted, it's gone out of business. Forever. The people that make it run have up and abandoned it" (I, 72). After "Perestroika" and the fall of the Berlin Wall, "the World's Oldest Living Bolshevik" decries the present as a "Sour Little Age" and regrets the loss of any "Grand" and "comprehensive [Theory]" to guide a new revolution (II, 13-14). Further, the planet is also wounded: "the Chernobyl Power Plant in Belarus is already by leagues the greatest nuclear catastrophe" (II, 129); Libby fears the radon escaping in Hannah's basement (I, 82); and Harper learns early on about "holes in the ozone layer. Over Antarctica. Skin burns, birds go blind, icebergs melt. The world's coming to an end" (I, 28).

As all these wounded bodies are analogues to the wounded body of Prior Walter, so too is the great wound in the body of the Judeo-Christian tradition: like Louis and Joe, who abandon their lovers, and those others who have abandoned the Halls of Justice, God has also abandoned the universe. The primal covenant is broken, and heaven *"has a deserted, derelict feel [. . .] rubble is strewn everywhere"* (II, 121). In a scene inspired perhaps by the "Parliament of Heaven" episode in the N-Town plays,[24] the angels announce that they have become mere "impotent witness[es]" longing for the return of God (II, 130-31). But while the N-Town Daughters of God prepare for the coming of Christ, Kushner's angels, like mouthpieces for the Religious Right, foresee a future filled with chaos, a chaos that can only be averted by embracing stasis. Here Kushner makes most evident that although the structure of his play is similar to that of the cycles, it is also quite obviously different. Instead of imitating the cycles in a slavish way, thereby producing only similarity, something "of no relevance to anything," Kushner imitates them so as to announce at the same time his distance from them. Rather than create something absolutely "new," Kushner keeps faithful to the principle of analogy: quite deliberately, and like Prior Walter, he enters into a conversation with his own usable (prior) past. Unlike his modernist monster, Roy Cohn, whose death is hastened by his uncompromising defense of utter difference ("Roy Cohn is a heterosexual man, Henry, who fucks around with guys" [I, 46]), Kushner shares with Prior and Harper (and, it might be added, with most medieval descriptions of the imagination)[25] the belief that because imagination is always in a conversation with memory, it "can't create anything new [. . .] It only recycles bits and pieces from the world and reassembles them into vision" (I, 32).

Distancing himself from the theological assumptions of the medieval cycles to comment on contemporary reality, however, does not necessarily make Kushner the unwitting heir of the Enlightenment, as Savran suggests. To see *Angels in America* built around "a host of binary oppositions," as Savran does, ignores the complexity of Kushner's fully analogical imagination and fails to consider what Tracy calls "that dialectical sense within analogy itself."[26] What Savran reads as an "elaboration of contradictions" ("heaven/hell . . . communitarianism/individualism, spirit/flesh," etc.)[27] Kushner's imagination holds in balance as dialectically aligned pairs. In his last scene, his "Doomsday," Kushner embodies the concordance of opposites, rather than their contradiction, in the Bethesda Fountain, "Prior's favorite place in the park" (II, 94), whose statuary angel dominates the scene. While Louis identifies the fountain as a monument to the "Naval dead of the Civil War" (II, 94), Belize sees it as a source of healing. Prior, the prophet of the impending age, however, sees it as both: "[it] commemorate[s] death but [. . .] suggest[s] a world without dying. [It is] made of the heaviest things on earth, stone and iron, [it] weigh[s] tons but [it is] winged" (II, 147). Incapable of understanding himself as independent of his body, and joined analogically to the community around him, Prior, unlike Roy Cohn and the ever-closeted Joe, is no representative of the detached, enlightened ego. Rather, more like a medieval holy man, Prior sees death not as the opposite of life, but as its complement and fulfillment. Conceived so, Prior's impending death, like the death of Christ in the mysteries, is not the occasion of despair but rather the springboard of hope.

Moreover, membership in the family which gathers around Prior at the end is dependent on a similar dialectical vision. Although Harper is absent, she is finally no more "pathologized" than is Prior Walter. She is clearly not the heir of Mary Tyrone and Blanche DuBois, as Savran suggests.[28] Unlike theirs, her disease and Prior's do not lead to isolation. Just as their diseases can never be understood in isolation from each other, disease itself roots them in a fragile and complex human condition that Joe and Roy, both absent from the final scenes, take great pains to deny. Moreover, for both Harper and Prior, disease can never be understood as independent of vision: her straight, Mormon, female vision always and everywhere the complement of his gay, secularist, male one. As she flies to San Francisco in a plane that also weighs tons and is winged, she has her own vision of apocalypse: "the souls of these departed joined hands, clasped ankles, and formed a web, a great net of souls, and the souls were three-atom oxygen molecules, of the stuff of ozone, and the outer rim absorbed them, and was repaired" (II, 144). If Roy and Joe are ineligible for membership in the new human family, it is precisely because they have failed to transcend Savran's binary oppositions: Joe's homosexual body remains the enemy of his Mormon spirit; Roy dies cursing life, gloating in the triumph of his will over Ethel Rosenberg (II, 115). Yet those who have loved Prior and join him around the Bethesda Fountain share in his analogical vision: while each remains independent of the other, they understand that the future of Prior's body is also their own. White, black; gay, straight; Jewish, Mormon; male, female: they retain their identities but share a common fate. While this final scene is indeed "utopian," it is not simply an image of an American utopia that "diffuse[s] or deflect[s] dissent," as Savran suggests.[29] It is, rather, an image of the new Jerusalem, which preserves the principle of analogy and where similarity and difference persist in constant and open conversation.

The credibility of this brief exploration of some medieval aspects of **Angels in America** was, unfortunately, nowhere supported by George C. Wolfe's New York production. Several foreign directors, however, seem to have appreciated the play's relationship to its medieval past. In doing so, they mounted productions that distanced themselves from the misguided attempts at psychological realism that marred Wolfe's production and thereby obscured Kushner's vision. Such a style could hardly convey what Bent Holm suggests is the

play's "allegorical nature" or support his view of the play as a "wake-up call to The Theater's 'reality.'"[30] In Neil Armfield's September 1994 Australian production, on the other hand, "all ropes and pulleys were clearly visible and almost every stage object was on wheels enabling the cast members to smoothly and swiftly run them in and out."[31] Most tellingly, at the Avignon theater festival in summer 1994, Brigitte Jacques staged the first part of the play outdoors in the medieval Cloître des Carmes. In a manner consistent with Kushner's original stage directions that the play be "actor-driven" (I, 5), French street kids visibly moved set pieces on and off stage in a production that one critic called "not only minimalist but basic."[32] Such a basic production, it seems to me, embodied the kind of interconnectedness the play longs for.

Notes

1. Harold Bloom, *The Western Canon: The Books and School of the Ages* (New York, 1994), 567.

2. Arlene Croce, "Discussing the Undiscussible," *New Yorker* (26 December 1994/2 January 1995), 55; Leo Bersani, *Homos* (Cambridge, MA, 1995), 69; David Savran, "Ambivalence, Utopia, and a Queer Sort of Materialism: How *Angels in America* Reconstructs the Nation," *Theatre Journal*, 47:2 (1995), 207-27.

3. Savran, "Ambivalence," 209. See note 1.

4. Arthur Lubow, "Tony Kushner's Paradise Lost," *New Yorker* (30 November 1992), 61.

5. Tony Kushner, "The Theatre of the Fabulous: An Interview with Tony Kushner," interview by David Savran, in *Essays on Kushner's Angels,* ed. Per Brask (Winnipeg, 1995), 134-35.

6. Thomas M. Greene, *The Light in Troy: Imitation and Discovery in Renaissance Poetry* (New Haven, CT, 1982), 40.

7. Savran, "Ambivalence," 211. See Walter Benjamin, "Theses on the Philosophy of History," in *Illumination,* ed. Hannah Arendt, trans. Harry Zohn (1968; rpt. with omissions, New York, 1969), 253-64.

8. Martin Stevens, "Medieval Drama: Genres, Misconceptions, and Approaches," in *Approaches to Teaching Medieval English Drama,* ed. Richard K. Emmerson (New York, 1990), 45-46.

9. David Stern, "The Man With Qualities: The Incongruous Achievement of Walter Benjamin," *The New Republic* (10 April 1995), 32.

10. Benjamin, 260, 254, 264, 257. See note 7.

11. Tony Kushner, *Angels in America: A Gay Fantasia on National Themes,* Part One, *Millennium Approaches* (hereafter I) and Part Two, *Perestroika* (hereafter II) (New York, 1992, 1994), I, 10. Subsequent references appear parenthetically in the text.

12. I Sam. 2: 1-10.

13. For example, Andrea Stevens, "Finding a Devil within to Portray Roy Cohn," interview with Ron Liebman and Ron Vawter, *New York Times* (18 April 1993), Arts and Leisure sec., 1. See also John R. Quinn, "*Corpus Juris Tertium*: Redemptive Jurisprudence in *Angels in America*," *Theatre Journal*, 48:1 (1996), 85: "the corporeality of Cohn and of Cohn's law are also inverted representations of the new law, a sort of Satan resurrected."

14. *The Fall of Lucifer* (The Tanners), Play I of *The Chester Mystery Cycle,* ed. R. M. Lumiansky and David Mills, Early English Text Society (London, 1974), II, 186-89.

15. *The Creation and the Fall of Lucifer* (The Bartiers), play I of *York Plays,* ed. Lucy Toulmin Smith (1885; rpt. New York, 1963), 156.

16. Savran, introduction to "Theatre of the Fabulous," 131. See note 5.

17. Rob Baker, *The Art of AIDS* (New York, 1994), 214.

18. Michel Foucault, *The Order of Things: An Archaeology of the Human Sciences* (New York, 1970), 17.

19. David Tracy, *The Analogical Imagination: Christian Theory and the Culture of Pluralism* (New York, 1981), 408.

20. Erich Auerbach, "Figura," trans. Ralph Manheim, in *Scenes from the Drama of European Literature* (New York, 1959), 52.

21. V. A. Kolve, *The Play Called Corpus Christi* (Stanford, CA, 1966), 67.

22. See Susan Sontag, *AIDS and Its Metaphors* (New York, 1989).

23. Charles Taylor, "The Dialogical Self," in *The Interpretive Turn: Philosophy, Science, Culture,* ed. David R. Hiley, James F. Bohman, and Richard Shusterman (Ithaca, 1991), 52.

24. See *The Parliament of Heaven; The Salutation and Conception*, play XI of *The N-Town Plays: Cotton MS Vespasin D.8,* ed. Stephen Spector, vol. I, *Introduction and Text*, Early English Text Society (Oxford, 1991), II. 1-216.

25. See, for example, the discussion in Richard Kearney, *The Wake of Imagination: Toward a Postmodern Culture* (Minneapolis, MN, 1988), 115-138.

26. Savran, "Ambivalence," 212-13; Tracy, 413 (see note 19).

27. Savran, "Ambivalence," 212.

28. Ibid., 215.

29. Savran, "Ambivalence," 224, quoting Sacvan Bercovitch, "The Problem of Ideology in American Literary History," *Critical Inquiry,* 12:4 (1985-86), 644.

30. Bent Holm, "Flying in Different Directions: *American Angels* in Denmark," trans. Per Brask, in *Essays on Kushner's Angels,* 30-31.

31. Ian Olorenshaw, "*Angels* in Australia," *Essays on Kushner's Angels,* 73.

32. Laszlo Szekrenyi, "*Angels* in Avignon," *TheaterWeek* (5-11 September 1994), 37.

Allen J. Frantzen (essay date 1998)

SOURCE: Frantzen, Allen J. "Alla, Angli, and *Angels.*" In *Before the Closet: Same-Sex Love from "Beowulf" to "Angels in America,"* pp. 264-92. Chicago: University of Chicago Press, 1998.

[*In the following essay, Frantzen examines the representation of Anglo-Saxon identity in* Angels in America *in terms of Kushner's sexual identity politics.*]

Rome, not Northumbria, is the center of *The Man of Law's Tale,* and celibacy, not marital bliss, is the Man of Law's preferred mode for Christ's holy ministers. Chaucer's text looks neither to the vernacular tradition of married clergy that the Wycliffites sought nor to the celibate clerical world demanded by Roman canon law and espoused earlier by the Anglo-Saxon church of Ælfric and by Norman reformers. Instead, the Man of Law's heroine is a product of Chaucerian compromise. She practices what might be thought of as serial chastity. Custance marries Alla, but after she becomes pregnant she lives without his company for all but the last year of his life. Clerical ideals dominate *The Man of Law's Tale,* much of its domestic sentiment notoriously devalued not only by the narrator's self-dramatizing interruptions but by Chaucer's debt to the work of a great reforming cleric, Pope Innocent III, whose "De miseriis humane conditionis" (On the misery of the human condition) is quoted in the prologue to the tale and elsewhere in the text.[1]

Chaucer makes much of the dependence of the English church on Rome. His reform-minded contemporaries, the Lollards, regarded Rome as a dangerous influence; in the Reformation the city became a symbol used to attack Catholicism. But for the Anglo-Saxons and for orthodox Christians of Chaucer's time, Rome was the center of the Church on earth. Correspondence with the pope and travel to and from Rome were means by which the church of the frontier established its authenticity. In this chapter I examine one small part of this traffic, an episode from Bede's *Ecclesiastical History of the English People,* which describes the sale of angelic English boys in Rome, a story subsequently retold by Wace, Laʒamon, and others, including John Bale, a Reformation historian. I compare the juxtaposition of angels and Angli, meaning "English," in these texts to angelic powers in Tony Kushner's ***Angels in America,*** a play in which the Anglo-Saxons, embodied in the stereotype of the WASP, play a small but significant role. For a moment, however, I return to Chaucer's Alla and a scene in which he too meets a boy in Rome.

ALLA AND ÆLLE

Alla registers a dim presence in *The Man of Law's Tale.* He is heard about after Custance converts Hermengyld and her husband but otherwise, except for letters to his mother, not heard from until a young boy (who proves to be his son) is set before him at a feast. This act is part of Custance's plan. She too has arrived in Rome but has refused to identify herself to the senator who rescued her from the ship on which she was set adrift from Northumbria. Now, in her husband's presence, she speaks through her son. "[A]t his moodres heeste / Biforn Alla, durynge the metes space, / The child stood, lookynge in the kynges face" (1013-15).[2] The child does not look like him, however, but "as lyk unto Custance / As possible is a creature to be" (1030-31). Because Alla has kept the faith (he is on a pilgrimage of repentance for killing his wicked mother), he realizes that Christ might have sent Custance to Rome just as he sent her to Northumbria. Shortly thereafter Alla and Custance are reconciled. Only then does she reveal herself to her father, the emperor, explaining for the first time who she is (1105-13).

The story of Custance reminds many readers of a saint's life and recalls some of the dynamics of stories about cross-dressed women saints recounted in chapter 2.[3] Like Euphrosyne, Custance is betrothed, in Custance's case to a sultan who becomes a Christian in order to marry her. His mother, outraged, kills him and sends Custance out to sea, a scenario repeated when Custance is expelled from Northumbria. Unlike Euphrosyne, Custance marries and has a child. But in many ways her life as a missionary is similar to the lives of the evangelizing saints commemorated in Anglo-Saxon texts. The moment at which Custance reveals herself to her father recalls the revelation made by both Euphrosyne and Eugenia to theirs. And, like Eugenia, Custance preaches the word of God from within a same-sex community. It is, of course, a tiny one, just Custance and Hermengyld, but their same-sex love, symbolized by the bed they share, is genuine and more warmly demonstrated than such love is in the Anglo-Saxon texts.

Having been reunited in Rome, Custance and Alla return to Northumbria for a year of wedded bliss. After Alla's death, Custance goes back to Rome and takes up a life of virtue and good works, never again parting from her father (1156-57). Chaucer rejoined his roving heroine to patriarchal structures identical to those governing the lives of Eugenia and Euphrosyne. The difference is that Chaucer's holy woman is not just a daughter but also a wife and mother—a married evangelist. To a surprising degree *The Man of Law's Tale* conforms to what might have been a Lollard vision of evangelism in the true church. Custance's language, for example, recognized as "a maner Latyn corrupt" in Northumbria, is what the Lollards thought Italians spoke—that is, a vernacular, albeit not English. The tale discreetly hints of controversies building in the Church in Chaucer's time by effecting a radical redescription of the origins of the Church in the Anglo-Saxon period. According to the Man of Law, Northumbria was converted by a woman who arrives from Rome by way of Syria, directed only by God's will and the winds. But as Bede's *Ecclesiastical History* makes clear, the territory was converted by Irish missionaries and by holy men who came at the pope's behest from Rome—Augustine sent by Gregory the Great in 596, Theodore and Hadrian sent by Pope Vitalian over half a century later. Equally bold is the Man of Law's revised account of Alla, Chaucer's version of the Northumbrian king Ælle, the only English character in the text who is known to have been a historical person. Chaucer's Alla is converted to Christianity by Custance and with her has a son, Maurice, who was crowned emperor by the pope (1122). Bede's Ælle was not Christian but rather served as a symbol of pagan kingship awaiting redemption. Ælle's son, Edwin, converted to Christianity because he wished to marry Æthelburh, the daughter of the Christian king Æthelberht.[4] Thereafter Edwin "held under his sway the whole realm of Britain, not only English kingdoms but those ruled over by the Britons as well."[5]

Ælle's role in Bede is much smaller on the historical level but much greater on the symbolic level. He appears in Bede's text but once, in a description of some boys who, like Maurice, ended up in Rome through circumstances not of their own choosing. They too looked into the face of an important man, Pope Gregory. Or I should say, rather, that he looked into their faces, and what he saw there, depending on whose account we accept, was either the image of a chosen people waiting to be converted (the preferred explanation)—or love.[6]

> It is said that one day, soon after some merchants had arrived in Rome, a quantity of merchandise was exposed for sale in the market place. Crowds came to buy and Gregory too amongst them. As well as other merchandise he saw some boys put up for sale, with fair complexions, handsome faces, and lovely hair. On seeing them he asked, so it is said, from what region or land they had been brought. He was told that they came from the island of Britain, whose inhabitants were like that in appearance. He asked again whether those islanders were Christians or still entangled in the errors of heathenism. He was told that they were heathen. Then with a deep-drawn sigh he said, "Alas that the author of darkness should have men so bright of face in his grip, and that minds devoid of inward grace

should bear so graceful an outward form." Again he asked for the name of the race. He was told that they were called *Angli.* "Good," he said, "they have the face of angels, and such men should be fellow-heirs of the angels in heaven." "What is the name," he asked, "of the kingdom from which they have been brought?" He was told that the men of the kingdom were called *Deiri.* "*Deiri,*" he replied, "*De ira!* good! snatched from the wrath of Christ and called to his mercy. And what is the name of the king of the land?" He was told that it was Ælle; and playing on the name, he said, "Alleluia! the praise of God the Creator must be sung in those parts."[7]

The story of the Anglian boys in Rome is found at the start of book 2 of the *Ecclesiastical History,* where Bede encloses a summary of Gregory's life within a larger narrative of the origins of the English nation. Like Gildas, Bede portrayed the early British as a Chosen People who violated their covenant with God and were destroyed as a result.[8] Bede effected a complete break between the histories of the lapsed early Christian communities of the British—the community that Custance encounters when she lands in Northumbria and reads a "Britoun book"—and the heathen tribes, the Anglo-Saxons, whom Gregory's missionaries would convert. Bede located his own origins in the Anglo-Saxons, the new rather than the old chosen people.

The boys whom Gregory saw in the marketplace were descendants of Anglo-Saxons who, 150 years after coming to Britain, were still pagan. Gregory and Bede call the boys "Angli," a term that generally means "English."[9] But Bede had a more particular understanding of the term, as his description of the settlements of Germanic tribes makes clear. Bede located the Jutes where the people of Kent live, and the Saxons where the West, East, and South Saxons live. He continued: "Besides this, from the country of the Angles, that is, the land between the kingdoms of the Jutes and the Saxons, which is called *Angulus,* came the East Angles, the Middle Angles, the Mercians, and all the Northumbrian race (that is those people who dwell north of the river Humber) as well as the other Anglian tribes. *Angulus* is said to have remained deserted from that day to this."[10] Bede seems to have meant "Anglian" in the more specific sense of "Northumbrian." He himself was born in the territory of Monkwearmouth-Jarrow, in Northumbria, and so was "Angli" in three senses— Northumbrian, Anglian, and English.[11] "Angli" also means "angels," of course, but Bede carefully understates this meaning, which in the anecdote is better left to Gregory. That the boys' beauty should make Gregory think of angels is significant, for it suggests a purely symbolic meaning for "angli" otherwise rare in Bede's *Ecclesiastical History.*

Bede affirms a natural affinity between Gregory and the Anglo-Saxons. It might seem curious that Gregory should find the boys attractive, since his admiration

suggests that he prefers their unfamiliar appearance (light-complected and light-haired) to that of his own people. The discrepancy strongly suggests that the anecdote originates with an English author whose views Gregory is made to express. The episode is a pretext for witty verbal play that valorizes the boys' race, their nation, and their king. Young, innocent, and beautiful, the boys themselves represent a benign and neglected heathendom. When Gregory recognizes all the signs of a chosen people awaiting God's blessing, Bede is permitted to foresee the new Christian age of the English people that arrived in England with Gregory's missionaries.

For all its piety, the encounter between Gregory and the boys reflects earthly and political concerns. Bede shows us Gregory's interest in establishing the Church in England and in complementing the churches that Rome had already fostered so successfully elsewhere in western Europe. Bede's chief aim was to bolster the success of that Church especially in the land of his birth; he dedicated the work to the Northumbrian king Ceolwulf.[12] The reference to angels promotes this aim, symbolically affiliating the Anglo-Saxon church with Rome. When Gregory announced that the people of Anglia, represented by angelic youth, were ready to be changed into "fellow-heirs of the angels in heaven," a new age—the history of Bede's own beginnings—came into being. But these unhappy boys were not its heralds, any more than they were angels. Other messengers— missionaries brought to England by Augustine at Gregory's command, long after the boys had been forgotten—were charged with bringing the faith to the Anglo-Saxons. That the boys could be compared to angels was not testimony to their proximity to the divine, a role Bede reserved for real angels, but to the angel-like state of their descendants, who would be newly baptized, newly converted, and newly saved.

The boys, Bede notes, were "put up for sale." Gregory saw them amid stacks of other merchandise. What were they doing there? Peter Hunter Blair warned that readers should not "jump to the romantic conclusion that the boys whose purchase was envisaged by Gregory were English slaves on sale in a market-place." The boys might also have been held in service, he suggested, as four English boys were held in the service of Jews at Narbonne, or prisoners of war, mercenaries, or "merely young men in some way bound to the soil on Merovingian estates."[13] A letter survives from Gregory to the priest Candidus (written in September 595), asking him to buy "English boys who are seventeen or eighteen years old, that they may be given to God and educated in the monasteries" ("pueros Anglos qui sunt ab annis decem et septem vel decem et octo, ut in Monasteriis dati Deo proficiant comparet").[14] The boys Gregory sees in the marketplace are not destined for education and clerical status, however. Those who have looked closely at the episode, including Bertram Colgrave, R. A. B. Mynors, and David Pelteret, identify the boys as slaves—although Bede does not—and relate the episode to the well-documented practice of slavery by the Anglo-Saxons.[15] "The custom of buying or ransoming slaves to turn them into missionaries was known," according to Colgrave, and both Aidan and Willibrord observed it.[16]

In the later Anglo-Saxon period opposition to slavery seemed to intensify. In 1014 Wulfstan denounced those who sold their children into foreign servitude.[17] But foreign trade in slaves persisted until the Norman Conquest, after which opposition to slavery continued. The Council of London of 1102 criticized the custom, even as servile tenure was becoming a more prevalent form of bondage.[18] In almost all cases in Anglo-Saxon sources the slaves in question are penal slaves forced into slavery because they could not pay debts or because they were being punished for some offense. The boys' status depended on their age; if they were seventeen or eighteen, they could have been sold as slave labor. But it is also possible that the boys Gregory saw in Rome were captives who were too young to be penal slaves and who merely represented a benign and neglected heathendom. Bede's narrative exalted their innocence, youth, and beauty, even though its real subject was their race, their nation, and Ælle, their king. What was their value in the market place? Ruth Mazo Karras points out that sexual exploitation was among the many unfortunate facts of life for women slaves. It is possible that boys were also sexually exploited and that their commercial value was directly related to their beauty and fairness, underscored by Gregory's focus on their faces (they are "bright of face," they have "the face of angels").[19] The boys would have been exploited by men, obviously, a kind of same-sex sex that, as we saw in chapter 4, was of particular concern to the Anglo-Saxons.

Any sexual resonance in the anecdote is, of course, suppressed by Bede and, in turn, by all those who retold the episode after him. In the version found in Laȝamon's *Brut,* the "angli" are men, not boys, whose response anticipates Gregory's discovery and spoils the drama of his curiosity and his good heart. "We are heathen men," they say, "and have been brought here, and we were sold in England, and we seek baptism from you if you would only free us" ("We beoð heðene men and hider beoð iladde, / and we weoren ut isalde of Anglene lond; / and fulluht we to þe ȝeorneð ȝef þe us wult ifreoiȝen," 14707-9). Gregory's reply is obliging. "[O]f all the peoples who live on earth, you English are assuredly most like angels; of all men alive your race is the fairest" ("Iwis ȝe beoð Ænglisce englen ilicchest / of alle þan folke þa wunieð uppen uolde; / eouwer cun is feȝerest of alle quike monnen," 14713-15).[20] Neither Laȝamon's nor other versions subsequent to Bede's include all of the episode's verbal play. Instead these versions overtly state points implied in Bede's account, showing, first, that the Angli desired baptism and requested it of Gregory, and, second, that they were captives who yearned to be free. But an ironic reading is also possible. Laȝamon's version, which makes nothing of Gregory's insight, might suggest that the Anglo-Saxons use the pope to effect a cynical exchange of baptism for freedom; conversion is their idea, not his.

The first modern reader to comment on the sexual subtext of Bede's story was John Boswell, who documented the Church's concern that abandoned children would be sold into slavery and used for sexual purposes. Some writers protested this practice, but not for the reasons we might expect. Their concern was that fathers who abandoned their children might later accidentally buy them as slaves and commit incest by having intercourse with them. Boswell noted that the public sale of slaves continued in Rome long after the empire was Christianized and illustrated the practice with the episode as Bede recounted it.[21] In the 1540s, some seven hundred years after Bede's death, Boswell's point was vividly anticipated by a remarkable figure named John Bale, the first reader to see a same-sex shadow in the story that has charmed so many.

BEDE AND BALE

Bale (1495-1563) was a Carmelite priest who left the Church of Rome in the 1530s. The author of several large-scale surveys of English authors and the first biographer of Chaucer, Bale was also a collector of early manuscripts, including those in Anglo-Saxon.[22] According to John N. King, Bale was "the most influential English Protestant author of his time."[23] He was also a prodigious instrument in the propaganda efforts of Thomas Cromwell.[24] Bale recounted the episode of Gregory and the slave boys in a revisionist narrative of English ecclesiastical history called *The Actes of Englysh Votaryes.*

> And as thys Gregorye behelde them fayre skynned and bewtyfullye faced, with heare upon their heades most comelye, anon he axed, of what regyon they were. And answere was made hym, that they were of an yle called Englande. Wele maye they be called *Angli* (sayth he) for they have verye Angelych vysages. Se how curyose these fathers were, in the wele eyenge of their wares. Here was no cyrcumstaunce unloked to, perteynynge to the sale. Yet have [has] thys Byshopp bene of all writers reckened the best sens hys tyme.[25]

Bale mockingly urged his readers to "[m]arke thys ghostlye mysterye, for the prelates had than no wyves." He plainly implied that Gregory had sexual designs on the boys. "[T]hese fathers" were "curyose" in the "wele eyenge" of the boys as "wares," he wrote, using an expression with strong sexual overtones. In sixteenth-century English, "ware" could mean "piece of goods" (an expression "jocularly applied to women," according to the *OED*) and "the privy parts of either sex."[26] Because priests were unmarried, Bale observes, with much sarcasm, "other spirytuall remedyes were sought out for them by their good prouvders and proctours, we maye (yf we wyll) call them apple squyres." "Apple-squires," according to the *OED*, means "pimp" or "panderer," thus further underscoring Bale's sexual innuendo. Stressing that this sale was not unique, Bale produces another witness, Machutus, who saw a similar event in Rome in AD 500 and bought the boys to protect them (23a). We are meant to conclude that Gregory, deprived of a wife by the Church's demand for clerical celibacy, sought out "other spirytuall remedyes" by purchasing boys for sex.

Bale's rewriting of the story of Gregory and the Anglian boys takes place in the context of an elaborate revision of England's Anglo-Saxon Christian history proposed in *The Actes of Englysh Votaryes* and *The Image of Bothe Churches*. In *The Actes of Englysh Votaryes* Bale boldly revised English history in order to describe the nation's struggles against the corrupt influences of the Church of Rome. The chief instrument of Roman domination, Bale argued, was clerical celibacy, which permitted the clergy to degrade marriage and advocate virginity, all the while using its own religious houses for immoral purposes. Bale vigorously defended the right of the clergy to wed and believed that the Roman clergy who claimed to be celibate had in fact indulged in every form of sexual corruption. In *The Image of Bothe Churches*, Bale set forth a thesis about the Church in England that, as it was later developed by his better-known contemporary, John Foxe, became a foundational strategy for Reformation anti-Roman polemic.[27] Bale argued that the Church had been divided during the reign of Constantine and that the See of Saint Peter stemmed from the corrupt division, while an isolated community of the faithful, who retained belief in the true Church, reestablished the true Church in England. Bale argued that the false Church of Rome had taken on the image of the true Church of antiquity and that from the time of St. Augustine's mission to the English (597) to the rejection of papal authority by Henry VIII (1533) the Church in England had been corrupt. Bale was among the historians who looked back to the Anglo-Saxon period, skipping over an internal period in which they perceived England as dominated by the Church of Rome to a point that they erroneously saw as a free, "native," English church unencumbered by Roman influence. This was an exercise in self-justification. Having recently thrown off Roman rule itself, the new "English" or "Anglican" church was searching for its origins in the Anglo-Saxon period, which was perceived as another time when England's Christians governed themselves justly and righteously.

For Bede, the mission of Augustine marked the permanent conversion of Britain. Bale reversed the significance of this event. He claimed that the English church had survived pure and uncorrupted until the coming of Roman missionaries. With them they brought pernicious doctrines such as clerical celibacy, and as a result they transformed the once-pure land and its church into a new Sodom. Seeking to open his readers' eyes to the false miracles used by "obstynate hypocrytes" still living under the pope's rules, Bale wrote *The Actes of Englysh Votaryes* in order to accuse Catholics of portraying "whoremongers, bawdes, brybers, idolaters, hypocrytes, traytors, and most fylthye Gomorreanes as Godlye men and women" (2a). His diatribes are laced with references to Sodom and Gomorrah. Although his definitions of the sins of these unholy places remain vague, they encompass theological error as well as sexual excess, including, at certain points, male homosexual intercourse.

Marriage, Bale wrote in *The Actes*, was the "first order of religion," created in order to protect against "beastlye abusyons of the fleshe that shuld after happen" if men and women disobeyed God's command to increase and multiply (7b). The Church sought to dissuade holy men and women from marriage, broke up existing marriages, venerated only unmarried saints, and demonized women as "spretes" ("sprites," 3a); these were the acts of "the Sodomytycall swarme or brode of Antichrist" (4a). According to Bale's extraordinary revision of the history of Anglo-Saxon holy men and women, clergymen fornicated with cloistered nuns and produced a race of bastards who were then venerated as saints, Cuthbert, Dunstan, Oswald, Anselm, and Becket among them (2b). Some did worse, since they refrained from women but "spared not to worke execrable fylthyness among themselves, and one to pollute the other," an obvious reference to male homosexual acts (12b). Devout in his praise of Mary, Bale was eager to insist that she was not abused by the clergy and that she was not a professed nun, "as the dottynge papystes have dreamed, to couer their sodometrye with a most precyouse coloure, but an honest mannys wyfe" (13a). Bale attacked "spirituall Sodomytes and knaves" who wrote the lives of these sinful saints (18a): "Come out of Sodome ye whoremongers and hypocrytes, popysh byshoppes and prestes" (18b). Bale used "sodometrie"—an obsolete word for sodomy, first used in 1530, according to the *OED*—to attack clergy who took the required vows of celibacy but who were unable to remain celibate: either men who had sex with each other because they could not have sex with women, or men who did have sex with cloistered nuns who were virtually the male clergy's sexual slaves. Shortly before he recounts the story about Gregory, Bale tells of a large group of women who joined a pilgrimage only to find that they had been taken from England to be forced to prostitute themselves to the clergy on the Continent (21a).

In leading up to his account of the boys, Bale followed Geoffrey of Monmouth, who embroidered Gildas's account into a claim that sodomy was pervasive among the early Britons, practiced by two of their kings (Malgo and Mempricius) and the cause of their overthrow by the Saxons. Gildas's version contains no hint of sexual slander, as we saw in chapter 5. Bale wrote that Malgo, who was possibly fashioned on William Rufus, was "the most comelye persone of all hys regyon," someone to whom God had given great victories against the "Saxons, Normeies, and Danes." But he was a sodomite. He imitated the ways of his predecessor Mempricius, who was "geuen to most abhomynable sodometrye, which he had lerned in hys youthe of the consecrate chastyte of the holie clergye" (21b-22a).[28] Thus the British were weak and were easily conquered by the Saxons. Bale believed that Roman Christianity entered England with the Saxons, who renamed the land England. "Then came therein a newe fashyoned christyanyte yet ones agayne from Rome with many more heythnysh yokes than afore." Bale then immediately introduced Gregory and told the story about the boys (22a-b, a section entitled "The Saxons entre with newe Christyanyte").

Elsewhere Bale underscored the charges of sodomy among Catholic clergy made in *The Image of Both Churches*. In his *Apology against a Rank Papist* (1550), Bale asked, "Whan the kynges grace of England by the autorite of Gods wurd, discharged the monkish sectes of his realme, from their vowed obedience to the byshop of Rome, did he not also discharge them in conscience of the vowe of Sodometry, whyche altogether made them Antichristes creatures?" Catholic clergy had set marriage and virginity "at variance" and replaced them with "two unhappy gestes, called whoredom and buggery."[29] In *The Pageant of Popes*, published in 1574 (after Bale's death), Bale recounted visitations to monasteries ordered by Henry VIII, which found "such swarmes of whoremongers, ruffians, filthie parsouns, giltye of sinne against nature, Ganimedes, and yet votaries and unmaryed all, so that thou wouldest thincke that there were a newer Gomorrah amonge them." At Battle Abbey, according to Bale, there were nearly twenty "gilty of sinne against nature" (their crimes included bigamy and adultery); at Canterbury there were eleven.[30] *The Pageant of Popes* shows that Bale saw another side to Gregory, casting him as the creator of a policy opposing clerical celibacy (no one could ever accuse Bale of consistency). Gregory was informed that priests "accompanied not only with virgins and wyves, but also even with their owne kindred, with mankind, yea and that whiche is horrible to be sayde, with brute beastes." ("Accompanied" is an obsolete euphemism for "cohabit with," according to the *OED*. Note that Bale regards bestiality as worse than same-sex acts.) Appalled at this conduct, Gregory revoked the canon requiring that priests not marry.[31]

Gregory was given credit for being "the best man of all these Romaine Patriarkes, for learning and good life," and Bale praised his humility and his learning.[32]

Like many polemicists, Bale was an idealist. His attack on the Roman clergy can be explained by his high regard for marriage and his ardent defense of women's position. When he was a Carmelite priest, in the 1520s, Bale carried out extensive research into Carmelite archives and took special interest in the Church's view of women, in part at least because of his interest in Mary, the patron of the Carmelite order.[33] His recruitment to the Church of England came in the 1530s, when he lived in London and could see the drastic impact of Henry's marriage and decrees on all monastic orders, including his own. It was also at this time—in 1536—that Bale married, and undoubtedly this change in his life fueled his polemics about the Roman Church's demand for clerical celibacy.[34] Bale identified the ideal of marriage for the clergy as an Anglo-Saxon custom that had been brought to an end with the Norman Conquest. "I omit to declare for lengthe of the matter," he wrote in *Apology against a Rank Papist* (xiii), "what mischefe and confusion, vowes [vows] brought to this realme by the Danes and Normannes, whan the lyves of the vowers in their monasteries were more beastlye than eyther amonge paganes or Turkes." Bale, who was unaware that the Danes were not Christian, believed that the monks and clergymen, once forced to give up wives, turned to "bestlye" lives worse than those lived by pagans or Turks. In other words, he thought they had become sodomites.

Sodomy also figured in Bale's plays, his best-known works. In *A Comedy concernynge Thre Lawes, of Nature, Moses, & Christ, Corrupted by the Sodomytes, Pharysees, and Papystes* (1538), written before the historical studies just sampled, Bale created a character named Sodomismus, an allegorical figure unique in sixteenth-century English drama.[35] Sodomismus is one of six vice characters in the play. Attired "lyke a monke of all sectes," according to Bale,[36] Sodomismus repeatedly associates himself with both monks and the pope.

> I dwelt amonge the Sodomytes,
> The Benjamytes and Madyantes
> And now the popish hypocrytes
>   Embrace me every where.
> I am now become all spyrytuall [i.e., taken over by
>   spiritual leaders],[37]
> For the clergye at Rome and over all
> For want of wyves, to me doth fall,
>   To God they have no feare.
>
>   (2:571-78)

Pederastic unions are listed among the forms of sodomy he promotes.

> In Rome to me they fall,
> Both byshopp and cardynall,

Monke, fryre, prest and all,
  More ranke they are than antes.
Example in Pope Julye,
Whych sought to have in hys furye
Two laddes, and to use them beastlye,
  From the Cardinall of Nantes.

(2:643-50)

Had he known about Gregory's letter to Candidus, Bale would have had an even more pertinent example of how a Roman pope allegedly abused innocent boys.

In *King Johan,* which casts the king as an opponent of clerical corruption, the king speaks for Bale's position. Johan (King John) regrets that the clergy

> Shuld thus bynd yowre selfe to the grett captyvyte Of blody Babulon the grownd and mother of whordom— The Romych Churche I meane, more vyle than ever was Sodom.[38]

For Bale, "sodomites" were not only the unjust and impious but also those who turned from the lawful union of marriage and had illicit intercourse either with the opposite sex or with their own. In *A Comedy concernynge Thre Lawes,* Sodomismus claims to have inspired all manner of sexual sinners, ranging from the fallen angels who fornicated with the daughters of men (Genesis 6:1-4) to Onan (Genesis 38:9; see *A Comedy,* 580-610). The offense that seems most closely connected to sodomy in Bale's mind is idolatry, represented in the play as Idolatria, an old woman. Idolatria is the companion of Sodomismus, who speaks to her in terms of endearment, calling her "myne owne swetehart of golde" (481). Sodomismus is sexually profligate, not exclusively or even primarily interested in same-sex intercourse. His accusations against monks and popes, however, conform precisely to those Bale himself made in his nondramatic works.

The inference that Bale had accused Gregory of sodomy was drawn by Bale's Catholic opponent, who recognized the unacknowledged source of Bale's story in Bede's *Ecclesiastical History.* In 1565, in the first translation of Bede's *Ecclesiastical History* in modern English, Thomas Stapleton listed "a number of diuersities between the pretended religion of Protestants, and the primitive faith of the english Church" (he counted forty-five points of difference in all). Stapleton contrasted the authority of Bede, who wrote without prejudice, with that of Bale, Foxe, and other "pretended refourmers." Stapleton discussed the episode involving Gregory and the Anglian boys in his preface. Bede, who was close to this event, had told a story contrasting outer beauty with inner lack of belief. Bale had deliberately misread the event in order to charge Gregory "with a most outrageous vice and not to be named." Stapleton obviously understood Bale to have accused Gregory of sodomy. Bede was a bee who made honey (beautiful meaning) out of this episode, said Stapleton, but Bale was a "venimous spider being filthy and uncleane himself," an "olde ribauld," and "another Nero" who found "poisonned sence and meaning" therein.[39]

To be fair, Bale's interpretation, admittedly harsh, is somewhat better than Stapleton allowed. Bale forces us to reconsider Bede's treatment of the anecdote and calls our attention to its dark side, its shadow. The episode about Gregory and the boys is animated by the contrast between light and dark, outside and inside. Gregory calls Satan "the author of darkness" who holds "men so bright of face in his grip." He finds the Anglians "devoid of inward grace" while admiring their "graceful . . . outward form[s]." Gregory's language clearly recognizes that physical and moral beauty exist in close proximity to the evil and the ugly. Bede did not look beyond Gregory's words for these malignant forces. Instead he saw the brightness of the episode, which marked the "Angli" as a people elevated by their likeness, at least in Gregory's mind, to angels. Bale saw around Gregory's words and, like Gregory himself, recognized how near evil was to the good. But Bale reversed the field of Gregory's vision, casting Gregory into the darkness where Gregory himself saw Satan. What lived in that darkness was same-sex desire, the unholy appetite of Gregory and other reluctant celibates for the sexual favors of young Englishmen. Such shadows, dark places of evil and corruption, are not the only kind of shadows where same-sex relations can be seen. They are not the kinds of shadows I think of when I think of the presence of same-sex love in a heterosexual world. All the same, Bale's vision of the shadow, however distasteful it might seem, is, in context, accurate. The sexual abuse of young boys was a danger to which life in the monastery exposed them, as the penitentials show. Slavery was another danger, not unrelated, that lurked in the episode Bede describes. It is difficult to deny that the shadows seen by Bale are places where "the author of darkness," as Gregory called him, held sway.

Bale's recasting of Anglo-Saxon history had a prominent sexual aspect, if not a primary sexual character. He saw the Anglo-Saxons as a people who naturally observed God's lawful commandment to be fruitful and multiply. Their Roman oppressors, on the other hand, were those who denied clergy the right to marry and, as a result, spread sexual corruption wherever they were to be found. Gregory's "wele eyenge" of the slave boys' "wares" vividly emblematizes this exploitation and situates it in the heart of Rome. For Bale, Anglo-Saxon identity was continuous with British identity that predated the arrival of the Anglo-Saxons. English identity emerged out of this combined British-Anglo-Saxon identity in a struggle against the enslaving bonds of Roman and then Norman domination. Racial differences are but vaguely registered by Bale, and his chronology, not unexpectedly, is confused. Malgo won victories over "Saxons, Normeies, and Danes," for example, even though it was the Saxons who subverted the realm (22a). Bale's historical discourse, punctuated with numerous references to Sodom and allegations of homosexual acts among the clergy, is entirely free of allegory (his plays, obviously, are not). Bale did not need a figurative discourse about angels or origins to celebrate what was, for him, the distinguishing feature of his sources. His sense of who was Saxon, Norman, or Dane was imprecise, but Bale unquestionably understood that Gildas, Bede, Geoffrey of Monmouth, Chaucer, and others, were not mythical figures but were instead his predecessors, righteous as he was himself.[40] He was sure that the history he chronicled was as English as he was. His association of corrupt sexual practices with foreign powers—Roman and Catholic especially—is therefore easily explained, however disagreeable we find it. His polemical use of sodomy strongly resembles that of the Anglo-Norman historians and chroniclers on whose work he drew. But whereas they directed their diatribes against their own princes and rulers, Bale directed his at the princes of the Catholic Church. Among their agents he numbered the Norman conquerors of England, the despoilers of the True Church of the British.

ANGELS AND ANGLI

Another polemicist and dramatist with a vague sense of the Anglo-Saxon past and strong views on its significance is Tony Kushner. His celebrated two-part drama, *Angels in America: A Gay Fantasia on National Themes,* approaches the Anglo-Saxons through the stereotype of the WASP. Kushner correlates same-sex relations with racial stereotypes and national heritage and makes revealing use of Anglo-Saxon culture that is seldom noticed by the play's admirers. Kushner's AIDS-infected hero is the play's only WASP, the thirty-second Prior Walter in a line traced to the Norman Conquest so that it can represent the Anglo-Saxon hegemony of the West. But *Angels* reverses a dynamic that operates in all the other texts I have examined throughout this study. Anglo-Saxon penitentials, histories, poems, and commentaries ultimately side with the angels. And so, for that matter, do Chaucer and Bale, Custance being Chaucer's angel, the English boys being Bede's and Bale's. Angels are pure, either above sex or, if involved with sexual relations, chastely married; they are on the side of order. Sodomites, however they have been defined, are not. They and same-sex relations are stigmatized and repressed because they subvert order, lack shame, and threaten to lead others into sin.

In order to express Kushner's millennial vision, *Angels in America* rewrites the social history of England (and America) in order to enable a new era in which same-sex relations thrive while heterosexual relations wither. Kushner does not take the side of the angels but rather represents them as weak, lost, and prejudiced. Amid their confusion, paradoxically, their saving grace is that they retain their sexual prowess. The Angel of America, as she will be known, enters the play as a messenger to a white, Anglo-Saxon, Protestant but exits taking advice because the WASP is also a PWA, a "person with AIDS," prophet of a new homosocial order and herald of a revolution so sweeping that it offers redemption even for angels.

Rich in references to migratory voyages and the Chosen People, *Angels in America* advances a broad argument about history and progress. The play is a multicultural juxtaposition of WASP, Jewish, black, and Mormon traditions, among others. David Savran has argued that the "spiritual geography" of Mormonism is central to the play's "conceptualization of America as the site of a blessed past and a millennial future." Savran demonstrates that Mormonism was among the evangelical, communitarian sects formed in reaction to the individualism fostered by Jacksonian democracy and the ideology of Manifest Destiny.[41] A key element in the racial basis of Manifest Destiny, which claimed for the chosen people "a preeminent social worth, a distinctively lofty mission, and consequently unique rights in the application of moral principles,"[42] is Anglo-Saxonism. The premise of Anglo-Saxonism (familiar in earlier forms in the works of Gildas, Bede, Chaucer, and Bale, as we have seen, and many others, of course) is that the English are a Chosen People and a superior race.[43] Numerous nineteenth-century accounts used the racial purity of the Anglo-Saxons to justify westward expansion and empire building. Anglo-Saxon culture was thought to have been inherently democratic and the Anglo-Saxons egalitarian, self-governing, and free. The descendants of a people who so perfectly embodied the principles of American democracy had, it appeared, natural rights over lesser peoples and their lands. Anglo-Saxonism enters *Angels in America* through the lineage of Prior Walter. He is a token of the WASP culture—the only white Anglo-Saxon Protestant in the play, according to Kushner[44]—against which the oppressed peoples of the play, Jews and blacks in particular, strive.

The Anglo-Saxon subtext of *Angels* emerges in both parts of the drama, *Millennium Approaches* and *Perestroika,* through the association of Prior Walter with the angel. Kushner locates Prior's origins in the mid-eleventh century, but the Anglo-Saxon characteristics that Prior represents are prior to the Normans, whose conquest of England constitutes a particularly troubled originary moment for the chief Anglo-Saxon of the play. An early scene in each of the three acts of *Millennium Approaches* reveals something about Prior's Anglo-Saxon identity (act 1, scene 4; act 2, scene 3; and act 3, scene 1). In the first of the scenes about his lineage,

Prior jokes with Louis, his Jewish lover, after a funeral service for Louis's grandmother. Prior comments on the difficulties that their relatives present for gay men: "Bloodlines," he says. "Jewish curses are the worst. I personally would dissolve if anyone ever looked me in the eye and said 'Feh.' Fortunately WASPs don't say 'Feh'" (1:20).[45] A few moments later he reveals his first AIDS lesions to Louis, who is horrified both by the lesions and by Prior's mordant jocularity about them. This scene establishes Prior's AIDS status and his WASP identity and introduces the largest of the cultural themes of *Angels in America:* the resistance that biological descent and inherited tradition, embodied here in the body of the WASP, pose to political change. Bloodlines are curses because they carry the past into the present, creating resistance to the possibilities of change that the present raises. WASP blood resists change because WASPs, as they are presented in this play, exist in a culture of stasis, while other races and creeds, denied that stability and permanence and driven by persecution and need from place to place, have developed migratory and transitional cultures open to, and indeed dependent on, change.

Having inherited a distinguished past, Prior faces an uncharacteristically grim future (for a WASP) because he carries a fatal new element in his bloodline, AIDS. The virus paradoxically reverses the deadening flow of WASP tradition and prepares for a new social order whose values the WASP himself will eventually espouse. The virus he bears is both literal (HIV) and figurative; it is eventually identified as "the virus of time," the "disease" of change and progress. The angel who appears to Prior at the end of *Millennium Approaches,* and who punctuates the play with intimations of her arrival, claims to herald a new age. When Prior receives his first intimation of the angelic, a feather drops into his room and an angelic voice ("an incredibly beautiful voice," the text specifies) commands, "Look up! . . . Prepare the way!" (1:34-35). But the side of the angels is not what we expect it to be. The angel is not pointing to a new age but instead calling for a return to a previous one. The tradition and stasis that constitute Prior's Anglo-Saxon heritage draw her. She believes that Prior will be a worthy prophet precisely because he is a worthy WASP.

Kushner happened on Prior's name when looking "for one of those WASP names that nobody gets called any more." Discussing Walter Benjamin with a friend so interested in the philosopher that she sometimes "thought she was Walter Benjamin reincarnated," Kushner referred to the real Benjamin as the "prior" Walter.[46] The significance of Prior's name unfolds in a subsequent dialogue between Louis and Emily, a nurse, after Prior has been hospitalized. "Weird name. Prior Walter," says Emily. "Like, 'The Walter before this one.'" Louis replies: "Lots of Walters before this one. Prior is an old

old family name is an old old family. The Walters go back to the Mayflower and beyond. Back to the Norman Conquest. He says there's a Prior Walter stitched into the Bayeux tapestry" (1:51). The oldest medieval record mentioned in *Angels in America,* the tapestry would seem designed to surround Prior's origins with an aura of great antiquity.

The appearance of Prior Walter's name on the tapestry validates Louis's claim that the Walter name is indeed an "old old" one. But the Bayeux tapestry is a record of the political and military events surrounding the Norman Conquest of Anglo-Saxon England in 1066. The tapestry testifies to the subjugation of the Anglo-Saxons and marks the point at which the government and official vernacular language of England were no longer English. Generations of Anglo-Saxonizing historians and writers regarded the arrival of the Normans as the pollution of the pure stock of the race.[47] Thus Kushner's announced aim of portraying Walter as a WASP is more than a little complicated by this decision to trace Walter's ancestry to a tapestry long accepted as a lucid statement of Norman claims to the English throne.[48] Notoriously ironic throughout *Angels in America,* Kushner might have chosen the tapestry to register precisely this compromised aspect of Prior's lineage.[49] But one's view of that lineage would seem to depend on the uses to which it is put in *Angels in America,* where it seems intended to represent the Anglo-Saxons as a monolithic, triumphant culture that has reached a symbolic end point in Prior's blood.

Emily (played by the actress who plays the angel) is somewhat baffled by Louis's high regard for Prior's ancient name and for the tapestry itself. Louis believes that the queen, "La Reine Mathilde," embroidered the tapestry while William was away fighting the English. In the long tradition of French historians and politicians who used the tapestry to arouse public sentiment to support nationalistic causes, including the Napoleonic wars against the English,[50] Louis pictures Mathilda waiting at home, "stitch[ing] for years," waiting for William to return. "And if he had returned mutilated, ugly, full of infection and horror, she would still have loved him," Louis says (1:52). He is thinking penitently of Prior, who is also "full of infection and horror," whom Louis will soon abandon for Joe, the married Mormon lawyer with whom Louis has an affair. Louis's view of when and where the tapestry was made is popular, but wrong. The tapestry was made in England, under the patronage of William's half-brother Odo, bishop of Bayeux and vice-regent of England, within a generation of 1066, not during the Conquest itself, and then taken to the Bayeux Cathedral.[51]

Kushner's mistaken ideas of when, where, and by whom the Bayeux tapestry was made have significant implications for his definition of "WASP." Kushner invokes the

Conquest as if its chief force were to certify the antiquity and authenticity of Prior's Anglo-Saxon credentials and heritage, a point of origin for *English* identity, although, as I have shown, it traditionally represented the very betrayal of the racial purity that "Anglo-Saxon" came to represent. Louis's assertion that the name of a "Prior Walter" is stitched into the tapestry is also without foundation. Only four minor characters are named in the tapestry, none of them Anglo-Saxons ("Turold," "Ælfgyva," "Wadard," and "Vital"). The rest are important figures (Harold, William, and others), most of them Norman and well-known from contemporary sources.[52] If Prior Walter were an Anglo-Saxon, it is highly unlikely that he would be commemorated in the tapestry, although it is possible he could have been an English retainer of Harold (who was defeated by William).

But "Prior Walter" is a singularly inappropriate name for an Anglo-Saxon. It strongly suggests an ecclesiastical, monastic context, as if "Prior Walter" were "Walter, prior of" some abbey, instead of the secular and heroic ethos usually called to mind by "Anglo-Saxon." Apart from the tapestry, there is no evidence either for or against an argument about Prior's origins. Although it is possible that his ancestors were Anglo-Saxon, it is more likely that they were Normans who, after the Conquest, settled in England and established the line from which the Walters descended. Few Anglo-Saxons would expect to find their ancestors mentioned in the tapestry, while Normans would want to boast of this testimony to a family's distinguished history. The original Prior Walter might have been a Norman who took part in the conquest of the English. His family would have been prosperous. As we saw in the last chapter, the Anglo-Saxons were less well-to-do than their conquerors and resented the superiority of French into the fourteenth century. If so, as the last in a line of thirty-one men of the same name (or, by an alternative count, if bastard sons are included, thirty-three [1:86]), Prior Walter claims Norman rather than Anglo-Saxon ancestry, or, more likely, a heritage in which Norman and Anglo-Saxon blood is mixed—in other words, Anglo-Norman. His long genealogy, to which Louis proudly points, is hybrid at its origins. Kushner's stereotype of the WASP is itself a further hybrid, obviously, since it is a post-Reformation construct in which P ("Protestant") is a new element. WASP, we can see, is not only a recent vehicle for the representation of "Anglo-Saxon" culture, but an exceedingly shallow one.[53]

We learn more about Prior's ancestry at the start of the third act, when two prior Priors appear to him in a dream (1:85-89). The first to appear, the "fifth of the name," is the thirteenth-century squire who is known as "Prior 1." He tells of the plague that wiped out whole villages, the "spotty monster" that killed him (1:86). (This is another sign of Kushner's shaky historical

sense; the first outbreak of the Black Death in England was a century later, in 1348.)[54] They are joined by "Prior 2," described as "an elegant 17th-century Londoner" (1:86), who preceded the current Prior by some seventeen others and also died of the plague, "Black Jack." Priors 1 and 2 are not merely ancient ancestors, however. They are also the forerunners of the angel whose arrival spectacularly concludes the play. To "distant, glorious music," they recite the language later used by the angel; her messengers, they are "sent to declare her fabulous incipience." "They [the angels] chose us," Prior 2 declares, "because of the mortal affinities. In a family as long-descended as the Walters there are bound to be a few carried off by plague" (1:87). Neither Prior 1 nor Prior 2 understands why Prior is unmarried and has no wife, although the second Prior understands that the plague infecting Prior is "the lamentable consequence of venery" (1:87). Only later, when they see him dancing with Louis, does Prior 1 understand: "Hah, Now I see why he's got no children. He's a sodomite" (1:114). Prior Walter is, therefore, the end of his line. After him the WASP hegemony of the Walters, apparently unbroken from the mid-eleventh century to the present, will cease to exist.

The vague and portentous sense of these genealogical relations is clarified in the next scene (1:89-96), in which Louis engages in a long, confused, and painfully naïve monologue about race and identity politics in America, much to the disgust of his friend Belize, a black nurse and ex-drag queen.[55] Louis describes a difference between American and European peoples that encapsulates the tension between Anglo-Saxons and other races. "Ultimately what defines us [in America] isn't race, but politics," he says. "Not like any European country where there's an insurmountable fact of a kind of racial, or ethnic, monopoly, or monolith, like all Dutchmen, I mean Dutch people, are, well, Dutch, and the Jews of Europe were never Europeans, just a small problem" (1:90). Significantly, Kushner chooses England as site for a scene in which, according to Louis, the "racial destiny," not the "political destiny," matters (1:91). A Jew in a gay bar in London, Louis found himself looked down upon by a Jamaican man who still spoke with a "lilt," even though his family had been in England for more than a century. At first this man, who complained that he was still treated as an outsider, struck Louis as a fellow traveler: "I said yeah, me too, these people are anti-Semites." But then the man criticized British Jews for keeping blacks out of the clothing business, and Louis realized how pervasive racial stereotypes could be (1:91). In America, Louis believes, there is no racial monopoly; in America the "monolith is missing," so "reaching out for a spiritual past in a country where no indigenous spirits exist" is futile (1:92). The native peoples have been killed off: "there are no angels in America, no spiritual past, no racial past, there's only the political and the decoys and the ploys to maneuver around the inescapable battle of politics, the shifting downwards and outwards of political power to the people" (1:92). Wiped clean of its indigenous spirits, the nation as Louis sees it would seem to be a blank slate not unlike England before the Anglo-Saxons, ready for migratory peoples (including Jews and Mormons) who bring their past with them as they seek to build a new future. Belize holds Louis's liberal interpretation of American government and culture in utter contempt. Kushner ensures that the naiveté of the Jew's liberalism will be exposed and contained by Belize's furious reply that in America race is more important than anything else.

Louis's speech reveals the meaning of Anglo-Saxon that is encapsulated in Prior's WASP identity. Even though Prior's mixed Norman and Anglo-Saxon genealogy contradicts Louis's point about the monolith of racial purity that the WASP supposedly represents, Prior is singled out as the recipient of the angel's visit because he is made to represent the cultural monolith of WASP America, fixed and unchanging, embodying what Louis calls "an insurmountable fact of a kind of racial, or ethnic, monopoly, or monolith" (1:90). WASP heritage stands conveniently juxtaposed both to Louis's vision and to Louis's own heritage of many small groups, "so many small problems" (1:90). Although Kushner might have wished to represent the Anglo-Saxons only as a hybrid people, and hence introduced evidence that points to the eleventh-century intermingling of Norman blood, it seems evident to me that the racial dynamics of the play require that the Anglo-Saxons represent the "monolith" about which Louis speaks. Only then can other races and groups be set up in opposition to them.

Indeed, even in motion, the Anglo-Saxons of *Angels in America* are oppressors. One of the most harrowing moments in *Millennium Approaches* is Prior's account of his ancestor, a ship's captain, who sent whale oil to Europe and brought back immigrants, "Irish mostly, packed in tight, so many dollars per head." The last ship he captained sank off Nova Scotia in a storm; the crew loaded seventy women and children onto an open boat but found that it was overcrowded and began throwing passengers overboard: "They walked up and down the longboat, eyes to the waterline, and when the boat rode low in the water they'd grab the nearest passenger and throw them into the sea" (1:41). The boat arrived in Halifax carrying nine people. Crewmen are the captain's agents; the captain is at the bottom of the sea, but his "implacable, unsmiling men, irresistibly strong, seize . . . maybe the person next to you, maybe you" (1:41-42). The agents of the Anglo-Saxons arbitrarily decide the fates of the Irish in their care. The episode is a stark political allegory, a nationally rendered reminder of the rights of one group to survive at the expense of another, a deft miniature that reveals

the power of the conquerors over the conquered, the interrelation of commerce and the immigration patterns of impoverished nations, and, most of all, "unique rights in the application of moral principles," a signature belief of Manifest Destiny.[56]

The point of the association of stasis with Anglo-Saxon heritage—the grand design of *Angels in America*—emerges fully in *Perestroika,* when the Angel of America articulates her ambitions for the WASP and discloses the assumed affiliations between the Anglo-Saxons and the angels. The angel attempts to persuade Prior to take up her prophecy. "IIII / Am the Bird of America," she proclaims, saying that she has come to expose the fallacy of change and progress (2:44), "the Virus of TIME" that God released in man (2:49), enabling humans to explore and migrate. Angels do not migrate; instead, they stand firm (2:49). God himself found time irresistible and began to prefer human time to life in heaven. The angel says:

Paradise itself Shivers and Splits
Each day when You awake, as though we are only
    the Dream of YOU.
PROGRESS! MOVEMENT!
Shaking *HIM*.

(2:50)

A few moments later she shouts, "YOU HAVE DRIVEN HIM AWAY! YOU MUST STOP MOVING!" (2:52). God became so bored with the angels that he abandoned them on the day of the 1906 San Francisco earthquake. And who could blame him? In the one scene that Kushner gives performers the permission to cut, if only in part (act 5, scene 5; see 2:9), the angels are shown sitting around heaven listening to a malfunctioning 1940s radio over which they hear the broadcast of the meltdown of the Chernobyl reactor. Their real concern, however, is the radio's malfunctioning vacuum tube (2:130). They are a picture of feckless paralysis, obviously unable to respond to the changes forced on them by human or heavenly time. "More nightmare than utopia, marooned in history," Savran writes, "Heaven commemorates disaster, despair, and stasis."[57] The purpose of the angel's visitation is to recruit Prior as the angels' prophet on earth. Angels, we see, are not messengers from the divine or heralds of change, although that is how we conventionally think of them, and how Kushner and the play's publicity represent them. Angels are instead associated with stasis and with the power of ancient spirits to resist change. Opposed to the flow of power "downward and outward," as Louis puts it, of "power to the people," the angels want God to return to his place so that they can return to theirs.

The angel's visit is not intended to save Prior from his disease but to use his disease against him, to try to persuade this "long descended" man (like the angel in this) to stop the phenomenon of human progress, to get him to turn back the clock. The angel says to him that she has written "The End" in his blood. This could mean that the AIDS virus is supposed to ensure his desire to stop time—stop the progress of the disease—and prompt him to proclaim her message (2:53), although what is written in his blood could also be his homosexuality, which writes "The End" in a different sense, since it means that he is the last of his line. Later in the scene in which the angel commands Prior to stand still, symbolically appealing to his Anglo-Saxon love of stability and tradition, Belize dismisses the vision as Prior recounts it: "This is just you, Prior, afraid of the future, afraid of time. Longing to go backwards so bad you made this angel up, a cosmic reactionary" (2:55). Prior and Belize were once lovers; Belize knows him well. Like Prior, three other figures—the angel, Sister Ella Chapter (a friend of Joe's mother in Salt Lake City), and the nurse (all played by the actress who plays the angel)—are fearful of movement. Emily does not want Louis to leave the hospital room (1:52). Before Joe's mother moves to New York to help Joe cope with his schizophrenic wife, Harper, Ella reminds her that Salt Lake City is "the home of the saints" and "the godliest place on earth," and then cautions, "Every step a Believer takes away from here is a step fraught with peril" (1:83). But Ella's is not a view that the play endorses. Joe's mother leaves anyway. All the chosen people do.

Like her, Prior rejects the advice to stay put. He ignores the angel's command precisely because "The End" is written in his blood. He interprets these words as the angel's wish that he die: "You want me dead" (2:53). No longer the Prior who joked fatalistically about his lesions outside the funeral home in act 1 of *Millennium Approaches,* he refuses to die. Because he has contracted "the virus of time," the WASP, who has the most to lose, turns from the past to the future. All the "good" characters in the play are already on the move, already evolving, even Joe's drug-maddened wife, just as all the valorized nations and races in the play have migrated. The prominence of migration and the movement away from racial purity are basic elements of Kushner's thesis about change, which is based on an idea of the Anglo-Saxons, the WASPS, as static, permanent, and fixed. Politics change racial makeup and break down pure races and their racism. Kushner explains:

> Prior is the only character in the play with a Yankee WASP background; he can trace his lineage back for centuries, something most Americans can't reliably do. African-American family trees have to start after ancestors were brought over as slaves. Jews emigrated from a world nearly completely destroyed by European genocide. And most immigrant populations have been from poor and oppressed communities among which accurate genealogy was a luxury or an impossibil-

ity. . . . a certain sense of rootlessness is part of the American character.[58]

Anglo-Saxon history prior to the Normans shows that "a certain sense of rootlessness" is also part of the Anglo-Saxon character. American rootlessness was inherited from the nation's Anglo-Saxon founders; the Anglo-Saxons in America were hardly a people who wanted to stay put. It is because of their restlessness and their desire to move westward that Louis, as Kushner's surrogate, can assert that there are no angels in America.[59]

Kushner's association of WASPs with stasis is his most interesting—but least accurate—reinterpretation of the historical record. Kushner seems to think that Anglo-Saxons—WASPs at least—are not a migratory people. At this point his play helps us see a truth in Bede's *Ecclesiastical History* that Bede himself did not acknowledge. Bede reported that after the migration of the Angles to Britain, the land of "Angulus" remained empty "from that day to this." Are there no angels in America? There are no angels in Angulus, either, because the entire population moved to Britain. Thus the Angles took *their* ancient spirits with them, just as did blacks, Jews, and other migrant peoples. Already in the eighth century the immigrants to Britain were known as Anglo-Saxons.[60]

Louis's tendentious view of history is easily discredited, and not only by Belize. The intermarrying of Anglo-Saxon and Norman families ended the pure monolith of "the English" that Prior Walter supposedly represents. What is true of Prior Walter and all WASPS was true for people in England even before the Conquest. "Apartheid is hard enough to maintain," Susan Reynolds writes, "even when physical differences are obvious, political control is firm, and records of births, deaths, and marriages are kept. After a generation or two of post-Roman Britain not everyone, perhaps comparatively few people, can have been of pure native or invading descent. Who can have known who was descended from whom?" Reynolds draws the inescapable conclusion that "those whom we call Anglo-Saxons were not consistently distinguishable from everyone else."[61] After the Conquest, of course, the Anglo-Saxons became less "Anglo-Saxon" than they had been earlier, but at no time were bloodlines in Anglo-Saxon England pure; like most bloodlines, they were even then more the consequence of politics than they were of race.

This severing of biological descent and culture is a denial of the power of race to unify a people. That is the good news of *Angels in America* for homosexuals, the new Chosen People of this epic (what epic does not have one?). Like Mormons, Jews, and other racial groups, gay people too are oppressed, without a homeland, and on the move. But unlike those groups, gays are, first of all, a *political* people, not bound by nation or race. They have no common descent; there is no link between their sexual identity, which the play sees as their central affiliation, and either their biological or their cultural ancestry. So seen, gays serve as a perfect prophetic vehicle for Kushner's newly multicultural America. Prior succeeds in subverting the angels' design and persuading them to become his messenger; he has refused to become theirs. Their message is that the clock should be turned back to old values and stasis, staying put. His message is that change is good. Won over to humanity's view of time and place, the angels sue God, resorting to time-bound human processes (litigation) to redress grievances. The joke apparently is that the angels' heavenly wishes are inferior to the desires of humanity. The new angels of America know better than the Angel of America because Prior, their WASP spokesman, resoundingly refutes the angel's call for stasis. God, however, will probably win; his lawyer is Roy Cohn, the demon in *Angels.* Discredited at this point, God is a disloyal lover who has abandoned his angels for (the men of?) San Francisco. The angels, in turn, are also discredited, for they have accepted Prior's suggestion that those who abandon their lovers should not be forgiven, just as Prior will not forgive or take back Louis (2:133, 136).

So Prior moves ahead, not in spite of AIDS but rather *because* of AIDS. The "virus of time" has jolted him out of torpor and self-pity and eventually transforms him into the play's strongest character, a position from which he waves an affectionate goodbye to the audience. This is an AIDS play with a difference—with a happy ending.[62] Because he is a WASP the angel singled him out, but because he is a PWA he rejects her. In *Angels in America,* AIDS retains its deadly force (Cohn and others die of it) without killing the play's central character. Obviously weakened, but strong nonetheless, Prior survives. Having been visited by an angel, Prior all but becomes one. "You are fabulous creatures, each and every one," he says to the audience. "And I bless you: *More Life.* The Great Work begins" (2:148). He recapitulates the last lines of *Millennium Approaches,* in which the Angel declares, "Greetings, Prophet. The Great Work begins. The Messenger has arrived" (1:119). Another messenger has arrived at the end of *Perestroika,* and his name is Prior Walter. Prior's farewell to the audience, however moving, is a remarkable banality to which I will return.

Savran argues that the play, like *The Book of Mormon,* "demonstrates that there are angels in America, that America is in essence a utopian and theological construction, a nation with a divine mission."[63] It is possible to suggest that Bede and Kushner share a political purpose, which is to create the idea of a unified people. Bede does this with the term—the concept—"Angli," which comes to mean "the English," a people elevated by their likeness to angels. Like Chaucer and Bale, Kushner is also out to unify a people, but more ambitiously and inclusively, and not a people to be compared to angels, but a people to replace them. The threat that unifies the English in Bede's work is the heathen past. The same might be said for Chaucer's ancient British Christians, at least as the Man of Law imagines them. Bale too imagined the British as overwhelmed by Roman Catholicism as brought by the Anglo-Saxons; he saw the British of his own time triumphing over the same evil force. The threat that unifies Kushner's new angels is not AIDS, which only menaces a small percentage of them, but the old regimes of race that divide and weaken people and prevent change, the very forces of conservative national and religious identity that Bede, Chaucer, and Bale advocated so powerfully. Those forces are routed at the end of *Angels in America,* and the boards are clear for a new age. The promised land of *Angels in America* is a multicultural, tolerant world in which biological descent counts for little (there are no successful marriages in the play) and cultural inheritance imparts defining characteristics to people without imposing barriers among them.

MILLENNIUM APPROACHES

I began thinking about this study in 1993, when I saw *Angels in America* for the first time. I was troubled by the conflation of Anglo-Saxon and Norman identities and unclear about how Kushner meant to align his vaguely sketched history of Prior's family with the play's sexual politics. It seemed obvious that he had merely used the WASP as a rhetorical trope and that he had not thought about the Anglo-Saxonism contained in that acronym or how Anglo-Saxonism might be related to his historical thesis about Mormons or, for that matter, angels in America. Kushner ignored the hybrid nature of WASP identity. Likewise, he missed the prominence of same-sex friendships in the nineteenth-century Mormon tradition. D. Michael Quinn has noted that Mormons, although sometimes seen as clannish and isolated, participated fully in what Quinn describes as the "extensive homocultural orientation among Americans generally" a century ago.[64] Same-sex relations, sexual and otherwise, figure prominently in the history of early Mormon leaders, male and female alike. Kushner's representation of the Mormons would lead one to believe otherwise, however, since his Mormons seem hardly aware that homosexuality exists.

In not knowing much about the Anglo-Saxons, Kushner shares a great deal with the authors I have examined in part 3 of this book. The Anglo-Norman chroniclers knew next to nothing about the Anglo-Saxons that they did not get from Bede's *Ecclesiastical History.* A few later writers, including thirteenth-century scholars, struggled to recover the Anglo-Saxons' language, but their efforts mostly reveal how quickly knowledge of the Anglo-Saxons' culture, even their ecclesiastical culture, had faded. Chaucer and his contemporaries knew even less, relying again on French chronicles to conjure images of the Anglo-Saxon past. For all his testy and repetitive declarations, Bale was closer than any of his predecessors to real knowledge of the Anglo-Saxons. Despite his errors and confusion, his knowledge of a continuous historical tradition and its sources shames both earlier and especially later efforts. The "scholarly recovery" of Anglo-Saxon language and texts advanced rapidly after Bale's time but did not, for many years, produce a representation of Anglo-Saxon culture any more accurate than his.

Kushner, unfortunately, did no better than the other authors I have named. I take *Angels in America* as a reasonable, if regrettable, reflection on popular understanding of Anglo-Saxon culture. Kushner seems to be more respectful of Mormon traditions than of Anglo-Saxon traditions. The play contains a diorama portraying the Mormons' westward journey but nothing about the migration of the Anglo-Saxons (2:62-72). Mormon culture seems alien to him and hence multiculturally significant; its history needs to be recaptured and represented. WASP culture, evidently, is familiar and does not need to be elaborated. But at least in the extended historical sense that Kushner evokes through his use of the Bayeux tapestry, WASP culture too is alien to him. Its multicultural significance is ignored, homogenized into stereotypical patterns and ideas. Absent the oversimplified WASP, would *Angels in America* have had a culture to demonize and denounce?

Angels in America is unique among the works I have discussed in not taking the side of the angels. More important, it is also unique in its perspective on same-sex love. As I showed in part 1, it is possible to glimpse satisfying moments of same-sex love—if not same-sex sex—in opera and dance, and even in a few Anglo-Saxon narrative texts. Gays and lesbians hoping to find representations of love as they know it can find it in these works, sometimes at a small cost (i.e., closing our eyes at the opera), often at no cost. But when we go to *Angels in America,* we have no need to deprive our senses in any way. This is a work that, like many others, not only aims to show gays and lesbians what the author assumes we want to see but even blesses its audience for showing up. There are many differences between the power of such a work and that of *Dido and Aeneas,* as danced by Mark Morris, and the power of *Der Rosenkavalier,* with its use of the convention of the trouser role. The central difference, it seems to me, conforms to the difference between liberation and legitimation as approaches to gay and lesbian rights. Kushner and Morris liberate a same-sex perspective; they emphasize the sexual—the homosexual—in a transgressive manner. That is one way to see homo-

sexual sensibility in the modern world, demanding its due. But finding same-sex love in works that are not about homosexual desire—for example, in operas using trouser roles—also legitimates same-sex love by pointing out that it can exist, plainly if unobtrusively, as the shadow of heteronormative desire.

The second time I saw *Angels in America* was New Year's Eve, 1995. My partner and I had bought tickets at a premium because the theater advertised a "party" to follow the performance, which concluded shortly before midnight. The "party" turned out to be glasses of cheap fizzy wine hurriedly passed out by staff members eager to clear the house. The cast reappeared to mock the management's fleecing of the audience and to lead us in "Auld Lang Syne," gracefully lifting the occasion above the circumstances provided for it. Shortly before midnight, in a light snowfall, we walked down a street filled with people who were rushing into bars and restaurants. It was a relief to board the train. The cars were also full—some couples, some groups, some singles, some straight, some gay—but oddly quiet, a capsule of greater Chicago heading to parties or to bed. Between one stop and another the new year arrived. The car's little communities acknowledged the moment without ceremony. Gay, straight, alone, together, we rode happily along. For me the calm—the indifference—made a welcome change from the excitement and intensity of the play and the hustle of the street. No angels crashed through the roof, no heterosexuals were chastised, no homosexuals turned into saints (or demons), no call to a great work of liberation sounded. This is all right, I thought to myself. This is how the millennium, Kushner's and any other, will come, and go.

That is also how I think same-sex love goes along in the world, how it works best for some of us at least—love that belongs in the picture, always there, an ever-present shadow. Political and social work will always be needed to win equal treatment for gays, lesbians, bisexuals, and others who make up sexual minority groups. But there are many ways in which that work can be undertaken. I know that many activists cannot see themselves resting until the difference between heterosexual and homosexual is obliterated and such institutions as marriage and the family are transformed and open partnerships and public sex become the new norms. These people see no reason why the institutions of heterosexual desire should be their institutions. Neither do I. Nor do I see why the institutions of homosexual desire should be mandated for all. My vision of same-sex love might seem tepid and diffuse, devoid of passion and revolutionary fervor, not queer enough. Perhaps it is. But I strongly believe that same-sex love cannot be reduced to genital sex, and I will always believe that life is more interesting, pleasurable, and meaningful if its erotic potential can be realized across a spectrum that includes but is not restricted to the sexual. A world that slowly gets used to that idea would seem a better home to me than any queer planet I have yet to see described.

Notes

1. See Robert P. Miller, ed., *Chaucer: Sources and Backgrounds* (New York: Oxford University Press, 1977), 484. On the narrator's many apostrophes, see the explanatory notes by Patricia J. Eberle in Geoffrey Chaucer, *The Riverside Chaucer,* ed. Larry D. Benson, 3d ed. (Boston: Houghton Mifflin, 1987), 856-58. Innocent's treatise was addressed to a deposed cardinal; Chaucer reported that he had translated this work himself. See the G Prologue to the *Legend of Good Women,* lines 414-15, in Benson, *Riverside Chaucer,* 600.

2. References to *The Man of Law's Tale* are given by line number from *Riverside Chaucer,* 89-103.

3. For an analysis of hagiographical tropes in *The Man of Law's Tale,* see Melissa M. Furrow, "The Man of Law's St. Custance: Sex and the Saeculum," *Chaucer Review* 24 (1990): 223-35.

4. Æthelburh was allowed to marry Edwin because he promised to allow her to worship as she wished and agreed to consider accepting her faith as his own. Eventually he did so, but only after letters to him and his wife from Pope Boniface and persuasions of other forms, including victory over his assailants, a vision, and the sage counsel of his wise men. See Bertram Colgrave and R. A. B. Mynors, eds. and trans., *Bede's Ecclesiastical History of the English People* (Oxford: Oxford University Press, 1969), book 2, where the saga of Edwin's conversion occupies chaps. 9-14, pp. 162-89.

5. Colgrave and Mynors, *Bede's Ecclesiastical History,* book 2, chap. 9, pp. 162-63.

6. Some of the Anglo-Saxon evidence discussed in this chapter appears in my essay "Bede and Bawdy Bale: Gregory the Great, Angels, and the 'Angli,'" in *Anglo-Saxonism and the Construction of Social Identity,* ed. Allen J. Frantzen and John D. Niles (Gainesville: University of Florida Press, 1997), 17-39.

7. Colgrave and Mynors, *Bede's Ecclesiastical History,* book 2, chap. 1, pp. 132-35. Gregory's puns were not original with Bede; a version of the story is found the anonymous Whitby *Life of St. Gregory,* probably written between 704 and 714 but unknown to Bede when he finished the *Ecclesiastical History* in 731. See Bertram Colgrave, ed. and trans., *The Earliest Life of Gregory the Great* (Cambridge: Cambridge University Press, 1985), 49, 144-45.

8. Gildas, *The Ruin of Britain and Other Documents,* ed. and trans. Michael Winter-bottom (London: Phillimore, 1978). See Nicholas Howe, *Migration and Myth-Making in Anglo-Saxon England* (New Haven: Yale University Press, 1989), 33-49, for a discussion of Gildas and the pattern of prophetic history.

9. Colgrave, *Earliest Life,* 144-45 note 42. See "Angles" and variants in the index to Colgrave and Mynors, *Bede's Ecclesiastical History,* 596. Recent studies on the meaning of "angli" in *Bede's Ecclesiastical History* do not discuss Gregory's role in choosing the name, presumably because it is seen as merely symbolic. See D. P. Kirby, *The Earliest English Kings* (London: Unwin Hyman, 1991), 13-15; and H. E. J. Cowdrey, "Bede and the 'English People,'" *Journal of Religious History* 11 (1981): 501-23. See also Patrick Wormald, "Bede, the *Bretwaldas,* and the Origins of the *Gens Anglorum,*" in *Ideal and Reality in Frankish and Anglo-Saxon Society,* ed. Patrick Wormald with Donald Bullough and Roger Collins (Oxford: Basil Blackwell, 1983), 121-24.

10. Colgrave and Mynors, *Bede's Ecclesiastical History,* book 1, chap. 15, p. 51. For an analysis of the ethnography operating in Bede's analysis, see John Hines, "The Becoming of the English: Identity, Material Culture, and Language in Early Anglo-Saxon England," *Anglo-Saxon Studies in Archaeology and History* 7 (1994): 49-59.

11. Colgrave and Mynors, *Bede's Ecclesiastical History,* book 5, chap. 24, pp. 566-67. Although Bede clearly wished to present the Angles (the angels) as the primary group in the migration, there was never a consensus about which group, the Angles or the Saxons, was primary, or even about where in England they settled. D. P. Kirby notes that Gregory believed that the Saxons settled in the north and the Angles in the south, reversing the usual assumptions about the pattern of distribution and pointing to its arbitrary nature. The *Life* of Wilfrid, who came from York, describes him as a Saxon bishop. See Kirby, *Earliest English Kings,* 12-13.

12. Colgrave and Mynors, *Bede's Ecclesiastical History,* preface, 2-3.

13. Peter Hunter Blair, *The World of Bede* (Cambridge: Cambridge University Press, 1970), 45. See also Hunter Blair, *An Introduction to Anglo-Saxon England* (Cambridge: Cambridge University Press, 1956), 116-17.

14. Colgrave and Mynors, *Bede's Ecclesiastical History,* 72 note 1; the letter is found in Arthur West Haddan and William Stubbs, eds., *Councils and Ecclesiastical Documents Relating to Great Britain and Ireland,* 3 vols. (Oxford: Clarendon, 1871), 3:5 (quoted here), and is translated in Dorothy Whitelock, ed., *English Historical Documents, c. 500-1042* (London: Eyre Methuen, 1979), no. 161, p. 790.

15. David Pelteret, "Slave Raiding and Slave Trading in Early England," *Anglo-Saxon England* 9 (1981): 104.

See also Pelteret, *Slavery in Early Mediaeval England: From the Reign of Alfred until the Twelfth Century* (Woodbridge, Suffolk: Boydell Press, 1995).

16. Colgrave, *Earliest Life,* 145 note 43.

17. Dorothy Whitelock, *The Beginnings of English Society* (Harmondsworth, Middlesex: Penguin, 1952), 111. The church allowed penitents to free or manumit slaves as a form of penance or as an act of mercy.

18. On the Council of London of 1102, dominated by Anselm, see the discussion in chapter 6. On the question of selling women who were wives of the clergy into slavery, see A. L. Poole, *From Domesday Book to Magna Carta, 1087-1216,* 2d ed. (Oxford: Oxford University Press, 1955), 40. The Normans' decrees did not affect the status of those who were already slaves, and it continued to be possible for individuals to voluntarily surrender their freedom when compelled by necessity to do so; see Marjorie Chibnall, *Anglo-Norman England, 1066-1166* (Oxford: Basil Blackwell, 1986), 188.

19. Ruth Mazo Karras comments on prostitution and female slaves in "Desire, Descendants, and Dominance: Slavery, the Exchange of Women, and Masculine Power," in *The Work of Work: Servitude, Slavery, and Labor in Medieval England,* ed. Allen J. Frantzen and Douglas Moffat (Glasgow: Cruithne, 1994), 16-29. See also Elizabeth Stevens Girsch, "Metaphorical Usage, Sexual Exploitation, and Divergence in the Old English Terminology for Male and Female Slaves," in *Work of Work,* 30-54. I raise the possibility that the Anglian boys were intended for sexual purposes in *Desire for Origins: New Language, Old English, and Teaching the Tradition* (New Brunswick: Rutgers University Press, 1990), 47.

20. G. L. Brook and R. F. Leslie, eds., *Laȝamon: "Brut,"* 2 vols., EETS, OS, 250, 277 (London: Oxford University Press, 1963, 1978), 2:770. For commentary on versions of the anecdote by Wace and Geoffrey of Monmouth, see Lawman, *Brut,* trans. Rosamond Allen (London: Dent, 1992), 463, notes to lines 14695-923.

21. John Boswell, *Christianity, Social Tolerance, and Homosexuality: Gay People in Western Europe from the Beginning of the Christian Era to the Fourteenth Century* (Chicago: University of Chicago Press, 1980), 144.

22. For an informative survey of Bale's achievement, see Leslie P. Fairfield, *John Bale: Mythmaker for the English Reformation* (West Lafayette, Ind.: Purdue University Press, 1976). See also Hugh A. MacDougall, *Racial Myth in English History: Trojans, Teutons, and Anglo-Saxon* (Hanover, N.H.: University Press of New England, 1982), 33-37. On Bale's Anglo-Saxon manuscripts, see David Dumville, "John Bale, Owner of St. Dunstan's Benedictional," *Notes and Queries* 41 (1994): 291-95.

23. John N. King, *English Reformation Literature: The Tudor Origins of the Protestant Tradition* (Princeton: Princeton University Press, 1982), 56. For recent commentary on Bale in the context of Renaissance humanism, see Alan Stewart, *Close Readers: Humanism and Sodomy in Early Modern England* (Princeton: Princeton University Press, 1997), 38-83.

24. See Fairfield, *John Bale,* 55-56, 121.

25. John Bale, *The Actes of Englysh Votaryes* (London, 1548), 22a-22b. Stewart comments briefly on this episode, *Close Readers,* 42.

26. Contemporary sources invite wordplay on "Angles" and "Ingles." In the sixteenth century "Ingles" meant both "English" and "a boy-favourite (in bad sense): a catamite" (*OED*), and was used to pun both on "angle" and on "angel." "Ingle" was also a term of abuse for boys who played women on the stage. See Patricia Parker, *Shakespeare from the Margins: Language, Culture, Context* (Chicago: University of Chicago Press, 1996), 143-46.

27. John Bale, *The Image of Bothe Churches* (Antwerp, 1545 or 1546). For Foxe's views, see William Haller, *The Elect Nation: The Meaning and Relevance of Foxe's "Book of Martyrs"* (New York: Harper and Row, 1963).

28. Ultimately these stories derive from Geoffrey of Monmouth, *History of the Kings of Britain,* trans. Sebastian Evans, revised by Charles W. Dunn (New York: Dutton, 1958), book 11, chap. 7, p. 238, for Malgo. Bale indicates a variety of sources, ranging from Gildas to Geoffrey of Monmouth, "Florence" (John) of Worcester, and others, including William Tyndale (22a). Bale's immediate source is probably the *Nova legenda Angliae* of John Capgrave, whose narratives of saints' lives he grossly distorted. See Fairfield, *John Bale,* 114, 121-22.

29. John Bale, *Apology against a Rank Papist* (London, 1550), xxvii, xii (v).

30. John Bale, *The Pageant of Popes* (London, 1574), 36.

31. Bale cites Gregory's "Epistle to Nicolas" (*Pageant of Popes,* 34v-35r).

32. Bale, *Pageant of Popes,* 32.

33. Fairfield, *John Bale,* 17-18, 42-43.

34. This summary is based on Fairfield's analysis, *John Bale,* 31-49.

35. Donald N. Mager, "John Bale and Early Tudor Sodomy Discourse," in *Queering the Renaissance,* ed. Jonathan Goldberg (Durham: Duke University Press, 1994), 141-61. See also Stewart, *Close Readers,* 52-62.

36. John Bale, *A Comedy concernynge Thre Lawes, of Nature, Moses, & Christ, Corrupted by the Sodomytes, Pharysees, and Papystes,* ed. Peter Happé, in

The Complete Plays of John Bale, 2 vols. (Cambridge: D. S. Brewer, 1986), 2:65-121. References to act and line number are for quotations from this text. On the attire for Sodomismus, see 121.

37. See Happé, *Complete Plays of John Bale,* 165, note to line 575.

38. Bale, *King Johan,* lines 368-70, in Happé, *Complete Plays of John Bale,* 1:39.

39. Thomas Stapleton, *The History of the Church of England Compiled by Venerable Bede, Englishman* (1565; reprint, Menston, England: Scolar, 1973), 3b. Stapleton's translation is used in the Loeb Classical Library, *Baedae opera historica,* ed. J. E. King (New York: Putnam, 1930).

40. John Bale, *Scriptorum illustrium Maioris Brytanniae* ("Ipswich," but really Wesel, 1548). For a list of Bede's works, including an English translation of the Gospel of John ("in patriam transtulit linguam"), see 50v-52r; for Chaucer's, see 198, unhelpfully alphabetized under *G* for "Galfridus Chaucer").

41. David Savran, "Ambivalence, Utopia, and a Queer Sort of Materialism: How *Angels in America* Reconstructs the Nation," *Theatre Journal* 47 (1995): 218. Some of the following material appears in my essay "Prior to the Normans: The Anglo-Saxons in *Angels in America,*" in *Approaching the Millennium: Essays on Tony Kushner's Angels in America,* ed. Deborah A. Geis and Steven F. Kruger (Ann Arbor: University of Michigan Press, 1997), 134-50.

42. Manifest Destiny had its roots in a theory of natural rights for a particular race that translates into nationalism and then imperialism. See Albert K. Weinberg, *Manifest Destiny* (1935; reprint, Chicago: Quadrangle, 1963), 8 (for the quote), 41.

43. Reginald Horsman, *Race and Manifest Destiny: The Origins of American Racial Anglo-Saxonism* (Cambridge: Harvard University Press, 1981); the phrase "Manifest Destiny" was not coined until 1845; see 219. On Anglo-Saxonism, see Frantzen, *Desire for Origins,* 15-18, and 27-61, where I comment on the phenomenon as a force in Anglo-Saxon studies from the Renaissance to the present.

44. Tony Kushner, "The Secrets of 'Angels,'" *New York Times,* 27 March 1994, H5.

45. Tony Kushner, *Angels in America: A Gay Fantasia on National Themes,* part 1, *Millennium Approaches* (New York: Theatre Communications Group, 1993); part 2, *Perestroika* (New York: Theatre Communications Group, 1994). References to volume and page number are given in the text (vol. 1 for *Millennium Approaches* and vol. 2 for *Perestroika*).

46. Savran, "Ambivalence," 212 note 14.

47. For an excellent summary of this issue, see Clare A. Simmons, *Reversing the Conquest: History and Myth in Nineteenth-Century British Literature* (New Brunswick: Rutgers University Press, 1990), 13-41.

48. The earl Harold was elected king of England at the death of Edward the Confessor in 1066; he was said to have given an oath of allegiance to William, duke of Normandy, and betrayed that oath when he claimed the throne of England. Harold was defeated at the Battle of Hastings by William the Conqueror. See Frank Stenton, *Anglo-Saxon England,* 3d ed. (Oxford: Oxford University Press, 1971), 576-80.

49. According to Savran, "The opposite of nearly everything you say about *Angels in America* will also hold true" ("Ambivalence," 208; see also 222).

50. David J. Bernstein, *The Mystery of the Bayeux Tapestry* (Chicago: University of Chicago Press, 1986), reports that Hitler, like Napoleon, studied the tapestry when he contemplated an invasion of England, 28-30.

51. Bernstein, *Mystery of the Bayeux Tapestry,* 8, 14.

52. Bernstein, *Mystery of the Bayeux Tapestry,* 30.

53. The term was originally used to describe American Protestantism. See E. Digby Baltzell, *The Protestant Establishment: Aristocracy and Caste in America* (New Haven: Yale University Press, 1964). Kushner's elaborate genealogy for Prior Walter attaches a far more ambitious historical and international sense to the term.

54. May McKisack, *The Fourteenth Century, 1307-1399* (Oxford: Oxford University Press, 1959), 219.

55. See Savran, "Ambivalence," 223-24, for an analysis of Kushner's treatment of identity politics and race in this scene.

56. Weinberg, *Manifest Destiny,* 8.

57. Savran, "Ambivalence," 213.

58. Kushner, "Secrets of 'Angels,'" H5.

59. Several reviewers have commented on the identification of Louis with Kushner's own views. See, for example, John Simon, "Angelic Geometry," *New York,* 6 December 1993, 130. Savran says that Louis is "constructed as the most empathetic character in the play" ("Ambivalence," 223).

60. Susan Reynolds, "What Do We Mean by 'Anglo-Saxon' and Anglo-Saxons'?" *Journal of British Studies* 24 (1985): 397-98.

61. Reynolds, "What Do We Mean by 'Anglo-Saxon'?" 402-3.

62. On the need for narratives that reverse the usual trajectory of the experience of AIDS, see Steven F. Kruger, *AIDS Narratives: Gender and Sexuality, Fiction and Science* (New York: Garland, 1996), 73-81.

63. Savran, "Ambivalence," 222-23.

64. D. Michael Quinn, *Same-Sex Dynamics among Nineteenth-Century Americans: A Mormon Example* (Urbana: University of Illinois Press, 1996), 2.

Matthew Wilson Smith (essay date 1999)

SOURCE: Smith, Matthew Wilson. "*Angels in America*: A Progressive Apocalypse." *Theater* 29, no. 3 (1999): 152-65.

[*In the following essay, Smith examines the conflict between apocalyptic and progressive impulses in* Angels in America.]

I. APOCALYPSE DESCENDING

Outside of Chekhov, I can think of no playwright whose characters *philosophize* so much about history as Tony Kushner's do; Kushner's characters are forever musing upon, arguing about, engaging with history. But while in Chekhov's plays such philosophizing talk is generally just that—talk, *mere* talk—in Kushner's it is urgent, of the essence. Which is to say that, for Kushner, talking about history functions not as a screen behind which the real but unstated (largely private, domestic) drama takes place, but rather *is* the "real drama," in surface and subtext. When Kushner's characters wonder, as they often do, whether the world is coming to an end, whether humanity has ceased to progress, whether a new age is just around the corner, we may psychologize their questions, but we may not psychologize them *away.* To do so would be to reduce them to mere interiorities, and thereby strip them of the political concerns that, as Kushner writes in the preface to *A Bright Room Called Day,* "are true passions for these people, not pretexts for private feelings."[1] At the risk of oversimplification: in Kushner's plays the political *is* the historical *is* the drama itself; we witness, in these plays, individuals and groups thrown into the midst of history, arguing the direction of the tide even as it pulls them under or along.

There are many visions of history in *Angels in America,* but none is so memorable, so shocking, as the apocalyptic. Harper tells us that "the world's coming to an end," and warns of an imminent "Judgment Day"; the Angels refer to "the grim Unfolding of these Latter Days," prophesy a catastrophe in which "millions" will die, and speak of "Apocalypse Descending"; Prior and Hannah look forward to the return of the waters of Bethesda fountain, "when the Millennium comes. . . . Not the year two thousand, but the Capital M Millennium."[2] Indeed, the whole play may be said to unfold like a landscape of ruins, of "beautiful systems dying, old fixed orders flying apart" (22). Sarah Ironson's burial at the outset of *Millennium Approaches* marks the disintegration of Jewish immigrant culture just as the Oldest Living Bolshevik's speech at the outset of *Perestroika* marks the end of Marxist Leninism. The AIDS crisis, though never permitted to serve as mere metaphor, takes on a decidedly apocalyptic tenor in the play, and becomes one of a larger web of catastrophes that reads like signs of the Endtime: the destruction of the environment, the ascendancy of the Reagan Right, the abandonment of Creation by God.

The apocalypticism of the work lies, too, in the significance of vision in the play. The poetics of apocalypse has always privileged vision over the other senses; the term *apokalypsis* means, literally, "to unveil," and originally connoted the marital stripping of a veiled virgin. Even as the word changed its dimensions and came to signify a divine revelation of the end of history, the poetics of apocalypse continued to emphasize sight and a certain erotics of disclosure.[3] In *Angels,* too, sight is privileged: Harper and Prior receive *visions* of the other world, whether in the form of angels, rising souls, or impossible dreamscapes. Harper is so thoroughly immersed in her eschatological visions (not to mention her depressants) that by the end of the play she is virtually defined by her "astonishing ability to see things." An even fuller sense of *apocalypse* is explored in Prior's visions, which are so erotically charged that his penis becomes a barometer of heavenly presence and orgasm a sign of revelation (a *sensus dei* he shares, incidentally, with Hannah). The explicit eroticism of Prior's visionary scenes recalls the erotic roots of apocalypticism and testifies to the sharp, and potentially dangerous, attraction of the apocalyptic blend: vision, violence, radical transformation, sublimity, sex.

Angels confronts us, as well, with two great modern millenarian faiths, one religious, one secular. Mormonism, a religion with its roots in the millenarian enthusiasms of nineteenth-century America, "lives on a threshold between this world and Millennium . . . and holds on hard to this world and the next."[4] Mormonism helps shape the apocalyptic discourse of the play through its influence on Harper, Joe, and Hannah, characters who retain a certain millennial fervor even as the influence of the Latter-day Saints over their lives slips away. While less prophetically inclined than his wife, Joe still brings to his admiration of the Reagan Right something of Harper's millennial mood: "America has rediscovered itself," he says of the 1980 election. "Its sacred position among nations. This is a great thing. The truth restored. Law restored" (32). Joe's admiration for Reaganism recalls the nativist impulses behind Mormon millenarianism, the emphasis in Mormon theology on America as the chosen nation, site of the New Jerusalem. Finally, Joe's mother Hannah takes the existence of angels for granted, exhibits an uncanny ability to recognize them, and by the end of the play (though now a New Yorker in dress and spirit) anticipates the coming of the angel of Bethesda and a New Jerusalem.

Mormonism shapes the play in other ways as well, most notably in the revelation of the apocalyptic tablets to Prior. The entire scenario of the angelic visitation, the command to unearth the sacred book, and the donning of magical glasses in order to read it are influenced by Joseph Smith's account of the discovery of the Book of Mormon. Smith's discovery was itself marked by apocalyptic overtones. One of the most frequently cited series of verses of the Book of Mormon is 3 Nephi 21:1-7, in which Jesus promises the Nephites "a sign that ye may know the time when these things shall be about to take place—that I shall gather in from their long dispersion, my people, O house of Israel." That sign, Jesus goes on to explain, is the discovery of the Book of Mormon itself, which shall serve as a millennial milestone. But just as Harper is no Joseph Smith, so Prior's apartment is no Palmyra, New York: the Book is located underneath the kitchen tiles, and Prior refuses to unearth it because he worries about losing his security deposit. This is a slip-shod revelation, one in which even the prophetic dreams that were supposed to prepare Prior for the event are lost in the heavenly bureaucracy. The signs of millennium are still there, but the religious myths that once supported them have declined into semiparody.

The same might be said of the other great modern millenarian faith of *Angels,* Bolshevism. This decaying system is chiefly presented through Aleksii Antedilluvianovich Prelapsarianov, the Oldest Living Bolshevik. It is a parodic personification, but, as with the Angel's visitation, it is touched with melancholy and a sense of shattered hope. The Bolshevik's evocation of the once-great promise of Soviet socialism is at the same time stirring and anachronistic: "You can't imagine," he tells us,

> when we first read the Classic Texts, when in the dark vexed night of our ignorance and terror the seed-words sprouted and shoved incomprehension aside, when the incredible bloody vegetable struggle up and through into Red Blooming gave us Praxis, True Praxis, True Theory married to Actual Life.

(166)

The "Classic Texts" the Bolshevik speaks of can no more be a source of redemption than can the Angel's sacred Book. But there is a poignancy at their loss, and a sense that the historical questions they pose are still before us. The millennial structures, secular and religious, may have broken down, but the millennial longings remain.

At the outset of *Perestroika,* it is the Oldest Living Bolshevik who poses these questions most pointedly: "The Great Question before us is: Are we doomed? The Great Question before us is: Will the Past release us? The Great Question before us is: Can we Change? In Time?" (165). The Bolshevik admits of the possibility of apocalypse ("Are we doomed?") at the same time that he contrasts it to another historical possibility, one

in which we are released from the past and able to "Change . . . In Time." We might be able to avoid collapse, he suggests, if we are able to reinvent ourselves, to evolve.

II. MILLENNIUM VERSUS PERESTROIKA

This second view of history is an optimistic, evolutionary one, one typified not by fate and doom but by human agency, the possibility of self-salvation. It is a view of history that we might term *progressive,* if we mean by that a sense of history as a gradual motion toward greater happiness, equality, and freedom. *Progressive* in this sense includes both liberalism and moderate forms of socialism. Broadly speaking, the socialist sense of history as a series of developmental stages toward ever greater emancipation may be termed *progressive,* while the occasional belief in the inevitable, history-ending nature of the revolution and the utopian nature of the state to follow is closer to the apocalyptic model. This often-uneasy combination of progressive and apocalyptic views of history has been at the heart of socialist theory since its inception, and is mirrored here in the musings of the Oldest Living Bolshevik—as well as those of Kushner himself.

On the face of it, the apocalyptic and the progressive are radically different visions of history. In the apocalyptic worldview, transformation is generally sudden and total: complete destruction and complete rebirth, eternal separation of the damned from the saved. At the same time, both the destruction and the rebirth of the world are unstoppable and externally motivated; mortals do not, ultimately, shape their own history. In the apocalyptic, it is only when history comes to an end that liberation is truly possible; the Kingdom of God lies outside of history, not within it. The progressive worldview might almost be defined as the precise opposite of such beliefs: instead of sudden, radical transformation, progressives tend to see the world evolving slowly, see history as a gradual, painful growth toward liberation. Humanity is a powerful agent in this upward drive, if not the only agent; self-liberation, self-salvation, in difficult stages, is the hope of the progressive. The progressive worldview, then, tends to embrace the fruits of human inventiveness, whether scientific, scholastic, technological, or industrial, as means toward the improvement of our collective condition.

The apocalypticism of *Angels* must be seen in the light of a contradictory impulse toward progressivism in the work. This rift inheres in the titles of the parts themselves: *Millennium Approaches* evokes an image of impending, mystical transformation, the ticking of an other-worldly clock, whereas *Perestroika* recalls a historical event, Gorbachev's attempt to liberalize the Soviet Union peaceably from within. Compare, too, the apocalyptic warnings of the Angels with, for example, the quote from Ralph Waldo Emerson that Kushner chooses to open "Perestroika": "Because the soul is progressive, it never quite repeats itself, but in every act attempts the production of a new and fairer whole" (163). The sentence might serve as a summation of the kind of trust in a process of gradual, intuitive awakening that is the very opposite of the apocalyptic. In John's Revelation, all was to be uprooted, suddenly, either transplanted into new ground or tossed into the everlasting fire; Emerson, on the other hand, imagined the soul opening like a rosebud, by degrees. If the Angels tend to take John's view, then Emerson's is also present in the play. We see it in somewhat parodic form in Louis's (self-described) "neo-Hegelian positivist sense of constant historical progress toward happiness or perfection or something," and, of course, in the cautious optimism of Prior, who insists on "More Life," and assures us, at the end of the play, that "the world only spins forward" (31; 298).

Often *Angels* gains its apocalyptic force from a sharp indictment of progress. Consider, for example, Harper's visions of the destruction of the ozone layer. Early on in the play, Harper speaks of the ozone layer as a spiritual realm, as "a kind of Gift, from God, the crowning touch to the creation of the world" (22). Its destruction is for Harper an eschatological sign, a signal that "everywhere, things are collapsing, lies surfacing, systems of defense giving way" (23). There is an implicit attack here on modern progress—the decay of the ozone layer, as we all know, is linked to the rising tide of industrial pollutants—and a spiritualization of that attack, a rendering of it in terms of Revelation. Harper returns to this image of the ozone layer at the end of the play, seeing its restoration in terms of the apocalyptic vision of the rising dead, so that the dead themselves are the stuff of ozone, healing the sacred skin by their ascension.

It would be wrong, though, to associate Harper too closely with any single position: her metier is closer to bewilderment than conviction, and her views change over time. The play's more consistent and unambiguous agents of antiprogressive apocalypticism are the Angels. When we first see them as a group, a radio is broadcasting a report of the Chernobyl disaster and the resulting environmental fallout ("radioactive debris contaminating over three hundred thousand hectares of topsoil for a minimum of thirty years" [279]). The Angels, listening with disgust to this report, find in it yet more evidence of "Apocalypse Descending," calling the modern age "the threnody chant of a Poet, / A dark-devising Poet whose only theme is Death," and predicting that "uncountable multitudes will die" (279). The Angels are the representatives of an antiprogressive, indeed antimodern, impulse taken to its furthest extent: "Surely you see towards what We are Progressing," says the Angel of America to Prior,

> The fabric of the sky unravels:
> Angels hover, anxious fingers worry
> The tattered edge.
> Before the boiling blood and the searing of skin
> Comes the Secret catastrophe.
>
> (196)

It is an indictment and a warning which recalls other modern apocalyptic dramas. There are echoes here of Georg Kaiser's *Gas* trilogy, in which prophetic characters warn that a world-ending explosion will result from the continued production of gas; there are echoes of Karl Kraus's *The Last Days of Mankind,* in which the author rails against the forces of "modern progress" that led to World War I and concludes that he has "written a tragedy whose doomed hero is mankind";[5] and there are echoes, too, of Rachel Rosenthal's *L.O.W. in Gaia,* in which an angry Mother Earth warns humanity that it is doomed to "crash."

The Angels' solution to this suicide-by-progress, however, goes beyond anything suggested by these earlier apocalyptic dramas. According to the Angels, humanity must reject intermingling, progression, migration, understanding:

> Forsake the Open Road:
> Neither Mix Nor Intermarry: Let Deep Roots Grow:
> If you do not MINGLE you will Cease to Progress:
> Seek Not to Fathom the World and its Delicate Particle Logic.
>
> (197)

In passages like this, the Angels are sublime, poetic reactionaries, a combination that forces us to question the status of sublimity, and poetry, in Kushner's world. Consumed by a terror of progress and the modern world, hurling versified warnings of the End from on high, the Angels come across as virtual parodies of modernist prophets of apocalypse, winged grotesques of Heidegger, Eliot, Pound. For the sake of humanity, they urge humanity to cease being human.

There is another irony as well to the apocalypticism of Kushner's Angels. Heaven, the site of the Angels' attack on human progress, is itself a ramshackle storehouse of the instruments of such progress. The table around which the Angels sit is covered with "an ancient map of the world" on which lie

> archaic and broken astronomical, astrological, mathematical and nautical objects of measurement and calculation; heaps and heaps and heaps of books and files and bundles of yellowing newspapers; inkpots, clay tablets, styli and quill pens. The great chamber is dimly lit by candles and a single great bulb overhead, the light of which pulses to the audible rhythmic surgings and waverings of a great unseen generator.

> At the center of the table is a single bulky radio, a 1940s model in very poor repair. It is switched on and glowing, and the Angels are gathered about it, intent upon its dim, crackly signal.
>
> (278)

This space at once presents a schema of the history of human knowledge (cartography, exploration, literacy, electricity, the radio) and recalls a dilapidated Eastern-bloc stateroom just before the collapse of the Wall. The Angels, then, appear to be complicit in the very systems of progress they condemn, an irony accentuated by the fact that the Angels receive their information about the Chernobyl disaster not through divine inspiration but through the bulky, crackling radio at the center of the table. Despite their aspiration to timelessness, the Angels are as dependent upon the instruments of progress as the mortals are.

Oddly enough, Prior's reply to the Angels may be unique in the literature of modern apocalyptic drama: while not denying the future horrors that the Angels predict, Prior refuses to relinquish his belief in progress. Returning the prophetic Book to the Angels, Prior explains,

> We can't just stop. We're not rocks—progress, migration, motion is . . . modernity. It's animate, it's what living things do. We desire. Even if all we desire is stillness, it's still desire *for.* Even if we go faster than we should. We can't *wait.* And wait for what? God . . .
>
> *(Thunderclap.)*
>
> God . . .
>
> *(Thunderclap.)*
>
> He isn't coming back.
>
> (282)

Even Prior's insistence that God "isn't coming back" is rendered here in progressive rather than apocalyptic terms. Compare the loss of God in Prior's account to that in Samuel Beckett. In Beckett, God's disappearance is final and irrevocable—Godot will never arrive, we know this, and there will be no miracles in Hamm's sunken bunker—and this total loss marks his play worlds as postapocalyptic. In Prior's account, on the other hand, God is not dead but off wandering, "sail-[ing] off on Voyages, no knowing where" (195). Though Kushner places the date of God's departure at the beginning of the twentieth century (in 1906, the year of the San Francisco earthquake), it seems that Kushner's God is not so much swept *away* by modernity as swept *up* in it: divinity wanders now "in Mortifying imitation of . . . his least creation" (195) and faces, it seems, all-too-human confusions in the face of the rapid transformation of our age. There is at least the suggestion in *Angels* that God, like so many of Kushner's characters, must wander off now in order to grow. Taking after his "least creation," God himself may need to progress in order to live.

But perhaps I am making too much of this dichotomy of *progressive* and *apocalyptic*—there is a sense, after all, in which *Angels* is profoundly *confused.* Almost every critic who has written on *Angels* has pointed to its "postmodern ambiguity," and it may well be that *Angels* is a work that, taken as a whole, reflects Harper's desperate millennial confusion at the outset of *Millennium Approaches.* "I'm undecided," she says,

> I feel . . . that something's going to give. It's 1985. Fifteen years till the third millennium. Maybe Christ will come again. Maybe seeds will be planted, maybe there'll be harvests then, maybe early figs to eat, maybe new life, maybe fresh blood, maybe companionship and love and protection, safety from what's outside, maybe the door will hold, or maybe . . . maybe the troubles will come, and the end will come, and the sky will collapse and there will be terrible rains and showers of poison and light, or maybe my life is really fine, maybe Joe loves me and I'm only crazy thinking otherwise, or maybe not, maybe it's even worse than I know, maybe . . . I want to know, maybe I don't. The suspense, Mr. Lies, it's killing me.

MR. LIES:

> I suggest a vacation.
>
> (24)

"Maybe. . . . maybe . . . maybe . . .": Harper's millennial dreaming here is a distinctly contemporary fantasia: a stream of references half-digested, at turns apocalyptic, progressive, pop psychological, paranoiac, utopian. To add to the confusion, Mr. Lies's response to the speech puts the lie to any reading of the play as a simple celebration of change against the reactionary forces of stasis. For though Mr. Lies is an agent of migration (indeed, he is a travel agent) the "vacation" he offers is mere escape without progression. In this sense he is the twin of the Angel, whose exhortations of stasis threaten life as much as Mr. Lies's seductions of motion. In Harper's early monologue, then, a complex of themes we have seen to be central (millennium, apocalypse, motion, progress) are rendered as "undecided" and, maybe, undecidable. Maybe, then, this is the mood of Kushner's work as a whole; maybe Harold Bloom is correct when he says about Prior that this "gallant, ill gay prophet simply has no prophecy to give us." It is, Bloom writes, "the ultimate aesthetic weakness" of the work.[6]

III. A Net of Souls

Bloom's reading would seem to fit with Kushner's skepticism toward any totalizing vision of history—progressive, apocalyptic, or otherwise. Kushner ultimately languishes in his own indecision, the argument would go, and his skepticism of universal historical claims makes genuine prophecy impossible. But behind this skepticism I wonder whether there doesn't lie a certain complex conviction, one that elevates the play above mere ambiguity. Indeed, *pace* Bloom, I would suggest that Prior does have a sort of prophecy, as does Harper, one that attempts to combine progressive and apocalyptic narratives into a single, overarching framework. In this respect, the visions of Prior and Harper at the end of the play echo a central theme of American religious history: postmillennialism. The term refers to the place assigned to the return of Christ, which was to occur after, rather than before, the coming of the millennium (hence *post-* rather than *pre*millennial). In an article entitled "Between Progress and Apocalypse," historian James H. Moorhead describes postmillennialism as "a compromise between a progressive, evolutionary view of history and the apocalyptic outlook of the Book of Revelation." According to Moorhead, the doctrine of postmillennialism was the dominant theological outlook of nineteenth-century America.[7] Though it would be too much of an imposition to call *Angels* a "postmillennial" drama, since the Christian theological debates that inform postmillennialism are simply not in evidence here, the play nevertheless exhibits a spirit of progressive apocalypticism that is reminiscent of this distinctly American theology.

We can begin to understand this composite vision by noting Harper's growth over the course of the play. Her early confusion gives way to the unambiguously millennial vision of her final speech, referred to earlier:

> But I saw something only I could see, because of my astonishing ability to see such things:
>
> Souls were rising, from the earth far below, souls of the dead, of people who had perished, from famine, from war, from the plague, and they floated up, like skydivers in reverse, limbs all akimbo, wheeling and spinning. And the souls of those departed joined hands, clasped ankles and formed a web, a great net of souls, and the souls were three-atom molecules, of the stuff of ozone, and the outer rim absorbed them, and was repaired.
>
> (293-94)

Harper's use of apocalyptic rhetoric here is far more assured than in her first speech. While her emphasis on the ozone layer, as discussed earlier, suggests a certain skepticism toward progress (a skepticism she shares with Prior), this skepticism is ultimately subsumed in a broader faith in the evolutionary nature of human history. Thus she follows this, her final revelation, with a sentiment reminiscent of the lines from Emerson that open *Perestroika*: "Nothing's lost forever," she says. "In this world there is a kind of painful progress" (294). It is a vision that exhibits both apocalyptic and progressive views of history.

Harper shares this outlook with Prior, whose final speech also combines the apocalyptic and the progressive. First Prior looks forward to the season when the Fountain of Bethesda will flow again, an event that has already been imbued with eschatological significance. After this millennial image, Prior turns to the AIDS

crisis and the struggle for gay rights, subjects that could easily be charged with apocalyptic intensity, but Prior renders them, instead, in a progressive mode:

> This disease will be the end of many of us, but not nearly all, and the dead will be commemorated and will struggle on with the living, and we are not going away. We won't die secret deaths anymore. The world only spins forward. We will be citizens. The time has come.
>
> (298)

Prior's painful progressivism at the end of *Angels* (reminiscent, like Harper's speech, of Emerson) is combined with an optimistic sort of apocalypticism that anticipates an age when Bethesda will flow again. Indeed, Prior "want[s] to be around to see" this new age (298). Prior does indeed have something to prophesy: he is the prophet, with Harper, of history as a slow, painful progress inspired by the promise of a New Jerusalem. This vision partakes of both apocalyptic and progressive elements; if they are not quite brought into synthesis, then neither are they totally opposed. Confronted with a seeming contradiction, Prior and Harper refuse to divest themselves of either the apocalyptic or the progressive; the composite visions they describe, however, are too uncertain, too fluid, to qualify as the new theory the Bolshevik searches for. We are left with only the instinctive (necessary?) belief in human progress, against so much historical evidence, and the hopeful (desperate?) revelation of an eventual utopia that is a genuine alternative to death: a society of change, of migration, of plurality, of "more life," whatever the cost.

It is this utopian society toward which the drama tends, not only in the visions of its prophetic characters, but in the structure of the work itself. For if *Angels* unfolds like a series of breakdowns, then these breakdowns lead not to chaos and utter fragmentation (as Rabbi Chemelwitz and the Oldest Living Bolshevik fear and—more frightening—Roy Cohn gleefully accepts) but to surprising reintegrations. "Imagination can't create anything new, can it?" asks Harper when she and Prior encounter each other in their respective dream states (38). The experience is the first of many such encounters, both surreal and unexpected: Prior and the Angel, Joe and Louis, Belize and Roy Cohn, Harper and the Mormon Mother, Prior and Hannah ("This is my ex-lover's lover's Mormon mother," says Prior [253]). Meanwhile, characters move in and out of communities in surprising ways: Hannah, for instance, begins her journey as a staunch Mormon matron; by the time the play is finished, she "is noticeably different—she looks like a New Yorker, and she is reading the *New York Times*" (295). If the world of *Angels* is coming undone, then it is just as rapidly being knit together again, being reconnected at the oddest points. The reknitting of *Angels* exposes the lie of Harper's early statement that "[imagination] only recycles bits and pieces from the worlds and reassembles them into visions" and Prior's claim that "it's All Been Done Before" (38-39); the visions that Prior and Harper experience together, and the "threshold of revelation" that they share, are signposts of an emergent, previously unimaginable, web of connections. It is a vision that is given expression, as we have seen, in Harper's closing image of a net of souls, and Kushner's own comments on the play that "Marx was right: The smallest human unit is two people, not one; one is a fiction. From such nets of souls societies, the social world, human life springs" (307). The millennialism of *Angels* is one that embraces "the weird interconnectedness" of us all, that accepts the knitting and tearing apart and reknitting of individuals and communities and envisions a net of souls, in motion, kaleidoscopic. Ironically, the emergence of such connections, visions, and prophecies amidst the collapse of older explanatory structures echoes the emergence of Mormonism itself. Historian Gordon Wood, for instance, explains the early growth of Mormonism by noting that "the disintegration of older structures of authority released torrents of popular religiosity into public life. Visions, dreams, prophesyings, and new emotion-soaked seekings acquired a validity they had not earlier possessed."[8]

It is this final, utopian vision that at once embraces apocalypticism and subverts the sort of totalizing, overarching Theory that the Oldest Living Bolshevik longs for. For what Theory, what Dogma, can incorporate the surprise of the radically Other, the unpredictability of "weird interconnectedness"? Insofar as apocalypticism has generally been associated with relentlessly totalizing schemes of human history, Kushner's apocalypse here is precisely an apocalypse of apocalypses, his "Capital M Millennium" an end to such all-encompassing units of time. A decentered apocalypse, a progressive millenarianism: it is the paradoxicality of such a vision that makes it so enticingly utopian in both the literal and the popular sense, at once a no-place and a paradise. And so Kushner's play leaves us with a quixotic sort of prophecy: that the millennium will continue to approach, and humanity to progress, long after Theory has passed away.

Notes

1. Tony Kushner, *A Bright Room Called Day* (New York: Theatre Communications Group; 1994), x.

2. Tony Kushner, *Angels in America* (New York: Theatre Communications Group, 1995), 34, 251, 283, 279, 283, 297.

3. Catherine Keller, *Apocalypse Now and Then* (Boston: Beacon, 1996), 1.

4. Harold Bloom, *Omens of Millennium* (New York: Riverhead Books, 1996), 225.

5. Karl Kraus, *The Last Days of Mankind,* trans. Max Knight and Joseph Fabry, in *In These Great Times: A Karl Kraus Reader,* ed. Harry Zohn (Chicago: University of Chicago Press, 1990), 255.

6. Bloom, *Omens of Millennium*, 225.

7. James H. Moorhead, "Between Progress and Apocalypse: A Reassessment of Millennialism in American Religious Thought, 1800-1880," *Journal of American History* 41 (1984): 524-42.

8. Gordon Wood, "Evangelical America and Early Mormonism," *New York History* 61 (1980): 368.

Daryl Ogden (essay date fall 2000)

SOURCE: Ogden, Daryl. "Cold War Science and the Body Politic: An Immuno/Virological Approach to *Angels in America*." *Literature and Medicine* 19, no. 2 (fall 2000): 241-61.

[*In the following essay, Ogden examines Kushner's representation of sexual identity in* Angels in America *in terms of the intersection of medical and political discourse around the AIDS epidemic.*]

Early on in *Millennium Approaches,* Part One of Tony Kushner's *Angels in America,* Roy Cohn's physician informs his patient that he's suffering from AIDS. Roy, the former assistant United States prosecuting attorney in the Rosenberg spy case and the right hand of Joseph McCarthy during the Senate Red Scare trials, feigns puzzlement with the diagnosis and outrage over his doctor's inference that he must be a homosexual:

> Your problem, Henry, is that you are hung up on words, on labels, that you believe they mean what they seem to mean. AIDS. Homosexual. Gay. Lesbian. You think these are names that tell you who someone sleeps with, but they don't tell you that. . . . Like all labels they tell you one thing and one thing only: where does an individual so identified fit in the food chain, in the pecking order? Not ideology, or sexual taste, but something much simpler: clout. Not who I fuck or who fucks me, but who will pick up the phone when I call, who owes me favors. This is what a label refers to. Now to someone who does not understand this, homosexual is what I am because I have sex with men. But really this is wrong. Homosexuals are not men who sleep with other men. Homosexuals are men who in fifteen years of trying cannot get a pissant antidiscrimination bill through City Council. Homosexuals are men who know nobody and who nobody knows. Who have zero clout. Does this sound like me, Henry?[1]

Despite his voracious sexual appetite for men, as a patron saint of right-wing politics Roy simply cannot occupy the ontological status of a homosexual. Roy recognizes that to be diagnosed with AIDS, a disease conflated with homosexuality, would signify the end of his powerbrokering ability in the high-Reagan era of the mid-eighties. It would also call ironic attention to his own closeted, socially subversive sexual identity from the 1940s forward, when his public life began in earnest. This identity is closely parallel to the politically and militarily subversive identity of the so-called communist infiltrators and homosexual federal employees whom he and his colleagues worked so hard to expose in that same era.

As far as Roy is concerned, AIDS is a homosexual disease. Therefore, to have contracted AIDS is an impossibility because he is a political insider who can "punch fifteen numbers" (*Millennium,* 45) and have Nancy Reagan on the other end of the telephone, because he is socially interpreted not as a homosexual but as "a heterosexual man . . . who fucks around with guys" (*Millennium,* 46). Homosexuality for Roy is incommensurate with clout. It is tantamount to being saddled with the leftist identity of Alger Hiss and Julius and Ethel Rosenberg in the United States of the 1940s and 1950s, three Americans who betrayed a decided lack of clout as far as the federal legal system was concerned. In fact, the ghost of Ethel Rosenberg herself haunts Roy in *Angels in America,* appearing to him at increasingly regular intervals as the play proceeds. Along with communists, homosexuals in the federal government were the other principal target of McCarthyism. This was the case, first, because their sexual preferences purportedly made them vulnerable to blackmail by foreign powers and, second, they were demonized as "perverts" neither morally worthy nor psychologically capable of holding government positions.[2] As one of the men tapped in the 1950s to hound both homosexuals and communists into oblivion, the actual Roy understood it is better to remain in the closet. In the mid-1980s, Kushner's fictional Roy recognizes it is even more important to cloak your sexual identity if you happen to be a homosexual with AIDS.

Angels in America: A Gay Fantasia on National Themes is a play in two parts whose titles, *Millennium Approaches* and *Perestroika,* suggest Kushner's grandiose themes. Set in New York City at the beginning of Ronald Reagan's second presidential term, the play explores the sexual, ethnic, political, and religious identities of five homosexual men, including Roy Cohn and Louis Ironson, a conservative and liberal Jew; Joe Pitt, a married Mormon still very much in the closet; Prior Walter, a WASP who can trace his lineage back to the Norman invasion of England; and Belize, an African American drag queen. These men are all afflicted to varying degrees by AIDS, ranging from the HIV infections of Roy and Prior to the responses of their friends and lovers, Louis, Joe, and Belize. Over the course of the play, Kushner masterfully weaves together realism, fantasy, and the supernatural and speculates on the nature of God, heaven, and the universe in the midst of

a gay holocaust. More specifically for the purposes of this essay, Kushner elaborates on the political and historical meanings of AIDS, medical science, and the Cold War persecution of marginalized Americans identified as sympathetic to the political left, including communists and homosexuals.

In all of Roy's appearances in *Angels in America,* Kushner makes visible a Cold War political discourse that underlines the ideological similarities between the McCarthyite 1950s and the Reaganite 1980s, calling attention to the parallels between communism and homosexuality as American identities of otherness and disempowerment.[3] Louis, Roy's liberal foil, understands this parallel well. He accuses Joe, his conservative lover (and Roy's protégé), of developing a legal argument for the Federal Court of Appeals, Second Circuit, to deny a gay army veteran benefits on the basis of his sexual identity. Despite his own gay identity, homosexuals, in Joe's view, are not entitled to Civil Rights protections. To make his case against Joe, Louis draws upon the famous words of Joseph Welch, special counsel to the Army during the McCarthy hearings: "Have you no decency, at long last, sir, have you no decency at all?"[4] In pursuing an argument that Louis calls "an important bit of legal fag-bashing" (*Perestroika,* 110), Joe reveals himself not only to be filled with self-loathing but also to be Roy's intellectual and ideological heir, continuing the McCarthy-era legal persecution of homosexuals.

Kushner portrays Reaganism polemically, as a version of neo-McCarthyism. It is surprising, then, that no critical attention has been given to the fact that the nascent Cold War decades of Roy's early professional history also proved crucial for the formation of the medical sciences of immunology and virology, sciences that would wield inordinate power during the 1980s in the race to inscribe culturally dominant metaphors on AIDS and homosexual sexual practices.[5] On one hand, reading Kushner's play within the context of the history of medicine highlights the central importance of immuno-virological metaphor to the political, social, and sexual identities of Kushner's characters and to the discourses of disease and identity generated by AIDS; on the other hand, reading *Angels in America* with an eye on the history of immunology and virology and their ideological relationship to American politics in the 1950s helps us to see the saturated Cold War consciousness of those two medical disciplines.

* * *

Immunology traces its early modern origins to the eighteenth-century Englishman Edward Jenner, whose successful experiments on cowpox eventually led to a smallpox innoculation that signaled a revolution in the ways that communicable diseases could be prevented.[6] Most medical historians, however, locate modern immunology's "birth" either in Claude Bernard's *An Introduction to the Study of Experimental Medicine* of 1865 or to Louis Pasteur's groundbreaking series of papers on the Germ Theory of Disease published in the 1880s.[7] Even though Pasteur's theory that germs were the principal causal factors in disease proved to be a medical dead end, his research cleared the ground for some of the early advances in immunological theory. The subsequent scientific internationalism in Europe that characterized the fin de siècle and early twentieth century made substantial theoretical gains in immunology possible, and science particularly benefited from promising developments shared between researchers in France, Germany, and Austria.[8] With the tragic advent of World War I, the significance of new discoveries in continental immunology were diminished as researchers of rival powers were cut off from one another and government resources were diverted to other areas of scientific research that might more directly benefit the war effort. While pre-war immunology generated first-time interest in autoantibodies and autoimmune diseases, for three decades following the conclusion of World War I theoretical and experimental advances in immunology advanced at a snail's pace.[9] For a variety of reasons, when they finally did advance, they predominantly did so during the Cold War.

Like immunology, virology also looks back to the experimental research of Jenner and Pasteur and their development of inoculations for two prominent viruses, smallpox and rabies.[10] Jenner's and Pasteur's discoveries amounted to two successful shots in the dark, however, because at the time of their research viruses remained quite misunderstood, principally because even the largest viruses could still not definitively be seen, even with the best optical microscopes that the eighteenth and nineteenth centuries had to offer. In the century between Jenner's and Pasteur's research, *virus* retained its generalized classical meaning of any poisonous substance that caused sickness. Finally, in the 1890s, one of the signature discoveries in modern virology was made by the Dutch scientist Martinus Beijerinck, who isolated tobacco mosaic virus (TMV). Beijerinck theorized the existence of cell-free filtrate—later known as a filterable virus—as a frequent cause of disease in tobacco plants. Beijerinck's accomplishment was made possible by his findings that TMV could be transmitted even after infected tobacco juice was absorbed by agar up to one tenth of an inch. Beijerinck reasoned that if infectious juice could be transmitted through solid jelly then the infectious agent must have the structure of a protein and not of a cell. Over the next decade other important viruses were isolated using modified versions of Beijerinck's technique, including foot-and-mouth disease in cattle by Friedrich Loeffler and Paul Frosch in 1898, and yellow-fever virus by Walter Reed and James Carroll in 1901. In the years following these discoveries bacteria-proof filters were

developed that allowed scientists to produce much less virulent versions of various viruses. These weakened viruses were in turn used to produce vaccines for a variety of plant, animal, and human diseases.

As a consequence of these theoretical and technological advances, the first third of the twentieth century proved to be a golden age for virology. Fueled by the research of Wendell Stanley, who became the first scientist to crystallize a virus, and Ernest Goodpasture, who inaugurated the technique of growing viruses in hen's eggs, virology enjoyed unprecedented success in determining the structure, size, and composition of viruses. These successes led to the production of vaccines for some of the deadliest diseases known to humanity, including yellow fever, influenza, measles, and, most famously in the research of Jonas Salk, polio.

Not until 1949, with the publication of Frank Fenner and Frank McFarlane Burnet's important *The Production of Antibodies,* did immunology achieve a theoretical breakthrough commensurate with those already realized by virology.[11] In their groundbreaking research, Fenner and Burnet proposed a theory as to how the body's immunological apparatus distinguished "self" from "nonself." Employing a hypothesis that eventually became known as the Clonal Selection Theory of Acquired Immunity, they argued that so-called normal or healthy cells possessed something called a self-marker, a distinguishing characteristic signaling to antibodies that the healthy cell in question was in fact part of the body, a non-threatening part of the self and should therefore be ignored and preserved. The Clonal Selection Theory proved to be one of the cornerstones upon which later research on immunologic tolerance relied, opening the door to developing drugs and protocols that made organ transplants, for instance, a realizable goal.[12]

Summing up their theoretical findings at the conclusion of *The Production of Antibodies*, Burnet and Fenner adopted a rhetoric that nearly jumps off the page if read within the terms of anti-communist, anti-homosexual political discourses of the post-World War II era:

1. The basis of our account is the recognition that the same system of cells is concerned both in the disposal of effete body cells (without antibody response) and of foreign organic material (with antibody response).

2. In order to allow this differentiation of function expendable body cells carry "self-marker" components which allow "recognition" of their "self" character.

What Burnet and Fenner describe here is a nearly perfect metaphor of how the American body politic, particularly in the McCarthy era, operated as a kind of large-scale human immune system, placing under surveillance and effectively eliminating citizens suspected of foreign sympathies that might weaken internal American resolve to fend off the debilitating disease of communism. Either consciously or not, Burnet, an Australian who would be knighted by Queen Elizabeth II after receiving the Nobel Prize in 1960 for his immunological research, continued to employ politicized medical rhetoric that complemented Cold War anxieties and responses. In 1970, for example, he published *Immunological Surveillance,* a book intended for a more popular audience than his earlier studies.[13] It goes without saying that Burnet's title, which resonates with the clandestine techniques employed against American citizens by the FBI of J. Edgar Hoover, couldn't provide a more powerful illustration of modern immunology's Cold War consciousness.[14]

Burnet and Fenner's reference in the passage cited above to the elimination of "effete" body cells appears to have been prescient, because it evokes cultural meanings important to the way that AIDS was pervasively interpreted in the early and mid-1980s as a "gay" disease. "Effete" is a value laden word, conjuring up images of decadence, physical depletion, and effeminacy, words with connotations stereotypically associated among American heterosexuals with homosexual men. When AIDS was first diagnosed, homosexual men were widely accused of excessive promiscuity, drug abuse, and unnatural sexual practices that had overloaded their immune systems to the point of exhaustion. This created an implicit double meaning in the way that AIDS could be read at the personal and cultural levels: their immune systems under assault by a deadly virus, the homosexual men afflicted with HIV and AIDS might just as well have been the useless effete cells expunged by the body's immune system. And those men diagnosed as HIV-positive in the early 1980s, many of whom held responsible the indifferent response of the Reagan administration for the accelerating crisis, must have felt exactly like expendable cells within what was widely perceived as an otherwise healthy body politic.

One need only recall Reagan's famous 1984 re-election slogan "It's Morning in America Again" and consider the fact that he went on to win the electoral votes of forty-nine states to agree that the majority of the country's citizens believed Reagan had the United States heading in the right direction, back to an America of the past, when homosexuality was a taboo word and homosexuals were safely hidden in the closet. In true conservative fashion, the 1984 Republican campaign hearkened back to a mythical golden age in American history. For Republicans, one of those golden ages was certainly the 1950s, a decade in which the grandfatherly Eisenhower twice defeated Adlai Stevenson in a landslide and thereby preserved American conservative values against an unreliable congress and the liberal Warren Supreme Court.

But the first years of the 1950s was also a dark period for Republicans, particularly those Republicans later identified with Joseph McCarthy's Senate investigations against Americans accused of an allegiance to communism and, more damning, of harboring sympathies for the Soviet Union. For example, in his infamous speech delivered at Wheeling, West Virginia, on 9 February 1950, Joseph McCarthy used the following language to describe the communist threat within U.S. borders: "The reason why we find ourselves in a position of impotency is not because our only powerful potential enemy has sent men to invade our shores, but rather because of the traitorous actions of those who have been treated so well by this Nation."[15] For the United States of the first half of the 1950s in particular, the "self-marker" of politics was equated with expressing in the strongest possible terms anti-communist sentiment. For Cold Warriors like Joseph McCarthy, Richard Nixon, and Roy Cohn, immunology's nascent language of the body's civil defenses and of identifiable markers of selfhood or loyal citizenship would have paralleled language they themselves would employ to root out whom they often imagined to be American spies and communist sympathizers in the service of the Soviets.[16]

For sociologists, theorists, and historians of science alike, it should come as no surprise that Fenner and Burnet's concept of the self-marker, which has proven to be among modern immunology's most powerful metaphors, occurred just as the Cold War was gaining the undivided attention of Americans from every political persuasion. While virology and its medical ancestor, microbiology, have long employed tropes of *hot* warfare to describe how enemy viruses invade or infiltrate the human host, immunology posited an entirely different set of metaphors and assumptions that paralleled if not parroted many post-World War II fears of communist traitors within the body politic.[17] Far from attributing disease to the power of an invading virus, immunology contended that sickness was primarily the fault of an individual's own failed immune system. At the risk of mixing political and biological metaphors, immunologists claimed that for the body to succeed against disease it had to do two things: 1) extirpate "effete" self-marked cells that weakened the body's own civil and border defenses and 2) eliminate non-self biological agents. As Burnet wrote in his 1962 book, *The Integrity of the Body:* "Antibody production or any other type of immunological reaction is against foreign material—against something that is not self."[18] Virology and immunology therefore emerged as explanatory models of sickness and disease that drew in large measure on two distinct yet complementary Cold War horrors. Virologists postulated the existence of powerful viruses, dangerous enemies beyond the body's borders, capable of violating those borders under favorable circumstances. Quite differently, immunologists warned healthy and sick Americans alike of formidable enemies within the body that appeared—like communist sympathizers and homosexuals—to constitute the Self but were, in fact, the Other. Understood in political terms, virology capitalized on fears of a hot war with America's communist adversaries whereas immunology was predicated on fear of disloyalty and subversion within the body (politic) itself.

* * *

As the preceding narrative suggests, an implicit competition, at least partly fueled by historical phenomena and what once seemed to be fundamental and irresolvable theoretical differences, exists between the sciences of immunology and virology and their respective understandings of bodily health and disease. Not until the early 1980s and the introduction of AIDS into the national consciousness were immunology and virology compelled to form a reluctant détente. Ironically, AIDS proved to be the perfect vehicle for a truce, however uneasy, to be called between the competing sciences. For example, when Henry, Roy's doctor, explains the nature of his patient's illness, he speaks fluently in a hybrid medical language of virology and immunology:

> The best theory is that we blame a retrovirus, the Human Immunodeficiency Virus. Its presence is made known to us by the useless antibodies which appear in reaction to its entrance into the blood-stream through a cut, or an orifice. The antibodies are powerless to protect the body against it. Why, we don't know. The body's immune system ceases to function. Sometimes the body even attacks itself. At any rate it's left open to a whole horror house of infections from microbes which it usually defends against.
>
> (*Millennium,* 42)

The extent of the truce between virology and immunology represented by Henry's speech should not be overstated, of course. When the AIDS crisis first began, immunologists and virologists clashed bitterly, with immunologists advocating that the new disease be named GRID for Gay Related Immune Deficiency and virologists arguing in favor of calling the same diagnosis HIV-Disease. An obvious tension between immunology and virology still exists in terms of the ways AIDS is read as sickness. For immunologists, to be HIV-positive is not necessarily to be sick until the body's immune system, finally diminished to dangerous levels, can no longer protect the host from disease and illness; by contrast, virologists argue that the disease begins with the infiltration of the virus into the body, not with what the American media dubbed for a while as "full-blown AIDS."

Yet the apparent "facts" of HIV compelled scientists from each discipline to work together to develop an adequate explanatory model because neither immunology nor virology alone could account for how HIV

works to produce AIDS. Though important etiological differences still existed between the two sciences, for the first time in their histories, immunology and virology had to depend more or less equally on one another to account for what was going on when it came to AIDS. For all intents and purposes, only when they finally did rely on one another to explain the basic causal factors of AIDS did the syndrome become, to employ the language of Bruno Latour, "black boxed" as scientific fact.[19] For Latour, once a scientific concept or technique is black boxed, researchers and lay persons alike need no longer concern themselves with how or why that concept or technique works specifically. It is simply a given that a particular input will result in a particular output.

In spite of the fact that a great deal of controversy still remained over the causes and consequences of HIV and AIDS, by the mid-eighties the "input" and "output" of HIV were more or less agreed upon: HIV was a virus passed from one host to another through bodily fluids. Once HIV was present in the human body, T-cell counts crucial to the success of the immunological system began to decline, eventually dropping to such a low figure that the body became increasingly vulnerable to opportunistic diseases such as Pneumocystis carinii, an unusual form of pneumonia, or Kaposi's sarcoma, a rare type of cancer that manifests itself in the form of painful skin lesions that, in the absence of sufficient T-cells, eventually leads to the death of the host.

Within this drastically simplified black-box picture of HIV and AIDS existed a large quantity of questions and uncertainties still too complex to be resolved definitively, but the picture represented what most in the scientific community accepted as certainties.[20] The black boxing of the syndrome explains why Prior, announcing to his lover Louis that he has AIDS, declares his life effectively to be over because there is "[n]o wall like the wall of hard scientific fact" (*Millennium,* 22). Prior, diagnosed with AIDS in the fall of 1985, draws his conclusions largely on the basis of mainstream findings at a relatively early stage in medical science's understanding of the syndrome. These findings unspokenly represented the initial compromise that immunology and virology had struck, a compromise that, as far as Prior is concerned, sentenced AIDS sufferers to an early death without any hope of a reprieve.

Angels in America uses the physical phenomenon of HIV, a virus that attacks the immune system, as a trope to investigate the degree to which homosexuals qualify as the Self or the Other in the United States. That is, Kushner asks a medical question that may just as usefully be paraphrased in the register of politics: do homosexuals strengthen or weaken the body politic? To recast the question more directly in terms of U.S. history: are homosexuals of the 1980s, particularly HIV-positive homosexuals, analogous to the communist sympathizers (and homosexual federal employees) of the 1950s, as Roy Cohn and his protégé, Joe Pitt (closeted homosexuals both), suggest they are? Are homosexuals themselves effete cells in an otherwise vigorous body politic, expendable for the health of the nation or are they, quite differently, a powerful national antibody capable of regenerating and making whole the body politic? More generally, is Kushner seeking to de-pathologize homosexuality to such a degree that gay identity is seen as inextricably linked to a healthy national identity? These questions form the political foundations of the complementary immuno-virological discourses of *Angels in America.*

* * *

Tony Kushner is a master of conflating a literal language of the diseased body and a metaphoric language of the body politic. In most cases these languages are spoken by, or associated with, the two characters directly afflicted with AIDS in the play, Roy and Prior. In Prior's case, his physical symptoms, particularly repeated references to blood and bleeding (fluid vehicles of transmission and infection) are intended to function as a metonymy of the devastation wreaked upon the entire American homosexual community by AIDS. Over and over, Prior is forced to face his blood. He informs Louis that he has "shat blood" (*Millennium,* 34). He later loses control of his bowels, whereupon Louis discovers an enormous quantity of blood in his stool (*Millennium,* 48). On another occasion, reflecting on his diagnosis, Prior observes, "My heart is pumping polluted blood" (*Millennium,* 34). Contrast this with Roy, the farthest thing possible from a bleeding-heart liberal, who informs us that his heart is a "[t]ough little muscle. Never bleeds" (*Perestroika,* 27).

Over the course of the play, a reluctant Prior is contacted by angels who invest him with the powers of a prophet of homosexuality and AIDS. Prior gradually acquires the status of a visionary who makes transparent the facades of the play's characters, particularly Joe Pitt, whom Prior rightly identifies to Harper Pitt, Joe's wife, as a closeted homosexual. In his prophetic relationship to the angels and in his eventual ascent to heaven and return to earth, Prior emerges as the play's figure of Christian redemption. The constant references to blood in fact associate him with Christ's bleeding wounds and the suffering that accompanies them.[21]

Important as blood is to Kushner's representation of Prior, the most emblematic signifier of AIDS found on the young man's body is a Kaposi's sarcoma (K.S.) lesion, what he calls "the wine-dark kiss of the angel of death" (*Millennium,* 21). In the early days of AIDS diagnosis, the frequent identification of K.S. among homosexual men was among the most puzzling symp-

toms for physicians to explicate. Well into the 1980s K.S. was still considered a rare and rather exotic form of skin cancer that afflicted mostly men with a Mediterranean heritage, particularly Jews. According to Louis, Prior can trace his WASP heritage back to 1066 and the Battle of Hastings in which the Norman invaders led by William the Conqueror defeated the Anglo-Saxon warriors of Prior's kin who fought under King Harold's banner.[22] As far as we know, nothing close to Mediterranean blood flows through Prior's veins. When Prior calls Louis's attention to the K.S., he playfully observes that the cancer is a "Foreign Lesion. An American Lesion. Lesionnaire's disease" (*Millennium,* 21).

But in Prior's joke there is also an important truth for the question of ethnic identity, otherness, and immunological metaphor in *Angels in America.* Normally alien to non-Jewish bodies, but now an all too frequent part of the bodies of American homosexual men, K.S. is paradoxically at once the most American and foreign of entities, Self and Other at the same time. In his lighthearted call for Louis to see the horrific lesion as intrinsically American, Prior strives to disrupt the otherness of K.S. and he does so, appropriately, with a Jew, someone who in a previous era would have had a much better chance of being afflicted with the cancer than Prior.

In many respects, Kushner gives Prior K.S.—which formerly marked those afflicted with the disease as Jewish, and in 1985 marked most sufferers as gay—in order to call attention to how the disease, informed consciously or not by immunological metaphors, impinges differently upon its victims' identity in the age of AIDS. Interestingly, Prior reveals the K.S. lesion to Louis immediately following the Orthodox Jewish funeral of Louis's grandmother, Sarah Ironson, a woman who migrated to the United States from Russia. This connection symbolically associates Prior, identified alone among the play's principal characters as a genuine WASP, as an eastern European Jew. The ethnic provenance of K.S. therefore links Louis and Prior, but it also links Prior with Louis's grandmother and with Ethel Rosenberg, another Jewish woman who would have been approximately the age of Sarah Ironson had she not been executed in 1953. By giving the gay and Jewish Roy K.S., Kushner drives home the double cultural association K.S. shares among physicians in a post-AIDS medical environment in which the cancer is most frequently diagnosed among HIV-infected homosexuals and Jewish men. Among homosexual men of WASP descent in general, and in Prior's case in particular, K.S. creates a tangible connection between WASP and Jewish identities.

Joe Pitt's Mormon identity bears a close relation to the connection between WASP and Jewish identities in the play. Ethnically a WASP, Joe's membership in the

Church of Jesus Christ of Latter-Day Saints makes him in some ways more like a Jew because Mormons and Jews each share a long history of persecution and prejudice. The Mormon faithful were originally hounded out of both Illinois and Missouri before embarking on an epic trek across the continent to Utah, their New Zion. Before their arrival in Utah, Mormons were widely regarded as pariahs by local and state governments and federal authorities, in large part because of the practice of polygamy pursued by the Church's male elders, most notoriously by Joseph Smith and the church's second leader, Brigham Young. Members of the Mormon faith—arguably the only important world religion that can boast an American origin—explicitly identified themselves as Mormons first, Americans second, and formally bracketed themselves off from American society by creating a closed, highly ceremonial, alternative society. Until 1890, Mormons flirted with Otherness in American culture before acceding to federal demands and stamping themselves with the self-marker of monogamy.

As a conservative Republican, Joe Pitt's political ideology is consonant with most of his Mormon brethren, but as a homosexual Joe reluctantly repudiates the enormous value that Mormons place on heterosexuality. Mormonism no doubt appealed to Kushner because it is a genuinely American religion that has, through much of its history, been marginalized as Other. Unafflicted with AIDS, Joe Pitt nonetheless suffers from a bleeding ulcer, which implicitly links him with Prior's bleeding and once again emphasizes Kushner's recurrence to medical metaphors to describe the degraded status of homosexuals in the American body politic.

Quite different from Prior and Joe—who both emphasize the shedding of their blood to drive home the situation of homosexuals in the 1980s—Roy employs metaphors of body to describe the law and politics. Roy ironically calls attention to the deteriorating status of his own body as well as to the utter corruptibility of the U.S. legal and political institutions he has manipulated from the beginning of his career:

> The whole Establishment. Their little rules. Because I know no rules. Because I don't see the Law as a dead and arbitrary collection of antiquated dictums, thou shall, thou shalt not, because, because I know the Law's a pliable, breathing, sweating . . . organ, because, because . . .
>
> (*Millennium*, 66, [Kushner's ellipses])

Disgusted with Joe's equivocation over whether to accept a job at the Department of Justice and help him to avoid disbarment after years of skirting legal ethics and protocol, Roy launches into a speech peppered with metaphors of body: "This is . . . this is gastric juices churning, this is enzymes and acids, this is intestinal is

what this is, bowel movement and blood-red meat—this stinks, this is politics, Joe, the game of being alive" (*Millennium*, 68, [Kushner's ellipsis]).

In a quasi-Nietzschean will to diagnosis, Roy insists that he be identified as a liver cancer patient so as not to have the indelible mark of homosexuality placed on him by a medical chart that reads "AIDS." By having the character whom Louis calls "the polestar of human evil" (*Perestroika*, 95) diagnose himself with liver cancer, Kushner cleverly recalls our introduction to Roy in Act I, Scene II of *Millennium Approaches,* where he devours a number of liver sandwiches, wildly punches the hold buttons on his office telephone, and wishes out loud to Joe that he were an octopus, "[e]ight loving arms and all those suckers. Know what I mean?" (p. 11). As Roy bites into one of the sandwiches and pleasurably responds, "Mmmmm, liver or some. . . ." (p. 12, [Kushner's ellipsis]), it anticipates his later intentionally erroneous self-diagnosis. In terms of immunological metaphors and their relation to a conservative body politic desirous of eradicating the other, liver cancer is, like AIDS, an ironically appropriate illness for Roy because the liver is responsible for purifying the blood against foreign elements and sending cleansed blood back into the body. When the liver ceases to function effectively the body is poisoned by toxins.

For Roy, the two elements of otherness that he tries to purify from American culture are homosexuality and communism, first by keeping his own and others' homosexuality in the closet, and second by pursuing and punishing those Americans ideologically identified with communism and marked as homosexual. In both cases Kushner shows Roy to have failed. First, with the exception of Joe, all of the other gay men in the play—and presumably also most New Yorkers who care—know definitively that Roy is gay, political clout or not. Furthermore, when Joe reveals to Roy, who is in rapid physical decline, that he is living with a man, his mentor demands that Joe return to his wife. Joe halfheartedly attempts to comply but cannot carry through because Roy's paternal admonishment is not strong enough to overcome Joe's desire for men. Second, although Roy successfully achieved Ethel Rosenberg's execution for her limited participation in relaying sensitive atomic bomb technology to the Soviets (Roy accomplished this, we learn, as a consequence of illegal *ex-parte* communication), Ethel's ghost haunts Roy throughout *Angels in America,* revealing to him just before he expires that he has been disbarred, thereby stripping him of the one identity that mattered most to his self-conception.

The cancer-ridden liver that Roy claims is his, which he symbolically cannibalizes in his first scene, is a double metaphor that highlights his growing incapacity to cleanse America of what he considers to be the undesirable political elements that have infiltrated it and of the cannibalization of the law ("because I know the Law's a pliable, breathing, sweating . . . organ,") that he has engaged in since the inception of his career. By drawing a connection between the Law as a metaphorical organ and attempting to make a cancer-ridden liver the bogus centerpiece of his illness, Roy ironically calls attention to the fact that the Law as he practices it is diseased and no longer able to expunge from the U.S. body politic genuine forces of corruption. As represented by Kushner, Roy embodies legal corruption.

Roy's growing physical and political weakness is well illustrated in his contentious bedside relationship with Belize, Roy's nurse and Prior's close friend, a man whom Roy identifies as "the Negro night nurse, my negation" (*Perestroika,* 76). Roy initially demands medical attention from a white nurse, but, soon attracted to the force of Belize's personality, lies back and accepts the IV needle that Belize menacingly wields with the threat that he can make it feel as if "I just hooked you up to a bag of Liquid Drano" (*Perestroika,* 27). Belize's victory with the needle is a harbinger of more victories to come. The former drag queen's medical knowledge, it turns out, exceeds that of Roy's "very expensive WASP doctor" (*Perestroika,* 29). Scheduled for radiation therapy to treat the telltale K.S. lesions, Roy is informed by Belize not to accept the therapy, under penalty of death. Belize, apparently well schooled in the discipline of AIDS immunology, tells Roy that "radiation will kill the T-cells and you don't have any you can afford to lose" (*Perestroika,* 29).

Belize's lines, indebted to immunological theory, are important precisely because of who speaks them and what they mean to the history of Cold War political metaphor in immunology. In the 1950s immunological metaphors relied largely on a Cold War discourse of Self and Other that targeted the Other—figured as leftists, communists, and homosexuals in American political terminology—for exclusion from the body politic. By contrast, the Other is here embodied by the gay, African-American Belize, who speaks in the language of immunological resistance to the ultimate conservative Cold Warrior and persecutor of American political Otherness. In giving Belize these lines, Kushner appropriates immunological tropes for leftists and homosexuals alike by showing that in this play those groups are not Other, but Selves crucial to the constitution of the healthy American body politic.

Roy's political conception of medical knowledge and power is conventional—he simply can't believe that a gay black nurse's knowledge can surpass a white doctor's—but, true to form, he omits an important variable in his calculations: the possibility that homosexuality could actually be a politically powerful identity, especially when it comes to circulating knowledge about

AIDS that can be translated into effective treatment. Although New York City's gay population might not have been able, in Roy's words, to pass a "pissant antidiscrimination bill in the city council," several branches of the U.S. homosexual community in the 1980s, determined to overcome what they regarded as governmental institutions, medical communities, and pharmaceutical companies unresponsive to the catastrophe befalling gay men, pursued alternative medical treatments, including foreign (especially French) treatments and in many cases generated their own therapeutic discourses by publishing in local newspapers targeted at gay audiences. These treatments and discourses both typically challenged conventional American medical wisdom on AIDS.[23] Among the most important challenges to mainstream AIDS research were passionate and politically effective attacks against double-blind drug testing of control groups that received nothing more than placebos.

Belize taps into this critique when he instructs Roy, on the heels of admonishing the ailing attorney not to accept radiation therapy, to demand actual AZT, the first effective drug to slow the advance of HIV, rather than risk the possibility of being treated with placebos that will "get the kind of statistics they can publish in the *New England Journal of Medicine*" (*Perestroika,* 30). Belize goes on to force upon Roy the sexual identity of homosexuality that he earlier rejected from his WASP physician. At the close of their first conversation Roy asks Belize what could possibly motivate him to divulge valuable information to a man who is his ideological adversary. Belize replies in a double-voiced language of leftist labor politics and gay appropriation of the vocabulary of oppression, "Consider it solidarity. One faggot to another" (*Perestroika,* 30), to which Roy responds with toothless threats. In his relationship with Belize, Roy isn't a heterosexual who fucks around with guys, he isn't even a homosexual—he's a "faggot," someone who may be able to telephone Nancy Reagan but without nearly enough clout to resist an African American drag queen.

But Roy still certainly has clout in Washington and, more specifically, in Bethesda, Maryland, where the National Institutes of Health is located and where AZT is administered. Later in *Perestroika,* Belize is astonished to discover that Roy is the beneficiary of his medical advice and, partly as a consequence of that advice, personally controls a huge private stash of AZT like "the dragon atop the golden horde" (p. 60). Belize manages, however, to turn this material illustration of Roy's political power into his own gain. Through Roy, Belize has access to the drugs that represent the last best chance for prolonging the lives of his friends afflicted with HIV/AIDS, most notably Prior. At first Roy flatly refuses Belize's request for the AZT, even though Belize assures him that "[i]f you live fifty more years you won't swallow all of those pills" (*Perestroika,* 60).

Both men turn belligerent, hurling racial, ethnic, and sexual epithets at one another. Significantly, Belize's utterance of "kike," an insult that forges linguistic and ethnic ties of solidarity between Roy, the Rosenbergs, the Ironsons, and all the rest of the "loser Jews" who in Roy's estimation "went Communist" (*Perestroika,* 27), turns out to be the key to the arch-conservative dragon's treasure. Roy subsequently ceases to resist Belize's entreaties and gives the nurse permission to take a single bottle, whereupon Belize removes three. Belize takes several more bottles in the short time that is left to Roy and, when the disbarred attorney dies, takes the remaining bottles. By giving Belize this important role of resistance to Roy, Kushner allows him to tap into governmental resources reserved for the vast minority of HIV/AIDS sufferers and to circumvent the experimental logic of double-blind testing.

* * *

Kushner wants us to read the overlapping medical and political discourses in *Angels in America* in terms of what it means to be a homosexual in contemporary America. Almost all of the homosexual characters in the play occupy an implied racial, ethnic, or religious position of marginality, if not of being a "nonself" in the American body politic at least of being a "less than full Self." These include the right-wing Roy and left-wing Louis, both Jews; Belize, an African American; and Joe, a Mormon.[24] Indeed, the only gay man who descends from the ethnic "mainstream" is Prior, a WASP of eminent bloodlines whose K.S. implicitly unites him to Jewish culture. Obviously, just as two Jews, one African American, one Mormon, and one ethnically identified WASP can't speak for everyone within their specific identity group, neither can one homosexual speak for all homosexuals. Nowhere is this more true than in a play where the so-called homosexual community is racially and ideologically divided along fault lines that can scarcely be negotiated. No character in *Angels in America* emerges as a mouthpiece for "all homosexuals."

Tony Kushner has long been an activist for the equal treatment of homosexuals. Yet to answer the question of whether or not in *Angels in America* he represents homosexuality as a healthy or diseased feature of American life, whether he sees homosexuals as Selves or Nonselves in the body politic, we must turn to the final pages of *Perestroika,* the parting words of his *Gay Fantasia on National Themes.* In those pages the work's right-wingers who deny their own homosexuality, Joe Pitt and Roy Cohn, are absent, Roy because he's dead and Joe because he has elected to cut off his

personal and political ties and forge out on his own in what Louis calls "the ego-anarchist-cowboys-shrilling-for-no-government part" of conservatism (p. 35). In their place are Hannah Pitt, Joe's mother, and Louis, Belize, and Prior, all seated at the Bethesda Fountain in Central Park. This fountain is an appropriate destination because in ancient Jerusalem Bethesda was a pool or public bath where miraculous cures were performed. Manhattan's version of the pool is appropriately dominated by a sculpture of the angel Bethesda, and it is surely no accident that the AZT procured by Roy, which has made its circuitous way into Prior's system, thus prolonging his life, originally comes from Bethesda, Maryland. While Louis and Belize debate the merits and deficiencies of liberal politics, Prior, still stricken with AIDS but having been granted a stay of execution never made available to the Rosenbergs, reserves his remarks for the status of HIV-positive homosexuals in national life: "This disease will be the end of many of us, but not nearly all, and the dead will be commemorated and will struggle on with the living, and we are not going away. We won't die secret deaths anymore. The world only spins forward. We will be citizens. The time has come" (*Perestroika,* 148).

Prior's concluding statement of gay citizenship, a medico-political discourse of full selfhood within the American body politic, deploys and revises the language of immunology that Burnet and Fenner proposed half a century ago. *Perestroika* is therefore less a title intended to remind us of the reform-minded Soviet Union of the Gorbachev era and more a manifesto calling for the kind of radical restructuring of U.S. society that would make Americans reflect seriously on their McCarthyite past as well as politically "naturalize" and medically depathologize gay Americans and other marginalized groups into full citizens. For Kushner, the American body politic may only be diagnosed as healthy when it finally embraces all of its citizens, all of its selves, not simply those endowed with the kind of *de facto* immunity achieved by circulating themselves within a straight and narrow political and sexual economy.

Notes

1. Tony Kushner, *Millennium Approaches,* Part One of *Angels in America: A Gay Fantasia on National Themes* (New York: Theatre Communications Group, 1992), 45. All subsequent citations to *Millennium Approaches* will appear parenthetically in the text by page number.

2. Homosexuals and communists shared common representational and discursive terrain in the 1950s. See, for instance, Jonathan Ned Katz, *Gay American History: Lesbians & Gay Men in the U.S.A., A Documentary History* (New York: Meridian, 1992); Robert J. Corber, *In the Name of National Security: Hitchcock, Homophobia, and the Political Construc-*

tion of Gender in Postwar America (Durham, N.C.: Duke Univ. Press, 1993); and John D'Emilo, *Sexual Politics, Sexual Communities: The Making of a Homosexual Minority in the United States, 1940-1970* (Chicago, Ill.: Univ. of Chicago Press, 1983). Communists and homosexuals alike were regarded as groups uniquely equipped to subvert U.S. security because they could "pass" as heterosexual and patriotic despite underlying identities regarded as subversive by the social and political mainstream. For more on the cultural, social, and medical history of homosexuality in the twentieth century, see David F. Greenberg, *The Construction of Homosexuality* (Chicago, Ill.: Univ. of Chicago Press, 1988); Domna C. Stanton, ed., *Discourses of Sexuality From Aristotle to AIDS* (Ann Arbor: Univ. of Michigan Press, 1992); and Henry Abelove, Michèle Aina Barale, and David Halperin, eds., *The Lesbian and Gay Studies Reader* (New York: Routledge, 1993).

3. The parallels between communism in the 1950s and homosexuality in the 1980s are discussed in Michael Cadden, "Strange Angel: The Pinklisting of Roy Cohn," in *Approaching the Millennium: Essays on Angels in America*, ed. Deborah R. Geis and Steven F. Kruger (Ann Arbor: Univ. of Michigan Press, 1997), 78-89. Cadden writes, "Kushner's play reflects a new gay self-recognition about the ways in which the oppression of gay men and lesbians, like the oppression of other minority groups, has been integral to majoritarian self-recognition, especially during the Reaganite 1980s, when antihomosexuality served many of the same purposes that anticommunism did in the 1950s" (pp. 83-84).

4. Tony Kushner, *Perestroika*, Part Two of *Angels in America* (New York: Theatre Communications Group, 1992), 110. All subsequent citations to *Perestroika* will appear parenthetically in the text by page number.

5. I am indebted to Cindy Patton, *Inventing AIDS* (New York: Routledge, 1990), for bringing my attention to the Cold War histories of immunology and virology. Patton, however, focuses on the immunological breakthroughs of the 1960s when, she observes, "[t]he idea of a delicately balanced internal ecology nicely mirrored the growing perception of the human being precariously perched in a world ecology. Immunology met the cultural needs of an 'America' fascinated by a return to homeopathic ideas, but unwilling to abandon the miracles of modern medical technology" (p. 59). While Patton is right to underline the cultural importance of immunology for Americans in the sixties, reading immunological metaphor in terms of *Angels in America* only makes sense when we focus our historical gaze on the immunological breakthroughs following World War II and during the McCarthy years when Roy Cohn was a key figure in the drive to identify communists within the U.S. body politic.

6. Edward Jenner, *An Inquiry into the Causes and Effects of the Variolae Vaccinae, a Disease Discovered in Some of the Western Counties of England, Particularly Gloucestershire, and Known by the Name of the Cow Pox* (London: Sampson Low, 1798).

7. See Claude Bernard, *An Introduction to the Study of Experimental Medicine* (1865), trans. Henry Copley (New York: Dover, 1957); and Louis Pasteur, "De l'atténuation du virus du choléra des poules," *Comptes Rendus. Academie des Sciences* 91 (1880):673-80, and "Méthode pour prevenir la rage après morsure," *Comptes Rendus. Academie des Sciences* 101 (1885):765-73.

8. Important immunological discoveries before World War I included, for example, Richard Pfeiffer's research on bacteriolysis, "Weitere Untersuchungen uber das Wesen der Choleraimmunitat und uber specifische baktericide Prozesse," *Zeitschrift fuer Hygiene und Infektionskrankheiten* 18 (1894):1-16; Max von Gruber and Herbert E. Durham's findings regarding specific agglutination, "Eine neue Methode zu raschen Erkennugn des Choleravibrio und des Typhusbacillus," *Deutsche Medizinal Zeitung Wochenschr* 43 (1896):285-86; Georges F. I. Widal and Arthur Sicard's test for the diagnosis of typhoid (the Widal test) on the basis of the Gruber-Durham reaction, "Recherches de la réaction agglutinate dans le sang et le sérum desséchés des typhiques et dans la sérosité des vésicatoires," *Bulletin et Memoires Société de Médecine de Paris* 13 (1896):681-82; and Paul Ehrlich's theory of antibody production, "On Immunity with Special Reference to Cell Life," *Proceedings of the Royal Society of London* 66 (1900):424-28.

9. To learn more about the history of immunology, see Arthur Silverstein, *A History of Immunology* (San Diego, Calif.: Harcourt Brace, 1989); and Emily Martin, *Flexible Bodies: Tracking Immunity in American Culture from the Days of Polio to the Age of AIDS* (Boston, Mass.: Beacon Press, 1994).

10. For more on the history of virology, see Greer Williams, *Virus Hunters* (New York: Knopf, 1959); A. P. Waterson and Lisa Wilkinson, *An Introduction to the History of Virology* (Cambridge: Cambridge Univ. Press, 1978); Peter Radetsky, *The Invisible Invaders: The Story of the Emerging Age of Viruses* (Boston, Mass.: Little, Brown, 1991); and Michael B. A. Oldstone, *Viruses, Plagues, and History* (New York: Oxford Univ. Press, 1998).

11. Frank Macfarlane Burnet and Frank Fenner, *The Production of Antibodies* (Melbourne: MacMillan, 1949). Burnet and Fenner's book was a revision of Burnet's single-authored *The Production of Antibodies* from 1941. All citations of the later edition will appear parenthetically in the text by page number.

12. The extent to which Burnet and Fenner's discovery shaped the rhetoric of immunology can be seen in

the title of Jan Klein's textbook, *Immunology: The Science of Self-Nonself Discrimination* (New York: Wiley, 1982).

13. Burnet was named a Fellow of the Royal Society in 1942 and later the President of the Australian Academy of Science. He shared the Nobel Prize for Physiology and Medicine with the British researcher Peter L. Medawar. Among the most highly decorated scientists in his lifetime, Burnet's other major honors included the two highest awards for research available to a British scientist, the Order of Merit, an award directly given by the Queen and which is limited to twenty-five living recipients at any one time, and the Copley Medal of the Royal Society. Only being elected to the Presidency is considered a higher honor within the Royal Society (see Sir Frank Macfarlane Burnet, *Immunological Surveillance* [London: Pergamon, 1970]).

14. Immunology and anti-communism's shared discursive preoccupation with surveillance also underlines a cultural disposition of western modernity, most comprehensively explored by Michel Foucault, to construct elaborate apparati of surveillance at both the molecular and molar levels. For the history of technologies and techniques of western cultural surveillance as understood by Foucault see, for instance, *The Birth of the Clinic: An Archaeology of Medical Perception,* trans. A. M. Sheridan Smith (New York: Vintage, 1975); *Discipline and Punish: The Birth of the Prison,* trans. Alan Sheridan (New York: Vintage, 1979); *History of Sexuality,* trans. Robert Hurley (New York: Vintage, 1980); and *Power/Knowledge: Selected Interviews & Other Writings 1972-1977,* ed. Colin Gordon (New York: Harvester, 1980).

15. Ellen Schrecker, ed., *The Age of McCarthyism: A Brief History with Documents* (New York: St. Martin's, 1994), 211.

16. In recalling the Alger Hiss case, Richard Nixon in *Six Crises* (New York: Doubleday, 1962) described Hiss—and the apparent unlikelihood that he could have been a communist—as follows: "Hiss . . . had come from a fine family, had made an outstanding record at Johns Hopkins and Harvard Law, had been honored by being selected for the staff of a great justice of the Supreme Court, had served as Executive Secretary to the big international monetary conference at Dumbarton Oaks in 1944, had accompanied President Roosevelt to Yalta, and had held a key post at the conference establishing the United Nations at San Francisco. Was it possible that a man with this background could have been a Communist whose allegiance was to the Soviet Union?" (p. 18). And finally, in *The Autobiography of Roy Cohn* (Secaucus, N.J.: Lyle Stuart, 1988), written in collaboration with Sidney Zion, Cohn describes William Walter Remington, a defendant in a perjury case that Cohn prosecuted, with the political language of

American Self and communist Other to emphasize Remington's guilt as a Soviet operative: "A handsome, brilliant WASP with everything going for him. Born in New York City in 1917, he was raised in Ridgewood, N.J., a picture postcard of a town that could have been the home of Judge Hardy. At 16, Remington enrolled in Dartmouth and made Phi Beta Kappa. Later he got a masters in economics at Columbia. In 1939, he married his college sweetheart, Ann Moos, and moved into her banker father's home in Croton-on-Hudson, New York. Then to Washington with the Commerce Department, the War Productions Board, the Navy, and after the war back to Commerce. Behind this All-American facade was a dedicated Communist who ultimately became a spy for the Kremlin" (p. 53). Nixon and Cohn both depend on a representational opposition between the "All-American" official biographies and seditious unofficial biographies of their nemeses. Cohn implicitly juxtaposes his own Jewish identity against Remington's markers of WASP respectability.

17. See Laura Otis, *Membranes: Metaphors of Invasion in Nineteenth-Century Literature, Science, and Politics* (Baltimore, Md.: The Johns Hopkins Univ. Press, 1999).

18. Frank Macfarlane Burnet, *The Integrity of the Body* (Cambridge, Mass.: Harvard Univ. Press, 1962), 68.

19. For a more complete explanation of the ways that science is black boxed, see Bruno Latour, *Science in Action: How to Follow Engineers and Scientists through Society* (Cambridge, Mass.: Harvard Univ. Press, 1987), 1-21.

20. Notwithstanding the objections of figures like Peter Duesberg, a research scientist on the faculty at the University of California at Berkeley in the Department of Molecular and Cell Biology (see Peter Duesberg, *Inventing the AIDS Virus* [Washington, D.C.: Regnery, 1996]). Duesberg utterly rejected the correlation between AIDS and HIV and was so confident of his position that he even offered to inject himself with HIV to prove that it was not the cause of AIDS. For more on Duesberg, his allies, and the controversy they stirred, see Steven Epstein, *Impure Science: AIDS, Activism, and the Politics of Knowledge* (Berkeley: Univ. of California, 1996). Epstein calls Duesberg the "premier 'HIV dissenter'" (p. 105).

21. In "Angels, Monsters, and Jews: Intersections of Queer and Jewish Identity in Kushner's *Angels in America,*" *PMLA* 113 (1998):90-102, Jonathan Freedman argues that Kushner, a Jew himself, actually engages in anti-Semitism in his metonymic portrayal of sexual deviance and Jewishness. Kushner, Freedman contends, eventually falls back on Christian imagery and teleology that assimilates the Jewish identity of the play.

22. Allen J. Frantzen, in his essay "Prior to the Normans: The Anglo-Saxons in *Angels in America,*" in *Approaching the Millennium: Essays on* Angels in

America, 134-50, informs us that Louis gets his history wrong. Louis bases his understanding of Prior's WASP genealogy on the fact that there is a Prior Walter depicted in the Bayeux Tapestry, presumably as an Anglo-Saxon defender. Frantzen writes, "Louis's view of when and where the tapestry was made is popular but wrong. The tapestry was made in England, under the patronage of William's half-brother Odo, bishop of Bayeux and vice-regent of England, within a generation of 1066, not during the conquest itself, and then taken to the Bayeux Cathedral. . . . The original Prior Walter might [therefore] . . . have been a Norman who took part in the conquest of the English. If so, in a line of thirty-one men of the same name . . . Prior Walter claims Anglo-Norman rather than Anglo-Saxon ancestry. His long genealogy, to which Louis proudly points, is hybrid in its origins" (pp. 140-41).

23. For more on the activism of AIDS treatment, see Epstein, 235-65.

24. Exploration of the play's Mormon themes can be found in David Savran, "Ambivalence, Utopia and a Queer Sort of Materialism: How *Angels in America* Reconstructs the Nation," in *Approaching the Millennium: Essays on* Angels in America, 13-39.

Roger Bechtel (essay date fall 2001)

SOURCE: Bechtel, Roger. "'A Kind of Painful Progress': The Benjaminian Dialectics of *Angels in America*." *Journal of Dramatic Theory and Criticism* 16, no. 1 (fall 2001): 99-121.

[*In the following essay, Bechtel examines the underlying political ideology of* Angels in America *in terms of the leftist cultural theories of Walter Benjamin. Bechtel asserts that Kushner's play ultimately achieves a "historical disruption" of status quo politics.*]

Broadway is, without a doubt, that which critics love to hate. Even without leveling sardonic broadsides at overproduced mega-musicals or overweening star turns, we can always count on Broadway to be our easiest target. Of course, historically speaking, we seem to have good cause: where once we could count on Broadway to nourish new plays and playwrights, we can now bemoan the economies that preclude most new American drama from ever making it north of 14th Street or east of 8th Avenue. These days, after all, our Pulitzer Prize winners are culled almost exclusively from the ranks of Off-Broadway, where they've often transferred after starting life in one or more of the regional theatres. The 90's did, however, witness one outstanding exception to this rule: the play that everyone loved to love, *Angels in America*.

There is bound to be something dubious, however, about a serious, ostensibly politically radical play, produced on Broadway, receiving uniform and unabashed adulation.[1] If at first the academic response was as sanguine as that in the popular press, with virtually every critic finding something different to admire, a kind of backlash has developed since. The turning point was conspicuously marked by David Savran's influential essay, "Ambivalence, Utopia, and a Queer Sort of Materialism: How *Angels in America* Reconstructs the Nation."[2] The unremitting accolades received by *Angels* is the very thing that, for Savran, makes the play itself suspect. "Why," he asks, "is [*Angels*] both popular and 'radical'?"[3] His answer is that the play isn't radical; despite its purported politics, ideologically *Angels* amounts to nothing more than a thinly veiled American liberal pluralism. Gone from the play, Savran argues, is any real sense of revolution, any trace of Kushner's avowed commitment to socialism. Formidable in its own right, Savran's argument was soon echoed or adopted by other scholars, creating a critical bandwagon which trumpeted the play's supposedly faulty politics.

Yet if *Angels* seems to fall short politically, it is important to examine the political bar it is so vehemently expected to clear. My goal in this essay is to perform this examination, primarily by looking at the play in the context of American realpolitik, and comparing it to the idealized leftist agenda marshaled against it by these critics. Primarily, however, I want to address their corresponding argument that *Angels* also fails to live up to its political and aesthetic inspiration, Walter Benjamin. Claims that *Angels* is insufficiently dialectical or opposed to Benjamin's derisory notion of progress prove false upon a closer reading of Benjamin and the play, which, I argue, exhibits a historical sensibility very much akin to Benjamin's.

THE CRITICAL RECEPTION

As Savran rightly points out, not only is the play's title and central conceit drawn from Walter Benjamin's famous "angel of history," but Kushner attempts to imbue his work with Benjamin's unique notion of historical dialectics (which I will examine shortly).[4] Kushner's failure, Savran claims, is that the play isn't actually dialectical at all. Instead, the political oppositions Kushner dramatizes either inevitably stand as ambivalent and/or "irreducibly contradictory," or collapse under the structural or rhetorical weight of one of the pair's terms.[5] What is missing is sublation, the essence of dialectical synthesis. As Savran argues, "*Angels* is carefully constructed so that communitarianism, rationalism, progress, etc., will be read as being preferable to their alternatives: individualism, indeterminacy, stasis, etc."[6] Of course, the real problem here is neither theoretical nor aesthetic but political; the terms into which these ostensible oppositions collapse coalesce into a liberal pluralist agenda.

The ultimate difference between Benjamin and Kushner, however, is the antithetical positions they take with regard to the notion of progress. According to Savran, "Unlike the Benjamin of the *Theses on the Philosophy of History,* for whom any concept of progress seems quite inconceivable, Kushner is devoted to rescuing Enlightenment epistemologies at a time when they are, to say the least, extremely unfashionable."[7] The problem, for Savran, in reasserting the concept of a progressive history is its subversion of the imperative for praxis. Averting the apocalypse in *Angels* amounts to the tacit implication that, in time, the "new Jerusalem" awaits all, regardless of class, race, ethnicity, or sexual preference. This is where *Angels'* seeming ambivalence comes into play. Although the binary terms of the play (communitarianism / individualism, progress / stasis, etc.) ultimately resolve one-sidedly, their appearance as functional oppositions serves to create the feeling and the vision of America as a potentially pluralist utopia. Ambivalence functions here in the same way dissensus functions in American culture: as the putative guard against conservative hegemony, and, at the same time, its most effective mask. In other words, both the play's ambivalence and the American culture's celebration of dissent that it mirrors promise a utopian future that obviates the need for revolutionary action, thus perpetuating the conservative status quo. What's left is a politics of identity that is reformist at best:

> . . . *Angels in America* assures the (liberal) theatergoing public that a kind of liberal pluralism remains the best hope for change. Revolution, in the Marxist sense, is rendered virtually unthinkable, oxymoronic. . . . In short: an identity politics comes to substitute for Marxist analysis. There is no clear sense that the political and social problems with which the characters wrestle might be connected to a particular economic system. . . . an alternative to capitalism, except in the form of an indefinitely deferred utopia, remains absent from the play's dialectic. Revolution, even in Benjamin's sense of the term, is evacuated of its political content, functioning less as a Marxist hermeneutic tool than a trope, a figure of speech (the oxymoron) that marks the place later to be occupied by a (liberal pluralist?) utopia.[8]

The problem with *Angels* on Broadway, Savran concludes, is that it generated not only "cultural capital" but "economic capital," which commits Kushner, even if only subconsciously, to perpetuating the system that rewarded him.[9]

Savran's views have begun to find support from other critics. In her essay "Notes on *Angels in America* as American Epic Theater," Janelle Reinelt echoes his argument in somewhat different terms:

> Rather than focusing on the reiteration of liberal themes, I regret Kushner's drift away from socialist themes. The replacement of class analysis by other identity categories, while useful and strategic in terms of contemporary exigencies, leaves the play with no other foundation for social change than the individual

subject, dependent on atomized agency. Since this subjectivity is contradictory and collapsed, the only horizon of hope must be transcendent.[10]

This last point is repeated by Charles McNulty in his essay, "*Angels in America:* Tony Kushner's Theses on the Philosophy of History."[11] Also citing Savran, McNulty makes much the same argument: that despite the historical materialist analysis of *Millennium Approaches, Perestroika* retreats into a "fairy tale of progress" and "religious fantasy."[12] McNulty, however, ends on a far harsher note:

> By the end of *Perestroika,* Kushner stops asking those pinnacle questions of our time, in order to dispense "answers" and bromides. . . . to be truly convincing, [they] must be passed through, dramatized, not eclipsed by celestial shenanigans peppered with *Wizard of Oz* insight.[13]

Needless to say, "*Wizard of Oz* insight" is a far cry from what *Newsweek* critic Jack Kroll called "the broadest, deepest, most searching American play of our time."[14]

What Savran, Reinelt, and McNulty all seem to be looking for in *Angels* is a statement of theory and praxis based on a revolutionary, or at least class, ideal that, discerning from their critical rejoinders, is best located in received modernist notions of "revolution." Savran's critique, however insightful it is in some respects, emits a positive air of nostalgia when it decries the absence of a revolutionary ethos in *Angels.* Yet what Kushner grapples with in his play is the very problem of effecting political praxis in the absence of theory; in a world where Marxism is struggling against its widely-perceived death-blow, realpolitik requires rethinking traditional approaches to "revolution," its theory, and its praxis. In our postmodern, poststructural, post Wall world, Kushner confronts the reality that, at least at the present moment, we are decidedly post-revolutionary, at least in the classical sense. Instead of recapitulating a revolutionary discourse that may not be presently useful, Kushner explores other options for a leftist politics at the millennium.

THE ANGEL OF HISTORY

Kushner has openly recognized the influence of Walter Benjamin on his thinking and writing, but it would be a mistake to see the Angels in Kushner's play as a simple theatrical translation of Benjamin's angel of history. In fact, the two representations can be read as dialectical opposites.[15] To examine the differences, the oft-cited passage from Benjamin's "Theses" is worth quoting again here:

> A Klee painting named "Angelus Novus" shows an angel looking as though he is about to move away from something he is fixedly contemplating. His eyes are

staring, his mouth is open, his wings are spread. This is how one pictures the angel of history. His face is turned toward the past. Where we perceive a chain of events, he sees one single catastrophe which keeps piling wreckage upon wreckage and hurls it in front of his feet. The angel would like to stay, awaken the dead, and make whole what has been smashed. But a storm is blowing from Paradise; it has got caught in his wings with such violence that the angel can no longer close them. This storm irresistibly propels him into the future to which his back is turned, while the pile of debris before him grows skyward. This storm is what we call progress.[16]

What Benjamin so arrestingly captures here is the forward thrust of progress without corresponding historical movement. The Enlightenment belief in progress has produced enormous destruction over time, but it has failed to produce "history," i.e., a substantial shift away from the ever-mounting catastrophe that has become the empirical constitutive of Enlightenment's reign. Benjamin's angel faces backwards, and although the vector of progress and time hurtle him forward, his fate is to be fixated on the historical past. Yet of history, he perceives only a single moment, unmarked by time, in which a single calamity piles its wreckage ever higher. The angel might perhaps be able to cease the carnage, to redeem this history, but he is ceaselessly propelled by the misguided notion that history is moving forward along the path of progress, that society is charting the course toward its own perfection. Thus Benjamin's angel longs to cease the "storm" of progress not so that he can settle into a comfortable stasis, but so that history can be wrested from the cycle of destruction that makes it synchronic and monolithic, and set on a new course. Only then will the angel be liberated from his forced retrospection, and with this new freedom of movement presumably be able to face, at his will and at any given moment, either the past or the future, gaining for the first time a perspective that is truly dialectical.

Kushner's *Angels,* on the other hand, is decidedly reactionary. Despite the Angel's dramatic entrance at the end of *Millennium Approaches,* it is only in *Perestroika* that her mission is made manifest when she explains to Prior the cosmic order. In his design of the human animal, God has incorporated the "virus of time" and thus the potential for change. However, the human compulsion for movement and progress has sent shock waves through Heaven, driving God away and leaving it resembling the ruins of San Francisco after the 1906 earthquake. In order to lure God back and to prevent earthly apocalypse, the Angel has anointed Prior as a prophet, entrusting him with the message that humankind must halt its movement and forbear all progress, mingling, and intermarriage. AIDS, presumably, is a form of reactionary angelic intervention, as the Angel announces to Prior, "On you in you in your blood we write have written STASIS! The END."[17] Ultimately,

however, Prior refuses the prophecy, announcing to the congregation of Angels, "We can't just stop. We're not rocks—progress, migration, motion is . . . modernity. It's *animate,* it's what living things do. We desire. Even if all we desire is stillness, it's still desire *for.* Even if we go faster than we should. We can't *wait*" (2.132).

Given Kushner's many affirming references to "progress" and "forward motion," it is easy to see how critics could read *Angels* as ideologically antithetical to Benjamin's critique of historicism. What these critics fail to do, however, is to historicize both Benjamin and Kushner. Placed in their proper historical contexts, the concepts of progress elicited by these two writers take on significantly different valences. For Benjamin, progress was the dangerous ideological foundation of social democracy, which, as embodied in the German SPD, had capitulated to fascism in the years leading to the Third Reich. He makes his argument against social democracy specific in the "Theses":

> Social Democratic theory, and even more its practice, have been formed by a conception of progress which did not adhere to reality but made dogmatic claims. Progress as pictured in the minds of Social Democrats was, first of all, the progress of mankind itself (and not just advances in men's ability and knowledge). Secondly, it was something boundless, in keeping with the infinite perfectibility of mankind. Thirdly, progress was regarded as irresistible, something that automatically pursued a straight or spiral course. Each of these predicates is controversial and open to criticism.[18]

Viewing progress as "irresistible" allowed the social democrats to tolerate fascism, however egregious its manifestation, as a historical phase destined ultimately to fall under the boots of history's forward march. Yet despite his attack on social democracy, Benjamin was denied the vantage of any real political position from which to launch his critique; as Terry Eagleton puts it, Benjamin was "stranded between social democracy and Stalinism."[19] Unable to embrace a communism mired in the abuses of Stalin, and at the same time philosophically opposed to the teleological certainties of social democracy, Benjamin was left to develop his own uniquely theological materialism.

As Savran implies, there is a Benjaminian concept of revolution that differs greatly from the classical Marxist formulation. In a sense, because history for Benjamin has no telos, it can exist in a more profoundly dialectical relationship with the present. Again in the "Theses" Benjamin writes, "History is the subject of a structure whose site is not homogeneous, empty time, but time filled by the presence of the now [*Jetztzeit*]. Thus, to Robespierre ancient Rome was a past charged with the time of the now which he blasted out of the continuum of history."[20] It is here we find both Benjamin's concept of revolution and its theological inflection. If history is not evolution, revolution can only be accomplished through an act of historical agency; the shock necessary to disrupt the catastrophic eternal recurrence that is history must come at the hands of one ready to make the "tiger's leap" into the past. Such a move, straining as it does against the closed history of the ruling class, requires not only historical consciousness but fortitude: "The historical materialist leaves it to others to be drained by the whore called 'Once upon a time' in historicism's bordello. He remains in control of his powers, man enough to blast open the continuum of history."[21]

Despite the "überman" sensibility of this last passage, couching historical agency in pointedly human (and masculine) terms allows Benjamin to prevent the key component of agency from being subsumed into his messianism. In other words, it reinforces the theory as materialism inflected by messianism rather than the converse. Indeed, what the revolutionary agent achieves in the act of exploding history is precisely a "*weak* Messianic power, a power to which the past has a claim."[22] For, unlike the Messiah, the historical materialist cannot through her mere appearance redeem all of history in a single stroke. Instead, the power she wields comes directly from the past, in the form of a discrete image or memory, by the rescue of which the rest of history might follow. As Terry Eagleton describes it:

> We repeat, as Freud taught us, what we cannot recollect; and we cannot recollect it because it is unpleasant. If we were able to recollect our ancestors, then in a moment of shock we might trigger the unpalatable memory trace at a ripe time, blast through the continuum of history and create the empty space in which the forces of tradition might congregate to shatter the present. That moment of shock is socialist revolution.[23]

This last sentence, however, somewhat overstates the case in that it might be read as reinserting the teleological moment into Benjamin's theory. It is perhaps a truer reading of Benjamin not to claim that the moment of shock is socialist revolution, but that socialist revolution "might" be able to congregate in the space voided by the shock. Indeed, earlier in Eagleton's essay, he explicitly argues against foreclosing the "'text' of revolutionary history" in the "symmetrical shape of narrative," and instead characterizes Marxism as a "transformative practice" of "ceaseless 'beginning.'"[24]

What should be apparent at this point is that Benjamin's theory of revolution posits only its moment of possibility and not its political form. Benjamin charges us to blast history open, but refuses to speculate as to how the revolution is to proceed through the breach. Indeed, the rhetoric of this particular charge implies a grand revolutionary gesture, but elsewhere Benjamin implies that the battle for control of history will not be won with a single blow but through the sustained efforts of

generational struggle: If the history ripe for exploding is the monolithic construction of bourgeois historicism, the explosion will detonate in a counterhistory constructed for just such a purpose. The past, for Benjamin, consists in flashes of memory that must be seized or risk being lost forever: "The same threat hangs over both [the content of the tradition and its receivers]: that of becoming a tool of the ruling classes. In every era the attempt must be made anew to wrest tradition away from a conformism that is about to overpower it . . . *even the dead* will not be safe from the enemy if he wins."[25] The dialectical working of agency and history becomes clearer here: man's weak messianic power is insufficient to break open history without the power of history itself working as his dialectical superior—this is the debt owed to the past. In other words, as a political practice, the received narrative of history must have wrested from it historical countermemories (to borrow from Foucault), which gain a kind of critical mass in accumulation. This critical mass is the power of counterhistory awaiting to be used to sunder its hegemonic opposite. What begins to reassert itself here is the concept of progress, but in a radically different form from the evolutionary Marxism of social democracy. For progress in this conceptual instance operates without teleology or preconceived narrative; it provides only a theory of praxis which aspires to write into history the "strait gate" through which revolution might enter. Benjamin's revolution now begins to come into focus as one of "ceaseless beginnings"; while the question of the precise political form of revolution remains unanswered, the "Theses" appear not quite as mute on the subject as first supposed. What emerges is a praxis of preparation ready to account for a prolonged series of discrete and local actions. Given the historical contingencies faced by Benjamin in 1940, such a praxis seems perhaps the only feasible alternative, a point elucidated by Eagleton:

> . . . [T]he *Jetztzeit* ceases to figure simply as a symbolic element within historical materialism and comes to stand in for the rigours of revolutionary practice. Between the coming of the masses and the coming of the Messiah, no third term is able to crystallize. The revolutionary prophet substitutes himself for the revolutionary party, able to fulfill its mnemonic but not its theoretical and organizational tasks, rich in wisdom partly because poor in practice. If Trotsky has the Transitional Programme, Benjamin is left with the "time of the now". No revolutionary movement can afford to ignore steady signs of progress, rhythms of gradual development, or (in a non-metaphysical sense of the term) questions of teleology. . . .[26]

If Benjamin was a revolutionary prophet, his foretelling of the Messiah's coming did not forestall his understanding of the real work needed to prepare for the arrival.

It would seem absurd to compare Benjamin's fascist Germany with Kushner's postmodern America, and yet, at least for Kushner, there are parallels. In his earlier play, *A Bright Room Called Day,* Kushner doesn't hesitate to compare Ronald Reagan to Adolf Hitler, although he hopes his audience will read into the comparison appropriate historical context: "I never indulged in fantasies of some archaic form of fascism goose-stepping down the streets of America. Reagan and the forces gathered about him seemed to me, in the flush of their demoralizing victory in 1984, the advance guard of a new and more dangerous and destructive form of barbarism." Citing Marcuse's admonishment that history would only repeat itself in a more highly-developed form, he goes on to say, "Postmodern, cybernetic, microwave, microchip fascism may not look anything like its modernist forbear."[27]

Whether the comparison between Nazi Germany and Reaganite America is apt is beside the point; what is relevant is that Kushner, like Benjamin, perceives the profound absence of any real platform for a meaningful politics of the left. If Benjamin's attack on the evolutionary ethos of social democracy was unremitting, it was because he perceived that ethos as standing in the way of what could have been a formidable revolutionary movement. That fascism was the enemy was clear; the existence of substantial popular support for the left was also clear. The challenge was to turn that support into substantive opposition, to ignite leftist sentiment into revolutionary fervor. To this end, and on the eve of Hitler's final ascent, all rhetoric of progress per se had to be abjured. Millennial America, however, poses an altogether different dilemma. Where Benjamin apprehended the misdirection of leftist political energy, Kushner perceives America's profound lack of any cohesive left whatsoever. Although we may strain to compare Reagan with Hitler, what remains strikingly similar between their historical moments is the political quietus engendered in response. It is the nature of that quietus, however, that differentiates the two eras. For Kushner, the battle is not against a quiescent left as it was for Benjamin, but to prompt a nascent leftist response by exposing the tyranny of the right. What both perhaps share is the fear that the left will soon disappear altogether. Kushner's response, as I will argue more fully later, is to urge counterhegemonic formations, beginning with identity politics, that have the potential to cohere into an organized left. Such a response can only be measured in terms of progress; to wish for a revolutionary realpolitik in America is to fantasize, or worse, to think of history in a nostalgic and undialectical way. Yet Kushner's concept of progress is not the progress of social democracy. If Kushner shuns a rhetoric of revolution, he also avoids backsliding into teleology and grand historical narrative. Although he may wear the idea of progress on his sleeve, his approach is much more Benjaminian than any of his critics have realized.

DIALECTICS AT A STANDSTILL

As previously discussed, Benjamin's method seems not to strain toward the untenable rescue of history in all its moments as if by the entrance of the Messiah, but to work toward the accumulation of counter-historical moments so that a revolutionary tradition may survive. Paradoxically, however, this is precisely the way to redeem the totality of history; from a dialectical perspective each moment of history sublates all others:

> A historical materialist approaches a historical subject only where he encounters it as a monad. . . . He takes cognizance of it in order to blast a specific era out of the homogenous course of history—blasting a specific life out of the era or a specific work out of the lifework. As a result of this method the lifework is preserved in this work and at the same time canceled; in the lifework, the era; and in the era, the entire course of history. The nourishing fruit of the historically understood contains time as a precious but tasteless seed.[28]

If this captures the dialectical essence of history's redemption, what remains is to elaborate on the nature of the historical subject.

Memory is the realm of the past, of history apprehended, and its medium is the image. "The past," Benjamin writes, "can be seized only as an image which flashes up at the instant when it can be recognized and is never seen again."[29] The importance of the image for Benjamin should not be underestimated; as he noted, "Only images in the mind vitalize the will. The mere word, by contrast, at most inflames it, to leave it smoldering, blasted. There is not intact will without exact pictorial imagination. No imagination without innervation."[30] These memory flashes, however, are not random but the product of the image's particular *Jetztzeit,* its embodiment of the presence of the now which reciprocally galvanizes both it and its present-time counterpart. Thus, to use Benjamin's example, Rome is redeemed by Robespierre and France ignited by Rome. It is not the historical image alone which embodies the charge, but the juxtaposition of past image and present moment, or of images and moments arrayed in constellation, which embodies a particular dialectical dynamic.

If Benjamin doesn't offer a term or phrase in his "Theses" to encompass this concept, his *Passegenwerk* suggests such configurations should be called "dialectical images." But, as Susan Buck-Morss points out, the dialectical image is "overdetermined in Benjamin's thought."[31] The most obvious difference between its conception in the "Theses" and in the *Passegenwerk* is that the latter locates these images in specific historical objects like the 19th century Parisian arcades. These objects still burst from the now-time of their historical milieu in dialectical tension with the present, but they also carry an inherent dialectical charge between their phenomenal presence as commodity fetishes and their embodiment of the collective desire for utopia. The shock or "illumination" gained from the dialectical image serves to awaken the viewer from the dreamscape of commodity capitalism, and thus has ontological as well as epistemological impact. While in the "Theses" the same operation obtains, the illumination does not necessarily issue from a "profane" object, but can be found in, for example, an entire era.

The concept of the dialectical image is bound up with another Benjaminian concept: "dialectics at a standstill." Benjamin's angel had the storm of progress caught in its wings, and we do as well. If there is any possibility of revolutionary change, we must be able to see history not as an irrepressible force which carries us helplessly along in its wake, but as a force open to our own use in shaping its future course. In this sense, the dialectics of history must be brought to a standstill to allow us that insight. Benjamin first alludes to this phenomenon in *One Way Street*:

> Again and again, in Shakespeare, in Calderon, battles fill the last act, and kings, princes, attendants and followers "enter fleeing." The moment in which they become visible to spectators *brings them to a standstill.* The flight of the *dramatis personae* is arrested by the stage. Their entry into the visual field of nonparticipating and truly impartial persons allows the harassed to draw breath, bathes them in new air. The appearance on stage of those who enter "fleeing" takes from this its hidden meaning. Our reading of this formula is imbued with expectation of a place, a light, a footlight glare, in which our flight through life may be likewise sheltered in the presence of onlooking strangers.
>
> (emphasis added)[32]

The theatre, appropriately enough, operates here as a metaphor for the alienation effect that Benjamin describes: by stopping both movement and time (or perhaps it is better to say the dialectical exchange between movement and time), and placing the object "on stage," we may observe and come to understand it in a way that is normally foreclosed to us. It is not simply the object, however, that becomes estranged, but the processes of movement and time that otherwise obscure both the object and themselves. In other words, history itself, both as a construction and a process of constructing, is dramatically displayed. Benjamin most clearly describes this moment in his "Theses":

> A historical materialist cannot do without the notion of a present which is not a transition, but in which time stands still and has come to a stop. For this notion defines the present in which he himself is writing history. . . . Materialist historiography, on the other hand, is based on the constructive principle. Thinking involves not only the flow of thoughts, but their arrest as well. Where thinking suddenly stops in a configuration pregnant with tensions, it gives that configuration a shock, by which it crystallizes into a monad. . . . In

this structure, he recognizes the sign of a Messianic cessation of happening, or, put differently, a revolutionary chance in the fight for the oppressed past.[33]

The monad Benjamin alludes to is the dialectical image; as Rolf Tiedemann points out, the content of the dialectical image is a dialectic at a standstill.[34]

It is precisely in its use of dialectical images that *Angels* embodies Benjamin's notion of history. *Perestroika* provides two scenes which are particularly good examples of how this concept is incorporated into Kushner's dramaturgy. The first of these scenes is set in the Diorama Room of the Mormon Visitor's Center, where Hannah has been working since her arrival in New York. At this point in the play, Joe has left Harper for Louis, and Harper has begun to spend her days with Hannah at the Center. Kushner describes the Diorama Room as "a little proscenium theatre" in which mannequins depicting a family of Mormons in 1847 are shown in tableau trekking across the desert in their covered wagon (2.62). A taped voice narrates the story of the great journey from Missouri to Salt Lake, and although only the father's face moves, taped dialogue is given to him and his sons, each being illuminated by a small spotlight when he speaks. The women in the tableau, it is important to note, the mother and daughter, neither move nor utter a word. On this particular day, Prior has come to the Center where he meets Harper—an uncanny encounter after their mutually hallucinatory interaction earlier in the play. When the mechanical theatre actually begins, the Mormon father is incarnated by Joe, and from nowhere Louis suddenly appears in the scene to question him about Mormonism and politics. Finally, the two of them leave the diorama to talk through their crisis, and Harper draws the curtain.

Kushner's Diorama Room is very much like the Parisian panoramas which figured prominently for Benjamin in the *Passegen-Werk*. According to Buck-Morss, panoramas were "artificially constructed, lifelike replicas of scenes from history and nature—everything from battlefields to alpine vistas—that were favorite attractions in the nineteenth century" (2.67). Like movie theatres at a contemporary shopping mall, the panoramas of Paris were often found in the arcades, where denizens would sit around a large, circular wall and look into individual viewing slots, watching history being literally unrolled before them. Not only was the content of this history ideologically charged, but the form of the panorama reflected the progressive idea of history so anathema to Benjamin: the panorama rolled inexorably forward, the spectators caught up in its irresistible acceleration.

This same dynamic is at play in *Angels*' Mormon diorama, which functions as a little theatre of history. The story it tells is Joseph Smith's leading the Mormons on the journey from New York across America to an unknown destination, the promised land. The rhetoric that bolstered the pilgrims on the way was, of course, one of religious faith, an ideology challenged by Harper as she comments on the staged conversation between the mannequin Father and his two sons, Orrin and Caleb:

ORRIN:

> When will we arrive in Zion, Father? When will our great exodus finally be done? All this wandering . . .

HARPER:

> Never. You'll die of snake bite and your brother looks like scorpion food to me.

FATHER:

> Soon boys, soon, just like the Prophet promised. The Lord leads the way.

CALEB:

> Will there be lots to eat there, Father?

HARPER:

> No, just sand.

CALEB:

> Will the desert flow with milk and honey? Will there be water there?

HARPER:

> Oh, there's a big lake but it's salt, that's the joke . . .

FATHER:

> The Lord will provide for us, son, he always has.

ORRIN:

> Well, not always . . .

HARPER:

> . . . they drag you on your knees through hell and when you get there the water of course is undrinkable. Salt. It's a Promised Land, but what a disappointing promise!

> (2.66)

Harper here is literally talking back to history, questioning the received narrative that still rules the Mormon Church. The scene becomes truly dialectical, however, when Louis enters the historical scenario to question Joe, still embedded in this narrative, about the theocratic nature of Mormonism, which conflicts with Louis's oft-espoused belief in pluralist democracy. The symbolism here is clear: Louis wants to pull Joe out of history, to free him from what Louis perceives as 150-year-old totalitarian religious dogma. Despite the fact that his Mormonism has long constrained him from exploring

his sexual identity, Joe protests and defends his faith; yet Louis prevails, at least in this scene, and the two exit the little proscenium stage. Even though Joe finally addresses his sexuality through Louis, at the end of the play he remains deeply divided, mired in the reactionary Reaganism that exists in tandem with the conservative strictures of his religious convictions. One of the central ironies here, indicative of his internal contradictions, is that Joe has reversed the pilgrimage of his probable namesake Joseph Smith: his repressed desire has fueled a migration away from the "promised land" of Utah, a dystopia of rigidity and conformity for a gay Mormon, to a relative utopia of freedom, New York. Yet while New York City allows Joe a sexual expression he could not enjoy in Salt Lake City, he cannot reconcile his new-found freedom with his Mormon past—like Joseph Smith's, his promised land is also a desert.

The dialectical tensions of the scene multiply when history begins to talk back to Harper in the figure of the Mormon Mother. If Joe mediated history in the form of the Mormon Father, allowing history to speak only indirectly in the guise of contemporary authority, Harper and the Mormon Mother participate in a direct historical exchange. After Prior leaves, Harper conjures the Mother, saying, "Bitter lady of the Plains, talk to me. Tell me what to do" (2.71). The Mother comes to life, steps out of the diorama, and gestures for Harper to follow her. Instead, Harper takes the Mother's place on the covered wagon. But when the Mother says simply, "Come on," Harper, too, steps out of this frozen historical model and follows her to the Brooklyn Heights Promenade. Without saying so directly, the Mormon Mother is telling Harper to leave Joe, just as she abandons her place alongside the doctrinaire Mormon Father in the Diorama Room. Harper's days in the Visitors' Center have been spent waiting for Joe to appear in the likeness of the diorama dummy, while, like the mounting debris faced by Benjamin's Angel of History, her discarded soda cans, candy wrappers, and potato chip bags pile up around her.[35] The moment is filled with the presence of the now, as Benjamin would say: both women, despite their historical separation of 150 years, are locked into a similar cycle of stasis and subjugation. Yet through their mutual interaction, the dialectical interpenetration of these two historical moments, history is cracked open—the dialectic is brought to a momentary standstill, and both women escape their historical inertia. Harper must call forth the Mormon Mother from her enforced silence and bid her to speak, but it is the voice of the Mother that beckons Harper away from her own historical entrapment. Together they leave the Mormon Center and all that it symbolizes.

The dialectic at a standstill is also evident in *Perestroika*'s epilogue. Until this final scene, Kushner's crisp dialogue and use of split and overlapping scenes give the play an unrelenting forward drive. But in the epilogue this forward motion wanes, and Kushner creates a moment that seems to be suspended both in time and space. The setting of the scene is the Bethesda fountain in Central Park, and as Prior describes it, it is a "sunny winter's day, warm and cold at once. The sky's a little hazy, so the sunlight has a physical presence, a character" (2.146). This contrasting matrix of attributes—warm and cold, bright and hazy—seems to arrest a moment and place it in perfect equipoise between seasons, temperatures, even conditions of light. The scene takes place in February, 1990, some four years after the previous scene, yet Prior himself seems to have stopped time, his AIDS having been in remission throughout this period. As he says, "I've been living with AIDS for five years. That's six whole months longer than I lived with Louis" (2.146). Finally, in this scene Kushner allows the characters to break the fourth wall and speak directly to the audience, a device he has not used at any previous moment in the play. By implicating the audience in the dramatic action, this use of direct address creates another level of suspension: the space becomes not just Central Park, but the theatre; the time not just February, 1990, but the present. In Prior's final monologue, the feeling of history standing still evoked by the dynamics of the scene finds its metaphor in the fountain: "The fountain's not flowing now, they turn it off in the winter, ice in the pipes. But in the summer it's a sight to see. I want to be around to see it. I plan to be. I hope to be" (2.148).

This "frozen" moment is the time-space in which history can be written, when the continuum of history can be disrupted and set on a new course. This scene, perhaps more than any other, embodies Kushner's description of his play as a "gay fantasia on national themes," for it allows and urges us to fantasize America as the "vehicle," to use Ron Scapp's term,[36] which might take us to a more genuinely democratic state (an argument which I will elaborate shortly). It allows us a glimpse of a realizable utopia. As Scapp urges, "*Angels in America* is an attempt to extend the political imagination of Americans through fantasy, that is to say, to broaden the fantasy of democracy. . . ." This fantasy, however, this new vision (it is significant that Prior appears in this scene for the first time wearing "thick glasses") can be gained only when the welter of history is momentarily halted and we can see, or foresee, as Prior does, beyond the present moment. Only then can we direct our action meaningfully; Prior's three declarative statements about "seeing" the fountain indicate the desire, the will, and the hope that inform his final assertion, "The Great Work Begins" (2.148).

PRAXIS, PROGRESS, AND PLURALISM

In addition to the diorama scene and the epilogue, the play is filled with countless other dialectical images.

The ghost of Ethel Rosenberg wanders the hospital where Roy Cohn is dying; the World's Oldest Bolshevik addresses the Kremlin; and prior Priors, ancestors from the 13th and 17th centuries, visit the bedside of their ailing namesake. While all of these elements, among others, create dialectical/historical tension, it is in the aforementioned scenes that we most clearly see history emerge as praxis. The exhortation to work that ends the play brings us back to the crucial place that agency occupies both in Kushner's play and in Benjamin's theory of history. In fact, Perestroika begins by framing the theory-praxis problematic.

Aleksii Antedilluvianovich Prelapsarianov, the World's Oldest Living Bolshevik, in a kind of prologue to the action proper, confronts what he considers to be the dire state of the world with a cry for theory:

> How are we to proceed without Theory? Do [these reformers] have, as we did, a beautiful Theory, as bold, as Grand, as comprehensive a construct. . . . ? You can't imagine, when we first read the Classic Texts, when in the dark vexed night of our ignorance and terror the seed-words sprouted and shoved incomprehension aside, when the incredible bloody vegetable struggle up and through into Red Blooming gave us Praxis, True Praxis, True Theory married to Actual Life . . . Have you, my little serpents, a new skin? Then we dare not, we cannot, we MUST NOT move ahead!

> (2.13-14)

The answer to Prelapsarianov's question is, of course, no—there is no grand new Theory, and if there were, it would certainly be suspect as the kind of metanarrative toward which Jean François Lyotard advises us to be incredulous.[37] Kushner's attitude toward the Oldest Living Bolshevik is anything but nostalgic, just as his Angels are anything but sentimental kitsch; both Prelapsarianov and the Angel suffer from the same defect: the urge toward stasis and inactivity, the surrender of agency vis-à-vis history. Kushner's Bolshevik and Angel are subversive, but only as dialectical images which undermine our preconceived nostalgia for a *sturm und drang* revolutionary left or a spiritually redemptive cultural icon. This nostalgic attitude is precisely the trap that Savran et al fall into: to critique *Angels* for lacking classical Marxist analysis is to be out of touch with the contemporary political zeitgeist. Instead, Kushner offers us a theory and praxis for a millennial America. Rather than a resigned paralysis in the absence of theory, or at least a conviction that praxis must follow theory, Kushner suggests a truly dialectical relationship between the two. As Hannah says in the epilogue, "You need an idea of the world to go out into the world. But it's the going into that makes the idea. You can't wait for a theory, but you have to have a theory" (2.147). Moreover, Kushner makes it clear that theory must have a use value, that it must translate into realpolitik, and that it can outlive its usefulness. Here again, Hannah is the voice of reason: "An angel is just a belief, with wings and arms that can carry you. It's naught to be afraid of. If it lets you down, reject it. Seek for something new" (2.105).

Seeking something new is precisely what Benjamin did when historical imperatives made classical Marxism seem untenable. Although often criticized in his own time for being inadequately materialist and insufficiently dialectical, Benjamin nevertheless attempted to negotiate a critical relationship with materialism throughout his last writings. It would be inappropriate to compare the nature of Benjamin's work with that of Kushner's, but apt to claim that Kushner, like Benjamin, is engaged in a negotiation with his own time. What Kushner finds in Benjamin is a theory of history that can also be used aesthetically, a means of reinvigorating our experience of history in an aesthetic mode. What has been leveled as a criticism of Benjamin can be turned to advantage in just this way. As Jürgen Habermas points out, "Benjamin also conceived the philosophy of history as a theory of experience."[38] While Habermas claims that Benjamin ultimately fails "to make his messianic theory of experience serviceable to historical materialism," nonetheless Benjamin becomes enormously useful in theorizing an experience of history that functions *as if* by messianic redemption.[39] History, as previously noted, exists for Benjamin in images, in flashes of memory, and must be liberated from the hegemonic narrative that we receive as history. We therefore *experience* history imagistically, which makes our relationship to history not just conceptual but ontological. This is the thrust of Benjamin's messianism, that the word of history can be made flesh through the image, that history can be redeemed in the presence of the now and not just represented in the past tense. This is the power of the dialectical image. It is through the accumulation of such images, wrested from a history that wants to level all countermemories before it, that a counterhistory can be written and gain critical mass. That Benjamin's theory rests on the image makes it symbiotic with the aesthetic, fulfilling the belief held by both him and Adorno that critique itself could only be "rescued" through the dialectical relationship of art and philosophy. Aesthetically, then, Benjamin's theory of the dialectical image becomes invaluable to the politicized artist, and certainly indispensable to the critical perspective of *Angels.* A silent Mormon Mother speaking after 150 years and Ethel Rosenberg returning to expose the crimes against her are both examples of counterhistorical images that crack open the continuum of history in Benjaminian fashion.

Realizing Benjamin's theory of history through dialectical stage images itself engenders the "idea of the world" needed to "go out into the world"; or, in other words, it constitutes not just theory but a kind of aesthetic praxis insofar as it stimulates our historical sensibility, a sensibility which operates as a kind of prerequisite to political action. Yet, for Kushner, this is not enough, the nature of that political action must be addressed as well. This is the arena in which he comes under attack, for it is here that ideas of progress and pluralism emerge. Progress and pluralism, however, need not be read as a liberal cop-out of leftist ideals. Instead of viewing these terms as irreconcilable with Marxist discourse, in an age and nation that lack a cohesive left it is better, in the words of Ernesto Laclau, to use them to establish a "living dialogue" with Marxism.[40] Like Kushner, Laclau recognizes the need to maintain a historical perspective, and to this end he advocates "creatively appropriat(ing) the past," reconstructing a radical tradition in which Marxism is but one part of the genealogy:

> It is clear that Marxism cannot be its only point of reference. The plurality of current social struggles, emerging in a radically different and more complex world than could have been conceived in the nineteenth century, entails the necessity of breaking with the provincial myth of the 'universal class.' The struggles of the working class, of women, gays, marginal populations, Third world masses, must result in the construction of their own reappropriations of tradition. . . .[41]

The "plurality of current social struggles" is readily apparent again in the epilogue to *Perestroika,* where we see, in just four characters, representations of men, women, the working class, whites, African-Americans, Jews, Wasps, Mormons, homosexuals, heterosexuals, youth, and maturity. Yet even drawing these categorical distinctions is problematic, since they combine and play off one another in their own dialectical constellation, making the location of "identity" a much more complex operation than such categories can accommodate. And from this complex plurality of identities arise the numerous social struggles the play encompasses. Gay politics, of course, predominate, but we shouldn't forget that Louis, Prior, and Belize are all working class—a point the play makes abundantly clear by portraying them at work. Joe and Louis first meet in the men's room at the Hall of Justice, where Louis has come to cry in private. Responding to Joe's confession that he doesn't know his name, Louis says, "Don't bother. Word processor. The lowest of the low" (1.28). Later he remarks that Joe was not the first to find him there, but was the first to show concern: "Three of your colleagues have preceded you to this baleful sight and you're the first one to ask. The others just opened the door, saw me, and fled. I hope they had to pee real bad" (1.29). We see this employer/employee (master/slave) hierarchy assert itself again between Belize, a nurse, and Roy's doctor. The doctor admonishes Belize for not wearing white, then later attempts to pull rank by asking Belize his name. Finally, when Belize correctly attempts to direct him toward the oncology ward (Roy insists he be listed as suffering from liver cancer), the doctor barks,

"I don't give a *fuck* what it *says*. *I* said this is the right floor. Got it?" (2.25). Of course, this abuse is nothing compared to what Roy himself dishes out: "Find the vein, you moron, don't start jabbing that goddamned spigot in my arm till you find the fucking vein or I'll sue you so bad they'll repossess your teeth you dim black motherf . . ." (2:26).

As Roy's tirade demonstrates, however, the source of his prejudice isn't just class, but a broader menu of biases including, at the very least, class and race, and most likely sexuality.[42] What class allows here is Roy's perceived license to exercise his pandemic hatred with impunity—although Belize will soon assert his own subversive power. Likewise, Joe's three colleagues might have avoided Louis for any number of reasons: his sexuality, his Jewishness, or his class. Issues, too, of racism and anti-Semitism arise in the several debates between Belize and Louis, and in Harper we see a woman struggle to free herself from a traditional gender role. The point is that Kushner represents the social struggles in the play as necessarily pluralistic, but not discrete, and not atomized. The boundaries that comprise the categories of class, race, gender, sexuality, etc. function here dialectically; they exist as important social and historical realities and markers, and at the same time are fluid enough to allow them to, in Kushner's words, mix, mingle, and intermarry.

What Laclau hopes for from just this kind of plurality is the galvanization of a new left, that these struggles born of identity politics will cohere into a counterhegemonic force. In *Hegemony and Socialist Strategy: Towards a Radical Democratic Politics,* written with Chantal Mouffe, liberal pluralism is viewed as the first step in a possible progression toward radical democracy:

> The task of the Left therefore cannot be to renounce liberal-democratic ideology, but on the contrary, to deepen and expand it in the direction of a radical and plural democracy . . . The very fact that it is possible arises out of the fact that the meaning of liberal discourse on individual rights is not definitively fixed; and just as this unfixity permits their articulation with elements of conservative discourse, it also permits different forms of articulation and redefinition which accentuate the democratic moment.[43]

Inherent in this formulation is the idea of a progressive transformation, and they are explicit in their desire to "redimension the revolutionary act itself."[44] Citing Gramsci's notion of a "war of position," they insist that every radical transformation is processual, and that "the revolutionary act is, simply, an internal moment of this process."[45] Thus any success in a liberatory struggle, whether anti-capitalist, anti-sexist, anti-racist, etc., is a victory in the war of position. However, anti-capitalism does not have *necessary* links to, for example, anti-sexism; they exist in separate spheres of the social. For these struggles to coalesce into a unified left, a hegemony must be articulated between them.

Kushner, too, understands the need for this articulation. Again in the epilogue to ***Perestroika*** we see not just pluralism, but a unified plurality of concerns. The scene begins with Louis and Belize debating politics, their talk ranging from Russia and the Balkans to the West Bank and the Gaza Strip. Gradually, however, as the scene progresses, a kind of harmony and consensus begin to form, until all the characters are working together to relate the story of the Bethesda Fountain and the Angel Bethesda to the audience. This cooperative effort emerges from an exchange about, of all things, theory:

LOUIS:

[Y]ou can't wait around for a theory. The sprawl of life, the weird . . .

HANNAH:

Interconnectedness . . .

LOUIS:

Yes.

BELIZE:

Maybe the sheer size of the terrain.

LOUIS:

It's all too much to be encompassed by a single theory now.

BELIZE:

The world is faster than the mind.

LOUIS:

That's what politics is. The world moving ahead. And only in politics does the miraculous occur.

BELIZE:

But that's a theory.

(2.146)

Rather than "rescuing Enlightenment epistemologies," Kushner here offers a theory that is also a non-theory: interconnectedness.[46] What he avoids are the grand narratives, the unified theories that have come under such harsh scrutiny, in favor of a praxis of plurality that will, in dialectical fashion, generate its own theory. Of course, precisely because progress is an ongoing dialectic, shortly after this moment, Louis and Belize return to their wrangling over politics, to the necessary and generative process of dissensus. But in this instant in which the dialectic freezes, this momentary picture of coalition, we can imagine an articulated counterhegemony of the left.

Finally, Laclau and Mouffe argue that recent decades have produced a dramatic interpenetration of the public and private spheres in terms of political space. As they put it:

Thus what has been exploded is the idea and the reality itself of a unique space of constitution of the political. What we are witnessing is a politicization far more radical than any we have known in the past, because it tends to dissolve the distinction between the public and the private, not in terms of the encroachment on the private by a unified public space, but in terms of a proliferation of radically new and different political spaces.[47]

If the private was historically considered apolitical, not only do we now understand its political valences, but it is increasingly becoming a political arena as highly charged as that of the public. Perhaps a better way to put it would be to say that the once rigid political barrier between the public and private is becoming more and more labile. The importance of this dynamic is that it multiplies the opportunity for a variety of divergent subjects to become politicized, increasing the impetus toward radical democratic pluralism.

The dissolution of public and private boundaries is integral as well to the dramaturgy of *Angels*—as Savran notes, *Angels* demonstrates throughout the "deconstruction" of the "opposition between public and private."[48] There are countless instances in *Angels* where we see the public/private boundary collapse—from the collision between Joe's politics and his sexual relationship with Louis, to Belize and Louis's debates about drag—but one particularly important example is the politics of AIDS evidenced in the play. Roy, wielding his political power like an axe, manages to acquire a considerable supply of AZT. This same treatment is unavailable to the politically impotent Prior. In 1986, the year in which the play is set, there was a two-year waiting list for AZT, and in this early experimental phase of the drug, patients were often administered placebos. The public/private distinction erodes in any number of ways in this scenario. Roy has public political power only by denying his private life; as he says, "Homosexuals are not men who sleep with other men. . . . Homosexuals are men who know nobody and who nobody knows. Who have zero clout" (1.45). Conversely, Prior's private affliction is subject to the politics of public funding for research and governmental restrictions on treatment distribution. Implicit in the play are several nagging questions: Why, in the face of a deadly epidemic, would there be a two-year waiting list for any potential treatment? Why would placebos be administered to patients in immediate danger of dying? If the population stricken with AIDS were not largely gay, would the public response be different? There is, however, a subversive irony at work here: Roy only knows about AZT and the placebo tests through Belize, who attributes his own knowledge to being "queer." Moreover, Belize steals several vials of AZT from the incapacitated Roy and gives them to Prior, who outlives Roy by years.

What we see in scenes like the one above is that the politics of the play range from pressing current issues to the larger questions of theory and praxis—indeed, as previously discussed, it is precisely the interconnectedness of the two that is the foundation of the play's politics. Similarly, on the spectrum of revolutionary theory, the messianic materialism of Walter Benjamin might seem to be far distant from the radical democracy of Laclau and Mouffe. Yet there is a commonality that binds them: assembly as a constitutive part of praxis. For Benjamin, it is the assembly of historical fragments into a present constellation rife with revolutionary potential. For Laclau and Mouffe, it is the assembly of local and fragmented struggles into a counterhegemonic force. That Kushner attempts to make bedfellows of these two theories is perhaps not so strange, for what both strive for is historical and political discontinuity, or political discontinuity as historical disruption. As Benjamin states in the notes to his "Theses": "[T]he classless society is not the final goal of progress in history, but its so frequently unsuccessful, yet ultimately accomplished interruption."[49] What Kushner understands, and what escapes his critics, is that progress can be a form of interruption, and democratic pluralism a form of progress. On this point the play is not ambivalent—even if the point is made on Broadway.

Notes

1. The response to Angels in the popular press was nothing short of ecstatic. In the *New York Times,* Frank Rich called *Angels* "miraculous . . . provocative, witty and deeply upsetting . . . a searching and radical rethinking of American political drama" (24 Nov. 1993: C11). Jack Kroll labeled it a "masterpiece" in *Newsweek,* and deemed it "the broadest, deepest, most searching American play of our time" (6 Dec. 1993: 83). John Lahr echoed this assessment in the *New Yorker*: "Not since Tennessee Williams has a playwright announced his vision with such authority on the Broadway stage. . . . *Perestroika* is a masterpiece" (13 Dec. 1993: 129-133).

2. David Savran, "Ambivalence, Utopia, and a Queer Sort of Materialism: How *Angels in America* Reconstructs the Nation," in *Approaching the Millennium: Essays on Angels in America,* eds. Deborah R. Geis and Steven F. Kruger (Ann Arbor: U of Michigan P, 1997), 13-39. Savran's article first appeared in *Theatre Journal* 47 (May 1995) 207-27.

3. Savran 14.

4. 16-17.

5. 17.

6. 22.

7. 21.

8. 32.

9. 34.

10. Janelle Reinelt, "Notes on *Angels in America* as American Epic Theatre," in Geis and Kruger 242.

11. Charles McNulty, "*Angels in America:* Tony Kushner's Theses on the Philosophy of History," *Modern Drama* 39 (1996) 84-96.

12. McNulty 92-93.

13. 95.

14. Kroll 83.

15. A similar point is made by Art Borreca in his essay "'Dramaturging' the Dialectic: Brecht, Benjamin, and Declan Donnellan's Production of *Angels in America*" (249). However, like Savran, Borreca reads *Angels,* contrary to Benjamin, as resorting to a "faith in enlightened historical progress" (249). Where Borreca differs from some other critics, however, is in viewing the non-realistic dramaturgical elements as creating a dialectic with the play's epic realism which ultimately "unmasks as false the possibility of redemption outside history" (251). Borreca, in Geis and Kruger 245-260.

16. Benjamin, "Theses" 257-58.

17. Tony Kushner, *Angels in America: Part Two: Perestroika* (New York: Theatre Communications Group, 1994) 54. All quotations from the play are from this edition, and from *Angels in America: Part One: Millennium Approaches.* Hereafter, page numbers will be cited in the text; those from *Millennium Approaches* will be preceded by the number one, and those from *Perestroika* by the number two.

18. Benjamin, "Theses" 260.

19. Terry Eagleton, *Walter Benjamin, or Toward a Revolutionary Criticism* (New York: Verso, 1981) 177.

20. Benjamin, "Theses" 261.

21. 262.

22. 254.

23. Eagleton 78.

24. 69.

25. Benjamin, "Theses" 255.

26. Eagleton 177.

27. Tony Kushner, *A Bright Room Called Day* (New York: Theatre Communications Group, 1994) 174-75.

28. Benjamin, "Theses" 263.

29. 255.

30. Qtd. in Susan Buck-Morss, *The Dialectics of Seeing: Walter Benjamin and the Arcades Project* (Cambridge: MIT Press, 1989) 290.

31. Buck-Morss 67. Rolf Tiedemann remarks, "Dialectical images and dialectic at a standstill are, without a doubt, the central categories of the *Passegen-Werk;* their meaning, however, remained iridescent, it never achieved any terminological consistency." See "Dialectics at a Standstill: Approaches to the *Passegen-Werk,*" in *On Walter Benjamin,* ed. Gary Smith (Cambridge: MIT Press, 1991) 284.

32. Walter Benjamin, "One Way Street," in *Reflections,* ed. Peter Demetz, trans. Edmund Jephcott (New York: Schocken, 1978) 91.

33. Benjamin, "Theses" 262-63.

34. Tiedemann describes dialectical images as "configurations of the Now and the Then; [Benjamin] defined their content as a 'dialectic at a standstill.'" See Tiedemann 284.

35. Juxtaposing the barren existence of the Mormon pioneers with contemporary urban culture serves to estrange this refuse. Like Benjamin's profane objects, they contain a dialectical charge: not only are they the detritus of commodity fetishism, but as the remains of consumption they refer back to the unfulfilled utopian desire that drives consumption.

36. Ron Scapp, "The Vehicle of Democracy: Fantasies toward a (Queer) Nation," in Geis and Kruger 90-100. Scapp also notes the dialectical nature of the scene: "This is one of the play's more Hegelian moments (*Aufheben*), for it compels us to face the negation of the state of things along with the preservation of the very 'spirit' of the state of things themselves, while the world continues to spin only forward, toward the future, toward a state that has yet to come" (92).

37. See Jean-François Lyotard, *The Postmodern Condition: A Report on Knowledge,* trans. Geoff Bennington and Brian Massumi (Minneapolis: U of Minnesota P, 1984) xxiv.

38. Jürgen Habermas, "Walter Benjamin: Consciousness-Raising or Rescuing Critique," in Smith 113.

39. 113.

40. Ernesto Laclau, "Politics and the Limits of Modernity," in *Postmodernism: A Reader,* ed. Thomas Docherty (New York: Columbia UP, 1993) 340.

41. Laclau 340.

42. For an excellent discussion of this issue see Framji Minwalla, "When Girls Collide: Considering Race in *Angels in America,*" in Geis and Kruger 103-117.

43. Ernesto Laclau and Chantal Mouffe, *Hegemony and Socialist Strategy: Towards a Radical Democratic Politics* (New York: Verso, 1985) 176.

44. 178.

45. 178.

46. Una Chaudhuri makes a similar point: "The characters gathered together—a miraculous social grouping in themselves—continue their dialogues with each other and with the audience. The new historiography that flows from this place is dialogic and site-specific—a matter of different voices, with no single or dominating voice, no source of a master narrative—not even Prior, who speaks from a specific place." *Staging Place: The Geography of Modern Drama* (Ann Arbor: U of Michigan P, 1995) 261.

47. 181.

48. Savran 26.

49. Qtd. in Buck-Morss 290.

Mark Steyn (review date February 2002)

SOURCE: Steyn, Mark. "Goin' to Afghanistan." *New Criterion* 20, no. 6 (February 2002): 35.

[*In the following review of* Homebody/Kabul, *Steyn comments that the characters are not well developed, the plot is unfocused, and the play lacks a clear sense of purpose.*]

There was an extraordinary picture in *Newsweek* the other day of some ferocious bearded warriors. They turned out to be Green Berets dropped in Afghanistan early in the war to liaise with anti-Taliban forces. All thirty-something, trained as soldiers, emergency workers, horsemen, and linguists, they speak at least four languages and on the ground muddled through with Arabic for the first few days until they picked up a working knowledge of Dari and Pashto. Some of them were seen in, I think, Kandahar shortly after liberation, enjoying a game of buzkashi with the natives. Buzkashi is the local equestrian sport played with a headless calf that the rider has to scoop off the ground and tuck under his arm. American special forces playing buzkashi: that's what I call multiculturalism in action.

It's easy to patronize soldiers, and our "artists" do it more easily than most, which is why those Green Berets are so startling: if a special forces commando turns up in an American play, chances are he won't be a multilingual sophisticate but a psychopath with a buzz cut. It is a given that in our society the artist holds a special status by virtue of his unique insight: that's why channel surfing in almost any western nation in the last four months you can stumble across a panel of novelists, poets, choreographers, and playwrights discussing the slaughter of September 11th and the war in Afghanistan. No one would think of convening a panel of soldiers to discuss the current off-Broadway season. But maybe that wouldn't be a bad idea. While Green Berets speak Dari and play buzkashi, America's playwrights have mostly retreated from the world, to a short checklist of familiar obsessions—growing up black in America, growing up gay in America, growing up gay in black America, etc.

This is where Tony Kushner comes in. Whatever else may be said, he's not parochial. Lots of guys were writing AIDS plays, but he decided to write the AIDS epic, and so, whatever one feels about it, *Angels in America* is *the* AIDS play, the play of the AIDS era. One reason for its success is that, in contrast to the authors of most AIDS plays, Kushner, though gay and a playwright, is not "a gay playwright" In these pages a few years ago, I compared him to David Belasco. Like Belasco with *Madam Butterfly,* he has an eye for the big subject, the broader canvas. The first Kushner play I saw, even before *Angels in America,* was *Slavs!,* a vaudeville peopled by gnarled old babushkas and the like rifting on the fall of Russian Communism. Put aside for a moment his views on the great issues of our time and give him credit for being engaged with the world in a way few other American dramatists are.

And now he and his remarkable sense of timing have pulled off their most ingenious *coup de theatre* yet. *Homebody/Kabul* (produced at the New York Theatre Workshop) was written well before September 11th and so has been credited for its almost eerie prescience, especially one line which seems like pure prophecy. An educated Afghan woman, blaming America for her country's oppressors, says, "You love the Taliban so much, bring them to New York. Well, don't worry, they're coming to New York. America!," she snorts. I reckon Kushner got lucky here, but, on the strength of that line, he's now being hailed as even more of a genius than he was previously. He's not, and he doesn't have to be. Three years ago, Kika Markham (the wife of Corin Redgrave and sister-in-law of Vanessa—please, no groans) asked Kushner to write her a monologue. He mulls it over, puts the map up in the operations room, and sticks a little pin in the Khyber Pass. Amazing. The biggest change across the century is that where once the ambitious writer thrust outward to the distant horizon now he looks inward, sunk in introspection. Not Kushner. He didn't foresee the scale of September nth, but then neither did the CIA or FBI. What he did do, as he worked and reworked his play from 1998 onwards, was identify the principal tributaries leading up to that dam burst: his script is woolly, wordy, and circuitous, but within its pages you'll find an awful lot about Afghan history, a little about Islamic culture, and a soupcon about the West's relationship to both. And, if you don't care for his take on these subjects (as some conservative critics don't), why blame Kushner? It's not his fault that there's no alternative view available on the New York stage: the fact is that, in the years since the Soviet retreat and the Taliban's rise and Osama's opening forays, no other working playwright thought any of these themes were worth writing about. What a place the New York theater would be if more writers could raise their eyes from their navels to the world, to embrace the big sweep of history. A decade or so back, in odd moments at London dinner parties, you could catch the various socialist colossi of Britain's subsidized theatrical establishment marveling at how they'd managed to miss completely the biggest story of the age—the fall of Communism. But in New York the irrelevance—the absence of anything to say—appears not even to have been felt, never mind acknowledged. Only Tony Kushner was curious enough to want to write a play about Afghanistan.

So take it as read that the motivation for that coming-to-New-York speech is a tiresome leftie's generic critique of his own country. Be aware, too, that this play is also very long-winded. Staged by Declan Donellan, the director of Angels's London production, *Homebody/Kabul* is a sprawling, languorous four hours, including passages in Pashto, French, Esperanto, and maybe a couple of languages I missed. Kushner never justifies the length for what is, narrative-wise, an underplotted and unresolved Agatha Christie on the North-West Frontier. But I see that even in disparaging it I've made it sound quite appealing, which it is.

Homebody/Kabul is divided into two sections: *Homebody* is an hour-long monologue delivered by the eponymous heroine in Britain; *Kabul* is a three-act play set in the eponymous capital after the Homebody has disappeared and her family has begun looking for her. Linda Emond's opening lines are riveting. "Our story begins at the very dawn of history, circa 3000 B.C.," she starts, and then explains: "I am reading from an outdated guidebook about the city of Kabul. In Afghanistan. In the valleys of the Hindu Kush mountains. A guidebook to a city which we all know, has . . . undergone change." The Homebody is at home in London, a garrulous English matron in pearls and cardigan, gushing over a travel guide from 1965, the last good time in Afghanistan, the final decade of King Zahir's reign. She speaks for the most part in long formal ornate meandering tapeworms of sentences, a cross between Mrs. Moore in *A Passage to India* and one of those rococo-erudite Afghan or Pakistani cabinet ministers who pop up on CNN to confound the anchors. When she lapses into the giddier sentiments of her own place and time, she sounds less convincing: "Oh, I love the world!," she trills. "I love love love love the world!" You'll have guessed she's on antidepressants, her own and her husband's.

Homebody is a piece of one-act exhibitionism by Kushner: he does it because he can, and he's been rewarded by glowing reviews in which even critics who dislike the ensuing three hours coo over the depth of character and command of language and "dreamlike quality" of this opening section. By this, they mean you have a tendency to nod off, as odd fragments from Afghanistan's Fascinating Fact File emerge and retreat and circle around each other and Linda Emond at times audibly struggles, not so much with the British accent as with the dilemma of being someone with a British accent speaking with an Afghan voice. As she reads, her stream of consciousness flows off into digressions, about hats, ten pacooli hats made by a fingered Afghan whom she meets in a London store. Kushner's maimed milliner captures very well both the cadences of Asian English and the almost genetic Afghan ambivalence to everything:

> It was hard work to get into the UK. I am happy here in the UK. I am terrified I will be made to leave the UK. I cannot wait to leave the UK. I despise the UK. I voted for John Major. I voted for Tony Blair. I did not, I cannot vote, I do not believe in voting, the people who ruined my hand were right to do so, they were wrong to do so, my hand is most certainly ruined, you will never understand, why are you buying so many hats?

Suddenly the English lady finds she can speak fluent Pashto, and, in her medication-fueled imagination, is whisked away by the hatseller to Kabul, where he makes love to her under a Chinar tree. The lovemaking over, she pays for her hats and leaves. The monologue ends with her singing along to Frank Sinatra's "It's Nice to go Trav'ling," a typical bit of Fifties pop exotica that sounds slightly dotty today:

> It's very nice to just wander
> The camel route to Iraq
> It's oh so nice to just wander
> But it's so much nicer
> Yes it's oh so nice to wander back.

I'll say. But not the Homebody. No sooner has she finished her singalong, then she gives us Sammy Cahn's sentiments through Persian eyes, a seventeenth-century poem on the raptures of the Afghan capital: "I sing to the gardens of Kabul./ Even Paradise is jealous of their greenery."

On the same album as "It's Nice to go Trav'ling," *Come Fly with Me*, Sinatra also recorded that great staple of British Empire concert parties "On the Road to Mandalay," but in a swinging Billy May arrangement flail of interpolated Frankisms:

> Ship me somewhere east of Suez
> Where the best is like the worst
> And there ain't no Ten Commandments
> And a cat can raise a thirst.

Kipling's daughter so disliked this take she managed to get it banned throughout the Commonwealth. But, whether serendipitously or otherwise, Kushner has hit upon a kind of Sinatrafied Kipling. East is East and West is West and the twain do meet in all manner of odd ways. Under the Taliban, all tunes Eastern or Western were banned, and so the potency of cheap music is all the more potent. The hat man longs to hear his English customer's Sinatra CD:

> Ah, beautiful song that will not die, stardust of yesterday, music of years gone by. Who may solve its mystery? Why shall it make a fool of me? Some few of these LPs my parents—may they have the perfect happiness of Paradise—have leave to me when they are dead, some I have myself to buy at souks in Egypt, Ashkabad, Tashkent, Alma-Ata, airplane tickets to romantic places, yes? They go to extremes with impossible dreams, yes? And so my record player is smashed and all each of the LPs of me, Popular Frank Sinatra Sings For Moderns. . . . Slips through a door a door marked nevermore that was not there before. It is hard you will find to be narrow of mind.

Very nice. An Afghan speech constructed from American song lyrics—"Stardust" "What Is This Thing Called Love?" "These Foolish Things." Even the album title is well-chosen—Frank Sinatra Sings *For Moderns*—for what could be more provocative to a regime at war with modernity? And once shattered, the past is impossible to rebuild: "A door marked nevermore/That wasn't there before."

That's Johnny Mercer from "Days of Wine and Roses." "It is hard you will find / To be narrow of mind" is Carolyn Leigh from "Young at Heart." Of course, if you're a Talib, it's not in the least bit hard to be narrow of mind. There's something very touching about a Sinatra-spouting Afghan retaining so many casual baubles of Tin Pan Alley whose easy rhymes encapsulate for him a whole world of lost promise.

For Kushner, the man represents a global pidgin culture, a world in which the great civilizations have not fused their glories but degraded each other. "All must be touched" says the Homebody. "All touch corrupts. All must be corrupted." Afghanistan is Kushner's case study: a put-upon land designated as a playing field for great-power rivalry, from the Moguls to the Russians to the British to the Soviets to the "American-backed" Taliban. There is a fevered summary of recent millennia. The British "seize" India. Hardly. Though the SAS commandos currently scouring Tora Bora are engaged in what's technically Britain's Fourth Afghan War, the previous three were comparatively short and, for the civilian population, relatively non-disruptive. If you'd been born in Afghanistan in 1887 and died there in 1973, you would have passed a long life in one of the most undisturbed corners of the planet—at least when compared to Germany or China, Russia or Japan, Ethiopia or Serbia.

But Kushner is not primarily interested in the world's impact on Afghanistan. A Pashtun with a pash on tunes by Sinatra is a jest, a conceit unlikely to be found anywhere between Bost and Kandahar. Kushner is more preoccupied by the Orient's impact on his Occidentals. By making his Westerners British, he's concocted a contemporary Kipling rematch: West and East, English and Pashtun, out on the North-West Frontier locked in a sordid reductio of the Great Game. The cosy English domestic setting (well conjured by the designer Nick Ormerod) is replaced by a shattered-brick set. We are in a Kabul hotel room, where the Homebody's husband and daughter are holed up trying to find out what's happened to her. It seems that, after her Afghan fantasy of Act One, she decided to go to Kabul for real. She went out for a stroll forgetting her burqa and accompanied only by forbidden Frank on her CD Walkman. What has happened to her? According to one version, she's been murdered by an anti-Western mob. This is 1998, just after Bill Clinton's diversionary raid on an empty al-Qaeda camp, when as Mr. Bush drolly put it he fired a $2 million missile at a $10 empty tent and hit a camel in the butt. It seems unlikely this would generate much "anti-Westernism" As the liberation of Kabul demonstrated, the Afghans didn't invest a lot of national pride in what was essentially a regime of colonial oppression, funded by Saudis and staffed by impressionable Pakistanis, Scots, and Californians. The other theory is that the Homebody has renounced her British identity and gone native, as the spouse of a good Muslim.

There's a vague familiarity to everything the minute we're in the hotel room. This is Graham Greene territory—expats, ethics, intrigue—and, either as in-joke or hommage, Kushner even gives one of the locals the same former occupation as Our Man In Havana: he was a salesman of vacuum cleaner parts. The Westerners are the Homebody's hubby Milton Ceiling (Dylan Baker), their adult daughter Priscilla (Kelly Hutchinson), and, since the British severed diplomatic relations, a kind of honorary consul-cum-aid-worker called Quango Twistleton (Bill Camp). "Twistleton" is one of those slightly twitty English names, being one third of the triple-barrel of the British explorer Sir Ranulph Twistleton-Wyckham-Fiennes. "Quango" sounds like P. G. Wodehouse but is in fact a British acronym, standing for Quasi-Autonomous Non-Governmental Organization. As an aid worker with various ancillary activities, Quango is literally his own QUANGO. He is the stereotypical seedy expat, even his opium addiction heady with the whiff of nostalgia. True, he puts Priscilla's knickers on his head and masturbates, which Somerset Maugham might have balked at. Milton is something in computers and loathes Priscilla. Priscilla, who got knocked up at eighteen and tried to kill herself, is a foul-mouthed harridan.

If Osama bin Laden met these three specimens in Kabul, mired as they are in a swamp of booze, drugs, and joyless sex, they would no doubt confirm all his fiercely held views on Western decadence. If there's any point to the exhaustive repulsiveness of the British half of the dramatis personae, it would seem to be that Kushner is inverting the perspective of traditional Imperial drama: the English are the primitive exotics, the Afghans are cultured, educated, artistic, urbane, articulate, poets, and librarians, masters of all the virtues the metropolitan power once claimed for itself. I found this argument, if such it is, somewhat undermined by the casting. The natives are mostly played by Asian-Americans—an odd distinction as Afghans are Caucasian, and Asian-Americans are mostly from Korea, Taiwan, Vietnam, etc. The only one who struck me as plausibly Afghan was the lady who gives that warning to New York, and she's played by a Briton—Rita Wolf, a British-Asian actress born in India who was in the film *My Beautiful Laundrette* fifteen years ago and has struggled to find prominent roles since. Miss Wolf's is the performance that stays with you—frenzied, gripping and disturbing, a Muslim librarian unhinged by life under the Taliban. "I have nothing to read!" she wails.

But this is thin reward for a four-hour investment. Kushner lacks Greene's interest in moral crisis, and no one seems to care very much about what happened to the Homebody, so it's hardly surprising we don't. Though we spend a long evening with these people, Miss Wolf's librarian is the only one who truly lives. The rest seem unformed, sketches for a play yet to be written.

So you come away feeling oddly cheated. Unlike Kim or John Buchan's *Greenmantle* or any other standard piece of Imp Lit, the world of **Homebody/Kabul** never seems to exist on its own terms. The characterizations and plot are full of holes: one lengthy subplot concerns a Muslim husband trying to figure out a way to get rid of his first wife. Say what you like about the Taliban, but that's one thing that's not a problem over there. And, even as emblems of all that is most sordid and pitiful about the West, Kushner's Brits are unsatisfactory: nobody here is as ghastly or "culturally insensitive" as Yvonne Ridley, the real-life Fleet Street hackette arrested by the Taliban, who kept moaning to her captors that she'd kill for a chilled Chardonnay. Back in London, she spent a fortnight cranking out a book about her experiences that reads like Bridget Jones's *Afghan Diary*. Modern Britons may indeed be as awful as Kushner says, but not usually so dull.

As for the history, the context, the big questions, the "root causes," they're all in there somewhere or other, alluded to on this page, back-referenced on that, but not in a way that invites us to re-think our preconceptions. At one level, it's puzzling: One of the reasons why the left's "peace movement" got nowhere after September nth was because they were obvious know-nothings, the lame generalities of their demo placards untroubled by anything so tiresome as a verifiable fact about the region. Here, in contrast, is a left-wing playwright who's taken the trouble to unearth ten-thousand facts and yet in the end has as little to say as the ignoramuses. **Homebody/Kabul** has a handful of piercing vignettes in search of a drama. As a playwright, Tony Kushner knows where to go but not what to do when he gets there.

James Reston Jr. (review date March 2002)

SOURCE: Reston, James, Jr. "A Prophet in His Time." *American Theatre* 19, no. 3 (March 2002): 28-30, 50-3.

[*In the following review, Reston offers praise for* Homebody/Kabul, *calling it a brilliant play and a major accomplishment.*]

Early in the second act of **Homebody/Kabul** Tony Kushner's brilliant play about Afghanistan, I gave up on my quest for a purely artistic evening. Foolishly, I had tried to imagine what this theatrical experience might have been if Sept. 11 had never happened; if America had not gone to Afghanistan—in truth and in its mind—through the fall of 2001; if I personally had not been so transfixed and paralyzed and fascinated by the faraway events, so that nothing else from September to January had seemed so important as to read every story about "the war," every profile about the innocent, vaporized victims, every new attempt to explain the mind of Osama bin Laden and the wrath of Islamic radicals against the West.

But it was no use. The connection of this play to the Recent Past (to borrow one of its early lines), was too intense, too immediate. Neither Kushner nor his audience could escape reality. There was no way to move back into the mind-set of just another evening out at the theatre. Much more than mere art was in play here.

"The Present is always an awful place to be," the loquacious British woman of a certain age known as the Homebody says at the play's beginning. And so it was: In early January, as **Homebody/Kabul** had just opened, Osama bin Laden and Mullah Omar were still at large. The flag-draped caskets of the first American casualties of war were coming home. The warlords and the thieves had taken over again, and the poppy fields were back in business, foreshadowing a flood of cheap Afghan heroin on the American streets next year. The calls for more American troops to engage in more dangerous operations, over a longer period of time, were growing more persistent, and the White House was talking about building permanent bases in central Asia.

No exit from this dreadful place is in sight.

The barren landscape of that tortured land had begun to look more and more like the quagmire that I had expected it would become from the beginning. Afghanistan was, had been, is and would always be in the future, "a populated disaster." But we were there, and it was here, everywhere. We could not avoid it.

"We shudder to recall the times through which we have lived," the wonderful, frumpy Homebody says as she sits next to her frilly lampshade, "the Recent Past, about which no one wants to think." We did not want to think about it, but we could think of nothing else. The blow had sucked all the wind out of us, and we were still gasping for breath months later. It had been hard to reach out for entertainment. Escapist distractions had seemed too trivial, and until this play, there had been few connections, few insights to this benighted, corrupt place halfway round the world with which suddenly our immediate destiny seemed intertwined.

To write so many prescient lines completely out of one's imagination, and then for colossal, unforeseen world events to impart such resonance to them . . . what an accomplishment! My admiration for the playwright soars. I am envious.

The day before my night at the theatre, I had contributed further to undermining my artistic evening. I thought it would be good preparation to see Mohsen Makhmalbaf's film *Kandahar.* There on the big screen was the real Afghanistan of sand dunes and jagged, desolate mountains, of chaos and thievery, of bird-like women behind their blue pleated bird-cage costumes, of primitive mullahs and hate-filled *madrassases,* of transportation by horse cart and bare feet, of bewildering, unfathomable, warring tribes—Tajiks, Uzbeks, Hazaras, Pashtunes—of ever-shifting loyalties, of mines and Mujahadeen, of bombed-out towns whose mud brick ruins are only suggested by the set of ***Homebody/Kabul***

So I bring the baggage of reality to the theatre on West 4th Street; but who in this theatre can leave that baggage at home? Toward the end of the play when the corrupted diplomat Quango says, "Have you noticed, nearly every other man you meet here is missing pieces?", the vision of the stumps of mine-shattered legs and arms that I had seen in *Khandahar* flashed into my mind.

And it is this populated disaster, this mutilated hand of a country that America has committed itself to embrace and to civilize and (could it really be?) to democratize. The Homebody uses the wonderful phrase "Universal Drift." But this is more about the American Drift. And our open-ended commitment as a nation to this terrible place is made by a president who had been elected on the platform that we could not go everywhere in the world as its policeman.

"I hold on tight to his ruined right hand," the Homebody says in her fantasy, "and he leads me on a guided tour through his city." And then a few lines later, once you understand the metaphor of the grossly dismembered hand, she says, "Would you make love to a stranger with a mutilated hand if the opportunity was offered to you?" And then, as if it were Bush or Rumsfeld answering: "Might do."

Kushner and I share an unusual bond. As he had written his play about an obscure place of medieval attitudes and barbaric practices that suddenly and unexpectedly became germane to a new American "war on terrorism," so I had written a book about an obscure 800-year-old story of a medieval crusade that had reportedly become required reading in the Bush White House. For, in his diatribes from the caves of Tora Bora, Osama bin Laden had railed against the "Jewish-Christian crusade" against Islam and all Arab peoples. In his construction, this was a struggle of believers versus infidels, East versus West, Christianity versus Islam, Godless secularism versus spiritualism, the United States versus al Qaeda. In his megalomania and narcissism, bin Laden had succeeded in personalizing the struggle. And President Bush had helped the villain mightily on Sept. 16 by declaring that America's struggle was a "crusade" against terrorism. Bush would use the word only once, but once was enough. It was a gift to bin Laden. Now it was bin Laden versus Bush.

And so people have been saying to me that, after reading about the 12th-century conflict in the Third Crusade between Richard the Lionheart and Saladin in *Warriors of God,* they understand the situation in the Middle East much better.

As I left the theatre after ***Homebody/Kabul,*** I overheard people saying the same thing. But what did they understand better? What insights did they glean after 3 hours and 45 minutes in the theatre? What could a stage play convey that we didn't already know from the newspapers and the television?

It begins with the power of romance. In her dusty and musty London flat, the Homebody sits alone in the absence of her waspish, uptight, priggish scientist-husband Milton and her screwed-up daughter Priscilla (in whose adolescent horrors the mother acknowledges responsibility and guilt).

"But guilt? Personal guilt?" she muses. "No more useful or impressive than adult nappy rash, and nearly as unsightly, and ought to be kept as private, ought guilt, as any other useless unimpressive unsightly inflammation. Not suitable for public exchange."

To divert herself from these unpleasant thoughts, the Homebody turns to her outdated guidebook. She reads with fascination and zest about great, virile men in long-forgotten wars, about the hill tribes of the Kabul

Valley in the times before Christ, about the Great Bactrian Confusion, whatever that was. (The mere words, falling off her limber tongue, excite her.)

Her boring life revolves around her safe kitchen and her comfy living-room table with its frilly shaded lamp. And then by chance, as she searches for funny hats to enliven a party she will give (and dreads) for her husband's dull friends—where the revelers are to celebrate some incomprehensible minor technical achievement—she has a chance encounter with an Afghan merchant who sells her 10 exotic hats. As he prepares her bill, she notices that three fingers of his hand have been evenly sliced off.

Back home, she spins an elaborate fantasy of how, beyond morbid fascination, she might have reacted. Magically, she acquires the facility to speak fluent Pashtu and musters up unthinkable courage to ask what happened to his fingers. His imaginary answer gives us one of the great moments of the Homebody's monologue. But the lines have resonance largely because of what we witnessed in our newspapers and on television last fall, as one warlord after another switched loyalties and told outrageous lies, and we gained the distinct impression that in this land where fundamental Islam was practiced, and where the Department for the Promotion of Virtue and Prevention of Vice held sway, no one believed in anything, much less the truth.

The Homebody's Confrontation with the terrible emptiness of her life leads to her disappearance. The playwright has her act on her romance, even if it means going to an unimaginably awful place, where she can take on the burqua, submit to a husband as his second or third wife, devote herself, unthinking like a teenager in a *madrassa,* to committing the entire Koran to memory. She acts on her romance, and she sticks to it. She has rejected the values of her home, of her life, of her society, of the West. In her act is the whiff of metaphysical treason.

The extraordinary act of the Homebody prefigures a similar act this past fall by a real-life romantic, who no doubt is every bit as screwed up as Priscilla. That is the American Taliban, John Walker. He also rejected the pleasures of his California culture of hot tubs and mood music, converted to Islam, joined the Taliban, fought at Masar-i-Sharif, was captured . . . and, perhaps most surprisingly, was uncontrite and unrepentant. He too sticks to his romance, however misguided and incomprehensible it may be to most of us. And the price of Walker's phantasmagoria has been a potential charge of treason.

The family agony of Milton and Priscilla in searching for the missing Homebody makes good theatre, especially Milton's descent into drugs under the tutelage of the dissipated diplomat-junkie, Quango. Quango reminded me of characters in the colonial novels of Graham Greene and Evelyn Waugh, and he is meant to represent the corruption of the colonial. Afghanistan, he claims, has broken his heart, as well as blown his mind to bits. "It's like a disease, this place," he tells Milton. If Milton does not really care whether he finds his estranged wife, Priscilla's search for her mother is real and powerful.

Indeed, family agony drives the entire second act, and it has about it the air of Greek tragedy. No doubt, a few years ago, when Kushner conceived of this play, he put his emphasis on the characterization of the family, never dreaming that the ambience around them could drive the play just as powerfully. In 1999, who really cared about the Taliban or the Pashtun?

The most original and telling characters of *Homebody/Kabul,* at least as the play is seen in the wake of Sept. 11, are two Afghan characters, the Taliban Mullah and the woman Mahala. Both the Mullah and Mahala would seem to be secondary roles, but they speak most pointedly to the situation America now faces in central Asia.

It is the monsters, of course, who always fascinate us. Who are these barbarians anyway who force women into cloth cages and deny them work, who chop off hands and arms for petty crime, who bake their victims in locked metal containers in the desert, who blow up 2,000-year-old statues, who have a special stadium for public executions? . . . and who for all that, purport to be holy men?

The Mullah Al Aftar Durranni makes his brief appearances on stage count. As Act 2 opens, we see him as the impresario of what seems to be an outrageous lie: that the Homebody is not only dead, but she literally has been torn limb from limb by the "rough boys" of Kabul, who have caught her improperly dressed without a burqua and in possession of debauched Western music. Frank Sinatra corrupts. Frank Sinatra is to be feared and suppressed. With wonderful menace, the Mullah says, "Impious music, which is an affront to Islam, to dress like so and then the music, these are regrettable."

Presenting the unfeeling face of the religious fanatic, his manner is cold, official, patronizing. "Kabul is not a city for Western tourist women," he says. Indeed, it is no place for a Western woman of any sort, as we saw countless times on our televisions this past fall, as intrepid women reporters braved the humiliations, the hardships and the real dangers to get the inside story. "We do not want them. No thing may be made or unmade unless Allah wills it. He fills our hearts with griefs, to see if we shall be strong. You are *kaafer,* you do not understand, but this is Allah's way." With such a credo, we see how atrocity is possible, everywhere, by anyone, for any reason. It is sanctioned, and even sanctified by God, just to see if the holy warrior is strong. As counterpoint to the Homebody's early reveling in history, the Mullah says blandly: "In Kabul now there is no history. There is only God."

Toward the end of the second act, the Mullah reappears in a dramatic and violent scene, and in it he delivers the rationale for the Taliban regime. When I read it in the script, the speech seemed simplistic and ignorant. But when played on the stage, his apologia has power and poignancy . . . and even a kind of truth to it.

"Afghanistan is Taliban and we shall save it," the Mullah says in his stylized patois. "No one else shall, no one else care. England betray us. United States betray us, bomb us, starve us to . . . distract [the world from the] adulterous debauch Clinton and his young whore. *This* is good for woman? U.S. and Russia destroy us as destroy Vietnam, Palestine, Chechnya, Bosnia. . . . As U.N. deny Taliban to be recognize. All plot against Islam. Iran plot against Islam. For four thousand years, no one shall save Afghan people. No one else but Allah may save it. We are servants of Allah."

In other words, the excuse for collective religious terror boils down to cruel order. The alternative, going back no doubt to the Great Bactrian Confusion, is chaos and exploitation.

My differing responses to the script and the performance suggest one way that the theatre trumps television and newsprint in making us understand. All fall, the newspapers and newsmagazines had been confounded by Arab wrath. Why do they hate us so? The question echoed from the building tops.

What the theatre can display, better than any other medium, is passion. This includes the passion of the Arab religious fanatic and the passion of his most immediate victims. That passion is something the West desperately needs to understand . . . in its own best interest. For this struggle has not been about ideas or religious tenets. In Arab psychology, everything is mixed together in an emotional stew: the oppression of history, the hatred of Israel and all European invaders going back to the 11th century, the ire against Israel's supporters, the envy of American wealth, self-loathing at the inability to master science and technology, the contempt for weak leadership of the Arab world itself, horror at the disparity between the princes and the paupers, and the sheer grinding poverty and backwardness of the entire region. All that is left is passion and religion . . . and in its worst despairing form, martyrdom.

It is from the mouth of the character Mahala in *Homebody/Kabul* that the counter-argument to the Taliban is forcefully delivered. She is a fascinating theatrical invention: the intelligent, bitter librarian, forced away from work, watching her library closed, losing her mind from disuse and her wits from the oppression both of her society and her household, the spurned wife of the doctor who has driven her from her house and (she is convinced) replaced her summarily with this docile, sentimental Westerner, the Homebody. Mahala is the most sympathetic of victims.

At Milton and Priscilla, the English travelers, she flies into a rage about the Taliban. They are occupiers, drug dealers, child murderers, torturers, Pashtun from the camps of Khandahar and Jalalabad who oppress all non-Pashtun. And then she turns her wrath on her Afghan translator. "And you call yourselves men. You suffer? We suffer more. You permit this? These criminals and savages to enslave and oppress your women? . . . I say women are braver than you men of Kabul."

Her rant is riveting, and as she turns her wrath on them all, Kushner can even squeeze a laugh from the scene.

"Usually she is cheerier," her Afghan companion whispers.

And when another witness suggests that she may be going mad, Priscilla interjects, "She isn't mad, she's fucking furious. It isn't at all the same."

For this audience in the East Village of New York, the city that is the ultimate Western victim of Afghanistan-bred terror, the tension is highest when Mahala turns on America for its role in the horror of Afghanistan. In the wake of Sept. 11, these thoughts are seldom expressed—especially since, as victims, we Americans like to think we occupy the high moral ground. Unlike the Homebody, Mahala has no qualms about assigning guilt. In the face of Taliban atrocity, where is America? she asks. And then the charges fly. Afghanistan was used as an instrument to topple the Soviet Union and end the Cold War, and then the instrument was discarded. The CIA funded the Taliban secretly through Pakistan, exploiting her land as a buffer for Iran, against whom the U.S. was still trying to settle a 20-year-old score. Always the frontline surrogate. Always someone else's tool. In the editorial pages and news magazines, these are familiar charges. And yet from the mouth of the female victim, they carry greater weight.

Of the Taliban, Mahala says, "They'll turn on their masters sooner or later."

And so they did, and for their complicity in the horrendous crime of Sept. 11, they have been destroyed as a result. But the conditions that led to their rise remain. The gangster bin Laden is mentioned only once in *Homebody/Kabul*; George Bush, the World Trade Center, the Pentagon, al Qaeda, Tora Bora, not at all.

We see no American flags fluttering on this stage, hear no macho one-liners from a Wild West American president. This is a play for those who are interested in the root causes that preceded Sept. 11, for those who can see through the fog of patriotism to the finer distinctions, who are finally ready to ask how on earth do we get out of this godforsaken place, who can bear to contemplate the thought that we have participated to some extent in our own tragedy.

The most shocking line of the play is left to Mahala.

"You love the Taliban so much. . . . Well, don't worry, they're coming to New York! Americans!"

Robert Brustein (review date 18 March 2002)

SOURCE: Brustein, Robert. "Angels in Afghanistan." *New Republic* 226, no. 10 (18 March 2002): 27-8.

[*In the following review, Brustein criticizes* Homebody/Kabul, *commenting that the events of the play seem inconsequential in light of the September 11, 2001 terrorist attacks on the United States, and asserts the play is lacking in focus, direction, and unity of theme.*]

Tony Kushner may be the luckiest and the unluckiest dramatist in town. Having had the foresight to write a play about Afghanistan before the September 11 attacks, he opened it last December, with America's presence in the area still dominating the front pages. That was the lucky part. It was also the unlucky part. The destruction of the World Trade Center and America's subsequent pursuit of the Taliban and Al Qaeda has radically altered our consciousness about that country in a way that no prophet could have possibly foreseen.

As a result, *Homebody/Kabul,* which recently completed a run at the New York Theatre Workshop, is a schizophrenic entity, at the same time relevant to the point of prescience and woefully out-of-date. Most of the play takes place in Kabul in 1998, and includes references to "another U.S. bombing" (of the terrorist camp at Khost) and how it missed Osama bin Laden and killed a number of innocents. But Kushner's account of a British father and daughter searching for a family member who disappeared after a tourist trip to Kabul seems particularly inconsequential against the background of the cataclysmic political events that have since transpired.

I saw the play twice, having attended a preview too early in the run to be allowed to review it. When I returned a few weeks later, after it had been exposed to the public and the critics, I could detect no major

changes, aside from the deepening of some performances. The problem is that the play was virtually crying out for revision after September 11. Although the action takes place three years earlier, it is now impossible to imagine these Western characters circulating among the Taliban without thinking of abductions, corpses, bomb craters, detention camps, and the recent terrorist attacks.

On second thought, instead of trying to update his play, Kushner might better have employed his energies trying to find some unity for it, or at least settling on what it was supposed to be about in the first place. I say this with profound respect for Kushner's talents. He is one of the very few dramatists now writing whose works are contributions to literature as well as to theater. (Stoppard is only a pretender to that crown.) What he lacks at present is not substance, eloquence, intelligence, or emotional power—he has those qualities in abundance, along with the Orwellian gift of being able to take the spiritual temperature of a people with a political thermometer.

Where Kushner falls short is in his formal control. Distracted by too many subjects at once, he often suffers from a divided focus. Beginning with the epic *Angels in America,* Kushner's plays have tended to be sprawling extravaganzas that suffer not so much from a deficit of sensibility as from a surplus of it. They display the literary equivalent of overacting: overwriting. (*Homebody/Kabul* is almost four hours long.) Kushner is one of the few playwrights who publicly acknowledge and even seem to advertise a need for a dramaturg—the current production boasts two.

Yet his material is still sorely in need of dramaturgical attention. As its odd title suggests, this is a bifurcated work in which the second part bears only a tangential relation to the first. What links them is a character, the Homebody, though by the time we get to Kabul she is just a hovering memory, having disappeared into the city after being brutally murdered and dismembered between the acts. (That is one explanation of how she vanished—Kushner provides some others.) Fully realized in the monologue that begins the play, she evaporates into a subject for regret and remorse in the longer section that ends it, which is far more preoccupied with a disintegrating family (widowed father and raging daughter) in an exotic country, losing their innocence among con men, junkies, fanatics, poets, and brutal despots.

This makes the opening monologue a bit of a tease—rather like the killing of Janet Leigh twenty minutes into *Psycho*. Finishing off the Homebody takes somewhat longer (her monologue lasts about an hour). But for the time that she is with us, she is an entirely winning presence. I suspect that this inveterate tourist was largely inspired by Mrs. Moore in *A Passage to India,* though there are echoes of the ruminating matrons of Virginia Woolf and perhaps the loquacious Violet Venable of Tennessee Williams's *Suddenly Last Summer.* A bit dotty, as infatuated with travel as she is intoxicated with language, the Homebody addresses us directly from a chair in her London home, using her guidebook to Afghanistan (based on Nancy Hatch Dupree's *An Historical Guide to Kabul*) as the basis for an investigation into the history, mores, and geography of this blighted land.

The Homebody's fascination with Afghanistan allows Kushner not only to turn his scholarly research into a theatrical metaphor, but also to make her compulsive nattering ("unregenerate chatterer that I am") into a medium for his own logorrhea. It is exhilarating to be engaged with this character's appetite for adventure, her embrace of life ("Oh, I love the world! I love love love love the world!"), though she has lost all feeling for a husband who is repelled by the very things about her that attract us most: "My husband cannot bear my—the sound of me and has threatened to leave on this account and so I rarely speak to him anymore." It is not surprising to learn that both are on anti-depressants. One way she fights her depression at this point is with her trip to Kabul.

What is most engaging about the Homebody is her intellectual curiosity. Her wandering mind has the capacity to go from the abstract and eternal to the specific and quotidian. A discourse on Third World hats ("abbreviated fez-like pillboxy attenuated yarmulkite millinarisms, um, *hats*") turns into a discourse on human history, on guilt and causality. And just as swiftly it becomes the occasion for an account of a real or imagined affair with a Muslim hatmaker in London after she bought one of his sartorial products. Her diction is pitch perfect, and so is her self-understanding: "Where stands the Homebody, safe in her kitchen, on her culpable shore, suffering uselessly watching others perishing in the sea, wringing her plump little maternal hands, oh, oh." (That self-denigrating "oh, oh" is particularly good.) This monologue, a major feat of memory and persistence, is delivered with force and grace by Linda Emond. It is the most nuanced writing and acting of the season.

The bridge to the second, less effective part of the play is a Frank Sinatra tune, "It's Nice to Go Trav'ling." The Homebody's passion for Sinatra ("such an awful man, such perfect perfect music"), combined with her love of travel, has proved to be fatal. Her headphones are now one of the few remaining relics of her existence (in addition to three hats and her guidebook). She was presumably murdered because of "this impious music which is an affront to Islam" and because she was not wearing a burqa while walking in the streets of Kabul listening to it.

The next three hours of the play are taken up with the consequences of this clash of cultures. Gathered in a hotel room in Kabul as if at a wake are the Homebody's husband, Milton; her daughter, Priscilla; a British aid worker named Quango Twistleton; a mullah; and a Muslim doctor. They are discussing the fate of the Homebody in gruesome detail, before Priscilla, like Isis preparing to piece together the remains of her mutilated brother Osiris, goes off on a quest for her mother's missing body (she ends up finding the putative grave of Cain). The suspense of the play lies in the question of whether the Homebody is dead or whether she has eloped with a Muslim. This question is never fully resolved, though the people who press for the second option are obviously conning the family. But it is not plot that absorbs the playwright's attention. Kushner seems more interested in examining the impact of Afghanistan's competing customs on the innocent Western consciousness.

His other interest is the impact of the Afghan atmosphere on the mental health of his central characters. Milton, an electronics engineer, comes increasingly under the influence of Quango, whose mind has been blown by the country and by the extremely cheap drugs he can acquire there. ("Why else would I be here? Afghanistan supplies the world.") He and Milton will share an opium pipe and a heroin needle before the evening is over. The obscene, angry, vaguely suicidal Priscilla—"a virago dedicated to punishing everyone she's indebted to"—falls under the influence of an Esperanto poet named Khwaja, who is probably using her to smuggle anti-Taliban codes out of the country.

Much incident follows without ever adding up to a coherent story, climaxed by the most dramatic scene in the play—Priscilla is apprehended by Taliban police for carrying military information (the poems in Esperanto) out of the country for the Northern Alliance, and the Kabuli woman whom she has agreed to take with her is almost shot. The final scene takes place back in London, with the Afghan woman living in the family's home, sleeping with Milton, and tending to the garden that the Homebody neglected, having replaced her in every possible way.

With the exception of the Homebody, all of the Western characters are singularly unappealing, and the occasional anti-Western sentiments that we overhear suggest that this is deliberate. Milton (Dylan Baker) is a sour drudge; Priscilla (Kelly Hutchinson) is a whining bore; and Quango (Bill Camp) is a self-hating drugged-out sexual opportunist out of Graham Greene. Under the pinpoint direction of Declan Donnellan, though, almost all the parts are filled by very good actors, not only those mentioned but also Joseph Kamal, Yusef Bulos, and Rita Wolf. (The exception is Hutchinson, who, unable to find any variety for her role—not surprisingly, given its one-dimensional character—settles for undifferentiated screeching.) Nick Ormerod's set, a decaying pile of bricks and rubble, makes excellent use of the New York Theatre Workshop stage in handling the multiple locations. Indeed, the entire production seems to have been fashioned by first-rate professionals.

But *Homebody/Kabul,* alas, is an errant and wandering play. I can think of no other writer who could have handled this difficult subject in such an intelligent manner. And it is encouraging to see that Kushner has other subjects on his mind than homoerotic relationships. But it is maddening to find Kushner's large talents dissipated in a work that never quite seems to know where it is going. Thanks to the Homebody, we leave the theater having learned a lot more about Afghanistan than we knew when we came. But it is knowledge that has not been sufficiently rooted in either the human events of the play or the events of recent history.

Richard Coles (review date 7 June 2002)

SOURCE: Coles, Richard. "Unveiling NW5." *Times Literary Supplement,* no. 5175 (7 June 2002): 18.

[*In the following review, Coles comments that* Homebody/Kabul *is an insightful and thought-provoking play.*]

Imagine a vast but indeterminate place, an artifice cobbled out of contending cultures and histories, at once civilized and barbarian, timely and timeless, impenetrably strange and startlingly familiar. *Homebody/Kabul* is itself a kind of theatrical Afghanistan; it is a demanding evening, although during the week in which another American import, Madonna, made her London stage debut, it was good to be reminded that a night in the theatre can be demanding in more than one way.

Tony Kushner's play, in Cheek By Jowl's production, is about how we, in the West, engage—or fail to engage—with the Great Other. It begins with a woman sitting at a table—a simple urban tableau, designed by Nick Ormerod, which could be anywhere in Tufnell Park. She is reading from an old guide to Kabul; we hear of the city's origins, the successive waves of invaders from north, south, east and west; we learn about the Graeco-Bactrian confusion. At frequent intervals she abandons the text to make fretful digressions into hermeneutics, her marriage, her medication, deploying a vocabulary that sounds like the clues from a gnostic crossword. She is Homebody, played indefatigably by Kika Markham, who somehow manages to be compellingly boring and engagingly irritating for an entire hour, supported only by a bag of Afghan hats. These she has

bought from a refugee. Afghanistan connects to the West, and as the first act ends, the stage cloth disappears down a tiny trapdoor, like water down a plughole, revealing a plain unvarnished wooden stage within a peeling stockade. Tufnell Park becomes Kabul.

It is only the first unveiling in a play full of guises, adopted and discarded, from the burkha that Homebody's daughter Priscilla is obliged to wear when she and her father Milton arrive in Kabul to look for his vanished spouse, to the unveiling of an Afghan woman who escapes to London in Act Three, only to be veiled again, differently, in a hair-do and cardigan. And Homebody's infuriating, footnoted monologue is just one example of how language itself conceals as it reveals. When we meet Milton at the beginning of Act Two, he is being addressed by an Afghan doctor, who describes with terrible, impersonal precision the state of Homebody's absent corpse; a little later, Priscilla encounters an Afghan poet, who writes in Esperanto so that "all people might be one". But if you are unfamiliar with Esperanto or the ghazal-form, how do you know what you're listening to, or reading? What use is a post-mortem on a person who might not be dead?

Kushner, with a typical flourish, uses the same device in reverse, to make the unintelligible intelligible. We encounter a character we recognize from news footage; an Afghan woman in a paroxysm of hair-tearing, breast-beating anguish—Mahala, played by Souad Faress—but it is she who makes sense. In another scene which recalls the news, Mahala trembles on the ground in her burkha while a Talib stands over her, aiming his Kalashnikov at her head. All is confusion, illuminated by moments of terrible clarity. Some of these moments take place off stage. September 11, which occurred after the play was written, is prefigured when Mahala rages: "You love the Taliban so much then bring them to New York! Well, don't worry. They're coming to New York!" Five hundred pairs of feet shifted uncomfortably.

Kushner has always had an extraordinary feel for the moment. His Pulitzer prize-winning two-part play *Angels in America* succeeded, like no other drama of the 1980s, in dramatizing the catastrophe of AIDS even as it was happening, connecting the progress of a virus to American domestic policy, to homosexuality and the Republican Party, to angelology in a secular age. In that play and in this, he sometimes fails to pay full price for his effects, beguiling us into an exchange of sympathies about which we may later feel uncomfortable. An idea (or an angel) appears and we are charmed, surprised, delighted, reassured; then, just as the temperature begins to drop, Kushner cleverly makes a joke, or points to its opposite. Priscilla makes a confession to her father and we feel the energies of that confession at work in the scene and in the audience; but her father, it turns out, is stoned beyond comprehension. We're let off the hook (we've had our fun anyway).

These strategies take time to unfold, which makes for a difficult and involved evening, although the director, Declan Donnellan, whose Avignon production of *Le Cid* was a miracle of freedom and organization, knows when to hold and when to release. It is worth turning out just for that; but to come away from a long evening in a London theatre thinking differently (thinking at all) about Tufnell Park and Kabul is a lot more than merely worthwhile.

Richard Hornby (review date summer 2002)

SOURCE: Hornby, Richard. "Free Association." *Hudson Review* 55, no. 2 (summer 2002): 286-92.

[*In the following review, Hornby asserts that, while* Homebody/Kabul *is written in a formless style, it is a major play by an important playwright.*]

George Bernard Shaw once said that when he wrote his plays, he never thought about plot. Instead, he just created some characters and "let 'em rip." This reaction against the well-made plays that dominated the late nineteenth-century stage continues in our own day, with playwrights spewing out dialog at random. Some, like Samuel Beckett, have consciously applied the free association technique of psychoanalysis, letting the talk go where it will, ad-lib, never censoring or revising. This risky method can of course result in pompous drivel when the writer lacks Beckett's discipline, intelligence, vast reading, and strong sense of characterization, but it can also yield a strange poetic intensity. Plot is all but dead in today's theatre; imagery, both visual and verbal, reigns supreme.

The plays of Tony Kushner exemplify the formless style. It is hard to say what *Angels in America* was about, much less describe its plot. At the beginning, Prior is diagnosed as having AIDS; after six hours of playing time, and several years of his life, he is still struggling along, the playwright unable to bring the obvious closure to his story. Diverse characters, including Roy Cohn, the ghost of Ethel Rosenberg, several of Prior's ancestors, and the Mormon angel Moroni, wander through. Even Shaw or Beckett would provide more focus. What makes the play work is the incredible *drive* the characters have. The speeches may ramble, but they are not mere reverie; the characters are obsessed with reaching an understanding, which they then drive home to their listeners. Narrative in drama works only when it is motivated for the speaker, and when it has a strong effect on the listeners. (Even with Beckett, we feel that the monologs are character-driven, rather than simply being eruptions from his unconscious mind.) When Roy Cohn rambles on that "homosexuals are not men who sleep with other men. Homosexuals

are men who in fifteen years of trying cannot get a pissant antidiscrimination bill through City Council. Homosexuals are men who know nobody and who nobody knows. Who have zero clout," he is not just making a philosophical observation, but creating a whole raison d'être, a rationalization for his own homosexuality, with which he overwhelms his listener. "Does that sound like me, Henry?" Roy sneers. He has sex with men, but by his definition he is categorically *not* homosexual, not a wimp.

Kushner's long-awaited new play, his first new full-length play in over a decade (unless you count his translation/adaptation of Corneille's *The Illusion*), awkwardly titled **Homebody/Kabul,** begins with a thirty-minute monolog by an Englishwoman, the homebody, in her London sitting room. "I speak elliptically, discursively," she admits, babbling about an obsolete guidebook to Kabul, Afghanistan, which she holds on her lap. The book is thirty-three years old, "long enough for Christ to have been born and died on the cross," a remark that is, typically, superfluous and soon forgotten. Heavily dosed with antidepressants (like Harper with her tranquilizers in **Angels**), she imagines her brain floating in a salt bath.

As usual with Kushner, this spontaneous gobbledygook is spellbinding. It is delivered directly to the audience, a departure for Kushner, whose previous monologs were never soliloquies. Yet in a sense this monolog is not a soliloquy either; we the audience become partners in the scene, like the silent Henry with the Roy Cohn monolog. At one point during the performance I witnessed, an audience member even gave out an audible, knowing "Ah!", as the homebody read from another book on the history of Afghanistan. She is obsessed with that exotic, sad country, and desperate to share her obsession with us. Of course, the scene was all the more poignant because of the September 11 atrocities and the subsequent, ongoing war, but that result was serendipitous. The play was written well before Afghanistan was in the news; in fact, I first saw the monolog, presented alone, three years ago in London, where it worked just as well as in the full-scale production.

The monolog ends with the homebody displaying ten Afghan caps she has bought. The shopkeeper who sold them to her appears, takes her hand, and leads her along a road; we have moved seamlessly to Kabul. This appears to be a drug-induced fantasy, but after an intermission we get a medical report with hard facts. The woman was dragged through the streets of Kabul, beaten by ten persons, and torn apart, all for not wearing a burka.

The remainder of the play, which goes on for several more hours, consists of the homebody's neurotic daughter in a quest to find her mother, or her dead body.

As with Dorothy on the road to Oz, however, the goal of her journey is not so important as the weird individuals and dangerous adventures she encounters en route. She is nearly killed for taking off her burka in the street and lighting up a cigarette, but is saved by an elderly Afghan who turns out to be an Esperanto poet. She meets her father, who is more interested in boozing and shooting up heroin (readily available in Afghanistan) with a diplomat friend than in his wife or daughter. There is a "madwoman" who is actually an Afghan feminist escaping to London, and the hat seller again, who quotes Sinatra lyrics like poems ("You can go to extremes with impossible dreams!"), while insisting that the homebody is alive and well, a happy convert to Islam, living the sequestered life of an Afghan woman under the Taliban.

Nothing, then, is ever what it seems in *Homebody/Kabul.* We never see the homebody again, though whether it is because she is dead, or because she has become an enthusiast for poverty and enslavement (Afghanistan is ranked only the fifth worst country in the world for women, "because they do not practice genital mutilation"), remains obscure. The madwoman escapes to London, but the Esperanto poet is killed, because the Taliban believed his poems were coded messages to the West.

Where *Angels* was subtitled *A Gay Fantasia on National Themes, Homebody/Kabul* might be subtitled "An American Fantasia on Orientalist Themes." We never learn much about Afghanistan, which remains exotic and ambiguous, but we learn a lot about American attitudes toward that benighted country, with its dysfunctional government and its obdurate religion. As in *Angels,* there are underlying motifs of drugs and dreams (e.g., the Sinatra song lyric), which are really what the play is about. We are thus never sure what we see is really happening, nor what we hear is true. Yet there is also a hard core of miscommunication, repression, and suffering. Our dreams about Islamic fundamentalism ultimately matter, as they did on September 11, when we all woke up with a series of bangs.

Homebody/Kabul is a major new play by one of our best playwrights. Despite the horrors of September, it did not get the attention it deserved, nor a particularly long run off-Broadway, where it ran for a few months last winter. This may be because the production, at the New York Theatre Workshop, was lackluster. Directing and designs were by Declan Donnellan and Nick Ormerod, two talented Englishmen with outstanding records in their native land, but whose talents did not weather the cross-Atlantic trip. Donnellan could not get much out of the American cast. None of the English accents was convincing, for example, while several of the performances were wooden. Bill Camp camped his way through the role of the diplomat, for example, though

the character is supposedly heterosexual, hot for the daughter; even worse, he played the entire role with a grimace frozen on his face. Linda Edmond did a nice job with the homebody's monolog, finding ample depths and contrasts in it, but she disappeared, as noted, after the first half-hour. In the role of her daughter, which becomes central, Kelly Hutchinson was weepy and monotonous, avoiding the considerable wit and strength in the role as it is written. None of the actors came anywhere near the depth and intensity of Joe Mantello and Stephen Spinella as the gay lovers in *Angels,* for instance, nor the astonishing swagger of Ron Leibman as Cohn.

The greatest weakness of the production, however, was in its designs. Ormerod showed resourcefulness and imagination in depicting the bleak landscape of Afghanistan, counterpointed by the sterile interiors of the tourist hotels, but succeeded only in making the play drably realistic. As in *Angels,* the true location of the play is in the dreams of its characters, who are typically on drugs or alcohol, or are neurotic, or are outright insane. Thus *Angels,* in its three separate productions in London, Los Angeles, and on Broadway in New York, had multi-million-dollar settings capable of extravagant, magical transformations. Kushner is not a playwright for low-budget, understated, off-Broadway renditions. Surely the granting agencies could have come up with some serious money, as they did in the past, for this important young American playwright! *Homebody/Kabul* is not a PBS documentary, but an *Arabian Nights* for our time.

James Fisher (essay date 2002)

SOURCE: Fisher, James. "Introduction: The Feathers and the Mirrors and the Smoke." In *The Theater of Tony Kushner: Living Past Hope,* pp. 1-20. New York: Routledge, 2002.

[*In the following essay, Fisher explains the significance of Kushner's work to American theater of the late twentieth century and turn of the millennium.*]

> Art is necessary in order that man should be able to recognize and challenge the world. But art is also necessary by virtue of the magic inherent in it.
>
> —Ernst Fischer (14)

Tony Kushner's sudden and conspicuous arrival on the international stage in the early 1990s was as surprising and jolting as the abrupt celestial appearance at the end of *Millennium Approaches,* the first of Kushner's two *Angels in America* plays. Together, these plays comprise a theatrical epic that critics compared favorably to the greatest plays of the twentieth century. In an era of increasing devaluation of the arts—and of the theater in particular—Kushner's self-described "gay fantasia on national themes" moved international audiences, generated controversy, and inspired activists and artists.

Kushner's apparently sudden prominence was not so sudden. He was established in regional theaters as a director, adaptor, and dramatist throughout the United States and England since the mid-1980s. *Angels* represented a remarkable culmination for a playwright laboring to develop a way of presenting political drama on American stages in the late twentieth century. Kushner writes that "since it's true that everything is political (though not exclusively so) it becomes meaningless to talk about political and nonpolitical theatre, and more useful to speak of a theatre that presents the world as it is, an interwoven web of the public and the private" (**"Notes about Political Theatre"** 22). Imagining a political theater is difficult, Kushner believes, because the theater is "a world that's many things but has always been tainted, tawdry, and superfluous. It's very important not to devalue the tainted, the tawdry, and the superfluous and indeed, the essential tackiness and falseness of the theatre is its greatest aesthetic asset and political strength" (**"Notes about Political Theatre"** 25). The theater, he believes, presents the sole realm in contemporary life where it is possible to explore the fact

> that things are not always what they seem to be; that the unpredictability and vibrancy of actual human presence contains an inimitable power and a subversive potential; that there is an impurity, a fluidity at the core of existence—these secrets speak to the liberationist, revolutionary agenda of our day. I continue to believe in this usefulness, and the effectiveness, of this increasingly marginalized profession and art. But I believe that for theatre, as for anything in life, its hope for survival rests in its ability to take a reading of the times, and change.
>
> (**"Notes about Political Theatre"** 34)

Angels in America examined these intangible but essential aspects of existence and, as a result, emerged as that rarest of theatrical ventures—a must-see event capturing many of the central issues of its time. It introduced a bold new theatricality to the American stage, as well as demonstrating a bracing intellectualism, lyricism, seriousness (tempered with the outrageously hilarious), and political activism. The tensions between popular mainstream theater and a drama of high purpose (a division that Kushner calls "invidious" [Vorlicky 64]) blends together in *Angels,* as well as in the rest of Kushner's dramatic work, in unique ways, and he recognizes the importance of the blending of art and the wonderment of the stage:

> The theater always has to function as popular entertainment. Or at least the theater that I do, because I don't

have the talent for doing anything else, I think . . . it has to have the jokes and it has to have the feathers and the mirrors and the smoke.
>
> (Vorlicky 63)

The feathers and the mirrors and the smoke, as well as the dynamic seriousness of *Angels,* thrust Kushner into the theatrical forefront, inviting comparison with earlier titans of American drama from Eugene O'Neill, Clifford Odets, and Thornton Wilder to Tennessee Williams and Edward Albee, while also making him a highly visible political and social activist both within the theater and outside its usual borders.

Comprised of two long plays, *Millennium Approaches* and *Perestroika, Angels* encompasses a complex and emotionally charged portrait of life in the United States in the midst of Ronald Reagan's presidency. Kushner presents this America as a place where present, past, and future intersect in a blur of reality, fantasy, and guardedly hopeful imagination. Written by Kushner during a time in which he despaired about America's sharp swing to the political right and its homophobic response to the mounting devastations of the AIDS crisis, *Angels* presents the mid-1980s as a critical transitional period in the history of the nation in which complicated questions about the future of American society are raised.

In *Angels,* as in most of his other plays, Kushner raises hard questions about morality in a diverse nation increasingly conflicted over moral, political, sexual, and spiritual views and values. Can we reckon with the past and constructively embrace the inevitability of change as we move into the future? Is America rushing headlong toward apocalypse or, despite failures and betrayals of its ideals, is it bound for a bright tomorrow? Kushner asks these questions through what has become his trademark mix of the hilarious and the tragic; his view is frequently dark, even frightening, but there is always a redeeming—and hard won—sense of hope. He is a cautious and questioning optimist, aware that there are no easy answers or completely happy endings, but always noting the possibility for change and progress. Examining individuals at moments of significant personal crisis (influenced, to a great extent, by societal conditions and the specters of the past and the future), Kushner probes the national conscience in ways that not only show him to be the equal of his dramatic predecessors and peers on the American stage, but also demonstrate his singularity in creating profoundly emotional and intellectually charged encounters with history, politics, and the personal.

In *Angels*—and in Kushner's lesser-known but equally challenging dramas—disparate, frequently self-contradictory characters are caught up in tragic personal situations that coincide with periods of significant social change. Their self-contradictions and the conflicts among the characters who, in Kushner's plays, always represent a mixed bag of classes, races, cultural backgrounds, and ideological principles, are explored in the plays. Kushner closely examines the contrasts and parallels between the characters and vividly establishes issues to debate on both the personal and universal levels. Like George Bernard Shaw and Bertolt Brecht, Kushner uses the stage as a platform for social, political, and religious argument, but in ways that neither Shaw nor Brecht, nor any other American dramatist, has. In Kushner's plays ideological debate emerges from a composite of rhetorical rationality, literary and cultural imagery drawn from the dogmas of the past, and wildly imaginative fantasy to unfold the complex cross-currents of history. Of history, Kushner acknowledges having "a kind of dangerously romantic reading of American history. I do think there is an advantage to not being burdened by history the way Europe is. This country has been, in a way, an improvisation of hastily assembled groups that certainly have never been together before and certainly have a lot of trouble being together" (Szentgyorgyi 19). It is, he believes, a "mongrel" nation made up of "the garbage, the human garbage that capitalism created: the prisoners and criminals and religiously persecuted and the oppressed and the slaves that were generated by the ravages of early capital" (Szentgyorgyi 19). Within the tensions inherent in these relationships, Kushner finds the pressure points of his drama:

> There are moments in history when the fabric of everyday life unravels, and there is this unstable dynamism that allows for incredible social change in short periods of time. People and the world they're living in can be utterly transformed, either for the good or for the bad, or some mixture of the two. I think that Russia in 1917 was one of the times, Chile under Allende was one of those times. It's a moment when the ground and the sky sort of split apart, and there's a space, a revolutionary space. During these sorts of periods all sorts of people—even people who are passive under the pressure of everyday life in capitalist society—are touched by the spirit of revolution and behave in extraordinary ways.
>
> (Szentgyorgyi 16)

Kushner found such a moment for *Angels* in the rise of the "new conservatism" of the late twentieth century. Kushner seeks out similar historical moments in all of his plays, finding them in the premodern rise of capitalism in the late seventeenth century in *Hydriotaphia, or The Death of Dr. Browne,* in the collision of the old world shtetls of Eastern Europe and the new technologies of the modern world in his adaptation of the Yiddish theater classic *A Dybbuk,* in the Nazi Party's seizure of power in 1930s Germany in *A Bright Room Called Day,* in the American Deep South of the 1960s in *Caroline, or Change,* in the collapse of the Soviet Union in *Slavs!,* and in the struggles for survival in the decaying American infrastructures of the late twentieth century in *Grim(m).*

Kushner's seemingly inexhaustible imagination, informed and fueled by a breathtakingly wide range of literary, cultural, historical, and religious sources, establishes his uniqueness within the traditions of U.S. drama. He is perhaps more successful than any of his predecessors or contemporaries in melding together an aesthetic drawn from aspects of postnaturalistic European theater, with elements of the traditions of America's lyrical dramatic realism. Influences from literature, art, and thought of the ancient world on through to the Renaissance blend together in Kushner's work, along with socialist politics inspired by Karl Marx and Leon Trotsky. In literary and dramatic terms, these political influences derive from Kushner's reading of Walter Benjamin and Brecht, his most important dramatic inspiration. Kushner's study of the great religions, from Christianity and Judaism (his own faith) to a variety of eastern religions, mingles with his love of a broad range of modern and postmodern literary influences including writers from the classical realm to nineteenth-century German classicism: poets ranging from Rilke to Stanley Kunitz; French Renaissance to Yiddish theater; modern dramatists from Brecht, O'Neill, and Williams to such contemporaries as John Guare, Richard Foreman, Maria Irene Fornes, Charles Ludlam, Robert Patrick, Harvey Fierstein, Larry Kramer, Terrence McNally, Suzan-Lori Parks, Paula Vogel, Connie Congdon, Mac Wellman, Ellen McLaughlin, Holly Hughes, David Greenspan, and their British counterparts like Edward Bond, Caryl Churchill, David Edgar, Howard Brenton, and David Hare, among others—all of whom Kushner refers to as part of "a kind of a weird little sort of tarnished golden age" (Vorlicky 210) of late-twentieth-century drama. From Williams to Hare, modern playwrights have attempted to find expressive ways to bring the fantasies and images of the historical past together with the real or imagined earlier lives of their characters, but few have done it with the dramatic potency, humor, and scope Kushner brings to the task.

An understanding of Kushner's political beliefs is essential to fully understanding his drama, as his socialist politics are never far from the surface. Although most critics and audiences think of Kushner almost solely as a "gay dramatist," it is truly the case that he is a "political dramatist" who happens to be gay. Kushner calls for a new brand of socialism that might better be labeled progressivism, a politics that he has called a "socialism of the skin," and one that honors the values and traditions of the past without a slavish adherence to belief systems whose traditions have excluded or oppressed diversity in culture, sexual orientation, and politics. For Kushner, socialism is about beginning to struggle in a really, really powerful way with why economic justice and equality are so incredibly uncomfortable for us, and why we still define our worth by how much money we individually can make at the expense of other people, and why we find sharing and collective enterprise and motivations that are not competitive so phenomenally difficult. It's a tremendously difficult struggle that one has to undertake. It has to do with unlearning privilege; it has to do with examining what sort of events and activities make you feel worthwhile as a human being. But I really believe that the world is doomed unless we can re-create ourselves as social beings as opposed to little ego-anarchists.

(Vorlicky 70)

Kushner insists that unshakable dogmas of any variety are dangerous and that viewing the world solely in rational ways is potentially catastrophic. Rather, he believes it is through the unspoken, the unseen, and a faith in the hard progress built of compassion and humanism that society can proceed most effectively into the unknowable future. Imagination is the true source of revelation for Kushner, particularly an imagination informed by an exposure to the workings of history, and the ways in which history has been understood, distorted, and manipulated over the centuries. Kushner engages with history, reevaluates its evidence and its ruins, its theories and its dictums, and its human toll, with the aim of illuminating those overlooked and misunderstood elements which might offer a valuable lesson for moving forward. Kushner is convinced that

the only politics that can survive an encounter with this world, and still speak convincingly of freedom and justice and democracy, is a politics that can encompass both the harmonics and the dissonance. The frazzle, the rubbed raw, the unresolved, the fragile and the fiery and the dangerous.

(***Thinking About the Longstanding Problems of Virtue and Happiness*** 10-11)

As an American playwright, Kushner's overt political voice makes him a nearly unique figure. Few contemporary dramatists in the United States, whatever their personal politics, examine political issues, theories, and historical figures as Kushner does, although collectives like the San Francisco Mime Troupe and the Bread and Puppet Theater offer interesting parallels to Kushner (whose own early experiences as a director and writer were in collective-style theater groups).

Contemporary British writers Caryl Churchill and David Hare attempt, in their different ways, to mount a similar assault on the collisions of history and politics with the personal and, as such, are obvious contemporaries of Kushner, although both British writers work on a smaller dramatic canvas. And despite the fact that there is little similarity in the theatrical styles employed, the

work of Nobel Prize-winning playwright and commedia dell'arte-inspired actor Dario Fo is connected to Kushner in that both draw their themes from left-wing politics and both have chosen, in their highly individual ways, to provide a voice for the oppressed and marginalized. Like Fo, Kushner tends toward inclusiveness in both his personal politics and in his art, and this extends even into the ways in which he makes plays. Kushner's plays borrow aspects of expressionism, Brechtian epic theater, realism/naturalism, fantasy, poetic drama, a rich brand of popular culture theatricalism, and a historical, linguistic, and universal thematic scope belonging more to classical and Renaissance dramatic traditions than to much of the theater of the twentieth century.

Much has been written about the importance of Brecht to Kushner's work: Kushner himself has frequently acknowledged the significance of Brecht to his evolution as a writer and theater artist. Reading Brecht's theories and plays "was a kind of revelation to me" (Weber 68), he recalls, and offered the first evidence that led him to believe

that people who are seriously committed political intellectuals could have a home in the theater, the first time I believed that theater, really good theater, had the potential for radical intervention, for effectual analysis. The things that were exciting me about Marx, specifically dialectics, I discovered in Brecht, in a wonderful witty and provocative form. I became very, very excited about doing theater as a result of reading Brecht.

(Weber 68)

As he began to write plays himself in the early 1980s, Kushner was profoundly influenced by Brecht's techniques, as well as the content of his plays. It might reasonably be expected that Kushner would be viewed as a logical heir to those few American dramatists with a political identity (Clifford Odets, Arthur Miller), but Kushner seems instead to descend directly from Ibsen, Shaw, and especially Brecht, believing deeply that "all theater is political" (Blanchard 42).

Kushner's political awakening had begun during his college days after reading Ernst Fischer's *The Necessity of Art. A Marxist Approach,* as well as the writings of Walter Benjamin, especially *Understanding Brecht.* From these writings, and from Brecht's plays themselves, Kushner gained a sense of the social responsibility of the artist. However, Kushner's initial response to Fischer was "incredibly angry, because I thought it was Stalinist and dangerous" (Vorlicky 247). Fischer, an Austrian who joined the Communist Party in 1934, was once described by Kenneth Tynan as the Aristotle of Marxism, and in *The Necessity of Art* he explores not only the nature of art, but the reasons it is needed by society. Fischer seems to be describing the impact of *Angels* while setting out Kushner's raison d'être when he writes:

In the alienated world in which we live, social reality must be presented in an arresting way, in a new light, through the "alienation" of the subject and the characters. The work of art must grip the audience not through passive identification but through an appeal to reason which demands action and decision.

(Fischer 10)

Fischer points out that even "a great didactic artist like Brecht does not act purely through reason and argument, but also through feeling and suggestion," with the goal of *"enlightening and stimulating action"* (Fischer 14). Kushner has obviously drawn on Fischer's concept of art and its purposes, and on Benjamin's conception of history. Kushner explains that his initial anger in response to Fischer's ideas led him to look at other works about art and Marxism, a choice that led him directly to Brecht and Benjamin. Widely regarded as the outstanding German literary critic of the twentieth century, Benjamin was described by Hannah Arendt as "the most peculiar Marxist" of his time, "whose spiritual existence had been formed and informed by Goethe," but who found in Brecht "a poet of rare intellectual powers and, almost as important for him at the time, someone on the Left who, despite all talk about dialectics, was no more of a dialectical thinker than he was, but whose intelligence was uncommonly close to reality" (Benjamin 11-15). Kushner shares these characteristics with Benjamin, and in Benjamin's essay, "Theses on the Philosophy of History," Kushner finds some grounding for his approach to historical drama. As Benjamin writes:

There is no document of civilization which is not at the same time a document of barbarism. And just as such a document is not free of barbarism, barbarism taints also the manner in which it was transmitted from one owner to another. A historical materialist therefore dissociates himself from it as far as possible. He regards it as his task to brush history against the grain.

(256-57)

This brushing against the grain of history is a guiding notion in those instances in which Kushner dramatizes actual events and characters, from the life and death of seventeenth-century writer and physician Sir Thomas Browne in *Hydriotaphia* to mid-twentieth-century political operative and ultraconservative lawyer Roy Cohn in *Angels.* It is perhaps too simple to suggest that Kushner's drama provides an alternative history—certainly with Cohn, his depiction seems not to depart very far from the realities of Cohn's life even as he fictionalizes specific events. Instead, Kushner probes into the unexplored corners of the historical figure and situation. He skews the angle of the life to crisis moments (the day of Browne's death or the moment at which Cohn learns that he has AIDS) and from this tilt, fresh visions of the history spill out.

Kushner—who for a time considered a career as a teacher of the literature and history of the Middle Ages—shares Benjamin's belief that history (social, political, and personal) teaches profound lessons and he understands that the concepts of apocalypse and the afterlife are fraught with the same struggles, confusions, and pain encountered in real life. Kushner is inspired by Benjamin's assertion that, as he describes it, one is "constantly looking back at the rubble of history. The most dangerous thing is to become set upon some notion of the future that isn't rooted in the bleakest, most terrifying idea of what's piled up behind you" (Savran 300). While Kushner looks to the past to help frame eternal questions about existence, he does not propose to simply recommit to old values. For Kushner, American society is in an age of intellectual stagnation and profound political and social crisis, but he views the greatest threats as internal—a moral emptiness stemming from what he views as a fundamental abandonment of commitment to justice, compassion, love, and mercy that is a requirement for moral survival in his universe.

There is little doubt that ideas from Benjamin's *Understanding Brecht* and other essays on art, theater and film, and literature permeate Kushner's work as a dramatist. "Theses on the Philosophy of History" not only provides central imagery for *Angels,* but it, along with Brecht's writings, illuminates all of Kushner's plays thus far. Kushner has also spoken of feeling intimidated by Brecht's dramatic achievement, that if he could not write a play equal to *Mother Courage and Her Children,* he did not want to write at all. However, while reading Shakespeare and Brecht at the same time, he found a dialectical method in the structure of the historical plays of these two vastly different dramatists and strove, at the beginning of his playwriting career, to emulate the lyricism and scope of Shakespeare while, at the same time, drawing on the epic qualities of Brecht. Even as a graduate student, Kushner wrote a couple of things that were heavily influenced by Brecht. Seeking an image of a politicized artist who successfully merged art and politics, Kushner found that Brecht offered "a really brilliant marriage of Marxist theory as theater practice" (Vorlicky 248). Brecht, who believed that "if we want a truly popular literature [and here, in regard to Kushner, one might interject theater], alive and fighting, completely gripped by reality and completely gripping reality, then we must keep pace with reality's headlong development" (Brecht 112), seems to imagine a Kushner carrying a Marx-inspired battle against oppression into the future.

Kushner's Brechtian style took fuller shape in his first two important plays, *A Bright Room Called Day* and *Hydriotaphia,* and flowered fully in *Angels* and in his own adaptation of Brecht's *The Good Person of Setzuan.* Kushner, however, has adapted Brecht's methods to suit his own particular voice, embellishing the method with his own devices. Kushner's major plays adopt a structure that is at once both cinematic (he has said that Robert Altman's 1974 epic film *Nashville* provided structural ideas for *Angels*) and Brechtian, but he couples the alienation techniques of Brecht with a fully realized emotional and personal strain drawn more from American lyrical realism than from Brecht (whose character's emotional struggles are often downplayed in his effort to keep the audience focused on the issues). These techniques combine with an often outrageous sense of humor (again, far bolder than the typical dry Brechtian ironies, owing much to Kushner's queering of his subjects), and a phantasmagoric theatricality (extending well beyond anything Brecht contemplated) to offer a completely original brand of American political theater. Much of this originality is already evident in Kushner's earliest plays, but it comes to full fruition between the writing of his first important play, the overtly Brechtian *A Bright Room Called Day,* and his masterfully original *Angels.*

As previously noted, the political dramatist is a comparative rarity in the American theater. Kushner's predecessors with political aims, including Odets and Miller, seem to have had little direct influence on Kushner, although he directed a production of Odets's *Golden Boy* at the Repertory Theatre of St. Louis in 1986. The profound influence of European politics, literature, and theater on Kushner is important, but he is, despite this, a quintessentially American figure. The stunning ambition (and length) of Kushner's plays calls to mind Eugene O'Neill, a dramatist whose life and work "excited and impressed" him, and, to a lesser extent, Wilder, but Kushner is closer in spirit to Tennessee Williams, "all-in-all my favorite playwright and probably all-in-all our greatest playwright" (Vorlicky 235).

Kushner also acknowledges some debt to contemporary gay dramatists like Larry Kramer and Harvey Fierstein, but they are less significant to Kushner's development as a dramatist than Williams. There are obvious similarities between Williams and Kushner in the lyricism of both writers and in the sexual identities that inform their work. Perhaps more significantly, Kushner and Williams present views of a changing sociopolitical environment—their characters are generally caught between two worlds: one that is dying and one that is being born. The friction of such transitions—and the attempt to survive in the confusing netherworld created by them—amplifies the emotions and struggles of their characters.

Of his predecessor, Kushner has said, "I've always loved Williams. The first time I read *Streetcar,* I was annihilated. I read as much Williams as I could get my hands on until the late plays started getting embarrassingly bad. . . . I'm really influenced by Williams" (Savran 297). Kushner is also drawn to the seriocomic plays of John Guare, who, like Williams, "has figured

out a way for Americans to do a kind of stage poetry. He's discovered a lyrical voice that doesn't sound horrendously twee and forced and phony" (Savran 297). Kushner aims for a similar sort of lyricism in *Angels,* both in language and in theme, weaving a tapestry of the crushing human and spiritual issues of the Reagan era—and beyond—with poignance (in the Williams and Guare senses) and epic stature (in both the differing O'Neillian and Brechtian senses). Kushner's less familiar but no less effective other plays, both full-length and one-act, are similar to *Angels* in this regard. Williams's passion for illusion, in his appreciation of the fragility of beauty and in the profound heartbreak of his most memorable characters, is certainly evident in Kushner's work. Prior Walter (who gets his name from Walter Benjamin) of *Angels* is a logical heir to Williams's delicate souls and Kushner, who gives Prior a famous Williams line to repeat in *Perestroika,* the second of the *Angels* plays, makes certain that the connection will not be missed—even if Prior turns out, despite his gentleness, to be a survivor, while Williams's Blanche DuBois cannot cope. The influence of Williams on Kushner could hardly be overlooked in the illusory and lyrical aspects of Kushner's work, as critic John Lahr writes:

> Not since Williams has a playwright announced his poetic vision with such authority on the Broadway stage. Kushner is the heir apparent to Williams' romantic theatrical heritage: he, too, has tricks in his pocket and things up his sleeve, and he gives the audience "truth in the pleasant disguise of illusion." And, also like Williams, Kushner has forged an original, impressionistic theatrical vocabulary to show us the heart of a new age.
>
> ("Earth Angels" 133)

An important connection between Kushner and Williams also lies in their homosexuality. Williams, who was guardedly open about his sexuality from the 1960s until his death, and featured gay characters in his drama from nearly the beginning of his playwriting career, could not be as "out" as Kushner can be. Still, a gay sensibility fuels the work of both writers. One of the great ironies of the success of *Angels* (and, for that matter, the plays of Williams) has been the enormous mainstream audience that has embraced it despite the fact that its politics, moral universe, and sexuality are, at least as measured by many of those elected to public office in the United States, incompatible with the beliefs of American society. It is perhaps in this irony that some of the questions that both Williams and Kushner explore meet: "What is the relationship between sexuality and power? Is sexuality merely an expression of power? Is there even such a thing as 'sexuality'?" (Savran 308).

As is true for Williams, not all—or even most—of Kushner's plays are *about* homosexuality. Even *Angels,* a play widely regarded as a milestone in gay drama—

and in the movement for gay rights and the war against AIDS—is not simply a gay play. It is about many facets of American life, of which sexuality and homophobia are traditionally, and certainly currently, divisive issues. Gay characters are usually present in Kushner's other plays, but often in secondary roles. However, regardless of the significance of a given character, sexuality informs Kushner's work, much as it does Williams's. If Williams can be said to sexualize American drama, Kushner queers it and the historical events he examines.

Kushner came of age in an era of dizzying changes in the American cultural landscape. Following some abortive efforts to find a "cure" for his sexual orientation, Kushner came to terms with his homosexuality and was inspired by gay activist writers and artists like Williams, and, even more so by those emerging from the Stonewall generation and after. Kushner's identity as a gay man not only led to the dramatic work for which he is most known, but has permeated all of his dramatic work and an increasing commitment to social activism, from a variety of leftist political issues to gay rights and AIDS to the role of controversial art in a society. Kushner was especially inspired by such gay rights organizations as ACT UP and Queer Nation, whose chant "We're here, we're queer, we're fabulous" pervades his drama, especially *Angels.* The social and political battles of the last four decades of the twentieth century are as important to understanding Kushner as are his literary and theatrical influences.

Kushner's reverence for great dramatic works of the past, many of which examine questions of religious faith in conflict with social reality, the complexities of politics, and the meeting of past and present, is important. As a gay man, Kushner also acknowledges some debt to pioneering gay dramatists Robert Patrick, Kramer, and Fierstein, as well as their logical predecessor, Williams, who dealt more frankly with this topic in later dramas—*Cat on a Hot Tin Roof* (1955), *Suddenly Last Summer* (1958), *Small Craft Warnings* (1972), *Something Cloudy, Something Clear* (1981), and *The Notebook of Trigorin* (1981). Williams paved the way for other gay dramatists to delve into gender matters with greater purpose, as with the outrageous camp sensibilities of Charles Ludlam and Charles Busch or in the politicized dramas of Kramer—and, ultimately, Kushner's plays. Kushner recognizes that Williams, with lyricism and compassion, brought sexuality out of the American theatrical closet.

Kushner's political activism is of central importance to an understanding of his work. It is also important to appreciate that he is both unmistakably American and strongly connected to his Eastern European roots and its cultural masterworks. As a Jew, Kushner is part of an ethnic heritage that has experienced harrowing losses—and has survived. He identifies parallels between the Jewish experience and what gays have contended with in American society. Kushner struggles with an ambivalence toward Judaism due to homophobic traditions within his faith. However, for him, the connections between Jews and homosexuals are most important in that he believes both groups have a shared a history of "oppression and persecution" that offers "a sort of false possibility of a kind of an assimilation" (Vorlicky 278). Kushner insists that "as Hannah Arendt says, it's better to be a pariah than a parvenu. If you're hated by a social order, don't try and make friends with it. Identify yourself as other, and identify your determining characteristics as those characteristics which make you other and unliked and despised" (Vorlicky 218).

Kushner began his dramatic career in earnest as the terrifying devastation of AIDS became all too clear, and it is against this background that Kushner emerged as a playwright and director. However, to see Kushner solely as a gay dramatist—either in *Angels* or Kushner's "queering" of history in other works—is far too limiting for a writer whose work is diverse in its subjects and characters. Other influences on him are at least as significant. Some of these can be seen in *Angels,* but they come into sharper relief in his lesser-known works written and produced both before and after the *Angels* phenomenon.

There is a sense of classical fatality in Kushner's plays, but there is also an unmistakable Ibsenite element—the idea that humanity may be proceeding on the wrong moral road and that the souls of the past and future will exact retribution. Kushner believes that tragedy—both real and fictional—teaches and changes people, a sentiment he shares with many modern dramatists and, in America, especially with the generation of post-World War II playwrights. American dramatists also supplied Kushner with a strong sense of the personal in drama. In bringing his own autobiography on to the stage, Kushner emphasizes that life is loss: "You can't conquer loss. You lose. To suggest otherwise would be to suggest a fantasy. . . . Life is about losing. Things are taken from you. People are taken from you. You just have to face it" (Pacheco 17). As a gay man, a Jew, and a political leftist, Kushner strives to express a capacity for forgiveness in the human spirit, but adds that the losses suffered by the groups of which he is a part make a forgiving spirit difficult. As he says, "Loss and forgiveness go hand in hand, and it's tricky" (Vorlicky 63).

If Williams provides Kushner with a powerful model of a dramatist struggling with issues of loss and forgiveness, other American dramatists offer different sorts of inspiration. Miller's plays share the Ibsenite moral quandaries, but Kushner professes not to admire much of Miller's drama except, grudgingly, the raw force of *Death of a Salesman,* despite his feeling that it is "melodramatic, and it has that awful, fifties kind of Herman Wouk-ish sexual morality that's disgusting and irritating" (Savran 296). However, at least on one level Kushner shares some thematic turf with Miller in questioning America's embracing of commerce—the relentless selling of a product, an image, or an idea as the measure of success—and that, for better or worse, this has been, and will likely continue to be, the driving aspect of the American national persona.

Like *Death of a Salesman* and its contemporary counterparts in David Mamet's *American Buffalo* and *Glengarry Glen Ross*, *Angels* sees the selling of America more in terms of a selling out—of the abandonment of principle, of the loss of compassion for the less fortunate, of a failure to believe in the fundamental connectedness of all members of humanity, despite the vast racial, ethnic, religious, and cultural diversity. Miller and Mamet both focus on the white heterosexual male as the center of society, while Kushner reflects the ever-changing American demographic, expanding it to include the full spectrum of American society. Miller's drama was born out of the crucible of the social struggles of the turbulent 1930s, an era in which America came closest to a socialist society and, as such, an era of significance to Kushner. However, Kushner's own formative era coincided with the turbulent late 1960s and early 1970s. The internalized moral battles of Miller's age, which exploded in the early 1950s during the witch hunts of the House Un-American Activities Committee, surely seem too constricting—even too narrow—for Kushner, an artist inspired to examine diverse issues on a broader and bolder level.

Angels, of course, provided Kushner with numerous awards and a fame usually unavailable to working American dramatists during the last half of the twentieth century. It also made him a leading spokesperson for gay rights and leftist politics in a contentious era for both. *Angels*, which has elicited both enthusiasm and controversy in productions around the world, is, at the very least, a defiant indictment of the hypocrisy of the American moral compass. Regarding politics, it is ironic that Kushner is perhaps the best-known dramatist of his generation in the United States as the result of representing viewpoints seemingly incompatible with a post-Reagan neoconservative age. Understanding Kushner's dramatic output, his conceptions of stage technique, his views of politics, religion, sexuality, and much else, may offer some insights into not only the drama of the past century, but also into the complex contradictions of American life at the dawn of a new millennium.

Much about Kushner's theatrical achievement, as well as his social and political beliefs, can be found in *Angels*. However, despite its remarkable impact, *Angels* is only a part of the rich and impressively diverse

dramatic output of a still youthful playwright. The twentieth-century American theater has produced only a few plays equal to *Angels*: *Long Day's Journey into Night*, *Our Town*, *A Streetcar Named Desire*, *Death of a Salesman*, *A Raisin in the Sun*, and *Who's Afraid of Virginia Woolf?* It is perhaps too soon to imagine Kushner's ultimate influence on American drama—and society—for at least a couple of reasons. Certainly, there is much more to come from his pen. More significantly, American theater at the dawn of the twenty-first century seems to be moving in several different directions at once. While it is obvious that Kushner provides a boldly epic, highly theatrical, politically engaged, and richly emotive model as a true alternative to the minimalist, densely constructed, and small-scale plays of such other leading contemporary dramatists as Albee, Mamet, McNally, and Sam Shepard, there is little doubt that Kushner has been a revitalizing force in American drama during the last decade of the twentieth century. His influence on the development of the American theater may ultimately equal that of O'Neill or Williams. His drama daringly mixes fantasy and reality—as well as tragedy and comedy—to blend together elements of the past, present, and future of the world of his play, the lives of his characters, and the society in which he lives.

The Theater of Tony Kushner: Living Past Hope is the first study to examine Kushner's entire dramatic output thus far. The phenomenon of *Angels*, while catapulting Kushner to prominence, has, at times, somewhat obscured the rest of his work as a dramatist (in both the full-length and one-act forms), adaptor, screenwriter, and librettist. His plays, produced and unproduced, offer a more staggering range of themes and characters than even the titanic *Angels* can encompass. In his own plays and his free adaptations, Kushner examines the nature of love as understood through the prisms of diverse cultures from seventeenth-century France to the shtetls of Eastern Europe, the rise of capitalism at the dawn of the industrial age, issues of spirituality and religion, the moral dilemmas of the Holocaust, the collapse of the Soviet Union, environmental catastrophe, psychoanalysis, grassroots tax revolt, the experience of immigrants coming to the United States, the struggles of gays within a homophobic society, the nature of art, and the meanings of death and the afterlife.

This book will examine all of these plays in an attempt to shed some light on the techniques and themes of Kushner's work and his place in millennial American and international drama. In exploring the profound moral, social, religious, and political questions that will shape the future of the United States in the world community, Kushner's ambitious output extends well beyond the impressive *Angels*. Single chapters are devoted to each of his produced full-length plays (*A Bright Room Called Day, Hydriotaphia, or The Death of Dr. Browne, Angels in America,* and *Slavs! Thinking About the Longstanding Problems of Virtue and Happiness*). Other chapters will examine a number of his one-act plays and his numerous adaptations including *The Illusion* (from Pierre Corneille's *L'Illusion comique*), *Stella* (from Goethe's play), *St. Cecilia, or The Power of Music* (adapted from a story by Heinrich von Kleist), *A Dybbuk* (from S. Ansky's Yiddish theater classic, *The Dybbuk*), Brecht's *The Good Person of Set-zuan,* and *Widows,* adapted in collaboration with Chilean novelist and political activist Ariel Dorfman. Kushner has also completed a number of unpublished and/or unproduced works that will be examined in this study, including the opera libretto *Caroline, or Change,* the screenplay *Grim(m),* and a number of works-in-progress, including a three-play cycle on economic history, the first play of which, *Henry Box Brown, or The Mirror of Slavery,* is expected to debut at the Royal National Theatre of Great Britain. Attention will also be paid to Kushner's essays, poetry, and political activism.

The Theater of Tony Kushner: Living Past Hope draws its subtitle from part of a speech spoken by Prior Walter in *Perestroika,* the second of the *Angels* plays: "We live past hope" (136). This line, more than any other in Kushner's oeuvre, captures the intent of his drama: a belief that despite centuries of historical and personal tragedy, we must progressively face the inevitabilities of a future we cannot know while, at the same time, learning from an often tragic and destructive past we know only too well. Belief in progress, in compassion, in the transformative power of love, in true community is the religion Kushner offers for the new millennium.

THE GREAT WORK BEGINS: A SHORT BIOGRAPHY

Tony Kushner is drunk on ideas, on language, on the possibility of changing the world. His talent and his heart are incendiary, combustible, explosive, heartbreakingly vital and on-target.

—Larry Kramer (Roca 32)

Tony Kushner was born in New York City on July 16, 1956, the second of three children of William and Sylvia (Deutscher) Kushner, both classically trained musicians who encouraged their son's interests in art and literature (they even named him after popular singer Tony Bennett as an added encouragement). From his parents, "New York-New Deal liberals transplanted to the Deep South," he inherited "a healthy appetite for politics, for history, for political theory," a hunger they, in turn, inherited from their parents, "all of us indebted to the insatiable curiosity, skepticism, pessimistic optimism, ethical engagement, and ardent pursuit of the millennium that is, for me, the most valuable heritage of nearly two thousand years of Diasporan Judaic culture" (**"Notes about Political Theatre"** 20).

Kushner spent most of his childhood in Lake Charles, Louisiana ("No one asked me if I wanted to go," Kushner jokes [Szentgyorgyi 18]), where his mother, a professional bassoonist, "one of the first American women to hold a principal chair in a major orchestra (the New York City Opera orchestra at the age of eighteen)" (**"Notes about Political Theatre"** 19), and an amateur actress, frequently performed in local plays, including *Death of a Salesman, The Diary of Anne Frank,* and *A Far Country.* It was in Louisiana, in "the culture of 'genteel' post-integration bayou-county racism" (*Thinking About the Longstanding Problems of Virtue and Happiness* 50), that Kushner became entranced by the emotional power of the theater and the arts in general—he would return to this setting for a semiautobiographical libretto, *Caroline, or Change,* and other of his works include similarly autobiographical strains most touchingly demonstrated in the sad bassoon music he employs in some in honor of his mother's memory. The stage, a place of "hysterical and historical conversion" ("Notes About Political Theatre" 20), provided an appealing world for a child who knew, even at an early age, that he was different: "I grew up very, very closeted, and I'm sure that the disguise of theater, the doubleness, and all that slightly tawdry stuff interested me" (Savran 293). As a child, he also acted occasionally in plays himself, but resisted the off-stage gay life of the theater which frightened him, becoming instead a high school debater because, "I had decided at a very early age that I would become heterosexual" (Savran 293). This painful struggle with his true self continued into Kushner's twenties.

Kushner moved to New York in 1974 to begin his college education at Columbia University, where he completed a Bachelor of Arts degree in English Literature in 1978. During his time at Columbia, he immersed himself in the New York theater scene, taking in as many Broadway shows as possible, as well as more experimental works by Spalding Gray, Lee Breuer, JoAnne Akalaitis, and especially Richard Schechner's production of *Mother Courage and Her Children* ("which I still think is the greatest play ever written") and Richard Foreman's staging of *The Threepenny Opera* ("which I saw about ninety-five times and which is one of my great theater experiences" [Savran 294]). Kushner's taste in theater began to mature, as did his "fairly standard liberal politics" (Savran 294) influenced by faculty and fellow students at Columbia, but more importantly through his growing interest in Brecht. He read Brecht's dramatic works, as well as his seminal essay, "A Short Organum for the Theater," along with Marx, Arnold Hauser, and Benjamin's *Understanding Brecht.* He was also drawn into study of medieval literature, including *Beowulf,* finding the "magic and the darkness of it very appealing" to his "fantastical, spiritual side" (Savran 295). His study of the classics included the Greeks and he found himself moved to realize that ancient plays by Aeschylus or Euripides did not seem at all primitive. Although he claims not to believe in fundamental universal truths, he discovered in reading ancient and medieval works that "there are certain human concerns" (Savran 295) that have always been part of the human experience.

In this period, Kushner grappled intensely with his sexual orientation, seeking therapy to find a so-called cure for his homosexuality, before facing it in various ways. One involved calling his mother from a New York City phone booth in September 1981 to tell her that he was gay, a scene he would powerfully recreate in *Angels*. In experiences recognized by many homosexuals, Kushner found himself struggling with his father's initial disapproval, though their battles eventually subsided as the senior Kushner accepted his son's orientation. Kushner himself came to embrace his sexuality and, as a dramatist, especially in the wake of *Angels,* became a prominent activist in the movement for gay and lesbian rights.

Following the completion of his degree at Columbia, Kushner worked as a switchboard operator at the United Nations Plaza Hotel beginning in 1979. During this period, he also directed small-scale theater productions of very big plays, ranging from stagings of Shakespeare's *The Tempest* and *A Midsummer Night's Dream* to Brecht's *The Baden-Baden Play for Learning*. Accepted to New York University's Tisch School of the Arts to pursue a Master of Fine Arts degree in directing, Kushner staged a short Brecht play as his audition for entrance into the program. At Tisch, he was trained under the guidance of Brecht specialist Carl Weber and aspired to follow the paths of such forerunning theatrical artists as Richard Foreman, Joanne Akalaitis, and Liz LeCompte, whose productions he found exceptional.

Kushner continued to work the switchboard to pay the rent, but in the summers he also worked at a school for gifted children in Louisiana, writing plays for them to perform and others which he produced with his fellow students at Tisch prior to completing his degree in directing in 1984. Some of these plays were also staged by the Imaginary Theatre Company at the Repertory Theatre of St. Louis and elsewhere. Kushner's plays from this period, beginning around 1982, demonstrate the breadth and virtuosity of his later playwriting, including a range of genres and styles, including an opera (*La Fin de la Baleine: An Opera for the Apocalypse* [1982]), some childrens' theater plays (*Historiomax* [1985], *Yes Yes No No* [1985], *The Protozoa Review* [1985], *The Heavenly Theatre: Hymns for Martyred Actors* [1985], *In Great Eliza's Golden Time* [1986]), one-act and full-length plays (*The Age of Assassins* [1986], *Last Gasp at the Cataract* [1986], and *Hydriotaphia, or The Death of Dr. Browne* [1987]), and an adaptation (Goethe's *Stella* [1987]). They also demonstrate elements of his later works in their lyricism, thematic sweep, and bold theatricality. For example, one of his earliest works, the 1982 *La Fin de la Baleine: An Opera for the Apocalypse* (translated from the French, the title means *The End of the Whale*), a theater-dance piece, features a scene in which a woman with a tuba dances on point while spouting water from her mouth. Imagination, ambition, and political commitment were Kushner's most evident traits as a beginning dramatist.

GRIEF PUSHES OUTWARD: *YES YES NO NO*

> It might be argued that, perhaps,
> Civilization would collapse
> Without us feeling that we had
> Collectively done something bad.
>
> —Actor 1, *Yes Yes No No* (5.19)

An especially illuminating example of Kushner's early works is his children's play, *Yes Yes No No* (subtitled *The Solace of Solstice Apogee/Perigee Bestial/Celestial Holiday Show*), which demonstrates that even within the often debased form of children's theater, and even at the beginning of his work as a dramatist, Kushner's imaginative poetic gifts and thematic ambition are present and, to a great extent, fully formed. Directed and designed by Kushner for the Repertory Theatre of St. Louis's Imaginary Theatre Company, and performed in shopping malls and hospitals from December 2-21, 1985 (with a brief December 23-27, 1985 run on the Rep's main stage), *Yes Yes No No* features a cast of four women, played in the original production by Kari Eli, Maggie Lerian, Lisa Raziq, and Jeanne Trevor. The roles can also be played by an all-male cast merely by changing a few pronouns in the text, but in either case cast members each play numerous roles.

Set during the winter solstice (at "various places around the universe" [stage directions]), *Yes Yes No No* announces that it is no ordinary children's play as its prologue establishes a seriocomic tone, an actor-centered technique, and explores themes no less significant than the creation of the universe and the meaning of good and evil. Beginning with a typically Kushnerian question, a tape-recorded voice (God?) asks, "Is it not wonder?" (Prologue. 1), as actors, playing shepherds and angels, ruminate on the beauty of the winter environment and remark that they are looking on

> The Face
> Of God, the Face
> Of Heaven, miracle face
> Of angels announcing in a language of Awe
> To a cold frightened hilltop
> Open vowels of . . .
>
> (Prologue. 1)

At which point they are interrupted by a chorus of sheep "ooh-ooh"-ing "The First Noel." This abrupt mixture of the portentous and the comic is a Kushner trademark that, along with his characteristically poetic language, is in ample evidence in this imaginative trip through religious myth and science. In the play's first part, God and Space converse about the creation of the first atom, and God has an idea:

> It will be VERY small.
> It will be VERY light.
> It will be HARD TO SEE
> And HARD TO TOUCH.
> It will not be much but
> It will be Something.
>
> (1.4)

Space thanks God for the atom's creation, noting that

> This could be the start
> Of Something b-b-b-
> Big.
>
> (1.5)

In part 2, the actors reflect on the multiplication of atoms and gases fusing to create the universe, with Kushner implanting a little political theory, as when all four actors proclaim

> From grains of sand to giant stars all things share one condition. The world we see would never be except for OPPOSITION.
>
> (2.8)

The complications of the making of the universe—and the existence of the human lives created ("Life is confusing" [3.8])—reveal, to some extent, Kushner's own childhood confusions and struggles, as in some counterpoint speeches in part 3:

> Sometimes, when I am
> sad, I can't remember what
> it's like to be happy, and I
> think I'll never be happy
> again.
>
> (3.9)

> Sometimes when I am
> happy, I can't remember what
> it's like to be sad, and I
> think I'll never be sad again.
>
> (3.10)

Part 4 explores the "contrariness" inherent in existence, as the angels, who are "very very nice," share a feast at the Table of Elements with the devils, who "live in Hell" (4.13). When a devil and an angel get into a fight, the angel's wings are broken off. God intervenes with a way of reinventing this damaged angelic being:

> I
> Have an idea.
> I will name it
> Something new.

> I will call it
> Human.
>
> (4.14-15)

The devil, feeling guilty, wants to know how he might atone for his sin, but begs the Human not to take his "badness" which "is all I have" (4.15), so the Human instead takes his guilt:

> While the angel, who was now
> A human being, was left
> Feeling guilty,
> And so became more human
> Than before.
>
> (4.16)

In part 5, Kushner examines the nature of guilt and its relation to human affairs ("Even the President feels guilty" [5.17]), which allows his young audience to experience the ways they feel when mistakes and their differences cause disturbance. Responses to guilt, apologizing, praying, talking to an analyst, singing, and eating are tested and found wanting, so Kushner proposes that it is possible that civilization might end without a collective human feeling of guilt. Even Santa Claus, it is revealed, feels guilty sometimes. One of the actors tells a tale in which a group of Santas give up their joyful dancing in the snow because they are too fat. Feeling greatly depressed:

> They all ate like little piggies
> Faster than they could digest.
> Ate the puddings, pears and figgies;
> Then they didn't feel depressed!
>
> (5.20)

At least not for the moment, until they are overwhelmed by feelings of despair much worse than what they felt before: "Why won't it ever let me be?" (5.21). Part 6 explores the meaning of despair, as Devil-Tempters play on human guilt, with the result that their souls are "slamming shut" (6.22) and

> Grief pushes outward
> And down to
> A dreamless deep slumber,
> Heavy and hollow
> And endlessly sad.
>
> (6.22)

For the final scene, the actors play "a BUSH, a PERSON, and two RAVENS" (6.23) crying at the coming of the sad, cold, and lonely winter. Person pricks his finger on a thorn from the Bush, leading all to marvel at the beauty of the "drop of red" (7.25) blood that, they imagine, is like the berries that come with springtime. They all feel better that "winter doesn't last forever" (7.25) and understand, as one of the actors explains in a final speech, that the spring is impossible without the winter:

Because this is a world that depends on FRICTION,
The Yes and the No and the CONTRADICTION.
The seed and the plant and the plant and the seed,
And is it not a wonder
Indeed?

(7.27)

Yes Yes No No was described by Don Shewey, who served on a panel selecting plays for an anthology of children's plays, as "the maddest piece of kid-lit I'd read since Ionesco's story for toddlers in which all the characters are named Jacqueline" (Shewey 32). Certainly few children's plays would attempt to deal, however lightheartedly and lyrically, with the issues in *Yes Yes No No.* Kushner typically takes his audience—even the young one this play is aimed at—into the depths of despair and pain from which he finds, through a belief in the wonder of existence, the essential spinning forward of progress and a hope earned through suffering and difficulty.

Yes Yes No No and Kushner's other early works explore themes and dramatic techniques that would remain evident, if more masterfully employed, in his plays through the end of the twentieth century. Beginning in the mid-1980s, Kushner's work, both as a director and a playwright, and as the artistic director of the Heat & Light Company, a political theater group, brought him awards and the support of several prestigious grants, including the Seidman Award in Directing from the New York University Tisch School of the Arts in 1983-84, a Directing Fellowship from the National Endowment for the Arts in 1985, the Princess Grace Award in 1986, a Playwriting Fellowship from the New York State Council for the Arts in 1987, and a Fellowship from the National Endowment for the Arts in 1988.

Kushner became assistant director of the St. Louis Repertory Theatre in 1985-86, and in 1987-88 he became artistic director of the New York Theatre Workshop. For NYTW he staged early versions of *A Bright Room Called Day* and his Goethe adaptation, *Stella,* and, that same year, directed the first version of his play, *Hydriotaphia, or The Death of Dr. Browne,* for the Home for Contemporary Theatre and Art in New York. Kushner also worked as Director of Literary Services for the Theatre Communications Group during 1989 and regularly taught at an array of universities, ultimately joining the permanent faculty of the Tisch School in 1996. However, Kushner's efforts as a director and teacher were superseded by his writing, adapting, and political activism in the late 1980s. Along with his own plays and adaptations, Kushner exercised his writing skills in a variety of ways, including contributing a narration to replace Paul Green's original text of *Johnny Johnson* to accompany Kurt Weill's music in a concert performance of the piece performed by Larry Kert on a program called *Voices of Change. American*

Music of Protest, Politics and Persuasion in September 1989. This breadth of activity suggests that in all aspects of his work—even from its beginnings—Kushner merged politics, literature, and music, as would be amply evident in all of his dramatic work.

In this period, Kushner lost his mother to cancer and he completed and produced his first important plays. It is at this point that *The Theater of Tony Kushner: Living Past Hope* begins, with the goal of serving as an introduction to Kushner's complete dramatic works to date and placing them beside the extraordinarily acclaimed *Angels.* Some of these works feature themes Kushner explored in *Angels,* while others move in different directions, both thematically and dramaturgically. Setting *Angels* within the context of Kushner's entire output as a working dramatic artist during an era of new energy, broader ethnic and gender diversity, and conspicuous theatricality on American stages will hopefully deepen understanding and appreciation of his dramatic journey to, as critic John Lahr describes it, "that most beautiful, divided, and unexplored country—the human heart" ("Angels on Broadway" 137).

Notes

0. Benjamin, Walter. *Illuminations. Essays and Reflections.* Edited and with an introduction by Hannah Arendt. Translated by Harry Zohn. New York: Schocken Books, 1968.

Blanchard, Bob. "Playwright of Pain and Hope," *Progressive,* vol. 58, October 1994, pp. 42-44.

Fischer, Ernst. *The Necessity of Art. A Marxist Approach.* Translated by Anna Bostock. New York: Penguin Books, 1963.

Kushner, Tony. *Angels in America. A Gay Fantasia on National Themes. Part Two: Perestroika.* New York: Theatre Communications Group, Inc., 1992, 1994.

———. "Notes about Political Theatre," *Kenyon Review,* vol. XIX, nos. 3/4, summer/fall 1997, pp. 19-34.

———. *Thinking About the Longstanding Problems of Virtue and Happiness, Essays, A Play, Two Poems and A Prayer.* New York: Theatre Communications Group, Inc., 1995.

———. "Yes Yes No No. The Solace of Solstice Apogee/Perigee Bestial/Celestial Holiday Show," in *Plays in Process. Three Plays for Young Audiences.* Vol. 7, no. 11. New York: Theatre Communications Group, 1987.

Lahr, John. "Angels on Broadway," *New Yorker,* May 23, 1993, p. 137.

———. "Earth Angels," *New Yorker,* December 13, 1993, pp. 129-33.

Pacheco, Patrick. "AIDS, Angels, Activism, and Sex in the Nineties," *Body Positive,* September 1993, pp. 17-28.

Roca, Octavio. "Kushner's Next Stage," *San Francisco Chronicle,* September 6, 1998, p. 32.

Savran, David. "Tony Kushner," in *Speaking on Stage. Interviews with Contemporary American Playwrights,* edited by Philip C. Kolin and Colby H. Kullman. Tuscaloosa: University of Alabama Press, 1996, pp. 291-313.

Shewey, Don. "Tony Kushner's Sexy Ethics," *Village Voice,* April 20, 1993, pp. 29-32, 36.

Szentgyorgyi, Tom. "Look Back—And Forward—In Anger," *Theater Week,* January 14-20, 1991, pp. 15-19.

Vorlicky, Robert, ed. *Tony Kushner in Conversation.* Ann Arbor: University of Michigan Press, 1998.

Weber, Carl. "I Always Go Back to Brecht," *Brecht Yearbook/Das Brecht-Jahrbuch,* vol. 25, 1995, pp. 67-88.

Peggy Phelan (review date March 2003)

SOURCE: Phelan, Peggy. Review of *Homebody/Kabul,* by Tony Kushner. *Theatre Journal* 55, no. 1 (March 2003): 166-68.

[*In the following review, Phelan compares productions of* Homebody/Kabul *staged in New York and in Berkeley, California. Phelan asserts that the first act of the play is stronger than the second act.*]

Tony Kushner's *Homebody/Kabul* was the winner of the Dramatists Guild Hull-Warriner award for best play of 2001. Kushner began writing *Homebody/Kabul* about three years before "Taliban," "Northern Alliance," "burqa," and "Afghanistan" became the *lingua franca* of denizens of the United States. Indelibly linked now with the events of 9/11/01, Kushner's play has been widely declared "eerily prescient." To his credit, Kushner dismisses this hype: "I'm not psychic. If you choose to write about current events there's a good chance you will find the events you've written about to be . . . well, current" (*Homebody/Kabul.* TCG 2002: 146). Kushner recognizes that plays must have something to say that exceeds the pressing tension of the present tense. I had the opportunity to see Kushner's play twice on opposite coasts in the space of eight months and this experience confirmed, once more, how accelerated the present tense is in an era of postmodernism.

In the New York Theatre Workshop production, directed by Declan Donnellan, the sheer length of the play—it was over four hours on opening night—led to a certain frustrated impatience on the audience's part. Even more dismaying was the fall in quality between the mesmerizing *Homebody* and the meandering plot of *Kabul.* In the production at the Berkeley Repertory Theatre, *Kabul* had been cut substantially, and Tony Taccone's direction was more aggressive and faster paced than Donnellan's. Moreover, in the eight months between the opening of the play and its Berkeley run, the situation in Kabul had been radically altered, making the political urgency of some of Kushner's comments about the Taliban's hold on the city seem already dated, rather than "eerily prescient." Finally, the psychological terrain between downtown New York twelve weeks after the destruction of the World Trade Center and Berkeley forty weeks later was also dramatically different. In New York, the play was seen primarily in terms of the attack on the city—there's a line in the play about the Taliban coming to New York—while in Berkeley, the reception of the play concerned Kushner's love affair with language.

The first hour and ten minutes of the play, the *Homebody* monologue, demonstrates Kushner's considerable gifts: his writing is fluent, evocative, and emotionally and intellectually expansive. Joining the aesthetics of theatrical minimalism—a woman sitting on a chair for seventy minutes talking—with language of such baroque intensity that the slightest physical gesture seems unbearably distracting, the monologue is completely captivating. The Homebody, an English woman who has an unhappy marriage, takes anti-depressants, worries about her daughter, "for whom alas nothing seems to go well," and reads and speaks obsessively. She begins the monologue quoting from Nancy Hatch Dupree's tour guide, *An Historical Guide to Kabul,* published in 1965 and thus completely out of date: "Our story begins at the very dawn of history, circa 3,000 BC. . . ." This sense of historical time-lag is crucial to Kushner's political polemic. To understand anything about the rise of the Taliban, Kushner insists, one needs to think through the extraordinarily brutal history of Afghanistan. The monologue places Kabul, a city now so newly near for US audiences, in a vast historical setting that continually displaces and defers the possibility of dramatic or political resolution. The sometimes maddeningly long sentences of the Homebody bespeak the difficulty of finding a way to reach closure about Kabul.

In New York, Linda Edmond was brilliant as Homebody. She performed the long monologue with verve and wit, and more impressively, she conveyed a profound sadness and despair about her loneliness even in—perhaps especially in—her most comic moments. In Berkeley, Michelle Moran emphasized the Homebody's frailty in physical terms. She had a cane placed in front of her chair, and when she moved at all, it seemed to require all of her attention. This approach also worked but it sometimes suggested that the Homebody's suffering was largely external. Edmond was so good she managed to make Kushner's beautiful, but perhaps somewhat naive, conceits seem plausible: that if we learn how to surrender without violence to the mystery of the unknown in the same way we surrender to the ineffable mystery of words, we might one day be—if not exactly saved—at least capable of finding and offering love, still a hugely transformative force in the world. The Homebody longs for love at least as much as she craves the right words. She, her husband, and daughter "all loved one another, once, but today it simply isn't so or isn't what it used to be, it's . . . well, love." The disappointment in that last "love" structures her indefatigable rhetorical aspirations; she knows that her husband and daughter resent her love for books, her way of speaking, and her interest in mystery. But because she loves the world, and the words that make up the world, she is unable to stop attempting to experience the world as precisely as language allows.

The Homebody's husband is a scientist, and her daughter is unemployed. All three are anxious. She and her husband both take "powerful antidepressants." She says, "his pills have one name and mine another. I frequently take his pills instead of mine so I can know what he's feeling. . . . [A]s far as I know he never takes my pills but ingests only his own, which are yellow and red, while mine are green and creamy-white; and I find his refusal to sample dull. A little dull" (13). Dullness is a vice to be avoided for the Homebody. She decides to have a party, even though her history as a successful party host has not been great. In the spirit of Virginia Woolf's Clarissa Dalloway, Homebody decides to buy, not the flowers, but the party hats, herself. She goes to a shop run by Afghan refugees and selects ten festive hats. As she pays for them she realizes that the shopkeeper has a mutilated hand: "Three fingers on his right hand have been hacked off, following the line of a perfect clean diagonal from middle to ring to little finger. . . ." She entertains many different possible causes, all contradictory—"my name is in the files if they haven't been destroyed, the names I gave are in the files, there are no more files"—until all the explanations seem both excessive and impoverished. Before long, the Homebody, suddenly fluent in Pushto, finds herself under a tree in Kabul where, she says, "the hat merchant and I make love beneath a chinair tree. . . . We kiss, his breath is very bitter; he places his hand inside me, it seems to me his whole hand inside me, it seems to me a whole hand." Then, just as suddenly, she is back in the London hat shop. The shift in time and space is startlingly and slightly unnerving, but it helps prepare us for the larger shift between the confined world of the Homebody's English living room and the war-torn city of Kabul, where the rest of the play takes place. But while the Homebody's (imaginative) journey to Kabul is motivated by some combination of love,

lust, curiosity, boredom, and hopefulness, her family's journey there is motivated by her apparent murder.

Act 2 begins in Kabul with a doctor explaining to the Homebody's husband and daughter that her body has been found. The doctor goes on at excruciating length explaining the nature of her injuries, which are brutal. The doctor's report is arranged by Quango Twistleton, an opium addict living in Kabul for the drugs who also works for a British NGO. Played with especial cunning by Bill Camp in the New York production, Quango is a fascinating character. He befriends the Homebody's husband, Milton Ceiling, and falls for Priscilla, their daughter. Milton, comically eager to get out of Kabul as fast as possible, readily accepts the doctor's explanations about his wife's death, but Priscilla finds everything about her mother's trip to Kabul incomprehensible and cannot believe anything the doctor says. She determines to investigate on her own. After a very complicated series of events, the Ceilings find themselves traveling back to England with neither the Homebody nor her corpse, but with the equally talkative Mahala, an Afghani librarian with no books to order. As Milton and Mahala begin to communicate tentatively, one sees Kushner's overall point more clearly. An exploration of the allure and impossibility of a universal language, *Homebody/Kabul* surveys the wreckage produced by faith-based wars, and the ruins produced by the hunger for power that we call colonialism and imperialism in the public sphere and call the family in the private sphere. But without these systems, Kushner is also honest enough to ask, what might save us from total brutality?

The Dewey decimal system, a universal language Kushner is willing to employ, tries to organize human knowledge coherently. It gives his play a rhizomic structure. Dewey's 000s are reserved for "facts and books about books." Hence, the bibliophile Homebody and the Librarian stand as bookends, quite literally, for the rest of the play's relationship to knowledge. The 100s are dedicated to materials "about great ideas and thinking": thus the Esperanto poet-philosopher and the Sufi mystic guide Priscilla thought great ideas. The 200s catalog books about God and religion: Kushner, in some of the best writing in the second part of the play, speculates about the relationship between Kabul and Cain—if Cain was buried there, as some evidence suggests, does the ghost of the first murderer curse the city? The 300s include materials about tourism, folklore, anthropology, and crime: *Kabul* concerns a crime allegedly committed against an English woman in Afghanistan, and the investigation, such as it is, is overseen by a British junkie. The 400s are devoted to languages; Kushner's play employs French, Russian, English, Pushto, and Dari. The 500s cover ideas about nature and physics: Kushner indexes them via Milton Ceiling's scientific discourse and Quango's analysis of the geoeconomics of oil and heroin. The 600s catalog works about medicine, and the Doctor's almost endless description of the Homebody's wounds represents that aspect of knowledge. The 700s concern material about art, and in addition to Kushner's own achievement as a playwright, the character Khwaja, the Esperanto poet who volunteers to be Priscilla's tour guide, the songs of Frank Sinatra, the poetry of anonymous seventh-century Persians, and the novels of P. G. Wodehouse are just some of the references to art in Kushner's play. The 800s are devoted to storytellers and their stories, and all of Kushner's characters are extraordinary storytellers, especially Quango and the Homebody. Finally in the 900s, one will find tour guides, and this is Kushner's point of departure.

Both productions did a better job staging **Homebody** than staging **Kabul.** The failure to sustain a coherent plot in a city overrun with plots is no sin. But Kushner is too valuable a voice in US theatre to forget, even momentarily, the difference between encounters with the ineffable and stories of imperialist and economic plunder. Kushner's habit of mind alerts him to the hideous violence the United States has done in the world, and while he continually reminds us of the vast complexity and long duration of the history of Afghanistan, all too often he wants to make the United States the "cause" of the disaster. But to place the United States as prime-mover everywhere and forever is to fall into the trap of considering it as it prefers to be considered: as only and forever the super-power. This falsifies the history of the world. Therefore, despite Kushner's best intentions, the agonizing drama of Afghanistan is not yet staged in **Homebody/Kabul.**

Natalie Meisner (essay date spring 2003)

SOURCE: Meisner, Natalie. "Messing with the Idyllic: The Performance of Femininity in Kushner's *Angels in America.*" *Yale Journal of Criticism* 16, no. 1 (spring 2003): 177-89.

[*In the following essay, Meisner examines Kushner's representations of women and femininity in* Angels in America.]

> We pay a high price for the maintenance of the myth of the individual.
>
> —Tony Kushner[1]

It may seem an odd project to focus on the female characters in Tony Kushner's two-part modern epic **Angels in America** since the plays' action revolves around Prior, Louis, Joe, and the other male characters. Kushner himself notes his plays' specificity by light-heartedly calling them "Jewish fag plays."[2] This is not

the whole story, however, as the plays do rely upon complex representations of femininity, femaleness, and biologically female-coded bodies for their coherence. The extent to which these plays have been used as source texts for queer theory throughout the 1990s makes them a rich site for investigation of the interstices between feminism and queer theory. If any texts could be termed venerable in a field as fledgling as queer theory **Millennium Approaches** and **Perestroika** would certainly be accorded this status. The plays, temporally and historically marked as they are, often serve as a kind of intimate shorthand for queer, performance, and theatre theorists.[3]

One of the most fascinating aspects of the plays is their ability to engage with and disrupt the bigoted rhetoric of blame that was aimed at gay men during the advent of the AIDS crisis in North America. The visible markings left by the disease on the very bodies that had transgressed the limits of compulsory heterosexuality provided all too convenient "proof" for those wishing to pathologize open, promiscuous, and indeed all gay sex. *Angels in America* dissolves this symbolic relationship, as David Savran has pointed out, by "turning one pole of a binarism relentlessly upon another."[4] The protagonist Prior, a gay man who in other circumstances might be condemned by the Christian right for his sexual choices, becomes a prophet; Roy Cohn, a rabidly antigay crusader, is himself suddenly thrust out of the closet. At the end of **Perestroika** the system of compulsory heterosexual marriage is abandoned, in favor of an idyllic new world of gay erotic affiliation. One binary that is not "turned relentlessly" is the one that polices the physical border between male and female bodies. Despite the ability of the plays, as Sue Ellen Case points out in *Queer Frontiers,* to stage "the convergence of so many different types of politics" the body politics of the border between man and woman, male and female remains remarkably stable.[5]

In works given the hopeful subtitle **"Gay Fantasia,"** one might expect to find gender roles denaturalized; male and female detached performatively from the biological bodies to which they are compelled to adhere in everyday life. While a spectrum of gender becomes available to most of the male characters through the performance of power and/or drag, the same is not available for the biologically female characters. It is somehow very important to the integrity of the plays' vision that The Angel of History, who is described as a "cosmic reactionary," be constructed as emphatically female despite being "Hermaphroditically Equipped . . . with a Bouquet of Phalli."[6]

The male characters in the plays gain power through the performance of a homoerotic, homo-social, and homo-political engagement. In the case of Joe this is underlined by his much-anticipated emergence from the closet. When he leaves his wife, Harper ("harp," of course, being a synonym for "nag"), she retreats further and further from the social, sexual, and political spheres. Harper's appearance as a sexually thwarted and politically detached female figure constructs Joe's emergence, by contrast, as all the more reasonable, brave, and lively. The character of Harper could be simply a foil and yet she represents a certain troubling female corporeal presence: A "messy" reminder/remainder that problematizes the plays for audiences, critics, and even for the playwright himself.

Although *Angels in America* trades in female iconicity, nearly all of the female characters are constructed as ghostly and/or disembodied. In their extra-terrestrial states, The Angel of History, Hannah, Ethel, and Louis's grandmother all rest comfortably as icons within the ideological framework of the plays. However, this is not the case with Harper, whose troublesome body—insofar as it appears biologically coded female—is subjected to a clinical and exhaustive set of restraints and strategies for containment. After her husband's departure, Harper escapes the disappointing circumstances of her failed marriage by retreating to her own absurd fantasy life. Her new prospect is a virtual travel agent appropriately named Mr. Lies. Harper's desires for travel, adventure, and sexual contact are thus titillated systematically and then thwarted by the smug figure of the travel agent. Not only is Mr. Lies an imaginary companion, he is also a failure of the imagination: incapable of providing even an engaging soporific. As such Mr. Lies provides a kind of asbestos insulation between Harper's desiring female body and the socio-political heart of the plays to which it seems to pose a menace.

No matter how many regimes of restraint the body is subjected to (this is particularly true of the female body with its sexualized and bloodied history on the stage), it resists being fully contained and inscribed by these regimes. Even as Harper is wrapped in layer after layer of dramatic barriers; as each scene in which she appears turns out to be yet another exit, she still makes demands upon the structure of the plays that threaten to disturb their so called natural order.[7] This is most evident in the warning issued to her by Mr. Lies, who tells her: "You keep messing with the idyllic, you're gonna wind up to your knees in slush" (2:19). The menace of this "slush" within the frame of Kushner's theatre of the fabulous—and within the masculine/liberal/humanist subject to which the plays default—is called forth by Harper, not only messing with the idyllic but imperiling the angelic binaries in these two most influential queer plays.

FROM A THEATRE OF THE RIDICULOUS TO A THEATRE OF THE FABULOUS: A KIND OF PAINFUL PROGRESS

It comes as no surprise that *Angels in America* should provide fertile ground for the exploration of queer vis-ibility, since the plays were written with the Queer Nation chant blasting in the background: "[w]e're here, we're queer. We're fabulous. Get used to it."[8] In an interview with David Savran, Kushner acknowledges that he advocates a shift for gay theatre from a theatre of the ridiculous to a theatre of the fabulous. He defines fabulous "in the sense of an evolutionary advance over the notion of being ridiculous" as well as "in the sense of being fabled, having a history."[9] A transition from the ridiculous to the fabulous in *Angels* creates gay male subjects with integrity. This integrity includes dignity and the shoring up of the porous borders of the self in favor of a sovereign subject. Harper, on the other hand, may tell us that people are like planets who need a thick skin, while her own "skin" is perpetually punctured and the borders of her self blurred as the first play commences; by the end of the second play there seems to be an eclipsing of her character's ability to think and act. Harper's permeability is emphasized by her decrepitude and dissolution when Joe leaves her. Even the slightest material demands of her life such as her personal hygiene seem an impossible task. Her discussion of her own body and the body of other female animals is encoded with loathing. Harper appears only to disappear. She fantasizes only to have her fantasies corrupted to the point that they appear even less satisfying than her life. As the only non-iconic female, she expresses embodied sexual desire solely to castigate herself from it. As such she presents a logjam in terms of what "female" means within Kushner's theatre of the fabulous that raises the question of the erasure of the biological female body within queer theory.

True to the binary logic of the plays, Joe, Louis, and Prior are located in the theatre of the fabulous while Harper remains marked by the "transference of disgust into humor [that] is the province of the grotesque and characteristic of the theatre of the ridiculous."[10] Similarly, the type of humor generated by Harper's dialogue is more consistent with a theatre of the ridiculous since on a textual level, audiences are encouraged to laugh *at*, not *with* her.

The association between being fabulous (being fabled, having a story, belonging to history) and "being citizens" (2:148) is such a profound one that it is very difficult to consider the un-fabulous characters as sentient beings or subjects. Harper speaks of "a kind of painful progress" (2:144) from which she is excluded since such an evolution is constructed as a departure from the ridiculous in favor of the fabulous. The exclusion of Harper from the sphere of the fabulous is related to the fact that fabulousness in *Angels* finds its highest expression in drag, which the plays showcase in the "girl-talk," ironic distancing, and pastiching of Belize and Prior. As Richard Cante points out, pleasure derived from female impersonation often depends upon "the conspicuous *absence of, ejection,* . . . and possibly even *hatred of* real female bodies."[11] Drag's celebratory and parodic explosion of femininity is potentially subversive of hegemonic representations of gender. However, one wonders why it is so often accompanied by an erasure and/or an aversion for female bodies. In other words why must a celebration of artifice be accompanied by denigration of a so-called original? Isn't this sacrificial model of identify much less "queer"—if we understand queer to mean a radicalized form of coalitional politics that questions identity-based activism—than a spectrum of bodies upon which masculine/feminine and male/female refuse to resolve themselves?

Separating the Men from the Boys and the Girls from Everyone

David Savran points out that in *Angels* the "utopia/dystopia coupling . . . plays itself out through a host of binary oppositions: heaven/hell, forgiveness/retribution, communitarianism/individualism, spirit/flesh, pleasure/pain, beauty/decay, future/past, homosexuality/heterosexuality, rationalism/indeterminacy, migration/staying put, progress/stasis, life/death."[12] There is, however, one pairing that Savran leaves out which, from the point of view of queer theory, could stand to be a little *more* paradoxical and a little *more* ambivalent: male/female. Theatrical convention calls for jokes to be set up by what is called a "straight man." In *Angels in America,* however, the jokes are consistently set up by super-straight women. Neither Harper nor Hannah, The Angel of History nor Emily, seem aware of the humor that surrounds them. Furthermore, when The Woman From the South Bronx cracks a joke it is accompanied by the flat declaration: "That was a joke" (1:104). If a kind of "painful progress" is possible for the citizens of the queer nation that *Angels* foretells it is only achievable through fabulous ironic distancing and savvy humor. The utter lack of these qualities in the female characters coupled with their persistent association to decay, stasis, death, and indeterminacy constructs them as threatening to the very principle of sociality. Progress has always been attainable for liberal humanism's highest subject—Man. Now this Man is "allowed" to be gay.

The binaries that haunt *Angels* are mirrored structurally by sets of symbolically paired characters. Roy (based on the infamous Roy Cohn) and Prior are both HIV positive. Roy refuses to claim his HIV status or any kind of homosexual identity, while Prior is not only out of the closet but performatively discloses his diagnosis. Roy is also paired with Ethel (based on Ethel Rosenberg) who haunts him for having campaigned tirelessly to send her to the electric chair. The plays expose the links between racism and homophobia by suggesting that Roy persecuted Ethel not because of her alleged spy activity but to expiate his own Jewishness.

Just as Roy uses Ethel as a scapegoat he also "saves" himself from accusations of homosexuality by championing regressive right-wing family values and attacking homosexuals in the public sphere. Prior and The Angel of History make another ghostly pair until Prior is visited by two earlier versions of himself, priors to Prior who situate him historically. Harper is, of course, visited by Mr. Lies who does not perform a similar function for her. Finally, to add the icing on the binary cake, Prior and Harper cross over into one another's dreams, acting as an ambassador for West Village gay culture on the one hand and Salt Lake City Mormonism on the other.

Savran maintains that "these pairings function not just as a set of conceptual poles but also as an oxymoron—a figure of indecidability whose contradictory being becomes an incitement to think the impossible—revolution!"[13] Yet some binaries are decidedly less oxymoronic than others. What seems to be Joe's journey from a dysfunctional heterosexual marriage to a homosexual awakening is elevated to his journey from stasis to movement; from living death to a life of desire. The sex scene between Joe and Louis blends politics, movement, risk, and subtext, creating opportunities for specular pleasure. This scene happens simultaneously with the one in which Harper sits "slumped in her chair" in an almost vegetable state declaring angrily that she misses "Joe's Penis" (2:37). This declaration is not contextualized by the conversation she is having with Hannah, but serves only to emphasize the point that she is demonstrably cut off from the social world around her and mystically absented of any life force by the removal of the penis/phallus.

There is an incitement to revolution in Prior's prediction at the end of *Perestroika.* He turns to the audience and says gravely and with great felicity that "[w]e will be citizens. The time has come." In the next breath he declares: "You are fabulous creatures, each and every one" (2:148). How should spectators relate to the separation of the female characters from every kind of community within the plays? Even Hannah, who is included in the final group, does not take part in the political discussion but only parrots unsolicited citations from the Bible. One wonders if there are any women who can play their parts sufficiently to become fabulous and hence to become citizens.

In the instances where the female characters are called upon to "hold down the fort" and provide ridiculous contrasts to their fabulous male counterparts, *Angels in America* relies upon what Alison Weir calls a "sacrificial logic that designates femininity as 'otherness,' nonidentity, and negativity."[14] Can Harper function as a critique of the liberal, humanist paradigm of an all-male theatre of the fabulous while she is ensconced in the same play under the mantle of the theatre of the ridiculous? Is *Angels* more easily absorbed by mainstream audiences (as well as by the traditions of epic and canonical literature with their male homosocial underpinnings) due to the fact that it does not challenge the relationship between the primacy of masculinity and capitalism? Its staging of women as socially and erotically thwarted and/or detached would seem to suggest so. When Harper insists on pursuing any erotic prospect she is warned that her actions will "tear a big old hole in the sky" and that she'll find herself "up to her knees in slush" (2:21). When her traditional "femininity" misfires, Harper is not fitted queerly into a complex grid of interlocking social and political relationships but rather spirals into a state of utter abjection. The question must then be asked why an embodied and untraditionally feminine woman in pursuit of sexual fulfillment must automatically pose a threat to the so-called natural order in contemporary queer plays in much the same way she did in those of Shakespeare.

By virtue of its sprawling and complex plot structure and its attempt to tackle Reagan-era nationalism, *Angels in America* strives to position itself as a candidate for canonicity as well as an heir to a tradition of epic theatre. The plays achieved the elusive feat of crossover in an incredible balancing act between commercial viability and sub-cultural subversion. *Angels* does not participate straightforwardly in post-WWII American literature's "war between style and content; between a feminized body in the text and a masculinized voice of authority that ceaselessly attempts to subjugate and master the body."[15] The plays do, however, perform a series of *sorting mechanisms* upon their female characters that serve to entrench hegemonic gender norms. Involvement in the sphere of politics, the pursuit of erotic fulfillment, the display of agency, and the negotiation between personal and political conflicts—traditionally the stage territory of men—remain emphatically so in *Angels in America.* Careful attention to the theatrical voice of Harper reveals the way that speech functions differently for men and women in these plays.

Harper speaks copiously and frequently but with far less felicity than Prior, Louis, Joe, or any other character. Stage directions are perhaps the most liminal and the least stable parts of a theatrical text; as such they provide a valuable "hot point" of interface between writer/director/actor/audience. It would not overstate the case to say that the theatrical text's precarious journey toward embodiment is mediated by these italicized asides. Stage directions never appear before audiences and may even be blacked out by a director at the beginning of a rehearsal process to avoid reductive choices by the actors. These texts nonetheless provide physical cues to which theatrical artists must assume a position. For this reason it is useful to look at the stage directions that introduce Harper. When we meet her, we are told she is "talking to herself, as she often does" (1:16).

Immediately after that we are told that Harper "speaks to the audience." Speaking directly to the audience can be a privileged position in drama. A character performing in the aside mode is afforded an extra layer of meaning and her words given added weight.[16] After a character breaks through any theatrical convention—especially the fourth wall—audiences expect her to "mean double" when she returns to a regular performance mode and resumes interaction with other characters. Harper frustrates this expectation since her subsequent interactions with other characters and her enunciatory positions elude multiplicity entirely. The performance style encouraged by Kushner's stage directions acts to inhibit any complicity the actor playing Harper might create with the audience. The effect of novelty and repetition in live performance cannot be overestimated. Unless directed otherwise, a theatre audience tends to give more attention to the uncommon utterance and overlooks the quotidian. Harper's delivery is noted to be "dull" and "flat" (2:33), pointing to a certain lifelessness and separating Harper from the theatre of the fabulous aesthetic. Other stage directions tell us that she is "sitting at home, all alone, with no lights on" and that "we can barely see her" (1:49). Harper's stylized speech, her tendency to numbly repeat snatches of television advertisement, her pill-popping, her agoraphobia, and her stereotyped hysterical fear of a "man with a knife" (1:24) increase throughout the plays in obsessive attempts to fix and/or freeze her. These factors coupled with her avoidance of conflict and tendency to contradict her own statements, such as, "maybe my life is really fine, maybe Joe loves me and I'm only crazy thinking otherwise, or maybe not, maybe it's even worse than I know, maybe . . . I want to know, maybe I don't" (1:18), tend to exile Harper even further from the nexus of the play. This very nexus is graphically defined by Roy in all its problematic intensity: "this is gastric juices churning, this is enzymes and acids, this is intestinal is what this is, bowel movement and blood-red meat—this stinks, this is politics, Joe, the game of being alive" (1:68).

Harper is certainly aware of the processes of history and politics when she notes that "everywhere things are collapsing, lies surfacing, systems of defense giving way" (1:17), and yet her most astute comments are invariably made when she is talking to herself. Her lack of awareness of her own performative potential generates laughter that is markedly different from the kind of comedic drive achieved by Belize or Prior or Louis. There are various facets to the male performance of power, ranging from the coercive, dangerous, and deranged figure of Roy Cohn to Belize and Prior's "girl-talk" (1:61). Not being included under the rubric of fabulousness leaves Harper in a strange place; a queer place, one might like to think. But time and again she is exhaustively proven to be deadly normal, empty of originality, and unworthy of our attention. This forced blandness may be what prompts Bruce McLeod to point out that Harper "appears to be rather asexual in a very sexy play."[17] Given that in *Angels* politics is sex and sex is being alive, the effect of cordoning off female bodies from any and all sexual pleasure is disastrous.

Angels not only moves its female characters away from erotic affiliation, it also systematically isolates each woman from any ties she may exploit through friendship. Friendship between women is treated as an anomaly in comments such as the one Sister Ella Chapter makes to Hannah: "I decided to like you 'cause you're the only unfriendly Mormon I ever met" (1:82). Friendship between men may not be perfect but it is necessary, like politics and oxygen. Friendship between women, on the other hand, is a matter of obscure taste and a perverse desire to go against the grain. The disavowal is complete in the passionless goodbye between the two women where Hannah limply agrees that she herself "wasn't ever much of a friend" (1:82).

Contrary to most popular representations of gay sexuality, the sex in *Angels* is not air-brushed to avoid offending a mainstream audience. Further, gay eroticism and gay sex are not demonized, but celebrated. The stiffening of Prior's penis and his subsequent ejaculation are greeted with a chorus from heaven. The staging of Prior's celestial orgasm, as it links gay male sexual pleasure with the angelic in a specifically Christian context, is a serious challenge to mind/body dualism, which has been one of the crucial factors in the history of sexual oppression. The repetition of gendered notions in philosophical discourse, however, means that Harper's dreams of fulfillment must transport her at the end of *Millennium Approaches* to the polar opposite of the celestial; literally to Antarctica "the Kingdom of ice, the bottommost part of the world" (1:101).

The constrained subjectivity offered to the female characters in *Angels* mirrors their status at the conjuncture of liberal humanism and late capitalism. Invoking discourses of male-dominated religion and nationalism, the Rabbi at the opening of *Millennium Approaches* pronounces: "I did not know this woman. I cannot accurately describe her attributes, nor do justice to her dimensions. She was . . . not a person, but a whole kind of person" (1:10).

Harper's refusal to abide as this "whole kind of person" may threaten the natural order established by the plays, creating trouble for the female spectator, for critics, and even the playwright himself. In interviews Kushner is ever willing to discuss the finer points of his character choices and even the compromises made to the demands of identity politics. When asked by Bruce McLeod to discuss his treatment of Harper, however, he forecloses upon the subject immediately:

TK:

> No. I reject all criticisms of Harper . . .

BM:

> So there have been other criticisms?

TK:

> I don't think there—perhaps I shouldn't say this in print, but I don't think the part has been played properly yet.[18]

Dissatisfaction with the way the part has been played may not be due to a lack of skill on the part of the actresses, but to Harper's contested status as an embodied female within a corporeal economy seemingly more comfortable with iconic, elemental, or mythic female presence. In the moments where Harper has the chance to interact with people, to partake of social contact, she is deprived of self-awareness. When she talks to herself her speech invokes the timeworn literary device of women's intuition. The force of Harper's speech acts is diminished considerably given her propensity to parrot television or radio discourse that frames her as insane. Insanity, however, is far from a simple matter in *Angels in America* given the variety of conditions the word is used to connote.

THE MENACE OF CRAZINESS

In *Angels* we are asked to simultaneously place a premium value on reason and to perceive the instability of the boundary between reason and insanity in American society. Insanity becomes both a lurking menace and a reason for hope. Many types of departures from reason are catalogued: schizophrenia, religious visitations, genealogical reincarnations, and chemically-induced hallucinations. Yet this plethora of madness adheres to some very strict gender lines. When insanity appears in Harper or in The Woman From The South Bronx it is framed as neurotic rather than visionary due to its lack of support by the events of the play. Harper repeatedly questions her own sanity with statements such as "I'm only crazy" (1:18). Louis says casually of his grandmother that "she was pretty crazy. She was up there in that home for ten years, talking to herself" (1:19). When Prior is menaced with unreason it is denaturalized. As he says, "the whole world is [crazy], why not me? It's 1986 and there's a plague, half my friends are dead and I'm only thirty-one" (1:55). Belize warns him immediately by saying; "You better not fucking flip out. This is not dementia. And this is not real. This is just you, Prior, afraid of the future, afraid of time" (1:55). When Prior and Harper meet at the Mormon visitors center and discuss their experiences of supernatural visions, Harper tells him "that sort of stuff" always happens to her. Prior, on the other hand, is afforded a logical explanation for his hallucinations: he has "a fever . . . and should be in bed" (1:64). Of the two, Prior alone gains self-knowledge from his visions.

Not only is his madness justifiable, it is proven productive when his status as a prophet is confirmed. His visions situate him as the center of the plays as he waves dominant culture's favorite sign—perhaps the only one that refuses to become detached from its signifier in *pomo homo culture*—the tumescent penis. Harper, on the other hand, may be "a witch" (2:43) whose visions are a waste of time since, as Deborah Geis claims, "each of the supposedly apocalyptic things she mentions has already (more or less) occurred within the narrative of the play."[19]

Given the forthright representation of sex and autoeroticism, the reticence that surrounds the female body is puzzling. It is interesting that the supposedly hermaphroditic Angel of History is still designated as "she" and that the didascalic cough that Kushner identifies as best for the Angel is "a variation on a cat hacking up a furball . . . sharp, simple and effectively nonhuman" (2:9). This non-humanity contributes to the notion that all the women in the plays sit at the "border of animal and machine."[20] These links between women, Harper particularly, and the animal world are pernicious. When Harper finally overcomes her agoraphobia and takes some action in the "real" world it amounts to her "imagining herself a beaver" (2:32) and chewing down a tree in a public park. The image of chewing echoes many other feminized images that invoke tearing holes in or puncturing the orderly world of the symbolic. Her connection to animals and animalistic connotations of female genitalia are reinforced when Harper appears later holding Prior's missing cat, whom he refers to as "le chat" (1:21). The choice of animals is telling since beaver is slang for vagina and "chat" has the same connotations in French that "pussy" does in English. A kind of essentialism is aimed at Harper as her body becomes de-humanized, de-sexualized and made ridiculous all in the same stroke. These terms double and redouble causing the essentialism to misfire in a hyperbolic frenzy of euphemism for female genitalia (beaver, chat, cooter, etc.). In tandem with the breakdown of the borders between female/human/animal this frenzy triggers a crisis of meaning around the term female and its currency in these plays. Border wars between the animal and human occur repeatedly at the site of Harper's body. She recounts a television program where "men in snowsuits videotaped . . . polar bears running to escape . . . and their tongues lolled and their eyes rolled in their stupid tiny heads and the men stabbed them in their huge butts with hypodermic needles, knocked them out. And then they shoved frozen polar bear sperm pencils up their cooters" (2:34). As Harper recounts the program the stage directions tell us she "makes the deep wheezy hooting of a panicky animal." The loathing expressed by Harper for female animals is mimetically extended to her own body when she vocalizes along with the polar bears. In another passage she expresses disdain: "there's your breasts, and your genitals, and they're amazingly stupid, like babies or faithful dogs" (2:20). This loathing is overshadowed by the bodily-inflected lateral violence aimed at Hannah by the Woman From the South Bronx who calls her a "loathsome whore" and screams "Slurp slurp slurp will you STOP that disgusting slurping! YOU DISGUSTING SLURPING FEEDING ANIMAL! Feeding yourself, just feeding yourself, what would it matter, to you or to ANYONE, if you just stopped. Feeding. And DIED?"[21] This imagined death echoes the breakdown of social ties and intersubjectivity between women. Furthermore the ensuing state of stillness mirrors Prior's comment about the angels when he declares that he "like(s) them best when they're statuary . . . they are made of the heaviest things on earth, stone and iron, they weigh tons but they're winged, they are engines and instruments of flight" (2:147). The angels he invokes are at once animated and dead—female, but disembodied. In most instances the departure of women from traditional femininity in *Angels in America* represents an "attack against Language and the Sign so totalizing as to be self destructive."[22]

In the end, the plays accession to the status of the fabulous relies upon the figure of the female to provide obstacles and impediments to the pursuit of male desire. This is what prompts David Savran to note that *Angels* "seems to replicate many of the structures that historically have produced female subjectivity as Other."[23]

DRAGGING HARPER OVER THE GENDER LINE

Angels at its most fabulous in the everyday "drag" of Prior and Belize that allows them to harness ironic self knowledge in order to perform their gender identities. This playfulness is constitutive of the theatre of the fabulous, whose elucidation of gay male subjectivity unfortunately is erected on the vestiges of the ridiculed and essentialized female body. None of the female characters in the play ever attain the status of a full speaking subject, but Harper at least (in her troublesome embodiment) offers a marker of sacrificial logics that are often operational in the production of male subjectivity.

In the plays, erotic desire and its free expression are not only the test for subjectivity but also for mental and physical health. This is highlighted by the fact that Joe gets a bleeding stomach ulcer when he tries to remain in the closet. The ghosting of Hannah, Ethel, The Angel, and The Woman From the South Bronx, condemns them to a realm devoid of desire. In pursuit of her own satisfaction, Harper succeeds against all odds in "messing with the idyllic." In a supposedly gender-bending play, one wonders why it is important that the double-sexed angel be played by a female actor as Kushner specified in his notes to the text. The whole, healthy, alive, conflicted, active, male subjects are created by their separation (under the logic of conflict and sacrifice), from the fragmented, pathological, passive female objects.

Does the exclusion of all the women from the political and sexual realms serve to construct a fabulous new world that either uses them as iconic presences or eclipses them entirely? Joseph Boone, in his introduction to *Queer Frontiers,* addresses exactly this kind of exclusion in another queer source text (the music video for the Pet Shop Boys "Go West") that also creates a brave new world of multicultural and erotic affiliation. Boone notes that the "visual omission in this panoply of queer difference, of course, is *women,* in the plural. What the video offers us, instead, is a single woman, the iconic representation of the Statue of Liberty . . . an exoticized diva who, in contrast to the moving men, remains frozen in place."[24]

Perhaps for **Angels in America** there is no "right" woman to play the part of Harper, an embodied female character who pursues her erotic desires. Whereas the other female characters in **Angels** dovetail easily with the ghostly, the disembodied, and the iconic "Woman," Harper remains stubbornly an inhabitant of her body. By remaining thus, she serves as a reminder that the price we pay "for the maintenance of the myth of the individual" (2:150) is, in some cases, far too high.

Notes

1. Tony Kushner, *Angels in America, Part One: Millennium Approaches* and *Part Two: Perestroika* (New York: Theatre Communications Group, 1992), 2:150. Hereafter cited parenthetically.

2. Bruce McLeod, "The Oddest Phenomena in Modern History," *Iowa Journal of Cultural Studies* 14.1 (1995): 143-153.

3. This is evidenced by the density of citation from and familiar reference to these plays in collectively authored books that deal with developments in queer theory such as the one edited by Joseph A. Boone et al., *Queer Frontiers: Millennial Geographies, Genders, and Generations* (Madison: University of Wisconsin Press, 2000).

4. David Savran, "Ambivalence, Utopia and a Queer Sort of Materialism: How *Angels In America* Reconstructs the Nation," *Theatre Journal* 47.2 (1995): 211.

5. Sue-Ellen Case, "Toward a Butch-Feminist Retro-Future," in *Queer Frontiers,* 330.

6. David Morgan, "You Too Can Have a Body Like Mine," in *Body Matters: Essays on the Sociology of the Body,* ed. Sue Scott and David Morgan (London: Falmer Press, 1993), 73.

7. For an excellent discussion of the way the term "nature" has been rhetorically employed as a containment strategy in response to different waves of the women's rights movement see Diana Fuss, *Essentially Speaking: Feminism, Nature and Difference* (New York: Routledge, 1989).

8. David Savran, "The Theatre of the Fabulous: An Interview with Tony Kushner," in *Essays on Kushner's Angels,* ed. Per Brask (Winnipeg: Blizzard Publishing, 1995), 139.

9. Ibid., 140.

10. Jane Arthurs, "Revolting Women: The Body in Comic Performance," in *Women's Bodies: Discipline and Transgression,* ed. Jane Arthurs and Jean Grimshaw, (London: Cassell, 1999), 137.

11. Richard Cante, "Pouring On the Past: Video Bars and the Emplacement of Gay Male Desire," in *Queer Frontiers,* 150. Original emphasis.

12. Savran, "Ambivalence," 212.

13. Ibid.

14. Alison Weir, *Sacrificial Logics: Feminist Theory and the Critique of Identity* (New York: Routledge, 1996), 138-39.

15. David Savran, *Taking it Like A Man: White Masculinity, Masochism, and Contemporary American Culture* (Princeton: Princeton University Press, 1998), 8.

16. Characters speaking in the aside mode may not always be reliable—think of the trickster—but are usually accorded a special status and often provide a conduit between the audience and the other characters or the characters and supernatural forces.

17. McLeod, "The Oddest Phenomena," 81.

18. Ibid., 140.

19. Deborah R. Geis, "The Delicate Ecology of your Delusions: Insanity, Theatricality, and the Thresholds of Revelation in Kushner's *Angels in America,*" in *Approaching the Millennium: Essays on Angels in America,* ed. Deborah R. Geis and Steven F. Kruger (Ann Arbor: University of Michigan Press, 1997), 200.

20. Donna Haraway, *Simians, Cyborgs, and Women: The Reinvention of Nature* (London: Free Association Books, 1991), 150.

21. Kushner, *Angels,* 1:104. Capitals are in the original.

22. Weir, *Sacrificial,* 147.

23. Savran, "Ambivalence," 215.

24. Boone, *Queer Frontiers,* 7.

Stephen Aiello (essay date October 2003)

SOURCE: Aiello, Stephen. "Aristotle and Angels: Tragedy in the Age of Anomie." *Florida English* (October 2003): 6-16.

[*In the following essay, Aiello compares* Angels in America *with Aristotle's* Poetics, *claiming that Kushner's play vitiates the form of tragedy.*]

It seems to be a contentious position throughout drama criticism that although there may be a tragic sense felt collectively in contemporary life that somehow such an experience when dramatized must be weighed against the classical tradition of tragedy. Thus, any reading of a modern drama as a tragedy dares to confront the same essentialist views as Arthur Miller did when he claimed a tragic dimension for his protagonist, Willy Loman, in *Death of a Salesman.* The playwright responded to critics who viewed *Death of a Salesman* in Aristotelian terms as a "pseudo-tragedy," (108) by distancing his play and a sense of modern tragedy from Aristotle and his *Poetics* and reminding these critics that "even a genius is limited by his time and the nature of society" (108).

Certainly at first glance an exegesis based on Aristotle's *Poetics* of another acclaimed drama written over four decades later than *Death of a Salesman* that also confronts a social issue commonly regarded as tragic—the AIDS epidemic—would appear to create an even worse collision between the classical theory and a modern dramatic work: Tony Kushner's Pulitzer Prize winning ***Angels in America: A Gay Fantasia on National Themes.*** What is apparent when the dust settles from a confrontation between Aristotle and ***Angels in America*** is that although Kushner's play retains elements of tragedy delineated in *Poetics,* it also vitiates the form, which Aristotle describes as so essential to the nature and purpose of Greek tragedy. Much of what distances the two works from each other, however, exists ironically in a common assumption—the correlation each presents between literary form and the view of the world expressed in a dramatic work. Thus, an examination of this interdependence between artistic form and culture in the two works may yield insight into how both classical theory and modern practice perceive and render tragedy.

Clearly, the connection between the homogeneous cultural experience of the ancient Greeks and its artistic representation in tragedy determines Aristotle's concept of mimesis. Aristotle emphatically posits each tenet of *Poetics* as a mode of achieving an imitation of an action both so experientially and emotionally credible that audiences would be completely absorbed into the tragedy. Therefore, what emerges as the salient characteristics of mimesis in *Poetics* is the necessity for the tragic form to be unified, consistent and ultimately plausible for audiences. Aristotle's argument contends that without such unity and plausibility, audiences would distance themselves intellectually and emotionally from the work, thus prohibiting the "cathartic" reaction so essential in making tragedy a pleasurable and edifying theatrical experience.

Moreover, although there exists enough ambiguity and flexibility in *Poetics* to allow for interpretation or "distortion" by the playwright, a point to which this essay will return, the delimitations of what was to become the neoclassical "unities" centuries later are evidently a consequence of the classical poets' desire to produce a literary form that necessarily reflects the perception of order within the Greek society. Indeed from a modern perspective it is very difficult to understand such a sense of social and aesthetic equipoise. As Raymond Williams explains in his *Modern Tragedy,* the ordered form of classical tragedy, "embodies not an isolable metaphysical stance, rooted in individual experience, but a shared and indeed collective experience, at once and indistinguishably metaphysical and social" (18). Tom Driver argues that this harmony of literary form and culture is most apparent in Sophocles' *Oedipus the King* in that "the play itself is such a masterpiece of orderly construction that its very form mirrors the cosmic order it wishes to disclose" (248). What this attention to strict literary form creates (although in the case of *Poetics* and *Oedipus the King* the expected chronological relationship between theory and practice is reversed: theory followed practice) is an understanding of the universal through an examination of the particular, a quality, according to Aristotle, that distinguishes poetry from history and philosophy (45; ch. 9). *Oedipus the King* is unified in its focus upon one incident in the life of a hero that has tragic implications for Oedipus but universal ones for Sophocles' audience.

Based on a story well-known to its audiences, *Oedipus the King* presents a conditional state of the world, a "what would happen if" situation, in which a "famous" but ordinary man, "someone like us," (Aristotle 49; ch. 13) who because of the mutability of Fate, his crimes of parricide and incest, and the predisposition of his own character, his hamartia, disrupts the "social and metaphysical order" (Williams 18). For this disruption a plague is cast upon Thebes by the gods. By recognizing the truth, Oedipus reverses the action of the play through his self-blinding and self-imposed exile from the social world. Even though audiences experience pity for the sufferings of a hero who in his attempt to save his nation and to seek the truth unwittingly causes his own downfall, they accept that such actions must be "redressed" by the gods, for "if it were not so, moral chaos would result; [. . .] in a world maintained by a balance of forces among the 'theoi,' [gods] chaos is unthinkable" (Driver 48).

Moreover, the tragedy of Oedipus evokes the fear that all are subject to the whims of Fate. As the play ends, order is restored, and the salutary effects of Oedipus' exile are felt throughout Thebes. The final chorus of the play helps to signify the "learning and inference" (Golden 44) in Sophocles' *Oedipus the King*—the vulnerability of the individual to Fate, a universal truth that neither society nor the gods are able to meliorate:

> Remember that death alone can end all sufferings;
> Go towards death, and ask for no greater
> Happiness than a life
> In which there has been no anger and no pain.
>
> (244)

Again, what *Poetics* effects in tragedy is a grounding of the dramatic action to the particular to reflect the universal. The "imitation" of one "object," (Aristotle 45; ch. 8) an incident that occurs within "one revolution of the sun" (Aristotle 42; ch. 6) is juxtaposed against the eternal, just as the chaotic and tragic actions of the isolated hero stand in contrast to the harmony of social and religious order symbolized by the chorus. What lingers from the tragedy after all have left the orchestra is "fixed, given, and unchangeable [. . .]" (Eagleton 64) existing beyond the grasp of history. It was through the aesthetics of classical tragedy that "the Greeks fought against time and won. They did it strangely by shutting out the future [. . .] the enemy of timelessness, as the past which is fixed, and the present, which is ineffable, are not" (Driver 250).

What exists in the penumbra created by the superimposition of *Poetics* upon *Angels in America* is this use of the particular as a means to reveal a universal vision; however, the contextual form in which the hero's search occurs shifts the focus of the tragedy away from the hero to the world in which he exists. Prior Walter, the central protagonist of *Angels in America,* in fact, possesses several Aristotelian and Oedipal dimensions. He is at once, like Oedipus, a descendant from a noble family (depicted on the Bayeux tapestry) and simply a "man whom we know" (Aristotle 39; ch. 4), "neither outstanding in virtue and righteousness [. . .]" [who] "falls into misfortune" (49; ch. 13). Furthermore, Prior, like Oedipus, suffers from a plague, the AIDS epidemic; and in the process of ridding himself of the effects of the plague, seeks both truth and meaning for his fate. Unlike Oedipus, however, Prior's search does not turn inward, resulting in a self-imposed blindness and isolation from the world. Although similarly blinded in his heroic transformation into a "prophet" for all those who have been abandoned by the "gods"—"I believe I've seen the end of things"[1] (II: 56) - Prior's journey is an expansive one, venturing into what Aristotle would most likely consider the realm of the "impossible" and "inexplicable" (58; ch. 24). In his search, Prior moves across time and space: from a discussion with his ances-

tors of centuries past to an interaction with the subconscious worlds of others; from wrestling with an angel in his hospital room to confronting the angels in heaven.

Prior's journey, therefore, is coterminous with the literary form of *Angels in America* that is so explicitly stated by Tony Kushner in the sub-title of the play: "A Gay Fantasia on National Themes." If we return to this essay's thesis that a "common assumption" of the intimate relationship between form and culture underscores an analysis of the tragic form described in Aristotle's *Poetics* and Kushner's *Angels in America,* then several questions emerge in regard to a "fantasia": What is the relationship between form and culture in *Angels in America*? Is *Angels in America* a tragic work? And lastly, does the form of a fantasia necessarily clash with the form and function of tragedy as Aristotle describes them?

First, of all, an Aristotelian disclaimer: in regard to the use of the supernatural and the previously stated "impossible and inexplicable," (58; ch. 24) Aristotle appears to subordinate considerations of form and content to the pleasurable, cathartic effect of "learning and inference" (Golden 44) through poetry: "Generally speaking, we must judge the impossible in relation to its poetic effect" (Aristotle 60; ch. 25). Thus, even though Aristotle states that "the plot should not consist of inexplicable incidents," (58; ch. 24) and that "the solution of the story itself . . . should not require the use of the supernatural," (52; ch. 15), Aristotle does seem to focus the objective of tragic poetry to the casual relationship between mimesis and the catharsis. Therefore, "what is impossible but can be believed should be preferred to what is plausible but unconvincing" (Aristotle 58; ch. 24). As previously stated in this essay, for the ancient Greeks the ordered aesthetic of classical tragedy almost perfectly reflects a harmonious view of the universe (Driver 48). Even though modern audiences may still realize universal truths from classical tragedy, its form and cathartic effects belong only to a specific culture and moment in history that produced them. Thus, as Raymond Williams explains, the development of Greek society had a deleterious effect on classical form:

> It is no accident that as this unique culture changed, the chorus was the crucial element of dramatic form which was weakened and eventually discarded. The structure of feeling which, in the great period, had developed and sustained it as the dramatized tension and resolution of collective and individual experience, weakened and was lost, and with it a unique meaning of tragedy.
>
> (18)

Consequently, what is considered as an "imitation, not of men, but of action and life, of happiness and misfortune" (42; ch. 6) and what is the literary "impossible" for each epoch would necessarily change in constancy with its social and ideological development.

Taken in this light, the form of a fantasia in ***Angels in America*** with its referencing of the "impossible and inexplicable" as its cultural context signifies a condition of the modern world that is in many ways the reverse of the ancient one Aristotle's *Poetics* reflects. As the Angel of America explains to Prior Walter, the epoch of the play is the "Age of Anomie," (II: 56) in which the plastic form of the fantasia so well accommodates the chaotic and vertiginous 1980's. This sense of a fragmented and almost surreal America is echoed in Harper Pitt's description of a disordered modern life as "beautiful systems dying, fixed orders falling apart . . . everywhere things are collapsing, lies surfacing, systems of defense are giving way [. . .]" (I: 16). A breaking apart of social and ideological rationality is visible as well as in the play's presentation of what can be described as a cinematic reality consisting of split scenes, simultaneous action scenes [an Aristotelian "no-no": "tragedy cannot represent different parts of the action at the same time" (58; ch. 24)], dream sequences, sub-plots and even a bifurcation into two distinct dramas: ***Millennium Approaches*** and ***Perestroika***. The two plays in one, which are sometimes performed separately or jointly, express an almost schizophrenic confusion as to what is real or illusory in the modern world. It may not seem possible but it doesn't seem totally inappropriate or unconvincing that the ghost of Ethel Rosenberg explains to a smug Roy Cohn that "history is about to crack wide open," (I: 112) or that Prior Walter and Harper Pitt for a moment share the same consciousness. Thus, as a "structure of feeling," (Williams 18) the fantasia makes the "impossible" seem plausible; whether the fantasia achieves enough of a mimetic description of life to create an Aristotelian cathartic reaction is doubtful.

However, what the form of a fantasia does allow in ***Angels in America*** is enough range and scope to explore fully its "national themes." Jointly stretching *Poetics* to the seams, ***Millennium Approaches*** and ***Perestroika,*** in their multiple sub-plots and cross-cultural and historical references to Mormons, Jewish immigrants, and Bolsheviks, as well as their conflation of angels and apparitions, gays and straights, and the powerless and the powerful, encompass many perspectives: historical, sexual, political, psychological, and spiritual. What results is a shift of the focus away from the particular, as in classical tragedy, to a general condition. Disorder is seen to originate not from the effect of fate on the individual but rather from society itself. If "revolution as such is in a common sense, tragedy, a time of chaos and suffering," (Williams 65) then a relationship between social upheaval and tragic form is a valid one.

Possibly George Bernard Shaw realized the same connection in similarly sub-titling *Heartbreak House* a "fantasia," for the play concludes with the resonance of Great War bombers raining destruction on England. As the millennium approaches in ***Angels in America,*** society itself acquires a tragic dimension.

In an Oedipal fashion, the social world, as Prior Walter learns, has been abandoned by what seems to be a conservative, anti-progressive God who blames humankind for creating history, the "virus of time," (II: 48) as his bureaucratic angels describe it. Cast out alone in the universe, society similarly suffers from blindness in its search for meaning, a condition of modern life cited by such political antipodes as the World's Oldest Living Bolshevik, whose speech at the Kremlin in "Perestroika" recounts the failure of past ideologies—"I promise the blind eyes will see again [. . .] show me the words that will reorder the world" (II: 14)—and the generation of the 80's, "Reagan's children," who are described by Louis Ironson as "selfish and greedy and loveless and blind" (I: 74). In the "Age of Anomie" blindness manifests itself as a world lost in its illusions in which truth, power, stability and community have become indeterminate. For Joe Pitt, the Reagan era "[. . .] is a great thing. The truth restored. Law restored. That's what President Reagan has done [. . .]. He says, 'Truth exists and can be spoken'" (I: 26). Pace Harper Pitt: "So when we think we have escaped the unbearable ordinariness and, well, untruthfulness of our lives, it's really the same old ordinariness and falseness rearranged into the appearance of novelty and truth" (I: 32).

Lies and illusions as a condition of a social tragedy also arise within the context of AIDS in ***Angels in America.*** AIDS as a metaphor for social tragedy exists not only in the pity and fear felt for the physical suffering of two characters, Prior Walter and Roy Cohn, and by implication, for all those stricken with the disease, but also for a group of protagonists who are specifically connected to them. In the unity formed around their suffering from a common lack of identity, these protagonists are reminiscent of the Greek chorus in their representation of an expression of a "shared and [. . .] collective experience" (Williams 18). What is essentially tragic about them—Joe Pitt, Harper Pitt, and Louis Ironson—is that each struggles with a state of false consciousness about him or herself, a group hamartia: for Joe, it exists in his conservative Mormon image as a straight man and husband belied by his true sexual identity; for Harper, it is in her role as a fulfilled wife and mother that is in truth a dream; and for Louis it is in his commitment as a lover to Prior Walter that is undermined by his inability to face life. For each of the group protagonists "to shed your skin, every old skin, one by one and then walk away unencumbered" (I:

72,73) requires the same kind of "moral choice" (52; ch. 15), which Aristotle felt necessary for the sole tragic figure. That moral choice, presented for each in a moment of Aristotelian recognition and reversal (Joe punches Louis and Harper slaps Joe), determines their "happiness and misfortune" (42; ch. 6). In Joe's situation, his choice leads him, like Oedipus, into isolation; while for Prior and Harper their decisions lead them to a greater sense of community.

Conversely, AIDS in *Angels in America* also lends itself as a metaphor for a tragic society that has lost its sense of community. Reagan-era individualism as a political force is personified in the play by the "power broker," Roy Cohn, who excoriates his own fate as an AIDS victim, not only because it labels him as a gay man and therefore relegates him to a lower, minority status as a "nobody [. . .] in the pecking order" (I: 45) of the power structure in Washington, but also because those in Cohn's view in the Reagan 80's who are considered the weak and therefore vulnerable are "booted out of the parade" (II: 62). Prior Walter, too, experiences feelings of isolation as a victim of the disease but with a different perspective. His reminiscence of a sea captain ancestor's shipwreck evokes a fearful image of a callous America as a lifeboat on a stormy sea in which those who lack authority because of disease are "pitched into freezing, turbulent water and salt and darkness to drown [. . .] by implacable, unsmiling men" (I: 42).

Despite the considerable pathos that both AIDS victims Prior Walter and Roy Cohn arouse, the juxtaposition of these two almost Manichean characters serves to inhibit any cathartic reaction. Placed within the form of the fantasia, Prior and Cohn's stories create the double-plot of the tragicomedy, which mitigates the emotional extremities of pity and fear. Prior's recognition of himself as a prophet reverses his action in the play, transforming his previous moribund feelings to those of transcendence in his wrestling from the angels his blessing for "more life" (II: 48). Cohn's experience of AIDS, however, directs him otherwise. As prophecies of "modern conservatism," (II: 81) Cohn's revelations to his young disciple, Joe Pitt, are those of existential terror. For Cohn AIDS avails him of no such recognition and reversal; instead what remains is that "life is full of horror; [and] nobody escapes, nobody, save yourself" (I: 58). Countering the movement of Prior Walter's "death" which brings him back to earth and community, Cohn dies alone, and any sense of pity for him is negated by the final hoax he plays on the ghost of Ethel Rosenberg, whom he entreats for comfort as his mother. However, the fantasia's last image of Cohn in heaven as God's lawyer is a humorous one (Cohn revels in insult comedy throughout both plays), exemplifying the Aristotelian rubric that tragedy, in Prior's case, imitates "the noble deeds of noble men" and comedy "the ac-

tions of meaner men" (39; ch. 4). The tragicomic fantasia mediates these forms, and in doing so enables *Angels in America* to achieve a harmonious conclusion with Cohn somewhat punished and Walter somewhat rewarded.

Again, working from our common assumption of the correlation between literary form and culture, we can see by distancing our two works from each other that diachronic movement underscores one and clashes with the other. For the Greeks, the mimetic form of tragedy prescribed in Aristotle's *Poetics* reveals universal truths that seem "incapable of being influenced by human initiative" (Esslin 134). Kushner's fantasia, on the other hand, brings the whole universe onto the stage to be wrestled with or altered however the playwright's imagination dictates. Whereas the more static form of *Poetics* uses history to achieve a credible connection to contemporary life, *Angels in America* extols an epic vision as a way to access and alter the future. Themes of the necessity of change and accepting responsibility for our actions are redolent in both *Millennium Approaches* and *Perestroika.* Moreover, they are expressed from equally divergent sources as well: the Rabbi Isidor Chemelwitz plays cards in heaven to continue the human experience of the "the Unknown, the Future," (II: 137) and Louis Ironson, who relishes a bloody lip gained from his confrontation with Joe Pitt, acknowledges that if he didn't suffer for abandoning Prior, "the universe would become unbalanced" (II: 33). Thus, what separates classical theory and modern practice in *Poetics* and *Angels in America* is that there is more to draw from the tragic in the contemporary world than an emotional catharsis and acceptance of the way things are; instead we must, too, wrestle with our angels.

Note

1. All references are to the following edition: Tony Kushner, *Angels in America, Part One: Millennium Approaches* and *Part Two: Perestroika.* New York: Theatre Communications Group, Inc., 1992, 1993, 1994).

Works Cited

Aristotle. The "Poetics." *Sources of Dramatic Theory.* Ed. Michael J. Sidnell. New York: Cambridge University Press, 1991. 32-61.

Driver, Tom F. "Oedipus the King." *Classical Tragedy: Greek and Roman.* Ed. Robert W. Corrigan. New York: Applause, 1990. 246-251.

Eagleton, Terry. *Marxism and Literary Criticism.* Berkeley, CA: University of California Press, 1976.

Esslin, Martin. *Brecht: The Man and His Work.* New York: Anchor Books, 1971.

Golden, Leon. "Aristotle." *The Johns Hopkins Guide to Literary Theory and Criticism.* Ed. Michael Groden and Martin Kreiswirth. Baltimore and London: Johns Hopkins University Press, 1994. 41-44.

Kushner, Tony. *Angels in America, Part One: Millennium Approaches. Part Two: Perestroika.* New York: Theatre Communications Group, Inc., 1992, 1993, 1994.

Miller, Arthur. "*Death of a Salesman*: A Modern Tragedy?" *Modern Theories of Drama.* Ed. George W. Brandt. Oxford: Clarendon Press, 1998. 106-112.

Williams, Raymond. *Modern Tragedy.* Stanford: Stanford University Press, 1996.

Publishers Weekly **(review date 3 November 2003)**

SOURCE: Review of *Brundibar,* by Tony Kushner. *Publishers Weekly* 250, no. 44 (3 November 2003): 72.

[*In the following review, the critic comments that the main story in* Brundibar *is ultimately one of hope, although it includes a darker subtext.*]

Pulitzer Prize-winning playwright Kushner adapts this allegorical tale from a Czech opera created by Hans Krása and Adolf Hoffmeister in 1938. [In *Brundibar,*] a doctor wearing the Star of David on his jacket dispatches siblings Aninku and Pepicek to town to find milk for their sick mother. Sendak, in a mix of fantasy and reality elements reminiscent of his *In the Night Kitchen* (especially the cameo appearance of a baker), thrusts the siblings—and readers—into an exotic backdrop of stone buildings topped by spires and turrets, but with familiar details such as a horse grazing behind a picket fence and a field of flowers. The two try to earn money to buy the milk, but their voices are drowned out by the noise of the "bellowing Brundibar"; Brundibar's refrain ("Little children, how I hate 'em/How I wish the bedbugs ate 'em") exemplifies Kushner's skill at tempering the potentially frightening with the comic. The dialogue and comments featured in balloons above the characters also inject an appealing spontaneity and levity to the proceedings. A trio of talking animals and 300 children come to the duo's aid. Working in colored pencils, crayons and brush pens, Sendak conjures bustling Slavic city streets and effectively juxtaposes innocence and evil in the cherubic visages of the children and Brundibar's ominously hyperbolic facial features (the villain's manicured mustache calls to mind the reigning tyrant of the time). Despite a final threat from Brundibar, the story is ultimately one of hope, as the children and their allies band together to defeat the evil foe. The collaborators wisely allow readers to appreciate the story on one level, yet those familiar with the opera's origins (a note in the flap copy tells of Krása's death at Auschwitz) will find a haunting subtext here. . . .

FURTHER READING

Criticism

Berstein, Andrea. "Tony Kushner." *Mother Jones* 20, no. 4 (July/August 1995): 59, 64.

Presents an interview with Kushner.

Fisher, James. Review of *The Good Person of Szechuan,* by Bertolt Brecht, adapted by Tony Kushner. *Theatre Journal* 52, no. 1 (March 2000): 120-01.

A review of *The Good Person of Szechuan,* asserting that Kushner's adaptation, while emphasizing the play's relevance to contemporary American society, is largely faithful to the original work by Bertolt Brecht.

Geis, Deborah R., and Steven F. Kruger, eds. *Approaching the Millennium: Essays on Angels in America.* Ann Arbor: University of Michigan Press, 1997.

A collection of essays by various authors on *Angels in America,* addressing such topics as sexual, racial, and ethnic identity, national politics, and religion.

Korn, Eric. "Slavs Are Us." *Times Literary Supplement,* no. 4788 (6 January 1995): 18.

A review of *Slavs!* that assesses the play as beautifully written and compelling, though poorly constructed and uneven in quality.

Kuharski, Allen J. Review of *Hydriotaphia, or, The Death of Dr. Browne,* by Tony Kushner. *Theatre Journal* 50, no. 3 (October 1998): 371-72.

A review of *Hydriotaphia,* describing the play as a provocative and chilling work that, despite elements of comedy, is ultimately a "deeply disturbing meditation on death."

Kushner, Tony, and Kim Myers. "Not on Broadway." In *Tony Kushner in Conversation,* edited by Robert Vorlicky, pp. 231-44. Ann Arbor: University of Michigan Press, 1998.

Presents an interview originally conducted on November 11, 1995 in which Kushner discusses his literary influences, the political nature of his plays, his work in theatrical production, and the role of theater in contemporary society.

Oppenheim, Irene. "Shedding More Light on *Bright Room.*" *American Theatre* 17, no. 7 (September 2000): 75-7.

A review of *A Bright Room Called Day* assessing the role of Zillah, the narrator of the play.

Additional coverage of Kushner's life and career is contained in the following sources published by Thomson Gale: *American Writers Supplement*, Vol. 9; *Contemporary American Dramatists*; *Contemporary Authors*, Vol. 144; *Contemporary Authors New Revision Series*, Vols. 74, 130; *Contemporary Dramatists*, Ed. 5; *Contemporary Literary Criticism*, Vol. 81; *Dictionary of Literary Biography*, Vol. 228; *DISCovering Authors 3.0*; *DISCovering Authors Modules: Dramatists*; *Drama Criticism*, Vol. 10; *Drama for Students*, Vol. 5; *Encyclopedia of World Literature in the 20th Century*, Ed. 3; *Gay & Lesbian Literature*, Ed. 1; *Literature and Its Times*, Vol. 5; *Literature Resource Center*; *Major 20th-Century Writers*, Ed. 2; and *Reference Guide to American Literature*, Ed. 4.

Martha Nussbaum
1947-

(Born Martha Craven; has also written as Martha Craven Nussbaum and Martha C. Nussbaum) American essayist, editor, and nonfiction writer.

The following entry provides criticism on Nussbaum's career through 2002.

INTRODUCTION

Nussbaum is a preeminent classicist and philosopher whose many works examine ancient Greek society and culture in relation to moral and ethical issues facing the modern world. In books such as *The Fragility of Goodness* (1986), *Love's Knowledge* (1990), and *Poetic Justice* (1995), Nussbaum has argued that reading great literature is central to the development of a "moral/political vision" of social justice. She has examined current liberal trends in American higher education in *Cultivating Humanity* (1997), in which she advocates college curricula that develop the notion of world citizenship as a foundation for social justice. In *Upheavals of Thought* (2001) and *Hiding from Humanity* (2004), Nussbaum argues that emotions are an important foundation for making ethical decisions about social justice. She expresses her political philosophy of "universalist liberal feminism" in *Sex and Social Justice* (1999).

BIOGRAPHICAL INFORMATION

Nussbaum was born on May 6, 1947, in New York City. She attended Wellesley College for two years before transferring to New York University, from which she graduated with a B.A. in 1969. That year, she married Alan J. Nussbaum, with whom she had a daughter, and whom she later divorced. Nussbaum received an M.A. and Ph.D. in classical philology from Harvard University, completing her graduate studies in 1975. She has since taught as a professor of philosophy and classics at several prestigious colleges and universities, including Harvard from 1975 to 1983, Wellesley from 1983 to 1984, and Brown University from 1985 to 1995. After serving as a visiting professor at Oxford University in 1996, Nussbaum took a post as professor of law and ethics at the University of Chicago. As her areas of research are interdisciplinary, she is associated with the school of law, divinity school, department of philosophy,

classics department, and Center for Gender Studies at the University of Chicago. Nussbaum has served in various capacities to promote her ideas of social justice on a national and international scale. Beginning in 1986, she served as an advisor at the United Nations University's World Institute for Development of Economics Research. In this capacity, she helped to develop a set of criteria for evaluating basic standards of human well-being that can be applied universally in international and cross-cultural contexts. As an advocate for lesbian and gay rights, she served as an expert witness in the court case of *Evans v. Romer,* which challenged a 1992 amendment to the Colorado constitution forbidding protection of the rights of homosexuals. Nussbaum provided testimony asserting that ancient Greek and Roman civilizations did not condemn homosexual conduct.

MAJOR WORKS

In *The Fragility of Goodness* Nussbaum examines the works of ancient Greek philosophers and poets in an effort to reconcile philosophical and literary ideas about moral thinking on the age-old question, "How should one live?" Nussbaum focuses particularly on the primacy of logic and reason in philosophy in contrast to the primacy of emotion and imagination in literature, illustrating her argument through close readings of classic philosophical texts as well as the tragic plays of ancient Greek theater. *Love's Knowledge* comprises a collection of essays in which she asserts that certain great literary texts are essential to moral and ethical thinking. She explains that literature extends the possibilities of human experience by evoking a capacity for sympathy in the reader, "making us reflect and feel about what might otherwise be too distant for feeling." She explores these ideas through close readings of novels by Charles Dickens, Henry James, and Marcel Proust, among others. Nussbaum continues this line of argument in *Poetic Justice,* in which she asserts that studying works of great literature is important to the development of an "ethical stance" which takes into account the experiences of marginalized segments of society. Through examination of such literary classics as Charles Dickens's *Hard Times* and Richard Wright's *Native Son,* Nussbaum puts forth the notion of a "literary imagination," by which readers learn to empathize with individuals whose conditions of life are different from their own. She asserts that this experience of sympathy which novels induce lays the foundation for a "moral/political vision" of social justice. She further suggests that this effect of literature on the reader's notions of social justice makes it crucial reading for those working in the legal profession, particularly judges. In *Cultivating Humanity* Nussbaum examines current trends of liberal reform in American higher education. She argues in favor of developments such as African American studies, women's studies, and gay/lesbian studies in college and university curricula, asserting that such courses represent a "new education." She states that the three core values of this new liberal education include critical self-examination, the idea of the world citizen, and the development of narrative imagination. Nussbaum goes on to discuss her findings in observing college courses throughout the United States in order to evaluate the extent to which specific curricula meet her own philosophical standards for "cultivating humanity" in students. *Sex and Social Justice* comprises fifteen essays in which Nussbaum advocates a "universalist liberal feminism." In these essays, she explores feminist issues such as pornography, prostitution, the rights of homosexuals, and the conditions of women in the Third World, as well as broader global issues of poverty, legal justice, religious freedom, and the rights of the individual. Nussbaum explains that the five "salient features" of her feminist philosophy are that "it is *internationalist, humanist, liberal, concerned with the social shaping of preference and desire,* and . . . *concerned with sympathetic understanding.*" In the opening

essay of *Sex and Social Justice,* Nussbaum describes her "capabilities" approach to international feminism, which developed out of her work for the United Nations. She identifies central human capacities which must be guaranteed in order to achieve justice for women on an international scale: longevity and bodily integrity; emotional, affective, social, and mental development; the ability to engage in practical reason and to form a conception of the good; the ability to live with concern for animals and the natural world; and control over one's political and material environment. In *Upheavals of Thought,* a work of over 700 pages, Nussbaum addresses questions about the role of emotion in the development of moral and ethical thinking. She further examines her previously stated assertions that: a) emotions are an expression of important evaluative judgments; b) compassion is central to the formation of an "ethical stance"; and c) literature is crucial to the development of a sense of compassion necessary for making moral and ethical evaluations that encompass the conditions of human life on a global scale. Nussbaum argues that emotions do not run counter to intelligence, but are in fact an important aspect of intelligent decision-making. In *Hiding from Humanity* she continues her ongoing exploration of the role of emotion in developing a sense of social justice. She argues that the emotions of fear, compassion, and indignation may be used as guidelines for creating a just legal system. However, the emotion of disgust, she contends, should not be used as a basis for legal decisions, because disgust is derived from fantasies of superhuman purity and omnipotence. On this ethical basis, Nussbaum discusses specific ongoing controversial legal issues, such as same-sex marriage and indecent exposure.

CRITICAL RECEPTION

Nussbaum's body of work is widely regarded as an important and original contribution to ethical philosophy and writings on social justice. Many reviewers have expressed admiration for her books, calling them ambitious, insightful, thought-provoking, and persuasive. Critics further praised her erudition in discussing works of ancient literature and philosophy. As Bernard Knox, in a review of *The Fragility of Goodness,* noted, "This long, intellectually demanding, and richly rewarding book must be almost unique in its expert analysis of both tragic and philosophical texts." Nussbaum has been widely praised for her eloquent, lucid, and accessible writing style. Thomas Frentz, for example, in a review of *The Therapy of Desire,* observed that Nussbaum's writing style "fuses argumentative rigor and unabashed feeling into a delicate balance that not only magically draws readers into her world, but also matches perfectly the spirit and temperament of whatever classical text she might be examining." Others critics, however, questioned the philosophical foundations on which Nussbaum's ideas are based, finding her arguments to be flawed and unconvincing.

PRINCIPAL WORKS

Aristotle's De motu animalium: Text with Translation, Commentary, and Interpretive Essay (nonfiction) 1978

Language and Logos: Studies in Ancient Greek Philosophy Presented to G. E. L. Owen [editor, with Malcolm Schofield] (nonfiction) 1982

The Fragility of Goodness: Luck and Ethics in Greek Tragedy and Philosophy (nonfiction) 1986

Logic, Science, and Dialectic: Collected Papers in Greek Philosophy by G. E. L. Owen [editor] (nonfiction) 1986

Internal Criticism and Indian Rationalist Traditions [co-author, with Amartya Sen] (nonfiction) 1987

Love's Knowledge: Essays on Philosophy and Literature (essays) 1990

Essays on Aristotle's De anima [editor, with Amelie Oksenberg Rorty] (essays) 1992

Passions & Perceptions: Studies in Hellenistic Philosophy of Mind: Proceedings of the Fifth Symposium Hellenisticum [editor, with Jacques Brunschwig] (nonfiction) 1993

The Quality of Life [editor, with Sen] (nonfiction) 1993

Virtue, Love & Form: Essays in Memory of Gregory Vlastos [editor, with Terence Irwin] (essays) 1993

The Therapy of Desire: Theory and Practice in Hellenistic Ethics (nonfiction) 1994

Poetic Justice: The Literary Imagination and Public Life (nonfiction) 1995

Women, Culture, and Development: A Study of Human Capabilities [editor, with Jonathan Glover] (nonfiction) 1995

For Love of Country: Debating the Limits of Patriotism [with respondents; edited by Joshua Cohen] (nonfiction) 1996

Cultivating Humanity: A Classical Defense of Reform in Liberal Education (nonfiction) 1997

Sex, Preference, and Family: Essays on Law and Nature [editor, with David M. Estlund] (essays) 1997

Clones and Clones: Facts and Fantasies about Human Cloning [editor, with Cass R. Sunstein] (essays) 1998

Sexual Orientation and Human Rights in American Religious Discourse [editor, with Saul M. Olyan] (nonfiction) 1998

Is Multiculturalism Bad for Women? [by Susan Moller Okin with respondents; edited by Nussbaum, Joshua Cohen, and Matthew Howard] (nonfiction) 1999

Sex and Social Justice (nonfiction) 1999

Women and Human Development: The Capabilities Approach (nonfiction) 2000

Upheavals of Thought: The Intelligence of Emotions (nonfiction) 2001

The Sleep of Reason: Erotic Experience and Sexual Ethics in Ancient Greece and Rome [editor, with Juha Sihvola] (nonfiction) 2002

Hiding from Humanity: Disgust, Shame, and the Law (nonfiction) 2004

CRITICISM

Jasper Griffin (review date 4 July 1986)

SOURCE: Griffin, Jasper. "Mastering the Irrational." *Times Literary Supplement* (4 July 1986): 730.

[*In the following review, Griffin asserts that* The Fragility of Goodness *is an important, ambitious book that is both formidably intelligent and persuasively emotional.*]

The subject of this long and closely written book [***The Fragility of Goodness: Luck and Ethics in Greek Tragedy and Philosophy***] (small type and large pages—561 of them) is an ambitious one: an investigation of the role played by luck in the area of human excellence and the activities associated with it. That means the whole nexus of questions about the role in moral thinking and in the good life of all those elements which cannot be reduced to rationality: external relationships such as love, friendship, political activity, attachment to possessions; and internal drives of a non-rational kind, the appetites, feelings, passions and needs. Martha Nussbaum develops a coherent argument as she goes through a range of Greek writings from the tragedians to Aristotle, which is worked out with great energy and force, and which makes the reader think hard about familiar texts and see them in new and very interesting lights. It is a prominent feature of the book that the author is not concerned only with a dispassionate exposition of ancient documents. On the contrary, she sees them as still morally illuminating, offering insights which are concealed in our conventional post-Kantian thinking. "We have discovered that we do live in the world that Aristotle describes", is her conclusion, and these Greek authors can help us to see how to understand and live in that world.

It is clearly true of human life that we are to a great extent at the mercy of external events and internal drives, and yet that we aspire, in a way and at least for some of the-time, to live in accordance with reason. The Greeks were intensely conscious of the tension. Plato, with his unflinching fearlessness of argument, made determined and consistent attempts to reduce to zero the power of the irrational, both from without and from within. The Socrates of dialogues like the *Phaedo* is completely detached from external needs: uninterested in possessions, physically ascetic, shoeless, tough and independent. He also, as we see in the *Symposium* is impregnably armoured against even the strongest temptations of sensuality. "No man ever saw Socrates drunk", and a determined assault on his virtue by the glamorous Alcibiades leaves the philosopher unmoved in his ironical superiority.

In the *Republic* Plato embeds this attitude in an elaborate system of metaphysics, which serves as the framework for a whole planned society: a society immune to chance, passion and change. The *Republic* insists on the suppression of the desires, except for privileged ones which relate to knowledge and truth: asceticism is to be the rule of society, where all is ordered and there is no room for chance. It is cardinal to the *Symposium* that all the objects of desire, which seem so different from each other, are in reality examples of the same single system of values. Seen in the true perspective, art and mathematics are really one, and so are physical love and political theory: there can be no incompatibility or conflict between any of them. The highest levels of abstract thought are also the most intense of pleasures. All aspirations and all desires tend, in reality, to the same end. Thus the *Symposium* goes even further than the *Republic* in removing the possibility of moral conflict. True values cannot be in conflict with each other; in fact, they are all interchangeable. The agony of the tragic hero, Hamlet or Orestes, is thus ruled out; and, quite consistently, Plato condemns and rejects the works of the tragedians.

There were of course people in the ancient world, as there are in the modern, who took the opposite course. Some said that happiness simply was good luck, nothing else; others that the only thing of value was pleasure. These people are not well represented in what survives of early literature, and it seems that only after Aristotle did a systematic philosophical hedonism come into existence. This view is hardly discussed in the present work.

Many scholars now find Plato's views repulsive or bizarre, and in some influential recent works he has taken a severe pounding. We want to insist on the variety of values, not all reducible to the same coin and interchangeable with each other, and on a greater importance of individual relationships and personal affections than seems to be allowed by this great theorist of love, who talks far more about the subject than modern philosophers do, yet who seems to regard it as a means rather than an end: a way of raising the soul to levels of vision and understanding which it cannot reach without the stimulus of passion, but which essentially are solitary and incommunicable.

Professor Nussbaum shows more sympathy and more understanding of the Platonic position than it often

receives. There is something in the human heart to which the Platonic demand for simplicity, clarity and independence makes a strong appeal. It will not do to dismiss it as merely eccentric. But it is possible to see how Plato's one-sided emphasis on this side of our nature can be redressed, without sinking into undistinguished blandness. She offers us a wide and synoptic account, which shows Plato first reacting against the views of the tragic poets, then himself developing in a more human and less ascetic direction. Finally the marvellous sanity of Aristotle restores the true balance between pure reason and passionate feeling, recognizing that neither is sufficient alone, but that rational moral choice involves both. Thus the reality of moral conflict, the clash of good with good, the importance of emotion and suffering over mistaken or constrained actions—all the elements vital to tragedy that Plato rejected are brought back by Aristotle. It is consistent with this that Aristotle was a great admirer of tragedy, keenly interested in the subject, and concerned to establish its intellectual respectability and significance after the Platonic denial.

This is an engrossing account and an important book. Its scope is very wide, in a world in which it has become sadly unusual for a scholar to tackle both tragedy and philosophy in a single work. It contains detailed discussions of two plays, the *Antigone* and the *Hecuba,* and it is prepared to tackle every aspect of the works it discusses, from the date and historical context of Plato's *Symposium* and *Phaedrus* to the real meaning of Aristotle's theory of catharsis (not purgation in the medical sense but "cognitive clarification").

It certainly contains things which will not command universal agreement. Probably the part most unlikely to be generally accepted is the discussion of the *Phaedrus.* This dialogue departs to some extent from the ascetic and self-controlled picture of love which, on the surface at least, characterizes the *Symposium*; it salutes madness as divine and a necessary part of human wellbeing. Whereas in earlier works of Plato desires were generally regarded as entirely bad, irrational distractions from the life of reason, in the *Phaedrus* they are granted an important role in the guidance of the soul. Coolness is now not enough. It is the view of this book that Plato here reinstates as central to successful living an erotic passion for a unique individual, studied in his uniqueness for his own sake and not as a means to an end: through shared experience and shared emotional struggle the soul learns and transcends itself. This reflects the profound impression made on Plato by his love for Dion, an impression confirmed by the great philosopher's verse epigrams. It is a comparatively small point that scholarly opinion has been convinced, ever since 1963, that none of these poems is genuine, though it is a surprise to find no mention of the view of Sir Denys Page in his magisterial edition of 1981: "Not one of these epigrams can be accepted as the work of Plato."

More important is that the view of love in this dialogue is less different, and less modern, than Nussbaum suggests. Love is still primarily "love of beauty", which is only embodied in the beloved person, and which enables the lover to rediscover and recapture the beauty which he knew before his birth; and the ways which the lover learns and imitates are not really those of the beloved but those of the patron god or goddess whom they both follow. The coolness of the *Symposium,* too, can be exaggerated: the atmosphere of the gathering described in the dialogue is electric with erotic tension, Alcibiades says to the company, "You have all shared in the madness and ecstasy of philosophy", and the stimulus of passion is necessary to the ascent of the Platonic ladder of perception and revelation.

Generally speaking it is right for scholars to write in a dryish tone. Embarrassment rather than inspiration is the effect produced, I suppose, by most scholarly books which seek to convey feelings along with the footnotes. This book is among the exceptions: a learned work which succeeds in communicating the urgency of the writer's feelings and the importance of her subject. Nussbaum's interest in the style of philosophical, discourse, as well as its substance, adds depth to her discussions. At moments the reader feels that the pull of modernity has slightly distorted the shape of the ancient texts, especially on questions concerned with women (though here too there are some very interesting discussions). It is sad that so sensitive a scholar has felt obliged to sprinkle her pages with "he or she": "to opt for 'he' everywhere seemed repugnant to my political sensibilities". It can only be with a heavy heart that the reader confronts a sentence like this (an uncharacteristic horror, it should in fairness be said): "The lovers' problem will arise for anyone who doubts that the external movements, gestures and speeches of his or her limbs, trunk, face, genitals, always fully and adequately express the person that [s]he feels himself or herself to be." And there is a quaintness about the compulsion which the author feels to let us know that she dissents from Plato's contemptuous attitude towards passive male homosexuals: "I'd like to leave no doubt that I dissociate myself from the social prejudices shown . . .". She herself points out that even Aristotle failed to achieve rationality in this area: "This judicious fair-minded man . . . shows us the tremendous power of sexual convention . . . in shaping a view of the world." That her own book, formidably intelligent and persuasively emotional, shares a blind spot of Aristotle as well as some of his virtues: that is a price which, in this imperfect world, she, and we, must be happy to pay.

Bernard Knox (review date 4 December 1986)

SOURCE: Knox, Bernard. "The Theater of Ethics." *New York Review of Books* (4 December 1986): 51-6.

[*In the following review, Knox asserts that Nussbaum's* The Fragility of Goodness *is unique in that it includes expert analysis of both philosophical and tragic literary texts. Knox observes that the book is intellectually demanding as well as richly rewarding.*]

"There is an ancient quarrel between philosophy and poetry," says Plato's Socrates, as, in Book X of the *Republic,* he reconfirms his decision to banish Homer and the tragic poets from his ideal city. And indeed it is true that long before Plato such philosophers as Xenophanes and Heraclitus had inveighed against the poets for, among other things, their presentation of gods engaged in unjust or immoral activities. Poets working in what Plato called the imitative poetic media, epic and tragedy, were of course unable to reply in kind (though some passages of tragic lyric reflect a critical reaction to current philosophical speculation), but Pindar complained that the natural philosophers (*tous physiologous*) were "harvesting the fruit of wisdom unripe."

Later on Aristophanes put on stage a scurrilous caricature of Socrates, and Plato himself was a favorite target of the comic poets when his Academy became a philosophical center in Athens. We have a fragment from a play of Epicrates, for example, which presents Plato and his students trying, without much success, to "distinguish" (a Platonic technical term) between "the life of animals, the nature of trees, and the species of vegetables." And in a comedy by Amphis a slave says to his master: "What good you expect to get from this, sir, I have no more idea of than I have of Plato's 'good.'"

This "quarrel" between poetry and philosophy tends to manifest itself also in modern scholarly and critical approaches to the two adversaries. Literary surveys of classical Greek culture usually pay too little attention to philosophical texts—and vice versa. Scholars who are not philosophically trained or inclined usually confine their reading of Plato (as Martha Nussbaum slyly remarks [in *The Fragility of Goodness*]) to the early and middle dialogues, where dramatic and poetic elements are given full play; as for Aristotle, they rarely venture outside the *Poetics,* the *Rhetoric,* and the *Nicomachean Ethics.* Students of philosophy, on the other hand, often seem unaware that many of the problems discussed by ancient philosophers, especially in the ethical field, are also posed, in a different but no less valid form, by lyric and especially by tragic poets.

An extreme case, of such disciplinary tunnel vision is the second volume of Michel Foucault's *Histoire de la sexualité,* recently published in English translation under the title *The Use of Pleasure.* Its subject is the "problematization" of sexual behavior in classical Greek culture but its evidence is drawn exclusively from the writings of Plato, Xenophon, Aristotle, and the Hippocratic physicians. It does not seem to have occurred to Foucault that for an understanding of the ways sexual behavior was conceived of in classical Greece, tragedies such as Sophocles' *Women of Trachis* and Euripides' *Hippolytus* and *Medea,* to cite only three of the relevant examples, might be just as revealing as the strictly homosexual erotic theorizing of Plato's *Symposium.*

Foucault's Olympian indifference to the evidence of tragedy is perhaps unique, but it is nevertheless "customary," as Nussbaum puts it, to regard tragic and philosophical texts as "of quite different sorts, bearing in quite different ways on human ethical questions." But this, as she goes on to point out, "was clearly not the view of the Greeks." Homer, Hesiod, and the poets of the tragic stage were in fact thought of as ethical teachers and Plato's indictment of them sprang from his conception of them not "as colleagues in another department, pursuing different aims, but as dangerous rivals." Nussbaum proposes to study the "works of the tragic poets as Plato studied them: as ethical reflections in their own right."

She is of course primarily a distinguished student of Greek philosophy, editor of a difficult Aristotelian text, *On the Motion of Animals,* and author not only of the first full-length commentary on that text to be published since the thirteenth century but also of a series of essays on the philosophical problems it raises.[1] But she is also the author of a remarkable article entitled **"Flawed Crystals: James's *The Golden Bowl* and Literature as Moral Philosophy"** as well as a penetrating essay on Sophoclean tragedy, **"Consequences and Character in Sophocles' *Philoctetes.*"**[2] She comes, then, well equipped for a book which opens with chapters on Aeschylus and the *Antigone* of Sophocles, proceeds to discussion of Plato's *Protagoras, Republic, Symposium,* and *Phaedrus,* follows this with five chapters on Aristotle, and ends with an epilogue devoted to Euripides' *Hecuba.* This long, intellectually demanding, and richly rewarding book must be almost unique in its expert analysis of both tragic and philosophical texts.

Nussbaum's argument is complex, occasionally technical, but always intelligible even for those who, like the reviewer, read Plato with pleasure as far as the *Phaedrus,* find the going tough in the *Parmenides* and *Politicus,* but get a second wind in *The Laws.* She recognizes that her chapter, "Rational Animals and the Explanation of Action" may "seem rather technical for the nonspecialist reader, who might prefer to turn directly to the chapter's concluding section (v), where the ethical implications of the explanatory project are described." In a short preface she gives the reader a choice: "This

book can be read in two ways." Since after the introductory chapter, which identifies the problems to be discussed, each chapter is devoted, except in the case of Aristotle, to a single work—tragedy or Platonic dialogue—"readers can . . . feel free to turn directly to the chapter or chapters that seem most pertinent to their own concerns." But the reader is also advised that "there is . . . an overall historical argument, concerning the development of Greek thought on our questions; this is closely linked to an overall philosophical argument about the merits of various proposals for self-sufficient life."

"Our questions" are those raised by the author's stated purpose: to examine "the aspiration to rational self-sufficiency in Greek ethical thought: the aspiration to make the goodness of a good human life safe from luck through the controlling power of reason." The word "luck" is a rough equivalent of the Greek word *tuche*— "rough" because *tuche* does not necessarily refer to "random or uncaused" events; *tuche* means simply "what just happens to a man" as opposed to "what he does or makes." Goodness, on the other hand, is used by Nussbaum in a double sense: the ethical quality of a human life and also the happiness, the enviability of that life. Clearly, goodness of the second kind is vulnerable to luck; the Greeks in general believed, contrary to modern Kantian ideas, that the first—the ethical quality of life—was vulnerable also. For one thing, the constituents of a happy life—love, friendship, attachment to property—may be "capable, in circumstances not of the agent's own making, of generating conflicting requirements that can themselves impair the goodness of the agent's life." And secondly there can be an inner conflict between a person's aspiration to self-sufficiency and the irrational forces in his own nature— "appetites, feelings, emotions"—sources of disorder, of what the Greeks called *mania,* "madness."

The attainment of complete immunity to luck would seem therefore to call for a renunciation not only of those vulnerable components of the good life that set it at risk but also a total suppression of the appetites and passions that might undermine a personal dedication to self-sufficiency. Even if such rigid self-control were possible for mere human creatures, the resultant life would seem, to most of us at least, limited and impoverished. And in fact it is only Plato, at the vertiginous height of his argument in *Phaedo, Republic,* and *Symposium,* who proposes "a life of self-sufficient contemplation, in which unstable activities and their objects have no intrinsic value."

The tragic poets, however, especially Aeschylus and Sophocles, present us with human characters exposed to fortune through their pursuit of those genuine human values that put us at risk—responsibility to others, loyalty to a community, devotion to the family. Nussbaum offers an impressive analysis of the tragic dilemmas of two Aeschylean heroes, Agamemnon at Aulis and Eteocles at the seventh gate of Thebes: in each case a "wrong action [is] committed without any direct physical compulsion and in full knowledge of its nature, by a person whose ethical character or commitments would otherwise dispose him to reject the act." Agamemnon, if he is to do his duty as commander of the expedition, must sacrifice his daughter; Eteocles, to save his city from destruction, must engage his brother in mortal combat. Agamemnon is placed by Zeus in a situation in which there is open to him no "guilt-free course." Modern critics have found contradiction and illogicality in the Aeschylean view of tragic necessity, a criticism for which Nussbaum has scant sympathy. "Such situations," she says, "may be repellent to practical logic; they are also familiar from the experience of life."

In Sophocles' *Antigone* the two principal characters attempt to avoid such dilemmas by "a ruthless simplification of the world of value which effectively eliminates conflicting obligations." Creon rules out all loyalties except that to the city; since Polynices, though a member of Creon's own family, has led a foreign assault on the city, he does not hesitate to order the exposure of his corpse, in spite of the fact that custom and religion assign him, as the only surviving male relative, responsibility for Polynices' proper burial.

Antigone too has her strategy of "avoidance and simplification"; her exclusive loyalty is to family obligations, specifically "duty to the family dead." Both of them come to grief, and though our sympathies are with Antigone the play clearly rejects the kind of rigid simplification of issues which inspired their actions. As Antigone is led off to her underground tomb, the chorus sings about others who have been similarly imprisoned, a song which Nussbaum, in a sensitive and convincing interpretation, sees as a repudiation of human action, a blind acceptance of passivity under the blows of fortune. The play seems to offer no escape from the choice between "Creon's violence against the external and complete helpless passivity before the external."

But this "paralyzing vision" is not the last word. In the speeches of Haemon and Tiresias a third possibility emerges, a prudent and intelligent moderation that makes it possible "to be flexibly responsive to the world, rather than rigid . . . a way of living in the world that allows an acceptable amount of safety and stability while still permitting recognition of the richness of value that is in the world." Creon concludes in the end that "it is best to keep to the established conventions (*nomous*)." These are "the traditions of a community, built up and established over time" which "offer a good guide to what, in the world, ought to be recognized and yielded to." They "preserve a rich

plurality of values" though they "offer no solution in bewildering tragic situations—except the solution that consists in being faithful to or harmonious with one's sense of worth by acknowledging the tension and disharmony."

The second choral ode of the *Antigone* begins with a famous celebration of the *technai,* the arts and sciences which have brought man, step by step, from helplessness to mastery of his environment and his crowning achievement, the creation of the state. *Techne,* the song seems to suggest, is the instrument by which man can make himself immune to *tuche.* In the event this proves to be a delusion; the messenger who announces the deaths of Antigone and Haemon proclaims the omnipotence of *tuche*—"Luck raises and luck humbles the lucky and the unlucky from day to day"—and the only successful *techne* mentioned in the play is that of the prophet Tiresias who reads the signs of divine wrath and comes to warn Creon that he stands "on the razor-edge of luck."

Discussion of *techne* and *tuche* was not a monopoly of the tragic poets, it was a major preoccupation of intellectual circles in Periclean Athens. The Sophists, the West's first professional educators, taught *technai,* especially the arts of persuasion, claiming they were the key to political advancement in democratic Athens; Protagoras, perhaps the greatest of them, says, in the Platonic dialogue that bears his name, that he can teach political *techne* and make men good citizens. This dialogue, one of Plato's greatest creations from the literary and dramatic point of view, is full of stumbling blocks for the admirers of Plato the philosopher; not only does Socrates use arguments that border on the fallacious, he also proposes an identification of pleasure and goodness which is specifically repudiated in nearly every other Platonic dialogue. Nussbaum's analysis of the dialogue is a subtle, finely argued attempt to set Plato's thought squarely in the context of her leitmotif: the aspiration to rational self-sufficiency.

Protagoras' science of practical reasoning can claim it is a *techne* that "increases our control over *tuche*" but, though it will go far toward "training the passions . . . it will not completely render them innocuous." Above all it will not eliminate the conflict of values and the possibility of tragedy since, against the argument of Socrates, it recognizes "a plurality of distinct values." Socrates' insistence on the unity of the virtues Nussbaum sees as a necessary base for his ethical science (*episteme*) of measurement which would remove the possibility of "serious value conflict. For instead of choosing, under circumstantial pressure, to neglect a distinct value with its own separate claims, one will merely be giving up a smaller amount of the same thing." His adoption of pleasure as "the single measuring-stick of value" Nussbaum sees as a temporary expedient, which is "undefended, even unexplored" and in effect discarded at the end of the dialogue. What is important is the formulation of a science of "deliberative measurement."

This reading of the argument of *Protagoras* is no more likely to win universal acceptance than any of its predecessors, but it is presented with persuasive skill and buttressed by footnotes addressed to professional colleagues dealing in depth with possible objections and conflicting interpretations. What is interesting about it from the point of view of the non-professional is the link to tragedy. Protagoras' program of practical reasoning is a *techne* which, as Nussbaum points out, "follows Tiresias' advice"; it is a "practical wisdom that bends responsively to the shape of the natural world, accommodating itself to, giving due recognition to, its complexities." It might be added that Socrates, in his insistence on a single value, seems to be following the pattern of Antigone and Creon, whose exclusive loyalty to one value armored them against normal human feelings that might conflict with it.

In later dialogues of the middle period Socrates abandons pleasure as the measuring stick but continues the search for a science concerned with "rendering diverse particulars qualitatively homogeneous and interchangeable" which will "undo several problems at once, transforming troublesome conflicts," and "cutting away our motivations for passional excess." The search leads in the *Republic* to the total rejection of passions and appetites in favor of the life of the philosopher, who "stands apart from human needs and limitations," and whose viewpoint is "detached and extra-human," and in the *Phaedo* it leads to the creation of a model life that is "practice for the separation of the soul from the body." This is, as a doctor might put it, a heroic remedy and Nussbaum might have pointed out that Plato's Socrates owes more than a little to tragedy's conception of the hero: he rejects compromises and goes to his death rather than change his way of life. In the *Apology,* Plato's version of his speech at his trial, Socrates compares himself to, of all people, Achilles, and even claims he is looking forward to conversing, in the next world, with the most stubborn, bloody, and revengeful of the heroes, Ajax son of Telamon.

Nussbaum's emphasis, however, is on the difference, not the resemblance. The tragic hero's single criterion of value has its roots in the passions; it involves him fatally in a nexus of human needs and interests—family, community, love of another person—which breeds conflict. Plato's hero on the other hand reaches his criterion through the exercise of reason, rejects the passions and appetites completely, and lives a life spent in contemplation of eternal unchanging truths, free from internal value conflicts and immune to luck.

Plato's intellectual heroism denies the premises of tragedy but, as Nussbaum reminds us in a brilliant interlude between chapters—"Plato's Anti-tragic Theater"—the medium he invented for the presentation of his ideas was much indebted to that tragic drama which he was eventually to banish from his ideal state. Not only did he develop along new lines the ethical themes that tragedy had embodied in its heroic protagonists, he also adapted for his own literary and philosophical ends tragedy's dramatic means—character, dialogue, and plot. The dramatic form of his philosophical treatises is a radical departure. Previous philosophers, whether they wrote verse like Parmenides and Empedocles or prose like Anaxagoras and Democritus, addressed their readers in their own persons and in a didactic tone; as Nussbaum observes, Parmenides claims that he is an initiate and Empedocles that he is a god on earth. These are the books that Socrates (so Plato tells us in the *Phaedrus*) compared to figures in paintings: "For if you ask them a question, they keep a solemn silence." The Platonic dialogue "puts before us the responsiveness of dialectical interaction, as tragedy has also shown us concerned moral communication and debate." Unlike the ex cathedra pronouncements of the philosophers or the artful rhetoric of the Sophists, the dialogues "might fairly claim that they awaken and enliven the soul, arousing it to rational activity rather than lulling it into drugged passivity. They owe this to their kinship with theater."

They are theater, but "theater purged and purified of theater's characteristic appeal to powerful emotions"; they are "a pure crystalline theater of the intellect." Like tragedy, the dialogues move toward recognition of the truth through *elenchos,* testing and refutation; they "share with tragic poetry its elenctic structure." But there is a fundamental difference between the tragic and the Platonic *elenchos.* Creon rejects the arguments of Antigone, Haemon, and Tiresias; It takes the death of his son, "the sudden rush of grief, the tug of loss to make him see an aspect of the world to which he had not done justice." Recognition of the truth comes through the emotions; it was his intellectual conviction that led him to disaster. For Plato, on the other hand, learning comes through the intellect alone; it "takes place when the interlocutor is enmeshed in logical contradiction." His emotions are not to be aroused; "the ascent of the soul towards true understanding, if it uses any texts at all, will . . . avoid any with an irrational or emotive character."

The most powerful and dangerous of the emotions is what the Greeks called Eros, an irrational, passionate attachment to another human being. If the philosophical life can be lived only with passions and emotions totally subdued Eros is clearly the most formidable adversary to be faced.

Plato recognizes this; he devotes to the problem of Eros the most richly dramatic of his dialogues, the *Symposium*. At a banquet in the house of the tragic poet Agathon, six speakers deliver an encomium of Eros; the last to speak is Socrates. Claiming that he is handing down the doctrine of the seer Diotima, he describes the progress of the lover, under the teacher's guidance, from love of an individual body and mind to contemplation of the beautiful itself, "unalloyed, pure, unmixed, not stuffed full of human flesh and colors and lots of other mortal rubbish" (211E, Nussbaum's translation). Anyone who can reach such a stage of unworldliness is obviously immune to luck, impervious to the sorrow that loss of the beloved person can inflict.

But to reach such heights is no easy matter. We shall be given later, when Alcibiades, an uninvited guest, speaks about Socrates, a picture of a man who has started to make the ascent. He is a man who, as Nussbaum puts it, "has so dissociated himself from his body that he genuinely does not feel its pain, or regard its sufferings as things genuinely happening to him." He is impervious to cold, to fatigue, to hardship of any kind; he can drink without fear of intoxication and he can resist "the most immediate and intense sexual temptation." This is a man "in the process of making himself self-sufficient," and it is not an inviting prospect. Socrates, as Alcibiades truly says, "is not like any human being."

When Alcibiades bursts in on the party just as Socrates concludes his exposition of Diotima's teaching, we are faced suddenly with the incarnation of everything Diotima, or rather Socrates, would have us renounce. Crowned with the ivy of Dionysus and the violets of Aphrodite, Alcibiades is a vibrant image of the splendors of this fleshly world—a man of extraordinary physical beauty, a rich aristocrat, a brilliant wit and forceful speaker, and also, at the dramatic time of the dialogue, 416 BC, indisputably the most admired man in Athens, the political leader who was shortly to persuade the Athenian assembly to send him in command of a fleet and army to conquer Sicily. The speech he makes is not, like those of the dinner guests, an encomium of Eros; it is a tragicomic account of his unsuccessful wooing of Socrates, this strange, fascinating, but incorruptible man.

Nussbaum sees in this speech more than a reluctant encomium of Socrates; it offers, she claims, an alternative to Diotima's progress from love of an individual to contemplation of universal truth. Her cogent analysis of the implications of the speech must be read in full for a real understanding of her thesis. Roughly speaking, she sees in Alcibiades a spokesman for the lover's understanding—an understanding "attained through the subtle interaction of sense, emotion, and intellect" and "yielding particular truths and particular judgements as a form of practical understanding." This is a position which

has an affinity with that of Tiresias, Haemon, and Protagoras, as well as that of Socrates in the *Phaedrus*. But its spokesman is himself, as every reader of Plato knew, a terrible example of lack of practical wisdom, a man "who will live, to the end, a disorderly, buffeted life, inconstant and wasteful of his excellent nature," to die at last in exile, murdered by order of the victorious Spartans or, according to another account, by the brothers of a girl he had seduced. On this reading, the *Symposium* does indeed seem to us "a harsh and alarming book . . . We see now that philosophy is not fully human; but we are terrified of humanity and what it leads to."

This comfortless vision of the human dilemma was something Plato himself was later to find too extreme; he tempered and modified it—so Nussbaum's argument proceeds—in the *Phaedrus*. In this dialogue Socrates first makes an attack on erotic passion as a form of degrading madness" and denies the passions any "role to play in our understanding of the good." Later on, however, he makes another speech, which begins with a quotation from the palinode of Stesichorus, the poet's recantation of his censure of Helen:

> *This story is not true.*
> *You did not board the benched ships,*
> *you did not come to the towers of*
> * Troy.*

It is a prelude to his own recantation of his first speech, a defense of the benefits of madness (*mania.)Mania* is a word that up to this point Plato has used to designate "the state of soul in which the nonintellectual elements—appetites and emotions—are in control and lead or guide the intellectual part," a state which Socrates has always rejected in favor of *sophrosune,* "the state of soul in which intellect rules securely over the other elements."

Socrates now finds some good in *mania* after all. It is a necessity for the inspired seer as also for the poet; it is also, he goes on to say, necessary for the lover. From the poetic speech that follows, famous because of its image of the soul as a charioteer with two horses, one good and one bad, there emerges a view of the role of the passions quite different from the total rejection of them characteristic of the earlier dialogues. It makes us

> see human sexuality as something much more complicated and deep, more aspiring, than the middle dialogues had suggested; and, on the other hand, to see intellect as something more sexual than they had allowed, more bound up with receptivity and motion.

This is not, of course, an endorsement of Alcibiades' position (though he too uses the word *mania*); the noblest lovers will stop short of sexual intercourse. Yet those who occasionally lose control of the bad horse are not condemned outright, and in any case Plato's acceptance of love for a particular person exposes the lover to luck, to the possibility of loss, to all those human emotions to which the Socratic lover of the *Symposium* has made himself immune. This dialogue, Nussbaum claims, is a work in which Plato "admits that he has been blind to something, conceived oppositions too starkly," a work in which "he seeks, through recantation and self-critical argument, to get back his sight," as Stesichorus did when he wrote his palinode to Helen. "In the *Phaedrus* philosophy itself is said to be a form of *mania,* of possessed, not purely intellectual activity, in which intellect is guided to insight by personal love itself and by a complex passion-engendered ferment of the entire personality."

Obviously such a dramatic volte-face cries out for explanation—"We feel like asking, what happened to Plato?" Nussbaum looks for it in the historical circumstances in which the work was composed. She has in fact been conscious of this element throughout her discussion of Plato. It was put to brilliant use in her evocation of what Alcibiades meant to the Athenian readers of the *Symposium* and provides the fascinating suggestion that the reason Protagoras can adopt a "conservative," compromising position is "satisfaction." He

> has lived the prime of his life in the greatest age of Athenian political culture. He still seems to us to be a part of this glorious, relatively happy past . . . He is not gripped by the sense of urgency about moral problems that will soon characterize the writing of younger thinkers.

In the case of the *Phaedrus,* the background factor is personal: it is Plato's love for his pupil Dion, the man who was to overthrow the tyranny in his native city of Syracuse, only to be assassinated later on by political rivals.

It has often been noticed that when Socrates in the *Phaedrus* speaks of the ideal lovers he juxtaposes two words that mean "of Zeus" and "brilliant" and in their original Greek form *dios dion* suggest a punning reference to Plato's pupil; the great German scholar Wilamowitz regarded the allusion as "beyond reasonable doubt." Nussbaum adds that Phaedrus's name also means "brilliant," and since she has suggested that we are to think of Socrates and Phaedrus as representing the ideal lovers of Socrates' speech she can go on to see them as "standing in for Plato and Dion." This gives the dialogue "the character of a love letter, an expression of passion, wonder, and gratitude." She is not of course saying anything as simple-minded as that love made Plato change his mind; she recognizes that "his experience of love was certainly also shaped by his developing thought." But she does claim firmly that the dialogue asks "us to recognize experience as one factor of importance."

Here, however, she may be carrying her legitimate and even admirable attempt to ground the Platonic arguments in the contemporary scene too far. An allusion to Dion there may well be, but, though Dion was Plato's pupil and the close relationship between the two men extended over a quarter of a century, the evidence for an erotic attachment is weak. Plutarch's very full biography of Dion, for example, gives no hint of it; the argument for it rests principally on the testimony of one Diogenes Laertius, whose gossipy compilation *The Lives and Opinions of the Philosophers* was put together some time in the third century AD. He cites from Book IV of Aristippus' *The Luxury of the Ancients* an epitaph for Dion written by Plato which concludes with the line: "O Dion, you who drove my soul mad with love." But since this same Aristippus announces that Plato was also in love with a boy named Aster ("Star") and produces a love poem addressed to him as well, following this up with the information that Plato was in love with Phaedrus too, many scholars, including the late Sir Denys Page, the most recent editor of these poems, have concluded that like the other Platonic love poems collected by Diogenes—addressed to Phaedrus, Alexis, Agathon, and two professional ladies called Archeanassa and Xanthippe—the Aristippus love poems, including the epitaph for Dion, are typical Hellenistic forgeries.[3]

Whatever may be thought of Nussbaum's tentative reconstruction of the emotions that prompted the composition of the *Phaedrus,* there can be no doubt that she offers a challenging new reading of it. When she moves on to Aristotle, whose "conception of ethical theory . . . is," she says, "roughly" her own, she presents us with an Aristotle whose vision of the good life has more affinity with the *Phaedrus* than with the middle dialogues. Her Aristotle

> develops a conception of a human being's proper relationship to *tuche* that returns to and further articulates many of the insights of tragedy. His philosophical account of the good human life is . . . an appropriate continuation and an explicit description of those insights.

Plato's earlier conception of philosophy as a *techne* that can lift the individual above the level of normal humanity and so free him from the tyranny of luck Aristotle rejects in favor of a nonscientific mode of practical reasoning, which recognizes that some components of a good life are vulnerable to catastrophe. Turning his back on the philosophical tradition which held that appearances are deceptive and the opinions of the many false, Aristotle "insists that he will find his truth *inside* what we say, see, and believe, rather than 'far from the beaten path of human beings' (in Plato's words) 'out there.'"

Nussbaum's limitation of the scope of Aristotle's ethical enquiry to the common beliefs and conceptions of humanity depends on her interpretation of the word *phainomena*, literally "appearances," which occurs in Aristotle's discussion of his method at the beginning of Book VI of the *Nicomachean Ethics*: The method consists of

> setting down the *phainomena*, dealing with the initial difficulties, and proceeding in this way to demonstrate the truth of all the common beliefs (*endoxa*) about these states of mind or, if that is impossible, the truth of the majority and the most important of them. For if the difficulties can be resolved and the beliefs (*endoxa*) still stand, the demonstration will have been adequate.

Shortly after this passage Aristotle dismisses Socrates' claim that no one acts wrongly knowing that his action is wrong, but only in ignorance as "manifestly in contradiction with the *phainomena*." Most interpreters and translators, some of them in one of these passages and some in both, have taken *phainomena* to mean "the facts," "the observed facts," "data of perception," "observations"—almost anything, as Nussbaum says, "*but* the literal 'appearances,' or the frequently interchangeable 'what we believe,' or 'what we say.'" The tendentious translations derive from a "long tradition in the interpretation of Aristotelian science," which sees Aristotle in Baconian terms: a scientist who gathers data through empirical observation and then searches for a theory that will explain the data. It is clear that in the texts quoted above such an interpretation of *phainomena* is not acceptable, since the *phainomena* are immediately identified with *endoxa*, "common conceptions or beliefs on the subject."

The correct interpretation of *phainomena* was established in what Nussbaum calls a "justly famous article" by G. E. L. Owen; according to her, however, he did not go far enough, since he understood the term in the Baconian sense in Aristotle's biological works and thus "forces us to charge Aristotle with equivocation concerning his method and several of its central terms." Finding this inadmissible, she devotes an important chapter, "Saving Aristotle's Appearances" to a "univocal general account" of *phainomena* in Aristotle's method of ethical enquiry.[4]

What is that method? The philosopher begins by "setting down" the relevant appearances, "the ordinary beliefs and sayings" and a "review of previous scientific or philosophical treatments of the problem, the views of 'the many and the wise.'" The next step is to sort out the confusions and contradictions such matter contains, to eliminate contradiction. But the process of bringing "the matter of life into perspicuous order" does not allow us to "follow a logical argument anywhere it leads." We must, in the end, show that the *phainomena*, or at any rate the greatest number and the most important of them, are true. "Theory must remain committed to the ways human beings live, act, see."

A more total rejection of Plato's fundamental precepts is hard to imagine, and Nussbaum quotes from, of all places, the *Posterior Analytics,* a "burst of exuberant malice that shows us aspects of Aristotle's temperament usually masked by a measured sobriety": "So goodbye to the Platonic Forms. They are *teretismata*" (the sort of sounds you make when you hum to yourself) "and have nothing to do with our speech."

Her next four chapters are devoted to an explanation and defense of Aristotle's articulation of "a conception of practical rationality that will make human beings self-sufficient in an appropriately human way." The chapter which she warns us "may seem rather technical for the non-specialist reader" is a discussion of Aristotle's theories of animal motion and motivation which is relevant to ethical theory because it is part of Aristotle's ethical view that "our shared animal nature is the ground of our ethical development. It is our nature to be animal, the sort of animal that is rational."

This is followed by Nussbaum's discussion of "nonscientific deliberation"; it deals with Aristotle's claim that, contrary to Platonic doctrine, practical wisdom is not scientific wisdom. It deals also with Aristotle's emphasis on the anthropomorphism of the search for the good life, his attack on the Platonic commensurability of values and the Platonic demand for generality, and his affirmation of the role of nonintellectual elements in deliberation (a point on which he comes close to Plato's position in the *Phaedrus*). He has eliminated those elements in the Platonic "science" which conferred invulnerability to outside contingency. Rejecting both extreme positions—that luck is the sole decisive factor in the living of a good life and that good living is invulnerable to luck—Aristotle admits the possibility of "disruption of good activity" and even "damage to good states of character." For the ethical values that constitute good living cannot exist except in a context of human activity; though for animals and gods such concepts as justice, courage, generosity are irrelevant, these central human values "cannot be found in a life without shortage, risk, need, and limitation." This is true also of the values of friendship and political activity, the subject of Nussbaum's final chapter of Aristotle's ethical theory. This chapter ends with an eloquent assessment of the Aristotelian achievement.

> Aristotle has attempted . . . by setting our various beliefs before us, to show us that they contain a conception of human good living that makes it something relatively stable, but still vulnerable, in its search for richness of value, to many sorts of accidents. We pursue and value both stability and the richness that opens us to risk. In a certain sense we value risk itself, as partially constitutive of some kinds of value. In our deliberations we must balance these competing claims. This balance will never be a tension-free harmony.

Good human deliberation is a "delicate balancing act . . . delicate, and never concluded, if the agent is determined, as long as he or she lives, to keep all the recognized human values in play." To those who find this picture of deliberation "mundane, messy, and lacking in elegance," Aristotle would reply "that we do well not to aim at a conception that is more elegant, or simpler, than human life is." This is one of several passages in the book which will seem to many readers to justify Nussbaum's belief "that Nietzsche was correct in thinking that a culture grappling with the widespread loss of Judaeo-Christian religious faith could gain insight into its own persisting intuitions about value by turning to the Greeks."

But this is not the end of her book. She began with tragedy and it is with tragedy that she ends. Plato rejected it as a corrupting influence, but Aristotle's ethical position clearly allows it a place, even an important place, in human life, since it "explores the gap between being good and living well." Under the heading "Luck and the Tragic Emotions" Nussbaum discusses Aristotle's treatise on tragedy and especially his remarks about pity and fear. "For Aristotle, pity and fear will be sources of illumination or clarification, as the agent, responding and attending to his or her responses, develops a richer self-understanding concerning the attachments and values that support the responses."

This interpretation of a much-disputed text depends on a new understanding of the key word *katharsis* in Aristotle's formula "through pity and fear to accomplish the *katharsis* of experiences of that kind." Developing an argument of Leon Golden, who pointed out that *katharsis* and related words, as used by Plato, have a strong connection with learning, occurring in connection with "the unimpeded or 'clear' rational state of the soul," Nussbaum looks at the history of these words and finds that their "primary, ongoing, central meaning is roughly one of 'cleaning up' or 'clarification.'" The meaning "purgation," usually adduced in explanation of this passage in Aristotle, is a special medical application of this general sense.

In an epilogue Nussbaum presents an analysis of a play which Plato, though he does not mention it, must have regarded with indignation, for it shows us the complete deterioration of moral character under the pressure of calamity. It is the *Hecuba* of Euripides, a play rarely discussed in the voluminous literature on Greek tragedy, one which from the nineteenth century on into our own has often been censured as "episodic," "melodramatic," even, by one influential critic, "poor and uninteresting."

Nussbaum offers a convincing defense of its dramatic and thematic unity: the two main episodes, the sacrifice of Polyxena and Hecuba's atrocious revenge on the murderer of her son Polydorus, are seen as dramatic embodiments of contrasting views on the stability of good character under adverse conditions. The nobility of Polyxena, who refuses to plead for her life and dies with dignity and courage, prompts Hecuba to reflect that "among human beings . . . the noble [is never] anything but noble, and is not corrupted in its nature by contingency, but stays good straight through to the end." But with the discovery of her son's body and the realization that he has been murdered by the guest-friend Polymestor to whom she has entrusted him for safe-keeping, Hecuba's conception of a world governed by *nomos,* "deep human agreements concerning value," is shattered. In exchange she embraces a *nomos* of a different nature: revenge, the old law—an eye for an eye and a tooth for a tooth. Using the same moral convention of guest-friendship that Polymestor has betrayed, and appealing to the greed which had prompted his murder of her son, she lures him and his infant sons into the tents of the captured Trojan women, where the children are killed and Polymestor blinded. Later Polymestor prophesies that she will fall from the yardarm of the ship on her way to Greece and be transformed into a dog, a creature which, as Nussbaum emphasizes, ranks, for the Greeks, "very low on the scale of animal nobility." But she is already something less than human. The destruction of the *nomos* of mutual trust can produce, even in a stable character, "bestiality, the utter loss of human relatedness and human language."

This is, as Nussbaum puts it, a "worst case," but Aristotle, though he might insist on the rarity of such a combination of disasters as that which overwhelms Hecuba, "cannot consistently close off the possibility of such events." He too, like Hecuba, "bases human excellence on the social nature of the human being" (*nomos*). He "stresses that all of excellence has an other-related aspect" and that "personal love and political association are not only important components of the good human life but also necessary for the continued flourishing of good character generally." And he "mentions explicitly that trust is required to reap the benefits of these associations."

Euripides' play does show us, in the person of Polyxena, an example of uncorrupted nobility, but, as Nussbaum puts it, she has the "good luck" to die before life can bring disillusionment—"to live on is to make contact in some way at some time with the possibility of betrayal." The Platonic alternative, to "put the world in good order by sealing off certain risks, closing ourselves to certain happenings," and still retain a world "relatively rich in value, since it would still contain the beauty of the Platonic contemplative life" seems, when we look at the world of the *Hecuba,* an attractive one. And yet, as Aristotle, and for that matter the *Phaedrus* and the *Antigone,* have made clear, "there is in fact a loss in value whenever the risks involved in specifically human virtue are closed off. . . . Each salient Aristotelian virtue seems inseparable from a risk of harm"—

courage for example exists only in a context of death or serious damage. "There are certain risks," Nussbaum concludes, "that we cannot close off without a loss in human value, suspended as we are between beast and god, with a kind of beauty available to neither."

This outline of Nussbaum's argument gives little idea of its originality, intellectual richness, and logical force, nor can quotations from her text convey more than a faint impression of the fluidity, grace, precision, and economy of her prose. In her opening pages she speaks of the problem facing a philosopher who chooses to deal with "competing conceptions of learning and writing, as embodied in poetic and philosophical texts": the decision whether to adopt "the hard 'philosophical' style" or "a mode of writing that lies closer to poetry and makes its appeal to more than one 'part' of the person," or else to "use different styles in different parts of the inquiry." Her choice is "to attempt to vary the way of writing so that it will be appropriate to the ethical conception to which it responds in each case; to try to show in my writing the full range of my responses to the texts and to evoke similar responses in the reader." She will "remain always committed to the critical faculties, to clarity and close argument" but will also "try to deal with tragic (and Platonic) images and dramatic situations in such a way that the reader will feel, as well as think, their force." Over the four hundred or so pages of text and the nearly one hundred pages of notes she succeeds handily in fulfilling these promises; this is a book which keeps a firm hold on the reader's attention, challenges the reader's intellectual capacity, and appeals, gravely and without fulsome rhetoric, to his or her deepest emotions.

It is also a book which, besides being required reading for anyone interested in Greek philosophy or literature, addresses a wider audience. It analyzes the attempts of poets and philosophers in the great creative age of Greek civilization to deal with problems that, as Nussbaum says in her opening chapter, are still problems for anyone who finds it hard to accept the Kantian view that the domain of moral value supersedes all other values and that it is altogether immune from the assaults of luck. "That much that I did not make goes towards making me whatever I shall be praised or blamed for being," she writes,

> that I must constantly choose among competing and apparently incommensurable goods and that circumstances may force me to a position in which I cannot help being false to something or doing some wrong; that an event that simply happens to me may, without my consent, alter my life; that it is equally problematic to entrust one's good to friends, lovers, or country and to try to have a good life without them—all these I take to be not just the material of tragedy, but everyday facts of lived practical reason.

Notes

1. Aristotle, *De Motu Animalium.* Text with translation, commentary, and interpretive essays (Princeton, 1978). Paperback edition with corrections, 1985.

2. *New Literary History* 15 (1983), pp. 25-50: *Philosophy and Literature* (1976-1977), pp. 25-53.

3. Aristippus of Cyrene was a contemporary of Plato so it is not likely that he would have included Plato's love affairs in a book called *The Luxury of the Ancients.* Even Wilamowitz, who accepts the Dion epitaph as genuine, assigns Diogenes "Aristippus" to the second century BC.

4. "If we do not insist on introducing an anachronistic scientific conception," she says later, "the alleged two senses and two methods can be one. When Aristotle sits on the shore of Lesbos taking notes on shellfish . . . he will be describing the world *as it appears to,* as it is experienced, by observers who are members of our kind."

Bernard Knox (review date 25 November 1990)

SOURCE: Knox, Bernard. "The Heart Has Its Reasons." *Washington Post Book World* (25 November 1990): 1, 10.

[*In the following review, Knox asserts that the essays in* Love's Knowledge *are persuasive, lucidly written, and accessible to a general readership.*]

What is one to make of a book called ***Love's Knowledge*** that offers detailed critical analyses of Platonic and Aristotelian ethical theory, critical discussions of Henry James's *Golden Bowl, Ambassadors* and *Princess Casamàssima* as well as of Beckett, Dickens and Proust, and also calls in to support its argument such texts as Homer's *Odyssey* and Sophocles's "Women of Trachis," not to mention Nietzsche, Kant and Wittgenstein? The reader's first reaction may well be skeptical. To move with authority over so wide a range of intellectual history, the author must be an unlikely combination: an acute and sensitive critic of ancient and modern literature, a professional philosopher and a trained scholar of ancient Greek. In this case skepticism can be dispensed with; Martha Nussbaum is all of these things.

She has published a critical edition of the Greek text of Aristotle's treatise *On the Movement of Animals,* and provided it with a commentary and a series of long and philosophically rich essays. She is the author of a brilliant and much admired book, ***The Fragility of Goodness,*** which examines the ethical problems addressed not only by Plato and Aristotle but also by Greek tragedy; it argues that we cannot understand the work of the philosophers in isolation from the moral concerns of the tragic poets, who make a distinctive contribution to ethical thought. She has also in the course of the last 10 years, published a number of essays on the relationship between literature, especially the modern novel, and philosophy. Twelve of them are included in the volume under review, together with two new essays and a substantial introduction entitled **"Form and Content, Philosophy and Literature."** Many of these essays, all written in her characteristically lucid style and addressed to the general literate public as well as to her professional colleagues, first appeared in periodicals the general public is not likely to come across; it is good to have them in a volume accessible to a wider audience.

This book is not, however, like many such collections, a roundup of whatever articles the author has happened to publish in recent years. She has omitted at least seven interesting pieces, some of them destined for a subsequent volume; those included have been revised and expanded, and also provided with end-notes that "make many specific remarks about the relationships of the articles to one another." And the long, thoughtful introduction serves to clarify the book's central themes and also to justify its intriguing title.

As a Philosopher she is concerned above all with ethical theory, moral philosophy—one section of her introduction is headed by a sentence from Plato's *Republic*: "It is no chance matter we are discussing, but how one should live." Plato rejected totally the validity of epic and tragic poetry as a medium for discussion of moral problems, pursuing what he called "the ancient quarrel between the poets and the philosophers" to its logical end: the banishment of the poets from his ideal city. Discussion of ethics was to be built on an intellectually sound basis of moral definitions, constructed according to logical principles and tested by dialectic—and so, from Socrates until quite recent times, it has been ever since.

Nussbaum finds that this approach has serious limitations. "There may be some views of the world and how one should live in it—views, especially, that emphasize the world's surprising variety, its complexity and mysteriousness, its flawed and imperfect beauty—that cannot be fully and adequately stated in the language of conventional philosophic prose, a style remarkably flat and lacking in wonder . . ." She calls for a style of philosophical writing that will express its ideas "in a language and forms . . . more complex, more allusive, more attentive to particulars." And she is also proposing that ethical philosophy should concentrate its attention on the great works of the imagination as well as on the classics of its own discipline. Her aim is to "establish that certain literary texts . . . are indispensable to a philosophical inquiry in the ethical sphere; not by any means sufficient, but sources of insight without which the inquiry cannot be complete."

Whether or not she can establish that claim in the court of her philosophical colleagues, her discussion of "how one should live," based on a penetrating analysis of some of the great modern fictions, is fascinating reading, for without abandoning philosophical standards of argument she writes in a style that shows how much she has learned from the masters of our prose.

Perhaps the most unruly and disconcerting element of "the world's . . . flawed and imperfect beauty" is the complex of emotions we call "love." It is, as she says, a "strange, unmanageable phenomenon or form of life, source at once of illumination and confusion, agony and beauty." It can play havoc with ethical standards. So, in Nussbaum's perceptive reading of *The Golden Bowl*, Maggie Verver comes to the realization that "to regain her husband she must damage Charlotte . . . Her love . . . must live on cunning and treachery; it requires the breaking of moral rules . . ." Love, in all its strange manifestations and amoral imperatives, is the major theme of these essays; Nussbaum develops its full diapason from the high refinement of Henry James to the lower depths of Beckett's Molloy trilogy. And in one extraordinary essay, that is presented in narrative form, she uses as her text Dora Carrington's desperate love for Lytton Strachey.

But why, the reader may ask, do we need these fictions, however admirable, in addition to moral philosophy in our search for the good life? Nussbaum poses that question and answers it by citing Aristotle, the philosopher she most admires. We need fiction because "we have never lived enough." Our experience, without it, is "too confined, and too parochial. Literature extends it, making us reflect and feel about what might otherwise be too distant for feeling." Her purpose in these essays is "to suggest, with Aristotle, that practical reasoning unaccompanied by emotion is not sufficient for practical wisdom"; that emotions are "frequently more reliable and less deceptively seductive" than intellectual calculation. It is a bold suggestion, but these essays make an eloquent and to this one reader convincing case for it.

Gordon D. Marino (review date 7 December 1991)

SOURCE: Marino, Gordon D. Review of *Love's Knowledge,* by Martha Nussbaum. *America* (7 December 1991): 442-43.

[*In the following review of* Love's Knowledge, *Marino observes that Nussbaum presents a strong case for expanding the concept of moral philosophy to include literature.*]

In her earlier work, **The Fragility of Goodness,** Martha Nussbaum gracefully established the futility of reading Plato and Aristotle in isolation from Greek tragedy. In

Love's Knowledge, Nussbaum continues her reflections on the relationship between philosophy and literature. For those concerned with the rank order of disciplines, Nussbaum, professor of philosophy and classics at Brown University, has some humbling news for philosophers. Where human excellence is the end, it is better to major in comparative literature than philosophy.

In a compelling chapter on Aristotle, Nussbaum argues that ethics is not a science and that there is no single standard of value by which all decisions can be cast. Forging a good life is more complicated than figuring out how best to maximize pleasure and meaning. Following Aristotle, Nussbaum argues for a multiplicity of ends (e.g., justice, friendship, courage), each of which is an irreducible component of human excellence. Some philosophers think that if the decisive choices in life are reduced to two, there can be no common denominator and thus no reasons for choosing one course of life over another. Defending what she takes to be an Aristotelian conception of rationality, Nussbaum disagrees. Practical wisdom, which is in large part choosing rightly, depends upon accurately and richly perceiving our situation and choices; hence, Nussbaum's case for the priority of perception over abstraction.

The philosophers preach that what is real is universal, but discernment demands being able to see and retain a vision of the uniqueness of the particular. As though they could provide us with supplementary experience, Nussbaum argues that novels and drama are the best materials for developing discernment.

For Nussbaum, discernment demands a lot more than 20/20 vision. As she explains it, a failure of feeling is a failure of perception. The person who can read about the myriad casualties of a war without some wrenching does not really perceive what is going on. *Love's Knowledge* charges the philosophical system builders and concept splitters with many crimes of negligence, not the least of which is peddling the myth that the heart is the mortal enemy of the mind. Most contemporary philosophers acknowledge that the emotions are not without cognitive content. After all, to feel something about someone is to believe something about them. Nussbaum, however, goes further. Consistently claiming to derive her insights from her favorite novels, she insists that there is much that can only be known feelingly. As her title indicates, to be without love is to be without a certain knowledge, or, to take a theme that Nussbaum positively harps upon, to be devoid of puzzlement is to fail to grasp the fundamental truth that the world is a very puzzling place.

Nussbaum appears to believe that what the abstracted moralists are missing is something Kant pointed to and Kierkegaard partially provided, namely, an aesthetic of morals, or, if you will, a glimpse of the concrete

implications of one's ideals. It is only through first-and second-hand experience that we can achieve clarity about what it means to believe what we only imagine ourselves to believe. Using Henry James's narratives, Nussbaum moralizes that achieving clarity of self may be our most pressing moral obligation. For all their fetishes about clarity of argument, philosophers, according to Nussbaum, are of scant assistance when it comes to helping people get clear about themselves. Literary artists are another story.

Nussbaum believes that we are often so preoccupied by self-interest that we do not see the most obvious truths about ourselves. Because of the combination of safe distance and emotional engagement the novel affords, it offers us a possibility of curing this blindness.

Love's Knowledge is an immense and arabesque book, unflinching in self-criticism and rich, perhaps even excessive, in content. Where the dissemination of knowledge about the good life is concerned, style and content are inextricable. Ironically, for a book so much concerned with style, the writing is prosaic and often rambles. Nussbaum's reflections on the proper curriculum for our sentimental education, nevertheless, are worth the effort it sometimes takes to read them. Nussbaum presents a strong case for expanding our concept of philosophy to include Austen, James and other artists who do their moralizing obliquely.

Mary Sirridge (review date winter 1992)

SOURCE: Sirridge, Mary. Review of *Love's Knowledge,* by Martha Nussbaum. *Journal of Aesthetics and Art Criticism* 50, no. 1 (winter 1992): 61-5.

[*In the following review, Sirridge asserts that* Love's Knowledge *lacks a clear central focus, and that Nussbaum's arguments are not persuasive because they are not based on sound philosophical foundations.*]

Love's Knowledge is a collection of essays, many of which have been published previously. These essays have a common rationale, however, and represent collectively an effort to develop and conduct ethical investigations in the way in which Nussbaum thinks ethics should proceed: by bringing philosophical awareness to bear upon the works of literary imagination.

Ethical inquiry, for Nussbaum, aims at an answer to the question: How should one live? She favors an answer to this question which she calls "Aristotelian." This conception of ethics involves, first of all, a recognition that objects of value do not differ just quantitatively, i.e., as different numbers of units of the same generic commodity, the good. Rather, such objects are qualitatively distinct, with the result that an agent who prefers one to the exclusion of another incurs a real loss. Thus, for Nussbaum's Aristotelian, the human ethical situation involves vulnerability to genuine loss; more generally, it is endemic to the good human life to be susceptible to being affected by factors beyond one's control. Consequently, the attempt to formulate ethical strategies which reduce or eliminate such vulnerability is completely misguided. For this "Aristotelian" conception, it is particular, practical contexts that are ethically significant; thus this "Aristotelian" approach to value requires a richly differentiated faculty of perception, "the ability to discern accurately and responsibly the salient features of one's particular situation" (p. 37). The emotions, as patterns of value response to the particular and the concrete, are not automatically suspect; indeed, according to Nussbaum, they have a "cognitive dimension in their very structure" (p. 41).

The opposite complex of views—commensurability of goods, the importance of the general and irrelevance of particularizing factors, the irrelevance or downright undesirability of emotion, the ideal of transcendence of the human—these are views which Nussbaum associates with Plato, though she notes that most of them are present to varying degrees and in diverse forms in a good deal of Western philosophy.

According to Nussbaum, this "Aristotelian" conception of ethical inquiry has specific consequences for a choice of philosophical style, for style is an important determinant of meaning. The typical Anglo-American analytic style, "correct scientific, abstract, hygienically pallid . . . a kind of all-purpose solvent" (p. 19), does not allow us to achieve fruitful investigations of the realm of individual choice, emotion, "our deepest practical searching" (p. 24). This arena of investigation crucially involves feeling and imagination. Thus the Aristotelian investigation of the human good requires that the narratives of literature, particularly the novel, be brought into the ethical search—"certain literary texts (or texts similar to these in certain relevant ways) are indispensable to a philosophical inquiry in the ethical sphere" (p. 23). "This would mean, in our argument, that the emotions, and their accomplices, the stories, would be not just permitted, but required, in a fully human philosophy" (p. 389). Stories are not sufficient, according to Nussbaum; this study of ethics also requires a philosophical awareness which is rich and discriminating, yet also potentially critical of the insights offered by literary narratives. Nussbaum seems also to subscribe to the further thesis that writing and reading narratives of this sort is, at least sometimes, moral activity. "The novel is itself a moral achievement" (p. 148), she says.

Love's Knowledge is an attempt to follow out the implications of this view of ethics by developing a mode of philosophical expression which includes narrative.

Nussbaum sets out to achieve her objective, first, by presenting the essays as parts of a philosophically reflective narrative about her own intellectual development; there is an autobiographical introduction, and the essays are connected with one another by a system of autobiographical-theoretical "epilogues." Second, most of the essays consist of Nussbaum's philosophical reflections about liberal chunks of narrative fiction, fiction which is for the most part already extremely morally and philosophically self-aware. Finally, and most daringly, in **"Love and the Individual,"** Nussbaum offers an interthreading of philosophical voice and narrative, a medley of reflections by and on a protagonist who works her way from the desolation of lost love to a more reflective sense of loss by way of a continued meditation (fictional?) on a passage from Dora Carrington's diary in which Carrington bewails the loss of her irreplaceable, irretrievably lost lover.

Nussbaum's presentation of Aristotle and Plato is a partial recapitulation of the longer and more detailed study in her earlier work, *The Fragility of Goodness* (Cambridge University Press, 1986). Nussbaum's emphasis on the cognitive significance of the particular and upon concrete ethical *praxis* is a result of taking *Nicomachean Ethics* as a point of departure; this pattern is found already among medieval Aristotelians. Moreover, Nussbaum takes Aristotle's *Poetics* seriously as a source of information about his views on the meaning of life, the nature of happiness and man's fate. Her view of Aristotle is somewhat more difficult to arrive at if one starts instead from *Posterior Analytics, Metaphysics,* and *De Anima,* as many current interpreters of Aristotle do; and readers who want to meet a very different Aristotle may wish to read Terence Irwin's *Aristotle's First Principles* (Oxford University Press, 1988). Nussbaum addresses some critics of her interpretation of Aristotle in the book's final essay, **"Transcending Humanity."**

From the point of view of aesthetics and the philosophy of literature, the philosophical foundations of Nussbaum's enterprise are sketchy, and those who are inclined to wring their hands about imprecision will find plenty to bemoan here. It is often difficult to determine what thesis, precisely, is being defended. Nussbaum sometimes seems to be claiming that the analytic style cannot give "a fully adequate *statement*" (p. 27) of moral realities. This seems wrong. What seems to be true is that a style which has the properties of studied dryness and impersonality is not likely to express or exemplify very many of the felt qualities of experience. Perhaps it follows from this that such a style cannot engender the relevant feelings. It may be true in addition, as Tolstoy seems to think, that a feeling or sentiment must be felt to be known; if so, we would have the conclusion that one cannot acquire knowledge of very many feelings from the likes of analytic philosophy. In fact, Nussbaum might be content with this conclusion, since on other occasions, she says that "there are candidates for moral truth which the plainness of traditional philosophy lacks the power to express" (p. 142). Incidentally, it does not follow from any of this that analytic philosophy cannot discourse profitably and informatively in its dry way about forms of feeling already known.

Similarly, the claim that narrative is indispensable to this sort of ethical endeavor is interesting if it is true, but the thesis is not effectively defended. It does not follow automatically from a conception of ethics which emphasizes practical wisdom and the ability to discern and respond to the particular, or from the fact, if it is one, that narrative (for Nussbaum an unexplicated primitive) is a prominent element in the shaping of the sensibility of a culture. Nussbaum's desired conclusion might follow from a clearly stated theory about the relationship between narrative and emotion and imagination; but we meet with considerable unclarity about what exactly the thesis concerning narrative and emotion is. Narrative forms are, she says, "the sources of emotional structure, the paradigms of what, for us, emotion *is*" (p. 296). "Narratives contain emotions in their very structure" (p. 310). These are very different claims, and there is no sustained attempt to distinguish among them and interconnect them.

Most of these problems strike me as relatively unimportant. As Nussbaum herself says about Smith's theory of the spectator, "We see the general shape of the argument well enough" (p. 341). Many of these claims about the special powers of literature are familiar ground, after all. For example, Kendall Walton's recent *Mimesis as Make-Believe: On the Foundations of the Representational Arts* (Harvard University Press, 1990) gives an extremely sophisticated presentation of the workings of representation and its connection with feeling.

In the case of the thesis that writing and reading novels is moral activity, however, one does miss clear statement and rigorous defense, since this is moderately unfamiliar turf in aesthetics and philosophy of literature. The thesis is unclear. Is *all* writing and reading of novels which is morally significant also morally beneficial? Perhaps so; perhaps there is some special perspective which is learned from these experiences which is good in itself. But probably not. In fact, it seems likely that on this view reading and writing certain sorts of novels is morally indictable, which may be a rather welcome conclusion. One wonders, though, just which ones they are, because two very different sorts of candidates put themselves forward. There are those novels which deaden the ability to differentiate and respond by particularly mind-numbing stereotypes and tear-jerking; the works of Barbara Cartland suggest themselves. And there are those novels which are richly differentiated

and express a powerful vision which is deformed. If Nussbaum's criticisms of Beckett are on target, his novels are a case in point.

The diverse strategies by which *Love's Knowledge* brings the concerns of ethics and moral psychology into collision with literature are not equally successful. The daring **"Love and the Individual"** is only moderately successful as an "experiment" in philosophy/narrative, despite some gorgeous writing. The problem is partly formal; Nussbaum's "philosophical plot" does not succeed as narrative. We do not really care very much about this protagonist, or believe in her as a character, despite the presence of a considerable amount of undigested feeling. Problems of form notwithstanding, the subject matter of the essay is enormously interesting: To what extent is personal loss complete and final, because it is the individual features of the person, the relationship, the history, which are essential, and to what extent are the characteristics of the object of love replaceable? The essay loses its nerve at the end, I think, and goes off into flippancy, because it comes up against that dimension of loss which has nothing to do with the characteristics of the object, replaceable or not: the experience of having something wrenched away, and the sense of emptiness. **"Love and the Individual"** makes very interesting progress; most interesting of all, perhaps, is the way it comes to a standstill.

The steadiest and most satisfactory strategy of *Love's Knowledge* consists of bringing philosophical reflection to bear on literary narratives. Here we find powerful and finely wrought criticism which centers on topics which are worth discussing. **"Narrative Emotions: Beckett's Genealogy of Love"** is a searching examination of the progress of Beckett's attempted dissolution of emotion, indeed of personal identity, and his attempt to decompose his own writing in *Molloy, Malone Dies, The Unnamable*. Nussbaum locates Beckett in the larger community of those who seek to purge and destroy some or all emotions, then mounts a criticism of his annihilating vision. Beckett is intolerant of shared forms of feeling and communication, she says, precisely because they are shared and common and human. He is "in the grip of a longing for the pure soul, hard as a diamond, individual and indivisible" and is one of those who "long for a pure language of the soul by itself" (p. 310). "The depth of Christian feeling in the construction of our narrative forms" (p. 310), she suggests, warns us to be philosophically wary of these conclusions. Nussbaum is, I think, almost completely on target here. In the works of Beckett, we are looking at a special and extravagant kind of misanthropy focused into corrosive hatred of the human in himself. As Nussbaum herself notes parenthetically, it is perhaps not precisely Christianity which is the culprit. "Jansenist" would be better than "Christian" here, I think; Dante, after all, was a Christian writer.

Several essays in this volume take novels by Henry James as their point of departure. They are central to Nussbaum's enterprise, since as a unit they deal with the Jamesian-Aristotelian view that "in good deliberation, the particular is in some sense prior to general rules and principles" (p. 165); and they undertake to examine a "morality of perception" (p. 189), particularly in connection with circumstances like strong emotion, which place the agent beyond the wholeness of vision demanded by such a morality.

"Finely Aware and Richly Responsible: Literature and the Moral Imagination" uses James's *The Golden Bowl* to develop the theme of the moral importance of fine-tuned perceiving, lucid imagination, and a finely diversified responsiveness to the particular person and situation at hand. Adam Verver's final responsive vision of his daughter as a free and shining sea creature who must be let go, Nussbaum calls "a moral achievement in its own right" (p. 151); in this vision, Adam accepts his responsibility as a moral agent. Maggie, too, has her achievement: "Her perceptions are necessary to her effort to give him up and to preserve his dignity. They are also moral achievements in their own right: expressions of love, protections of the loved, creations of a new and richer bond between them" (p. 153). The Ververs are in the process of becoming the sort of persons "on whom nothing is lost," so richly aware and responsive are they to every nuance of their situation, and so fully do they take responsibility for the effect of their vision and their responses on each other.

Nussbaum's analysis of the significance of this scene between Maggie and Adam is deep and telling. Still, it seems to me that we can see their interaction as morally ideal only if we share Maggie and Adam's mutual self-absorption, if, that is, we look away from Charlotte and Amerigo. The scene in the boat, of course, invites us to do just this, i.e., to think of Maggie and Adam as if they were the only people in the world, and wholly to accept their vision of their relationship. But, are Maggie and Adam, then, good examples of the ethic of perception and the "Aristotelian" ideal? It seems to me that they are rather closer to the position which Nussbaum ascribes to Maggie in **"Flawed Crystals: James' *The Golden Bowl* and Literature as Moral Philosophy"**; strong emotion causes their moral vision to narrow. According to Nussbaum, this at least constitutes a fracture in the ethical point of view. Or perhaps they merit the more extreme treatment suggested by the essay **"Steerforth's Arm: Love and the Moral Point of View"**; perhaps she should say that they have been placed beyond the moral point of view by their love.

The Princess Casamassima and the fate of Hyacinth, who is truly someone on whom nothing is lost, call the "morality of perception" into question more straightforwardly. Hyacinth ends by shooting himself through the heart, of no use to himself or anyone else; we need, then, to question the ethical value of his most salient characteristic. Finely developed perceptual abilities and responsiveness are surely important in the moral life; but it also seems that emotional maturity is a matter of becoming the sort of person on whom a good deal is lost—because repetition makes some things too routine to merit notice, because a broader perspective makes some things less valuable, because a sense of humor about oneself undercuts some responses. In one scene which Nussbaum considers very important, Hyacinth and Aurora, both "taken up" and dropped by the Princess Casamassima, are silent, communing in full awareness of something in a shared consciousness that was "inconsistent with the grossness of accusation" (p. 210). "Hyacinth and Aurora love the Princess, love her in a perceiving way, seeing her in all her tangled complexity. To complain about her would be, then, too blindly self-proclaiming, too crudely unloving and self-absorbed" (p. 210). But the Princess is a monster, just as Hyacinth's revolutionary friend Paul Muniment says. Surely by this time Hyacinth and Aurora should be able to put the Princess's charm and tangled complexity and the rest of it into perspective, perhaps while acknowledging ruefully her continued fascination and their susceptibility. Of course, within the framework of the novel, Hyacinth cannot do this. Unlike Maggie Verver—in **"Flawed Crystals,"** Nussbaum very insightfully stresses Maggie's intense activity and her ability to distance herself—Hyacinth is wholly passive and wholly absorbed. There are any number of ways in which a more active, more distanced, Hyacinth could deal with his moral predicament: his promise to the revolution and genuine sympathy for the downtrodden *versus* his appreciation for art and beauty and the finer mode of existence of the nobility. As it is, his pure responsiveness kills him. It is very difficult to share Nussbaum's view that he is admirable, let alone her claim that he is a political ideal. Moreover, though I have no interpretation handy of the parting vision of Hyacinth which James offers us, "There was something on [the bed], something ambiguous, something outstretched. . . . Hyacinth lay there as if asleep, but there was a horrible thing, a mess of blood, on the counterpane, in his side, in his heart" (Henry James, *The Golden Bowl* [Harper and Row 1962] p. 510), I feel fairly certain that James does not intend it to affect us positively.

Thus reflection on James's novels casts some doubt on the sovereignty and self-sufficiency of an ethic of perception, and perhaps even on Nussbaum's Aristotelian conception of ethics. Nussbaum herself is nagged by her intuition that the characteristic perspective of this ethic is dissolved and submerged by love; an examination of *The Golden Bowl* suggests that this problem is a good deal more pervasive than she thinks. There is, however, a more serious problem that she does not seem to see, one which is introduced by *The Princess Casamassima*: fine awareness and rich responsiveness do not seem to be self-justifying. Rather, they seem to be, in moderation, an indispensable part of ethical reasoning, which may in the end also involve general norms. Those general norms may well conflict in some cases with unconditional indulgence in the ethic of perception.

It is obviously not possible to reflect on all the questions raised by the essays in *Love's Knowledge* in one breath. Other essays on related topics are those on Proust, of which **"Love's Knowledge"** is the more nuanced and critical. Here Nussbaum takes on the central Proustian anti-intellectualist theme that cataleptic emotion, paradigmatically suffering, reveals infallibly the realities of the soul. She finds even a weak interpretation of this thesis extremely questionable. **"Steerforth's Arm: Love and the Moral Point of View"** uses David Copperfield's love for Steerforth in all its warmth and poignancy to raise the theme of values which, as Nussbaum sees it, may lie beyond the moral point of view. This essay succeeds in giving us a nontraditional Dickens, one who is a subtle and deep moralist.

Love's Knowledge is a provoking book, mainly in the praiseworthy sense that it is bound to start up fresh debate on some old issues and start some discussions which are long overdue. There is a great deal of overlapping material, as one would expect from a collection of essays written to advance the same point of view, but on different occasions and for different audiences. It has an adequate index, but a book of this sort should certainly have been provided with a bibliography.

Donald G. Marshall (review date spring 1994)

SOURCE: Marshall, Donald G. Review of *Love's Knowledge,* by Martha Nussbaum. *Comparative Literature* 46, no. 2 (spring 1994): 195-97.

[*In the following review of* Love's Knowledge, *Marshall questions the theoretical and philosophical foundations of Nussbaum's arguments.*]

Moral philosophy has flourished in recent years, and Martha Nussbaum has been one of its most vivid practitioners. Like several other philosophers, she argues [in *Love's Knowledge: Essays on Philosophy and Literature*] that the attentive reading of literary works, specifically novels, is an indispensable aid for moral reflection. Ways of thinking and writing that developed in the analytic tradition are appropriate to some inquiries, such as epistemology and philosophy of science, but they cannot accomplish what is necessary for moral philosophy.

This defect demarcates the positive philosophical content of moral philosophy. Following Aristotle, Nussbaum concedes important roles to general rules. They can aid moral development by serving as a summary of others' wise judgments. When time is too short to analyze a complex situation, they may identify the best available decision. When we fear that interest or bias may distort our own or others' judgments, rules may give stability and consistency. They help underscore key features in a given case. But moral reflection requires more than discovering general rules, and cannot be convincingly characterized as the dispassionate and disinterested application of general rules in particular cases. Genuine moral reflection requires sensitivity to new and unanticipated features of a situation, to the ways features are embedded in a specific context, and to the relations among the specific persons involved. A sound moral decision includes what our emotions—our hopes, fears, loves—discern and offers us an ideal to which we as emotional beings can commit ourselves. In logical terms, the philosophical interest of moral reflection is that here the particular is prior to the general and universal and that this kind of reflection involves our whole human being, encompassing perception, reason, and emotion.

For Nussbaum, novels provide rich emotive and concrete situations thought out with accountability to the actual complexities of experience. By contrast, the examples invented by philosophers are thin and unconvincing. Readers and critics should not attempt to extract general principles from novels or apply them directly. Rather, novels provide our best opportunities to exercise and thus sharpen moral thinking outside our immediate situation. Quite consistently, in discussing novels Nussbaum mainly draws out insights about the process of moral thinking in the particular situations, not general moral rules.

Nussbaum conceives moral philosophy neither as the formulation and systematization of rules; nor as the identification of "virtues" constitutive of a good character. For her, moral philosophy is an inquiry focused on the question, "what is the good life for a human being?" It aims to achieve insights that will be put into practice, but it also already incarnates ethical insights. Thus, Nussbaum's way of reading novels is itself moral. It incarnates an intelligence that implies a certain way of life—one attentive to nuance, implication, metaphor, the interaction of parts and features in contextual wholes—one capable of taking in subtleties of language and of entering imaginatively and respectfully into the lives of others. It exhibits a knowledge that is the fruit of her love of the novels, a fruit harvested with the help of a philosophically trained mind.

Nussbaum's project orbits elliptically around two points: the defense of reflection on the literary particular against Kantians, utilitarians, Platonists, analytic philosophers, and any other one-sided champions of the general and universal; and actual commentaries on scenes from novels she loves and finds particularly significant. Her contribution is to revivify our conviction that literary texts are traversed by engagements with experience that enter into our ongoing practical and emotional life in ways that justifiably inflect that life and persist within it. Yet from the literary side, even someone who respects and sympathizes with her achievement may be uneasy at her project's Aristotelianism and Arnoldianism, her sophisticated representationalism and high moral seriousness. Wesley Trimpi and Kathy Eden have provided the detailed account Nussbaum needs of how the Aristotelian tradition analyzed literature's capacity to articulate the structure of moral experience. Obviously, deconstruction, extreme conventionalisms, and other widespread contemporary anti-representationalist relativisms challenge that tradition. In two chapters whose tone borders on irritation Nussbaum firmly rejects such critical theories, but her arguments are not elaborated nor does she reflect much on the moral offense these theories seem to give her.

She grants the novels she discusses an unexamined aura of classic grandeur. Henry James is the presiding genius with supporting roles by Proust, Dickens, Beckett, and the *Odyssey*. This is not exactly a stacked deck, but it would be ethically interesting to see her wrestling with works she finds extremely uncongenial. She endorses enlarging the canon but argues that the shared reading of certain particularly intelligent authors nurtures ethical communities, and she thinks that extending the canon to a wider range would not fundamentally alter the style of close reading she practices. And yet, how would some of the claims advanced here about literature and the moral life sound amidst a discussion of Céline, William Burroughs, Swift, Bataille, Duras, Sade, Pauline Réage, or even some hilariously slippery skeptic like Robert Musil or François Rabelais? Is only some literature usable and then only in some kinds of moral reflection?

Moreover, what conception of the good life for a human being is implicit in taking Henry James as exemplary? What are the material and social conditions for the moral agent he posits as ideal? Does contemporary life make that ideal, however desirable in the abstract, unrealizable? Are there moral issues or intensities beyond its scope? Nussbaum mentions Nietzsche in passing but does not really face the risk he and heirs like Derrida raise that the "ethical" as such may be extremely problematic, in fact utterly self-deceiving, particularly wherever terms like "love" are freely used. One gets little feeling here for the possibility that there may exist incommensurable moral perspectives, a radi-

cal problem of evil, or a clash between a moral perspective and the deliberate, amoral or anti-moral refusal of any such perspective. Hers is not a suspicious hermeneutics.

Charles Taylor has objected that Nussbaum's understanding of ethics precludes seeing transcending humanity as a coherent ethical ideal. In the book's final essay, Nussbaum concedes her preference for Aristotle's earthbound practicality and her suspicion of religious motives. But what if we aim to be not good, but holy; not morally upright, but justified, in St. Paul's sense? Suppose one's ideal is not Lambert Strether, but St. Francis? Christianity seems closer to Nussbaum's project than she recognizes. Paul and all his heirs also criticize the generality of law and insist on the particularity of love—God's love for the individual and our love for one another. For a Christian, moral rules are secondary to contemplating a narrative, the life of Jesus. The centrality Nussbaum accords love as well as qualities like humility, self-sacrifice, the examination of conscience, confession and apology for one's wrongdoing, forgiveness even of those who repeatedly and unrepentantly injure one, the formulation of ethical problems in terms of friendship and family relations—all seem more consonant with Christianity than with Aristotle. Given Kierkegaard's themes and literary practice, one is surprised to find no mention of him nor of such contemporaries as Buber and Levinas.

Yet the measure of this book's power is that it stimulates us to raise serious questions like these, not as rhetorical, but as genuinely inviting Nussbaum's response.

Ronald L. Hall (essay date September 1994)

SOURCE: Hall, Ronald L. "Transcending the Human: A Kierkegaardian Reading of Martha Nussbaum." *International Philosophical Quarterly* 34, no. 3 (September 1994): 361-73.

[*In the following essay, Hall discusses Kierkegaardian dialectics in relation to the philosophical ideas put forth by Nussbaum. Hall focuses particularly on Nussbaum's essay "Transcending Humanity" and Kierkegaard's* Fear and Trembling.]

I. INTRODUCTION

In this essay, I propose to show that and how Kierkegaardian dialectics can be put to hermeneutical good work. My immediate purpose is to show this in relation to the thought of a contemporary American philosopher, Martha Nussbaum. More generally, I hope to suggest the positive heuristic value of Kierkegaardian hermeneutics; more concretely, I hope to imply the positive existential value of a Kierkegaardian dialectical framework for interpreting life.

I will focus here on Kierkegaard's resignation/faith dialectic, my understanding of which is derived mostly from *Fear and Trembling*.[1] Here Kierkegaard, writing under the pseudonym Johannes De Silentio, recounts and analyzes the biblical story of Abraham and Isaac. Kierkegaard considers that Abraham, at least from the Christian point of view, is a knight of faith, a perfect embodiment of faith. Abraham's faith is found in his unflinching, unhesitant, response to God's command to sacrifice his son Isaac: for God's sake he was willing to give up his son, and in absolute trust in God's promises, he believed that he would receive his son back.

From this story it is clear that for Kierkegaard, resignation is an essential element in faith. Resignation, however, is not faith, but faith is not faith apart from resignation. Kierkegaard's way of putting this is to say that resignation is but the first step in the double movement of faith. For me (and any concrete individual) to make this double movement, to answer the call of God to live in faith, I must first resign from the finite world, turn away from, go beyond, all that is relative; I must foreswear all of my idolatrous relations to finitude.

This first movement of faith is not faith, however, until its second movement is made. In this, where faith becomes fully actual, the whole of the finite world, every inch, is "given" back at the very dialectical moment it is given up. In faith a new relation to finitude is thus established—a personal relation. This new personal relation lies on the other side of resignation, but it does not leave it completely behind. Actually going through the movement of resignation brings with it the concrete existential awareness of my power (my freedom) to turn away from the world. Such an awareness prepares the way for faith, insofar as faith is realized in the existential movement (moment) in which I receive back—from the hands of the Eternal—every inch of the finite that I have willingly given up. Faith receives and embraces the world just as Abraham was enabled by faith to receive and embrace Isaac when God stayed his willing hand. I can be said only to be able to receive the world, to be able to embrace it, to be able to choose it, and hence to be able to make it my own in a deeply personal way, if I have the power to turn away, the power of renouncement, the will to resignation. For this reason the element of resignation is a permanent structural element within faith. I have learned from Kierkegaard's *Sickness Unto Death* to think of resignation's place within faith, its permanent presence within it, in terms of his notion of an *annulled possibility*.[2]

The primary issue in *Sickness Unto Death* is the relation between faith and despair. Here Kierkegaard says something about their relation that seems structurally similar to what he says (in *Fear and Trembling*) about the relation between faith and resignation, namely, that the movement of resignation *simpliciter* (the movement of the knight of infinite resignation) could not be further from faith, from the movements that the knight of faith makes. His famous definition of faith seems to presuppose such a relation of absolute mutual exclusion between despair and faith, a relation in which despair has no place at all within faith. His prefatory remark that introduces his definition of faith is as follows: "The formula that describes the state of the self [the self in faith] when *despair is completely rooted out* is . . ." (SUD 4, italics added). Faith, then, is a state, we might call it a state of spiritual health, in which it seems there is no trace of despair; for despair is after all, a sickness, the sickness unto death!

On the other hand, in his usual maddening dialectic, Kierkegaard says that despair is an essential element within faith. He says: "Note that here despair over sin is dialectically understood as pointing towards faith. The existence of this dialectic must never be forgotten (even though this book deals only with despair as sickness); in fact, it is implied in despair's also being the first element in faith" (SUD 116). So it seems that even though despair is the very opposite of faith, as resignation is the opposite of faith, or at least, far removed from it, it is also, again like resignation, an element within faith—indeed, an indispensable element. How can Kierkegaard have it both ways?

I suggest that if we are to make sense out of this, if we are to find a way to save what some might dismiss as a blatant contradiction, we must turn to the notion of *annulled possibility*. Kierkegaard remarks: "Not to be in despair must signify the destroyed possibility of being able to be in despair; if a person is truly not to be in despair, he must at every moment destroy the possibility" (SUD 15). If a person cannot be in despair, if he or she does not have this capacity to be, then the person cannot exist in faith. It is in this way that despair figures essentially in the structure of faith, for it is what faith, at every moment, destroys, negates, annuls, as a possibility. As such, to the extent that despair is not possible, neither is faith. Despair, then, like resignation, is an essential dialectical moment in faith: despair, like resignation, is present within faith, dialectically present as absent; despair, like resignation, is present within faith as an annulled possibility.

I am convinced that this dialectic makes sense, and further, that it helps us to make sense of the unique qualities of our human existence. But rather than trying to make out this case in terms of Kierkegaard's work only, I will show in the following how this tricky notion of annulled possibility can both illumine and be illuminated by the recent work of Martha Nussbaum.

II. Transcending Humanity

In her article **"Transcending Humanity,"**[3] Martha Nussbaum says that it seems perfectly intelligible that human beings often find themselves dreaming of, longing for, wishing for, a form of existence that is other than their own, an existence that transcends the human one. Such a longing may well be for a god-like transcendence, that is, immortal, omniscient, omnipotent, ageless, griefless, painless, etc. Who would not want to live so transcendently? Would it not in fact be perverse not to want this?

At the same time, she wonders about the intelligibility, the coherence of this wish, its own intrinsic perversion. This question of the coherency of the human wish to transcend the human, the coherency of the lure of resignation, is generated by her recognition that it is also intelligible that human beings would refuse or reject this other-than-human existence were it ever actually offered to us as more than a dream, more than a fantasy. Would we really want to have what we sometimes think that we want to have? Would we really resign from our own finitude, our own humanity? Would we really want to be gods if this were more than an idle fantasy?

Nussbaum puts this question in terms of an offer made to Odysseus by Calypso to stay with her and become a god, immortal and ageless. The offer would require that Odysseus turn away from his quest to return home, that he resign from the concerns of human finitude. He refuses the offer, though he has already stayed with Calypso for some time, and even though he stays one more year. The reasons he offers are as follows:

> Goddess and queen, do not make this a cause of anger with me. I know the truth of everything that you say. I know that my wise Penelope, when a man looks at her, is far beneath you in form and stature; she is a mortal, you are immortal and unageing. Yet, notwithstanding, my desire and longing day by day is still to reach my own home and to see the day of my return. And if this or that divinity should shatter my craft on the wine-dark ocean, I will bear it and keep a bold heart within me. Often enough before this time have war and wave oppressed and plagued me; let new tribulations join the old.
>
> **(TH 365)**[4]

So Odysseus chooses his own life, his own human existence with all of its vulnerability to change, to ageing, to death; he chooses a real ageing and mortal woman over an ageless, deathless, beautiful nymph. And this seems not only intelligible, but somehow admirable, perhaps more so than Abraham who chooses God over his own son, over his own hopes for the future. Why?

Human existence, its loves, fears, hopes, griefs, dangers, joys, presupposes a context of, is conditioned by, time and hence contingency and uncertainty. Such a context places human beings in risk and in need, and so requires relations of dependency; but the human condition of contingency also calls for courage, for resourcefulness,

for love, hope, and trust, the human virtues we admire, the virtues we reckon as human excellences. It is just these features of our existence that give it its intrinsic worth. Yet it is just these features that would be lost in the timeless, changeless, deathless eternity of divine transcendence. What we admire in Odysseus' choice of his own human finitude, a choice he makes at the price of his own mortality, are precisely those qualities of finite contingent existence that make human existence itself of intrinsic value.

But let us come full circle. Does the lure of god-like transcendence have its proper human place? Who is right here? Abraham who is willing to turn his back on the world, his only son, or Odysseus who will not turn his back on his earthly home, his ageing wife, his humanness. Must we resist the lure of transcendence for the sake of our humanity? Or, more subtly and more paradoxically, is it the case that the wish to transcend our humanity is a wish constitutive of, intrinsic to, our humanness? Is it the case that only human beings can (have the capacity to) wish to be something other than they are? If so, would not the complete repression of this longing to, or at least of this temptation to long to, transcend our humanity for the sake of fully embracing it, be in some paradoxical way a repression of our humanness, as much so as the wish for transcending it?

Herein is the problematic of the dialectic of resignation and faith: how do we reckon with the human lure to divinity, with the human temptation to want to transcend itself, without destroying the human, without destroying ourselves? Nussbaum helps us sort through this problematic by introducing two conceptions of transcendence, what she calls—I think unfortunately—external and internal forms of transcendence.[5]

Nussbaum makes this distinction in response to a question that Charles Taylor asks her in his review of her book *The Fragility of Goodness*.[6] His question is simply this: where does she stand on the issue between Plato and Aristotle on the point of whether the Platonic aspiration to transcend the human must be excluded from an Aristotelian eudaimonia? Taylor presents two positions and asks which Nussbaum thinks is correct: (1) the inclusive view that the good life, Aristotle's eudaimonia (happiness), includes, even though it is in tension with, the Platonic aspiration for transcendence; (2) the exclusive view that the good life (Aristotelian eudaimonia) is only, that is, purely, human, with no place for extrahuman transcendence. Before we can see what her answer to this is, we must turn briefly to summarize the difference that she sees between Plato and Aristotle on this issue of transcendence.[7]

III. Aristotle's Critique of Plato

For Nussbaum, Plato's philosophical enterprise, at least as that is reflected in the early and middle dialogues,[8] is motivated by his wish to find a *technē,* a science or art of control, that would take the sting out of *tuchē*, that human, all too human, condition of being subject to ungoverned contingency, to luck, to that which simply happens to us as human beings. Such an exposure to *tuchē* exposes us to pain, to uncertainty, makes us vulnerable to chance, vulnerable to loss, the ultimate such loss being death, and hence to grief. His effort was directed at finding a way to make human existence safer, more predictable, more under control. Nussbaum puts it as follows: "*Technē,* then, is a deliberate application of human intelligence to some part of the world, yielding some control over *tuchē*; it is concerned with the management of need and with prediction and control concerning future contingencies" (**FG** 95).

In summary, Nussbaum says that Plato is searching for a form of goodness (the good human life) without fragility, without vulnerability to mortality, to the deception of appearances, to the consuming demands of the appetites and madness of the passions, to the distractions of bodily existence, etc. This, Nussbaum claims, is the argument of the *Phaedo* and is consistent with the other dialogues of this period. Again, I quote: "Socrates defends as the best life a life which he calls a practice for death; a life of philosophical contemplation in which the philosopher dissociates himself as much as possible from the desires and pursuits of the human body, according them no positive value at all" (**FG** 139).

The Platonic aspiration, the aspiration to live well, is to live as a god, aloof from the concerns of the earth, of bodily existence, from appearances, from passions: it is an aspiration to live absolutely without need, and so without any dependency on others, to live as absolutely self-sufficient, absolutely alone. So self-sufficient is the philosopher who is practicing death, that even sexual arousal is resisted:

> It is not without reason that Alcibiades compares Socratic virtues to statues of the gods. For, as we have seen, Socrates, in his ascent towards form, has become himself, very like a form, hard, indivisible, unchanging. . . . It is not only Socrates' dissociation from his body. It is not only that he sleeps all night with the naked Alcibiades without arousal. There is, along with this remoteness, a deeper impenetrability of spirit. Words launched 'like bolts' have no effect . . . Socrates refuses to be affected. He is stone; and he also turns others to stone.
>
> (**FG** 195)

It is no wonder why Alcibiades committed his famous sacrilege. One night he went for a walk, drunk on the divine madness of eros and frustrated by the impenetrability of Socrates-the-stone, and in a rage of madness mutilated the statues of the gods, smashing their faces and genitals. Here we see a human being rejecting Socrates' cold and inhuman definition of the best human life; here we see a human being raging against the lure

of the inhuman. To live as a stone, as a god, frees us from the conflicts of passion, from the vulnerability to loss, from dependence, from neediness, but at what price? For Alcibiades, as for Odysseus, that price is too dear.

A different attitude toward the gods, to god-like existence is reflected in Greek tragedy and in Aristotle. This different attitude probably accounts for why Plato thought so little of tragedy and Aristotle thought so highly of it. In contradistinction to Plato, what we see in popular Greek culture, especially as that is reflected in the tragedies, is a deep ambivalence felt towards the gods, towards a god-like existence. The ambivalence concerns two very different ways of thinking about the gods, about a god-like existence. One way to understand the gods would be to think that they are *better* than humans, superior. This is Plato. Their existence is better because the gods lack what we call human limitations. On the other hand, the gods may be thought to be simply and strangely *different*; different as an alien might be, different as some superhuman from some other planet, some other place, another species perhaps, not human; as different from human beings as apes, and as similar. This is Aristotle. To want to live among such beings, as such an alien being, would entail forfeiting our human existence; it would be to live another way. Some (Aristotle and Odysseus) recognize and contend that such an existence would not be worth living. Others wonder: would it be? Does transcendence betoken a freedom from the bitters of human existence (its socalled limitations) but at the expense of the loss of its sweets?

This ancient debate is really the subject of the popular film Cocoon. Here the issue is simply put: we, ageing and dying human beings, have a chance to leave St. Petersburg, the nursing home, to have our health and youthful vigor, including sexual potency and desire, restored, and to live forever; all we have to do is to go somewhere else, all we have to do is to leave the earth. Do we want this? In the film, most who are invited to leave reckon that they would be crazy not to. But there is one hold-out; one character who refuses, who takes this rocket flight to be a metaphysical flight from humanness; one character who chooses to stay, to die (he is, I might point out, a Jew). In the sequel, one couple changes their mind and decides to return to the earth, to their grandchildren, their children, even if this means that they must die. And somehow this seems the noble, the human choice, a kind of confirmation that Odysseus was right.

What, from the Aristotelian point of view, would we miss if we could actually become gods? Nussbaum considers some interesting examples. (1) First, athletics. Would not the value of, the glory of, achieving excellence in athletics vanish if we were unlimited? Is it not the case that it is the structure of the human body and the conditions of space and time, etc. that provide the necessary conditions for making sense of athletic excellence? Athletic excellence is species-specific; we do not think of it in terms of races or contests with other animals; or aliens, or robots. We frown on that which is outside of, that which is unnatural to the human species; we do not admire something that would give an unfair advantage, say drugs or bionics. What makes athletic excellence excellent is determined by the natural possibilities of the human species as such—by the kind of beings that we are. The offer of Calypso, then, appears not an offer of a better human life but a radically different *kind* of existence, a non-human one.

(2) Consider political associations. One thing, a point Aristotle forcefully makes, that marks human beings off from both the beast and the gods is that we are political beings. What is the glory of this? Nussbaum says: "Politics is about using human intelligence to support human neediness; so to be truly human you have to have both elements. Beasts fail on the one count, gods on the other" (**TH** 372). Aristotle does not allow the idea of a completely self-sufficient life—a life that would not depend on the presence of others, a solitary life—to count as a fully human life; for him, the relationships of care and dependency that bind citizens together in the state, that bind families and friends together, are intrinsic to the good human life; a complete human existence must include them, even though such an inclusion will generate risks, vulnerabilities, disappointments, pain, as an essential part of the good life, as an intrinsic part of happiness.

And (3), what about the virtues that Aristotle thinks are ingredient to the good life? Courage, for example? Nussbaum remarks: "Homeric gods usually cannot and do not have it, since there is nothing grave for them to risk. On the other hand courageous action seems to be a fine *human* achievement" (**TH** 374). And of moderation, she says: "Moderation will go out too, since for a being who cannot get ill or become overweight or alcoholic, there is not only little motivation to moderate intake, but also little intelligibility to the entire concept. On the other hand, moderation is a challenge and a fine thing in human life: there are so many ways to go wrong here, so few ways of finding what is truly appropriate" (**TH** 374). And what about justice?

> Aristotle seems right that the whole notion of the gods making contracts and returning deposits is ludicrous, makes no sense at all. . . . Human beings are in a sense worse off than the gods because they suffer; but they also know how to deal with suffering, and their morality is a response to the fact of suffering. The gods are better because they *can* simply overlook, look over, the sufferings of human beings, without involvement or response.
>
> (**TH** 375)

If justice requires us to recognize the needs of others, to have compassion for them, to want to put a stop to suffering where we can, then human beings are better off than the gods in terms of their capacity to understand, to pursue, and to achieve justice.

Not only do the gods seem worse off in important ways in comparison to human beings; they also seem to know this, that is, to envy human existence. The Greek gods do fall in love, but not with each other, but with mortals. It seems that: "They long . . . for that which displays effort and longing, need and striving, achievement against odds. . . . So the transcendent ones long, it seems for a certain sort of transcendence: for transcendence of their own limit, which is to lack limit and therefore to be incapable of virtue" (**TH** 377).

IV. Two Forms of Transcendence

Now back to the issue that Taylor raised for Nussbaum: which view does she support? "The view that our proper human goal is activity according to complete human excellence plus some form of transcending? Or the view that, in order to pursue appropriately the whole human good, we must leave aside our desire for transcendence?" (**TH** 378). Refusing to identify herself with either of these views, Nussbaum goes on to say: "It may appear that I am in fact supporting, as Taylor suspected, the second view. But I believe that matters are more complex" (**TH** 378).

In what way are these matters more complex? At this point she introduces the distinction between two forms of transcendence, internal and external. The internal form of transcendence does not aim at some other-worldly, extrahuman existence, nor does it hover above this world in a kind of abstract philosophical detachment from it. Internal transcendence enlivens the ordinary, the everyday, by introducing into it a sense of spirit—a sense of spontaneity, surprise, novelty, improvisation, freedom, and so forth—that keeps the human life from becoming banal. As she puts it, such a transcendence takes us "above the dullness and obtuseness of the everyday" (**TH** 379). But it is more than this: internal transcendence has a moral and political dimension. Internal transcendence is more than an aesthetic rising above; it is a rising above in moral and political excellence; it is the transcendence of practical wisdom. This sort of transcendence does not aim at transcending our humanity. Quite to the contrary, it aims to deepen our sense of humanness, it makes us more aware of the riches of our human existence. This is the sense of transcendence that we must cultivate for a life of complete virtue.

The second form of transcendence she calls external. In its every manifestation, the lure of external transcendence is the wish to depart human life altogether. It is this form of transcendence that Nussbaum is particularly concerned to reject as incoherent. She says: ". . . what my argument urges us to reject as incoherent is the aspiration to leave behind altogether the constitutive conditions of our humanity and to seek for a life that is really the life of another sort of being—as if it were a higher and better life for us" (**TH** 379).

Nussbaum cautions, however, that it is not always easy to draw the line between these two forms of transcendence: "The puzzle then is, when does the aspiration to internal transcendence become the aspiration to depart from human life altogether?" (**TH** 380).

At one point, she seems to me to be very Greek in her suggestion that what we need to do is to moderate the lure of external transcendence, to keep it from going too far, to keep it in check, as it were. She invokes here the Greek idea of pride (*hubris*).

> There is a kind of striving that is appropriate to a human life; and there is a kind of striving that consists in trying to depart from that life to another life. This is what *hubris* is—the failure to comprehend what sort of life one has actually got, the failure to live within its limits (which are also possibilities), the failure, being mortal, to think mortal thoughts. Correctly understood, the injunction to avoid *hubris* is not a penance or denial—it is an instruction as to where the valuable things *for us* are to be found.
>
> (**TH** 381)

But then she takes a different tack; more dialectical, I would say, perhaps more biblical: now the terms she uses are the terms of tension, even contradiction. She asks: "Does this mean that one should actually not want the people one loves to live forever?" Her response: "Yes and no." She even admits that this tension is close to being a contradiction, but asserts that it "seems to be a part of the best human life" (**TH** 381). In summary: ". . . the best human life in my own conception contains more tension and conflict around the issue of transcendence than Aristotle's best life, in which the fear of death plays a very small role. Not enough, perhaps, to make it Taylor's 'inclusive view.' But more than his 'narrow view,' insofar as he identifies that with Aristotle's" (**TH** 381).

So, does she or does she not? Does she or does she not reject altogether the place of external transcendence within a fully human life, and specifically the Platonic version of this transcendence, the aspiration to divinity? Does she reject this lure to divinity as figuring in the good human life as Aristotle seemed to? Granting that transcendence of the internal sort is necessary for a good human existence, what, if any, role does the lure of external transcendence, or, at least, the wish for immortality, play in the good life? On the one hand, she seems to want to reject it altogether as incoherent; and

on the other, she seems to want to say that it is a constitutive element in the good human life. Is it coherent to want to live forever? "Yes and no," she says. Can she have it both ways? What would it mean to have it both ways?

V. Plato's Contribution

But before we address these matters, we must ask what it is, if anything, that Nussbaum wants to save from the Platonic aspiration to divinity? What, if anything, does she think is worth saving here?

At the time she wrote *Fragility* (chapter 5), it was quite clear that she did want to save something, even though by the time of the writing of **"Transcending Humanity"** she seems to have abandoned altogether the thought that such a transcendence has any coherent role to play in a fully human life. I think that her original position and her current one betoken what I would call Nussbaum's undialectical imagination. It is precisely at this point that she could learn from Kierkegaard.

In *Fragility,* it is clear that Nussbaum thinks that if we were unequivocally to reject the Platonic aspiration for immortality, we would flatten our existence. She calls on Nietzsche, an anti-Platonist, to support this positive dimension of the Platonic aspiration to divinity. Nietzsche's description of the "last man" (*Zarathustra*) envisions the extinction of humanity as the result of "the extinction of the Platonic longing for self-transcendence" (**FG** 163). That is, we had better be careful when we reject the Platonic aspiration for divinity that we do not throw out with it something that is essentially human, something that, if missing, would result in the extinction of our humanness. For Plato, the longing for immortality is part of the nobleness of our humanness. He saw clearly: "the humanness of denial and dissatisfaction, the depth of our human longing for something better than what we are. Plato would say that to cease to see and feel these things would be to cease, in some way to be human" (**FG** 163).[9]

At this point in Nussbaum's evolution therefore, she thinks that the Platonic aspiration for the extrahuman is not all bad. Her way of thinking about the positive function of such a transcendence is, however, completely undialectical. As she thinks about it at this point, it is as though contemplation or transcendence of the Platonic sort were a nice capstone to a fully human life, at least, if not taken too far; as though a fully human life needs a little of the salt of transcendence, though too much will make it unsavory. In Kierkegaardian terms, this would be a little like saying that a sprinkling of despair—but not too much mind you—is good for the life of faith.

But by the time of the writing of **"Transcending Humanity,"** Nussbaum completely rejects any positive place for Platonic transcendence within the fully human life. This categorical rejection shows clearly that she will have nothing to do with dialectics. Again, however, she is unsettled. You might think that this absolute rejection of Platonic transcendence would lead her unequivocally into the arms of Aristotle. Not quite so. Aristotle, she thinks, does not have a healthy fear of death, and so does not feel the drive to press the limits of human mortality. We need to press in just this direction. But is not this to press for immortality? And are we not right back into the Platonic longing for divinity? Nussbaum thinks that her position comes comes close to being a contradiction, yet she embraces it and refuses to identify her position with Aristotle's *simpliciter.* So, are we left with the earlier position wherein the good life must strive to establish some sort of equilibrium between giving in completely to the Platonic aspiration to immortality and simply and categorically rejecting such an aspiration? Or, are we left with the later position which finds no place at all for extrahuman transcendence within the fully human life?

My question in all of this simply is: why must we settle for these as the exclusive options? Why must our choice be either (1) the good, fully human, life needs a little, but not too much, Platonic transcendence, or (2) the good life has no place at all for, indeed, cannot coherently wish for, such a Platonic aspiration? That is, why must we settle with Nussbaum for the idea that internal transcendence—now understood as a modification, almost a Platonic modification, of Aristotle's conception of the virtuous life—is sufficient for the fully human life?

What Nussbaum flirts with, but does not seriously consider, I contend, is the plausibility of a third, dialectical approach to the issue: is it not possible coherently to say that the Platonic aspiration to divinity must be rejected completely and absolutely in a fully human existence and at the same time say that it must also figure positively as a constitutive element in the good human life? I turn to Kierkegaard to try to make the case that this third alternative is not only not nonsense, but it illuminates what Nussbaum is struggling to say; in particular, I turn to Kierkegaard's discussion of the dialectic involved in resignation and faith and in despair and faith.

VI. A KIERKEGAARDIAN DIALECTIC

I suggest that the Platonic aspiration to extrahuman transcendence figures positively within human existence in just the same way that resignation (and despair) figures within faith for Kierkegaard, namely, dialectically, as an annulled possibility. To be fully human, it is necessary that we be able to wish for, that we be able to think about, that we be able to want, that we be able to conceive of, something other than our human existence. To be fully human, that is, to live in faith, it is neces-

sary, dialectically, to be able to resign from everything that is human, to be able to refuse human existence. Why is this necessary? This is complicated and tricky.

For Kierkegaard it is possible to be a self only if it is possible not to be; but one can actually be a self, that is, be the self that one already is, if and only if this latter possibility (that is, the possibility of not being a self, or one's self) is annulled by faith. Faith thus requires a certain transcendence, a level of self-consciousness in terms of which the self may become problematic, or distanced, divorced, or otherwise separated from itself. This is why beasts are not subject to despair and, a fortiori, not capable of existing in faith. Kierkegaard in fact defines despair, the opposite of faith, as a condition of not being, or not willing to be, or willing not to be, the self that one is. Despair is that state of human existence in which the self is alienated from itself. This possibility of alienation, this wedge that separates me from myself, provides the space, the conditions as it were, that enable me to come to myself, to embrace my existence as my own—at least insofar as this possibility is concretely realized. This is why Kierkegaard is insistent that despair is an element *within* faith, but at the same time the opposite of faith; why he defines faith as a condition in which despair is completely rooted out.

Let me close by returning to Abraham and Odysseus. Both Abraham and Odysseus are called to resign from their human existence, to give up what is valuable to them, and to do this for some higher calling. Recall that in the biblical story this resignation/faith dialectic is played out in the demand God places on Abraham, the demand that Abraham sacrifice, or at least be wiling to sacrifice, his own and only son; and along with this, his hope to be the father of a great nation—that hope which first uprooted him from his ancestral home, that had made of him a nomad, a wanderer in history. The lesson here seems to be something like this: faith requires an uprooting from nature, it requires that the faithful finds his or her absolute center of gravity outside of his or her natural home in the finite world; that the faithful finds his or her place in history, before God, and hence, in its primary orientation, outside of the relative, in the Absolute, the absolutely other, in the divine. Faith requires, in summary, transcendence. Transcendence implies a break with finitude; infinite resignation provides this break.

But this is not all: faith also entails receiving the finite back, every inch. What is given back to the faithful self (the finite, Isaac) is the same as what was given up, but the relationship is radically transformed; transformed from what we might call a natural relation to a personal one. This latter relation to finitude is personal insofar as it is qualified by radical contingency and choice, by an existentially felt vulnerability to loss, by a consciousness of the finite as relative. No longer is finitude thought to be ours by default, by natural right, as it were. Rather, finitude can now belong to us, of our own free and responsible choice; now we can embrace it as our own, as a gift from the hands of the Eternal. It is just this difference that allowed Isaac to belong to Abraham in a more deeply personal way than before the knife had been raised to him.

Resignation drives us toward transcendence; drives us from the world; faith drives us, as spirit, back into the world. But we do not come back from Mt. Moriah the same. The movement of resignation, when it is really made, irreversibly transforms our relation to finitude. The paradoxical result of resignation is that finitude becomes exponentially higher in value. It is ever so much more precious because on the other side of resignation it becomes ever so much our own, just as Isaac came to belong to Abraham so much more intensely after he had given him up.

Odysseus, on the other hand, refuses the offer to resign from his humanity, to give up his adventure, his wife, his home. Unlike Abraham, therefore, he does not, is not willing to, make the first movement of faith, the movement of resignation. Indeed, it seems that under no conditions would he make such a sacrifice. He is ethical through and through. It seems that he could not seriously entertain the possibility of doing what Abraham did, lifting the knife to his son, his wife? Odysseus has, we might say, no distance on his humanness.

Yes, Odysseus is a human being. But does he choose his humanness, as Nussbaum thinks he does? Only in a qualified sense, a less than radical, less than personal sense. It is almost as if Odysseus were being given two options, one of which was inconceivable for him actually to take. In this context, the choice of the other option seems to lack the force of a real choice; and despite the meaning of Odysseus' name, his choice seems not to reflect any real struggle, any real suffering. It is almost as though there were no *real* possibility for him to annul, to refuse. Yes, the temptation to Odysseus is there, to become a god (or, perhaps to retreat into Calypso's cave), but he never goes so far as to let that possibility become more than a dreaming fantasy; more than one more obstacle to his return home. He was not able to allow it to take on the actuality it took on in the story of Abraham. But precisely because Odysseus could not conceive of giving up Penelope, he was in no position to relate to her as one would relate to someone who has been dialectically given up and miraculously restored.

Nussbaum thinks that Odysseus has chosen life, decided that the human is better than the life of a god. But if I am right, he never allowed the possibility of resignation to have its full existential power and force. As such, his reunion with Penelope does not have the passion that it seems to have in the case of Abraham and Isaac.

My speculation is that this is what Nussbaum actually wants to say, but lacks the dialectical resources to pull off: she tries to capture a very deeply un-Greek dialectic within Greek categories. She rightly recognizes that the issue is transcendence; that the issue is choosing what is ours, ultimately choosing our world, our finite mortal home. She thinks that this is exactly what Odysseus did. What she fails to see, however, is the more dialectical Kierkegaardian point that such a radical choice is inextricably tied not just to the abstract possibility of resignation, but to the concrete realization of that possibility. Indeed what faith does is to embrace what we can turn away from, but only after that possibility has been made radically concrete. And it is this concrete realization that faith constantly carries inside itself and constantly annuls.

To reject the urge to transcend our humanity is an easy move, if the urge is not played out as a real possibility in one's life, if the knife is, as it were, never really lifted, if the will to resignation is only a pious self-deception. In this case, what is ours cannot be chosen as ours in any radical sense, and so remains less than ours in any deeply personal sense.

Notes

1. Søren Kierkegaard, *Fear and Trembling/Repetition,* ed. and trans. Howard V. and Edna H. Hong (Princeton, NJ: Princeton Univ. Press, 1983); hereafter FT.

2. Søren Kierkegaard, *Sickness Unto Death: A Christian Psychological Exposition for Upbuilding and Awakening,* ed. and trans. by Howard V. and Edna H. Hong (Princeton, NJ: Princeton Univ. Press, 1980), p. 116n; hereafter SUD.

3. Martha Nussbaum, "Transcending Humanity," in *Love's Knowledge: Essays on Philosophy and Literature* (New York: Oxford Univ. Press, 1990), pp. 365-91; hereafter TH. These essays develop many of the ideas of Nussbaum's earlier work, *The Fragility of Goodness: Luck and Ethics in Greek Tragedy and Philosophy* (New York: Cambridge Univ. Press, 1986); hereafter FG.

4. It is interesting to note here that Calypso's offer to Odysseus to remain with her is an offer not to transcend the natural order, but precisely the opposite. She is tempting Odysseus to refuse to stand out from nature. It is true that the temptation she offers is a temptation to depart from human existence, but this departure is not in the direction of an aloof god. Rather, her temptation draws Odysseus in the opposite direction, the direction of the Earth Mother, we might say (Calypso is portrayed by Homer as a nymph not a goddess). Odysseus resists the temptation to be engulfed by the immanent, to re-enter the womb, her cave, to live wholly within the natural order, even if such an existence would be as deathless as nature.

I owe this insight to my colleague, R. Taylor Scott. In fairness to Professor Nussbaum, however, I must note that she does think of the lure of transcending the human as a lure in two directions, upwards to the gods or downwards to the beasts. She says: ". . . the human being is also the being that can most easily cease to be itself—either by moving (Platonically) upwards towards the self-sufficiency of the divine, or by slipping downward towards the self-sufficiency of doggishness . . . both involve the closing-off of important human things" (FG 417). In fairness though to Professor Scott, she does make it seem that Odysseus is tempted in the Platonic direction, which, on her own terms, may not be the case, or at least, it certainly need not be.

5. I take this to be unfortunate because the idea of internal transcendence may be construed as a retreat into oneself. This sort of transcendence is as much a wish to depart from our humanness as is the transcendence of the external sort. Indeed, the risk of interpreting internal transcendence in this way is particularly acute in our own time where everything is subject to being psychologized. What Nussbaum wants to say, I think correctly, is that transcendence, in some form, is intrinsic to our humanness: this is human transcendence. What she does not seem to resolve is the place of extrahuman transcendence within the human. Is this also intrinsic to human existence?

6. See Charles Taylor's review of *The Fragility of Goodness* in *Canadian Journal of Philosophy* 18 (1988), 805-14.

7. Nussbaum says that she will not pursue a point that Taylor raises about her placing the issue of transcendence exclusively in the context of Greek polytheism. Taylor wants to know why she does not consider transcendence in the Judaeo-Christian context. This, I think, is an important point. Søren Kierkegaard argues that it was Christianity that introduced radical transcendence into the world: he called this concept of transcendence "spirit," a concept that Greek consciousness lacked: the Greek understanding of spirit was as psyche, not pneuma. See "The Immediate Erotic Stages," in *Either/Or I*, ed, and trans. Howard V. and Edna H. Hong (Princeton, NJ: Princeton Univ. Press, 1987), pp. 47ff; also, see my own *Word and Spirit: A Kierkegaardian Critique of the Modern Age* (Bloomington, IN: Indiana Univ. Press, 1993). Nussbaum may be guilty of reading a Judaeo-Christian concept of transcendence into Greek polytheism and Greek philosophy. If Kierkegaard is correct, the Greeks had a notion of transcendence, but it was finite—a kind of higher form of finitude; this is transcendence as psyche. For Greek consciousness, the idea of a radically other-than-the-finite was not available, or what is the same thing, the Greeks lacked the idea of spirit, of the infinite. One reason that the Greeks lacked the conception of spirit is that they lacked the biblical conception of the universe as

a creation; it simply was inconceivable to the Greek imagination that the cosmos had come into being, and a fortiori that it came into being as the result of a free, contingent act. As such, the Greek mind could not imagine the radical transcendence of such a creator vis à vis the creation; such a transcendence imagines the creator as radically other than the creation.

8. This persistent attempt of Plato to root out of existence every trace of contingency, passion, vulnerability, and so forth, finds its exception in his late dialogue *Phaedrus*. See the chapter of *Fragility* subtitled: "Madness, Reason, and Recantation in the *Phaedrus*," pp. 200ff.

9. Strangely enough, the remarks that Nussbaum makes about the positive contribution of Plato's aspiration to divinity, a kind of striving to make things better, a striving to live a noble life devoted to truth, goodness, and beauty, make it seem that what she really admires in Plato is what could well fit into her notion of "internal transcendence," that human form of transcendence that deepens our humanity, and keeps our ordinary lives from degenerating into banality.

Robert P. George (essay date winter 1995-96)

SOURCE: George, Robert P. "'Shameless Acts' Revisited: Some Questions for Martha Nussbaum." *Academic Questions* 9, no. 1 (winter 1995-96): 24-42.

[*In the following essay, George puts forth a critique of Nussbaum's expert testimony in a court case,* Evans v. Romer, *concerning the rights of homosexuals.*]

Author's Note: This article is dedicated to the late Barry Gross, whose devotion to the ideal of scholarly integrity was exemplary, and who insisted that the matters discussed in this article not be passed over in silence.

* * *

In *Evans v. Romer,* the *Colorado Amendment 2 Case,*[1] so called, Martha Nussbaum, then University Professor and professor of philosophy, classics, and comparative literature at Brown University,[2] offered expert testimony in court and by affidavit purporting to show that moral objections to homosexual conduct did not exist, or were, in any event, not significant, in pre-Christian Greek and Roman civilizations or in the major philosophical traditions associated with them. According to her, such objections originated in the West with Christianity. Moral theories that condemn homosexual conduct as contrary to natural law or the natural human good are, she asserted, "inherently theological."[3]

I offered testimony to contradict these claims, as did John Finnis, professor of law and legal philosophy at Oxford University. In a subsequent article,[4] Finnis argued that Professor Nussbaum's testimony under oath in the Amendment 2 case amounted to a series of misrepresentations, distortions, and deceptions. He accused her of falsifying the positions not only of Plato and Aristotle but also of such modern commentators on Greek philosophy and public morality as Sir Kenneth Dover, A. W. Price, and Gregory Vlastos. Indeed, he accused her of misrepresenting her own published work. He alleged, moreover, that she had engaged in an act of gross deception of the court by attempting to pass off as "the authoritative dictionary relied on by all scholars in this area," viz. classics, a definitively superseded nineteenth-century edition of Liddell and Scott's *A Greek-English Lexicon.* Finally, he accused her of dissembling about the scholarly credentials of Professor David Cohen, whose work Professor Finnis had introduced to show that the public morality of classical Athens in fact condemned homosexual conduct.

Professor Nussbaum has now published a lengthy article of her own on the question of classics scholarship in the Amendment 2 case. It appears in *Virginia Law Review,*[5] where it occupies 137 pages, and contains 486 footnotes.[6] The article, which is based on a lecture Professor Nussbaum presented at the University of Virginia Law School, criticizes the testimony of various witnesses for the state of Colorado (including Professor Finnis and me) and purports to answer some of Finnis's allegations against her. It includes an appendix coauthored with Sir Kenneth Dover,[7] and cites as "on file with the Virginia Law Review Association" letters from various classics scholars.

Readers of the *Virginia Law Review,* particularly those who have not read Finnis's article in *Academic Questions,* will likely not realize that Professor Nussbaum offers no reply at all to the great majority of the very serious allegations of abuse of scholarship that Finnis made against her.[8] And, even with respect to the small number of charges she does purport to answer, readers will likely not know that her answers—albeit (apparently)[9] supported by such scholars as Dover and Price (whose work Finnis had accused her of misrepresenting)—do not exonerate her of the misconduct alleged by Finnis. Let me give some particulars.[10]

Consider, first of all, Professor Nussbaum's treatment of the historian of ancient law and classics scholar David Cohen. In his affidavit, Finnis had introduced Cohen's book *Law, Sexuality, and Society: The Enforcement of Morals in Classical Athens*[11] to explain "what is questionable about the picture, in certain respects sound and illuminating, drawn in works such as Dover's *Greek Homosexuality* (which is foundational for contemporary pro-'gay' classical scholarship)."[12] According to Cohen, classical Athenian public morality was far from unambiguously accepting of homosexual conduct. Though such conduct was not punishable as a matter of

criminal law, there was a wide range of views in Athenian society on homosexual activity, and those who adhered to some imposed their moral judgment against it in a variety of formal and informal ways. If Cohen is right about Athenian public morality, then Professor Nussbaum's claim that Christianity introduced moral objections to homosexual conduct in the West immediately collapses.

So, how did Professor Nussbaum deal with Cohen? She alleged that "Cohen . . . is not a classicist." She claimed that he "has never been employed by a department of Classics." "He is," she stated, "a Professor in a department of Rhetoric, with a degree in law." His "well-intentioned" book on Athenian public morality, she declared, "falls sadly short in its coverage of the evidence." For Cohen had not, she said, discussed the "dream book" of Artemidorus, "presumably because it was not available in English translation at the time he wrote the book."[13]

The facts, however, are as follows: Professor Cohen *is* a classicist (and, in truth, a scholar of considerable distinction in the field). He holds appointments in the departments of rhetoric *and classics* at the University of California at Berkeley. He holds a Ph.D. *in classics* from Cambridge University. And, contrary to what Finnis termed Professor Nussbaum's "sly, defamatory suggestion," he *can* (and does) read Greek at the high level of proficiency necessary to conduct original scholarship in Greek history. Had he considered Artemidorus—who lived four centuries after the period Cohen was concerned with in his book—in any way relevant to understanding classical Athenian law and public morality, he would not have required a translation of the "dream book." Cohen had explained that he considered Artemidorus irrelevant in a review essay published prior to the Colorado litigation. Professor Nussbaum must have known this, for she cites this essay later in the very paragraph of her affidavit which suggests that Cohen ignored Artemidorus because it was not available to him in translation. (Incidentally, as Finnis and others have pointed out, a competent English translation of Artemidorus has, in fact, been available for many years.)

Since Professor Nussbaum testified under oath, her misrepresentations, if she knew them to be such, probably constituted perjury. Did she know that Cohen in fact possesses the scholarly qualifications she told the court he lacked? Finnis reports that "[a]ll these facts about Cohen should, he told me, be well known to Professor Nussbaum, since he personally recounted them, in answer to her questions, during a long conversation they had in Chicago in 1992."[14] Professor Nussbaum testified in Colorado in October 1993.

In her *Virginia Law Review* article, Professor Nussbaum, while retracting none of her disparagements of Cohen's scholarly credentials, treats him more gently and, by way of citation, invites her readers to "see" his letter to her of 27 April 1994, "on file with the Virginia Law Review Association." She reports that "Cohen holds that the proper way to use his book in the context of these public issues is to argue that the state has no business trying to use the law to enforce morality."[15] The suggestion, one supposes, is that Cohen shares Professor Nussbaum's moral and political views about sodomy statutes and other morals laws (none of which were at issue in Colorado) and, perhaps, her view as to which side had the better Constitutional argument in the Amendment 2 litigation. But none of this is relevant to the question of whether David Cohen teaches in a classics department, holds a doctorate in classics (in addition to a degree in law), or reads Greek. Either he does or he doesn't. And since he does, and had told Professor Nussbaum that he does, she should explain why she, while under oath, stated or plainly implied that he doesn't.

Professor Nussbaum's use of the letter from Cohen turns out to be typical. Finnis argued that she had misrepresented the published views of various scholars, many of whom hold moral and political views like her own and unlike Finnis's and mine. She obtained letters from some of these scholars, which she cites in a way so as to leave the impression that they support her position *generally* in her dispute with Finnis and me. In some cases, perhaps, scholars have attempted to support her even on questions of the integrity of the use of their work; this seems to be true, for example, of Sir Kenneth Dover, the author of three letters that she cites and the co-author of the aforementioned appendix to her article. These efforts, however, fail to get Professor Nussbaum off the hook. In the end, they simply make clear what knowledgeable readers of Finnis's affidavit and article have known all along, namely, that many of the late twentieth-century scholars he cites to show that Greek civilization and Greek philosophers had moral objections to homosexual conduct do not themselves have such objections.

The appendix co-authored by Professor Nussbaum and Sir Kenneth Dover says that "because Professor Finnis' citation of Dover as if he supports Finnis' position has made public clarification of Dover's position urgent, we jointly state our position below."[16] But for which of his positions did Finnis cite Dover? Finnis manifestly did not cite Dover as someone who personally objected to homosexuality or who holds that Athenian public morality was marked by substantial moral objections to homosexual conduct. Indeed, Finnis noted that Dover's work on the latter point is "foundational for contemporary pro-'gay' classical scholarship," and he introduced Cohen's work precisely to "explain what was questionable" in the picture of Athenian attitudes drawn by Dover. So it comes as no surprise to find Dover opposing Finnis's views in this respect.

What is surprising is Dover's apparent willingness to offer some measure of support for Professor Nussbaum's claims regarding his position on *Socrates'* (and *Plato's*) view of homosexual conduct. This was one of the most egregious of her misrepresentations to the court in Colorado. The story is worth telling in some detail.

On the witness stand, Professor Nussbaum was asked point-blank by the attorney for the State of Colorado defending Amendment 2 whether Sir Kenneth Dover, author of *Greek Homosexuality,* had reached the conclusion that Socrates, among others, "condemned homosexual conduct." Her answer was unequivocal:

> No, he didn't reach that conclusion. He reached the conclusion that they condemned certain forms of conduct, in particular, that Socrates condemned the seduction of students; the conclusion that in Plato's dialogues we find condemnation of sex where bribery or prostitution is involved.[17]

Testifying as a rebuttal witness the next day, I simply read aloud to the court from Dover's book:

> Xenophon's Socrates lacks the sensibility and urbanity of the Platonic Socrates, but there is no doubt that both of them condemn homosexual copulation.[18]

Readers will note, as the judge no doubt did, that there is no suggestion in this unequivocal statement that, in Dover's view, Socrates condemned homosexual conduct only in the particular relationship of teacher and student. What is "condemned" is homosexual conduct ("copulation") as such.[19]

When I returned from Colorado to Princeton, I found waiting for me a fax from Professor Nussbaum demanding a retraction of my claim that she had misrepresented the position of Sir Kenneth Dover, asserting that it was "(a) false, (b) produced with reckless disregard for the truth . . . [and] (c) damaging to [her] reputation as a scholar."[20] Was she claiming that Dover had abandoned the view he had expressed so unambiguously in *Greek Homosexuality*?

In a passage from an affidavit that she was then preparing, and which she attached to her letter to me, Professor Nussbaum stated that "George, though making clear on the stand that he was reading from the *second* edition of Dover's book, did not inform the court that it is the *Postscript* to the second edition (pp. 168-70) in which Dover explains the changes in his views, among which is Dover's express rejection of many of his earlier restrictive statements on anal and oral sex."[21] This suggested to the court, as it was undoubtedly designed to do, that Dover had in fact rejected, indeed expressly rejected in his postscript, the views he had published in his first edition about Socrates' position on homosexual acts. And this suggestion is utterly false. As I pointed out to the court in a reply to Professor Nussbaum's affidavit, "Here Nussbaum implies—though she is careful not to state—that in his postscript Dover retracts or modifies his view that Plato's Socrates, no less than Xenophon's, condemns homosexual copulation. In fact, the postscript does not even mention Socrates, much less his views on homosexual acts."[22] Actually, Dover's short postscript retracts *none* of what he said about the moral conclusions drawn by any Greek philosopher regarding homosexual conduct. Professor Nussbaum's sworn suggestion to the contrary was simply outrageous.

In her letter to me and in her affidavit, Professor Nussbaum claimed that "when one reads the rest of what Dover writes, the condemnation is in the nature of the pupil-teacher relationship."[23] However, when one reads "the rest of what Dover writes," one finds nothing of the kind. Dover's unambiguous conclusion regarding Socrates' condemnation of homosexual copulation is nowhere in his writings retracted or even qualified. So, again, Professor Nussbaum's testimony was false. Did she know it to be false when she gave it? I do not know. However, because I suspected that Nussbaum might attempt to induce Sir Kenneth Dover (whose liberal sympathies regarding the morality and the politics of homosexuality are well known) to provide some cover for the testimony she gave regarding his views, I urged Finnis, with whom I was working on a reply to Professor Nussbaum, to write to Sir Kenneth and ask about his views.

On 19 January 1994, Finnis wrote to him, asking, among other things

> —whether your statement on p. 160 of *Greek Homosexuality* that Socrates, as portrayed by Plato and Xenophon, condemned homosexual copulation really says no more than that Socrates condemned homosexual copulation within pupil-teacher relationships [as Nussbaum had testified], or rather (as I think) conveys your judgment that Socrates, as so portrayed, condemned such conduct (rightly or wrongly) without limiting the condemnation either by type of copulation or type of context or relationship; [and]

> —whether *Greek Homosexuality* (as I think) maintains that Plato (rightly or wrongly) rejected all copulation between males, and not simply acts involving bribery or prostitution [as Nussbaum had also testified was Dover's view].[24]

On 23 January 1994, Dover replied to Finnis:

> Many thanks for your letter. I think I can give pretty definite answers to your questions.

> 1. It is certainly my opinion that the Socrates of Plato and Xenophon condemned homosexual copulation as such, and did not confine the prohibition to any particular relationships. I certainly meant to say that on

pp. 159f. of my book. At the same time he expected any normal male to experience homosexual *desire,* and he did not think that occasional copulation 'in an unguarded moment' completely vitiated a non-physical relationship (p. 163). It is like a temptation to commit adultery or various forms of dishonesty or violence; natural and normal to experience the temptation, but wrong to yield to it.

> 2. Where one can distinguish Plato from his 'Socrates,' i.e., in *Laws,* Plato condemns all homosexual copulation (pp. 165-68 in my book).[25]

Dover's answers are indeed "pretty definite."

What, then, are we to make of Dover's willingness to sign on as co-author of an appendix to Professor Nussbaum's *Virginia Law Review* article containing the following claim:[26]

> In *Greek Homosexuality*, Dover stated that the Socrates of both Plato and Xenophon "condemns" homosexual copulation. Moreover, in a letter to Finnis, Dover wrote: "It is certainly my opinion that the Socrates of Plato and Xenophon condemned homosexual copulation as such. . . ."[27] First of all, however, Dover never claimed that Socrates condemns this copulation as wicked, shameful, and depraving; he said quite clearly that it was condemned *as inferior to the pursuit of wisdom,* on the grounds that one should not pursue an inferior good when one might pursue a superior good.[28] "Inferior" does not mean "wicked," nor does "condemns" mean "condemns as wicked and depraving." Someone who says, "Polonius condemns borrowing," does not imply that Polonius regards borrowing as wicked or depraved. Thus, Finnis' use of Dover's letter to support Finnis' own position is inappropriate.[29]

This passage suggests that Dover, in *Greek Homosexuality,* says (indeed, says "quite clearly") that Plato condemned homosexual conduct merely as an inferior "good" to the superior good of the pursuing of wisdom. As readers of pages 153-70 (and especially pages 159-60) of *Greek Homosexuality* will see, this is worse than an oversimplification; it distorts the account of Socrates's views presented in that book. Nowhere in *Greek Homosexuality* (or, as far as I can tell, in any of his other writings) does Dover present Socrates as describing or treating homosexual conduct as a *good* of any kind. Rather, he consistently portrays Socrates as treating such conduct as bad, wrong, dishonorable, and, as such, to be avoided. (Contrary to what the Nussbaum-Dover appendix here and elsewhere insinuates, Finnis has never attributed to Dover the view that Socrates condemned homosexual activity or other immoral sexual conduct in stronger terms, such as "wicked" and "depraving.")

According to the account of Socrates' views Dover gives in *Greek Homosexuality,* homosexual conduct is bad in a way that merits *condemnation.* One may accept or decline to accept Dover's speculative explanation of Socrates' reasons for condemning such conduct, viz., that it is an "inferior end" (not a "good") that vitiates the soul's capacity to pursue the higher (indeed highest) end of wisdom. Either way, homosexual conduct differs radically from other non-wisdom-pursuing activities that may nevertheless legitimately and honorably be pursued, and which Socrates never suggests are (1) not honorable, (2) like pigs scratching against stones, or (3) like a poisonous spider's bite, as the Socrates of Dover's *Greek Homosexuality* suggests homosexual acts are. This explains why Dover, in his "pretty definite" answers to Finnis's questions about the accuracy of Finnis's interpretation of his book (which, as the reader will recall, Dover had the opportunity to consider in light of Professor Nussbaum's interpretation of it as expounded in her affidavit), likened the temptation to engage in homosexual conduct to the temptation to engage in such manifest evils as *adultery, dishonesty,* and *violence.* For Socrates, he says, succumbing to the temptation to engage in homosexual conduct is *wrong* just as giving in to the temptation to deal dishonestly is wrong. Surely Dover does not now mean to suggest that Socrates thought it "wrong to yield to" any of these temptations merely because they are "inferior goods" to the pursuit of wisdom?[30]

An incautious reader of the passage I have quoted from the coauthored appendix might take away the impression that Socrates's condemnation of homosexual acts, as presented in Dover's book, was not a *moral* condemnation. Read carefully, however, the passage avoids denying what even a casual reader of *Greek Homosexuality* knows, namely, that Socrates, according to Dover, considered homosexual conduct to be (like adultery and dishonesty) *morally* wrong. Professor Nussbaum's testimony was, however, by her own account, to show that "prior to the Christian tradition, there is no evidence that natural law theories regarded same-sex erotic attachments as immoral, 'unnatural,' or improper."[31] (Theories that reach such judgments, she claimed, are "inherently theological.") So, despite Dover's willingness to join Professor Nussbaum in declaring that Finnis's "use" of his letter is somehow "inappropriate," nothing he is prepared to join her in saying exonerates her of the precise allegation Finnis has cited that letter to support, namely, that Nussbaum did not tell the truth when she testified that, according to Dover, Socrates did not condemn homosexual conduct.

Indeed, the appendix would not have exonerated Professor Nussbaum of this charge even if Dover had been willing to deny that Socrates' condemnation of homosexual conduct was a moral condemnation. The lawyer for the state of Colorado who cross examined Professor Nussbaum asked her, not whether Dover had concluded that Socrates (and Plato) condemned homosexual conduct "as wicked or depraving," or even "as immoral," but rather, simply, whether Dover had concluded

that Socrates (and Plato) "condemned homosexual conduct." Her answer, under oath, was "No." And that answer was false. Its falsity was clear from Dover's book and is confirmed by his letter to Finnis. Nothing in what Dover joins Nussbaum in saying in the coauthored appendix alters that.

Another point on which Finnis, in his article in *Academic Questions,* accused Professor Nussbaum of misconduct concerned statements she made, again under oath, in defense of her claim that Plato's *Laws,* Book 1, 636c, appears to contain a condemnation of homosexual conduct only because translators, under the influence of Christianity, imported prejudices against homosexuality into their translations. Although the dispute in the courtroom involved the question whether the relevant passage in *Laws,* properly translated, in fact condemns homosexual conduct, the issue Finnis raised in his article concerns Professor Nussbaum's honesty in defending her position.

For example, the passage in *Laws* 636c describes homosexual acts as *para phusin,* which all translations that I have been able to discover render as "unnatural" or "contrary to nature."[32] Here is Professor Nussbaum's sworn testimony in the face of these translations:

> the terms tendentiously translated "according to nature" and "unnatural" or "contrary to nature" actually refer (in my own expert opinion and the consensus of recent scholars such as Price, whose study of the passage has been widely accepted) to "birth" and not "nature" in any normative sense.[33]

By "Price" is meant the classicist A.W. Price; his study is contained in his book *Love and Friendship in Plato and Aristotle.*[34] As the passage I just quoted from Professor Nussbaum's affidavit makes clear, she invokes his work in a way that unmistakably suggested to the court that, in line with "the consensus of recent scholars," he rejects the standard translations of *para phusin* in Plato's *Laws* as "tendentious" and would render the term as something like "contrary to birth" (in the sense of being inconsistent with a policy aimed at combatting underpopulation). As Finnis pointed out, however, when one actually looks at Price's study, one finds him unhesitatingly employing the standard translation of *para phusin* as "unnatural," and translating the passage in question as "homosexual intercourse, between males or females, seems to be an *unnatural* crime of the first rank" (p. 230, emphasis added).

Finnis further observed:

> The conclusions of the book's long appendix "Plato's Sexual Morality" are squarely based on Price's reasoned judgment that "unnatural" in these passages both conveyed and entailed Plato's essential *moral* judgments on sexual conduct, yet Professor Nussbaum swears that it supports her denial that the term had

"any normative moral sense" and her assertion that it signified for Plato no more than inconsistency with a temporary pro-natalist colonial politics.[35]

Price's political and moral views regarding homosexual conduct, like those of Dover, resemble Professor Nussbaum's rather than Finnis's or mine. Yet, what she describes as his widely accepted study turns out to contain a devastating counterwitness to her claims that moral objections to homosexual conduct were a Christian innovation—a counterwitness whose existence she withheld from view even as she implied to the court that Price's translation of *para phusin* in *Laws* 636c eliminated the quality of moral condemnation of homosexual conduct conveyed by the "tendentious" rendering of the phrase as "unnatural." Indeed, as Finnis put it, "Price's book in fact argues, prominently and very explicitly, that Plato's main positions on the morality of sexual conduct, as evidenced by the *Republic* and the *Phaedrus* as well as by the *Laws,* were (rather to Price's regret) substantially the same as the positions maintained in the Catholic tradition."[36]

In giving testimony under oath, had Professor Nussbaum merely forgotten that Price, in perfect harmony with other translators, had translated *para phusin* as "unnatural"? Did she not recall Price's *lament* that Plato's main positions on sexual morality were essentially those of the Catholic tradition, as reaffirmed by Pope Paul VI? Her *Virginia Law Review* article does not say, despite the fact that she had a long memorandum from Finnis and me raising these issues—and containing many more allegations of misrepresentation, distortion, and deception—in plenty of time to include some discussion of it in the article. The article does, however, cite two letters from Price ("on file with the Virginia Law Review Association").[37] This gives the appearance that Price somehow supports Nussbaum, and in one sense—albeit an utterly irrelevant one—he does.

In the portion of his first letter quoted by Professor Nussbaum, Price makes two criticisms of Finnis.[38] First, he claims that Finnis and others on his side of the Colorado litigation "are well aware that what motivated popular support for Amendment 2 was not respect for the natural law as they interpret it, but attitudes of prejudice and antipathy[39] that contradict the heart of Christian morality." Second, noting dissent among many Catholics regarding the Church's teaching on contraception (teaching which Finnis and I, notoriously, support), he says that "to call Finnis's argument sectarian would be to *exaggerate* its acceptability." Now, neither of these criticisms provides Professor Nussbaum with any defense against Finnis's charge that she deceived the court in suggesting that Price's book rejects, as "tendentious," the standard translation of *"para phusin"* as "unnatural" and instead translates the phrase in some fashion that avoids negative moral connotations. Nor do

these criticisms excuse her withholding from the court the fact that Price's book concludes that Plato, to the author's regret, held views regarding sexual morality remarkably similar to those of the Catholic tradition (hundreds of years later).

The reader will recall that Price translated the noun *"tolmema,"* as it appears in Plato's *Laws* 636c, as "crime of the first rank." In *Greek Homosexuality,* Dover had translated *"tolmema"* as "crime" and "crime of the first order." In rendering the term pejoratively, the translations of Dover and Price were consistent with most other translations, including the one by Bury, which Finnis used (along with Dover's) in his original affidavit introducing *Laws* 636c as an example of Plato's moral disapprobation of homosexual conduct. In her testimony in court, Professor Nussbaum had criticized Finnis's reliance on the Bury translation, which she cited as an example of a mistranslation that imported a "personal opinion" against homosexual acts into the text of a classical author. She claimed that Finnis himself "has access to the ancient texts only through translations,"[40] and is "repeatedly tripped up by things that are not in the Greek."[41]

Professor Nussbaum asserted as her solitary evidence to support those claims that the correct translation of *"tolmema,"* indeed the only reasonable one, was a morally neutral one, such as "venture" or "deed of daring." "Enormity," which had been Bury's translation, or any other pejorative translation (e.g., Dover's "crime" and "crime of the first order"), she claimed, was not a legitimate scholarly possibility. "There are some reasonable disagreements about meanings of words," she declared in response to a cross examiner's inquiry, "but the issues that I've raised with Finnis are—they're not a disagreement. Those sentences [*sic*] just are not there in the Greek."[42]

Now, the question is not, and has never been, whether a nonpejorative translation of *"tolmema"* in *Laws* 636c is reasonable; Finnis has remarked that "venture"

> is indeed a quite possible translation, albeit a rather timid and unilluminating one. It leaves entirely intact the condemnation of homosexual acts conveyed by the sentence as a whole.[43]

The question was whether a pejorative translation, such as Bury's, was *un*reasonable, outside the scope of scholarly possibility, so that, as Professor Nussbaum alleged, it falsified the sentence by importing into it a condemnation not in the Greek text.

Her claim was doomed from the start because Finnis had cited not only Bury but, in the same line of his affidavit, also Dover, whose *Greek Homosexuality* gives an even more condemnatory and pejorative translation.[44] But, in any event, having chosen her line of attack,

Professor Nussbaum sought to establish her claim by introducing, *inter alia,* a definition of *"tolmema"* from a lexicon that she identified in the version of her affidavit filed with the defendant State of Colorado on 22 October 1993, as

> Liddle [*sic*], Scott, & Jones *Lexicon of the Ancient Greek Language,* the authoritative dictionary relied on by all scholars in this area . . .

and, in the version filed with the court the same day, as

> Liddle [*sic*], Scott, *Lexicon of the Ancient Greek Language,* the authoritative dictionary relied on by all scholars in this area . . .

That *Lexicon,* she alleged in both versions, gives no pejorative translations for *"tolmema"*; it offers only the neutral definitions "an adventure, enterprise, deed of daring." Her purpose in introducing it, obviously, was to support her claim that *"tolmema"* in *Laws* 636c could not reasonably be translated pejoratively, since the "authoritative dictionary relied on by all scholars in this area" did not include a pejorative translation.

The shocking fact is that Liddell, Scott & Jones, *A Greek-English Lexicon,* the truly authoritative dictionary relied on by all classicists (including, notably, Professor Nussbaum herself in her published writings), includes, in addition to the meanings given for *"tolmema"* cited by her, the manifestly pejorative "shameless act."[45] The whiting out of the ampersand and the word "Jones" in the version of her affidavit served on the court enabled her to claim, *ex post facto,* that she was actually citing an earlier edition of the Lexicon, one that does not include an explicitly pejorative definition. The difficulty for Professor Nussbaum, however, is that the earlier edition is, in truth, a long-superseded edition, which can in no way be considered "the authoritative dictionary relied on by all scholars in this area."[46] So she has managed to trap herself: The version of her affidavit served on the State is a falsification, because Liddell, Scott & Jones, *A Greek-English Lexicon* contains precisely what she denies it contains, namely, a pejorative definition of *"tolmema."* The version served on the court is equally a falsification, because the pre-Jones edition is not "the authoritative dictionary." Either way, what Professor Nussbaum told the court just isn't true.

In a letter to me dated 29 October 1993,[47] Professor Nussbaum claimed that the whiting out of the ampersand and the name "Jones" in the version of her affidavit filed with the court was attributable to the fact that the lawyers for her side

> who filled up the footnotes and references, didn't realize that I use the edition without the supplementation by Jones, since it is more reliable on authors of the classical period. . . . I don't even have the Jones [edition] around, so it would have been absurd to cite that.

As a lawyer myself, and having seen the form of her affidavit, I find it odd to imagine it falling to the lawyers, rather than to Professor Nussbaum, to "fill up" references to classical texts and lexicographical tools, but let that pass for now. The important thing is that she apparently cited the pre-Jones edition of Liddell and Scott with full knowledge that the Jones edition *includes* the pejorative definition of *"tolmema."* If so, this was no mere negligence, no innocent mistake. To have revealed to the court the definition of *"tolmema"* given in the truly authoritative Jones edition, far from advancing her case, would badly have damaged it.

As I pointed out in a letter responding to her,[48] the Jones edition is the one that she herself regularly cites in her published scholarship, including her work on authors of the classical period from Homer to Aristotle. For example, in her influential book *The Fragility of Goodness,*[49] Professor Nussbaum refers to the Jones edition, not the nineteenth-century edition it superseded, for the meaning of *"biazesthai"* and of *"hubris"* in Plato's *Symposium,* for the meaning of *"orego"* from Homer to Plato, and for the meaning of *"katharsis"* in Plato and Aristotle.[50]

After a lecture[51] at Princeton on 2 December 1993 Professor Nussbaum was asked by Barry R. Gross, a philosopher at York College of The City University of New York, who had himself submitted an affidavit for the State in the Amendment 2 case, about her citing the pre-Jones edition of the *Lexicon,* and her failure to inform the court that the authoritative Jones edition actually contained the pejorative definition whose reasonableness she denied. Here is her reply:

> I considered it to be an absolutely useless entry, which supplies no guidance about the meaning of any particular passage. I would never dream of submitting such a sloppy and useless entry to a court.

She went on to say, falsely, that the procedure employed by Jones "as he described it, was not to change Liddell's renderings for the authors that Liddell did study, but rather to add renderings for authors that Liddell didn't study." As Finnis says "That was entirely untrue. Jones's description of the revision says nothing of the sort."[52] The truth, which I invite the reader to confirm by simply looking at Jones's own account of the matter in the *Lexicon's* Preface, is that he considered that "the references to Plato and Aristotle [in the old edition] needed careful revision and some amplification" (p. viii). So this excuse for citing the pre-Jones edition as "the authoritative dictionary relied on by all scholars in this area," and for hiding from the court the pejorative definition contained in the Jones edition, does not get Professor Nussbaum off the hook either.

In the *Virginia Law Review,* Professor Nussbaum attempts to defend herself against Finnis's charge of "reckless irresponsibility" in her use of the *Lexicon:*

[L]ater does not always mean better. . . . A nineteenth-century scholar such as Liddell could perfectly well be a better Platonist than a lexicographer of recent date. . . . There is not linear progress in scholarship in this field. . . .

In short, if a lexicon is cited, it has no weight without an independent linguistic argument, though in connection with such an argument it may have some corroborative value.[53]

A few pages later, she says that "Finnis points to the fact that the most recent edition of the Liddell and Scott lexicon, as revised by Jones, includes 'shameless act' as one possible meaning for the noun *tolmema*."[54] Some readers may get the impression from this and other statements that Finnis introduced Liddell and Scott's *Lexicon* into the litigation. He did not. *Professor Nussbaum herself introduced the Lexicon.* She did so precisely to show that it did not identify a pejorative translation of *"tolmema"* and thus supported *her* claim that such a translation was not a reasonable possibility. Finnis pointed out that Professor Nussbaum was able to create the appearance of such support only by citing as "authoritative" and "relied on by all scholars in this area" a dictionary long superseded—the later editions, misleadingly now called by Professor Nussbaum "the most recent edition," having in fact been around for more than fifty years—and cited rarely, if at all, by contemporary classicists, including Professor Nussbaum herself.

One can take any position one wishes on the proper or best translation of *"tolmema,"* on the question of whether Plato's *Laws* contains a condemnation of homosexual conduct, on the issue of whether moral objections to homosexual acts are a Christian innovation, on the morality of homosexual acts, on the Constitutionality of Colorado's Amendment 2, or on any other substantive question in the case and still feel the force of these questions: Why did Professor Nussbaum state, under oath, that "Liddle, Scott, the authoritative dictionary relied on by all scholars in this area"—as she described it (giving no date or edition) in the version of her affidavit lodged with the court—contains no pejorative definition of the term *"tolmema"?* Why did she fail to reveal to the court that Liddell, Scott, & Jones, "the authoritative dictionary relied on by all scholars in this area"—as she (rightly!) described it in the version of her affidavit served on the State—contained a manifestly pejorative definition? The explanations she has given so far are too lame to credit.[55]

Professor Nussbaum reports in her *Virginia Law Review* article what Finnis had learned in correspondence with Dover (and what he was careful to mention in n. 35 of "'Shameless Acts' in Colorado,") namely, that Dover and Price have in correspondence with her withdrawn their explicitly pejorative translations of *"tolmema"* in

Laws 636c. Neither, so far as I can determine, has stated a position on the question of whether Professor Nussbaum behaved responsibly in her citation of the pre-Jones edition of the *Lexicon* as "authoritative" and "relied on by all scholars in this area." In any event, the fact remains that Dover and Price, however their opinions have evolved in the aftermath of the Amendment 2 trial, were firmly on record as translating the term pejoratively at the point at which Professor Nussbaum testified. And even now Dover declines to endorse her claim that a pejorative definition (such as "shameless act") is "unreasonable," though such a translation "would not be my preferred translation; I would go for 'audacious' rather than 'shameless.'"[56] Of course, the question before us now is not what one might say for or against Professor Nussbaum's translation or the one Finnis prefers—it is, rather, whether Professor Nussbaum observed the canons of scholarly honesty in defending her translation and her related claim that the alternative translation was not a reasonable scholarly option. It is important not to conflate these questions. Professor Nussbaum could be correct in her assertions, and, at the same time, be guilty of Finnis's charge of "(at best) reckless irresponsibility" in the means she employed to defend those assertions.

Although, as I informed the court, I do not myself read Greek, I am confident from what Dover says and what I have been told by other distinguished classicists that Professor Nussbaum is wrong in claiming that a pejorative translation is not a reasonable option. As for the truth of Finnis's charge of dishonesty, one needs no knowledge of Greek to form a sound judgment; as Barry Gross said, "English will do nicely."

Notes

1. In *Evans,* the plaintiffs "are seeking . . . to invalidate a State constitutional amendment passed by referendum in 1992. It provided that no official body in Colorado may adopt any law or policy 'whereby homosexual, lesbian or bisexual orientation, conduct, practices or relationships shall constitute or otherwise be the basis of . . . a claim to minority status, quota preferences, protected status or claim of discrimination.'" John Finnis, "'Shameless Acts' in Colorado: Abuse of Scholarship in Constitutional Cases," *Academic Questions, (Fall 1994): 19.*

2. Professor Nussbaum has since left Brown for the University of Chicago, where she holds appointments in the divinity and law schools.

3. Anyone familiar with the Supreme Court's jurisprudence of religion will immediately recognize the import of this claim. According to prevailing doctrine, laws or policies lacking a "secular purpose" must be invalidated, as contrary to the Constitutional prohibition of laws respecting an establishment of religion. Thus, Professor Nussbaum's testimony, if she could make her claim stick, was likely to be extremely valuable to opponents of Amendment 2.

4. Finnis.

5. Martha C. Nussbaum, "Platonic Love and Colorado Law: The Relevance of Ancient Greek Norms to Modern Sexual Controversies," *80 Virginia Law Review* (hereinafter *"VLR"*) 1515-1651 (1994).

6. The length and level of detail of Professor Nussbaum's article creates a thick fog for readers interested in the truth of Finnis's allegations against her of scholarly abuses. Such readers must examine the article, and its numerous citations, with great care, always bearing in mind Finnis's precise allegations, and noting instances in which Professor Nussbaum, in purporting to respond to them, merely changes the subject.

7. "Dover and Nussbaum Respond to Finnis," 80 VLR 1641-1651. Prior to its publication, a draft of Professor Nussbaum's article was sent to me by a third party. Noting that it contained criticism of my own testimony as well as criticism of Finnis and responses to some of Finnis's claims against her, I got in touch with the *VLR* to request space to reply. When this was denied, I offered to draft a reply and submit it for consideration like any other uncommissioned piece. I expressed the hope that the student editors would publish my response if, in their judgment, it met the established standard for publication in *VLR*. The student editor to whom I spoke initially indicated that there was no reason why I could not make a submission "on spec," though he could not assure publication even if my work met the review's standard. A few days later, however, I received a message from him on my voice mail informing me that there was no point in my making a submission because, he had determined, the editorial board would not consider publishing a reply to Professor Nussbaum's article.

8. When she was writing her *VLR* article, Professor Nussbaum probably did not have a copy of the Finnis article. However, she did have a 6,500-word memorandum that Finnis and I compiled, and which Finnis, as a courtesy, sent to her on 26 January 1994. It made substantially all the allegations against her that were to appear in his article, as well as others that considerations of space did not permit him to include. (The memorandum is on file with the editor of *Academic Questions*.) In reply to Finnis's cover letter inviting her to identify "any point on which you think it is mistaken," she wrote:

> I have looked at it, and I do indeed find numerous errors in it. Since I have received legal advice not to correspond with you and Professor George about these issues beyond the point represented by this letter, I regret that I am unable to point them out to you. My associates and I will inform you of them on an appropriate occasion.

Martha C. Nussbaum to John Finnis, letter, 3 February 1994 (on file with the editor of *Academic Questions*).

9. As this article goes to press, I have had no reply to a written request to the editor-in-chief of the *VLR* for copies of the letters cited by Professor Nussbaum in her article as "on file with the Virginia Law Review Association." Obviously, this makes it exceedingly difficult to assess the legitimacy of Professor Nussbaum's claims that these letters support the case she is trying to make in her article. Since her honesty in the use of sources is precisely what is called into question in Professor Finnis's article, her critics naturally wish to examine anything she cites.

10. I am here concerned with the question of whether Professor Nussbaum was dishonest, or otherwise behaved irresponsibly, in her sworn testimony as an expert in the Amendment 2 case. I do not here respond to criticisms of my philosophical views (or Finnis's) by Professor Nussbaum or others she cites. Nor do I respond to criticisms by her or others of interpretations of classical thinkers or modern commentators except insofar as these touch upon allegations of misconduct by Professor Nussbaum. It is true that I, like Finnis, hold what are today thought of as very conservative moral views and that I, not entirely like Finnis, hold many conservative political views. Many readers will prefer the quite different moral and political views held by Professor Nussbaum, particularly as they pertain to the moral and Constitutional questions at stake in the Amendment 2 case. However, the differences in moral and political viewpoint between Professor Nussbaum, on the one side, and Finnis and me, on the other, are not my concern in the present essay.

11. David Cohen, *Law, Sexuality, and Society: The Enforcement of Morals in Classical Athens* (New York: Cambridge University Press, 1991).

12. Finnis, 20 (note omitted).

13. Affidavit of Martha C. Nussbaum (in *Evans v. Romer*) sworn to on 21 October 1993 (hereinafter "Nussbaum Affidavit"), paragraph 30.

14. Finnis, 34.

15. Nussbaum, "Platonic Love," 1548, n. 120.

16. Ibid., 1641 (note omitted).

17. Reporter's Transcript, Testimony of Martha Craven Nussbaum, Ph.D., 15 October 1993 (hereinafter "Nussbaum Transcript"), 23.

18. Kenneth J. Dover, *Greek Homosexuality,* updated and with a new postscript (Cambridge, Mass.: Harvard University Press, 1989), 160.

19. Commenting on Socrates and Plato, Dover noted that "[c]ondemnation of homosexual acts as contrary to nature was destined to have a profound effect on the history of morality," *Greek Homosexuality,* p. 168. Indeed it was. How odd, therefore, to find Professor Nussbaum associating Dover with the view that the

general condemnation of homosexual acts was no part of the thinking of such pre-Christian philosophers as Socrates and Plato. Incidentally, since Dover made clear in the preface to *Greek Homosexuality* that he personally does not share the general condemnation of homosexual acts, his witness to the fact that Socrates (and Plato) did have moral objections to homosexual conduct is all the more impressive.

20. Martha C. Nussbaum to Robert P. George, letter, 20 October 1993 (on file with the editor of *Academic Questions*).

21. Nussbaum Affidavit, paragraph 11.

22. Rebuttal Affidavit of Robert P. George, sworn to on 22 October 1993, paragraph 5.

23. Nussbaum to George, letter, 20 October 1993.

24. John Finnis, FBA, to Sir Kenneth Dover, letter, 19 January 1994 (on file with the Editor of *Academic Questions*).

25. Sir Kenneth Dover to John Finnis, letter, 23 January 1994 (on file with the editor of *Academic Questions*). It is perhaps worth noting here that Finnis concluded his letter to Dover of 19 January 1994, as follows:

> I am writing to you, giving these indications of how I interpret *Greek Homosexuality,* in the hope that if in any respect I am misinterpreting it, you will send me a line to say so. I would not quote such a communication, or use either it or its absence to advance my case by suggesting that you either tacitly or expressly have indicated your support of my understanding on these points (or any others!). My wish is to correct, if you say it needs correction, my understanding of your positions on these points.

In a postscript, Finnis said, "I enclose the relevant page of an affidavit of October 1993 by Professor Nussbaum, to which I am preparing a response." On that page, Professor Nussbaum repeats her testimony that Socrates, according to Dover, disapproved of homosexual acts only in a pupil-teacher relationship.

In concluding his response of 23 January 1994 to Finnis, unequivocally confirming Finnis's view that, according to Dover, Socrates (and Plato) condemn homosexual conduct as such and not merely (as Professor Nussbaum had alleged) in a pupil-teacher relationship, Dover invited Finnis to "by all means quote any part of this letter that you may wish to quote in any connection."

26. I have already remarked on the differences between Dover's moral views regarding homosexual conduct and Finnis's (and my own). In her *VLR* article, Professor Nussbaum, too, calls attention to these differences: "In his forthcoming autobiography, Dover comments on [the theme of the arousal of the soul by a visual response to bodily beauty] in a manner that makes evident the wide difference between his own moral intuitions and those of Finnis. See Kenneth J. Dover, Marginal Comment (forthcoming Nov. 1994)," Nussbaum, "Platonic Love," 1572, n. 235. Dover's autobiography has since appeared and it indeed "makes evident" the profound differences between Dover's moral views and those of someone like Finnis in a number of areas. See, especially, chapter 26, "The Aston Affair 1980-1985."

27. Readers should note what is left out in the ellipsis: the words "and did not confine the prohibition to any particular relationships." Remember, Professor Nussbaum's testimony was precisely to assert that Socrates, according to Dover, condemned homosexual conduct only in the particular relationship of pupil and teacher, and to deny that he condemned homosexual conduct *tout court*.

28. Here no citation is given. I would direct readers to pages 153-70 of Dover's book and, particularly, to pages 159-60, and ask them to judge whether Dover here "said quite clearly," or said at all, that Socrates condemned homosexual copulation merely as an inferior "good" to the pursuit of wisdom.

29. Nussbaum, "Platonic Love," 1645.

30. Even if Dover now claims that his account of *Socrates* in *Greek Homosexuality* should be read down in this way, he could not, and does not, make the same claim about his account of *Plato* in that work, which begins its treatment of Plato as distinct from Socrates by portraying him as "no longer in the mood for compromise or tolerance such as he shows for the [homosexual] pair who 'lapse' in Phaedrus," and goes on to quote, precisely as summarizing Plato's views, the condemnation of homosexual pleasuring as "a crime caused by failure to control the desire for pleasure," *Greek Homosexuality,* p. 165.

31. Expert Witness Summary for Professor Martha Nussbaum, p. 1.

32. Here the reader will recall Professor Nussbaum's statement, in her Expert Witness Summary, that "prior to Christian tradition, there is no evidence that natural law theories regarded same-sex erotic attachments [by which, the context makes clear, she means to include conduct] as immoral, '*unnatural,*' or improper" (emphasis added).

33. Nussbaum Affidavit, paragraph 54.

34. A.W. Price, *Love and Friendship in Plato and Aristotle* (New York: Oxford University Press, 1990).

35. Finnis, "'Shameless Acts,'" 29.

36. Ibid.

37. She cites the first as an "Open Letter from Anthony Price, Lecturer in Philosophy, University of York, to Martha Nussbaum (Dec. 12, 1993) (on file with the Virginia Law Review Association)," "Platonic Love," 1528, n. 37, though neither Finnis nor I have seen it or have been told where it appeared.

38. Professor Nussbaum cites, but does not quote from, a second letter from Price, dated 12 May 1994 "(on file with the Virginia Law Review Association)," Ibid. 1578, n. 271, which, as far as I can tell, relates to a problem in the interpretation of Plato's *Phaedrus* not relevant to Finnis's allegations of misconduct in her use of Price's work.

39. Although it has no bearing whatever on the question whether Finnis's allegations of misconduct against Professor Nussbaum are valid, I cannot help but remark that the charge Price is here quoted as making against supporters of Colorado Amendment 2 seems itself to reflect "prejudice and antipathy" against the many sincere Christians, Jews, and others whose moral and political views regarding homosexual conduct and issues pertaining thereto deviate from his own. There is, no doubt, an element of "prejudice and antipathy" in the motives of some people on both sides of this moral and political debate. I have been to Colorado and spoken with many supporters of Amendment 2, and it strikes me as a smear to suggest in wholesale fashion that "popular support" for the amendment was motivated by such emotions. Reasonable people can and do disagree about these issues.

40. Nussbaum Transcript, 10. Professor Nussbaum was here speaking from ignorance. Finnis in fact is a skilled Latinist and possesses a sufficiently good understanding of Greek to confirm the quality of the translations on which he relies, even if his Greek is not as good as, say, David Cohen's. In her *VLR* article, Professor Nussbaum acknowledges Finnis's claims in this regard, and responds by (1) saying that the Greek texts of Plato used by Finnis (viz. the Loeb editions) "are well known . . . to contain very poor editions . . . not supplied with the extensive critical apparatus that a scholar requires for serious work on the text," and (2) expressing doubt about whether someone can assess a translation made by a translator whose knowledge of the language of the text is generally superior to one's own (1533, n. 54). Her responses overlook the fact that, as Finnis's affidavit indicated, Finnis had compared translations and only cited Loeb texts where they were substantially in line with translations by other scholars, such as Dover. What an expert witness in Finnis's position needs to do is quote translations that have sound scholarly support and, where there is dispute, to be able to follow the argument between the translators and their critics.

Moreover, as Kevin Flannery has pointed out to me, Professor Nussbaum's talk of the Loeb volume's "very poor" text and lack of "extensive critical apparatus" is a red herring. That volume's text of *Laws* 636c1-7 (which Nussbaum chose to make central to her attack on Finnis) differs in absolutely no relevant way from the texts to which she herself appeals. Her discussion of textual matters in the *VLR* article at pages 1625-34 seems tacitly to acknowledge as

much. (Readers who have followed this affair will not be surprised to discover further scholarly offenses in her discussion of translation and text-critical issues on the pages just referenced in the *VLR*, see n. 44, *infra.*)

41. Ibid., 11. The procedure adopted by Finnis (who did not hold himself out to the court as a classicist)—of cautiously comparing texts and translations in several languages, and then quoting translations whose substance was fully confirmed by other versions acceptable to the opposing witnesses—proved eminently sound and serviceable compared with Professor Nussbaum's confident reliance on her own translating skills. (In a letter to me of 29 October 1993, cited at n. 47, *infra.*, she asserted that her selection as assessor of the philosophical texts by the Loeb Library indicated that she is "the living scholar in the Anglo-American community whose knowledge of the Greek of the philosophical authors was judged to be the best." Having "steeped" herself in Plato and Aristotle, she further claimed to "have a sense of the Greek that is some-what like a native speaker's sense after twenty-seven years, and probably as good a sense, where these authors are concerned, as any living person has.") This reliance spectacularly tripped her up, leaving her to a desperate defensive retreat that could be managed only by the falsifications of modern classical scholarship (e.g., her alleged modern consensus around Price, whom she imagines rejecting as "tendentious" the standard translation of *para phusin* as "unnatural"), in which she was soon detected by Finnis, and that has ended with her tacitly surrendering key linguistic claims she made to the court.

42. Ibid., 22.

43. Finnis, "'Shameless Acts,'" 23. The rumor circulating in some quarters, that Finnis accused Nussbaum of dishonesty because she disagreed with his translation of a Greek word, is preposterous. Finnis's allegations against her pertaining to *"tolmema"* have to do, not with the reasonableness of her preferred (neutral) translation, but rather with statements she made under oath (in English and about English-speaking works of scholarship) in support of her claim that the competing (pejorative) translations were unreasonable. It is to these statements that the present essay now turns.

44. The mass of scholarly opinion in favor of a translation that Professor Nussbaum had declared to be outside the range of scholarly possibilities makes it difficult for her to defend her position without further manipulations of the evidence. Thus, on page 1627 of the *VLR*, she says that "all other translations known to me" (i.e., other than Dover's) take the two words immediately following *"tolmema"* in the Greek (*"ton proton"*) to mean "the first people who did it." But on page 1625 she has appealed to "the major philological commentary on the *Laws*," *The*

Laws of Plato, edited by E. B. England (1921). England, having stated that those two words seem at first sight to have the meaning that Professor Nussbaum favors, argued carefully that they have another meaning (which is neither the one she favors nor the one favored by Dover), and concluded in favor of the following translation: "and that the audacity is in an especial degree due to unbridled lust" (231).

Again, the *VLR* article extends her attack on Bury from the issue of translation to that of the Greek text (see footnote 40 *supra*). This is a smokescreen. When she gets to textual issues in relation to the passage that she made the focus of her attack, she is unable to point to anything to fault, great or small, in the Bury text of the passage. To cover this embarrassing fact, she diverts attention by launching a sweeping assault on the Oxford Classical Text (OCT) of *Laws* (not Bury's Loeb text); and when she comes to identify the point at which the OCT differs from the text she regards as sound in relation to *Laws* 636b1-d4, she gives a list of editors and translators who favor the text she favors, and from that list carefully omits *Bury.*

45. Thus, the definitive "Jones" edition of what classicists refer to as "Liddell and Scott" would have been useless to Professor Nussbaum precisely because it contained the pejorative definition she was alleging to be outside the realm of possibility for reasonable translators. That meaning was introduced as one of a vast number of revisions, supplementations, and amplifications in the twentieth-century revised edition of the original Liddell & Scott *Lexicon,* undertaken in 1911 and completed in 1940 by a large team of scholars under the direction of Henry Stuart Jones, and since supplemented. Please note that Liddell (not "Liddle") and Scott has always had the title *A Greek-English Lexicon* (not *A Lexicon of the Ancient Greek Language*).

46. If we allow that her citation "Liddle [*sic*], Scott & Jones" in the version of her affidavit served on the State was in fact a mistake, then, as Finnis remarks, "Professor Nussbaum put a dictionary before the court precisely as 'the authoritative dictionary relied on by all scholars in this area,' but the quotation that, she said, was from that dictionary is in fact from one that is not authoritative or relied on by all scholars, or indeed any scholars," "'Shameless Acts,'" 25-26. Finnis goes on, incidentally, to argue that Professor Nussbaum's claims about *"tolmema"* are "in substance a falsification *even of the 1897 edition's entry* for *tolmema."* Loc. cit., p. 26.

47. Martha C. Nussbaum to Robert P. George, letter, 29 October 1993 (on file with the editor of *Academic Questions*).

48. Robert P. George to Martha C. Nussbaum, letter, 17 November 1993 (on file with the editor of *Academic Questions*).

49. Martha C. Nussbaum, *The Fragility of Goodness* (Cambridge: Cambridge University Press, 1986).

50. Of course, it doesn't matter whether Professor Nussbaum *owns* a copy of the Jones edition or "has it around." It is freely available in university libraries to which she has access. Judging from her frequent citations to it in her published writings, she has no difficulty getting hold of it when she needs it. So what is truly absurd is her claim that, since she doesn't "have it around," it would have been "absurd" for her to cite it.

51. The James A. Moffett Lecture in Ethics.

52. Finnis, "'Shameless Acts,'" 26.

53. Nussbaum, "Platonic Love," 1621-1622. In her n. 389, on 1620 ff., Professor Nussbaum quotes an open letter from Richard Sorabji, director of the Institute for Classical Studies at the University of London, "on file with the Virginia Law Review Association," to the effect that the Liddell and Scott *Lexicon* (by which, I assume, he means the Jones edition, referred to by classicists and in the Jones edition itself as "Liddell and Scott"), though "the best of the available dictionaries for the purposes of learning Ancient Greek, [] has to be used with caution in matters of scholarship, and can serve at best as an initial source of opinions." (Sorabji's letter is quoted earlier, n. 64, 1535, as critical of Bury's translations for lacking "the kind of accuracy required for understanding precise philosophical meaning." No indication is given, however, whether Sorabji supports Professor Nussbaum's contention that a pejorative rendering of *"tolmema"* in Plato's *Laws* 636c is beyond the scope of reasonable scholarly possibility. Nor is any indication given whether Sorabji states an opinion regarding her honesty in citing the *Lexicon* in her sworn affidavit.) Professor Nussbaum also cites A. W. Price's first letter (see n. 37) to the effect that lexicographers can make mistakes, so "[i]t would be . . . erroneous to cite some particular edition of a Greek lexicon as if that was gospel." Of course, none of this gives any cover to Professor Nussbaum. To repeat: *She* introduced the *Lexicon,* telling the court, under oath, that it was "the authoritative dictionary relied on by all scholars in this area," while hiding the fact that the Jones edition, which she and all other scholars regularly cite as the authoritative dictionary, even exists. Since that edition, as she apparently knew, contradicted her contention regarding the reasonableness of pejorative translations of *"tolmema,"* she had a strict obligation to inform the court of the difference between the nineteenth- and twentieth-century editions and to state her reasons (if she could identify any) for preferring, in this case, the nineteenth-century edition.

54. Ibid., 1629 (note omitted).

55. Finnis's article made several other allegations against Professor Nussbaum of misconduct in her use of sources in testimony given under oath in the Amend-

ment 2 case. These allegations she has, as far as I can determine, thus far ignored in published writings. One hopes that she will take them up in the future. At that time, perhaps, she will also answer some of the questions I have put to her in this essay.

56. Sir Kenneth Dover to Finnis, letter, 9 July 1994 (on file with the editor of *Academic Questions*).

Jack Abecassis (essay date September 1995)

SOURCE: Abecassis, Jack. "The Fragility of Philosophy: Passions, Ancient and Modern." *MLN* 110, no. 4 (September 1995): 918-42.

[*In the following essay, Abecassis compares Nussbaum's* The Therapy of Desire *with* Le Philosophe et les Passions *by Michel Meyer, contending each examines the concept of passion in moral philosophy. Abecassis observes that Nussbaum's is a polemical book full of brilliant and insightful analysis.*]

> *Les hommes sont si nécessairement fous, que ce serait être fou, par un autre tour de folie, de n'être pas fou.*
>
> Pascal, *Pensées*, B 414

The *sophia* in philo-sophia is the antonym of *pathos*. Thus philosophers are, for the most part, the enemies of the *phil-pathé*, the tragedians. If, as Epictetus defines it, "tragedy is uniquely the narration in tragic verse of passions experienced by men fascinated by external objects,"[1] philosophy seems by its very self-definition to be the overcoming of passion by Reason. Indeed, from its inception, philosophy conceived of passion as its radical other, the difference by which it fashioned its own identity (Meyer, 293). Hence the semantic dissonance we experience when confronted by a concept such as 'philosophy of passions.' This ironic dissonance would become all the more evident if we consider a tragedy whose subject is philosophical practice. The *Clouds* of Aristophanes, let us not forget, is a comedy.

Moral philosophy (ethics) is clearly on the defensive here. Its traditional role having been challenged and supplanted first by the Moralists (Montaigne, Pascal, La Rochefoucauld) and then by social scientists, moral philosophy is in want of a discourse capable of constructively accounting for passion. "Passion" here does not refer necessarily to grandiose excesses (*thumos*) depicted by Homer or Wagner, but quite simply it refers to our mundane daily psycho-drama: hate and love, fear and confidence, calm and anger, shame and impudence, compassion, emulation, jealousy, good will, indignation and contempt (Meyer, 75). Although very different in nature, the two books considered here set themselves the identical tasks of creating (Meyer) or rediscovering (Nussbaum) a philosophical practice which will make

an adequate description and analysis of the passions possible and which, by the inclusion of passion in the categories susceptible of philosophical analysis, would henceforth overcome the perennial dichotomy between *logos* and *pathos*.

Le Philosophe et les Passions [by Michel Meyer] and ***The Therapy of Desire*** [by Martha Nussbaum] share a common anxiety about the state of contemporary philosophy. Both evidently seek to go beyond nihilism, facile relativism, historicism and psychoanalysis; both challenge the apparent sterility of academic moral philosophy, be it analytically or continentally inspired; and, finally, both share a common allegiance to some form of cognitive rationality in their attempt at a conceptual corralling of passions. But the similarities end here. Nussbaum's book is an idiosyncratic account of Hellenistic philosophy in which she advances a polemical argument regarding the relationship between reason and passion and the role of philosophy as the true healer of excessive emotions or passions. This argument challenges virtually all the anti-foundationalist critique of metaphysics from Nietzsche down to Rorty. Meyer's book is both a history and a critique of the concept of passion in western philosophy from Plato to Kant (part I) and a cohesive theory of passions (part II). Nussbaum argues, to a large extent, for a philosophical return to a Hellenistic form of rationality and pragmatic commitment to a philosophical therapeutics, while Meyer axiomatically rejects all concepts of passion arising out of the Plato-Kant tradition. Meyer offers us "problematology"—a philosophical practice which rejects propositionalism, postulating a form of questioning which does not obliterate foundational questions.[2] Finally, these two books are particularly well suited for comparison because each conceives of itself as the critique of the other. Nussbaum's substantial acceptance of the Hellenistic conception of the *logos* represents a form of propositional rationalism which Meyer explicitly rejects. On the other hand, Meyer's skepticism (antifoundationalism), linguistic pragmatism and phenomenology would place him in a modern perspective to which Nussbaum is acutely averse.

The Therapy of Desire is a polemical book. It is not simply an antiquarian gloss which tries to reconstruct the historical, philological and philosophical cohesiveness of ancient texts. Although such an effort is also a major component of Nussbaum's book, and here as in her previous work brilliant and insightful analyses abound (especially regarding Lucretius), the interdisciplinary and conceptual interest lies rather with the theoretical assumptions and the polemical anti-modern conceptual models which generate the entire subsequent argument.

Nussbaum makes to initial cases for the study of Hellenistic philosophy. The historical case is convincing. In most philosophy departments a gaping hole exists between Aristotle and Descartes. Epicureanism, Skepticism and Stoicism (not to mention Augustine, Aquinas and Maimondes and Renaissance philosophy *in toto*) are rarely part of the curriculum, yet they are absolutely crucial for the understanding of all subsequent history of thought, in particular the history of Medieval and Renaissance thought. *The Therapy of Desire,* being in part an engaging and accessible exposition of the ethics and cultural history of Hellenistic philosophy, should contribute to the ongoing rediscovery of this post-classical philosophy.

But the interest of the book lies in what Nussbaum calls the "transcontextual ethical truths" (8) of Hellenistic philosophy. Whatever legitimacy historicism, and its corollary relativism, are allowed, the insights of the Epicureans and Stoics[3] cannot be reduced, as Foucault asserts, to a *biou techné* (art of life or *technique de soi*).[4] This would obviously reduce Hellenistic philosophical theory and practice to the level of "religious and magical/superstitious movements" (p. 5), and thereby undermine its permanent claims to truth. "What is distinctive," writes Nussbaum, "about the contribution of the philosophers is that they assert that *philosophy,* and not anything else, is the art we require, an art that deals in valid and sound arguments, an art that is committed to the truth" (ibid.). Given his view that "knowledge and argument are themselves tools of power" (ibid.), Foucault argues that these techniques are another variation of power politics. Nussbaum, on the other hand, contends that such a commitment to transcendental truth is anything but one more trick in a panoply of power tools, and that this particular type of philosophical rationality is ontologically and epistemologically different from non-philosophical modes of knowledge.

Similarly, Nussbaum criticizes John Rawls because of his belief that ethical theorizing is a matter of practical reasoning, an historical, culture-specific activity, without any claim for transcendental reality.[5] "[Rawls] concludes that the notion of truth can be appropriate only in an inquiry that is a search for the nature of an altogether independent reality. Ethical theories, lacking such an independent goal, cannot claim to embody truth" (22). While Nussbaum also denies the possible existence of supra-human Platonic ethical truths, she wants to preserve the notion of truth ("transcontextual ethical truths") understood in terms of her main analytical tool and the metaphor which generates the entire argument: the medical analogy. Since the whole argument of the *Therapy of Desire* rests on the validity of this analogy, I shall concentrate exclusively here on its two aspects: first, the competence of the physician, and second, the disease, the passion, of the patient.

Simply put, the medical analogy is predicated on the following argument: the relationship between physician and patient is analogous to the relationship between philosopher and ordinary human being. The analogy is certainly historically valid. Unlike their classical predecessors, Epicureans and Stoics have a much more pragmatic attitude toward the applicability of philosophical concepts *hic et nunc* for the amelioration of individual lives. The goal of their philosophy is *eudaimonia,* human flourishing through the use of reason. To clarify this concept, Nussbaum contrasts the medical model of ethics to the Platonic approach and to the approach based on ordinary belief. Plato errs in postulating ethical norms "independently of human being, human ways of life, human desires" (17). Besides being empirically wrong, such suprahuman categories would obviously make the Platonic physician "sadistic and callous" (20). In contrast, ordinary belief-based ethics involves the notion that "ethical inquiry and teaching are simply the recording of traditional social belief and have no legitimate goal beyond this. Ethics, in this view, begins from what we might call an assumption of social health, the assumption that, for the most part, people have been brought up to have true ethical beliefs and reliable intuitions, and that ordinary beliefs and intuitions can be treated as criteria of ethical truth and rightness" (24). But such an ethics, based on a common, historically secreted consensus as to the *true good,* would be anathema to the Epicureans and Stoics. Being a passive follower of custom, the non-philosopher is a victim of the ordinary rather than being a happy participant in it. Ordinary beliefs provide a starting point, a place where the problems are located, but they do not offer a normative model. The *nomos* is the disease and not the cure. In short, "moral medical philosophy" seeks to reproduce the a-symmetry which predicates the physician-patient situation. Like the physician, the philosopher knows the truth and is capable through the practice of an art of curing the patient. And like physicians Epicureans, and Stoics take into account the real, individual and specific subjectivity of their patients, their beliefs and desires, hopes and fears. This, then, would be a philosophical practice far more human than any abstract philosophy of Being, whence its attraction for Nussbaum.

Let us return to the notion of truth. Within the logic of the medical analogy, truth is claimed through appeal to the following criteria: 1) internal consistency 2) correspondence 3) broad coherence and fit (23). *Internal consistency,* namely the surveying and sorting out of "beliefs toward the end of consistency" (ibid), is a necessary but not sufficient condition for healing. "By bringing to light the hidden contradictions and tensions in a system of beliefs, a pragmatic medical ethics can claim to be doing something that is at least necessary in the search for truth" (23-24). This survey completed, the philosopher/physician proceeds to evaluate the correspondence of the survey data with his "normative yet empirical" (ibid) positive knowledge of Nature.

The second criterion, *correspondence,* presupposes not only the aforementioned self-transparency of the subject (e.g. ability to harmonize contradictions through the use of Reason), or the transparency of the patient to the philosopher, but also the transparency of nature. Epicureans and Stoics, although in very different ways, ground their ethics in a normative account of Nature. Epicurus, for example, holds that "an account of the ethical end is inseparable from his general epistemology, according to which the senses are themselves entirely reliable, and all error comes from beliefs" (108). Hence, Epicurus sees consciousness as capable of being a reflective screen of external reality, a true mirror of the Real, were it not for the obfuscation of false beliefs. In the case of the philosopher, the correspondence between phenomena, somatic sensation and intellection is complete. More importantly, a correct reading of Nature, of natural signs, conveys a prescriptive code of ethics. Correspondence, therefore, implies the possible symbolic adequation of two independent sets: (m_1, m_2, m_3, . . . m_n) for the mind, and (n_1, n_2, n_3, . . . n_n) for Nature. The tragic, existential opacity of Man in Nature vanishes to oblivion in this ideal adequation. Everything being transparent and normative and teleological (in a diffused sense with Epicurus and in a grand narratological sense with Zeno), the "therapy of desire" would consist in the imposition upon the patient of the apodictic and prescriptive Truth of Nature. To arrive at this ideal, the Epicurean student will be confronted with "a process of argument [. . .] often called *diorthosis,* 'correcting'" (131).

The truth criterion of *coherence and general fit* proves to be just as problematic. As we saw, Nussbaum rebuts Foucault by asserting that Hellenistic ethics, since it constitutes itself as a *systematic* philosophical inquiry with strong transcendental truth claims, is not to be reduced to a *biou techné,* a form of psychological *bricolage* lacking theoretical coherence and fit and bearing only incidental and localized relationship to truth. In other words, Nussbaum holds fast to the distinction between *logos* and *nomos* and does not allow for a relativizing of the former into the latter. It must be remembered that Epicureanism and Stoicism presented themselves as complete systems of thought. From the beginning to the end they insisted that no part of the system could be independent of or superior to any other part.[6] Logic, physics and ethics form one coherent system, the premises of which are always dogmatically asserted (e.g. atomism in Lucretius; cosmos, providence, logic, physics in Stoicism). In Stoicism, as Goldschmidt demonstrates, "The conquest [. . .] is a passage from the *same* to the *same* [un passage du même au même]. In the structural movement of the system, the starting point coincides with the finishing line."[7] Stoicism is not a deductive system; the initial founding "proposition" regards the whole of Being and the Real. In other words, it is impossible to isolate one argument within the

system for a particular truth-claim; it all stands and falls together, logic as much as physics and ethics. Truth, consequently, can then be claimed on two distinct levels: internal logic within the system and/or adequation to the Real, the fit between *logos* and phenomena. Despite the arguments that both the Hellenistic philosophers and Nussbaum make, the inherent tension between a dogmatic and totalizing philosophical system and the contingency and individuality of the medical situation becomes evident. The philosopher-physician possesses total knowledge; he only wonders about how to move his sick patient along from point *a* to point *b*. Whatever is contingent and individual is not the analysis of the problem or the solution, but simply the tactics required in a particular cure. The philosopher here is clinical in that he is willing to deal with individual cases *hic et nunc*. But, in real clinical medicine, the good clinician never possesses this totalizing and universal medical semiology, never infers natural apodicticity in every aspect of existence, and never worries too much about the coherence and fit of a given remedy with metaphysics, cosmology and logic.

It is now clear why Nussbaum needs to attack all manner of historical (Foucault) or ontological (Rawls) relativism. Even if one only partially subscribes to this medical conception of Hellenistic philosophy (as at times she herself does intimate), its *entire* validity rests on the acceptability of the a-symmetry between the philosopher and the commoner. And, in turn, this a-symmetry depends wholly on the availability of "transcontextual [ethical] truths" to the philosopher. Yet, nowhere are we told how a Zeno or an Epicurus attains this higher knowledge. We return to the foundational paradox of the *Meno*[8], as Meyer will continuously insist: how is the passage from ignorance to knowledge possible? How can I ignore yet know at the same time? In short, how can the philosopher, living in the sensible, contingent world, like all other humans, arrive at a true and total knowledge and meaning of all sensible phenomena (Epicurus) or understand his role within the Cosmos and its providence (Zeno)? How does one arrive at this meta-positionality vis-à-vis Being and Nature?

Furthermore, a close scrutiny of the three criteria guiding the Hellenistic medical conception of philosophy suggests a number of other problems. The notion of consistency, for one, presupposes the (possible) transparency of the subject to him/her self. Can we speak today of harmonizing all "contradictions and beliefs" within our subjectivity? Is it possible, as Descartes and the rationalists still thought, to achieve simultaneously this empirical adequation between knowledge and Being? Certainly, a Socratic introspective search, an Aristotelian gradual acquisition of good habits or even a psychoanalytical slow process of self-discovery, are conceivable as positive and partially achievable goals, but never the total self-adequation with Nature. Even more disturbing for me is Nussbaum's evasion of the contemporary debates (e.g. Rorty) regarding the viability of a theory of meaning based on *general fit, correspondence* and *cohesion.*

To be sure, Nussbaum does seem to be somewhat troubled with the dogmatic epistemology and ethics of the Stoics and Epicureans. But her solution of "using Aristotle's ethical thought as a background and a foil" (8) seems, from a modern polemical point of view, to be equally problematic. This Aristotelian critique certainly points to core problems in Stoic and Epicurean epistemologies but for a contemporary reader it does so insufficiently, since Nussbaum's polemical argument is *not* limited to a comparative history of ancient ethics but extends to a critique of anti-foundationalism. Aristotle conducts inquiries; he starts with not knowing and sifts his way toward a partial understanding by dialectics, by deduction and by induction. Stoics and Epicureans move from dogmatic knowledge to prescription. The tension between the two practices is obvious. This Aristotelian "foil" may be interesting from a striclty historical point of view, but is insufficient in the polemical context of championing Epicurean and Stoic theory and practice against Rawls and Foucault. Nussbaum passionately argues here for an Aristotelicized version of Hellenistic philosophical practice as a counter practice to the paralyzing impotence and nihilism of modernity. Yet I wonder whether Nussbaum's Aristotelicized revisionism of Hellenistic philosophy really constitutes that *magic bullet* sufficient to do away with the gnawing skepticism of the Derridas and Rortys? As in the case of truth criteria discussed above, Nussbaum does not directly tackle the core problems which animate modern critique. On the contrary it seems that for Nussbaum Reason corresponds *only* to its Greek Aristotelian variety; all critiques of this type of reason are then automatically assigned to the domain of the "irrational." The foundational hypotheses of Epicurus and Zeno are never questioned or justified *per se*: How do they arrive at their insights into the true nature of things and the universe as a whole? How is the passage made from Nature to apodictic reason? How is human subjectivity and contingency the grand disease to be cured by the *logoi* of the philosophers? How is Nature to be the transparent guide in all things?

The paradox of virtue-based, naturalist ethics is just a more exacerbated case of the paradox of ethical naturalism in general. Be they *strict* or *liberal* naturalism, they all suffer from varying degrees of (false) argument from unproven hypothesis, circular logic and anthropomorphic projection. With the exception of early Hebrew thought and (perhaps) strict Platonism, virtually all Greek, Roman and later European philosophy seeks to ground itself in one form or another of naturalism. Modern liberal philosophy, for example, grounds itself

in a philosophy of Natural Right. Circular argumentation here is inevitable: all positive proofs are predicated upon and proven by unfounded presuppositions: i.e. *x* is bad because it is contrary to Nature; and it is so because I hold *y* to be the true state of Nature; the State of Nature being always a confounding matrix of cognitive data and anthropomorphic projection. For every (natural) instance of piety offered by Lucretius and Rousseau there is a corresponding instance of (natural) cruelty offered by Euripides and De Sade. Ideology consists in creating *necessary* adequations of a particular idiosyncratic custom with Nature. Plato circumvents naturalism by inventing the theory of forms, so that the Real of Nature is but the shadow of the Real. Early Hebrew thought circumvents naturalism by grounding the Law in the word of God, in strict opposition to the horror of Nature. The medical analogy can only be sustained by the Epicurean and Stoic metaphysician at the price of turning Nature into a metaphorical sign system containing its own apodictic moral imperatives, all of which are then exclusively known to the philosopher. Only then can the a-symmetry between patient and doctor be theoretically sustained as a viable analogy. Let us now, then, turn to the patient and her disease, the passions. For the sake of economy and clarity, I will henceforth limit my comments to Stoic therapeutics.

Nussbaum creates a fictional character who is the patient. Her name is Nikidion (small victory). She is a Greek *hetaira,* a courtesan. In a surprising move for an academic book, Nikidion is the imaginary student/ patient of the three Hellenistic schools. Through her eyes, her imagined subjectivity, her imagined experiences, the reader is introduced to the multiple therapies of desire offered by each school. Through Nikidion we shall imagine ourselves as Hellenistic Greeks trying to cure our excessive desires by the therapy of the physician-philosophers. With this rhetorical device two complementary aims are achieved: first, the reader is in the text because he or she identifies with Nikidion and, second, the distance between our philosophical horizons and those of the Greeks diminishes by our identification with the "victim," who experiences the same universal problems experienced in our own daily life. Nikidion symbolizes victory over abstractness (philosophy) and over difference (Greek/Modern).

Nikidion's disease is passion. As in Epictetus' definition of tragedy and the tragic hero, the patients of passion suffer from false judgments and beliefs which induce excessive ascription of importance to externals. The description of passion starts on firm Aristotlelian grounds. Unlike Freud, who believes that emotions are "a mindless surge of affect" (88) or "some kind of a mindless process" (101) (an apparent reference to Freud's drive and instinct theory), Aristotle offers a cognitive view of the emotions which erases the difference between emotion (involuntary) and thinking (voluntary). Aristotle postulates that emotions are states of "intentional awareness, containing a view of their object" (81). Aristotle's analysis rests on the consensus of Greek philosophy concerning the emotions: 1) "Emotions are forms of intentional awareness [. . .] directed at or about subjects". 2) "Emotions have a very intimate relationship to beliefs, and can be modified by a modification of belief. [. . .]" 3) ". . . Emotions may appropriately be assessed as rational or irrational, and also (independently) as true or false, depending on the beliefs that are their basis or ground [. . .]" (80-1). As examples of Aristotelian analysis of passion (with implicit reference to identity, non-contradiction and causality), Nussbaum discusses the emotions of fear and pity, demonstrating that in both these basic emotions there must be a "rich intentional awareness of its objects, resting on beliefs and judgments of many sorts, both general and concrete" (86). That is, I fear x of which I am intentionally aware and the reason I fear x as opposed to say loving x is that I hold certain beliefs about its nature. Thus emotions are cognitive responses to my subjective perception of the Real. From the purely subjective point of view they are eminently rational. They may, however, be true or false or objectively rational or irrational depending on my beliefs. If my beliefs correspond to the truth, then my emotions are both rational and true; if my beliefs are false, then emotions are false. "Emotions [in Aristotle] [. . .] are individuated by reference to their characteristic beliefs" (88), and, thus, it is not surprising that Aristotle, unlike Plato and the Stoics, does not categorically condemn passions and emotions.

Thus Nussbaum's "Greek" cognitive scheme seems to be: external stimulus → perception → intentional awareness → [existing belief] → judgment → action-emotion. With the exception of the ability of the therapist to change emotions simply by modifying belief, this scheme corresponds in a rough manner to the concept of emotion advanced by Marcia Cavel in her recent book *The Psychoanalytic Mind, From Freud to Philosophy.*[9] For Cavel "belief is a particular sort of attitude toward a proposition, since other attitudes toward the same proposition are possible."[10] The cognitivist view of emotions, asserts Cavell, "show[s] us in our guise as organisms interacting with the world around us, which makes for confusion about both perception and emotion."[11] Without challenging this fundamental cognitivist scheme, it is possible to wonder about the nature of the concepts of *belief* and *judgment.* In other words, does belief result *exclusively* from a conscious cognitivist activity or is it an opaque combinatory sedimentation comprised of cognition, deep cultural structures and practices (*habitus*), unconscious behavioral adaptation and primate social biology—*as well as* billiard-like conscious cognition?

With these questions in mind, I would like to zero in on the crucial theoretical moment in the *Therapy of Desire*: the transition from Aristotle to Chrysippus. There are "four theses that are defended within this [Stoic] tradition about the relationship between belief or judgment and passion. 1. Necessity. The relevant belief is necessary for the passion. 2. Constituent element. The belief is a (necessary) constituent element in the passion. 3. Sufficiency. The belief is sufficient for the passion. 4. Identity. The belief is identical to the passion" (371). Aristotle holds (1) and (2) to be true; his position concerning (3) is unclear. Now, in order to make the case for Stoic psychology as a model of "transcontextual [ethical] truth," a model of *perennis philosophia,* partially endorsed by Nussbaum against modernity, the reader, who intuitively assents to a mild version of (1) and (2), would have somehow to swallow steps (3) and (4). For *all* Stoic psychology of the passions down to Marcus Aurelius, relies on this Chrysippian scheme whose stated aim is the complete extirpation of the passions.

Now Nussbaum explains very carefully all the subtleties of this position (different sorts of judgments, beliefs, appetites, innate dispositions, etc.). But however we turn the question, and whatever "common sense" and "plausibility" arguments are advanced, from a modern point of view, the identification of passion with judgment cannot be ironed out by generous *subtilitas.* In Stoicism, all passions, in the final analysis, are identical with mistakes in judgments based on false belief; they are all condemnable over-valuing of "externals." Nikidion will be told repeatedly that all emotions stem from her inability to extricate herself from the world of the *stulti,* fools. Even were she sincerely grieving for the loss of a loved one, her emotion would be condemned for ascribing to the lost person too much importance (379). She will become a sage once she assents only to representations philosophically consistent with the Stoic world view. At that moment, controlling her representation to herself of external stimuli, withholding assent from all things not philosophical, she would live in an eternal present of the sage, undisturbed by all things external, entirely autonomous.

The disease of passion is then a cognitive sickness of the weak-minded. Not only drunkard fools and noble tragic heroes suffer the disease of passion but all of humanity save the (Stoic) philosophers. Nikidion, like us, to escape her sickness, must transform reality into an all embracing *cognitive* matrix. As Goldschmidt insists, Stoicism, unlike Platonism, accepts reality as it is (its vaunted naturalism and sensualism, acceptance of the *sensible*) but only at the price of transforming reality through and through (Nature is Reason). Consequently, the a-symmetry between the (meta) physician and the (alleged) patient is not relative but massive. As the Stoic sage has access to a transformed reality, he can guide the rest of us who are prisoners of raw reality, assenters to raw representations. The Platonic omniscience is completely reproduced here, except that it is the world *hic et nunc* that is transformed in Stoicism and not a supra-lunar reality in the realm of forms. The medical analogy, upon which rests the whole of Nussbaum's argument, can only be sustained as a polemical model, as a model of compassionate philosophical practice for us today, at the price of entertaining the plausibility of *both* the omniscient *cogito* of the philosopher and the exclusively cognitive nature of the patient's disease.

In reading **The Therapy of Desire** I am struck by how Nussbaum reproduces in her book exactly what Goldschmidt cautioned against in the fourth and final postface to his *Le Système Stoïcien et l'Idée du Temps*: first, explaining Stoicism against the background of Aristotle; second, isolating one element within the Stoic system; third, trying to understand Stoicism in "analytic terms," canceling thereby the utter otherness of Stoic rationality to us moderns.[12] Nussbaum's style of argumentation is to start with "plausible and intuitive" premises (i.e. Aristotle "reasonable" cognitivism) and argue that Stoic arguments are simply their radicalization. Arguing from Aristotle, appealing to common sense, concentrating within the Stoic system solely on psychology, inducing a personal identification with Nikidion, all have the same strategic objective of doing away with the radical otherness of Stoicism. This otherness consists precisely in the definition of Reason as the understanding of the order of the universe (*cosmos*) and the *necessity* of adjusting all human actions and thoughts to the order of the universe, to the thoughts of god (cosmic *sympathy*). "This consciousness of the self," writes Pierre Hadot, "is not only a moral consciousness, it is also a cosmic consciousness: the 'attentive' man lives without interruption in the presence of God in the 'memory of god,' consenting joyfully to the will of Universal Reason and seeing all things with the same gaze of god himself."[13] There is no break between physics and morality: it is as if carved out of one block of *logos*.

The Stoics always insisted that each element in their philosophy must cohere with the rest: *ad singula respondere* [. . .] *totam sententiam explicare*, insists Cicero.[14] Thus when Nussbaum writes that "A motivation for me in writing about them [Epicureans and Stoics] was to discover whether it was possible to accept their arguments about the elimination of anger, while still rejecting their more general attack on passions such as love, fear and grief" (509), one wonders what is the possible connection among this very limited interest and the vaunted "transcontextual ethical truths" and the three truth criteria mentioned at the beginning as an alternative to modern relativism. Nussbaum not only isolates morality within Stoicism, but also within this Stoic moral theory she finally rejects the equation of all

passion with error of judgment while seeming to accept the possibility of the extirpation of anger, as if anger as a passion had an ontology and a global functional logic different from that of other passions. Ironically, this *à la carte* acceptance of Stoic morality, with only casual regard to its coherence within Stoic cosmic rationalism, has the effect of reducing it to a type of a subjectively seen 'timeless wisdom,' a spiritual coping mechanism, a tranquilizer (as Paul Veyne would say)[15] that is precisely what Foucault meant by a *biou techne*. After all the theoretical concessions, qualifications, historicizations and outright "cherry picking" are taken into account—within Nussbaum's anti-anti-foundationalism polemical context—what "Hellenistic medical therapeutics" offers us is another *pharmacon* of the *biou techne* variety for the unsuccessful treatment of our post-modern blues.

Michel Meyer places the problem of passion at the heart of the western philosophical project. Passion is the Other of reason, its imaginary nemesis, the projection of its own (passionate) impulse, its real yet denied *raison d'être*. Greek philosophical culture (save Socrates and the Skeptics) provides answers which often obliterate the foundational questions. From the theory of reminiscence in Plato's *Meno*, to the absoluteness of the principle of non-contradiction in Aristotle, and to the dogmatic shift from the same to the same in Stoicism, through Hobbes' *Leviathan*, Descartes' *cogito* and the Kantian *a-priori*—all are variations of attempts to create a rational philosophy forming its own *causa sui*. Propositionalism had both to obliterate the question at the origin of the inquiry (in Plato, how can I know if I do not know where to search? In Descartes, am I deceived by the senses?) and invent a guarantor of ultimate rational veracity (the Forms in Plato; rationally proven God in Descartes; the arbitrary a-priori in Kant). In opposition to religious beliefs, myths, social customs, superstitions, tragic theater, and so on (all effective answers to human questioning), Greek rationalism demarcates its claim to absolute Truth, its answer, by the notion of apodicticity—the absolute cosmic and natural necessity of its propositions and answers. Meyer defines the classical Greek project as the idea that "the logos could have access, by its internal resources, to the apodicticity of the order of things, to their nature, of which man is a part and which he should then reflect to be what he really is" (96). Nussbaum's criteria of correspondence and coherence clearly constitute a strong version of this logos.

At its heart, philosophical rationalism constitutes a response to the human existential demand for certitude. Twenty-five centuries of philosophy notwithstanding, this ideal adequation between nature and humanity is yet to be achieved. Progress in fact has been so questionable that virtually all philosophers since Descartes have tried to re-establish philosophy on firm grounding once and for all. Nussbaum, for one, seems to be so distraught over the state of modern philosophy that she prescribes a rethinking of philosophical practice along the lines of an Aristotelized reading of Hellenistic philosophy.

As far as we know, humans are the only organisms in nature whose *telos* is not a given. Unlike plants and animals, human beings experience almost every facet of existence as a form of conscious or unconscious questioning to which culture is an answer; human beings are the only phenomenon in nature who experience the problem of means and ends as an open question. That is why we are the only entities in nature in need of a self-generated ethics. Between Being and the Real there is an inadequation which, according to Meyer, only passion can mediate. Philosophy desires to short circuit the endless and necessary questioning, as well as obliterate the answers which custom provides, answers to the unbearable weight of human indeterminancy, with its own rational necessity: the necessity of its answers to the exclusion of all others. But, perennially, there lies an enemy who foils this imperial project—passion, the obstacle between the pure concept and the practice of real beings in the world.

"Propositionalism," writes Meyer, "answers the most fundamental question there is: what does it mean to answer? This question governs all the other [questions], it models them, because the solution brought will be valid for any possible solution, since it is precisely a matter of determining that which constitutes a solution in general. As the questioning is open to a multiplicity of options, the answer, being one of them, does away at once with any alternative, therefore with any problem" (289). If the principle of non-contradiction is my a-priori guarantee of the veracity of any proposition, then all that which contradicts this absolute truth would be rejected as "irrational". Since philosophy is cognitive by nature, the move to rationalize passion, rendering it in this manner a proper subject of intelligible properties (i.e. judgment) is inevitable within the internal logic of Greek philosophy. In the world of the intelligible, properties must *necessarily* be what they are; in the world of the sensible, properties are contingent. The whole struggle of philosophy is to somehow reduce the ontological difference between the intelligible and the sensible; to pretend that what holds for intelligible properties (logic, grammar, mathematics) must also encompass the variable, contingent multiplicity of the sensible. Passion, being at the heart of the unpredictable contingency in humanity, becomes the radical Other of propositionalism: "Propositionalism, at heart, has only the fault of its absolutes. Demonstration, necessity, are certainly excellent forms of discourse, but could not pretend to be the only ones, without having to relegate all others to the darkness of the irrational. And there, propositionalism is destroyed by itself, because it only conceives of itself as exclusive of its exclusions.

The reason for this is simple: to accept plurality in answerhood means admitting that the problematic and the multiple can inscribe themselves in it, and resurface under the form of questions in the answers themselves. But, propositionalism is born of necessity, which thus affirms itself circularly, but also excludes all that is not apodictic" (291).

Now this critique of traditional philosophy is not original. What is new is Meyer's attempt to go beyond a purely negative critique of philosophy and ground philosophy in what he calls "problematology"—a philosophy of questioning, a rational skepticism which poses questions having no answers in advance; a philosophy built around the problematological difference, meaning that it always keeps alive the difference between questions and answers (300). For Meyer the opposition should not be between (Greek) rationalism and post modern irrationalism, as it is in Nussbaum, but between propositional rationalism and interrogative rationalism. And passion, being that theoretical monkey on philosophy's back, would naturally prove to be the perfect subject for the exploration of the difference between the two approaches.

Throughout *Le Philosophe et les Passions,* Meyer poses three interrelated questions: 1) What is Man? i.e. what specifically can passion reveal about the human condition? 2) What is passion if we are to define it positively and not simply in opposition to an idiosyncratic (e.g. Greek) form of rationality? 3) What is it precisely about traditional philosophical discourse which necessitates the exclusion of passion from "the philosophical life"? These questions are explored within two contexts, first, that of an examination of a series of problems relating to philosophy and passion from Plato to Kant; and second, that of an exposition of what could be a positive phenomenology of passions. By way of continuation and contrast to Nussbaum, I will first briefly sketch Meyer's analysis of passion in Aristotle and then explore some aspects of Meyer's own functional understanding of the passions.

We saw earlier that Nussbaum noted the indecisiveness in Aristotle's view of passion (cognitivism but without necessity), leaving the explanation for it open. Meyer insists on the fact that this indecision springs from tension within Aristotle's philosophy in general. There are in fact two Aristotles: one, close to Platonism, wants to resolve the duality of the intelligible and the sensible in a generalized apodictic system. This Aristotle rejects passion almost along Platonic lines (cf. *Metaphysics,* 1022b15). The other Aristotle accepts man as an entity "free as to its choices of ends, plunged in the contingent, assigning itself each time particular objectives which he is driven to redefine" (65-6). This is the Aristotle of the *Rhetoric.* Aristotle, Meyer insists, holds simultaneously two moralities: a morality of the apodictic *logos* and a morality of contingency.

The objective of the *Rhetoric* is to teach the orator how to manipulate the emotions of the jurors. To do so, the orator must first know what emotions are. Meyer reads the rhetoric of the passions in Aristotle within the framework of intersubjective phenomenology. He is aware of the fact that one cannot speak of consciousness and subjectivity in a pre-Cartesian context—Greek philosophy is a philosophy of Being and not of subjectivity—but, nevertheless, decides that for the modern reader, with this caution always in mind, the conceptual transposition is instructive. Passion, therefore, is the instantiation of the dialectic of identity and difference which is constantly negotiated within any social group. "Passion is the consciousness I have of the consciousness of the Other concerning me, and at once, it is an image of our rapport which I interiorize, a difference which fuses or which explodes" (72). I am with a given person and I perceive (I make the judgment would say Nussbaum) that he or she disdains me; a hostile image of our rapport forms in my imagination; this interiorized hostile difference with the Other renders our rapport hostile. Passion is that which I suffer from the Other; it is "the Other in me so long that he has an image of me against which I react." This intersubjective consciousness, declares Meyer, is "the essence of passion in the Aristotelian Rhetoric" (72).

The political implications here are obvious. A community that resolves to renounce violence must find a way to negotiate difference so that there might exist a minimum of common identity. But common identity is a result of negotiations whose ultimate product is an equilibrium which is in turn always menaced by excess of passion. Excessive difference in the dialectic of identity can become harmful, whence the doctrine of the mean in Aristotle. At the heart of the political pact there lies the micro-intersubjective Sartrian hell: to have an identity I must be different; but if everybody asserts this difference how can we coexist politically? "Each wanting to be one self, each becomes inevitably the same as the other, who wants the same thing while wanting to be different" (173). The drama of this (ego) negotiation is the drama of the passions—the sign of the contingent in a political animal whose *telos* is never a natural given. To talk of politics is to talk of passion; to talk of community is to talk about the negotiation of passion. That is why the understanding of passion is the single most important element in the (courtroom) judicial process. The other political alternative is a totalitarian dictatorship of the *logos* as fantasized by Plato and Zeno. There real debate is absent since all problems have been resolved in advance, and passion is circumvented by the apodictic *logos*. To a large extent the political and social marginalization of philosophy is a function of philosophy's unwillingness to acknowledge the rhetorical reality of human intersubjectivity. The so-called "sophists," recognizing that *logos* itself in matters human is part of the mutable, contingent reality, lacking from a human point of view any cosmic necessity, being never in correspondence with the order of things, insisted upon a practice of philosophy which is consistent with this lack of adequation and correspondence. Only then, based on a shrewd assessment of the reality of human affairs, its passionate substratum, could philosophy become pertinent to the *agora*.

For Meyer the subjective *a-priori* is passion. The theory of *reminiscence,* the *cogito,* the Kantian *a-priori* are all products of the passionate quest for the answer to a perennial question: where, in the final analysis, can the contingent subject anchor his or her existential need for certitude? Desire to know, impulse to search, these are manifestations of the original passion, the degree zero of the philosophical quest, and, according to Meyer, the only possible solution to the paradox of the *Meno*: "Passion is at once the obstacle to the truth and that which pushes me toward it" (294).[16] The more dogmatic the rationalism, the more transparent its passion: Stoicism.

No longer seen as the opposite of reason, no longer excluded as the menace to the immutable stability of thought, passion constitutes the space of the *interface* between the subject and reality. It is the filter, the valve, which mediates between the continual shock of the real and the subject's desire for permanent stability. From the subjective point of view, reality presents itself as an endless series of questions for which passion functions as an answer. "Passion assures the continuity of the real. How is this continuity assured? Each new problem is seen on the basis of questions already resolved, and apprehended in function of answers which were brought to them in the past. The new questions become then rhetorical questions, in the sense that they present themselves as interrogative forms of already accepted truths. [. . .] if the question was able to be suppressed as such [. . .] this has to do [. . .] with the human desire to live in self-assurance and security. This nourishes an "I am right" ceaselessly re-enacted, and upon which are transplanted all ideologies and unconscious constructions" (302). Hence notions such as *common sense* and *plausibility* are seen for what they are: not the shared, timeless, universal mental substratum of humanity, but historical and culture-specific responses to the questions of the Real. *Common sense* is the common filter a culture imposes upon its interpretation of reality so that the illusion of a stable, timeless continuity between subjectivity and the Real is accomplished. Common sense, like all passionate phenomena, is an homeostatic mechanism assuring the cohesion of the subject (and the culture) in that menacing sea of change that is the Real. For Meyer common sense represents the "essentialized passion" of a culture, the self-imposed filter between its consciousness and reality, its responses to the questions of reality crystalized into unquestioned timeless truisms.

Taking his cue from psychoanalysis, Meyer asserts that "As long as we will have not understood that the self is a story (histoire), we will not have resolved any of the grand problems that the concept of subjectivity poses since Descartes and Kant" (305). Storytelling involves a narrative reduction where raw data (the Real) is reduced into a sequence having its own internal dynamics and its own logic. But the psychoanalytic inspiration stops here. Echoing Nussbaum, Meyer entitles his theoretical chapter "For a critique of pure passion", meaning a critique of passion seen as a dark, innate and unconscious mechanism which, by definition, escapes all rational discourse. For Meyer rhetoric, pragmatics, and phenomenology (all done within the problematological framework) are capable of a rational discourse concerning the passions.

What then is the rhetoric driving this subjective storytelling? Its social framework, as we said, is common sense and ideology. On the micro-level Meyer identifies three rhetorical devices capital for the construction of the *barrier* against the real: *deliteralization, denomination, hierarchization.* These mechanisms are not symptoms of a cognitive disease, susceptible to 'correction' once they are understood. Rather they indicate the basic paradox of the passions in that there is a "certain refusal of the real in the act of getting a grip of the real, so that we can live it and live in it. But reality is a function, and not a content" (303).

Deliteralization is chief among these mechanisms: signs, stimuli from the outside do not possess their corresponding necessary interpretation. If such were the case, most human passion would then indeed be errors in judgment. But, in fact, most passion around us today such as the videos of Rodney King and Reginald Denney, to cite just the most obvious examples, demonstrate that a video graphic representation, the closest thing we have in the domain of representation to the Real, can still give rise to a wide variety of genuine deliteratization on the part of the viewing subject. These extreme examples illustrate the rhetorical process in which we engage countless times every day. A stable ego ideal is incompatible with the cognitive requirements of the Real. We cannot function if our basic assumptions about the Real are constantly challenged by contrary data. That is why integral skepticism is a psychological impossibility. By deliteralizing the real, we can reduce difference to sameness, assuring thus the stability of the subject. The questions of the Real, its problematicity, are nullified in favor of an illusion, but a very potent and functional illusion, of changeless, timeless stability. The criterion of the success of passion is not truth but efficacy. It is precisely this feature of *nomos* which so terrified Greek philosophers: instead of deliterazing the real through myth and custom, they wanted to create new cosmically apodictic criteria of judgment that would escape the arbitrariness of custom

and opinion. Instead of the perception of reality as a function of *nomos,* philosophy wished to eradicate this functionality by the discovery of a necessary and absolute identity of judgment with what is. Within this logic, passion is necessarily the enemy, the eternal foil for those searching for a supra-human order.

Denomination and *hierarchization* represent the same subjective act of ordering. To name an act is to imply a judgment. For some Brutus was a murderer, for others a liberator. Violent acts may be named riots or uprisings. The name, at any case, reveals a judgment, that is a reduction of the Real to its subjective and passionate expression. This is why language and metaphors communicate instantly a mentality and an ethics. Naming is closely connected to the more general concept of hierarchization. The act of deliteralization and denomination express the subjective passionate interpretation of the real, a process accomplished by a (necessary) preestablished hierarchy of meaning and value assigned to events. "This circularity [between passion and perception] functions in that the chosen denomination anticipates implications which must follow, these implications being known by other means" (320). This is the subjective *a-priori* of consciousness; the buffer zone between the desire for stability and the ruthless demands of the real. In order to tell a story, the story of the Self, passionate reduction is inevitable. Some narratives, certainly, are better than others. But, given our existential inadequation with the Real, the act of passionate reduction *per se* is inevitable. In short "Passion reflects this discrepancy between the metaphorical and the literal" (341).

This rhetoric of the passions exhibits an underlying logic. It is the logic of the "Amalgam between properties and subjects of properties, a logic of contagiousness and contiguity: x is a but "to be a" applies also to y, which is b, and then even to z and so on." (326). Muslims are our (e.g. Serbs) traditional enemies (x is a), this also applies to one named Mohammed who was my neighbor and dated my sister (to be a applies to y); being Muslim he should then be viewed as my mortal enemy, etc. Being a logic of substitution, the amalgam can seem absurd to somebody looking at a rhetorical-historical situation from the outside. Indeed the discrepancy between the literal and the figurative, which is the space of passion, can result in fantastic amalgams and substitutions. But it is only 'fantastic' to someone looking in from the outside; for the subject, however, this amalgam is eminently rational. Thus, amalgam and substitution result in syllogistic reasoning which in turn reveals the thorough subjectivity of perception and judgment.

But beyond its rhetorical and logical aspects, passion should be understood in relation to existential problems. First is the notion of consciousness itself. Traditionally, two theories of consciousness have emerged: consciousness of the object (Descartes) and consciousness of the self (Romanticism). Between Classicism and Romanticism, the criterion of truth has been displaced from the Real to the self. The transparent consciousness implied in Descartes has the following problem: how is it possible at the same time for consciousness to be submerged irreflexively in the world and to have a critical consciousness of itself? There is a sequential time difference here that remains a perennial problem. Meyer locates this problematic time difference as the space where passion integrates a cohesiveness to consciousness: "The temporal difference is the identity of consciousness. The unreflected consciousness is distinct from the consciousness of the self, while being the same, therefore consciousness, because it is not at the same instant that the return to the self and the forgetfulness of the self take place. Passion worms its way into this [temporal] discrepancy and reveals itself by this act as the time of consciousness. To live one's passion, is to live one's temporality" (347). Passion is then the index of this hesitation between the absolute of the Real and the contingency of the subject. And here we see clearly why passion is so inextricably tied to the notion of time. The acceptance of one is a function of the acceptance of the other. For the Stoics "to conquer passion means abolishing time: [creating] a coincidence among the consciousness of the self and the consciousness of things external, and that time of their discrepancy [being] abolished. The unity of Reason gives man then a present without age, as if he wanted to extirpate himself from the flux of time" (347). Goldschmidt shows that Stoicism's entire project could be understood as a concentrated effort to cancel out the paradoxical and passionate whirlwind of time (i.e. we are either absorbed in regrets of the past or fear of the future, but never in touch with the present)[17] and somehow to live in the eternal present of the sage. According to Meyer, Stoicism here (as in so many other aspects) expresses in a forcefully dogmatic fashion the fundamental human desire to see the problem of time and change neutralized in favor of an immutable *logos* (for the philosopher) or common sense (for the commoner).

Much the same can be said about history: *Plus ça change plus ça reste la même chose* says the popular proverb. The self strives to possess a stable identity, an autonomy vis-à-vis time and history. Passionately we erect an identity against time (348). To accomplish this feat there must be a denial of change, a denial of that which threatens my ego ideal. As we said, *common sense* and *plausibility* serve the function of erecting a fiction of timeless and history-less 'analytic' continuity. The stronger the culture, the more stable its consensus as to its consciousness of the real and its negotiation of the problem of means and ends in ethics. Strong cultures create a tight correspondence between questions and answers. Given that we are all today sons and daughters

of Romanticism, Meyer is correct in insisting that this *bon pensant sens commun* is equally a passionate discourse to which subjects cling with as much passion as to any discourse of revolutionary rapture.

But in the West the time when a Descartes could still imagine denying historical and temporal change is long gone (348).[18] The acceleration of history has made it increasingly more difficult to deny what Meyer calls the *shock of the real*. From Cartesian passion for a *mathesis universalis* we pass to a Hegelian passion for History. The *logos* as it were changed optics from geometry to history. Increasingly the rupture between historical change and personal ethos becomes apparent. Cervantes writes the great novel of this rupture. It is the first great novel about the discrepancy between personal ethos and history, between questions of the self and answers of the Real.[19] The novel, a specifically modern western phenomenon, becomes the genre representing this passionate difference between individual consciousness and objective history. Passion then no longer functions mostly as a cultural homeostatic buffering mechanism but increasingly as the mark of the individual revolt against historical *common sense*: the passion of Madame Bovary against the passion of Monsieur Homais.

The logic of passion governs three large domains: the rapport to the self (the story of the self), to the other (inter subjective consciousness) and to things (history, events, etc.) (380). A filter between the subject and the real; a valve regulating their interaction; a rampart against the passage of time, change, history; a catalyst of change, knowledge, quest; a source of automatic answers and the origin of revolutionary questions; an inter subjective "hell"—these are its paradoxical realities and functions. Paradoxical, because no one single proposition could conceptualize passion's essence. We can not say that passion is A and not -A thereby creating its identity. Starting with the paradox of the *Meno*, Meyer shows that each time propositionalism deals with passion, the result is inevitably paradoxical. Passion has a rhetorical and not a propositional reality: it "works with the conflict between propositions".[20] To seize the reality of passion, its multiple facets must be brought to the surface. But because it is so often for us a concept of projection—"I am reasonable, you are passionate"—we are blind to the pervasiveness of passion. Meyer's contention is that we must first critique propositional thought, showing that while it is adequate for most scientific reasoning, it falls short in the understanding of human contingency. Second, within a rhetorical framework that is eminently rational, but not propositional, using pragmatics, language theory, rhetoric, psychology, phenomenology, it is possible to conceptualize passion without falling into the traditional philosophical trap of seeing it as the other of Reason, as the obstacle which humanity, if it is to "grow up" must surmount. Passion for Meyer is the specificity of humanity: "Passion is, because we are, and must be" (380).

In sum, Nussbaum's neo-Aristotelian critique of anti-foundationalism has two unhappy results: first, an endorsement of a specifically Greek form of rational-ism, to the exclusion of all others; second, the (perhaps unintended) re-activation of the age-old metaphysical opposition between *logos* and *pathos*. Meyer, on the other hand, seeks to form a new rationality which, by its problematological foundation and openness to rhetoric and linguistics, circumvents the problems of propositionalism. Meyer's analysis of passion is the fruit of a close empirical study of contingency. Within this optic, passion assumes a positive role—it is the mark of humanity, Reason being but one of its manifes-tations. To be sure, neither Nussbaum nor Meyer (nor perhaps anybody else) can account within their schemes of passion for the Augustinian-Freudian problematics of absolute evil—so pertinent to this twentieth century. Nevertheless, Meyer's "problematology" of passion represents a serious attempt to bridge the gulfs between philosophy, literature and science.[21] If passion is no longer seen as the enemy, philosophy, literature and criticism may at last recognize each other as manifesta-tions of a shared problematic—Passion.

Notes

1. Epictetus, Diss. I, IV, 26, cited in Victor Gold-schmidt, *Le Système Stoïcien et l'Idée du Temps* (Paris: Vrin [1952], 1976), 178. See also Augustine, *Confessions,* III, 2 for an extensive discussion of passion, representation/imitation, theater and philoso-phy.

2. Meyer's substantial discussion of "problématologie" is in his book, *De la Problématologie* (Bruxelles: Mardaga, 1986). For a more synoptic discussion in English see: Michel Meyer, *Rhetoric, Language and Reason* (University Park: Pennsylvania State Univer-sity Press, 1994).

3. I shall henceforth refer particularly to Epicureans and Stoics and not to the Hellenistic schools *in toto* because the Skeptics, as Nussbaum admits ("skeptics always excepted" [22]), are essentially different from the dogmatic schools and indeed occupy little space in *The Therapy of Desire.*

4. Michel Foucault. *Histoire de la Sexualité Vol. 3, Le Souci de Soi,* (Paris: Gallimard, 1984).

5. John Rawls, *A Theory of Justice* (Cambridge: Cambridge University Press, 1971) and "Kantian Constructivism in Moral Theory: The Dewey Lec-tures," *Journal of Philosophy,* 77, 1980.

6. Goldschmidt, p. 63.

7. Ibid., p. 63. All translations from the French are my own.

8. Plato, *Meno,* 80, d-e.

9. Marcia Cavell, *The Psychoanalytic Mind: From Freud to Philosophy* (Cambridge: Harvard University Press, 1993).

10. Ibid., p. 10.

11. Ibid., p. 144.

12. Goldschmidt, pp. 264-65

13. Pierre Hadot, *Exercises Sprituels et Philosophie An-tique* (Paris: Etudes Augustiniennes, 1981), 63.

14. *De finibus,* III, iv, 14.

15. *The History of Private Life* (Vol. I), ed. Paul Veyne (Cambridge: Harvard UP, 1987), pp. 207-33.

16. The relationship between memory, passion and the quest for the truth are masterfully analyzed by Au-gustine in *Confessions,* X. In purely Platonic terms, Augustine insists that it is passion (love, grace, inspiration, etc.) which propels us to ask the right questions of the inner self, our memory, where all knowledge is permanently stored.

17. See Pascal, *Pensées,* B 172.

18. On Cartesian philosophy being specifically a philosophy constructed against Time and History see: Stephen Toulmin, *Cosmopolis: The Hidden Agenda of Modernity* (New York: The Free Press, 1990).

19. See Meyer, *Meaning and Reading* (Amsterdam: John Benjamins Publishing Co, 1983), 132-37.

20. See Meyer, *Rhetoric, Language, and Reason,* p. 68.

21. For a recent scientific debunking of the opposition of Emotion to Reason, see Antonio R. Damasio, *Des-cartes' Error: Emotion, Reason and the Human Brain* (New York, G. P. Putnam's Sons, 1994).

Maureen McLane (review date spring 1996)

SOURCE: McLane, Maureen. Review of *Poetic Justice,* by Martha Nussbaum. *Chicago Review* 42, no. 2 (spring 1996): 95-100.

[*In the following review of* Poetic Justice, *McLane expresses admiration for Nussbaum's ideas, but points out various shortcomings in the author's arguments.*]

The University of Chicago is perhaps better known as the home of Milton Friedman, patron saint and theorist of Reagan's revolution, than the *habitus* of Martha Nussbaum, philosopher and recently-appointed Profes-sor of Law, Literature and Ethics at the Law and Divin-ity Schools of the University of Chicago. If we are lucky this reputation will change. Nussbaum's **Poetic Justice** may be read as a salvo against the hegemony of free-market ideology and utilitarian calculation in public discourse. More precisely, Nussbaum challenges the unphilosophical, pseudo-scientific claims of rational-choice theorists who, as she notes, increasingly dominate economic discourse, public policy disputes, and legal reasoning. In its most extreme forms, rational-choice theory posits persons as mere aggregates of preferences, mere sites for the calculation of utilities. According to such a model, you are what you prefer, and what you prefer is your choice. Each of your preferences (for this car, that sex act, this political candidate, that CD) is equally measurable, quantifiable—a bit of data to be entered in the charts or computer programs of economists and other social scientists. Nussbaum denounces this abject thralldom to objectivity, facticity, mathematical description and prediction. Even within economics, she observes, other models more conducive to "quality of life" assessment have emerged. She invokes the economists and philosophers (Amartya Sen is one) who, in the development sphere, have defended "an approach to quality of life measurement based on a notion of human functioning or human capability, rather than on either opulence or utility" (51). Yet it is the rational-choice theorists who have had the most profound impact on public life, as illustrated by, for example, the ascendancy of the law-and-economics school of thought.

How else should we be imagining persons, and on what other grounds might public life and reasoning be conducted? Nussbaum proposes the literary imagination, especially as manifested in the nineteenth-century Anglo-American realist novel, as the basis for another kind of richly qualitative reasoning. Novel-reading, Nussbaum argues, invites identification and sympathy; the novel's capacity to establish and populate a vivid and varied world offers a better, or at least a fuller, vision of life than that produced by economic treatises and other nonfiction documents. Although she begins her book with an epigraph from Whitman's *Song of Myself,* it is Dickens's *Hard Times* that serves as the most notable case in her argument. With its satirical yet ultimately sympathetic portrait of the arch-utilitarian pedant, Gradgrind, *Hard Times* directly confronts the stakes of theorizing persons as mere sites of utility.

What Gradgrind (and his twentieth-century heirs such as Richard Posner and Gary Becker) undervalue, according to Nussbaum, is the power of "fancy," of the compassionate "metaphorical imagination" (36). Novels explicitly address and cultivate this capacity. Nussbaum believes that policy makers and judges would do well to cultivate fancy, since it is the faculty which allows us to recognize and value the quality, complexity, and specificity of human experience. Nussbaum's choice of the word "fancy" is perhaps unfortunate, bringing as it

does connotations of whimsy and Tinkerbellish insubstantiality. Yet she takes care to distinguish fancy from simple sentiment; nor does she advocate any jettisoning of rule-governed morality. What she is really arguing for is a kind of hard fancy, a committed imagination. In this, as in her apparently pre-Marxian vision of a public sphere, Nussbaum reveals her affinities with certain luminaries of the Scottish Enlightenment, particularly Adam Smith. Smith's *Theory of Moral Sentiments* proposes the figure of the sympathetic yet "impartial spectator"; it is this engaged spectatorship which Nussbaum wishes to re-imagine in public life, and which the novel more than other cultural forms best fosters.

The necessary defense of novels and novel-reading entailed by Nussbaum's argument may be the strangest aspect of the book—strange not because novels don't need defending, but because Nussbaum's commitment to and implicit theory of literature seem to come from an earlier time. One would think modernism never happened, or that the so-called postmodern condition was an invention of mischievous academics. Is the realist novel an anachronism? If so, is its commitment to liberal individualism also anachronistic? I certainly don't think so, but I also don't think it is possible to avoid these questions, which Nussbaum largely does. Nussbaum remarks that "films may also make contributions to public life" (6); in this way her argument should not stand or fall on whether one privileges the novel as a "living form." And she also notes that novels may dehumanize as well as humanize: the depiction of the working poor in *Hard Times,* as she notes, leaves something to be desired. Yet Nussbaum insists that the novel is a genre the structure of which "invites concern and respect for any story to which it directs the reader's attention" (129, note 34). In its traditional immersion in the concrete, the novel offers, in Nussbaum's view, a model of public reasoning which is context-specific without being relativistic. It seems to me, however, that Nussbaum's argument works better as a defense of fancy than as a defence of the novel. Novels may go the way of the heroic epistle, a more or less obsolete cultural form; but moral and aesthetic imagination will find new forms and offer new possibilities for contributing to public life.

Nussbaum invokes Wayne Booth's theory of "coduction," by which critical reflection and conversation should accompany and inform the pleasures of reading; only through such comparative and informed reflection will the full ethical possibilities of novel-reading be realized. Obviously this second requirement—that one not only read but also discuss, compare, and critically reflect on one's reading—presents a further demand on readers and on reading communities. There is something of the romance of the eighteenth-century coffeehouse or perhaps of the salon of *philosophes* in Nussbaum's musings. Yet it may be that engaged and cooperative reading (or moviegoing, or poetry-slamming) is already happening or is at least possible in late twentieth-century America. The proliferation of book groups suggests that there is a hunger for some kind of intellectual community outside of academia. And the endless parade of articles on the death or rebirth or dislocation of the "public intellectual" indexes the interest (however pernicious) the mainstream media has in discovering another site of thoughtful contribution to public life and reasoning.

Having introduced the "literary imagination" and its possible contribution to reasoning, Nussbaum turns to the supposed enemy of reason: emotion. Should emotions be components of reasoning? Nussbaum argues both that they are and should be such a component. Her third chapter, "Rational Emotions," elaborates her primary philosophical argument, a defense of the emotions. As Nussbaum notes, emotions, like literature, "badly need defending" (54). Rational-choice theorists insist that, for choices to be rational, emotions must be excluded. Nussbaum invokes Richard Posner, who in his 1981 book *The Economics of Justice* announced that he would assume "'that people are rational maximizers of satisfactions'" (54). Nussbaum unpacks Posner's position to mean that "we can respect people's choices as rational in the normative sense only if we can show that they conform to the utilitarian rational-maximizing conception and do not reflect the influence of emotional factors" (55). Such a view, as Nussbaum remarks, tends to confuse descriptive and normative uses of "reason" and "rational" and relies on an unexamined opposition of "emotion" to "reason"—an opposition which has historically devolved into the asymmetrical binary, "feminine/masculine."

Nussbaum quickly dispenses with theories that equate emotion with irrationality; she reserves both her intellectual firepower and respect for the Greek and Roman Stoics. These "antiemotion philosophers" (57) acknowledged emotions to be judgments yet considered them *false* judgments. These thinkers imagined that "the good person is completely self-sufficient"; they expressed a profound hostility to anything which revealed humans to be "needy and incomplete" (57). Virtue lay in curing oneself of those attachments (e.g. to beloved people) which would subject one to the contingent, or to forces beyond one's control. Such a position is crystallized, Nussbaum writes, in Socrates's pronouncement, "The good person cannot be harmed." It is quite clear that Nussbaum believes passionately that the good person *may* be harmed, that he or she is in fact harmed every day, whether we see the evidence for this in novels, newspapers, or Amnesty International reports. Nussbaum argues, *contra* the Stoics, that emotions may well be accurate perceptions of value; moreover, she concludes that "if we reject the Stoic tradition in the matter of self-sufficiency, we must, to be consistent,

reject its normative arguments for the dismissal of emotion" (67). The fantasy of self-sufficiency, which seems to me heavily freighted by its repression of childhood and mothering (and perhaps fathering), precludes the judicious recognition of our common human claims and vulnerabilities. No man is an island, to invoke the cliché, and it is a moral defeat to imagine that he should be.

Yet neither are people simply units in a grand collective, such as class. When Nussbaum addresses the Marxist critique of the novel as an excessively individualistic cultural form, we see another aspect of her moral reasoning. Just as she criticizes utilitarians for aggregating "pleasures" and "pains" (which can only be experienced by individuals, not *en masse*), so too she resists a premature collectivization, as it were, of the individual into larger or broader units such as class (and, we must assume, race, gender, nationality, region). She is deeply committed to the particularity of the individual, however marked, constructed, situated, or historicizable that individual (or the concept of the "individual") may be. While she is a strong critic of the reification and quantification of individuals in rational-choice theory and of the fantasy of "self-sufficiency" in antiemotion philosophy, Nussbaum refuses to renounce the individual as the basis for moral thinking, address, and compassionate imagination. And since it is, in first-world democracies if not in Stalinist states, individuals and not classes of individuals who commit crimes and submit to trial, a philosophical defense of compassionate and rigorous imagination thus has especial relevance for the judge and jury confronted with the accused.

Nussbaum's final chapter, "Poets as Judges," takes up Whitman's concept of the poet as "the equable man." She puts her model of the judicious spectator to the test. Such a spectator, reader, or jurist must sympathetically imagine and critically reason: "both empathetic participation and external assessment are crucial in determining the degree of compassion it is rational to have for the person" (73). When Nussbaum turns to legal reasoning, she imagines a "literary judge" (82) as preferable to "three rivals" (82): the skeptically detached judge, the scientist judge, and the distantiated abstract judge. Again, Nussbaum takes care not to propose the literary not as a substitute for legal reasoning but rather as a supplement to or component thereof. As she writes,

> In order to be fully rational, judges must also be capable of fancy and sympathy. They must educate not only their technical capacities but also their capacity for humanity. In the absence of that capacity, their impartiality will be obtuse and their justice blind.
>
> (121)

Such conclusions, unsurprising at the end of a book which sutures "fancy" and "sympathy" to reasoning and judgment, nevertheless ring a bit hollow. Who would call for less humane judges? (I will overlook, for the moment, the possibility that some fellow citizens would enumerate hanging judges and chain gangs as among the last true defenses of "humanity" in America.) How to assess and promote "humanity" is, of course, the crux of the dispute.

More substantial than this homage to humanity are Nussbaum's readings of three court opinions, two of which demonstrate, in her opinion, the salutary influence of literary imagination in judging, and the third of which (a sodomy case) exemplifies the woeful failure of such imagination. Anyone interested in the vexed and vexing legal reasoning concerning sodomy should read Nussbaum's account of the 1986 case *Bowers v. Hardwick.* Here, as in her reading of Richard Wright's *Native Son,* Nussbaum shows that failures of imagination—whether homophobic or racist—contribute to a blighting of personal freedom, potential community, and democratic life. At the other end of the spectrum is the triumphant legal imagining of *Mary J. Carr v. Allison Gas Turbine Division, General Motors Corporation,* U.S. Court of Appeals for the Seventh Circuit, July 26, 1994. This opinion comes from the pen of none other than Richard Posner, who elsewhere appears as the law-and-economics bogeyman of this book. Posner's sardonic and lucid obliteration of General Motors is a delight to read; more important, in Nussbaum's view, is the role sympathy and fancy play in the very substance of his reasoning. Vividly recreating in his opinion the predicament of Mary Carr, a female tinsmith who was sexually harassed for years, Posner moves to the heart of the case, exposes General Motors' protestations of helplessness (boys will be boys, and what could we do?) as the sham they were, and effectively diagnoses the asymmetry of gender and power relations in this particular worksite. Not every judge writes as brilliantly as Posner, but literary skill is not the point, Nussbaum argues: the point lies rather in the habits of mind cultivated by exposure to and participation in the literary imagination.

If the chapters of this book seem a bit associatively connected, it may be that *Poetic Justice* has not transcended its origins as the Alexander Rosenthal Lectures for 1991 at the Northwestern University Law School. Each of Nussbaum's chapters could launch its own book, and in fact the chapter on "Rational Emotions" draws on another book she is currently writing. After re-reading *Poetic Justice,* I am still not persuaded that it is necessary to locate, as Nussbaum does, the literary imagination in the Anglo-American realist novel, although I think it is one fine example; another might be found in the writings, for example, of Percy Shelley, who strongly advocated an informed, passionate, and critical imagination in his poetry and in numerous essays, among them *A Philosophical View of Reform* and *A Defence of Poetry.* Nussbaum's book implicitly

imagines several figures in a common conversation: rational-choice theorists, judges, Dickens, Aristotle, Adam Smith, Richard Wright—these and others mingle in her brilliant common room. Yet I suspect that humanists, wherever they are, already agree with Martha Nussbaum, and that rational-choice theorists won't be too bothered by her critique. Maybe the best hope for Nussbaum's vision appears in the anecdote she includes in her acknowledgements: Nussbaum met Richard Posner, the arch-villain of her first lecture, on the night before it was to be given. They apparently both survived the awkwardness and developed a vital friendship: indeed the book is dedicated to him. Whether such amicable if oppositional friendship may serve as a model for a reconstructed public sphere remains to be seen.

John Plotz (review date fall 1996)

SOURCE: Plotz, John. "A Sympathetic Social Science." *Novel* 30, no. 1 (fall 1996): 132-34.

[*In the following review, Plotz asserts that* Poetic Justice *is persuasive and tremendously thought-provoking. Plotz, however, points out various flaws in Nussbaum's arguments, and contends that she fails to adequately develop the implications of her central ideas.*]

Charles Dickens begins *Bleak House* with a lament that establishes the central importance of *sympathy* to the nineteenth-century novel: "nobody knew about Miss Flite, because nobody cared." When he goes on to recount Miss Flite's fate—and Jo's death, and all the rest—in sometimes excruciating physical and emotional detail, the novel delivers what it calls for: nine hundred pages of caring. The reader proceeds, via an initial sympathy, to the knowledge that in turn ensures a deeper sympathy.

In *Poetic Justice,* Martha Nussbaum goes to bat for Dickens, arguing that knowledge sometimes is not really knowledge unless it proceeds through sympathy. This claim is part of Nussbaum's long-term project on the role that emotions have to play in approaching various philosophical and political questions: aside from work on the topic in *Love's Knowledge* and *The Therapy of Desire,* she has edited two books on related topics, *The Quality of Life* and *Women, Culture and Development.* Her *Upheavals of Thought: A Theory of the Emotions* is also forthcoming. Her ethical ambition is to convince philosophical opponents—particularly the "law and economics" movement, which preaches a sort of radically free-market utilitarianism as a panacea for the liberal state's ills—that "an ethics of impartial respect for human dignity will fail to engage real human beings unless they are made capable of entering imaginatively into the lives of others and to have emotions related to that participation." To sympathize with all is to dignify all.

Nussbaum calls convincingly for treating sympathy as an inextricable component of understanding, rather than a threat to reason. She chooses her guides well: because her theory of emotions rests on a "common sense" notion of sympathy, she brings into play Adam Smith's remarkable *Theory of Moral Sentiments,* which argues that a necessary emotionality is the only reliable road to true fellow feeling—and, Nussbaum adds, true action for social equality or the betterment of all. In Smith's terms, it is only by training as "judicious spectators" that we learn to imagine others from their own viewpoint, rather than from our own. And the best way our own culture has devised to cultivate judicious spectatorship, Nussbaum argues, is novel-reading.

Nussbaum has a legitimate and serious quarrel with the current practice of the social sciences, which she argues are divorced from any interest (imaginative or otherwise) in how other human beings, as individuals, feel and think. But is she right to turn to novels as the genre best designed to induce compensatory fellow-feeling? Novel-reading, she argues, is how our culture cultivates sympathy—presumably it replaces tragedy for the Greeks, or Bible-reading for Reformation Protestants. The production of sympathy is the best work of novels, and for that reason they are the best of literary works (Whitman's poems function very like novels for the purpose of her argument). Her test cases, including Whitman, Dickens, and E. M. Forster's *Maurice,* are "literary works that promote identification and emotional reaction . . . requiring us to see and to respond to many things that may be difficult to confront—and they make this process palatable by giving us pleasure in the very act of confrontation" (6). There is an inherent appeal to this claim. Almost immediately, however, problems arise. Take, for example, the apparently straightforward problem of translating the feelings that novel-reading produces to encounters in the real world. The pleasure that Nussbaum mentions here is presumably related to the very *fictionality* of the sympathy she describes.

But there is a good case to be made that fictional sympathy is easier to train, and easier to maintain, than sympathy with real people. Catherine Gallagher argued recently, in her magisterial and compelling *Nobody's Story,* that "it is easier to identify with nobody than it is with somebody." Gallagher's work suggests that novels (at least before the advent of Modernism, and arguably even after) are filled with sites where one can jump in, and start identifying—with a character narrating or narrated, seen or heard, similar or dissimilar to oneself. These sites might be called, to borrow a phrase from the Apple computer control panels, "points of insertion." It is not too hard to see how such sympathy might become a dangerous thing. Augustine warned Romans not to weep for the imaginary death of an imaginary Dido, and Rousseau declared that citizens of an ethical city-state should reserve their sympathy for suffering fellow-citizens, not waste it on painted players.

Nussbaum could certainly argue that the novel's purely fictional beings (not quite human, but not quite inhuman) are essential in instructing us to care about, and to care for, others. Unfortunately, the most interesting implications of that argument never quite get played out in this book. Nussbaum's writings on ancient literature, like her articles on Henry James, bespeak a terrific sensitivity to the powers of literature. But *Poetic Justice* goes oddly astray in its extended reading of Dickens's polemic on utilitarianism, *Hard Times.* The choice is a poor one: *Hard Times* is as tendentious in its own way as the law and economics textbooks that Nussbaum thunders against. *Hard Times* only *says* it is reminding us of the mistake of applying any single set of cut-and-dried laws to human behavior and the "maximization" of utility or of happiness. By contrast, *Bleak House*'s enormous diversity of sympathy-inducing stories would seem to offer a perfect test case for the novel's ability to represent the permanent human condition of sharing a linguistic realm, but having our own bodies—sick and well, old and young—always to ourselves.

Nussbaum is certainly asking the right questions about the classic nineteenth-century novel's interest in making readers feel individuated sympathy for suffering characters. For example, Nussbaum points out that *Hard Times*'s credo of emotional individualism at the expense of any sort of mass movement leads Dickens to denounce trade unions bitterly. Here she touches on one of the most interesting implications of the novel's hostility toward other forms of sympathetic identification, such as the fellow-feeling produced by a trade union.

But can't this hostility also be construed as a form of jealousy? Couldn't it be argued that the sort of highly individuated sympathy novels engender may cause readers to *give up* on common feeling with larger groups? Nussbaum is on fascinating ground here: what are the implications of the vicarious empathy that the classic realist novel aimed to produce? It might well be argued that the sort of distant interest that the novel promotes works in our society to *inhibit* other forms of sympathy. With the romantic turmoil of a novel to retreat to, what need is there to contemplate the (sociological) problems of one's own city? Better leave that to the social scientists. The more convincing the sympathetic emotions induced by the novel are, the less that one will need to look for sympathy in the public realm. Curling up with a Harlequin or with Proust is a sort of political statement.

Nussbaum does not reckon with the novel's long and complex history, much of which has nothing at all to do with the production of sympathy: a thriller thrills, historical epics immerse the reader in a lost world, pornography titillates, and so on. Even within her chosen scope, she seems unwilling to consider the nineteenth-century novel's attempts both to *deny* and to *replace* the forms of mass organization that Dickens denounces in *Hard Times*. The realist novel's disabling mixture of readerly pleasure and sympathy is not far from the"pity and terror" that Aristotle praised in tragedy, or the "false tears for Dido" that Augustine and Rousseau denounced—but it is also intimately connected to a new (largely bourgeois) ethos of spatial isolation and distant sympathy.

What Nussbaum has written already is tremendously thought-provoking, but is only half the story: the responses she inspires are the other. Nussbaum's interdisciplinary foray will only count as fully successful if it encourages a close examination of the boundary between the anti-emotional assumptions of social science and the narrow, subjectivist ambitions of a certain sort of literature. If Nussbaum's manifesto succeeds, novelistic sympathy will have to be imported into other disciplines (though many would argue that the sympathy she has in mind has little to do with the contemporary novel). Ironically, Nussbaum appears to agree, on this one point, with one of the novel's harshest critics, Hannah Arendt. Forty years ago Arendt argued that the reign of novelistic sympathy was tied to our society's loss of a public space in which *political* solidarity could emerge. Arendt's response was to reject the novel's sorts of emotionality, while Nussbaum wants to see it spread everywhere. Both seem certain, though, that sympathizing only with nobody is getting us nowhere.

Daniel McInerny (essay date March 1997)

SOURCE: McInerny, Daniel. "'Divinity Must Live within Herself': Nussbaum and Aquinas on Transcending the Human." *International Philosophical Quarterly* 37, no. 1 (March 1997): 65-82.

[*In the following essay, McInerny examines Nussbaum's thinking on transcendence and "virtue-ethics," as expressed in her essay* "Transcending Humanity."]

> Why should she give her bounty to the dead?
> What is divinity if it can come
> Only in silent shadows and in dreams?
> Shall she not find in comforts of the sun,
> In pungent fruit and bright, green wings, or else
> In any balm or beauty of the earth,
> Things to be cherished like the thought of heaven?
> Divinity must live within herself:
> Passions of rain, or moods in falling snow;
> Grievings in loneliness, or unsubdued
> Elations on wet roads on autumn nights;
> All pleasures and all pains, remembering
> The bough of summer and the winter branch.
> These are the measures destined for her soul.
>
> Wallace Stevens, "Sunday Morning"

Throughout her writings on ethics Martha Nussbaum has expounded a notion of transcendence meant to be the corrective to those notions expounded by religious traditions of ethical inquiry. In her essay **"Transcending Humanity,"**[1] for example, Nussbaum accuses of incoherence any conception of transcendence that takes as the standard for human excellence anything other than human life itself.[2] Her defense of this claim is in some ways Aristotelian both in its concentration on the human good and in its view of practical reason. The crux of the defense, put simply, is that "Human limits structure the human excellences, and give excellent action its significance" (**TH** 378). To prescind from risk, and from limit and fragility in general, is to prescind from the conditions of human virtue itself, so that it is incoherent for a human being to conceive of his or her good as measured by a being that transcends limit and fragility. As Nussbaum observes, Aristotle denies to divinity the ethical virtues, and political life in general, precisely because for a god such attributes are unintelligible (**TH** 374).[3] Courage, for instance, is not a virtue of divinity because for a being never in danger of death there is nothing grave to risk. For human beings, on the other hand, courage is not only an important good but an inherently valuable one.

While Nussbaum does argue for "a certain sort of aspiration to transcend our ordinary humanity" (**TH** 378), she is clear that this will be transcendence "of an *internal* and human sort" (**TH** 379). Like religious conceptions of transcendence, Nussbaum's own notion abounds in spatial metaphor: transcendence is *internal* to human thoughts, motivations, and feelings; it will involve a *descent,* "delving more deeply into oneself and one's humanity, and becoming deeper and more *spacious* as a result" (**TH** 379, italics added). What the fragility of human goodness calls for is not, then, a metamorphosis into some other kind of being but rather greater attention paid to what it means to live a fully human life.

More precisely, what Nussbaum has in mind by this internal and human sort of transcendence is an Aristotelian-like notion of virtue as a mean of action and passion. Such excellence in deliberation and choice is a very difficult business, and although she does not believe human beings are originally evil or sinful, "it is all too plain that most people are much of the time lazy, inattentive, unreflective, shallow in feeling" (**TH** 378). Hitting the mean, however, requires "much experience and practice, much flexibility and refinement of thought and feeling" (**TH** 378) and thus manifests transcendence of the lax and atrophied sensibility which characterizes too many human beings. We might summarize this notion of internal transcendence, to borrow a phrase that Nussbaum borrows from Henry James, as the act of being "finely aware and richly responsible."[4] The link with James is important, for Nussbaum strongly believes great literary works, and James's in particular, evince just the sort of transcendence she is proposing. In a passage she quotes with much approval from James's preface to *The Golden Bowl,* he compares excellent literary works to angels, angels that in Nussbaum's words "soar above the dullness and obtuseness of the everyday, offering their readers a glimpse of a more compassionate, subtler, more responsive, more richly human world" (**TH** 379). Such Jamesian angels "of fine-tuned perception and bewildered human grace" herald for Nussbaum the revelation of a "transcendent descent" into human being itself and its aspirations and fulfillments.

But we might wonder whether this notion of internal transcendence does not too easily devolve into a multiplex of disparate perspectives on what comprises peculiarly *human* fulfillment. What basis does Nussbaum leave, in short, for agreement on what it means to live a more compassionate, more subtle, more responsive, and more richly human life? And especially since her ethical view hopes to recapture, against the remoteness of Kantian and utilitarian ethical theory, a more Aristotelian conception of the virtues, the question is even more firmly pressed whether her virtue-ethics, as contemporary virtue-ethics is wont to do, takes a turn toward relativism. In no way am I suggesting that Nussbaum is unattuned to these questions. Indeed, she has set the very problems to herself and responded to them in thoughtful and provocative fashion, arguing in the end for a non-relative account of the virtues.[5] It is this response and how it relates to the issue of transcendence which I plan to address in what follows.

An important preliminary distinction should first be made concerning the term *transcendence*. Transcendence does not necessarily imply the supernatural, although more often than not this is what is meant by it and it is this sense of transcendence which Nussbaum critiques most forcefully in **"Transcending Humanity."** But another important and often related sense of transcendence refers to the grounding of practical reason in goods which are not simply the "artifacts" of one's own desire for fulfillment. *Immanence,* we can say in contrast to this, refers to that which persists within oneself, be it a power, a wish, or an experience.[6] Now, it is already clear that Nussbaum rejects as incoherent the first sense of transcendence, at least as it applies to the human good. So the question becomes: does Nussbaum subscribe to transcendence in the *second* sense, that is, as a ground of practical reason irreducible to human wishes, possibilities, and fulfillments? If not, then we must ask ourselves whether Nussbaum is really propounding an ethical view driven by a coherent notion of transcendence or whether she is propounding, rather, a notion of *immanence* under the guise of transcendent principle.[7] Her arguments on behalf of a non-relative account of the virtues seem to be the

perfect place to look for an answer to this question, for, as we have seen, it is an Aristotelian-style exercise of practical wisdom and virtue which she believes manifests the sort of internal transcendence she is advocating. If Nussbaum's arguments for non-relative virtues are sound, then it must follow that she has an argument for a real transcendent ground of practical reason.

My examination and analysis of Nussbaum's arguments will consist of three steps: first, a summary of her Aristotelian-style defense of virtue-ethics against the claims of relativism; second, a discussion of some objections to this defense; and lastly, a different kind of test of her account of non-relative virtues by way of a comparison of her treatment of the virtue of magnanimity with that of St. Thomas Aquinas. Magnanimity, I will claim, is *the* virtue to spotlight in regard to these issues, for, as Nussbaum herself points out, magnanimity is the relativist's favorite target in exposing Aristotle's list of virtues to be as culture-bound as any other.[8] Thus it will be crucial for Nussbaum's non-relative account of the virtues, as well as for any rival to it, to show how a thinker like Aquinas can justify a claim in his moral theology for what seems like such a peculiarly Greek and even anti-Christian virtue.

I

In taking up Nussbaum's defense of non-relative virtues, I should make it clear right away that in arguing thus she in no way makes an appeal to an Archimedean point outside of what she deems, following Aristotle, the "appearances" of the ethical life.[9] In settling disputes about the virtues, accordingly, she believes that there is "no pure access to unsullied 'nature'—even, here, human nature—as it is in itself. There is just human life as it is lived" (**NRV** 49). How, then, can she provide against the charge of relativism? Nussbaum's answer to this question relies upon her analysis of the relevant passages of *Nicomachean Ethics* Book II where Aristotle first outlines the structures of the various virtues. She sees Aristotle introducing his list of virtues in two steps: first, by isolating "a sphere of human experience that figures in more or less any human life, and in which more or less any human being will have to make *some* choices rather than others, and act in *some* way rather than some other" (**NRV** 35); and second, by dialectically establishing a concrete specification, by the consideration of various alternatives, of what it would mean to choose well within this particular sphere. In this way Nussbaum sees Aristotle moving from a "thin" conception of a given virtue (meaning whatever it is to be stably disposed to act well within a certain sphere of choice) toward a "thick" definition of that virtue, a depiction of how *best* to act within that sphere.

An example will help. Begin by considering the pervasiveness of mankind's fear of important changes, especially death. Experiences and choices regarding the fear of death are obviously universal and transcultural, and it is from such a universally experienced sphere of action and choice that the Aristotelian, on Nussbaum's account, begins his search for the virtue appropriate to this fear. Already, it is argued, the Aristotelian can lay claim to a certain degree of objectivity, for everyone has *some* attitude and behavior toward the fear of death. Of course, differing ways of handling what Nussbaum calls the "grounding experience" of the fear of death will crop up within differing cultures—how is the Aristotelian to confront these rival attitudes and behaviors?

First of all, Nussbaum would not have us so quickly overlook the fact that rival conceptions of the appropriate way to regard the fear of death (*i.e.,* rival conceptions of the virtue of *courage*) will be competing descriptions of the *same* phenomenon. There is, in other words, a fixed reference for the various "thick" descriptions of courage which serves as the *substratum* for these differing descriptions and for arguments concerning which description is best. But still we want to know what it is that will allow us to assess, for example, the archaic Greek notion of courage against what Nussbaum describes as "a more civic and communally attuned understanding of proper behavior toward the fear of death" (**NRV** 38).

Nussbaum's reply to this question brings to light her *non-teleological functionalism*. This view understands the virtues (1) as essentially plural, irreducible, and incommensurable and (2) as qualities of well-functioning that are "appropriate to the common life" of a particular community.[10] From the functionalist point of view it comes down to a shared conception of what is "appropriate" to the common life which determines whatever "thick" conceptions of the virtues are to reign supreme. The "common life," however, is for Nussbaum an analogous if not equivocal term. Differing cultures will be able to assess differing conceptions of courage on the basis of an ever-developing conception of what is well-functioning in the human sphere. But criticism of local and traditional moralities will remain possible, taking place "in the name of a more inclusive account of the circumstances of human life, and of the needs for human functioning that these circumstances call forth" (**NRV** 39). So, for example, certain ways of managing the fear of death will be found to be "more in keeping with the totality of our evidence and with the totality of our wishes for flourishing life than others" (**NRV** 46). Against the relativists, therefore, Nussbaum *denies* "that all world interpretations are equally valid and altogether non-comparable, that there are no good standards of assessment and 'anything goes'" (**NRV** 46). What she affirms is that "[the] standards used in

such criticisms must come from inside human life" (**NRV** 46), from a heightened, more inclusive awareness of what motivates us within our shared grounding experiences.

We are beginning to see how Nussbaum's arguments attest to a theory of ethical progress. Early in the essay "Non-Relative Virtues" she considers why those believing in ethical progress might shy away from virtue-ethics due to its apparently relativistic approach. "If the position of women," she writes, "as established by local traditions in many parts of the world, is to be improved, if traditions of slave holding and racial inequality, if religious intolerance, if aggressive and warlike conceptions of manliness, if unequal norms of material distribution are to be criticized in the name of practical reason, this criticizing (one might easily suppose) will have to be done from a Kantian or utilitarian viewpoint, not through the Aristotelian approach" (**NRV** 33). Highlighted in this comment are several ethical conclusions—for example, racial equality, less aggressive and warlike conceptions of manliness—which Nussbaum apparently regards as progressive and sufficiently so. And against those who might understand virtue-ethics as unable to bear such objectively grounded progressions, Nussbaum articulates a virtue-ethic which aspires to defend such conceptions against their rivals by means of a real standard, that is, the notion of the *human good.*[11] Determining the peculiarly human good once again will consist in first recognizing the various spheres of choice, or grounding experiences, from which a "thick" account is ultimately desirable based upon an inclusive understanding of the goods pursued in these grounding experiences.

This inclusivism, I take it, is the linchpin of Nussbaum's argument for a non-relative conception of the virtues. Progress in our understanding of the virtues, she writes, "is aided by a perspicuous mapping of the sphere of the grounding experiences" (**NRV** 37). Such perspicuity seems to be the effort of including in one's view of the human good as wide an array of goods as possible. As cited earlier, Nussbaum speaks of certain ways of managing the fear of death as "more in keeping with the totality of our evidence and with the totality of our wishes for flourishing life than others" (**NRV** 46). To keep the *totality* of our wishes and their possible fulfillments in mind is thus crucial to Nussbaum's view of the good. Also crucial to this view is the incommensurability-thesis, which submits, in short, that any one inherently valuable good is neither equal to nor better than another. So what Nussbaum understands as Platonic asceticism would commit a trespass against the thesis; for in assimilating the good of bodily appetite and its pleasures to the good of philosophical contemplation, the Platonic Socrates fails to respect the intrinsic goodness found in one of our most basic grounding experiences. Not to respect the intrinsic and incommensurable goodness of the totality of our grounding experiences is, for Nussbaum, not to respect the basic needs of human functioning. In the end, therefore, and with at least verbal irony, Nussbaum professes the lack of commensurability among the human goods—that is, the lack of any essential standard by which to order and arrange them—to be itself the standard to be used in assessing competing conceptions of a single virtue and of virtues in general.

II

The goal of ethics according to Nussbaum is to answer the broad, inclusive, and Socratic question of how one should live. In searching for the answer, she advises, different conceptions of the human good should be held up against each other "and also against the participants' beliefs and feelings, their active sense of life."[12] Consensus among disparate "senses of life" depends not upon some Archimedean point founded in God, nature, or human nature, not upon "correspondence to some extra-human reality," but upon "the best overall fit between a view and what is deepest in human lives."[13] Nussbaum's functionalism, however, demands an inherent connection between what is "deepest" for human beings and a view of the human good as inclusive of a variety of inherently valuable and incommensurable goods.

But if the goal of such an approach to ethics is to attain a non-relative answer to the Socratic question, and one which furthermore highlights human virtue, then there are at least three problems which must be addressed.

First, I have said that Nussbaum's functionalism regards the virtues as essentially plural, irreducible, and incommensurable. Yet, more than one writer on this topic has argued that no virtue can be adequately characterized, much less assessed, without reference to some overall pattern or teleology within which a given virtue comes to life.[14] A functionalist table of "thick" conceptions of the virtues, in other words, is like a laundry-list of discrete items with no necessary co-ordination between them. In fact, however, virtues arise only within the ordering schemes of various moral outlooks. Alasdair MacIntyre has shown how in the *Laws,* for example, Plato speaks of at least three forms of the virtue of *sōphrosunē,* or temperance.[15] As *sōphrosunē* appears in Spartan culture, its duties are subsumed under the Spartan conception of courage as the comprehensive virtue.[16] For a Spartan tempering one's bodily appetites implies a particular regard for military excellence as the ultimate good for man. The citizens of the perfectly just *polis* display a second type of *sōphrosunē.* This is the habit of calculating in terms of pleasure and pain, a habit fostered by the positive laws of that city.[17] Thus for these citizens pleasure serves as the measuring rod for virtuous choice. This sort of conditioning is inap-

propriate, however, for the rulers themselves of the ideal city, who exercise a third sort of *sōphrosunē* which is the result of the possession of another virtue altogether, *epistēmē.*[18] What MacIntyre shows in referring to these texts is simply the fact that virtues and goods manifest themselves only insofar as they are ordered to other goods and virtues. Aristotelian virtue likewise depends on such ordering. What moral virtue, for instance, is possible for Aristotle without the intellectual virtue of prudence? In Aristotle's eyes a virtue such as temperance is nourished by prudence and prudence by this and the other moral virtues.

My point is that a *pattern* of goods is necessary for the manifestation of goodness, whether that goodness be instrumental or intrinsic. But in saying this I should not be taken to mean that the order of one intrinsically valuable good to another in effect renders the former merely instrumental. To be well-disposed toward situations of grave risk is always an intrinsically valuable good, no matter how that disposition is ordered to other goods. The point I am pressing is that *how* one understands good disposition in regard to situations of grave risk will depend on one's overall ordering of goods. Achilles, who understands honor as that for the sake of which everything else is pursued, will thereby find different situations worthy of risk, or similar risky situations as calling for different sorts of response, than will Socrates, who understands philosophical contemplation as man's ultimate end. Indeed, unless Achilles comes to understand Socrates's complex arguments in the *Crito* and *Phaedo,* it may well be that he will find Socrates's taking of the hemlock cowardly, whereas for Plato it is an act of supreme heroism far surpassing anything in Homer. This argument is only to remind ourselves of Aristotle's claim in the *Nicomachean Ethics* that a good can be desired both for its own sake *and* for the sake of something else.[19] And it is precisely in terms of its being desirable for the sake of something else that the *ratio* of the intrinsic goodness of a virtue comes to light.[20]

Virtues and other intrinsically valuable goods, then, do not co-exist "side by side" with each other with no inherent connection between them; they exist "linked" together in complex networks of subordination and superorientation. But in Nussbaum's view the virtues and other intrinsically valuable goods are not only naturally untethered from each other but even possess an inherent *dis*connection, coming into conflict in ways that are tantamount to contradiction in our pursuit of the good.[21]

Nussbaum might object at this point that nothing about inclusivism precludes a given agent, set of agents, or culture at large from constructing a pattern out of the menu of intrinsically valuable goods. She might argue that her Aristotelian approach to virtue agrees with my view that different "thick" conceptions of the virtues and other intrinsically valuable goods become "thick" only within the context of a pattern of life. She might even go on to say that some of these goods and virtues will be seen as subordinate to others, will be assigned a certain weight different from others in an overall pattern of life. Indeed, she might add that, insofar as a given pattern of life maintains a respect for each intrinsically valuable good, it deserves consideration as a non-relative conception of human functioning. We have already seen how Nussbaum provides us with a glimpse of what she understands as the right pattern of life for a *polis*; it will include, for example, racial equality, religious tolerance, equal norms of material distribution, less aggressive and warlike conceptions of manliness, and so forth.

This objection prompts me to address a second problem concerning Nussbaum's inclusivist ethic. If it is the case that the virtues and other intrinsically valuable goods are truly incommensurable, then considered in and of themselves there is no means by which to order these goods which is not wholly arbitrary. Take again, for example, the two intrinsically valuable goods of honor and courage. A given conception of human life might assign the good of honor priority over the virtue of courage. The Achilles of Homer's *Iliad* might be understood in this way. A slight against his honor is enough for him, at the beginning of that narrative, to forsake exhibitions of courage on the battlefield. But if Achilles understands honor and courage to be incomparable *in se,* then his decision to value honor more than courage can only be a statement of preference. This being the case, for anyone to argue with Achilles is impossible; for in fact there is no basis upon which to build an argument if Achilles's only claim is that honor is his most "deeply held" commitment. Real comparisons between goods, and not mere statements of preference, cannot be made without there being some standard by which to evaluate them. On a non-inclusivist reading of Aristotle, the good of honor can be compared with courage according to the measuring rod of *eudaimonia*: activity in accord with virtue. On this reading honor is subordinated to courage as an external good of fortune concomitant to virtuous action. This point is important for the further reason that it shows how intrinsically valuable goods can be compared without resorting to a *single* standard of ethical value. Honor can be subordinated to courage not because its own intrinsic goodness is *subsumed* into the intrinsic goodness of courage, thereby rendering honor merely instrumental; rather, honor is maintained as an intrinsic good, yet one which can be further ordered to a higher good, as courage itself can be further ordered to intellectual virtue.

It is because the incommensurability-thesis cannot ensure any one view of the good that even Nussbaum's non-relative argument is forced to conclude to the possibility of several specifications of a given virtue: "the

Aristotelian position that I wish to defend need not insist, in every case, on a single answer to the request for a specification of a virtue. The answer might well turn out to be a disjunction" (**NRV** 43). Thus there is no one specification of what honor or courage or justice shall be like; it simply comes down to the ordering principles of agents and cultures. But granted the incommensurability-thesis, these ordering principles cannot be other than preference, yielding not only various but possibly also *disjunctive* conceptions of the goods. This latter occasion leaves open the possibility that two members of a disjunction will be mutually exclusive. A conception of courage based on warlike aggressiveness might come into conflict with one based upon pacifism. How, then, could one not merely prefer but *justify* the notion of one against the other if the overall patterns of goods in which these conceptions of courage arise are in essence artificially constructed aggregates of preference?

But if we remember that Nussbaum's inclusivism has set a certain standard of assessment, are we not then being unfair in saying that *any* pattern of life made from within the inclusivist point of view is mere artifice? The inclusivist hope would seem to be that, if we are equally respectful of all intrinsically valuable goods, then we will have, by dint of that respect, a pretty good and fairly objective idea of how we are to entertain grave risks or to temper our bodily appetites. In this event we would neither entertain grave risks to the exclusion of practicing justice nor pursue certain toothsome delights to the exclusion of our responsibilities at work because in either case we would know that we would thereby commit injustice and thus disrespect the intrinsic goodness of just activity. Maintenance of respect for all intrinsically valuable goods helps us shape our approaches to the various grounding experiences which Nussbaum outlines.

At least one objection to this argument is that it assumes that what Nussbaum calls a grounding experience is like a permanent node confronting any view of human life. So a third problem arising from Nussbaum's non-relative account of the virtues, and one which she herself takes to be the most profound objection to it, is its vulnerability to the charge that in some forms of human life even certain grounding experiences, upon which for Nussbaum all hope of debate and possible consensus hinge, seem to melt away. Both Aristotle and Marx, Nussbaum writes, observe that societies which eliminate private ownership do away with opportunities for generous action and thereby with the virtues of liberality and magnificence. Or to borrow another example from MacIntyre, in consumer-societies like our own the virtue of temperance is becoming increasingly less prevalent since the grounding experience of moderating one's tactile desires is ever increasingly spurned.[22]

Nussbaum's response to this objection is twofold. The central question as she formulates it is, if the virtues are defined relatively to certain problems, limitations, and endowments peculiar to individual ethical cultures, how are we to tell which ones "are sufficiently central that their removal would make us into different beings, and open up a wholly new and different debate about the good?" (**NRV** 50). For Nussbaum there is no way to answer this question "but [to] ask ourselves which elements of our experience seem to us so important that they count, for us, as part of who we are" (**NRV** 50). Included in her list of these elements are morality itself (and the limitations on human agency which morality presupposes), needs for food, drink, and assistance from others, cognitive functioning, and practical reasoning. These are elements "of any life that we would regard as human" (**NRV** 50). We should take note here of the prevalence of the first person plural in Nussbaum's sentences; for it is not at all clear who this "we" is supposed to represent. If it is taken to represent those who maintain Nussbaum's inclusivist view of the good, then it cannot include, for example, the Epicurean. For the philosophy expressed in the Letter to Menoeceus is meant to *relieve* the seeker of the happy life from the fear of death: "Accustom yourself to the belief that death is of no concern to us, since all good and evil lie in sensation and sensation ends with death. . . . Death, the most dreaded of evils, is therefore of no concern for us."[23] Nussbaum's view of the good, however, sees the fear of death as an *ineliminable* grounding experience, most intimately associated with "our" sense of the fragility of the human good, which the virtue of courage is meant to organize according to the demands of practical reason. But Epicurus does not view the fear of death as an ineliminable grounding experience at all. In fact, he takes it as quite eliminable and its elimination as the necessary condition of human happiness. The point for us, however, is not so much which one of these contending views is the true one but how Nussbaum proposes to adjudicate between them.[24]

Nussbaum recognizes the force of the problem, though in the light of the Marxist quest to eliminate private property rather than in regard to the fear of death. One can certainly imagine "forms of human life that do not contain the holding of private property—and, therefore, not those virtues that have to do with its proper management. And this means that it remains an open question whether these virtues ought to be regarded as virtues, and kept upon our list" (**NRV** 50). But in the end, Nussbaum can only advise a skeptical attitude toward those transformations of human life which seek to steamroll commonly-held grounding experiences. Aristotle's outlook on such transformations, she argues, is that they usually have a tragic dimension: "If we remove one sort of problem—say, by removing private property—we frequently do so by introducing another—say, the absence of a certain sort of freedom of choice, the

freedom that makes it possible to do fine and generous actions for others" (**NRV** 50).

But this advice (and advice is all it can really amount to) assumes that there will be a sort of remainder, or residue, of regret or even tragedy when one seeks to eliminate one or another grounding experience which helps make up the inclusivist view of the good. Such a residue could be felt of course only from "inside" the inclusivist viewpoint. It is presumption to say that the Marxist will somehow feel regret at what is lost by the removal of private property. This would be the case only if he valued what is lost as much as he did the elimination of property, and there is nothing to guarantee this for the Marxist. The same goes for the Epicurean, whose view of man insists that the fear of important changes, especially death, is exactly what keeps the common run from living the best kind of life. Specific notions of God, man, and nature yield specific tables of goods and virtues, *as well as* what is to count as a grounding experience of human activity; and the only way to counteract such tables of goods is to disclose the poverty of the conceptions which drive them. It is not clear to me that Nussbaum, in the end and especially insofar as she merely posits an array of grounding experiences ineliminable from any pursuit of the truly human good, is doing anything more than asserting her own most deeply held commitments against those of her rivals.

Still, Nussbaum expresses a great deal of confidence in the ability of "us" ultimately to come to consensus about that which is most important for us in living human lives. She seems to expect that certain "deeply" held wishes for our fulfillment will eventually work their way to the fore, and in this hope is the Archimedean point she uses to support her claim for non-relative virtues. My objections have argued that this support is just that, a hope, and therefore cannot claim any more persuasive power than any other hope deeply held by "us" or "them" or anyone else seeking to achieve the human good.

In raising these objections I have not myself argued for any specific table of goods and virtues nor for the specific notions of God, man, and nature which organize it. What I have tried to indicate is that any approach that does not depend upon some extrinsic principle of human acts, that is, which does not understand the importance for practical reason of an order "we" do not make, can successfully assess in the way Nussbaum desires competing notions of the human good. And as we have seen, not only assessment but also the notion of virtue itself, as well as the grounding experiences which make up the field of human achievement, depend—at least if relativism is to be avoided—upon an ordering principle which transcends human wishes for fulfillment. This thesis will remain unconvincing, however, if I cannot show how such principles are in play in manifesting the non-relativity of particular virtues. The proposal for my final section, therefore, is to take up the relativist's favorite target, the Aristotelian virtue of *megalopsychia,* understood by many to be Aristotle's rather idiosyncratic and supercilious portrait of a Greek "gentleman," and to show how this virtue can be assimilated to an ethical culture quite alien to Aristotle's, and in a way that does not annihilate the integrity of the Aristotelian virtue. Thus let us turn to Aquinas's discussion of the virtue he calls *magnanimitas.*

III

The prospects for a 13th-century Dominican theologian's having much affinity for Aristotle's *megalopsychos* might seem especially bleak. Yet, it is strange that nowhere in Thomas's commentary on Aristotle's chapter on *megalopsychia* is there any hint that Thomas finds this seemingly most pagan of virtues to be precluded by Christianity or in tension with the Christian virtue of humility, with which magnanimity seems especially to be in conflict. If it is surmised that the reason for this is that Thomas is only commenting here and not giving his own opinion, then one only has to turn to question 129 of the *Secunda secundae* of the *Summa theologiae* to find Thomas articulating the place of this virtue within his own exposition of theology. How does Aquinas account for the assimilation of this virtue to Christianity, and are its affinities with its Aristotelian cousin any more than merely nominal?

First a look at the text of Aristotle. At *Nicomachean Ethics* IV.3.1123a33 Aristotle indicates that the magnanimous man is concerned primarily with "great" objects (*peri megala*), which, as the discussion proceeds, are revealed to be great honors. We have been arguing that even grounding experiences evince a certain level of ordering, and the external good of honor (external, that is, to virtuous activity) especially indicates that he who values it is also valuing a certain ordering of things to a *best.* This is true of both praise and honor. Everything that is praised, Aristotle explains at I.12 of the *Ethics,* "seems to be praised because it is of a certain kind and is related somehow to something else" (1101b13-14). Praise has both a *ratio* and an *ordinatio* to other goods. Honor also has a certain *ratio* and an *ordinatio* to other goods, but honor is reserved for that which occupies the seat at the top of the hierarchy of goods. So for Aristotle honor among human beings is reserved for virtuous activity and, optimally, for contemplation; but in the *kosmos* as a whole it is reserved for god.[25]

For Aristotle the concern of the magnanimous man is thus for a special type of praise beyond praise which is due to those who exercise the virtues. Aristotle speaks of magnanimity as a certain adornment to the virtues (*kosmos tis*) because it deals with the honor that is due

great acts of all the other virtues.[26] On this general picture of magnanimity Aquinas and Aristotle are in substantial agreement. That agreement is made possible by generally shared conceptions of man, God, and nature, which recognize that both the grounding experience of magnanimity as well as the specification of the virtue involve a hierarchical ordering of goods. Let us turn now to see this agreement from Aquinas's perspective.

For Aquinas, magnanimity is understood most fundamentally as one of the "potential parts" of the virtue of courage. He explains this by noting that the action of courage involves both attack and endurance; and in terms of attack two things are required, one of which is what Cicero calls "confidence" and Aristotle magnanimity, that is, the attribute by which the mind puts great trust and hope in itself to perform great and honorable deeds. Now, a potential part of courage regards in lesser matters what courage maintains in regard to the most difficult ones, such as the fear of death. So, while magnanimity will not concern itself primarily with the fear of death, it will concern itself with lesser matters which demand great trust and hope in order to perform great deeds.[27]

In *ST* II-II.129 Aquinas addresses the virtue of magnanimity more specifically. In article 1 he asks whether magnanimity is concerned with honors. The core of his response is that the specific act of magnanimity is the spirit for some great act ("principaliter dicitur aliquis magnanimus quod animum habet ad aliquem magnum actum"[28]). But an act can be called great in two ways, either proportionately or absolutely: proportionately, if it makes great use of something small or modest; absolutely, if it makes the best use of something very great. Now, the things which man makes use of are external objects, among which the greatest absolutely speaking, is honor. Aquinas gives three reasons for honor's pre-eminence among the external goods: (1) honor is closest to virtue because it bears positive witness to a man's virtue (cf. *EN* I.5.1095b26-29); (2) honor is that which is extended to God and to the noblest members of society (an echo of *EN* I.12); and (3) the pursuit of honor and avoidance of censure are those standards by which men regulate everything else. Therefore, on the presumption that the magnanimous man has the spirit for some great act and that the greatness of this act will be considered absolutely, it is clear the magnanimous man will concern himself with those acts which make the best use of the very greatest of external goods, namely, honor.

In the first objection of article 1 it is further clarified that magnanimity is a perfection of the irascible appetite, for the spirit (*animus*) in *magnanimitas* expressly connotes the irascible appetite in man. This is important because the magnanimous man's regard for honor is for a desirable good, which is normally in the bailiwick of the concupiscible appetite. But, as Aquinas explains in his reply, insofar as the idea of the difficult enters the idea of a good, that good engages the irascible, not the concupiscible, appetite. And the irascible appetite finds the good of honor difficult to obtain because great virtue itself is difficult. This last point is underscored in Aquinas's reply to the third objection of this article. The magnanimous man is concerned with honor only in that he desires to perform acts worthy of it. His concern with honor, accordingly, will not drive him to do base acts in order to obtain it, nor will he despise honor to the extent of *not* performing great acts worthy of it.

In article 2 Aquinas asks whether magnanimity is concerned with great honors (*magnos honores*). We have just seen that magnanimity has to do with a mean by which men regulate the irascible appetite for honor. I pointed out that the difficulty confronting the irascible appetite in regard to magnanimity is the difficulty of virtue itself. More precisely, as Aquinas explains in the body of article 2, the magnanimous man is faced with the difficulty of shaping a passion for an external good which is especially enticing. Certain feelings, Thomas notes, strongly resist reason because of their external objects; and because these external objects produce feelings so strongly resistant to reason, it is necessary to acquire virtues that govern not only great instances of these objects but also moderate or slight instances of them. For this reason Aquinas, following Aristotle, posits two virtues concerned with honor, and that concerned with great honors is magnanimity.

In regard to my argument against Nussbaum's non-relative conception of the virtues, the most salient point of Aquinas's agreement with Aristotle is his understanding of what constitutes the grounding experience of magnanimity. Clearly, both Aristotle and Aquinas see this grounding experience as involving a hierarchical structure of goods. For what the irascible appetite desires, in either the magnanimous or non-magnanimous soul, is honor; and a conception of honor entails the recognition that certain actions or goods are the *best*. So, despite the obvious and at points vast differences in their conceptions of God, man, and nature, it is because Aristotle and Aquinas share basic principles of order regarding honor and virtue that magnanimity is included in both of their *schemata* of the virtues.

Nussbaum's inclusivism, by contrast, fails to perceive the real agreement between Aristotle and Aquinas on the virtue of magnanimity. This is so because what she deems the grounding experience of magnanimity—"Attitudes and actions with respect to one's own worth"—is worlds apart from the experience known to Aristotle and Aquinas. This will be recognized by those attuned to the transformations which have occurred in conceptions of identity and self-worth from the ancient and medieval world to the modern and post-modern one. Insofar as the modern world conceives of the self as defined essentially apart from archetypal and hierarchically-arranged social roles, practices, and institutions, it tends to regard its own self-worth more in terms of notions of human *dignity* rather than as linked to public recognition and honor.[29] What Nussbaum misses, then, in calling the basic grounding experience related to magnanimity "Attitudes and actions with respect to one's own worth" is the correlation that such attitudes and actions have, at least for Aristotle and medieval Christianity, with the concept of *honor*. And to make a place for honor within the experience of one's sense of self-worth is necessarily to make a place for a hierarchical system of goods and activities which Nussbaum has no interest in maintaining. So here we have another instance of the problem of order running all the way down to the grounding experiences.

Moreover, insofar as Nussbaum dismisses honor from the initial demarcation of the sphere of choice, she allows for magnanimity to disappear altogether from a Christian conception of the virtues. Magnanimity, in fact, on Nussbaum's reading of Christianity, is utterly displaced by what she calls "humility."

To understand how Nussbaum arrives at this conclusion, recall that in her Aristotelian-style analysis the grounding experiences fix the reference of the virtue-term which neutrally characterizes what appropriate choice within that grounding experience is. Nussbaum complains that Aristotle does not always do this carefully, and this comes to light in the language he uses to characterize certain virtue-terms. There is no problem with such terms as "temperance" and "justice" and "courage," which according to Nussbaum seem "vaguely normative but relatively empty, so far, of concrete moral content" (**NRV** 38). Rather, problems arise when Aristotle uses phrases like "mildness of temper" and "greatness of soul," phrases that do not imply a relative "emptiness" in regard to concrete moral content. Quite the contrary, "mildness of temper" connotes a very particular attitude toward the grounding experience which Nussbaum calls "Attitude to slights and damages." Aristotle seems to be stacking the deck of the discussion in favor of his own preference for a "mild" reaction when it comes to slights and damages. A similar situation arises with the term "greatness of soul," a term, Nussbaum writes, "which implies in its very name an attitude to one's own worth that is more Greek than universal." A Christian, she continues, "will feel that the proper attitude to one's own worth requires understanding one's lowness, frailty, and sinfulness. The virtue of humility requires considering oneself *small,* not great" (*ibid.*). What Nussbaum's non-relative account of the virtues demands, therefore, is a term for the proper behavior toward one's worth that is more truly neutral toward competing specifications, such as those represented by Aristotle and by Christianity. Then, she concludes, "we could regard the competing conceptions as rival accounts of one and the same thing, so that, for example, Christian humility would be a rival specification of the same virtue whose Greek specification is given in Aristotle's account of *megalopsychia,* namely, the proper way to behave toward the question of one's own worth" (**NRV** 38-39).

But if the Christian specification of "Attitudes and actions with respect to one's own worth" is the virtue of humility rather than of magnanimity, it is at least strange that the most revered of Christian moral thinkers finds a prominent place for magnanimity within his moral theology, and one which does not put it in conflict with the virtue of humility. This fact is not so strange, however, when one realizes that Nussbaum's account of Christianity fails to recognize certain transcendent principles of order shared by the pagan and Christian worlds. Because of this Nussbaum is forced to concede a great deal of relativity to Aristotelian *megalopsychia* and to Christian *humilitas,* while she eliminates Christian *magnanimitas* altogether.

One objection to my argument might recognize that, while Aquinas does indeed assimilate *some* virtue called magnanimity to Christian moral theology, it is certainly not anything like the virtue Aristotle knew as *megalopsychia.* The claim is that in regard to this virtue Aquinas is accommodating Aristotle overmuch. The claim is put forward by an appeal to the various features of Aristotelian magnanimity which are apparently at odds with Christian character, especially Christian humility. What is to be made of this objection?

The first thing that ought to be said is that Thomas himself is well aware of it. Article 3 of *ST* II-II 129, which asks whether magnanimity is a virtue, contains two objections which expressly raise the issue. The first, objection 4, claims that no virtue is opposed to a second virtue but that magnanimity is the opposite of humility. The objection then refers to *EN* IV.3.1124b29 where Aristotle says that the magnanimous man *disdains* other men. Thomas's reply is distinctly Christian, though not in a way that undermines the core of his agreement with Aristotle. He says that in man there is found a certain greatness possessed as a gift from God, while at the same time a certain defect which comes from the infirmity of his nature. Magnanimity is the estimation that man has of himself according to the greatness of God's gift in him, while humility is the estimation that man has of himself according to his weakness. For this reason magnanimity condemns others insofar as they fall short of God's gifts since the magnanimous man will not esteem others so much as to do or favor some unworthy act. In this context Aquinas quotes the fourth verse of Psalm 14 where it is said of the just man, "In his eyes the reprobate is despised."

The sense of disdain which Aquinas traces here, despite its Christian inheritance, is not without its Aristotelian foundation. For in being a man of perfect virtue (1124a8) the *megalopsychos* will not look down on others merely for the sake of sport. It is his virtue which compels him to look with disdain on others, yet only insofar as they are lacking in virtue. If he looks down on them for any other reason, his concern will not be with virtue, and so he can hardly be called a magnanimous man. This is not to deny the difference in Aquinas's conception of the magnanimity introduced by the workings of divine providence. But whether the ultimate source of excellence is providence or man's own doing, it is clear that the magnanimous man's estimation of himself is not beyond that which is his due and thus not opposed to humility. Aristotle in fact criticizes those who would ape magnanimity by thinking themselves superior to others without possessing virtue itself (1124a26-b6).

In objection 5 of article 3 Aquinas mentions five further qualities of Aristotelian magnanimity which all seem, from the Christian point of view, worthy of censure rather than of praise: (1) the magnanimous man does not remember kindnesses (1124b13); (2) he is idle and slow (1124b24); (3) he addresses the common man with irony (in the sense of affectation of ignorance) (1124b30); (4) he cannot associate with others (1124b31); (5) he prefers to have possessions which are useless rather than productive (1125a12-1414). In his reply to this objection Aquinas begins by stating, surprisingly, that these qualities of the magnanimous man call not for blame but for abundant praise ("non sunt vituperabiles, sed superexced-enter laudabiles"). His aim is to show that these qualities, as understood by the objector, are misunderstood as affronts to Christian humility if they are taken out of their proper context of the magnanimous man's exclusive concern with virtue. Since (1), (3), and (4) seem to be for the Christian objector the most damning features of magnanimity, let us see, in turn, Thomas's explanations of how these qualities are rightly to be understood.

In regard to the first, that the magnanimous man does not remember kindnesses, Aquinas reminds us that the magnanimous man gets no pleasure from receiving benefits unless he is able to make a still greater benefit in return. And this is typical of perfect gratitude, in which the magnanimous man also desires to excel. So it is not the case that the magnanimous man will snub those who benefit him. Rather, Aristotle's point seems to be that the magnanimous man is so concerned with benefitting others that he is not assiduous in remembering those who have benefited him. If this indeed is a fault, it is at least a fault of charity.

Concerning the third quality, that the magnanimous man addresses the common man with irony, Aquinas makes clear that this in no way implies that the magnanimous man will oppose the truth by belittling himself or by denying some of his great qualities. He will only refrain from manifesting the whole of his greatness, especially to the mass of those who do not possess great virtue. As to the fourth quality, that he cannot associate with others, Aquinas quickly adds, quoting Aristotle, that the magnanimous man cannot associate with others, except with his friends. Thus both Aristotle and Thomas indicate that, while magnanimity is concerned with cooperation in virtuous acts, the magnanimous man will not seek associations for the sake of being flattered by those who are lacking in virtue.

So Aquinas, in the end, makes several plausible arguments that the virtue of magnanimity which he expounds in *ST* II-II, 129 is substantially identical with its Aristotelian forebearer. This agreement remains intact, I would argue, even if some skepticism remains that Aquinas has not shown that every feature of Aristotelian magnanimity is compatible with Christianity.[30] Once again, what is needed for that substantial agreement is, first, a view of the grounding experience of magnanimity as involving the good of honor, and so a hierarchical arrangement of goods; second, a specification of that grounding experience which views magnanimity as the spirit for some great act of virtue worthy of the greatest honor. Of course, agreement on these two issues would be impossible if Aristotle and Thomas did not also share the same general transcendent principles of order.

IV

In the Third Essay of *On the Genealogy of Morals,* Nietzsche exhorts his dear philosophers to be on their guard not only against the dangerous old conceptual fictions that posited a "pure, will-less, painless, timeless knowing subject" but also against such contradictory notions as "pure reason," "absolute spirituality," and "knowledge in itself." Although one might like to argue with the terms by which Nietzsche formulates this dichotomy, his often uncanny insight is nonetheless correct to discern a fundamental "either/or" between the so-called "dangerous" efforts of the old philosophers to theorize about the human good by positing an underlying nature for human being and the aspiration of Nietzsche's new race of philosophers to abolish that fiction once and for all. My effort in this essay has been to analyze Martha Nussbaum's attempt to navigate a *media via* between this dichotomy, an attempt I have judged to be ultimately unsuccessful. The major liability of the attempt, I have argued, is its inability to justify the principles of order essential to the virtue-ethic it tries to promote. Nussbaum's attempt to find a real transcendent ground for practical reason without an appeal to conceptions of God, nature, and human nature fails to see what Nietzsche sees to clearly: that minus an extrinsic principle of human action there is *only* a perspective

seeing, *only* a perspective knowing. *Tertium non datur.* Nussbaum's exhortation to "internal" transcendence seeks to rouse those who, like the woman in Stevens's poem "Sunday Morning," feel a complacency toward life produced, at least in part, by a desire to become another sort of being. In the end, however, the chilling effect of internal transcendence is to make divinities of ourselves, to ratify the "measures" of our souls by the mere assertion that without them we cannot live a properly human life. Yet a race of such divinities, armed with these assertions, can expect, like the divinities of ancient myth, to live only in constant and interminable strife.

Notes

1. Chapter 15 of her volume *Love's Knowledge* (New York: Oxford Univ. Press, 1990); hereafter TH.

2. "On the other side, what my argument urges to reject as incoherent is the aspiration to leave behind altogether the constitutive conditions of our humanity, and to seek for a life that is really the life of another sort of being—as if it were a higher and better life for *us*" (TH 379).

3. The Aristotelian text in question is *EN* VII.1.1145a25ff. Nussbaum also refers the reader to *Pol.* I.2.1253a8ff.

4. Further elucidation of Nussbaum's notion of internal transcendence can be found, among other essays, in her Introduction to *Love's Knowledge* and in chapters 2 and 5 of that volume, entitled respectively "The Discernment of Perception: An Aristotelian Conception of Private and Public Rationality" and "'Finely Aware and Richly Responsible': Literature and the Moral Imagination."

5. Nussbaum's arguments for this claim are put forward in her essay "Non-Relative Virtues: An Aristotelian Approach," *Midwest Studies in Philosophy* 13 (1988) 32-53; hereafter NRV.

6. I borrow this distinction from Russell Hittinger as he expounds it in *A Critique of the New Natural Law Theory* (Notre Dame: Univ. of Notre Dame Press, 1984) pp. 65 and 85. Hittinger's book is an analysis and critique of the Finnis-Grisez theory of natural law, and the distinction I am borrowing is made in regard to the question of whether that theory maintains a notion of transcendence. The student of the Finnis-Grisez theory will find many affinities between it and Nussbaum's understanding of practical reason, not only in respect to the issue of transcendence but also in their shared inclusivist account of human happiness, based upon a view of human goods as plural and incommensurable.

7. In setting up the problem in this way it should not be understood that there is necessarily a hard and fast distinction between these two senses of transcendence. In Thomistic natural-law theory, to take one

example, the natural inclination to be like God is simply one manifestation of the natural law, *i.e.,* the transcendent ground of practical reason. But for Nussbaum the two senses of transcendence do not so neatly coalesce. She certainly does not fail to account for such commonplace human experiences as the fear of death and its consequent wish that we might live forever; that is, she does not deny that humans *have* at certain times desires to live an other than human life. What she does deny, however, is that the *object* of such desires (an immortal life) can be desired coherently by humans. On the one hand, Nussbaum recognizes desires to go beyond the limits of human life; on the other hand, she takes desires for peculiarly human goodness to make up the constituent terms of a paradox: "The larger problem has, it seems, something like the same shape as the paradox of the athlete. She shouldn't wish to be without the human body and its limits altogether, since then there is no athletic achievement and no goal; but it seems perfectly reasonable, in any particular case, to want, always, to be better, stronger, faster, to push against those limits more successfully. It is the paradox of a struggle for victory in which *complete* 'victory' would be disaster and emptiness— or, at any rate, a life so different from our own that we could no longer find ourselves and our valued activities in it" (TH 381).

8. Nussbaum cites, in example, Bernard Williams, *Ethics and the Limits of Philosophy* (Cambridge: Harvard Univ. Press, 1985) pp. 34-36, and Stuart Hampshire, *Morality and Conflict* (Cambridge: Harvard Univ. Press, 1983) pp. 150ff.

9. An indispensable source for Nussbaum's views on Aristotle's method of "saving the appearances" and how they relate to our issues is chapter 8 of her book *The Fragility of Goodness: Luck and Ethics in Greek Tragedy and Philosophy* (Cambridge: Cambridge Univ. Press, 1986).

10. Nussbaum discusses her view of non-teleological functionalism in the 1st and 4th of her interpretive essays on her text and translation of Aristotle's *De Motu Animalium* (Princeton: Princeton Univ. Press, 1978), and in ch. 10 of *The Fragility of Goodness.*

11. An important text for Nussbaum in this regard is *Pol.* II.8, 1268b38ff. In the midst of a discussion of change in human positive law, Aristotle writes: "And, if politics be an art, change must be necessary in this as in any other art. That improvement has occurred is shown by the fact that old customs are exceedingly simple and barbarous. For the ancient Hellenes went about armed and bought their brides from each other. The remains of ancient laws which have come down to us are quite absurd; for example, at Cumae there is a law about murder, to the effect that if the accuser produce a certain number of witnesses from among his kinsmen, the accused shall be held guilty. *Again, men in general desire the good, and not merely what*

their fathers had" (emphasis added). This translation is from the revised Oxford text found in *The Complete Works of Aristotle,* vol. 2, ed. Barnes (Princeton: Princeton Univ. Press, 1984); all translations from Aristotle's texts will be taken from this source.

12. Introduction to *Love's Knowledge*: "Form and Content, Philosophy and Literature," p. 26.

13. *Ibid.*

14. See the following two works to which my argument is generally indebted: Russell Hittinger, "After MacIntyre: Natural Law Theory, Virtue Ethics, and Eudaimonia," *International Philosophical Quarterly* 29 (1989) 449-61; and Alasdair MacIntyre "Sōphrosunē: How a Virtue Can Become Socially Disruptive," *Midwest Studies in Philosophy* 13 (1988) 1-11.

15. MacIntyre, pp. 3-4.

16. *Laws* 633d.

17. *Laws* 644c-d.

18. *Laws* 900d.

19. *EN* I.7.1097a30ff. To my knowledge Nussbaum has never commented on this crucial passage in the argument of the *Nicomachean Ethics.*

20. Richard Kraut articulates the same idea when he claims, in commenting upon the argument of *EN* I.1, that the for-the-sake-of relation which Aristotle speaks of has not only a causal element but a *normative* one as well: "But it should also be kept in mind that the for-the-sake-of relation has a normative component: when A is pursued for the sake of B, then B provides a norm that guides A. The bridle-maker decides how to treat his raw material by looking to a paradigm of the finished product, and the proper design of his product is determined by the expert rider. The horseman tells the bridlemaker what sort of bridle he needs; so the activity of riding provides a standard for determining how bridles should be made. And in turn the military leader tells his cavalry which sorts of maneuvers they need to master. The bridlemaker puts himself at the service of the rider, who puts himself at the service of the general; each lower discipline plays a causal role in the pursuit of each higher discipline, and the higher disciplines in turn provide the norms for the proper pursuit of lower disciplines. The for-the-sake-of relation is accordingly a mixture of causal and normative elements." *Aristotle on the Human Good* (Princeton: Princeton Univ. Press, 1989) pp. 200-01. This schema should be regarded as applying to the way in which the moral virtues for Aristotle are ordered to, are "for-the-sake-of," prudence and, in turn, to philosophical wisdom and its contemplative activity.

21. For Nussbaum the possibility of inherent contradiction between "values" manifests itself on the practi-

cal level in what she understands as the situation of tragedy. In chs. 10-12 of *The Fragility of Goodness* she draws support for this position from the Aristotelian ethics.

22. MacIntyre, p. 6.

23. Epicurus, "Letter to Menoeceus," trans. Russell M. Geer, in *Epicurus: Letters, Principal Doctrines, and Vatican Sayings* (New York: MacMillan, 1988) 124b1-3, 125a7-8.

24. To be more precise, near the beginning of "Non-Relative Virtues" Nussbaum claims that the grounding experience associated with death is described by Aristotle more or less as "Fear of important changes, esp. death" (NRV 35), whereas near the end of the essay, when she re-formulates the basic grounding experiences in a way "closely related to Aristotle's original list," she says about mortality that "No matter how death is understood, all human beings face it and (after a certain age) know that they face it. This fact shapes every aspect of more or less every human life" (NRV 48). The latter formulation could of course accommodate Epicurus, but at the same time its universality loses Aristotle. For courage in Aristotle's view is not simply a perfection of our *notion* that we are going to die, but of our *fear* that we are going to die and, what is more, in noble circumstances. Nussbaum concedes that understanding of the grounding experiences will always be interpretive (*cf.* NRV 48) but fails to tell us, despite appeals to the commonality of human experience, on what basis certain interpretations should prevail over others.

25. "But if praise is for things such as we have described, clearly what applies to the best things is not praise, but something greater and better, as is indeed obvious; for what we do to the gods and most godlike men is to call them blessed and happy. And so too with good things; no one praises happiness as he does justice, but rather calls it blessed, as being something more divine and better" (1101b21-26).

26. For an excellent discussion of magnanimity throughout the Aristotelian text, one which patiently outlines Aristotle's focus on the integrity of virtuous action, see Stephen White, *Sovereign Virtue* (Stanford: Stanford Univ. Press, 1992) esp. pp. 247-71.

27. These distinctions are taken from *ST* II-II.128 where Thomas distinguishes between the integral and potential parts of courage. The integral parts of courage are those which comprise the constituents of the act of courage. In this regard magnanimity may be an integral part of courage insofar as it is enjoined to effect a reasonable response to the fear of death.

28. *ST* II-II.129.1, *corp.* All translations from the *Summa theologiae* are from the Blackfriars edition (New York: McGraw-Hill, 1966).

29. A provocative account of this transformation is provided by Peter Berger in his essay "On the Obsolescence of the Concept of Honor" in *Revisions,* ed. Hauerwas and MacIntyre (Notre Dame: Univ. of Notre Dame Press, 1983) pp. 172-81.

30. For more on the interrelationship and harmony that Aquinas sees between magnanimity and humility, see *ST* II-II.161.

Finbarr McCarthy (review date winter 1998)

SOURCE: McCarthy, Finbarr. Review of *Poetic Justice,* by Martha Nussbaum. *College Literature* 25, no. 1 (winter 1998): 290-96.

[*In the following review of* Poetic Justice, *McCarthy evaluates Nussbaum's arguments regarding the role of compassion in legal decisions made by judges.*]

To learn how to regard others as fully human, to identify sympathetically with others the better to promote a vision of social justice as complex and democratic, legal thinkers, particularly judges, must, argues Martha Nussbaum in *Poetic Justice: The Literary Imagination and Public Life,* immerse themselves in literature. Particularly by reading such realist novels as *Hard Times* and *Native Son,* and perhaps by watching movies, and by then comparing their responses, the judiciary can develop, insists Nussbaum, the truly sophisticated ethical stance that judging other people demands. More than other narrative genres, novels, Nussbaum believes, enable such a stance. Their form and style compel readers to evaluate, against certain very general notions of human flourishing, characters whose emotions and actions they set in detailed personal, social, and economic circumstances. Such evaluating, Nussbaum assumes, will then incline readers to identify sympathetically with others, many of whose hopes, desires, and fears but not whose social and material circumstances they share. Sympathy is ultimately for Nussbaum the social emotion that best promotes a "moral / political vision" that is "democratic, compassionate, committed to complexity, choice and qualitative differences." It is this activity leading to sympathetic identification with others that Nussbaum wants judges self-consciously to observe if they are to appreciate the nature of truly moral and rational public decision making. Because literature produces engaged, responsive readers, judges will, Nussbaum hopes, forge in the smithy of their souls the uncreated conscience of their race.

Though pleading a moral role for literature in public life has a long, controversial history, Nussbaum is particularly well trained to tackle it afresh. A professor of philosophy, she brings to the task the broad interdisciplinary training that many scholars in the humanities now embrace. She is engaged on a long term project analyzing the role of belief and thought in the emotions. Nussbaum has worked with economists from the World Institute for Development Economics Research devising a measure to assess the quality of life in developing countries. In recent years, her work has especially appealed to legal scholars because, she surmises, the common law has traditionally promoted a humanistic conception of public rationality. She has taught a course in law and literature at the University of Chicago Law school. Indeed, *Poetic Justice* originated in a series of lectures that Nussbaum delivered at various law schools here and abroad. In discussing the appropriate content of public rationality, it draws upon her knowledge of philosophy, economics, literature, and law.

A slim volume whose intermittent redundancy reveals its origin in lectures, *Poetic Justice* consists of three parts. The first contrasts the narrow moral vision of utilitarian economics with the much more capacious and generous one that Nussbaum believes literary texts offer. The second tackles the pervasive attitude, part of the legacy the Puritans bequeathed this country, that the emotions have no place in fully rational public decision-making. The third illustrates at work in three judicial opinions the sympathetic identification that Nussbaum believes literature nurtures.

Good judging demands a sophisticated ethical stance. But that stance presently eludes judges because, Nussbaum believes, the useful but limited perspective of utilitarian economics dominates not only public policy generally, but legal decision making particularly. Because it offers, in Nussbaum's opinion, too parched a sense of human flourishing and too pinched a sense of the role of emotions, economics cannot sufficiently ground moral judgment. Because of these shortcomings, Nussbaum contends that the many judges whom economics unduly influences too often promote the welfare of the group over that of the individual.

Because utilitarian economics takes little interest in real individuals, it can never, Nussbaum believes, adequately inform public decision making. Nussbaum repeats many of the familiar criticisms of economics. In its models, individuals are not truly individuals. They display little of the complex social life and none of the inner emotional and moral life that makes a person unique. They seem denied the freedom to do anything but pursue preferences and utility, avidly and single-mindedly. Moreover, these preferences seem never tied to particular social conditions. Everybody lives in a colorless, raceless, sexless, aspiritual world. There they measure their satisfaction with life quantitatively, not qualitatively, so more is always better.

The shortcomings of economic theory particularly trouble Nussbaum because that theory no longer confines its desiccated characters to the traditional

marketplace. Many economists now seek to have them colonize noncommercial areas of social life—the relationships between the sexes, for instance, to which Richard Posner, a federal judge, has applied economic models. Apparently, utilitarians accept the grandiloquent claim of the Chicago economist George Stigler that "all of man's deliberative, forward-looking behavior follows the principles of economics." But though correct in her descriptions of the shortcomings of economic theory, Nussbaum considerably overestimates, I suspect, the influence of economics on legal practice. Certainly, it has influenced legal scholarship and, to a far lesser degree, legal teaching. Several specialized, peer-reviewed journals have indeed emerged. A couple of the more influential among the discipline's acolytes are the *Journal of Law and Economics* associated with the University of Chicago and the *Journal of Law, Economics, and Organization.* Much of what the latter journal in particular publishes is inaccessible to readers untrained in economics. Frequently, less recondite articles appear in general student-edited reviews.

As for the teaching of law from an economic perspective, many casebooks include an obligatory excerpt from the theory. Many teachers mention the concepts of efficiency and waste, which some lawyers undoubtedly recall as useful sources of argument. But aside from those who write about law and economics, few teachers, I suspect, rigorously incorporate the subject into their courses. Many ignore it, some because they know little about it and so fear teaching it, and some because they believe it largely inappropriate for the humanistic tasks of lawyering.

The degree to which scholars have influenced legal practice seems difficult to measure. Indeed, how little legal scholarship influences practice and public policy generally might surprise scholars from other disciplines. Certainly, legal scholarship has influenced antitrust law. But other, less market-oriented areas seem unaffected. Perhaps the main influence of the law and economics movement has been to contribute to the current political cycle a theory to which politicians and public policy makers can turn to legitimize their emphasizing the bottom line. But whether the movement shapes the climate or the climate nurtures the movement remains hard to say. I suspect that the influence moves both ways.

Even were we to accept that complex behavior indeed corresponded to the simple principles of utilitarian economics, we would still have to question whether they alone should guide public decision-making. People with very complex emotions actually live their lives in concrete social and political circumstances which they would want considered in any judgment either of their actions or of their best interests.

To understand how inadequately the rational economic individual provides information on which to base moral decisions in a complex world, Nussbaum suggests comparing the typical utilitarian text to a realist novel such as Dickens's *Hard Times*. In the rich, dense and textured world of such novels, the individuals who inhabit utilitarian communities would serve only as flat, one-dimensional minor characters. They would be of passing interest, readers understanding that the author has limited their ability to understand and judge the motives and actions of these characters. Besides, more complex, more distinct, characters located in a densely described physical, economic, and social world await the readers. The detail aims to compel readers to analyze and evaluate in some depth both the choices that these more rounded characters make and the ways in which social and personal circumstances limit those choices. Any resulting judgments, generalizations, and prescriptions will, therefore, emerge from a detailed knowledge of both the individual and his or her social world.

But since sketchy, detached characters inhabiting a rather shallow world are all that economic models allow readers to analyze, the resulting evaluations are highly abstract. They may, Nussbaum hesitantly concedes, serve useful predictive purposes. But, she cautions, such abstract evaluations should not be taken, as too often they are, either to predict the whole of reality or to be merely descriptive. They are, she insists, normative. To call the decisions of these economic actors rational is, she argues, to imply that the decisions of other more human actors may not be. But in claiming that decisions that shun emotional content epitomize rational thought, economists are, as Nussbaum points out, making normative claims about self sufficiency and detachment that are very contestable.

Showing that public deliberations should embrace the emotions because they contain important cognitive information about the value, the moral worth, of the object of the emotion occupies the second part of Nussbaum's text. This important section constitutes the theoretical foundation of the book's thesis that literature serves a public function. Those who would deny the emotions a public role have usually relied on four reasons: the emotions are impulsive forces that neither embody reflection nor respond to reason; emotions generate false judgments because they overvalue persons and things which an individual cannot control, thereby rendering that individual dependent and vulnerable, neither self-sufficient nor virtuous (for which reason Plato banned literature from the ideal republic); emotions focus on people tied closely to the self, and not on distant lives; and, finally, emotions are much too concerned with individuals and not with classes.

The essence of Nussbaum's response to these arguments is that cognition, not impulse, produces emotions. Emotions, Nussbaum states, are ways of perceiving objects. An emotion focuses on an object that figures in that emotion as the person experiencing it sees that object. Moreover, so intimately connected are emotions with beliefs about the value of the object that without those beliefs, the emotion would not exist. Consequently, says Nussbaum, the real issue is not whether emotions have a role in public life, but whether a particular emotional response is appropriate to the object and situation. Deliberations in the public arena particularly require that participants monitor and then exclude those responses that self-concern generates from those that an other-regarding stance generates.

Criminal law, as Nussbaum notes, but civil law too, has long taken such a stance: did the defendant, the law often asks, act as a reasonable person would have acted in the situation? This question assumes that in the community a behavioral norm exists of which people are aware. It implies that their awareness should, if necessary, induce them to modify their behavior, which may depend upon adjusting their emotional response. Judges and juries strive to determine whether individual behavior coincided with the community norm. If it did not coincide, then they seek to measure the extent of the discrepancy between the individual response and the community's sense of an appropriate response. These efforts acknowledge the cognitive content of the emotions and their role in judging people. But they also recognize the need to circumscribe the emotions.

Many judges, Nussbaum believes, need practice not only in admitting the emotions to their deliberations but in evaluating the appropriateness of particular emotions in context. Too many judges, she thinks, either strive for a scientific objectivity in their reasoning or remain skeptically detached or loftily remote from the particulars of the case. To get that practice, Nussbaum argues in the final third of *Poetic Justice* that judges should not only read literature, but closely observe themselves doing so. They will discover, she believes, that the very structure of the literary experience compels readers to consider how inequalities in society impoverish the lives of individuals through no fault of their own. The wealth of detail in which reading realist novels immerses readers leads them to identify sympathetically with characters. In turn, that identification with individuals can undermine the facile generalizations about groups which often produce the discrimination and prejudice which individuals must bear. As Nussbaum illustrates, in generating considerable sympathy in the reader for Bigger Thomas, a young black man, Richard Wright's *Native Son* underscores how perniciously racism affects individual lives. In a similar manner, E. M. Forster's *Maurice* underscores how homophobia diminishes the lives of gay men.

But, insists Nussbaum, such sympathetic identifying with characters does not mean, as those who closely observe themselves reading will discover, that readers necessarily hold fictional characters morally worthy or blameless. Sympathy does not mandate any particular result. Ultimately, practiced readers of fiction tend, Nussbaum believes, to judge characters as would Walt Whitman's poet, the god-like "equable man," who is "arbiter of the diverse . . . equalizer of his age and land." He "judges not as the judge judges but as the sun falling around a helpless thing . . . He sees eternity in men and women, he does not see men and women as dreams and dots." In other words, readers, just like the distant sun to a rock, subject the lives of characters to the full, clear glare of their scrutiny. Like the sun, readers of fiction tend, Nussbaum implies, to be neutral. Their not being personally involved in the events of the narrative enables them to measure the lives of the characters in a more detached manner. But readers do not exercise the absolute judgment of Whitman's poet because part of their assessment involves comparing their views of characters to that of other readers. Reading, therefore, ultimately produces some evaluation of characters against some fairly general norms of human flourishing.

This readerly plunging into the details of individual lives followed by the more detached, neutral assessing of those lives mimics the activity that Nussbaum would have good judges adopt. Judges too, she accepts, cannot join Whitman's poet on his lofty, numinous bench. Just as the insights of others informs a reader's judgment of fictional characters, so too does the legal world within which judicial decisions occur act as a check on a judge. Precedent and legal rules set the confines within which judges must strive to understand the actions of individuals. They must then judge those actions, assigning responsibility when due, but letting neither personal bias nor group interest direct the outcome. The final pages of *Poetic Justice* provide three judicial opinions to illustrate both the literary judging that Nussbaum advocates and the unimaginative judging that she denounces. Somewhat ironically, an opinion of Richard Posner, a leading advocate of the law and economics movement, exemplifies the former.

Here for legal readers *Poetic Justice* stops before the truly difficult question. Fostering in judges a sympathetic understanding for others does not, as Nussbaum intuitively grasps, necessarily conflict with the principle of charging people with responsibility for their actions. Far more crucially for her legal readers, Nussbaum fails to address how judges should resolve the conflict between a decision mandated by legal precedent and one mandated by the literary imagination formed by the reading of realist fiction. Clearly she recognizes the presence of the principle of legal precedent. But she never tackles the thorny issues it raises—particularly what a judge should do who believes that precedent should not control in a particular instance. Former Supreme Court Justice William Brennan has implied

that the emotions should trump precedent. He is on record as saying that in crafting opinions he preferred to draw upon a wide range of emotions rather than upon what he called cold reasoning. In his opinion in *Carr*, Posner circumvented precedent by holding the district court's finding of facts to be clearly erroneous. But that is a strategy that judges may only infrequently use if they are not to undermine either their credibility or respect for the legal system. The issue is a highly charged one, generating charges of judicial activism when judges overrule precedent. But the emotions, as Nussbaum shows, properly play a role in legal decisions. The more difficult issue is where we should circumscribe them. Discussion on that issue is, however, rarely broached.

In *Poetic Justice* Nussbaum's plea is essentially that reading fiction is good training for a lawyer, judges included. She is updating the argument that a lawyer should bring to the profession a broad humanistic education. In this sense, *Poetic Justice* is unlikely to provoke much controversy. Reading can expose readers to worlds with which they have had little contact. Towards the people portrayed, fiction may create a favorable predisposition that may positively influence future relations. Of course, fiction might also generate in readers other emotions such as disgust and even hatred. So readers must search for appropriate sympathy-inducing novels.

Reading fiction is an important means of creating sympathy because our society tends not to tolerate people demanding it directly. We extend it to those we believe have been harmed through no fault of their own, but we limit how often and how long they may directly make such demands. Witness the treatment of race over the last thirty years. At first, demands to rectify the injustices of the past generated such legislation as the Civil Rights Act of 1964. But more recently a backlash has occurred. A vocal segment of the white majority believes enough sympathy has been extended to the victims of racism and that various minorities ought to take responsibility for improving their situation. In such a climate fiction can indirectly state the plea for understanding and sympathy.

Reading fiction for a knowledge of others may also particularly inform those judges too busy and too isolated from the general population to acquire this knowledge in any other way. In a society where work occupies an increasing amount of time, where people live in areas divided by class, race, and even religion and school, the opportunities to have contact with others who differ from a reader seem increasingly narrowed. But the audience to whom Nussbaum implicitly addresses her plea seem especially isolated from the disadvantaged. Federal appellate judges, and especially Supreme Court judges, are an elite group—still mostly upper middle-class, aging white males. Many were appointed during the Reagan and Bush eras when personal responsibility, not sympathetic understanding, was a key phrase. Federal appellate judges typically maintain a low public profile. They have little contact with others outside their own small world. Most of the time they work independently with a few clerks and a few secretaries. Moreover, outside the confines of the courtroom and chambers, many insist on being addressed as "judge," as if further to distance themselves from most of the population they serve. If people do, in fact, tend to empathize more with those most like themselves and less with those to whom society accords low esteem, then federal appellate judges should be especially vigilant in broadening their knowledge of the lives of others.

But most trial judges, I suspect, and especially elected state judges, who far outnumber federal appellate judges, probably fairly accurately dispense or withhold sympathy in accordance with society's rules for doing so. Sympathy is, after all, a social construct, as sociologists and anthropologists have proven—in some societies it does not exist. Historically, our society has promoted individual responsibility, so we typically grant sympathy only to those of whom we can say they have not caused their own harm. Our society has, by the time most people reach adulthood, well schooled its members in the rules for when to extend sympathy and when to withhold it. People are always assessing against a societal norm whether they have correctly sympathized or not. Consider all the occasions that require such calibration—deaths not only of close relatives, but of coworkers and of their relatives, various degrees of sickness and even the small daily slights that besiege most of us. Consider then the different rules that apply for each of these situations. If people sympathize too readily or too often or for the wrong reasons or if, on the other hand, they have not done so generously enough, others will sharply criticize and label them. They will lose credibility. Others will suspect their judgment. Consequently, elected judges are probably fairly good barometers of society's attitudes, at any given moment, towards sympathy. Their own interests demand that they be.

For these reasons, were all judges to read fiction, few decisions would, I suspect, change. But to predict this result is not to minimize the importance of sympathetic identification. Reading may change the way in which judges undertake their onerous duties. A capacity to empathize and then to sympathize may induce judges to allow parties to tell their stories in court. Even if they then have to rule against a party, as they must in civil cases, the display of sympathy has a value. It suggests to its recipients that they have moral worth.

But Nussbaum, I suspect, might consider such an end rather pallid. She has, I believe, a larger goal. She seems genuinely to want to extend the sympathy boundaries, particularly to encompass those whom racism, sexism and homophobia exclude or treat as less worthy of the law's notice. Though Nussbaum acknowledges that sympathetically identifying with someone does not mandate a particular result, she clearly implies that if reading engenders sympathy more decisions will favor those whom she champions. But to achieve that goal more rapidly she has addressed the wrong audience. Legislators, to whom she only perfunctory attends, are, theoretically at least, much closer to the source from which sympathy rules spring. Their interests mandate that they, like elected judges, be attuned to the climate for sympathy. But, unlike judges, they may much more actively and openly shape an environment with wider sympathy margins. Over the last few centuries, legislators have often embraced such a role. They have outlawed the practice of treating children as cheap labor, a stance for which Dickens is partly responsible. Similarly, various civil rights laws have sent a message that our society no longer tolerates discrimination against certain groups. Social behavior has, consequently, changed dramatically. Legislation has even sanctioned the granting of sympathy to animals in a way unimaginable two centuries ago.

The public forges the social rules of which the laws are often a reflection. They also serve on juries where they might exercise the moral judgment that Nussbaum desires. So Nussbaum might much more profitably have argued that legislators and public policy makers and, indeed, the general public turn to literature. When the general public read fiction, independence of thought, toleration and, ultimately, democracy thrive, as totalitarian regimes have long understood.

Dennis O'Brien (review date 10 April 1998)

SOURCE: O'Brien, Dennis. "Socrates Didn't Have Tenure." *Commonweal* 125, no. 7 (10 April 1998): 26-7.

[*In the following review of* Cultivating Humanity, *O'Brien discusses the philosophy of Socrates in relation to Nussbaum's arguments about education.*]

[In **Cultivating Humanity**] Martha Nussbaum, one of our most distinguished philosophers and classical scholars, has fashioned a "report card" on contemporary liberal education: not failure, certainly not a "gentleman's" C (politically incorrect), perhaps not A+, but very much alive and lively in an astonishing array of academic settings. Her reassurance about the vitality of liberal arts is particularly striking coming as a classical defense of liberal education because it would seem that it is precisely the classical that has been eroded by contemporary interest in non Western culture, African-American studics, women's studies, and gay studies. To external critics, none of these educational turns, fashions, or fads look at all like the traditional classical curriculum, for example, "the Great Books" (from Sophocles to Shakespeare to—well, maybe T. S. Eliot). Nussbaum assures us that despite apparent change the spirit of liberal education remains strong.

Unlike most philosophers setting out to prove a case, Nussbaum actually cites empirical evidence. She has personally tracked the practices of liberal arts teachers in such varied settings (among others) as Bentley College (essentially a business school), Notre Dame (a Catholic university), Brigham Young (Mormon), Randolph-Macon (small residential), University of Pittsburgh (large, state-related institution with significant commuter population). At each of these institutions, she salutes individuals and/or programs which challenge students to think openly and creatively, to resist the "idols of the marketplace," to make up their own minds. The new—supposedly anticlassical—curricula do exactly what one hopes the liberal arts will accomplish: liberation of the human mind.

That at least is one version of the liberal arts. In his meticulous and indispensable study of the history of the liberal arts tradition (*Orators & Philosophers: A History of the Idea of Liberal Education*), Bruce Kimball delineates two strikingly different ideologies of "the liberal arts." The oratorical liberal arts emphasize the tradition, recovery of a civic value. The philosophical liberal arts opt for the critical, continual re-examination of inculcated cultural assumptions. Kimball distinguishes an *artes liberales* tradition (orators) and the "liberal free" tradition (philosophers). It is the "liberal free" tradition that Nussbaum finds healthy and well on campus.

Nussbaum's nominal hero, representing the "liberal free" liberal arts, is Socrates. Chapter 1 is titled "Socratic Self-Examination" and the teachers and programs singled out for praise in one way or another replicate the persistent questioning of the great Athenian "gadfly." "The central task of education . . . is to confront the passivity of the student, challenging the mind to take charge of its own thought." To that end, "tradition is one foe of Socratic reason." So much for right-wing critics who think that "liberal arts" is just all those dead, white, European males so long (too long) revered by the "classical curriculum." The other "foes" of Socrates are those left-wing progressives who view "reason" as the claptrap invention of male hierarchy. Nussbaum is firm in upholding universal reason as the great device for the critical appraisal essential to the liberal arts (in their liberalfree guise).

I am deeply sympathetic to Nussbaum's views, and I offer hearty congratulations to all those present-day gadflies out on the front-line classrooms, yet there are limitations to her Socratic overlay on higher education. Socrates is never without his ironies! I point to two

significant ironies: Socrates' distrust of "professors"; Socrates' civic piety.

It is not incidental that Socrates practiced his critical art in the market place, in the gymnasium, and at drunken feasts. It was Plato who invented the (our) academy, a sheltered spot for philosophers to practice their trade. Socrates believed that in the search for wisdom the best he could do was confess his own ignorance while querying merchants, generals, poets, religious prophets and whatall for any scraps of wisdom they might have come upon. What Socrates seems to have distrusted most were the Sophists, those who professed to have a knowledge or skill which they could pass on for a fee to willing pupils. Socrates would be amazed—probably amused—that there are Socratic-like professors, that is, certified and tenured gadflies.

It is also not incidental that when push came to hemlock, Socrates refused to go into exile. In the *Crito* he imagines the Athenian laws speaking to him as the mother and father who shaped him and whom he could not now flaunt by abandoning the city. Nussbaum's text shapes Socrates in terms of the later Stoics who advocated an ideal of the universal citizenship of reason and humanity beyond the confines of Athens or Rome.

One problem with Socrates plus higher education is that for us higher education is through and through institutionalized. Higher education is the Academy—a place set apart with professional standards, tenure, credentialing, certification, and so on, none of which makes much sense in the Socratic life-search for wisdom. Are professors specially qualified, more than poets, politicians, or people of practice to offer a "guide to life"? A second and contrary paradox is that Socrates does not seem (at least in the *Crito* nor in his life practice) to have been a proto-Stoic universalist. To be sure, he was critical of Athenian torpor, but he seemed to believe that the problem was not discovering the truth of reason above, but in waking up the embedded pieties of the existing polis. In sum, Nussbaum's Socratic ideal—noble as it is—either does not sit easily with the institutional reality of higher education, or Socrates' allegiance of a sort to an embedded civic wisdom does not sit well with Nussbaum's fundamental critical transcendence of tradition in the realm of reason. We should bless our Socrateses in and out of our colleges and universities, but the issues of higher-education-as-institution go beyond (or below) the great gadfly.

Henry S. Richardson (essay date October 1998)

SOURCE: Richardson, Henry S. "Nussbaum: Love and Respect." *Metaphilosophy* 29, no. 4 (October 1998): 254-62.

[*In the following essay, Richardson discusses the tension between concepts of love and respect in Nussbaum's theories of institutional justice.*]

Immanuel Kant insisted that we must not regard human beings as subject only to the laws of empirical nature. Nonetheless, he admired the precise symmetries of Newton's celestial mechanics. In the striking passage in his *Doctrine of Virtue* which sets my theme, he applies a Newtonian analogy to relations among persons:

> According to the principle of *mutual love* [persons] are directed constantly to approach one another; by the principle of *respect* which they owe one another they are directed to keep themselves at a distance. Should one of these great moral forces sink, "so then would nothingness (immorality) with gaping throat drink up the whole realm of (moral) beings like a drop of water."
>
> (Kant 1983, Ak. 449; emphasis in original)

The picture is a vivid one: without the centrifugal force of respect, human beings, in perhaps their vain quests to reunite themselves with their lost halves, or in any case captured by love's overwhelming attraction, would collide with one another. The result would be immoral and destructive. Yet without love's centripetal attraction to hold them together, people would fly out of their orbits and lose all stable connection with one another. The result would be anarchic and immoral. A well-regulated human life, according to Kant, must carefully balance these opposing forces with each other. We must find an equipoise of love and respect.

Kant's theory of virtue, which makes a place for love and respect as coordinate moral principles, purports to locate such a balance. It maintains respect-based constraints on intimacy even for the closest of friends. His account also features an inverse correlation between the intimacy of a relationship and the stringency of the duty of practical love therein. Love of humankind, which Kant champions, pulls upon us like the gravitational fields of the stars in the heavens: measurably but weakly and diffusely. In our relationships with strangers, it is instead the strict duties of justice, embodying respect alone, that principally control us.

We know in advance that such a tidy and cautious resolution would not be Martha Nussbaum's. Informed by the ancients' unflinching explorations of *eros,* she has little patience for the sorts of fastidiousness among intimates that Kant recommends. She has recently drawn on Kant to develop a cosmopolitan universalism; but her attention to the plight of those in the globe's poorest countries carries and demands an intensity of response that upsets Kant's circumspect model of attraction at a distance. At the intimate end of the spectrum, love resists the constraints of respect, while at the universal end, love remains ardent.

Since Nussbaum has now embraced universal respect in addition to particularistic love, I want to raise the question of how, in her moral philosophy, these two elemental forces are to be reconciled. Before we

consider the possibilities for their conciliation, however, we need to examine how Nussbaum has made the problem harder than it was for Kant. It is more difficult because, on Nussbaum's view, *both* love and respect are more demanding than they are for Kant. Let me explain.

For Kant, what is involved in respecting persons may be set out in terms of universal principles. In the section of the *Metaphysical Principles of Virtue* titled "Concerning the Moral Duties to Other Men Issuing from the Respect Due Them," Kant (1983) gives some examples. One must not treat the opinions of others with contempt, but must be willing to assume that there is a grain of truth in what each person says. One must not inflict punishments, such as cutting off noses and ears, that assault their dignity as persons. And quite generally, one must act in a way that recognizes their dignity as rational persons; that is, one must obey the moral law in one's behavior toward them. The Kantian account of what respect requires, then, is quite general and schematic. It suggests two tiers of requirement, each equally universal: first, one must not treat others in any way that wholly flouts their nature as rational beings, and, second, one must otherwise act toward them in universalizable ways. The requirements of respect, then, are captured by the moral law.

To be sure, contemporary Kantians such as Barbara Herman (1993) have correctly pointed out that working out, in any instance, what respect so interpreted requires will demand situational judgment. One delicate issue discussed by Kant himself is how to render aid to someone without humiliating him or her. The benefactor, writes Kant (1983, Ak. 453),

> must carefully avoid any appearance of intending to obligate the other person, lest he not render a true benefit, inasmuch as by his act he expresses that he wants to lay an obligation upon the receiver (which always humbles the one obligated in his own eyes). Rather, the benefactor must express himself as being obligated or honored by the other's acceptance, treating the duty merely as a debt he owes, if he cannot . . . carry out his beneficence completely in secret.

The delicate balance between the opposing forces of love and respect, then, demands concrete discernment. Love bids one approach and help, but one must maintain a respectful distance so as not to humiliate one's beneficiary. The moral law, though, still stands behind the situational judgment, providing a general principle of respect for persons—the principle whose implications need to be worked out case by case. What ought to be done is that persons should be respected in universalizable ways; the case of giving charity indicates that judgment is needed in working out *how* to abide by the moral law.

Nussbaum's work on moral discernment carries this theme of situational discernment much farther. As she has described moral perception in such essays as **"'Finely Aware and Richly Responsible'"** (in 1990b), it is no longer simply a handmaiden to a resolution that can be independently described in principle. The literary imagination, and the genre of the novel, Nussbaum has argued, are essential contributors to sound moral judgment precisely because there exists no sound, fully general, and in-principle statement of *what* ought to be done. In the essay I just mentioned, Nussbaum writes,

> A good action is not flat and toneless and lifeless like my paraphrase—whose use of the "standing terms" of moral discourse, words like "mutual sacrifice," makes it too blunt for the highest value. It is an "alert wingèd creature," soaring above these terms in flexibility and lucidity of vision. The only way to paraphrase this passage without loss of value would be to write another work of art.
>
> (1990b, 154-55)

To bring home her point that discernment of the moral particulars cannot be paraphrased in terms of a principle that it serves to implement, Nussbaum several times invokes the simile of jazz musicians, whose sensitive responses to their fellows are not dictated by any score, but rather reflect true improvisation (1990b, 94, 155). Improvising well in response to the improvisations of others requires, she notes, that one be "far *more* keenly attentive to what is given by the other actors and by the situation" than where there is a script (1990b, 94; emphasis in original).

If "respect" must be given a Kantian interpretation, then Nussbaum's stress on moral particularism moves against it. Central to perceptive attunement to particular others, she rightly emphasizes, is an awareness of them as embodied persons—of their bodies and of their emotions, which have bodily aspects. Thus, in her essay on James's *Golden Bowl,* Nussbaum describes Maggie Verver's love as

> requir[ing] the breaking of moral rules and a departure from the comfortable garden. . . . The departure from Eden brings with it the possibility of certain moral emotions that were unknown in that garden. . . . From having seen only clear, splendid objects, Maggie learns, inhabiting a human world, to be a "mistress of shades" . . . , a reader of nuance and complexity.
>
> (1990b, 134)

In Henry James's world, the contrasting point of view of equal respect is exhibited by Mrs. Newsome in *The Ambassadors,* who, in Nussbaum's words, "would never wear her dress cut down, encouraging Strether to perceive her as a surprisingly particular physical being and so to surrender his own dignity before her" (1990b, 178). Love motivates a risky attunement to embodied particulars, whereas a Kantian respect maintains a safe distance.

But of course what I want to say is that at this point in our story love and respect cooperate; for we must not admit that Kant's Newtonian metaphor has the last word on respect.[1] While there has been a deep tendency for "the moral point of view" to point us upward, toward the transcendent, and hence to contrast and compete with the sensuous and earthly gestures of human love for which Steerforth's arm is Nussbaum's emblem, her overriding effort in these essays, it seems to me, is to shift our conception of what the moral point of view actually requires of us. Respect that requires the shield of Mrs. Newsome's black ruched dress, I hear Nussbaum telling us, is no proper respect for human beings. Truly to respect human beings as the vulnerable, embodied, and emotional beings that we are requires a willingness to descend from the philosopher's imaginary Eden and engage in a riskier and more responsive improvisation. *That* is what morality requires of us.

Although this particularistic respect flows from a better understanding of what morality demands of us, it nonetheless sits in an uneasy relationship with the more general and defining elements of the moral point of view. Nussbaum recognizes this in various ways and places. In the essay on Steerforth's arm, she calls on David Copperfield's novelizing voice, or Dickens's novel-writing art, to finesse the tension between Agnes's arm uplifted toward heaven and Steerforth's languid limb (1990b, 348). Even more explicit is her discussion in the essay "Perceptive Equilibrium" of whether the perceptions of a fine-tuned particular awareness may simply be folded into a broader effort at achieving a reflective equilibrium on moral matters. If we take seriously the improvisatory and shifting nature of the perceptive responses we are called upon to have, Nussbaum suggests, we will see that instead of equilibrium we must expect "an unsteady oscillation between blindness and openness, exclusivity and general concern, fine reading of life and the immersion of love." The unavoidable and proper state of moral thinking, she writes, "might not be equilibrium at all, but a dynamic tension between two irreconcilable visions" (1990b, 190).

At this level, then, which concerns the proper interpretation of respect within the moral point of view, Nussbaum herself articulates the problem. More than that: she suggests a solution. As her introduction to ***Love's Knowledge*** carefully explains, the particularism of the essays on James and Dickens is to be seen as part of a broader view about ethics and practical reasoning. This broader view, this "framing method" as she puts it (1990b, 104n.), pursues, in a way inspired by Aristotle, the question, How should a human being live? The Aristotelian general answer to this question that Nussbaum has herself articulated and defended in a range of essays orients the moral perceiver and indicates how the situational, emotional responsiveness of an agent to particulars can nonetheless be the actualization of a virtuous character the outlines of which are established by a general account of the human good. Within this Aristotelian picture, the tension between general norm and particular perceptiveness can become a fruitful and productive tension, as the discernment of the *phronimos,* the person of practical wisdom, contributes to a more exact specification of the norm of virtuous action. Love is tamed by being put in harness for morality—not, indeed, by being converted into the chaste *agapê* of the Christians, but by being made a powerful engine of particularistic concern for others. Respect is softened by this moral particularism, and no longer seems to demand that we hold our distance, as Kant had thought. The two poles will produce some helpful oscillation, but the Aristotelian framing conception will hold them together.

Had Nussbaum rested here, she would have given us an attractively revised and filled-in version of Kant's delicate balance between love and respect. She has not rested, however. As she has turned her attention from personal ethics to global justice and from literary imagination to social welfare assessment, she has increasingly emphasized the importance of universal claims. She has recently written in favor of "the life of the cosmopolitan, who puts right before country and universal reason before the symbols of national belonging" (1996, 17). Is this not to follow Agnes's upward-pointing finger, forgetting Steerforth's bed-nestled arm? For Nussbaum, the theme of cosmopolitan reason is above all a Kantian one. In a recent essay (1997a), she has traced in detail the parallels between the Stoics' view of universal reason and Kant's, which was strongly influenced by them. Her aim, in these writings, is the noble and practical one of inciting more of us to believe that we have important and demanding duties to aid distant people who are less fortunate than ourselves. In taking this position, she has retained the element of latitude which, Kant (1983, Ak. 390, 393) had insisted, applied to the duties of beneficence he described. That is, it is not at the outset, simply from the abstract characterization of her moral position, clear what, exactly, we must do to help others. In this regard her view differs, as she has made clear, from the simplistic sort of utilitarian view proposed by Peter Unger in his *Living High and Letting Die,* from which one can immediately deduce that one ought to sign over all one's assets to OXFAM and be willing to give one's life to save that of any other pair of people (cf. Nussbaum 1997b). Rather, it will require the sustained attention of a loving attitude—a Jamesian fine-tuned responsiveness to particular problems in order to figure out how best to fulfill and interpret our obligations to those distant people. Yet—and here is my present concern—if this loving attention is in the service of *universal* respect, is it really love anymore?

In a recent essay on love in the Stoics, Nussbaum (1995) has characteristically anticipated this question, and has answered it in the negative. To be sure, she criticizes Plutarch for the superficiality of his negative answer: it is not simply the universalism of the Stoics, demanding that we transcend our typical narrowness of attachment and bind ourselves to all rational beings, which rules out love. Rather, it is the claim that this universal love will be measured, impartial, and serene, for while this stance might count as empathetic or sympathetic, it is incompatible with the madness, the ferocious attachment to the particular, which Plato rightly discerned in love—in *eros.* To claim, with the Christians, that the attitude of loving can reconcile the urgent claims of particular loved ones with the duties of impartial respect is, Nussbaum is in effect suggesting, a cheat. If the *eros* that binds us to our mates were the same as the *agapê* with which we might be linked to humanity at large, then invoking love as the reconciling rubric might be helpful; but these two attitudes, these two psychological forces, are sharply distinct. Furthermore, Nussbaum's earlier work strongly suggests, erotic love with its devotion to particulars is a morally valuable attitude, both in itself and for the insight that it brings. We ought, then, to maintain a loving attitude toward (certain) particulars, and we cannot reconcile this with a demand for universal respect by pretending that it may be identified with philanthropy, a general love of humankind.

So Nussbaum has heightened the potential tension between love and respect by strengthening what each requires. Can we imagine an equipoise between love and respect within Nussbaum's view? I think that we can, but that the balance will have to take a quite different form than it did for Kant.

On the Kantian picture, recall that the tension is at least nominally resolved by a theory of optimal distance. Love bids us approach others, respect bids us hold our distance, and a proper equilibrium between the two (as settled by the moral law) will determine the optimal distance. Nussbaum's view, thankfully, is more complicated than this simple Newtonian model of balanced forces. On her account, love underwrites a discernment of particulars that amounts to an intimate form of respect. Respect, by contrast, demands of us a response to distant people that is less tepid than a general and distance-diluted philanthropy. Our response to the plight of women in Bangladesh, for instance, ought not to be divided by the square of the miles between us.

In my brief account, I have treated this tension merely thematically. Clearly, however, the issues of justice with respect to those in developing countries is one place at which this tension, if unresolved, will generate conflicting views about what we ought to do. Conflicts will arise concerning both what our duties are and when we are justified in intervening in other countries' affairs.

With regard to duties, Nussbaum has sensibly rejected the immoderate universalism of a position such as Peter Unger's—the view that none of us should be here now because we should have devoted the resources we used to get here to help starving people abroad; but she has not specified what it is that we do owe. Concerning the grounds for intervention, she has indicated how the Aristotelian conception of the human good will provide a basis for avoiding the paralysis that occurs when a loving respect for the particulars of other cultures yields a nonjudgmental deference. We must not forget, she says, that we can have a normative basis for discounting an individual's claim that he or she is doing fine. With intervention as with justice, though, we need more guidance than this about when we ought to act on the basis of such a critical stance.

I see no direct, general, and specifiable way to reconcile these refined attitudes of love and respect within the individual psyche. Nussbaum's rich elaborations of each have made this too difficult. However, I do think I see a promising, non-Kantian route to reconciliation. This would be to rest more heavily on the normative theory of social institutions. Issues about global justice cannot be adequately settled by the theory of individual virtue or by the theory of individual duty. Instead, we need an account of just social institutions. Schematically: this is to cope with a conflict between Aristotelian particularism and Kantian universalism by turning to Hegel's conception of the subject matter of ethics, in which the structure of *sittlich* institutions frames individual virtues and rights. Taking social institutions as the subject matter of ethical reflection was not new with Hegel. Nussbaum (1990a) has herself explored an Aristotelian account of social justice which centers on the claim that the duty of the politician is to see to it that each citizen has available the basic materials for living a good life. As with most traditional theories of justice, however, this took for granted that distributive justice stops at home. What I am urging is that as Nussbaum presses the cause of distributive justice in the international realm, institutions must come into focus (cf. Pogge 1994).

My schematic suggestion, then, has a negative aspect and a positive one. To begin with the negative: the conflict between love and respect as moral attitudes incumbent on individuals will not be resolved so long as one sticks to posing questions solely about individual duty and virtue. The positive aspect is that a shift to the institutional level should help. This is for three reasons. First, a set of just institutions will provide a series of varied contexts in which different mixes of universal respect and particular devotion would be appropriate. I would like to illustrate this by reference to actual institutions which may or may not be just: how one ought to reconcile one's particularistic understanding of local customs in Bangladesh with a universally grounded commitment to helping women there may appropriately vary according to whether one is acting as a private individual, an official of the World Bank, or a consultant to the World Institute for Development Economics Research. Second, reforming institutions can be a powerful way of mediating our actions toward others, especially distant others. Perhaps the most important thing we can do to express love for distant others is not to write one check that will then be diluted into a multitude of parts, but instead to fight for a more just scheme for taxing international financial transactions or natural resource extraction (cf. Pogge 1994). Finally, institutions also extend our particular awareness, contributing to a moral division of responsibility and attention that becomes crucial as soon as it is recognized that no one individual, in isolation, can meet the cognitive demands for a respectful love for all others. Those of us who have not traveled to Bangladesh must rely upon the lovingly respectful and critical moral discernment of those who have. Reading OXFAM's newsletters may be as morally important as sending them money.

I do not know if Nussbaum will find focusing on institutions an attractive way to synthesize particularistic, loving respect with respectful, universal love. I am sure that she has heightened the tension between them sufficiently that they will not resolve themselves into equipoise the way Kant's opposed forces do. And I am confident that since each side of the tension is fully alive within her, Nussbaum will continue to seek ways not to deny the true moral demands either of respect or of love.

Note

1. Intriguingly, in a forthcoming article, Marcia Baron argues that the passage with which I began should not be taken to be the Kantian's last word on love and respect, either.

References

Baron, Marcia. (Forthcoming). "Love and Respect in the *Doctrine of Virtue*." *Southern Journal of Philosophy*.

Herman, Barbara. (1993). *The Practice of Moral Judgment*. Cambridge: Harvard University Press.

Kant, Immanuel. (1983). *Metaphysical Principles of Virtue [Tugendlehre]*. Trans. by James W. Ellington. Indianapolis: Hackett. Cited by the standard Akademie edition pagination.

Nussbaum, Martha C. (1990a). "Aristotelian Social Democracy." In *Liberalism and the Good*, edited by R. B. Douglass, G. Mara, and H. S. Richardson, 203-52. New York: Routledge.

———. (1990b). *Love's Knowledge*. New York: Oxford University Press.

————. (1995). "Eros and the Wise." In *Oxford Studies in Philosophy,* Vol. XIII, edited by C. C. W. Taylor, 231-67. Oxford: Oxford University Press.

————. (1996). "Patriotism and Cosmopolitanism." In *For Love of Country,* edited by J. Cohen, 3-17. Boston: Beacon Press.

————. (1997a). "Kant and Stoic Cosmopolitanism." *Journal of Political Philosophy,* 5, 1-25.

————. (1997b). Review of *Living High and Letting Die* by Peter Unger. *London Review of Books,* Sept. 4, 1997, 18-19.

Pogge, Thomas. (1994). "An Egalitarian Law of Peoples." *Philosophy & Public Affairs,* 23, 195-224.

Bryan Appleyard (review date 9 October 1998)

SOURCE: Appleyard, Bryan. "Well, Hello Dolly—and Goodbye." *New Statesman* (9 October 1998): 45-6.

[*In the following review of* Clones and Clones, *a collection of essays edited by Nussbaum and Cass R. Sunstein, Appleyard concludes that the book as a whole is not convincing.*]

This book [*Clones and Clones*] contains a great comic sentence. It is at the start of Richard Dawkins' essay, "What's Wrong with Cloning?" Here it is (the punchline is the parenthesis): "Science and logic cannot tell us what is right and what is wrong (Dawkins, 1998)." So there you have it: the great crisis of the Enlightenment, the shocking thought that an "ought" cannot be derived from an "is". But you don't have to read Kant or trouble yourself with Hume, you don't even have to read *early* Dawkins. No, "Dawkins '98" should see you right. As with all the best gags, you don't know whether to laugh or cry.

The ensuing essay does not sustain these comic heights and concludes, unamazingly, that freedom should allow people to clone themselves unless somebody can come up with a good reason why they shouldn't. The problem with this argument is that it permits Dawkins to define "good reason". In the course of this book, many arguments are advanced against human cloning. If we are honest, we don't know which of them are good and which bad. But that is the point—we have to decide. Dawkins' essay goes nowhere and should have been omitted.

But how do you go somewhere in this debate? Human cloning is not, as far as we know, likely in the immediate future. What exactly happened with Dolly the sheep is still in dispute. As Stephen Jay Gould points out in his essay, "Dolly's Fashion and Louis' Passion", the

cell from which she was cloned may have been an embryo-like, undifferentiated cell from her donor's/ mother's swollen mammary glands. This would mean adult cloning had not, in fact, been achieved—we have long been able to clone from undifferentiated cells. And, in any case, nobody quite knows how it worked, nor if the resulting clone will suffer from premature senescence as a result of the elderly and certainly mutated DNA from which she sprang. Yet Dolly did, undoubtedly, raise the possibility of human cloning and this book is an anthology of responses to that state of affairs.

It is somewhat quirky—there are four short stories and no fewer than eight of the 23 contributors are connected with the editors' own University of Chicago. In addition, as so often happens, writers have tended to adapt the terms of the brief to their own interests. So, typically excellent as Gould's essay is, it does not really address the issue. He prefers to use the opportunity once more to advance the case of nurture against nature. And Andrea Dworkin's sentimental and diseased—there is no other word—essay says, predictably enough: "Cloning is the absolute power over reproduction that men have wanted and have destroyed generations upon generations of women to approximate." Oh, sure.

More to the point is a very odd but profound piece by William Ian Miller, a professor of law. Miller writes in a rather airy, almost whimsical style, but he has a tough point to make: "cloning appals us, unnerves us, disgusts, horrifies and revolts us precisely because it engages our deepest concerns about personhood, identity, life and sex." Miller is, essentially, saying "yuk" in a rather highbrow way. And his version of yuk is based on, for me, the central truth that "there are certain large constraints on being human and we have certain emotions that tell us when we are pressing against those constraints in a dangerous way".

One can argue against this kind of studied irrationalism, as many here do, by saying that it overinterprets the science of cloning. As far as we know, nuclear DNA is only half—or somewhat less or somewhat more—of the story. We also have mitochondrial DNA which is not cloned by the Dolly technique. And, more importantly, the environment—from the womb to the family, the school, the whole life—is certainly a crucial factor in determining the nature of the self. To express disgust about cloning because it is an invasion of the self can, therefore, be seen as naive.

But I don't think so. After all, Dawkins wants to be cloned. Why, if it does not, in some sense, represent a replication of the self? And, as Eric A Posner and Richard A Posner point out in their shrewd essay, "The Demand for Human Cloning", narcissists, psychotics, felons, especially rich ones, would, because of their difficulty in forming stable relationships, be likely to want to clone themselves. So, too, would the congenitally infertile, and they would pass their infertility on to their clones. Since the fertile would continue to produce mutations causing infertility, there would be significant selection pressure in favour of infertility. Over time cloning would destroy sex. And, over a much longer time, it would dangerously reduce the variety of the human gene pool. Is that a good enough reason for Dawkins?

The conflict is between individual freedom and the greater social good. In "Queer Clones", William N Estridge and Edward Stein put the strong freedom case in terms that suggest it would benefit the greater good in a very specific sense—it would allow homosexuals to reproduce more freely, it would "expand gay people's options for family formation, 'normalise' queer people as more of them become parents as well as partners, and perhaps even contribute in some modest way to the erosion of gender, sex, and sexual orientation as stigmatising traits". This is the full-blooded Utopian view of cloning as libertarian social engineering.

Between that and the Miller view, these essayists oscillate. None quite draws the whole issue together in a convincing way. The point about cloning is that it is the most graphic vision we have yet been offered of science's gathering assault on the human self. As such, it becomes an issue that expands to take in everything that we are and believe ourselves to be. For me, extending Miller's point, to want to be cloned is a symptom of a high degree of solipsistic disgust. Personally, I like other people more than I like me. More importantly, I value the specific social, sexual and imaginative history that has made us what we are. If we throw it away we will become a lesser species. So hello, Dolly—and, I hope, goodbye.

George Scialabba (review date fall 1998)

SOURCE: Scialabba, George. "Pollyanna and Cassandra." *Dissent* (fall 1998): 128-31.

[*In the following review, Scialabba discusses two books on the dwindling status of classical Greek in higher education:* Cultivating Humanity *by Nussbaum, and* Who Killed Homer?, *by Victor Davis Hanson and John Heath. Scialabba comments that Nussbaum's assertions about education are merely bland, over-generalized, platitudinous restatements of widely accepted values.*]

In "Literature and Science" (1883), a lecture delivered in America during the high noon of the Victorian culture wars, Matthew Arnold defended the study of Greek against utilitarian educational reformers and a newly as-

sertive commercial class. "Literature may perhaps be needed in education," he imagines these Philistines conceding grudgingly, "but why on earth should it be Greek literature?" Because, he replies, we crave it.

> The instinct for beauty is set in human nature, as surely as the instinct for knowledge is set there, or the instinct for [right] conduct. If the instinct for beauty is served by Greek literature and art as it is served by no other literature and art, we may trust to the instinct of self-preservation in humanity for keeping Greek as part of our culture. We may trust to it for even making the study of Greek more prevalent than it is now. . . . So long as human nature is what it is, [its] attractions will remain irresistible.

Apparently human nature is no longer what it was. Around six hundred undergraduates currently major in classics each year at American colleges and universities, fewer than one in sixteen hundred new B.A.s—a figure that probably warrants designating them an endangered species. On the other hand, though unknown in Matthew Arnold's time, business majors now account for roughly a quarter of the graduating class. Greek, it would seem, is history.

So what? Is there still any reason to read the Greeks? Martha Nussbaum thinks so, and so do Victor Davis Hanson and John Heath. That, however, is nearly all they agree on. Nussbaum is upbeat, engaged, optimistic about the current academic scene; Hanson and Heath are angry, marginal, apocalyptic: Cassandras to her Pollyanna. Their new books make a curious pair.

[In *Cultivating Humanity*] Nussbaum champions cosmopolitanism: wider knowledge of the great variety of human cultures and institutions, enlivened by imaginative sympathy and brought to bear in rational and vigorous but mutually respectful deliberation about the common good, of which the Greeks were exemplary practitioners. Education for world citizenship is her theme. "A new and broader focus for knowledge is necessary to adequate citizenship in a world now characterized by complicated interdependencies. We cannot afford to be ignorant of the traditions of one half of the world, if we are to grapple well with the economic, political, and human problems that beset us." This means cultivating humanity. "Three capacities, above all," she writes, "are essential to the cultivation of humanity in today's world. First is the capacity for critical examination of oneself and one's traditions—for living what, following Socrates, we may call 'the examined life.'" The second is "an ability to see ourselves not simply as citizens of some local region or group but also, and above all, as human beings bound to all other human beings by ties of recognition and concern." The third is "an ability to think what it might be like to be in the shoes of a person different from oneself, to be an intelligent reader of that person's story, and to understand the emotions and wishes and desires that someone so placed might have."

As these examples suggest, Nussbaum is prone to platitude—she writes like a dean or a foundation officer or the chair of the National Endowment for the Humanities. No one could disagree with her bland and contentless cosmopolitanism; and indeed no one does disagree with it, just as no one professes principled opposition to peace, justice, freedom, love, rationality, or compassion. The disagreements come when one gets down to cases. Of course there's no harm in restating (in good prose, that is; bad prose always does harm) even the most respectable and uncontroversial ideal. But it doesn't help much, either.

Nussbaum does get down to cases. She has gone around the country for several years looking at curricular developments, and by and large she likes what she's seen. Ideologues may rail at political correctness on campus, and pessimists may lament pervasive dumbing down, but these complaints "bear little resemblance to the daily reality of higher education in America." On the contrary, "higher education in America is in a healthy state. Never before have there been so many talented and committed young faculty so broadly dispersed in institutions of so many different kinds, thinking about different ways of connecting education with citizenship." They are doing this good work in courses on non-European societies and cultures, the history of women, the history of sexuality, and other nontraditional subjects. Much of the book describes these courses and programs, for the most part sympathetically. And they do sound . . . nice. But they also sound a touch banal. Here is the statement of purpose for a course Nussbaum cites as a "very successful example" of an "ambitious, . . . arduous, but potentially more satisfying approach" to multicultural education:

> [The] goal of the course is to develop within students a sense of informed, active citizenship as they enter an American society of increasing diversity by focusing on contemporary and historical issues of race, ethnicity, gender, social class, and religious sectarianism in American life . . . to provide students with an intellectual awareness of the causes and effects of structured inequalities and prejudicial exclusion in American society . . . to provide students with increased self-awareness of what it means in our culture to be a person of their own gender, race, class, ethnicity, and religion as well as an understanding of how these categories affect those who are different from themselves . . . to expand students' ability to think critically, and with an open mind, about controversial contemporary issues that stem from the gender, race, class, ethnic, and religious differences that pervade American society.

Thanks, but I think I'd rather study Plato with Allan Bloom, or even join the Great Books discussion group at my local public library. Yes, it is vitally important to recognize and acknowledge that one's own values and traditions are not the only ones worthy of respect—that other human beings are indeed human beings, however different. But although the acknowledgment may sometimes be morally demanding, the recognition is not, intellectually speaking, very difficult or interesting. Once you've got it, you've got it. We're not talking poetry criticism or higher mathematics.

Besides, isn't there perhaps a filament of connection between the drive for diversity and the culture of consumption? Students are increasingly seen primarily as customers by universities today; isn't the emphasis on "difference" at least partly a marketing tool? To what extent are students attracted to nontraditional subjects by an appetite for novelty, or simply by mental laziness? In the hyperstimulated world of the American campus (by the way, *Cultivating Humanity* takes very little notice of the equally vast but less stimulating world of community and junior colleges), isn't depth rather than breadth the more pressing need?

Nussbaum, however, has chosen a different text for her sermon:

> To unmask prejudice and secure justice, we need argument, an essential tool of civic freedom.

> Education must promote the ability to doubt the unqualified goodness of one's own ways, as we search for what is good in human life the world over.

> A central role of art is to challenge conventional wisdom and values.

> If literature is a representation of human possibilities, the works of literature we choose will inevitably respond to, and further develop, our sense of who we are and might be.

> However we order our varied loyalties, we should still be sure that we recognize the worth of human life wherever it occurs and see ourselves as bound by common human abilities and problems to people who lie at a great distance from us.

Amen. Yet as one endures these pious exhortations, one is reminded of Norman Mailer's exasperated comment on Paul Goodman in *The Armies of the Night.* "Mailer, of course, was not without respect for Goodman. He thought Goodman had had an enormous influence in the colleges and much of it had been, from his own point of view, very much to the good. . . . But, oh, the style! It set Mailer's teeth on edge to read it; he was inclined to think that the body of students who followed Goodman must have something de-animalized to put up with the style, or at least such was Mailer's bigoted view."

If Nussbaum is a slightly sententious Socrates, Hanson and Heath are savagely indignant Jeremiahs. "On the whole, higher education in America is in a healthy state," Nussbaum opines. [In *Who Killed Homer?*] Hanson and Heath take a different view. Their immediate grievance is the imminent demise of classics as a discipline. "The Greeks, unfamiliar to the general public, are now also dead in the university. Today Classics embraces a body of knowledge and a way of looking at the world that are virtually unrecognized, an almost extinct species even in its own protected habitat, the academic department. We Classicists are the dodo birds of academia."

True, the rate of publication in classics is at an all-time high: upwards of sixteen thousand articles, monographs, and books in one recent year, nearly thirty for each graduating senior in the field. This, however, is part of the problem. Most of this stuff, according to Hanson and Heath, is "silly, boring, mostly irrelevant," and above all, self-serving. "All of us who teach the Greeks anywhere, according to our station, confront daily a set of realities that say the opposite of what we learn from the Greeks: obscure and narrow publication, travel, title, pelf, and university affiliation are everything, undergraduate teaching, matching word with deed, living like Greeks relatively nothing."

"Living like Greeks"—what can that mean today? To the postmodernist left, it means the unthinkable: slavery, patriarchy, imperialism. To Nussbaum, it appears to mean an open-ended, society-wide philosophy seminar (led, presumably, by philosophy professors). To Hanson and Heath, it means something far less genteel and now scarcely comprehensible. For them, the Greeks' main legacy is not Socratic dialectic or cosmopolitan humanism—valuable though these things are—but rather a "hard and peculiar way of looking at the world": austere, rooted, stoical, individualistic, plainspoken, egalitarian, mistrustful of novelty, contemptuous of luxury and vanity, jealous of economic and political independence, regardful of physical courage and mother wit. The heroic ideal and the tragic sense are what they mean by "Homer" and what they consider just about dead.

Who's to blame? Hanson and Heath's indictment names names (including Nussbaum's) and cites documents (dozens of passages of wretched prose by academic feminists, postcolonialists, and deconstructionists). By the end there is as much blood on the floor as there was in Ithaca, in the Great Hall, after Odysseus killed the suitors. But of course the problems transcend classics. In every field, the star system means that senior faculty avoid teaching, junior faculty resent teaching, and both frantically publish more and more worth less and less. Financial troubles have turned university administrators into shills. French fads bemuse students; the therapeutic ethos coddles them; mass culture distracts them; and the global economy scares the bejesus out of them (hence all those business majors).

As Hanson and Heath acknowledge, all this has been said before (though rarely so well, in my opinion). What is perhaps most valuable in *Who Killed Homer?* is its continuation of the themes of Hanson's remarkable *The Other Greeks* (1995) and *Fields without Dreams* (1996). The former is a radical reappraisal of Greek culture, which seeks to displace our interpretive focus from the polis to the countryside. "Greece alone," Hanson argues, "first created 'agrarianism,' an ideology in which the production of food and, above all, the actual people who own the land and do the farmwork, are held to be of supreme social importance. The recovery of this ancient ideology . . . explains both the beginning and the end of the Greeks' greatest achievement, the classical city-state."

Fields without Dreams is even more original and radical: a *Works and Days* of California raisin farming (Hanson is, I have neglected to mention, a sixth-generation small farmer, and not primarily an academic), a bitter lament for American agriculture, and a fierce, despairing brief for agrarian populism. Hanson's portrait of the vanishing small farmer—"this bothersome, queer oddball"—is clear-eyed and unromantic; and his skepticism about the hollow abundance that has followed is free of condescension and nostalgia. As a diagnosis of contemporary cultural weightlessness, *Fields without Dreams* ranks with the best of Christopher Lasch and Wendell Berry.

Hanson and Heath's Greeks are not Allan Bloom's aristocratic youths and esoteric sages nor Martha Nussbaum's proto-"world citizens"—nor, for that matter, Matthew Arnold's immortal poets and sculptors. They are *hoi mesoi,* a "society of small independent yeomen," a "republic of hoplite soldiers," each one claiming "an equal slot in the phalanx, a voice in the assembly, and a plot in the countryside." These "middling ones" created "the first freeholding citizenry in civilization" and then "crafted war and invented politics to preserve their discovery of agrarian egalitarianism." That all this sounds strikingly like late eighteenth-century and early nineteenth-century America—the high-water mark of democratic republicanism in modern history—is probably not a coincidence.

Is it necessary to choose between cosmopolitanism and agrarian populism? Let us hope not. The liberal virtues and the republican virtues are both indispensable. But that does not mean they are, at this moment, equally urgent or equally vulnerable. The apparently irresistible thrust of global capitalism threatens the latter virtues far more than the former, rootedness and psychological integrity far more than mobility and personal growth, perhaps even—to stretch a point—independence and self-reliance more than impartial benevolence. The "heroic ideal" and the "tragic sense": these phrases already sound archaic. But our civilization has not outgrown what they signify; it has merely forgotten. Cultural amnesia is not the same thing as progress. Or is it, as the critics of "progress" allege?

Thomas Nagel (review date 8 March 1999)

SOURCE: Nagel, Thomas. "Equality's Pleasures." *New Republic* 220, no. 10 (8 March 1999): 33-6.

[*In the following review of* Sex and Social Justice, *Nagel evaluates Nussbaum's arguments concerning feminism and sexual equality.*]

Any society concerned with fairness must try to decide what general structures or modes of treatment, applied to persons who differ greatly one from another, will qualify morally as a form of equal treatment, or at least as not egregiously unequal treatment. In some cases, such as the vote, identical treatment will do. In other cases, such as taxation or maternity leave, it clearly will not. Sex is one of the most important dimensions in which people differ; they come in two sexes and a variety of sexual roles and orientations. Apart from being one of the most important things in life, sex is at the heart of the structure of families and responsibility for children, and therefore at the heart of everyone's socioeconomic status. So it is hard to tell what laws, practices, and institutions would come closest to meeting the conditions of normative equality or equal consideration of persons against the background of such deep differences and inequalities.

In the face of such a problem, there almost inevitably develops an opposition between liberal and radical approaches. Liberals attempt to discover a way of taking the differences into account in the design of fair institutions without hoping to transcend the differences themselves, because they are considered part of the human complexity and diversity that cannot be abolished without tyranny. Radicals are more optimistic about eliminating the source of the problem, root and branch, persuaded that differences that many find natural or inevitable are really the social product of temporary conditions, to be transformed by a revolution in conventions, mores, or human self-understanding. The conflict within feminism between liberals and radicals is an example of this classic problem.

[In *Sex and Social Justice*] Martha C. Nussbaum presents a broadly liberal outlook in this rich though uneven collection of essays about feminism, homosexuality, the subjection of women in the Third World, and the social, historical, and religious variations in sexual consciousness. The political theory upon which she relies is derived from John Rawls, Susan Okin, and Amartya Sen, and contains no surprises. It is an egalitarian but individualistic liberalism that aims to secure for everyone the basic capacities, opportunities, and freedoms that will allow them to pursue a good life. What is of interest is the application of this idea to the complexities of sex and their wide variation across cultures. Nussbaum considers important issues about the degree to which sexual desire and sexual norms are socially shaped, and about the relation between liberal tolerance of religious and cultural differences and liberal concern for equality of status and treatment. She engages with radical feminists, cultural relativists, and anti-gay conservatives. Nussbaum is a compulsive writer and often goes on too long, but one gets a useful picture of the contemporary battlefield.

Her most sobering chapters are those that deal with the situation faced by women in parts of Asia and Africa, where cultural and religious traditions of crushing subordination and restriction are pervasive and powerful. In this era of international recognition of human rights, the oppression of women deserves equal status with racial or religious persecution and police-state methods as a target of protest. This oppression may be imposed by the state, as in Afghanistan, but it is often privately enforced. Nussbaum describes a widow in India subject to beatings by her in-laws if she breaks the ban applicable to women of her caste on leaving the house, even to work the plot of land that provides the only food for herself and her children. In Pakistan, she reports, conviction for rape requires four male witnesses, and an unsuccessful accusation of rape constitutes a confession to fornication, an offense punishable by whipping. There is a grim chapter on female genital mutilation, widespread in Africa, and designed to make sexual pleasure a male monopoly, so that women can be trusted to leave the house and work in the fields without being led astray by uncontrollable lust. Think about the diabolical genius who invented those procedures of cutting off the clitoris and labia. And think about the sexuality of men who prefer to take their pleasure with a numb partner.

In another chapter, Nussbaum documents the important point that often, though not always, the disabilities of women are imposed with the authority of religion, particularly Islam; but there are very serious Hindu examples as well, and a few milder Jewish and Christian ones. Nussbaum discusses the dilemma that this poses for liberalism, which is committed to both religious toleration and individual rights. India and Bangladesh, though they have liberal democratic constitutions, allow religious law to govern certain aspects of private life. (To a degree, the same is true of Israel.) This can result in severe disadvantages to women in regard to marriage, divorce, property, child custody, and so forth. Toleration of religious pluralism can overshadow concern for equal treatment of individuals. She also observes that, when it comes to the international response to the maltreatment of women, "these violations do not always receive the intense public concern and condemnation that other systematic atrocities against groups often receive—and there is reason to think that liberal respect for religious difference is involved in this neglect."

As she astutely notes, the Supreme Court's 1972 decision in *Wisconsin v. Yoder,* which permitted the Amish on religious grounds to withdraw their children from school after the eighth grade, provides an American example of the link between respect for religion and sexual inequality. It did more damage to the freedom of girls than of boys, since the boys learn marketable skills such as carpentry that make it easy for them to leave the community later if they choose—a further reason why it was a bad decision.

In the worst cases, such as Afghanistan, Iran, and Sudan, religious law is imposed by a tyrannical state, so there is no question of defending it out of respect for religious pluralism. But elsewhere the attitude toward religion poses a real problem for liberalism—a problem of the limits of toleration. It is a difficult question of priorities. Right now, in the United States, most religions teach that homosexuality is sinful, promoting torments of guilt, concealment, and self-denial among their members who discover after puberty that their primary sexual attraction is to members of their own sex. Given its effect on individuals, how much toleration should liberals want to accord to groups that form the lives and the minds of children as well as adults?

The anticlerical impulse is a real test for the liberal inhibition against imposing one's own values across the board. The French ban against girls wearing the Islamic head-scarf to school would be unimaginable here, but its motivation is understandable. Nussbaum's horror stories show that there is a hard question about where to draw the line between respect for religious communities and protection of individual autonomy. And she takes a fairly tough line, which seems right.

Her position starts from the principle that "the fundamental bearer of rights is the individual human being." This means that the state should not enforce religious rules about marriage, divorce, and education, and that it should not discriminate between the sexes, even if it does so in a system that treats all religions symmetrically. But active state interference is a trickier matter. Nussbaum would not allow anti-discrimination law to require the Catholic Church to admit women to the priesthood; but she thinks that conduct by a religion that does not lie within what she calls "the core of worship" should be subject to review for violation of equal rights. One might add that it is essential that anyone should be free to leave a religion, and that policies that affect non-members should be much more vulnerable to public scrutiny than policies that do not.

The inferior status of women in America and other Western democratic societies pales by comparison with much of the world, but in spite of recent progress, it displays a stubborn persistence. This raises the question how deep beneath the surface of legal and institutional structures it is necessary or possible to extend a movement of social reconstruction. Institutional change is essential, of course, to overcome political, legal, and above all economic inequality between men and women. And much remains to be done: even if conditions of employment, child care, child support, and divorce can be improved by governmental action, the most basic institution, the family, will alter its division of labor and power only by the transformation of habits and conventions over generations. Progress in all these respects is under way, and widely regarded as a good thing. What is more controversial is the question of transformations in sex itself—in sexual life, feelings, conduct, and the understanding that people have of their sexuality.

The controversy is connected with the issue of how much sexual desire is socially shaped, or "constructed." Nussbaum is far more sympathetic to the radicalism represented by Catharine MacKinnon and Andrea Dworkin than most liberals are. She credits them with having exposed deep-seated attitudes that support the inequality of power between men and women while concealing those inequalities from view, particularly in the treatment of rape, domestic violence, and sexual harassment, but not only there. Fortunately, we are getting rid of the idea that it is the role of men to try to impose themselves sexually on women, and the role of virtuous women to resist until marriage, and then to submit; that it is a mark of general lasciviousness in a woman, and a forfeiture of protection against being forced, if she ever willingly has sex outside of marriage. This conception was responsible for the requirement of active resistance, even at the risk of physical injury, to sustain a charge of rape, for the admission of evidence about the sexual history of the victim in rape trials, for the nonrecognition of marital rape, for the indifference to sexual harassment as a serious offense in the workplace or other institutional settings. The blend of excitement, fascination, and contempt aroused in unreconstructed males by female desire is one of the ugliest elements of this syndrome.

Even if radical feminists have contributed to the decline of these attitudes, it is part of a wider sexual revolution in which others have been just as important. But Nussbaum expresses particular sympathy with the claim that social injustice invades and shapes sexual feelings themselves. Just how far she is prepared to go with MacKinnon and Dworkin is not clear. She says at one point that "certainly we may agree with MacKinnon and Dworkin that sexual intercourse is, in crucial respects, a meeting of socially constructed fantasies and role enactments more than it is of uninterpreted bodies," but this is too vague to count as a significant agreement.

In another essay, however, she says that Dworkin should have been "more circumspect" in her rhetoric, to avoid giving the impression that she thinks all heterosexual intercourse is rape:

> Examining her rhetoric with care, one may discern a far more plausible and interesting thesis: that the sexualization of dominance and submission, and the perpetuation of these structures through unequal laws (such as the failure to criminalize marital rape or to prosecute domestic violence effectively), have so pervasively infected the development of desire in our society that "you cannot separate the so-called abuses of women from the so-called normal uses of women." This sentence certainly does not say that all acts of intercourse are abuses. It does say that the dominant paradigms of the normal are themselves culpable, so we can't simply write off the acts of rapists and batterers by saying that they are "abnormal." Gendered violence is too deep in our entire culture.

It is not perfectly clear what Nussbaum is saying, but she seems to be endorsing the claim that rape and battery are just fuller and franker expressions of the feelings present at the core of most heterosexual relations in our society.

MacKinnon and Dworkin have gotten a lot of mileage out of this charge, and they have been helped along by the discreditable thrill that too many men feel at being portrayed as dangerous rapists: they all want to hear about how terrible they are. I think that the idea is nonsense, though without looking into the souls of my fellow Americans, I can't prove it. Anyone who does not flee from self-awareness knows that the inner life is a jungle, most of it never expressed. Apparently some women and some men are aroused by fantasies of rape and degradation, and there is pornography addressed to such fantasies; but it is simple-minded to regard this as a matter for societal concern.

The socially important features of sexual consciousness are more mainstream and closer to the surface, and these have responded to criticism. It is now impossible not to cringe at even the best movies from the 1950s, with their thoughtless assumption that women would be passive, unprincipled, and subjected to hilarious humiliation at the hands of men. (The same is true of the portrayal of blacks as childish and ridiculous.) The fact that these conventions which were once second nature now seem benighted shows that things can improve. Still, to overcome the maltreatment of women and the refusal to take them seriously it should not be necessary to attack all asymmetries in the sexual relation, as infections of "dominance."

Nussbaum has a lengthy discussion of the charge of "objectification," in which she comes down in favor of D. H. Lawrence's way of seeing women as sex objects and against *Playboy*'s. "One cannot even imagine Mellors boasting in the locker room of the 'hot number' he had the previous night, or regarding the tits and ass or the sexual behavior of Connie as items of display in the male world." This is rather high-minded, and it is uncharitable to the readers of *Playboy,* whose drooling over the centerfold need not be incompatible with treating women with respect, and even more important, with regarding the sexual desire and sexual behavior of women without contempt. Women's bodies are great erotic vessels, and there is nothing wrong with erotic art that displays them as such, and arouses the physical imagination.

We all speak inevitably out of our own experience in discussing these matters. Being a man and not a woman, and inhabiting a relatively feminized corner of this society, I may underrate both the sexual solipsism of most American males and the sense of violation on the part of most American women on receiving their gross attentions. Certainly the appeal to many women of Dworkin's and MacKinnon's violent images reveals something—if only that there is a great deal of sexual unhappiness out there. As Nussbaum observes, however, one kind of sexual objectification, the surrender of autonomy and control during sex, can be personally and sexually fulfilling for women. Sexual dismantlement drives all of us, men and women alike, deeper into our bodies, and thereby reunifies the multiple layers from the most civilized to the least civilized.

The mere fact that sexual desire and sexual relations are socially shaped does not mean that they have to be infected with injustice. Other natural appetites, for food and drink, are subject to elaborate socially created forms of expression and fulfillment without carrying much of a message, except when they become vehicles for conspicuous consumption. Of course, sex is a relation between people, and more likely to be entangled with their other relations. Yet sexual feelings are powerful enough to determine a good deal in their own right, whatever the social setting. It is not a mere convention that men and women are anatomically and sexually different, and that in sexual intercourse these differences are imaginatively and physically expressed and acted out. Social structures can reach deep into the core of the self, but they usually do not replace it—certainly not in the case of anything as fundamental and powerful as sexuality.

It is almost impossible to get reliable information about this subject, because the motives and the opportunities for concealment of what really goes on in the minds and the bodies of people in bed are nearly unlimited. What is revealed will be strongly influenced by whatever social norm holds public sway. Yet there is a datum that convinces me that social construction is relatively powerless over sexual desire, and it is the unquenchable survival of homosexuality in the face of the most severe repression and public obloquy. Nussbaum is sensibly skeptical about the social explanation of basic sexual orientation, invoking "the feeling of determination and constraint that is such a common feature of self-reports concerning homosexuality in our society." We must distinguish, she rightly says, between the social explanation of norms and the social explanation of desires. One of her essays offers a heart-felt defense of gay and lesbian rights. It seems to me that the much-maligned desires of horny heterosexual males deserve comparable understanding.

Norms and practices can change rapidly, as we have seen in recent years with regard to everything from extra-marital cohabitation to oral sex. (The latter is considered among the young, we are told, as less "intimate" than intercourse.) But there always seem to be taboos of some sort. In ancient Athens, for example, where sexual relations between men were common, actual penetration, anal or oral, was socially condemned, and the younger partner, while submitting to intercourse between the thighs, was not supposed to experience sexual pleasure himself.

Nussbaum is a specialist in ancient philosophy, and some parts of her book deploy this expertise at numbing length. The information about Greek homosexuality, for example, appears in a chapter based on her testimony before a Colorado court on the merits of Colorado's notorious Amendment 2 (subsequently found unconstitutional by the Supreme Court) which denied anti-discrimination protection to homosexuals. She says that she was called in only to rebut historical and philosophical testimony offered in defense of the amendment, and that she thinks all this material is irrelevant to the case. That is a relief to hear; but then she goes on for many pages about the views of Socrates, Plato, and Aristotle on homosexuality. She seems to be straining to show that Plato never condemned sex between men.

A comic example of her classical piety is the invocation of Seneca's argument, in *On Anger,* for mercy and against retribution, which is offered as a response to Dworkin's bloodcurdling fantasies (in the novel *Mercy*) of kicking men to death to avenge the crimes committed against women. Nussbaum's writings tend to be bloated with references; in this book the endnotes go on for eight-eight pages. There is too much heavy cultural artillery being trained on the problems of the day. Yet on most of the topics treated here Nussbaum is a voice of good sense and goodwill, and a reminder, for those who need it, that sex is the scene of some of the worst injustices in the world.

Veit Bader (essay date June 1999)

SOURCE: Bader, Veit. "For Love of Country." *Political Theory* 27, no. 3 (June 1999): 379-97.

[*In the following essay, Bader compares* For Love of Country: Debating the Limits of Patriotism, *by Nussbaum, with* For Love of Country: An Essay on Patriotism and Nationalism, *by Maurizio Viroli.*]

Nationalism and patriotism seem to gain momentum in our times of globalization and decreasing importance of the (nation-)state. Likewise, multiculturalism is becoming predominant while real differences of ethnic cultures are decreasing globally as well as inside traditionally multiethnic states such as the United States. Among the growing stream of publications concerning nationalism or cosmopolitanism, two recent American books deserve special attention. *For Love of Country* (edited by Joshua Cohen) contains Martha Nussbaum's essay **"Patriotism and Cosmopolitanism,"** which first appeared in the Boston Review (October/November 1994) together with eleven of the twenty-nine replies she originally provoked and five new contributions, all "debating the limits of patriotism." This volume is of special interest because leading American political theorists succeeded in getting broad public attention for problems excluded from the political agenda for so long. *For Love of Country: An Essay on Patriotism and Nationalism,* by Maurizio Viroli, adds historical depth and a comparative European perspective to these discussions, which focus mainly on the United States. Therefore, it makes sense that it be presented and discussed first. As is true of most of the contributors to Cohen's volume, Viroli tries to find a third way between "nasty" ethnocentristic nationalism and "abstract" cosmopolitanism by adapting "noble" patriotism to recent conditions of multiethnic and multicultural states and global problems and obligations.

Maurizio Viroli tries to achieve two goals not easily to be combined. As a historian of political language or discourse, he aims "at understanding what scholars, agitators, poets and prophets have meant when they spoke of love of country" (pp. 4f). As a political philosopher and vivid defender of "true" patriotism, he tries to convince us that his patriotism of liberty is the best attitude to respond to the challenges of multiethnic diversity and of globalization. These two goals are intertwined by his conviction that an underlying, fairly consistent intellectual tradition of true patriotism exists in modern and early modern political thought, which only has to be brought to the surface. His true patriotism of liberty, consequently, has to be distinguished as sharply as possible from nationalism, conceptually as well as historically. Patriotism as the "love of political institutions," the "common liberty of a people," or "the republic" is exclusively civic or political and completely opposed to nationalism, which was forged in late eighteenth-century Europe, assuming the existence of or striving for linguistic, cultural, religious, ethnic or even racial unity, homogeneity, and purity (pp. 1ff, 6, 13, 185).

Chapter 1 traces the "Legacy of Republican Patriotism" in ancient, mainly Roman, sources where love of country was pietas and republican political patriotism was intertwined with religion. The basis for a distinctive republican language of patriotism was developed in the fourteenth century in the Italian city-republics by theorists of communal self-government and by civic humanists. Florentine fifteenth-century patriotism, however, was also a celebration of the city's military and civic superiority, meaning that the rhetoric of republicanism served to legitimate exclusions and aggression abroad (p. 29). Machiavelli elaborated a different version, without the same parochialism or exaggerated sense of civic pride.

The "Decline and Revival" of the language of republican patriotism in the late sixteenth and seventeenth centuries is sketched in chapter 2. It survived in the few republics in Venice, Holland, and Naples, but this could not arrest its decline in the unfavorable context of absolute monarchies and principalities and the burgeoning language of raison d'etat. The republican content was lost; patria and liberty parted company. Republican patriotism regained a central place again during the English revolution. Monarchical patriotism replaced love of liberty with loyalty to the king but could not weaken the continuing actuality of republican patriotism.

In continental Europe, the language of patriotism also flourished in the eighteenth century due to the renaissance of republican thought and, more important, due to concrete experiences of political and military resistance against absolutism (chap. 3, "Patriotism and the Politics of the Ancients"). In opposition to the politics of the moderns (of states, princes, the king), patriotism again meant res publica and good government. As a response to Vico's criticism that the ancient patriotism of heroic societies offends our sense of justice and humanity, Montesquieu "rescued" that patriotism by presenting it as a virtue suitable only for ancient citizens of ancient republics. He introduced a distinction between political virtue and private interest (La douce commerce), which one does not find in earlier republican writings. For the "cosmopolitan" Encyclopedists and Voltaire, patrie is also synonymous with republic and liberty (as opposed to the newly invented "oriental despotism"). It has, however, no essential reference to a particular culture or ethnicity but is reduced to its essential political and legal structure (rule of law, liberty, and self-government): "the place does not matter, and history matters even less" (p. 78). To resolve Montesquieu's contrast between political virtues and private interests,

love of country is interpreted as enlightened or rational selflove. Rousseau uses patrie as equivalent of republic but parts company from Montesquieu (also for the "modems") and Voltaire (not only "rational selfinterest" but also passion). For him, love of country means not only purely political love of an impersonal, abstract entity but attachment to particular people as well.

"The Birth of the Language of Nationalism" (chap. 4) is situated at the end of the eighteenth century. In England, the language of patriotism was established as a major intellectual tradition, integrating ancient republicanism and modern natural law tradition (the "boundaries that justice imposes on compassion"; p. 95). Issues of social justice and of integrating the "lower classes" increasingly came to the fore. In Italy and Germany, "the language of patriotism . . . proved inadequate as a means of helping peoples to find their way to liberty. The purely abstract ideal of patrie sounded too abstract" (pp. 106f). This criticism of "culturally remote" patriots appealed to a different idea of country (cultural unity) and a different love (pride or esteem). Love of country should be political and cultural, and liberty demands cultural unity. In Germany, as a reaction to French Enlightenment cosmopolitism and German cosmopolitans, a more radical critique of the language of patriotism was developed, which rejected the priority of civic and political liberty in favor of cultural and spiritual unity and ethnic identity. "Nation means oneness" (p. 118). This language of cultural nationalism was used, at least in Herder's and in Fichte's case, as a premise or preparation for a call to struggle for political liberty (p. 129). The emphasis on unity and purity more than on liberty and equality also infected Michelet and other French patriots.

This "Nationalization of Patriotism" (chap. 5) during the nineteenth century infected even England, where working-class radical patriotism lost from the Gladstonian and Disraelian project (p. 156). In an age of imperialism, it seemed impossible to promote cosmopolitanism or proletarian internationalism. In Italy, Mazzini could not effectively prevent the language of patriotism from assuming nationalistic and monarchical tones, and the same happened in France and Germany. Ernest Renan, however, showed that "even in the age of imperialism," the nation "must be understood as a political community founded on the free consent of the citizens" (p. 159).

Finally, after this historical reconstruction, Viroli intervenes in his epilogue in contemporary debates on "Patriotism without Nationalism" (Habermas, Gian Enrico Rusconi, MacIntyre, Walzer, Schaar, Taylor).

Viroli's vividly written essay presents a valuable reconstruction of the language of patriotism. It reminds us that recent discussions have their historical forerunners and that solutions to the many dilemmas involved do not have to be invented from scratch. It also serves as a counterweight against historically uninformed normative theory still so prominent in America. The specific way, however, in which he combines writing history with normative theorizing is the reason why his historical study is not completely convincing and why he often simply reproduces old and unconvincing normative claims. Let me start with the first point.

As a historian, Viroli is confronted with the well-known "Protean" nature of the concepts of patriotism and nationalism (pp. 4f). Patriotism (and nationalism) show many faces: monarchical, republican, proletarian, liberal, communitarian, Christian, ethnocentristic, nationalist, imperialist. The same holds for cosmopolitanism: it can be stoic, humanist, catholic, professional, socialist, and so on. How to construct one story of one patriotism out of the many localized and contextualized stories? Viroli claims the historical existence of one and the same intellectual tradition of patriotism, which only has to be brought to the surface by rereading the texts, following the line of references, and cleansing this "true," "right sort of patriotism," "properly understood" (p. 8) from all "degenerated" forms (pp. 69, 96), from the historical "misuse" (p. 2) of this language, and from its "misunderstandings" (p. 7) by historians and social scientists. This cleansing operation allows him a dubious normative criticism of historical actors as well as of fellow researchers such as Deutsch, Benedict Anderson, Kohn, and Greenfeld, who use other concepts of nationalism instead of his "historically accurate distinction" (pp. 5, 7f). He does not explicate the pros and cons of his own normative or ideal model of patriotism for historical research.

The construction of this noble patriotism as a love of "liberty," "patria," and "the republic" is not very helpful in spelling out the distinctive historical forms of patriotism itself and the shifts in the meaning of liberty, patria, and the republic. We learn something about the enemies of patriotism in general (tyranny, dictatorship, oppression, conquest, corruption), but we learn very little about historical contexts and power positions. This may be a general weakness of the history of discourses in which contexts and practices enter only marginally to explain shifts in linguistic meaning, much less in social or political meaning. In his critique of Rousseau's "nationalist" patriotism, Viroli mentions that the appeal to cultural unity of a people depends on the fact of whether a people is already politically free and united or, to put it in traditional language, has already achieved sovereignty by way of state-nation building (pp. 91ff): "Divided and politically unfree people must above all else love and be proud of its own national culture to be able one day to be free," traditionally by way of building a "nation-state." And the appeal to cultural unity also depends on resistance to external cultural threats of enforced cultural assimilation and "against the tendency to absorb them in a uniformly European or cosmopolitan way of life" (see p. 93 for Rousseau's fears). Still, every appeal to cultural unity, be it in the case of the Polish people by Rousseau or in the case of the Germans by Herder and Fichte, is, according to Viroli, a vice[1]. On the other side, Ernest Renan's political patriotism is naively presented without even mentioning the rhetorical battle about Alsace, enforced French cultural assimilationism, and "chauvinist universalism." Thus, Viroli mentions contexts without appropriately pointing out that roughly the same rhetoric of patriotism and of nationalism, which often are used synonymously, can have divergent or even contrary social and political meaning depending on positions in asymmetric power relations. The same holds for his abstract treatment of questions such as "how much and which type of unity" is required. According to Viroli, "cultural unity," projects of cultural unification, and "democratic nationalism" from below are "vices" (p. 13), regardless of power positions. These abstract statements benefit powerful states and dominant majorities, which have reached political unity earlier and present their culturally unified nations as neutral and universal. But this does not seem to worry Viroli. Cultural diversity is good, unity is bad; patriots are the good guys and nationalists the bad ones.

Let me now turn to my second normative line of criticism. Viroli's plea for a true patriotism of liberty or diversity contains at least three endemic problems that, in my view, are not treated in a wholly satisfying way: (1) how to combine reason and history, the universal and the particular, the political and the ethnic-cultural; (2) how to combine reason and passion; and (3) how the presumed transformation of parochial into global obligations and allegiances works.

(1) Viroli rightly draws a sharp analytical line separating universal, civic, and political principles of liberty and democracy, of the rule of law, selfgovernment, and good government from particular places or soils, from ethnic and "racial" descent (blood), as well as from language, ethnic culture and tradition, and history. Patriotism as opposed to cosmopolitanism and to ethnocentric nationalism implies a specific, contested combination of the universal and the particular: one "must enter into the dangerous world of particularity" (p. 12). It turns out to be very difficult to "adequately connect" (p. 175) the civic-political and the ethnic-cultural, not only for historical patriots but for Viroli as a normative theorist as well. On one hand, he criticizes all positions that neglect or try to disemphasize the spatial (Toland, Shaftesbury), ethnocultural, and historical (Voltaire) aspect as much as possible.[2] On the other hand, and contrary to his own critical remarks, he seems to applaud the Habermasian strict separation or disentanglement of political, "constitutional patriotism"

from all "pre-political community of language and culture" (p. 170). Rusconi's criticism of Habermas's strategy reclaiming a "synthesis" of universalistic principles and ethnocultural values, of cultural and political community (pp. 172f -is firmly rejected by Viroli: "a love of common liberty should be all that we need. We need, to put it simply, patriotism and we must at the same time help to reduce, rather than invoke, identification with ethnocultural values" (p. 174). If history enters this project at all, it has to be history cleansed from all ethnic aspects: the purely political history of a people (pp. 16f) or its republic (p. 13), its political institutions and practices, and its struggle for liberty.

Viroli's own normative concept of patriotism eventually seems to be "sustained by politics alone," accepting no "pre-political" bases of love of country. It very much resembles the old myth of American exceptionalism: "to love one's country means to love the republic as a political community based on the principle of common liberty, with its own culture and way of life" (p. 183 with Walzer, Schaar, de Tocqueville, Taylor). But one may wonder what remains of "its own culture and way of life" if all "ethnocultural values" are left out. Viroli's patriotism, in the end, is nearly indistinguishable from the "purely" political patriotism he himself started to question. This patriotism has a hard time as soon as one recognizes that (1) the borders of all political units—be it empires, city-states, modern "nation"-states or immigration-states—cannot be derived from political principles of liberty or democracy and that the borders of "nation"-states as well as those of immigration-states more or less explicitly refer to prepolitical, ethnic concepts of the nation(s) and (2) that universalist "political" principles get particularized as soon as one looks at their interpretation, at their institutional translation, and at civic and political cultures, virtues, and traditions of good practices.[3]

Viroli's "adequate connection" of the ethnic and political aspects boils down to a matter of right "emphasis" (pp. 2, 139), which means the "priority" or "primacy" of the political. He can only repeat well-known magic formulas like "love of liberty" in which love is "particularist" and liberty is "inclusive" or universal (p. 12). Such a strand is too malleable. It allows him to criticize both cosmopolitanism and more nationalist patriotism without specifying exactly what would be required. If one chooses the "thin" political version of his patriotism, one may ask Viroli himself whether this can still be called "love of country." There may be a patriotism without nationalism, but there is no patriotism without patria, which most of the time includes a lot of ethnonational values. There is, therefore, no patriotism without "natio" in modern times, and such a "patriotism" would be indistinguishable from cosmopolitanism. If one chooses the "thicker" version, one can allude to

"colors," "flavor," "warmth" and to places, customs, traditions, and ways of life. To each what she or he wants to hear.

Which cultural politics and which institutions would Viroli recommend? I seriously doubt whether his patriotism of liberty, sharing so much with traditional republicanism, can really live up to the conditions of multiethnic, multinational, and multicultural states. In its "thin" version, it may make enough room to "organize diversity" as so many neorepublicans try.[4] However, I cannot find any sign that such a cultural pluralism would be accommodated by institutional pluralism, a concept and project fiercely rejected by traditional republicans as well as by neorepublicans.[5]

(2) The magic formula "love of liberty" also has to answer the old question of how to combine reason and passion. Liberty and justice stand for reason, which is loosely associated with truth, universalist principles, rights, and obligations, appealing to anonymous, disinterested, dispassionate, rational moral agents; impersonal observers; or ideal speakers. It remains cold, distant, and general and cannot mobilize a motivating force, which are crucial weaknesses of "rationalist," "enlightened" liberalism or cosmopolitanism. It is opposed to love as a passion loosely associated with "the real world" of particularist people in time and places. Love's language is rhetorical, warm, nearby. It appeals to the virtues that are presented as particularist feelings (p. 176), sentiments, emotions, and compassion. It can mobilize people to sacrifice their lives. Republican patriotism claims that "between the ideal worlds of rational moral agents . . . and the real world of exclusive and narrow passions there is space for a possible politics for the republic" (p. 17). Following Barber and others, republican patriotism is presented by Viroli as an alternative to both liberalism aiming at a moral foundation of politics and communitarianism aiming at a culturalist foundation. Against "bloodless" liberalism and cosmopolitanism, however, patriotism and nationalism "compete on the same terrain of passions and particularity" (p. 8; see p. 14). Both are eminently rhetorical, playing on the passions of particular people, their cultural and historical identity. Both "possess a unifying and mobilizing force that others lack." Patriotism is thus a "formidable opponent of nationalism" and should be embraced by "the democratic left" in search of a language "capable of countering nationalistic and communitarian languages" (p. 15, praising Rorty). Though patriotism and nationalism appeal to the passions, they try to mold "different types of love": the love of patriots is "inclusive" (pp. 58, 98), "expansive," "charitable," "generous," "intelligent," "defensive," and full of "compassion" and of "tolerance" and "respect" for diversity. The love of nationalists is "exclusive," "invidious," "deaf and blind," "offensive," and full of "contempt," "intolerance," "hatred," "fear," and "resent-

ment." It longs for "uniqueness," "pride," "glory," "grandeur," "domination," "oppression," and "exclusion." Against nationalism "one must find ways of encouraging and sustaining the right sort of passions and love" (p. 12) by working "on bonds of solidarity and fellowship that like feels toward like to transmute them into forces that sustain liberty instead of fomenting exclusion or aggression" (p. 8).

Viroli's version of this old saga of reasonable patriotic love rests on three highly questionable assumptions: Virtues are not a privileged terrain of republicans, communitarians, or nationalists (see Macedo, O'Neill). The crucial question is, Which virtues? In this regard, it is doubly misleading that Viroli identifies "civic virtue" with "a love of the republic" (p. 183) because, first of all, virtues are specific competences to act in a normatively praised way, not feelings or passions.[6] Second, pace MacIntyre, not all virtues are "particularistic" (p. 176): civic and political virtues are universalistic or "generic" (see O'Neill).

If not virtue, is then not love essentially "particularistic": whom can we love? Only particular individuals or also a people or even humanity? Only people or also institutions, states, and so on? Only persons or also ideas, principles? If Viroli, following Rousseau, really believes that "one cannot love strangers, or unknown or anonymous individuals" (p. 81), then his love of country has a hard time in modem states where most compatriots are anonymous strangers.

If one can also be fiercely attached or committed to universalistic principles, it becomes less obvious that "justice" and "liberty" are unable to mobilize any motivational force at all. Their motivational force may be "weak,' and it certainly is weaker than the hot republican language of "sacrifice." Even if Viroli does not ask for "heroic self-abnegation" (p.185), a bit more distance to "white-hot" republican motivations may be healthy.

(3) How does the transformation of parochial into national and global obligations and allegiances work? All true patriots hope and expect that some such transformation takes place, and historical references can be found throughout Viroli's essay. "We have to appeal to the feelings of compassion and solidarity that are—when they are—rooted in bonds of language, culture, and history. The work to be done is to translate these bonds into love of common liberty. To make this alchemy of passions possible, we surely need moral arguments that appeal to reason and interests, but we must also be able to resort, as good rhetoricians do, to stories, images, and visions" (p. 10).

Patriotism "works on the already existing ethnic and cultural bonds that somehow connect members of the same people to transform them into a generous commit-ment against oppression, political corruption, and discrimination" (p. 14). "Patriotism tries to translate a particular attachment between people who are culturally similar into a commitment to a good—the republic—which is still particular as it is the republic of a particular people, although it encompasses cultural diversity" (pp. 16f, see "direct," "shape" [p. 171; "transform sordid and ignoble passions into higher and more generous ones" [pp. 17, 162]; "translate" [pp. 77, 175]; "enlarge" [p. 55]; "love's expansive drive" [p. 100]). Viroli, like all patriotic authors, follows the same logic or paradigmatic argument of concentric circles: love, attachment, commitment, allegiances, and obligations develop first and are most intense or "fundamental" with regard to family and intimates. Love of country is "a passion that pushed him to embrace and enlarge his affection for other peoples beyond the sphere of family and to extend respect and understanding to peoples beyond the boundaries of his own country" (p. 55, for Milton). This logic is never questioned (see below), but even if one accepts it for the moment, the argument remains inconclusive. In fact, one can detect two different types of argument. The first "appeals to the [political] culture that grows out of the practice of citizenship" (p. 13). This traditional republican argument can explain, to a certain degree, how and why familial, local, and regional allegiances are transformed into "national ones." The love of country may "stimulate sharing" and may "breed solidarity" (p. 37) inside the country, but it cannot explain how and why this sharing and solidarity should stretch beyond the borders[7] at least as long as these practices of citizenship are not also transformed in a transnational direction. In Viroli's essay, one looks in vain for any political or institutional proposals in this direction. On the contrary, one gets the impression that he agrees with Mazzini's famous statement, "only citizens can successfully demand social justice. . . . Without country you have neither name, token, voice, nor rights" (p.149)[8]

The second argument appeals to global moral principles and obligations. This "liberal" argument stresses the same universal principles of liberty and justice, whatever the "embodiment": "In labouring according to true principles for our country we are labouring for humanity" (Mazzini, p.151). Here, "our most fundamental moral obligations are to humanity" (p. 150). No appeal to the specific color, flavor, and warmth of the "embodiments" of "equal liberty" (p. 13) and social justice can help here. When it comes to global obligations, not only all references to "ethnocultural" values but also all references to purely "political" history and love of "patria" are counterproductive. This argument is much more plausible, but here patriotism dissolves into cosmopolitanism that, by the way, knows its own rhetoric and tells its own stories, images, and visions. The conflicting tendencies of the "republican" and the "liberal" argument cannot really be reconciled by arranging them under the catholic roof of "common liberty." An appeal to common liberty cannot do the job, and "love of the common liberty of one's people" in no way "naturally" (pp. 59, 77) or "easily extends beyond national boundaries and translates into solidarity" (p. 12).

Why, how, and under which conditions such a transformation is possible and has worked historically is never questioned or explained. Transformation resembles juggling, and it is no coincidence that the metaphor of "alchemy" is frequently used (pp. 5, 10, 98; see Barber, p. 35, for the "American trick"). To explain chemical processes, scientists don't use alchemist models and engineers don't rely on alchemy in the production of synthetics. Why should social scientists believe in alchemy when it comes to explaining how, when, in which degree, and under which conditions parochial allegiances have been or can be translated into global ones? Why should political theorists do it when it comes to designing institutions and policies to stimulate and develop this transformation?

II

Martha Nussbaum clearly does not believe in this alchemy of transformation. "A bottom nationalism and ethnocentric particularism are not alien to one another but akin" (p. 5). Rejecting fine-grained distinctions between nationalism and patriotism, she holds that appeal to particularist national sentiments "subverts . . . the substantive universal values of justice and right" (p. 5), that patriotic pride is "subversive of some of the worthy goals patriotism sets out to serve" (p. 4). Her plea for cosmopolitanism, for the "possibility of a more international basis for political emotions and concern" (p. 4) where the "primary allegiance is to the community of human beings in the entire world" (p. 4), is motivated by two concerns: By "international quality of life issues" (hunger, extreme poverty, extreme inequalities, and ecological problems). She reminds us of "moral obligations to the rest of the world" and criticizes "moral hypocrites who talk the language of universability but whose universe has a self-servingly narrow scope" (p. 13).

By a "renewal of appeals to the nation" among American liberals like Rorty and Hackney, who, in their opposition against multiculturalist "politics of difference," argue for a new "politics of nationalism" and try to regain the language of patriotism for "the American Left" (just as Viroli recommends). Such appeals to patriotic pride "undercut the very case for multicultural respect" (p. 14). Nussbaum clearly does not rely on any automatic or naturally "universalizing tendencies" of patriotic values, and she does not see why universalistic values of liberal democracy, like liberty and justice, "lose steam when they get to the borders of the nation" (p. 14).

Patriotic allegiances seem counterproductive to her in both regards, and consequently, she asks for a reversal of our primary allegiances and obligations from citizens of a (nation-)state to "citizens of the world," for a radical, decisive shift in emphasis or "priority" from national toward global commitments. Although it may sometimes look as if she argues—in an either/or way—for a complete replacement of particularist (local, national) obligations by global or universalist ones, no such replacement strategy is really defended (see p. 9, "no need to give up" and the "concentric circles" imagery; see p. 13, "special degree of concern . . . is justifiable in universalist terms"). For four reasons, we should make "world citizenship, rather than democratic or national citizenship, the focus for civic education" (p. 11): to "learn more about ourselves" (pp. 11 If), to be able to solve problems that require international cooperation" (p. 12), to "recognize moral obligations to the rest of the world that are real and that otherwise would go unrecognized" (pp. 12ff), and to be able to make "a consistent and coherent argument based on distinction we are prepared to defend" (pp. 14f).

Nussbaum's essay provoked many critical reactions from American patriots and only few positive ones embracing the project of a decisive shift toward transnational and global obligations and allegiances. Criticism focused on (1) conceptual, (2) moral, and (3) legal/political issues.

(1) Conceptual criticism highlighted the importance of distinguishing patriotism from nationalism, chauvinism, and jingoism in the same way as Viroli did (see Bernan and Blum in Boston Review [BR]; Glazer, p. 61, for many). Patriotism as well as cosmopolitanism has many forms with different social and political meanings in different contexts (Lloyd Rudolph and Charles Beitz in BR; Wallerstein, pp. 122ff; Glazer, p. 64). It is one-sided and unfair to focus only on the "pathologies" of patriotism (Barber) and not also on the "perversions" of cosmopolitanism (Walzer, pp. 126f). And finally, Nussbaum, intentionally or not, seduces us into making the wrong choices of "either" cosmopolitanism "or" patriotism (McConnell, p. 79; Taylor, p. 119) and of replacing democratic or national citizenship by world citizenship.

Falk and Wallerstein point to the many forms of patriotism and cosmopolitanism and criticize context-independent "choices." Falk also declares both options unsatisfactory in recent global capitalism: the "ethical viability of patriotism depends on sufficient political space at the level of the state" (p. 55) and the "cosmopolitan orientation is not much more satisfactory on these matters" (p. 56). It should be supplemented by "a critique of the ethically deficient" neoliberal globalization. Wallerstein generally opposes an "abstract" or "universal" evaluation of both patriotism and cosmopolitanism in our "deeply unequal world": "our options vary according to social location" in power structures (see also Rudolph, Lerner, and Connolly in BR). The strong and rich have xenophobic options as well as "magnanimous comprehension of 'difference'" but remain privileged, and the weak and poor need "group equality" and may stimulate "nationalism" or "ethnic assertiveness" (pp. 122ff). Consequently, the "stance of citizenship of the world" is a deeply ambiguous response. Instead, we have to "break down existing inequalities and help to create a more democratic, egalitarian world" (p. 124).

(2) Such sociological and historical criticism is resumed by postmodern critics of the universalism of morality itself. Butler places "universality in culture": a "ready made universalist perspective" is misleading because "the meaning of 'the universal' proves to be culturally variable" (p. 45); it has no "transcultural status." Hilary Putnam finds the "notion of universal reason as something independent of all traditions" (p. 95) indefensible. It is a "strange" "overreacting to Rorty" (p. 93) not in line with the many wonderful books Nussbaum has written previously. He refutes her cosmopolitanism as well as Rortian tribalism and defends a notion of situated, critical intelligence in our endless renegotiations of our understanding of reason itself. Yet he misses Nussbaum's crucial point that a decisive shift toward global obligations is urgent. Himmelfarb bluntly states that the presumed universalism of cosmopolitan values is an illusion. Justice, rights and reason, and the even more "culture-" and "polity-bound" values of democracy and liberty "are . . . predominantly, perhaps even uniquely, Western values" (pp. 75f), a claim that is clearly refuted by Sen (pp.117f).

Against Nussbaum's universalist moral point of view, defenders of patriotism have fired the traditional battery of critical arguments: (i) Her cosmopolitanism with its appeal to reason and universal principles is seen as dispassionate, abstract, disembodied, and lacking the motivational force of patriotic passions (Barber, see Leo Marx, A. Schlesinger Jr. in BR). Nussbaum halfheartedly nourishes this impression by accrediting patriotism "special power among the motivations" but still holds that cosmopolitanism "need not be boring, flat, or lacking in love" (p. 17; see "Reply," p. 139 vs. "bloodless," "characterless"). Charles Beitz (in BR) offers a more aggressive argument by treating patriotism as a question of self-conception or identity and rescuing the idea that moral principles can be "powerful, even revolutionary." Instead of powerless reason of cosmopolitanism versus irrational passions of patriotism, the discussion should focus on matters of degree, kinds of passion, and shifting emphasis.

(ii) Her cosmopolitanism abstractly confronts universal reason with the particularities of history and nation and thus fails to combine them productively.[9] Gutmann op-

poses Nussbaum from a more interesting angle in this regard. A defense of democratic citizenship and democratic education includes a commitment to liberty and justice for all, to basic human rights. It should not be misunderstood as opting for "national values." It is not "a weak concession to anything," certainly not to a "nationalistic view" (p. 67). It is as universalist as anything and can be associated with "nationalism" only in one sense in which Nussbaum's cosmopolitanism is also "nationalist": that it is taught within states.

(iii) Nussbaum's statement that borders are "morally arbitrary" (p. 14) and state membership is "a morally irrelevant characteristic" (p. 5) elicited many critical reactions. Bok uses William Godwin's example of two drowning persons, one of whom is a relative, to argue against the moral irrelevance of special relations. Nussbaum did not succeed in mediating between the two conflicting perspectives, leading to a "glaringly different conclusion about domestic and international politics" (p. 39), already recognized by Sidgwick "to threaten any coherent view of ethics" (p. 40): the "universalist view" stressing the moral irrelevance of all particular, special relations and identities, particularly the "accident of where one is born" (p. 7); the "bounded view" emphasizing particular allegiances that "cannot be over-ridden" by global obligations.

In her first contribution, Nussbaum already stated that special attention, care, and concern and special obligations are "justifiable in universalist terms" (p. 13). In her reply, she tries to explicate the moral point of view, clearly misunderstood by Gintis (BR) and others: "To count people as moral equals is to treat nationality, ethnicity, religion, class, race, and gender as 'morally irrelevant'—as irrelevant to that equal standing" (p. 133). The "equal worth of all human beings" has to work "as a regulative constraint" on particular allegiances. Instead of "either" global "or" particular moral obligations, the question, then, becomes one of shifting emphasis in specific contexts. In Nussbaum's treatment, however, the realm of normative or "practical reason" is unduly limited to moral arguments, and most contributors use such a "flat" frame, which does not even allow posing the right questions of how to balance moral, ethical, prudential, and realist normative arguments.[10]

(iv) The imagery of "a series of concentric circles" (p. 9) points to such a direction under the condition that three traditional dogmas—normally linked with it—are criticized. First, it suggests a ready-made answer to questions of priority of moral obligations: there is just one throw of one pebble, and the obligations are strongest the closest by, getting weaker and weaker the farther away from this center.[11] Second, this presumably natural priority of moral obligations toward intimates and compatriots is mixed up with the dogma of an

equally natural logic of the development of moral sentiments and obligations: first parents, then other relatives,
then local, regional, national, and "finally, if at all, we
get to humanity on the outside" (pp. 141 f). In her reply,
Nussbaum refutes such a simplistic "account of moral
development that makes a mystery out of familiar
experiences of commonality" (p. 141), offering an
alternative account in which experiences and recognition of universal needs and of particular people develop
"at the same time." "All circles develop simultaneously,
in a complex and interlacing movement. But surely the
outer circle is not the last to form" (p. 143). Third, a
criticism of these double dogmas of "diminishing"
moral obligations and sequential moral development
has consequences for moral education. Bok rightly
states that educational programs "that declare either a
global or a more bounded perspective to be the only
correct one are troubling insofar as they short-circuit
reflection concerning" the question "how, and on what
grounds, to weigh these claims when they conflict" (p.
42). In educational practice, we are confronted with
"agonizing choices . . . because syllabi, like canons,
are not infinitely expandable" (Rachel Hadas in BR).
We need to be selective and to begin somewhere: "Is it
better for parents and teachers to begin at the outer
edges and move inward, to move back and forth
between the two, or to begin with the inner circles and
move outward?" (Bok, p. 42). To argue for simultaneous
teaching does not mean to deprive children "of a culturally rooted education" (Bok, p. 43). If one does not
trust the patriotic alchemy of passions, if one is
convinced that moral development and moral education
"from part to whole" is not "a by-product" (McConnell,
p. 80), not natural or easy, let alone automatic, one
should be more critical with regard to the sequential
logic than all patriotic critics of Nussbaum. Finally, it is
astonishing that none of the contributors distinguishes
between development and teaching of sentiments, feelings, identifications and identities, affiliation, loyalty,
and commitment, on one hand, and moral principles
and obligations, on the other hand. As if all were the
same, all followed one evolutionary logic in all contexts.
And only few contributors explicitly"[12] criticize
traditional assumptions about "one," "static" fairly
"homogeneous" identity and culture so common to
many patriots and so at odds with multilayered ties,
relations, identities, and commitments on so many levels
in recent multicultural, global society.

To be sure, Nussbaum's argument in favor of a decisive
moral shift toward universal, global obligations could
have been much stronger if she had avoided many
terminological ambiguities and suggestions of a replacement of particular by universal allegiances that have
been interpreted as "either/or" and then, rightly, have
been criticized as wrong choices. It nevertheless remains
astonishing that the basic thrust of her essay in favor of
such a decisive shift has found so little enthusiastic

response, particularly with regard to the moral scandal
of hunger, poverty, and global inequality. Sissela Bok at
least explicitly states the challenge: "This widening gap
between haves and have-nots, and the sheer magnitude
and intensity of present suffering, challenge, I suggest,
all existing conceptions of human rights and duties and
obligations. What does it require in practice, under
today's conditions, to give priority either to world
citizenship or to national or community allegiances? . . . And whose obligation is it to offer assistance on the scale now needed, or to protect rights
. . . when violated by others abroad?" (pp. 41 f).

(3) The fact that this shift has not been applauded more
broadly may not only have to do with the specific
parochialism of American patriots. It may also be the
consequence of two serious legal and political weaknesses of Nussbaum's position, clearly criticized by
many contributors: her sloppy, metaphorical use of the
language of citizenship and her neglect of principles
and practices of democratic polities.

It has been widely, and rightly, noted that the language
of "worldcitizenship" is highly misleading: Walzer is
"not a citizen of the world. . . . I am not even aware
that there is a world such that one could be a citizen of
it. No one has ever offered me citizenship, or described
the naturalization process, or enlisted me in the world's
institutional structures, or given me an account of its
decision procedures (I hope they are democratic), or
provided me with a list of the benefits and obligations
of citizenship, or shown me the world's calendar and
the common celebrations and commemorations of its
citizens" (p. 125; see, similarly, Glazer, pp. 62f; Gutmann, pp. 68ff; Himmelfarb, pp. 74ff for many). Sen's
defense (pp. 112, 116) and Nussbaum's reply (pp. 132ff)
try to clarify that the language of "citizenship of the
world" should be understood in the moral sense only
(as a "postlegal" as well as a "prelegal" concept) and
not as "a legal form of language that excludes" the possibility to be a citizen of the world without there being
a world state. But even such a clarification has two
obvious disadvantages. First, in a substantive sense,
"citizen of the world" would be identical with "human
being," and citizenship rights would be identical with
human rights. This, however, is not a harmless, though
superficial, duplication of terminology because, second,
the actual relationship between human rights and
citizenship rights in our era is obscured. Increasingly,
civic rights, social rights, and even some political rights
are not only claimed but also guaranteed regardless of
citizenship status or nationality in the legal sense.
Specific political rights such as the right to vote and get
elected, however, are reserved to "nationals" and cannot
even be thought of independently of political units of
decision making.[13] Not only in our present world but
also in all institutional designs of better worlds, a great
variety of separate political units have to exist beside

and above each other. Instead of opting for a second decisive, institutional shift toward new transnational and global political institutions, on one hand, and toward a devolution of power to more regional and local institutions, on the other hand,[14] Nussbaum neglects institutional concerns completely, and this weakens the practical political force of her moral appeal considerably. Still, it remains astonishing that so few commentators try to fill this gap to rescue the institutional dimension of the shift toward more global institutions.

The weakness of politics and democracy in her cosmopolitanism criticized by Gutman (p. 69) and Himmelfarb (pp. 75f; see Beitz in BR) follows from Nussbaum's specific (neo)stoic version of cosmopolitanism. Specific democratic principles—autonomy, political freedom and equality, participation—are absent from her list of universal values, and the question of the adequate political units for democratic self-government is never raised. "Liberal" principles of "liberty and justice" may not easily be combined with democratic principles. They may point to different directions in policies of first admission and international redistribution (see Baubock 1994; Bader 1995, 1997). This should be no reason, however, to neglect or de-emphasize them completely, particularly if one recognizes that not only internal policies "to forestall excessive inequality . . . require a high degree of mutual commitment" (Taylor, p. 120; see Fletcher in BR) but transnational and global policies as well. The absence of democratic politics and democratic commitment also contributes to the moralistic weakness of Nussbaum's cosmopolitan intervention.[15]

Many of her American critics appeal to the outworn story of American exceptionalism that, so it is said, is able to combine strong democratic commitment with global moral obligations (see Barber, pp. 30-33; McConnell, pp. 83f; Pinsky, pp. 86, 90; Leo Marx and Anthony Kronman in BR). To a foreign commentator, this rhetorical move is understandable but still somewhat strange. It has to be pointed out that American republican patriotism has not adequately addressed, let alone resolved, the two burning questions that have motivated Nussbaum's essay. First, how to respond adequately to longstanding national, "racial," and ethnic diversity inside the United States? American patriotism, implicitly or explicitly (see Lind), requires too much "national" cultural unity and has difficulties accepting institutional diversity and separation.[16] Viroli's hope that it would be easy to develop a patriotism of "liberty or diversity" remains a far cry. Second, how to live up to minimal global moral obligations? Even in a comparative perspective, American foreign policy, particularly with regard to foreign aid, ecology, and international trade, does near to nothing to address the moral scandals of our times. A lot has to be done by noble American patriots to criticize American "chauvinist universal-

ism,"[17] which still promotes a "self servingly narrow scope" as Nussbaum rightly reminded her readers and, it seems to me, most of her critics.

Notes

1. Herder's cultural nationalism, his opposition against cosmopolitanism and cultural assimilation, and his condemnation of conquest and imperialism (pp. 119, 123) are not adequately understood in the context of German Kleinstaaterei, predominant French culture of German aristocracy, and oppositional bildungsbirgerlicher Kultur versus French "civilisation." Fichte's republican nationalism is not understood as a specific reaction to the French revolution and the Napoleontic conquest. Viroli's standard-type criticism—Herder "did not teach them to look at it [the nation] from the right angle and he did not teach them to love it in the best way" (p. 124) is not corroborated by a historical counterfactual or by historical examples (why not Forster?). In the case of the Left, supposedly "fleeing the field" of patriotism in the "age of imperialism," he presents such a completely unelaborated counterfactual conditional questioning "whether the left did all it could" (p. 157). Again, he fails to discuss historical examples of socialist patriotism and the reasons why they too "would probably not have worked." Marx and Engels on nationalism, patriotism, and cosmopolitanism are absent throughout and, implicitly, accused of abstract proletarian internationalism. But why is the explicitly "patriotic socialism" of Lassalle and others not even mentioned? The whole history of "socialist patriotism" in all its varieties is lacking: from English patriotic socialists, the patriotic socialism of A. de Leeuw or the AustroMarxists (most prominently Otto Bauer) until the VIIth World Congress of the Communist International, and the rhetoric of socialist patriotism of the so-called really existing socialist (RES) countries. This is particularly astonishing if one takes into account that Viroli has dedicated his book to Norberto Bobbio and explicitly wants to reconsider Left thought and attitude regarding patriotism. The example of the rhetoric of RES— "socialist patriotism"—could also work as a reminder that one should more often look at the huge discrepancies between rhetoric and practices. It also reminds us that it is important to recognize whether one speaks in exile (as Mazzini), in the resistance (as Carlo Rosselli, pp. 161ff, or Simone Weil, pp. 163ff), in opposition, or in power—a fact generally neglected by Viroli.

2. See pp. 14-16 versus "liberalism." Toland's and Shaftesbury's purely political, "true" patriotism is criticized for making "the gap between the patriotism of the soil and political patriotism too wide." It gives "no indication as to how to incorporate natural attachment to a place into a moral and general political patriotism" (pp. 59f). In his "attempt to separate love

of country from cultural rootedness," Toland "did not recognize that liberty found in another country cannot have the same flavour. . . . A pure love of country . . . is a different love. One may wonder whether a purely political love can still be called 'love of country'" (p. 56). Viroli's argument that "one can be attached to but one soil" (p. 56) and that "one can be hardly attached to the soil of the world or any other country as to one's native soil" (p. 56) shows the traditional weaknesses: (1) why so much fuss about "soil" instead of "people" or "community" (see Rousseau: "amour des Citoyens plut'ot que celui de la terre," p. 83)? (2) People can be attached to more than one soil (as they can be attached to more than one person) and increasingly are in an age of migration. (3) If anything, one's "native" soil is local rather than "national." (4) Why has the enlargement of this supposed attachment to the soil to stop at the boundaries of national territory?

3. See Veit Bader, "The Cultural Conditions of Transnational Citizenship," *Political Theory* 25, no. 6 (1997): 783-89. Viroli, strangely enough, eventually seems to adhere to what Joe Carens has aptly called the "hands-off' approach to cultural fairness.

4. See Michael Lind, *The Next American Nation* (New York: Free Press, 1995); David Hollinger, *Post-Ethnic America* (New York: Basic Books, 1995); Herman van Gunsteren, *Organizing Plurality: Citizenship in Post 1989 Democracies* (Boulder, CO: Westview, 1998).

5. See Veit Bader, "Egalitarian Multiculturalism: Institutional Separation and Cultural Pluralism." In *Blurred Boundaries,* eds. R. Baubock and R. Rundell (Aldershot, UK: Ashgate, 1998), 185-220. Indicative is Viroli's criticism of Walzer's pluralism, which is treated as just another version of the liberty of the moderns (pp. 1 Of).

6. See Bader, "The Cultural Conditions," 786.

7. Quite to the contrary, it proved to be very difficult to prevent that the "tie which holds together . . . those who live under the same government" and the internal solidarity of "one people" (if and to the degree in which it really exists) excludes the "common interests of outsiders" (see, for completely reverse "priorities:' p. 29 for Bruni, p. 32 for Machiavelli, and p. 90 for Rousseau). Viroli's rejection of Todorov's claim that acts of solidarity are at the same time acts of exclusion (p. 12) is apodictical and waves away the problem to be addressed: "citizenship as exclusion" does not really enter Viroli's reasoning.

8. See Veit Bader, "Conclusion." In *Citizenship and Exclusion,* ed. Veit Bader (Houndsmills, UK: Macmillan, 1997), 182-84.

9. See Pinsky (pp. 85, 89f), Putnam (pp. 95f), and Kronman in BR.

10. See Veit Bader, "Conclusion," 176f, with Habermas and Raz. See Beitz in BR for the distinction between moral and ethical arguments.

11. See the examples of this dogmatic logic of "first-second," "part-whole:' which automatically gives priority, primacy to the "most fundamental" obligations toward intimates. This automatically seems to stretch to "strangers" within state boundaries treated as "compatriots" and automatically excludes or de-emphasizes strangers beyond borders: Barber, pp. 34f; Bok, p. 43 (only God's love not from part to whole); Glazer, pp. 63f; McConnel, pp. 79ff; and Walzer, p.126 ("start with the center," "begin by," "to open the inner one's out:' "then we extend," "ultimately to all," and "commitments and obligations are diminished as they are extended"). Excellent criticism of the metaphor itself and, particularly, of the inconsistent treatment of strangers inside and outside the modern state is articulated by Henry Shue, "Mediating Duties:' Ethics 98 (1998): 687-704.

12. See Nussbaum, p.135, asking for "tough thinking"; Appiah, Butler, and Taylor, p.121; Sen, pp.113f. See my treatment of the problem: Veit Bader, "Fairly Open Borders." In *Citizenship and Exclusion,* ed. Veit Bader (Houndsmill, UK: Macmillan, 1997), 28-60.

13. See my "Citizenship of the European Union: Human Rights, Rights of Citizens of the Union and of Member-States," Ratio Juris, forthcoming, 1999.

14. See Bader, "Conclusion," 184. See Charles Beitz in BR. See Falk's second proposal "to disengage the practice of democracy from its traditional state/society nexus" (p. 59).

15. In her most recent book, *Cultivating Humanity,* she discusses the role universities can play in educating cosmopolitan citizens in liberal democratic societies, stressing deliberation and learning to argue. Still, no attention is paid to specific democratic institutions and politics.

16. Sociological, liberal, and republican dogmas of "unity" are criticized by Richard Sennett (in BR) as "errors" and "exercises in nostalgia" diverting from the contemporary questions "how to live in difference, not how to transcend difference." See my more extensive treatment in Bader, "Unity and Stability in Modern Societies and Recent Political Philosophy." In *Individualism, Civil Society, and Civil Religion,* eds. A. V. Harskamp and A. W. Musschenga (Leuven, Belgium: Peeters, 1999).

17. See Wallerstein for the uneasy mix of "narrow nationalism," "nationalism of the wealthy," and "the hypocrisy of American Kantianism": "America is the defender of the universal values of individual liberty and freedom of opportunity" (pp. 123f).

Gardner Fair (review date summer 1999)

SOURCE: Fair, Gardner. Review of *Sex and Social Justice*, by Martha Nussbaum. *Social Theory and Practice* 25, no. 2 (summer 1999): 344-52.

[*In the following review of* Sex and Social Justice, *Fair asserts that, while Nussbaum carefully balances different sides of the questions she addresses, she fails to reconcile her abstract theories with historically specific realities.*]

In recent years, at least two distinct tendencies within contemporary Western feminist debates have emerged. The first involves the internationalization of feminist theory and politics, and the second involves a critique of "victimization." Both of these tendencies have influenced the feminist arguments found in Martha Nussbaum's recent book, *Sex and Social Justice.*

Feminist theory is only one of several areas that Nussbaum has written on, and in our age of academic specialization, her interdisciplinary breadth is intriguing. She began her career in the classics of Greek and Roman antiquity, writing *The Fragility of Goodness: Luck and Ethics in Greek Tragedy and Philosophy* (1986) and later *The Therapy of Desire: Theory and Practice in Hellenistic Ethics* (1994). She extended her research to contemporary literature (*Love's Knowledge: Essays on Philosophy and Literature,* 1990) as well as to legal issues (*Poetic Justice: The Literary Imagination and Public Life,* 1996). Meanwhile, she was a research adviser from 1986 to 1993 at the World Institute for Development Economics Research, Helsinki which led to her work *The Quality of Life (Studies in Development Economics),* co-authored with Amartya Sen. Responding to the Gulf War in a *Boston Review* essay, she wrote a critique of patriotism that provoked several responses by other thinkers, leading to *For Love of Country: Debating the Limits of Patriotism* (edited by Nussbaum and Joshua Cohen in 1996). In the recent *Cultivating Humanity: A Classical Defense of Radical Reform in Higher Education* (1997), she defended liberal reform within education against the likes of Allan Bloom, William Bennet, and Dinesh D'Souza. Most recently, she is primarily concerned with feminism. *Sex and Social Justice* (1999) will be followed by *Feminist Internationalism* as well as *Upheavals of Thought: A Theory of the Emotions.*

What is one to think of this astonishing breadth of concerns that include the classics, literature, ethics, politics, law, economic development, educational reform, psychology of the emotions, and finally, feminism? *Sex and Social Justice* alone is a good representation of Nussbaum's style of thought. In a densely packed text, she covers a wide variety of topics. All but two or three of the fifteen chapters were published as articles, and as much as she reworked them for the present volume, the topics hang only loosely together. While avoiding eclecticism, Nussbaum's attempt at breadth and attention to a plurality of issues succeeds only partially, especially in regard to the unique demands of contemporary feminist theory.

Anyone familiar with Nussbaum's earlier work will be prepared for her adroit balancing of various sides of a question. The mark of Nussbaum's feminism is her balancing of international issues of economic and legal development with the ethical importance of the emotions. To begin with, in *Sex and Social Justice* utilitarianism and relativism are rejected, while a more subtle balance between equality and freedom is defended. Contrasting her own "capabilities model" to Rawls's similar position on primary goods, Nussbaum carefully considers the challenge, on the one hand, of a utilitarian's avoidance of discussing any qualitative, thick theory of the good, and on the other hand, of a relativist's refusal to judge other cultures at all. Her difference with Rawls is that being a neo-Aristotelian, she risks a more substantive theory of justice than he does. But as a liberal, she agrees with Rawls that a line has to be carefully drawn, somehow, between state intervention and individual rights, or in short, between equality and freedom. Thus, while she supports strong public legislation prohibiting female genital mutilation, she disagrees with Catharine MacKinnon—who is the main feminist against whose views she compares and contrasts her own—that violent, misogynist pornography should be criminalized. Although MacKinnon tries to prevent her anti-porn civic ordinance strategy from being opportunistically used by conservatives (as in shutting down gay and lesbian bookstores), the protection is not sufficient for Nussbaum (and many other feminists) to insure that our private freedoms of sexual expression and literary taste will not be infringed upon.

Within feminist debates, the way that the conflict between equality and freedom is often played out is through the contrast between victimization and agency. Reacting to MacKinnon's and Andrea Dworkin's characterization of women as victims, several recent works have over-emphasized women's agency. Camille Paglia, Katie Rophie, Rene Denfeld, and Christina Hoff Sommers all offer a simplistic gloss of the problems of feminism, with MacKinnon's and Dworkin's "hysterical male bashing" directly in mind, while defending their own media-savvy, quick-fix turn to female empowerment and individual agency. But Nussbaum is careful not to let these popular readings of MacKinnon get away with a simple dismissal of her as an authoritarian puritan. Curiously, Nussbaum defends MacKinnon's stance as Kantian: "MacKinnon, far from turning women into victims, is making the Kantian demand that women be treated as ends in themselves, centers of agency and freedom rather than merely as adjuncts to the plans of men" (20).

Many critics have interpreted the work of poststructuralist feminist Judith Butler as a defense of agency (as gender performativity) against any condescending appeal to victimization. Against any structuralist, Marxist, or psychoanalytic notion of economic or libidinal determinism, this reading of Butler argues that one must deconstruct all forms of essentialism to open up room for individual agency and the play of micro-politics. This, of course, is a false reading of Butler: she is not so crude as to merely invert the binary, as she might put it, between individual agency and social victimization. Rather, the individual for Butler is a very problematic social construct that claims to be able to transcend social power through an imaginary grounding in some "state of nature" or "original position." Slippages and disruptions occur, for Butler, not through an individual's autonomous agency, but despite one's own interests. In the very repetition of the status quo's power relations, subversion occurs as accidental, unintended by-products. Subversion for Butler is an incalculable effect—and the more uncontrolled and incalculable it is by both the individual and society at large, the greater its subversive force.

For reasons very different from those of Butler, Nussbaum is also not so crude as to think that feminists must prioritize either agency or victimization in analyses of patriarchy. Nussbaum begins *Sex and Social Justice* with the case study of Saleha Begum's struggles in Bangladesh. When her husband became so physically disabled that he could not work, they lost their farmland because local communal norms prohibited women from working outside their homes. Threatened by increasing poverty, Saleha Begum eventually braved ostracism and started to work the fields herself at night by moonlight. While local criticism eventually abated, allowing her and other women to work the fields during the day, local officials legally blocked their employment at government sponsored food-for-work sites. Two years later, Saleha Begum organized a group of women, and with the help of the United Nations World Food Program, the national Ministry of Relief and Rehabilitation, and another non-governmental organization, they won both the right to work and access to educational programs and loans. In response to examples like this, Nussbaum concludes: "Women do overcome the greatest obstacles, showing an amazing courage and resourcefulness. So much was true of Saleha Begum. But this is no reason not to change the conditions that placed these obstacles in their way, especially when the conditions are unequally experienced by women just because they are women" (18-19). As we witness in her discussion of Saleha Begum, Nussbaum is a clear supporter of individual rationality and agency. But against what she

views to be Butler's position, this does not lead her to a libertarian rejection of law as authoritarian and invasive. Rejecting this Nietzschean view that she considers adolescent, she states: "Legal guarantees do not erode agency: They create a framework within which people can develop and exercise agency" (19).

Nussbaum's internationalism and interest in law leads her to focus on non-Western examples of patriarchy such as female genital mutilation and prohibition on education and work outside the home. With this focus, she intends to humble U.S. feminists' preoccupation with what she views as less urgent issues such as eating disorders (122-25) as well as Butler's over-exaggerated and self-involved radical constructionism.[1] But as a liberal, she also distances herself from the conservative arguments in Christina Hoff Sommers's *Who Stole Feminism: How Women Have Betrayed Women.* Drawing from statistics provided by *Human Development Reports* and blatantly ignoring racial and economic differences between U.S. women, Nussbaum argues that basic health, nutrition, and life expectancy are not serious concerns for U.S. women (134). This may sound similar to Sommers's position that U.S. women have little reason to complain, but Nussbaum argues that economic and political representation is still an important issue for women. But most important for Nussbaum, there is the fact that the U.S. may even lead the world in sexual violence incidents. Again taking MacKinnon's side, Nussbaum defends the advances that MacKinnon has achieved with her legislation against rape and sexual harassment in the workplace (136-53). Here she tries to strike yet another balance, this time in an international focus that does not neglect a local focus on one's own country. But in this attempt to be inclusive and to avoid a self-involved onesidedness, she amazingly neglects U.S. black feminist theory that is centrally concerned with linking women of color's health issues, for example, to the racialized poverty of an indifferent global capitalist order.

I mention these attempted balances between relativism and utilitarianism, the private and public, freedom and equality, agency and victimization, and the local and global for two reasons. First, the way Nussbaum negotiates these balances in part reveals the position she will take toward MacKinnon, Butler, and Sommers. More generally, they also give an opening summary of Nussbaum's overall political approach. While ignoring race and post-colonial theory, Nussbaum turns to issues faced, for example, by poor women in Bangladesh. From this top-down perspective, what becomes apparent is the need to defend a high degree of state intervention and involvement by non-governmental organizations, national governments, and the United Nations to guarantee a fundamental safety net below which no one, anywhere in the world, should fall. Given her attention to feminist legalism, Nussbaum ends up sounding much like MacKinnon despite their differences of focus and disagreements over specifics concerning the role of pornography in society. Nussbaum clearly has great sympathy for MacKinnon's project. Nussbaum merely shifts her focus away from local U.S. issues and turns her attention to human rights and international law (which MacKinnon also recently did when she addressed the use of rape in the war in Bosnia). Here, law is applied to issues that she argues are more ethically unambiguous and thus safer: rather than pornography and the issue of censorship, Nussbaum focuses on the banning, for example, of female genital mutilation and of obstacles discouraging women's public participation.

But Nussbaum, better than MacKinnon, can draw out the Kantian principles at play, specifically by beginning to compare her view with Rawls. In her attention to legal solutions, Nussbaum also is able to consider longstanding debates within legal theory. In her chapter "Equity and Mercy," Nussbaum criticizes Andrea Dworkin's "angry refusal of mercy, her determination to exact retribution without concern for the identity of the particulars" (155). The balance that Nussbaum now strikes is between a liberal defense of law in terms of deterrence and a radical use of law in terms of retribution. Drawing freely from Aristotle and Seneca, she contrasts her position with both Andrea Dworkin's angry call for retribution and Richard Posner's careful defense of a behaviorist-measured, deterrence theory of justice. Readers of *Poetic Justice* will find this view of jurisprudence overly familiar. As important as legal niceties are, and as clear-cut and determinate as they in fact are in many cases, Nussbaum tirelessly argues that the judge must be adroit at also drawing in a "literary" (which for her means merely a narrative) imagination and sympathy. For her, an attention to the actual person would displace any behaviorist, deterrence-based dismissal of the accused's inner states as advocated by Posner. It would equally override any vindictive, retributive-based fixation on the harm done that also dehumanizes the accused. In the case of Dworkin's fixation on criminal patriarchal behavior, Nussbaum would prevent the judge from sinking into the angry view of all men as criminals, where a victim of male power could not "tell him from him from him" (155).

Thus, law is an important focus for Nussbaum, but a focus that is qualified with her characteristic attention to our inner life of emotions and desires. To support her international focus and her critique of both utilitarianism and relativism, it is important for Nussbaum to defend the idea that women's preferences are not to be taken at face value. Both a utilitarian measurement of a community's prosperity and interests and a relativist hands-off approach take preferences at face value. By contrast, Nussbaum argues in several separate chapters

that preferences, and desires and emotions in general, are socially constructed to a significant degree. In the moment, within the threatening oversight of others, a girl might desire genital mutilation, or disdain getting an education or working outside of the family. But given freedom from immediate ostracism and room to think through for herself what she really wants, Nussbaum claims that the girl would quickly change her mind.

Yet as can be expected, Nussbaum does not flip to the other extreme of what she considers Butler's irresponsible, radical constructivism. Again, she is careful to balance different sides of a question. While defending the degree to which our preferences are socially constructed, she equally defends the courage of individuals to define their own desires against the grain of society, however much a victim of socialization they may be. As much as Nussbaum defends the importance of passion and analyzes how it is socially constructed, she vehemently defends the individual. In a chapter entitled "The Feminist Critique of Liberalism," she even claims that from a feminist perspective, "liberal political thought has not been nearly individualistic enough" (63).

Nussbaum is thus a solid, liberal neo-Aristotelian, attempting always to strike the right balance and find the right mean between the extremes. And in addition to this dialectical sensitivity that leads her to try to do justice to a variety of interdisciplinary issues, she is equally skilled at being analytically precise. Nussbaum's analytic training is indeed striking. The clarity of her prose style and the precision of her thinking is unmistakable. But at points, this becomes a detriment to her thought, for example, in her critique of MacKinnon.

In the central chapter, "Objectification," Nussbaum faults MacKinnon for her lack of analytic preciseness when it comes to defining just what the objectification of women means. Delineating seven distinct forms of treating a person as a thing, Nussbaum examines several possible examples of objectification, ranging from passages drawn from Lawrence, Joyce, James, *Playboy,* a hardcore novel, and Alan Hollinghurst's homoerotic novel. Nussbaum concludes that there is no univocal definition of objectification:

> The concept of objectification is complex and requires much further investigation, as does its relationship to other concepts, such as autonomy, exploitation, and commodification. This preliminary mapping, however, shows, at least, how much work there is to be done; in that way it indicates that analytic philosophy (of, admittedly, an expanded and rather atypical kind) is not without its benefits for feminist politics.

(239)

Her critique of MacKinnon's overly simplistic use of the concept of objectification is to the point. But this is a small point that most feminist theories take for granted today. Nussbaum's neglect of other trends of feminism is surprising for a thinker who is so broad in her scope. In this case, she neglects psychoanalytic feminism that has developed ideas far beyond both MacKinnon's legalism and Nussbaum's own oddly anachronistic critique. That she ignores psychoanalysis is especially strange given her focus on the importance of our emotions. While she refers in passing to Carol Gilligan and Nel Noddings, nowhere is there a reference to Julia Kristeva, Luce Irigaray, Jessica Benjamin, or Teresa Brennan, for example.

Being a good Aristotelian, Nussbaum tries to combine analytic preciseness, dialectical balancing of various disciplines and sides of a question, and rhetorical attention to the emotions. But her chapter on objectification, for example, betrays the limits, on the one hand, of her exaggerated analytic clarity and, on the other hand, of her neglect of dark emotional and rhetorically explosive issues that psychoanalysts, literary critics, and thinkers like Butler explore. Nussbaum is much better than MacKinnon not only in introducing issues from legal and political philosophy but also in exploring just the opposite: non-legal, private issues of emotion, desire, and preference. One could never imagine MacKinnon writing the last chapter of Nussbaum's work, which gives a reading of Virginia Woolf's *To the Lighthouse* that is especially sensitive to the philosophical question of solipsism. But Nussbaum does not extend herself nearly far enough beyond her analytic clarity into the complex and personal issues of the self and our emotional life.

Failing to achieve a true balance of analysis and rhetoric in particular, Nussbaum's thought lacks a full dialectical sense of balance in general. MacKinnon, who attempted to come up with a "feminist theory of the state," at least recognized the need to compare her theory to Marx's comprehensive theory that includes reflection on its own preconditioned place within the practical everyday. For all of her neo-Aristotelian dialectical balances, Nussbaum fails to integrate this most important balance: that of reflexively balancing theory with practice. At times she gestures in passing to the human rights movement and the importance of international agencies. But these are only gestures, and nowhere else in her thought is she attentive to the contingent historical location of this practice—other than in her abstract, jet-setting response to cultural relativism's equally abstract, jet-setting critique of ethnocentric universalism.

Perhaps one should not be surprised by Nussbaum's blind spots. Neglecting history and our own historical moment in favor of trying to analytically specify the universal and trans-historical issue at hand is a common failure in Nussbaum's other works. For example, Morris Dickstein highlights her neglecting of the historical hour of novels in a review of *Poetic Justice.* For him, the "major misstep" of her book is that "Nussbaum's argument depends too much on novels up-to-date in their politics but strictly 19th-century in their storytelling conventions."[2] Like her literary theory, her claim on feminism is up-to-date in some respects, but in other respects oddly anachronistic when compared to other contemporary feminist theorists. While explicitly focused on how even the most private of our emotions are shaped by society, Nussbaum ignores how political ideologies such as her own are also shaped by the historical moment. Paralleling her ahistorical treatment of realistic novels, her defense of a liberalism rejuvenated by international feminism is highly insensitive to its possible historical hour.

Nussbaum, to be sure, is not alone in failing to think one's own specific place within the bad totality of our times. But because it is a pervasive error, we must be especially critical. Against cultural relativists, she with others remarks how no culture is monolithic and how each culture has many different trends and counter-trends, and traditions and counter-traditions, from which to draw. But Nussbaum, like many others today, fails to question just what these trends and traditions might be outside this abstract claim to pluralism. She fails to examine how they might conflict, and in this conflict, what space (other than that of the abstract individual) might be opened for the growth of certain types of liberatory movements. Instead of settling down into these difficult historical, sociological, and political questions that draw upon philosophy, race and post-colonial theory, psychoanalysis, and literary theory, Nussbaum speaks abstractly about the importance of human rights and international law as well as of the epistemological relevance of the emotions and novels in our ethical lives. Like so many others, Nussbaum attempts to be interdisciplinary, but when examined closely, one quickly finds whole areas of thought—areas that are intensely relevant to the issues at hand—strangely ignored. As a result, Nussbaum claims that her feminism constructively reveals problems within liberalism, but the truth is her liberalism blinds her to what insights the full array of feminism has to offer.

Notes

1. Nussbaum's actual critique of Butler is not included within *Sex and Social Justice.* It was published first in a *New Republic* article, and one can only hope that she will include this and other relevant material in her forthcoming *Feminist Internationalism.*

2. Morris Dickstein, "Moral Fictions," *New York Times Book Review,* April 1, 1996, pp. 14-15.

Miranda Fricker (review date August 2000)

SOURCE: Fricker, Miranda. Review of *Sex and Social Justice,* by Martha Nussbaum. *Journal of Philosophy* 97, no. 8 (August 2000): 471-75.

[*In the following review, Fricker offers praise for* Sex and Social Justice, *calling it an impressive, wonderfully diverse, and enormously rewarding collection of essays.*]

The final essay in this impressive volume **Sex and Social Justice,** Martha Nussbaum is a discussion of the quotidian yet complex interpretive enterprise of understanding other people. It presents, in domestic microcosm, many of the themes treated at a more general level in the preceding essays. The focus is on the couple at the center of Virginia Woolf's *To The Lighthouse,* who communicate without giving voice, and concede or hold their ground over their differences without making anything explicit. They sustain a subtle, if fallible, working understanding of each other's thoughts and experiences by drawing silently on their intimate history together. Although most of the rather noisier contexts in which human beings may try to understand each other do not involve any such history of intimacy, Nussbaum's concluding essay appropriately directs one's attention backward through the volume so that one momentarily rereads it whole as an elaboration on our human capacity for sympathetic, sometimes critical, understanding—not only of other individuals but also of other cultures. One must avoid romanticism, of course. Interpersonal understanding between individuals who share a way of life is one thing, and crosscultural understanding another. The question of crosscultural understanding tends to present itself in Western thought as either a hope or an anxiety as to whether we may succeed in understanding others well enough to avoid doing them any harm. (Thinking from a position of power means that the question whether others may be able to understand *us* well enough so that we might avoid being harmed tends not to be raised.) Whether in the form of anxiety or hope, the philosophical question demands attention; but it must not be allowed to paralyze first-order ethical thought. Thus it is right that Nussbaum should address the issue principally at the first-order level. Not, then, by engaging in extended a priori argument about the very idea of crosscultural understanding, but rather through paying close attention to specific cases (the most relevant essay in this connection perhaps being **"Judging Other Cultures: The Case of Genital Mutilation"**). The task is to look and see whether or not the response that a certain practice is unjust constitutes a sensitively informed judgment, or merely an ethical-imperialist reaction. If some particular practice deprives girls and women of realizing a fundamental human capability (the capability for bodily integrity, for example), then one will have found that

something humanly universal is offended and the practice is unjust. The idea of a common humanity is at the heart of Nussbaum's position, and is specified as a set of basic human functional capabilities. The capabilities approach (which, as she says, has also been developed by Amartya Sen) is really the starting point of the book, and the explicit subject matter of the first essays, in which she presents and defends her universalist feminist position.

On Nussbaum's view, there are a number of basic functional capabilities possessed universally by human beings, which justice requires must not be thwarted. If the universalism is to be sound, these capabilities must be described so that they are constant through historical and cultural diversity. But then the list of "Central Human Functional Capabilities" as it is presented here includes two or three things that do not belong. It includes capabilities described in a way that makes them dependent on culturally and historically contingent institutions. The third entry on the list includes "marital rape," which presupposes an institution of marriage; the tenth includes "being able to hold property" and "the right to seek employment on an equal basis with others," which presuppose institutions of private property and competitive employment which belong specifically to capitalist economic systems. These are glitches in an otherwise very plausible and ethically powerful list. But I think they are worth noting, not because they must cast doubt on the overall project—they could surely be reexpressed in more neutral terms, or, if not, the list would in any case remain substantial enough without them—but rather because confidence in the universalist project must be earned precisely by showing that historical and cultural specificity can be kept from creeping into the description of the purportedly universal capabilities.

Nussbaum's feminism "has five salient features: It is *internationalist, humanist, liberal, concerned with the social shaping of preference and desire,* and, finally, *concerned with sympathetic understanding*" (6). It is interesting to reflect on how these features fit together. Many of the essays here contain empirical data and individual case studies (Nussbaum worked for some years for a development agency connected with the United Nations). The empirically informed and politically engaged character of her internationalism affords the theoretical features of her approach their full weight in a deeply convincing ethical position. The engaged stance is a particular strength in staving off the automated skeptical responses of those in the grip of an a priori skepticism about universalist or (as Nussbaum uses the term) humanist projects. One of the conclusions to be drawn from this book, I think, is that any responsible skepticism to the effect that such projects are inevitably culturally imperialist will not be a skepticism a priori. Philosophical skepticism about the very idea of universal human capabilities, or of universal rights to safeguard them, is intellectually facile and ethically obnoxious when clung to in the face of social realities in which women are asymmetrically deprived of the basic education they need for minimal material independence (30), or in which they are prohibited from working outside the home even when staying there means virtual starvation (29). Rather, if there is a responsible skepticism to be reckoned with here, it will be more a historical than a philosophical one, consisting principally of a worldly pessimism at anyone's (and perhaps especially the West's) chances of managing to shape a universalism that avoids doing violence to cultural difference. But a skepticism of pessimism, combined with a practical commitment to justice, is not something to make one give up on a universalism of basic human capabilities and their defense. On the contrary, it is something to make one pursue it with careful and self-conscious attention to particulars—hence the importance of the concern with sympathetic understanding.

The connection between Nussbaum's liberalism and the concern with the social shaping of preference and desire is particularly interesting, not least because the connection is surely not quite as presented. An awareness of the power of ideology (if I may put it that way) in shaping preferences serves as an important corrective to liberalism's asocializing individualist drift. As Nussbaum nicely puts it:

> Any living culture contains plurality and argument; it contains relatively powerful voices, relatively silent voices, and voices that cannot speak at all in the public space. Often some of these voices would speak differently, too, if they had more information or were less frightened—so part of a culture, too, is what its members *would* say if they were freer or more fully informed.
>
> (8)

Quite. As I see it, then, Nussbaum's liberalism takes from feminism what feminism took from socialism: most particularly, the insight that what oppressed people want is not always what is in their interests, that is, not always what they would want if they had access to the bigger picture. One of the essays is entirely devoted to the feminist critique of liberalism, and Nussbaum's espousal of liberalism is explicitly informed by that critique—specifically, by the idea that desires and preferences, and indeed emotions quite generally, are socially formed. But it is odd that the only precedents traced for this idea are precursors in the liberal tradition. It is well worth having it drawn to one's attention that Jean-Jacques Rousseau, Adam Smith, and J. S. Mill (78) all expressed views about the social shaping of emotions, and that so did the Greek and Roman Stoics (Introduction, 12). But the liberalism that Nussbaum espouses surely owes a direct debt to socialist thought—

most notably the insights expressed there in terms of ideology and false consciousness—and this debt is obscured by the emphasis on liberal and ancient precursors. Nussbaum's feminism, then, surely has a more mixed intellectual inheritance than she represents. But the result is no less exciting: a liberal feminist position which (like some other liberal feminist work—for instance, that of Susan Okin) is properly inflected by an awareness that inequalities of power can create an uneven pitch for the actual exercise of individual freedoms.

This is a wonderfully diverse volume of essays, so much so that one is forced to discuss it in the broad; and yet one cannot hope to do justice to its breadth, or its depth, by attending to the general ethical trajectory alone. There is some slight repetition, chiefly in discussions of Catharine MacKinnon and Andrea Dworkin. This is perhaps inevitable in essays written over a span of seven years, and would not be worth mentioning except that it is also in part the result of what I am personally inclined to consider an unduly exclusive attention to MacKinnon's and Dworkin's work (the exclusivity can create the false impression that the feminist insight into power's conditioning of sexual desire is owed uniquely to them; see 78). Be that as it may, this volume is a feast, with essays treating matters arising directly from development work, from the reading of fiction, from first-order political commitments, from competing philosophical conceptions of justice, and also from more personal autobiographical concerns. Thus, there are discussions of women's literacy, genital mutilation, the moral authority of religion, the place of mercy within justice, lesbian and gay rights, prostitution, and sexual objectification; and there is also a personal discussion of Kenneth Dover's life, to whom the volume is dedicated. All make enormously rewarding reading, and the philosophy is lit up by Nussbaum's sensitive and perceptive drawing on real-life stories. The two parts of the book—"Justice" and "Sex"—give a broad division of themes, but the essays are bound together as a whole by a family of thematic relations: sex, gender, sexuality, and justice. What emerges from these luminous writings is a sense of an utterly authentic ethical outlook whose commitment to the dignity of human life, in all its diverse cultural forms, may well be enough to put paid to the skepticism of pessimism with which some readers, not altogether without reason, might approach it.

Hilary Charlesworth (essay date October 2000)

SOURCE: Charlesworth, Hilary. "Martha Nussbaum's Feminist Internationalism." *Ethics* 111, no. 1 (October 2000): 64-78.

[*In the following essay, Charlesworth examines two major challenges facing feminist internationalism: state hostility to feminist internationalism and differences among women within the global community. Charles-worth evaluates the extent to which Nussbaum's "capabilities" approach to feminist internationalism adequately addresses these issues.*]

The term 'feminist internationalism' generally means the elaboration of transnational principles and standards to advance the position of women. The move to define international benchmarks to improve women's globally disadvantaged situation has a long history. For example, international women's groups were established in the late nineteenth and early twentieth centuries to deal with issues such as equal access to education and training and women's suffrage.[1] Women's groups lobbied the League of Nations and the International Labour Organisation to develop standards and practices relating to matters such as the nationality of married women, trafficking in women and girls, women's suffrage, and the working conditions of women.[2] Since the founding of the United Nations in 1945, the international arena has become increasingly attractive for women's groups, which have worked to persuade states to adopt treaties and resolutions dealing with many aspects of women's lives. The most significant of these international standards is the 1979 Convention on the Elimination of All Forms of Discrimination against Women.

Feminist internationalism has encountered considerable controversy and resistance from various quarters. A major source of antipathy is from states (whether "liberal" or "religious") which regard recourse to international standards with respect to women as illegitimate because they may challenge national culture, traditions, policies, and laws. A different form of resistance to feminist internationalism comes from some feminist activists and scholars who regard it as dependent on essentialist accounts of women, obliterating differences of race, class, wealth, sexuality, and so on.

Prompted by her work as a research adviser at the United Nations University's World Institute for Development Economics Research, beginning in 1986, Martha Nussbaum has developed a theory of human capabilities to inform feminist internationalism. From evidence of the second-class status of women across the developing and developed country divide and their consistently lower quality of life when measured by access to health, education, political liberty and participation, employment, self-respect, and life itself, Nussbaum argues [in *Sex and Social Justice*] that "the situation of women in the contemporary world calls urgently for moral standtaking."[3] Nussbaum considers utilitarianism to be an unsatisfactory basis for such moral standtaking because it is unable to adequately account for the pressures of tradition in the measurement of individual preferences or desires.[4] Rawlsian liberalism is also deficient as a basis for determining justice in

this context, according to Nussbaum, because of its focus on the distribution of resources such as wealth and its failure to pay attention to the links between having particular resources and the capacity to function as a human being.[5]

Nussbaum's response to the injustice of women's position is a version of the "capabilities" approach to the measurement of the quality of life and the development of public policy. This approach has been cultivated in development economics by Amartya Sen and has guided the United Nations Development Programme's annual *Human Development Reports* in the 1990s. The capabilities approach concentrates on the actual functioning of individuals and groups in areas deemed central to the quality of life. It is less interested than utilitarianism in the stated preferences of people, because it regards such preferences as affected by traditions of oppression; and it is less concerned than liberalism with the distribution of resources, because it regards resources as of value only insofar as they contribute to human functioning.[6]

Nussbaum's capabilities approach to feminist internationalism then focuses on women's abilities to do and be certain things deemed valuable.[7] The approach is concerned with capability to function, rather than functioning itself, because it emphasizes the role of practical reason and choice in exploiting the capability.[8] The central human capacities identified by Nussbaum (which are all inter related) are longevity and bodily integrity (clauses 1-3), emotional, affective, social, and mental development (clauses 4, 5, 7, and 9), the ability to engage in practical reason and to form a conception of the good (clause 6), the ability to live with concern for animals and the natural world (clause 8), and control over one's political and material environment (clause 10). The list of central human capabilities has evolved considerably since Nussbaum first began writing about them.[9] The idea is that a person who lacks any of the capabilities cannot be said to have a good human life. Thus development and preservation of the capabilities must be the central goal of all public policy making. In the context of the inequalities women experience across the world, the capacities become claims that can be made by women, which generate concomitant political duties.[10]

I want to consider two different types of challenges to feminist internationalism in the context of international law and to examine how far Nussbaum's capabilities approach can respond to these issues. The first category of challenge arises from the antipathy of particular states to claims of women's equality. The second group is the product of differences among women and the significance that feminists attach to these differences.

State Hostility to Feminist
Internationalism

The traditional understanding of international law is that it is universally applicable and binds all states, whatever their specific national circumstances. There have been a range of challenges to this account of international law: for example, developing nations have argued at various times that particular norms of international environmental law, trade law, and human rights law were Western constructs whose effect was to impose unfair restraints on governmental action. Despite these challenges, certain norms of international law have been widely accepted as fundamental to the international community and global in their application. These include the norm of nondiscrimination on the basis of race, the prohibition on slavery, and the prohibition on torture. These laws are regularly flouted in practice, but no state or international institution would now question their legal nature and significance.

Although it has an apparently similar legal pedigree to the prohibition of racial discrimination, expressed in treaty provisions, the norm of nondiscrimination on the basis of sex has in practice a much reduced status in international law. When international law and lawyers address the issues of women's global inequality, they are prepared to accept arguments and positions that would not be tolerated in other areas. Claims of culture and religion readily trump women's rights. One example of this is the position taken by the international community with respect to reservations to the United Nations' Convention on the Elimination of All Forms of Discrimination against Women of 1979 (the Women's Convention), the most detailed international expression of the principle of sex equality. Although the convention is widely ratified (with 162 states parties in January 2000), it is subject to an extraordinary number of formal reservations made by states when ratifying the treaty. The legal effect of a reservation is to modify a state's obligation to implement the treaty. Many of the reservations are in the name of preserving a state's religious or cultural traditions.[11] Typical of these reservations is that of Egypt. With respect to article 16 of the Women's Convention, which requires that states observe equality between men and women in all matters concerning marriage and family relations, Egypt's reservation states that this matter must be subject to Islamic Shari'a law.

Some states have made even more sweeping reservations. For example, the Maldives' reservation commits it to comply with the convention's provisions "except those which the Government may consider contradictory to the principles of the Islamic Shari'a upon which the laws and the traditions of the Maldives is founded." Moreover, the reservation goes on to say, "the Republic of Maldives does not see itself bound by any provisions of the Convention which obliges it to change its Constitutions and laws in any manner." While there is little question that this type of reservation is technically invalid at international law because it undermines the object and purpose of the treaty,[12] there are no satisfactory mechanisms in international law to challenge reservations adequately. A number of states have objected to the reservations, but the objections have been rejected by the Islamic states as a form of religious intolerance, and there the matter rests.[13] Thus Islamic states are still considered parties to the Women's Convention although they have rejected the equality provisions that are at its heart. Israel, India, and the United Kingdom also have entered reservations making the laws of religious communities immune to the convention's guarantee of sex equality. Other states, such as Australia, have not formally made reservations precluding the application of the principle of sex equality to religious communities, but they have exempted religions from the principle in legislation designed to implement the Women's Convention.[14] The pattern of reservations to and implementation of the International Convention on the Elimination of Racial Discrimination of 1965 (CERD) provides a striking contrast. Although similar numbers of states have accepted both the Women's Convention and CERD, few reservations have been made to the substance of the obligation of nondiscrimination on the basis of race.

How can feminist internationalism effectively challenge the power of claims of culture and religion in international law? One method is to analyze the political uses of claims of culture. In other words, we need to ask whose culture is being invoked, what the status of the interpreter is, in whose name the argument is advanced, and who the primary beneficiaries of the invocation of culture are.[15] In the case of Islamic states, for example, "culture" is regularly used as an interchangeable rationale with "the rule of law," "public order and morality," and "state policy" to suppress any activism by women.[16] An example of this was the reported statement by the governor of Kandahar, a province of Afghanistan, rejecting attempts by the Grameen bank of Bangladesh to lend money to rural women to start their own businesses. He was quoted as saying that "the motive of the bank was to lead Moslems away from Islam and to promote shamelessness among women."[17]

The capabilities approach elaborated by Martha Nussbaum offers a detailed method to challenge invocations of culture in international law to justify the denial of women's equality. Although Nussbaum does not address the relationship of the central human fundamental capabilities to the existing body of international human rights law, many of the capabilities she identifies have a counterpart in the rights recognized in international law. For example the capability of "being able to live to the end of a human life of normal length" (clause 1) is closely linked to the right to life set out in article 6 of the International Covenant on Civil and Political Rights (ICCPR). Some of Nussbaum's capabilities extend and develop existing human rights guarantees. Thus the capability of senses, imagination, and thought (clause 4) appears to build on the right to education recognized in the International Covenant on Economic, Social and Cultural Rights (ICESCR) and the right to freedoms of expression and religious exercise contained in the IC-CPR but also covers abilities that have no international legal protection such as that to have pleasurable experiences and to avoid nonbeneficial pain. Other of the capabilities are not articulated in the human rights treaties, such as the ability to live with concern for and in relation to animals, plants, and the world of nature (clause 8). Nussbaum's list of capabilities, then, is a more detailed, and modern, prescription than offered by international human rights treaties.

The current system of monitoring a state's performance of its human rights obligations under United Nations treaties is primarily through periodic reporting by states to expert committees. The treaty-monitoring committees review the reports and question the representatives of states about problems they identify. The final step in this monitoring process is the adoption of a formal statement of conclusions by the relevant committee, which is forwarded to the United Nations General Assembly. The rationale for the reporting system is both to encourage states to scrutinize critically national practices in the preparation of reports (perhaps leading to reform) and to expose (and perhaps eradicate) human rights violations through international monitoring.[18] These aims have not been met in practice. The reporting process has been criticized for its weakness, allowing states to paper over bad human rights records with references to fine legislative guarantees.[19] The "constructive dialogue" engaged in between committees and state representatives is often a dialogue of the deaf, with states either ignoring evidence of inadequate protection of human rights or sloughing it off with bland reassurances. Most of the states' reports present the existence of legal protection, constitutional or otherwise, as proof of implementation of the international standards. The significance of the capabilities approach is that it moves the focus of rights protection from the provision of legal guarantees, which may be of limited utility, to the way that national legal and policy systems actually ensure the quality of life of individuals and groups—in Nussbaum's words, "What are the people of the group or country in question actually able to do and to be?"[20] While the various human rights treaty-monitoring committees vary in their practices and efficacy, the idea of central human capabilities could be readily absorbed into their work.

For example, economic, social, and cultural rights, such as the right to food and shelter, have often been regarded as particularly difficult to protect because they require positive action rather than restraints on government action (the traditional account of the protection of civil and political rights). In periodic reports under the ICESCR, states tend simply to list laws and practices touching on these rights as proof of their protection. Australia's 1998 report under ICESCR is a paradigm of this approach.[21] Viewed from the perspective of human capabilities, the lengthy Australian report provides no information at all. It does not address how any of the relevant capabilities identified by Nussbaum are fulfilled—what people within Australia are actually able to do and to be. How many people are adequately nourished? How many have adequate shelter?

The Committee on Economic, Social and Cultural Rights, which monitors the ICESCR, has been in fact the most exigent of all the human rights treaty bodies. It has developed the idea of "minimum core entitlements" under the ICESCR in these terms: "A State party in which any significant number of individuals is deprived of essential foodstuffs, of essential primary health care, of basic shelter and housing, or of the most basic forms of education is, prima facie, failing to discharge its obligations under the Covenant."[22] While this notion has some affinity with the capabilities approach, the latter is considerably broader. The term 'minimum core entitlements' suggests mere survival, a "bare humanness."[23] Nussbaum's account of central human capabilities is, by contrast, built on a commitment to full human functioning and flourishing. The capabilities approach would therefore extend the boundaries of current understandings of economic, social, and cultural rights.

In the specific context of women's rights, the capabilities approach could similarly broaden and make more concrete the obligations contained in the Women's Convention. States' reports under the Convention typically set out nondiscrimination provisions in constitutions and legislation with little or no assessment of their impact in practice. If the question asked by the Committee on the Elimination of Discrimination against Women is to what extent are women in a particular society capable of performing the central human functions identified by Nussbaum, the investigation must shift from formal guarantees to structural barriers to equality. Thus economic data indicating that, in all societies, women live in greater poverty than men will be of greater significance in measuring implementation of the Women's Convention than legal commitments to equality.[24] The capabilities approach would require the treaty bodies to seek and consider broader forms of evidence and to devise empirical strategies to define and measure rights.[25]

The capabilities approach could also inform the assessment of reservations to the Women's Convention made in the name of culture and religion. If the effect of reservations is to reduce women's opportunities to live a fully human life, for example, by preventing effective participation in political choices governing one's life (clause 10), the reservation cannot be considered compatible with the treaty obligations. Nussbaum's insistence that "a woman's affiliation with a certain group or culture should not be taken as normative for her unless, on due consideration, with all the capabilities at her disposal, she makes that norm her own" offers a method to counter resort to claims of culture to trump women's rights in international law.[26] It is not clear, however, what type of evidence would be necessary to establish that a woman has not made a particular communal norm "her own." Does it require active rejection and protest, or is Nussbaum proposing an assumption that any practice that does not treat women in the same way as men could not be taken as normative for women without proof of active embrace of the practice?

The United Nations treaty-monitoring committees all use "general comments" or "general recommendations" to elaborate their jurisprudence on particular rights as a guide to states, and these comments are regularly reviewed and updated. These statements could provide a vehicle for introducing the notion of capabilities and analyzing their relationship with the open-textured treaty statements of rights. In the case of the capabilities proposed by Nussbaum that have no direct treaty counterpart, such as that to have the opportunity for sexual satisfaction and for choice in matters of reproduction (clause 3), the capabilities approach would provoke more controversy. The idea that women have these capabilities has been strongly resisted, for example, by a coalition of Islamic and Catholic states at the 1995 Beijing conference.

The capabilities approach also has significance outside the context of treaty obligations. It offers a method to consider all cases where women's rights are trumped by claims of culture and tradition. For example, in a 1999 decision of the Supreme Court of Zimbabwe, *Venia Magaya v. Nakayi Shonhiwa Magayavenia,* Shona traditional customs were relied on to prevent a woman from inheriting her father's estate.[27] The Zimbabwe Constitution prohibits discrimination, although not specifically discrimination based on sex. It also excludes African customary law from the nondiscrimination principle. The court resisted arguments to interpret the constitution in the light of international law on the basis that "allowing female children to inherit in a broadly patrilineal society . . . would disrupt the African customary laws of that society." It also stated "there is a need to advance gender equality in all spheres of society . . . [but] great care must be taken when African customary law is under consideration . . . The application of customary law is in a way voluntary. It could therefore be argued that there should be no or little interference with a person's choice." Nussbaum's ac-

count of the capabilities approach offers a response to these arguments. A woman must be shown to have accepted the norms of a particular culture through the exercise of practical reason, with all the central human capabilities available to her, before those norms can be held to bind her. The Zimbabwe case however also highlights the problematic notion of choice in Nussbaum's theory. Can a woman authentically choose to accept discriminatory practices that reduce her human capabilities? Nussbaum's version of feminist internationalism is built on the significance of choice in liberal philosophy, and yet there is the implication that the choice of inequality would be irrational in some way.[28]

DIFFERENCES AMONG WOMEN

A second type of challenge facing feminist internationalism in international law arises from the differences in the position of women worldwide. Can we use the term 'women' as a global category when women's positions and interests vary so widely? Factors such as class, race, wealth, sexuality, nationality, social and economic position, and physical and mental disabilities affect women's lives in important ways and may be more significant than sex in determining a particular woman's quality of life. In an international context, feminists have dealt with the issue of differences among women by focusing on problems women appear to face whatever their situation.[29] In practice, women from very different backgrounds have worked successfully together at an international level to raise awareness of oppressive and discriminatory practices. For example, the four United Nations conferences on women (Mexico [1975], Copenhagen [1980], Nairobi [1985], and Beijing [1995]), and particularly their respective associated nongovernment forums, indicate that women are able to use international arenas to negotiate a great range of differences to support both common projects and common concerns of particular groups. The campaign for recognition of violence against women, prevalent in all countries and cultures, as a violation of women's human rights has been particularly effective as a unifying force in international feminism.

The tactic of identifying and addressing common global issues for women is, however, complex and sometimes hazardous. For example, there are disagreements about whether specific practices constitute violence against women, and there are deep divisions over the appropriate methods to deal with a problem. The debate over the appropriate feminist responses to female genital mutilation illustrates this. No other issue has attracted such controversy and passion. Some international lawyers have argued that female genital mutilation is morally comparable to cosmetic surgery undertaken by women in the developed world, and they have replaced the pejorative terminology 'mutilation' with 'surgery'.[30] Others have rejected such parallels and argued for international legal prohibition.

More generally, the search for "universal" women's predicaments can obscure differences among women and homogenize women's experiences. Feminists from the developing world often charge Western feminists with being overly concerned with the acquisition of civil and political rights while ignoring the significance of economic and social rights, such as the right to food and to housing, or collective rights such as the right to self-determination and development. Emphasis on universal issues can also sideline the situation of women who suffer from multiple forms of discrimination, for example, because of their race, class, age, and sexual orientation. Certainly, the international legal system has been slow to accommodate ideas of diversity of women. The Fourth World Conference on Women in Beijing in 1995 paid some attention to the intersection of a variety of obstacles to women's empowerment, for example, race, age, language, ethnicity, culture, religion, disability, indigeneity, family, and socioeconomic status, or status as refugees or displaced persons or as victims of environmental damage, disease, or violence, although it ultimately failed to acknowledge sexual orientation as an aspect of women's identity.[31] But, apart from this listing, no further attention was given to diversity between women in the official Beijing documents. In any event, the acknowledgment of some forms of women's diversity was undermined by the limited vision of women's roles in the Beijing Platform for Action. Debate in Beijing about what might constitute "balanced and nonstereotyped" images of women resulted in a paragraph referring to women's experiences as including "balancing work and family responsibilities, as mothers, as professionals, as managers, as entrepreneurs."[32] In other words, the traditional role of mother remains crucial for women, and all that is added is the need to participate in the free market economy.[33]

How does Nussbaum's capabilities approach respond to the question of differences among women and the charge that the international human rights system cannot deliver a contextualized form of justice for women everywhere? Nussbaum has usefully drawn attention to the dangers of confusing differences among women with the way that women are treated in particular societies. For example, she has observed that, in the name of antiessentialism, some scholars, otherwise committed to the advancement of women, have espoused reactionary, oppressive, and sexist positions.[34] The capabilities approach with its regularly revised list of central human capabilities also responds to the often-voiced criticism of the international human rights system by feminists from the developing world that it gives priority to civil and political rights. It transcends the traditional division of civil and political rights on the one hand and economic and social rights on the other. Nussbaum's list of central human functional capabilities includes a range of civil and political rights (freedom of expression [clause 4], liberty of conscience [clause 6], as well

as rights to health, food, and shelter [clause 3]). At the same time, the silences of some versions of the list may be taken to reflect a limited notion of differences among women: for example, nondiscrimination on the basis of race, sex, and sexual orientation is considered central but non-discrimination on the basis of disability is not.[35]

A related concern for feminist internationalism in the context of international law is the issue of how far it needs to rely on the language of universalism. Claims based on universal values increasingly generate tensions and objections in international law-making forums because the vocabulary of universalism is associated with Western traditions. The development of international law relied on European ideals as universals and these standards were imposed by colonialism and conequest.[36] The term 'universal' thus carries with it considerable baggage in international law: it implies a worldview of the economically dominant and does not give emphasis to the significance of interpretation (or 'phronesis', in Aristotle's terms) in the local application of international legal norms. There have been longstanding, and rather sterile, debates between international lawyers about whether legal principles are based on relative or universal values. The extremes of both positions do not, however, acknowledge the complex interdependence of the local and the universal in international law.

Nussbaum firmly links the ideas of universalism and feminist internationalism, but is this critical to her project? She is clearly using the notion of universality in a broader way than most international lawyers because of the emphasis she places on the revisability of her list of central human capabilities. A more useful guide for feminist internationalism than the language of universals may be the idea of commitments developed through dialogue. One such technique is that of "world traveling," which depends upon what Maria Lugones has called a "loving perception" of other women.[37] This involves three steps in a multicultural conversation: first, the need to be explicit about our own historical and cultural context; second, an attempt to understand how other women might see us; and third, a recognition of the complexities of the contexts of other women, in other words, to try to see them through their own eyes.[38] A similar method is that of "rooting" and "shifting" described by some European feminists. Each woman remains "rooted" in her own history and identity while "shifting" to understand the roots of other women in the dialogue. This process of what has been termed "transversalism" has two conditions: it should not mean losing one's own roots and values nor should it homogenize "other" women.[39] Transversalism differs from universalism by allowing multiple points of departure rather than assuming that there is a universal bedrock of values in all societies.

The value of the idea of world traveling in the context of international law is its emphasis on the multiplicity of women's stories and the range of their cultural, national, religious, economic, and social concerns and interests. Analysis of this discipline means confronting the inevitable tension between general theories and local experience, being receptive to a diversity of voices and perspectives. In other words, world travelers must use different modes of transport according to the terrain. As Elizabeth Grosz has observed, "feminists are not faced with pure and impure options. All options are in their various ways bound by the constraints of patriarchal power. The crucial political question is which commitments remain, in spite of their patriarchal alignments, of use to feminists in their political struggles? What kind of feminist strategy do they make possible or hinder?"[40]

Chandra Mohanty has proposed the idea of an "imagined community" (borrowed from Benedict Anderson) that has implications for feminist analysis of international law.[41] Mohanty has developed the notion in the context of problems of writing about Third World feminisms in a general but worthwhile way, but it can be usefully extended to all women in an international context. The epithet "imagined" is used in contrast to existing boundaries—of nation, color, sexuality, and so on—to indicate the potential for collaborative endeavour across them; the term 'community' refers to the possibility of a "horizontal comradeship" across existing hierarchies. An "imagined community" of feminist interests does not imply a single set of feminist concerns but, rather, a strategic, political alliance.

In the context of international law, then, I think that feminists need to attend to the complex structures of domination that affect women differently rather than invoke a single, universal notion of oppression. Donna Haraway has wryly observed the difficulty of this task: "It has seemed very rare for feminist theory to hold race, sex/gender and class analytically together—all the best intentions, hues of authors, and remarks in prefaces notwithstanding."[42]

Despite her attachment to the vocabulary of universality, Nussbaum's capabilities approach is a concrete version of "world traveling"—an internationally applicable baseline to measure women's progress toward equality, which is derived from considerable consultation with women in many different situations. Nussbaum has spoken of her search for a "subtle balance between perception of the particular and recognition of the common."[43] The term 'feminism' has little meaning if it does not extend beyond purely local concerns, but the use of feminist theories on a global level requires attention to the way that these theories can privilege some women's experiences over others.

Do the "central human functional capabilities" identified by Nussbaum meet this standard? As I have noted above, they transcend the standard Western obsession with civil and political liberties at the expense of economic and social equity. The vocabulary of the list, however, may indicate that greater weight is accorded to civil and political rights. For example, the language of "guarantees of freedoms" is used only with respect to freedom of expression and freedom of religious exercise (clause 4), and the term 'right' is used only with respect to political participation, protection of free speech and association (clause 10), and not in other contexts. Freedoms of speech and association are described as "fundamental." The status of group rights is also not clear in the capabilities approach, which appears interested primarily in the lives of individuals. For example, how can the claims of groups of indigenous peoples to self-determination be understood?[44] Another human rights concern prompted by Nussbaum's list of capabilities is that it appears applicable only to citizens of a country.[45] This leaves open the question, of increasing significance all around the world, of the rights of noncitizens to the conditions of a reasonable life.

A crucial issue for the capabilities approach is how conflicts between different central capabilities will be resolved. For example, freedom of religious exercise will regularly clash with the norm of nondiscrimination on the basis of sex and sexuality. At the international political and legal level such conflicts are almost invariably resolved in favor of religious freedom. Nussbaum takes a different tack, arguing that religious laws cannot be allowed to trump the "basic human rights of citizens," which include nondiscrimination on the basis of sex.[46] She implies a hierarchy in the central capabilities, with nondiscrimination taking precedence over all others, although her parallel insistence on the fundamental nature of freedom of speech and association to human functioning generates a tension at the top of the hierarchy.

From the perspective of international law, some of the capabilities identified by Nussbaum are described in language whose force has been whittled away. For example, the capability of affiliation includes the ability "to be treated as a dignified being whose worth is equal to that of others" (clause 7). Nussbaum observes that this capability requires guarantees of nondiscrimination. However, the interpretation of the norm of nondiscrimination in international law indicates that in practice this is a weak conceptual tool to counter systemic, large-scale oppression.[47] By contrast, notions of equality of outcome, which allow for positive measures to benefit marginalized groups, may be of greater value for women. More generally, the rights of political participation, free speech, and freedom of association (clause 10), referred to in Nussbaum's list, have been interpreted in narrow ways in the international human rights system and would need considerable development to have transformative outcomes.

CONCLUSION

The international legal system has not responded adequately to the global situation of women. It has acknowledged inequality only in very limited contexts and in any event has allowed states to justify their treatment of women on the basis of tradition and culture. Nussbaum's version of feminist internationalism with its statement of commitments to particular central human capabilities offers a focus for activism and development of the law. It allows us to understand the barriers to women's equality as not simply the product of inadequate resources but as the product of curtailment of women's capabilities imposed by tradition and culture. On a broader level, Nussbaum's approach encourages a shift in direction in international law by placing human needs rather than state priorities at its center. In my view, feminist internationalism requires us to rethink the accepted dichotomy between national sovereignty and international concern. We need to investigate the way that the structure of the state and its sovereignty are gendered and the barriers they create for real justice for women.

Notes

1. Deborah Stienstra, *Women's Movements and International Organisations* (London: Macmillan, 1994), pp. 48-51.

2. Ibid., pp. 65-75; Carol Lubin and Anne Winslow, *Social Justice for Women: The International Labor Organization and Women* (Durham, N.C.: Duke University Press, 1990), pp. 21-30.

3. Martha Nussbaum, *Sex and Social Justice* (Oxford: Oxford University Press, 1999), p. 31.

4. Ibid., p. 33.

5. Ibid., p. 34.

6. Ibid.

7. A recent statement of this approach is in ibid., pp. 39-42. References to clauses are to the list at pp. 41-42.

8. Ibid., pp. 42-44.

9. Nussbaum has emphasized the dynamic nature of the list. See her "Capabilities and Human Rights," *Fordham Law Review* 66 (1997): 273-300 For example, earlier versions included more specific attention to standard of living, measured by income relative to the poverty level.

10. Nussbaum, *Sex and Social Justice,* p. 43.

11. For the text of reservations, see http://www.un.org/depts/treaty. For a discussion of the issue of reservations in the context of the Women's Convention, see

R. Cook, "Reservations to the Convention on the Elimination of All Forms of Discrimination against Women," *Virginia Journal of International Law* 30 (1990): 643-716, pp. 673-78.

12. United Nations, Conference on the Law of Treaties, *Vienna Convention on the Law of Treaties,* 1969, 1155 UNTS, U.N. Document A/Conf. 39/27, p. 331, arts. 19-21.

13. States that have objected to the reservations include Austria, Canada, Denmark, Finland, Portugal, and Sweden. The objections can be found at http://www.un.org/depts/treaty. On the objections as a form of religious intolerance, see Ann Elizabeth Mayer, "Cultural Particularism as a Bar to Women's Rights: Reflections on the Middle East Experience," in *Women's Rights, Human Rights,* ed. Julie Peters and Andrea Wolper (New York: Routledge, 1995), pp. 176-88, p. 178.

14. Commonwealth of Australia, Sex Discrimination Act, 1984, sec. 37.

15. Arati Rao, "The Politics of Gender and Culture in International Human Rights Discourse," in Peters and Wolper, eds., pp. 167-75, p. 174.

16. Mayer, p. 182.

17. *The Bulletin* (Sydney) (September 23, 1997).

18. Anne Bayefsky, "Making the Human Rights Treaty Bodies Work," in *Human Rights: An Agenda for the Next Century,* ed. Louis Henkin and John Lawrence Hargrove (Washington, D.C.: American Society of International Law, 1994), pp. 229-95, p. 232.

19. Ibid., p. 231.

20. Nussbaum, *Sex and Social Justice,* p. 34.

21. See http://www.austlii.edu.au/ofat/reports/Icescr.html.

22. United Nations, Committee on Economic, Social and Cultural Rights, *The Nature of States Parties Obligations,* General Comment no. 3, 1990, E/C.12/1990/8.

23. Nussbaum, *Sex and Social Justice,* p. 40.

24. For economic data on women's poverty as compared with men, see Clair Apodaca, "Measuring Women's Economic and Social Rights Achievement," *Human Rights Quarterly* 20 (1998): 139-72, pp. 154-56.

25. Ibid.

26. Nussbaum, *Sex and Social Justice,* p. 46.

27. *Venia Magaya v. Nakayi Shonhiwa Magayavenia,* Civil Appeal No. 635/92, Harare, February 16, 1999.

28. Anne Phillips, "Feminism and Liberalism Revisited: Has Martha Nussbaum Got It Right?" (paper presented at the Workshop on Feminist and Social Political Theory, Australian National University, Canberra, March 28, 2000).

29. For example, Dorothy Thomas and R. Levi, "Common Abuses against Women," in *Women and International Human Rights Law,* ed. Kelly Askin and Dorean Koenig (New York: Transnational, 1999), pp. 139-76, p. 139.

30. For example, Isabelle Gunning, "Arrogant Perception, World-Travelling and Multicultural Feminism: The Case of Female Genital Surgeries," *Columbia Human Rights Law Review* 23 (1991-92): 189-248.

31. Fourth World Conference on Women, *Beijing Platform for Action* (New York: United Nations Division for the Advancement of Women, 1995), par. 46 (http://www.un.org/womenwatch/daw/beijing/platform/index.ht).

32. Ibid., par. 245 (b).

33. Dianne Otto, "Holding up Half the Sky, but for Whose Benefit? A Critical Analysis of the Fourth World Conference on Women," *Australian Feminist Law Journal* 6 (1996): 7-28, p. 27.

34. Martha Nussbaum, "Human Functioning and Social Justice: In Defense of Aristotelian Essentialism," *Political Theory* 20 (1992): 202-46, p. 212.

35. The version of the list used by M. Nussbaum in a lecture at the Australian National University, Canberra, June 15, 1999.

36. Antony Anghie, "Universality and the Concept of Governance in International Law," in *Legitimate Governance in Africa,* ed. E. K. Quashigah and O. C. Okafor (The Hague: Kluwer Law International, 1999), pp. 21-40, pp. 31-33.

37. Maria Lugones, "Playfulness, 'World-Travelling,' and Loving Perception," *Hypatia* 2 (1987): 3-19, p. 18.

38. Gunning, p. 191.

39. See, generally, Hilary Charlesworth and Christine Chinkin, *The Boundaries of International Law* (Manchester: Manchester University Press, 2000), pp. 51-52.

40. Elizabeth Grosz, "A Note on Essentialism and Difference," in *Feminist Knowledge: Critique and Construct,* ed. Sneja Gunew (London: Routledge, 1990), pp. 332-44, pp. 342-43.

41. Benedict Anderson, *Imagined Communities: Reflections on the Origins and Spread of Nationalism,* rev. ed. (London: Verso, 1991); Chandra Mohanty, "Cartographies of Struggle," in *Third World Women and the Politics of Feminism,* ed. Chandra Mohanty, Ann Russo, and Lourdes Torres (Bloomington: Indiana University Press, 1991), pp. 1-47, p. 4.

42. Donna Haraway, *Simians, Cyborgs and Women: The Reinvention of Nature* (New York: Routledge, 1991), p. 129.

43. Nussbaum, *Sex and Social Justice,* p. 380, n. 42.

44. Ibid., p. 42.

45. Ibid., p. 43.

46. Ibid., p. 103.

47. Charlesworth and Chinkin, pp. 214-16.

Iris Marion Young (review date July 2001)

SOURCE: Young, Iris Marion. Review of *Sex and Social Justice,* by Martha Nussbaum. *Ethics* 111, no. 4 (July 2001): 819-23.

[*In the following review, Young calls Nussbaum's* Sex and Social Justice *a significant achievement that addresses pressing contemporary and moral problems.*]

This collection of fifteen essays [*Sex and Social Justice*], all previously published in some form, ranges over issues of contemporary politics, policy, and law concerning gender and sexuality, as well as reflects on themes of knowledge and emotion in ancient and modern philosophy and literature. Certain of the essays recalled for me the pleasure and admiration I felt for Nussbaum's earlier work interpreting ancient thought. **"Equity and Mercy,"** for example, develops ideas of Aristotle and Seneca to argue against strongly retributive impulses in both criminal law and the politics of oppressed people. In **"Constructing Love, Desire, and Care,"** Nussbaum endorses claims that the meanings of love and sexuality are socially constructed and culturally variable, usefully elaborating the claim by discussing ancient Greek understandings of sexual norms and feelings of familial caring.

"Platonic Love and Colorado Law: The Relevance of Ancient Greek Norms to Modern Sexual Controversies" expands this attention to the social specificity of sexual norms, focusing specifically on the ideas of Socrates, Plato, and Aristotle about homosexuality. This essay grows out of Nussbaum's testimony in a series of court proceedings that eventually resulted in the 1996 U.S. Supreme Court decision against the constitutionality of Colorado Amendment 2. The Colorado law had made it illegal for any state or local government agent to institute regulations or ordinances forbidding discrimination based on sexual orientation. Nussbaum was asked to testify before the Colorado State Supreme Court as an expert witness concerning whether Great Thinkers of the Western World—Socrates, Plato, and Aristotle—really did condone homosexuality. Thoroughly and sometimes dramatically, Nussbaum answers emphatically yes. While the great thinkers made many distinctions between praiseworthy and blameworthy sexual conduct, none of them (with the possible exception of Plato in the *Laws*) condemned homosexual conduct as such, and in some ways praised it. Nussbaum further argues that the Athenians did not even distinguish between heterosexual and homosexual orientations, much less normalize heterosexuality. This essay is fun to read because Nussbaum documents her claims almost to the point of ironic overkill.

Several of the essays in this volume apply the particular vision of liberalism which Nussbaum advocates in her introduction to moral analysis of important contemporary sexuality issues—lesbian and gay rights, pornography and sexual objectification, and prostitution. In **"Objectification,"** and **"Rage and Reason,"** Nussbaum successfully tempers several polemical feminist overgeneralizations, notably that all objectification is morally problematic or that anger is always and only the appropriate response to sexism. **"Whether from Reason or Prejudice: Taking Money for Bodily Services"** passionately and cogently defends the liberty of women to work as prostitutes without fear of legal prosecution or harassment. Nussbaum thereby skillfully reconstructs the moral issues of prostitution as about work: the morality of wage labor, circumstances that foster desperate labor contracts, evaluation of working conditions, and so on. This essay is one of the finest moral analytical works on prostitution that I have read.

There is much worth praising and endorsing in this collection. For the remainder of this review, however, I would like to concentrate on the several essays where I find some aspects of the arguments and rhetoric more problematic. The book's first four essays stake out Nussbaum's cosmopolitan liberal feminism, defend this framework against what she constructs as antiliberal and relativist feminism, and apply this framework to judgments of injustice toward women in other cultures, particularly Africa and Asia.

Some of Nussbaum's most important philosophical and practical work of the last decade has been with the United Nations sponsored World Institute for Development Economic Research (WIDER) in a series of meetings to develop a universal cross-cultural concept of basic standards of human well-being that can be used by international organizations and governments to assess how well people are doing in particular locales. The lead essay in this volume, **"Women and Cultural Universals,"** documents some of Nussbaum's contribution to this effort. Here Nussbaum offers a list of ten functional capabilities which she argues are essential for human life in whatever cultural and social context is lived. The main task of the essay is to defend such a bold essentialism against recent critiques of universalism and essentialism.

Although Nussbaum's immediate targets are particular conference participants who resist universalist claims, I read this essay as a general response to post-modernism as an approach. In my view, Nussbaum here wrongly construes what is primarily a critical theory as a positive moral theory of cultural relativism. Perhaps some critics of essentialist anthropological and moral discourse do aim positively to assert moral relativism, but I would contend that most do not. By moving so fast to answer the antiessentialists with her own positive moral arguments, Nussbaum does not give enough weight to the hazards of conceptual blindness or structural social bias that attend such a generalizing project.

Recent critiques of moral universalism are usually *epistemological.* They call attention to the fact that assertions of universal norms or standards are liable to mask an origin in the particular experience and perspective of persons located in structurally privileged positions—positions privileged by masculinity, of ownership power, or whiteness, or legacies of imperialism. The critique suspects that there is no neutral point of view from which universal norms or human attributes might be named. Cultural relativism does not follow from such critique. What should follow, in my opinion, is a method of social criticism in which people in a particular social context discuss the details of their practices as they do or do not promote well-being, both with one another and with those from different contexts. Nussbaum intends her list of universal human functional capabilities as a guide for such discussions. Given her description of them as corresponding to an essential human "core" underlying what she calls accidents of historical and cultural location, such discussion of well-being-in-context seems to be conceptualized as applying the same forms to different contexts. This gives too little recognition to how specific histories, practices, and patterns of interaction unavoidably and properly give differing meanings, priorities, and pragmatic implications to abstract norms.

In **"Feminist Critiques of Liberalism,"** I find that Nussbaum similarly reconstructs critical ontological arguments as arguments for positive moral and political positions. Here Nussbaum affirms many of the most important criticisms feminist theorists have directed at many mainstream liberal theorists: their implicit or explicit assumptions of a public-private distinction that leaves issues of justice in the family unexamined; reliance on a rational choice model of the individual agent who chooses in the self-interest of himself or his household; and the model of moral reason for which emotion is a distraction or a danger. Since Nussbaum agrees with many other feminists that the public-private distinction helps sanction sexism, that emotion often serves as a source of moral knowledge, and that rational economic man is too narrow and biased a concept of the citizen, one wonders if there remains anything of the substance of liberal thought.

Nussbaum insists, however, that the core values of liberalism remain untouched by these correct critiques of the ideas of some liberals. These core values include "a twofold intuition about human beings: namely that all, just by being human, are of equal dignity and worth, no matter where they are situated in society, and that the primary source of this worth is a power of moral choice within them, a power that consists in the ability to plan a life in accordance with one's own evaluation of ends" (p. 57). These values are threatened, Nussbaum believes, by feminist criticisms that claim to reject liberalism as such rather than perform immanent critique. Nussbaum constructs feminist critiques of liberal individualism that she is worried about as arguments for collectivism as an alternative and then shows why any view that takes a group as prior to the individual is wrong. She also constructs some of the theories she criticizes as arguments either for Marxist socialism or a care-based political theory and then defends the virtues of a model of liberal rights as against these other models. I think that she has at least partly misconstrued the aim of the critiques and thus defends a point of view that few feminists reject.

Most of the feminist criticisms of liberalism to which Nussbaum responds are not taken by their authors as arguments for alternative moral and political theories. Feminist criticisms of liberalism, for example, do not aim to argue for a collectivist alternative that would take groups as more important morally than individuals, as Nussbaum suggests they do. Instead, they aim to question the idea that the individual person is a "self-originating source of value." In contrast to a tendency toward ontological atomism and voluntarism they find in much modern and contemporary moral and political theory, these feminists theorize the individual person's identity as conditioned by her concrete interactive context. They argue that much liberalism takes relationships of exchange or contract as paradigmatic of the context of moral obligation, thereby missing the degree to which the obligations of all persons derive to a significant degree from nonvoluntary relationships such as family and community. While she is right to criticize Nel Noddings's interpretation of this self-in-relation view as valuing too self-sacrificing a norm of women's caring practice, Nussbaum does not respond to more nuanced feminist reinterpretations of autonomy-in-relation such as those by Diana Meyers and Jennifer Nedelsky.

Feminist criticisms of the abstraction and oppressiveness of many applications of liberal law, moreover, are not for the most part arguments for wholly different economic or political systems that would be opposed to the values Nussbaum endorses. Insofar as they argue for radically altered economic and political arrangements, it is partly on grounds that these values of equal worth and autonomy can only be realized with such

changes. More often the arguments remain critical rather than positive, however, calling into question a propensity in liberal law and policy to construe equal consideration as treating everyone in the same way.

"Religion and Women's Human Rights" and **"Judging Other Cultures"** both apply Nussbaum's universalist liberal feminism to issues of the attitude moral judgment and law should take toward practices that appeal to religious or other traditional beliefs to justify restrictive or harmful treatment of women. I agree with Nussbaum that respect for the basic rights of women ought to constrain religious practice and expression in any social context. Religious justifications for violence against or abuse of women should not excuse such harms. Both these essays nevertheless can appear to adopt the stance of enlighteners coming from outside that Nussbaum herself warns against, because they focus on particular non-Western religions and practices, and because their rhetoric suggests an "us-them" opposition.

Although **"Religion and Women's Human Rights"** briefly mentions ways that Roman Catholic or Orthodox Jewish beliefs sometimes conflict with women's freedom, Nussbaum's main analysis in this essay is directed at the influence of Islam and Hinduism on law and custom that affect women. Most of her examples of harms to women foreground events and practices in Africa and South Asia that have become exoticized and oversensationalized in the West, such as so-called "dowry murder," physical abuse of unveiled women, and female genital mutilation. Some of Nussbaum's rhetoric, moreover, suggests that religions per se are responsible for harms to women. We should not forget, she says, "that religions (like many nonreligious political actors) can propose atrocities" (p. 85). I think there needs to be more balance here, both in the acknowledgment that nearly *all* religions have *some* patriarchal interpreters, that sometimes these interpreters have significant power, and that it is the people rather than the religions as such that "propose atrocities."

The distancing effect of relatively exotic examples and categorical statements about religion is reinforced by a rhetoric that tends to distinguish "we" who make judgments from "they" whose actions we criticize and aim to stop. The very title of the essay, **"Judging Other Cultures,"** implies such an us-them opposition. That impression is reinforced by passages like this: "Why should we give a particular group of men licence to put women down, just because they have managed to use power in some group that would like to put women down, if we have concluded that women should have guarantees of equal protection in our nation generally?" (p. 109). "We" find no shortage of feminist criticism of beauty ideals in American society, Nussbaum says, but there is a reluctance to criticize the sexism of other cultures. "We indulge in moral narcissism when we flagellate ourselves for our own errors while neglecting to attend to the needs of those who ask our help from a distance" (p. 122), namely, women seeking protection from female genital mutilation. Such rhetoric evokes a discourse of accusation and defense that can make "us" less open than we should be to listening to the others we are judging explain their understanding of the situation. Nussbaum neither tells us in what forum or through what channels some of the others make a call on us, nor what we concretely can and should do to enforce human rights for and over them.

These problems with some of the discourse in this collection do not negate the significant achievement of this book. *Sex and Social Justice* contains a good deal of wisdom and sensitivity. Few writers can match the extent of Nussbaum's philosophical, legal, and factual knowledge, and her skill in bringing this knowledge to analysis of pressing contemporary moral problems.

Anne Norton (review date October 2001)

SOURCE: Norton, Anne. "Review Essay on Euben, Okin, and Nussbaum." *Political Theory* 29, no. 5 (October 2001): 736-49.

[*In the following review, Norton discusses Nussbaum's* Sex and Social Justice *in comparison to* The Enemy in the Mirror, *by Roxanne Euben, and* Is Multiculturalism Bad for Women?, *by Susan Okin. Norton criticizes both Nussbaum and Okin for failing to account for the works of post-colonial feminist scholars in formulating their arguments.*]

The Enemy in the Mirror: Islamic Fundamentalism and the Limits of Modern Rationalism [by Roxanne Euben] is a book written with learning, brilliance, and judgment. We are fortunate to have it.

In a more sensible academy, in a more just world, Roxanne Euben would be able to say that she has written a work of political theory—not "comparative political theory." In fiction, in critical studies in comparative literature, and in political theory, there are now those, educated beyond the conventional limits of the academy, who draw syncretically on Western and non-Western theorists, who write of, on, and through theorists from diverse traditions, who cross not only the boundary between East and West but the often greater divide between theory and politics.[1] Euben's work goes some way-as far as it can, I think-to opening a way for such works to enter and be recognized, breaching the walls that confine the work of the other within the pale of area studies and comparative politics.

The Enemy in the Mirror provides a unique and invaluable perspective on the relation of Western liberalism, rationalism, and modernity to Muslim political thought,

but it is not without a history or without ancestors. In it, Euben furthers earlier enterprises that were left incomplete. Her work continues a project begun in Albert Hourani's magisterial Arabic Thought in the Liberal Age. Hourani provided an elegant narrative account of the reception of and resistance to liberalism in the Arab Middle East, charting the intellectual genealogy that ran from Jamal al-din al Afghani to Hassan al-Banna. Hourani's book had a surface of cool disinterestedness, maintained by unimpeachable scholarship. Beneath the cool prose and the elegant style was an unrelenting insistence on the intellectual merits of these figures and their debates and an unyielding commitment to the world historical importance of the Arab critiques of liberalism and modernity. Hourani succeeded. His book was read—is-read—by those studying the Arab world and those studying Islamic political philosophy, by theorists and comparativists, and by students of comparative literature and contemporary politics. Hourani's enterprise was furthered by Leonard Binder, whose study of the Egyptian constitutionalist Ali Abd al-Raziq was central to Islamic Liberalism, and by Vali Nasr's writing on Maududi. Studies by Hamid Algar, Patrick Gaffney, Gilles Kepel, Lila Abu Lughod, and others on elements of contemporary political Islam have also made the agonistic renaissance of Islamic political thought more accessible to those without Arabic, Turkish, or Farsi.[2] The former have not, however, received adequate attention from political theorists, and the latter studies tend to concern themselves more with social context, rhetoric, performance, and political effects. Muslim political thought has remained alien territory, until Euben. Her work comes in the wake not only of Hourani but of colonial and postcolonial studies, of Said's Orientalism, and the work of a generation of transcultural scholars. Her continuance of Hourani's enterprise will fall, consequently, on ground more fertile and more fully prepared. Euben's book is as useful as Hourani's. I hope that it will be as widely read. Euben provides, as Hourani did, an intellectual context for the philosophic efflorescence that now, as then, is shaping Arab thought and politics.[3] The relation of Arab political philosophy to liberalism and an all-too-Western modernity remains central to her time, as it was to Hourani's.[4]

Euben centers her study on a single theorist, and one whose intellectual merits are not above question. Sayyid Qutb is, by Euben's account, a problematic figure to occupy the position of political and philosophic primacy that contemporary politics and culture accord him. He is a writer whose political and theoretic centrality is absolutely uncontested but whose originality and intellectual eminence are not quite as firmly established. Euben may concede more ground than she should here. Qutb is (correctly) placed by Euben in one of the most important of the intellectual lineages Hourani described: from Jamal al din al Afghani to Hassan al Banna. Hassan al Banna was, as Euben writes, "more activist than theorist, he committed little systematic doctrine to paper" (p. 55).[5] Qutb forged "al Banna's legacy into a systematic ideology that would outlast the passing of his charismatic leadership." Qutb has has more than popular political influence. As the principal theorist of the Muslim Brothers, Qutb has an intellectual heir in Hassan Turabi, whose work is worthy of study in its own right.

Euben observes that Qutb's commanding theoretical and political position is due, in part, "to the ways in which the events of Qutb's life and death have become an extension and symbol of his life's work" (p. 56). She explicitly disavows the project of establishing a "causal relationship between personal, political, and historical events and specific moments in Qutb's political thought, as if there were a meaningful dichotomy between thought and context" (p. 57). Euben leaves us in no doubt that there is meaning in the relation of thought and context, but she leads us, through Qutb, to a still more valuable double question: whether that meaning is properly located "between" and whether the relation is dichotomous. This fundamental question, directed by an alien and enlightening example, could lead us to think differently about theory and practice, one of the constitutive dichotomies of Western political theory and one that has too often been crippling and confining. In thinking of Qutb in this way, Euben is acting under a license, if not an imperative, given to her in Muslim thought. In assessing a claim, one is instructed to consider the merits of the claimant as some warrant for its acceptance. The knowledge that Qutb was exiled to the United States-in the hope that exposure to its robust, enthusiastic, and, perhaps, seductive modernity would win him over and returned to write the indicting Signposts along the Way informs that text. Qutb's private and public conduct, including steadfastness under repeated episodes of imprisonment and torture, are read as informing his work broadly. So too is his execution. The term for martyr in Arabic shares a root with the term for witness.[6] In quite practical terms, Qutb bore witness to—answered for—his work in his death.

Thinking differently of the relation of theory and practice would enable us to see theory as practice and practice as theoretical. Occasionally, political theorists in the West have evaded the dichotomy of theory and practice to treat a largely practical figure as a theorist. Lincoln, Jefferson, and the authors of the Federalist Papers are perhaps the most common examples in the United States. More often, consideration of the life informs the text, albeit implicitly and obliquely, as in the cases of Gramsci and Benjamin, Schmitt, Heidegger, DeMan, and Negri. We would profit, I think, from doing this less obliquely and more mindfully. Perhaps more important (and how much of the Western academy

rests in that "perhaps") would be the rupture that altered habits of thinking would make in the wall that divides theory and practical politics.

Euben discusses the (Western) perception that Muslim thought is curiously devoid of discussions of institutions. At one level, this is simply nonsense. Islam has an elaborate scholarship on jurisprudence. Ibn Khaldun's theory of institutional strength and decline has influenced European as well as Muslim scholars for centuries. There are superb treatments of constitutionalism in Abd al-Raziq, Maududi, and Iqbal. Euben, though she knows this well, is both generous and inquisitive enough to translate it into a more interesting question, one that recognizes the differences in Muslim approaches to questions of political order and authority and makes the form and language of these approaches accessible. Central to this aspect of the enterprise is her discussion of the umma and ijtihad.

The umma is the Islamic community and has a decisive legitimating role. Following the prophet's declaration "my community will not be agreed upon an error," it is seen as sovereign in legitimation and interpretation. This conception of the community can, of course, be used conservatively or radically to forward or preclude democracy. The umma may also be understood to refer to a historical or a transcendent community, in space and time, or beyond it. "As used by Qutb," Euben writes, "the umma is thus a transcendent, ahistorical ideal, waiting to be actualized at any moment in history." In Qutb's words, it is "a demand of the present and hope for the future" (p. 61). The jahiliyya, similarly, was understood to refer not (as has conventionally been the case) to a specific "period of ignorance" before Islam but to a condition that might prevail at any time (and does prevail in our own). In Qutb's thought, not only Islam but the human is outside history, outside time. Here and throughout the book, Euben's readings serve not only to make Qutb's thought accessible but to open new perspectives.

Euben recognizes that Sayyid Qutb has a genealogy in Muslim thought, linking him to certain lines of thought, and a political position (varying from his time to our own, and no doubt to alter more). Neither is simply representative of Islam or Muslim thought. This is most visible in Qutb's position on ijtihad. This position is central to Euben's analysis, for it is here that Qutb's recognition of "the limits of modern rationalism" is most pronounced. This position places him at odds with much of the classical tradition of Muslim thought (e.g., al Farabi, Ibn Sina, though one might find an ancestor for him in Ibn Tufayl) and with important currents in modern Muslim thought as well. Euben provides a discussion of Jamal al din al Afghani and Mohammed Abduh that is invaluable in several respects. She enables us to see Qutb in a complex theoretical terrain and to locate him more precisely within that, giving us an appreciation of the depth of the intellectual tradition in which he is embedded. She enables us to see the rupture effected by Qutb's rejection of rationalism. We are then in a position to recognize the presence and force of this against alternatives. As Euben's account makes clear, Afghani and Abduh's intellectual positions granted reason "an extraordinarily wide scope," a position that was continued by Abduh's student Rashid Rida. My own teacher, Fazlur Rahman, represented another profound and learned alternative to Qutb's position.[7] As Qutb's position continues, so do these, albeit in altered and disseminate forms.

Euben recalls Hourani in her firm insistence that the Western academy take seriously the critiques of rationalist modernity forwarded by thinkers like Qutb, as well as in her provision of a guide to the central debates and theorists in Arabic thought in the liberal age. She departs from Hourani in providing a more explicit consideration of the challenge posed by these theorists to the Western academy in which she writes. One of her strategies for doing so is to render the alien familiar, by providing an account of the resonances between critics of that modernity in Islam and the West. Thus, she examines Arendt and Arendtians such as Schaar and Villa on the crisis of authority and the loss of the commons; MacIntyre, Taylor, and John Neuhaus on the decay of morality; and Daniel Bell and Robert Bellah on the decline of community.

As Euben notes,

> Historicizing such notions about "essential cores" suggests that the relationship between religious and political thought in both traditions is not easily captured, and, concomitantly, that the putative distance between "Islam" and "the West" is not so easily defined and measured.
>
> (P. 50)

The comparative enterprise that finds and details resonances between arguments in contemporary Islamic and Western political thought similarly undermines assumptions about the distance between those "civilizations," discourses, or systems of thought in the present.

She leaves us with our problem: the problem of "we." Euben does well to refuse the category "non-Western . . . a misleading convention," but she has not yet surrendered the West. "I want to specify," she writes at the outset, "that all future uses of 'we,' 'us' and 'our' in this text should be taken to refer to Western students of politics, and students of politics trained in Western methods of scholarship." This category is no more useful than the category she rejects. I belong easily in this category, but I inhabit it with Talal Asad, Homi Bhabha, Uday Mehta, Magda al Nowaihi, and Geeta Patel. I was

taught al Farabi and al Ghazali by Ralph Lerner and Islamic law and Koranic interpretation by Fazlur Rahman, all in the course of my altogether Western education. The Ramayana furnished many of the stories of my childhood, and I hear Arabic often now. There may have been a West once to which these worlds were alien. If there were such a place, its inhabitants are fewer now, and they should not be encouraged to believe that our universities belong to them. Euben acknowledges, with Francis Robinson, the interpenetration, intellectual indebtedness, and cultural imbrication of Western and Eastern political theory in these fictive monoliths. There is no reason for her to defer to the fictions of cultural purity preferred by our more parochial colleagues (see pp. 12, 50).

This is a work that, in its clear-sightedness, its thorough commitment to the work of thinking as an enterprise not confined to one's own, its discipline, its care, and its brilliance, gives one faith in the future of academic work. Roxanne Euben has done a greater service to the academy with this book than many have done with entire careers. There is a certain sadness, consequently, about reviewing this book with the others I have been asked to consider.

Is Multiculturalism Bad for Women? the title of a volume with a lead essay by Susan Moller Okin, followed by several responses, is a profoundly misguided question, one asked so long and so often and so often answered that to hear it again is to be filled with a vague despair. The question is only a half step beyond the presumption that "all the blacks are men, all the women are white." If the women are not always white here, they are nevertheless marked as alien and other to the concerns of multiculturalism, which cannot, the formula presumes, be their own. The question collapses cultural differences into a simple dichotomy of an unstated universal and a muddled, inchoate category of otherness. Finally, and perhaps most insidiously, the question presumes an alternative to multiculturalism that serves as the standard by which gender (if not sexual) justice is to be assessed. The hard-won lessons of an older feminism, Moraga to McKinnon, seem to have been forgotten here.

It is in the assumption of liberalism as an unjustified standard that the asymmetries on which the force of the question depends reveal themselves. Okin (and Joshua Cohen, Matthew Howard, and Martha C. Nussbaum) counterpose liberalism to multiculturalism and group rights but in a highly asymmetric fashion. Liberalism is presented as a set of ideas and principles, despite the fact that the practices of Western liberal cultures may not accord with these. Other cultures, not of the West (or not, at least, included in Okin's West), are assessed not according to their principles but according to their practices. When men in the United States beat their wives, it is an aberration, counter to the liberal principles that govern here. When Muslim men beat their wives, it is an act representative of the principles of Islam—whatever Koran or hadith may say.

Similar asymmetries appear throughout the argument. "Advocates of group rights for minorities within liberal states" are faulted for their tendency "to treat cultural groups as monoliths," ignoring differences within them. Okin falls repeatedly to the same intellectual temptation. The use of multiculturalism as a blanket term for all self-consciously culturally situated critiques of liberal universalism is the most conspicuous. The one I find most interesting, however, is Okin's tendency to assume a critical unity among women with regard to cultures and cultural practices she finds distasteful or contemptible. Sometimes the degree of imputed cultural consensus is still greater, uniting men and women.

Clitoridectomy, for example, is presented as a practice understood, by those who accept and reject it alike, as intended to diminish or eliminate a woman's sexual pleasure and increase her marriageability. There are certainly other justifications offered for this practice. Bhikhu Parekh observes that "adult, sane and educated women" may engage in the practice "as a way of regulating their sexuality, or reminding themselves that they are from now onward primarily mothers rather than wives, or as a religious sacrifice of what they greatly value . . . or as a symbolic break with one phase of life" (p. 71). Among the justifications I have heard are hygiene, tradition, and providing women access to a wider array of religious practices. The first two arguments should be familiar for they are those most frequently employed in defense of male circumcision. I encountered the last when, I heard to my astonishment, that female circumcision in Egypt (which does not generally entail clitoridectomy) was referred to as sunnah, the term used for religious law.[8] Knowing that the practice is not Koranic, I asked about this and was told that by making circumcision available to women as well as men, it brought women within the law on terms equal to men. While the argument appears to me as somewhat, shall we say, jesuitical, it did remind me that I was all too prepared to judge a practice whose social origins and effects I did not know. History and politics (or, failing these, Foucault) ought to have taught us that the social origins and effects of a practice are not easily inferred from the practice itself.

Okin also tells us that "French African immigrant women deny that they like polygamy and say that not only are they given 'no choice' in the matter, but their female forebears in Africa did not like it either." The source she gives for this is the "news section" of the *International Herald Tribune*. As I read this, I recalled more than one article on the Church of Latter Day Saints that could enable one to refer to the "news sec-

tion" of the *New York Times* and declare that "women in the United States like polygamy." One could, using the same source, recapitulate their arguments in favor of the practice and their opposition to the prevailing laws and practices of this country. I can recall, moreover, a conversation in which a North African scholar (male and Muslim) argued against polygamy only to meet the dissent of a (female, secular, and liberal) scholar from the United States. The American, moreover, argued (in the liberal tradition) for choice and the possibility (visible in certain Mormon households) that a polygamous marriage might free one—or more—wives from the necessity of child rasing and enable her to pursue a career outside the home. The North African quoted Koran. Opinions on polygamy vary: among men and women in cultures that permit or ratify it and among men and women in cultures that outlaw and condemn it. A closer look at those opinions and the arguments for them would have been both more interesting and more valuable. For Okin, however, the matter is already settled. Polygamy, like clitoridectomy, is a practice supported by (other) men because "it accords with their self-interest and is a means of controlling women" (p. 15).

This argument has an interesting, informative, and ultimately disturbing precursor in the literature on sati in India. Sati is the practice in which a bereaved wife immolates herself on the funeral pyre of her husband. It is related to the practice of johar, in which the wives of a defeated army immolate themselves collectively. The practice has connotations of heroism and fortitude as well as submission and fidelity, and satis, like martial heroes, are remembered in stone monuments. The practice has been contested throughout the nineteenth and twentieth centuries into the present. Critics argued in terms virtually identical to those employed by Okin: sati accorded with the self-interest of men and served as a means of controlling women. Women who practiced it went either unwilling (drugged or coerced or both) or deluded to their deaths. The practice marked women as inferior and served as proof of their oppressed (and their culture's degraded and inferior) status. For generations, sati served as a liberal feminist shibboleth: marking the limit of the male appetite for domination and the point at which cultural relativism must bow before moral imperatives. Historical research suggested, however, that the issue was not quite that simple. It appeared that with sati, as with other cultural practices, the frequency, significance, and political effects of the practice changed in response to changes in the surrounding political and cultural context. Instances of sati increased rather than declined under the colonial rule that outlawed, opposed, and stigmatized it. The debate over sati was an extended and important moment in feminist studies, postcolonial studies, and social history. It produced an extensive literature, engaged important scholars, and was conducted in highly visible venues. It effected dramatic changes in how many of us thought about normative political theory and the uses of history. This was exciting and controversial scholarship; it speaks directly to Okin's concerns, yet Okin's essay proceeds as if this debate never occurred.

Throughout Okin's essay, the arguments made on behalf of liberal principles are drawn from the work of liberal scholars. Characterizations, praise, and condemnations of the practices Okin deprecates as foreign, illiberal, and unjust are taken from the newspaper. Why this double asymmetry? Why are the condemned practices assigned to others and unacknowledged where they occur in the United States? Why is liberalism given a scholarly voice, while its opponents are spoken of and spoken for in the popular press? There was (and, in some circles, there remains) a vigorous debate about the consonance of polygamy with liberal institutions-in the United States. There has been—and remains—a rich literature on polygamy in the work of Muslim philosophers and jurists. If liberal theorists wish to treat these matters, they should do their homework.

Those who read history as well as political theory might be struck by another, more ironic, asymmetry, the silence of the following question: "Is liberalism good for women?" This question animated a generation of scholars examining the French and American revolutions. The answer they returned was a reluctant but resounding no. More recently, the question has been fielded by feminist scholars examining Europe after 1989 and the effects of "liberalization" on women in the Middle East and North Africa (p. 9).[9] Again, the answer has been no.

The asymmetries that trouble Okin's analysis are dealt with very effectively by her respondents. I am occasionally tempted to agree with Okin that "most cultures have as one of their principal aims the control of women by men," though I can think of no persuasive reason why this should be the case, and I shudder at the ammunition it gives to the likes of Edmund Wilson and Lionel Tiger (p. 13). I therefore found it particularly bracing to be reminded by Bonnie Honig's essay that "such efforts are usually matched by efforts to control male sexuality as well" (p. 37). In critiques of veiling, for example, corresponding constraints on male dress and bodily display go undisputed and unremarked. Honig also knows that "many Muslim feminists . . . see veiling as an empowering practice" (p. 19).[10] Honig recognizes that "the cultures Okin mentions are less univocally patriarchal than she suggests" (pp. 36-37).

Honig's sensible essay points the reader toward the importance of learning: learning the role of a practice within a given political and social context, learning its genealogy, inquiring into occurrences of the practice elsewhere, and questioning the assumptions that impel condemnations of the practice here. She also provides a salutary caution: "an analysis of the tense relations between feminism and multiculturalism must be careful not to conflate 'different' with 'culture' and 'culture' with foreignness" (p. 39). Difference occurs within, as well as between, cultures. Honig observes that Okin mentions, to great effect, the "case of an immigrant from rural Iraq [who] married his two daughters, aged 13 and 14, to two of his friends, aged 28 and 34" and justified the practice as commonplace in his native village. "Perhaps," Honig writes, "the mere mention of Jerry Lee Lewis's famous (but not unusual) marriage to his 13 year old cousin will suffice to remind us that such practices are not exactly unheard-of in the United States" (p. 39). A turn to history in Sander Gilman's essay indicates the politics that may be at work in the rhetorical association of practices with "others." As he notes, male circumcision goes unquestioned at present in the debate over "female genital mutilation," but Okin's "language and images" echo those deployed against male circumcision—and its Jewish, and therefore alien, practitioners—150 years ago.

Azizah al-Hibri and Abdullahi An-Nai' im point out, generously and tolerantly, that the nominal universalism championed by liberals is a covert particularism; that it has not and, indeed, cannot deliver on its claims; and that its nominal ends of justice and inclusion can often be well (if not better) pursued outside its confines. Homi Bhabha furnishes a similar reminder, though he sounded to me as if he were (understandably) at the end of his tether.

One can assume, as Okin does, that all cultures (with the possible exception of liberalism) treat women badly, structuring the social order in a way that advantages men. One might, however, conclude with equal justice that all cultures are capable of advancing sexual justice and that all have done so, at different times and in different venues. This suggests that a better strategy might be to ask, "How does this (particular) culture serve women?" or "When is liberalism good for women?" A still better approach would be to ask which women, in which venues and under which circumstances, prosper and advance. Such a strategy would avoid the reduction of all other cultures to the vacuous single category "multiculturalism." It would open the critique to Western liberal cultures, on equal terms. It would require us to consider differences of class and race. Most important, this strategy would oblige us to go to other cultures as students rather than instructors, and it would also enable us to come away with something that might be of use not only to them but to ourselves.

The work done by many of Okin's respondents is learned, clear-sighted, and even influential. None of this, it appears, has been enough to set this question aside. That the question, "Is multiculturalism good for women?" is well intentioned I have no doubt, but it leads very surely down the road to hell.

Having gone down the road of good intentions, I find myself in the company of Martha Nussbaum's **Sex and Social Justice.** Nussbaum's passion for social justice, her commitment to improving the lives of women, and her fortitude in working toward this are admirable. Her arrogant conviction that she knows, better than we or they, what women want is much less so. She resembles nothing so much as a nineteenth-century colonial missionary bringing sustenance to the starving and the gospel to the heathen. I expect that her work will prove as useful as theirs.

There is quite a lot to use. Nussbaum gives us some 460 pages, in which she provides accounts of many legal cases, interesting synopses of the reports of the United Nations Commission on Women and the work of other institutions and nongovernmental organizations, many anecdotes (of which, more later), and some quite interesting and elegant remarks on ancient philosophers and philosophic movements.

One might ask, then, why I write of Nussbaum in such condemnatory terms. She is well intentioned, she is learned in certain fields, and she has a passionate commitment to justice. If she is misguided, that is a fault most of us share. I would answer by pointing to an early passage. When I first read this passage, I thought it was generous. I was mistaken. Nussbaum acknowledges that

> universalist views, applied to women, are frequently suspected of being the projections of a male view onto women, or of the views of well-educated white women onto women of diverse backgrounds and cultures. I try to answer this concern through my method, which lets the voices of many women speak.
>
> (P. 9)

Much might be written of this passage, which so calmly and unthinkingly aligns whiteness with education, diversity with racial others. The first and simplest thing to say, however, is that it is not true. There are very few women's voices here. Few feminist theorists are cited; the most powerful critics (by Nussbaum's own accounts elsewhere) go wholly unmentioned. The many women not of the West who write on sex and social justice are neither read nor recognized: one looks in vain for Gayatri Spivak, Assia Djebbar, Nawal al Sadawi, Fatima Mernissi, Nilufer Gole, Chandra Mohanty, Aiwa Ong, Suha Sabbagh, Mervat Hatem, and Rey Chow, much less Zeinab al Ghazali. Veena Das is given one citation, to a brief passage in which Nussbaum observes that Das has made "a similar argument" to that of a Western woman whom Nussbaum treats at length. There is no justice in failing to acknowledge the prominence these women have in feminist debates.

When Nussbaum writes that she lets many women speak, I suspect she has in mind those moments when she quotes "Rohima of West Shanbandha" or "Metha Bai, a young widow in Rajasthan." These moments are infrequent (most chapters have none at all), and when they appear they have a curious and unsettling effect. One reads the stories with admiration for the women and shame for Nussbaum. Their status is invariably inferior to hers. They are made to speak at her behest and in support of her contentions.

Nussbaum's persistent failure to acknowledge the work of women scholars in South Asia, Africa, and the Middle East is an act of scholarly irresponsibility and social injustice. If she does not know that work, then she has failed in the ordinary obligations of a scholar. If she knows it and does not cite it, then she is engaged in an act of deliberate silencing that is a shameful betrayal of the values she pretends to espouse.

Nussbaum has not troubled herself to read much of those on whom she writes, or if she has, she has not seen fit to trouble us with it. She does furnish substitutions, and these, like the lacunae, are extraordinarily revealing. Turning away from the work of postcolonial feminists and other postcolonial scholars, Nussbaum supplies her own views on the position of women in Africa and Asia, occasionally ratified by the approval of unnamed natives. In the midst of a rich literature of feminist theory and queer theory, Nussbaum turns consistently to heterosexual men, many only peripherally interested in (or relevant to) the work she has under discussion. Gay men are praised for praising heterosexuality as Chinese feminists (not cited by name) are praised for praising Mill. Apart from the ethical propriety of consulting gays, lesbians, bisexuals, and people of still more complex or transgressive sexual orientations, much of the literature in queer theory speaks directly to the issues Nussbaum raises. Nussbaum opens her chapter on "A Defense of Gay and Lesbian Rights" with a consideration of the contradictions that bedevil attempts to define homosexuality, gay, lesbian, and the other terms that designate the aberrant in the discourses of law and social policy. She proceeds from this to a discussion of the difficulties of classifying sexuality or sexual orientation. She concludes, however, with an ambiguous affirmation of the categories employed that, though she appears to retain her doubts about their value, has the effect of reifying them. A little more attention to the work of other scholars might have enabled her to avoid this expedient, which she rightly finds unsatisfying. One does not need to read far or thoroughly to find works that enable one to escape this cycle of reification. Foucault, in a brief and elegant essay on friendship, makes an argument that speaks directly to the difficulties Nussbaum experiences in this chapter. That essay, which has classical resonances Nussbaum would appreciate, argues that sex is

not the issue in persecution, homophobia, or more diffuse anxieties about gay and lesbian relations. I wish
Nussbaum had turned to it, for classical references appear to elicit a degree of scholarly care, reflection, and
generosity that is too often absent from her readings of
more modern works. She is ill served here by her
animus against Judith Butler, for Butler's reasoned and
compassionate inquiries into our troubled conceptions
of gender and sexuality might also have served to guide
her through the field she has found so difficult.

The selective silencing Nussbaum practices serves her
in another respect. She is given to recounting exchanges
at conferences in which she identifies people as holders
of positions critical to her own, characterizes their positions, and disputes, ridicules, or dismisses them (pp. 35-
36).[11] This approach has several strategic advantages.
She need not mention the names of those she ridicules,
shielding herself from responses by them or by others
present at the time. She is free to characterize the argument as she will, uncorrected, and without the informing context that mention of her opponents' names might
bring. She is free to employ rhetorical strategies that
would, if names were given to the figures, be seen as
the lowest sort of ad hominem attacks. She fashions a
world in which—literally—she has no peer. Others occupy political positions or play roles, while she remains
the only named individual, exercising independent
reason.

Reading Nussbaum and Okin has been deeply disturbing. In her work on the ancients, Nussbaum has written
with sensitivity and understanding of a people distant
from her in culture as well as time. Okin opened the
gates to a form of scholarship once closed to us all.
Both Nussbaum and Okin evince a passion for justice
that is admirable. Yet when they write of cultures not
their own, both abandon the scholarly care and passion
for justice that elevate their work. This would be
altogether disheartening if it were not for work like Euben's. Here we see a young scholar, moving with ease
between worlds, reading Arabs in Arabic, and reading
them with the attention that Nussbaum or Okin—or Euben herself—would give to J. S. Mill or Isaiah Berlin.
If this is the new shape of the academy, it will be more
learned and more just than what we leave behind.

Notes

1. I have in mind works by Homi Bhabha, Dipesh
   Chakrabarty, Partha Chatterjee, Alev Cinar, Faisal
   Devji, Assia Djebbar, Nilufer Gole, Mahmoud Mam-
   dani, Pratap Mehta, Uday Mehta, Fatima Memissi,
   Magda al Nowaihi, Abdullahi an-Naim, Vali Nasr,
   and Fadwa Tuqan. There are more works of this kind
   than I mention here and, no doubt, many more than
   are known to me.

2. Leonard Binder, *Islamic Liberalism: A Critique of
   Development Ideologies* (Chicago: University of
   Chicago Press, 1988); Gilles Kepel, *Prophet and*

Pharaoh: Muslim Extremism in Egypt, trans. Jon
Rothschild (London: Al Saqi Books/Zed, 1985);
Patrick Gaffney, *The Prophet's Pulpit: Islamic
Preaching in Contemporary Egypt* (Berkeley: Univer-
sity of California Press, 1994); Hamid Algar, trans.,
*Islam and Revolution: Writings and Declarations of
Imam Khomeini 1941-1980* (Berkeley, CA: Mizan
Press, 1981). See also R. Scott Appleby, ed., *Spokes-
men for the Despised: Fundamentalist Leaders of the
Middle East* (Chicago: University of Chicago Press,
1997), and Lila Abu Lughod, ed., *Remaking Women:
Feminism and Modernity in the Middle East*
(Princeton, NJ: Princeton University Press, 1998),
esp. her essay "The Marriage of Feminism and Is-
lamism in Egypt: Selective Repudiation as a Dynamic
of Postcolonial Cultural Politics," 243-69.

3. This vast and tumultuous philosophic renaissance is
   often almost invisible in the Anglo-American
   academy, and those (like myself) who lack competence in Arabic, Turkish, and Farsi are obliged to
   rely on French and English translations, some clearly
   defective. Nevertheless, there are many works by
   major figures (e.g., Khomeini, Iqbal, Maududi, Qutb,
   Rahman, Taha) and active participants (e.g., Ahmed,
   An-Naim, Gole, Mernissi, Turabi) readily available
   in English in the United States.

4. One might ask "her time or the time she studies?"
   Euben and Hourani both have a dual presence in this
   regard. Hourani wrote both in and of a time when
   these questions had political and intellectual primacy.
   Euben does so as well. Her time and the time of her
   principal subject, Sayyid Qutb, are likewise marked
   by the primacy of the engagement with Western
   liberal modernism.

5. For accounts of Hassan al Banna and Jamal al din al
   Afghani, see Hourani, *Arabic Thought in the Liberal
   Age 1789-1939* (Cambridge, UK: Cambridge Univer-
   sity Press, 1983).

6. The Hebrew term is similarly resonant. I believe that
   this resonance, in Arabic as well as Hebrew, informs
   the readings of witnessing and testimony in Derrida
   and Levinas.

7. Fazlur Rahman, *Islam and Modernity: Transformation of an Intellectual Tradition* (Chicago: University
   of Chicago Press, 1982).

8. I am indebted to Diane Singerman for first telling me
   of this. Singerman is the author of *Avenues of
   Participation: Family, Politics and Networks in
   Urban Quarters of Cairo* (Princeton, NJ: Princeton
   University Press, 1995), which provides a rich and
   discerning account of the complexities of family and
   gender roles in Cairene political and economic life.

9. Joan Scott, *Only Paradoxes to Offer: French
   Feminists and the Rights of Man* (Cambridge, MA:
   Harvard University Press, 1996); Joan Scott, Cora
   Kaplan, and Debra Keates, *Transitions, Environ-*

ments, Translations: Feminisms in International Politics (New York: Routledge Kegan Paul, 1997); Louise Tilly and Jytte Klausen, *European Integration in Social and Historical Perspective* (Lanham, MD: Rowman and Littlefield, 1997); Laurie Brand, *Women, the State, and Political Liberalization: The Middle East and North African Experience* (New York: Columbia University Press, 1998); Christine Faure, *Democratie sans les femmes: essai sur le liberalisme en France* (Paris: Presses Universitaires de France, 1985).

10. Muslim feminists do indeed exist, with the same intensity of conflict and wide variations that trouble and enrich feminism among Christians and Jews or, as Gayatri Spivak once said, "my class, international bourgeois feminists." They have not been adequately studied. A good primer on veiling and a valuable and highly accessible introduction to debates on feminist issues in the Muslim world can be found in Elizabeth Warnock Fernea, *Women and the Family in the Middle East: New Voices of Change* (Dallas: University of Texas Press, 1985), and in her documentary "Veiled Revolution." Nilufer Gole has a superb treatment of feminist issues in the Turkish Islamist discourse on veiling in *The Forbidden Modern: Civilization and Veiling* (Ann Arbor: University of Michigan Press, 1996).

11. In a note on this passage, Nussbaum locates these views in the published work of Frederique Apffel and S. A. Marglin without identifying them as the figures under discussion. This may be because she acknowledges having taken some liberties with her report of these confrontations (p. 379, n28).

Monique Deveaux (essay date July 2002)

SOURCE: Deveaux, Monique. "Political Morality and Culture: What Difference Do Differences Make?" *Social Theory and Practice* 28, no. 3 (July 2002): 503-18.

[*In the following essay, Deveaux discusses Nussbaum's* Women and Human Development *in comparison to* Multicultural Jurisdictions *by Ayelet Shachar, contending that each addresses questions regarding the significance of cultural pluralism to concepts of social justice.*]

INTRODUCTION

Can a conception of political morality—specifically, a conception of justice—be said to be valid across cultures? Few contemporary philosophers explicitly claim that their account of political morality enjoys legitimacy in all societies. The universalizability of a particular conception of justice is, however, typically assumed, without adequate justification or argumentation. By contrast, social and cultural anthropologists

have more readily explored the challenges that cultural diversity poses for any understanding of moral behavior and systems of ethics. Anthropologists' charge that morality is culturally bounded or coded[1] is a claim few philosophers have been eager to face head-on, despite the obvious normative significance of cultural differences for ethics. Notwithstanding the lack of systematic attention to issues of culture, the relationship of morality to social and cultural diversity has been a subject of intermittent interest and controversy for moral and political philosophers since the eighteenth century, when philosophical musings and travel writings by Europeans about the mores and customs of foreigners first emerged.

Analytic philosophers reluctant to engage questions of culture generally reject the suggestion that a *descriptive* account of *actual* moral differences among social groups ought to have any bearing at all on a *normative* account of morality, including a conception of justice. But this may be changing. John Rawls's shift from a strictly moral (and hypothetical) justification of justice as fairness in *A Theory of Justice*[2] to a justificatory framework that appeals to the fit or resonance of principles of political liberalism with the actual beliefs and intuitions of citizens in liberal democratic societies, for instance, marked a significant departure from this view. With his *Political Liberalism,*[3] Rawls cleared a space for political philosophers in the Anglo-American analytic tradition to count practical social and political conditions, including circumstances of cultural diversity, as important to both the conceptualization and application of a conception of justice. To the extent that deep differences among social and cultural norms are understood to raise questions about the universal applicability and moral legitimacy of ethical principles, however, we should perhaps not be surprised that more systematic moral thinkers remain reluctant to engage with these challenges. Kant and neo-Kantians in particular are vulnerable to the charge that an ethical-political conception founded on the ideal of moral autonomy, the inviolability of human dignity, and the test of moral universalizability is both too strenuous and too culturally bounded to hold much significance for a wide range of societies, especially non-liberal, non-European ones.

For those contemporary political philosophers who, like (recent) Rawls, link the legitimacy of political principles of justice to their wide (actual) acceptability by—and applicability to—a plurality of citizens, the increasing social and cultural diversity of liberal democratic societies presents obvious challenges. If the resonance of moral ideals and rules with diverse persons is held to be of real, justificatory significance, then the question of whether or not particular moral principles hold universal validity cannot be answered strictly in normative terms. That is, it also has an empirical aspect. Whether equal moral worth and equal human dignity are truly universal principles, for example, is not a question that can be answered in isolation from reflection on deeply held values and beliefs in diverse, often non-liberal, cultures, many of which exist within the borders of liberal states. Such a suggestion of course opens up the possibility that certain moral systems will be revealed to simply formalize culturally bounded or specific rules and concepts, but it need not lead to this conclusion.

CULTURE'S CHALLENGE TO MORAL UNIVERSALISM

As political claims for recognition and accommodation by cultural minorities in numerous liberal democracies have steadily increased, moral and political philosophers have come to focus greater attention on the significance of cultural differences for a conception of political morality. In recent years, a range of diverse thinkers have explored aspects of the broad question of political morality's scope and limits in light of cultural plural-ism.[4] Two metaethical questions emerge as paramount in the discussions of the relationship of morality to culture by these and other writers: Should the norma-tive coherence and success of a conception of political morality—particularly a conception of justice—depend upon its acceptability to moral agents from diverse cultural communities, and to its "fit" with circumstances of deep cultural pluralism? And does a social context of cultural diversity make the very articulation of a universal moral system less plausible, conceptually or practically?

Philosopher Martha Nussbaum, in two recent books that address the theme of gender justice, seeks to offer answers to these and other questions. The position she develops, known as the human capabilities approach, claims to combine a sensitivity to social and cultural pluralism with a moral conception of human needs and human flourishing boasting universal applicability. In both *Sex and Social Justice*[5] and *Women and Human Development,* Nussbaum steadfastly rejects suggestions that circumstances of cultural diversity make the search for a common view of the requirements of human well-being and social justice in any way less viable. As Nuss-baum writes in *Women and Human Development,* "legitimate concerns for diversity, pluralism, and personal freedom are not incompatible with the recogni-tion of universal norms; indeed, universal norms are required if we are to protect diversity, pluralism, and freedom, treating each human being as an agent and an end" (6). Nussbaum is certainly not alone in her view. There is no shortage of contemporary political philoso-phers seeking to rescue liberal universalism and broadly neo-Kantian justice from attack by a range of critics, from post-colonial and post-modern thinkers to skepti-cal pragmatists. Among the defenders, political liberals (which Nussbaum counts herself among) are persuasive proponents of the need to reject criticisms of individual

rights frameworks as well as to resist the introduction of culturally differentiated collective rights for cultural minority groups. We ought instead, political liberals argue, to fashion universal principles of justice that enjoy wide legitimacy in culturally plural liberal societ-ies.

Brian Barry's recent polemic on the perils of policies of multiculturalism from the point of view of political liberalism is perhaps the most forceful example of this view. In *Culture and Equality,*[6] Barry makes a passion-ate plea for the enduring value of liberal principles and individual rights over what he sees as misguided and dangerous moves towards a framework of multicultural-ism in liberal democracies. Rather than capitulating to the demands of multiculturalists and cultural interest groups, Barry suggests that we need to hold fast to a liberal conception of justice and address persistent group inequalities through broader policies of social and economic redistribution.

Similarly, prominent liberal political theorist Susan Mol-ler Okin, in an essay entitled "Is Multiculturalism Bad for Women?," defends a liberal egalitarian framework of justice over proposals to pluralize—and so, in her view, dilute and weaken—liberal values.[7] The resulting dichotomy that Okin's article trades in—in which demands for cultural recognition, especially by non-liberal groups, are pitted against the re-affirmation of liberal universalist values—raises yet another critical dilemma for political philosophers. This dilemma is best articulated in terms of the following questions: Where the practices and norms of traditional, non-liberal minorities (often religious groups) conflict sharply with principles and arrangements in a given liberal demo-cratic state, what accommodation, if any, are such minorities entitled to? And what state interference, if any, is warranted in order to protect vulnerable group members from discrimination and injustice at the hands of more powerful members of the group?

The first question is of course a version of the classic liberal paradox or dilemma of toleration, namely, are the intolerant to be tolerated? A common response by contemporary liberals is simply to say that such illiberal minorities might be owed minimal tolerance but not any substantive form of recognition or accommodation.[8] The second question poses the problem of internal discrimination *within* minority groups, a scenario that may arise when non-liberal groups are granted limited autonomy over their communities' practices and social arrangements. In response to this concern, liberals tend to argue that so long as the right of exit—so central to liberal political theory—is guaranteed, then there exists a bulwark against the abuse and oppression of vulner-able group members.

Gender Justice and Cultural Rights

Both of these questions and the problems they describe provide the focus for legal theorist Ayelet Shachar's recent book, *Multicultural Jurisdictions: Cultural Differences and Women's Rights.* Shachar challenges the view that the practices and arrangements of non-liberal minorities within liberal states do not merit respect or protection, as well as the assumption that such accommodation would be politically dangerous. Both the threat of outright prohibition of group practices by the liberal state and the last-ditch solution of exit held out to members of cultural minority groups do little more than present individuals with a tragic and unjust ultimatum: "either your culture or your rights!" (5). Assuming that no such tragic choice between one's culture and one's individual rights is strictly necessary—at least not at a general level—the task then becomes one of reconciling the normative and, most especially, the practical tensions between group cultural practices and arrangements and the norms of the constitutional liberal states in which such groups reside. As Shachar's book demonstrates, this is an enormous task, and one well known among constitutional law specialists in culturally plural liberal states.

Perhaps the greatest point of friction between the norms and customs of distinct cultural communities on the one hand and liberal principles on the other concerns the role and status of women. The principle of sex equality, conceived as a protection of a woman's individual right to equality, may conflict sharply with local cultural practices, many of which require sharp sex role differentiation and questionable treatment of women. This is not a phenomenon unique to cultural minority communities, of course: a central function of all cultures is the shaping of gender roles through cultural expectations and rules governing family and social practices. But the tensions between a social group's arrangements and the norm of sex equality may be particularly acute in the case of traditional cultures. Where cultural communities face unwanted forms of assimilation and so seek to preserve their language, identity, and distinct ways of life, the pressures on members of the group to conform to traditional gender roles can also be enormous. Shachar shows that family law, governing matters of marriage, divorce, custody, and inheritance, is most often the site where the customs of religious and cultural minorities clash with the principles of liberal society. In those states where particular ethnic groups are left to administer their own family law (such as India, Israel, and South Africa), the stage is set for conflict with constitutional principles of non-discrimination and sex equality.

The belief that cultures can unjustly prevent women from achieving social, political, and economic equality is a common point of departure point for Nussbaum and Shachar. Both ***Women and Human Development*** and *Multicultural Jurisdictions* offer welcome and long-overdue discussions of the issue of gender and justice in an era of multiculturalism. Although this problem appears to be a rapidly growing area of research interest for feminist political theorists, surprisingly little of this scholarship has reached publication. To date, there have been only two other such books: the aforementioned volumes by Okin and her respondents (***Is Multiculturalism Bad for Women?***) and Nussbaum (***Sex and Social Justice***), which cover some of the same ground. Rounding this picture out is a small selection of articles on the issue by political theorists.[9] In the two volumes under review, the authors pay particular attention to the tensions that the practices and arrangements of more *traditional* cultures pose for liberal justice and in particular for the prospects of sex equality for women of those cultures.

Culture and Sex Oppression: Shachar's Joint Governance Solution

Shachar's emphasis on the implications for gender equality of policies of multicultural accommodation in liberal democratic states is especially welcome, for it raises a number of important questions that contemporary proponents of cultural pluralism have tended to ignore. Foremost among these are the consequences of collective rights and arrangements for *individual group members,* particularly for vulnerable individuals within cultural communities, such as women. To illustrate some of the unjust effects of culturally specific political arrangements and group rights, Shachar skillfully introduces examples of discriminatory family law policies and practices in such culturally plural states as Israel and India. These contextual discussions illustrate why, as Shachar argues, political theorists need to address the three participants involved in legal and political arrangements—the group, the state, and the individual—rather than focusing exclusively on state-group interactions. Shachar aims to highlight the plight of "individuals who are put at risk at the hands of their own culture" (5), women most especially.

As someone who is broadly in favor of greater accommodation for cultural minorities yet who also fully supports gender equality and justice for women, Shachar has her work cut out for her. In laying the groundwork for her argument that cultural rights and gender justice can indeed be combined, Shachar dismisses two common responses to what we might call the "internal discrimination" problem. First, she criticizes proposals for a "re-universalized citizenship," which simply shores up individual rights at the expense of claims for cultural rights and recognition. This view, which Shachar rightly attributes to Susan Okin, Brian Barry, and Amy Gutmann, presents "the relationship between multiculturalism and feminism . . . [as] a zero-sum game" (65).

Critically, such an approach overlooks the extent to which cultures can and do change over time, and also tends to treat women as victims of culture, with no agency to resist, modify, or affirm social and cultural practices and arrangements (66-67). Most obviously, however, this view is problematic in that it simply refuses to engage the legitimate justice claims of cultural minorities.

Shachar also reveals the inadequacy of the reverse position, namely, a non-interventionist stance that is resigned to the "unavoidable costs" of cultural autonomy. Note that proponents of this view may or may not support cultural rights per se—they may simply be opposed to state intervention in citizens' private and social arrangements. Shachar is surely right to point out that such a laissez-faire attitude towards possible mistreatment of individuals at the hands of their cultures—a view that she attributes primarily to political philosopher Chandran Kukathas—relies on two false assumptions (68-70). First, it presumes that all membership in cultural communities is essentially voluntary, and that therefore members should be expected to shoulder the risks of such membership. And second, it relies on the related belief that members can always "opt out" of their community, thereby making state intervention either redundant or heavy-handed as a response to rights abuses. Surely such a conclusion is problematic in that it leaves vulnerable members of groups—many of whom cannot leave their families or communities, for reasons ranging from economic hardship to fear of physical violence—without recourse to broader state resources. From the standpoint of the justice claims of minorities within minorities, the belief that the "right of exit" from one's cultural community suffices as protection from egregious abuses may also undercut dissenters' constitutional claims for reform, for example, to prevent sex and religious discrimination within indigenous groups.

The tendency to place unwarranted faith in the significance and protective effect of the right to exit without fully considering either the difficulty or the cost of exit is evident in a recent article by Jeff Spinner-Halev. Arguing that "avoiding the injustice of imposing reform on oppressed groups is often more important than avoiding the injustice of discrimination against women," Spinner-Halev contends that the possibility of exit that exists for members of minority group members in democratic states affords them "a minimal but important level of autonomy."[10] Given the personal consequences of departure from one's community and the dangers of exit for the most vulnerable members (consider the phenomenon of "honor killings" of women accused of sexual misconduct in some Muslim communities), this seems arguable. The point here is not that members of more traditional, illiberal minority groups in liberal democratic states have no agency whatsoever, but rather

that it is important to attend to the actual circumstances and social contexts in which options are presented or denied, chosen or shunned.[11] One of the key strengths of Martha Nussbaum's recent work, as I shall shortly discuss, is that it rejects blanket statements about the presence or absence of autonomy, focusing instead on a more nuanced study of agents' *capabilities* for freedom and "functioning."

As suggested by her focus on the problem of internal discrimination, Shachar's discussion of the "perils of multicultural accommodation" centers on traditional or conservative cultural communities. She pays particular attention to the dangers posed when liberal states permit such communities to hold exclusive authority over matters of family and personal law, domains in which sex discrimination is often felt most keenly. Through an incisive discussion of the discriminatory features of marriage and divorce law in Israel, which come under the jurisdiction of religious authorities, Shachar shows that women can be left uniquely vulnerable by community rights. A more adequate set of legal and political arrangements governing diverse communities requires a more complex conception of governance, in Shachar's view. Such a conception, if realized, could extend limited powers of self-governance to culturally distinct communities at the same time as ensuring protection for vulnerable members of those groups. By contrast, the key flaw of both the "re-universalized citizenship" view and the "unavoidable costs" position is that both are based on an "oversimplified 'either/or'-type understanding of legal authority which is not tailored to respect individuals' manifold identities" (12).

The solution to the problem of internal discrimination that Shachar advances is essentially one of legal power-sharing, or what she calls the "joint governance approach." It is only by "re-examining the question of jurisdiction," Shachar claims, that constitutional democracies can adequately and *justly* accommodate cultural minorities without leaving some members vulnerable and unprotected. Although she discusses several forms of joint governance, the one she singles out as most promising is that of "transformative accommodation," less of a technical description than it is an aspirational one. This approach comes with conditions attached that are designed to prevent egregious abuses of power, such as the "no monopoly rule" and the requirement of "clearly delineated choice options" for group members.[12] More generally, it aims at a transformation of group practices and mores: "Instead of forceful intervention or full immunity, transformative accommodation seeks to create institutional conditions where the group recognizes that its own survival depends on its revoking certain discriminatory practices . . ." (125).

The idea that a more complex division of legal authority or jurisdictional powers could prevent a host of abuses and systematic forms of discrimination enabled by state-protected cultural arrangements is certainly plausible. In part this is because Shachar's "joint governance" model relies on a quid-pro-quo bargain: cultural groups may receive the support and concessions they seek from the liberal democratic state provided they agree to reduce or eliminate internally discriminatory practices that cannot justly be defended (7-8). In Shachar's words, the joint governance approach "ties the mechanisms for reducing sanctioned in-group rights violations to the very same accommodation structure that enhances the jurisdictional autonomy of the *nomoi* group in the first place" (8). Her proposal is strikingly similar in this regard to Will Kymlicka's argument in *Multicultural Citizenship* that liberal states ought to encourage forms of accommodation that increase the equality of minority cultural groups vis-à-vis the rest of society (via "external protections") but reject those arrangements whose purpose or effect is to maintain or exacerbate discrimination within the group (via "internal restrictions").[13]

Shachar ultimately develops and defends a highly legalistic framework—her joint governance approach— whose value rests precariously on the task of securing the right balance of power between the state, cultural groups, and individuals. Ironically, however, questions of power are largely overlooked by her approach. Shachar's suggestion that structures of joint governance would force both state and groups alike to "abandon their perfectionist and maximalist jurisdictional aspirations, which are so often the source of conflict" (143) is savvy, if optimistic. However, she says little about what might transpire when both the state and a cultural group seek jurisdictional authority over the same institutions or practices. Instead, Shachar proposes that "contested social arenas are internally divisible into 'sub-matters',' which suggests a neat demarcation of micro-areas of jurisdiction. As she writes, "In cases where both the state and group have a legitimate claim to authority, the specific allocation of power between them depends on the justifications that each provide for its preferred position in governing a specific sub-matter" (128). Surely, however, the precise outcome will depend less on considerations of justice than it will on the relative power of the agents involved? Some wishful thinking and naïve rationalism are evident in Shachar's approach, though both are admittedly hard to avoid (as anyone brave enough to venture solutions to problems of justice and pluralism will surely acknowledge). The problem here is that Shachar seems to expect that the problem of contested domains can be resolved through Kantian-style rational dialogue, without explaining why, or exploring issues of force and capitulation, compliance and non-compliance.

Related to this reluctance to engage issues of power and compliance head-on, Shachar's joint governance approach also sidesteps important normative questions

about the justice or injustice of particular practices and arrangements. Granted, such a task is treacherous at the best of times, for it is not clear how, as a pluralist liberal democrat, one can ask about the permissibility of practices in the abstract without re-inscribing pernicious power relations reminiscent of colonial relations. Nevertheless, some of these questions must be asked: Should arranged marriage, including more forceful variants, be permitted in liberal democratic polities? Ought polygamy to be permitted? Should religious schooling that separates girls out and limits their education to preparation for more conventional, restricted roles be allowed? Despite her clear criticisms of family law policies that enable systematic discrimination against women, Shachar all but avoids these hard cases. Instead, she hopes and expects that over time, the arrangements forged by joint governance will transform community practices and expectations. As noted, the quid-pro-quo bargain that underlies the joint governance approach aspires to "transformative accommodation," in that it is "designed to encourage group authorities themselves to reduce discriminatory internal restrictions" (14). But again, such an explanation partly sidesteps the key normative questions at stake, and gives us little sense of what to do in the hard cases.

Shachar's highly legalistic, prudential approach is in many ways admirable, and displays a healthy skepticism about the propensity of philosophers and political theorists to resolve cultural and political disputes at an ethical or metaethical level. However, some guidance on the normative front is surely necessary, for even in the disputes over jurisdictional authority that Shachar fully expects will arise, citizens need some way of determining just what counts as a *good justification* for choosing whether a group or a state apparatus should control particular institutions or practices.

UNIVERSALISM REVISITED: NUSSBAUM'S CAPABILITIES APPROACH

In this regard, Martha Nussbaum's work offers a much farther-reaching and unabashedly normative response to the question, "What social conditions, arrangements, and practices foster gender justice, and which do not?" On Nussbaum's view, social justice requires that our basic human capabilities be fostered and supported. This implicates not only the state, but also structures in civil society, including the family. Practically speaking, Nussbaum's approach requires that all citizens have real access to the resources they need to develop and sustain their basic human capabilities. What is important here is the "idea of a threshold level of each capability, beneath which it is held that truly human functioning is not available to citizens" (5). To this end, she provides a list of core capabilities that contribute significantly to one's capacity to lead a life of well-being. Among these capabilities are those of life; bodily health; bodily integrity; capabilities relating to the senses, imagination, thought, and to emotions and emotional attachments; and capabilities for practical reason, social affiliation, and political engagement. These capabilities in turn require a range of concrete social circumstances and opportunities for their development: for instance, the capability for affiliation is dependent on "having the social bases of self-respect and non-humiliation"; the capability for practical reason implies the need for "protection for the liberty of conscience," and so on (78-80).

Nussbaum stresses that the list of capabilities is "a partial and not a comprehensive conception of the good" (96). It is also "emphatically, a list of separate components," such that a "larger amount" of one good cannot be expected to replace another good (81). The list of capabilities becomes politically meaningful when joined with a social and political commitment to the "principle of each person's capability," by which every individual person's capabilities are to be counted seriously. And indeed, Nussbaum conceives of the capabilities approach as a way to inform and redirect government policy around the world. She writes that "the approach is recommended as a good idea to politicians in India or any other nation who want to make it the basis of national or local policy," and that "the primary role for the capabilities account remains that of providing political principles that can underlie national constitutions" (104-5).

For Nussbaum's claim to the universal applicability of the capabilities approach to hold any water, it must of course show that it is at least potentially compatible with diverse ways of life—that it does not simply reinscribe culturally specific, Western understandings of flourishing and well-being. It is not surprising, then, that this is one of the first claims Nussbaum makes in support of her theory. The capability approach, she argues, "yields a form of universalism that is sensitive to pluralism and cultural difference" (8). It is useful to unpack this claim here. The basis of Nussbaum's assertion seems to be that the list of capabilities she provides does not in any way constitute a comprehensive conception of the good. Even leaving aside the question of the thick Aristotelianism evident in the list of goods and capabilities, it is noteworthy that she fully expects that the capabilities approach can and should be used to make "comparisons of life equality." Yet as Nussbaum herself rightly notes, we need a normative conception in order to make such comparisons worthwhile. Circumstances of social diversity surely complicate the task of delineating a culturally neutral conception of the good life. Is such a conception even possible?

One way around this problem is to emphasize, as Nussbaum does, that people can use the basic capabilities to choose very different kinds of lives. Here Nussbaum's

distinction between human capabilities and the *actual functionings* of persons becomes important. Whereas a list of actual *functionings* would be too prescriptive, a list of capabilities is not, Nussbaum argues; this is because capabilities are simply a measure of someone's capacity to live a life of choice and well-being, however defined. Another answer that Nussbaum gives to the criticisms she anticipates concerning the cultural thickness of the human capabilities model is that a person can choose to ignore a good of the list of central human capabilities, or choose a non-list good, without necessarily risking a substandard life (95). But these qualifications of course only take us so far.

The normative thickness of Nussbaum's conception of the good comes into sharp relief when she discusses roles and arrangements that bind women in many traditional societies, which are largely incompatible with her list of capabilities. She is admirably upfront about the extent to which capabilities theory and the conception of respect for persons as ends in themselves will require that people "take a stand against some very common ways of treating women—as child-like, as incompetent in matters of property and contract, as mere adjuncts of a family line, as reproducers and care givers rather than as having their own lives to live" (58). But what of the cases where women seem to embrace these subordinate roles? Here Nussbaum raises, as she must, the possibility that some women, especially those in traditional societies, might not choose or want certain of the basic capabilities enumerated in the list— namely, those that conflict with their customary roles. An interesting but ultimately unsatisfying discussion of the problem of adaptive preferences ensues (in chapter 2), wherein Nussbaum contends that the apparent preferences of women in restrictive cultures are in any case mostly adaptive, and so can change. This discussion calls to mind classical Marxist arguments about the malleability of the working classes' consciousness and allegiances, which were said to closely reflect and also to *change along with* prevailing social and economic conditions.[14]

The adaptive preferences rationale does provide Nussbaum with a conceptual wedge with which to argue that women's choices can and likely will change once they have the full range of capabilities and attendant opportunities. This is presumably what leads her to insist that in facing the prospect of women who reject one or more of the basic capabilities or who agree to a practice or custom that permanently jeopardizes a list good, a stringent test must be applied: "What we would need to show is that women who have experienced the full range of the central capabilities choose, with full information and without intimidation . . . to deny these capabilities, politically, to all women" (153). This test, seemingly inspired by Kant's maxim of moral universalizability, would no doubt lead to the prohibition of a wide range of traditional roles and practices in which women find themselves. The implications of such a test on traditional ways of life, and the possibility that such a rule might be perceived by communities as unjust interference, however, is not a matter that Nussbaum much dwells on.

How does Nussbaum manage to paint herself into this corner? Integral to her list are those capabilities that one needs in order to make uncoerced choices about one's life. These capabilities in turn require the support of political rights and liberties, which reflect a political demand for a certain basic treatment vis-à-vis important capabilities. Rights (or the demand for them) reinforce "the basic role of the spheres of ability" and emphasize "people's choice and autonomy" (98-101). The emphasis on choice and autonomy, and the reinforcing role of political rights, suggests that nothing short of a fully liberal egalitarian framework for the sexes can supply the requirements of social justice. One of the first examples of a practice that fails the capabilities test is that of restrictive, traditional marriage: insofar as such marriages remove or make impossible the development of important capabilities, Nussbaum argues that they ought not to be tolerated (94).

Nussbaum's particular conception of the good life is a curious combination of Aristotelian idealism, political liberalism, and Kantian ethics (she emphasizes that treating "each person as an end" becomes a "principle of each person's capability"). It is not an unattractive vision. Common to all three ideals, of course, is the pivotal value of autonomy. Nor is there much to quibble with here: Nussbaum is surely right that people generally prefer more choice and control over the circumstances of their lives than not. The conversations with poor Indian women that Nussbaum invokes to illustrate the role of capabilities in well-being, in which they almost uniformly praise the positive effects of greater choice in their lives, certainly resonate as true. However, the difficulty of Nussbaum's conception is that it doesn't merely assert that choice is an important good; rather, it claims that choice—and the capabilities and opportunities that support choice—is an ultimate good. This claim, if it can be defended at all, will require extensive normative justification, particularly if it is to apply to diverse social groups. But no such justification is forthcoming. Instead, more claims are piled on top of this one. If choice and the capabilities that support it are critical components of a good life, then our social and political arrangements must, as a matter of justice, reflect this. For Nussbaum, this rule holds even if someone seems to collude in their own subordination: in the case of a person who seems to choose to "sign away a major capability in a permanent way," often state intervention is warranted in order "to protect the capability" (93-94).

The determinate nature of Nussbaum's conception of the good life, despite her protests to the contrary, is thus further reinforced by her insistence that one cannot rationally choose to (permanently) give up an important capability. If highly traditional, restrictive marriages—particularly arranged marriages—warrant intervention in the form of social policy, one can imagine a long list of other practices and arrangements that are simply intolerable from the standpoint of core capabilities. An adult African woman who elects to undergo female circumcision after the birth of her children—a real-life example that Bhikhu Parekh has discussed—is thus incomprehensible and insupportable, since to do so is to permanently give up capability central to human flourishing (the capacity for sexual pleasure). Presumably, to elect to become the second or third wife of Muslim man is also to risk compromising one's core capabilities for choice and autonomy, since polygamous marriages frequently render women financially vulnerable and weaken their individual decision-making power.

As it turns out, then, certain choices are simply not choices at all in Nussbaum's capability scheme. Women cannot freely choose to participate in practices or arrangements that will jeopardize their well-being (and if they do, the state ought to step in to prevent them. On Nussbaum's rationalist view, women will seek to secure their own basic physical and material well-being, and that of their children, before they venture out to seek a wider range of goods or to develop other capabilities. But what of choices that do not fall into line, such as a life of religious devotion, which may include deliberate sacrifice of several of the capabilities Nussbaum cites, and even suffering? A faint echo of the Marxist, materialist conception of self-interest can be heard here, together with a hint of the possibility of false consciousness (wherein women fail to recognize their own rational self-interest).

Given Nussbaum's claim that the capabilities approach is widely, indeed universally, applicable across culturally plural societies, the normative thickness of her list is potentially problematic. If Nussbaum were to offer better justification for her substantive conception of the good life as reflected by the list of capabilities, we could at least grapple with that. Not only is such an argument not forthcoming, however, but the conception of flourishing Nussbaum sets out depends upon a normative *ordering* of choices that she does not acknowledge. Women will (or ought to) first choose to develop and maintain capabilities that enhance their ability to make choices and lead reasonably self-directed lives, according to the theory. They will (or ought to) choose to secure basic capabilities and the circumstances that support these (nutrition, shelter) before they pursue other capabilities and goods (religious fulfillment, say). It is merely assumed that women will make rational choices in the order suggested by the degree of critical importance of the capability in question, as elaborated by Nussbaum. We do not have to look very far to see that this ordering of preferences and choices is simply not to be counted on.

HOW SHOULD CULTURAL GROUP NORMS AND LIBERAL PRINCIPLES BE RECONCILED?

While compelling and well intentioned, both Nussbaum's Aristotelian capabilities approach and Shachar's joint governance proposal may strike readers as overly optimistic, and possibly counterfactual. This isn't to say that democratic approaches to resolving tensions between cultural practices and the goal of justice for women are necessarily naïve or impractical. It is to say, however, that neither approach offered in these books holds out an adequate answer to the *practical* dilemmas at hand. Shachar may come closer in that she begins to explore the merits of a more dialogue-based approach to resolving normative and legal tensions between traditional cultural communities and liberal principles. Moreover, her approach takes seriously, as it must, the identity claims and self-government aspirations (especially in the case of Aboriginal peoples) of the cultures in question. However, to date, no feminist discussions of the issue of "culture versus sex equality" has argued in a systematic way for a dialogical approach sensitive to the claims of cultural groups. Indeed, in response to conflicts between (minority) cultural norms and practices and sex equality, both Nussbaum and Susan Okin argue for the application of principles of justice that do not take much account of the values and normative commitments of members of traditional cultures: Nussbaum argues for an essentially Aristotelian response to gender injustice, and Okin merely re-asserts the primacy of liberal individual rights.[15] Shachar, though more open to discursive or deliberative solutions, retreats to a legalistic remedy for conflicts of culture, leaving unresolved the profound normative questions that are certain to arise.

Despite, or perhaps because of, Shachar's and Nussbaum's engaging discussion of the problem of gender and justice in plural societies, we are left with the same broad questions that surely motivated their studies in the first place: What happens when cultural and ethical norms and frameworks collide in democratic societies? Should liberal norms and principles prevail when traditional cultures clash with liberal ones? If so, what normative justification can be offered for this move? If not, what persuasive justifications can we offer for permitting traditional values and arrangements to prevail, unchallenged, in certain communities? These questions inevitably invite us to weigh the merits of both moral universalism and cultural relativism as possible approaches to dilemmas of difference. Yet respect for cultural group differences need not entail a stance of extreme cultural or moral relativism, the sort that would permit grave mistreatment of persons, all in the name of culture; indeed, such a position is surely indefensible in liberal democratic societies. Nor is it clear, however, that the way to reconciling the sometimes competing claims for cultural group recognition and gender equality lies in shoring up a framework of individual rights that may be increasingly at odds with citizens' deeply held beliefs and norms in culturally plural liberal democratic societies. Perhaps we would do better instead to develop practices of judgment and decision-making that are sensitive to the competing normative claims of different cultural communities, and to adopt truly pluralistic political norms—provided that some can be discovered.

Notes

1. Some leading texts by anthropologists that assert the cultural embeddedness of social and moral norms include Melville Herskovits, *Cultural Relativism: Perspectives in Cultural Pluralism* (New York: Random House, 1972), and Renato Rosaldo, *Culture and Truth: The Remaking of Social Analysis* (Boston: Beacon Press, 1989/1993).

2. John Rawls, *A Theory of Justice* (Cambridge, Mass.: Harvard University Press, 1971).

3. John Rawls, *Political Liberalism* (New York: Columbia University Press, 1993).

4. Some examples include David Archard (ed.), *Philosophy and Pluralism* (Cambridge: Cambridge University Press, 1996); Monique Deveaux, *Cultural Pluralism and Dilemmas of Justice* (Ithaca, N. Y.: Cornell University Press, 2000); Samuel Fleischacker, *The Ethics of Culture* (Ithaca, N. Y.: Cornell University Press, 1994); Thomas Hill, Jr., *Respect, Pluralism, and Justice* (Oxford: Oxford University Press, 2000); Anthony Laden, *Reasonably Radical: Deliberative Liberalism and the Politics of Identity* (Ithaca, N. Y.: Cornell University Press, 2001); Onora O'Neill, *The Bounds of Justice* (Cambridge: Cambridge University Press, 2000); Bhikhu Parekh, *Rethinking Multiculturalism: Cultural Diversity and Political Theory* (Cambridge, Mass.: Harvard University Press, 2000); Richard Rorty, *Contingency, Irony and Solidarity* (Cambridge: Cambridge University Press, 1989); Amartya Sen, *Development as Freedom* (New York: Knopf, 1999); Charles Taylor et al., *Multiculturalism: Examining the Politics of Recognition,* ed. Amy Gutmann (Princeton: Princeton University Press, 1994); Jim Tully (ed.) with Daniel Weinstock, *Philosophy in an Age of Pluralism: The Philosophy of Charles Taylor in Question* (Cambridge: Cambridge University Press, 1994); and James Tully, *Strange Multiplicity: Constitutionalism in an/Age of Diversity* (Cambridge: Cambridge University Press, 1995).

5. Martha Nussbaum, *Sex and Social Justice* (Cambridge, Mass.: Harvard University Press, 1999).

6. Brian Barry, *Culture and Equality: An Egalitarian Critique of Multiculturalism* (Cambridge, Mass.: Harvard University Press, 2001).

7. In Susan Moller Okin and respondents, *Is Multiculturalism Bad for Women?*, ed. J. Cohen, M. Howard, and M.C. Nussbaum (Princeton: Princeton University Press, 1999), pp. 7-24. Also see her reply to critics in the same volume.

8. This is the position Charles Larmore defends, for example, in his *Patterns of Moral Complexity* (Cambridge: Cambridge University Press, 1987).

9. Some examples include Jeff Spinner-Halev, "Feminism, Multiculturalism, Oppression, and the State," *Ethics* 112 (2001): 84-113; Monique Deveaux, "Conflicting Equalities? Cultural Group Rights and Sex Equality," *Political Studies* 48 (2000): 522-39; and Avigail Eisenberg, "Diversity and Equality: Three Approaches to Cultural and Sexual Difference," *Journal of Political Philosophy,* forthcoming. Material from Shachar's book was previously published as articles in the *Journal of Political Philosophy* and *Political Theory,* and elsewhere.

10. Spinner-Halev, "Feminism, Multiculturalism," pp. 86 and 106.

11. For a critique of the liberal conception of the right to exit from a feminist perspective, see Susan Moller Okin, "'Mistresses of Their Own Destiny': Group Rights, Gender, and Realistic Rights of Exit," *Ethics* 112 (2002): 205-30.

12. See chapter 6 generally, esp. pp. 117-18 and p. 127.

13. Will Kymlicka, *Multicultural Citizenship* (Oxford: Oxford University Press, 1995), esp. chapters 3 and 5. Despite the seeming complementarity of Shachar's view, she criticizes Kymlicka's distinction between "external and internal aspects of accommodation" for "failing to provide a workable solution in practice for certain real-life situations involving accommodated groups" (18).

14. Thanks to Roger Gottlieb for this insight.

15. Here I refer to the Nussbaum volume under discussion, and to Okin's "Is Multiculturalism Bad for Women?"

FURTHER READING

Criticism

Beaty, Michael, and Anne-Marie Bowery. "Cultivating Christian Citizenship: Martha Nussbaum's Socrates, Augustine's *Confessions,* and the Modern University." *Christian Scholar's Review* 33, no. 1 (fall 2003): 23-54.

Critique of Nussbaum's model of liberal education in which the authors propose instead a model for Christian education based upon Augustine's *Confessions.*

Christiansen, Bryce. Review of *Hiding from Humanity,* by Martha Nussbaum. *Booklist* 100, no. 13 (1 March 2004): 1117.

Review of Nussbaum's *Hiding from Humanity.*

Davis, Lennard J. "Are Novels Good for Us?" *Nation* 263, no. 3 (15 July 1996): 40-2.

Review of Nussbaum's *Poetic Justice.*

Frentz, Thomas. Review of *The Therapy of Desire,* by Martha Nussbaum. *Quarterly Journal of Speech* 82, no. 2 (May 1996): 189-91.

Asserts that *The Therapy of Desire* is an important book for scholars of rhetoric, yet faults Nussbaum for failing to adequately address issues of rhetoric in her arguments.

Griswold, Charles L., "Cool Hand Socrates." *American Scholar* (spring 1988): 314-20.

Review of Nussbaum's *The Fragility of Goodness.*

Harpham, Geoffrey Galt. "The Hunger of Martha Nussbaum." *Representations,* no. 77 (winter 2002): 52-81.

Harsh and extensive criticism of the ideas underlying Nussbaum's prolific output of books and essays.

Kingwell, Mark. "The Depths of Feeling." *American Scholar* 74, no. 1 (winter 2002): 142-45.

Review of Nussbaum's *Upheavals of Thought.*

Kopff, Christian. "News from the Thinkery." *National Review* 50, no. 2 (9 February 1998): 56-8.

Review of Nussbaum's *Cultivating Humanity.*

Leget, Carol. "Martha Nussbaum and Thomas Aquinas on the Emotions." *Theological Studies* 64, no. 3 (September 2003): 558-81.

Examines Nussbaum's *Upheavals of Thought* in light of ideas put forth by Thomas Aquinas.

Ruprecht, Louis A. Review of *Love's Knowledge,* by Martha Nussbaum. *Journal of Religion* 73, no. 3 (July 1993): 463-65.

Review of Nussbaum's *Love's Knowledge.*

Solomon, Robert C. Review of *Upheavals of Thought,* by Martha Nussbaum. *Mind* 111, no. 444 (October 2002): 897-901.

Provides a review of *Upheavals of Thought,* calling it a magnificent, ambitious achievement that represents the culmination of Nussbaum's work to date.

Spelman, Elizabeth. "How Do They See You?" *London Review of Books* (16 November 2000): 11-13.

Presents a review of Nussbaum's *Sex and Social Justice* and *Women and Human Development.*

Additional coverage of Nussbaum's life and career is contained in the following sources published by Thomson Gale: *Contemporary Authors,* **Vol. 134;** *Contemporary Authors New Revision Series,* **Vol. 102; and** *Literature Resource Center.*

How to Use This Index

The main references

> **Calvino, Italo**
>   1923-1985 .... **CLC 5, 8, 11, 22, 33, 39,**
>   **73; SSC 3, 48**

list all author entries in the following Gale Literary Criticism series:

AAL = *Asian American Literature*
BG = *The Beat Generation: A Gale Critical Companion*
BLC = *Black Literature Criticism*
BLCS = *Black Literature Criticism Supplement*
CLC = *Contemporary Literary Criticism*
CLR = *Children's Literature Review*
CMLC = *Classical and Medieval Literature Criticism*
DC = *Drama Criticism*
HLC = *Hispanic Literature Criticism*
HLCS = *Hispanic Literature Criticism Supplement*
HR = *Harlem Renaissance: A Gale Critical Companion*
LC = *Literature Criticism from 1400 to 1800*
NCLC = *Nineteenth-Century Literature Criticism*
NNAL = *Native North American Literature*
PC = *Poetry Criticism*
SSC = *Short Story Criticism*
TCLC = *Twentieth-Century Literary Criticism*
WLC = *World Literature Criticism, 1500 to the Present*
WLCS = *World Literature Criticism Supplement*

The cross-references

> See also CA 85-88, 116; CANR 23, 61;
> DAM NOV; DLB 196; EW 13; MTCW 1, 2;
> RGSF 2; RGWL 2; SFW 4; SSFS 12

list all author entries in the following Gale biographical and literary sources:

AAYA = *Authors & Artists for Young Adults*
AFAW = *African American Writers*
AFW = *African Writers*
AITN = *Authors in the News*
AMW = *American Writers*
AMWR = *American Writers Retrospective Supplement*
AMWS = *American Writers Supplement*
ANW = *American Nature Writers*
AW = *Ancient Writers*
BEST = *Bestsellers*
BPFB = *Beacham's Encyclopedia of Popular Fiction: Biography and Resources*
BRW = *British Writers*
BRWS = *British Writers Supplement*
BW = *Black Writers*
BYA = *Beacham's Guide to Literature for Young Adults*
CA = *Contemporary Authors*
CAAS = *Contemporary Authors Autobiography Series*
CABS = *Contemporary Authors Bibliographical Series*
CAD = *Contemporary American Dramatists*
CANR = *Contemporary Authors New Revision Series*
CAP = *Contemporary Authors Permanent Series*
CBD = *Contemporary British Dramatists*
CCA = *Contemporary Canadian Authors*
CD = *Contemporary Dramatists*
CDALB = *Concise Dictionary of American Literary Biography*
CDALBS = *Concise Dictionary of American Literary Biography Supplement*
CDBLB = *Concise Dictionary of British Literary Biography*

CMW = *St. James Guide to Crime & Mystery Writers*
CN = *Contemporary Novelists*
CP = *Contemporary Poets*
CPW = *Contemporary Popular Writers*
CSW = *Contemporary Southern Writers*
CWD = *Contemporary Women Dramatists*
CWP = *Contemporary Women Poets*
CWRI = *St. James Guide to Children's Writers*
CWW = *Contemporary World Writers*
DA = *DISCovering Authors*
DA3 = *DISCovering Authors 3.0*
DAB = *DISCovering Authors: British Edition*
DAC = *DISCovering Authors: Canadian Edition*
DAM = *DISCovering Authors: Modules*
   DRAM: Dramatists Module; MST: Most-studied Authors Module;
   MULT: Multicultural Authors Module; NOV: Novelists Module;
   POET: Poets Module; POP: Popular Fiction and Genre Authors Module
DFS = *Drama for Students*
DLB = *Dictionary of Literary Biography*
DLBD = *Dictionary of Literary Biography Documentary Series*
DLBY = *Dictionary of Literary Biography Yearbook*
DNFS = *Literature of Developing Nations for Students*
EFS = *Epics for Students*
EXPN = *Exploring Novels*
EXPP = *Exploring Poetry*
EXPS = *Exploring Short Stories*
EW = *European Writers*
FANT = *St. James Guide to Fantasy Writers*
FW = *Feminist Writers*
GFL = *Guide to French Literature,* Beginnings to 1789, 1798 to the Present
GLL = *Gay and Lesbian Literature*
HGG = *St. James Guide to Horror, Ghost & Gothic Writers*
HW = *Hispanic Writers*
IDFW = *International Dictionary of Films and Filmmakers: Writers and Production Artists*
IDTP = *International Dictionary of Theatre: Playwrights*
LAIT = *Literature and Its Times*
LAW = *Latin American Writers*
JRDA = *Junior DISCovering Authors*
MAICYA = *Major Authors and Illustrators for Children and Young Adults*
MAICYAS = *Major Authors and Illustrators for Children and Young Adults Supplement*
MAWW = *Modern American Women Writers*
MJW = *Modern Japanese Writers*
MTCW = *Major 20th-Century Writers*
NCFS = *Nonfiction Classics for Students*
NFS = *Novels for Students*
PAB = *Poets: American and British*
PFS = *Poetry for Students*
RGAL = *Reference Guide to American Literature*
RGEL = *Reference Guide to English Literature*
RGSF = *Reference Guide to Short Fiction*
RGWL = *Reference Guide to World Literature*
RHW = *Twentieth-Century Romance and Historical Writers*
SAAS = *Something about the Author Autobiography Series*
SATA = *Something about the Author*
SFW = *St. James Guide to Science Fiction Writers*
SSFS = *Short Stories for Students*
TCWW = *Twentieth-Century Western Writers*
WLIT = *World Literature and Its Times*
WP = *World Poets*
YABC = *Yesterday's Authors of Books for Children*
YAW = *St. James Guide to Young Adult Writers*

Literary Criticism Series
Cumulative Author Index

Armatrading, Joan 1950- .... **CLC 17**
See also CA 114; 186

Armitage, Frank
See Carpenter, John (Howard)

Armstrong, Jeannette (C.) 1948- .... **NNAL**
See also CA 149; CCA 1; CN 7; DAC;
SATA 102

Arnette, Robert
See Silverberg, Robert

Arnim, Achim von (Ludwig Joachim von Arnim) 1781-1831 ..... **NCLC 5; SSC 29**
See also DLB 90

Arnim, Bettina von 1785-1859 ...... **NCLC 38, 123**
See also DLB 90; RGWL 2, 3

Arnold, Matthew 1822-1888 ..... **NCLC 6, 29, 89, 126; PC 5; WLC**
See also BRW 5; CDBLB 1832-1890; DA;
DAB; DAC; DAM MST, POET; DLB 32,
57; EXPP; PAB; PFS 2; TEA; WP

Arnold, Thomas 1795-1842 .... **NCLC 18**
See also DLB 55

Arnow, Harriette (Louisa) Simpson 1908-1986 .... **CLC 2, 7, 18**
See also BPFB 1; CA 9-12R; 118; CANR
14; DLB 6; FW; MTCW 1, 2; RHW;
SATA 42; SATA-Obit 47

Arouet, Francois-Marie
See Voltaire

Arp, Hans
See Arp, Jean

Arp, Jean 1887-1966 .... **CLC 5; TCLC 115**
See also CA 81-84; 25-28R; CANR 42, 77;
EW 10

Arrabal
See Arrabal, Fernando

Arrabal, Fernando 1932- ... **CLC 2, 9, 18, 58**
See Arrabal (Teran), Fernando
See also CA 9-12R; CANR 15; EWL 3;
LMFS 2

Arrabal (Teran), Fernando 1932-
See Arrabal, Fernando
See also CWW 2

Arreola, Juan Jose 1918-2001 .... **CLC 147; HLC 1; SSC 38**
See also CA 113; 131; 200; CANR 81;
CWW 2; DAM MULT; DLB 113; DNFS
2; EWL 3; HW 1, 2; LAW; RGSF 2

Arrian c. 89(?)-c. 155(?) .... **CMLC 43**
See also DLB 176

Arrick, Fran .... **CLC 30**
See Gaberman, Judie Angell
See also BYA 6

Arrley, Richmond
See Delany, Samuel R(ay), Jr.

Artaud, Antonin (Marie Joseph) 1896-1948 .... **DC 14; TCLC 3, 36**
See also CA 104; 149; DA3; DAM DRAM;
DLB 258; EW 11; EWL 3; GFL 1789 to
the Present; MTCW 1; RGWL 2, 3

Arthur, Ruth M(abel) 1905-1979 ..... **CLC 12**
See also CA 9-12R; 85-88; CANR 4; CWRI
5; SATA 7, 26

Artsybashev, Mikhail (Petrovich) 1878-1927 .... **TCLC 31**
See also CA 170; DLB 295

Arundel, Honor (Morfydd) 1919-1973 .... **CLC 17**
See also CA 21-22; 41-44R; CAP 2; CLR
35; CWRI 5; SATA 4; SATA-Obit 24

Arzner, Dorothy 1900-1979 .... **CLC 98**

Asch, Sholem 1880-1957 .... **TCLC 3**
See also CA 105; EWL 3; GLL 2

Ascham, Roger 1516(?)-1568 .... **LC 101**
See also DLB 236

Ash, Shalom
See Asch, Sholem

Ashbery, John (Lawrence) 1927- .. **CLC 2, 3, 4, 6, 9, 13, 15, 25, 41, 77, 125; PC 26**
See Berry, Jonas
See also AMWS 3; CA 5-8R; CANR 9, 37,
66, 102, 132; CP 7; DA3; DAM POET;
DLB 5, 165; DLBY 1981; EWL 3; INT
CANR-9; MTCW 1, 2; PAB; PFS 11;
RGAL 4; WP

Ashdown, Clifford
See Freeman, R(ichard) Austin

Ashe, Gordon
See Creasey, John

Ashton-Warner, Sylvia (Constance) 1908-1984 .... **CLC 19**
See also CA 69-72; 112; CANR 29; MTCW
1, 2

Asimov, Isaac 1920-1992 ..... **CLC 1, 3, 9, 19, 26, 76, 92**
See also AAYA 13; BEST 90:2; BPFB 1;
BYA 4, 6, 7, 9; CA 1-4R; 137; CANR 2,
19, 36, 60, 125; CLR 12, 79; CMW 4;
CPW; DA3; DAM POP; DLB 8; DLBY
1992; INT CANR-19; JRDA; LAIT 5;
LMFS 2; MAICYA 1, 2; MTCW 1, 2;
RGAL 4; SATA 1, 26, 74; SCFW 2; SFW
4; SSFS 17; TUS; YAW

Askew, Anne 1521(?)-1546 .... **LC 81**
See also DLB 136

Assis, Joaquim Maria Machado de
See Machado de Assis, Joaquim Maria

Astell, Mary 1666-1731 .... **LC 68**
See also DLB 252; FW

Astley, Thea (Beatrice May) 1925-2004 .... **CLC 41**
See also CA 65-68; 229; CANR 11, 43, 78;
CN 7; DLB 289; EWL 3

Astley, William 1855-1911
See Warung, Price

Aston, James
See White, T(erence) H(anbury)

Asturias, Miguel Angel 1899-1974 .... **CLC 3, 8, 13; HLC 1**
See also CA 25-28; 49-52; CANR 32; CAP
2; CDWLB 3; DA3; DAM MULT, NOV;
DLB 113, 290; EWL 3; HW 1; LAW;
LMFS 2; MTCW 1, 2; RGWL 2, 3; WLIT
1

Atares, Carlos Saura
See Saura (Atares), Carlos

Athanasius c. 295-c. 373 .... **CMLC 48**

Atheling, William
See Pound, Ezra (Weston Loomis)

Atheling, William, Jr.
See Blish, James (Benjamin)

Atherton, Gertrude (Franklin Horn) 1857-1948 .... **TCLC 2**
See also CA 104; 155; DLB 9, 78, 186;
HGG; RGAL 4; SUFW 1; TCWW 2

Atherton, Lucius
See Masters, Edgar Lee

Atkins, Jack
See Harris, Mark

Atkinson, Kate 1951- .... **CLC 99**
See also CA 166; CANR 101; DLB 267

Attaway, William (Alexander) 1911-1986 .... **BLC 1; CLC 92**
See also BW 2, 3; CA 143; CANR 82;
DAM MULT; DLB 76

Atticus
See Fleming, Ian (Lancaster); Wilson,
(Thomas) Woodrow

Atwood, Margaret (Eleanor) 1939- ... **CLC 2, 3, 4, 8, 13, 15, 25, 44, 84, 135; PC 8; SSC 2, 46; WLC**
See also AAYA 12, 47; AMWS 13; BEST
89:2; BPFB 1; CA 49-52; CANR 3, 24,
33, 59, 95, 133; CN 7; CP 7; CPW; CWP;
DA; DA3; DAB; DAC; DAM MST, NOV,
POET; DLB 53, 251; EWL 3; EXPN; FW;

INT CANR-24; LAIT 5; MTCW 1, 2;
NFS 4, 12, 13, 14, 19; PFS 7; RGSF 2;
SATA 50; SSFS 3, 13; TWA; WWE 1;
YAW

Aubigny, Pierre d'
See Mencken, H(enry) L(ouis)

Aubin, Penelope 1685-1731(?) .... **LC 9**
See also DLB 39

Auchincloss, Louis (Stanton) 1917- .. **CLC 4, 6, 9, 18, 45; SSC 22**
See also AMWS 4; CA 1-4R; CANR 6, 29,
55, 87, 130; CN 7; DAM NOV; DLB 2,
244; DLBY 1980; EWL 3; INT CANR-
29; MTCW 1; RGAL 4

Auden, W(ystan) H(ugh) 1907-1973 . **CLC 1, 2, 3, 4, 6, 9, 11, 14, 43, 123; PC 1; WLC**
See also AAYA 18; AMWS 2; BRW 7;
BRWR 1; CA 9-12R; 45-48; CANR 5, 61,
105; CDBLB 1914-1945; DA; DA3;
DAB; DAC; DAM DRAM, MST, POET;
DLB 10, 20; EWL 3; EXPP; MTCW 1, 2;
PAB; PFS 1, 3, 4, 10; TUS; WP

Audiberti, Jacques 1899-1965 .... **CLC 38**
See also CA 25-28R; DAM DRAM; EWL 3

Audubon, John James 1785-1851 . **NCLC 47**
See also ANW; DLB 248

Auel, Jean M(arie) 1936- .... **CLC 31, 107**
See also AAYA 7, 51; BEST 90:4; BPFB 1;
CA 103; CANR 21, 64, 115; CPW; DA3;
DAM POP; INT CANR-21; NFS 11;
RHW; SATA 91

Auerbach, Erich 1892-1957 .... **TCLC 43**
See also CA 118; 155; EWL 3

Augier, Emile 1820-1889 .... **NCLC 31**
See also DLB 192; GFL 1789 to the Present

August, John
See De Voto, Bernard (Augustine)

Augustine, St. 354-430 .... **CMLC 6; WLCS**
See also DA; DA3; DAB; DAC; DAM
MST; DLB 115; EW 1; RGWL 2, 3

Aunt Belinda
See Braddon, Mary Elizabeth

Aunt Weedy
See Alcott, Louisa May

Aurelius
See Bourne, Randolph S(illiman)

Aurelius, Marcus 121-180 .... **CMLC 45**
See Marcus Aurelius
See also RGWL 2, 3

Aurobindo, Sri
See Ghose, Aurabinda

Aurobindo Ghose
See Ghose, Aurabinda

Austen, Jane 1775-1817 ...... **NCLC 1, 13, 19, 33, 51, 81, 95, 119, 150; WLC**
See also AAYA 19; BRW 4; BRWC 1;
BRWR 2; BYA 3; CDBLB 1789-1832;
DA; DA3; DAB; DAC; DAM MST, NOV;
DLB 116; EXPN; LAIT 2; LATS 1:1;
LMFS 1; NFS 1, 14, 18, 20; TEA; WLIT
3; WYAS 1

Auster, Paul 1947- .... **CLC 47, 131**
See also AMWS 12; CA 69-72; CANR 23,
52, 75, 129; CMW 4; CN 7; DA3; DLB
227; MTCW 1; SUFW 2

Austin, Frank
See Faust, Frederick (Schiller)
See also TCWW 2

Austin, Mary (Hunter) 1868-1934 . **TCLC 25**
See Stairs, Gordon
See also ANW; CA 109; 178; DLB 9, 78,
206, 221, 275; FW; TCWW 2

Averroes 1126-1198 .... **CMLC 7**
See also DLB 115

Avicenna 980-1037 .... **CMLC 16**
See also DLB 115

Baratynsky, Evgenii Abramovich
1800-1844 .... **NCLC 103**
See also DLB 205
Barbauld, Anna Laetitia
1743-1825 .... **NCLC 50**
See also DLB 107, 109, 142, 158; RGEL 2
Barbellion, W. N. P. .... **TCLC 24**
See Cummings, Bruce F(rederick)
Barber, Benjamin R. 1939- .... **CLC 141**
See also CA 29-32R; CANR 12, 32, 64, 119
Barbera, Jack (Vincent) 1945- .... **CLC 44**
See also CA 110; CANR 45
Barbey d'Aurevilly, Jules-Amedee
1808-1889 .... **NCLC 1; SSC 17**
See also DLB 119; GFL 1789 to the Present
Barbour, John c. 1316-1395 .... **CMLC 33**
See also DLB 146
Barbusse, Henri 1873-1935 .... **TCLC 5**
See also CA 105; 154; DLB 65; EWL 3; RGWL 2, 3
Barclay, Alexander c. 1475-1552 .... **LC 109**
See also DLB 132
Barclay, Bill
See Moorcock, Michael (John)
Barclay, William Ewert
See Moorcock, Michael (John)
Barea, Arturo 1897-1957 .... **TCLC 14**
See also CA 111; 201
Barfoot, Joan 1946- .... **CLC 18**
See also CA 105
Barham, Richard Harris
1788-1845 .... **NCLC 77**
See also DLB 159
Baring, Maurice 1874-1945 .... **TCLC 8**
See also CA 105; 168; DLB 34; HGG
Baring-Gould, Sabine 1834-1924 ... **TCLC 88**
See also DLB 156, 190
Barker, Clive 1952- .... **CLC 52; SSC 53**
See also AAYA 10, 54; BEST 90:3; BPFB
1; CA 121; 129; CANR 71, 111, 133;
CPW; DA3; DAM POP; DLB 261; HGG;
INT CA-129; MTCW 1, 2; SUFW 2
Barker, George Granville
1913-1991 .... **CLC 8, 48**
See also CA 9-12R; 135; CANR 7, 38;
DAM POET; DLB 20; EWL 3; MTCW 1
Barker, Harley Granville
See Granville-Barker, Harley
See also DLB 10
Barker, Howard 1946- .... **CLC 37**
See also CA 102; CBD; CD 5; DLB 13, 233
Barker, Jane 1652-1732 .... **LC 42, 82**
See also DLB 39, 131
Barker, Pat(ricia) 1943- ...... **CLC 32, 94, 146**
See also BRWS 4; CA 117; 122; CANR 50,
101; CN 7; DLB 271; INT CA-122
Barlach, Ernst (Heinrich)
1870-1938 .... **TCLC 84**
See also CA 178; DLB 56, 118; EWL 3
Barlow, Joel 1754-1812 .... **NCLC 23**
See also AMWS 2; DLB 37; RGAL 4
Barnard, Mary (Ethel) 1909- .... **CLC 48**
See also CA 21-22; CAP 2
Barnes, Djuna 1892-1982 .... **CLC 3, 4, 8, 11,
29, 127; SSC 3**
See Steptoe, Lydia
See also AMWS 3; CA 9-12R; 107; CAD;
CANR 16, 55; CWD; DLB 4, 9, 45; EWL
3; GLL 1; MTCW 1, 2; RGAL 4; TUS
Barnes, Jim 1933- .... **NNAL**
See also CA 108; 175; CAAE 175; CAAS
28; DLB 175
Barnes, Julian (Patrick) 1946- . **CLC 42, 141**
See also BRWS 4; CA 102; CANR 19, 54,
115; CN 7; DAB; DLB 194; DLBY 1993;
EWL 3; MTCW 1

Barnes, Peter 1931-2004 .... **CLC 5, 56**
See also CA 65-68; CAAS 12; CANR 33,
34, 64, 113; CBD; CD 5; DFS 6; DLB
13, 233; MTCW 1
Barnes, William 1801-1886 .... **NCLC 75**
See also DLB 32
Baroja (y Nessi), Pio 1872-1956 .... **HLC 1;
TCLC 8**
See also CA 104; EW 9
Baron, David
See Pinter, Harold
Baron Corvo
See Rolfe, Frederick (William Serafino
Austin Lewis Mary)
Barondess, Sue K(aufman)
1926-1977 .... **CLC 8**
See Kaufman, Sue
See also CA 1-4R; 69-72; CANR 1
Baron de Teive
See Pessoa, Fernando (Antonio Nogueira)
Baroness Von S.
See Zangwill, Israel
Barres, (Auguste-)Maurice
1862-1923 .... **TCLC 47**
See also CA 164; DLB 123; GFL 1789 to
the Present
Barreto, Afonso Henrique de Lima
See Lima Barreto, Afonso Henrique de
Barrett, Andrea 1954- .... **CLC 150**
See also CA 156; CANR 92
Barrett, Michele .... **CLC 65**
Barrett, (Roger) Syd 1946- .... **CLC 35**
Barrett, William (Christopher)
1913-1992 .... **CLC 27**
See also CA 13-16R; 139; CANR 11, 67;
INT CANR-11
Barrett Browning, Elizabeth
1806-1861 ... **NCLC 1, 16, 61, 66; PC 6,
62; WLC**
See also BRW 4; CDBLB 1832-1890; DA;
DA3; DAB; DAC; DAM MST, POET;
DLB 32, 199; EXPP; PAB; PFS 2, 16;
TEA; WLIT 4; WP
Barrie, J(ames) M(atthew)
1860-1937 .... **TCLC 2**
See also BRWS 3; BYA 4, 5; CA 104; 136;
CANR 77; CDBLB 1890-1914; CLR 16;
CWRI 5; DA3; DAB; DAM DRAM; DFS
7; DLB 10, 141, 156; EWL 3; FANT;
MAICYA 1, 2; MTCW 1; SATA 100;
SUFW; WCH; WLIT 4; YABC 1
Barrington, Michael
See Moorcock, Michael (John)
Barrol, Grady
See Bograd, Larry
Barry, Mike
See Malzberg, Barry N(athaniel)
Barry, Philip 1896-1949 .... **TCLC 11**
See also CA 109; 199; DFS 9; DLB 7, 228;
RGAL 4
Bart, Andre Schwarz
See Schwarz-Bart, Andre
Barth, John (Simmons) 1930- ... **CLC 1, 2, 3,
5, 7, 9, 10, 14, 27, 51, 89; SSC 10**
See also AITN 1, 2; AMW; BPFB 1; CA
1-4R; CABS 1; CANR 5, 23, 49, 64, 113;
CN 7; DAM NOV; DLB 2, 227; EWL 3;
FANT; MTCW 1; RGAL 4; RGSF 2;
RHW; SSFS 6; TUS
Barthelme, Donald 1931-1989 ... **CLC 1, 2, 3,
5, 6, 8, 13, 23, 46, 59, 115; SSC 2, 55**
See also AMWS 4; BPFB 1; CA 21-24R;
129; CANR 20, 58; DA3; DAM NOV;
DLB 2, 234; DLBY 1980, 1989; EWL 3;
FANT; LMFS 2; MTCW 1, 2; RGAL 4;
RGSF 2; SATA 7; SATA-Obit 62; SSFS
17

Barthelme, Frederick 1943- ...... **CLC 36, 117**
See also AMWS 11; CA 114; 122; CANR
77; CN 7; CSW; DLB 244; DLBY 1985;
EWL 3; INT CA-122
Barthes, Roland (Gerard)
1915-1980 .... **CLC 24, 83; TCLC 135**
See also CA 130; 97-100; CANR 66; DLB
296; EW 13; EWL 3; GFL 1789 to the
Present; MTCW 1, 2; TWA
Bartram, William 1739-1823 .... **NCLC 145**
See also ANW; DLB 37
Barzun, Jacques (Martin) 1907- ..... **CLC 51,
145**
See also CA 61-64; CANR 22, 95
Bashevis, Isaac
See Singer, Isaac Bashevis
Bashkirtseff, Marie 1859-1884 .... **NCLC 27**
Basho, Matsuo
See Matsuo Basho
See also PFS 18; RGWL 2, 3; WP
Basil of Caesaria c. 330-379 .... **CMLC 35**
Basket, Raney
See Edgerton, Clyde (Carlyle)
Bass, Kingsley B., Jr.
See Bullins, Ed
Bass, Rick 1958- .... **CLC 79, 143; SSC 60**
See also ANW; CA 126; CANR 53, 93;
CSW; DLB 212, 275
Bassani, Giorgio 1916-2000 .... **CLC 9**
See also CA 65-68; 190; CANR 33; CWW
2; DLB 128, 177, 299; EWL 3; MTCW 1;
RGWL 2, 3
Bastian, Ann .... **CLC 70**
Bastos, Augusto (Antonio) Roa
See Roa Bastos, Augusto (Antonio)
Bataille, Georges 1897-1962 .... **CLC 29;
TCLC 155**
See also CA 101; 89-92; EWL 3
Bates, H(erbert) E(rnest)
1905-1974 .... **CLC 46; SSC 10**
See also CA 93-96; 45-48; CANR 34; DA3;
DAB; DAM POP; DLB 162, 191; EWL
3; EXPS; MTCW 1, 2; RGSF 2; SSFS 7
Bauchart
See Camus, Albert
Baudelaire, Charles 1821-1867 . **NCLC 6, 29,
55; PC 1; SSC 18; WLC**
See also DA; DA3; DAB; DAC; DAM
MST, POET; DLB 217; EW 7; GFL 1789
to the Present; LMFS 2; PFS 21; RGWL
2, 3; TWA
Baudouin, Marcel
See Peguy, Charles (Pierre)
Baudouin, Pierre
See Peguy, Charles (Pierre)
Baudrillard, Jean 1929- .... **CLC 60**
See also DLB 296
Baum, L(yman) Frank 1856-1919 .. **TCLC 7,
132**
See also AAYA 46; BYA 16; CA 108; 133;
CLR 15; CWRI 5; DLB 22; FANT; JRDA;
MAICYA 1, 2; MTCW 1; NFS 13;
RGAL 4; SATA 18, 100; WCH
Baum, Louis F.
See Baum, L(yman) Frank
Baumbach, Jonathan 1933- .... **CLC 6, 23**
See also CA 13-16R; CAAS 5; CANR 12,
66; CN 7; DLBY 1980; INT CANR-12;
MTCW 1
Bausch, Richard (Carl) 1945- .... **CLC 51**
See also AMWS 7; CA 101; CAAS 14;
CANR 43, 61, 87; CSW; DLB 130
Baxter, Charles (Morley) 1947- . **CLC 45, 78**
See also CA 57-60; CANR 40, 64, 104, 133;
CPW; DAM POP; DLB 130; MTCW 2
Baxter, George Owen
See Faust, Frederick (Schiller)
Baxter, James K(eir) 1926-1972 .... **CLC 14**
See also CA 77-80; EWL 3

Benda, Julien 1867-1956 .... **TCLC 60**
　See also CA 120; 154; GFL 1789 to the
　Present

Benedict, Ruth (Fulton)
　1887-1948 .... **TCLC 60**
　See also CA 158; DLB 246

Benedikt, Michael 1935- .... **CLC 4, 14**
　See also CA 13-16R; CANR 7; CP 7; DLB
　5

Benet, Juan 1927-1993 .... **CLC 28**
　See also CA 143; EWL 3

Benet, Stephen Vincent 1898-1943 ... **SSC 10;**
　TCLC 7
　See also AMWS 11; CA 104; 152; DA3;
　DAM POET; DLB 4, 48, 102, 249, 284;
　DLBY 1997; EWL 3; HGG; MTCW 1;
　RGAL 4; RGSF 2; SUFW; WP; YABC 1

Benet, William Rose 1886-1950 ..... **TCLC 28**
　See also CA 118; 152; DAM POET; DLB
　45; RGAL 4

Benford, Gregory (Albert) 1941- ..... **CLC 52**
　See also BPFB 1; CA 69-72, 175; CAAE
　175; CAAS 27; CANR 12, 24, 49, 95,
　134; CSW; DLBY 1982; SCFW 2; SFW
　4

Bengtsson, Frans (Gunnar)
　1894-1954 .... **TCLC 48**
　See also CA 170; EWL 3

Benjamin, David
　See Slavitt, David R(ytman)

Benjamin, Lois
　See Gould, Lois

Benjamin, Walter 1892-1940 .... **TCLC 39**
　See also CA 164; DLB 242; EW 11; EWL
　3

Ben Jelloun, Tahar 1944-
　See Jelloun, Tahar ben
　See also CA 135; CWW 2; EWL 3; RGWL
　3; WLIT 2

Benn, Gottfried 1886-1956 .. **PC 35; TCLC 3**
　See also CA 106; 153; DLB 56; EWL 3;
　RGWL 2, 3

Bennett, Alan 1934- .... **CLC 45, 77**
　See also BRWS 8; CA 103; CANR 35, 55,
　106; CBD; CD 5; DAB; DAM MST;
　MTCW 1, 2

Bennett, (Enoch) Arnold
　1867-1931 .... **TCLC 5, 20**
　See also BRW 6; CA 106; 155; CDBLB
　1890-1914; DLB 10, 34, 98, 135; EWL 3;
　MTCW 2

Bennett, Elizabeth
　See Mitchell, Margaret (Munnerlyn)

Bennett, George Harold 1930-
　See Bennett, Hal
　See also BW 1; CA 97-100; CANR 87

Bennett, Gwendolyn B. 1902-1981 .... **HR 2**
　See also BW 1; CA 125; DLB 51; WP

Bennett, Hal .... **CLC 5**
　See Bennett, George Harold
　See also DLB 33

Bennett, Jay 1912- .... **CLC 35**
　See also AAYA 10; CA 69-72; CANR 11,
　42, 79; JRDA; SAAS 4; SATA 41, 87;
　SATA-Brief 27; WYA; YAW

Bennett, Louise (Simone) 1919- .... **BLC 1;**
　CLC 28
　See also BW 2, 3; CA 151; CDWLB 3; CP
　7; DAM MULT; DLB 117; EWL 3

Benson, A. C. 1862-1925 .... **TCLC 123**
　See also DLB 98

Benson, E(dward) F(rederic)
　1867-1940 .... **TCLC 27**
　See also CA 114; 157; DLB 135, 153;
　HGG; SUFW 1

Benson, Jackson J. 1930- .... **CLC 34**
　See also CA 25-28R; DLB 111

Benson, Sally 1900-1972 .... **CLC 17**
　See also CA 19-20; 37-40R; CAP 1; SATA
　1, 35; SATA-Obit 27

Benson, Stella 1892-1933 .... **TCLC 17**
　See also CA 117; 154, 155; DLB 36, 162;
　FANT; TEA

Bentham, Jeremy 1748-1832 .... **NCLC 38**
　See also DLB 107, 158, 252

Bentley, E(dmund) C(lerihew)
　1875-1956 .... **TCLC 12**
　See also CA 108; DLB 70; MSW

Bentley, Eric (Russell) 1916- .... **CLC 24**
　See also CA 5-8R; CAD; CANR 6, 67;
　CBD; CD 5; INT CANR-6

ben Uzair, Salem
　See Horne, Richard Henry Hengist

Beranger, Pierre Jean de
　1780-1857 .... **NCLC 34**

Berdyaev, Nicolas
　See Berdyaev, Nikolai (Aleksandrovich)

Berdyaev, Nikolai (Aleksandrovich)
　1874-1948 .... **TCLC 67**
　See also CA 120; 157

Berdyayev, Nikolai (Aleksandrovich)
　See Berdyaev, Nikolai (Aleksandrovich)

Berendt, John (Lawrence) 1939- ...... **CLC 86**
　See also CA 146; CANR 75, 93; DA3;
　MTCW 1

Beresford, J(ohn) D(avys)
　1873-1947 .... **TCLC 81**
　See also CA 112; 155; DLB 162, 178, 197;
　SFW 4; SUFW 1

Bergelson, David (Rafailovich)
　1884-1952 .... **TCLC 81**
　See Bergelson, Dovid
　See also CA 220

Bergelson, Dovid
　See Bergelson, David (Rafailovich)
　See also EWL 3

Berger, Colonel
　See Malraux, (Georges-)Andre

Berger, John (Peter) 1926- .... **CLC 2, 19**
　See also BRWS 4; CA 81-84; CANR 51,
　78, 117; CN 7; DLB 14, 207

Berger, Melvin H. 1927- .... **CLC 12**
　See also CA 5-8R; CANR 4; CLR 32;
　SAAS 2; SATA 5, 88; SATA-Essay 124

Berger, Thomas (Louis) 1924- .. **CLC 3, 5, 8,**
　11, 18, 38
　See also BPFB 1; CA 1-4R; CANR 5, 28,
　51, 128; CN 7; DAM NOV; DLB 2;
　DLBY 1980; EWL 3; FANT; INT CANR-
　28; MTCW 1, 2; RHW; TCWW 2

Bergman, (Ernst) Ingmar 1918- ...... **CLC 16,**
　72
　See also CA 81-84; CANR 33, 70; CWW
　2; DLB 257; MTCW 2

Bergson, Henri(-Louis) 1859-1941 . **TCLC 32**
　See also CA 164; EW 8; EWL 3; GFL 1789
　to the Present

Bergstein, Eleanor 1938- .... **CLC 4**
　See also CA 53-56; CANR 5

Berkeley, George 1685-1753 .... **LC 65**
　See also DLB 31, 101, 252

Berkoff, Steven 1937- .... **CLC 56**
　See also CA 104; CANR 72; CBD; CD 5

Berlin, Isaiah 1909-1997 .... **TCLC 105**
　See also CA 85-88; 162

Bermant, Chaim (Icyk) 1929-1998 ... **CLC 40**
　See also CA 57-60; CANR 6, 31, 57, 105;
　CN 7

Bern, Victoria
　See Fisher, M(ary) F(rances) K(ennedy)

Bernanos, (Paul Louis) Georges
　1888-1948 .... **TCLC 3**
　See also CA 104; 130; CANR 94; DLB 72;
　EWL 3; GFL 1789 to the Present; RGWL
　2, 3

Bernard, April 1956- .... **CLC 59**
　See also CA 131

Bernard of Clairvaux 1090-1153 .. **CMLC 71**
　See also DLB 208

Berne, Victoria
　See Fisher, M(ary) F(rances) K(ennedy)

Bernhard, Thomas 1931-1989 ..... **CLC 3, 32,**
　61; DC 14
　See also CA 85-88; 127; CANR 32, 57; CD-
　WLB 2; DLB 85, 124; EWL 3; MTCW 1;
　RGWL 2, 3

Bernhardt, Sarah (Henriette Rosine)
　1844-1923 .... **TCLC 75**
　See also CA 157

Bernstein, Charles 1950- .... **CLC 142,**
　See also CA 129; CAAS 24; CANR 90; CP
　7; DLB 169

Bernstein, Ingrid
　See Kirsch, Sarah

Berriault, Gina 1926-1999 .... **CLC 54, 109;**
　SSC 30
　See also CA 116; 129; 185; CANR 66; DLB
　130; SSFS 7,11

Berrigan, Daniel 1921- .... **CLC 4**
　See also CA 33-36R, 187; CAAE 187;
　CAAS 1; CANR 11, 43, 78; CP 7; DLB 5

Berrigan, Edmund Joseph Michael, Jr.
　1934-1983
　See Berrigan, Ted
　See also CA 61-64; 110; CANR 14, 102

Berrigan, Ted .... **CLC 37**
　See Berrigan, Edmund Joseph Michael, Jr.
　See also DLB 5, 169; WP

Berry, Charles Edward Anderson 1931-
　See Berry, Chuck
　See also CA 115

Berry, Chuck .... **CLC 17**
　See Berry, Charles Edward Anderson

Berry, Jonas
　See Ashbery, John (Lawrence)
　See also GLL 1

Berry, Wendell (Erdman) 1934- ... **CLC 4, 6,**
　8, 27, 46; PC 28
　See also AITN 1; AMWS 10; ANW; CA
　73-76; CANR 50, 73, 101, 132; CP 7;
　CSW; DAM POET; DLB 5, 6, 234, 275;
　MTCW 1

Berryman, John 1914-1972 ... **CLC 1, 2, 3, 4,**
　6, 8, 10, 13, 25, 62
　See also AMW; CA 13-16; 33-36R; CABS
　2; CANR 35; CAP 1; CDALB 1941-1968;
　DAM POET; DLB 48; EWL 3; MTCW 1,
　2; PAB; RGAL 4; WP

Bertolucci, Bernardo 1940- ...... **CLC 16, 157**
　See also CA 106; CANR 125

Berton, Pierre (Francis Demarigny)
　1920-2004 .... **CLC 104**
　See also CA 1-4R; CANR 2, 56; CPW;
　DLB 68; SATA 99

Bertrand, Aloysius 1807-1841 .... **NCLC 31**
　See Bertrand, Louis oAloysiusc

Bertrand, Louis oAloysiusc
　See Bertrand, Aloysius
　See also DLB 217

Bertran de Born c. 1140-1215 .... **CMLC 5**

Besant, Annie (Wood) 1847-1933 ..... **TCLC 9**
　See also CA 105; 185

Bessie, Alvah 1904-1985 .... **CLC 23**
　See also CA 5-8R; 116; CANR 2, 80; DLB
　26

Bestuzhev, Aleksandr Aleksandrovich
　1797-1837 .... **NCLC 131**
　See also DLB 198

Bethlen, T. D.
　See Silverberg, Robert

Beti, Mongo .... **BLC 1; CLC 27**
　See Biyidi, Alexandre
　See also AFW; CANR 79; DAM MULT;
　EWL 3; WLIT 2

Betjeman, John 1906-1984 ...... **CLC 2, 6, 10, 34, 43**
See also BRW 7; CA 9-12R; 112; CANR 33, 56; CDBLB 1945-1960; DA3; DAB; DAM MST, POET; DLB 20; DLBY 1984; EWL 3; MTCW 1, 2

Bettelheim, Bruno 1903-1990 .... **CLC 79; TCLC 143**
See also CA 81-84; 131; CANR 23, 61; DA3; MTCW 1, 2

Betti, Ugo 1892-1953 .... **TCLC 5**
See also CA 104; 155; EWL 3; RGWL 2, 3

Betts, Doris (Waugh) 1932- ..... **CLC 3, 6, 28; SSC 45**
See also CA 13-16R; CANR 9, 66, 77; CN 7; CSW; DLB 218; DLBY 1982; INT CANR-9; RGAL 4

Bevan, Alistair
See Roberts, Keith (John Kingston)

Bey, Pilaff
See Douglas, (George) Norman

Bialik, Chaim Nachman
1873-1934 .... **TCLC 25**
See also CA 170; EWL 3

Bickerstaff, Isaac
See Swift, Jonathan

Bidart, Frank 1939- .... **CLC 33**
See also CA 140; CANR 106; CP 7

Bienek, Horst 1930- .... **CLC 7, 11**
See also CA 73-76; DLB 75

Bierce, Ambrose (Gwinett)
1842-1914(?) ..... **SSC 9, 72; TCLC 1, 7, 44; WLC**
See also AAYA 55; AMW; BYA 11; CA 104; 139; CANR 78; CDALB 1865-1917; DA; DA3; DAC; DAM MST; DLB 11, 12, 23, 71, 74, 186; EWL 3; EXPS; HGG; LAIT 2; RGAL 4; RGSF 2; SSFS 9; SUFW 1

Biggers, Earl Derr 1884-1933 .... **TCLC 65**
See also CA 108; 153; DLB 306

Billiken, Bud
See Motley, Willard (Francis)

Billings, Josh
See Shaw, Henry Wheeler

Billington, (Lady) Rachel (Mary)
1942- .... **CLC 43**
See also AITN 2; CA 33-36R; CANR 44; CN 7

Binchy, Maeve 1940- .... **CLC 153**
See also BEST 90:1; BPFB 1; CA 127; 134; CANR 50, 96, 134; CN 7; CPW; DA3; DAM POP; INT CA-134; MTCW 1; RHW

Binyon, T(imothy) J(ohn) 1936- .... **CLC 34**
See also CA 111; CANR 28

Bion 335B.C.-245B.C. .... **CMLC 39**

Bioy Casares, Adolfo 1914-1999 ... **CLC 4, 8, 13, 88; HLC 1; SSC 88**
See Casares, Adolfo Bioy; Miranda, Javier; Sacastru, Martin
See also CA 29-32R; 177; CANR 19, 43, 66; CWW 2; DAM MULT; DLB 113; EWL 3; HW 1, 2; LAW; MTCW 1, 2

Birch, Allison .... **CLC 65**

Bird, Cordwainer
See Ellison, Harlan (Jay)

Bird, Robert Montgomery
1806-1854 .... **NCLC 1**
See also DLB 202; RGAL 4

Birkerts, Sven 1951- .... **CLC 116**
See also CA 128; 133, 176; CAAE 176; CAAS 29; INT CA-133

Birney, (Alfred) Earle 1904-1995 .. **CLC 1, 4, 6, 11; PC 52**
See also CA 1-4R; CANR 5, 20; CP 7; DAC; DAM MST, POET; DLB 88; MTCW 1; PFS 8; RGEL 2

Biruni, al 973-1048(?) .... **CMLC 28**

Bishop, Elizabeth 1911-1979 ..... **CLC 1, 4, 9, 13, 15, 32; PC 3, 34; TCLC 121**
See also AMWR 2; AMWS 1; CA 5-8R; 89-92; CABS 2; CANR 26, 61, 108; CDALB 1968-1988; DA; DA3; DAC; DAM MST, POET; DLB 5, 169; EWL 3; GLL 2; MAWW; MTCW 1, 2; PAB; PFS 6, 12; RGAL 4; SATA-Obit 24; TUS; WP

Bishop, John 1935- .... **CLC 10**
See also CA 105

Bishop, John Peale 1892-1944 ..... **TCLC 103**
See also CA 107; 155; DLB 4, 9, 45; RGAL 4

Bissett, Bill 1939- .... **CLC 18; PC 14**
See also CA 69-72; CAAS 19; CANR 15; CCA 1; CP 7; DLB 53; MTCW 1

Bissoondath, Neil (Devindra)
1955- .... **CLC 120**
See also CA 136; CANR 123; CN 7; DAC

Bitov, Andrei (Georgievich) 1937- ... **CLC 57**
See also CA 142; DLB 302

Biyidi, Alexandre 1932-
See Beti, Mongo
See also BW 1, 3; CA 114; 124; CANR 81; DA3; MTCW 1, 2

Bjarme, Brynjolf
See Ibsen, Henrik (Johan)

Bjoernson, Bjoernstjerne (Martinius)
1832-1910 .... **TCLC 7, 37**
See also CA 104

Black, Robert
See Holdstock, Robert P.

Blackburn, Paul 1926-1971 .... **CLC 9, 43**
See also BG 2; CA 81-84; 33-36R; CANR 34; DLB 16; DLBY 1981

Black Elk 1863-1950 .... **NNAL; TCLC 33**
See also CA 144; DAM MULT; MTCW 1; WP

Black Hawk 1767-1838 .... **NNAL**

Black Hobart
See Sanders, (James) Ed(ward)

Blacklin, Malcolm
See Chambers, Aidan

Blackmore, R(ichard) D(oddridge)
1825-1900 .... **TCLC 27**
See also CA 120; DLB 18; RGEL 2

Blackmur, R(ichard) P(almer)
1904-1965 .... **CLC 2, 24**
See also AMWS 2; CA 11-12; 25-28R; CANR 71; CAP 1; DLB 63; EWL 3

Black Tarantula
See Acker, Kathy

Blackwood, Algernon (Henry)
1869-1951 .... **TCLC 5**
See also CA 105; 150; DLB 153, 156, 178; HGG; SUFW 1

Blackwood, Caroline 1931-1996 .... **CLC 6, 9, 100**
See also BRWS 9; CA 85-88; 151; CANR 32, 61, 65; CN 7; DLB 14, 207; HGG; MTCW 1

Blade, Alexander
See Hamilton, Edmond; Silverberg, Robert

Blaga, Lucian 1895-1961 .... **CLC 75**
See also CA 157; DLB 220; EWL 3

Blair, Eric (Arthur) 1903-1950 .... **TCLC 123**
See Orwell, George
See also CA 104; 132; DA; DA3; DAB; DAC; DAM MST, NOV; MTCW 1, 2; SATA 29

Blair, Hugh 1718-1800 .... **NCLC 75**

Blais, Marie-Claire 1939- .... **CLC 2, 4, 6, 13, 22**
See also CA 21-24R; CAAS 4; CANR 38, 75, 93; CWW 2; DAC; DAM MST; DLB 53; EWL 3; FW; MTCW 1, 2; TWA

Blaise, Clark 1940- .... **CLC 29**
See also AITN 2; CA 53-56; CAAS 3; CANR 5, 66, 106; CN 7; DLB 53; RGSF 2

Blake, Fairley
See De Voto, Bernard (Augustine)

Blake, Nicholas
See Day Lewis, C(ecil)
See also DLB 77; MSW

Blake, Sterling
See Benford, Gregory (Albert)

Blake, William 1757-1827 . **NCLC 13, 37, 57, 127; PC 12; WLC**
See also AAYA 47; BRW 3; BRWR 1; CD-BLB 1789-1832; CLR 52; DA; DA3; DAB; DAC; DAM MST, POET; DLB 93, 163; EXPP; LATS 1:1; LMFS 1; MAICYA 1, 2; PAB; PFS 2, 12; SATA 30; TEA; WCH; WLIT 3; WP

Blanchot, Maurice 1907-2003 .... **CLC 135**
See also CA 117; 144; 213; DLB 72, 296; EWL 3

Blasco Ibanez, Vicente 1867-1928 . **TCLC 12**
See also BPFB 1; CA 110; 131; CANR 81; DA3; DAM NOV; EW 8; EWL 3; HW 1, 2; MTCW 1

Blatty, William Peter 1928- .... **CLC 2**
See also CA 5-8R; CANR 9, 124; DAM POP; HGG

Bleeck, Oliver
See Thomas, Ross (Elmore)

Blessing, Lee 1949- .... **CLC 54**
See also CAD; CD 5

Blight, Rose
See Greer, Germaine

Blish, James (Benjamin) 1921-1975 . **CLC 14**
See also BPFB 1; CA 1-4R; 57-60; CANR 3; DLB 8; MTCW 1; SATA 66; SCFW 2; SFW 4

Bliss, Frederick
See Card, Orson Scott

Bliss, Reginald
See Wells, H(erbert) G(eorge)

Blixen, Karen (Christentze Dinesen)
1885-1962
See Dinesen, Isak
See also CA 25-28; CANR 22, 50; CAP 2; DA3; DLB 214; LMFS 1; MTCW 1, 2; SATA 44; SSFS 20

Bloch, Robert (Albert) 1917-1994 .... **CLC 33**
See also AAYA 29; CA 5-8R, 179; 146; CAAE 179; CAAS 20; CANR 5, 78; DA3; DLB 44; HGG; INT CANR-5; MTCW 1; SATA 12; SATA-Obit 82; SFW 4; SUFW 1, 2

Blok, Alexander (Alexandrovich)
1880-1921 .... **PC 21; TCLC 5**
See also CA 104; 183; DLB 295; EW 9; EWL 3; LMFS 2; RGWL 2, 3

Blom, Jan
See Breytenbach, Breyten

Bloom, Harold 1930- .... **CLC 24, 103**
See also CA 13-16R; CANR 39, 75, 92, 133; DLB 67; EWL 3; MTCW 1; RGAL 4

Bloomfield, Aurelius
See Bourne, Randolph S(illiman)

Bloomfield, Robert 1766-1823 ..... **NCLC 145**
See also DLB 93

Blount, Roy (Alton), Jr. 1941- .... **CLC 38**
See also CA 53-56; CANR 10, 28, 61, 125; CSW; INT CANR-28; MTCW 1, 2

Blowsnake, Sam 1875-(?) .... **NNAL**

Bloy, Leon 1846-1917 .... **TCLC 22**
See also CA 121; 183; DLB 123; GFL 1789 to the Present

Blue Cloud, Peter (Aroniawenrate)
1933- .... **NNAL**
See also CA 117; CANR 40; DAM MULT

Bowles, Jane Auer
See Bowles, Jane (Sydney)
See also EWL 3

Bowles, Paul (Frederick) 1910-1999 . **CLC 1, 2, 19, 53; SSC 3**
See also AMWS 4; CA 1-4R; 186; CAAS 1; CANR 1, 19, 50, 75; CN 7; DA3; DLB 5, 6, 218; EWL 3; MTCW 1, 2; RGAL 4; SSFS 17

Bowles, William Lisle 1762-1850 . **NCLC 103**
See also DLB 93

Box, Edgar
See Vidal, (Eugene Luther) Gore
See also GLL 1

Boyd, James 1888-1944 .... **TCLC 115**
See also CA 186; DLB 9; DLBD 16; RGAL 4; RHW

Boyd, Nancy
See Millay, Edna St. Vincent
See also GLL 1

Boyd, Thomas (Alexander)
1898-1935 .... **TCLC 111**
See also CA 111; 183; DLB 9; DLBD 16

Boyd, William 1952- .... **CLC 28, 53, 70**
See also CA 114; 120; CANR 51, 71, 131; CN 7; DLB 231

Boyesen, Hjalmar Hjorth
1848-1895 .... **NCLC 135**
See also DLB 12, 71; DLBD 13; RGAL 4

Boyle, Kay 1902-1992 .... **CLC 1, 5, 19, 58, 121; SSC 5**
See also CA 13-16R; 140; CAAS 1; CANR 29, 61, 110; DLB 4, 9, 48, 86; DLBY 1993; EWL 3; MTCW 1, 2; RGAL 4; RGSF 2; SSFS 10, 13, 14

Boyle, Mark
See Kienzle, William X(avier)

Boyle, Patrick 1905-1982 .... **CLC 19**
See also CA 127

Boyle, T. C.
See Boyle, T(homas) Coraghessan
See also AMWS 8

Boyle, T(homas) Coraghessan
1948- .... **CLC 36, 55, 90; SSC 16**
See Boyle, T. C.
See also AAYA 47; BEST 90:4; BPFB 1; CA 120; CANR 44, 76, 89, 132; CN 7; CPW; DA3; DAM POP; DLB 218, 278; DLBY 1986; EWL 3; MTCW 2; SSFS 13, 19

Boz
See Dickens, Charles (John Huffam)

Brackenridge, Hugh Henry
1748-1816 .... **NCLC 7**
See also DLB 11, 37; RGAL 4

Bradbury, Edward P.
See Moorcock, Michael (John)
See also MTCW 2

Bradbury, Malcolm (Stanley)
1932-2000 .... **CLC 32, 61**
See also CA 1-4R; CANR 1, 33, 91, 98; CN 7; DA3; DAM NOV; DLB 14, 207; EWL 3; MTCW 1, 2

Bradbury, Ray (Douglas) 1920- .... **CLC 1, 3, 10, 15, 42, 98; SSC 29, 53; WLC**
See also AAYA 15; AITN 1, 2; AMWS 4; BPFB 1; BYA 4, 5, 11; CA 1-4R; CANR 2, 30, 75, 125; CDALB 1968-1988; CN 7; CPW; DA; DA3; DAB; DAC; DAM MST, NOV, POP; DLB 2, 8; EXPN; EXPS; HGG; LAIT 3, 5; LATS 1:2; LMFS 2; MTCW 1, 2; NFS 1; RGAL 4; RGSF 2; SATA 11, 64, 123; SCFW 2; SFW 4; SSFS 1, 20; SUFW 1, 2; TUS; YAW

Braddon, Mary Elizabeth
1837-1915 .... **TCLC 111**
See also BRWS 8; CA 108; 179; CMW 4; DLB 18, 70, 156; HGG

Bradfield, Scott (Michael) 1955- .... **SSC 65**
See also CA 147; CANR 90; HGG; SUFW 2

Bradford, Gamaliel 1863-1932 .... **TCLC 36**
See also CA 160; DLB 17

Bradford, William 1590-1657 .... **LC 64**
See also DLB 24, 30; RGAL 4

Bradley, David (Henry), Jr. 1950- .... **BLC 1; CLC 23, 118**
See also BW 1, 3; CA 104; CANR 26, 81; CN 7; DAM MULT; DLB 33

Bradley, John Ed(mund, Jr.) 1958- . **CLC 55**
See also CA 139; CANR 99; CN 7; CSW

Bradley, Marion Zimmer
1930-1999 .... **CLC 30**
See Chapman, Lee; Dexter, John; Gardner, Miriam; Ives, Morgan; Rivers, Elfrida
See also AAYA 40; BPFB 1; CA 57-60; 185; CAAS 10; CANR 7, 31, 51, 75, 107; CPW; DA3; DAM POP; DLB 8; FANT; FW; MTCW 1, 2; SATA 90, 139; SATA-Obit 116; SFW 4; SUFW 2; YAW

Bradshaw, John 1933- .... **CLC 70**
See also CA 138; CANR 61

Bradstreet, Anne 1612(?)-1672 ...... **LC 4, 30; PC 10**
See also AMWS 1; CDALB 1640-1865; DA; DA3; DAC; DAM MST, POET; DLB 24; EXPP; FW; PFS 6; RGAL 4; TUS; WP

Brady, Joan 1939- .... **CLC 86**
See also CA 141

Bragg, Melvyn 1939- .... **CLC 10**
See also BEST 89:3; CA 57-60; CANR 10, 48, 89; CN 7; DLB 14, 271; RHW

Brahe, Tycho 1546-1601 .... **LC 45**
See also DLB 300

Braine, John (Gerard) 1922-1986 . **CLC 1, 3, 41**
See also CA 1-4R; 120; CANR 1, 33; CDBLB 1945-1960; DLB 15; DLBY 1986; EWL 3; MTCW 1

Braithwaite, William Stanley (Beaumont)
1878-1962 .... **BLC 1; HR 2; PC 52**
See also BW 1; CA 125; DAM MULT; DLB 50, 54

Bramah, Ernest 1868-1942 .... **TCLC 72**
See also CA 156; CMW 4; DLB 70; FANT

Brammer, William 1930(?)-1978 ...... **CLC 31**
See also CA 77-80

Brancati, Vitaliano 1907-1954 .... **TCLC 12**
See also CA 109; DLB 264; EWL 3

Brancato, Robin F(idler) 1936- .... **CLC 35**
See also AAYA 9; BYA 6; CA 69-72; CANR 11, 45; CLR 32; JRDA; MAICYA 2; MAICYAS 1; SAAS 9; SATA 97; WYA; YAW

Brand, Dionne 1953- .... **CLC 192**
See also BW 2; CA 143; CWP

Brand, Max
See Faust, Frederick (Schiller)
See also BPFB 1; TCWW 2

Brand, Millen 1906-1980 .... **CLC 7**
See also CA 21-24R; 97-100; CANR 72

Branden, Barbara .... **CLC 44**
See also CA 148

Brandes, Georg (Morris Cohen)
1842-1927 .... **TCLC 10**
See also CA 105; 189; DLB 300

Brandys, Kazimierz 1916-2000 .... **CLC 62**
See also EWL 3

Branley, Franklyn M(ansfield)
1915-2002 .... **CLC 21**
See also CA 33-36R; 207; CANR 14, 39; CLR 13; MAICYA 1, 2; SAAS 16; SATA 4, 68, 136

Brant, Beth (E.) 1941- .... **NNAL**
See also CA 144; FW

Brant, Sebastian 1457-1521 .... **LC 112**
See also DLB 179; RGWL 2, 3

Brathwaite, Edward Kamau
1930- .... **BLCS; CLC 11; PC 56**
See also BW 2, 3; CA 25-28R; CANR 11, 26, 47, 107; CDWLB 3; CP 7; DAM POET; DLB 125; EWL 3

Brathwaite, Kamau
See Brathwaite, Edward Kamau

Brautigan, Richard (Gary)
1935-1984 .... **CLC 1, 3, 5, 9, 12, 34, 42; TCLC 133**
See also BPFB 1; CA 53-56; 113; CANR 34; DA3; DAM NOV; DLB 2, 5, 206; DLBY 1980, 1984; FANT; MTCW 1; RGAL 4; SATA 56

Brave Bird, Mary .... **NNAL**
See Crow Dog, Mary (Ellen)

Braverman, Kate 1950- .... **CLC 67**
See also CA 89-92

Brecht, (Eugen) Bertolt (Friedrich)
1898-1956 ..... **DC 3; TCLC 1, 6, 13, 35; WLC**
See also CA 104; 133; CANR 62; CDWLB 2; DA; DA3; DAB; DAC; DAM DRAM, MST; DFS 4, 5, 9; DLB 56, 124; EW 11; EWL 3; IDTP; MTCW 1, 2; RGWL 2, 3; TWA

Brecht, Eugen Berthold Friedrich
See Brecht, (Eugen) Bertolt (Friedrich)

Bremer, Fredrika 1801-1865 .... **NCLC 11**
See also DLB 254

Brennan, Christopher John
1870-1932 .... **TCLC 17**
See also CA 117; 188; DLB 230; EWL 3

Brennan, Maeve 1917-1993 ... **CLC 5; TCLC 124**
See also CA 81-84; CANR 72, 100

Brent, Linda
See Jacobs, Harriet A(nn)

Brentano, Clemens (Maria)
1778-1842 .... **NCLC 1**
See also DLB 90; RGWL 2, 3

Brent of Bin Bin
See Franklin, (Stella Maria Sarah) Miles (Lampe)

Brenton, Howard 1942- .... **CLC 31**
See also CA 69-72; CANR 33, 67; CBD; CD 5; DLB 13; MTCW 1

Breslin, James 1930-
See Breslin, Jimmy
See also CA 73-76; CANR 31, 75; DAM NOV; MTCW 1, 2

Breslin, Jimmy .... **CLC 4, 43**
See Breslin, James
See also AITN 1; DLB 185; MTCW 2

Bresson, Robert 1901(?)-1999 .... **CLC 16**
See also CA 110; 187; CANR 49

Breton, Andre 1896-1966 .. **CLC 2, 9, 15, 54; PC 15**
See also CA 19-20; 25-28R; CANR 40, 60; CAP 2; DLB 65, 258; EW 11; EWL 3; GFL 1789 to the Present; LMFS 2; MTCW 1, 2; RGWL 2, 3; TWA; WP

Breytenbach, Breyten 1939(?)- .. **CLC 23, 37, 126**
See also CA 113; 129; CANR 61, 122; CWW 2; DAM POET; DLB 225; EWL 3

Bridgers, Sue Ellen 1942- .... **CLC 26**
See also AAYA 8, 49; BYA 7, 8; CA 65-68; CANR 11, 36; CLR 18; DLB 52; JRDA; MAICYA 1, 2; SAAS 1; SATA 22, 90; SATA-Essay 109; WYA; YAW

Bridges, Robert (Seymour)
1844-1930 .... **PC 28; TCLC 1**
See also BRW 6; CA 104; 152; CDBLB 1890-1914; DAM POET; DLB 19, 98

Bush, Ronald 1946- .... **CLC 34**
See also CA 136
Bustos, F(rancisco)
See Borges, Jorge Luis
Bustos Domecq, H(onorio)
See Bioy Casares, Adolfo; Borges, Jorge
Luis
Butler, Octavia E(stelle) 1947- .. **BLCS; CLC 38, 121**
See also AAYA 18, 48; AFAW 2; AMWS
13; BPFB 1; BW 2, 3; CA 73-76; CANR
12, 24, 38, 73; CLR 65; CPW; DA3;
DAM MULT, POP; DLB 33; LATS 1:2;
MTCW 1, 2; NFS 8; SATA 84; SCFW 2;
SFW 4; SSFS 6; YAW
Butler, Robert Olen, (Jr.) 1945- ...... **CLC 81, 162**
See also AMWS 12; BPFB 1; CA 112;
CANR 66; CSW; DAM POP; DLB 173;
INT CA-112; MTCW 1; SSFS 11
Butler, Samuel 1612-1680 .... **LC 16, 43**
See also DLB 101, 126; RGEL 2
Butler, Samuel 1835-1902 .... **TCLC 1, 33; WLC**
See also BRWS 2; CA 143; CDBLB 1890-
1914; DA; DA3; DAB; DAC; DAM MST,
NOV; DLB 18, 57, 174; RGEL 2; SFW 4;
TEA
Butler, Walter C.
See Faust, Frederick (Schiller)
Butor, Michel (Marie Francois)
1926- .... **CLC 1, 3, 8, 11, 15, 161**
See also CA 9-12R; CANR 33, 66; CWW
2; DLB 83; EW 13; EWL 3; GFL 1789 to
the Present; MTCW 1, 2
Butts, Mary 1890(?)-1937 .... **TCLC 77**
See also CA 148; DLB 240
Buxton, Ralph
See Silverstein, Alvin; Silverstein, Virginia
B(arbara Opshelor)
Buzo, Alex
See Buzo, Alexander (John)
See also DLB 289
Buzo, Alexander (John) 1944- .... **CLC 61**
See also CA 97-100; CANR 17, 39, 69; CD
5
Buzzati, Dino 1906-1972 .... **CLC 36**
See also CA 160; 33-36R; DLB 177; RGWL
2, 3; SFW 4
Byars, Betsy (Cromer) 1928- .... **CLC 35**
See also AAYA 19; BYA 3; CA 33-36R,
183; CAAE 183; CANR 18, 36, 57, 102;
CLR 1, 16, 72; DLB 52; INT CANR-18;
JRDA; MAICYA 1, 2; MAICYAS 1;
MTCW 1; SAAS 1; SATA 4, 46, 80;
SATA-Essay 108; WYA; YAW
Byatt, A(ntonia) S(usan Drabble)
1936- .... **CLC 19, 65, 136**
See also BPFB 1; BRWC 2; BRWS 4; CA
13-16R; CANR 13, 33, 50, 75, 96, 133;
DA3; DAM NOV, POP; DLB 14, 194;
EWL 3; MTCW 1, 2; RGSF 2; RHW;
TEA
Byrd, Willam II 1674-1744 .... **LC 112**
See also DLB 24, 140; RGAL 4
Byrne, David 1952- .... **CLC 26**
See also CA 127
Byrne, John Keyes 1926-
See Leonard, Hugh
See also CA 102; CANR 78; INT CA-102
Byron, George Gordon (Noel)
1788-1824 ..... **DC 24; NCLC 2, 12, 109, 149; PC 16; WLC**
See also BRW 4; BRWC 2; CDBLB 1789-
1832; DA; DA3; DAB; DAC; DAM MST,
POET; DLB 96, 110; EXPP; LMFS 1;
PAB; PFS 1, 14; RGEL 2; TEA; WLIT 3;
WP
Byron, Robert 1905-1941 .... **TCLC 67**
See also CA 160; DLB 195

C. 3. 3.
See Wilde, Oscar (Fingal O'Flahertie Wills)
Caballero, Fernan 1796-1877 .... **NCLC 10**
Cabell, Branch
See Cabell, James Branch
Cabell, James Branch 1879-1958 .... **TCLC 6**
See also CA 105; 152; DLB 9, 78; FANT;
MTCW 1; RGAL 4; SUFW 1
Cabeza de Vaca, Alvar Nunez
1490-1557(?) .... **LC 61**
Cable, George Washington
1844-1925 .... **SSC 4; TCLC 4**
See also CA 104; 155; DLB 12, 74; DLBD
13; RGAL 4; TUS
Cabral de Melo Neto, Joao
1920-1999 .... **CLC 76**
See Melo Neto, Joao Cabral de
See also CA 151; DAM MULT; DLB 307;
LAW; LAWS 1
Cabrera Infante, G(uillermo) 1929- . **CLC 5, 25, 45, 120; HLC 1; SSC 39**
See also CA 85-88; CANR 29, 65, 110; CD-
WLB 3; CWW 2; DA3; DAM MULT;
DLB 113; EWL 3; HW 1, 2; LAW; LAWS
1; MTCW 1, 2; RGSF 2; WLIT 1
Cade, Toni
See Bambara, Toni Cade
Cadmus and Harmonia
See Buchan, John
Caedmon fl. 658-680 .... **CMLC 7**
See also DLB 146
Caeiro, Alberto
See Pessoa, Fernando (Antonio Nogueira)
Caesar, Julius .... **CMLC 47**
See Julius Caesar
See also AW 1; RGWL 2, 3
Cage, John (Milton, Jr.)
1912-1992 .... **CLC 41; PC 58**
See also CA 13-16R; 169; CANR 9, 78;
DLB 193; INT CANR-9
Cahan, Abraham 1860-1951 .... **TCLC 71**
See also CA 108; 154; DLB 9, 25, 28;
RGAL 4
Cain, G.
See Cabrera Infante, G(uillermo)
Cain, Guillermo
See Cabrera Infante, G(uillermo)
Cain, James M(allahan) 1892-1977 .. **CLC 3, 11, 28**
See also AITN 1; BPFB 1; CA 17-20R; 73-
76; CANR 8, 34, 61; CMW 4; DLB 226;
EWL 3; MSW; MTCW 1; RGAL 4
Caine, Hall 1853-1931 .... **TCLC 97**
See also RHW
Caine, Mark
See Raphael, Frederic (Michael)
Calasso, Roberto 1941- .... **CLC 81**
See also CA 143; CANR 89
Calderon de la Barca, Pedro
1600-1681 .... **DC 3; HLCS 1; LC 23**
See also EW 2; RGWL 2, 3; TWA
Caldwell, Erskine (Preston)
1903-1987 .... **CLC 1, 8, 14, 50, 60; SSC 19; TCLC 117**
See also AITN 1; AMW; BPFB 1; CA 1-4R;
121; CAAS 1; CANR 2, 33; DA3; DAM
NOV; DLB 9, 86; EWL 3; MTCW 1, 2;
RGAL 4; RGSF 2; TUS
Caldwell, (Janet Miriam) Taylor (Holland)
1900-1985 .... **CLC 2, 28, 39**
See also BPFB 1; CA 5-8R; 116; CANR 5;
DA3; DAM NOV, POP; DLBD 17; RHW
Calhoun, John Caldwell
1782-1850 .... **NCLC 15**
See also DLB 3, 248

Calisher, Hortense 1911- ..... **CLC 2, 4, 8, 38, 134; SSC 15**
See also CA 1-4R; CANR 1, 22, 117; CN
7; DA3; DAM NOV; DLB 2, 218; INT
CANR-22; MTCW 1, 2; RGAL 4; RGSF
2
Callaghan, Morley Edward
1903-1990 ..... **CLC 3, 14, 41, 65; TCLC 145**
See also CA 9-12R; 132; CANR 33, 73;
DAC; DAM MST; DLB 68; EWL 3;
MTCW 1, 2; RGEL 2; RGSF 2; SSFS 19
Callimachus c. 305B.C.-c.
240B.C. .... **CMLC 18**
See also AW 1; DLB 176; RGWL 2, 3
Calvin, Jean
See Calvin, John
See also GFL Beginnings to 1789
Calvin, John 1509-1564 .... **LC 37**
See Calvin, Jean
Calvino, Italo 1923-1985 .... **CLC 5, 8, 11, 22, 33, 39, 73; SSC 3, 48**
See also CA 85-88; 116; CANR
23, 61, 132; DAM NOV; DLB 196; EW
13; EWL 3; MTCW 1, 2; RGSF 2; RGWL
2, 3; SFW 4; SSFS 12
Camara Laye
See Laye, Camara
See also EWL 3
Camden, William 1551-1623 .... **LC 77**
See also DLB 172
Cameron, Carey 1952- .... **CLC 59**
See also CA 135
Cameron, Peter 1959- .... **CLC 44**
See also AMWS 12; CA 125; CANR 50,
117; DLB 234; GLL 2
Camoens, Luis Vaz de 1524(?)-1580
See Camoes, Luis de
See also EW 2
Camoes, Luis de 1524(?)-1580 . **HLCS 1; LC 62; PC 31**
See Camoens, Luis Vaz de
See also DLB 287; RGWL 2, 3
Campana, Dino 1885-1932 .... **TCLC 20**
See also CA 117; DLB 114; EWL 3
Campanella, Tommaso 1568-1639 .... **LC 32**
See also RGWL 2, 3
Campbell, John W(ood, Jr.)
1910-1971 .... **CLC 32**
See also CA 21-22; 29-32R; CANR 34;
CAP 2; DLB 8; MTCW 1; SCFW; SFW 4
Campbell, Joseph 1904-1987 .... **CLC 69; TCLC 140**
See also AAYA 3; BEST 89:2; CA 1-4R;
124; CANR 3, 28, 61, 107; DA3; MTCW
1, 2
Campbell, Maria 1940- .... **CLC 85; NNAL**
See also CA 102; CANR 54; CCA 1; DAC
Campbell, (John) Ramsey 1946- ..... **CLC 42; SSC 19**
See also AAYA 51; CA 57-60, 228; CAAE
228; CANR 7, 102; DLB 261; HGG; INT
CANR-7; SUFW 1, 2
Campbell, (Ignatius) Roy (Dunnachie)
1901-1957 .... **TCLC 5**
See also AFW; CA 104; 155; DLB 20, 225;
EWL 3; MTCW 2; RGEL 2
Campbell, Thomas 1777-1844 .... **NCLC 19**
See also DLB 93, 144; RGEL 2
Campbell, Wilfred .... **TCLC 9**
See Campbell, William
Campbell, William 1858(?)-1918
See Campbell, Wilfred
See also CA 106; DLB 92
Campion, Jane 1954- .... **CLC 95**
See also AAYA 33; CA 138; CANR 87
Campion, Thomas 1567-1620 .... **LC 78**
See also CDBLB Before 1660; DAM POET;
DLB 58, 172; RGEL 2

Cassill, R(onald) V(erlin)
1919-2002 .... **CLC 4, 23**
See also CA 9-12R; 208; CAAS 1; CANR
7, 45; CN 7; DLB 6, 218; DLBY 2002
Cassiodorus, Flavius Magnus c. 490(?)-c.
583(?) .... **CMLC 43**
Cassirer, Ernst 1874-1945 .... **TCLC 61**
See also CA 157
Cassity, (Allen) Turner 1929- .... **CLC 6, 42**
See also CA 17-20R, 223; CAAE 223;
CAAS 8; CANR 11; CSW; DLB 105
Castaneda, Carlos (Cesar Aranha)
1931(?)-1998 .... **CLC 12, 119**
See also CA 25-28R; CANR 32, 66, 105;
DNFS 1; HW 1; MTCW 1
Castedo, Elena 1937- .... **CLC 65**
See also CA 132
Castedo-Ellerman, Elena
See Castedo, Elena
Castellanos, Rosario 1925-1974 .... **CLC 66;
HLC 1; SSC 39, 68**
See also CA 131; 53-56; CANR 58; CD-
WLB 3; DAM MULT; DLB 113, 290;
EWL 3; FW; HW 1; LAW; MTCW 1;
RGSF 2; RGWL 2, 3
Castelvetro, Lodovico 1505-1571 .... **LC 12**
Castiglione, Baldassare 1478-1529 ...... **LC 12**
See Castiglione, Baldesar
See also LMFS 1; RGWL 2, 3
Castiglione, Baldesar
See Castiglione, Baldassare
See also EW 2
Castillo, Ana (Hernandez Del)
1953- .... **CLC 151**
See also AAYA 42; CA 131; CANR 51, 86,
128; CWP; DLB 122, 227; DNFS 2; FW;
HW 1; LLW 1; PFS 21
Castle, Robert
See Hamilton, Edmond
Castro (Ruz), Fidel 1926(?)- .... **HLC 1**
See also CA 110; 129; CANR 81; DAM
MULT; HW 2
Castro, Guillen de 1569-1631 .... **LC 19**
Castro, Rosalia de 1837-1885 ... **NCLC 3, 78;
PC 41**
See also DAM MULT
Cather, Willa (Sibert) 1873-1947 . **SSC 2, 50;
TCLC 1, 11, 31, 99, 132, 152; WLC**
See also AAYA 24; AMW; AMWC 1;
AMWR 1; BPFB 1; CA 104; 128; CDALB
1865-1917; CLR 98; DA; DA3; DAB;
DAC; DAM MST, NOV; DLB 9, 54, 78,
256; DLBD 1; EWL 3; EXPN; EXPS;
LAIT 3; LATS 1:1; MAWW; MTCW 1,
2; NFS 2, 19; RGAL 4; RGSF 2; RHW;
SATA 30; SSFS 2, 7, 16; TCWW 2; TUS
Catherine II
See Catherine the Great
See also DLB 150
Catherine the Great 1729-1796 .... **LC 69**
See Catherine II
Cato, Marcus Porcius
234B.C.-149B.C. .... **CMLC 21**
See Cato the Elder
Cato, Marcus Porcius, the Elder
See Cato, Marcus Porcius
Cato the Elder
See Cato, Marcus Porcius
See also DLB 211
Catton, (Charles) Bruce 1899-1978 . **CLC 35**
See also AITN 1; CA 5-8R; 81-84; CANR
7, 74; DLB 17; SATA 2; SATA-Obit 24
Catullus c. 84B.C.-54B.C. .... **CMLC 18**
See also AW 2; CDWLB 1; DLB 211;
RGWL 2, 3
Cauldwell, Frank
See King, Francis (Henry)

Caunitz, William J. 1933-1996 .... **CLC 34**
See also BEST 89:3; CA 125; 130; 152;
CANR 73; INT CA-130
Causley, Charles (Stanley)
1917-2003 .... **CLC 7**
See also CA 9-12R; 223; CANR 5, 35, 94;
CLR 30; CWRI 5; DLB 27; MTCW 1;
SATA 3, 66; SATA-Obit 149
Caute, (John) David 1936- .... **CLC 29**
See also CA 1-4R; CAAS 4; CANR 1, 33,
64, 120; CBD; CD 5; CN 7; DAM NOV;
DLB 14, 231
Cavafy, C(onstantine) P(eter) .... **PC 36;
TCLC 2, 7**
See Kavafis, Konstantinos Petrou
See also CA 148; DA3; DAM POET; EW
8; EWL 3; MTCW 1; PFS 19; RGWL 2,
3; WP
Cavalcanti, Guido c. 1250-c.
1300 .... **CMLC 54**
See also RGWL 2, 3
Cavallo, Evelyn
See Spark, Muriel (Sarah)
Cavanna, Betty .... **CLC 12**
See Harrison, Elizabeth (Allen) Cavanna
See also JRDA; MAICYA 1; SAAS 4;
SATA 1, 30
Cavendish, Margaret Lucas
1623-1673 .... **LC 30**
See also DLB 131, 252, 281; RGEL 2
Caxton, William 1421(?)-1491(?) .... **LC 17**
See also DLB 170
Cayer, D. M.
See Duffy, Maureen
Cayrol, Jean 1911- .... **CLC 11**
See also CA 89-92; DLB 83; EWL 3
Cela (y Trulock), Camilo Jose
See Cela, Camilo Jose
See also CWW 2
Cela, Camilo Jose 1916-2002 .... **CLC 4, 13,
59, 122; HLC 1; SSC 71**
See Cela (y Trulock), Camilo Jose
See also BEST 90:2; CA 21-24R; 206;
CAAS 10; CANR 21, 32, 76; DAM
MULT; DLBY 1989; EW 13; EWL 3; HW
1; MTCW 1, 2; RGSF 2; RGWL 2, 3
Celan, Paul .... **CLC 10, 19, 53, 82; PC 10**
See Antschel, Paul
See also CDWLB 2; DLB 69; EWL 3;
RGWL 2, 3
Celine, Louis-Ferdinand .. **CLC 1, 3, 4, 7, 9,
15, 47, 124**
See Destouches, Louis-Ferdinand
See also DLB 72; EW 11; EWL 3; GFL
1789 to the Present; RGWL 2, 3
Cellini, Benvenuto 1500-1571 .... **LC 7**
Cendrars, Blaise .... **CLC 18, 106**
See Sauser-Hall, Frederic
See also DLB 258; EWL 3; GFL 1789 to
the Present; RGWL 2, 3; WP
Centlivre, Susanna 1669(?)-1723 .... **DC 25;
LC 65**
See also DLB 84; RGEL 2
Cernuda (y Bidon), Luis
1902-1963 .... **CLC 54; PC 62**
See also CA 131; 89-92; DAM POET; DLB
134; EWL 3; GLL 1; HW 1; RGWL 2, 3
Cervantes, Lorna Dee 1954- ..... **HLCS 1; PC
35**
See also CA 131; CANR 80; CWP; DLB
82; EXPP; HW 1; LLW 1
Cervantes (Saavedra), Miguel de
1547-1616 .... **HLCS; LC 6, 23, 93; SSC
12; WLC**
See also AAYA 56; BYA 1, 14; DA; DAB;
DAC; DAM MST, NOV; EW 2; LAIT 1;
LATS 1:1; LMFS 1; NFS 8; RGSF 2;
RGWL 2, 3; TWA

Cesaire, Aime (Fernand) 1913- .... **BLC 1;
CLC 19, 32, 112; DC 22; PC 25**
See also BW 2, 3; CA 65-68; CANR 24,
43, 81; CWW 2; DAM MULT,
POET; EWL 3; GFL 1789 to the Present;
MTCW 1, 2; WP
Chabon, Michael 1963- ... **CLC 55, 149; SSC
59**
See also AAYA 45; AMWS 11; CA 139;
CANR 57, 96, 127; DLB 278; SATA 145
Chabrol, Claude 1930- .... **CLC 16**
See also CA 110
Chairil Anwar
See Anwar, Chairil
See also EWL 3
Challans, Mary 1905-1983
See Renault, Mary
See also CA 81-84; 111; CANR 74; DA3;
MTCW 2; SATA 23; SATA-Obit 36; TEA
Challis, George
See Faust, Frederick (Schiller)
See also TCWW 2
Chambers, Aidan 1934- .... **CLC 35**
See also AAYA 27; CA 25-28R; CANR 12,
31, 58, 116; JRDA; MAICYA 1, 2; SAAS
12; SATA 1, 69, 108; WYA; YAW
Chambers, James 1948-
See Cliff, Jimmy
See also CA 124
Chambers, Jessie
See Lawrence, D(avid) H(erbert Richards)
See also GLL 1
Chambers, Robert W(illiam)
1865-1933 .... **TCLC 41**
See also CA 165; DLB 202; HGG; SATA
107; SUFW 1
Chambers, (David) Whittaker
1901-1961 .... **TCLC 129**
See also CA 89-92; DLB 303
Chamisso, Adelbert von
1781-1838 .... **NCLC 82**
See also DLB 90; RGWL 2, 3; SUFW 1
Chance, James T.
See Carpenter, John (Howard)
Chance, John T.
See Carpenter, John (Howard)
Chandler, Raymond (Thornton)
1888-1959 .... **SSC 23; TCLC 1, 7**
See also AAYA 25; AMWC 2; AMWS 4;
BPFB 1; CA 104; 129; CANR 60, 107;
CDALB 1929-1941; CMW 4; DA3; DLB
226, 253; DLBD 6; EWL 3; MSW;
MTCW 1, 2; NFS 17; RGAL 4; TUS
Chang, Diana 1934- .... **AAL**
See also CA 228; CWP; EXPP
Chang, Eileen 1921-1995 .... **AAL; SSC 28**
See Chang Ai-Ling; Zhang Ailing
See also CA 166
Chang, Jung 1952- .... **CLC 71**
See also CA 142
Chang Ai-Ling
See Chang, Eileen
See also EWL 3
Channing, William Ellery
1780-1842 .... **NCLC 17**
See also DLB 1, 59, 235; RGAL 4
Chao, Patricia 1955- .... **CLC 119**
See also CA 163
Chaplin, Charles Spencer
1889-1977 .... **CLC 16**
See Chaplin, Charlie
See also CA 81-84; 73-76
Chaplin, Charlie
See Chaplin, Charles Spencer
See also DLB 44
Chapman, George 1559(?)-1634 . **DC 19; LC
22**
See also BRW 1; DAM DRAM; DLB 62,
121; LMFS 1; RGEL 2

NOV; DFS 2; DLB 13, 77, 245; MSW;
MTCW 1, 2; NFS 8; RGEL 2; RHW;
SATA 36; TEA; YAW

Christie, Philippa .... **CLC 21**
See Pearce, Philippa
See also BYA 5; CANR 109; CLR 9; DLB
161; MAICYA 1; SATA 1, 67, 129

Christine de Pizan 1365(?)-1431(?) .... **LC 9**
See also DLB 208; RGWL 2, 3

Chuang Tzu c. 369B.C.-c.
286B.C. .... **CMLC 57**

Chubb, Elmer
See Masters, Edgar Lee

Chulkov, Mikhail Dmitrievich
1743-1792 .... **LC 2**
See also DLB 150

Churchill, Caryl 1938- .... **CLC 31, 55, 157;
DC 5**
See Churchill, Chick
See also BRWS 4; CA 102; CANR 22, 46,
108; CBD; CWD; DFS 12, 16; DLB 13;
EWL 3; FW; MTCW 1; RGEL 2

Churchill, Charles 1731-1764 .... **LC 3**
See also DLB 109; RGEL 2

Churchill, Chick
See Churchill, Caryl
See also CD 5

Churchill, Sir Winston (Leonard Spencer)
1874-1965 .... **TCLC 113**
See also BRW 6; CA 97-100; CDBLB
1890-1914; DA3; DLB 100; DLBD 16;
LAIT 4; MTCW 1, 2

Chute, Carolyn 1947- .... **CLC 39**
See also CA 123; CANR 135

Ciardi, John (Anthony) 1916-1986 . **CLC 10,
40, 44, 129**
See also CA 5-8R; 118; CAAS 2; CANR 5,
33; CLR 19; CWRI 5; DAM POET; DLB
5; DLBY 1986; INT CANR-5; MAICYA
1, 2; MTCW 1, 2; RGAL 4; SAAS 26;
SATA 1, 65; SATA-Obit 46

Cibber, Colley 1671-1757 .... **LC 66**
See also DLB 84; RGEL 2

Cicero, Marcus Tullius
106B.C.-43B.C. .... **CMLC 3**
See also AW 1; CDWLB 1; DLB 211;
RGWL 2, 3

Cimino, Michael 1943- .... **CLC 16**
See also CA 105

Cioran, E(mil) M. 1911-1995 .... **CLC 64**
See also CA 25-28R; 149; CANR 91; DLB
220; EWL 3

Cisneros, Sandra 1954- .... **CLC 69, 118, 193;
HLC 1; PC 52; SSC 32, 72**
See also AAYA 9, 53; AMWS 7; CA 131;
CANR 64, 118; CWP; DAM MULT;
DLB 122, 152; EWL 3; EXPN; FW; HW
1, 2; LAIT 5; LATS 1:2; LLW 1; MAI-
CYA 2; MTCW 2; NFS 2; PFS 19; RGAL
4; RGSF 2; SSFS 3, 13; WLIT 1; YAW

Cixous, Helene 1937- .... **CLC 92**
See also CA 126; CANR 55, 123; CWW 2;
DLB 83, 242; EWL 3; FW; GLL 2;
MTCW 1, 2; TWA

Clair, Rene .... **CLC 20**
See Chomette, Rene Lucien

Clampitt, Amy 1920-1994 .... **CLC 32; PC 19**
See also AMWS 9; CA 110; 146; CANR
29, 79; DLB 105

Clancy, Thomas L., Jr. 1947-
See Clancy, Tom
See also CA 125; 131; CANR 62, 105;
DA3; INT CA-131; MTCW 1, 2

Clancy, Tom .... **CLC 45, 112**
See Clancy, Thomas L., Jr.
See also AAYA 9, 51; BEST 89:1, 90:1;
BPFB 1; BYA 10, 11; CANR 132; CMW
4; CPW; DAM NOV, POP; DLB 227

Clare, John 1793-1864 .. **NCLC 9, 86; PC 23**
See also DAB; DAM POET; DLB 55, 96;
RGEL 2

Clarin
See Alas (y Urena), Leopoldo (Enrique
Garcia)

Clark, Al C.
See Goines, Donald

Clark, (Robert) Brian 1932- .... **CLC 29**
See also CA 41-44R; CANR 67; CBD; CD
5

Clark, Curt
See Westlake, Donald E(dwin)

Clark, Eleanor 1913-1996 .... **CLC 5, 19**
See also CA 9-12R; 151; CANR 41; CN 7;
DLB 6

Clark, J. P.
See Clark Bekederemo, J(ohnson) P(epper)
See also CDWLB 3; DLB 117

Clark, John Pepper
See Clark Bekederemo, J(ohnson) P(epper)
See also AFW; CD 5; CP 7; RGEL 2

Clark, Kenneth (Mackenzie)
1903-1983 .... **TCLC 147**
See also CA 93-96; 109; CANR 36; MTCW
1, 2

Clark, M. R.
See Clark, Mavis Thorpe

Clark, Mavis Thorpe 1909-1999 ...... **CLC 12**
See also CA 57-60; CANR 8, 37, 107; CLR
30; CWRI 5; MAICYA 1, 2; SAAS 5;
SATA 8, 74

Clark, Walter Van Tilburg
1909-1971 .... **CLC 28**
See also CA 9-12R; 33-36R; CANR 63,
113; DLB 9, 206; LAIT 2; RGAL 4;
SATA 8

Clark Bekederemo, J(ohnson) P(epper)
1935- .... **BLC 1; CLC 38; DC 5**
See Clark, J. P.; Clark, John Pepper
See also BW 1; CA 65-68; CANR 16, 72;
DAM DRAM, MULT; DFS 13; EWL 3;
MTCW 1

Clarke, Arthur C(harles) 1917- .... **CLC 1, 4,
13, 18, 35, 136; SSC 3**
See also AAYA 4, 33; BPFB 1; BYA 13;
CA 1-4R; CANR 2, 28, 55, 74, 130; CN
7; CPW; DA3; DAM POP; DLB 261;
JRDA; LAIT 5; MAICYA 1, 2; MTCW 1,
2; SATA 13, 70, 115; SCFW; SFW 4;
SSFS 4, 18; YAW

Clarke, Austin 1896-1974 .... **CLC 6, 9**
See also CA 29-32; 49-52; CAP 2; DAM
POET; DLB 10, 20; EWL 3; RGEL 2

Clarke, Austin C(hesterfield) 1934- .. **BLC 1;
CLC 8, 53; SSC 45**
See also BW 1; CA 25-28R; CAAS 16;
CANR 14, 32, 68; CN 7; DAC; DAM
MULT; DLB 53, 125; DNFS 2; RGSF 2

Clarke, Gillian 1937- .... **CLC 61**
See also CA 106; CP 7; CWP; DLB 40

Clarke, Marcus (Andrew Hislop)
1846-1881 .... **NCLC 19**
See also DLB 230; RGEL 2; RGSF 2

Clarke, Shirley 1925-1997 .... **CLC 16**
See also CA 189

Clash, The
See Headon, (Nicky) Topper; Jones, Mick;
Simonon, Paul; Strummer, Joe

Claudel, Paul (Louis Charles Marie)
1868-1955 .... **TCLC 2, 10**
See also CA 104; 165; DLB 192, 258; EW
8; EWL 3; GFL 1789 to the Present;
RGWL 2, 3; TWA

Claudian 370(?)-404(?) .... **CMLC 46**
See also RGWL 2, 3

Claudius, Matthias 1740-1815 .... **NCLC 75**
See also DLB 97

Clavell, James (duMaresq)
1925-1994 .... **CLC 6, 25, 87**
See also BPFB 1; CA 25-28R; 146; CANR
26, 48; CPW; DA3; DAM NOV, POP;
MTCW 1, 2; NFS 10; RHW

Clayman, Gregory .... **CLC 65**

Cleaver, (Leroy) Eldridge
1935-1998 .... **BLC 1; CLC 30, 119**
See also BW 1, 3; CA 21-24R; 167; CANR
16, 75; DA3; DAM MULT; MTCW 2;
YAW

Cleese, John (Marwood) 1939- .... **CLC 21**
See Monty Python
See also CA 112; 116; CANR 35; MTCW 1

Cleishbotham, Jebediah
See Scott, Sir Walter

Cleland, John 1710-1789 .... **LC 2, 48**
See also DLB 39; RGEL 2

Clemens, Samuel Langhorne 1835-1910
See Twain, Mark
See also CA 104; 135; CDALB 1865-1917;
DA; DA3; DAB; DAC; DAM MST, NOV;
DLB 12, 23, 64, 74, 186, 189; JRDA;
LMFS 1; MAICYA 1, 2; NCFS 4; NFS
20; SATA 100; SSFS 16; YABC 2

Clement of Alexandria
150(?)-215(?) .... **CMLC 41**

Cleophil
See Congreve, William

Clerihew, E.
See Bentley, E(dmund) C(lerihew)

Clerk, N. W.
See Lewis, C(live) S(taples)

Cleveland, John 1613-1658 .... **LC 106**
See also DLB 126; RGEL 2

Cliff, Jimmy .... **CLC 21**
See Chambers, James
See also CA 193

Cliff, Michelle 1946- .... **BLCS; CLC 120**
See also BW 2; CA 116; CANR 39, 72; CD-
WLB 3; DLB 157; FW; GLL 2

Clifford, Lady Anne 1590-1676 .... **LC 76**
See also DLB 151

Clifton, (Thelma) Lucille 1936- .... **BLC 1;
CLC 19, 66, 162; PC 17**
See also AFAW 2; BW 2, 3; CA 49-52;
CANR 2, 24, 42, 76, 97; CLR 5; CP 7;
CSW; CWP; CWRI 5; DA3; DAM MULT,
POET; DLB 5, 41; EXPP; MAICYA 1, 2;
MTCW 1, 2; PFS 1, 14; SATA 20, 69,
128; WP

Clinton, Dirk
See Silverberg, Robert

Clough, Arthur Hugh 1819-1861 ... **NCLC 27**
See also BRW 5; DLB 32; RGEL 2

Clutha, Janet Paterson Frame 1924-2004
See Frame, Janet
See also CA 1-4R; 224; CANR 2, 36, 76,
135; MTCW 1, 2; SATA 119

Clyne, Terence
See Blatty, William Peter

Cobalt, Martin
See Mayne, William (James Carter)

Cobb, Irvin S(hrewsbury)
1876-1944 .... **TCLC 77**
See also CA 175; DLB 11, 25, 86

Cobbett, William 1763-1835 .... **NCLC 49**
See also DLB 43, 107, 158; RGEL 2

Coburn, D(onald) L(ee) 1938- .... **CLC 10**
See also CA 89-92

Cocteau, Jean (Maurice Eugene Clement)
1889-1963 ...... **CLC 1, 8, 15, 16, 43; DC
17; TCLC 119; WLC**
See also CA 25-28; CANR 40; CAP 2; DA;
DA3; DAB; DAC; DAM DRAM, MST,
NOV; DLB 65, 258; EW 10; EWL 3; GFL
1789 to the Present; MTCW 1, 2; RGWL
2, 3; TWA

Cooke, John Esten 1830-1886 .... NCLC 5
See also DLB 3, 248; RGAL 4

Cooke, John Estes
See Baum, L(yman) Frank

Cooke, M. E.
See Creasey, John

Cooke, Margaret
See Creasey, John

Cooke, Rose Terry 1827-1892 ...... NCLC 110
See also DLB 12, 74

Cook-Lynn, Elizabeth 1930- .... CLC 93;
NNAL
See also CA 133; DAM MULT; DLB 175

Cooney, Ray .... CLC 62
See also CBD

Cooper, Anthony Ashley 1671-1713 .. LC 107
See also DLB 101

Cooper, Dennis 1953- .... CLC 203
See also CA 133; CANR 72, 86; GLL 1; St.
James Guide to Horror, Ghost, and Gothic
Writers.

Cooper, Douglas 1960- .... CLC 86

Cooper, Henry St. John
See Creasey, John

Cooper, J(oan) California (?)- .... CLC 56
See also AAYA 12; BW 1; CA 125; CANR
55; DAM MULT; DLB 212

Cooper, James Fenimore
1789-1851 .... NCLC 1, 27, 54
See also AAYA 22; AMW; BPFB 1;
CDALB 1640-1865; DA3; DLB 3, 183,
250, 254; LAIT 1; NFS 9; RGAL 4; SATA
19; TUS; WCH

Cooper, Susan Fenimore
1813-1894 .... NCLC 129
See also ANW; DLB 239, 254

Coover, Robert (Lowell) 1932- ...... CLC 3, 7,
15, 32, 46, 87, 161; SSC 15
See also AMWS 5; BPFB 1; CA 45-48;
CANR 3, 37, 58, 115; CN 7; DAM NOV;
DLB 2, 227; DLBY 1981; EWL 3;
MTCW 1, 2; RGAL 4; RGSF 2

Copeland, Stewart (Armstrong)
1952- .... CLC 26

Copernicus, Nicolaus 1473-1543 .... LC 45

Coppard, A(lfred) E(dgar)
1878-1957 .... SSC 21; TCLC 5
See also BRWS 8; CA 114; 167; DLB 162;
EWL 3; HGG; RGEL 2; RGSF 2; SUFW
1; YABC 1

Coppee, Francois 1842-1908 .... TCLC 25
See also CA 170; DLB 217

Coppola, Francis Ford 1939- ... CLC 16, 126
See also AAYA 39; CA 77-80; CANR 40,
78; DLB 44

Copway, George 1818-1869 .... NNAL
See also DAM MULT; DLB 175, 183

Corbiere, Tristan 1845-1875 .... NCLC 43
See also DLB 217; GFL 1789 to the Present

Corcoran, Barbara (Asenath)
1911- .... CLC 17
See also AAYA 14; CA 21-24R, 191; CAAE
191; CAAS 20; CANR 11, 28, 48; CLR
50; DLB 52; JRDA; MAICYA 2; MAIC-
YAS 1; RHW; SAAS 20; SATA 3, 77;
SATA-Essay 125

Cordelier, Maurice
See Giraudoux, Jean(-Hippolyte)

Corelli, Marie .... TCLC 51
See Mackay, Mary
See also DLB 34, 156; RGEL 2; SUFW 1

Corinna c. 225B.C.-c. 305B.C. ...... CMLC 72

Corman, Cid .... CLC 9
See Corman, Sidney
See also CAAS 2; DLB 5, 193

Corman, Sidney 1924-2004
See Corman, Cid
See also CA 85-88; 225; CANR 44; CP 7;
DAM POET

Cormier, Robert (Edmund)
1925-2000 .... CLC 12, 30
See also AAYA 3, 19; BYA 1, 2, 6, 8, 9;
CA 1-4R; CANR 5, 23, 76, 93; CDALB
1968-1988; CLR 12, 55; DA; DAB; DAC;
DAM MST, NOV; DLB 52; EXPN; INT
CANR-23; JRDA; LAIT 5; MAICYA 1,
2; MTCW 1, 2; NFS 2, 18; SATA 10, 45,
83; SATA-Obit 122; WYA; YAW

Corn, Alfred (DeWitt III) 1943- .... CLC 33
See also CA 179; CAAE 179; CAAS 25;
CANR 44; CP 7; CSW; DLB 120, 282;
DLBY 1980

Corneille, Pierre 1606-1684 ... DC 21; LC 28
See also DAB; DAM MST; DLB 268; EW
3; GFL Beginnings to 1789; RGWL 2, 3;
TWA

Cornwell, David (John Moore)
1931- .... CLC 9, 15
See le Carre, John
See also CA 5-8R; CANR 13, 33, 59, 107,
132; DA3; DAM POP; MTCW 1, 2

Cornwell, Patricia (Daniels) 1956- . CLC 155
See also AAYA 16, 56; BPFB 1; CA 134;
CANR 53, 131; CMW 4; CPW; CSW;
DAM POP; DLB 306; MSW; MTCW 1

Corso, (Nunzio) Gregory 1930-2001 . CLC 1,
11; PC 33
See also AMWS 12; BG 2; CA 5-8R; 193;
CANR 41, 76, 132; CP 7; DA3; DLB 5,
16, 237; LMFS 2; MTCW 1, 2; WP

Cortazar, Julio 1914-1984 ... CLC 2, 3, 5, 10,
13, 15, 33, 34, 92; HLC 1; SSC 7, 76
See also BPFB 1; CA 21-24R; CANR 12,
32, 81; CDWLB 3; DAM MULT,
NOV; DLB 113; EWL 3; EXPS; HW 1,
2; LAW; MTCW 1, 2; RGSF 2; RGWL 2,
3; SSFS 3, 20; TWA; WLIT 1

Cortes, Hernan 1485-1547 .... LC 31

Corvinus, Jakob
See Raabe, Wilhelm (Karl)

Corwin, Cecil
See Kornbluth, C(yril) M.

Cosic, Dobrica 1921- .... CLC 14
See also CA 122; 138; CDWLB 4; CWW
2; DLB 181; EWL 3

Costain, Thomas B(ertram)
1885-1965 .... CLC 30
See also BYA 3; CA 5-8R; 25-28R; DLB 9;
RHW

Costantini, Humberto 1924(?)-1987 . CLC 49
See also CA 131; 122; EWL 3; HW 1

Costello, Elvis 1954- .... CLC 21
See also CA 204

Costenoble, Philostene
See Ghelderode, Michel de

Cotes, Cecil V.
See Duncan, Sara Jeannette

Cotter, Joseph Seamon Sr.
1861-1949 .... BLC 1; TCLC 28
See also BW 1; CA 124; DAM MULT; DLB
50

Couch, Arthur Thomas Quiller
See Quiller-Couch, Sir Arthur (Thomas)

Coulton, James
See Hansen, Joseph

Couperus, Louis (Marie Anne)
1863-1923 .... TCLC 15
See also CA 115; EWL 3; RGWL 2, 3

Coupland, Douglas 1961- .... CLC 85, 133
See also AAYA 34; CA 142; CANR 57, 90,
130; CCA 1; CPW; DAC; DAM POP

Court, Wesli
See Turco, Lewis (Putnam)

Courtenay, Bryce 1933- .... CLC 59
See also CA 138; CPW

Courtney, Robert
See Ellison, Harlan (Jay)

Cousteau, Jacques-Yves 1910-1997 .. CLC 30
See also CA 65-68; 159; CANR 15, 67;
MTCW 1; SATA 38, 98

Coventry, Francis 1725-1754 .... LC 46

Coverdale, Miles c. 1487-1569 .... LC 77
See also DLB 167

Cowan, Peter (Walkinshaw)
1914-2002 .... SSC 28
See also CA 21-24R; CANR 9, 25, 50, 83;
CN 7; DLB 260; RGSF 2

Coward, Noel (Peirce) 1899-1973 . CLC 1, 9,
29, 51
See also AITN 1; BRWS 2; CA 17-18; 41-
44R; CANR 35, 132; CAP 2; CDBLB
1914-1945; DA3; DAM DRAM; DFS 3,
6; DLB 10, 245; EWL 3; IDFW 3, 4;
MTCW 1, 2; RGEL 2; TEA

Cowley, Abraham 1618-1667 .... LC 43
See also BRW 2; DLB 131, 151; PAB;
RGEL 2

Cowley, Malcolm 1898-1989 .... CLC 39
See also AMWS 2; CA 5-8R; 128; CANR
3, 55; DLB 4, 48; DLBY 1981, 1989;
EWL 3; MTCW 1, 2

Cowper, William 1731-1800 ..... NCLC 8, 94;
PC 40
See also BRW 3; DA3; DAM POET; DLB
104, 109; RGEL 2

Cox, William Trevor 1928-
See Trevor, William
See also CA 9-12R; CANR 4, 37, 55, 76,
102; DAM NOV; INT CANR-37; MTCW
1, 2; TEA

Coyne, P. J.
See Masters, Hilary

Cozzens, James Gould 1903-1978 . CLC 1, 4,
11, 92
See also AMW; BPFB 1; CA 9-12R; 81-84;
CANR 19; CDALB 1941-1968; DLB 9,
294; DLBD 2; DLBY 1984, 1997; EWL
3; MTCW 1, 2; RGAL 4

Crabbe, George 1754-1832 .... NCLC 26, 121
See also BRW 3; DLB 93; RGEL 2

Crace, Jim 1946- .... CLC 157; SSC 61
See also CA 128; 135; CANR 55, 70, 123;
CN 7; DLB 231; INT CA-135

Craddock, Charles Egbert
See Murfree, Mary Noailles

Craig, A. A.
See Anderson, Poul (William)

Craik, Mrs.
See Craik, Dinah Maria (Mulock)
See also RGEL 2

Craik, Dinah Maria (Mulock)
1826-1887 .... NCLC 38
See Craik, Mrs.; Mulock, Dinah Maria
See also DLB 35, 163; MAICYA 1, 2;
SATA 34

Cram, Ralph Adams 1863-1942 ..... TCLC 45
See also CA 160

Cranch, Christopher Pearse
1813-1892 .... NCLC 115
See also DLB 1, 42, 243

Crane, (Harold) Hart 1899-1932 .... PC 3;
TCLC 2, 5, 80; WLC
See also AMW; AMWR 2; CA 104; 127;
CDALB 1917-1929; DA; DA3; DAB;
DAC; DAM MST, POET; DLB 4, 48;
EWL 3; MTCW 1, 2; RGAL 4; TUS

Crane, R(onald) S(almon)
1886-1967 .... CLC 27
See also CA 85-88; DLB 63

Crane, Stephen (Townley)
1871-1900 ...... SSC 7, 56, 70; TCLC 11,
17, 32; WLC
See also AAYA 21; AMW; AMWC 1; BPFB
1; BYA 3; CA 109; 140; CANR 84;
CDALB 1865-1917; DA; DA3; DAB;
DAC; DAM MST, NOV, POET; DLB 12,

Dacre, Charlotte c. 1772-1825? ... **NCLC 151**

Dafydd ap Gwilym c. 1320-c. 1380 ..... **PC 56**

Dagerman, Stig (Halvard)
1923-1954 .... **TCLC 17**
See also CA 117; 155; DLB 259; EWL 3

D'Aguiar, Fred 1960- .... **CLC 145**
See also CA 148; CANR 83, 101; CP 7;
DLB 157; EWL 3

Dahl, Roald 1916-1990 .... **CLC 1, 6, 18, 79**
See also AAYA 15; BPFB 1; BRWS 4; BYA
5; CA 1-4R; 133; CANR 6, 32, 37, 62;
CLR 1, 7, 41; CPW; DA3; DAB; DAC;
DAM MST, NOV, POP; DLB 139, 255;
HGG; JRDA; MAICYA 1, 2; MTCW 1,
2; RGSF 2; SATA 1, 26, 73; SATA-Obit
65; SSFS 4; TEA; YAW

Dahlberg, Edward 1900-1977 .. **CLC 1, 7, 14**
See also CA 9-12R; 69-72; CANR 31, 62;
DLB 48; MTCW 1; RGAL 4

Daitch, Susan 1954- .... **CLC 103**
See also CA 161

Dale, Colin .... **TCLC 18**
See Lawrence, T(homas) E(dward)

Dale, George E.
See Asimov, Isaac

Dalton, Roque 1935-1975(?) ..... **HLCS 1; PC 36**
See also CA 176; DLB 283; HW 2

Daly, Elizabeth 1878-1967 .... **CLC 52**
See also CA 23-24; 25-28R; CANR 60;
CAP 2; CMW 4

Daly, Mary 1928- .... **CLC 173**
See also CA 25-28R; CANR 30, 62; FW;
GLL 1; MTCW 1

Daly, Maureen 1921- .... **CLC 17**
See also AAYA 5, 58; BYA 6; CANR 37,
83, 108; CLR 96; JRDA; MAICYA 1, 2;
SAAS 1; SATA 2, 129; WYA; YAW

Damas, Leon-Gontran 1912-1978 .... **CLC 84**
See also BW 1; CA 125; 73-76; EWL 3

Dana, Richard Henry Sr.
1787-1879 .... **NCLC 53**

Daniel, Samuel 1562(?)-1619 .... **LC 24**
See also DLB 62; RGEL 2

Daniels, Brett
See Adler, Renata

Dannay, Frederic 1905-1982 .... **CLC 11**
See Queen, Ellery
See also CA 1-4R; 107; CANR 1, 39; CMW
4; DAM POP; DLB 137; MTCW 1

D'Annunzio, Gabriele 1863-1938 ... **TCLC 6, 40**
See also CA 104; 155; EW 8; EWL 3;
RGWL 2, 3; TWA

Danois, N. le
See Gourmont, Remy(-Marie-Charles) de

Dante 1265-1321 .... **CMLC 3, 18, 39, 70; PC 21; WLCS**
See also DA; DA3; DAB; DAC; DAM
MST, POET; EFS 1; EW 1; LAIT 1;
RGWL 2, 3; TWA; WP

d'Antibes, Germain
See Simenon, Georges (Jacques Christian)

Danticat, Edwidge 1969- .... **CLC 94, 139**
See also AAYA 29; CA 152, 192; CAAE
192; CANR 73, 129; DNFS 1; EXPS;
LATS 1:2; MTCW 1; SSFS 1; YAW

Danvers, Dennis 1947- .... **CLC 70**

Danziger, Paula 1944-2004 .... **CLC 21**
See also AAYA 4, 36; BYA 6, 7, 14; CA
112; 115; 229; CANR 37, 132; CLR 20;
JRDA; MAICYA 1, 2; SATA 36, 63, 102,
149; SATA-Brief 30; WYA; YAW

Da Ponte, Lorenzo 1749-1838 .... **NCLC 50**

Dario, Ruben 1867-1916 .... **HLC 1; PC 15; TCLC 4**
See also CA 131; CANR 81; DAM MULT;
DLB 290; EWL 3; HW 1, 2; LAW;
MTCW 1, 2; RGWL 2, 3

Darley, George 1795-1846 .... **NCLC 2**
See also DLB 96; RGEL 2

Darrow, Clarence (Seward)
1857-1938 .... **TCLC 81**
See also CA 164; DLB 303

Darwin, Charles 1809-1882 .... **NCLC 57**
See also BRWS 7; DLB 57, 166; LATS 1:1;
RGEL 2; TEA; WLIT 4

Darwin, Erasmus 1731-1802 .... **NCLC 106**
See also DLB 93; RGEL 2

Daryush, Elizabeth 1887-1977 ...... **CLC 6, 19**
See also CA 49-52; CANR 3, 81; DLB 20

Das, Kamala 1934- .... **CLC 191; PC 43**
See also CA 101; CANR 27, 59; CP 7;
CWP; FW

Dasgupta, Surendranath
1887-1952 .... **TCLC 81**
See also CA 157

**Dashwood, Edmee Elizabeth Monica de la
Pasture** 1890-1943
See Delafield, E. M.
See also CA 119; 154

da Silva, Antonio Jose
1705-1739 .... **NCLC 114**

Daudet, (Louis Marie) Alphonse
1840-1897 .... **NCLC 1**
See also DLB 123; GFL 1789 to the Present;
RGSF 2

d'Aulnoy, Marie-Catherine c.
1650-1705 .... **LC 100**

Daumal, Rene 1908-1944 .... **TCLC 14**
See also CA 114; EWL 3

Davenant, William 1606-1668 .... **LC 13**
See also DLB 58, 126; RGEL 2

Davenport, Guy (Mattison, Jr.)
1927-2005 .... **CLC 6, 14, 38; SSC 16**
See also CA 33-36R; CANR 23, 73; CN 7;
CSW; DLB 130

David, Robert
See Nezval, Vitezslav

Davidson, Avram (James) 1923-1993
See Queen, Ellery
See also CA 101; 171; CANR 26; DLB 8;
FANT; SFW 4; SUFW 1, 2

Davidson, Donald (Grady)
1893-1968 .... **CLC 2, 13, 19**
See also CA 5-8R; 25-28R; CANR 4, 84;
DLB 45

Davidson, Hugh
See Hamilton, Edmond

Davidson, John 1857-1909 .... **TCLC 24**
See also CA 118; 217; DLB 19; RGEL 2

Davidson, Sara 1943- .... **CLC 9**
See also CA 81-84; CANR 44, 68; DLB
185

Davie, Donald (Alfred) 1922-1995 .... **CLC 5, 8, 10, 31; PC 29**
See also BRWS 6; CA 1-4R; 149; CAAS 3;
CANR 1, 44; CP 7; DLB 27; MTCW 1;
RGEL 2

Davie, Elspeth 1919-1995 .... **SSC 52**
See also CA 120; 126; 150; DLB 139

Davies, Ray(mond Douglas) 1944- ... **CLC 21**
See also CA 116; 146; CANR 92

Davies, Rhys 1901-1978 .... **CLC 23**
See also CA 9-12R; 81-84; CANR 4; DLB
139, 191

Davies, (William) Robertson
1913-1995 .... **CLC 2, 7, 13, 25, 42, 75, 91; WLC**
See Marchbanks, Samuel
See also BEST 89:2; BPFB 1; CA 33-36R;
150; CANR 17, 42, 103; CN 7; CPW;
DA; DA3; DAB; DAC; DAM MST, NOV,
POP; DLB 68; EWL 3; HGG; INT CANR-
17; MTCW 1, 2; RGEL 2; TWA

Davies, Sir John 1569-1626 .... **LC 85**
See also DLB 172

Davies, Walter C.
See Kornbluth, C(yril) M.

Davies, William Henry 1871-1940 ... **TCLC 5**
See also CA 104; 179; DLB 19, 174; EWL
3; RGEL 2

Da Vinci, Leonardo 1452-1519 ..... **LC 12, 57, 60**
See also AAYA 40

Davis, Angela (Yvonne) 1944- .... **CLC 77**
See also BW 2, 3; CA 57-60; CANR 10,
81; CSW; DA3; DAM MULT; FW

Davis, B. Lynch
See Bioy Casares, Adolfo; Borges, Jorge
Luis

Davis, Frank Marshall 1905-1987 ...... **BLC 1**
See also BW 2, 3; CA 125; 123; CANR 42,
80; DAM MULT; DLB 51

Davis, Gordon
See Hunt, E(verette) Howard, (Jr.)

Davis, H(arold) L(enoir) 1896-1960 . **CLC 49**
See also ANW; CA 178; 89-92; DLB 9,
206; SATA 114

Davis, Rebecca (Blaine) Harding
1831-1910 .... **SSC 38; TCLC 6**
See also CA 104; 179; DLB 74, 239; FW;
NFS 14; RGAL 4; TUS

Davis, Richard Harding
1864-1916 .... **TCLC 24**
See also CA 114; 179; DLB 12, 23, 78, 79,
189; DLBD 13; RGAL 4

Davison, Frank Dalby 1893-1970 ..... **CLC 15**
See also CA 217; 116; DLB 260

Davison, Lawrence H.
See Lawrence, D(avid) H(erbert Richards)

Davison, Peter (Hubert) 1928- .... **CLC 28**
See also CA 9-12R; CAAS 4; CANR 3, 43,
84; CP 7; DLB 5

Davys, Mary 1674-1732 .... **LC 1, 46**
See also DLB 39

Dawson, (Guy) Fielding (Lewis)
1930-2002 .... **CLC 6**
See also CA 85-88; 202; CANR 108; DLB
130; DLBY 2002

Dawson, Peter
See Faust, Frederick (Schiller)
See also TCWW 2, 2

Day, Clarence (Shepard, Jr.)
1874-1935 .... **TCLC 25**
See also CA 108; 199; DLB 11

Day, John 1574(?)-1640(?) .... **LC 70**
See also DLB 62, 170; RGEL 2

Day, Thomas 1748-1789 .... **LC 1**
See also DLB 39; YABC 1

Day Lewis, C(ecil) 1904-1972 . **CLC 1, 6, 10; PC 11**
See Blake, Nicholas
See also BRWS 3; CA 13-16; 33-36R;
CANR 34; CAP 1; CWRI 5; DAM POET;
DLB 15, 20; EWL 3; MTCW 1, 2; RGEL
2

Dazai Osamu .... **SSC 41; TCLC 11**
See Tsushima, Shuji
See also CA 164; DLB 182; EWL 3; MJW;
RGSF 2; RGWL 2, 3; TWA

de Andrade, Carlos Drummond
See Drummond de Andrade, Carlos

de Andrade, Mario 1892(?)-1945
See Andrade, Mario de
See also CA 178; HW 2

Deane, Norman
See Creasey, John

Deane, Seamus (Francis) 1940- .... **CLC 122**
See also CA 118; CANR 42

**de Beauvoir, Simone (Lucie Ernestine Marie
Bertrand)**
See Beauvoir, Simone (Lucie Ernestine
Marie Bertrand) de

de Beer, P.
See Bosman, Herman Charles

Derry Down Derry
See Lear, Edward
Dersonnes, Jacques
See Simenon, Georges (Jacques Christian)
Desai, Anita 1937- .... **CLC 19, 37, 97, 175**
See also BRWS 5; CA 81-84; CANR 33, 53, 95, 133; CN 7; CWRI 5; DA3; DAB; DAM NOV; DLB 271; DNFS 2; EWL 3; FW; MTCW 1, 2; SATA 63, 126
Desai, Kiran 1971- .... **CLC 119**
See also BYA 16; CA 171; CANR 127
de Saint-Luc, Jean
See Glassco, John
de Saint Roman, Arnaud
See Aragon, Louis
Desbordes-Valmore, Marceline
1786-1859 .... **NCLC 97**
See also DLB 217
Descartes, Rene 1596-1650 ..:......... **LC 20, 35**
See also DLB 268; EW 3; GFL Beginnings to 1789
Deschamps, Eustache 1340(?)-1404 .. **LC 103**
See also DLB 208
De Sica, Vittorio 1901(?)-1974 .... **CLC 20**
See also CA 117
Desnos, Robert 1900-1945 .... **TCLC 22**
See also CA 121; 151; CANR 107; DLB 258; EWL 3; LMFS 2
Destouches, Louis-Ferdinand
1894-1961 .... **CLC 9, 15**
See Celine, Louis-Ferdinand
See also CA 85-88; CANR 28; MTCW 1
de Tolignac, Gaston
See Griffith, D(avid Lewelyn) W(ark)
Deutsch, Babette 1895-1982 .... **CLC 18**
See also BYA 3; CA 1-4R; 108; CANR 4, 79; DLB 45; SATA 1; SATA-Obit 33
Devant, William 1606-1649 .... **LC 13**
Devkota, Laxmiprasad 1909-1959 . **TCLC 23**
See also CA 123
De Voto, Bernard (Augustine)
1897-1955 .... **TCLC 29**
See also CA 113; 160; DLB 9, 256
De Vries, Peter 1910-1993 ..... **CLC 1, 2, 3, 7, 10, 28, 46**
See also CA 17-20R; 142; CANR 41; DAM NOV; DLB 6; DLBY 1982; MTCW 1, 2
Dewey, John 1859-1952 .... **TCLC 95**
See also CA 114; 170; DLB 246, 270; RGAL 4
Dexter, John
See Bradley, Marion Zimmer
See also GLL 1
Dexter, Martin
See Faust, Frederick (Schiller)
See also TCWW 2
Dexter, Pete 1943- .... **CLC 34, 55**
See also BEST 89:2; CA 127; 131; CANR 129; CPW; DAM POP; INT CA-131; MTCW 1
Diamano, Silmang
See Senghor, Leopold Sedar
Diamond, Neil 1941- .... **CLC 30**
See also CA 108
Diaz del Castillo, Bernal
1496-1584 .... **HLCS 1; LC 31**
See also LAW
di Bassetto, Corno
See Shaw, George Bernard
Dick, Philip K(indred) 1928-1982 ... **CLC 10, 30, 72; SSC 57**
See also AAYA 24; BPFB 1; BYA 11; CA 49-52; 106; CANR 2, 16, 132; CPW; DA3; DAM NOV, POP; DLB 8; MTCW 1, 2; NFS 5; SCFW; SFW 4

Dickens, Charles (John Huffam)
1812-1870 .... **NCLC 3, 8, 18, 26, 37, 50, 86, 105, 113; SSC 17, 49; WLC**
See also AAYA 23; BRW 5; BRWC 1, 2; BYA 1, 2, 3, 13, 14; CDBLB 1832-1890; CLR 95; CMW 4; DA; DA3; DAB; DAC; DAM MST, NOV; DLB 21, 55, 70, 159, 166; EXPN; HGG; JRDA; LAIT 1, 2; LATS 1:1; LMFS 1; MAICYA 1, 2; NFS 4, 5, 10, 14, 20; RGEL 2; RGSF 2; SATA 15; SUFW 1; TEA; WCH; WLIT 4; WYA
Dickey, James (Lafayette)
1923-1997 .... **CLC 1, 2, 4, 7, 10, 15, 47, 109; PC 40; TCLC 151**
See also AAYA 50; AITN 1, 2; AMWS 4; BPFB 1; CA 9-12R; 156; CABS 2; CANR 10, 48, 61, 105; CDALB 1968-1988; CP 7; CPW; CSW; DA3; DAM NOV, POET, POP; DLB 5, 193; DLBD 7; DLBY 1982, 1993, 1996, 1997, 1998; EWL 3; INT CANR-10; MTCW 1, 2; NFS 9; PFS 6, 11; RGAL 4; TUS
Dickey, William 1928-1994 .... **CLC 3, 28**
See also CA 9-12R; 145; CANR 24, 79; DLB 5
Dickinson, Charles 1951- .... **CLC 49**
See also CA 128
Dickinson, Emily (Elizabeth)
1830-1886 ... **NCLC 21, 77; PC 1; WLC**
See also AAYA 22; AMW; AMWR 1; CDALB 1865-1917; DA; DA3; DAB; DAC; DAM MST, POET; DLB 1, 243; EXPP; MAWW; PAB; PFS 1, 2, 3, 4, 5, 6, 8, 10, 11, 13, 16; RGAL 4; SATA 29; TUS; WP; WYA
Dickinson, Mrs. Herbert Ward
See Phelps, Elizabeth Stuart
Dickinson, Peter (Malcolm de Brissac)
1927- .... **CLC 12, 35**
See also AAYA 9, 49; BYA 5; CA 41-44R; CANR 31, 58, 88, 134; CLR 29; CMW 4; DLB 87, 161, 276; JRDA; MAICYA 1, 2; SATA 5, 62, 95, 150; SFW 4; WYA; YAW
Dickson, Carr
See Carr, John Dickson
Dickson, Carter
See Carr, John Dickson
Diderot, Denis 1713-1784 .... **LC 26**
See also EW 4; GFL Beginnings to 1789; LMFS 1; RGWL 2, 3
Didion, Joan 1934- . **CLC 1, 3, 8, 14, 32, 129**
See also AITN 1; AMWS 4; CA 5-8R; CANR 14, 52, 76, 125; CDALB 1968-1988; CN 7; DA3; DAM NOV; DLB 2, 173, 185; DLBY 1981, 1986; EWL 3; MAWW; MTCW 1, 2; NFS 3; RGAL 4; TCWW 2; TUS
di Donato, Pietro 1911-1992 .... **TCLC 159**
See also CA 101; 136; DLB 9
Dietrich, Robert
See Hunt, E(verette) Howard, (Jr.)
Difusa, Pati
See Almodovar, Pedro
Dillard, Annie 1945- .... **CLC 9, 60, 115**
See also AAYA 6, 43; AMWS 6; ANW; CA 49-52; CANR 3, 43, 62, 90, 125; DA3; DAM NOV; DLB 275, 278; DLBY 1980; LAIT 4, 5; MTCW 1, 2; NCFS 1; RGAL 4; SATA 10, 140; TUS
Dillard, R(ichard) H(enry) W(ilde)
1937- .... **CLC 5**
See also CA 21-24R; CAAS 7; CANR 10; CP 7; CSW; DLB 5, 244
Dillon, Eilis 1920-1994 .... **CLC 17**
See also CA 9-12R, 182; 147; CAAE 182; CAAS 3; CANR 4, 38, 78; CLR 26; MAICYA 1, 2; MAICYAS 1; SATA 2, 74; SATA-Essay 105; SATA-Obit 83; YAW
Dimont, Penelope
See Mortimer, Penelope (Ruth)

Dinesen, Isak ..... **CLC 10, 29, 95; SSC 7, 75**
See Blixen, Karen (Christentze Dinesen)
See also EW 10; EWL 3; EXPS; FW; HGG; LAIT 3; MTCW 1; NCFS 2; NFS 9; RGSF 2; RGWL 2, 3; SSFS 3, 6, 13; WLIT 2
Ding Ling .... **CLC 68**
See Chiang, Pin-chin
See also RGWL 3
Diphusa, Patty
See Almodovar, Pedro
Disch, Thomas M(ichael) 1940- ... **CLC 7, 36**
See Disch, Tom
See also AAYA 17; BPFB 1; CA 21-24R; CAAS 4; CANR 17, 36, 54, 89; CLR 18; CP 7; DA3; DLB 8; HGG; MAICYA 1, 2; MTCW 1, 2; SAAS 15; SATA 92; SCFW; SFW 4; SUFW 2
Disch, Tom
See Disch, Thomas M(ichael)
See also DLB 282
d'Isly, Georges
See Simenon, Georges (Jacques Christian)
Disraeli, Benjamin 1804-1881 ... **NCLC 2, 39, 79**
See also BRW 4; DLB 21, 55; RGEL 2
Ditcum, Steve
See Crumb, R(obert)
Dixon, Paige
See Corcoran, Barbara (Asenath)
Dixon, Stephen 1936- .... **CLC 52; SSC 16**
See also AMWS 12; CA 89-92; CANR 17, 40, 54, 91; CN 7; DLB 130
Djebar, Assia 1936- .... **CLC 182**
See also CA 188; EWL 3; RGWL 3; WLIT 2
Doak, Annie
See Dillard, Annie
Dobell, Sydney Thompson
1824-1874 .... **NCLC 43**
See also DLB 32; RGEL 2
Doblin, Alfred .... **TCLC 13**
See Doeblin, Alfred
See also CDWLB 2; EWL 3; RGWL 2, 3
Dobroliubov, Nikolai Aleksandrovich
See Dobrolyubov, Nikolai Alexandrovich
See also DLB 277
Dobrolyubov, Nikolai Alexandrovich
1836-1861 .... **NCLC 5**
See Dobroliubov, Nikolai Aleksandrovich
Dobson, Austin 1840-1921 .... **TCLC 79**
See also DLB 35, 144
Dobyns, Stephen 1941- .... **CLC 37**
See also AMWS 13; CA 45-48; CANR 2, 18, 99; CMW 4; CP 7
Doctorow, E(dgar) L(aurence)
1931- .... **CLC 6, 11, 15, 18, 37, 44, 65, 113**
See also AAYA 22; AITN 2; AMWS 4; BEST 89:3; BPFB 1; CA 45-48; CANR 2, 33, 51, 76, 97, 133; CDALB 1968-1988; CN 7; CPW; DA3; DAM NOV, POP; DLB 2, 28, 173; DLBY 1980; EWL 3; LAIT 3; MTCW 1, 2; NFS 6; RGAL 4; RHW; TUS
Dodgson, Charles L(utwidge) 1832-1898
See Carroll, Lewis
See also CLR 2; DA; DA3; DAB; DAC; DAM MST, NOV, POET; MAICYA 1, 2; SATA 100; YABC 2
Dodsley, Robert 1703-1764 .... **LC 97**
See also DLB 95; RGEL 2
Dodson, Owen (Vincent) 1914-1983 .. **BLC 1; CLC 79**
See also BW 1; CA 65-68; 110; CANR 24; DAM MULT; DLB 76
Doeblin, Alfred 1878-1957 .... **TCLC 13**
See Doblin, Alfred
See also CA 110; 141; DLB 66

2; NCFS 5; PAB; PFS 1, 7, 20; RGAL 4; RGEL 2; TUS; WLIT 4; WP

Elizabeth 1866-1941 .... **TCLC 41**

Elkin, Stanley L(awrence)
1930-1995 .. **CLC 4, 6, 9, 14, 27, 51, 91; SSC 12**
See also AMWS 6; BPFB 1; CA 9-12R; 148; CANR 8, 46; CN 7; CPW; DAM NOV, POP; DLB 2, 28, 218, 278; DLBY 1980; EWL 3; INT CANR-8; MTCW 1, 2; RGAL 4

Elledge, Scott .... **CLC 34**

Elliott, Don
See Silverberg, Robert

Elliott, George P(aul) 1918-1980 .... **CLC 2**
See also CA 1-4R; 97-100; CANR 2; DLB 244

Elliott, Janice 1931-1995 .... **CLC 47**
See also CA 13-16R; CANR 8, 29, 84; CN 7; DLB 14; SATA 119

Elliott, Sumner Locke 1917-1991 ..... **CLC 38**
See also CA 5-8R; 134; CANR 2, 21; DLB 289

Elliott, William
See Bradbury, Ray (Douglas)

Ellis, A. E. .... **CLC 7**

Ellis, Alice Thomas .... **CLC 40**
See Haycraft, Anna (Margaret)
See also DLB 194; MTCW 1

Ellis, Bret Easton 1964- ..... **CLC 39, 71, 117**
See also AAYA 2, 43; CA 118; 123; CANR 51, 74, 126; CN 7; CPW; DA3; DAM POP; DLB 292; HGG; INT CA-123; MTCW 1; NFS 11

Ellis, (Henry) Havelock
1859-1939 .... **TCLC 14**
See also CA 109; 169; DLB 190

Ellis, Landon
See Ellison, Harlan (Jay)

Ellis, Trey 1962- .... **CLC 55**
See also CA 146; CANR 92

Ellison, Harlan (Jay) 1934- ... **CLC 1, 13, 42, 139; SSC 14**
See also AAYA 29; BPFB 1; BYA 14; CA 5-8R; CANR 5, 46, 115; CPW; DAM POP; DLB 8; HGG; INT CANR-5; MTCW 1, 2; SCFW 2; SFW 4; SSFS 13, 14, 15; SUFW 1, 2

Ellison, Ralph (Waldo) 1914-1994 .... **BLC 1; CLC 1, 3, 11, 54, 86, 114; SSC 26, 79; WLC**
See also AAYA 19; AFAW 1, 2; AMWC 2; AMWR 2; AMWS 2; BPFB 1; BW 1, 3; BYA 2; CA 9-12R; 145; CANR 24, 53; CDALB 1941-1968; CSW; DA; DA3; DAB; DAC; DAM MST, MULT, NOV; DLB 2, 76, 227; DLBY 1994; EWL 3; EXPN; EXPS; LAIT 4; MTCW 1, 2; NCFS 3; NFS 2; RGAL 4; RGSF 2; SSFS 1, 11; YAW

Ellmann, Lucy (Elizabeth) 1956- ..... **CLC 61**
See also CA 128

Ellmann, Richard (David)
1918-1987 .... **CLC 50**
See also BEST 89:2; CA 1-4R; 122; CANR 2, 28, 61; DLB 103; DLBY 1987; MTCW 1, 2

Elman, Richard (Martin)
1934-1997 .... **CLC 19**
See also CA 17-20R; 163; CAAS 3; CANR 47

Elron
See Hubbard, L(afayette) Ron(ald)

El Saadawi, Nawal 1931- .... **CLC 196**
See al'Sadaawi, Nawal; Sa'adawi, al-Nawal; Saadawi, Nawal El; Sa'dawi, Nawal al-
See also CA 118; CAAS 11; CANR 44, 92

Eluard, Paul .... **PC 38; TCLC 7, 41**
See Grindel, Eugene
See also EWL 3; GFL 1789 to the Present; RGWL 2, 3

Elyot, Thomas 1490(?)-1546 .... **LC 11**
See also DLB 136; RGEL 2

Elytis, Odysseus 1911-1996 .... **CLC 15, 49, 100; PC 21**
See Alepoudelis, Odysseus
See also CA 102; 151; CANR 94; CWW 2; DAM POET; EW 13; EWL 3; MTCW 1, 2; RGWL 2, 3

Emecheta, (Florence Onye) Buchi
1944- .... **BLC 2; CLC 14, 48, 128**
See also AFW; BW 2, 3; CA 81-84; CANR 27, 81, 126; CDWLB 3; CN 7; CWRI 5; DA3; DAM MULT; DLB 117; EWL 3; FW; MTCW 1, 2; NFS 12, 14; SATA 66; WLIT 2

Emerson, Mary Moody
1774-1863 .... **NCLC 66**

Emerson, Ralph Waldo 1803-1882 . **NCLC 1, 38, 98; PC 18; WLC**
See also AAYA 60; AMW; ANW; CDALB 1640-1865; DA; DA3; DAB; DAC; DAM MST, POET; DLB 1, 59, 73, 183, 223, 270; EXPP; LAIT 2; LMFS 1; NCFS 3; PFS 4, 17; RGAL 4; TUS; WP

Eminescu, Mihail 1850-1889 .. **NCLC 33, 131**

Empedocles 5th cent. B.C.- .... **CMLC 50**
See also DLB 176

Empson, William 1906-1984 ... **CLC 3, 8, 19, 33, 34**
See also BRWS 2; CA 17-20R; 112; CANR 31, 61; DLB 20; EWL 3; MTCW 1, 2; RGEL 2

Enchi, Fumiko (Ueda) 1905-1986 ..... **CLC 31**
See Enchi Fumiko
See also CA 129; 121; FW; MJW

Enchi Fumiko
See Enchi, Fumiko (Ueda)
See also DLB 182; EWL 3

Ende, Michael (Andreas Helmuth)
1929-1995 .... **CLC 31**
See also BYA 5; CA 118; 124; 149; CANR 36, 110; CLR 14; DLB 75; MAICYA 1, 2; MAICYAS 1; SATA 61, 130; SATA-Brief 42; SATA-Obit 86

Endo, Shusaku 1923-1996 ..... **CLC 7, 14, 19, 54, 99; SSC 48; TCLC 152**
See Endo Shusaku
See also CA 29-32R; 153; CANR 21, 54, 131; DA3; DAM NOV; MTCW 1, 2; RGSF 2; RGWL 2, 3

Endo Shusaku
See Endo, Shusaku
See also CWW 2; DLB 182; EWL 3

Engel, Marian 1933-1985 .... **CLC 36; TCLC 137**
See also CA 25-28R; CANR 12; DLB 53; FW; INT CANR-12

Engelhardt, Frederick
See Hubbard, L(afayette) Ron(ald)

Engels, Friedrich 1820-1895 .. **NCLC 85, 114**
See also DLB 129; LATS 1:1

Enright, D(ennis) J(oseph)
1920-2002 .... **CLC 4, 8, 31**
See also CA 1-4R; 211; CANR 1, 42, 83; CP 7; DLB 27; EWL 3; SATA 25; SATA-Obit 140

Enzensberger, Hans Magnus
1929- .... **CLC 43; PC 28**
See also CA 116; 119; CANR 103; CWW 2; EWL 3

Ephron, Nora 1941- .... **CLC 17, 31**
See also AAYA 35; AITN 2; CA 65-68; CANR 12, 39, 83

Epicurus 341B.C.-270B.C. .... **CMLC 21**
See also DLB 176

Epsilon
See Betjeman, John

Epstein, Daniel Mark 1948- .... **CLC 7**
See also CA 49-52; CANR 2, 53, 90

Epstein, Jacob 1956- .... **CLC 19**
See also CA 114

Epstein, Jean 1897-1953 .... **TCLC 92**

Epstein, Joseph 1937- .... **CLC 39**
See also AMWS 14; CA 112; 119; CANR 50, 65, 117

Epstein, Leslie 1938- .... **CLC 27**
See also AMWS 12; CA 73-76, 215; CAAE 215; CAAS 12; CANR 23, 69; DLB 299

Equiano, Olaudah 1745(?)-1797 . **BLC 2; LC 16**
See also AFAW 1, 2; CDWLB 3; DAM MULT; DLB 37, 50; WLIT 2

Erasmus, Desiderius 1469(?)-1536 ..... **LC 16, 93**
See also DLB 136; EW 2; LMFS 1; RGWL 2, 3; TWA

Erdman, Paul E(mil) 1932- .... **CLC 25**
See also AITN 1; CA 61-64; CANR 13, 43, 84

Erdrich, Louise 1954- .... **CLC 39, 54, 120, 176; NNAL; PC 52**
See also AAYA 10, 47; AMWS 4; BEST 89:1; BPFB 1; CA 114; CANR 41, 62, 118; CDALBS; CN 7; CP 7; CPW; CWP; DA3; DAM MULT, NOV, POP; DLB 152, 175, 206; EWL 3; EXPP; LAIT 5; LATS 1:2; MTCW 1; NFS 5; PFS 14; RGAL 4; SATA 94, 141; SSFS 14; TCWW 2

Erenburg, Ilya (Grigoryevich)
See Ehrenburg, Ilya (Grigoryevich)

Erickson, Stephen Michael 1950-
See Erickson, Steve
See also CA 129; SFW 4

Erickson, Steve .... **CLC 64**
See Erickson, Stephen Michael
See also CANR 60, 68; SUFW 2

Erickson, Walter
See Fast, Howard (Melvin)

Ericson, Walter
See Fast, Howard (Melvin)

Eriksson, Buntel
See Bergman, (Ernst) Ingmar

Eriugena, John Scottus c.
810-877 .... **CMLC 65**
See also DLB 115

Ernaux, Annie 1940- .... **CLC 88, 184**
See also CA 147; CANR 93; NCFS 3, 5

Erskine, John 1879-1951 .... **TCLC 84**
See also CA 112; 159; DLB 9, 102; FANT

Eschenbach, Wolfram von
See Wolfram von Eschenbach
See also RGWL 3

Eseki, Bruno
See Mphahlele, Ezekiel

Esenin, Sergei (Alexandrovich)
1895-1925 .... **TCLC 4**
See Yesenin, Sergey
See also CA 104; RGWL 2, 3

Eshleman, Clayton 1935- .... **CLC 7**
See also CA 33-36R, 212; CAAE 212; CAAS 6; CANR 93; CP 7; DLB 5

Espriella, Don Manuel Alvarez
See Southey, Robert

Espriu, Salvador 1913-1985 .... **CLC 9**
See also CA 154; 115; DLB 134; EWL 3

Espronceda, Jose de 1808-1842 ..... **NCLC 39**

Esquivel, Laura 1951(?)- ... **CLC 141; HLCS 1**
See also AAYA 29; CA 143; CANR 68, 113; DA3; DNFS 2; LAIT 3; LMFS 2; MTCW 1; NFS 5; WLIT 1

Esse, James
See Stephens, James

Esterbrook, Tom
See Hubbard, L(afayette) Ron(ald)
Estleman, Loren D. 1952- .... **CLC 48**
See also AAYA 27; CA 85-88; CANR 27,
74; CMW 4; CPW; DA3; DAM NOV,
POP; DLB 226; INT CANR-27; MTCW
1, 2
Etherege, Sir George 1636-1692 . **DC 23; LC
78**
See also BRW 2; DAM DRAM; DLB 80;
PAB; RGEL 2
Euclid 306B.C.-283B.C. .... **CMLC 25**
Eugenides, Jeffrey 1960(?)- .... **CLC 81**
See also AAYA 51; CA 144; CANR 120
Euripides c. 484B.C.-406B.C. .... **CMLC 23,
51; DC 4; WLCS**
See also AW 1; CDWLB 1; DA; DA3;
DAB; DAC; DAM DRAM, MST; DFS 1,
4, 6; DLB 176; LAIT 1; LMFS 1; RGWL
2, 3
Evan, Evin
See Faust, Frederick (Schiller)
Evans, Caradoc 1878-1945 ... **SSC 43; TCLC
85**
See also DLB 162
Evans, Evan
See Faust, Frederick (Schiller)
See also TCWW 2
Evans, Marian
See Eliot, George
Evans, Mary Ann
See Eliot, George
See also NFS 20
Evarts, Esther
See Benson, Sally
Everett, Percival
See Everett, Percival L.
See also CSW
Everett, Percival L. 1956- .... **CLC 57**
See Everett, Percival
See also BW 2; CA 129; CANR 94, 134
Everson, R(onald) G(ilmour)
1903-1992 .... **CLC 27**
See also CA 17-20R; DLB 88
Everson, William (Oliver)
1912-1994 .... **CLC 1, 5, 14**
See also BG 2; CA 9-12R; 145; CANR 20;
DLB 5, 16, 212; MTCW 1
Evtushenko, Evgenii Aleksandrovich
See Yevtushenko, Yevgeny (Alexandrovich)
See also CWW 2; RGWL 2, 3
Ewart, Gavin (Buchanan)
1916-1995 .... **CLC 13, 46**
See also BRWS 7; CA 89-92; 150; CANR
17, 46; CP 7; DLB 40; MTCW 1
Ewers, Hanns Heinz 1871-1943 ..... **TCLC 12**
See also CA 109; 149
Ewing, Frederick R.
See Sturgeon, Theodore (Hamilton)
Exley, Frederick (Earl) 1929-1992 .... **CLC 6,
11**
See also AITN 2; BPFB 1; CA 81-84; 138;
CANR 117; DLB 143; DLBY 1981
Eynhardt, Guillermo
See Quiroga, Horacio (Sylvestre)
Ezekiel, Nissim (Moses) 1924-2004 .. **CLC 61**
See also CA 61-64; 223; CP 7; EWL 3
Ezekiel, Tish O'Dowd 1943- .... **CLC 34**
See also CA 129
Fadeev, Aleksandr Aleksandrovich
See Bulgya, Alexander Alexandrovich
See also DLB 272
Fadeev, Alexandr Alexandrovich
See Bulgya, Alexander Alexandrovich
See also EWL 3
Fadeyev, A.
See Bulgya, Alexander Alexandrovich
Fadeyev, Alexander .... **TCLC 53**
See Bulgya, Alexander Alexandrovich

Fagen, Donald 1948- .... **CLC 26**
Fainzilberg, Ilya Arnoldovich 1897-1937
See Ilf, Ilya
See also CA 120; 165
Fair, Ronald L. 1932- .... **CLC 18**
See also BW 1; CA 69-72; CANR 25; DLB
33
Fairbairn, Roger
See Carr, John Dickson
Fairbairns, Zoe (Ann) 1948- .... **CLC 32**
See also CA 103; CANR 21, 85; CN 7
Fairfield, Flora
See Alcott, Louisa May
Fairman, Paul W. 1916-1977
See Queen, Ellery
See also CA 114; SFW 4
Falco, Gian
See Papini, Giovanni
Falconer, James
See Kirkup, James
Falconer, Kenneth
See Kornbluth, C(yril) M.
Falkland, Samuel
See Heijermans, Herman
Fallaci, Oriana 1930- .... **CLC 11, 110**
See also CA 77-80; CANR 15, 58, 134; FW;
MTCW 1
Faludi, Susan 1959- .... **CLC 140**
See also CA 138; CANR 126; FW; MTCW
1; NCFS 3
Faludy, George 1913- .... **CLC 42**
See also CA 21-24R
Faludy, Gyoergy
See Faludy, George
Fanon, Frantz 1925-1961 .... **BLC 2; CLC 74**
See also BW 1; CA 116; 89-92; DAM
MULT; DLB 296; LMFS 2; WLIT 2
Fanshawe, Ann 1625-1680 .... **LC 11**
Fante, John (Thomas) 1911-1983 .... **CLC 60;
SSC 65**
See also AMWS 11; CA 69-72; 109; CANR
23, 104; DLB 130; DLBY 1983
Far, Sui Sin .... **SSC 62**
See Eaton, Edith Maude
See also SSFS 4
Farah, Nuruddin 1945- ...... **BLC 2; CLC 53,
137**
See also AFW; BW 2, 3; CA 106; CANR
81; CDWLB 3; CN 7; DAM MULT; DLB
125; EWL 3; WLIT 2
Fargue, Leon-Paul 1876(?)-1947 .... **TCLC 11**
See also CA 109; CANR 107; DLB 258;
EWL 3
Farigoule, Louis
See Romains, Jules
Farina, Richard 1936(?)-1966 .... **CLC 9**
See also CA 81-84; 25-28R
Farley, Walter (Lorimer)
1915-1989 .... **CLC 17**
See also AAYA 58; BYA 14; CA 17-20R;
CANR 8, 29, 84; DLB 22; JRDA; MAI-
CYA 1, 2; SATA 2, 43, 132; YAW
Farmer, Philip Jose 1918- .... **CLC 1, 19**
See also AAYA 28; BPFB 1; CA 1-4R;
CANR 4, 35, 111; DLB 8; MTCW 1;
SATA 93; SCFW 2; SFW 4
Farquhar, George 1677-1707 .... **LC 21**
See also BRW 2; DAM DRAM; DLB 84;
RGEL 2
Farrell, J(ames) G(ordon)
1935-1979 .... **CLC 6**
See also CA 73-76; 89-92; CANR 36; DLB
14, 271; MTCW 1; RGEL 2; RHW; WLIT
4
Farrell, James T(homas) 1904-1979 . **CLC 1,
4, 8, 11, 66; SSC 28**
See also AMW; BPFB 1; CA 5-8R; 89-92;
CANR 9, 61; DLB 4, 9, 86; DLBD 2;
EWL 3; MTCW 1, 2; RGAL 4

Farrell, Warren (Thomas) 1943- ...... **CLC 70**
See also CA 146; CANR 120
Farren, Richard J.
See Betjeman, John
Farren, Richard M.
See Betjeman, John
Fassbinder, Rainer Werner
1946-1982 .... **CLC 20**
See also CA 93-96; 106; CANR 31
Fast, Howard (Melvin) 1914-2003 .. **CLC 23,
131**
See also AAYA 16; BPFB 1; CA 1-4R, 181;
214; CAAE 181; CAAS 18; CANR 1, 33,
54, 75, 98; CMW 4; CN 7; CPW; DAM
NOV; DLB 9; INT CANR-33; LATS 1:1;
MTCW 1; RHW; SATA 7; SATA-Essay
107; TCWW 2; YAW
Faulcon, Robert
See Holdstock, Robert P.
Faulkner, William (Cuthbert)
1897-1962 .... **CLC 1, 3, 6, 8, 9, 11, 14,
18, 28, 52, 68; SSC 1, 35, 42; TCLC
141; WLC**
See also AAYA 7; AMW; AMWR 1; BPFB
1; BYA 5, 15; CA 81-84; CANR 33;
CDALB 1929-1941; DA; DA3; DAB;
DAC; DAM MST, NOV; DLB 9, 11, 44,
102; DLBD 2; DLBY 1986, 1997; EWL
3; EXPN; EXPS; LAIT 2; LATS 1:1;
LMFS 2; MTCW 1, 2; NFS 4, 8, 13;
RGAL 4; RGSF 2; SSFS 2, 5, 6, 12; TUS
Fauset, Jessie Redmon
1882(?)-1961 .. **BLC 2; CLC 19, 54; HR
2**
See also AFAW 2; BW 1; CA 109; CANR
83; DAM MULT; DLB 51; FW; LMFS 2;
MAWW
Faust, Frederick (Schiller)
1892-1944(?) .... **TCLC 49**
See Austin, Frank; Brand, Max; Challis,
George; Dawson, Peter; Dexter, Martin;
Evans, Evan; Frederick, John; Frost, Fred-
erick; Manning, David; Silver, Nicholas
See also CA 108; 152; DAM POP; DLB
256; TUS
Faust, Irvin 1924- .... **CLC 8**
See also CA 33-36R; CANR 28, 67; CN 7;
DLB 2, 28, 218, 278; DLBY 1980
Faustino, Domingo 1811-1888 ...... **NCLC 123**
Fawkes, Guy
See Benchley, Robert (Charles)
Fearing, Kenneth (Flexner)
1902-1961 .... **CLC 51**
See also CA 93-96; CANR 59; CMW 4;
DLB 9; RGAL 4
Fecamps, Elise
See Creasey, John
Federman, Raymond 1928- .... **CLC 6, 47**
See also CA 17-20R, 208; CAAE 208;
CAAS 8; CANR 10, 43, 83, 108; CN 7;
DLBY 1980
Federspiel, J(uerg) F. 1931- .... **CLC 42**
See also CA 146
Feiffer, Jules (Ralph) 1929- ...... **CLC 2, 8, 64**
See also AAYA 3; CA 17-20R; CAD; CANR
30, 59, 129; CD 5; DAM DRAM; DLB 7,
44; INT CANR-30; MTCW 1; SATA 8,
61, 111
Feige, Hermann Albert Otto Maximilian
See Traven, B.
Feinberg, David B. 1956-1994 .... **CLC 59**
See also CA 135; 147
Feinstein, Elaine 1930- .... **CLC 36**
See also CA 69-72; CAAS 1; CANR 31,
68, 121; CN 7; CP 7; CWP; DLB 14, 40;
MTCW 1

Fleming, Thomas (James) 1927- ...... **CLC 37**
See also CA 5-8R; CANR 10, 102; INT
CANR-10; SATA 8

Fletcher, John 1579-1625 .... **DC 6; LC 33**
See also BRW 2; CDBLB Before 1660;
DLB 58; RGEL 2; TEA

Fletcher, John Gould 1886-1950 .... **TCLC 35**
See also CA 107; 167; DLB 4, 45; LMFS
2; RGAL 4

Fleur, Paul
See Pohl, Frederik

Flieg, Helmut
See Heym, Stefan

Flooglebuckle, Al
See Spiegelman, Art

Flora, Fletcher 1914-1969
See Queen, Ellery
See also CA 1-4R; CANR 3, 85

Flying Officer X
See Bates, H(erbert) E(rnest)

Fo, Dario 1926- .... **CLC 32, 109; DC 10**
See also CA 116; 128; CANR 68, 114, 134;
CWW 2; DA3; DAM DRAM; DLBY
1997; EWL 3; MTCW 1, 2

Fogarty, Jonathan Titulescu Esq.
See Farrell, James T(homas)

Follett, Ken(neth Martin) 1949- .... **CLC 18**
See also AAYA 6, 50; BEST 89:4; BPFB 1;
CA 81-84; CANR 13, 33, 54, 102; CMW
4; CPW; DA3; DAM NOV, POP; DLB
87; DLBY 1981; INT CANR-33; MTCW
1

Fondane, Benjamin 1898-1944 ..... **TCLC 159**

Fontane, Theodor 1819-1898 .... **NCLC 26**
See also CDWLB 2; DLB 129; EW 6;
RGWL 2, 3; TWA

Fontenot, Chester .... **CLC 65**

Fonvizin, Denis Ivanovich
1744(?)-1792 .... **LC 81**
See also DLB 150; RGWL 2, 3

Foote, Horton 1916- .... **CLC 51, 91**
See also CA 73-76; CAD; CANR 34, 51,
110; CD 5; CSW; DA3; DAM DRAM;
DFS 20; DLB 26, 266; EWL 3; INT
CANR-34

Foote, Mary Hallock 1847-1938 .. **TCLC 108**
See also DLB 186, 188, 202, 221

Foote, Samuel 1721-1777 .... **LC 106**
See also DLB 89; RGEL 2

Foote, Shelby 1916- .... **CLC 75**
See also AAYA 40; CA 5-8R; CANR 3, 45,
74, 131; CN 7; CPW; CSW; DA3; DAM
NOV, POP; DLB 2, 17; MTCW 2; RHW

Forbes, Cosmo
See Lewton, Val

Forbes, Esther 1891-1967 .... **CLC 12**
See also AAYA 17; BYA 2; CA 13-14; 25-
28R; CAP 1; CLR 27; DLB 22; JRDA;
MAICYA 1, 2; RHW; SATA 2, 100; YAW

Forche, Carolyn (Louise) 1950- .... **CLC 25,
83, 86; PC 10**
See also CA 109; 117; CANR 50, 74; CP 7;
CWP; DA3; DAM POET; DLB 5, 193;
INT CA-117; MTCW 1; PFS 18; RGAL 4

Ford, Elbur
See Hibbert, Eleanor Alice Burford

Ford, Ford Madox 1873-1939 ... **TCLC 1, 15,
39, 57**
See Chaucer, Daniel
See also BRW 6; CA 104; 132; CANR 74;
CDBLB 1914-1945; DA3; DAM NOV;
DLB 34, 98, 162; EWL 3; MTCW 1, 2;
RGEL 2; TEA

Ford, Henry 1863-1947 .... **TCLC 73**
See also CA 115; 148

Ford, Jack
See Ford, John

Ford, John 1586-1639 .... **DC 8; LC 68**
See also BRW 2; CDBLB Before 1660;
DA3; DAM DRAM; DFS 7; DLB 58;
IDTP; RGEL 2

Ford, John 1895-1973 .... **CLC 16**
See also CA 187; 45-48

Ford, Richard 1944- .... **CLC 46, 99**
See also AMWS 5; CA 69-72; CANR 11,
47, 86, 128; CN 7; CSW; DLB 227; EWL
3; MTCW 1; RGAL 4; RGSF 2

Ford, Webster
See Masters, Edgar Lee

Foreman, Richard 1937- .... **CLC 50**
See also CA 65-68; CAD; CANR 32, 63;
CD 5

Forester, C(ecil) S(cott) 1899-1966 . **CLC 35;
TCLC 152**
See also CA 73-76; 25-28R; CANR 83;
DLB 191; RGEL 2; RHW; SATA 13

Forez
See Mauriac, Francois (Charles)

Forman, James
See Forman, James D(ouglas)

Forman, James D(ouglas) 1932- .... **CLC 21**
See also AAYA 17; CA 9-12R; CANR 4,
19, 42; JRDA; MAICYA 1, 2; SATA 8,
70; YAW

Forman, Milos 1932- .... **CLC 164**
See also CA 109

Fornes, Maria Irene 1930- .... **CLC 39, 61,
187; DC 10; HLCS 1**
See also CA 25-28R; CAD; CANR 28, 81;
CD 5; CWD; DLB 7; HW 1, 2; INT
CANR-28; LLW 1; MTCW 1; RGAL 4

Forrest, Leon (Richard)
1937-1997 .... **BLCS; CLC 4**
See also AFAW 2; BW 2; CA 89-92; 162;
CAAS 7; CANR 25, 52, 87; CN 7; DLB
33

Forster, E(dward) M(organ)
1879-1970 ...... **CLC 1, 2, 3, 4, 9, 10, 13,
15, 22, 45, 77; SSC 27; TCLC 125;
WLC**
See also AAYA 2, 37; BRW 6; BRWR 2;
BYA 12; CA 13-14; 25-28R; CANR 45;
CAP 1; CDBLB 1914-1945; DA; DA3;
DAB; DAC; DAM MST, NOV; DLB 34,
98, 162, 178, 195; DLBD 10; EWL 3;
EXPN; LAIT 3; LMFS 1; MTCW 1, 2;
NCFS 1; NFS 3, 10, 11; RGEL 2; RGSF
2; SATA 57; SUFW 1; TEA; WLIT 4

Forster, John 1812-1876 .... **NCLC 11**
See also DLB 144, 184

Forster, Margaret 1938- .... **CLC 149**
See also CA 133; CANR 62, 115; CN 7;
DLB 155, 271

Forsyth, Frederick 1938- .... **CLC 2, 5, 36**
See also BEST 89:4; CA 85-88; CANR 38,
62, 115; CMW 4; CN 7; CPW; DAM
NOV, POP; DLB 87; MTCW 1, 2

Forten, Charlotte L. 1837-1914 .... **BLC 2;
TCLC 16**
See Grimke, Charlotte L(ottie) Forten
See also DLB 50, 239

Fortinbras
See Grieg, (Johan) Nordahl (Brun)

Foscolo, Ugo 1778-1827 .... **NCLC 8, 97**
See also EW 5

Fosse, Bob .... **CLC 20**
See Fosse, Robert Louis

Fosse, Robert Louis 1927-1987
See Fosse, Bob
See also CA 110; 123

Foster, Hannah Webster
1758-1840 .... **NCLC 99**
See also DLB 37, 200; RGAL 4

Foster, Stephen Collins
1826-1864 .... **NCLC 26**
See also RGAL 4

Foucault, Michel 1926-1984 . **CLC 31, 34, 69**
See also CA 105; 113; CANR 34; DLB 242;
EW 13; EWL 3; GFL 1789 to the Present;
GLL 1; LMFS 2; MTCW 1, 2; TWA

**Fouque, Friedrich (Heinrich Karl) de la
Motte** 1777-1843 .... **NCLC 2**
See also DLB 90; RGWL 2, 3; SUFW 1

Fourier, Charles 1772-1837 .... **NCLC 51**

Fournier, Henri-Alban 1886-1914
See Alain-Fournier
See also CA 104; 179

Fournier, Pierre 1916- .... **CLC 11**
See Gascar, Pierre
See also CA 89-92; CANR 16, 40

Fowles, John (Robert) 1926- . **CLC 1, 2, 3, 4,
6, 9, 10, 15, 33, 87; SSC 33**
See also BPFB 1; BRWS 1; CA 5-8R;
CANR 25, 71, 103; CDBLB 1960 to
Present; CN 7; DA3; DAB; DAC; DAM
MST; DLB 14, 139, 207; EWL 3; HGG;
MTCW 1, 2; RGEL 2; RHW; SATA 22;
TEA; WLIT 4

Fox, Paula 1923- .... **CLC 2, 8, 121**
See also AAYA 3, 37; BYA 3, 8; CA 73-76;
CANR 20, 36, 62, 105; CLR 1, 44, 96;
DLB 52; JRDA; MAICYA 1, 2; MTCW
1; NFS 12; SATA 17, 60, 120; WYA;
YAW

Fox, William Price (Jr.) 1926- .... **CLC 22**
See also CA 17-20R; CAAS 19; CANR 11;
CSW; DLB 2; DLBY 1981

Foxe, John 1517(?)-1587 .... **LC 14**
See also DLB 132

Frame, Janet .. **CLC 2, 3, 6, 22, 66, 96; SSC
29**
See Clutha, Janet Paterson Frame
See also CN 7; CWP; EWL 3; RGEL 2;
RGSF 2; TWA

France, Anatole .... **TCLC 9**
See Thibault, Jacques Anatole Francois
See also DLB 123; EWL 3; GFL 1789 to
the Present; MTCW 1; RGWL 2, 3;
SUFW 1

Francis, Claude .... **CLC 50**
See also CA 192

Francis, Richard Stanley 1920- ... **CLC 2, 22,
42, 102**
See also AAYA 5, 21; BEST 89:3; BPFB 1;
CA 5-8R; CANR 9, 42, 68, 100; CDBLB
1960 to Present; CMW 4; CN 7; DA3;
DAM POP; DLB 87; INT CANR-9;
MSW; MTCW 1, 2

Francis, Robert (Churchill)
1901-1987 .... **CLC 15; PC 34**
See also AMWS 9; CA 1-4R; 123; CANR
1; EXPP; PFS 12

Francis, Lord Jeffrey
See Jeffrey, Francis
See also DLB 107

Frank, Anne(lies Marie)
1929-1945 .... **TCLC 17; WLC**
See also AAYA 12; BYA 1; CA 113; 133;
CANR 68; CLR 101; DA; DA3; DAB;
DAC; DAM MST; LAIT 4; MAICYA 2;
MAICYAS 1; MTCW 1, 2; NCFS 2;
SATA 87; SATA-Brief 42; WYA; YAW

Frank, Bruno 1887-1945 .... **TCLC 81**
See also CA 189; DLB 118; EWL 3

Frank, Elizabeth 1945- .... **CLC 39**
See also CA 121; 126; CANR 78; INT CA-
126

Frankl, Viktor E(mil) 1905-1997 ...... **CLC 93**
See also CA 65-68; 161

Franklin, Benjamin
See Hasek, Jaroslav (Matej Frantisek)

Franklin, Benjamin 1706-1790 .... **LC 25;
WLCS**
See also AMW; CDALB 1640-1865; DA;
DA3; DAB; DAC; DAM MST; DLB 24,
43, 73, 183; LAIT 1; RGAL 4; TUS

Gawsworth, John
See Bates, H(erbert) E(rnest)

Gay, John 1685-1732 .... **LC 49**
See also BRW 3; DAM DRAM; DLB 84, 95; RGEL 2; WLIT 3

Gay, Oliver
See Gogarty, Oliver St. John

Gay, Peter (Jack) 1923- .... **CLC 158**
See also CA 13-16R; CANR 18, 41, 77; INT CANR-18

Gaye, Marvin (Pentz, Jr.)
1939-1984 .... **CLC 26**
See also CA 195; 112

Gebler, Carlo (Ernest) 1954- .... **CLC 39**
See also CA 119; 133; CANR 96; DLB 271

Gee, Maggie (Mary) 1948- .... **CLC 57**
See also CA 130; CANR 125; CN 7; DLB 207

Gee, Maurice (Gough) 1931- .... **CLC 29**
See also AAYA 42; CA 97-100; CANR 67, 123; CLR 56; CN 7; CWRI 5; EWL 3; MAICYA 2; RGSF 2; SATA 46, 101

Geiogamah, Hanay 1945- .... **NNAL**
See also CA 153; DAM MULT; DLB 175

Gelbart, Larry (Simon) 1928- .... **CLC 21, 61**
See Gelbart, Larry
See also CA 73-76; CANR 45, 94

Gelbart, Larry 1928-
See Gelbart, Larry (Simon)
See also CAD; CD 5

Gelber, Jack 1932-2003 ...... **CLC 1, 6, 14, 79**
See also CA 1-4R; 216; CAD; CANR 2; DLB 7, 228

Gellhorn, Martha (Ellis)
1908-1998 .... **CLC 14, 60**
See also CA 77-80; 164; CANR 44; CN 7; DLBY 1982, 1998

Genet, Jean 1910-1986 . **DC 25; CLC 1, 2, 5, 10, 14, 44, 46; TCLC 128**
See also CA 13-16R; CANR 18; DA3; DAM DRAM; DFS 10; DLB 72; DLBY 1986; EW 13; EWL 3; GFL 1789 to the Present; GLL 1; LMFS 2; MTCW 1, 2; RGWL 2, 3; TWA

Gent, Peter 1942- .... **CLC 29**
See also AITN 1; CA 89-92; DLBY 1982

Gentile, Giovanni 1875-1944 .... **TCLC 96**
See also CA 119

Gentlewoman in New England, A
See Bradstreet, Anne

Gentlewoman in Those Parts, A
See Bradstreet, Anne

Geoffrey of Monmouth c.
1100-1155 .... **CMLC 44**
See also DLB 146; TEA

George, Jean
See George, Jean Craighead

George, Jean Craighead 1919- .... **CLC 35**
See also AAYA 8; BYA 2, 4; CA 5-8R; CANR 25; CLR 1; 80; DLB 52; JRDA; MAICYA 1, 2; SATA 2, 68, 124; WYA; YAW

George, Stefan (Anton) 1868-1933 . **TCLC 2, 14**
See also CA 104; 193; EW 8; EWL 3

Georges, Georges Martin
See Simenon, Georges (Jacques Christian)

Gerald of Wales c. 1146-c. 1223 ... **CMLC 60**

Gerhardi, William Alexander
See Gerhardie, William Alexander

Gerhardie, William Alexander
1895-1977 .... **CLC 5**
See also CA 25-28R; 73-76; CANR 18; DLB 36; RGEL 2

Gerson, Jean 1363-1429 .... **LC 77**
See also DLB 208

Gersonides 1288-1344 .... **CMLC 49**
See also DLB 115

Gerstler, Amy 1956- .... **CLC 70**
See also CA 146; CANR 99

Gertler, T. .... **CLC 34**
See also CA 116; 121

Gertsen, Aleksandr Ivanovich
See Herzen, Aleksandr Ivanovich

Ghalib .... **NCLC 39, 78**
See Ghalib, Asadullah Khan

Ghalib, Asadullah Khan 1797-1869
See Ghalib
See also DAM POET; RGWL 2, 3

Ghelderode, Michel de 1898-1962 ..... **CLC 6, 11; DC 15**
See also CA 85-88; CANR 40, 77; DAM DRAM; EW 11; EWL 3; TWA

Ghiselin, Brewster 1903-2001 .... **CLC 23**
See also CA 13-16R; CAAS 10; CANR 13; CP 7

Ghose, Aurabinda 1872-1950 .... **TCLC 63**
See Ghose, Aurobindo
See also CA 163

Ghose, Aurobindo
See Ghose, Aurabinda
See also EWL 3

Ghose, Zulfikar 1935- .... **CLC 42, 200**
See also CA 65-68; CANR 67; CN 7; CP 7; EWL 3

Ghosh, Amitav 1956- .... **CLC 44, 153**
See also CA 147; CANR 80; CN 7; WWE 1

Giacosa, Giuseppe 1847-1906 .... **TCLC 7**
See also CA 104

Gibb, Lee
See Waterhouse, Keith (Spencer)

Gibbon, Edward 1737-1794 .... **LC 97**
See also BRW 3; DLB 104; RGEL 2

Gibbon, Lewis Grassic .... **TCLC 4**
See Mitchell, James Leslie
See also RGEL 2

Gibbons, Kaye 1960- .... **CLC 50, 88, 145**
See also AAYA 34; AMWS 10; CA 151; CANR 75, 127; CSW; DA3; DAM POP; DLB 292; MTCW 1; NFS 3; RGAL 4; SATA 117

Gibran, Kahlil 1883-1931 . **PC 9; TCLC 1, 9**
See also CA 104; 150; DA3; DAM POET, POP; EWL 3; MTCW 2

Gibran, Khalil
See Gibran, Kahlil

Gibson, William 1914- .... **CLC 23**
See also CA 9-12R; CAD 2; CANR 9, 42, 75, 125; CD 5; DA; DAB; DAC; DAM DRAM, MST; DFS 2; DLB 7; LAIT 2; MTCW 2; SATA 66; YAW

Gibson, William (Ford) 1948- ... **CLC 39, 63, 186, 192; SSC 52**
See also AAYA 12, 59; BPFB 2; CA 126; 133; CANR 52, 90, 106; CN 7; CPW; DA3; DAM POP; DLB 251; MTCW 2; SCFW 2; SFW 4

Gide, Andre (Paul Guillaume)
1869-1951 ..... **SSC 13; TCLC 5, 12, 36; WLC**
See also CA 104; 124; DA; DA3; DAB; DAC; DAM MST, NOV; DLB 65; EW 8; EWL 3; GFL 1789 to the Present; MTCW 1, 2; RGSF 2; RGWL 2, 3; TWA

Gifford, Barry (Colby) 1946- .... **CLC 34**
See also CA 65-68; CANR 9, 30, 40, 90

Gilbert, Frank
See De Voto, Bernard (Augustine)

Gilbert, W(illiam) S(chwenck)
1836-1911 .... **TCLC 3**
See also CA 104; 173; DAM DRAM, POET; RGEL 2; SATA 36

Gilbreth, Frank B(unker), Jr.
1911-2001 .... **CLC 17**
See also CA 9-12R; SATA 2

Gilchrist, Ellen (Louise) 1935- .. **CLC 34, 48, 143; SSC 14, 63**
See also BPFB 2; CA 113; 116; CANR 41, 61, 104; CN 7; CPW; CSW; DAM POP; DLB 130; EWL 3; EXPS; MTCW 1, 2; RGAL 4; RGSF 2; SSFS 9

Giles, Molly 1942- .... **CLC 39**
See also CA 126; CANR 98

Gill, Eric 1882-1940 .... **TCLC 85**
See Gill, (Arthur) Eric (Rowton Peter Joseph)

Gill, (Arthur) Eric (Rowton Peter Joseph)
1882-1940
See Gill, Eric
See also CA 120; DLB 98

Gill, Patrick
See Creasey, John

Gillette, Douglas .... **CLC 70**

Gilliam, Terry (Vance) 1940- .... **CLC 21, 141**
See Monty Python
See also AAYA 19, 59; CA 108; 113; CANR 35; INT CA-113

Gillian, Jerry
See Gilliam, Terry (Vance)

Gilliatt, Penelope (Ann Douglass)
1932-1993 .... **CLC 2, 10, 13, 53**
See also AITN 2; CA 13-16R; 141; CANR 49; DLB 14

Gilman, Charlotte (Anna) Perkins (Stetson)
1860-1935 ...... **SSC 13, 62; TCLC 9, 37, 117**
See also AMWS 11; BYA 11; CA 106; 150; DLB 221; EXPS; FW; HGG; LAIT 2; MAWW; MTCW 1; RGAL 4; RGSF 2; SFW 4; SSFS 1, 18

Gilmour, David 1946- .... **CLC 35**

Gilpin, William 1724-1804 .... **NCLC 30**

Gilray, J. D.
See Mencken, H(enry) L(ouis)

Gilroy, Frank D(aniel) 1925- .... **CLC 2**
See also CA 81-84; CAD; CANR 32, 64, 86; CD 5; DFS 17; DLB 7

Gilstrap, John 1957(?)- .... **CLC 99**
See also CA 160; CANR 101

Ginsberg, Allen 1926-1997 .... **CLC 1, 2, 3, 4, 6, 13, 36, 69, 109; PC 4, 47; TCLC 120; WLC**
See also AAYA 33; AITN 1; AMWC 1; AMWS 2; BG 2; CA 1-4R; 157; CANR 2, 41, 63, 95; CDALB 1941-1968; CP 7; DA; DA3; DAB; DAC; DAM MST, POET; DLB 5, 16, 169, 237; EWL 3; GLL 1; LMFS 2; MTCW 1, 2; PAB; PFS 5; RGAL 4; TUS; WP

Ginzburg, Eugenia .... **CLC 59**
See Ginzburg, Evgeniia

Ginzburg, Evgeniia 1904-1977
See Ginzburg, Eugenia
See also DLB 302

Ginzburg, Natalia 1916-1991 .... **CLC 5, 11, 54, 70; SSC 65; TCLC 156**
See also CA 85-88; 135; CANR 33; DFS 14; DLB 177; EW 13; EWL 3; MTCW 1, 2; RGWL 2, 3

Giono, Jean 1895-1970 .... **CLC 4, 11; TCLC 124**
See also CA 45-48; 29-32R; CANR 2, 35; DLB 72; EWL 3; GFL 1789 to the Present; MTCW 1; RGWL 2, 3

Giovanni, Nikki 1943- ...... **BLC 2; CLC 2, 4, 19, 64, 117; PC 19; WLCS**
See also AAYA 22; AITN 1; BW 2, 3; CA 29-32R; CAAS 6; CANR 18, 41, 60, 91, 130; CDALBS; CLR 6, 73; CP 7; CSW; CWP; CWRI 5; DA; DA3; DAB; DAC; DAM MST, MULT, POET; DLB 5, 41; EWL 3; EXPP; INT CANR-18; MAICYA 1, 2; MTCW 1, 2; PFS 17; RGAL 4; SATA 24, 107; TUS; YAW

Guillen, Jorge 1893-1984 . **CLC 11; HLCS 1; PC 35**
 See also CA 89-92; 112; DAM MULT, POET; DLB 108; EWL 3; HW 1; RGWL 2, 3

Guillen, Nicolas (Cristobal) 1902-1989 .... **BLC 2; CLC 48, 79; HLC 1; PC 23**
 See also BW 2; CA 116; 125; 129; CANR 84; DAM MST, MULT, POET; DLB 283; EWL 3; HW 1; LAW; RGWL 2, 3; WP

Guillen y Alvarez, Jorge
 See Guillen, Jorge

Guillevic, (Eugene) 1907-1997 .... **CLC 33**
 See also CA 93-96; CWW 2

Guillois
 See Desnos, Robert

Guillois, Valentin
 See Desnos, Robert

Guimaraes Rosa, Joao 1908-1967 .... **HLCS 2**
 See Rosa, Joao Guimaraes
 See also CA 175; LAW; RGSF 2; RGWL 2, 3

Guiney, Louise Imogen 1861-1920 .... **TCLC 41**
 See also CA 160; DLB 54; RGAL 4

Guinizelli, Guido c. 1230-1276 ...... **CMLC 49**

Guiraldes, Ricardo (Guillermo) 1886-1927 .... **TCLC 39**
 See also CA 131; EWL 3; HW 1; LAW; MTCW 1

Gumilev, Nikolai (Stepanovich) 1886-1921 .... **TCLC 60**
 See Gumilyov, Nikolay Stepanovich
 See also CA 165; DLB 295

Gumilyov, Nikolay Stepanovich
 See Gumilev, Nikolai (Stepanovich)
 See also EWL 3

Gump, P. Q.
 See Card, Orson Scott

Gunesekera, Romesh 1954- .... **CLC 91**
 See also BRWS 10; CA 159; CN 7; DLB 267

Gunn, Bill .... **CLC 5**
 See Gunn, William Harrison
 See also DLB 38

Gunn, Thom(son William) 1929-2004 . **CLC 3, 6, 18, 32, 81; PC 26**
 See also BRWS 4; CA 17-20R; 227; CANR 9, 33, 116; CDBLB 1960 to Present; CP 7; DAM POET; DLB 27; INT CANR-33; MTCW 1; PFS 9; RGEL 2

Gunn, William Harrison 1934(?)-1989
 See Gunn, Bill
 See also AITN 1; BW 1, 3; CA 13-16R; 128; CANR 12, 25, 76

Gunn Allen, Paula
 See Allen, Paula Gunn

Gunnars, Kristjana 1948- .... **CLC 69**
 See also CA 113; CCA 1; CP 7; CWP; DLB 60

Gunter, Erich
 See Eich, Gunter

Gurdjieff, G(eorgei) I(vanovich) 1877(?)-1949 .... **TCLC 71**
 See also CA 157

Gurganus, Allan 1947- .... **CLC 70**
 See also BEST 90:1; CA 135; CANR 114; CN 7; CPW; CSW; DAM POP; GLL 1

Gurney, A. R.
 See Gurney, A(lbert) R(amsdell), Jr.
 See also DLB 266

Gurney, A(lbert) R(amsdell), Jr. 1930- .... **CLC 32, 50, 54**
 See Gurney, A. R.
 See also AMWS 5; CA 77-80; CAD; CANR 32, 64, 121; CD 5; DAM DRAM; EWL 3

Gurney, Ivor (Bertie) 1890-1937 ... **TCLC 33**
 See also BRW 6; CA 167; DLBY 2002; PAB; RGEL 2

Gurney, Peter
 See Gurney, A(lbert) R(amsdell), Jr.

Guro, Elena (Genrikhovna) 1877-1913 .... **TCLC 56**
 See also DLB 295

Gustafson, James M(oody) 1925- ... **CLC 100**
 See also CA 25-28R; CANR 37

Gustafson, Ralph (Barker) 1909-1995 .... **CLC 36**
 See also CA 21-24R; CANR 8, 45, 84; CP 7; DLB 88; RGEL 2

Gut, Gom
 See Simenon, Georges (Jacques Christian)

Guterson, David 1956- .... **CLC 91**
 See also CA 132; CANR 73, 126; DLB 292; MTCW 2; NFS 13

Guthrie, A(lfred) B(ertram), Jr. 1901-1991 .... **CLC 23**
 See also CA 57-60; 134; CANR 24; DLB 6, 212; SATA 62; SATA-Obit 67

Guthrie, Isobel
 See Grieve, C(hristopher) M(urray)

Guthrie, Woodrow Wilson 1912-1967
 See Guthrie, Woody
 See also CA 113; 93-96

Guthrie, Woody .... **CLC 35**
 See Guthrie, Woodrow Wilson
 See also DLB 303; LAIT 3

Gutierrez Najera, Manuel 1859-1895 .... **HLCS 2; NCLC 133**
 See also DLB 290; LAW

Guy, Rosa (Cuthbert) 1925- .... **CLC 26**
 See also AAYA 4, 37; BW 2; CA 17-20R; CANR 14, 34, 83; CLR 13; DLB 33; DNFS 1; JRDA; MAICYA 1, 2; SATA 14, 62, 122; YAW

Gwendolyn
 See Bennett, (Enoch) Arnold

H. D. .... **CLC 3, 8, 14, 31, 34, 73; PC 5**
 See Doolittle, Hilda

H. de V.
 See Buchan, John

Haavikko, Paavo Juhani 1931- .. **CLC 18, 34**
 See also CA 106; CWW 2; EWL 3

Habbema, Koos
 See Heijermans, Herman

Habermas, Juergen 1929- .... **CLC 104**
 See also CA 109; CANR 85; DLB 242

Habermas, Jurgen
 See Habermas, Juergen

Hacker, Marilyn 1942- ...... **CLC 5, 9, 23, 72, 91; PC 47**
 See also CA 77-80; CANR 68, 129; CP 7; CWP; DAM POET; DLB 120, 282; FW; GLL 2; PFS 19

Hadewijch of Antwerp fl. 1250- ... **CMLC 61**
 See also RGWL 3

Hadrian 76-138 .... **CMLC 52**

Haeckel, Ernst Heinrich (Philipp August) 1834-1919 .... **TCLC 83**
 See also CA 157

Hafiz c. 1326-1389(?) .... **CMLC 34**
 See also RGWL 2, 3

Hagedorn, Jessica T(arahata) 1949- .... **CLC 185**
 See also CA 139; CANR 69; CWP; RGAL 4

Haggard, H(enry) Rider 1856-1925 .... **TCLC 11**
 See also BRWS 3; BYA 4, 5; CA 108; 148; CANR 112; DLB 70, 156, 174, 178; FANT; LMFS 1; MTCW 2; RGEL 2; RHW; SATA 16; SCFW; SFW 4; SUFW 1; WLIT 4

Hagiosy, L.
 See Larbaud, Valery (Nicolas)

Hagiwara, Sakutaro 1886-1942 .... **PC 18; TCLC 60**
 See Hagiwara Sakutaro
 See also CA 154; RGWL 3

Hagiwara Sakutaro
 See Hagiwara, Sakutaro
 See also EWL 3

Haig, Fenil
 See Ford, Ford Madox

Haig-Brown, Roderick (Langmere) 1908-1976 .... **CLC 21**
 See also CA 5-8R; 69-72; CANR 4, 38, 83; CLR 31; CWRI 5; DLB 88; MAICYA 1, 2; SATA 12

Haight, Rip
 See Carpenter, John (Howard)

Hailey, Arthur 1920- .... **CLC 5**
 See also AITN 2; BEST 90:3; BPFB 2; CA 1-4R; CANR 2, 36, 75; CCA 1; CN 7; CPW; DAM NOV, POP; DLB 88; DLBY 1982; MTCW 1, 2

Hailey, Elizabeth Forsythe 1938- ..... **CLC 40**
 See also CA 93-96, 188; CAAE 188; CAAS 1; CANR 15, 48; INT CANR-15

Haines, John (Meade) 1924- .... **CLC 58**
 See also AMWS 12; CA 17-20R; CANR 13, 34; CSW; DLB 5, 212

Hakluyt, Richard 1552-1616 .... **LC 31**
 See also DLB 136; RGEL 2

Haldeman, Joe (William) 1943- .... **CLC 61**
 See Graham, Robert
 See also AAYA 38; CA 53-56, 179; CAAE 179; CAAS 25; CANR 6, 70, 72, 130; DLB 8; INT CANR-6; SCFW 2; SFW 4

Hale, Janet Campbell 1947- .... **NNAL**
 See also CA 49-52; CANR 45, 75; DAM MULT; DLB 175; MTCW 2

Hale, Sarah Josepha (Buell) 1788-1879 .... **NCLC 75**
 See also DLB 1, 42, 73, 243

Halevy, Elie 1870-1937 .... **TCLC 104**

Haley, Alex(ander Murray Palmer) 1921-1992 .... **BLC 2; CLC 8, 12, 76; TCLC 147**
 See also AAYA 26; BPFB 2; BW 2, 3; CA 77-80; 136; CANR 61; CDALBS; CPW; CSW; DA; DA3; DAB; DAC; DAM MST, MULT, POP; DLB 38; LAIT 5; MTCW 1, 2; NFS 9

Haliburton, Thomas Chandler 1796-1865 .... **NCLC 15, 149**
 See also DLB 11, 99; RGEL 2; RGSF 2

Hall, Donald (Andrew, Jr.) 1928- ...... **CLC 1, 13, 37, 59, 151**
 See also CA 5-8R; CAAS 7; CANR 2, 44, 64, 106, 133; CP 7; DAM POET; DLB 5; MTCW 1; RGAL 4; SATA 23, 97

Hall, Frederic Sauser
 See Sauser-Hall, Frederic

Hall, James
 See Kuttner, Henry

Hall, James Norman 1887-1951 ..... **TCLC 23**
 See also CA 123; 173; LAIT 1; RHW 1; SATA 21

Hall, Joseph 1574-1656 .... **LC 91**
 See also DLB 121, 151; RGEL 2

Hall, (Marguerite) Radclyffe 1880-1943 .... **TCLC 12**
 See also BRWS 6; CA 110; 150; CANR 83; DLB 191; MTCW 2; RGEL 2; RHW

Hall, Rodney 1935- .... **CLC 51**
 See also CA 109; CANR 69; CN 7; CP 7; DLB 289

Hallam, Arthur Henry 1811-1833 .... **NCLC 110**
 See also DLB 32

Higginson, Thomas Wentworth
1823-1911 .... **TCLC 36**
See also CA 162; DLB 1, 64, 243
Higgonet, Margaret ed. .... **CLC 65**
Highet, Helen
See MacInnes, Helen (Clark)
Highsmith, (Mary) Patricia
1921-1995 .... **CLC 2, 4, 14, 42, 102**
See Morgan, Claire
See also AAYA 48; BRWS 5; CA 1-4R; 147;
CANR 1, 20, 48, 62, 108; CMW 4; CPW;
DA3; DAM NOV, POP; DLB 306; MSW;
MTCW 1, 2
Highwater, Jamake (Mamake)
1942(?)-2001 .... **CLC 12**
See also AAYA 7; BPFB 2; BYA 4; CA 65-
68; 199; CAAS 7; CANR 10, 34, 84; CLR
17; CWRI 5; DLB 52; DLBY 1985;
JRDA; MAICYA 1, 2; SATA 32, 69;
SATA-Brief 30
Highway, Tomson 1951- ...... **CLC 92; NNAL**
See also CA 151; CANR 75; CCA 1; CD 5;
DAC; DAM MULT; DFS 2; MTCW 2
Hijuelos, Oscar 1951- .... **CLC 65; HLC 1**
See also AAYA 25; AMWS 8; BEST 90:1;
CA 123; CANR 50, 75, 125; CPW; DA3;
DAM MULT, POP; DLB 145; HW 1, 2;
LLW 1; MTCW 2; NFS 17; RGAL 4;
WLIT 1
Hikmet, Nazim 1902(?)-1963 .... **CLC 40**
See also CA 141; 93-96; EWL 3
Hildegard von Bingen 1098-1179 . **CMLC 20**
See also DLB 148
Hildesheimer, Wolfgang 1916-1991 .. **CLC 49**
See also CA 101; 135; DLB 69, 124; EWL
3
Hill, Geoffrey (William) 1932- ...... **CLC 5, 8,**
18, 45
See also BRWS 5; CA 81-84; CANR 21,
89; CDBLB 1960 to Present; CP 7; DAM
POET; DLB 40; EWL 3; MTCW 1; RGEL
2
Hill, George Roy 1921-2002 .... **CLC 26**
See also CA 110; 122; 213
Hill, John
See Koontz, Dean R(ay)
Hill, Susan (Elizabeth) 1942- ...... **CLC 4, 113**
See also CA 33-36R; CANR 29, 69, 129;
CN 7; DAB; DAM MST, NOV; DLB 14,
139; HGG; MTCW 1; RHW
Hillard, Asa G. III .... **CLC 70**
Hillerman, Tony 1925- .... **CLC 62, 170**
See also AAYA 40; BEST 89:1; BPFB 2;
CA 29-32R; CANR 21, 42, 65, 97, 134;
CMW 4; CPW; DA3; DAM POP; DLB
206, 306; MSW; RGAL 4; SATA 6;
TCWW 2; YAW
Hillesum, Etty 1914-1943 .... **TCLC 49**
See also CA 137
Hilliard, Noel (Harvey) 1929-1996 ... **CLC 15**
See also CA 9-12R; CANR 7, 69; CN 7
Hillis, Rick 1956- .... **CLC 66**
See also CA 134
Hilton, James 1900-1954 .... **TCLC 21**
See also CA 108; 169; DLB 34, 77; FANT;
SATA 34
Hilton, Walter .(?)-1396 .... **CMLC 58**
See also DLB 146; RGEL 2
Himes, Chester (Bomar) 1909-1984 .. **BLC 2;**
CLC 2, 4, 7, 18, 58, 108; TCLC 139
See also AFAW 2; BPFB 2; BW 2; CA 25-
28R; 114; CANR 22, 89; CMW 4; DAM
MULT; DLB 2, 76, 143, 226; EWL 3;
MSW; MTCW 1, 2; RGAL 4
Himmelfarb, Gertrude 1922- .... **CLC 202**
See also CA 49-52; CANR 28, 66, 102;
Hinde, Thomas .... **CLC 6, 11**
See Chitty, Thomas Willes
See also EWL 3

Hine, (William) Daryl 1936- .... **CLC 15**
See also CA 1-4R; CAAS 15; CANR 1, 20;
CP 7; DLB 60
Hinkson, Katharine Tynan
See Tynan, Katharine
Hinojosa(-Smith), Rolando (R.)
1929- .... **HLC 1**
See Hinojosa-Smith, Rolando
See also CA 131; CAAS 16; CANR 62;
DAM MULT; DLB 82; HW 1, 2; LLW 1;
MTCW 2; RGAL 4
Hinton, S(usan) E(loise) 1950- .. **CLC 30, 111**
See also AAYA 2, 33; BPFB 2; BYA 2, 3;
CA 81-84; CANR 32, 62, 92, 133;
CDALBS; CLR 3, 23; CPW; DA; DA3;
DAB; DAC; DAM MST, NOV; JRDA;
LAIT 5; MAICYA 1, 2; MTCW 1, 2; NFS
5, 9, 15, 16; SATA 19, 58, 115; WYA;
YAW
Hippius, Zinaida (Nikolaevna) .... **TCLC 9**
See Gippius, Zinaida (Nikolaevna)
See also DLB 295; EWL 3
Hiraoka, Kimitake 1925-1970
See Mishima, Yukio
See also CA 97-100; 29-32R; DA3; DAM
DRAM; GLL 1; MTCW 1, 2
Hirsch, E(ric) D(onald), Jr. 1928- .... **CLC 79**
See also CA 25-28R; CANR 27, 51; DLB
67; INT CANR-27; MTCW 1
Hirsch, Edward 1950- .... **CLC 31, 50**
See also CA 104; CANR 20, 42, 102; CP 7;
DLB 120
Hitchcock, Alfred (Joseph)
1899-1980 .... **CLC 16**
See also AAYA 22; CA 159; 97-100; SATA
27; SATA-Obit 24
Hitchens, Christopher (Eric)
1949- .... **CLC 157**
See also CA 152; CANR 89
Hitler, Adolf 1889-1945 .... **TCLC 53**
See also CA 117; 147
Hoagland, Edward 1932- .... **CLC 28**
See also ANW; CA 1-4R; CANR 2, 31, 57,
107; CN 7; DLB 6; SATA 51; TCWW 2
Hoban, Russell (Conwell) 1925- ... **CLC 7, 25**
See also BPFB 2; CA 5-8R; CANR 23, 37,
66, 114; CLR 3, 69; CN 7; CWRI 5; DAM
NOV; DLB 52; FANT; MAICYA 1, 2;
MTCW 1, 2; SATA 1, 40, 78, 136; SFW
4; SUFW 2
Hobbes, Thomas 1588-1679 .... **LC 36**
See also DLB 151, 252, 281; RGEL 2
Hobbs, Perry
See Blackmur, R(ichard) P(almer)
Hobson, Laura Z(ametkin)
1900-1986 .... **CLC 7, 25**
See Field, Peter
See also BPFB 2; CA 17-20R; 118; CANR
55; DLB 28; SATA 52
Hoccleve, Thomas c. 1368-c. 1437 ...... **LC 75**
See also DLB 146; RGEL 2
Hoch, Edward D(entinger) 1930-
See Queen, Ellery
See also CA 29-32R; CANR 11, 27, 51, 97;
CMW 4; DLB 306; SFW 4
Hochhuth, Rolf 1931- .... **CLC 4, 11, 18**
See also CA 5-8R; CANR 33, 75; CWW 2;
DAM DRAM; DLB 124; EWL 3; MTCW
1, 2
Hochman, Sandra 1936- .... **CLC 3, 8**
See also CA 5-8R; DLB 5
Hochwaelder, Fritz 1911-1986 .... **CLC 36**
See Hochwalder, Fritz
See also CA 29-32R; 120; CANR 42; DAM
DRAM; MTCW 1; RGWL 3
Hochwalder, Fritz
See Hochwaelder, Fritz
See also EWL 3; RGWL 2

Hocking, Mary (Eunice) 1921- .... **CLC 13**
See also CA 101; CANR 18, 40
Hodgins, Jack 1938- .... **CLC 23**
See also CA 93-96; CN 7; DLB 60
Hodgson, William Hope
1877(?)-1918 .... **TCLC 13**
See also CA 111; 164; CMW 4; DLB 70,
153, 156, 178; HGG; MTCW 2; SFW 4;
SUFW 1
Hoeg, Peter 1957- .... **CLC 95, 156**
See also CA 151; CANR 75; CMW 4; DA3;
DLB 214; EWL 3; MTCW 2; NFS 17;
RGWL 3; SSFS 18
Hoffman, Alice 1952- .... **CLC 51**
See also AAYA 37; AMWS 10; CA 77-80;
CANR 34, 66, 100; CN 7; CPW; DAM
NOV; DLB 292; MTCW 1, 2
Hoffman, Daniel (Gerard) 1923- . **CLC 6, 13,**
23
See also CA 1-4R; CANR 4; CP 7; DLB 5
Hoffman, Eva 1945- .... **CLC 182**
See also CA 132
Hoffman, Stanley 1944- .... **CLC 5**
See also CA 77-80
Hoffman, William 1925- .... **CLC 141**
See also CA 21-24R; CANR 9, 103; CSW;
DLB 234
Hoffman, William M(oses) 1939- ..... **CLC 40**
See Hoffman, William M.
See also CA 57-60; CANR 11, 71
Hoffmann, E(rnst) T(heodor) A(madeus)
1776-1822 .... **NCLC 2; SSC 13**
See also CDWLB 2; DLB 90; EW 5; RGSF
2; RGWL 2, 3; SATA 27; SUFW 1; WCH
Hofmann, Gert 1931- .... **CLC 54**
See also CA 128; EWL 3
Hofmannsthal, Hugo von 1874-1929 ... **DC 4;**
TCLC 11
See also CA 106; 153; CDWLB 2; DAM
DRAM; DFS 17; DLB 81, 118; EW 9;
EWL 3; RGWL 2, 3
Hogan, Linda 1947- ..... **CLC 73; NNAL; PC**
35
See also AMWS 4; ANW; BYA 12; CA 120;
226; CAAE 226; CANR 45, 73, 129;
CWP; DAM MULT; DLB 175; SATA
132; TCWW 2
Hogarth, Charles
See Creasey, John
Hogarth, Emmett
See Polonsky, Abraham (Lincoln)
Hogarth, William 1697-1764 .... **LC 112**
See also AAYA 56
Hogg, James 1770-1835 .... **NCLC 4, 109**
See also BRWS 10; DLB 93, 116, 159;
HGG; RGEL 2; SUFW 1
Holbach, Paul Henri Thiry Baron
1723-1789 .... **LC 14**
Holberg, Ludvig 1684-1754 .... **LC 6**
See also DLB 300; RGWL 2, 3
Holcroft, Thomas 1745-1809 .... **NCLC 85**
See also DLB 39, 89, 158; RGEL 2
Holden, Ursula 1921- .... **CLC 18**
See also CA 101; CAAS 8; CANR 22
Holderlin, (Johann Christian) Friedrich
1770-1843 .... **NCLC 16; PC 4**
See also CDWLB 2; DLB 90; EW 5; RGWL
2, 3
Holdstock, Robert
See Holdstock, Robert P.
Holdstock, Robert P. 1948- .... **CLC 39**
See also CA 131; CANR 81; DLB 261;
FANT; HGG; SFW 4; SUFW 2
Holinshed, Raphael fl. 1580- .... **LC 69**
See also DLB 167; RGEL 2
Holland, Isabelle (Christian)
1920-2002 .... **CLC 21**
See also AAYA 11; CA 21-24R; 205; CAAE
181; CANR 10, 25, 47; CLR 57; CWRI

5; JRDA; LAIT 4; MAICYA 1, 2; SATA
8, 70; SATA-Essay 103; SATA-Obit 132;
WYA

Holland, Marcus
See Caldwell, (Janet Miriam) Taylor
(Holland)

Hollander, John 1929- .... **CLC 2, 5, 8, 14**
See also CA 1-4R; CANR 1, 52; CP 7; DLB
5; SATA 13

Hollander, Paul
See Silverberg, Robert

Holleran, Andrew 1943(?)- .... **CLC 38**
See Garber, Eric
See also CA 144; GLL 1

Holley, Marietta 1836(?)-1926 .... **TCLC 99**
See also CA 118; DLB 11

Hollinghurst, Alan 1954- .... **CLC 55, 91**
See also BRWS 10; CA 114; CN 7; DLB
207; GLL 1

Hollis, Jim
See Summers, Hollis (Spurgeon, Jr.)

Holly, Buddy 1936-1959 .... **TCLC 65**
See also CA 213

Holmes, Gordon
See Shiel, M(atthew) P(hipps)

Holmes, John
See Souster, (Holmes) Raymond

Holmes, John Clellon 1926-1988 ...... **CLC 56**
See also BG 2; CA 9-12R; 125; CANR 4;
DLB 16, 237

Holmes, Oliver Wendell, Jr.
1841-1935 .... **TCLC 77**
See also CA 114; 186

Holmes, Oliver Wendell
1809-1894 .... **NCLC 14, 81**
See also AMWS 1; CDALB 1640-1865;
DLB 1, 189, 235; EXPP; RGAL 4; SATA
34

Holmes, Raymond
See Souster, (Holmes) Raymond

Holt, Victoria
See Hibbert, Eleanor Alice Burford
See also BPFB 2

Holub, Miroslav 1923-1998 .... **CLC 4**
See also CA 21-24R; 169; CANR 10; CD-
WLB 4; CWW 2; DLB 232; EWL 3;
RGWL 3

Holz, Detlev
See Benjamin, Walter

Homer c. 8th cent. B.C.- .... **CMLC 1, 16, 61;
PC 23; WLCS**
See also AW 1; CDWLB 1; DA; DA3;
DAB; DAC; DAM MST, POET; DLB
176; EFS 1; LAIT 1; LMFS 1; RGWL 2,
3; TWA; WP

Hongo, Garrett Kaoru 1951- .... **PC 23**
See also CA 133; CAAS 22; CP 7; DLB
120; EWL 3; EXPP; RGAL 4

Honig, Edwin 1919- .... **CLC 33**
See also CA 5-8R; CAAS 8; CANR 4, 45;
CP 7; DLB 5

Hood, Hugh (John Blagdon) 1928- . **CLC 15,
28; SSC 42**
See also CA 49-52; CAAS 17; CANR 1,
33, 87; CN 7; DLB 53; RGSF 2

Hood, Thomas 1799-1845 .... **NCLC 16**
See also BRW 4; DLB 96; RGEL 2

Hooker, (Peter) Jeremy 1941- .... **CLC 43**
See also CA 77-80; CANR 22; CP 7; DLB
40

Hooker, Richard 1554-1600 .... **LC 95**
See also BRW 1; DLB 132; RGEL 2

hooks, bell
See Watkins, Gloria Jean

Hope, A(lec) D(erwent) 1907-2000 .... **CLC 3,
51; PC 56**
See also BRWS 7; CA 21-24R; 188; CANR
33, 74; DLB 289; EWL 3; MTCW 1, 2;
PFS 8; RGEL 2

Hope, Anthony 1863-1933 .... **TCLC 83**
See also CA 157; DLB 153, 156; RGEL 2;
RHW

Hope, Brian
See Creasey, John

Hope, Christopher (David Tully)
1944- .... **CLC 52**
See also AFW; CA 106; CANR 47, 101;
CN 7; DLB 225; SATA 62

Hopkins, Gerard Manley
1844-1889 .... **NCLC 17; PC 15; WLC**
See also BRW 5; BRWR 2; CDBLB 1890-
1914; DA; DA3; DAB; DAC; DAM MST,
POET; DLB 35, 57; EXPP; PAB; RGEL
2; TEA; WP

Hopkins, John (Richard) 1931-1998 .. **CLC 4**
See also CA 85-88; 169; CBD; CD 5

Hopkins, Pauline Elizabeth
1859-1930 .... **BLC 2; TCLC 28**
See also AFAW 2; BW 2, 3; CA 141; CANR
82; DAM MULT; DLB 50

Hopkinson, Francis 1737-1791 .... **LC 25**
See also DLB 31; RGAL 4

Hopley-Woolrich, Cornell George 1903-1968
See Woolrich, Cornell
See also CA 13-14; CANR 58; CAP 1;
CMW 4; DLB 226; MTCW 2

Horace 65B.C.-8B.C. .... **CMLC 39; PC 46**
See also AW 2; CDWLB 1; DLB 211;
RGWL 2, 3

Horatio
See Proust, (Valentin-Louis-George-Eugene)
Marcel

Horgan, Paul (George Vincent
O'Shaughnessy) 1903-1995 .. **CLC 9, 53**
See also BPFB 2; CA 13-16R; 147; CANR
9, 35; DAM NOV; DLB 102, 212; DLBY
1985; INT CANR-9; MTCW 1, 2; SATA
13; SATA-Obit 84; TCWW 2

Horkheimer, Max 1895-1973 .... **TCLC 132**
See also CA 216; 41-44R; DLB 296

Horn, Peter
See Kuttner, Henry

Horne, Frank (Smith) 1899-1974 .... **HR 2**
See also BW 1; CA 125; 53-56; DLB 51;
WP

Horne, Richard Henry Hengist
1802(?)-1884 .... **NCLC 127**
See also DLB 32; SATA 29

Hornem, Horace Esq.
See Byron, George Gordon (Noel)

Horney, Karen (Clementine Theodore
Danielsen) 1885-1952 .... **TCLC 71**
See also CA 114; 165; DLB 246; FW

Hornung, E(rnest) W(illiam)
1866-1921 .... **TCLC 59**
See also CA 108; 160; CMW 4; DLB 70

Horovitz, Israel (Arthur) 1939- .... **CLC 56**
See also CA 33-36R; CAD; CANR 46, 59;
CD 5; DAM DRAM; DLB 7

Horton, George Moses
1797(?)-1883(?) .... **NCLC 87**
See also DLB 50

Horvath, odon von 1901-1938
See von Horvath, Odon
See also EWL 3

Horvath, Oedoen von -1938
See von Horvath, Odon

Horwitz, Julius 1920-1986 .... **CLC 14**
See also CA 9-12R; 119; CANR 12

Hospital, Janette Turner 1942- .... **CLC 42,
145**
See also CA 108; CANR 48; CN 7; DLBY
2002; RGSF 2

Hostos, E. M. de
See Hostos (y Bonilla), Eugenio Maria de

Hostos, Eugenio M. de
See Hostos (y Bonilla), Eugenio Maria de

Hostos, Eugenio Maria
See Hostos (y Bonilla), Eugenio Maria de

Hostos (y Bonilla), Eugenio Maria de
1839-1903 .... **TCLC 24**
See also CA 123; 131; HW 1

Houdini
See Lovecraft, H(oward) P(hillips)

Houellebecq, Michel 1958- .... **CLC 179**
See also CA 185

Hougan, Carolyn 1943- .... **CLC 34**
See also CA 139

Household, Geoffrey (Edward West)
1900-1988 .... **CLC 11**
See also CA 77-80; 126; CANR 58; CMW
4; DLB 87; SATA 14; SATA-Obit 59

Housman, A(lfred) E(dward)
1859-1936 .... **PC 2, 43; TCLC 1, 10;
WLCS**
See also BRW 6; CA 104; 125; DA; DA3;
DAB; DAC; DAM MST, POET; DLB 19,
284; EWL 3; EXPP; MTCW 1, 2; PAB;
PFS 4, 7; RGEL 2; TEA; WP

Housman, Laurence 1865-1959 .... **TCLC 7**
See also CA 106; 155; DLB 10; FANT;
RGEL 2; SATA 25

Houston, Jeanne (Toyo) Wakatsuki
1934- .... **AAL**
See also AAYA 49; CA 103; CAAS 16;
CANR 29, 123; LAIT 4; SATA 78

Howard, Elizabeth Jane 1923- ..... **CLC 7, 29**
See also CA 5-8R; CANR 8, 62; CN 7

Howard, Maureen 1930- .... **CLC 5, 14, 46,
151**
See also CA 53-56; CANR 31, 75; CN 7;
DLBY 1983; INT CANR-31; MTCW 1, 2

Howard, Richard 1929- .... **CLC 7, 10, 47**
See also AITN 1; CA 85-88; CANR 25, 80;
CP 7; DLB 5; INT CANR-25

Howard, Robert E(rvin)
1906-1936 .... **TCLC 8**
See also BPFB 2; BYA 5; CA 105; 157;
FANT; SUFW 1

Howard, Warren F.
See Pohl, Frederik

Howe, Fanny (Quincy) 1940- .... **CLC 47**
See also CA 117, 187; CAAE 187; CAAS
27; CANR 70, 116; CP 7; CWP; SATA-
Brief 52

Howe, Irving 1920-1993 .... **CLC 85**
See also AMWS 6; CA 9-12R; 141; CANR
21, 50; DLB 67; EWL 3; MTCW 1, 2

Howe, Julia Ward 1819-1910 .... **TCLC 21**
See also CA 117; 191; DLB 1, 189, 235;
FW

Howe, Susan 1937- .... **CLC 72, 152; PC 54**
See also AMWS 4; CA 160; CP 7; CWP;
DLB 120; FW; RGAL 4

Howe, Tina 1937- .... **CLC 48**
See also CA 109; CAD; CANR 125; CD 5;
CWD

Howell, James 1594(?)-1666 .... **LC 13**
See also DLB 151

Howells, W. D.
See Howells, William Dean

Howells, William D.
See Howells, William Dean

Howells, William Dean 1837-1920 ... **SSC 36;
TCLC 7, 17, 41**
See also AMW; CA 104; 134; CDALB
1865-1917; DLB 12, 64, 74, 79, 189;
LMFS 1; MTCW 2; RGAL 4; TUS

Howes, Barbara 1914-1996 .... **CLC 15**
See also CA 9-12R; 151; CAAS 3; CANR
53; CP 7; SATA 5

Hrabal, Bohumil 1914-1997 ...... **CLC 13, 67;
TCLC 155**
See also CA 106; 156; CAAS 12; CANR
57; CWW 2; DLB 232; EWL 3; RGSF 2

Hrotsvit of Gandersheim c. 935-c.
   1000 .... **CMLC 29**
      See also DLB 148

Hsi, Chu 1130-1200 .... **CMLC 42**

Hsun, Lu
   See Lu Hsun

Hubbard, L(afayette) Ron(ald)
   1911-1986 .... **CLC 43**
      See also CA 77-80; 118; CANR 52; CPW;
      DA3; DAM POP; FANT; MTCW 2; SFW
      4

Huch, Ricarda (Octavia)
   1864-1947 .... **TCLC 13**
      See also CA 111; 189; DLB 66; EWL 3

Huddle, David 1942- .... **CLC 49**
      See also CA 57-60; CAAS 20; CANR 89;
      DLB 130

Hudson, Jeffrey
   See Crichton, (John) Michael

Hudson, W(illiam) H(enry)
   1841-1922 .... **TCLC 29**
      See also CA 115; 190; DLB 98, 153, 174;
      RGEL 2; SATA 35

Hueffer, Ford Madox
   See Ford, Ford Madox

Hughart, Barry 1934- .... **CLC 39**
      See also CA 137; FANT; SFW 4; SUFW 2

Hughes, Colin
   See Creasey, John

Hughes, David (John) 1930- .... **CLC 48**
      See also CA 116; 129; CN 7; DLB 14

Hughes, Edward James
   See Hughes, Ted
      See also DA3; DAM MST, POET

Hughes, (James Mercer) Langston
   1902-1967 ..... **BLC 2; CLC 1, 5, 10, 15,
   35, 44, 108; DC 3; HR 2; PC 1, 53;
   SSC 6; WLC**
      See also AAYA 12; AFAW 1, 2; AMWR 1;
      AMWS 1; BW 1, 3; CA 1-4R; 25-28R;
      CANR 1, 34, 82; CDALB 1929-1941;
      CLR 17; DA; DA3; DAB; DAC; DAM
      DRAM, MST, MULT, POET; DFS 6, 18;
      DLB 4, 7, 48, 51, 86, 228; EWL 3; EXPP;
      EXPS; JRDA; LAIT 3; LMFS 2; MAI-
      CYA 1, 2; MTCW 1, 2; PAB; PFS 1, 3, 6,
      10, 15; RGAL 4; RGSF 2; SATA 4, 33;
      SSFS 4, 7; TUS; WCH; WP; YAW

Hughes, Richard (Arthur Warren)
   1900-1976 .... **CLC 1, 11**
      See also CA 5-8R; 65-68; CANR 4; DAM
      NOV; DLB 15, 161; EWL 3; MTCW 1;
      RGEL 2; SATA 8; SATA-Obit 25

Hughes, Ted 1930-1998 . **CLC 2, 4, 9, 14, 37,
   119; PC 7**
      See Hughes, Edward James
      See also BRWC 2; BRWR 2; BRWS 1; CA
      1-4R; 171; CANR 1, 33, 66, 108; CLR 3;
      CP 7; DAB; DAC; DLB 40, 161; EWL 3;
      EXPP; MAICYA 1, 2; MTCW 1, 2; PAB;
      PFS 4, 19; RGEL 2; SATA 49; SATA-
      Brief 27; SATA-Obit 107; TEA; YAW

Hugo, Richard
   See Huch, Ricarda (Octavia)

Hugo, Richard F(ranklin)
   1923-1982 .... **CLC 6, 18, 32**
      See also AMWS 6; CA 49-52; 108; CANR
      3; DAM POET; DLB 5, 206; EWL 3; PFS
      17; RGAL 4

Hugo, Victor (Marie) 1802-1885 .... **NCLC 3,
   10, 21; PC 17; WLC**
      See also AAYA 28; DA; DA3; DAB; DAC;
      DAM DRAM, MST, NOV, POET; DLB
      119, 192, 217; EFS 2; EW 6; EXPN; GFL
      1789 to the Present; LAIT 1, 2; NFS 5,
      20; RGWL 2, 3; SATA 47; TWA

Huidobro, Vicente
   See Huidobro Fernandez, Vicente Garcia
      See also DLB 283; EWL 3; LAW

Huidobro Fernandez, Vicente Garcia
   1893-1948 .... **TCLC 31**
      See Huidobro, Vicente
      See also CA 131; HW 1

Hulme, Keri 1947- .... **CLC 39, 130**
      See also CA 125; CANR 69; CN 7; CP 7;
      CWP; EWL 3; FW; INT CA-125

Hulme, T(homas) E(rnest)
   1883-1917 .... **TCLC 21**
      See also BRWS 6; CA 117; 203; DLB 19

Humboldt, Wilhelm von
   1767-1835 .... **NCLC 134**
      See also DLB 90

Hume, David 1711-1776 .... **LC 7, 56**
      See also BRWS 3; DLB 104, 252; LMFS 1;
      TEA

Humphrey, William 1924-1997 .... **CLC 45**
      See also AMWS 9; CA 77-80; 160; CANR
      68; CN 7; CSW; DLB 6, 212, 234, 278;
      TCWW 2

Humphreys, Emyr Owen 1919- .... **CLC 47**
      See also CA 5-8R; CANR 3, 24; CN 7;
      DLB 15

Humphreys, Josephine 1945- ..... **CLC 34, 57**
      See also CA 121; 127; CANR 97; CSW;
      DLB 292; INT CA-127

Huneker, James Gibbons
   1860-1921 .... **TCLC 65**
      See also CA 193; DLB 71; RGAL 4

Hungerford, Hesba Fay
   See Brinsmead, H(esba) F(ay)

Hungerford, Pixie
   See Brinsmead, H(esba) F(ay)

Hunt, E(verette) Howard, (Jr.)
   1918- .... **CLC 3**
      See also AITN 1; CA 45-48; CANR 2, 47,
      103; CMW 4

Hunt, Francesca
   See Holland, Isabelle (Christian)

Hunt, Howard
   See Hunt, E(verette) Howard, (Jr.)

Hunt, Kyle
   See Creasey, John

Hunt, (James Henry) Leigh
   1784-1859 .... **NCLC 1, 70**
      See also DAM POET; DLB 96, 110, 144;
      RGEL 2; TEA

Hunt, Marsha 1946- .... **CLC 70**
      See also BW 2, 3; CA 143; CANR 79

Hunt, Violet 1866(?)-1942 .... **TCLC 53**
      See also CA 184; DLB 162, 197

Hunter, E. Waldo
   See Sturgeon, Theodore (Hamilton)

Hunter, Evan 1926- .... **CLC 11, 31**
      See McBain, Ed
      See also AAYA 39; BPFB 2; CA 5-8R;
      CANR 5, 38, 62, 97; CMW 4; CN 7;
      CPW; DAM POP; DLB 306; DLBY 1982;
      INT CANR-5; MSW; MTCW 1; SATA
      25; SFW 4

Hunter, Kristin
   See Lattany, Kristin (Elaine Eggleston)
      Hunter

Hunter, Mary
   See Austin, Mary (Hunter)

Hunter, Mollie 1922- .... **CLC 21**
      See McIlwraith, Maureen Mollie Hunter
      See also AAYA 13; BYA 6; CANR 37, 78;
      CLR 25; DLB 161; JRDA; MAICYA 1,
      2; SAAS 7; SATA 54, 106, 139; SATA-
      Essay 139; WYA; YAW

Hunter, Robert (?)-1734 .... **LC 7**

Hurston, Zora Neale 1891-1960 .... **BLC 2;
   CLC 7, 30, 61; DC 12; HR 2; SSC 4,
   80; TCLC 121, 131; WLCS**
      See also AAYA 15; AFAW 1, 2; AMWS 6;
      BW 1, 3; BYA 12; CA 85-88; CANR 61;
      CDALBS; DA; DA3; DAC; DAM MST,
      MULT, NOV; DFS 6; DLB 51, 86; EWL

   3; EXPN; EXPS; FW; LAIT 3; LATS 1:1;
   LMFS 2; MAWW; MTCW 1, 2; NFS 3;
   RGAL 4; RGSF 2; SSFS 1, 6, 11, 19;
   TUS; YAW

Husserl, E. G.
   See Husserl, Edmund (Gustav Albrecht)

Husserl, Edmund (Gustav Albrecht)
   1859-1938 .... **TCLC 100**
      See also CA 116; 133; DLB 296

Huston, John (Marcellus)
   1906-1987 .... **CLC 20**
      See also CA 73-76; 123; CANR 34; DLB
      26

Hustvedt, Siri 1955- .... **CLC 76**
      See also CA 137

Hutten, Ulrich von 1488-1523 .... **LC 16**
      See also DLB 179

Huxley, Aldous (Leonard)
   1894-1963 .... **CLC 1, 3, 4, 5, 8, 11, 18,
   35, 79; SSC 39; WLC**
      See also AAYA 11; BPFB 2; BRW 7; CA
      85-88; CANR 44, 99; CDBLB 1914-1945;
      DA; DA3; DAB; DAC; DAM MST, NOV;
      DLB 36, 100, 162, 195, 255; EWL 3;
      EXPN; LAIT 5; LMFS 2; MTCW 1, 2;
      NFS 6; RGEL 2; SATA 63; SCFW 2;
      SFW 4; TEA; YAW

Huxley, T(homas) H(enry)
   1825-1895 .... **NCLC 67**
      See also DLB 57; TEA

Huysmans, Joris-Karl 1848-1907 ... **TCLC 7,
   69**
      See also CA 104; 165; DLB 123; EW 7;
      GFL 1789 to the Present; LMFS 2; RGWL
      2, 3

Hwang, David Henry 1957- .... **CLC 55, 196;
   DC 4, 23**
      See also CA 127; 132; CAD; CANR 76,
      124; CD 5; DA3; DAM DRAM; DFS 11,
      18; DLB 212, 228; INT CA-132; MTCW
      2; RGAL 4

Hyde, Anthony 1946- .... **CLC 42**
      See Chase, Nicholas
      See also CA 136; CCA 1

Hyde, Margaret O(ldroyd) 1917- ..... **CLC 21**
      See also CA 1-4R; CANR 1, 36; CLR 23;
      JRDA; MAICYA 1, 2; SAAS 8; SATA 1,
      42, 76, 139

Hynes, James 1956(?)- .... **CLC 65**
      See also CA 164; CANR 105

Hypatia c. 370-415 .... **CMLC 35**

Ian, Janis 1951- .... **CLC 21**
      See also CA 105; 187

Ibanez, Vicente Blasco
   See Blasco Ibanez, Vicente

Ibarbourou, Juana de
   1895(?)-1979 .... **HLCS 2**
      See also DLB 290; HW 1; LAW

Ibarguengoitia, Jorge 1928-1983 ..... **CLC 37;
   TCLC 148**
      See also CA 124; 113; EWL 3; HW 1

Ibn Battuta, Abu Abdalla
   1304-1368(?) .... **CMLC 57**
      See also WLIT 2

Ibn Hazm 994-1064 .... **CMLC 64**

Ibsen, Henrik (Johan) 1828-1906 .... **DC 2;
   TCLC 2, 8, 16, 37, 52; WLC**
      See also AAYA 46; CA 104; 141; DA; DA3;
      DAB; DAC; DAM DRAM, MST; DFS 1,
      6, 8, 10, 11, 15, 16; EW 7; LAIT 2; LATS
      1:1; RGWL 2, 3

Ibuse, Masuji 1898-1993 .... **CLC 22**
      See Ibuse Masuji
      See also CA 127; 141; MJW; RGWL 3

Ibuse Masuji
   See Ibuse, Masuji
      See also CWW 2; DLB 180; EWL 3

Ichikawa, Kon 1915- .... **CLC 20**
      See also CA 121

2; NFS 12, 16, 19; RGAL 4; RGEL 2;
RGSF 2; SSFS 9; SUFW 1; TUS

James, M. R.
See James, Montague (Rhodes)
See also DLB 156, 201

James, Montague (Rhodes)
1862-1936 .... **SSC 16; TCLC 6**
See James, M. R.
See also CA 104; 203; HGG; RGEL 2;
RGSF 2; SUFW 1

James, P. D. .... **CLC 18, 46, 122**
See White, Phyllis Dorothy James
See also BEST 90:2; BPFB 2; BRWS 4;
CDBLB 1960 to Present; DLB 87, 276;
DLBD 17; MSW

James, Philip
See Moorcock, Michael (John)

James, Samuel
See Stephens, James

James, Seumas
See Stephens, James

James, Stephen
See Stephens, James

James, William 1842-1910 .... **TCLC 15, 32**
See also AMW; CA 109; 193; DLB 270,
284; NCFS 5; RGAL 4

Jameson, Anna 1794-1860 .... **NCLC 43**
See also DLB 99, 166

Jameson, Fredric (R.) 1934- .... **CLC 142**
See also CA 196; DLB 67; LMFS 2

James VI of Scotland 1566-1625 .... **LC 109**
See also DLB 151, 172

Jami, Nur al-Din 'Abd al-Rahman
1414-1492 .... **LC 9**

Jammes, Francis 1868-1938 .... **TCLC 75**
See also CA 198; EWL 3; GFL 1789 to the
Present

Jandl, Ernst 1925-2000 .... **CLC 34**
See also CA 200; EWL 3

Janowitz, Tama 1957- .... **CLC 43, 145**
See also CA 106; CANR 52, 89, 129; CN
7; CPW; DAM POP; DLB 292

Japrisot, Sebastien 1931- .... **CLC 90**
See Rossi, Jean-Baptiste
See also CMW 4; NFS 18

Jarrell, Randall 1914-1965 .... **CLC 1, 2, 6, 9,**
13, 49; PC 41
See also AMW; BYA 5; CA 5-8R; 25-28R;
CABS 2; CANR 6, 34; CDALB 1941-
1968; CLR 6; CWRI 5; DAM POET;
DLB 48, 52; EWL 3; EXPP; MAICYA 1,
2; MTCW 1, 2; PAB; PFS 2; RGAL 4;
SATA 7

Jarry, Alfred 1873-1907 .... **SSC 20; TCLC 2,**
14, 147
See also CA 104; 153; DA3; DAM DRAM;
DFS 8; DLB 192, 258; EW 9; EWL 3;
GFL 1789 to the Present; RGWL 2, 3;
TWA

Jarvis, E. K.
See Ellison, Harlan (Jay)

Jawien, Andrzej
See John Paul II, Pope

Jaynes, Roderick
See Coen, Ethan

Jeake, Samuel, Jr.
See Aiken, Conrad (Potter)

Jean Paul 1763-1825 .... **NCLC 7**

Jefferies, (John) Richard
1848-1887 .... **NCLC 47**
See also DLB 98, 141; RGEL 2; SATA 16;
SFW 4

Jeffers, (John) Robinson 1887-1962 .. **CLC 2,**
3, 11, 15, 54; PC 17; WLC
See also AMWS 2; CA 85-88; CANR 35;
CDALB 1917-1929; DA; DAC; DAM
MST, POET; DLB 45, 212; EWL 3;
MTCW 1, 2; PAB; PFS 3, 4; RGAL 4

Jefferson, Janet
See Mencken, H(enry) L(ouis)

Jefferson, Thomas 1743-1826 . **NCLC 11, 103**
See also AAYA 54; ANW; CDALB 1640-
1865; DA3; DLB 31, 183; LAIT 1; RGAL
4

Jeffrey, Francis 1773-1850 .... **NCLC 33**
See Francis, Lord Jeffrey

Jelakowitch, Ivan
See Heijermans, Herman

Jelinek, Elfriede 1946- .... **CLC 169**
See also CA 154; DLB 85; FW

Jellicoe, (Patricia) Ann 1927- .... **CLC 27**
See also CA 85-88; CBD; CD 5; CWD;
CWRI 5; DLB 13, 233; FW

Jelloun, Tahar ben 1944- .... **CLC 180**
See Ben Jelloun, Tahar
See also CA 162; CANR 100

Jemyma
See Holley, Marietta

Jen, Gish .... **AAL; CLC 70, 198**
See Jen, Lillian
See also AMWC 2

Jen, Lillian 1956(?)-
See Jen, Gish
See also CA 135; CANR 89, 130

Jenkins, (John) Robin 1912- .... **CLC 52**
See also CA 1-4R; CANR 1, 135; CN 7;
DLB 14, 271

Jennings, Elizabeth (Joan)
1926-2001 .... **CLC 5, 14, 131**
See also BRWS 5; CA 61-64; 200; CAAS
5; CANR 8, 39, 66, 127; CP 7; CWP;
DLB 27; EWL 3; MTCW 1; SATA 66

Jennings, Waylon 1937- .... **CLC 21**

Jensen, Johannes V(ilhelm)
1873-1950 .... **TCLC 41**
See also CA 170; DLB 214; EWL 3; RGWL
3

Jensen, Laura (Linnea) 1948- .... **CLC 37**
See also CA 103

Jerome, Saint 345-420 .... **CMLC 30**
See also RGWL 3

Jerome, Jerome K(lapka)
1859-1927 .... **TCLC 23**
See also CA 119; 177; DLB 10, 34, 135;
RGEL 2

Jerrold, Douglas William
1803-1857 .... **NCLC 2**
See also DLB 158, 159; RGEL 2

Jewett, (Theodora) Sarah Orne
1849-1909 .... **SSC 6, 44; TCLC 1, 22**
See also AMW; AMWC 2; AMWR 2; CA
108; 127; CANR 71; DLB 12, 74, 221;
EXPS; FW; MAWW; NFS 15; RGAL 4;
RGSF 2; SATA 15; SSFS 4

Jewsbury, Geraldine (Endsor)
1812-1880 .... **NCLC 22**
See also DLB 21

Jhabvala, Ruth Prawer 1927- . **CLC 4, 8, 29,**
94, 138
See also BRWS 5; CA 1-4R; CANR 2, 29,
51, 74, 91, 128; CN 7; DAB; DAM NOV;
DLB 139, 194; EWL 3; IDFW 3, 4; INT
CANR-29; MTCW 1, 2; RGSF 2; RGWL
2; RHW; TEA

Jibran, Kahlil
See Gibran, Kahlil

Jibran, Khalil
See Gibran, Kahlil

Jiles, Paulette 1943- .... **CLC 13, 58**
See also CA 101; CANR 70, 124; CWP

Jimenez (Mantecon), Juan Ramon
1881-1958 .... **HLC 1; PC 7; TCLC 4**
See also CA 104; 131; CANR 74; DAM
MULT, POET; DLB 134; EW 9; EWL 3;
HW 1; MTCW 1, 2; RGWL 2, 3

Jimenez, Ramon
See Jimenez (Mantecon), Juan Ramon

Jimenez Mantecon, Juan
See Jimenez (Mantecon), Juan Ramon

Jin, Ha .... **CLC 109**
See Jin, Xuefei
See also CA 152; DLB 244, 292; SSFS 17

Jin, Xuefei 1956-
See Jin, Ha
See also CANR 91, 130; SSFS 17

Joel, Billy .... **CLC 26**
See Joel, William Martin

Joel, William Martin 1949-
See Joel, Billy
See also CA 108

John, Saint 10(?)-100 .... **CMLC 27, 63**

John of Salisbury c. 1115-1180 ..... **CMLC 63**

John of the Cross, St. 1542-1591 .... **LC 18**
See also RGWL 2, 3

John Paul II, Pope 1920- .... **CLC 128**
See also CA 106; 133

Johnson, B(ryan) S(tanley William)
1933-1973 .... **CLC 6, 9**
See also CA 9-12R; 53-56; CANR 9; DLB
14, 40; EWL 3; RGEL 2

Johnson, Benjamin F., of Boone
See Riley, James Whitcomb

Johnson, Charles (Richard) 1948- .... **BLC 2;**
CLC 7, 51, 65, 163
See also AFAW 2; AMWS 6; BW 2, 3; CA
116; CAAS 18; CANR 42, 66, 82, 129;
CN 7; DAM MULT; DLB 33, 278;
MTCW 2; RGAL 4; SSFS 16

Johnson, Charles S(purgeon)
1893-1956 .... **HR 3**
See also BW 1, 3; CA 125; CANR 82; DLB
51, 91

Johnson, Denis 1949- . **CLC 52, 160; SSC 56**
See also CA 117; 121; CANR 71, 99; CN
7; DLB 120

Johnson, Diane 1934- .... **CLC 5, 13, 48**
See also BPFB 2; CA 41-44R; CANR 17,
40, 62, 95; CN 7; DLBY 1980; INT
CANR-17; MTCW 1

Johnson, E. Pauline 1861-1913 .... **NNAL**
See also CA 150; DAC; DAM MULT; DLB
92, 175

Johnson, Eyvind (Olof Verner)
1900-1976 .... **CLC 14**
See also CA 73-76; 69-72; CANR 34, 101;
DLB 259; EW 12; EWL 3

Johnson, Fenton 1888-1958 .... **BLC 2**
See also BW 1; CA 118; 124; DAM MULT;
DLB 45, 50

Johnson, Georgia Douglas (Camp)
1880-1966 .... **HR 3**
See also BW 1; CA 125; DLB 51, 249; WP

Johnson, Helene 1907-1995 .... **HR 3**
See also CA 181; DLB 51; WP

Johnson, J. R.
See James, C(yril) L(ionel) R(obert)

Johnson, James Weldon 1871-1938 .. **BLC 2;**
HR 3; PC 24; TCLC 3, 19
See also AFAW 1, 2; BW 1, 3; CA 104;
125; CANR 82; CDALB 1917-1929; CLR
32; DA3; DAM MULT, POET; DLB 51;
EWL 3; EXPP; LMFS 2; MTCW 1, 2;
PFS 1; RGAL 4; SATA 31; TUS

Johnson, Joyce 1935- .... **CLC 58**
See also BG 3; CA 125; 129; CANR 102

Johnson, Judith (Emlyn) 1936- .... **CLC 7, 15**
See Sherwin, Judith Johnson
See also CA 25-28R, 153; CANR 34

Johnson, Lionel (Pigot)
1867-1902 .... **TCLC 19**
See also CA 117; 209; DLB 19; RGEL 2

Johnson, Marguerite Annie
See Angelou, Maya

Johnson, Mel
See Malzberg, Barry N(athaniel)

Kalidasa fl. c. 400-455 .... **CMLC 9; PC 22**
See also RGWL 2, 3
Kallman, Chester (Simon)
1921-1975 .... **CLC 2**
See also CA 45-48; 53-56; CANR 3
Kaminsky, Melvin 1926-
See Brooks, Mel
See also CA 65-68; CANR 16
Kaminsky, Stuart M(elvin) 1934- ..... **CLC 59**
See also CA 73-76; CANR 29, 53, 89;
CMW 4
Kamo no Chomei 1153(?)-1216 .... **CMLC 66**
See also DLB 203
Kamo no Nagaakira
See Kamo no Chomei
Kandinsky, Wassily 1866-1944 .... **TCLC 92**
See also CA 118; 155
Kane, Francis
See Robbins, Harold
Kane, Henry 1918-
See Queen, Ellery
See also CA 156; CMW 4
Kane, Paul
See Simon, Paul (Frederick)
Kanin, Garson 1912-1999 .... **CLC 22**
See also AITN 1; CA 5-8R; 177; CAD;
CANR 7, 78; DLB 7; IDFW 3, 4
Kaniuk, Yoram 1930- .... **CLC 19**
See also CA 134; DLB 299
Kant, Immanuel 1724-1804 ..... **NCLC 27, 67**
See also DLB 94
Kantor, MacKinlay 1904-1977 .... **CLC 7**
See also CA 61-64; 73-76; CANR 60, 63;
DLB 9, 102; MTCW 2; RHW; TCWW 2
Kanze Motokiyo
See Zeami
Kaplan, David Michael 1946- .... **CLC 50**
See also CA 187
Kaplan, James 1951- .... **CLC 59**
See also CA 135; CANR 121
Karadzic, Vuk Stefanovic
1787-1864 .... **NCLC 115**
See also CDWLB 4; DLB 147
Karageorge, Michael
See Anderson, Poul (William)
Karamzin, Nikolai Mikhailovich
1766-1826 .... **NCLC 3**
See also DLB 150; RGSF 2
Karapanou, Margarita 1946- .... **CLC 13**
See also CA 101
Karinthy, Frigyes 1887-1938 .... **TCLC 47**
See also CA 170; DLB 215; EWL 3
Karl, Frederick R(obert)
1927-2004 .... **CLC 34**
See also CA 5-8R; 226; CANR 3, 44
Karr, Mary 1955- .... **CLC 188**
See also AMWS 11; CA 151; CANR 100;
NCFS 5
Kastel, Warren
See Silverberg, Robert
Kataev, Evgeny Petrovich 1903-1942
See Petrov, Evgeny
See also CA 120
Kataphusin
See Ruskin, John
Katz, Steve 1935- .... **CLC 47**
See also CA 25-28R; CAAS 14, 64; CANR
12; CN 7; DLBY 1983
Kauffman, Janet 1945- .... **CLC 42**
See also CA 117; CANR 43, 84; DLB 218;
DLBY 1986
Kaufman, Bob (Garnell) 1925-1986 . **CLC 49**
See also BG 3; BW 1; CA 41-44R; 118;
CANR 22; DLB 16, 41

Kaufman, George S. 1889-1961 ...... **CLC 38;**
DC 17
See also CA 108; 93-96; DAM DRAM;
DFS 1, 10; DLB 7; INT CA-108; MTCW
2; RGAL 4; TUS
Kaufman, Sue .... **CLC 3, 8**
See Barondess, Sue K(aufman)
Kavafis, Konstantinos Petrou 1863-1933
See Cavafy, C(onstantine) P(eter)
See also CA 104
Kavan, Anna 1901-1968 .... **CLC 5, 13, 82**
See also BRWS 7; CA 5-8R; CANR 6, 57;
DLB 255; MTCW 1; RGEL 2; SFW 4
Kavanagh, Dan
See Barnes, Julian (Patrick)
Kavanagh, Julie 1952- .... **CLC 119**
See also CA 163
Kavanagh, Patrick (Joseph)
1904-1967 .... **CLC 22; PC 33**
See also BRWS 7; CA 123; 25-28R; DLB
15, 20; EWL 3; MTCW 1; RGEL 2
Kawabata, Yasunari 1899-1972 ..... **CLC 2, 5,**
9, 18, 107; SSC 17
See Kawabata Yasunari
See also CA 93-96; 33-36R; CANR 88;
DAM MULT; MJW; MTCW 2; RGSF 2;
RGWL 2, 3
Kawabata Yasunari
See Kawabata, Yasunari
See also DLB 180; EWL 3
Kaye, M(ary) M(argaret)
1908-2004 .... **CLC 28**
See also CA 89-92; 223; CANR 24, 60, 102;
MTCW 1, 2; RHW; SATA 62; SATA-Obit
152
Kaye, Mollie
See Kaye, M(ary) M(argaret)
Kaye-Smith, Sheila 1887-1956 .... **TCLC 20**
See also CA 118; 203; DLB 36
Kaymor, Patrice Maguilene
See Senghor, Leopold Sedar
Kazakov, Iurii Pavlovich
See Kazakov, Yuri Pavlovich
See also DLB 302
Kazakov, Yuri Pavlovich 1927-1982 . **SSC 43**
See Kazakov, Iurii Pavlovich; Kazakov,
Yury
See also CA 5-8R; CANR 36; MTCW 1;
RGSF 2
Kazakov, Yury
See Kazakov, Yuri Pavlovich
See also EWL 3
Kazan, Elia 1909-2003 .... **CLC 6, 16, 63**
See also CA 21-24R; 220; CANR 32, 78
Kazantzakis, Nikos 1883(?)-1957 .... **TCLC 2,**
5, 33
See also BPFB 2; CA 105; 132; DA3; EW
9; EWL 3; MTCW 1, 2; RGWL 2, 3
Kazin, Alfred 1915-1998 ..... **CLC 34, 38, 119**
See also AMWS 8; CA 1-4R; CAAS 7;
CANR 1, 45, 79; DLB 67; EWL 3
Keane, Mary Nesta (Skrine) 1904-1996
See Keane, Molly
See also CA 108; 114; 151; CN 7; RHW
Keane, Molly .... **CLC 31**
See Keane, Mary Nesta (Skrine)
See also INT CA-114
Keates, Jonathan 1946(?)- .... **CLC 34**
See also CA 163; CANR 126
Keaton, Buster 1895-1966 .... **CLC 20**
See also CA 194
Keats, John 1795-1821 ...... **NCLC 8, 73, 121;**
PC 1; WLC
See also AAYA 58; BRW 4; BRWR 1; CD-
BLB 1789-1832; DA; DA3; DAB; DAC;
DAM MST, POET; DLB 96, 110; EXPP;
LMFS 1; PAB; PFS 1, 2, 3, 9, 17; RGEL
2; TEA; WLIT 3; WP

Keble, John 1792-1866 .... **NCLC 87**
See also DLB 32, 55; RGEL 2
Keene, Donald 1922- .... **CLC 34**
See also CA 1-4R; CANR 5, 119
Keillor, Garrison .... **CLC 40, 115**
See Keillor, Gary (Edward)
See also AAYA 2; BEST 89:3; BPFB 2;
DLBY 1987; EWL 3; SATA 58; TUS
Keillor, Gary (Edward) 1942-
See Keillor, Garrison
See also CA 111; 117; CANR 36, 59, 124;
CPW; DA3; DAM POP; MTCW 1, 2
Keith, Carlos
See Lewton, Val
Keith, Michael
See Hubbard, L(afayette) Ron(ald)
Keller, Gottfried 1819-1890 .... **NCLC 2; SSC**
26
See also CDWLB 2; DLB 129; EW; RGSF
2; RGWL 2, 3
Keller, Nora Okja 1965- .... **CLC 109**
See also CA 187
Kellerman, Jonathan 1949- .... **CLC 44**
See also AAYA 35; BEST 90:1; CA 106;
CANR 29, 51; CMW 4; CPW; DA3;
DAM POP; INT CANR-29
Kelley, William Melvin 1937- .... **CLC 22**
See also BW 1; CA 77-80; CANR 27, 83;
CN 7; DLB 33; EWL 3
Kellogg, Marjorie 1922- .... **CLC 2**
See also CA 81-84
Kellow, Kathleen
See Hibbert, Eleanor Alice Burford
Kelly, M(ilton) T(errence) 1947- ...... **CLC 55**
See also CA 97-100; CAAS 22; CANR 19,
43, 84; CN 7
Kelly, Robert 1935- .... **SSC 50**
See also CA 17-20R; CAAS 19; CANR 47;
CP 7; DLB 5, 130, 165
Kelman, James 1946- .... **CLC 58, 86**
See also BRWS 5; CA 148; CANR 85, 130;
CN 7; DLB 194; RGSF 2; WLIT 4
Kemal, Yasar
See Kemal, Yashar
See also CWW 2; EWL 3
Kemal, Yashar 1923(?)- .... **CLC 14, 29**
See also CA 89-92; CANR 44
Kemble, Fanny 1809-1893 .... **NCLC 18**
See also DLB 32
Kemelman, Harry 1908-1996 .... **CLC 2**
See also AITN 1; BPFB 2; CA 9-12R; 155;
CANR 6, 71; CMW 4; DLB 28
Kempe, Margery 1373(?)-1440(?) ... **LC 6, 56**
See also DLB 146; RGEL 2
Kempis, Thomas a 1380-1471 .... **LC 11**
Kendall, Henry 1839-1882 .... **NCLC 12**
See also DLB 230
Keneally, Thomas (Michael) 1935- ... **CLC 5,**
8, 10, 14, 19, 27, 43, 117
See also BRWS 4; CA 85-88; CANR 10,
50, 74, 130; CN 7; CPW; DA3; DAM
NOV; DLB 289, 299; EWL 3; MTCW 1,
2; NFS 17; RGEL 2; RHW
Kennedy, A(lison) L(ouise) 1965- ... **CLC 188**
See also CA 168, 213; CAAE 213; CANR
108; CD 5; CN 7; DLB 271; RGSF 2
Kennedy, Adrienne (Lita) 1931- .... **BLC 2;**
CLC 66; DC 5
See also AFAW 2; BW 2, 3; CA 103; CAAS
20; CABS 3; CANR 26, 53, 82; CD 5;
DAM MULT; DFS 9; DLB 38; FW
Kennedy, John Pendleton
1795-1870 .... **NCLC 2**
See also DLB 3, 248, 254; RGAL 4

Kirk, Russell (Amos) 1918-1994 .. **TCLC 119**
See also AITN 1; CA 1-4R; 145; CAAS 9; CANR 1, 20, 60; HGG; INT CANR-20; MTCW 1, 2

Kirkham, Dinah
See Card, Orson Scott

Kirkland, Caroline M. 1801-1864 . **NCLC 85**
See also DLB 3, 73, 74, 250, 254; DLBD 13

Kirkup, James 1918- .... **CLC 1**
See also CA 1-4R; CAAS 4; CANR 2; CP 7; DLB 27; SATA 12

Kirkwood, James 1930(?)-1989 .... **CLC 9**
See also AITN 2; CA 1-4R; 128; CANR 6, 40; GLL 2

Kirsch, Sarah 1935- .... **CLC 176**
See also CA 178; CWW 2; DLB 75; EWL 3

Kirshner, Sidney
See Kingsley, Sidney

Kis, Danilo 1935-1989 .... **CLC 57**
See also CA 109; 118; 129; CANR 61; CD-WLB 4; DLB 181; EWL 3; MTCW 1; RGSF 2; RGWL 2, 3

Kissinger, Henry A(lfred) 1923- ..... **CLC 137**
See also CA 1-4R; CANR 2, 33, 66, 109; MTCW 1

Kivi, Aleksis 1834-1872 .... **NCLC 30**

Kizer, Carolyn (Ashley) 1925- ... **CLC 15, 39, 80**
See also CA 65-68; CAAS 5; CANR 24, 70, 134; CP 7; CWP; DAM POET; DLB 5, 169; EWL 3; MTCW 2; PFS 18

Klabund 1890-1928 .... **TCLC 44**
See also CA 162; DLB 66

Klappert, Peter 1942- .... **CLC 57**
See also CA 33-36R; CSW; DLB 5

Klein, A(braham) M(oses)
1909-1972 .... **CLC 19**
See also CA 101; 37-40R; DAB; DAC; DAM MST; DLB 68; EWL 3; RGEL 2

Klein, Joe
See Klein, Joseph

Klein, Joseph 1946- .... **CLC 154**
See also CA 85-88; CANR 55

Klein, Norma 1938-1989 .... **CLC 30**
See also AAYA 2, 35; BPFB 2; BYA 6, 7, 8; CA 41-44R; 128; CANR 15, 37; CLR 2, 19; INT CANR-15; JRDA; MAICYA 1, 2; SAAS 1; SATA 7, 57; WYA; YAW

Klein, T(heodore) E(ibon) D(onald)
1947- .... **CLC 34**
See also CA 119; CANR 44, 75; HGG

Kleist, Heinrich von 1777-1811 ...... **NCLC 2, 37; SSC 22**
See also CDWLB 2; DAM DRAM; DLB 90; EW 5; RGSF 2; RGWL 2, 3

Klima, Ivan 1931- .... **CLC 56, 172**
See also CA 25-28R; CANR 17, 50, 91; CDWLB 4; CWW 2; DAM NOV; DLB 232; EWL 3; RGWL 3

Klimentev, Andrei Platonovich
See Klimentov, Andrei Platonovich

Klimentov, Andrei Platonovich
1899-1951 .... **SSC 42; TCLC 14**
See Platonov, Andrei Platonovich; Platonov, Andrey Platonovich
See also CA 108

Klinger, Friedrich Maximilian von
1752-1831 .... **NCLC 1**
See also DLB 94

Klingsor the Magician
See Hartmann, Sadakichi

Klopstock, Friedrich Gottlieb
1724-1803 .... **NCLC 11**
See also DLB 97; EW 4; RGWL 2, 3

Kluge, Alexander 1932- .... **SSC 61**
See also CA 81-84; DLB 75

Knapp, Caroline 1959-2002 .... **CLC 99**
See also CA 154; 207

Knebel, Fletcher 1911-1993 .... **CLC 14**
See also AITN 1; CA 1-4R; 140; CAAS 3; CANR 1, 36; SATA 36; SATA-Obit 75

Knickerbocker, Diedrich
See Irving, Washington

Knight, Etheridge 1931-1991 ... **BLC 2; CLC 40; PC 14**
See also BW 1, 3; CA 21-24R; 133; CANR 23, 82; DAM POET; DLB 41; MTCW 2; RGAL 4

Knight, Sarah Kemble 1666-1727 .... **LC 7**
See also DLB 24, 200

Knister, Raymond 1899-1932 .... **TCLC 56**
See also CA 186; DLB 68; RGEL 2

Knowles, John 1926-2001 ... **CLC 1, 4, 10, 26**
See also AAYA 10; AMWS 12; BPFB 2; BYA 3; CA 17-20R; 203; CANR 40, 74, 76, 132; CDALB 1968-1988; CLR 98; CN 7; DA; DAC; DAM MST, NOV; DLB 6; EXPN; MTCW 1, 2; NFS 2; RGAL 4; SATA 8, 89; SATA-Obit 134; YAW

Knox, Calvin M.
See Silverberg, Robert

Knox, John c. 1505-1572 .... **LC 37**
See also DLB 132

Knye, Cassandra
See Disch, Thomas M(ichael)

Koch, C(hristopher) J(ohn) 1932- .... **CLC 42**
See also CA 127; CANR 84; CN 7; DLB 289

Koch, Christopher
See Koch, C(hristopher) J(ohn)

Koch, Kenneth (Jay) 1925-2002 .... **CLC 5, 8, 44**
See also CA 1-4R; 207; CAD; CANR 6, 36, 57, 97, 131; CD 5; CP 7; DAM POET; DLB 5; INT CANR-36; MTCW 2; PFS 20; SATA 65; WP

Kochanowski, Jan 1530-1584 .... **LC 10**
See also RGWL 2, 3

Kock, Charles Paul de 1794-1871 . **NCLC 16**

Koda Rohan
See Koda Shigeyuki

Koda Rohan
See Koda Shigeyuki
See also DLB 180

Koda Shigeyuki 1867-1947 .... **TCLC 22**
See Koda Rohan
See also CA 121; 183

Koestler, Arthur 1905-1983 ... **CLC 1, 3, 6, 8, 15, 33**
See also BRWS 1; CA 1-4R; 109; CANR 1, 33; CDBLB 1945-1960; DLBY 1983; EWL 3; MTCW 1, 2; NFS 19; RGEL 2

Kogawa, Joy Nozomi 1935- ...... **CLC 78, 129**
See also AAYA 47; CA 101; CANR 19, 62, 126; CN 7; CWP; DAC; DAM MST, MULT; FW; MTCW 2; NFS 3; SATA 99

Kohout, Pavel 1928- .... **CLC 13**
See also CA 45-48; CANR 3

Koizumi, Yakumo
See Hearn, (Patricio) Lafcadio (Tessima Carlos)

Kolmar, Gertrud 1894-1943 .... **TCLC 40**
See also CA 167; EWL 3

Komunyakaa, Yusef 1947- .. **BLCS; CLC 86, 94; PC 51**
See also AFAW 2; AMWS 13; CA 147; CANR 83; CP 7; CSW; DLB 120; EWL 3; PFS 5, 20; RGAL 4

Konrad, George
See Konrad, Gyorgy

Konrad, Gyorgy 1933- .... **CLC 4, 10, 73**
See also CA 85-88; CANR 97; CDWLB 4; CWW 2; DLB 232; EWL 3

Konwicki, Tadeusz 1926- .... **CLC 8, 28, 54, 117**
See also CA 101; CAAS 9; CANR 39, 59; CWW 2; DLB 232; EWL 3; IDFW 3; MTCW 1

Koontz, Dean R(ay) 1945- .... **CLC 78**
See also AAYA 9, 31; BEST 89:3, 90:2; CA 108; CANR 19, 36, 52, 95; CMW 4; CPW; DA3; DAM NOV, POP; DLB 292; HGG; MTCW 1; SATA 92; SFW 4; SUFW 2; YAW

Kopernik, Mikolaj
See Copernicus, Nicolaus

Kopit, Arthur (Lee) 1937- ...... **CLC 1, 18, 33**
See also AITN 1; CA 81-84; CABS 3; CD 5; DAM DRAM; DFS 7, 14; DLB 7; MTCW 1; RGAL 4

Kopitar, Jernej (Bartholomaus)
1780-1844 .... **NCLC 117**

Kops, Bernard 1926- .... **CLC 4**
See also CA 5-8R; CANR 84; CBD; CN 7; CP 7; DLB 13

Kornbluth, C(yril) M. 1923-1958 .... **TCLC 8**
See also CA 105; 160; DLB 8; SFW 4

Korolenko, V. G.
See Korolenko, Vladimir Galaktionovich

Korolenko, Vladimir
See Korolenko, Vladimir Galaktionovich

Korolenko, Vladimir G.
See Korolenko, Vladimir Galaktionovich

Korolenko, Vladimir Galaktionovich
1853-1921 .... **TCLC 22**
See also CA 121; DLB 277

Korzybski, Alfred (Habdank Skarbek)
1879-1950 .... **TCLC 61**
See also CA 123; 160

Kosinski, Jerzy (Nikodem)
1933-1991 .... **CLC 1, 2, 3, 6, 10, 15, 53, 70**
See also AMWS 7; BPFB 2; CA 17-20R; 134; CANR 9, 46; DA3; DAM NOV; DLB 2, 299; DLBY 1982; EWL 3; HGG; MTCW 1, 2; NFS 12; RGAL 4; TUS

Kostelanetz, Richard (Cory) 1940- .. **CLC 28**
See also CA 13-16R; CAAS 8; CANR 38, 77; CN 7; CP 7

Kostrowitzki, Wilhelm Apollinaris de
1880-1918
See Apollinaire, Guillaume
See also CA 104

Kotlowitz, Robert 1924- .... **CLC 4**
See also CA 33-36R; CANR 36

Kotzebue, August (Friedrich Ferdinand) von
1761-1819 .... **NCLC 25**
See also DLB 94

Kotzwinkle, William 1938- ..... **CLC 5, 14, 35**
See also BPFB 2; CA 45-48; CANR 3, 44, 84, 129; CLR 6; DLB 173; FANT; MAICYA 1, 2; SATA 24, 70, 146; SFW 4; SUFW 2; YAW

Kowna, Stancy
See Szymborska, Wislawa

Kozol, Jonathan 1936- .... **CLC 17**
See also AAYA 46; CA 61-64; CANR 16, 45, 96

Kozoll, Michael 1940(?)- .... **CLC 35**

Kramer, Kathryn 19(?)- .... **CLC 34**

Kramer, Larry 1935- .... **CLC 42; DC 8**
See also CA 124; 126; CANR 60, 132; DAM POP; DLB 249; GLL 1

Krasicki, Ignacy 1735-1801 .... **NCLC 8**

Krasinski, Zygmunt 1812-1859 .... **NCLC 4**
See also RGWL 2, 3

Kraus, Karl 1874-1936 .... **TCLC 5**
See also CA 104; 216; DLB 118; EWL 3

Kreve (Mickevicius), Vincas
1882-1954 .... **TCLC 27**
See also CA 170; DLB 220; EWL 3

CPW; DA3; DAM NOV, POP; DLB 206; DLBY 1980; MTCW 1, 2; RGAL 4

Lampedusa, Giuseppe (Tomasi) di .... **TCLC 13**
See Tomasi di Lampedusa, Giuseppe
See also CA 164; EW 11; MTCW 2; RGWL 2, 3

Lampman, Archibald 1861-1899 ... **NCLC 25**
See also DLB 92; RGEL 2; TWA

Lancaster, Bruce 1896-1963 .... **CLC 36**
See also CA 9-10; CANR 70; CAP 1; SATA 9

Lanchester, John 1962- .... **CLC 99**
See also CA 194; DLB 267

Landau, Mark Alexandrovich
See Aldanov, Mark (Alexandrovich)

Landau-Aldanov, Mark Alexandrovich
See Aldanov, Mark (Alexandrovich)

Landis, Jerry
See Simon, Paul (Frederick)

Landis, John 1950- .... **CLC 26**
See also CA 112; 122; CANR 128

Landolfi, Tommaso 1908-1979 .... **CLC 11, 49**
See also CA 127; 117; DLB 177; EWL 3

Landon, Letitia Elizabeth
1802-1838 .... **NCLC 15**
See also DLB 96

Landor, Walter Savage
1775-1864 .... **NCLC 14**
See also BRW 4; DLB 93, 107; RGEL 2

Landwirth, Heinz 1927-
See Lind, Jakov
See also CA 9-12R; CANR 7

Lane, Patrick 1939- .... **CLC 25**
See also CA 97-100; CANR 54; CP 7; DAM POET; DLB 53; INT CA-97-100

Lang, Andrew 1844-1912 .... **TCLC 16**
See also CA 114; 137; CANR 85; CLR 101; DLB 98, 141, 184; FANT; MAICYA 1, 2; RGEL 2; SATA 16; WCH

Lang, Fritz 1890-1976 .... **CLC 20, 103**
See also CA 77-80; 69-72; CANR 30

Lange, John
See Crichton, (John) Michael

Langer, Elinor 1939- .... **CLC 34**
See also CA 121

Langland, William 1332(?)-1400(?) ..... **LC 19**
See also BRW 1; DA; DAB; DAC; DAM MST, POET; DLB 146; RGEL 2; TEA; WLIT 3

Langstaff, Launcelot
See Irving, Washington

Lanier, Sidney 1842-1881 . **NCLC 6, 118; PC 50**
See also AMWS 1; DAM POET; DLB 64; DLBD 13; EXPP; MAICYA 1; PFS 14; RGAL 4; SATA 18

Lanyer, Aemilia 1569-1645 .... **LC 10, 30, 83; PC 60**
See also DLB 121

Lao-Tzu
See Lao Tzu

Lao Tzu c. 6th cent. B.C.-3rd cent.
B.C. .... **CMLC 7**

Lapine, James (Elliot) 1949- .... **CLC 39**
See also CA 123; 130; CANR 54, 128; INT CA-130

Larbaud, Valery (Nicolas)
1881-1957 .... **TCLC 9**
See also CA 106; 152; EWL 3; GFL 1789 to the Present

Lardner, Ring
See Lardner, Ring(gold) W(ilmer)
See also BPFB 2; CDALB 1917-1929; DLB 11, 25, 86, 171; DLBD 16; RGAL 4; RGSF 2

Lardner, Ring W., Jr.
See Lardner, Ring(gold) W(ilmer)

Lardner, Ring(gold) W(ilmer)
1885-1933 .... **SSC 32; TCLC 2, 14**
See Lardner, Ring
See also AMW; CA 104; 131; MTCW 1, 2; TUS

Laredo, Betty
See Codrescu, Andrei

Larkin, Maia
See Wojciechowska, Maia (Teresa)

Larkin, Philip (Arthur) 1922-1985 ... **CLC 3, 5, 8, 9, 13, 18, 33, 39, 64; PC 21**
See also BRWS 1; CA 5-8R; 117; CANR 24, 62; CDBLB 1960 to Present; DA3; DAB; DAM MST, POET; DLB 27; EWL 3; MTCW 1, 2; PFS 3, 4, 12; RGEL 2

La Roche, Sophie von
1730-1807 .... **NCLC 121**
See also DLB 94

La Rochefoucauld, Francois
1613-1680 .... **LC 108**

Larra (y Sanchez de Castro), Mariano Jose de 1809-1837 .... **NCLC 17, 130**

Larsen, Eric 1941- .... **CLC 55**
See also CA 132

Larsen, Nella 1893(?)-1963 .... **BLC 2; CLC 37; HR 3**
See also AFAW 1, 2; BW 1; CA 125; CANR 83; DAM MULT; DLB 51; FW; LATS 1:1; LMFS 2

Larson, Charles R(aymond) 1938- ... **CLC 31**
See also CA 53-56; CANR 4, 121

Larson, Jonathan 1961-1996 .... **CLC 99**
See also AAYA 28; CA 156

La Sale, Antoine de c. 1386-1460(?) . **LC 104**
See also DLB 208

Las Casas, Bartolome de
1474-1566 .... **HLCS; LC 31**
See Casas, Bartolome de las
See also LAW

Lasch, Christopher 1932-1994 .... **CLC 102**
See also CA 73-76; 144; CANR 25, 118; DLB 246; MTCW 1, 2

Lasker-Schueler, Else 1869-1945 ... **TCLC 57**
See Lasker-Schuler, Else
See also CA 183; DLB 66, 124

Lasker-Schuler, Else
See Lasker-Schueler, Else
See also EWL 3

Laski, Harold J(oseph) 1893-1950 . **TCLC 79**
See also CA 188

Latham, Jean Lee 1902-1995 .... **CLC 12**
See also AITN 1; BYA 1; CA 5-8R; CANR 7, 84; CLR 50; MAICYA 1, 2; SATA 2, 68; YAW

Latham, Mavis
See Clark, Mavis Thorpe

Lathen, Emma .... **CLC 2**
See Hennissart, Martha; Latsis, Mary J(ane)
See also BPFB 2; CMW 4; DLB 306

Lathrop, Francis
See Leiber, Fritz (Reuter, Jr.)

Latsis, Mary J(ane) 1927-1997
See Lathen, Emma
See also CA 85-88; 162; CMW 4

Lattany, Kristin
See Lattany, Kristin (Elaine Eggleston) Hunter

Lattany, Kristin (Elaine Eggleston) Hunter 1931- .... **CLC 35**
See also AITN 1; BW 1; BYA 3; CA 13-16R; CANR 13, 108; CLR 3; CN 7; DLB 33; INT CANR-13; MAICYA 1, 2; SAAS 10; SATA 12, 132; YAW

Lattimore, Richmond (Alexander)
1906-1984 .... **CLC 3**
See also CA 1-4R; 112; CANR 1

Laughlin, James 1914-1997 .... **CLC 49**
See also CA 21-24R; 162; CAAS 22; CANR 9, 47; CP 7; DLB 48; DLBY 1996, 1997

Laurence, (Jean) Margaret (Wemyss)
1926-1987 . **CLC 3, 6, 13, 50, 62; SSC 7**
See also BYA 13; CA 5-8R; 121; CANR 33; DAC; DAM MST; DLB 53; EWL 3; FW; MTCW 1, 2; NFS 11; RGEL 2; RGSF 2; SATA-Obit 50; TCWW 2

Laurent, Antoine 1952- .... **CLC 50**

Lauscher, Hermann
See Hesse, Hermann

Lautreamont 1846-1870 .. **NCLC 12; SSC 14**
See Lautreamont, Isidore Lucien Ducasse
See also GFL 1789 to the Present; RGWL 2, 3

Lautreamont, Isidore Lucien Ducasse
See Lautreamont
See also DLB 217

Lavater, Johann Kaspar
1741-1801 .... **NCLC 142**
See also DLB 97

Laverty, Donald
See Blish, James (Benjamin)

Lavin, Mary 1912-1996 . **CLC 4, 18, 99; SSC 4, 67**
See also CA 9-12R; 151; CANR 33; CN 7; DLB 15; FW; MTCW 1; RGEL 2; RGSF 2

Lavond, Paul Dennis
See Kornbluth, C(yril) M.; Pohl, Frederik

Lawler, Ray
See Lawler, Raymond Evenor
See also DLB 289

Lawler, Raymond Evenor 1922- .... **CLC 58**
See Lawler, Ray
See also CA 103; CD 5; RGEL 2

Lawrence, D(avid) H(erbert Richards)
1885-1930 .... **PC 54; SSC 4, 19, 73; TCLC 2, 9, 16, 33, 48, 61, 93; WLC**
See Chambers, Jessie
See also BPFB 2; BRW 7; BRWR 2; CA 104; 121; CANR 131; CDBLB 1914-1945; DA; DA3; DAB; DAC; DAM MST, NOV, POET; DLB 10, 19, 36, 98, 162, 195; EWL 3; EXPP; EXPS; LAIT 2, 3; MTCW 1, 2; NFS 18; PFS 6; RGEL 2; RGSF 2; SSFS 2, 6; TEA; WLIT 4; WP

Lawrence, T(homas) E(dward)
1888-1935 .... **TCLC 18**
See Dale, Colin
See also BRWS 2; CA 115; 167; DLB 195

Lawrence of Arabia
See Lawrence, T(homas) E(dward)

Lawson, Henry (Archibald Hertzberg)
1867-1922 .... **SSC 18; TCLC 27**
See also CA 120; 181; DLB 230; RGEL 2; RGSF 2

Lawton, Dennis
See Faust, Frederick (Schiller)

Layamon fl. c. 1200- .... **CMLC 10**
See Laȝamon
See also DLB 146; RGEL 2

Laye, Camara 1928-1980 ..... **BLC 2; CLC 4, 38**
See Camara Laye
See also AFW; BW 1; CA 85-88; 97-100; CANR 25; DAM MULT; MTCW 1, 2; WLIT 2

Layton, Irving (Peter) 1912- .... **CLC 2, 15, 164**
See also CA 1-4R; CANR 2, 33, 43, 66, 129; CP 7; DAC; DAM MST, POET; DLB 88; EWL 3; MTCW 1, 2; PFS 12; RGEL 2

Lazarus, Emma 1849-1887 ...... **NCLC 8, 109**

Lazarus, Felix
See Cable, George Washington

Lazarus, Henry
See Slavitt, David R(ytman)

Lea, Joan
See Neufeld, John (Arthur)

MacEwen, Gwendolyn (Margaret)
1941-1987 .... **CLC 13, 55**
See also CA 9-12R; 124; CANR 7, 22; DLB
53, 251; SATA 50; SATA-Obit 55

Macha, Karel Hynek 1810-1846 .... **NCLC 46**

Machado (y Ruiz), Antonio
1875-1939 .... **TCLC 3**
See also CA 104; 174; DLB 108; EW 9;
EWL 3; HW 2; RGWL 2, 3

Machado de Assis, Joaquim Maria
1839-1908 .... **BLC 2; HLCS 2; SSC 24;**
TCLC 10
See also CA 107; 153; CANR 91; DLB 307;
LAW; RGSF 2; RGWL 2, 3; TWA; WLIT
1

Machaut, Guillaume de c.
1300-1377 .... **CMLC 64**
See also DLB 208

Machen, Arthur .... **SSC 20; TCLC 4**
See Jones, Arthur Llewellyn
See also CA 179; DLB 156, 178; RGEL 2;
SUFW 1

Machiavelli, Niccolo 1469-1527 ... **DC 16; LC**
8, 36; WLCS
See also AAYA 58; DA; DAB; DAC; DAM
MST; EW 2; LAIT 1; LMFS 1; NFS 9;
RGWL 2, 3; TWA

MacInnes, Colin 1914-1976 .... **CLC 4, 23**
See also CA 69-72; 65-68; CANR 21; DLB
14; MTCW 1, 2; RGEL 2; RHW

MacInnes, Helen (Clark)
1907-1985 .... **CLC 27, 39**
See also BPFB 2; CA 1-4R; 117; CANR 1,
28, 58; CMW 4; CPW; DAM POP; DLB
87; MSW; MTCW 1, 2; SATA 22; SATA-
Obit 44

Mackay, Mary 1855-1924
See Corelli, Marie
See also CA 118; 177; FANT; RHW

Mackay, Shena 1944- .... **CLC 195**
See also CA 104; CANR 88; DLB 231

Mackenzie, Compton (Edward Montague)
1883-1972 .... **CLC 18; TCLC 116**
See also CA 21-22; 37-40R; CAP 2; DLB
34, 100; RGEL 2

Mackenzie, Henry 1745-1831 .... **NCLC 41**
See also DLB 39; RGEL 2

Mackey, Nathaniel (Ernest) 1947- .... **PC 49**
See also CA 153; CANR 114; CP 7; DLB
169

MacKinnon, Catharine A. 1946- .... **CLC 181**
See also CA 128; 132; CANR 73; FW;
MTCW 2

Mackintosh, Elizabeth 1896(?)-1952
See Tey, Josephine
See also CA 110; CMW 4

MacLaren, James
See Grieve, C(hristopher) M(urray)

Mac Laverty, Bernard 1942- .... **CLC 31**
See also CA 116; 118; CANR 43, 88; CN
7; DLB 267; INT CA-118; RGSF 2

MacLean, Alistair (Stuart)
1922(?)-1987 .... **CLC 3, 13, 50, 63**
See also CA 57-60; 121; CANR 28, 61;
CMW 4; CPW; DAM POP; DLB 276;
MTCW 1; SATA 23; SATA-Obit 50;
TCWW 2

Maclean, Norman (Fitzroy)
1902-1990 .... **CLC 78; SSC 13**
See also AMWS 14; CA 102; 132; CANR
49; CPW; DAM POP; DLB 206; TCWW
2

MacLeish, Archibald 1892-1982 ... **CLC 3, 8,**
14, 68; PC 47
See also AMW; CA 9-12R; 106; CAD;
CANR 33, 63; CDALBS; DAM POET;
DFS 15; DLB 4, 7, 45; DLBY 1982; EWL
3; EXPP; MTCW 1, 2; PAB; PFS 5;
RGAL 4; TUS

MacLennan, (John) Hugh
1907-1990 .... **CLC 2, 14, 92**
See also CA 5-8R; 142; CANR 33; DAC;
DAM MST; DLB 68; EWL 3; MTCW 1,
2; RGEL 2; TWA

MacLeod, Alistair 1936- .... **CLC 56, 165**
See also CA 123; CCA 1; DAC; DAM
MST; DLB 60; MTCW 2; RGSF 2

Macleod, Fiona
See Sharp, William
See also RGEL 2; SUFW

MacNeice, (Frederick) Louis
1907-1963 .... **CLC 1, 4, 10, 53; PC 61**
See also BRW 7; CA 85-88; CANR 61;
DAB; DAM POET; DLB 10, 20; EWL 3;
MTCW 1, 2; RGEL 2

MacNeill, Dand
See Fraser, George MacDonald

Macpherson, James 1736-1796 .... **LC 29**
See Ossian
See also BRWS 8; DLB 109; RGEL 2

Macpherson, (Jean) Jay 1931- .... **CLC 14**
See also CA 5-8R; CANR 90; CP 7; CWP;
DLB 53

Macrobius fl. 430- .... **CMLC 48**

MacShane, Frank 1927-1999 .... **CLC 39**
See also CA 9-12R; 186; CANR 3, 33; DLB
111

Macumber, Mari
See Sandoz, Mari(e Susette)

Madach, Imre 1823-1864 .... **NCLC 19**

Madden, (Jerry) David 1933- .... **CLC 5, 15**
See also CA 1-4R; CAAS 3; CANR 4, 45;
CN 7; CSW; DLB 6; MTCW 1

Maddern, Al(an)
See Ellison, Harlan (Jay)

Madhubuti, Haki R. 1942- ... **BLC 2; CLC 6,**
73; PC 5
See Lee, Don L.
See also BW 2, 3; CA 73-76; CANR 24,
51, 73; CP 7; CSW; DAM MULT, POET;
DLB 5, 41; DLBD 8; EWL 3; MTCW 2;
RGAL 4

Madison, James 1751-1836 .... **NCLC 126**
See also DLB 37

Maepenn, Hugh
See Kuttner, Henry

Maepenn, K. H.
See Kuttner, Henry

Maeterlinck, Maurice 1862-1949 ..... **TCLC 3**
See also CA 104; 136; CANR 80; DAM
DRAM; DLB 192; EW 8; EWL 3; GFL
1789 to the Present; LMFS 2; RGWL 2,
3; SATA 66; TWA

Maginn, William 1794-1842 .... **NCLC 8**
See also DLB 110, 159

Mahapatra, Jayanta 1928- .... **CLC 33**
See also CA 73-76; CAAS 9; CANR 15,
33, 66, 87; CP 7; DAM MULT

Mahfouz, Naguib (Abdel Aziz Al-Sabilgi)
1911(?)- .... **SSC 66**
See Mahfuz, Najib (Abdel Aziz al-Sabilgi)
See also AAYA 49; BEST 89:2; CA 128;
CANR 55, 101; DA3; DAM NOV;
MTCW 1, 2; RGWL 2, 3; SSFS 9

Mahfuz, Najib (Abdel Aziz al-Sabilgi)
.... **CLC 52, 55**
See Mahfouz, Naguib (Abdel Aziz Al-
Sabilgi)
See also AFW; CWW 2; DLBY 1988; EWL
3; RGSF 2; WLIT 2

Mahon, Derek 1941- .... **CLC 27; PC 60**
See also BRWS 6; CA 113; 128; CANR 88;
CP 7; DLB 40; EWL 3

Maiakovskii, Vladimir
See Mayakovski, Vladimir (Vladimirovich)
See also IDTP; RGWL 2, 3

Mailer, Norman (Kingsley) 1923- . **CLC 1, 2,**
3, 4, 5, 8, 11, 14, 28, 39, 74, 111
See also AAYA 31; AITN 2; AMW; AMWC
2; AMWR 2; BPFB 2; CA 9-12R; CABS
1; CANR 28, 74, 77, 130; CDALB 1968-
1988; CN 7; CPW; DA; DA3; DAB;
DAC; DAM MST, NOV, POP; DLB 2,
16, 28, 185, 278; DLBD 3; DLBY 1980,
1983; EWL 3; MTCW 1, 2; NFS 10;
RGAL 4; TUS

Maillet, Antonine 1929- .... **CLC 54, 118**
See also CA 115; 120; CANR 46, 74, 77,
134; CCA 1; CWW 2; DAC; DLB 60;
INT CA-120; MTCW 2

Mais, Roger 1905-1955 .... **TCLC 8**
See also BW 1, 3; CA 105; 124; CANR 82;
CDWLB 3; DLB 125; EWL 3; MTCW 1;
RGEL 2

Maistre, Joseph 1753-1821 .... **NCLC 37**
See also GFL 1789 to the Present

Maitland, Frederic William
1850-1906 .... **TCLC 65**

Maitland, Sara (Louise) 1950- .... **CLC 49**
See also CA 69-72; CANR 13, 59; DLB
271; FW

Major, Clarence 1936- ... **BLC 2; CLC 3, 19,**
48
See also AFAW 2; BW 2, 3; CA 21-24R;
CAAS 6; CANR 13, 25, 53, 82; CN 7;
CP 7; CSW; DAM MULT; DLB 33; EWL
3; MSW

Major, Kevin (Gerald) 1949- .... **CLC 26**
See also AAYA 16; CA 97-100; CANR 21,
38, 112; CLR 11; DAC; DLB 60; INT
CANR-21; JRDA; MAICYA 1, 2; MAIC-
YAS 1; SATA 32, 82, 134; WYA; YAW

Maki, James
See Ozu, Yasujiro

Makine, Andrei 1957- .... **CLC 198**
See also CA 176; CANR 103

Malabaila, Damiano
See Levi, Primo

Malamud, Bernard 1914-1986 .. **CLC 1, 2, 3,**
5, 8, 9, 11, 18, 27, 44, 78, 85; SSC 15;
TCLC 129; WLC
See also AAYA 16; AMWS 1; BPFB 2;
BYA 15; CA 5-8R; 118; CABS 1; CANR
28, 62, 114; CDALB 1941-1968; CPW;
DA; DA3; DAB; DAC; DAM MST, NOV,
POP; DLB 2, 28, 152; DLBY 1980, 1986;
EWL 3; EXPS; LAIT 4; LATS 1:1;
MTCW 1, 2; NFS 4, 9; RGAL 4; RGSF
2; SSFS 8, 13, 16; TUS

Malan, Herman
See Bosman, Herman Charles; Bosman,
Herman Charles

Malaparte, Curzio 1898-1957 .... **TCLC 52**
See also DLB 264

Malcolm, Dan
See Silverberg, Robert

Malcolm, Janet 1934- .... **CLC 201**
See also CA 123; CANR 89; NCFS 1

Malcolm X .... **BLC 2; CLC 82, 117; WLCS**
See Little, Malcolm
See also LAIT 5; NCFS 3

Malherbe, Francois de 1555-1628 .... **LC 5**
See also GFL Beginnings to 1789

Mallarme, Stephane 1842-1898 ...... **NCLC 4,**
41; PC 4
See also DAM POET; DLB 217; EW 7;
GFL 1789 to the Present; LMFS 2; RGWL
2, 3; TWA

Mallet-Joris, Francoise 1930- .... **CLC 11**
See also CA 65-68; CANR 17; CWW 2;
DLB 83; EWL 3; GFL 1789 to the Present

Malley, Ern
See McAuley, James Phillip

Mallon, Thomas 1951- .... **CLC 172**
See also CA 110; CANR 29, 57, 92

Mallowan, Agatha Christie
See Christie, Agatha (Mary Clarissa)
Maloff, Saul 1922- .... **CLC 5**
See also CA 33-36R
Malone, Louis
See MacNeice, (Frederick) Louis
Malone, Michael (Christopher)
1942- .... **CLC 43**
See also CA 77-80; CANR 14, 32, 57, 114
Malory, Sir Thomas 1410(?)-1471(?) . **LC 11, 88; WLCS**
See also BRW 1; BRWR 2; CDBLB Before 1660; DA; DAB; DAC; DAM MST; DLB 146; EFS 2; RGEL 2; SATA 59; SATA-Brief 33; TEA; WLIT 3
Malouf, (George Joseph) David
1934- .... **CLC 28, 86**
See also CA 124; CANR 50, 76; CN 7; CP 7; DLB 289; EWL 3; MTCW 2
Malraux, (Georges-)Andre
1901-1976 .... **CLC 1, 4, 9, 13, 15, 57**
See also BPFB 2; CA 21-22; 69-72; CANR 34, 58; CAP 2; DA3; DAM NOV; DLB 72; EW 12; EWL 3; GFL 1789 to the Present; MTCW 1, 2; RGWL 2, 3; TWA
Malthus, Thomas Robert
1766-1834 .... **NCLC 145**
See also DLB 107, 158; RGEL 2
Malzberg, Barry N(athaniel) 1939- ... **CLC 7**
See also CA 61-64; CAAS 4; CANR 16; CMW 4; DLB 8; SFW 4
Mamet, David (Alan) 1947- .. **CLC 9, 15, 34, 46, 91, 166; DC 4, 24**
See also AAYA 3, 60; AMWS 14; CA 81-84; CABS 3; CANR 15, 41, 67, 72, 129; CD 5; DA3; DAM DRAM; DFS 2, 3, 6, 12, 15; DLB 7; EWL 3; IDFW 4; MTCW 1, 2; RGAL 4
Mamoulian, Rouben (Zachary)
1897-1987 .... **CLC 16**
See also CA 25-28R; 124; CANR 85
Mandelshtam, Osip
See Mandelstam, Osip (Emilievich)
See also EW 10; EWL 3; RGWL 2, 3
Mandelstam, Osip (Emilievich)
1891(?)-1943(?) .... **PC 14; TCLC 2, 6**
See Mandelshtam, Osip
See also CA 104; 150; MTCW 2; TWA
Mander, (Mary) Jane 1877-1949 ... **TCLC 31**
See also CA 162; RGEL 2
Mandeville, Bernard 1670-1733 .... **LC 82**
See also DLB 101
Mandeville, Sir John fl. 1350- ...... **CMLC 19**
See also DLB 146
Mandiargues, Andre Pieyre de .... **CLC 41**
See Pieyre de Mandiargues, Andre
See also DLB 83
Mandrake, Ethel Belle
See Thurman, Wallace (Henry)
Mangan, James Clarence
1803-1849 .... **NCLC 27**
See also RGEL 2
Maniere, J.-E.
See Giraudoux, Jean(-Hippolyte)
Mankiewicz, Herman (Jacob)
1897-1953 .... **TCLC 85**
See also CA 120; 169; DLB 26; IDFW 3, 4
Manley, (Mary) Delariviere
1672(?)-1724 .... **LC 1, 42**
See also DLB 39, 80; RGEL 2
Mann, Abel
See Creasey, John
Mann, Emily 1952- .... **DC 7**
See also CA 130; CAD; CANR 55; CD 5; CWD; DLB 266
Mann, (Luiz) Heinrich 1871-1950 ... **TCLC 9**
See also CA 106; 164, 181; DLB 66, 118; EW 8; EWL 3; RGWL 2, 3

Mann, (Paul) Thomas 1875-1955 .... **SSC 5, 80; TCLC 2, 8, 14, 21, 35, 44, 60; WLC**
See also BPFB 2; CA 104; 128; CANR 133; CDWLB 2; DA; DA3; DAB; DAC; DAM MST, NOV; DLB 66; EW 9; EWL 3; GLL 1; LATS 1:1; LMFS 1; MTCW 1, 2; NFS 17; RGSF 2; RGWL 2, 3; SSFS 4, 9; TWA
Mannheim, Karl 1893-1947 .... **TCLC 65**
See also CA 204
Manning, David
See Faust, Frederick (Schiller)
See also TCWW 2
Manning, Frederic 1882-1935 .... **TCLC 25**
See also CA 124; 216; DLB 260
Manning, Olivia 1915-1980 .... **CLC 5, 19**
See also CA 5-8R; 101; CANR 29; EWL 3; FW; MTCW 1; RGEL 2
Mano, D. Keith 1942- .... **CLC 2, 10**
See also CA 25-28R; CAAS 6; CANR 26, 57; DLB 6
Mansfield, Katherine . **SSC 9, 23, 38; TCLC 2, 8, 39; WLC**
See Beauchamp, Kathleen Mansfield
See also BPFB 2; BRW 7; DAB; DLB 162; EWL 3; EXPS; FW; GLL 1; RGEL 2; RGSF 2; SSFS 2, 8, 10, 11; WWE 1
Manso, Peter 1940- .... **CLC 39**
See also CA 29-32R; CANR 44
Mantecon, Juan Jimenez
See Jimenez (Mantecon), Juan Ramon
Mantel, Hilary (Mary) 1952- .... **CLC 144**
See also CA 125; CANR 54, 101; CN 7; DLB 271; RHW
Manton, Peter
See Creasey, John
Man Without a Spleen, A
See Chekhov, Anton (Pavlovich)
Manzoni, Alessandro 1785-1873 ... **NCLC 29, 98**
See also EW 5; RGWL 2, 3; TWA
Map, Walter 1140-1209 .... **CMLC 32**
Mapu, Abraham (ben Jekutiel)
1808-1867 .... **NCLC 18**
Mara, Sally
See Queneau, Raymond
Maracle, Lee 1950- .... **NNAL**
See also CA 149
Marat, Jean Paul 1743-1793 .... **LC 10**
Marcel, Gabriel Honore 1889-1973 . **CLC 15**
See also CA 102; 45-48; EWL 3; MTCW 1, 2
March, William 1893-1954 .... **TCLC 96**
See also CA 216
Marchbanks, Samuel
See Davies, (William) Robertson
See also CCA 1
Marchi, Giacomo
See Bassani, Giorgio
Marcus Aurelius
See Aurelius, Marcus
See also AW 2
Marguerite
See de Navarre, Marguerite
Marguerite d'Angouleme
See de Navarre, Marguerite
See also GFL Beginnings to 1789
Marguerite de Navarre
See de Navarre, Marguerite
See also RGWL 2, 3
Margulies, Donald 1954- .... **CLC 76**
See also AAYA 57; CA 200; DFS 13; DLB 228
Marie de France c. 12th cent. - ..... **CMLC 8; PC 22**
See also DLB 208; FW; RGWL 2, 3

Marie de l'Incarnation 1599-1672 ...... **LC 10**
Marier, Captain Victor
See Griffith, D(avid Lewelyn) W(ark)
Mariner, Scott
See Pohl, Frederik
Marinetti, Filippo Tommaso
1876-1944 .... **TCLC 10**
See also CA 107; DLB 114, 264; EW 9; EWL 3
Marivaux, Pierre Carlet de Chamblain de
1688-1763 .... **DC 7; LC 4**
See also GFL Beginnings to 1789; RGWL 2, 3; TWA
Markandaya, Kamala .... **CLC 8, 38**
See Taylor, Kamala (Purnaiya)
See also BYA 13; CN 7; EWL 3
Markfield, Wallace 1926-2002 .... **CLC 8**
See also CA 69-72; 208; CAAS 3; CN 7; DLB 2, 28; DLBY 2002
Markham, Edwin 1852-1940 .... **TCLC 47**
See also CA 160; DLB 54, 186; RGEL 4
Markham, Robert
See Amis, Kingsley (William)
Markoosie .... **NNAL**
See Patsauq, Markoosie
See also CLR 23; DAM MULT
Marks, J.
See Highwater, Jamake (Mamake)
Marks, J
See Highwater, Jamake (Mamake)
Marks-Highwater, J
See Highwater, Jamake (Mamake)
Marks-Highwater, J.
See Highwater, Jamake (Mamake)
Markson, David M(errill) 1927- .... **CLC 67**
See also CA 49-52; CANR 1, 91; CN 7
Marlatt, Daphne (Buckle) 1942- ... **CLC 168**
See also CA 25-28R; CANR 17, 39; CN 7; CP 7; CWP; DLB 60; FW
Marley, Bob .... **CLC 17**
See Marley, Robert Nesta
Marley, Robert Nesta 1945-1981
See Marley, Bob
See also CA 107; 103
Marlowe, Christopher 1564-1593 . **DC 1; LC 22, 47; PC 57; WLC**
See also BRW 1; BRWR 1; CDBLB Before 1660; DA; DA3; DAB; DAC; DAM DRAM, MST; DFS 1, 5, 13; DLB 62; EXPP; LMFS 1; RGEL 2; TEA; WLIT 3
Marlowe, Stephen 1928- .... **CLC 70**
See Queen, Ellery
See also CA 13-16R; CANR 6, 55; CMW 4; SFW 4
Marmion, Shakerley 1603-1639 .... **LC 89**
See also DLB 58; RGEL 2
Marmontel, Jean-Francois 1723-1799 .. **LC 2**
Maron, Monika 1941- .... **CLC 165**
See also CA 201
Marquand, John P(hillips)
1893-1960 .... **CLC 2, 10**
See also AMW; BPFB 2; CA 85-88; CANR 73; CMW 4; DLB 9, 102; EWL 3; MTCW 2; RGAL 4
Marques, Rene 1919-1979 .. **CLC 96; HLC 2**
See also CA 97-100; 85-88; CANR 78; DAM MULT; DLB 305; EWL 3; HW 1, 2; LAW; RGSF 2
Marquez, Gabriel (Jose) Garcia
See Garcia Marquez, Gabriel (Jose)
Marquis, Don(ald Robert Perry)
1878-1937 .... **TCLC 7**
See also CA 104; 166; DLB 11, 25; RGAL 4
Marquis de Sade
See Sade, Donatien Alphonse Francois
Marric, J. J.
See Creasey, John
See also MSW

Maurhut, Richard
  See Traven, B.
Mauriac, Claude 1914-1996 .... **CLC 9**
  See also CA 89-92; 152; CWW 2; DLB 83;
  EWL 3; GFL 1789 to the Present
Mauriac, Francois (Charles)
  1885-1970 .... **CLC 4, 9, 56; SSC 24**
  See also CA 25-28; CAP 2; DLB 65; EW
  10; EWL 3; GFL 1789 to the Present;
  MTCW 1, 2; RGWL 2, 3; TWA
Mavor, Osborne Henry 1888-1951
  See Bridie, James
  See also CA 104
Maxwell, William (Keepers, Jr.)
  1908-2000 .... **CLC 19**
  See also AMWS 8; CA 93-96; 189; CANR
  54, 95; CN 7; DLB 218, 278; DLBY
  1980; INT CA-93-96; SATA-Obit 128
May, Elaine 1932- .... **CLC 16**
  See also CA 124; 142; CAD; CWD; DLB
  44
Mayakovski, Vladimir (Vladimirovich)
  1893-1930 .... **TCLC 4, 18**
  See also Maiakovskii, Vladimir; Mayakovsky,
  Vladimir
  See also CA 104; 158; EWL 3; MTCW 2;
  SFW 4; TWA
Mayakovsky, Vladimir
  See Mayakovski, Vladimir (Vladimirovich)
  See also EW 11; WP
Mayhew, Henry 1812-1887 .... **NCLC 31**
  See also DLB 18, 55, 190
Mayle, Peter 1939(?)- .... **CLC 89**
  See also CA 139; CANR 64, 109
Maynard, Joyce 1953- .... **CLC 23**
  See also CA 111; 129; CANR 64
Mayne, William (James Carter)
  1928- .... **CLC 12**
  See also AAYA 20; CA 9-12R; CANR 37,
  80, 100; CLR 25; FANT; JRDA; MAI-
  CYA 1, 2; MAICYAS 1; SAAS 11; SATA
  6, 68, 122; SUFW 2; YAW
Mayo, Jim
  See L'Amour, Louis (Dearborn)
  See also TCWW 2
Maysles, Albert 1926- .... **CLC 16**
  See also CA 29-32R
Maysles, David 1932-1987 .... **CLC 16**
  See also CA 191
Mazer, Norma Fox 1931- .... **CLC 26**
  See also AAYA 5, 36; BYA 1, 8; CA 69-72;
  CANR 12, 32, 66, 129; CLR 23; JRDA;
  MAICYA 1, 2; SAAS 1; SATA 24, 67,
  105; WYA; YAW
Mazzini, Guiseppe 1805-1872 .... **NCLC 34**
McAlmon, Robert (Menzies)
  1895-1956 .... **TCLC 97**
  See also CA 107; 168; DLB 4, 45; DLBD
  15; GLL 1
McAuley, James Phillip 1917-1976 .. **CLC 45**
  See also CA 97-100; DLB 260; RGEL 2
McBain, Ed
  See Hunter, Evan
  See also MSW
McBrien, William (Augustine)
  1930- .... **CLC 44**
  See also CA 107; CANR 90
McCabe, Patrick 1955- .... **CLC 133**
  See also BRWS 9; CA 130; CANR 50, 90;
  CN 7; DLB 194
McCaffrey, Anne (Inez) 1926- .... **CLC 17**
  See also AAYA 6, 34; AITN 2; BEST 89:2;
  BPFB 2; BYA 5; CA 25-28R, 227; CAAE
  227; CANR 15, 35, 55, 96; CLR 49;
  CPW; DA3; DAM NOV, POP; DLB 8;
  JRDA; MAICYA 1, 2; MTCW 1, 2; SAAS
  11; SATA 8, 70, 116, 152; SATA-Essay
  152; SFW 4; SUFW 2; WYA; YAW

McCall, Nathan 1955(?)- .... **CLC 86**
  See also AAYA 59; BW 3; CA 146; CANR
  88
McCann, Arthur
  See Campbell, John W(ood, Jr.)
McCann, Edson
  See Pohl, Frederik
McCarthy, Charles, Jr. 1933-
  See McCarthy, Cormac
  See also CANR 42, 69, 101; CN 7; CPW;
  CSW; DA3; DAM POP; MTCW 2
McCarthy, Cormac .... **CLC 4, 57, 101**
  See McCarthy, Charles, Jr.
  See also AAYA 41; AMWS 8; BPFB 2; CA
  13-16R; CANR 10; DLB 6, 143, 256;
  EWL 3; LATS 1:2; TCWW 2
McCarthy, Mary (Therese)
  1912-1989 .. **CLC 1, 3, 5, 14, 24, 39, 59;
  SSC 24**
  See also AMW; BPFB 2; CA 5-8R; 129;
  CANR 16, 50, 64; DA3; DLB 2; DLBY
  1981; EWL 3; FW; INT CANR-16;
  MAWW; MTCW 1, 2; RGAL 4; TUS
McCartney, (James) Paul 1942- . **CLC 12, 35**
  See also CA 146; CANR 111
McCauley, Stephen (D.) 1955- .... **CLC 50**
  See also CA 141
McClaren, Peter .... **CLC 70**
McClure, Michael (Thomas) 1932- ... **CLC 6,
  10**
  See also BG 3; CA 21-24R; CAD; CANR
  17, 46, 77, 131; CD 5; CP 7; DLB 16;
  WP
McCorkle, Jill (Collins) 1958- .... **CLC 51**
  See also CA 121; CANR 113; CSW; DLB
  234; DLBY 1987
McCourt, Frank 1930- .... **CLC 109**
  See also AMWS 12; CA 157; CANR 97;
  NCFS 1
McCourt, James 1941- .... **CLC 5**
  See also CA 57-60; CANR 98
McCourt, Malachy 1931- .... **CLC 119**
  See also SATA 126
McCoy, Horace (Stanley)
  1897-1955 .... **TCLC 28**
  See also AMWS 13; CA 108; 155; CMW 4;
  DLB 9
McCrae, John 1872-1918 .... **TCLC 12**
  See also CA 109; DLB 92; PFS 5
McCreigh, James
  See Pohl, Frederik
McCullers, (Lula) Carson (Smith)
  1917-1967 .... **CLC 1, 4, 10, 12, 48, 100;
  SSC 9, 24; TCLC 155; WLC**
  See also AAYA 21; AMW; AMWC 2; BPFB
  2; CA 5-8R; 25-28R; CABS 1, 3; CANR
  18, 132; CDALB 1941-1968; DA; DA3;
  DAB; DAC; DAM MST, NOV; DFS 5,
  18; DLB 2, 7, 173, 228; EWL 3; EXPS;
  FW; GLL 1; LAIT 3, 4; MAWW; MTCW
  1, 2; NFS 6, 13; RGAL 4; RGSF 2; SATA
  27; SSFS 5; TUS; YAW
McCulloch, John Tyler
  See Burroughs, Edgar Rice
McCullough, Colleen 1938(?)- .. **CLC 27, 107**
  See also AAYA 36; BPFB 2; CA 81-84;
  CANR 17, 46, 67, 98; CPW; DA3; DAM
  NOV, POP; MTCW 1, 2; RHW
McCunn, Ruthanne Lum 1946- .... **AAL**
  See also CA 119; CANR 43, 96; LAIT 2;
  SATA 63
McDermott, Alice 1953- .... **CLC 90**
  See also CA 109; CANR 40, 90, 126; DLB
  292
McElroy, Joseph 1930- .... **CLC 5, 47**
  See also CA 17-20R; CN 7

McEwan, Ian (Russell) 1948- .... **CLC 13, 66,
  169**
  See also BEST 90:4; BRWS 4; CA 61-64;
  CANR 14, 41, 69, 87, 132; CN 7; DAM
  NOV; DLB 14, 194; HGG; MTCW 1, 2;
  RGSF 2; SUFW 2; TEA
McFadden, David 1940- .... **CLC 48**
  See also CA 104; CP 7; DLB 60; INT CA-
  104
McFarland, Dennis 1950- .... **CLC 65**
  See also CA 165; CANR 110
McGahern, John 1934- ... **CLC 5, 9, 48, 156;
  SSC 17**
  See also CA 17-20R; CANR 29, 68, 113;
  CN 7; DLB 14, 231; MTCW 1
McGinley, Patrick (Anthony) 1937- . **CLC 41**
  See also CA 120; 127; CANR 56; INT CA-
  127
McGinley, Phyllis 1905-1978 .... **CLC 14**
  See also CA 9-12R; 77-80; CANR 19;
  CWRI 5; DLB 11, 48; PFS 9, 13; SATA
  2, 44; SATA-Obit 24
McGinniss, Joe 1942- .... **CLC 32**
  See also AITN 2; BEST 89:2; CA 25-28R;
  CANR 26, 70; CPW; DLB 185; INT
  CANR-26
McGivern, Maureen Daly
  See Daly, Maureen
McGrath, Patrick 1950- .... **CLC 55**
  See also CA 136; CANR 65; CN 7; DLB
  231; HGG; SUFW 2
McGrath, Thomas (Matthew)
  1916-1990 .... **CLC 28, 59**
  See also AMWS 10; CA 9-12R; 132; CANR
  6, 33, 95; DAM POET; MTCW 1; SATA
  41; SATA-Obit 66
McGuane, Thomas (Francis III)
  1939- .... **CLC 3, 7, 18, 45, 127**
  See also AITN 2; BPFB 2; CA 49-52;
  CANR 5, 24, 49, 94; CN 7; DLB 2, 212;
  DLBY 1980; EWL 3; INT CANR-24;
  MTCW 1; TCWW 2
McGuckian, Medbh 1950- .... **CLC 48, 174;
  PC 27**
  See also BRWS 5; CA 143; CP 7; CWP;
  DAM POET; DLB 40
McHale, Tom 1942(?)-1982 .... **CLC 3, 5**
  See also AITN 1; CA 77-80; 106
McHugh, Heather 1948- .... **PC 61**
  See also CA 69-72; CANR 11, 28, 55, 92;
  CP 7; CWP
McIlvanney, William 1936- .... **CLC 42**
  See also CA 25-28R; CANR 61; CMW 4;
  DLB 14, 207
McIlwraith, Maureen Mollie Hunter
  See Hunter, Mollie
  See also SATA 2
McInerney, Jay 1955- .... **CLC 34, 112**
  See also AAYA 18; BPFB 2; CA 116; 123;
  CANR 45, 68, 116; CN 7; CPW; DA3;
  DAM POP; DLB 292; INT CA-123;
  MTCW 2
McIntyre, Vonda N(eel) 1948- .... **CLC 18**
  See also CA 81-84; CANR 17, 34, 69;
  MTCW 1; SFW 4; YAW
McKay, Claude .... **BLC 3; HR 3; PC 2;
  TCLC 7, 41; WLC**
  See McKay, Festus Claudius
  See also AFAW 1, 2; AMWS 10; DAB;
  DLB 4, 45, 51, 117; EWL 3; EXPP; GLL
  2; LAIT 3; LMFS 2; PAB; PFS 4; RGAL
  4; WP
McKay, Festus Claudius 1889-1948
  See McKay, Claude
  See also BW 1, 3; CA 104; 124; CANR 73;
  DA; DAC; DAM MST, MULT, NOV,
  POET; MTCW 1, 2; TUS
McKuen, Rod 1933- .... **CLC 1, 3**
  See also AITN 1; CA 41-44R; CANR 40

**Morgenstern, Christian (Otto Josef
 Wolfgang)** 1871-1914 .... **TCLC 8**
  See also CA 105; 191; EWL 3

Morgenstern, S.
  See Goldman, William (W.)

Mori, Rintaro
  See Mori Ogai
  See also CA 110

Moricz, Zsigmond 1879-1942 .... **TCLC 33**
  See also CA 165; DLB 215; EWL 3

Morike, Eduard (Friedrich)
  1804-1875 .... **NCLC 10**
  See also DLB 133; RGWL 2, 3

Mori Ogai 1862-1922 .... **TCLC 14**
  See Ogai
  See also CA 164; DLB 180; EWL 3; RGWL
  3; TWA

Moritz, Karl Philipp 1756-1793 .... **LC 2**
  See also DLB 94

Morland, Peter Henry
  See Faust, Frederick (Schiller)

Morley, Christopher (Darlington)
  1890-1957 .... **TCLC 87**
  See also CA 112; 213; DLB 9; RGAL 4

Morren, Theophil
  See Hofmannsthal, Hugo von

Morris, Bill 1952- .... **CLC 76**
  See also CA 225

Morris, Julian
  See West, Morris L(anglo)

Morris, Steveland Judkins 1950(?)-
  See Wonder, Stevie
  See also CA 111

Morris, William 1834-1896 . **NCLC 4; PC 55**
  See also BRW 5; CDBLB 1832-1890; DLB
  18, 35, 57, 156, 178, 184; FANT; RGEL
  2; SFW 4; SUFW

Morris, Wright 1910-1998 .. **CLC 1, 3, 7, 18,
  37; TCLC 107**
  See also AMW; CA 9-12R; 167; CANR 21,
  81; CN 7; DLB 2, 206, 218; DLBY 1981;
  EWL 3; MTCW 1, 2; RGAL 4; TCWW 2

Morrison, Arthur 1863-1945 .... **SSC 40;
  TCLC 72**
  See also CA 120; 157; CMW 4; DLB 70,
  135, 197; RGEL 2

Morrison, Chloe Anthony Wofford
  See Morrison, Toni

Morrison, James Douglas 1943-1971
  See Morrison, Jim
  See also CA 73-76; CANR 40

Morrison, Jim .... **CLC 17**
  See Morrison, James Douglas

Morrison, Toni 1931- ..... **BLC 3; CLC 4, 10,
  22, 55, 81, 87, 173, 194**
  See also AAYA 1, 22; AFAW 1, 2; AMWC
  1; AMWS 3; BPFB 2; BW 2, 3; CA 29-
  32R; CANR 27, 42, 67, 113, 124; CDALB
  1968-1988; CLR 99; CN 7; CPW; DA;
  DA3; DAB; DAC; DAM MST, MULT,
  NOV, POP; DLB 6, 33, 143; DLBY 1981;
  EWL 3; EXPN; FW; LAIT 2, 4; LATS
  1:2; LMFS 2; MAWW; MTCW 1, 2; NFS
  1, 6, 8, 14; RGAL 4; RHW; SATA 57,
  144; SSFS 5; TUS; YAW

Morrison, Van 1945- .... **CLC 21**
  See also CA 116; 168

Morrissy, Mary 1957- .... **CLC 99**
  See also CA 205; DLB 267

Mortimer, John (Clifford) 1923- ..... **CLC 28,
  43**
  See also CA 13-16R; CANR 21, 69, 109;
  CD 5; CDBLB 1960 to Present; CMW 4;
  CN 7; CPW; DA3; DAM DRAM, POP;
  DLB 13, 245, 271; INT CANR-21; MSW;
  MTCW 1, 2; RGEL 2

Mortimer, Penelope (Ruth)
  1918-1999 .... **CLC 5**
  See also CA 57-60; 187; CANR 45, 88; CN
  7

Mortimer, Sir John
  See Mortimer, John (Clifford)

Morton, Anthony
  See Creasey, John

Morton, Thomas 1579(?)-1647(?) .... **LC 72**
  See also DLB 24; RGEL 2

Mosca, Gaetano 1858-1941 .... **TCLC 75**

Moses, Daniel David 1952- .... **NNAL**
  See also CA 186

Mosher, Howard Frank 1943- .... **CLC 62**
  See also CA 139; CANR 65, 115

Mosley, Nicholas 1923- .... **CLC 43, 70**
  See also CA 69-72; CANR 41, 60, 108; CN
  7; DLB 14, 207

Mosley, Walter 1952- .... **BLCS; CLC 97, 184**
  See also AAYA 57; AMWS 13; BPFB 2;
  BW 2; CA 142; CANR 57, 92; CMW 4;
  CPW; DA3; DAM MULT, POP; DLB
  306; MSW; MTCW 2

Moss, Howard 1922-1987 . **CLC 7, 14, 45, 50**
  See also CA 1-4R; 123; CANR 1, 44; DAM
  POET; DLB 5

Mossgiel, Rab
  See Burns, Robert

Motion, Andrew (Peter) 1952- .... **CLC 47**
  See also BRWS 7; CA 146; CANR 90; CP
  7; DLB 40

Motley, Willard (Francis)
  1909-1965 .... **CLC 18**
  See also BW 1; CA 117; 106; CANR 88;
  DLB 76, 143

Motoori, Norinaga 1730-1801 .... **NCLC 45**

Mott, Michael (Charles Alston)
  1930- .... **CLC 15, 34**
  See also CA 5-8R; CAAS 7; CANR 7, 29

Mountain Wolf Woman 1884-1960 . **CLC 92;
  NNAL**
  See also CA 144; CANR 90

Moure, Erin 1955- .... **CLC 88**
  See also CA 113; CP 7; CWP; DLB 60

Mourning Dove 1885(?)-1936 .... **NNAL**
  See also CA 144; CANR 90; DAM MULT;
  DLB 175, 221

Mowat, Farley (McGill) 1921- .... **CLC 26**
  See also AAYA 1, 50; BYA 2; CA 1-4R;
  CANR 4, 24, 42, 68, 108; CLR 20; CPW;
  DAC; DAM MST; DLB 68; INT CANR-
  24; JRDA; MAICYA 1, 2; MTCW 1, 2;
  SATA 3, 55; YAW

Mowatt, Anna Cora 1819-1870 ..... **NCLC 74**
  See also RGAL 4

Moyers, Bill 1934- .... **CLC 74**
  See also AITN 2; CA 61-64; CANR 31, 52

Mphahlele, Es'kia
  See Mphahlele, Ezekiel
  See also AFW; CDWLB 3; DLB 125, 225;
  RGSF 2; SSFS 11

Mphahlele, Ezekiel 1919- ... **BLC 3; CLC 25,
  133**
  See Mphahlele, Es'kia
  See also BW 2, 3; CA 81-84; CANR 26,
  76; CN 7; DA3; DAM MULT; EWL 3;
  MTCW 2; SATA 119

Mqhayi, S(amuel) E(dward) K(rune Loliwe)
  1875-1945 .... **BLC 3; TCLC 25**
  See also CA 153; CANR 87; DAM MULT

Mrozek, Slawomir 1930- .... **CLC 3, 13**
  See also CA 13-16R; CAAS 10; CANR 29;
  CDWLB 4; CWW 2; DLB 232; EWL 3;
  MTCW 1

Mrs. Belloc-Lowndes
  See Lowndes, Marie Adelaide (Belloc)

Mrs. Fairstar
  See Horne, Richard Henry Hengist

M'Taggart, John M'Taggart Ellis
  See McTaggart, John McTaggart Ellis

Mtwa, Percy (?)- .... **CLC 47**

Mueller, Lisel 1924- .... **CLC 13, 51; PC 33**
  See also CA 93-96; CP 7; DLB 105; PFS 9,
  13

Muggeridge, Malcolm (Thomas)
  1903-1990 .... **TCLC 120**
  See also AITN 1; CA 101; CANR 33, 63;
  MTCW 1, 2

Muhammad 570-632 .... **WLCS**
  See also DA; DAB; DAC; DAM MST

Muir, Edwin 1887-1959 . **PC 49; TCLC 2, 87**
  See Moore, Edward
  See also BRWS 6; CA 104; 193; DLB 20,
  100, 191; EWL 3; RGEL 2

Muir, John 1838-1914 .... **TCLC 28**
  See also AMWS 9; ANW; CA 165; DLB
  186, 275

Mujica Lainez, Manuel 1910-1984 ... **CLC 31**
  See Lainez, Manuel Mujica
  See also CA 81-84; 112; CANR 32; EWL
  3; HW 1

Mukherjee, Bharati 1940- ..... **AAL; CLC 53,
  115; SSC 38**
  See also AAYA 46; BEST 89:2; CA 107;
  CANR 45, 72, 128; CN 7; DAM NOV;
  DLB 60, 218; DNFS 1, 2; EWL 3; FW;
  MTCW 1, 2; RGAL 4; RGSF 2; SSFS 7;
  TUS; WWE 1

Muldoon, Paul 1951- .... **CLC 32, 72, 166**
  See also BRWS 4; CA 113; 129; CANR 52,
  91; CP 7; DAM POET; DLB 40; INT CA-
  129; PFS 7

Mulisch, Harry (Kurt Victor)
  1927- .... **CLC 42**
  See also CA 9-12R; CANR 6, 26, 56, 110;
  CWW 2; DLB 299; EWL 3

Mull, Martin 1943- .... **CLC 17**
  See also CA 105

Muller, Wilhelm .... **NCLC 73**

Mulock, Dinah Maria
  See Craik, Dinah Maria (Mulock)
  See also RGEL 2

Munday, Anthony 1560-1633 .... **LC 87**
  See also DLB 62, 172; RGEL 2

Munford, Robert 1737(?)-1783 .... **LC 5**
  See also DLB 31

Mungo, Raymond 1946- .... **CLC 72**
  See also CA 49-52; CANR 2

Munro, Alice 1931- .... **CLC 6, 10, 19, 50, 95;
  SSC 3; WLCS**
  See also AITN 2; BPFB 2; CA 33-36R;
  CANR 33, 53, 75, 114; CCA 1; CN 7;
  DA3; DAC; DAM MST, NOV; DLB 53;
  EWL 3; MTCW 1, 2; RGEL 2; RGSF 2;
  SATA 29; SSFS 5, 13, 19; WWE 1

Munro, H(ector) H(ugh) 1870-1916 .... **WLC**
  See Saki
  See also AAYA 56; CA 104; 130; CANR
  104; CDBLB 1890-1914; DA; DA3;
  DAB; DAC; DAM MST, NOV; DLB 34,
  162; EXPS; MTCW 1, 2; RGEL 2; SSFS
  15

Murakami, Haruki 1949- .... **CLC 150**
  See Murakami Haruki
  See also CA 165; CANR 102; MJW; RGWL
  3; SFW 4

Murakami Haruki
  See Murakami, Haruki
  See also CWW 2; DLB 182; EWL 3

Murasaki, Lady
  See Murasaki Shikibu

Murasaki Shikibu 978(?)-1026(?) ... **CMLC 1**
  See also EFS 2; LATS 1:1; RGWL 2, 3

Murdoch, (Jean) Iris 1919-1999 ... **CLC 1, 2,
  3, 4, 6, 8, 11, 15, 22, 31, 51**
  See also BRWS 1; CA 13-16R; 179; CANR
  8, 43, 68, 103; CDBLB 1960 to Present;

CN 7; CWD; DA3; DAB; DAC; DAM
MST, NOV; DLB 14, 194, 233; EWL 3;
INT CANR-8; MTCW 1, 2; NFS 18;
RGEL 2; TEA; WLIT 4

Murfree, Mary Noailles 1850-1922 .. **SSC 22;**
TCLC 135
See also CA 122; 176; DLB 12, 74; RGAL
4

Murnau, Friedrich Wilhelm
See Plumpe, Friedrich Wilhelm

Murphy, Richard 1927- .... **CLC 41**
See also BRWS 5; CA 29-32R; CP 7; DLB
40; EWL 3

Murphy, Sylvia 1937- .... **CLC 34**
See also CA 121

Murphy, Thomas (Bernard) 1935- ... **CLC 51**
See also CA 101

Murray, Albert L. 1916- .... **CLC 73**
See also BW 2; CA 49-52; CANR 26, 52,
78; CSW; DLB 38

Murray, James Augustus Henry
1837-1915 .... **TCLC 117**

Murray, Judith Sargent
1751-1820 .... **NCLC 63**
See also DLB 37, 200

Murray, Les(lie Allan) 1938- .... **CLC 40**
See also BRWS 7; CA 21-24R; CANR 11,
27, 56, 103; CP 7; DAM POET; DLB 289;
DLBY 2001; EWL 3; RGEL 2

Murry, J. Middleton
See Murry, John Middleton

Murry, John Middleton
1889-1957 .... **TCLC 16**
See also CA 118; 217; DLB 149

Musgrave, Susan 1951- .... **CLC 13, 54**
See also CA 69-72; CANR 45, 84; CCA 1;
CP 7; CWP

Musil, Robert (Edler von)
1880-1942 .... **SSC 18; TCLC 12, 68**
See also CA 109; CANR 55, 84; CDWLB
2; DLB 81, 124; EW 9; EWL 3; MTCW
2; RGSF 2; RGWL 2, 3

Muske, Carol .... **CLC 90**
See Muske-Dukes, Carol (Anne)

Muske-Dukes, Carol (Anne) 1945-
See Muske, Carol
See also CA 65-68, 203; CAAE 203; CANR
32, 70; CWP

Musset, (Louis Charles) Alfred de
1810-1857 .... **NCLC 7, 150**
See also DLB 192, 217; EW 6; GFL 1789
to the Present; RGWL 2, 3; TWA

Mussolini, Benito (Amilcare Andrea)
1883-1945 .... **TCLC 96**
See also CA 116

Mutanabbi, Al-
See al-Mutanabbi, Ahmad ibn al-Husayn
Abu al-Tayyib al-Jufi al-Kindi

My Brother's Brother
See Chekhov, Anton (Pavlovich)

Myers, L(eopold) H(amilton)
1881-1944 .... **TCLC 59**
See also CA 157; DLB 15; EWL 3; RGEL
2

Myers, Walter Dean 1937- .. **BLC 3; CLC 35**
See also AAYA 4, 23; BW 2; BYA 6, 8, 11;
CA 33-36R; CANR 20, 42, 67, 108; CLR
4, 16, 35; DAM MULT, NOV; DLB 33;
INT CANR-20; JRDA; LAIT 5; MAICYA
1, 2; MAICYAS 1; MTCW 2; SAAS 2;
SATA 41, 71, 109; SATA-Brief 27; WYA;
YAW

Myers, Walter M.
See Myers, Walter Dean

Myles, Symon
See Follett, Ken(neth Martin)

Nabokov, Vladimir (Vladimirovich)
1899-1977 .... **CLC 1, 2, 3, 6, 8, 11, 15,**
23, 44, 46, 64; SSC 11; TCLC 108;
WLC
See also AAYA 45; AMW; AMWC 1;
AMWR 1; BPFB 2; CA 5-8R; 69-72;
CANR 20, 102; CDALB 1941-1968; DA;
DA3; DAB; DAC; DAM MST, NOV;
DLB 2, 244, 278; DLBD 3; DLBY 1980,
1991; EWL 3; EXPS; LATS 1:2; MTCW
1, 2; NCFS 4; NFS 9; RGAL 4; RGSF 2;
SSFS 6, 15; TUS

Naevius c. 265B.C.-201B.C. .... **CMLC 37**
See also DLB 211

Nagai, Kafu .... **TCLC 51**
See Nagai, Sokichi
See also DLB 180

Nagai, Sokichi 1879-1959
See Nagai, Kafu
See also CA 117

Nagy, Laszlo 1925-1978 .... **CLC 7**
See also CA 129; 112

Naidu, Sarojini 1879-1949 .... **TCLC 80**
See also EWL 3; RGEL 2

Naipaul, Shiva(dhar Srinivasa)
1945-1985 .... **CLC 32, 39; TCLC 153**
See also CA 110; 112; 116; CANR 33;
DA3; DAM NOV; DLB 157; DLBY 1985;
EWL 3; MTCW 1, 2

Naipaul, V(idiadhar) S(urajprasad)
1932- .... **CLC 4, 7, 9, 13, 18, 37, 105,**
199; SSC 38
See also BPFB 2; BRWS 1; CA 1-4R;
CANR 1, 33, 51, 91, 126; CDBLB 1960
to Present; CDWLB 3; CN 7; DA3; DAB;
DAC; DAM MST, NOV; DLB 125, 204,
207; DLBY 1985, 2001; EWL 3; LATS
1:2; MTCW 1, 2; RGEL 2; RGSF 2;
TWA; WLIT 4; WWE 1

Nakos, Lilika 1903(?)-1989 .... **CLC 29**

Napoleon
See Yamamoto, Hisaye

Narayan, R(asipuram) K(rishnaswami)
1906-2001 . **CLC 7, 28, 47, 121; SSC 25**
See also BPFB 2; CA 81-84; 196; CANR
33, 61, 112; CN 7; DA3; DAM NOV;
DNFS 1; EWL 3; MTCW 1, 2; RGEL 2;
RGSF 2; SATA 62; SSFS 5; WWE 1

Nash, (Frediric) Ogden 1902-1971 . **CLC 23;**
PC 21; TCLC 109
See also CA 13-14; 29-32R; CANR 34, 61;
CAP 1; DAM POET; DLB 11; MAICYA
1, 2; MTCW 1, 2; RGAL 4; SATA 2, 46;
WP

Nashe, Thomas 1567-1601(?) .... **LC 41, 89**
See also DLB 167; RGEL 2

Nathan, Daniel
See Dannay, Frederic

Nathan, George Jean 1882-1958 .... **TCLC 18**
See Hatteras, Owen
See also CA 114; 169; DLB 137

Natsume, Kinnosuke
See Natsume, Soseki

Natsume, Soseki 1867-1916 .... **TCLC 2, 10**
See Natsume Soseki; Soseki
See also CA 104; 195; RGWL 2, 3; TWA

Natsume Soseki
See Natsume, Soseki
See also DLB 180; EWL 3

Natti, (Mary) Lee 1919-
See Kingman, Lee
See also CA 5-8R; CANR 2

Navarre, Marguerite de
See de Navarre, Marguerite

Naylor, Gloria 1950- ..... **BLC 3; CLC 28, 52,**
156; WLCS
See also AAYA 6, 39; AFAW 1, 2; AMWS
8; BW 2, 3; CA 107; CANR 27, 51, 74,
130; CN 7; CPW; DA; DA3; DAC; DAM

MST, MULT, NOV, POP; DLB 173; EWL
3; FW; MTCW 1, 2; NFS 4, 7; RGAL 4;
TUS

Neff, Debra .... **CLC 59**

Neihardt, John Gneisenau
1881-1973 .... **CLC 32**
See also CA 13-14; CANR 65; CAP 1; DLB
9, 54, 256; LAIT 2

Nekrasov, Nikolai Alekseevich
1821-1878 .... **NCLC 11**
See also DLB 277

Nelligan, Emile 1879-1941 .... **TCLC 14**
See also CA 114; 204; DLB 92; EWL 3

Nelson, Willie 1933- .... **CLC 17**
See also CA 107; CANR 114

Nemerov, Howard (Stanley)
1920-1991 ... **CLC 2, 6, 9, 36; PC 24;**
TCLC 124
See also AMW; CA 1-4R; 134; CABS 2;
CANR 1, 27, 53; DAM POET; DLB 5, 6;
DLBY 1983; EWL 3; INT CANR-27;
MTCW 1, 2; PFS 10, 14; RGAL 4

Neruda, Pablo 1904-1973 .. **CLC 1, 2, 5, 7, 9,**
28, 62; HLC 2; PC 4; WLC
See also CA 19-20; 45-48; CANR 131; CAP
2; DA; DA3; DAB; DAC; DAM MST,
MULT, POET; DLB 283; DNFS 2; EWL
3; HW 1; LAW; MTCW 1, 2; PFS 11;
RGWL 2, 3; TWA; WLIT 1; WP

Nerval, Gerard de 1808-1855 ... **NCLC 1, 67;**
PC 13; SSC 18
See also DLB 217; EW 6; GFL 1789 to the
Present; RGSF 2; RGWL 2, 3

Nervo, (Jose) Amado (Ruiz de)
1870-1919 .... **HLCS 2; TCLC 11**
See also CA 109; 131; DLB 290; EWL 3;
HW 1; LAW

Nesbit, Malcolm
See Chester, Alfred

Nessi, Pio Baroja y
See Baroja (y Nessi), Pio

Nestroy, Johann 1801-1862 .... **NCLC 42**
See also DLB 133; RGWL 2, 3

Netterville, Luke
See O'Grady, Standish (James)

Neufeld, John (Arthur) 1938- .... **CLC 17**
See also AAYA 11; CA 25-28R; CANR 11,
37, 56; CLR 52; MAICYA 1, 2; SAAS 3;
SATA 6, 81, 131; SATA-Essay 131; YAW

Neumann, Alfred 1895-1952 .... **TCLC 100**
See also CA 183; DLB 56

Neumann, Ferenc
See Molnar, Ferenc

Neville, Emily Cheney 1919- .... **CLC 12**
See also BYA 2; CA 5-8R; CANR 3, 37,
85; JRDA; MAICYA 1, 2; SAAS 2; SATA
1; YAW

Newbound, Bernard Slade 1930-
See Slade, Bernard
See also CA 81-84; CANR 49; CD 5; DAM
DRAM

Newby, P(ercy) H(oward)
1918-1997 .... **CLC 2, 13**
See also CA 5-8R; 161; CANR 32, 67; CN
7; DAM NOV; DLB 15; MTCW 1; RGEL
2

Newcastle
See Cavendish, Margaret Lucas

Newlove, Donald 1928- .... **CLC 6**
See also CA 29-32R; CANR 25

Newlove, John (Herbert) 1938- .... **CLC 14**
See also CA 21-24R; CANR 9, 25; CP 7

Newman, Charles 1938- .... **CLC 2, 8**
See also CA 21-24R; CANR 84; CN 7

Newman, Edwin (Harold) 1919- ...... **CLC 14**
See also AITN 1; CA 69-72; CANR 5

Newman, John Henry 1801-1890 . **NCLC 38, 99**
See also BRWS 7; DLB 18, 32, 55; RGEL 2

Newton, (Sir) Isaac 1642-1727 ...... **LC 35, 53**
See also DLB 252

Newton, Suzanne 1936- .... **CLC 35**
See also BYA 7; CA 41-44R; CANR 14; JRDA; SATA 5, 77

New York Dept. of Ed. .... **CLC 70**

Nexo, Martin Andersen
1869-1954 .... **TCLC 43**
See also CA 202; DLB 214; EWL 3

Nezval, Vitezslav 1900-1958 .... **TCLC 44**
See also CA 123; CDWLB 4; DLB 215; EWL 3

Ng, Fae Myenne 1957(?)- .... **CLC 81**
See also BYA 11; CA 146

Ngema, Mbongeni 1955- .... **CLC 57**
See also BW 2; CA 143; CANR 84; CD 5

Ngugi, James T(hiong'o) . **CLC 3, 7, 13, 182**
See Ngugi wa Thiong'o

Ngugi wa Thiong'o
See Ngugi wa Thiong'o
See also DLB 125; EWL 3

Ngugi wa Thiong'o 1938- ... **BLC 3; CLC 36, 182**
See Ngugi, James T(hiong'o); Ngugi wa Thiong'o
See also AFW; BRWS 8; BW 2; CA 81-84; CANR 27, 58; CDWLB 3; DAM MULT, NOV; DNFS 2; MTCW 1, 2; RGEL 2; WWE 1

Niatum, Duane 1938- .... **NNAL**
See also CA 41-44R; CANR 21, 45, 83; DLB 175

Nichol, B(arrie) P(hillip) 1944-1988 . **CLC 18**
See also CA 53-56; DLB 53; SATA 66

Nicholas of Cusa 1401-1464 .... **LC 80**
See also DLB 115

Nichols, John (Treadwell) 1940- .... **CLC 38**
See also AMWS 13; CA 9-12R, 190; CAAE 190; CAAS 2; CANR 6, 70, 121; DLBY 1982; LATS 1:2; TCWW 2

Nichols, Leigh
See Koontz, Dean R(ay)

Nichols, Peter (Richard) 1927- .... **CLC 5, 36, 65**
See also CA 104; CANR 33, 86; CBD; CD 5; DLB 13, 245; MTCW 1

Nicholson, Linda ed. .... **CLC 65**

Ni Chuilleanain, Eilean 1942- .... **PC 34**
See also CA 126; CANR 53, 83; CP 7; CWP; DLB 40

Nicolas, F. R. E.
See Freeling, Nicolas

Niedecker, Lorine 1903-1970 ..... **CLC 10, 42; PC 42**
See also CA 25-28; CAP 2; DAM POET; DLB 48

Nietzsche, Friedrich (Wilhelm)
1844-1900 .... **TCLC 10, 18, 55**
See also CA 107; 121; CDWLB 2; DLB 129; EW 7; RGWL 2, 3; TWA

Nievo, Ippolito 1831-1861 .... **NCLC 22**

Nightingale, Anne Redmon 1943-
See Redmon, Anne
See also CA 103

Nightingale, Florence 1820-1910 ... **TCLC 85**
See also CA 188; DLB 166

Nijo Yoshimoto 1320-1388 .... **CMLC 49**
See also DLB 203

Nik. T. O.
See Annensky, Innokenty (Fyodorovich)

Nin, Anais 1903-1977 ..... **CLC 1, 4, 8, 11, 14, 60, 127; SSC 10**
See also AITN 2; AMWS 10; BPFB 2; CA 13-16R; 69-72; CANR 22, 53; DAM NOV, POP; DLB 2, 4, 152; EWL 3; GLL 2; MAWW; MTCW 1, 2; RGAL 4; RGSF 2

Nisbet, Robert A(lexander)
1913-1996 .... **TCLC 117**
See also CA 25-28R; 153; CANR 17; INT CANR-17

Nishida, Kitaro 1870-1945 .... **TCLC 83**

Nishiwaki, Junzaburo
See Nishiwaki, Junzaburo
See also CA 194

Nishiwaki, Junzaburo 1894-1982 .... **PC 15**
See Nishiwaki, Junzaburo; Nishiwaki Junzaburo
See also CA 194; 107; MJW; RGWL 3

Nishiwaki Junzaburo
See Nishiwaki, Junzaburo
See also EWL 3

Nissenson, Hugh 1933- .... **CLC 4, 9**
See also CA 17-20R; CANR 27, 108; CN 7; DLB 28

Nister, Der
See Der Nister
See also EWL 3

Niven, Larry .... **CLC 8**
See Niven, Laurence Van Cott
See also AAYA 27; BPFB 2; BYA 10; DLB 8; SCFW 2

Niven, Laurence Van Cott 1938-
See Niven, Larry
See also CA 21-24R, 207; CAAE 207; CAAS 12; CANR 14, 44, 66, 113; CPW; DAM POP; MTCW 1, 2; SATA 95; SFW 4

Nixon, Agnes Eckhardt 1927- .... **CLC 21**
See also CA 110

Nizan, Paul 1905-1940 .... **TCLC 40**
See also CA 161; DLB 72; EWL 3; GFL 1789 to the Present

Nkosi, Lewis 1936- .... **BLC 3; CLC 45**
See also BW 1, 3; CA 65-68; CANR 27, 81; CBD; CD 5; DAM MULT; DLB 157, 225; WWE 1

Nodier, (Jean) Charles (Emmanuel)
1780-1844 .... **NCLC 19**
See also DLB 119; GFL 1789 to the Present

Noguchi, Yone 1875-1947 .... **TCLC 80**

Nolan, Christopher 1965- .... **CLC 58**
See also CA 111; CANR 88

Noon, Jeff 1957- .... **CLC 91**
See also CA 148; CANR 83; DLB 267; SFW 4

Norden, Charles
See Durrell, Lawrence (George)

Nordhoff, Charles Bernard
1887-1947 .... **TCLC 23**
See also CA 108; 211; DLB 9; LAIT 1; RHW 1; SATA 23

Norfolk, Lawrence 1963- .... **CLC 76**
See also CA 144; CANR 85; CN 7; DLB 267

Norman, Marsha 1947- . **CLC 28, 186; DC 8**
See also CA 105; CABS 3; CAD; CANR 41, 131; CD 5; CSW; CWD; DAM DRAM; DFS 2; DLB 266; DLBY 1984; FW

Normyx
See Douglas, (George) Norman

Norris, (Benjamin) Frank(lin, Jr.)
1870-1902 .... **SSC 28; TCLC 24, 155**
See also AAYA 57; AMW; AMWC 2; BPFB 2; CA 110; 160; CDALB 1865-1917; DLB 12, 71, 186; LMFS 2; NFS 12; RGAL 4; TCWW 2; TUS

Norris, Leslie 1921- .... **CLC 14**
See also CA 11-12; CANR 14, 117; CAP 1; CP 7; DLB 27, 256

North, Andrew
See Norton, Andre

North, Anthony
See Koontz, Dean R(ay)

North, Captain George
See Stevenson, Robert Louis (Balfour)

North, Captain George
See Stevenson, Robert Louis (Balfour)

North, Milou
See Erdrich, Louise

Northrup, B. A.
See Hubbard, L(afayette) Ron(ald)

North Staffs
See Hulme, T(homas) E(rnest)

Northup, Solomon 1808-1863 ...... **NCLC 105**

Norton, Alice Mary
See Norton, Andre
See also MAICYA 1; SATA 1, 43

Norton, Andre 1912- .... **CLC 12**
See Norton, Alice Mary
See also AAYA 14; BPFB 2; BYA 4, 10, 12; CA 1-4R; CANR 68; CLR 50; DLB 8, 52; JRDA; MAICYA 2; MTCW 1; SATA 91; SUFW 1, 2; YAW

Norton, Caroline 1808-1877 .... **NCLC 47**
See also DLB 21, 159, 199

Norway, Nevil Shute 1899-1960
See Shute, Nevil
See also CA 102; 93-96; CANR 85; MTCW 2

Norwid, Cyprian Kamil
1821-1883 .... **NCLC 17**
See also RGWL 3

Nosille, Nabrah
See Ellison, Harlan (Jay)

Nossack, Hans Erich 1901-1978 .... **CLC 6**
See also CA 93-96; 85-88; DLB 69; EWL 3

Nostradamus 1503-1566 .... **LC 27**

Nosu, Chuji
See Ozu, Yasujiro

Notenburg, Eleanora (Genrikhovna) von
See Guro, Elena (Genrikhovna)

Nova, Craig 1945- .... **CLC 7, 31**
See also CA 45-48; CANR 2, 53, 127

Novak, Joseph
See Kosinski, Jerzy (Nikodem)

Novalis 1772-1801 .... **NCLC 13**
See also CDWLB 2; DLB 90; EW 5; RGWL 2, 3

Novick, Peter 1934- .... **CLC 164**
See also CA 188

Novis, Emile
See Weil, Simone (Adolphine)

Nowlan, Alden (Albert) 1933-1983 ... **CLC 15**
See also CA 9-12R; CANR 5; DAC; DAM MST; DLB 53; PFS 12

Noyes, Alfred 1880-1958 ...... **PC 27; TCLC 7**
See also CA 104; 188; DLB 20; EXPP; FANT; PFS 4; RGEL 2

Nugent, Richard Bruce 1906(?)-1987 ... **HR 3**
See also BW 1; CA 125; DLB 51; GLL 2

Nunn, Kem .... **CLC 34**
See also CA 159

Nussbaum, Martha 1947- .... **CLC 203**
See also CA 134; CANR 102

Nwapa, Flora (Nwanzuruaha)
1931-1993 .... **BLCS; CLC 133**
See also BW 2; CA 143; CANR 83; CD-WLB 3; CWRI 5; DLB 125; EWL 3; WLIT 2

Nye, Robert 1939- .... **CLC 13, 42**
See also BRWS 10; CA 33-36R; CANR 29, 67, 107; CN 7; CP 7; CWRI 5; DAM NOV; DLB 14, 271; FANT; HGG; MTCW 1; RHW; SATA 6

Nyro, Laura 1947-1997 .... **CLC 17**
See also CA 194

6, 9, 11, 12, 16, 20; DLB 7; EWL 3; LAIT 3; LMFS 2; MTCW 1, 2; RGAL 4; TUS

Onetti, Juan Carlos 1909-1994 ... **CLC 7, 10; HLCS 2; SSC 23; TCLC 131**
See also CA 85-88; 145; CANR 32, 63; CD-WLB 3; CWW 2; DAM MULT, NOV; DLB 113; EWL 3; HW 1, 2; LAW; MTCW 1, 2; RGSF 2

O Nuallain, Brian 1911-1966
See O'Brien, Flann
See also CA 21-22; 25-28R; CAP 2; DLB 231; FANT; TEA

Ophuls, Max 1902-1957 .... **TCLC 79**
See also CA 113

Opie, Amelia 1769-1853 .... **NCLC 65**
See also DLB 116, 159; RGEL 2

Oppen, George 1908-1984 ..... **CLC 7, 13, 34; PC 35; TCLC 107**
See also CA 13-16R; 113; CANR 8, 82; DLB 5, 165

Oppenheim, E(dward) Phillips
1866-1946 .... **TCLC 45**
See also CA 111; 202; CMW 4; DLB 70

Opuls, Max
See Ophuls, Max

Orage, A(lfred) R(ichard)
1873-1934 .... **TCLC 157**
See also CA 122

Origen c. 185-c. 254 .... **CMLC 19**

Orlovitz, Gil 1918-1973 .... **CLC 22**
See also CA 77-80; 45-48; DLB 2, 5

Orris
See Ingelow, Jean

Ortega y Gasset, Jose 1883-1955 ...... **HLC 2; TCLC 9**
See also CA 106; 130; DAM MULT; EW 9; EWL 3; HW 1, 2; MTCW 1, 2

Ortese, Anna Maria 1914-1998 .... **CLC 89**
See also DLB 177; EWL 3

Ortiz, Simon J(oseph) 1941- .... **CLC 45; NNAL; PC 17**
See also AMWS 4; CA 134; CANR 69, 118; CP 7; DAM MULT, POET; DLB 120, 175, 256; EXPP; PFS 4, 16; RGAL 4

Orton, Joe ...... **CLC 4, 13, 43; DC 3; TCLC 157**
See Orton, John Kingsley
See also BRWS 5; CBD; CDBLB 1960 to Present; DFS 3, 6; DLB 13; GLL 1; MTCW 2; RGEL 2; TEA; WLIT 4

Orton, John Kingsley 1933-1967
See Orton, Joe
See also CA 85-88; CANR 35, 66; DAM DRAM; MTCW 1, 2

Orwell, George ...... **SSC 68; TCLC 2, 6, 15, 31, 51, 128, 129; WLC**
See Blair, Eric (Arthur)
See also BPFB 3; BRW 7; BYA 5; CDBLB 1945-1960; CLR 68; DAB; DLB 15, 98, 195, 255; EWL 3; EXPN; LAIT 4, 5; LATS 1:1; NFS 3, 7; RGEL 2; SCFW 2; SFW 4; SSFS 4; TEA; WLIT 4; YAW

Osborne, David
See Silverberg, Robert

Osborne, George
See Silverberg, Robert

Osborne, John (James) 1929-1994 .... **CLC 1, 2, 5, 11, 45; TCLC 153; WLC**
See also BRWS 1; CA 13-16R; 147; CANR 21, 56; CDBLB 1945-1960; DA; DAB; DAC; DAM DRAM, MST; DFS 4, 19; DLB 13; EWL 3; MTCW 1, 2; RGEL 2

Osborne, Lawrence 1958- .... **CLC 50**
See also CA 189

Osbourne, Lloyd 1868-1947 .... **TCLC 93**

Osgood, Frances Sargent
1811-1850 .... **NCLC 141**
See also DLB 250

Oshima, Nagisa 1932- .... **CLC 20**
See also CA 116; 121; CANR 78

Oskison, John Milton
1874-1947 .... **NNAL; TCLC 35**
See also CA 144; CANR 84; DAM MULT; DLB 175

Ossian c. 3rd cent. - .... **CMLC 28**
See Macpherson, James

Ossoli, Sarah Margaret (Fuller)
1810-1850 .... **NCLC 5, 50**
See Fuller, Margaret; Fuller, Sarah Margaret
See also CDALB 1640-1865; FW; LMFS 1; SATA 25

Ostriker, Alicia (Suskin) 1937- .... **CLC 132**
See also CA 25-28R; CAAS 24; CANR 10, 30, 62, 99; CWP; DLB 120; EXPP; PFS 19

Ostrovsky, Aleksandr Nikolaevich
See Ostrovsky, Alexander
See also DLB 277

Ostrovsky, Alexander 1823-1886 .. **NCLC 30, 57**
See Ostrovsky, Aleksandr Nikolaevich

Otero, Blas de 1916-1979 .... **CLC 11**
See also CA 89-92; DLB 134; EWL 3

O'Trigger, Sir Lucius
See Horne, Richard Henry Hengist

Otto, Rudolf 1869-1937 .... **TCLC 85**

Otto, Whitney 1955- .... **CLC 70**
See also CA 140; CANR 120

Otway, Thomas 1652-1685 ... **DC 24; LC 106**
See also DAM DRAM; DLB 80; RGEL 2

Ouida .... **TCLC 43**
See De la Ramee, Marie Louise (Ouida)
See also DLB 18, 156; RGEL 2

Ouologuem, Yambo 1940- .... **CLC 146**
See also CA 111; 176

Ousmane, Sembene 1923- ... **BLC 3; CLC 66**
See Sembene, Ousmane
See also BW 1, 3; CA 117; 125; CANR 81; CWW 2; MTCW 1

Ovid 43B.C.-17 .... **CMLC 7; PC 2**
See also AW 2; CDWLB 1; DA3; DAM POET; DLB 211; RGWL 2, 3; WP

Owen, Hugh
See Faust, Frederick (Schiller)

Owen, Wilfred (Edward Salter)
1893-1918 ... **PC 19; TCLC 5, 27; WLC**
See also BRW 6; CA 104; 141; CDBLB 1914-1945; DA; DAB; DAC; DAM MST, POET; DLB 20; EWL 3; EXPP; MTCW 2; PFS 10; RGEL 2; WLIT 4

Owens, Louis (Dean) 1948-2002 .... **NNAL**
See also CA 137, 179; 207; CAAE 179; CAAS 24; CANR 71

Owens, Rochelle 1936- .... **CLC 8**
See also CA 17-20R; CAAS 2; CAD; CANR 39; CD 5; CP 7; CWD; CWP

Oz, Amos 1939- ...... **CLC 5, 8, 11, 27, 33, 54; SSC 66**
See also CA 53-56; CANR 27, 47, 65, 113; CWW 2; DAM NOV; EWL 3; MTCW 1, 2; RGSF 2; RGWL 3

Ozick, Cynthia 1928- .... **CLC 3, 7, 28, 62, 155; SSC 15, 60**
See also AMWS 5; BEST 90:1; CA 17-20R; CANR 23, 58, 116; CN 7; CPW; DA3; DAM NOV, POP; DLB 28, 152, 299; DLBY 1982; EWL 3; EXPS; INT CANR-23; MTCW 1, 2; RGAL 4; RGSF 2; SSFS 3, 12

Ozu, Yasujiro 1903-1963 .... **CLC 16**
See also CA 112

Pabst, G. W. 1885-1967 .... **TCLC 127**

Pacheco, C.
See Pessoa, Fernando (Antonio Nogueira)

Pacheco, Jose Emilio 1939- .... **HLC 2**
See also CA 111; 131; CANR 65; CWW 2; DAM MULT; DLB 290; EWL 3; HW 1, 2; RGSF 2

Pa Chin .... **CLC 18**
See Li Fei-kan
See also EWL 3

Pack, Robert 1929- .... **CLC 13**
See also CA 1-4R; CANR 3, 44, 82; CP 7; DLB 5; SATA 118

Padgett, Lewis
See Kuttner, Henry

Padilla (Lorenzo), Heberto
1932-2000 .... **CLC 38**
See also AITN 1; CA 123; 131; 189; CWW 2; EWL 3; HW 1

Page, James Patrick 1944-
See Page, Jimmy
See also CA 204

Page, Jimmy 1944- .... **CLC 12**
See Page, James Patrick

Page, Louise 1955- .... **CLC 40**
See also CA 140; CANR 76; CBD; CD 5; CWD; DLB 233

Page, P(atricia) K(athleen) 1916- ...... **CLC 7, 18; PC 12**
See Cape, Judith
See also CA 53-56; CANR 4, 22, 65; CP 7; DAC; DAM MST; DLB 68; MTCW 1; RGEL 2

Page, Stanton
See Fuller, Henry Blake

Page, Stanton
See Fuller, Henry Blake

Page, Thomas Nelson 1853-1922 .... **SSC 23**
See also CA 118; 177; DLB 12, 78; DLBD 13; RGAL 4

Pagels, Elaine Hiesey 1943- .... **CLC 104**
See also CA 45-48; CANR 2, 24, 51; FW; NCFS 4

Paget, Violet 1856-1935
See Lee, Vernon
See also CA 104; 166; GLL 1; HGG

Paget-Lowe, Henry
See Lovecraft, H(oward) P(hillips)

Paglia, Camille (Anna) 1947- .... **CLC 68**
See also CA 140; CANR 72; CPW; FW; GLL 2; MTCW 2

Paige, Richard
See Koontz, Dean R(ay)

Paine, Thomas 1737-1809 .... **NCLC 62**
See also AMWS 1; CDALB 1640-1865; DLB 31, 43, 73, 158; LAIT 1; RGAL 4; RGEL 2; TUS

Pakenham, Antonia
See Fraser, Antonia (Pakenham)

Palamas, Costis
See Palamas, Kostes

Palamas, Kostes 1859-1943 .... **TCLC 5**
See Palamas, Kostis
See also CA 105; 190; RGWL 2, 3

Palamas, Kostis
See Palamas, Kostes
See also EWL 3

Palazzeschi, Aldo 1885-1974 .... **CLC 11**
See also CA 89-92; 53-56; DLB 114, 264; EWL 3

Pales Matos, Luis 1898-1959 .... **HLCS 2**
See Pales Matos, Luis
See also DLB 290; HW 1; LAW

Paley, Grace 1922- .. **CLC 4, 6, 37, 140; SSC 8**
See also AMWS 6; CA 25-28R; CANR 13, 46, 74, 118; CN 7; CPW; DA3; DAM POP; DLB 28, 218; EWL 3; EXPS; FW; INT CANR-13; MAWW; MTCW 1, 2; RGAL 4; RGSF 2; SSFS 3, 20

Roberts, Kate 1891-1985 .... **CLC 15**
 See also CA 107; 116
Roberts, Keith (John Kingston)
 1935-2000 .... **CLC 14**
 See also BRWS 10; CA 25-28R; CANR 46;
 DLB 261; SFW 4
Roberts, Kenneth (Lewis)
 1885-1957 .... **TCLC 23**
 See also CA 109; 199; DLB 9; RGAL 4;
 RHW
Roberts, Michele (Brigitte) 1949- .... **CLC 48,**
 178
 See also CA 115; CANR 58, 120; CN 7;
 DLB 231; FW
Robertson, Ellis
 See Ellison, Harlan (Jay); Silverberg, Robert
Robertson, Thomas William
 1829-1871 .... **NCLC 35**
 See Robertson, Tom
 See also DAM DRAM
Robertson, Tom
 See Robertson, Thomas William
 See also RGEL 2
Robeson, Kenneth
 See Dent, Lester
Robinson, Edwin Arlington
 1869-1935 .... **PC 1, 35; TCLC 5, 101**
 See also AMW; CA 104; 133; CDALB
 1865-1917; DA; DAC; DAM MST,
 POET; DLB 54; EWL 3; EXPP; PFS 4; RGAL 4; WP
Robinson, Henry Crabb
 1775-1867 .... **NCLC 15**
 See also DLB 107
Robinson, Jill 1936- .... **CLC 10**
 See also CA 102; CANR 120; INT CA-102
Robinson, Kim Stanley 1952- .... **CLC 34**
 See also AAYA 26; CA 126; CANR 113;
 CN 7; SATA 109; SCFW 2; SFW 4
Robinson, Lloyd
 See Silverberg, Robert
Robinson, Marilynne 1944- ...... **CLC 25, 180**
 See also CA 116; CANR 80; CN 7; DLB
 206
Robinson, Mary 1758-1800 .... **NCLC 142**
 See also DLB 158; FW
Robinson, Smokey .... **CLC 21**
 See Robinson, William, Jr.
Robinson, William, Jr. 1940-
 See Robinson, Smokey
 See also CA 116
Robison, Mary 1949- .... **CLC 42, 98**
 See also CA 113; 116; CANR 87; CN 7;
 DLB 130; INT CA-116; RGSF 2
Rochester
 See Wilmot, John
 See also RGEL 2
Rod, Edouard 1857-1910 .... **TCLC 52**
Roddenberry, Eugene Wesley 1921-1991
 See Roddenberry, Gene
 See also CA 110; 135; CANR 37; SATA 45;
 SATA-Obit 69
Roddenberry, Gene .... **CLC 17**
 See Roddenberry, Eugene Wesley
 See also AAYA 5; SATA-Obit 69
Rodgers, Mary 1931- .... **CLC 12**
 See also BYA 5; CA 49-52; CANR 8, 55,
 90; CLR 20; CWRI 5; INT CANR-8;
 JRDA; MAICYA 1, 2; SATA 8, 130
Rodgers, W(illiam) R(obert)
 1909-1969 .... **CLC 7**
 See also CA 85-88; DLB 20; RGEL 2
Rodman, Eric
 See Silverberg, Robert
Rodman, Howard 1920(?)-1985 .... **CLC 65**
 See also CA 118
Rodman, Maia
 See Wojciechowska, Maia (Teresa)

Rodo, Jose Enrique 1871(?)-1917 .... **HLCS 2**
 See also CA 178; EWL 3; HW 2; LAW
Rodolph, Utto
 See Ouologuem, Yambo
Rodriguez, Claudio 1934-1999 .... **CLC 10**
 See also CA 188; DLB 134
Rodriguez, Richard 1944- .... **CLC 155; HLC**
 2
 See also AMWS 14; CA 110; CANR 66,
 116; DAM MULT; DLB 82, 256; HW 1,
 2; LAIT 5; LLW 1; NCFS 3; WLIT 1
Roelvaag, O(le) E(dvart) 1876-1931
 See Rolvaag, O(le) E(dvart)
 See also CA 117; 171
Roethke, Theodore (Huebner)
 1908-1963 .... **CLC 1, 3, 8, 11, 19, 46,**
 101; PC 15
 See also AMW; CA 81-84; CABS 2;
 CDALB 1941-1968; DA3; DAM POET;
 DLB 5, 206; EWL 3; EXPP; MTCW 1, 2;
 PAB; PFS 3; RGAL 4; WP
Rogers, Carl R(ansom)
 1902-1987 .... **TCLC 125**
 See also CA 1-4R; 121; CANR 1, 18;
 MTCW 1
Rogers, Samuel 1763-1855 .... **NCLC 69**
 See also DLB 93; RGEL 2
Rogers, Thomas Hunton 1927- .... **CLC 57**
 See also CA 89-92; INT CA-89-92
Rogers, Will(iam Penn Adair)
 1879-1935 .... **NNAL; TCLC 8, 71**
 See also CA 105; 144; DA3; DAM MULT;
 DLB 11; MTCW 2
Rogin, Gilbert 1929- .... **CLC 18**
 See also CA 65-68; CANR 15
Rohan, Koda
 See Koda Shigeyuki
Rohlfs, Anna Katharine Green
 See Green, Anna Katharine
Rohmer, Eric .... **CLC 16**
 See Scherer, Jean-Marie Maurice
Rohmer, Sax .... **TCLC 28**
 See Ward, Arthur Henry Sarsfield
 See also DLB 70; MSW; SUFW
Roiphe, Anne (Richardson) 1935- .. **CLC 3, 9**
 See also CA 89-92; CANR 45, 73; DLBY
 1980; INT CA-89-92
Rojas, Fernando de 1475-1541 ... **HLCS 1, 2;**
 LC 23
 See also DLB 286; RGWL 2, 3
Rojas, Gonzalo 1917- .... **HLCS 2**
 See also CA 178; HW 2; LAWS 1
Roland, Marie-Jeanne 1754-1793 .... **LC 98**
Rolfe, Frederick (William Serafino Austin
 Lewis Mary) 1860-1913 .... **TCLC 12**
 See Al Siddik
 See also CA 107; 210; DLB 34, 156; RGEL
 2
Rolland, Romain 1866-1944 .... **TCLC 23**
 See also CA 118; 197; DLB 65, 284; EWL
 3; GFL 1789 to the Present; RGWL 2, 3
Rolle, Richard c. 1300-c. 1349 ...... **CMLC 21**
 See also DLB 146; LMFS 1; RGEL 2
Rolvaag, O(le) E(dvart) .... **TCLC 17**
 See Roelvaag, O(le) E(dvart)
 See also DLB 9, 212; NFS 5; RGAL 4
Romain Arnaud, Saint
 See Aragon, Louis
Romains, Jules 1885-1972 .... **CLC 7**
 See also CA 85-88; CANR 34; DLB 65;
 EWL 3; GFL 1789 to the Present; MTCW
 1
Romero, Jose Ruben 1890-1952 .... **TCLC 14**
 See also CA 114; 131; EWL 3; HW 1; LAW
Ronsard, Pierre de 1524-1585 . **LC 6, 54; PC**
 11
 See also EW 2; GFL Beginnings to 1789;
 RGWL 2, 3; TWA

Rooke, Leon 1934- .... **CLC 25, 34**
 See also CA 25-28R; CANR 23, 53; CCA
 1; CPW; DAM POP
Roosevelt, Franklin Delano
 1882-1945 .... **TCLC 93**
 See also CA 116; 173; LAIT 3
Roosevelt, Theodore 1858-1919 ..... **TCLC 69**
 See also CA 115; 170; DLB 47, 186, 275
Roper, William 1498-1578 .... **LC 10**
Roquelaure, A. N.
 See Rice, Anne
Rosa, Joao Guimaraes 1908-1967 ... **CLC 23;**
 HLCS 1
 See Guimaraes Rosa, Joao
 See also CA 89-92; DLB 113, 307; EWL 3;
 WLIT 1
Rose, Wendy 1948- . **CLC 85; NNAL; PC 13**
 See also CA 53-56; CANR 5, 51; CWP;
 DAM MULT; DLB 175; PFS 13; RGAL
 4; SATA 12
Rosen, R. D.
 See Rosen, Richard (Dean)
Rosen, Richard (Dean) 1949- .... **CLC 39**
 See also CA 77-80; CANR 62, 120; CMW
 4; INT CANR-30
Rosenberg, Isaac 1890-1918 .... **TCLC 12**
 See also BRW 6; CA 107; 188; DLB 20,
 216; EWL 3; PAB; RGEL 2
Rosenblatt, Joe .... **CLC 15**
 See Rosenblatt, Joseph
Rosenblatt, Joseph 1933-
 See Rosenblatt, Joe
 See also CA 89-92; CP 7; INT CA-89-92
Rosenfeld, Samuel
 See Tzara, Tristan
Rosenstock, Sami
 See Tzara, Tristan
Rosenstock, Samuel
 See Tzara, Tristan
Rosenthal, M(acha) L(ouis)
 1917-1996 .... **CLC 28**
 See also CA 1-4R; 152; CAAS 6; CANR 4,
 51; CP 7; DLB 5; SATA 59
Ross, Barnaby
 See Dannay, Frederic
Ross, Bernard L.
 See Follett, Ken(neth Martin)
Ross, J. H.
 See Lawrence, T(homas) E(dward)
Ross, John Hume
 See Lawrence, T(homas) E(dward)
Ross, Martin 1862-1915
 See Martin, Violet Florence
 See also DLB 135; GLL 2; RGEL 2; RGSF
 2
Ross, (James) Sinclair 1908-1996 ... **CLC 13;**
 SSC 24
 See also CA 73-76; CANR 81; CN 7; DAC;
 DAM MST; DLB 88; RGEL 2; RGSF 2;
 TCWW 2
Rossetti, Christina (Georgina)
 1830-1894 .... **NCLC 2, 50, 66; PC 7;**
 WLC
 See also AAYA 51; BRW 5; BYA 4; DA;
 DA3; DAB; DAC; DAM MST, POET;
 DLB 35, 163, 240; EXPP; LATS 1:1;
 MAICYA 1, 2; PFS 10, 14; RGEL 2;
 SATA 20; TEA; WCH
Rossetti, Dante Gabriel 1828-1882 . **NCLC 4,**
 77; PC 44; WLC
 See also AAYA 51; BRW 5; CDBLB 1832-
 1890; DA; DAB; DAC; DAM MST,
 POET; DLB 35; EXPP; RGEL 2; TEA
Rossi, Cristina Peri
 See Peri Rossi, Cristina
Rossi, Jean-Baptiste 1931-2003
 See Japrisot, Sebastien
 See also CA 201; 215

Rossner, Judith (Perelman) 1935- . **CLC 6, 9, 29**
See also AITN 2; BEST 90:3; BPFB 3; CA 17-20R; CANR 18, 51, 73; CN 7; DLB 6; INT CANR-18; MTCW 1, 2

Rostand, Edmond (Eugene Alexis) 1868-1918 .... **DC 10; TCLC 6, 37**
See also CA 104; 126; DA; DA3; DAB; DAC; DAM DRAM, MST; DFS 1; DLB 192; LAIT 1; MTCW 1; RGWL 2, 3; TWA

Roth, Henry 1906-1995 ..... **CLC 2, 6, 11, 104**
See also AMWS 9; CA 11-12; 149; CANR 38, 63; CAP 1; CN 7; DA3; DLB 28; EWL 3; MTCW 1, 2; RGAL 4

Roth, (Moses) Joseph 1894-1939 ... **TCLC 33**
See also CA 160; DLB 85; EWL 3; RGWL 2, 3

Roth, Philip (Milton) 1933- ... **CLC 1, 2, 3, 4, 6, 9, 15, 22, 31, 47, 66, 86, 119, 201; SSC 26; WLC**
See also AMWR 2; AMWS 3; BEST 90:3; BPFB 3; CA 1-4R; CANR 1, 22, 36, 55, 89, 132; CDALB 1968-1988; CN 7; CPW 1; DA; DA3; DAB; DAC; DAM MST, NOV, POP; DLB 2, 28, 173; DLBY 1982; EWL 3; MTCW 1, 2; RGAL 4; RGSF 2; SSFS 12, 18; TUS

Rothenberg, Jerome 1931- .... **CLC 6, 57**
See also CA 45-48; CANR 1, 106; CP 7; DLB 5, 193

Rotter, Pat ed. .... **CLC 65**

Roumain, Jacques (Jean Baptiste) 1907-1944 .... **BLC 3; TCLC 19**
See also BW 1; CA 117; 125; DAM MULT; EWL 3

Rourke, Constance Mayfield 1885-1941 .... **TCLC 12**
See also CA 107; 200; YABC 1

Rousseau, Jean-Baptiste 1671-1741 ...... **LC 9**

Rousseau, Jean-Jacques 1712-1778 .... **LC 14, 36; WLC**
See also DA; DA3; DAB; DAC; DAM MST; EW 4; GFL Beginnings to 1789; LMFS 1; RGWL 2, 3; TWA

Roussel, Raymond 1877-1933 .... **TCLC 20**
See also CA 117; 201; EWL 3; GFL 1789 to the Present

Rovit, Earl (Herbert) 1927- .... **CLC 7**
See also CA 5-8R; CANR 12

Rowe, Elizabeth Singer 1674-1737 ..... **LC 44**
See also DLB 39, 95

Rowe, Nicholas 1674-1718 .... **LC 8**
See also DLB 84; RGEL 2

Rowlandson, Mary 1637(?)-1678 .... **LC 66**
See also DLB 24, 200; RGAL 4

Rowley, Ames Dorrance
See Lovecraft, H(oward) P(hillips)

Rowley, William 1585(?)-1626 .... **LC 100**
See also DLB 58; RGEL 2

Rowling, J(oanne) K(athleen) 1966- .... **CLC 137**
See also AAYA 34; BYA 11, 13, 14; CA 173; CANR 128; CLR 66, 80; MAICYA 2; SATA 109; SUFW 2

Rowson, Susanna Haswell 1762(?)-1824 .... **NCLC 5, 69**
See also DLB 37, 200; RGAL 4

Roy, Arundhati 1960(?)- .... **CLC 109**
See also CA 163; CANR 90, 126; DLBY 1997; EWL 3; LATS 1:2; WWE 1

Roy, Gabrielle 1909-1983 .... **CLC 10, 14**
See also CA 53-56; 110; CANR 5, 61; CCA 1; DAB; DAC; DAM MST; DLB 68; EWL 3; MTCW 1; RGWL 2, 3; SATA 104

Royko, Mike 1932-1997 .... **CLC 109**
See also CA 89-92; 157; CANR 26, 111; CPW

Rozanov, Vasilii Vasil'evich
See Rozanov, Vassili
See also DLB 295

Rozanov, Vasily Vasilyevich
See Rozanov, Vassili
See also EWL 3

Rozanov, Vassili 1856-1919 .... **TCLC 104**
See Rozanov, Vasilii Vasil'evich; Rozanov, Vasily Vasilyevich

Rozewicz, Tadeusz 1921- ...... **CLC 9, 23, 139**
See also CA 108; CANR 36, 66; CWW 2; DA3; DAM POET; DLB 232; EWL 3; MTCW 1, 2; RGWL 3

Ruark, Gibbons 1941- .... **CLC 3**
See also CA 33-36R; CAAS 23; CANR 14, 31, 57; DLB 120

Rubens, Bernice (Ruth) 1923-2004 . **CLC 19, 31**
See also CA 25-28R; CANR 33, 65, 128; CN 7; DLB 14, 207; MTCW 1

Rubin, Harold
See Robbins, Harold

Rudkin, (James) David 1936- .... **CLC 14**
See also CA 89-92; CBD; CD 5; DLB 13

Rudnik, Raphael 1933- .... **CLC 7**
See also CA 29-32R

Ruffian, M.
See Hasek, Jaroslav (Matej Frantisek)

Ruiz, Jose Martinez .... **CLC 11**
See Martinez Ruiz, Jose

Ruiz, Juan c. 1283-c. 1350 .... **CMLC 66**

Rukeyser, Muriel 1913-1980 . **CLC 6, 10, 15, 27; PC 12**
See also AMWS 6; CA 5-8R; 93-96; CANR 26, 60; DA3; DAM POET; DLB 48; EWL 3; FW; GLL 2; MTCW 1, 2; PFS 10; RGAL 4; SATA-Obit 22

Rule, Jane (Vance) 1931- .... **CLC 27**
See also CA 25-28R; CAAS 18; CANR 12, 87; CN 7; DLB 60; FW

Rulfo, Juan 1918-1986 .. **CLC 8, 80; HLC 2; SSC 25**
See also CA 85-88; 118; CANR 26; CD-WLB 3; DAM MULT; DLB 113; EWL 3; HW 1, 2; LAW; MTCW 1, 2; RGSF 2; RGWL 2, 3; WLIT 1

Rumi, Jalal al-Din 1207-1273 ...... **CMLC 20; PC 45**
See also RGWL 2, 3; WP

Runeberg, Johan 1804-1877 .... **NCLC 41**

Runyon, (Alfred) Damon 1884(?)-1946 .... **TCLC 10**
See also CA 107; 165; DLB 11, 86, 171; MTCW 2; RGAL 4

Rush, Norman 1933- .... **CLC 44**
See also CA 121; 126; CANR 130; INT CA-126

Rushdie, (Ahmed) Salman 1947- .... **CLC 23, 31, 55, 100, 191; WLCS**
See also BEST 89:3; BPFB 3; BRWS 4; CA 108; 111; CANR 33, 56, 108, 133; CN 7; CPW 1; DA3; DAB; DAC; DAM MST, NOV, POP; DLB 194; EWL 3; FANT; INT CA-111; LATS 1:2; LMFS 2; MTCW 1, 2; RGEL 2; RGSF 2; TEA; WLIT 4; WWE 1

Rushforth, Peter (Scott) 1945- .... **CLC 19**
See also CA 101

Ruskin, John 1819-1900 .... **TCLC 63**
See also BRW 5; BYA 5; CA 114; 129; CD-BLB 1832-1890; DLB 55, 163, 190; RGEL 2; SATA 24; TEA; WCH

Russ, Joanna 1937- .... **CLC 15**
See also BPFB 3; CA 5-28R; CANR 11, 31, 65; CN 7; DLB 8; FW; GLL 1; MTCW 1; SCFW 2; SFW 4

Russ, Richard Patrick
See O'Brian, Patrick

Russell, George William 1867-1935
See A.E.; Baker, Jean H.
See also BRWS 8; CA 104; 153; CDBLB 1890-1914; DAM POET; EWL 3; RGEL 2

Russell, Jeffrey Burton 1934- .... **CLC 70**
See also CA 25-28R; CANR 11, 28, 52

Russell, (Henry) Ken(neth Alfred) 1927- .... **CLC 16**
See also CA 105

Russell, William Martin 1947-
See Russell, Willy
See also CA 164; CANR 107

Russell, Willy .... **CLC 60**
See Russell, William Martin
See also CBD; CD 5; DLB 233

Russo, Richard 1949- .... **CLC 181**
See also AMWS 12; CA 127; 133; CANR 87, 114

Rutherford, Mark .... **TCLC 25**
See White, William Hale
See also DLB 18; RGEL 2

Ruyslinck, Ward .... **CLC 14**
See Belser, Reimond Karel Maria de

Ryan, Cornelius (John) 1920-1974 ..... **CLC 7**
See also CA 69-72; 53-56; CANR 38

Ryan, Michael 1946- .... **CLC 65**
See also CA 49-52; CANR 109; DLBY 1982

Ryan, Tim
See Dent, Lester

Rybakov, Anatoli (Naumovich) 1911-1998 .... **CLC 23, 53**
See Rybakov, Anatolii (Naumovich)
See also CA 126; 135; 172; SATA 79; SATA-Obit 108

Rybakov, Anatolii (Naumovich)
See Rybakov, Anatoli (Naumovich)
See also DLB 302

Ryder, Jonathan
See Ludlum, Robert

Ryga, George 1932-1987 .... **CLC 14**
See also CA 101; 124; CANR 43, 90; CCA 1; DAC; DAM MST; DLB 60

S. H.
See Hartmann, Sadakichi

S. S.
See Sassoon, Siegfried (Lorraine)

Sa'adawi, al- Nawal
See El Saadawi, Nawal
See also AFW; EWL 3

Saadawi, Nawal El
See El Saadawi, Nawal
See also WLIT 2

Saba, Umberto 1883-1957 .... **TCLC 33**
See also CA 144; CANR 79; DLB 114; EWL 3; RGWL 2, 3

Sabatini, Rafael 1875-1950 .... **TCLC 47**
See also BPFB 3; CA 162; RHW

Sabato, Ernesto (R.) 1911- .... **CLC 10, 23; HLC 2**
See also CA 97-100; CANR 32, 65; CD-WLB 3; CWW 2; DAM MULT; DLB 145; EWL 3; HW 1, 2; LAW; MTCW 1, 2

Sa-Carneiro, Mario de 1890-1916 . **TCLC 83**
See also DLB 287; EWL 3

Sacastru, Martin
See Bioy Casares, Adolfo
See also CWW 2

Sacher-Masoch, Leopold von 1836(?)-1895 .... **NCLC 31**

Sachs, Hans 1494-1576 .... **LC 95**
See also CDWLB 2; DLB 179; RGWL 2, 3

Sachs, Marilyn (Stickle) 1927- .... **CLC 35**
See also AAYA 2; BYA 6; CA 17-20R; CANR 13, 47; CLR 2; JRDA; MAICYA 1, 2; SAAS 2; SATA 3, 68; SATA-Essay 110; WYA; YAW

Sachs, Nelly 1891-1970 .... **CLC 14, 98**
See also CA 17-18; 25-28R; CANR 87;
CAP 2; EWL 3; MTCW 2; PFS 20;
RGWL 2, 3

Sackler, Howard (Oliver)
1929-1982 .... **CLC 14**
See also CA 61-64; 108; CAD; CANR 30;
DFS 15; DLB 7

Sacks, Oliver (Wolf) 1933- .... **CLC 67, 202**
See also CA 53-56; CANR 28, 50, 76;
CPW; DA3; INT CANR-28; MTCW 1, 2

Sackville, Thomas 1536-1608 .... **LC 98**
See also DAM DRAM; DLB 62, 132;
RGEL 2

Sadakichi
See Hartmann, Sadakichi

Sa'dawi, Nawal al-
See El Saadawi, Nawal
See also CWW 2

Sade, Donatien Alphonse Francois
1740-1814 .... **NCLC 3, 47**
See also EW 4; GFL Beginnings to 1789;
RGWL 2, 3

Sade, Marquis de
See Sade, Donatien Alphonse Francois

Sadoff, Ira 1945- .... **CLC 9**
See also CA 53-56; CANR 5, 21, 109; DLB
120

Saetone
See Camus, Albert

Safire, William 1929- .... **CLC 10**
See also CA 17-20R; CANR 31, 54, 91

Sagan, Carl (Edward) 1934-1996 .... **CLC 30,
112**
See also AAYA 2; CA 25-28R; 155; CANR
11, 36, 74; CPW; DA3; MTCW 1, 2;
SATA 58; SATA-Obit 94

Sagan, Francoise .... **CLC 3, 6, 9, 17, 36**
See Quoirez, Francoise
See also CWW 2; DLB 83; EWL 3; GFL
1789 to the Present; MTCW 2

Sahgal, Nayantara (Pandit) 1927- .... **CLC 41**
See also CA 9-12R; CANR 11, 88; CN 7

Said, Edward W. 1935-2003 .... **CLC 123**
See also CA 21-24R; 220; CANR 45, 74,
107, 131; DLB 67; MTCW 2

Saint, H(arry) F. 1941- .... **CLC 50**
See also CA 127

St. Aubin de Teran, Lisa 1953-
See Teran, Lisa St. Aubin de
See also CA 118; 126; CN 7; INT CA-126

Saint Birgitta of Sweden c.
1303-1373 .... **CMLC 24**

Sainte-Beuve, Charles Augustin
1804-1869 .... **NCLC 5**
See also DLB 217; EW 6; GFL 1789 to the
Present

**Saint-Exupery, Antoine (Jean Baptiste
Marie Roger) de** 1900-1944 .... **TCLC 2,
56; WLC**
See also BPFB 3; BYA 3; CA 108; 132;
CLR 10; DA3; DAM NOV; DLB 72; EW
12; EWL 3; GFL 1789 to the Present;
LAIT 3; MAICYA 1, 2; MTCW 1, 2;
RGWL 2, 3; SATA 20; TWA

St. John, David
See Hunt, E(verette) Howard, (Jr.)

St. John, J. Hector
See Crevecoeur, Michel Guillaume Jean de

Saint-John Perse
See Leger, (Marie-Rene Auguste) Alexis
Saint-Leger
See also EW 10; EWL 3; GFL 1789 to the
Present; RGWL 2

Saintsbury, George (Edward Bateman)
1845-1933 .... **TCLC 31**
See also CA 160; DLB 57, 149

Sait Faik .... **TCLC 23**
See Abasiyanik, Sait Faik

Saki .... **SSC 12; TCLC 3**
See Munro, H(ector) H(ugh)
See also BRWS 6; BYA 11; LAIT 2; MTCW
2; RGEL 2; SSFS 1; SUFW

Sala, George Augustus 1828-1895 . **NCLC 46**

Saladin 1138-1193 .... **CMLC 38**

Salama, Hannu 1936- .... **CLC 18**
See also EWL 3

Salamanca, J(ack) R(ichard) 1922- .. **CLC 4,
15**
See also CA 25-28R, 193; CAAE 193

Salas, Floyd Francis 1931- .... **HLC 2**
See also CA 119; CAAS 27; CANR 44, 75,
93; DAM MULT; DLB 82; HW 1, 2;
MTCW 2

Sale, J. Kirkpatrick
See Sale, Kirkpatrick

Sale, Kirkpatrick 1937- .... **CLC 68**
See also CA 13-16R; CANR 10

Salinas, Luis Omar 1937- ... **CLC 90; HLC 2**
See also AMWS 13; CA 131; CANR 81;
DAM MULT; DLB 82; HW 1, 2

Salinas (y Serrano), Pedro
1891(?)-1951 .... **TCLC 17**
See also CA 117; DLB 134; EWL 3

Salinger, J(erome) D(avid) 1919- .. **CLC 1, 3,
8, 12, 55, 56, 138; SSC 2, 28, 65; WLC**
See also AAYA 2, 36; AMW; AMWC 1;
BPFB 3; CA 5-8R; CANR 39, 129;
CDALB 1941-1968; CLR 18; CN 7; CPW
1; DA; DA3; DAB; DAC; DAM MST,
NOV, POP; DLB 2, 102, 173; EWL 3;
EXPN; LAIT 4; MAICYA 1, 2; MTCW
1, 2; NFS 1; RGAL 4; RGSF 2; SATA 67;
SSFS 17; TUS; WYA; YAW

Salisbury, John
See Caute, (John) David

Sallust c. 86B.C.-35B.C. .... **CMLC 68**
See also AW 2; CDWLB 1; DLB 211;
RGWL 2, 3

Salter, James 1925- .. **CLC 7, 52, 59; SSC 58**
See also AMWS 9; CA 73-76; CANR 107;
DLB 130

Saltus, Edgar (Everton) 1855-1921 . **TCLC 8**
See also CA 105; DLB 202; RGAL 4

Saltykov, Mikhail Evgrafovich
1826-1889 .... **NCLC 16**
See also DLB 238:

Saltykov-Shchedrin, N.
See Saltykov, Mikhail Evgrafovich

Samarakis, Andonis
See Samarakis, Antonis
See also EWL 3

Samarakis, Antonis 1919-2003 .... **CLC 5**
See Samarakis, Andonis
See also CA 25-28R; 224; CAAS 16; CANR
36

Sanchez, Florencio 1875-1910 .... **TCLC 37**
See also CA 153; DLB 305; EWL 3; HW 1;
LAW

Sanchez, Luis Rafael 1936- .... **CLC 23**
See also CA 128; DLB 305; EWL 3; HW 1;
WLIT 1

Sanchez, Sonia 1934- .... **BLC 3; CLC 5, 116;
PC 9**
See also BW 2, 3; CA 33-36R; CANR 24,
49, 74, 115; CLR 18; CP 7; CSW; CWP;
DA3; DAM MULT; DLB 41; DLBD 8;
EWL 3; MAICYA 1, 2; MTCW 1, 2;
SATA 22, 136; WP

Sancho, Ignatius 1729-1780 .... **LC 84**

Sand, George 1804-1876 ..... **NCLC 2, 42, 57;
WLC**
See also DA; DA3; DAB; DAC; DAM
MST, NOV; DLB 119, 192; EW 6; FW;
GFL 1789 to the Present; RGWL 2, 3;
TWA

Sandburg, Carl (August) 1878-1967 . **CLC 1,
4, 10, 15, 35; PC 2, 41; WLC**
See also AAYA 24; AMW; BYA 1, 3; CA
5-8R; 25-28R; CANR 35; CDALB 1865-
1917; CLR 67; DA; DA3; DAB; DAC;
DAM MST, POET; DLB 17, 54, 284;
EWL 3; EXPP; LAIT 2; MAICYA 1, 2;
MTCW 1, 2; PAB; PFS 3, 6, 12; RGAL
4; SATA 8; TUS; WCH; WP; WYA

Sandburg, Charles
See Sandburg, Carl (August)

Sandburg, Charles A.
See Sandburg, Carl (August)

Sanders, (James) Ed(ward) 1939- .... **CLC 53**
See Sanders, Edward
See also BG 3; CA 13-16R; CAAS 21;
CANR 13, 44, 78; CP 7; DAM POET;
DLB 16, 244

Sanders, Edward
See Sanders, (James) Ed(ward)
See also DLB 244

Sanders, Lawrence 1920-1998 .... **CLC 41**
See also BEST 89:4; BPFB 3; CA 81-84;
165; CANR 33, 62; CMW 4; CPW; DA3;
DAM POP; MTCW 1

Sanders, Noah
See Blount, Roy (Alton), Jr.

Sanders, Winston P.
See Anderson, Poul (William)

Sandoz, Mari(e Susette) 1900-1966 .. **CLC 28**
See also CA 1-4R; 25-28R; CANR 17, 64;
DLB 9, 212; LAIT 2; MTCW 1, 2; SATA
5; TCWW 2

Sandys, George 1578-1644 .... **LC 80**
See also DLB 24, 121

Saner, Reg(inald Anthony) 1931- .... **CLC 9**
See also CA 65-68; CP 7

Sankara 788-820 .... **CMLC 32**

Sannazaro, Jacopo 1456(?)-1530 .... **LC 8**
See also RGWL 2, 3

Sansom, William 1912-1976 . **CLC 2, 6; SSC
21**
See also CA 5-8R; 65-68; CANR 42; DAM
NOV; DLB 139; EWL 3; MTCW 1;
RGEL 2; RGSF 2

Santayana, George 1863-1952 .... **TCLC 40**
See also AMW; CA 115; 194; DLB 54, 71,
246, 270; DLBD 13; EWL 3; RGAL 4;
TUS

Santiago, Danny .... **CLC 33**
See James, Daniel (Lewis)
See also DLB 122

**Santillana, Íñigo López de Mendoza,
Marqués de** 1398-1458 .... **LC 111**
See also DLB 286

Santmyer, Helen Hooven
1895-1986 .... **CLC 33; TCLC 133**
See also CA 1-4R; 118; CANR 15, 33;
DLBY 1984; MTCW 1; RHW

Santoka, Taneda 1882-1940 .... **TCLC 72**

Santos, Bienvenido N(uqui)
1911-1996 ... **AAL; CLC 22; TCLC 156**
See also CA 101; 151; CANR 19, 46; DAM
MULT; EWL; RGAL 4; SSFS 19

Sapir, Edward 1884-1939 .... **TCLC 108**
See also CA 211; DLB 92

Sapper .... **TCLC 44**
See McNeile, Herman Cyril

Sapphire
See Sapphire, Brenda

Sapphire, Brenda 1950- .... **CLC 99**

Sappho fl. 6th cent. B.C.- ... **CMLC 3, 67; PC
5**
See also CDWLB 1; DA3; DAM POET;
DLB 176; PFS 20; RGWL 2, 3; WP

Saramago, Jose 1922- ..... **CLC 119; HLCS 1**
See also CA 153; CANR 96; CWW 2; DLB
287; EWL 3; LATS 1:2

Schwarz-Bart, Simone 1938- . **BLCS; CLC 7**
  See also BW 2; CA 97-100; CANR 117;
  EWL 3

Schwerner, Armand 1927-1999 .... **PC 42**
  See also CA 9-12R; 179; CANR 50, 85; CP
  7; DLB 165

Schwitters, Kurt (Hermann Edward Karl
  Julius) 1887-1948 .... **TCLC 95**
  See also CA 158

Schwob, Marcel (Mayer Andre)
  1867-1905 .... **TCLC 20**
  See also CA 117; 168; DLB 123; GFL 1789
  to the Present

Sciascia, Leonardo 1921-1989 .. **CLC 8, 9, 41**
  See also CA 85-88; 130; CANR 35; DLB
  177; EWL 3; MTCW 1; RGWL 2, 3

Scoppettone, Sandra 1936- .... **CLC 26**
  See Early, Jack
  See also AAYA 11; BYA 8; CA 5-8R;
  CANR 41, 73; GLL 1; MAICYA 2; MAI-
  CYAS 1; SATA 9, 92; WYA; YAW

Scorsese, Martin 1942- .... **CLC 20, 89**
  See also AAYA 38; CA 110; 114; CANR
  46, 85

Scotland, Jay
  See Jakes, John (William)

Scott, Duncan Campbell
  1862-1947 .... **TCLC 6**
  See also CA 104; 153; DAC; DLB 92;
  RGEL 2

Scott, Evelyn 1893-1963 .... **CLC 43**
  See also CA 104; 112; CANR 64; DLB 9,
  48; RHW

Scott, F(rancis) R(eginald)
  1899-1985 .... **CLC 22**
  See also CA 101; 114; CANR 87; DLB 88;
  INT CA-101; RGEL 2

Scott, Frank
  See Scott, F(rancis) R(eginald)

Scott, Joan .... **CLC 65**

Scott, Joanna 1960- .... **CLC 50**
  See also CA 126; CANR 53, 92

Scott, Paul (Mark) 1920-1978 ...... **CLC 9, 60**
  See also BRWS 1; CA 81-84; 77-80; CANR
  33; DLB 14, 207; EWL 3; MTCW 1;
  RGEL 2; RHW; WWE 1

Scott, Ridley 1937- .... **CLC 183**
  See also AAYA 13, 43

Scott, Sarah 1723-1795 .... **LC 44**
  See also DLB 39

Scott, Sir Walter 1771-1832 .... **NCLC 15, 69,**
  110; PC 13; SSC 32; WLC
  See also AAYA 22; BRW 4; BYA 2; CD-
  BLB 1789-1832; DA; DAB; DAC; DAM
  MST, NOV, POET; DLB 93, 107, 116,
  144, 159; HGG; LAIT 1; RGEL 2; RGSF
  2; SSFS 10; SUFW 1; TEA; WLIT 3;
  YABC 2

Scribe, (Augustin) Eugene 1791-1861 . **DC 5;**
  NCLC 16
  See also DAM DRAM; DLB 192; GFL
  1789 to the Present; RGWL 2, 3

Scrum, R.
  See Crumb, R(obert)

Scudery, Georges de 1601-1667 .... **LC 75**
  See also GFL Beginnings to 1789

Scudery, Madeleine de 1607-1701 .. **LC 2, 58**
  See also DLB 268; GFL Beginnings to 1789

Scum
  See Crumb, R(obert)

Scumbag, Little Bobby
  See Crumb, R(obert)

Seabrook, John
  See Hubbard, L(afayette) Ron(ald)

Seacole, Mary Jane Grant
  1805-1881 .... **NCLC 147**
  See also DLB 166

Sealy, I(rwin) Allan 1951- .... **CLC 55**
  See also CA 136; CN 7

Search, Alexander
  See Pessoa, Fernando (Antonio Nogueira)

Sebald, W(infried) G(eorg)
  1944-2001 .... **CLC 194**
  See also BRWS 8; CA 159; 202; CANR 98

Sebastian, Lee
  See Silverberg, Robert

Sebastian Owl
  See Thompson, Hunter S(tockton)

Sebestyen, Igen
  See Sebestyen, Ouida

Sebestyen, Ouida 1924- .... **CLC 30**
  See also AAYA 8; BYA 7; CA 107; CANR
  40, 114; CLR 17; JRDA; MAICYA 1, 2;
  SAAS 10; SATA 39, 140; WYA; YAW

Sebold, Alice 1963(?)- .... **CLC 193**
  See also AAYA 56; CA 203

Second Duke of Buckingham
  See Villiers, George

Secundus, H. Scriblerus
  See Fielding, Henry

Sedges, John
  See Buck, Pearl S(ydenstricker)

Sedgwick, Catharine Maria
  1789-1867 .... **NCLC 19, 98**
  See also DLB 1, 74, 183, 239, 243, 254;
  RGAL 4

Seelye, John (Douglas) 1931- .... **CLC 7**
  See also CA 97-100; CANR 70; INT CA-
  97-100; TCWW 2

Seferiades, Giorgos Stylianou 1900-1971
  See Seferis, George
  See also CA 5-8R; 33-36R; CANR 5, 36;
  MTCW 1

Seferis, George .... **CLC 5, 11**
  See Seferiades, Giorgos Stylianou
  See also EW 12; EWL 3; RGWL 2, 3

Segal, Erich (Wolf) 1937- .... **CLC 3, 10**
  See also BEST 89:1; BPFB 3; CA 25-28R;
  CANR 20, 36, 65, 113; CPW; DAM POP;
  DLBY 1986; INT CANR-20; MTCW 1

Seger, Bob 1945- .... **CLC 35**

Seghers, Anna .... **CLC 7**
  See Radvanyi, Netty
  See also CDWLB 2; DLB 69; EWL 3

Seidel, Frederick (Lewis) 1936- .... **CLC 18**
  See also CA 13-16R; CANR 8, 99; CP 7;
  DLBY 1984

Seifert, Jaroslav 1901-1986 . **CLC 34, 44, 93;**
  PC 47
  See also CA 127; CDWLB 4; DLB 215;
  EWL 3; MTCW 1, 2

Sei Shonagon c. 966-1017(?) .... **CMLC 6**

Sejour, Victor 1817-1874 .... **DC 10**
  See also DLB 50

Sejour Marcou et Ferrand, Juan Victor
  See Sejour, Victor

Selby, Hubert, Jr. 1928-2004 ..... **CLC 1, 2, 4,**
  8; SSC 20
  See also CA 13-16R; 226; CANR 33, 85;
  CN 7; DLB 2, 227

Selzer, Richard 1928- .... **CLC 74**
  See also CA 65-68; CANR 14, 106

Sembene, Ousmane
  See Ousmane, Sembene
  See also AFW; EWL 3; WLIT 2

Senancour, Etienne Pivert de
  1770-1846 .... **NCLC 16**
  See also DLB 119; GFL 1789 to the Present

Sender, Ramon (Jose) 1902-1982 ...... **CLC 8;**
  HLC 2; TCLC 136
  See also CA 5-8R; 105; CANR 8; DAM
  MULT; EWL 3; HW 1; MTCW 1; RGWL
  2, 3

Seneca, Lucius Annaeus c. 4B.C.-c.
  65 .... **CMLC 6; DC 5**
  See also AW 2; CDWLB 1; DAM DRAM;
  DLB 211; RGWL 2, 3; TWA

Senghor, Leopold Sedar 1906-2001 ... **BLC 3;**
  CLC 54, 130; PC 25
  See also AFW; BW 2; CA 116; 125; 203;
  CANR 47, 74, 134; CWW 2; DAM
  MULT, POET; DNFS 2; EWL 3; GFL
  1789 to the Present; MTCW 1, 2; TWA

Senior, Olive (Marjorie) 1941- .... **SSC 78**
  See also BW 3; CA 154; CANR 86, 126;
  CN 7; CP 7; CWP; DLB 157; EWL 3;
  RGSF 2

Senna, Danzy 1970- .... **CLC 119**
  See also CA 169; CANR 130

Serling, (Edward) Rod(man)
  1924-1975 .... **CLC 30**
  See also AAYA 14; AITN 1; CA 162; 57-
  60; DLB 26; SFW 4

Serna, Ramon Gomez de la
  See Gomez de la Serna, Ramon

Serpieres
  See Guillevic, (Eugene)

Service, Robert
  See Service, Robert W(illiam)
  See also BYA 4; DAB; DLB 92

Service, Robert W(illiam)
  1874(?)-1958 .... **TCLC 15; WLC**
  See Service, Robert
  See also CA 115; 140; CANR 84; DA;
  DAC; DAM MST, POET; PFS 10; RGEL
  2; SATA 20

Seth, Vikram 1952- .... **CLC 43, 90**
  See also BRWS 10; CA 121; 127; CANR
  50, 74, 131; CN 7; CP 7; DA3; DAM
  MULT; DLB 120, 271, 282; EWL 3; INT
  CA-127; MTCW 2; WWE 1

Seton, Cynthia Propper 1926-1982 .. **CLC 27**
  See also CA 5-8R; 108; CANR 7

Seton, Ernest (Evan) Thompson
  1860-1946 .... **TCLC 31**
  See also ANW; BYA 3; CA 109; 204; CLR
  59; DLB 92; DLBD 13; JRDA; SATA 18

Seton-Thompson, Ernest
  See Seton, Ernest (Evan) Thompson

Settle, Mary Lee 1918- .... **CLC 19, 61**
  See also BPFB 3; CA 89-92; CAAS 1;
  CANR 44, 87, 126; CN 7; CSW; DLB 6;
  INT CA-89-92

Seuphor, Michel
  See Arp, Jean

Sevigne, Marie (de Rabutin-Chantal)
  1626-1696 .... **LC 11**
  See Sevigne, Marie de Rabutin Chantal
  See also GFL Beginnings to 1789; TWA

Sevigne, Marie de Rabutin Chantal
  See Sevigne, Marie (de Rabutin-Chantal)
  See also DLB 268

Sewall, Samuel 1652-1730 .... **LC 38**
  See also DLB 24; RGAL 4

Sexton, Anne (Harvey) 1928-1974 ..... **CLC 2,**
  4, 6, 8, 10, 15, 53, 123; PC 2; WLC
  See also AMWS 2; CA 1-4R; 53-56; CABS
  2; CANR 3, 36; CDALB 1941-1968; DA;
  DA3; DAB; DAC; DAM MST, POET;
  DLB 5, 169; EWL 3; EXPP; FW;
  MAWW; MTCW 1, 2; PAB; PFS 4, 14;
  RGAL 4; SATA 10; TUS

Shaara, Jeff 1952- .... **CLC 119**
  See also CA 163; CANR 109

Shaara, Michael (Joseph, Jr.)
  1929-1988 .... **CLC 15**
  See also AITN 1; BPFB 3; CA 102; 125;
  CANR 52, 85; DAM POP; DLBY 1983

Shackleton, C. C.
  See Aldiss, Brian W(ilson)

Shacochis, Bob .... **CLC 39**
  See Shacochis, Robert G.

Shacochis, Robert G. 1951-
  See Shacochis, Bob
  See also CA 119; 124; CANR 100; INT CA-
  124

Shvarts, Elena 1948- .... **PC 50**
See also CA 147

Sidhwa, Bapsy (N.) 1938- .... **CLC 168**
See also CA 108; CANR 25, 57; CN 7; FW

Sidney, Mary 1561-1621 .... **LC 19, 39**
See Sidney Herbert, Mary

Sidney, Sir Philip 1554-1586 . **LC 19, 39; PC 32**
See also BRW 1; BRWR 2; CDBLB Before 1660; DA; DA3; DAB; DAC; DAM MST, POET; DLB 167; EXPP; PAB; RGEL 2; TEA; WP

Sidney Herbert, Mary
See Sidney, Mary
See also DLB 167

Siegel, Jerome 1914-1996 .... **CLC 21**
See Siegel, Jerry
See also CA 116; 169; 151

Siegel, Jerry
See Siegel, Jerome
See also AAYA 50

Sienkiewicz, Henryk (Adam Alexander Pius) 1846-1916 .... **TCLC 3**
See also CA 104; 134; CANR 84; EWL 3; RGSF 2; RGWL 2, 3

Sierra, Gregorio Martinez
See Martinez Sierra, Gregorio

Sierra, Maria (de la O'LeJarraga) Martinez
See Martinez Sierra, Maria (de la O'LeJarraga)

Sigal, Clancy 1926- .... **CLC 7**
See also CA 1-4R; CANR 85; CN 7

Siger of Brabant 1240(?)-1284(?) . **CMLC 69**
See also DLB 115

Sigourney, Lydia H.
See Sigourney, Lydia Howard (Huntley)
See also DLB 73, 183

Sigourney, Lydia Howard (Huntley) 1791-1865 .... **NCLC 21, 87**
See Sigourney, Lydia H.; Sigourney, Lydia Huntley
See also DLB 1

Sigourney, Lydia Huntley
See Sigourney, Lydia Howard (Huntley)
See also DLB 42, 239, 243

Siguenza y Gongora, Carlos de 1645-1700 .... **HLCS 2; LC 8**
See also LAW

Sigurjonsson, Johann
See Sigurjonsson, Johann

Sigurjonsson, Johann 1880-1919 ... **TCLC 27**
See also CA 170; DLB 293; EWL 3

Sikelianos, Angelos 1884-1951 .... **PC 29; TCLC 39**
See also EWL 3; RGWL 2, 3

Silkin, Jon 1930-1997 .... **CLC 2, 6, 43**
See also CA 5-8R; CAAS 5; CANR 89; CP 7; DLB 27

Silko, Leslie (Marmon) 1948- .... **CLC 23, 74, 114; NNAL; SSC 37, 66; WLCS**
See also AAYA 14; AMWS 4; ANW; BYA 12; CA 115; 122; CANR 45, 65, 118; CN 7; CP 7; CPW 1; CWP; DA; DA3; DAC; DAM MST, MULT, POP; DLB 143, 175, 256, 275; EWL 3; EXPP; EXPS; LAIT 4; MTCW 2; NFS 4; PFS 9, 16; RGAL 4; RGSF 2; SSFS 4, 8, 10, 11

Sillanpaa, Frans Eemil 1888-1964 ... **CLC 19**
See also CA 129; 93-96; EWL 3; MTCW 1

Sillitoe, Alan 1928- .. **CLC 1, 3, 6, 10, 19, 57, 148**
See also AITN 1; BRWS 5; CA 9-12R, 191; CAAE 191; CAAS 2; CANR 8, 26, 55; CDBLB 1960 to Present; CN 7; DLB 14, 139; EWL 3; MTCW 1, 2; RGEL 2; RGSF 2; SATA 61

Silone, Ignazio 1900-1978 .... **CLC 4**
See also CA 25-28; 81-84; CANR 34; CAP 2; DLB 264; EW 12; EWL 3; MTCW 1; RGSF 2; RGWL 2, 3

Silone, Ignazione
See Silone, Ignazio

Silver, Joan Micklin 1935- .... **CLC 20**
See also CA 114; 121; INT CA-121

Silver, Nicholas
See Faust, Frederick (Schiller)
See also TCWW 2

Silverberg, Robert 1935- .... **CLC 7, 140**
See also AAYA 24; BPFB 3; BYA 7, 9; CA 1-4R, 186; CAAE 186; CAAS 3; CANR 1, 20, 36, 85; CLR 59; CN 7; CPW; DAM POP; DLB 8; INT CANR-20; MAICYA 1, 2; MTCW 1, 2; SATA 13, 91; SATA-Essay 104; SCFW 2; SFW 4; SUFW 2

Silverstein, Alvin 1933- .... **CLC 17**
See also CA 49-52; CANR 2; CLR 25; JRDA; MAICYA 1, 2; SATA 8, 69, 124

Silverstein, Shel(don Allan) 1932-1999 .... **PC 49**
See also AAYA 40; BW 3; CA 107; 179; CANR 47, 74, 81; CLR 5, 96; CWRI 5; JRDA; MAICYA 1, 2; MTCW 2; SATA 33, 92; SATA-Brief 27; SATA-Obit 116

Silverstein, Virginia B(arbara Opshelor) 1937- .... **CLC 17**
See also CA 49-52; CANR 2; CLR 25; JRDA; MAICYA 1, 2; SATA 8, 69, 124

Sim, Georges
See Simenon, Georges (Jacques Christian)

Simak, Clifford D(onald) 1904-1988 . **CLC 1, 55**
See also CA 1-4R; 125; CANR 1, 35; DLB 8; MTCW 1; SATA-Obit 56; SFW 4

Simenon, Georges (Jacques Christian) 1903-1989 .... **CLC 1, 2, 3, 8, 18, 47**
See also BPFB 3; CA 85-88; 129; CANR 35; CMW 4; DA3; DAM POP; DLB 72; DLBY 1989; EW 12; EWL 3; GFL 1789 to the Present; MSW; MTCW 1, 2; RGWL 2, 3

Simic, Charles 1938- .... **CLC 6, 9, 22, 49, 68, 130**
See also AMWS 8; CA 29-32R; CAAS 4; CANR 12, 33, 52, 61, 96; CP 7; DA3; DAM POET; DLB 105; MTCW 2; PFS 7; RGAL 4; WP

Simmel, Georg 1858-1918 .... **TCLC 64**
See also CA 157; DLB 296

Simmons, Charles (Paul) 1924- .... **CLC 57**
See also CA 89-92; INT CA-89-92

Simmons, Dan 1948- .... **CLC 44**
See also AAYA 16, 54; CA 138; CANR 53, 81, 126; CPW; DAM POP; HGG; SUFW 2

Simmons, James (Stewart Alexander) 1933- .... **CLC 43**
See also CA 105; CAAS 21; CP 7; DLB 40

Simms, William Gilmore 1806-1870 .... **NCLC 3**
See also DLB 3, 30, 59, 73, 248, 254; RGAL 4

Simon, Carly 1945- .... **CLC 26**
See also CA 105

Simon, Claude (Eugene Henri) 1913-1984 .... **CLC 4, 9, 15, 39**
See also CA 89-92; CANR 33, 117; CWW 2; DAM NOV; DLB 83; EW 13; EWL 3; GFL 1789 to the Present; MTCW 1

Simon, Myles
See Follett, Ken(neth Martin)

Simon, (Marvin) Neil 1927- ... **CLC 6, 11, 31, 39, 70; DC 14**
See also AAYA 32; AITN 1; AMWS 4; CA 21-24R; CANR 26, 54, 87, 126; CD 5;

DA3; DAM DRAM; DFS 2, 6, 12, 18; DLB 7, 266; LAIT 4; MTCW 1, 2; RGAL 4; TUS

Simon, Paul (Frederick) 1941(?)- ..... **CLC 17**
See also CA 116; 153

Simonon, Paul 1956(?)- .... **CLC 30**

Simonson, Rick ed. .... **CLC 70**

Simpson, Harriette
See Arnow, Harriette (Louisa) Simpson

Simpson, Louis (Aston Marantz) 1923- .... **CLC 4, 7, 9, 32, 149**
See also AMWS 9; CA 1-4R; CAAS 4; CANR 1, 61; CP 7; DAM POET; DLB 5; MTCW 1, 2; PFS 7, 11, 14; RGAL 4

Simpson, Mona (Elizabeth) 1957- ... **CLC 44, 146**
See also CA 122; 135; CANR 68, 103; CN 7; EWL 3

Simpson, N(orman) F(rederick) 1919- .... **CLC 29**
See also CA 13-16R; CBD; DLB 13; RGEL 2

Sinclair, Andrew (Annandale) 1935- . **CLC 2, 14**
See also CA 9-12R; CAAS 5; CANR 14, 38, 91; CN 7; DLB 14; FANT; MTCW 1

Sinclair, Emil
See Hesse, Hermann

Sinclair, Iain 1943- .... **CLC 76**
See also CA 132; CANR 81; CP 7; HGG

Sinclair, Iain MacGregor
See Sinclair, Iain

Sinclair, Irene
See Griffith, D(avid Lewelyn) W(ark)

Sinclair, Mary Amelia St. Clair 1865(?)-1946
See Sinclair, May
See also CA 104; HGG; RHW

Sinclair, May .... **TCLC 3, 11**
See Sinclair, Mary Amelia St. Clair
See also CA 166; DLB 36, 135; EWL 3; RGEL 2; SUFW

Sinclair, Roy
See Griffith, D(avid Lewelyn) W(ark)

Sinclair, Upton (Beall) 1878-1968 ..... **CLC 1, 11, 15, 63; TCLC 160; WLC**
See also AMWS 5; BPFB 3; BYA 2; CA 5-8R; 25-28R; CANR 7; CDALB 1929-1941; DA; DA3; DAB; DAC; DAM MST, NOV; DLB 9; EWL 3; INT CANR-7; LAIT 3; MTCW 1, 2; NFS 6; RGAL 4; SATA 9; TUS; YAW

Singe, (Edmund) J(ohn) M(illington) 1871-1909 .... **WLC**

Singer, Isaac
See Singer, Isaac Bashevis

Singer, Isaac Bashevis 1904-1991 .. **CLC 1, 3, 6, 9, 11, 15, 23, 38, 69, 111; SSC 3, 53, 80; WLC**
See also AAYA 32; AITN 1, 2; AMW; AMWR 2; BPFB 3; BYA 1, 4; CA 1-4R; 134; CANR 1, 39, 106; CDALB 1941-1968; CLR 1; CWRI 5; DA; DA3; DAB; DAC; DAM MST, NOV; DLB 6, 28, 52, 278; DLBY 1991; EWL 3; EXPS; HGG; JRDA; LAIT 3; MAICYA 1, 2; MTCW 1, 2; RGAL 4; RGSF 2; SATA 3, 27; SATA-Obit 68; SSFS 2, 12, 16; TUS; TWA

Singer, Israel Joshua 1893-1944 .... **TCLC 33**
See also CA 169; EWL 3

Singh, Khushwant 1915- .... **CLC 11**
See also CA 9-12R; CAAS 9; CANR 6, 84; CN 7; EWL 3; RGEL 2

Singleton, Ann
See Benedict, Ruth (Fulton)

Singleton, John 1968(?)- .... **CLC 156**
See also AAYA 50; BW 2, 3; CA 138; CANR 67, 82; DAM MULT

Solomos, Dionysios 1798-1857 .... **NCLC 15**
Solwoska, Mara
    See French, Marilyn
Solzhenitsyn, Aleksandr I(sayevich)
    1918- .. **CLC 1, 2, 4, 7, 9, 10, 18, 26, 34,
    78, 134; SSC 32; WLC**
    See Solzhenitsyn, Aleksandr Isaevich
    See also AAYA 49; AITN 1; BPFB 3; CA
    69-72; CANR 40, 65, 116; DA; DA3;
    DAB; DAC; DAM MST; DLB 302;
    EW 13; EXPS; LAIT 4; MTCW 1, 2; NFS
    6; RGSF 2; RGWL 2, 3; SSFS 9; TWA
Solzhenitsyn, Aleksandr Isaevich
    See Solzhenitsyn, Aleksandr I(sayevich)
    See also CWW 2; EWL 3
Somers, Jane
    See Lessing, Doris (May)
Somerville, Edith Oenone
    1858-1949 .... **SSC 56; TCLC 51**
    See also CA 196; DLB 135; RGEL 2; RGSF
    2
Somerville & Ross
    See Martin, Violet Florence; Somerville,
    Edith Oenone
Sommer, Scott 1951- .... **CLC 25**
    See also CA 106
Sommers, Christina Hoff 1950- ...... **CLC 197**
    See also CA 153; CANR 95
Sondheim, Stephen (Joshua) 1930- . **CLC 30,
    39, 147; DC 22**
    See also AAYA 11; CA 103; CANR 47, 67,
    125; DAM DRAM; LAIT 4
Sone, Monica 1919- .... **AAL**
Song, Cathy 1955- .... **AAL; PC 21**
    See also CA 154; CANR 118; CWP; DLB
    169; EXPP; FW; PFS 5
Sontag, Susan 1933- .... **CLC 1, 2, 10, 13, 31,
    105, 195**
    See also AMWS 3; CA 17-20R; CANR 25,
    51, 74, 97; CN 7; CPW; DA3; DAM POP;
    DLB 2, 67; EWL 3; MAWW; MTCW 1,
    2; RGAL 4; RHW; SSFS 10
Sophocles 496(?)B.C.-406(?)B.C. .... **CMLC 2,
    47, 51; DC 1; WLCS**
    See also AW 1; CDWLB 1; DA; DA3;
    DAB; DAC; DAM DRAM, MST; DFS 1,
    4, 8; DLB 176; LAIT 1; LATS 1:1; LMFS
    1; RGWL 2, 3; TWA
Sordello 1189-1269 .... **CMLC 15**
Sorel, Georges 1847-1922 .... **TCLC 91**
    See also CA 118; 188
Sorel, Julia
    See Drexler, Rosalyn
Sorokin, Vladimir .... **CLC 59**
    See Sorokin, Vladimir Georgievich
Sorokin, Vladimir Georgievich
    See Sorokin, Vladimir
    See also DLB 285
Sorrentino, Gilbert 1929- .. **CLC 3, 7, 14, 22,
    40**
    See also CA 77-80; CANR 14, 33, 115; CN
    7; CP 7; DLB 5, 173; DLBY 1980; INT
    CANR-14
Soseki
    See Natsume, Soseki
    See also MJW
Soto, Gary 1952- ... **CLC 32, 80; HLC 2; PC
    28**
    See also AAYA 10, 37; BYA 11; CA 119;
    125; CANR 50, 74, 107; CLR 38; CP 7;
    DAM MULT; DLB 82; EWL 3; EXPP;
    HW 1, 2; INT CA-125; JRDA; LLW 1;
    MAICYA 2; MAICYAS 1; MTCW 2; PFS
    7; RGAL 4; SATA 80, 120; WYA; YAW
Soupault, Philippe 1897-1990 .... **CLC 68**
    See also CA 116; 147; 131; EWL 3; GFL
    1789 to the Present; LMFS 2

Souster, (Holmes) Raymond 1921- .... **CLC 5,
    14**
    See also CA 13-16R; CAAS 14; CANR 13,
    29, 53; CP 7; DA3; DAC; DAM POET;
    DLB 88; RGEL 2; SATA 63
Southern, Terry 1924(?)-1995 .... **CLC 7**
    See also AMWS 11; BPFB 3; CA 1-4R;
    150; CANR 1, 55, 107; CN 7; DLB 2;
    IDFW 3, 4
Southerne, Thomas 1660-1746 .... **LC 99**
    See also DLB 80; RGEL 2
Southey, Robert 1774-1843 .... **NCLC 8, 97**
    See also BRW 4; DLB 93, 107, 142; RGEL
    2; SATA 54
Southwell, Robert 1561(?)-1595 .... **LC 108**
    See also DLB 167; RGEL 2; TEA
Southworth, Emma Dorothy Eliza Nevitte
    1819-1899 .... **NCLC 26**
    See also DLB 239
Souza, Ernest
    See Scott, Evelyn
Soyinka, Wole 1934- .. **BLC 3; CLC 3, 5, 14,
    36, 44, 179; DC 2; WLC**
    See also AFW; BW 2, 3; CA 13-16R;
    CANR 27, 39, 82; CD 5; CDWLB 3; CN
    7; CP 7; DA; DA3; DAB; DAC; DAM
    DRAM, MST, MULT; DFS 10; DLB 125;
    EWL 3; MTCW 1, 2; RGEL 2; TWA;
    WLIT 2; WWE 1
Spackman, W(illiam) M(ode)
    1905-1990 .... **CLC 46**
    See also CA 81-84; 132
Spacks, Barry (Bernard) 1931- .... **CLC 14**
    See also CA 154; CANR 33, 109; CP 7;
    DLB 105
Spanidou, Irini 1946- .... **CLC 44**
    See also CA 185
Spark, Muriel (Sarah) 1918- ..... **CLC 2, 3, 5,
    8, 13, 18, 40, 94; SSC 10**
    See also BRWS 1; CA 5-8R; CANR 12, 36,
    76, 89, 131; CDBLB 1945-1960; CN 7;
    CP 7; DA3; DAB; DAC; DAM MST,
    NOV; DLB 15, 139; EWL 3; FW; INT
    CANR-12; LAIT 4; MTCW 1, 2; RGEL
    2; TEA; WLIT 4; YAW
Spaulding, Douglas
    See Bradbury, Ray (Douglas)
Spaulding, Leonard
    See Bradbury, Ray (Douglas)
Speght, Rachel 1597-c. 1630 .... **LC 97**
    See also DLB 126
Spelman, Elizabeth .... **CLC 65**
Spence, J. A. D.
    See Eliot, T(homas) S(tearns)
Spencer, Anne 1882-1975 .... **HR 3**
    See also BW 2; CA 161; DLB 51, 54
Spencer, Elizabeth 1921- ..... **CLC 22; SSC 57**
    See also CA 13-16R; CANR 32, 65, 87; CN
    7; CSW; DLB 6, 218; EWL 3; MTCW 1;
    RGAL 4; SATA 14
Spencer, Leonard G.
    See Silverberg, Robert
Spencer, Scott 1945- .... **CLC 30**
    See also CA 113; CANR 51; DLBY 1986
Spender, Stephen (Harold)
    1909-1995 .... **CLC 1, 2, 5, 10, 41, 91**
    See also BRWS 2; CA 9-12R; 149; CANR
    31, 54; CDBLB 1945-1960; CP 7; DA3;
    DAM POET; DLB 20; EWL 3; MTCW 1,
    2; PAB; RGEL 2; TEA
Spengler, Oswald (Arnold Gottfried)
    1880-1936 .... **TCLC 25**
    See also CA 118; 189
Spenser, Edmund 1552(?)-1599 ..... **LC 5, 39;
    PC 8, 42; WLC**
    See also AAYA 60; BRW 1; CDBLB Before
    1660; DA; DA3; DAB; DAC; DAM MST,
    POET; DLB 167; EFS 2; EXPP; PAB;
    RGEL 2; TEA; WLIT 3; WP

Spicer, Jack 1925-1965 .... **CLC 8, 18, 72**
    See also BG 3; CA 85-88; DAM POET;
    DLB 5, 16, 193; GLL 1; WP
Spiegelman, Art 1948- .... **CLC 76, 178**
    See also AAYA 10, 46; CA 125; CANR 41,
    55, 74, 124; DLB 299; MTCW 2; SATA
    109; YAW
Spielberg, Peter 1929- .... **CLC 6**
    See also CA 5-8R; CANR 4, 48; DLBY
    1981
Spielberg, Steven 1947- .... **CLC 20, 188**
    See also AAYA 8, 24; CA 77-80; CANR
    32; SATA 32
Spillane, Frank Morrison 1918-
    See Spillane, Mickey
    See also CA 25-28R; CANR 28, 63, 125;
    DA3; MTCW 1, 2; SATA 66
Spillane, Mickey .... **CLC 3, 13**
    See Spillane, Frank Morrison
    See also BPFB 3; CMW 4; DLB 226;
    MSW; MTCW 2
Spinoza, Benedictus de 1632-1677 .. **LC 9, 58**
Spinrad, Norman (Richard) 1940- ... **CLC 46**
    See also BPFB 3; CA 37-40R; CAAS 19;
    CANR 20, 91; DLB 8; INT CANR-20;
    SFW 4
Spitteler, Carl (Friedrich Georg)
    1845-1924 .... **TCLC 12**
    See also CA 109; DLB 129; EWL 3
Spivack, Kathleen (Romola Drucker)
    1938- .... **CLC 6**
    See also CA 49-52
Spoto, Donald 1941- .... **CLC 39**
    See also CA 65-68; CANR 11, 57, 93
Springsteen, Bruce (F.) 1949- .... **CLC 17**
    See also CA 111
Spurling, (Susan) Hilary 1940- .... **CLC 34**
    See also CA 104; CANR 25, 52, 94
Spyker, John Howland
    See Elman, Richard (Martin)
Squared, A.
    See Abbott, Edwin A.
Squires, (James) Radcliffe
    1917-1993 .... **CLC 51**
    See also CA 1-4R; 140; CANR 6, 21
Srivastava, Dhanpat Rai 1880(?)-1936
    See Premchand
    See also CA 118; 197
Stacy, Donald
    See Pohl, Frederik
Stael
    See Stael-Holstein, Anne Louise Germaine
    Necker
    See also EW 5; RGWL 2, 3
Stael, Germaine de
    See Stael-Holstein, Anne Louise Germaine
    Necker
    See also DLB 119, 192; FW; GFL 1789 to
    the Present; TWA
Stael-Holstein, Anne Louise Germaine
    Necker 1766-1817 .... **NCLC 3, 91**
    See Stael; Stael, Germaine de
Stafford, Jean 1915-1979 .. **CLC 4, 7, 19, 68;
    SSC 26**
    See also CA 1-4R; 85-88; CANR 3, 65;
    DLB 2, 173; MTCW 1, 2; RGAL 4; RGSF
    2; SATA-Obit 22; TCWW 2; TUS
Stafford, William (Edgar)
    1914-1993 .... **CLC 4, 7, 29**
    See also AMWS 11; CA 5-8R; 142; CAAS
    3; CANR 5, 22; DAM POET; DLB 5,
    206; EXPP; INT CANR-22; PFS 2, 8, 16;
    RGAL 4; WP
Stagnelius, Eric Johan 1793-1823 . **NCLC 61**
Staines, Trevor
    See Brunner, John (Kilian Houston)
Stairs, Gordon
    See Austin, Mary (Hunter)
    See also TCWW 2

Stone, Ruth 1915- .... **PC 53**
See also CA 45-48; CANR 2, 91; CP 7;
CSW; DLB 105; PFS 19

Stone, Zachary
See Follett, Ken(neth Martin)

Stoppard, Tom 1937- ... **CLC 1, 3, 4, 5, 8, 15,
29, 34, 63, 91; DC 6; WLC**
See also BRWC 1; BRWR 2; BRWS 1; CA
81-84; CANR 39, 67, 125; CBD; CD 5;
CDBLB 1960 to Present; DA; DA3;
DAB; DAC; DAM DRAM, MST; DFS 2,
5, 8, 11, 13, 16; DLB 13, 233; DLBY
1985; EWL 3; LATS 1:2; MTCW 1, 2;
RGEL 2; TEA; WLIT 4

Storey, David (Malcolm) 1933- . **CLC 2, 4, 5,
8**
See also BRWS 1; CA 81-84; CANR 36;
CBD; CD 5; CN 7; DAM DRAM; DLB
13, 14, 207, 245; EWL 3; MTCW 1;
RGEL 2

Storm, Hyemeyohsts 1935- ... **CLC 3; NNAL**
See also CA 81-84; CANR 45; DAM MULT

Storm, (Hans) Theodor (Woldsen)
1817-1888 .... **NCLC 1; SSC 27**
See also CDWLB 2; DLB 129; EW; RGSF
2; RGWL 2, 3

Storni, Alfonsina 1892-1938 . **HLC 2; PC 33;
TCLC 5**
See also CA 104; 131; DAM MULT; DLB
283; HW 1; LAW

Stoughton, William 1631-1701 .... **LC 38**
See also DLB 24

Stout, Rex (Todhunter) 1886-1975 ..... **CLC 3**
See also AITN 2; BPFB 3; CA 61-64;
CANR 71; CMW 4; DLB 306; MSW;
RGAL 4

Stow, (Julian) Randolph 1935- ... **CLC 23, 48**
See also CA 13-16R; CANR 33; CN 7;
DLB 260; MTCW 1; RGEL 2

Stowe, Harriet (Elizabeth) Beecher
1811-1896 .... **NCLC 3, 50, 133; WLC**
See also AAYA 53; AMWS 1; CDALB
1865-1917; DA; DA3; DAB; DAC; DAM
MST, NOV; DLB 1, 12, 42, 74, 189, 239,
243; EXPN; JRDA; LAIT 2; MAICYA 1,
2; NFS 6; RGAL 4; TUS; YABC 1

Strabo c. 64B.C.-c. 25 .... **CMLC 37**
See also DLB 176

Strachey, (Giles) Lytton
1880-1932 .... **TCLC 12**
See also BRWS 2; CA 110; 178; DLB 149;
DLBD 10; EWL 3; MTCW 2; NCFS 4

Stramm, August 1874-1915 .... **PC 50**
See also CA 195; EWL 3

Strand, Mark 1934- .... **CLC 6, 18, 41, 71**
See also AMWS 4; CA 21-24R; CANR 40,
65, 100; CP 7; DAM POET; DLB 5; EWL
3; PAB; PFS 9, 18; RGAL 4; SATA 41

Stratton-Porter, Gene(va Grace) 1863-1924
See Porter, Gene(va Grace) Stratton
See also ANW; CA 137; CLR 87; DLB 221;
DLBD 14; MAICYA 1, 2; SATA 15

Straub, Peter (Francis) 1943- ... **CLC 28, 107**
See also BEST 89:1; BPFB 3; CA 85-88;
CANR 28, 65, 109; CPW; DAM POP;
DLBY 1984; HGG; MTCW 1, 2; SUFW
2

Strauss, Botho 1944- .... **CLC 22**
See also CA 157; CWW 2; DLB 124

Strauss, Leo 1899-1973 .... **TCLC 141**
See also CA 101; 45-48; CANR 122

Streatfeild, (Mary) Noel
1897(?)-1986 .... **CLC 21**
See also CA 81-84; 120; CANR 31; CLR
17, 83; DLB 160; CWRI 5; MAICYA 1,
2; SATA 20; SATA-Obit 48

Stribling, T(homas) S(igismund)
1881-1965 .... **CLC 23**
See also CA 189; 107; CMW 4; DLB 9;
RGAL 4

Strindberg, (Johan) August
1849-1912 ... **DC 18; TCLC 1, 8, 21, 47;
WLC**
See also CA 104; 135; DA; DA3; DAB;
DAC; DAM DRAM, MST; DFS 4, 9;
DLB 259; EW 7; EWL 3; IDTP; LMFS
2; MTCW 2; RGWL 2, 3; TWA

Stringer, Arthur 1874-1950 .... **TCLC 37**
See also CA 161; DLB 92

Stringer, David
See Roberts, Keith (John Kingston)

Stroheim, Erich von 1885-1957 ..... **TCLC 71**

Strugatskii, Arkadii (Natanovich)
1925-1991 .... **CLC 27**
See Strugatsky, Arkadii Natanovich
See also CA 106; 135; SFW 4

Strugatskii, Boris (Natanovich)
1933- .... **CLC 27**
See Strugatsky, Boris (Natanovich)
See also CA 106; SFW 4

Strugatsky, Arkadii Natanovich
See Strugatskii, Arkadii (Natanovich)
See also DLB 302

Strugatsky, Boris (Natanovich)
See Strugatskii, Boris (Natanovich)
See also DLB 302

Strummer, Joe 1953(?)- .... **CLC 30**

Strunk, William, Jr. 1869-1946 ...... **TCLC 92**
See also CA 118; 164; NCFS 5

Stryk, Lucien 1924- .... **PC 27**
See also CA 13-16R; CANR 10, 28, 55,
110; CP 7

Stuart, Don A.
See Campbell, John W(ood, Jr.)

Stuart, Ian
See MacLean, Alistair (Stuart)

Stuart, Jesse (Hilton) 1906-1984 ... **CLC 1, 8,
11, 14, 34; SSC 31**
See also CA 5-8R; 112; CANR 31; DLB 9,
48, 102; DLBY 1984; SATA 2; SATA-
Obit 36

Stubblefield, Sally
See Trumbo, Dalton

Sturgeon, Theodore (Hamilton)
1918-1985 .... **CLC 22, 39**
See Queen, Ellery
See also AAYA 51; BPFB 3; BYA 9, 10;
CA 81-84; 116; CANR 32, 103; DLB 8;
DLBY 1985; HGG; MTCW 1, 2; SCFW;
SFW 4; SUFW

Sturges, Preston 1898-1959 .... **TCLC 48**
See also CA 114; 149; DLB 26

Styron, William 1925- .... **CLC 1, 3, 5, 11, 15,
60; SSC 25**
See also AMW; AMWC 2; BEST 90:4;
BPFB 3; CA 5-8R; CANR 6, 33, 74, 126;
CDALB 1968-1988; CN 7; CPW; CSW;
DA3; DAM NOV, POP; DLB 2, 143, 299;
DLBY 1980; EWL 3; INT CANR-6;
LAIT 2; MTCW 1, 2; NCFS 1; RGAL 4;
RHW; TUS

Su, Chien 1884-1918
See Su Man-shu
See also CA 123

Suarez Lynch, B.
See Bioy Casares, Adolfo; Borges, Jorge
Luis

Suassuna, Ariano Vilar 1927- .... **HLCS 1**
See also CA 178; DLB 307; HW 2; LAW

Suckert, Kurt Erich
See Malaparte, Curzio

Suckling, Sir John 1609-1642 . **LC 75; PC 30**
See also BRW 2; DAM POET; DLB 58,
126; EXPP; PAB; RGEL 2

Suckow, Ruth 1892-1960 .... **SSC 18**
See also CA 193; 113; DLB 9, 102; RGAL
4; TCWW 2

Sudermann, Hermann 1857-1928 .. **TCLC 15**
See also CA 107; 201; DLB 118

Sue, Eugene 1804-1857 .... **NCLC 1**
See also DLB 119

Sueskind, Patrick 1949- .... **CLC 44, 182**
See Suskind, Patrick

Suetonius c. 70-c. 130 .... **CMLC 60**
See also AW 2; DLB 211; RGWL 2, 3

Sukenick, Ronald 1932-2004 ..... **CLC 3, 4, 6,
48**
See also CA 25-28R; 209; 229; CAAE 209;
CAAS 8; CANR 32, 89; CN 7; DLB 173;
DLBY 1981

Suknaski, Andrew 1942- .... **CLC 19**
See also CA 101; CP 7; DLB 53

Sullivan, Vernon
See Vian, Boris

Sully Prudhomme, Rene-Francois-Armand
1839-1907 .... **TCLC 31**
See also GFL 1789 to the Present

Su Man-shu .... **TCLC 24**
See Su, Chien
See also EWL 3

Sumarokov, Aleksandr Petrovich
1717-1777 .... **LC 104**
See also DLB 150

Summerforest, Ivy B.
See Kirkup, James

Summers, Andrew James 1942- .... **CLC 26**

Summers, Andy
See Summers, Andrew James

Summers, Hollis (Spurgeon, Jr.)
1916- .... **CLC 10**
See also CA 5-8R; CANR 3; DLB 6

**Summers, (Alphonsus Joseph-Mary
Augustus) Montague**
1880-1948 .... **TCLC 16**
See also CA 118; 163

Sumner, Gordon Matthew .... **CLC 26**
See Police, The; Sting

Sun Tzu c. 400B.C.-c. 320B.C. ...... **CMLC 56**

Surrey, Henry Howard 1517-1574 ...... **PC 59**
See also BRW 1; RGEL 2

Surtees, Robert Smith 1805-1864 .. **NCLC 14**
See also DLB 21; RGEL 2

Susann, Jacqueline 1921-1974 .... **CLC 3**
See also AITN 1; BPFB 3; CA 65-68; 53-
56; MTCW 1, 2

Su Shi
See Su Shih
See also RGWL 2, 3

Su Shih 1036-1101 .... **CMLC 15**
See Su Shi

Suskind, Patrick .... **CLC 182**
See Sueskind, Patrick
See also BPFB 3; CA 145; CWW 2

Sutcliff, Rosemary 1920-1992 .... **CLC 26**
See also AAYA 10; BYA 1, 4; CA 5-8R;
139; CANR 37; CLR 1, 37; CPW; DAB;
DAC; DAM MST, POP; JRDA; LATS
1:1; MAICYA 1, 2; MAICYAS 1; RHW;
SATA 6, 44, 78; SATA-Obit 73; WYA;
YAW

Sutro, Alfred 1863-1933 .... **TCLC 6**
See also CA 105; 185; DLB 10; RGEL 2

Sutton, Henry
See Slavitt, David R(ytman)

Suzuki, D. T.
See Suzuki, Daisetz Teitaro

Suzuki, Daisetz T.
See Suzuki, Daisetz Teitaro

Suzuki, Daisetz Teitaro
1870-1966 .... **TCLC 109**
See also CA 121; 111; MTCW 1, 2

Suzuki, Teitaro
See Suzuki, Daisetz Teitaro

Svevo, Italo .... **SSC 25; TCLC 2, 35**
See Schmitz, Aron Hector
See also DLB 264; EW 8; EWL 3; RGWL
2, 3

Tremblay, Michel 1942- .... **CLC 29, 102**
See also CA 116; 128; CCA 1; CWW 2;
DAC; DAM MST; DLB 60; EWL 3; GLL
1; MTCW 1, 2

Trevanian .... **CLC 29**
See Whitaker, Rod(ney)

Trevor, Glen
See Hilton, James

Trevor, William .. **CLC 7, 9, 14, 25, 71, 116;**
SSC 21, 58
See Cox, William Trevor
See also BRWS 4; CBD; CD 5; CN 7; DLB
14, 139; EWL 3; LATS 1:2; MTCW 2;
RGEL 2; RGSF 2; SSFS 10

Trifonov, Iurii (Valentinovich)
See Trifonov, Yuri (Valentinovich)
See also DLB 302; RGWL 2, 3

Trifonov, Yuri (Valentinovich)
1925-1981 .... **CLC 45**
See Trifonov, Iurii (Valentinovich); Trifonov, Yury Valentinovich
See also CA 126; 103; MTCW 1

Trifonov, Yury Valentinovich
See Trifonov, Yuri (Valentinovich)
See also EWL 3

Trilling, Diana (Rubin) 1905-1996 . **CLC 129**
See also CA 5-8R; 154; CANR 10, 46; INT
CANR-10; MTCW 1, 2

Trilling, Lionel 1905-1975 ..... **CLC 9, 11, 24;**
SSC 75
See also AMWS 3; CA 9-12R; 61-64;
CANR 10, 105; DLB 28, 63; EWL 3; INT
CANR-10; MTCW 1, 2; RGAL 4; TUS

Trimball, W. H.
See Mencken, H(enry) L(ouis)

Tristan
See Gomez de la Serna, Ramon

Tristram
See Housman, A(lfred) E(dward)

Trogdon, William (Lewis) 1939-
See Heat-Moon, William Least
See also CA 115; 119; CANR 47, 89; CPW;
INT CA-119

Trollope, Anthony 1815-1882 .... **NCLC 6, 33,**
101; SSC 28; WLC
See also BRW 5; CDBLB 1832-1890; DA;
DA3; DAB; DAC; DAM MST, NOV;
DLB 21, 57, 159; RGEL 2; RGSF 2;
SATA 22

Trollope, Frances 1779-1863 .... **NCLC 30**
See also DLB 21, 166

Trollope, Joanna 1943- .... **CLC 186**
See also CA 101; CANR 58, 95; CPW;
DLB 207; RHW

Trotsky, Leon 1879-1940 .... **TCLC 22**
See also CA 118; 167

Trotter (Cockburn), Catharine
1679-1749 .... **LC 8**
See also DLB 84, 252

Trotter, Wilfred 1872-1939 .... **TCLC 97**

Trout, Kilgore
See Farmer, Philip Jose

Trow, George W. S. 1943- .... **CLC 52**
See also CA 126; CANR 91

Troyat, Henri 1911- .... **CLC 23**
See also CA 45-48; CANR 2, 33, 67, 117;
GFL 1789 to the Present; MTCW 1

Trudeau, G(arretson) B(eekman) 1948-
See Trudeau, Garry B.
See also AAYA 60; CA 81-84; CANR 31;
SATA 35

Trudeau, Garry B. .... **CLC 12**
See Trudeau, G(arretson) B(eekman)
See also AAYA 10; AITN 2

Truffaut, Francois 1932-1984 ... **CLC 20, 101**
See also CA 81-84; 113; CANR 34

Trumbo, Dalton 1905-1976 .... **CLC 19**
See also CA 21-24R; 69-72; CANR 10;
DLB 26; IDFW 3, 4; YAW

Trumbull, John 1750-1831 .... **NCLC 30**
See also DLB 31; RGAL 4

Trundlett, Helen B.
See Eliot, T(homas) S(tearns)

Truth, Sojourner 1797(?)-1883 ...... **NCLC 94**
See also DLB 239; FW; LAIT 2

Tryon, Thomas 1926-1991 .... **CLC 3, 11**
See also AITN 1; BPFB 3; CA 29-32R; 135;
CANR 32, 77; CPW; DA3; DAM POP;
HGG; MTCW 1

Tryon, Tom
See Tryon, Thomas

Ts'ao Hsueh-ch'in 1715(?)-1763 .... **LC 1**

Tsushima, Shuji 1909-1948
See Dazai Osamu
See also CA 107

Tsvetaeva (Efron), Marina (Ivanovna)
1892-1941 .... **PC 14; TCLC 7, 35**
See also CA 104; 128; CANR 73; DLB 295;
EW 11; MTCW 1, 2; RGWL 2, 3

Tuck, Lily 1938- .... **CLC 70**
See also CA 139; CANR 90

Tu Fu 712-770 .... **PC 9**
See Du Fu
See also DAM MULT; TWA; WP

Tunis, John R(oberts) 1889-1975 ..... **CLC 12**
See also BYA 1; CA 61-64; CANR 62; DLB
22, 171; JRDA; MAICYA 1, 2; SATA 37;
SATA-Brief 30; YAW

Tuohy, Frank .... **CLC 37**
See Tuohy, John Francis
See also DLB 14, 139

Tuohy, John Francis 1925-
See Tuohy, Frank
See also CA 5-8R; 178; CANR 3, 47; CN 7

Turco, Lewis (Putnam) 1934- ..... **CLC 11, 63**
See also CA 13-16R; CAAS 22; CANR 24,
51; CP 7; DLBY 1984

Turgenev, Ivan (Sergeevich)
1818-1883 ..... **DC 7; NCLC 21, 37, 122;**
SSC 7, 57; WLC
See also AAYA 58; DA; DAB; DAC; DAM
MST, NOV; DFS 6; DLB 238, 284; EW
6; LATS 1:1; NFS 16; RGSF 2; RGWL 2,
3; TWA

Turgot, Anne-Robert-Jacques
1727-1781 .... **LC 26**

Turner, Frederick 1943- .... **CLC 48**
See also CA 73-76, 227; CAAE 227; CAAS
10; CANR 12, 30, 56; DLB 40, 282

Turton, James
See Crace, Jim

Tutu, Desmond M(pilo) 1931- .. **BLC 3; CLC**
80
See also BW 1, 3; CA 125; CANR 67, 81;
DAM MULT

Tutuola, Amos 1920-1997 ..... **BLC 3; CLC 5,**
14, 29
See also AFW; BW 2, 3; CA 9-12R; 159;
CANR 27, 66; CDWLB 3; CN 7; DA3;
DAM MULT; DLB 125; DNFS 2; EWL
3; MTCW 1, 2; RGEL 2; WLIT 2

Twain, Mark .... **SSC 6, 26, 34; TCLC 6, 12,**
19, 36, 48, 59, 161; WLC
See Clemens, Samuel Langhorne
See also AAYA 20; AMW; AMWC 1; BPFB
3; BYA 2, 3, 11, 14; CLR 58, 60, 66; DLB
11; EXPN; EXPS; FANT; LAIT 2; NCFS
4; NFS 1, 6; RGAL 4; RGSF 2; SFW 4;
SSFS 1, 7; SUFW; TUS; WCH; WYA;
YAW

Tyler, Anne 1941- . **CLC 7, 11, 18, 28, 44, 59,**
103
See also AAYA 18, 60; AMWS 4; BEST
89:1; BPFB 3; BYA 12; CA 9-12R; CANR
11, 33, 53, 109, 132; CDALBS; CN 7;
CPW; CSW; DAM NOV, POP; DLB 6,
143; DLBY 1982; EWL 3; EXPN; LATS
1:2; MAWW; MTCW 1, 2; NFS 2, 7, 10;
RGAL 4; SATA 7, 90; SSFS 17; TUS;
YAW

Tyler, Royall 1757-1826 .... **NCLC 3**
See also DLB 37; RGAL 4

Tynan, Katharine 1861-1931 .... **TCLC 3**
See also CA 104; 167; DLB 153, 240; FW

Tyndale, William c. 1484-1536 .... **LC 103**
See also DLB 132

Tyutchev, Fyodor 1803-1873 .... **NCLC 34**

Tzara, Tristan 1896-1963 ..... **CLC 47; PC 27**
See also CA 153; 89-92; DAM POET; EWL
3; MTCW 2

Uchida, Yoshiko 1921-1992 .... **AAL**
See also AAYA 16; BYA 2, 3; CA 13-16R;
139; CANR 6, 22, 47, 61; CDALBS; CLR
6, 56; CWRI 5; JRDA; MAICYA 1, 2;
MTCW 1, 2; SAAS 1; SATA 1, 53; SATA-
Obit 72

Udall, Nicholas 1504-1556 .... **LC 84**
See also DLB 62; RGEL 2

Ueda Akinari 1734-1809 .... **NCLC 131**

Uhry, Alfred 1936- .... **CLC 55**
See also CA 127; 133; CAD; CANR 112;
CD 5; CSW; DA3; DAM DRAM, POP;
DFS 11, 15; INT CA-133

Ulf, Haerved
See Strindberg, (Johan) August

Ulf, Harved
See Strindberg, (Johan) August

Ulibarri, Sabine R(eyes)
1919-2003 .... **CLC 83; HLCS 2**
See also CA 131; 214; CANR 81; DAM
MULT; DLB 82; HW 1, 2; RGSF 2

Unamuno (y Jugo), Miguel de
1864-1936 .. **HLC 2; SSC 11, 69; TCLC**
2, 9, 148
See also CA 104; 131; CANR 81; DAM
MULT, NOV; DLB 108; EW 8; EWL 3;
HW 1, 2; MTCW 1, 2; RGSF 2; RGWL
2, 3; SSFS 20; TWA

Uncle Shelby
See Silverstein, Shel(don Allan)

Undercliffe, Errol
See Campbell, (John) Ramsey

Underwood, Miles
See Glassco, John

Undset, Sigrid 1882-1949 ..... **TCLC 3; WLC**
See also CA 104; 129; DA; DA3; DAB;
DAC; DAM MST, NOV; DLB 293; EW
9; EWL 3; FW; MTCW 1, 2; RGWL 2, 3

Ungaretti, Giuseppe 1888-1970 ... **CLC 7, 11,**
15; PC 57
See also CA 19-20; 25-28R; CAP 2; DLB
114; EW 10; EWL 3; PFS 20; RGWL 2,
3

Unger, Douglas 1952- .... **CLC 34**
See also CA 130; CANR 94

Unsworth, Barry (Forster) 1930- .... **CLC 76,**
127
See also BRWS 7; CA 25-28R; CANR 30,
54, 125; CN 7; DLB 194

Updike, John (Hoyer) 1932- . **CLC 1, 2, 3, 5,**
7, 9, 13, 15, 23, 34, 43, 70, 139; SSC 13,
27; WLC
See also AAYA 36; AMW; AMWC 1;
AMWR 1; BPFB 3; BYA 12; CA 1-4R;
CABS 1; CANR 4, 33, 51, 94, 133;
CDALB 1968-1988; CN 7; CP 7; CPW 1;
DA; DA3; DAB; DAC; DAM MST, NOV,
POET, POP; DLB 2, 5, 143, 218, 227;
DLBD 3; DLBY 1980, 1982, 1997; EWL
3; EXPP; HGG; MTCW 1, 2; NFS 12;
RGAL 4; RGSF 2; SSFS 3, 19; TUS

Upshaw, Margaret Mitchell
See Mitchell, Margaret (Munnerlyn)

Upton, Mark
See Sanders, Lawrence

MAICYA 1, 2; RGWL 2, 3; SATA 21;
SCFW; SFW 4; TWA; WCH

Verus, Marcus Annius
See Aurelius, Marcus

Very, Jones 1813-1880 .... **NCLC 9**
See also DLB 1, 243; RGAL 4

Vesaas, Tarjei 1897-1970 .... **CLC 48**
See also CA 190; 29-32R; DLB 297; EW
11; EWL 3; RGWL 3

Vialis, Gaston
See Simenon, Georges (Jacques Christian)

Vian, Boris 1920-1959(?) .... **TCLC 9**
See also CA 106; 164; CANR 111; DLB
72; EWL 3; GFL 1789 to the Present;
MTCW 2; RGWL 2, 3

Viaud, (Louis Marie) Julien 1850-1923
See Loti, Pierre
See also CA 107

Vicar, Henry
See Felsen, Henry Gregor

Vicente, Gil 1465-c. 1536 .... **LC 99**
See also DLB 287; RGWL 2, 3

Vicker, Angus
See Felsen, Henry Gregor

Vidal, (Eugene Luther) Gore 1925- .. **CLC 2,
4, 6, 8, 10, 22, 33, 72, 142**
See Box, Edgar
See also AITN 1; AMWS 4; BEST 90:2;
BPFB 3; CA 5-8R; CAD; CANR 13, 45,
65, 100, 132; CDALBS; CN 7;
CPW; DA3; DAM NOV, POP; DFS 2;
DLB 6, 152; EWL 3; INT CANR-13;
MTCW 1, 2; RGAL 4; RHW; TUS

Viereck, Peter (Robert Edwin)
1916- .... **CLC 4; PC 27**
See also CA 1-4R; CANR 1, 47; CP 7; DLB
5; PFS 9, 14

Vigny, Alfred (Victor) de
1797-1863 .... **NCLC 7, 102; PC 26**
See also DAM POET; DLB 119, 192, 217;
EW 5; GFL 1789 to the Present; RGWL
2, 3

Vilakazi, Benedict Wallet
1906-1947 .... **TCLC 37**
See also CA 168

Villa, Jose Garcia 1914-1997 .... **AAL; PC 22**
See also CA 25-28R; CANR 12, 118; EWL
3; EXPP

Villa, Jose Garcia 1914-1997
See Villa, Jose Garcia

Villa, Jose Garcia 1914-1997 .... **AAL; PC 22**
See also CA 25-28R; CANR 12, 118; EWL
3; EXPP

Villard, Oswald Garrison
1872-1949 .... **TCLC 160**
See also CA 113, 162; DLB 25, 91

Villaurrutia, Xavier 1903-1950 ...... **TCLC 80**
See also CA 192; EWL 3; HW 1; LAW

Villaverde, Cirilo 1812-1894 .... **NCLC 121**
See also LAW

Villehardouin, Geoffroi de
1150(?)-1218(?) .... **CMLC 38**

Villiers, George 1628-1687 .... **LC 107**
See also DLB 80; RGEL 2

**Villiers de l'Isle Adam, Jean Marie Mathias
Philippe Auguste** 1838-1889 ... **NCLC 3;
SSC 14**
See also DLB 123, 192; GFL 1789 to the
Present; RGSF 2

Villon, Francois 1431-1463(?) . **LC 62; PC 13**
See also DLB 208; EW 2; RGWL 2, 3;
TWA

Vine, Barbara .... **CLC 50**
See Rendell, Ruth (Barbara)
See also BEST 90:4

Vinge, Joan (Carol) D(ennison)
1948- .... **CLC 30; SSC 24**
See also AAYA 32; BPFB 3; CA 93-96;
CANR 72; SATA 36, 113; SFW 4; YAW

Viola, Herman J(oseph) 1938- .... **CLC 70**
See also CA 61-64; CANR 8, 23, 48, 91;
SATA 126

Violis, G.
See Simenon, Georges (Jacques Christian)

Viramontes, Helena Maria 1954- .... **HLCS 2**
See also CA 159; DLB 122; HW 2; LLW 1

Virgil
See Vergil
See also CDWLB 1; DLB 211; LAIT 1;
RGWL 2, 3; WP

Visconti, Luchino 1906-1976 .... **CLC 16**
See also CA 81-84; 65-68; CANR 39

Vitry, Jacques de
See Jacques de Vitry

Vittorini, Elio 1908-1966 .... **CLC 6, 9, 14**
See also CA 133; 25-28R; DLB 264; EW
12; EWL 3; RGWL 2, 3

Vivekananda, Swami 1863-1902 .... **TCLC 88**

Vizenor, Gerald Robert 1934- .... **CLC 103;
NNAL**
See also CA 13-16R, 205; CAAE 205;
CAAS 22; CANR 5, 21, 44, 67; DAM
MULT; DLB 175, 227; MTCW 2; TCWW
2

Vizinczey, Stephen 1933- .... **CLC 40**
See also CA 128; CCA 1; INT CA-128

Vliet, R(ussell) G(ordon)
1929-1984 .... **CLC 22**
See also CA 37-40R; 112; CANR 18

Vogau, Boris Andreyevich 1894-1938
See Pilnyak, Boris
See also CA 123; 218

Vogel, Paula A(nne) 1951- ... **CLC 76; DC 19**
See also CA 108; CAD; CANR 119; CD 5;
CWD; DFS 14; RGAL 4

Voigt, Cynthia 1942- .... **CLC 30**
See also AAYA 3, 30; BYA 1, 3, 6, 7, 8;
CA 106; CANR 18, 37, 40, 94; CLR 13,
48; INT CANR-18; JRDA; LAIT 5; MAI-
CYA 1, 2; MAICYAS 1; SATA 48, 79,
116; SATA-Brief 33; WYA; YAW

Voigt, Ellen Bryant 1943- .... **CLC 54**
See also CA 69-72; CANR 11, 29, 55, 115;
CP 7; CSW; CWP; DLB 120

Voinovich, Vladimir (Nikolaevich)
1932- .... **CLC 10, 49, 147**
See also CA 81-84; CAAS 12; CANR 33,
67; CWW 2; DLB 302; MTCW 1

Vollmann, William T. 1959- .... **CLC 89**
See also CA 134; CANR 67, 116; CPW;
DA3; DAM NOV, POP; MTCW 2

Voloshinov, V. N.
See Bakhtin, Mikhail Mikhailovich

Voltaire 1694-1778 . **LC 14, 79, 110; SSC 12;
WLC**
See also BYA 13; DA; DA3; DAB; DAC;
DAM DRAM, MST; EW 4; GFL Begin-
nings to 1789; LATS 1:1; LMFS 1; NFS
7; RGWL 2, 3; TWA

von Aschendrof, Baron Ignatz
See Ford, Ford Madox

von Chamisso, Adelbert
See Chamisso, Adelbert von

von Daeniken, Erich 1935- .... **CLC 30**
See also AITN 1; CA 37-40R; CANR 17,
44

von Daniken, Erich
See von Daeniken, Erich

von Hartmann, Eduard
1842-1906 .... **TCLC 96**

von Hayek, Friedrich August
See Hayek, F(riedrich) A(ugust von)

von Heidenstam, (Carl Gustaf) Verner
See Heidenstam, (Carl Gustaf) Verner von

von Heyse, Paul (Johann Ludwig)
See Heyse, Paul (Johann Ludwig von)

von Hofmannsthal, Hugo
See Hofmannsthal, Hugo von

von Horvath, Odon
See von Horvath, Odon

von Horvath, Odon
See von Horvath, Odon

von Horvath, Odon 1901-1938 .... **TCLC 45**
See von Horvath, Oedoen
See also CA 118; 194; DLB 85, 124; RGWL
2, 3

von Horvath, Oedoen
See von Horvath, Odon
See also CA 184

von Kleist, Heinrich
See Kleist, Heinrich von

**von Liliencron, (Friedrich Adolf Axel)
Detlev**
See Liliencron, (Friedrich Adolf Axel) De-
tlev von

Vonnegut, Kurt, Jr. 1922- . **CLC 1, 2, 3, 4, 5,
8, 12, 22, 40, 60, 111; SSC 8; WLC**
See also AAYA 6, 44; AITN 1; AMWS 2;
BEST 90:4; BPFB 3; BYA 3, 14; CA
1-4R; CANR 1, 25, 49, 75, 92; CDALB
1968-1988; CN 7; CPW 1; DA; DA3;
DAB; DAC; DAM MST, NOV, POP;
DLB 2, 8, 152; DLBD 3; DLBY 1980;
EWL 3; EXPN; EXPS; LAIT 4; LMFS 2;
MTCW 1, 2; NFS 3; RGAL 4; SCFW;
SFW 4; SSFS 5; TUS; YAW

Von Rachen, Kurt
See Hubbard, L(afayette) Ron(ald)

von Rezzori (d'Arezzo), Gregor
See Rezzori (d'Arezzo), Gregor von

von Sternberg, Josef
See Sternberg, Josef von

Vorster, Gordon 1924- .... **CLC 34**
See also CA 133

Vosce, Trudie
See Ozick, Cynthia

Voznesensky, Andrei (Andreievich)
1933- .... **CLC 1, 15, 57**
See Voznesensky, Andrey
See also CA 89-92; CANR 37; CWW 2;
DAM POET; MTCW 1

Voznesensky, Andrey
See Voznesensky, Andrei (Andreievich)
See also EWL 3

Wace, Robert c. 1100-c. 1175 .... **CMLC 55**
See also DLB 146

Waddington, Miriam 1917-2004 .... **CLC 28**
See also CA 21-24R; 225; CANR 12, 30;
CCA 1; CP 7; DLB 68

Wagman, Fredrica 1937- .... **CLC 7**
See also CA 97-100; INT CA-97-100

Wagner, Linda W.
See Wagner-Martin, Linda (C.)

Wagner, Linda Welshimer
See Wagner-Martin, Linda (C.)

Wagner, Richard 1813-1883 ..... **NCLC 9, 119**
See also DLB 129; EW 6

Wagner-Martin, Linda (C.) 1936- .... **CLC 50**
See also CA 159; CANR 135

Wagoner, David (Russell) 1926- .... **CLC 3, 5,
15; PC 33**
See also AMWS 9; CA 1-4R; CAAS 3;
CANR 2, 71; CN 7; CP 7; DLB 5, 256;
SATA 14; TCWW 2

Wah, Fred(erick James) 1939- .... **CLC 44**
See also CA 107; 141; CP 7; DLB 60

Wahloo, Per 1926-1975 .... **CLC 7**
See also BPFB 3; CA 61-64; CANR 73;
CMW 4; MSW

Wahloo, Peter
See Wahloo, Per

Wain, John (Barrington) 1925-1994 . **CLC 2,
11, 15, 46**
See also CA 5-8R; 145; CAAS 4; CANR
23, 54; CDBLB 1960 to Present; DLB 15,
27, 139, 155; EWL 3; MTCW 1, 2

Watkins, Paul 1964- .... **CLC 55**
　　See also CA 132; CANR 62, 98
Watkins, Vernon Phillips
　　1906-1967 .... **CLC 43**
　　See also CA 9-10; 25-28R; CAP 1; DLB
　　20; EWL 3; RGEL 2
Watson, Irving S.
　　See Mencken, H(enry) L(ouis)
Watson, John H.
　　See Farmer, Philip Jose
Watson, Richard F.
　　See Silverberg, Robert
Watts, Ephraim
　　See Horne, Richard Henry Hengist
Watts, Isaac 1674-1748 .... **LC 98**
　　See also DLB 95; RGEL 2; SATA 52
Waugh, Auberon (Alexander)
　　1939-2001 .... **CLC 7**
　　See also CA 45-48; 192; CANR 6, 22, 92;
　　DLB 14, 194
Waugh, Evelyn (Arthur St. John)
　　1903-1966 .. **CLC 1, 3, 8, 13, 19, 27, 44,
　　107; SSC 41; WLC**
　　See also BPFB 3; BRW 7; CA 85-88; 25-
　　28R; CANR 22; CDBLB 1914-1945; DA;
　　DA3; DAB; DAC; DAM MST, NOV;
　　POP; DLB 15, 162, 195; EWL 3; MTCW
　　1, 2; NFS 13, 17; RGEL 2; RGSF 2; TEA;
　　WLIT 4
Waugh, Harriet 1944- .... **CLC 6**
　　See also CA 85-88; CANR 22
Ways, C. R.
　　See Blount, Roy (Alton), Jr.
Waystaff, Simon
　　See Swift, Jonathan
Webb, Beatrice (Martha Potter)
　　1858-1943 .... **TCLC 22**
　　See also CA 117; 162; DLB 190; FW
Webb, Charles (Richard) 1939- .... **CLC 7**
　　See also CA 25-28R; CANR 114
Webb, Frank J. .... **NCLC 143**
　　See also DLB 50
Webb, James H(enry), Jr. 1946- ...... **CLC 22**
　　See also CA 81-84
Webb, Mary Gladys (Meredith)
　　1881-1927 .... **TCLC 24**
　　See also CA 182; 123; DLB 34; FW
Webb, Mrs. Sidney
　　See Webb, Beatrice (Martha Potter)
Webb, Phyllis 1927- .... **CLC 18**
　　See also CA 104; CANR 23; CCA 1; CP 7;
　　CWP; DLB 53
Webb, Sidney (James) 1859-1947 .. **TCLC 22**
　　See also CA 117; 163; DLB 190
Webber, Andrew Lloyd .... **CLC 21**
　　See Lloyd Webber, Andrew
　　See also DFS 7
Weber, Lenora Mattingly
　　1895-1971 .... **CLC 12**
　　See also CA 19-20; 29-32R; CAP 1; SATA
　　2; SATA-Obit 26
Weber, Max 1864-1920 .... **TCLC 69**
　　See also CA 109; 189; DLB 296
Webster, John 1580(?)-1634(?) ...... **DC 2; LC
　　33, 84; WLC**
　　See also BRW 2; CDBLB Before 1660; DA;
　　DAB; DAC; DAM DRAM, MST; DFS
　　17, 19; DLB 58; IDTP; RGEL 2; WLIT 3
Webster, Noah 1758-1843 .... **NCLC 30**
　　See also DLB 1, 37, 42, 43, 73, 243
Wedekind, (Benjamin) Frank(lin)
　　1864-1918 .... **TCLC 7**
　　See also CA 104; 153; CANR 121, 122;
　　CDWLB 2; DAM DRAM; DLB 118; EW
　　8; EWL 3; LMFS 2; RGWL 2, 3
Wehr, Demaris .... **CLC 65**
Weidman, Jerome 1913-1998 .... **CLC 7**
　　See also AITN 2; CA 1-4R; 171; CAD;
　　CANR 1; DLB 28

Weil, Simone (Adolphine)
　　1909-1943 .... **TCLC 23**
　　See also CA 117; 159; EW 12; EWL 3; FW;
　　GFL 1789 to the Present; MTCW 2
Weininger, Otto 1880-1903 .... **TCLC 84**
Weinstein, Nathan
　　See West, Nathanael
Weinstein, Nathan von Wallenstein
　　See West, Nathanael
Weir, Peter (Lindsay) 1944- .... **CLC 20**
　　See also CA 113; 123
Weiss, Peter (Ulrich) 1916-1982 .. **CLC 3, 15,
　　51; TCLC 152**
　　See also CA 45-48; 106; CANR 3; DAM
　　DRAM; DFS 3; DLB 69, 124; EWL 3;
　　RGWL 2, 3
Weiss, Theodore (Russell)
　　1916-2003 .... **CLC 3, 8, 14**
　　See also CA 9-12R; 189; 216; CAAE 189;
　　CAAS 2; CANR 46, 94; CP 7; DLB 5
Welch, (Maurice) Denton
　　1915-1948 .... **TCLC 22**
　　See also BRWS 8, 9; CA 121; 148; RGEL
　　2
Welch, James (Phillip) 1940-2003 ..... **CLC 6,
　　14, 52; NNAL; PC 62**
　　See also CA 85-88; 219; CANR 42, 66, 107;
　　CN 7; CP 7; CPW; DAM MULT, POP;
　　DLB 175, 256; LATS 1:1; RGAL 4;
　　TCWW 2
Weldon, Fay 1931- . **CLC 6, 9, 11, 19, 36, 59,
　　122**
　　See also BRWS 4; CA 21-24R; CANR 16,
　　46, 63, 97; CDBLB 1960 to Present; CN
　　7; CPW; DAM POP; DLB 14, 194; EWL
　　3; FW; HGG; INT CANR-16; MTCW 1,
　　2; RGEL 2; RGSF 2
Wellek, Rene 1903-1995 .... **CLC 28**
　　See also CA 5-8R; 150; CAAS 7; CANR 8;
　　DLB 63; EWL 3; INT CANR-8
Weller, Michael 1942- .... **CLC 10, 53**
　　See also CA 85-88; CAD; CD 5
Weller, Paul 1958- .... **CLC 26**
Wellershoff, Dieter 1925- .... **CLC 46**
　　See also CA 89-92; CANR 16, 37
Welles, (George) Orson 1915-1985 .. **CLC 20,
　　80**
　　See also AAYA 40; CA 93-96; 117
Wellman, John McDowell 1945-
　　See Wellman, Mac
　　See also CA 166; CD 5
Wellman, Mac .... **CLC 65**
　　See Wellman, John McDowell; Wellman,
　　John McDowell
　　See also CAD; RGAL 4
Wellman, Manly Wade 1903-1986 ... **CLC 49**
　　See also CA 1-4R; 118; CANR 6, 16, 44;
　　FANT; SATA 6; SATA-Obit 47; SFW 4;
　　SUFW
Wells, Carolyn 1869(?)-1942 .... **TCLC 35**
　　See also CA 113; 185; CMW 4; DLB 11
Wells, H(erbert) G(eorge) 1866-1946 . **SSC 6,
　　70; TCLC 6, 12, 19, 133; WLC**
　　See also AAYA 18; BPFB 3; BRW 6; CA
　　110; 121; CDBLB 1914-1945; CLR 64;
　　DA; DA3; DAB; DAC; DAM MST, NOV;
　　DLB 34, 70, 156, 178; EWL 3; EXPS;
　　HGG; LAIT 3; LMFS 2; MTCW 1, 2;
　　NFS 17, 20; RGEL 2; RGSF 2; SATA 20;
　　SCFW; SFW 4; SSFS 3; SUFW 1; TEA;
　　WCH; WLIT 4; YAW
Wells, Rosemary 1943- .... **CLC 12**
　　See also AAYA 13; BYA 7, 8; CA 85-88;
　　CANR 48, 120; CLR 16, 69; CWRI 5;
　　MAICYA 1, 2; SAAS 1; SATA 18, 69,
　　114; YAW
Wells-Barnett, Ida B(ell)
　　1862-1931 .... **TCLC 125**
　　See also CA 182; DLB 23, 221

Welsh, Irvine 1958- .... **CLC 144**
　　See also CA 173; DLB 271
Welty, Eudora (Alice) 1909-2001 .. **CLC 1, 2,
　　5, 14, 22, 33, 105; SSC 1, 27, 51; WLC**
　　See also AAYA 48; AMW; AMWR 1; BPFB
　　3; CA 9-12R; 199; CABS 1; CANR 32,
　　65, 128; CDALB 1941-1968; CN 7; CSW;
　　DA; DA3; DAB; DAC; DAM MST, NOV;
　　DLB 2, 102, 143; DLBD 12; DLBY 1987,
　　2001; EWL 3; EXPS; HGG; LAIT 3;
　　MAWW; MTCW 1, 2; NFS 13, 15; RGAL
　　4; RGSF 2; RHW; SSFS 2, 10; TUS
Wen I-to 1899-1946 .... **TCLC 28**
　　See also EWL 3
Wentworth, Robert
　　See Hamilton, Edmond
Werfel, Franz (Viktor) 1890-1945 ... **TCLC 8**
　　See also CA 104; 161; DLB 81, 124; EWL
　　3; RGWL 2, 3
Wergeland, Henrik Arnold
　　1808-1845 .... **NCLC 5**
Wersba, Barbara 1932- .... **CLC 30**
　　See also AAYA 2, 30; BYA 6, 12, 13; CA
　　29-32R, 182; CAAE 182; CANR 16, 38;
　　CLR 3, 78; DLB 52; JRDA; MAICYA 1,
　　2; SAAS 2; SATA 1, 58; SATA-Essay 103;
　　WYA; YAW
Wertmueller, Lina 1928- .... **CLC 16**
　　See also CA 97-100; CANR 39, 78
Wescott, Glenway 1901-1987 .. **CLC 13; SSC
　　35**
　　See also CA 13-16R; 121; CANR 23, 70;
　　DLB 4, 9, 102; RGAL 4
Wesker, Arnold 1932- .... **CLC 3, 5, 42**
　　See also CA 1-4R; CAAS 1, 33;
　　CBD; CD 5; CDBLB 1960 to Present;
　　DAB; DAM DRAM; DLB 13; EWL 3;
　　MTCW 1; RGEL 2; TEA
Wesley, John 1703-1791 .... **LC 88**
　　See also DLB 104
Wesley, Richard (Errol) 1945- .... **CLC 7**
　　See also BW 1; CA 57-60; CAD; CANR
　　27; CD 5; DLB 38
Wessel, Johan Herman 1742-1785 .... **LC 7**
　　See also DLB 300
West, Anthony (Panther)
　　1914-1987 .... **CLC 50**
　　See also CA 45-48; 124; CANR 3, 19; DLB
　　15
West, C. P.
　　See Wodehouse, P(elham) G(renville)
West, Cornel (Ronald) 1953- .... **BLCS; CLC
　　134**
　　See also CA 144; CANR 91; DLB 246
West, Delno C(loyde), Jr. 1936- .... **CLC 70**
　　See also CA 57-60
West, Dorothy 1907-1998 .. **HR 3; TCLC 108**
　　See also BW 2; CA 143; 169; DLB 76
West, (Mary) Jessamyn 1902-1984 ... **CLC 7,
　　17**
　　See also CA 9-12R; 112; CANR 27; DLB
　　6; DLBY 1984; MTCW 1, 2; RGAL 4;
　　RHW; SATA-Obit 37; TCWW 2; TUS;
　　YAW
West, Morris
　　See West, Morris L(anglo)
　　See also DLB 289
West, Morris L(anglo) 1916-1999 ..... **CLC 6,
　　33**
　　See West, Morris
　　See also BPFB 3; CA 5-8R; 187; CANR
　　24, 49, 64; CN 7; CPW; MTCW 1, 2
West, Nathanael 1903-1940 .. **SSC 16; TCLC
　　1, 14, 44**
　　See also AMW; AMWR 2; BPFB 3; CA
　　104; 125; CDALB 1929-1941; DA3; DLB
　　4, 9, 28; EWL 3; MTCW 1, 2; NFS 16;
　　RGAL 4; TUS

461

Wilding, Michael 1942- ...... **CLC 73; SSC 50**
See also CA 104; CANR 24, 49, 106; CN 7; RGSF 2

Wiley, Richard 1944- .... **CLC 44**
See also CA 121; 129; CANR 71

Wilhelm, Kate .... **CLC 7**
See Wilhelm, Katie (Gertrude)
See also AAYA 20; BYA 16; CAAS 5; DLB 8; INT CANR-17; SCFW 2

Wilhelm, Katie (Gertrude) 1928-
See Wilhelm, Kate
See also CA 37-40R; CANR 17, 36, 60, 94; MTCW 1; SFW 4

Wilkins, Mary
See Freeman, Mary E(leanor) Wilkins

Willard, Nancy 1936- .... **CLC 7, 37**
See also BYA 5; CA 89-92; CANR 10, 39, 68, 107; CLR 5; CWP; CWRI 5; DLB 5, 52; FANT; MAICYA 1, 2; MTCW 1; SATA 37, 71, 127; SATA-Brief 30; SUFW 2

William of Malmesbury c. 1090B.C.-c. 1140B.C. .... **CMLC 57**

William of Ockham 1290-1349 ..... **CMLC 32**

Williams, Ben Ames 1889-1953 ..... **TCLC 89**
See also CA 183; DLB 102

Williams, C(harles) K(enneth)
1936- .... **CLC 33, 56, 148**
See also CA 37-40R; CAAS 26; CANR 57, 106; CP 7; DAM POET; DLB 5

Williams, Charles
See Collier, James Lincoln

Williams, Charles (Walter Stansby)
1886-1945 .... **TCLC 1, 11**
See also BRWS 9; CA 104; 163; DLB 100, 153, 255; FANT; RGEL 2; SUFW 1

Williams, Ella Gwendolen Rees
See Rhys, Jean

Williams, (George) Emlyn
1905-1987 .... **CLC 15**
See also CA 104; 123; CANR 36; DAM DRAM; DLB 10, 77; IDTP; MTCW 1

Williams, Hank 1923-1953 .... **TCLC 81**
See Williams, Hiram King

Williams, Helen Maria
1761-1827 .... **NCLC 135**
See also DLB 158

Williams, Hiram Hank
See Williams, Hank

Williams, Hiram King
See Williams, Hank
See also CA 188

Williams, Hugo (Mordaunt) 1942- ... **CLC 42**
See also CA 17-20R; CANR 45, 119; CP 7; DLB 40

Williams, J. Walker
See Wodehouse, P(elham) G(renville)

Williams, John A(lfred) 1925- . **BLC 3; CLC 5, 13**
See also AFAW 2; BW 2, 3; CA 53-56, 195; CAAE 195; CAAS 3; CANR 6, 26, 51, 118; CN 7; CSW; DAM MULT; DLB 2, 33; EWL 3; INT CANR-6; RGAL 4; SFW 4

Williams, Jonathan (Chamberlain)
1929- .... **CLC 13**
See also CA 9-12R; CAAS 12; CANR 8, 108; CP 7; DLB 5

Williams, Joy 1944- .... **CLC 31**
See also CA 41-44R; CANR 22, 48, 97

Williams, Norman 1952- .... **CLC 39**
See also CA 118

Williams, Sherley Anne 1944-1999 ... **BLC 3; CLC 89**
See also AFAW 2; BW 2, 3; CA 73-76; 185; CANR 25, 82; DAM MULT, POET; DLB 41; INT CANR-25; SATA 78; SATA-Obit 116

Williams, Shirley
See Williams, Sherley Anne

Williams, Tennessee 1911-1983 . **CLC 1, 2, 5, 7, 8, 11, 15, 19, 30, 39, 45, 71, 111; DC 4; WLC**
See also AAYA 31; AITN 1, 2; AMW; AMWC 1; CA 5-8R; 108; CABS 3; CAD; CANR 31, 132; CDALB 1941-1968; DA; DA3; DAB; DAC; DAM DRAM, MST; DFS 17; DLB 7; DLBD 4; DLBY 1983; EWL 3; GLL 1; LAIT 4; LATS 1:2; MTCW 1, 2; RGAL 4; TUS

Williams, Thomas (Alonzo)
1926-1990 .... **CLC 14**
See also CA 1-4R; 132; CANR 2

Williams, William C.
See Williams, William Carlos

Williams, William Carlos
1883-1963 .... **CLC 1, 2, 5, 9, 13, 22, 42, 67; PC 7; SSC 31**
See also AAYA 46; AMW; AMWR 1; CA 89-92; CANR 34; CDALB 1917-1929; DA; DA3; DAB; DAC; DAM MST, POET; DLB 4, 16, 54, 86; EWL 3; EXPP; MTCW 1, 2; NCFS 4; PAB; PFS 1, 6, 11; RGAL 4; RGSF 2; TUS; WP

Williamson, David (Keith) 1942- ..... **CLC 56**
See also CA 103; CANR 41; CD 5; DLB 289

Williamson, Ellen Douglas 1905-1984
See Douglas, Ellen
See also CA 17-20R; 114; CANR 39

Williamson, Jack .... **CLC 29**
See Williamson, John Stewart
See also CAAS 8; DLB 8; SCFW 2

Williamson, John Stewart 1908-
See Williamson, Jack
See also CA 17-20R; CANR 23, 70; SFW 4

Willie, Frederick
See Lovecraft, H(oward) P(hillips)

Willingham, Calder (Baynard, Jr.)
1922-1995 .... **CLC 5, 51**
See also CA 5-8R; 147; CANR 3; CSW; DLB 2, 44; IDFW 3, 4; MTCW 1

Willis, Charles
See Clarke, Arthur C(harles)

Willy
See Colette, (Sidonie-Gabrielle)

Willy, Colette
See Colette, (Sidonie-Gabrielle)
See also GLL 1

Wilmot, John 1647-1680 .... **LC 75**
See Rochester
See also BRW 2; DLB 131; PAB

Wilson, A(ndrew) N(orman) 1950- .. **CLC 33**
See also BRWS 6; CA 112; 122; CN 7; DLB 14, 155, 194; MTCW 2

Wilson, Angus (Frank Johnstone)
1913-1991 . **CLC 2, 3, 5, 25, 34; SSC 21**
See also BRWS 1; CA 5-8R; 134; CANR 21; DLB 15, 139, 155; EWL 3; MTCW 1, 2; RGEL 2; RGSF 2

Wilson, August 1945- ... **BLC 3; CLC 39, 50, 63, 118; DC 2; WLCS**
See also AAYA 16; AFAW 2; AMWS 8; BW 2, 3; CA 115; 122; CAD; CANR 42, 54, 76, 128; CD 5; DA; DA3; DAB; DAC; DAM DRAM, MST, MULT; DFS 3, 7, 15, 17; DLB 228; EWL 3; LAIT 4; LATS 1:2; MTCW 1, 2; RGAL 4

Wilson, Brian 1942- .... **CLC 12**

Wilson, Colin 1931- .... **CLC 3, 14**
See also CA 1-4R; CAAS 5; CANR 1, 22, 33, 77; CMW 4; CN 7; DLB 14, 194; HGG; MTCW 1; SFW 4

Wilson, Dirk
See Pohl, Frederik

Wilson, Edmund 1895-1972 .. **CLC 1, 2, 3, 8, 24**
See also AMW; CA 1-4R; 37-40R; CANR 1, 46, 110; DLB 63; EWL 3; MTCW 1, 2; RGAL 4; TUS

Wilson, Ethel Davis (Bryant)
1888(?)-1980 .... **CLC 13**
See also CA 102; DAC; DAM POET; DLB 68; MTCW 1; RGEL 2

Wilson, Harriet
See Wilson, Harriet E. Adams
See also DLB 239

Wilson, Harriet E.
See Wilson, Harriet E. Adams
See also DLB 243

Wilson, Harriet E. Adams
1827(?)-1863(?) .... **BLC 3; NCLC 78**
See Wilson, Harriet; Wilson, Harriet E.
See also DAM MULT; DLB 50

Wilson, John 1785-1854 .... **NCLC 5**

Wilson, John (Anthony) Burgess 1917-1993
See Burgess, Anthony
See also CA 1-4R; 143; CANR 2, 46; DA3; DAC; DAM NOV; MTCW 1, 2; NFS 15; TEA

Wilson, Lanford 1937- .. **CLC 7, 14, 36, 197; DC 19**
See also CA 17-20R; CABS 3; CAD; CANR 45, 96; CD 5; DAM DRAM; DFS 4, 9, 12, 16, 20; DLB 7; EWL 3; TUS

Wilson, Robert M. 1941- .... **CLC 7, 9**
See also CA 49-52; CAD; CANR 2, 41; CD 5; MTCW 1

Wilson, Robert McLiam 1964- .... **CLC 59**
See also CA 132; DLB 267

Wilson, Sloan 1920-2003 .... **CLC 32**
See also CA 1-4R; 216; CANR 1, 44; CN 7

Wilson, Snoo 1948- .... **CLC 33**
See also CA 69-72; CBD; CD 5

Wilson, William S(mith) 1932- .... **CLC 49**
See also CA 81-84

Wilson, (Thomas) Woodrow
1856-1924 .... **TCLC 79**
See also CA 166; DLB 47

Wilson and Warnke eds. .... **CLC 65**

Winchilsea, Anne (Kingsmill) Finch
1661-1720
See Finch, Anne
See also RGEL 2

Windham, Basil
See Wodehouse, P(elham) G(renville)

Wingrove, David (John) 1954- .... **CLC 68**
See also CA 133; SFW 4

Winnemucca, Sarah 1844-1891 .... **NCLC 79; NNAL**
See also DAM MULT; DLB 175; RGAL 4

Winstanley, Gerrard 1609-1676 .... **LC 52**

Wintergreen, Jane
See Duncan, Sara Jeannette

Winters, Janet Lewis .... **CLC 41**
See Lewis, Janet
See also DLBY 1987

Winters, (Arthur) Yvor 1900-1968 .... **CLC 4, 8, 32**
See also AMWS 2; CA 11-12; 25-28R; CAP 1; DLB 48; EWL 3; MTCW 1; RGAL 4

Winterson, Jeanette 1959- .... **CLC 64, 158**
See also BRWS 4; CA 136; CANR 58, 116; CN 7; CPW; DA3; DAM POP; DLB 207, 261; FANT; FW; GLL 1; MTCW 2; RHW

Winthrop, John 1588-1649 .... **LC 31, 107**
See also DLB 24, 30

Wirth, Louis 1897-1952 .... **TCLC 92**
See also CA 210

Wiseman, Frederick 1930- .... **CLC 20**
See also CA 159

Wister, Owen 1860-1938 .... **TCLC 21**
See also BPFB 3; CA 108; 162; DLB 9, 78, 186; RGAL 4; SATA 62; TCWW 2

Yakamochi 718-785 .... **CMLC 45; PC 48**

Yakumo Koizumi
See Hearn, (Patricio) Lafcadio (Tessima Carlos)

Yamada, Mitsuye (May) 1923- .... **PC 44**
See also CA 77-80

Yamamoto, Hisaye 1921- .... **AAL; SSC 34**
See also CA 214; DAM MULT; LAIT 4; SSFS 14

Yamauchi, Wakako 1924- .... **AAL**
See also CA 214

Yanez, Jose Donoso
See Donoso (Yanez), Jose

Yanovsky, Basile S.
See Yanovsky, V(assily) S(emenovich)

Yanovsky, V(assily) S(emenovich)
1906-1989 .... **CLC 2, 18**
See also CA 97-100; 129

Yates, Richard 1926-1992 .... **CLC 7, 8, 23**
See also AMWS 11; CA 5-8R; 139; CANR 10, 43; DLB 2, 234; DLBY 1981, 1992; INT CANR-10

Yau, John 1950- .... **PC 61**
See also CA 154; CANR 89; CP 7; DLB 234

Yeats, W. B.
See Yeats, William Butler

Yeats, William Butler 1865-1939 . **PC 20, 51; TCLC 1, 11, 18, 31, 93, 116; WLC**
See also AAYA 48; BRW 6; BRWR 1; CA 104; 127; CANR 45; CDBLB 1890-1914; DA; DA3; DAB; DAC; DAM DRAM, MST, POET; DLB 10, 19, 98, 156; EWL 3; EXPP; MTCW 1, 2; NCFS 3; PAB; PFS 1, 2, 5, 7, 13, 15; RGEL 2; TEA; WLIT 4; WP

Yehoshua, A(braham) B. 1936- .. **CLC 13, 31**
See also CA 33-36R; CANR 43, 90; CWW 2; EWL 3; RGSF 2; RGWL 3

Yellow Bird
See Ridge, John Rollin

Yep, Laurence Michael 1948- .... **CLC 35**
See also AAYA 5, 31; BYA 7; CA 49-52; CANR 1, 46, 92; CLR 3, 17, 54; DLB 52; FANT; JRDA; MAICYA 1, 2; MAICYAS 1; SATA 7, 69, 123; WYA; YAW

Yerby, Frank G(arvin) 1916-1991 ..... **BLC 3; CLC 1, 7, 22**
See also BPFB 3; BW 1, 3; CA 9-12R; 136; CANR 16, 52; DAM MULT; DLB 76; INT CANR-16; MTCW 1; RGAL 4; RHW

Yesenin, Sergei Alexandrovich
See Esenin, Sergei (Alexandrovich)

Yesenin, Sergey
See Esenin, Sergei (Alexandrovich)
See also EWL 3

Yevtushenko, Yevgeny (Alexandrovich)
1933- ...... **CLC 1, 3, 13, 26, 51, 126; PC 40**
See Evtushenko, Evgenii Aleksandrovich
See also CA 81-84; CANR 33, 54; DAM POET; EWL 3; MTCW 1

Yezierska, Anzia 1885(?)-1970 .... **CLC 46**
See also CA 126; 89-92; DLB 28, 221; FW; MTCW 1; RGAL 4; SSFS 15

Yglesias, Helen 1915- .... **CLC 7, 22**
See also CA 37-40R; CAAS 20; CANR 15, 65, 95; CN 7; INT CANR-15; MTCW 1

Yokomitsu, Riichi 1898-1947 .... **TCLC 47**
See also CA 170; EWL 3

Yonge, Charlotte (Mary)
1823-1901 .... **TCLC 48**
See also CA 109; 163; DLB 18, 163; RGEL 2; SATA 17; WCH

York, Jeremy
See Creasey, John

York, Simon
See Heinlein, Robert A(nson)

Yorke, Henry Vincent 1905-1974 ..... **CLC 13**
See Green, Henry
See also CA 85-88; 49-52

Yosano Akiko 1878-1942 .... **PC 11; TCLC 59**
See also CA 161; EWL 3; RGWL 3

Yoshimoto, Banana .... **CLC 84**
See Yoshimoto, Mahoko
See also AAYA 50; NFS 7

Yoshimoto, Mahoko 1964-
See Yoshimoto, Banana
See also CA 144; CANR 98; SSFS 16

Young, Al(bert James) 1939- ... **BLC 3; CLC 19**
See also BW 2, 3; CA 29-32R; CANR 26, 65, 109; CN 7; CP 7; DAM MULT; DLB 33

Young, Andrew (John) 1885-1971 ...... **CLC 5**
See also CA 5-8R; CANR 7, 29; RGEL 2

Young, Collier
See Bloch, Robert (Albert)

Young, Edward 1683-1765 .... **LC 3, 40**
See also DLB 95; RGEL 2

Young, Marguerite (Vivian)
1909-1995 .... **CLC 82**
See also CA 13-16; 150; CAP 1; CN 7

Young, Neil 1945- .... **CLC 17**
See also CA 110; CCA 1

Young Bear, Ray A. 1950- ... **CLC 94; NNAL**
See also CA 146; DAM MULT; DLB 175

Yourcenar, Marguerite 1903-1987 ... **CLC 19, 38, 50, 87**
See also BPFB 3; CA 69-72; CANR 23, 60, 93; DAM NOV; DLB 72; DLBY 1988; EW 12; EWL 3; GFL 1789 to the Present; GLL 1; MTCW 1, 2; RGWL 2, 3

Yuan, Chu 340(?)B.C.-278(?)B.C. . **CMLC 36**

Yurick, Sol 1925- .... **CLC 6**
See also CA 13-16R; CANR 25; CN 7

Zabolotsky, Nikolai Alekseevich
1903-1958 .... **TCLC 52**
See Zabolotsky, Nikolay Alekseevich
See also CA 116; 164

Zabolotsky, Nikolay Alekseevich
See Zabolotsky, Nikolai Alekseevich
See also EWL 3

Zagajewski, Adam 1945- .... **PC 27**
See also CA 186; DLB 232; EWL 3

Zalygin, Sergei -2000 .... **CLC 59**

Zalygin, Sergei (Pavlovich)
1913-2000 .... **CLC 59**
See also DLB 302

Zamiatin, Evgenii
See Zamyatin, Evgeny Ivanovich
See also RGSF 2; RGWL 2, 3

Zamiatin, Evgenii Ivanovich
See Zamyatin, Evgeny Ivanovich
See also DLB 272

Zamiatin, Yevgenii
See Zamyatin, Evgeny Ivanovich

Zamora, Bernice (B. Ortiz) 1938- .. **CLC 89; HLC 2**
See also CA 151; CANR 80; DAM MULT; DLB 82; HW 1, 2

Zamyatin, Evgeny Ivanovich
1884-1937 .... **TCLC 8, 37**
See Zamiatin, Evgenii; Zamiatin, Evgenii Ivanovich; Zamyatin, Yevgeny Ivanovich
See also CA 105; 166; EW 10; SFW 4

Zamyatin, Yevgeny Ivanovich
See Zamyatin, Evgeny Ivanovich
See also EWL 3

Zangwill, Israel 1864-1926 ... **SSC 44; TCLC 16**
See also CA 109; 167; CMW 4; DLB 10, 135, 197; RGEL 2

Zappa, Francis Vincent, Jr. 1940-1993
See Zappa, Frank
See also CA 108; 143; CANR 57

Zappa, Frank .... **CLC 17**
See Zappa, Francis Vincent, Jr.

Zaturenska, Marya 1902-1982 ..... **CLC 6, 11**
See also CA 13-16R; 105; CANR 22

Zayas y Sotomayor, Maria de 1590-c. 1661 .... **LC 102**
See also RGSF 2

Zeami 1363-1443 .... **DC 7; LC 86**
See also DLB 203; RGWL 2, 3

Zelazny, Roger (Joseph) 1937-1995 . **CLC 21**
See also AAYA 7; BPFB 3; CA 21-24R; 148; CANR 26, 60; CN 7; DLB 8; FANT; MTCW 1, 2; SATA 57; SATA-Brief 39; SCFW 4; SFW 4; SUFW 1, 2

Zhang Ailing
See Chang, Eileen
See also CWW 2; RGSF 2

Zhdanov, Andrei Alexandrovich
1896-1948 .... **TCLC 18**
See also CA 117; 167

Zhukovsky, Vasilii Andreevich
See Zhukovsky, Vasily (Andreevich)
See also DLB 205

Zhukovsky, Vasily (Andreevich)
1783-1852 .... **NCLC 35**
See Zhukovsky, Vasilii Andreevich

Ziegenhagen, Eric .... **CLC 55**

Zimmer, Jill Schary
See Robinson, Jill

Zimmerman, Robert
See Dylan, Bob

Zindel, Paul 1936-2003 ...... **CLC 6, 26; DC 5**
See also AAYA 2, 37; BYA 2, 3, 8, 11, 14; CA 73-76; 213; CAD; CANR 31, 65, 108; CD 5; CDALBS; CLR 3, 45, 85; DA; DA3; DAB; DAC; DAM DRAM, MST, NOV; DFS 12; DLB 7, 52; JRDA; LAIT 5; MAICYA 1, 2; MTCW 1, 2; NFS 14; SATA 16, 58, 102; SATA-Obit 142; WYA; YAW

Zinn, Howard 1922- .... **CLC 199**
See also CA 1-4R; CANR 2, 33, 90

Zinov'Ev, A. A.
See Zinoviev, Alexander (Aleksandrovich)

Zinov'ev, Aleksandr (Aleksandrovich)
See Zinoviev, Alexander (Aleksandrovich)
See also DLB 302

Zinoviev, Alexander (Aleksandrovich)
1922- .... **CLC 19**
See Zinov'ev, Aleksandr (Aleksandrovich)
See also CA 116; 133; CAAS 10

Zizek, Slavoj 1949- .... **CLC 188**
See also CA 201

Zoilus
See Lovecraft, H(oward) P(hillips)

Zola, Emile (Edouard Charles Antoine)
1840-1902 ...... **TCLC 1, 6, 21, 41; WLC**
See also CA 104; 138; DA; DA3; DAB; DAC; DAM MST, NOV; DLB 123; EW 7; GFL 1789 to the Present; IDTP; LMFS 1, 2; RGWL 2; TWA

Zoline, Pamela 1941- .... **CLC 62**
See also CA 161; SFW 4

Zoroaster 628(?)B.C.-551(?)B.C. ... **CMLC 40**

Zorrilla y Moral, Jose 1817-1893 .... **NCLC 6**

Zoshchenko, Mikhail (Mikhailovich)
1895-1958 .... **SSC 15; TCLC 15**
See also CA 115; 160; EWL 3; RGSF 2; RGWL 3

Zuckmayer, Carl 1896-1977 .... **CLC 18**
See also CA 69-72; DLB 56, 124; EWL 3; RGWL 2, 3

Zuk, Georges
See Skelton, Robin
See also CCA 1

Literary Criticism Series
Cumulative Topic Index

This index lists all topic entries in Gale's *Children's Literature Review* (CLR), *Classical and Medieval Literature Criticism* (CMLC), *Contemporary Literary Criticism* (CLC), *Drama Criticism* (DC), *Literature Criticism from 1400 to 1800* (LC), *Nineteenth-Century Literature Criticism* (NCLC), *Short Story Criticism* (SSC), and *Twentieth-Century Literary Criticism* (TCLC). The index also lists topic entries in the Gale Critical Companion Collection, which includes the following publications: *The Beat Generation* (BG), and *Harlem Renaissance* (HR).

Topic Index

CLC Cumulative Nationality Index

479

CONTEMPORARY LITERARY CRITICISM

Nationality Index

Nationality Index

CLC-203 Title Index